W9-BLS-812

"The 2000 presidential election was such a close call— how does that happen? I wonder if it has happened before."

"How am I going to be sure I know all this material for the test? I feel confident now, but..."

"I understand that the Bill of Rights is important, but how is it used in real life?"

mypoliscilab™

Where participation leads to action!

with LongmanParticipate.com 3.0 inside!

This **TIMELINE ACTIVITY** examines other close-call elections in our history.

PRE-TESTS, POST-TESTS, CHAPTER EXAMS and **STUDY GUIDES** for each chapter of your book help students prepare for exams.

This **SIMULATION ACTIVITY** helps students judge whether a police officer who is breaking and entering is violating civil rights.

Available in CourseCompass, Web CT, & Blackboard

mypoliscilab™
Where participation leads to action!

with LongmanParticipate.com 3.0 inside!

From **simulations** that place students in the role of campaign manager to **timeline activities**, from **pre- and post-chapter tests** to a fully integrated **Ebook**, MyPoliSciLab brings together an amazing collection of resources for both students and instructors. See a demo now at **www.mypoliscilab.com**!

Here's what's in MyPoliSciLab—

Pre-Test, Post Test, and Chapter Exam.
For each chapter of the text, students will navigate through a pre-test, post-test, and a full chapter exam—all fully integrated with the online Ebook so students can assess, review, and improve their understanding of the material in each chapter.

Ebook.
Matching the exact layout of the printed textbook, the Ebook contains multimedia icons in the margins that launch a wealth of exciting resources.

Chapter Review.
For each chapter, students will find additional resources, such as a complete study guide, learning objectives, a summary, and Web explorations.

Research Navigator™.
This database provides thousands of articles from popular periodicals like *Newsweek* and *USA Today* that give students and professors access to topical content from a variety of sources.

New York Times Online Feed & The New York Times Search by Subject™ Archive.
Both provide free access to the full text of *The New York Times* and articles from the world's leading journalists of the *Times*. The online feed provides students with updated headlines and political news on an hourly basis.

LongmanParticipate.com 3.0
Our well-known and highly respected online tool is now fully updated. Students will find over 100 simulations, interactive timelines, comparative exercises and more—all integrated with the online ebook. Available inside MyPoliSciLab or as a website alone.

LongmanParticipate.com 3.0
Inside!

Go to mypoliscilab.com for a free demo.

www.longmanparticipate.com

LongmanParticipate.com version 3.0 inside MyPoliSciLab or as a website alone!

Within the margins of your textbook you will find these icons directing students to the LongmanParticipate.com activities, which will correspond to the chapter content. Now fully updated with brand new activities!

Longman Participate Activities:

 SIMULATION. Students are given a role to play —such as Congress member, lobbyist, or police officer—and experience the challenges and excitement of politics firsthand.

 VISUAL LITERACY. Students interpret and apply data about intriguing political topics. Each activity begins with an interactive primer on reading graphics.

 TIMELINE. With an abundance of media and graphics, students can step through the evolution of an aspect of government.

 PARTICIPATION. Bringing the importance of politics home, these activities appear as three types: 1.) Debates, 2.) Surveys, and 3.) Get Involved activities.

 COMPARATIVE. Students compare the U.S. political system to that of other countries.

INSTRUCTORS:

Course Management System—

MyPoliSciLab is available in different versions to fit your needs:
- MyPoliSciLab in CourseCompass™
- MyPoliSciLab in Blackboard
- MyPoliSciLab in WebCT

Website alone—
If you do not want a course management system, the LongmanParticipate.com 3.0 activities are available in a website-alone version.

STUDENTS:

If your text did not come with an access code to MyPoliSciLab, you can still get this amazing resource to help you succeed in the course. Just go to www.mypoliscilab.com and click on "How do I get access to mypoliscilab?"

Go to mypoliscilab.com for a free demo.

mypoliscilab™
Where participation leads to action!

American Government

American Government

CONTINUITY AND CHANGE

Alternate 2006 Edition

KAREN O'CONNOR

Professor of Government
American University

LARRY J. SABATO

University Professor
and Robert Kent Gooch Professor of Politics
University of Virginia

PEARSON
Longman

New York San Francisco Boston
London Toronto Sydney Tokyo Singapore Madrid
Mexico City Munich Paris Cape Town Hong Kong Montreal

Executive Editor: Eric Stano
Development Editor: Barbara A. Conover
Senior Marketing Manager: Elizabeth Fogarty
Media and Supplements Editor: Kristi Olson
Production Manager: Eric Jorgensen
Project Coordination, Text Design, and Electronic Page Makeup:
    Electronic Publishing Services Inc., NYC
Art Sudio: Electronic Publishing Services Inc., NYC
Cover Designer/Manager: Nancy Danahy
Cover Images: Getty Images, Inc.
Cover Image Montage: Keithley & Associates, Inc.
Photo Researcher: Photosearch, Inc.
Senior Manufacturing Buyer: Alfred C. Dorsey
Printer and Binder: RR Donnelley & Sons Co.
Cover Printer: Phoenix Color Corp.

Library of Congress Cataloging-in-Publication Data

O'Connor, Karen,
    American government : continuity and change / Karen O'Connor, Larry J. Sabato.—2006
        alternate ed.
        p. cm.
    Includes bibliographical references and index.
    ISBN 0-321-31710-6 (paperbound)
        1. United States—Politics and government. I. Sabato, Larry. II. Title.

JK276 .023 2006b
320.473—dc22

                                                                    2004026407

Copyright © 2006 by Pearson Education, Inc.

All rights reserved. No part of this publication may be reproduced, stored in a retrieval system, or transmitted, in any form or by any means, electronic, mechanical, photocopying, recording, or otherwise, without the prior written permission of the publisher. Printed in the United States.

Please visit us at http://www.ablongman.com.

ISBN 0–321–31710-6 (paperback)

1 2 3 4 5 6 7 8 9 10—DOW—08 07 06 05

To Meghan,
who grew up with this book

Karen O'Connor

To my Government 101 students
over the years, who all know that
"politics is a good thing"

Larry Sabato

Brief Contents

Detailed Contents

Preface

It has happened again. As we have prepared every new edition of this book over the last decade, we find ourselves unfailingly surprised, challenged, and ultimately riveted by the dramatic changes that continue to take place across our political landscape. In 1992, the year this book first saw print, we experienced the "Year of the Woman" that produced record numbers of women elected to national office. Then, in 1994, we were greeted with the "Year of the Angry Male Voter" that produced a Republican revolution in Congress. The editions that followed those years appeared during various phases of the Clinton scandals, including the second impeachment trial of a U.S. president. Then came the 2000 election, when the outcome did not occur until December and appeared to be decided by a single Supreme Court Justice; the terrorist attacks of September 11, 2001; and the history-bucking 2002 midterm elections that returned control of both houses of Congress to the Republicans.

Little did we realize that, not long after those midterm elections, one of the longest, most expensive, divisive, and impassioned campaigns ever for the presidency was about to get underway. The 2004 national elections were dominated by heated discussion of the preemptive war in Iraq and debates about security and terrorism, the economy, and social issues such as same-sex marriage. We saw the emergence of so-called 527s as a powerful (and well-financed) political force, unprecedented "get out the vote" efforts by both Republicans and Democrats, and a closely divided and hotly charged electorate that returned George W. Bush to office for a second term with a majority of the popular vote and a solid win in the Electoral College.

It can never be said that American politics is boring. For every edition of this text, something unexpected or extraordinarily unusual has occurred, giving question to the old adage, "Politics as usual." At least on the national level, there appears to be little that is usual. Politics and policy form a vital, fascinating process that affects all our daily lives, and we hope that this text reflects that phenomenon and provides you with the tools to understand politics as an evolutionary process where history matters.

In less than a decade, our perceptions of politics, the role of the media, and the utility of voting appear to have undergone tremendous change. Since its inception, this text has tried diligently to reflect those changes and to present information about politics in a manner to engage students actively—many of whom have little interest in politics when they come into the classroom. In this edition, we build on a solid, tried-and-true base and at the same time present information about how politics now seems to be changing ever more rapidly. Thus, we present new information that we hope will whet students' appetites to learn more about politics while providing them with all of the information they need to make informed decisions about their government, politics, and politicians. We very much want our students to make such decisions. We very much want them to *participate*. Our goal with this text is to transmit just this sort of practical, useful information while creating and fostering student interest in American politics despite growing national skepticism about government and government officials at all levels. In fact, we hope that this new edition of our text will explain the national mood about politics and put it in a better context for students to understand their important role in a changing America.

APPROACH

We believe that one cannot fully understand the actions, issues, and policy decisions facing the U.S. government, its constituent states, or "the people" unless these issues are examined from the perspective of how they have evolved over time. Consequently, the title of this book is *American Government: Continuity and Change*. In its pages, we try to examine how the United States is governed today by looking not just at present behavior but also at the *Framers' intentions and how they have been implemented and adapted over the years.* For example, we believe that it is critical to an understanding of the role of political parties in the United States to understand the Framers' fears of factionalism, how parties evolved, and when and why realignments in party identification occurred.

In addition to questions raised by the Framers, we explore issues that the Framers could never have envisioned, and how the basic institutions of government have changed in responding to these new demands. For instance, no one more than two centuries ago could have foreseen election campaigns in an age when nearly all American homes contain television sets, and the Internet and fax machines allow instant access to information. Moreover, increasing citizen demands and expectations have routinely forced government reforms, making an understanding of the dynamics of change essential for introductory students.

Our overriding concern is that students understand their government as it exists today, so that they may become better citizens and make better choices. We believe that by providing students with information about government, explaining why it is important, and why their participation counts, students will come to see that politics can be a good thing.

To understand their government at all levels, students must understand how it was designed in the Constitution. Each chapter, therefore, approaches its topics from a combination of perspectives, which we believe will facilitate this approach. We have also included a full, *annotated* Constitution of the United States and a new boxed feature, "The Living Constitution," both of which are new to this edition, to further increase students' understanding and appreciation of the role of the Constitution in our government and every-day lives. (More on this in the "Features" section of this Preface.) In writing this book, we chose to put the institutions of government (Part II) before political behavior (Part III). Both sections, however, were written independently, making them easy to switch for those who prefer to teach about the actors in government and elections before discussing its institutions. To test the book, each of us has taught from it in both orders, with no pedagogical problems.

WHAT'S CHANGED IN THIS EDITION?

In this 2006 Edition of *American Government: Continuity and Change*, we have retained our basic approach to the study of politics as a constantly changing and often unpredictable enterprise. But we also discuss the dizzying array of important events that have taken place since the book last published. Most importantly, we include in-depth coverage of the 2004 campaign for the presidency and its results. We discuss the issues that were paramount during the long election season, including debates over the war in Iraq, leadership and terrorism, the economy, and issues such as same-sex marriage and "moral values." We examine the financing of elections in the wake of campaign finance reform and the emergence of so-called 527 groups, and we include analysis and tallies of both the expenditures and votes for George W. Bush and John Kerry.

Chapter Changes

Many of these changes and others are reflected in this 2006 Edition. **Chapter 1** contains updated figures on the changing demographics of the United States and new information on voter turnout. **Chapter 2** includes an expanded discussion of the Constitutional Convention debate over the question of slavery. **Chapter 3** discusses the state of state budgets, marriage in the federal system, and the issue of access to abortion. **Chapter 4** includes a new discussion of the growing strength of the Republican Party in state legislatures and governor's offices in the South and an analysis of the impact of state and local taxes. **Chapter 5** includes a completely revised discussion of obscenity as well as updates on the assault weapon ban, Partial Birth Abortion Ban Act, and the impact of

Lawrence v. *Texas*. **Chapter 6** has been revised to update coverage of gay rights and affirmative action. **Chapter 7** includes complete coverage of the membership of the 109th Congress, the 2004 elections, a new "Politics Now" box on a minority bill of rights, and judicial nominations. **Chapter 8** begins with a new vignette on Ronald Reagan's funeral and includes updated coverage of the first term of the George W. Bush administration. **Chapter 9** begins with a new vignette on Robert Mueller, John Ashcroft, and The Department of Homeland Security. It also includes updated figures and data on the federal workforce and new coverage of e-government. **Chapter 10** offers updates on the Supreme Court's 2003-2004 term, William H. Rehnquist's illness, judicial appointments, and the charateristics of appointees. **Chapter 11** includes updates on American's political knowledge, political behavior in the 2004 election (including exit poll data), tracking polls, exit polling, and the National Election Pool. **Chapter 12** begins with a new vignette on party conventions and contains updated data on party unity, fund-raising, identification, and an exploration of "Red and Blue" America. **Chapter 13** features an opening vignette on the 2004 presidential election campaign and contains new data and updated figures on election results, voter turnout, and demographics. **Chapter 14** examines the highly contentious 2004 presidential election, with special attention to new campaign finance regulations, 527s, and the advertising strategies utilized by both campaigns. **Chapter 15** evaluates the media coverage of major news events in 2004 and also features and updated discussion of how politicians use the media, including a discussion about argumentative news shows like CNN's (now cancelled) *Crossfire*. **Chapter 16** begins with a new vignette on MoveOn.org and Swift Boat Veterans for Truth, provides updates on interest group activity in the 2004 election (including the efforts of the Christian Coalition, NRA, and organized labor).

We have also made a major effort to make certain that this edition contains the most up-to-date scholarship by political scientists, not only on how government works, but what they have said on contemporary debates.

FEATURES

The 2006 Edition has retained the best features and pedagogy from previous editions, enhanced or revised others, and added exciting new ones.

Historical Perspective

Every chapter uses history to serve three purposes: first, to show how institutions and processes have evolved to their present states; second, to provide some of the color that makes information memorable; and third, to provide students with a more thorough appreciation that our government was born amid burning issues of representation and power, issues that continue to smolder today. A richer historical texture helps to explain the present.

Comparative Perspective

Changes in the Middle East, Russia and Eastern Europe, North America, South America, and Asia all remind us of the preeminence of democracy, in theory if not always in fact. As new democratic experiments spring up around the globe (e.g. Iraq), it becomes increasingly important for students to understand the rudiments of presidential versus parliamentary government and of multiparty versus two-party systems. To put American government in perspective, we continue to draw comparisons with Great Britain within the text discussion. *Global Perspective* boxes, all of which have been substantially revised for this edition, compare issues, politics and institutions in the U.S., with those of both industrialized democracies and non-Western countries such as Russia, Iraq, Egypt, India, Iran, and China.

Enhanced Pedagogy

We have revised and enhanced many pedagogical features to help students become stronger political thinkers and to echo the book's theme of evolution and change.

Preview and Review.   To pique students' interest and draw them into each chapter, we begin each chapter with a contemporary vignette. These vignettes, including the California gubernatorial recall, the Iraqi war protest at the United Nations, and the concern about outsourcing of jobs, frequently deal with issues of high interest to students, which we hope will whet their appetites to read the rest of the chapter. Each vignette is followed by a bridge paragraph linking the vignette with the chapter's topics and by an outline previewing the chapter's major headings. Chapter summaries at the conclusion of each chapter restate the major points made under each of these same major headings.

Key Terms.   Glossary definitions are included in the margins of the text for all bold-faced key terms. Key terms are listed once more at the end of each chapter, with page references for review and study.

Special Features.   Throughout the text there are several boxed features in keeping with its theme of continuity and change. In addition to chapter-by-chapter changes, we have developed new features designed to enhance student understanding of the political processes, institutions, and policies of American government:

- ***Annotated Constitution of the United States*** New to this edition and appearing between chapters 2 and 3, this copy of the Constitution is integrated a comprehensive primer on the meaning and context of its most significant articles, sections, and amendments. Students will understand not only what the language of the Constitution says but *why* it was fashioned as it was and how it is relevant today. For instance, students learn everything from why Article I is the longest and most detailed portion of the Constitution to why the "Full Faith and Credit" clause, rarely controversial, now becomes so in the context of gay marriage. The Constitution was annotated here with the significant help of a Constitutional expert, Gregg Ivers, of American University.

- ***The Living Constitution*** New to this edition and appearing in every chapter, these boxes examine the Constitutional context of that chapter's topic. Each box excerpts and explains a relevant portion of the Constitution, analyzes what the Framers were responding to when it was written, and examines how it is still relevant today. For instance, chapter 5 includes a box on the Ninth Amendment, a discussion of the impossibility of enumerating every fundamental liberty and right, and the Supreme Court's ruling—nonetheless—in favor of a host of fundamental liberties since 1965.

- ***On Campus*** These popular boxes, which have been expanded in this edition to appear in most chapters, focus in particular on material that we believe will be of great interest to college students. To that end, this feature examines issues of concern to college campuses, as well as issues, events, or legislation that were initiated on college campuses and that had an impact on the larger arena of American politics. Chapter 3, for example, questions whether legislation protecting women from violence is a casualty of the devolution revolution. Chapter 6 describes how college students can help others to attain their civil rights.

- ***Join the Debate*** To engage students in critical thinking, foster interest in important issues, and help inspire their participation through involvement in decision making and taking a stand, we developed a *Join the Debate* feature. Heavily revised to remain current and resonant to both instructors and students, this feature introduces provocative issues under debate today and explores those issues by suggesting arguments for and against them. Topics such as chapter 3's "No Child

Left Behind Act," chapter 5's "The USA Patriot Act," or chapter 13's "Lowering the Voting Age" are accompanied by supporting questions and guidance from the authors and are designed to prompt students to examine various arguments in the debate, consider larger context, and take a position on issues that matter in American government today.

- **Global Perspective** To put American government in perspective, these boxes compare issues and U.S. politics with other nations. Many of these boxes now include comparisons to non-Western nations such as Iran, Iraq, Egypt, India, China, Russia, and Indonesia; some focus on specific issues of particular interest today such as chapter 15's "Al-Jareeza: The CNN of the Arab World?"

- **Politics Now** These contemporary boxes act as a counterpoint to the text's traditional focus on the "roots of government." Based on current clippings, editorials, and moments in time, these boxes are designed to encourage students to think about current issues in the context of the continuing evolution of the American political system. Chapter 1, for example, examines "Deepening Disapproval of U.S. Involvement in Iraq." Chapter 6 examines how Native Americans are using diverse ways to reverse the economic adversity of discrimination.

- **Analyzing Visuals** A feature designed to encourage visual literacy, *Analyzing Visuals* helps students make sense of quantitative and qualitative information presented visually and enables them to get the most out of graphic representations. This feature examines a wide variety of images, including news photographs and political cartoons, as well as tables, bar graphs, line graphs, maps, and charts. In addition, students are encouraged to analyze and interpret the visual information themselves, using the introductory captions, pointers, and critical thinking questions provided to guide them. An introductory section, *Analyzing Visuals: A Brief Guide* (see pages xxxvi–xxxix), offers a foundation for analyzing and interpreting different kinds of visuals that students will encounter in the text. In addition to helping students examine the *Analyzing Visuals* features throughout the book, this introduction offers valuable strategies and suggested questions that can be applied to all the visuals in the text as well as those found in daily newspapers, weekly magazines, etc. These visual learning features appear twice per chapter.

- **Roots of Government** These historical boxes appear in half of the text's chapters and highlight the role that a particular institution, process, or person has played in the course of American politics as it has evolved to the present. Chapter 5, for example, examines the American Civil Liberties Union, while chapter 16 looks at "pressure politics" of the past.

Web Explorations

The end of each chapter contains several links to the World Wide Web through our book-specific Web site. Web Explorations encourage students to learn more and think critically about a specific issue or concept.

MyPoliSciLab and LongmanParticipate.com 3.0   MyPoliSciLab is a state of the art, interactive online solution for your course. Available in CourseCompass, Blackboard, and WebCT, MyPoliSciLab offers students a wealth of simulations, interactive exercises, and assessment tools—all intergrated with the printed text and an online e-book. For each chapter of the text, students can navigate through a pre-test, post-test, chapter review, and a full chapter exam, so they can assess, review, and improve their understanding of the concepts within the chapters. In addition to the online chapter content and assessment, students will have access to LongmanParticipate.com (updated 3.0 version), Longman's best-selling, interactive online tool, which provides over one hundred exercises for students. LongmanParticipate.com (3.0) is also available as a Web site alone.

Throughout the text students will find icons (see opposite page for samples) in the margins that direct them to relevant simulations, visual literacy exercises and other activities—*all of which appear in both MyPoliSciLab and LongmanParticipate.com 3.0.* Students will know which site to use by using the access card that came packaged with this text.

THE ANCILLARY PACKAGE

The ancillary package for *American Government: Continuity and Change, 2006 Edition,* reflects the pedagogical goals of the text: to provide information in a useful context and with colorful examples. We have tried especially hard to provide materials that are useful for instructors and helpful to students.

Instructor Supplements for Qualified College Adopters

Instructor's Manual.   Written by Sue Davis of Denison University. Includes chapter overviews, chapter outlines, learning objectives, key terms, and valuable teaching suggestions for all chapters.

Test Bank.   Written by Paul W. Cooke of Cy-Fair College. Contains hundreds of thoroughly revised and challenging multiple choice, true-false, and essay questions along with an answer key.

TestGen EQ CD-ROM.   The printed Test Bank is also available through our computerized testing system, TestGen-EQ. This fully networkable, user-friendly program enables instructors to view and edit questions, add their own questions, and print tests in a variety of formats.

MyPoliSciLab and LongmanParticipate.com 3.0 Faculty Teaching Guide. Written by Scott Furlong of University of Wisconsin. Contains chapter-by-chapter detailed summaries for each of the sites' interactive activities, as well as a list of concepts covered, recommendations about how to integrate the sites into coursework, and discussion questions and paper topics for every exercise. Instructors may use the table of contents in the front of the guide to locate information on a given activity icon that appears in the margin of their adopted textbook. This guide also provides faculty with detailed instructions and screen shots showing how to use MyPoliSciLab or LongmanParticipate.com, how to register on the sites, and how to set up and use any available administrative features. The introductory chapter describes the numerous additional resources included on the websites.

Digital Media Archive Presentation CD-ROM.   This complete multimedia presentation tool provides instructors with the following: a built-in presentation-maker, approximately 100 photos and 150 figures, graphs, and tables from Longman American government textbooks, 40 video clips, and more! All items can be imported into an instructor's existing presentation program, such as PowerPoint®.

Companion Website (CW) www.ablongman.com/oconnor.   This online course companion provides a wealth of resources for instructors using *American Government: Continuity and Change.*

PowerPoint® Presentation.   A lecture outline presentation to accompany all the chapters of this new edition along with complete graphics from the book. See the companion Web site at *www.ablongman.com/oconnor* to download the presentations.

Transparencies.   Full-color acetates of the figures from all chapters of the book.

Interactive American Government Video.   Contains twenty-seven video segments on topics ranging from the term limit debate to Internet pornography to women in the Citadel. Critical thinking questions accompany each clip, encouraging students to "interact" with the videos by analyzing their content and the concepts they address.

Politics in Action Video.   Eleven "lecture-launchers" covering subjects from conducting a campaign to the passage of a bill. Includes narrated videos, interviews, edited documentaries, original footage, and political ads.

American Government Video Program.   Qualified adopters can peruse our list of videos for the American government classroom at www.ablongman.com/irc.

Student Supplements for Qualified College Adopters

MyPoliSciLab for American Government with LongmanParticipate.com 3.0. MyPoliSciLab is a state-of -the art, interactive online solution for your course. Available in CourseCompass WebCt, or Blackboard with this text, MyPoliSciLab offers a wealth of simulations, interactive excercises, and assessment tools—all integrated with an online e-book version of this text. For each chapter, students will navigate through a pre-test, post-test, chapter review, and a full chapter exam, allowing them to assess, review, and improve their understanding of key concepts. In addition to the online chapter content, students will have access to LongmanParticipate.com (updated 3.0 version), Longman's best-selling interactive online tool, which offers over 100 exercises for students. These exercises include:

- Simulations putting students in the role of a political actor;
- Visual Literacy exercises getting students interpreting, manipulating, and applying data in visual form;
- Interactive Timelines enabling students to experience the evolution of an aspect of government;
- Participation activities that personalize politics by either getting students involved (e.g. in a debate) or exploring their own thoughts and opinions about our system;
- Comparative exercises that have students compare aspects of our system to those of other countries.

Students receive feedback at every step, and instructors can track student work through the gradebook feature. The activities for the sites were written and revised by Quentin Kidd, *Christopher Newport University* and William Field, *Temple University.*

Activities and content for previous versions of the sites were written by: James Brent, *San Jose State University;* Laura Roselle, *Elon College;* Denise Scheberle, *University of Wisconsin;* B. Thomas Schuman, *University of New Hampshire;* Sharon Spray, *Elon College;* Cara Strebe, *San Francisco State University;* Ruth Ann Strickland, *Appalachian State University;* Kaare Strøm, *University of California, San Diego;* David Tabb, *San Francisco State University;* Paul Benson, *Tarrant County Community College;* Stephen Sandweiss, *Tacoma Community College.*

LongmanParticipate.com 3.0 is also available as a website alone, for instructors who do not wish to use a course management system such as CourseCompass.

A free six-month subscription to MyPoliSciLab or LongmanParticipate.com 3.0 is available when access cards to either site are ordered packaged with this text. To find out more about MyPoliSciLab, go to *www.mypoliscilab.com.* To find out more about LongmanParticipate.com 3.0 go to *www.longmanparticipate.com.*

Companion Website (cw) www.ablongman.com/oconnor.   This online course companion provides a wealth of resources for students using *American Government: Continuity and Change,* including learning objectives, practice tests, vocabulary flashcards, an online glossary, and more.

Study Guide.   Written by John Ben Sutter of Houston Community College. The printed study guide features chapter outlines, key terms, a variety of practice tests, and critical thinking questions to help students learn.

StudyWizard CD-ROM.   Written by David Dupree of Victor Valley College. This interactive study guide helps students master concepts in the text through practice tests, chapter and topic summaries, and a comprehensive interactive glossary. Students receive immediate feedback on practice tests in the form of answer explanations and page references in the text to go to for extra help. FREE when ordered packaged with the text.

Discount Subscription to The *New York Times*.   A ten-week subscription for only $20! Contact your local Allyn & Bacon/Longman representative for more information.

Discount Subscription to *Newsweek* Magazine.   Students receive twelve issues of *Newsweek* at more than 80% off the regular price. An excellent way for students to keep up with current events.

Culture War? The Myth of a Polarized America.   By Morris P. Fiorina, Stanford University, Samuel J. Abrams, Harvard University, and Jeremy C. Pope, Stanford University. The first book in the "Great Questions in Politics" series, *Culture War? The Myth of a Polarized America* combines polling data with a compelling narrative to debunk commonly believed myths about American politics—particularly the claim that Americans are deeply divided in their fundamental political views.

You Decide! Current Debates in American Politics, 2005 Edition.   Edited by John T. Rourke, University of Connecticut, this exciting new debate-style reader examines provocative issues in American politics today—from same-sex marriage and abortion to the electoral college and the war on terror. The topics have been selected for their currency, importance, and student interest, and the pieces that argue various sides of a given issue come from recent journals, congressional hearings, think tanks, and periodicals. Free when packaged with this text.

Voices of Dissent: Critical Readings in American Politics, Sixth Edition. Edited by William F. Grover, St. Michael's College, and Joseph G. Peschek, Hamline University, this collection of critical essays goes beyond the debate between mainstream liberalism and conservatism to fundamentally challenge the status quo. Available at a discount when ordered packaged with the text.

American Government: Readings and Cases, Sixteenth Edition. Edited by Peter Woll, Brandeis University, this longtime bestseller offers a strong focus on the major cases and readings that define our thinking about American government and politics.

As it has since its first edition, this reader provides a strong, balanced blend of classics that illustrate and amplify important concepts in American government, along with extremely current readings and cases drawn from today's literature. The sixteenth edition continues to put students directly in touch with the great authors and political leaders who have shaped—and are shaping—American government.

Ten Things That Every American Government Student Should Read.   Edited by Karen O'Connor, American University. We asked American government instructors across the country to vote for ten things beyond the text that they believe every student should read and put them in this brief and useful reader. Free when ordered packaged with the text.

Choices: An American Government Database Reader.   This customizable reader allows instructors to choose from a database of over 300 readings to create a reader that exactly matches their course needs. Go to *www.pearsoncustom.com/database/ choices.html* for more information.

Penguin–Longman Value Bundles.   Longman offers twenty-five Penguin Putnam titles at more than a 60% discount when packaged with any Longman text. A totally unique offer and a wonderful way to enhance students' understanding of concepts in American Government. Please go to *www.ablongman.com/penguin* for more information.

Writing in Political Science, Third Edition.   By Diane Schmidt, this book takes students step-by-step through all aspects of writing in political science. Available at a discount when ordered packaged with any Longman textbook.

Getting Involved: A Guide to Student Citizenship.   By Mark Kann, Todd Belt, Gabriela Cowperthwaite, and Steven Horn. A unique and practical handbook that guides students through political participation with concrete advice and extensive sample material—letters, telephone scripts, student interviews, and real-life anecdotes—for getting involved and making a difference in their lives and communities.

Texas Politics Supplement, 3/e.   By Debra St. John, Collin County Community College. A ninety-page primer on state and local government and issues in Texas. Free when shrink-wrapped with the text.

California Politics Supplement, 4/e.   By Pamela Fiber, California State University–Long Beach. A seventy-page primer on state and local government and issues in California. Free when shrink-wrapped with the text.

Florida Politics Supplement.   By John Bertalan, Hillsborough Community College. A fifty-page primer on state and local government and issues in Florida. Free when shrink-wrapped with the text.

ACKNOWLEDGMENTS

Karen O'Connor thanks the thousands of students in her American Government courses at Emory and American University who, over the years, have pushed her to learn more about American government and to have fun in the process. She especially thanks her American

University colleagues who offered books and suggestions for this most recent revision—especially Gregg Ivers and David Lublin. Her former professor and longtime friend and co-author, Nancy E. McGlen, has offered support for more than two decades. Her former students, too, have contributed in various ways to this project, especially John R. Hermann, Paul Fabrizio, Bernadette Nye, Sue Davis, Laura van Assendelft, and Sarah Brewer.

For this edition of the book, Ali Yanus, a brilliant undergraduate, offered invaluable assistance. Her fresh perspectives on politics and ideas about things of interest to students, as well as her keen eye for the typo, have greatly benefited the book. Her unbelievably hard work has made this a much better book.

Larry J. Sabato would like to acknowledge all of the students from his University of Virginia Introduction to American Politics classes, who have offered valuable suggestions and thoughtful feedback. A massive textbook project like this one needs the very best assistance an author can find, and this author was lucky enough to find some marvelously talented people. Matthew V. Smyth of the UVA Center for Politics worked endless hours researching the new edition and weaving together beautifully constructed sections on recent American politics. In this, his reliable and exceptionally skillful colleague was James M. Patterson, a graduate student in politics at UVA and the head teaching assistant for a class of 500 that utilizes the textbook. Completing this duo's efforts were Joshua J. Scott and Molly Clancy, who also toiled diligently in the days after the 2004 election to make this text the most up-to-date volume on the market. Other current and former staff members, interns, and colleagues who helped with this and previous editions include, but are not limited to: Colin Allen, Jonathan Carr, Zach Courser, Howard Ernst, Rakesh Gopalan, Bruce Larson, Gregg Lindskog, Ryan Rakness, Greg Smith, and Matthew Wikswo. Finally, he extends his thanks to the faculty and staff of the Department of Politics at UVA, especially Debbie Best and Sid Milkis.

Particular thanks from both of us go to James Strandberg, who revised chapter 4 (State and Local Government) and chapters 17-19 (Social Welfare Policy, Economic Policy, and Foreign and Defense Policy) for this edition. Our continued thanks go to the previous authors of these chapters, whose work served as such a strong foundation on which James could build in this edition: Dennis L. Dresang at the University of Wisconsin-Madison, Steven Koven at the University of Louisville, and Daniel S. Papp of the University System of Georgia. We also thank Glenn Hastedt of James Madison University, who prepared the Global Perspectives features, and Brian Bearry of the University of Texas at Dallas for his help with many of the Join the Debate features.

In the now many years we have been writing and rewriting this book, we have been blessed to have been helped by many people at Macmillan, Allyn & Bacon, and now Longman. Eric Stano has been a fantastic editor as well as fun to work with. Our development editor, Barbara Conover, and our marketing manager, Elizabeth Fogarty, have also done terrific jobs and made this a better book. We would also like to acknowledge the tireless efforts of the Pearson Education sales force. In the end, we hope that all of these talented people see how much their work and support have helped us to write a better book.

Many of our peers reviewed past editions of the book and earned our gratitude in the process:

Danny Adkison, *Oklahoma State University*

Weston H. Agor, *University of Texas at El Paso*

Victor Aikhionbare, *Salt Lake Community College*

James Anderson, *Texas A&M University*

Judith Baer, *Texas A&M University*

Ruth Bamberger, *Drury College*

Christine Barbour, *Indiana University*

Jon Bond, *Texas A&M University*

Stephen A. Borrelli, *University of Alabama*

Ann Bowman, *University of South Carolina*

Robert C. Bradley, *Illinois State University*

Gary Brown, *Montgomery College*

John Francis Burke, *University of Houston–Downtown*

Kevin Buterbaugh, *Northwest Missouri State University*

Greg Caldeira, *Ohio State University*

David E. Camacho, *Northern Arizona University*

Alan R. Carter, *Schenectady County Community College*

Carl D. Cavalli, *North Georgia College and State University*

Steve Chan, *University of Colorado*

Richard Christofferson Sr. *University of Wisconsin–Stevens Point*

David Cingranelli, *State University of New York, Binghamton*

Clarke E. Cochran, *Texas Tech University*

Anne N. Costain, *University of Colorado*

Cary Covington, *University of Iowa*

Lorrie Clemo, *State University of New York, Oswego*

Stephen C. Craig, *University of Florida*

Lane Crothers, *Illinois State University*

Abraham L. Davis, *Morehouse College*

Robert DiClerico, *West Virginia University*

John Dinan, *Wake Forest University*

John Domino, *Sam Houston State University*

Keith L. Doughtery, *St. Mary's College of Maryland*

David E. Dupree, *Victor Valley College*

Craig F. Emmert, *Texas Tech University*

Walle Engedayehu, *Prairie View A&M University*

Alan S. Engel, *Miami University*

Timothy Fackler, *University of Nevada Las Vegas*

Frank B. Feigert, *University of North Texas*

Evelyn Fink, *University of Nebraska*

Scott R. Furlong, *University of Wisconsin–Green Bay*

James D. Gleason, *Victoria College*

Sheldon Goldman, *University of Massachusetts, Amherst*

Doris Graber, *University of Illinois at Chicago*

Jeffrey D. Green, *University of Montana*

Roger W. Green, *University of North Dakota*

Charles Hadley, *University of New Orleans*

Mel Hailey, *Abilene Christian University*

William K. Hall, *Bradley University*

Robert L. Hardgrave Jr. *University of Texas at Austin*

Chip Hauss, *George Mason University/University of Reading*

Stacia L. Haynie, *Louisiana State University*

John R. Hermann, *Trinity University*

Marjorie Hershey, *Indiana University*

Steven Alan Holmes, *Bakersfield College*

Jon Hurwitz, *State University of New York at Buffalo*

Thomas Hyde, *Pfeiffer University*

Joseph Ignagni, *University of Texas at Arlington*

Willoughby Jarrell, *Kennesaw State College*

Susan M. Johnson, *University of Wisconsin–Whitewater*

Dennis Judd, *University of Missouri–St. Louis*

Carol J. Kamper, *Rochester Community College*

Kenneth Kennedy, *College of San Mateo*

Donald F. Kettl, *University of Wisconsin*

Quentin Kidd, *Christopher Newport University*

John Kincaid, *Lafayette College*

Karen M. King, *Bowling Green State University*

Alec Kirby, *University of Wisconsin–Stout*

Jonathan E. Kranz, *John Jay College of Criminal Justice*

John C. Kuzenski, *The Citadel*

Mark Landis, *Hofstra University*

Sue Lee, *North Lake College*

Ted Lewis, *Collin County Community College*

Brad Lockerbie, *University of Georgia*

Cecilia Manrique, *University of Wisconsin–La Crosse*

Larry Martinez, *California State University–Long Beach*

Lynn Mather, *Dartmouth College*

Laurel A. Mayer, *Sinclair Community College*

Steve Mazurana, *University of Northern Colorado*

Clifton McCleskey, *University of Virginia*

James L. McDowell, *Indiana State University*

Carl E. Meacham, *State University of New York, Oneonta*

Stephen S. Meinhold, *University of North Carolina–Wilmington*

Mark C. Miller, *Clark University*

Kenneth F. Mott, *Gettysburg College*

Joseph Nogee, *University of Houston*

John O'Callaghan, *Suffolk University*

Bruce Oppenheimer, *Vanderbilt University*

Richard Pacelle, *Georgia Southern University*

Marian Lief Palley, *University of Delaware*

David R. Penna, *Gallaudet University*

Richard M. Pious, *Columbia University*

David H. Provost, *California State University–Fresno*

Lawrence J. Redlinger, *University of Texas at Dallas*

James A. Rhodes, *Luther College*

Leroy N. Rieselbach, *Indiana University*

David Robertson, *Public Policy Research Centers, University of Missouri–St. Louis*

David Robinson, *University of Houston–Downtown*

David W. Rohde, *Michigan State University*

Frank Rourke, *Johns Hopkins University*

Donald Roy, *Ferris State University*

Ronald Rubin, *City University of New York, Borough of Manhattan Community College*

Bruce L. Sanders, *MacComb Community College*

Denise Scheberle, *University of Wisconsin–Green Bay*

Gaye Lynn Scott, *Austin Community College*

Martin P. Sellers, *Campbell University*

Daniel M. Shea, *University of Akron*

John N. Short, *University of Arkansas–Monticello*

Michael Eric Siegel, *American University*

Mark Silverstein, *Boston University*

James R. Simmons, *University of Wisconsin–Oshkosh*

Andrea Simpson, *University of Washington*

Philip M. Simpson, *Cameron University*

Elliott E. Slotnick, *Ohio State University*

Michael W. Sonnleitner, *Portland Community College*

Frank J. Sorauf, *University of Minnesota*

Gerald Stanglin, *Cedar Valley College*

C. S. Tai, *University of Arkansas–Pine Bluff*

Richard J. Timpone, *State University of New York, Stony Brook*

Brian Walsh, *University of Maryland*

Shirley Anne Warshaw, *Gettysburg College*

Matt Wetstein, *San Joaquin Delta College*

Richard Whaley, *Marian College*

Rich Whisonant, *York Technical College*

Martin Wiseman, *Mississippi State University*

Kevan Yenerall, *Bridgewater College*

Finally, we'd also like to thank our peers who reviewed and aided in the development of the current edition:

Albert C. Waite, *Central Texas College*

Ken Baxter, *San Joaquin Delta College*

Kevin Corder, *Western Michigan University*

John F. Kozlowicz, *University of Wisconsin–Whitewater*

Mark Byrnes, *Middle Tennessee State University*

Paul W. Cook, *Cy-Fair College*

Dana K. Glencross, *Oklahoma City Community College*

James Michael Greig, *University of North Texas*

Brian Bearry, *University of Texas at Dallas*

Norman Rodriguez, *John Wood Community College*

Justin Holmes, *University of Minnesota*

John Mercurio, *San Diego State University*

Terri S. Fine, *University of Central Florida*

John H. Calhoun, *Palm Beach Atlantic University*

John C. Hughes, *Oklahoma City Community College*

Tim Howard, *North Harris College*

David Kennedy, *Montgomery College*

Leena Thacker-Kumer, *University of Houston–Downtown*

Analyzing Visuals: A Brief Guide

The information age requires a new, more expansive definition of literacy. Visual literacy—the ability to analyze, interpret, synthesize, and apply visual information—is essential in today's world. We receive much information from the written and spoken word, but much also comes from visual forms. We are used to thinking about reading written texts critically—for example, reading a textbook carefully for information, sometimes highlighting or underlining as we go along—but we do not always think about "reading" visuals in this way. We should, for images and informational graphics can tell us a lot if we read and consider them carefully. In order to emphasize these skills, this edition of *American Government: Continuity and Change* contains two *Analyzing Visuals* features in each chapter. The features are intended to prompt you to think about the images and informational graphics you will encounter throughout this text, as well as those you see every day in the newspaper, in magazines, on the Web, on television, and in books. We provide critical thinking questions to assist you in learning how to analyze visuals. Though we focus on a couple of visuals in each chapter, we encourage you to examine carefully and ask similar questions of *all* the visuals in this text, and those you encounter elsewhere in your study of and participation in American government.

We look at several types of visuals in the chapters: tables, graphs and charts, maps, news photographs, and political cartoons. This brief guide provides some information about these types of visuals and offers a few questions to guide your analysis of each type.

TABLES

Tables are the least "visual" of the visuals we explore. Tables consist of textual information and/or numerical data arranged in tabular form, in columns and rows. Tables are frequently used when exact information is required and when orderly arrangement is necessary to locate and, in many cases, to compare the information. For example, a table presenting the estimated life expectancy, education levels, earnings, and number of single parents among men and women in 1970 and 2003 would make comparisons of the data visually accessible.

TABLE 1.2 Men and Women in a Changing Society	1970		2003	
	Men	*Women*	*Men*	*Women*
Estimated life expectancy	67	74	74	80
% high school graduates	53	52	45	65
% of BAs awarded	56	43	43	56
% of MAs awarded	60	40	41	59
% of PhDs awarded	87	13	55.1	44.9
% of JDs awarded	95	5	52.7	47.3
Median earnings	$26,760	$14,232	$29,101	$16,614
Single parents	1.2 million	5.6 million	4.4 million	13.1 million

Sources: 1970 data: U.S. Census Bureau, *1996 Statistical Abstract of the United States.* U.S. Department of Commerce, Economics and Statistics Administration, Bureau of the Census. 2003 data: U.S. Census Bureau, *2003 Statistical Abstract of the United States.*

Here are a few questions to guide your analysis:

- What is the purpose of the table? What information does it show? There is usually a title that offers a sense of the table's purpose.

- What information is provided in the column headings (provided in the top row)? How are the rows labeled?

- Is there a time period indicated, such as January to June 2005? Or, are the data as of a specific date, such as June 30, 2005?

- If the table shows numerical data, what do these data represent? In what units? Dollars a special interest lobby provides to a political party? Percentages of men and women responding in a particular way to a poll question about the president's performance? Estimated life expectancy in years?

- What is the source of the information presented in the table?

CHARTS AND GRAPHS

Charts and graphs depict numerical data in visual forms. The most common kinds of graphs plot data in two dimensions along horizontal and vertical axes. Examples that you will encounter throughout this text are line graphs, pie charts, and bar graphs. These kinds of visuals emphasize data relationships: at a particular point in time, at regular intervals over a fixed period of time, or, sometimes, as parts of a whole. Line graphs show a progression, usually over time (as in Political Party Finances, 1978–2004). Pie charts (such as the distribution of federal civilian employment) demonstrate how a whole (total federal civilian employment) is divided into its parts (employees in each branch). Bar graphs compare values across categories, showing how proportions are related to each other (as in the numbers of women and minorities in Congress). Bar graphs can present data either horizontally or vertically.

Here are a few questions to guide your analysis:

- What is the purpose of the chart or graph? What information does it provide? Or, what is being measured? There is usually a title that indicates the subject and purpose of the figure.

- Is there a time period shown, such as January to June 2005? Or, are the data as of a specific date, such as June 30, 2005? Are the data shown at multiple intervals over a fixed period, or at one particular point in time?

- What do the units represent? Dollars a candidate spends on a campaign? Number of voters versus number of nonvoters in Texas? If there are two or more sets of figures, what are the relationships among them?

- What is the source? Is it government information? Private polling information? A newspaper? A private organization? A corporation? An individual?

- Is the type of chart or graph appropriate for the information that is provided? For example, a line graph assumes a smooth progression from one data point to the next. Is that assumption valid for the data shown?

- Is there distortion in the visual representation of the information? Are the intervals equal? Does the area shown distort the actual amount or the proportion?

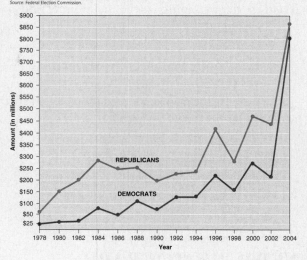

FIGURE 12.4 Political Party Finances, 1978–2004: Total Receipts. Note how the Republican Party has consistently taken in substantially higher receipts than their Democratic competitors, especially in the 1980s, when the Republican Party consolidated and prospered during Ronald Reagan's administration. Not until 1996 did Democrats reach levels long enjoyed by the Republicans. ■

Source: Federal Election Commission.

FIGURE 9.1 Distribution of Federal Civilian Employment by Branch, May 2002

Source: Office of Personnel Management, *The Fact Book*, 2003.

FIGURE 7.3 Numbers of Women and Minorities in Congress

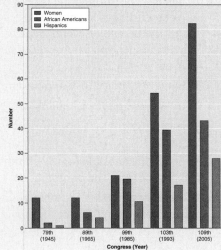

MAPS

Maps—of the United States, of particular regions, or of the world—are frequently used in political analysis to illustrate demographic, social, economic, and political issues and trends.

Here are a few questions to guide your analysis:

■ Is there a title that identifies the purpose or subject of the map?

■ What does the map key/legend show? What are the factors that the map is analyzing?

■ What is the region being shown?

■ What source is given for the map?

■ Maps usually depict a specific point in time. What is the point in time being shown on the map?

FIGURE 4.1   Party of State Governors, 2005
Republicans control a majority of the governorships, including the four most populous states. ■
Source: http://www.ncsl.org/statevote2002/govParty_post2002.htm, and updates by the authors.

NEWS PHOTOGRAPHS

If a picture is worth a thousand words, it is no wonder that our newspapers, magazines, and television news broadcasts rely on photographs as well as words to report and analyze the news. Photos can have a dramatic—and often immediate—impact on politics and government. Think about some photos that have political significance. For example, do you remember photos from the September 11, 2001, terrorist attack on the World Trade Center? Visual images usually evoke a stronger emotional response from people than do written descriptions. For this reason, individuals and organizations have learned to use photographs as a means to document events, make arguments, offer evidence, and even in some cases to manipulate the viewer into having a particular response.

Here are a few questions to guide your analysis:

■ When was the photograph taken? (If there is no date given for the photograph in its credit line or caption, you may be able to approximate the date according to the people or events depicted in the photo. If the photograph appears in a newspaper, you can usually assume that the shot is fairly current with publication.)

■ What is the subject of the photograph?

■ Why was the photo taken? What appears to be the purpose of the photograph?

■ Is it spontaneous or posed? Did the subject know he or she was being photographed?

■ Who was responsible for the photo? (An individual, an agency, or organization?) Can you discern the photographer's attitude toward the subject?

■ Is there a caption? If so, what kind of information does it provide? Does it identify the subject of the photo? Does it provide an interpretation of the subject?

POLITICAL CARTOONS

Political cartoons have a long history in America. Some of the most interesting commentary on American politics takes place in the form of political cartoons, which usually exaggerate physical and other qualities of the persons depicted and often rely on a kind of visual shorthand to announce the subject or set the scene—visual cues, clichés, or stereotypes that are instantly recognizable. For example, a greedy corporate executive might be depicted as an individual in professional clothing with paper currency sticking out of his or her pockets. In another cartoon, powdered wigs and quill pens might signal a historical setting. The cartoonist's goal is to comment on and/or criticize political figures, policies, or events. The cartoonist uses several techniques to accomplish this goal, including exaggeration, irony, and juxtaposition. For example, the cartoonist may point out how the results of governmental policies are the opposite of their intended effects (irony). In other cartoons, two people, ideas, or events that don't belong together may be joined to make a point (juxtaposition). Because cartoons comment on political situations and events, you generally need some knowledge of current events to interpret political cartoons.

Here are a few questions to guide your analysis:

- Study the cartoon element by element. Political cartoons are often complex. If the cartoon is in strip form, you also need to think about the relationship of the frames in sequence.

- What labels appear on objects or people in the cartoon? Cartoonists will often label some of the elements. For example, a building with columns might be labeled "U.S. Supreme Court." Or, an individual might be labeled "senator" or "Republican."

(Photo courtesy: DOONESBURY © G.B. Trudeau. Reprinted by permission of UNIVERSAL PRESS SYNDICATE. All rights reserved.)

- Is there a caption or title to the cartoon? If so, what does it contribute to the meaning or impact of the cartoon?

- Can you identify any of the people shown? Presidents, well-known members of Congress, and world leaders are often shown with specific characteristics that help to identify them. Jimmy Carter was often shown with an exaggerated, toothy smile. George W. Bush is often shown with large ears, small eyes, and bushy eyebrows—sometimes with a "W." or a "43" label.

- Can you identify the event being depicted? Historical events, such as the American Revolution, or contemporary events, such as the 2004 presidential election, are often the subject matter for cartoons.

- What are the elements of the cartoon? Objects often represent ideas or events. For example, a donkey is often used to depict the Democratic Party. Or, an eagle is used to represent the United States.

- How are the characters interacting? What do the speech bubbles contribute to the cartoon?

- What is the overall message of the cartoon? Can you determine what the cartoonist's position is on the subject?

American Government

Photo courtesy: Eric L. Wheate/Lonely Planet Images

The Political Landscape

WE THE PEOPLE of the United States, in Order to form a more perfect Union, establish Justice, insure domestic Tranquility, provide for the common defence, promote the general Welfare, and secure the Blessings of Liberty to ourselves and our Posterity, do ordain and establish this Constitution for the United States of America.

These are the words that begin the Preamble to the United States Constitution. Written in 1787 by a group of men we today refer to as the Framers, this document has guided our nation, its government, its politics, its institutions, and its inhabitants for over 200 years.

When the Constitution was written, the phrases "We the People" and "ourselves" meant something very different from what they do today. After all, voting largely was limited to property-owning white males. Indians, slaves, and women could not vote. Today, through the expansion of the right to vote, the phrase "the People" encompasses men and women of all races, ethnic origins, and social and economic statuses—a variety of peoples and interests. The Framers could not have imagined the range of people today who are eligible to vote.

In the goals it outlines, the Preamble to the Constitution describes what the people of the United States can expect from their government. In spite of the wave of nationalism that arose in the wake of the September 11, 2001, terrorist attacks, some continue to question how well the U.S. government can deliver on the goals set out in the Preamble. Few Americans today classify the union as "perfect"; many feel excluded from "Justice" and the "Blessings of Liberty," and even our leaders do not believe that our domestic situation is particularly tranquil, as evidenced by the creation of the Department of Homeland Security and calls for a national intelligence director. Furthermore, recent poll results and economic statistics indicate that many Americans believe their general welfare is not particularly well promoted by their government. Others simply do not care much at all about government. Many believe that they have no influence in its decision making, or they do not see any positive benefits from it in their lives.

If there has been one constant in the life of the United States, it is change. The Framers would be astonished to see the current forms and functions of the institutions they so carefully outlined in the Constitution, as well as the number of additional political institutions that have arisen to support and fuel the functioning of the national government. The Framers also would be amazed at the array of services and programs the government—especially the national government—provides. They further would be surprised to see how the physical boundaries and the composition of the population have changed over the past 200 plus years. And, they might well wonder, "How did we get here?"

It is part of the American creed that each generation should hand down to the next not only a better America, but an improved economic, educational, and social status. In general, Americans long have been optimistic about our nation, its institutions, and its future. Thomas Jefferson saw the United States as the world's "best hope"; Abraham Lincoln echoed these sentiments when he called it the "last, best hope on earth."[1] But, beginning in the 1990s, for the first time in decades, some of that optimism faded. Many Americans were dismayed by the Clinton/Lewinsky affair, campaign finance abuses, the negative presidential campaigns, and often even government in general. While their lives are better than their parents' and most are optimistic about the future, in the aftermath of terrorist attacks, 2001's stock market collapse, the war in Iraq, and the continued loss of jobs to firms outside the United States, many Americans are uncertain about what the future holds.

IN THIS TEXT, WE PRESENT you with the tools that you need to understand how our political system has evolved and to prepare you to understand the changes that are yet to come. If you approach the study of American government and politics with an open mind, it should help you become a better citizen. We hope that you learn to ask questions, to understand how various issues have come to be important, and to see why a particular law was enacted and how it was implemented. With such understanding, we further hope that you will learn not to accept at face value everything you see on the television news, hear on the radio, or read in the newspaper or on the Internet. Work to understand your government, and use your vote and other forms of participation to help ensure that your government works for you.

We recognize that the discourse of politics has changed dramatically in just the last few years, and that many Americans—especially the young—are turned off to politics, especially at the national level. We also believe that a thorough understanding of the workings of government will allow you to question and think about the system—the good parts and the bad—and decide for yourself the advantages and disadvantages of possible changes and reforms. Equipped with such an understanding, we hope you will become better informed and more active participants in the political process.

Every long journey begins with a single step. In this chapter, we will examine the following topics:

- First, we will discuss *government: what it is and why we need it*. Governments perform a range of well-known and not so well-known functions that affect citizens' lives on a daily basis.

- Second, we will look at *the roots of American government*. To understand how the U.S. government and our political system work today, it is critical to understand the philosophies that guided the American colonists as they created a system of governance different from those then in existence.

- Third, we will explore *American political culture and the characteristics of American democracy*. Several enduring characteristics have defined American democracy since its beginning and continue to influence our nation's government and politics today.

- Fourth, we will explore *the changing characteristics of the American people*. Because the government derives its power from the people, an understanding of who the American people are and their changing age, racial, and ethnic composition is critical to an understanding of American politics.

- Fifth, we will discuss the political *ideology of the American public*. Political ideology has a profound impact on the government policies that Americans support or oppose.

- Finally, we will discuss *current American attitudes toward government* and the role that government plays in their lives.

THE ORIGINS OF AMERICAN GOVERNMENT: WHAT IT IS AND WHY WE NEED IT

THROUGHOUT HISTORY, ALL SORTS OF SOCIETIES have organized themselves into a variety of governments, small and large, simple and complex, democratic and nondemocratic, elected and nonelected.

Governments, which are made up of individuals and institutions, are the vehicles through which policies are made and affairs of state are conducted. In fact, the term "government" is derived from the Greek for "to pilot a ship," which is appropriate, since we expect governments to guide "the ship of state."

Unlike schools, banks, or corporations, the actions of government are binding on all of its citizens. **Citizens,** by law, are members of the political community who by nature of being born in a particular nation or having become a naturalized citizen are entitled to all of the freedoms guaranteed by the government. In exchange for these freedoms, citizens must obey the government, its laws, and its constitution. Citizens also are expected to support their governments through exercising their right to vote, paying taxes due, and, if they are eligible, submitting themselves to military service.

Only governments can legitimately use force to keep order, and without governments, societies may descend into chaos. The fall of Baghdad, Iraq, in April 2003, vividly portrayed the need for government. With the end of Saddam Hussein's government, Baghdad and other areas throughout Iraq experienced looting and violence. The U.S. military immediately attempted to help Iraqis establish a government.

As we explore governments, especially American government, in this text, we are referring to the web of formal administrative structures that exist on the national, state, and local levels. But, these governments do not exist in a vacuum. Indeed, as we explore throughout this text, these governments were a result of trial and error, experiment, compromise, and sometimes bloodshed. Governments, then, must be discussed in the context of **politics,** the study of what has been called "who gets what, when, and how," or more simply, the process of how policy decisions get made.

The study of "who gets what, when, and how" can be a fascinating process. While all governments share to greater or lesser degrees the need to provide certain key functions, to whom they provide these benefits, which benefits they provide, when they provide them, and how they are provided vary tremendously across as well as within nations. (See Global Perspective: American Uniqueness in the World: Are We Number One?) One need only look to recent debates on tax policy to realize that there are many questions involving who, what, when, and how during policy debates.

Functions of Government

The Framers of the U.S. Constitution clearly recognized the need for a new government. As our opening vignette underscores, in attempting "to form a more perfect

government
A collective of individuals and institutions, the formal vehicles through which policies are made and affairs of state are conducted.

citizen
Member of the political community to whom certain rights and obligations are attached.

politics
The study of who gets what, when, and how—or how policy decisions are made.

Roots of Government

THE PHILOSOPHIES OF THOMAS HOBBES AND JOHN LOCKE: THE PROPER SCOPE OF GOVERNMENT

IN ALMOST any newspaper or television news report, on any given day, you can find stories that show Americans grappling with questions about the proper role of government in their lives. These questions are not new. Centuries ago, Thomas Hobbes and John Locke both wrote extensively on these issues. Their ideas, however, differed remarkably. For Hobbes, who viewed humans as basically evil, a government that regulated all kinds of conduct was necessary. Locke, who was more optimistic, saw the need only for limited government.

Hobbes: Government to Save People from Themselves

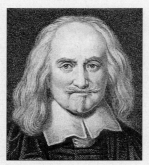

Thomas Hobbes was born in 1588 in Gloucestershire, England, and began his formal education at the age of four. By the age of six he was learning Latin and Greek, and by the age of nineteen he had obtained his bachelor's degree from Oxford University. In 1608, Hobbes accepted a position as a family tutor with the earl of Devonshire, a post he retained for the rest of his life.

Hobbes was greatly influenced by the chaos of the English Civil War during the mid-seventeenth century. Its impact is evident in his most famous work, *Leviathan* (1651), a treatise on governmental theory that states his views on man and citizen. *Leviathan* is commonly described as a book about politics, but it also deals with religion and moral philosophy.

Hobbes characterized humans as selfishly individualistic and constantly at war with one another. Thus, he believed that people must surrender themselves to rulers in exchange for protection from their neighbors.

Locke: Government Through Consent of the People

John Locke, born in England in 1632, was admitted to an outstanding public school at the age of fifteen. It was there that he began to question his upbringing in the Puritan faith. At twenty, he went on to study at Oxford, where he later became a lecturer in Aristotelian philosophy. Soon, however, he found a new interest in medicine and experimental science.

In 1666, Locke met Anthony Ashley Cooper, the first earl of Shaftsbury, a politician who believed in individual rights and parliamentary reform. It was through Cooper that Locke discovered his own talent for philosophy. In 1689, Locke published his most famous work, *Second Treatise on Civil Government*, in which he set forth a theory of natural rights. He used natural rights to support his "social contract [theory]—the view that the consent of the people is the only true basis of any sovereign's right to rule." A government exists, he argued, because individuals agree, through a contract, to form a government to protect their rights under natural law. By agreeing to be governed, individuals agree to abide by decisions made by majority vote in the resolution of disputes.

Both men, as you can see, relied on wealthy royal patrons to allow them the time to work on their philosophies of government. While Hobbes and Locke agreed that government was a social contract between the people and their rulers, they differed significantly about the proper scope of government. Which man's views about government (and people) reflect your views?

Union," the Framers set out several key functions of government that continue to be relevant today, over 200 years later. As discussed below, several of the Framers' ideas centered on their belief that the major function of government was creating mechanisms to allow individuals to solve conflicts in an orderly and peaceful manner. Just how much authority one must give up to governments in exchange for this kind of security, however, has vexed political philosophers as well as politicians for ages.

Establishing Justice.   One of the first things expected from governments is a system of laws that allows individuals to abide by a common set of principles. Societies adhering to what is called the rule of law allow for the rational dispensing of justice by acknowledged legal authorities. Thus, today, the Bill of Rights entitles people to a trial by jury, to know what the charges against them are, and to be tried in a courtroom presided over by an impartial judge. The U.S. Constitution created a federal judicial system to dispense justice, but the Bill of Rights specified a host of rights guaranteed to all citizens in an effort to establish justice.

Ensuring Domestic Tranquility.   As we will discuss throughout this text, the role of government in ensuring domestic tranquility is a subject of much debate. In times of crisis such as the terrorist attacks of September 11, 2001, the U.S. government, as well as states and local governments, took extraordinary measures to contain the threat of terrorism from abroad as well as within the United States. The creation of the Department of Homeland Security as well as the passage of legislation giving the national government nearly unprecedented ability to ferret out potential threats shows the degree to which the government takes seriously its charge to preserve domestic tranquility. On an even more practical front, local governments have police forces, the states have national guards, and the federal government can always call up troops to quell any threats.

Providing for the Common Defense.   The U.S. Constitution calls for the president to be the commander in chief of the armed forces, and the Congress was given the authority to raise an army. The Framers recognized that one of the major purposes of government was to provide for the defense of its citizens, who alone had no ability to protect themselves from other governments. As highlighted in Figure 1.1, the defense budget is a considerable proportion of all federal outlays.

Promoting the General Welfare.   When the Framers added "promoting the general welfare" to their list of key government functions, they never envisioned how the involvement of the government at all levels would expand so tremendously. In fact, promoting the general welfare was more of an ideal than a mandate for government. Over time, however, our notions of what the government should do have expanded along with the size of government. As we discuss throughout this text, however, there is no universal agreement on the scope of what governments should do. There is no doubt that Social Security income programs as well as governmental programs providing health care are designed to promote the general welfare. These programs make up a significant proportion of the federal budget, as highlighted in Figure 1.1.

Securing the Blessings of Liberty.   A well-functioning government that enjoys the support of its citizenry is one of the best ways to secure the blessings of liberty on its people. In a free society, citizens enjoy a wide range of liberties and freedoms and feel free to prosper. They are free to criticize the government as well as to petition it when they disagree with its policies or have a grievance.

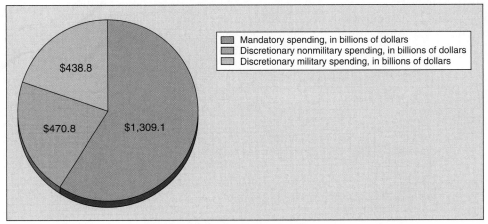

FIGURE 1.1
Allocation of the Federal Budget, 2005. ■

Source: Fiscal Year 2005 Budget, http://www.whitehouse.gov/omb/budget/fy2005/pdf/spec.pdf.

■ Former Iraqi President Saddam Hussein ruled Iraq as a totalitarian state. Here, Hussein was in court to hear the lengthy list of charges against him.

Photo courtesy: Pool/Getty Images

Taken together, these principal functions of government permeate our lives. Whether it is your ability to obtain a low-interest student loan, buy a formerly prescription-only allergy drug, Claritin, over the counter, or drive a car at a particular age, government has played a major role. Similarly, without government-sponsored research, we would not have cellular telephones, the Internet, four-wheel drive vehicles, or even Velcro.

Types of Government

monarchy
A form of government in which power is vested in hereditary kings and queens who govern in the interests of all.

totalitarianism
An economic system in which the government has total control over the economy.

oligarchy
A form of government in which the right to participate is conditioned on the possession of wealth, social status, military position, or achievement.

As early as Plato and Aristotle, theorists have tried to categorize governments by who participates, who governs, and how much authority those who govern enjoy. As revealed in Table 1.1, a **monarchy,** the type of government rejected by the Framers, is defined by the rule of one in the interest of all of his or her subjects. In contrast is **totalitarianism,** as was the case in Iraq under Saddam Hussein. In a totalitarian system, the leader exercises unlimited power and individuals have no personal rights or liberties. Generally, these systems tend to be ruled in the name of a particular religion or orthodoxy, an ideology, or a personality cult organized around the supreme leader. In an **oligarchy,** participation in government is conditioned on the possession of wealth, social status, military position, or achievement. Oligarchies are rare today.

TABLE 1.1	Types of Government	
	Whose Interests Are Represented	
Rulers	*The Ruled*	*The Rulers*
Government by one	Monarchy	Totalitarian
Government by a few	Aristocracy	Oligarchy
Government by many	Citizenry	Democracy

Source: Adapted from Albert B. Saye, Merritt B. Pound, and John F. Allums, *Principles of American Government,* 5th ed. (Englewood Cliffs, NJ: Prentice Hall, 1966): 9.

A **democracy,** from the Greek words *demos* (the people) and *kratia* (power or authority), is a system of government that gives power to the people either directly or through their elected representatives. As we will explore below, this was the form of government favored by the Framers.

democracy
A system of government that gives power to the people, whether directly or through their elected representatives.

ROOTS OF AMERICAN GOVERNMENT: WHERE DID THE IDEAS COME FROM?

THE CURRENT AMERICAN POLITICAL SYSTEM did not spring into being overnight. It is the result of philosophy, trial and error, and even luck. To begin our examination of why we have the type of government we have today, we will look at the theories of government that influenced the Framers who drafted the Constitution and created the United States of America.

The Reformation and the Enlightenment: Questioning the Divine Right of Kings

In the third century, as the Roman Empire began to fall, kings throughout Europe began to rule their countries absolutely, claiming their right to govern came directly from God. Thus, since it was thought to be God's will that a particular monarch ruled a country, the people in that country had no right to question their monarch's authority or agitate for a voice in their government's operation.

During the Enlightenment period, the ideas of philosophers and scientists such as Isaac Newton (1642–1727) radically changed people's views of government. Newton and others argued that the world could be improved through the use of human reason, science, and religious toleration. He and other theorists directly challenged earlier notions that fate alone controlled an individual's destiny and that kings ruled by divine right.

Photo courtesy: SIPA Press

■ Sir Isaac Newton and other Enlightenment thinkers challenged people's ideas about the nature of government.

The intellectual and religious developments of the Reformation and Enlightenment periods of the sixteenth and seventeenth centuries encouraged people to seek alternatives to absolute monarchies and to ponder new methods of governance. In the late sixteenth century, radical Protestants split from the Church of England (which was created by King Henry VIII when the Roman Catholic Church forbade him to divorce and remarry). These Protestants or Puritans believed in their ability to speak one on one to God and established self-governing congregations. They were persecuted for their religious beliefs by the English monarchy. The Pilgrims were the first group of these Protestants to flee religious persecution and settle in America. There they established self-governing congregations and were responsible for the first widespread appearance of self-government in the American colonies. The Mayflower Compact, the document setting up the new government, was deemed sufficiently important to be written while the Pilgrims were still at sea. It took the form of a **social contract,** or agreement between the people and their government signifying their consent to be governed.

social contract
An agreement between the people and their government signifying their consent to be governed.

Hobbes, Locke, and a Social Contract Theory of Government

Two English theorists of the seventeenth century, Thomas Hobbes (1588–1679) and John Locke (1632–1704), built on conventional notions about the role of government and the relationship of the government to the people in proposing a **social contract theory** of government (see Roots of Government: The Philosophies of Thomas Hobbes and John Locke). They argued that all individuals were free and equal by natural right. This freedom, in turn, required that all men and women give their consent to be governed.

social contract theory
The belief that people are free and equal by God-given right and that this in turn requires that all people give their consent to be governed; espoused by John Locke and influential in the writing of the Declaration of Independence.

Global Perspective

AMERICAN UNIQUENESS IN THE WORLD: ARE WE NUMBER ONE?

Is the United States unique—or is it merely ordinary? Most Americans consider this question at some point in their lives as they ponder the meaning and significance of their citizenship and identity. After all, if the United States is ordinary, then by implication Americans are probably ordinary, too. Most Americans, not satisfied with this answer, prefer to think of their country as unique.

In fact, American uniqueness—or exceptionalism—has been a pervasive theme in American political rhetoric since before the founding. Americans in the nineteenth century routinely described the nation as a "City on a Hill"—a reference to a passage in the New Testament in which Jesus Christ urges his followers to be an example for the rest of the world. Others have declared that the United States has a manifest destiny to occupy large swaths of land and exert significant influence in the world. As expressed by Joseph S. Nye Jr.'s 1991 classic, *Bound to Lead: The Changing Nature of American Power,*[a] U.S. foreign policy has for many years been guided by the idea that America is "bound to lead"—in the dual sense that its leadership is both an obligation it owes to the world and an inevitable role, given its strength and abilities.

Throughout this text we will consider, in these brief Global Perspective features, the question of American uniqueness. Study the figure included here, which shows how the United States compares to the rest of the world in a variety of dimensions. Then, you can begin to judge for yourself whether the United States is truly exceptional.

The data seem to reveal that the United States has amassed a tremendous amount of wealth, technology, political stability, human and natural resources, and military might,

while at the same time the health and well-being of the American people are merely average. It is ironic, for example, that a country with the most powerful military—capable of projecting its presence and influence around the planet and beyond—is doing worse than fifty-eight other countries in ensuring that every adult can read. Likewise, it seems odd that the country with the highest gross domestic product (the sum of all goods and services generated in a given year) has a harder time distributing this wealth than do sixty-six other countries.

As you study each chapter of this text, it will be important for you to consider whether this situation is a matter of choice or of circumstance. In other words, can the American people, acting privately or through government, change the rankings that we find here, or are they the product of structural forces that are impervious to change?

Questions

1. If you were surprised by any of the rankings in the figure, why were you under the impression that the United States was worse (or better) than you thought?
2. How is the U.S. image presented to the world and to American citizens? Assuming that this image does not always fit reality, where would you go for more accurate information?

[a] Joseph S. Nye Jr. *Bound to Lead: The Changing Nature of American Power* (New York: Basic Books, 1990).

Sources: Figure data are taken from various sources, compiled by Globastat.com. In most cases, the total number of countries listed is 192. The data are from 2001 and 2002.

How the U.S. Compares to Other Countries of the World

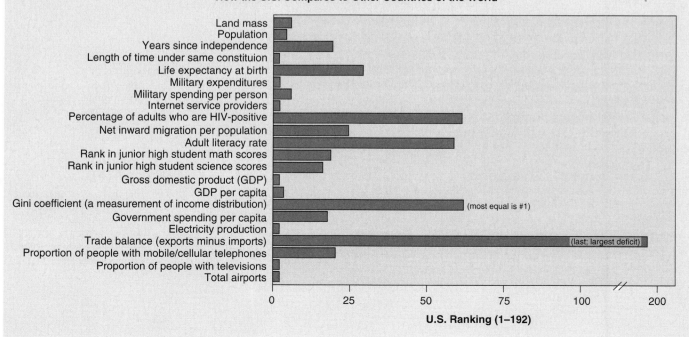

In Hobbes's now classic political treatise, *Leviathan* (1651), he argued pessimistically that man's* natural state was war. Government, Hobbes theorized, particularly a monarchy, was necessary to restrain man's bestial tendencies because life without government was but a "state of nature." Without written, enforceable rules, people would live like animals—foraging for food, stealing, and killing when necessary. To escape the horrors of the natural state and to protect their lives, Hobbes argued, people must give up certain rights to government. Without government, Hobbes warned, life would basically be "solitary, poor, nasty, brutish, and short"—a constant struggle to survive against the evil of others. For these reasons, governments had to intrude on people's rights and liberties to better control society and to provide the necessary safeguards for property.

Hobbes argued strongly for a single ruler, no matter how evil, to guarantee the rights of the weak against the strong. Leviathan, a biblical sea monster, was his characterization of an all-powerful government. Strict adherence to Leviathan's laws, however all-encompassing or intrusive on liberty, was but a small price to pay for living in a civilized society.

In contrast to Hobbes, John Locke, like many other political philosophers of the era, took the basic survival of humanity for granted. He argued that a government's major responsibility was the preservation of private property, an idea that ultimately found its way into the U.S. Constitution. In two of his works (*Essay Concerning Human Understanding* [1690] and *Second Treatise on Civil Government* [1689]), Locke not only denied the divine right of kings to govern but argued that men were born equal and with natural rights that no king had the power to void. Under Locke's conception of social contract theory, the consent of the people is the only true basis of any sovereign's right to rule. According to Locke, people form governments largely to preserve life, liberty, and property, and to assure justice. If governments act improperly, they break their contract with the people and therefore no longer enjoy the consent of the governed. Because he believed that true justice comes from laws, Locke argued that the branch of government that makes laws—as opposed to the one that enforces or interprets laws—should be the most powerful.

Locke believed that having a chief executive to administer laws was important, but that he should necessarily be limited by law or by the social contract with the governed. Locke's writings influenced many American colonists, especially Thomas Jefferson, whose original draft of the Declaration of Independence noted the rights to "life, liberty, and property" as key reasons to split from England.[2] This document was "pure Locke" because it based the justification for the split with England on the English government's violation of the social contract with the American colonists.

Photo courtesy: Bettmann/CORBIS

■ The title page from Thomas Hobbes's *Leviathan* (1651) depicts a giant ruler whose body consists of the bodies of his subjects. This is symbolic of the people coming together under one ruler.

Devising a National Government in the American Colonies

Although social contract theorists agreed on the need for government, they did not necessarily agree on the form that a government should take. Thomas Hobbes argued for a single leader; John Locke and Jean-Jacques Rousseau, a French philosopher (1712–1778), saw the need for less centralized power.

---

*The term "man" is used here because only males were considered fit to vote.

The American colonists rejected a system with a strong ruler, as in the British monarchy, as soon as they declared their independence. Many of the colonists had fled Great Britain to avoid religious persecution and other harsh manifestations of power wielded by King George II, whom they viewed as a malevolent despot who failed to govern in their interests. They naturally were reluctant to put themselves in the same position in their new nation.

The colonists also were fearful of replicating the landed and titled system of the British aristocracy. They viewed the formation of a representative form of government as far more in keeping with the ideas of social contract theorists.

As evidenced by the creation in 1619 of the Virginia House of Burgesses as the first representative assembly in North America, and its objections to "taxation without representation," the colonists were quick to create participatory forms of government in which most men were allowed to take part. The New England town meeting, where all citizens gather to discuss and decide issues facing the town, today stands as a surviving example of a **direct democracy,** such as was used in ancient Greece when all free, male citizens came together periodically to pass laws and "elect" leaders by lot.

Direct democracies, in which the people rather than their elected representatives make political decisions, soon proved unworkable in the colonies. But, as more and more settlers came to the New World, many town meetings were replaced by a system called an **indirect democracy** (this is also called representative democracy). This system of government, in which representatives of the people are chosen by ballot, was considered undemocratic by ancient Greeks, who believed that all citizens must have a direct say in their governance.[3] Later, in the 1760s, Jean-Jacques Rousseau also would argue that true democracy is impossible unless all citizens participate in governmental decision making. Nevertheless, indirect democracy was the form of government opted for throughout most of the colonies.

Representative or indirect democracies, which call for the election of representatives to a governmental decision-making body, were formed first in the colonies and then in the new union. Many citizens were uncomfortable with the term democracy because it implied a direct democracy that conjured up Hobbesian fears of the people and mob rule. Instead, they preferred the term **republic,** which implied a system of government in which the interests of the people were represented by more educated or wealthier citizens who were responsible to those who elected them. Today, representative democracies are more commonly called republics, and the words democracy and republic often are used interchangeably.

AMERICAN POLITICAL CULTURE AND THE CHARACTERISTICS OF AMERICAN DEMOCRACY

AS SHOWN ABOVE, the Framers devised a representative democratic system to govern the United States. This system is based on a number of underlying concepts and distinguishing characteristics that sometimes conflict with one another. Taken together, these ideas lie at the core of American political culture. More specifically, **political culture** can be defined as commonly shared attitudes, beliefs, and core values about how government should operate. American political culture emphasizes the values of personal liberty, equality, popular consent and majority rule, popular sovereignty, civil society, and individualism.

Personal Liberty

Personal liberty is perhaps the single most important characteristic of American democracy. The Constitution itself was written to ensure life and liberty. Over the years, however, our concepts of liberty have changed and evolved from freedom *from* to

---

direct democracy
A system of government in which members of the polity meet to discuss all policy decisions and then agree to abide by majority rule.

indirect (representative) democracy
A system of government that gives citizens the opportunity to vote for representatives who will work on their behalf.

republic
A government rooted in the consent of the governed; a representative or indirect democracy.

political culture
Commonly shared attitudes, beliefs, and core values about how government should operate.

personal liberty
A key characteristic of U.S. democracy. Initially meaning freedom from governmental interference, today it includes demands for freedom to engage in a variety of practices free from governmental discrimination.

freedom to. The Framers intended Americans to be free from governmental infringements on freedom of religion and speech, from unreasonable search and seizure, and so on (see chapter 5). The addition of the Fourteenth Amendment to the Constitution and its emphasis on equal protection of the laws and subsequent passage of laws guaranteeing civil rights, however, expanded Americans' concept of liberty to include demands for freedom to work or go to school free from discrimination. Debates over how much the government should do to guarantee these rights or liberties illustrate the conflicts that continue to occur in our democratic system.

Equality

Another key characteristic of our democracy is political equality. This emphasis reflects Americans' stress on the importance of the individual. Although some individuals clearly wield more political clout than others, the adage "one person, one vote" implies a sense of political equality for all.

Popular Consent and Majority Rule

Popular consent, the idea that governments must draw their powers from the consent of the governed, is one distinguishing characteristic of American democracy. Derived from John Locke's social contract theory, the notion of popular consent was central to the Declaration of Independence. A citizen's willingness to vote represents his or her consent to be governed and is thus an essential premise of democracy. Growing numbers of nonvoters can threaten the operation and legitimacy of a truly democratic system.

Majority rule, another core political value, means that the majority (normally 50 percent of the total votes cast plus one) of citizens in any political unit should elect officials and determine policies. This principle holds for both voters and their elected representatives. Yet, the American system also stresses the need to preserve minority rights, as evidenced by the myriad protections of individual rights and liberties found in the Bill of Rights.

The concept of the preservation of minority rights has changed dramatically in the United States. It wasn't until after the Civil War that slaves were freed and African Americans began to enjoy minimal citizenship rights. By the 1960s, however, rage at America's failure to guarantee minority rights in all sections of the nation fueled the civil rights movement. This ultimately led to congressional passage of the Civil Rights Act of 1964 and the Voting Rights Act of 1965, both designed to further minority rights.

Popular Sovereignty

The notion of **popular sovereignty,** the right of the majority to govern themselves, has its basis in **natural law.** Ultimately, political authority rests with the people, who can create, abolish, or alter their governments. The idea that all governments derive their power from the people is found in the Declaration of Independence and the U.S. Constitution, but the term popular sovereignty did not come into wide use until pre–Civil War debates over slavery. At that time, supporters of popular sovereignty argued that the citizens of new states seeking admission to the Union should be able to decide whether or not their states would allow slavery within their borders.

Civil Society

Several of these hallmarks of our political culture also are fundamentals of what many now term **civil society.** This term is used to describe the "nongovernmental, not-for-profit, independent nature" of people and groups who can express their views publicly and engage in an open debate about public policy.[4] The fall of the Soviet Union "accelerated the global trend toward democracy . . . which pushed democracy to the top of the political agenda."[5] In Russia, for example, the U.S. government has used a variety of initiatives to train people how to act in a new democratic system.

popular consent
The idea that governments must draw their powers from the consent of the governed.

majority rule
The central premise of direct democracy in which only policies that collectively garner the support of a majority of voters will be made into law.

popular sovereignty
The right of the majority to govern themselves.

natural law
A doctrine that society should be governed by certain ethical principles that are part of nature and, as such, can be understood by reason.

civil society
Society created when citizens are allowed to organize and express their views publicly as they engage in an open debate about public policy.

Independent and politically active citizens are key to the success of any democracy, yet people who have not lived in democratic systems often are unschooled, reluctant, or afraid to participate after years in communist or totalitarian systems. The U.S. government routinely makes grants to nongovernmental organizations, professional associations, civic education groups, and women's groups to encourage the kind of participation in the political system that Americans often take for granted. U.S. efforts to assist Afghanistan and Iraq, for example, include not only public works projects but also development of the new democratic government.

Individualism

Simulation
What Are American Civic Values?

Although many core political values concern protecting the rights of others, tremendous value is placed on the individual in American democracy. All individuals are deemed rational and fair, and endowed, as Thomas Jefferson proclaimed in the Declaration of Independence, "with certain unalienable rights." Even today, many view individualism, which holds that the primary function of government is to enable the individual to achieve his or her highest level of development, as a mixed blessing. It is also a concept whose meaning has changed over time. The rugged individualism of the western frontier, for example, was altered as more citizens moved westward, cities developed, and demands for government services increased as many individuals no longer could exist independently of others.

CHANGING CHARACTERISTICS OF THE AMERICAN PEOPLE

AMERICANS HAVE MANY THINGS IN COMMON in addition to their political culture. Most Americans share a common language—English—and have similar aspirations for themselves and their families. Most agree that they would rather live in the United States than anywhere else, and that democracy, with all of its warts, is still the best system for most. Most Americans highly value education and want to send their children to the best schools possible, viewing an education as the key to success.

Despite these similarities, politicians, media commentators, and even the citizenry itself tend to focus on differences among Americans, in large part because these differences contribute to political conflicts among the electorate. Although it is true that America and its population are undergoing rapid change, this is not necessarily a new phenomenon. It is simply new to most of us. In the pages that follow, we take a look at some of the characteristics of the American populace. Because the people of the United States are the basis of political power and authority, their characteristics and attitudes have important implications for how America is governed and how and what policies are made.

Changing Size and Population

One year after the Constitution was ratified, fewer than 4 million Americans lived in the thirteen states. They were united by a single language, most shared a similar Protestant-Christian heritage, and those who voted were white male property owners. The Constitution mandated that each of the sixty-five members of the original House of Representatives should represent 30,000 people. However, because of rapid growth, that number often was much higher. Anti-Federalists, who opposed a strong national government during the founding period, at least took solace in the fact that members of the House of Representatives, who generally represented far fewer people than senators, would be more in touch with "the People."

As revealed in Figure 1.2, as the nation grew with the addition of new states, the population also grew. Although the physical size of the United States has remained stable since the addition of Alaska and Hawaii in 1959, in 2005 there were more than 293

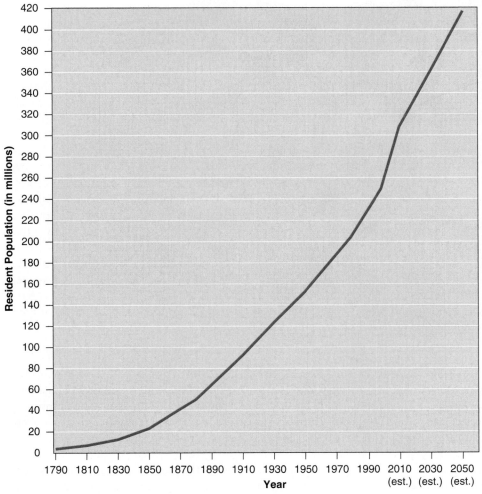

FIGURE 1.2 U.S. Population, 1790–2050

Since around 1890, when large numbers of immigrants began arriving in America, the United States has seen a sharp increase in population. The major reasons for this increase are new births and increased longevity, although immigration has also been a contributing factor. ■

Source: U.S. Census Bureau, *2003 Statistical Abstract of the United States.*

million Americans. In 2005, a single member of the House of Representatives from Montana represented more than 905,000 people. As a result of this growth, most citizens today feel far removed from the national government and their elected representatives. Members of Congress, too, feel this change. Often they represent diverse constituencies with a variety of needs, concerns, and expectations, and they can meet only a relative few of these people face to face.

Changing Demographics of the U.S. Population

As the physical size and population of the United States have changed, so have many of the assumptions on which it was founded. Some of the dynamism of the American system actually stems from the racial and ethnic changes that have taken place throughout our history, a notion that often gets lost in debates about immigration policy. Moreover, for the first time, the U.S. population is getting much older. This graying of America also will lead assuredly to changes in our expectations of government and in our public policy demands. The debate that took place in 2003 over Medicare prescription drug coverage illustrates this phenomenon. Below, we look at some demographic facts (that is, information on characteristics of America's population) and then discuss some implications of these changes for how our nation is governed and what policy issues might arise.

Understanding Who We Are

Changes in Racial and Ethnic Composition.   From the start, the population of America has been changed constantly by the arrival of various kinds of immigrants

from various regions to its shores—Western Europeans fleeing religious persecution in the 1600s to early 1700s, Chinese laborers arriving to work on the railroads following the Gold Rush in 1848, Irish Catholics escaping the potato famine in the 1850s, Northern and Eastern Europeans from the 1880s to 1910s, and, most recently, Southeast Asians, Cubans, and Mexicans, among others.

Immigration to the United States peaked in the first decade of the 1900s, when nearly 9 million people, many of them from Eastern

Photo courtesy: Chris Steele-Perkins/Magnum Photos

■ American Muslims celebrate Muslim Day Parade in New York City. From St. Patrick's Day to Chinese New Year celebrations, Americans often honor their immigrant origins.

Participation

The Debate over Immigration

Europe, entered the country. The United States did not see another major wave of immigration until the late 1980s, when nearly 2 million immigrants were admitted in one year.

While immigration has been a continual source of changing demographics in America, race has also played a major role in the development and course of politics in the United States. As revealed in Figure 1.3, the racial balance in America is changing dramatically. In 2003, for example, non-Hispanic whites made up 68.3 percent of the U.S. population, African Americans 12.7 percent, and Hispanics 13.4 percent, surpassing the number of African Americans in the United States for the first time. Originally, demographers did not anticipate Hispanics would surpass African Americans until 2050.

Changes in Age Cohort Composition. Just as the racial and ethnic composition of the American population is changing, so too is the average age of the population (See Analyzing Visuals: Changing Age Composition in the United States.) "For decades, the U.S. was described as a nation of the young because the number of persons under the age of twenty greatly outnumber[ed] those sixty-five and older,"[6] but this is no

Photo courtesy: New York Public Library

■ Concern over immigration is not a new phenomenon, as this cartoon from the early 1900s depicts.

16

FIGURE 1.3   Race and Ethnicity in America: 2005 and Beyond. ■

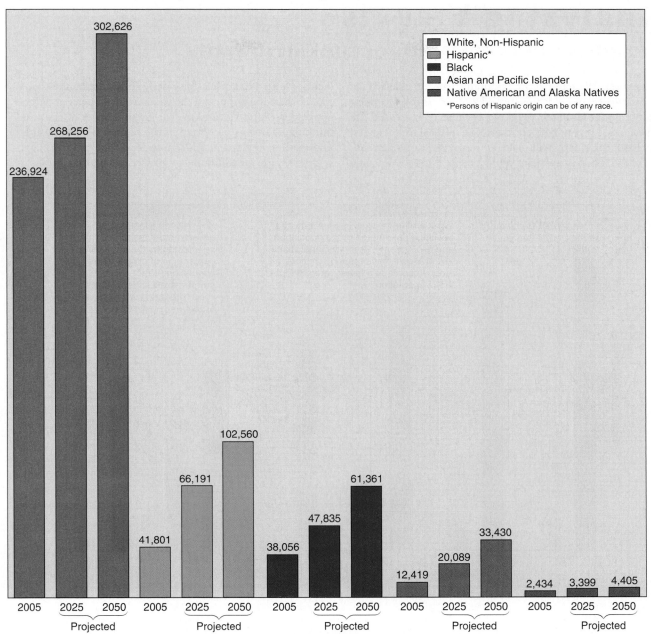

U.S. Population (in thousands)

Source: U.S. Census Bureau, *2003 Statistical Abstract of the United States.*

longer the case. Because of changes in patterns of fertility, life expectancy, and immigration, the nation's age profile has changed drastically.[7] When the United States was founded, the average life expectancy was thirty-five years; by 2004, it was nearly eighty years for women and seventy-four and a half years for men.

As people live longer, the types of services and policies they demand from government differ dramatically. In Florida, for example, which leads the nation in the percentage of its population over age sixty-five, citizens are far less concerned with the quality of public schools (especially if they are being taxed for those schools) than are the citizens in states with far lower proportions of the elderly.[8]

Simulation
How to Satisfy
Aunt Martha

Analyzing Visuals

CHANGING AGE COMPOSITION OF THE UNITED STATES

Between 1990 and 2000, the number of the elderly (age sixty-five and older) increased at a rate similar to those people under eighteen years old because of increased life expectancy, immigration, and advanced medical technologies. By 2040, the elderly will make up nearly the same percentage of the U.S. population as young people. This is a dramatic increase from 1900, when the elderly constituted only 4 percent of the population, and the young were 40 percent of the population. After viewing the bar graph, answer the critical thinking questions presented in the pointer bubbles, using information provided in this chapter. See Analyzing Visuals: A Brief Guide for additional guidance in analyzing graphs.

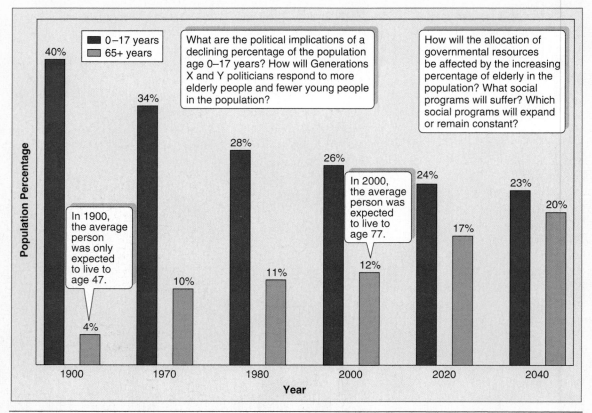

What are the political implications of a declining percentage of the population age 0–17 years? How will Generations X and Y politicians respond to more elderly people and fewer young people in the population?

How will the allocation of governmental resources be affected by the increasing percentage of elderly in the population? What social programs will suffer? Which social programs will expand or remain constant?

In 1900, the average person was only expected to live to age 47.

In 2000, the average person was expected to live to age 77.

Sources: 1900–1980 data from Susan A. MacManus, *Young v. Old: Generational Combat in the 21st Century.* © 1995 by Westview Press, Inc. Reprinted by permission of Westview Press, a member of Perseus Books, L.L.C. 2000 data from Julie Meyer, "Age: 2000," U.S. Census Bureau, C2KBR/01–12, October 2001. Accessed June 30, 2002, http://www.census.gov/population/www/cen2000/briefs.html. 2020–2040 data from U.S. Census Bureau, National Population Projections, Detailed Files, revised November 2, 2000. Accessed June 30, 2002, http://www.census.gov/population/www/projections/natdetD1A.html.

As the age profile of the U.S. population has changed, political scientists and others have found it useful to assign labels to various generations. Such labels can help us to understanding the various pressures put on our nation and its government, because when people are born and the events they experience can have important consequences on how they view other political, economic, and social events. For example, those 76.8 million people born after World War II (1946–1964) often are referred to as Baby Boomers. These individuals, who grew up in an America very different from that of their parents, now are reaching retirement age, which will put a major strain on the already overburdened Social Security and Medicare systems.[9]

In contrast, the children of the Baby Boomers, the 50 million who were born in the late 1960s through the mid-1970s, often are called Generation X, the name of an early 1980s punk band and, later, a novel.[10] This group experienced the economic downturn of the late 1980s. Jobs were scarce when Generation X-ers graduated from college, and many initially had a hard time paying off their college loans. They overwhelmingly believe that political leaders ignore them, and they distrust the political process. X-ers work longer hours, are better educated, and are more grassroots oriented politically than their parents.[11] Moreover, it is a very libertarian generation. According to one commentator, a difference between Generation X-ers and the liberal Baby Boomers is that X-ers "see capitalism as something that's not necessarily evil." X-ers believe they "can use capitalism for social change. It's one way to make government and big business stand up and take notice."[12]

The fastest growing group under age sixty-five is called Generation Y, those people born from 1977 to 1994 (26 percent of the U.S. population). Members of this group, unlike their Generation X predecessors, have "grown up in good times and have nothing but optimism about their future."[13] Generation Y is very Internet savvy and much more globally focused than any generation preceding it.

Changes in Family and Family Size.   Family size and household arrangements can be affected by several factors, including age at first marriage, divorce rates, economic conditions, longevity rates, and improvements in health care. In the past, large families were the norm (in part because so many children died early) and gender roles were clearly defined. Women did housework and men worked in the fields. Large families were imperative; children were a source of cheap farm labor.

Industrialization and knowledge of birth control methods began to put a dent in the size of American families by the early 1900s. No longer needing children to work for the survival of the household unit on the farm, couples began to limit the sizes of their families.

By 1949, 49 percent of those polled thought that four or more children was the "ideal" family size; in 1997, only 8 percent favored large families, and 54 percent responded that no children to two children were the "best."[14] As chronicled in the popular press as well as by the U.S. Department of Commerce, the American family also no longer looks like *The Cosby Show* or even *The Brady Bunch*. While the actual number of households in the United States grew from 93.3 million in 1970 to 103 million in 2000, what those households looked like has changed dramatically. In 1940, nine out of ten households were traditional family households; by 2003, only 72.2 percent were two-parent family households, 27.8 percent of all households were headed by a single parent, and more than 25 percent of all households consisted of a single person. Less than one-half of the family households had children under the age of eighteen. Since 1970, the number of female-headed households has more than doubled from 5.5 million to 12.9 million.

These changes in composition of households, lower birthrates, and prevalence of single-parent families, especially single-female-headed families, affect the kinds of demands people place on government as well as their perceptions of the role that government should play in their lives.

■ With the tagline "Everyone has a little dirty laundry," the hit television show "Desperate Housewives" satirizes the idea of the perfect suburban family. The plot revolves around the concept that if a family seems ideal on the outside, there is most likely much hidden behind the façade.

Photo courtesy: ABC Photo Archives

THE HUNTINGTON THEORY OF HISPANIZATION

OVERVIEW: Many observers of American culture and politics argue that one of the United States' greatest strengths is its ability to absorb and assimilate into the social body the diverse customs and values of different peoples. These commentators highlight the contributions to politics, the arts and sciences, national defense, and the common good by various waves of immigrants—and by those brought against their will during the years of slavery. Traditionalists such as Harvard professor Samuel Huntington contend that the American "melting pot" has been successful in part because, historically, the new Americans have absorbed the fundamental political principles of the United States as their own. Though there are numerous cultures within the country, Huntington insists that there is one shared American culture based on the values espoused in the Declaration of Independence— that is, American political culture is based on the fundamental principles of equality, individual rights, and government by consent. In order for the love of freedom and self-government to be nurtured and maintained, American core principles must be accepted and protected by all citizens.

Huntington argues that during the latter part of the twentieth and into the twenty-first century, there has been a new wave of immigration into the United States unlike any other; he considers immigration from Mexico in particular, and Latin America in general, to be potentially destructive of original American political principles. According to Huntington's highly controversial thesis, this immigration wave is unique in that there is a political agenda within part of the Hispanic community to "reclaim" the lands ceded to the United States after both the Texas war for independence and the Mexican-American War, thus giving Hispanic immigrants a political claim no other group of immigrants have had.

Furthermore, Huntington argues, no other nation has had to contend with a long, contiguous border that immigrants can rather freely cross to maintain familial, economic, and cultural ties, thereby fostering a type of dual national or cultural allegiance (or, at worst, immigrant loyalty to the home country) that can weaken ties to American core values. Finally, he contends, Hispanic immigrants have created linguistic and cultural enclaves within the United States (Los Angeles and Miami, for example) in which there is no need to learn the language, history, and political values of their adopted nation, thus further eroding social and political bonds between citizens.

Huntington's thesis raises serious questions. Are American core ideals so exceptional that only persons who share those values should be allowed citizenship? Can immigrants whose political and social beliefs differ from or oppose America's core values be assimilated into American society? If not, what corrective policy measures should be implemented? Has American history shown that, ultimately, most immigrants and their descendents embrace the principles that underlie the U.S. Constitution and American political culture?

Arguments for Huntington's Thesis

- **The core political values found in the Declaration of Independence and Constitution are essential to**

Implications of These Changes

The varied races, ethnic origins, sizes of the various age cohorts, family types, and even gender roles of Americans have important implications for government and politics. Today, most Americans (76 percent) believe that the number of legal immigrants should be kept below current levels.[15] (See Join the Debate: The Huntington Theory of Hispanization.) Eighty-five percent believe that illegal immigration is a serious problem, and several states have attempted to deny drivers licenses or access to other public services to undocumented immigrants. Many believe that the numbers of immigrants, legal and illegal, flooding onto our shores will lead to disastrous consequences. Such anti-immigration sentiments are hardly new. In fact, American history is replete with examples of Americans set against any new immigration. In the 1840s, for example, the Know Nothing Party arose in part to oppose immigration from Roman Catholic nations, charging that the pope was going to organize the slaughter of all Protestants in the United States. In the 1920s, the Ku Klux Klan, which had over 5 million members, called for barring immigration to stem the tide of Roman Catholics and Jews into the nation.

Changing racial, ethnic, and even age and family demographics also seem to intensify—at least for some—an us versus them attitude. For example, government affirma-

maintain freedom and protect rights. It may be that original American principles run the risk of being replaced by ideals that advocate forms of government or politics opposed to liberty, self-government, and individual rights, thus changing the character of the American regime.

- **American institutions and political culture pursue "Justice as the end of government . . . as the end of civil society."** American ideals can be a guide for all to live together effectively in peace and harmony, rather than an end in themselves. These principles allow most individuals to pursue their unique conception of the American dream, relatively free from interference by the government and others.
- **A shared language and civic education bind citizens together.** Teaching multiple languages and cultural viewpoints while denying a common civic education and political origin can create competing sources of identity that will weaken citizens' attachments to one another and to their government.

Arguments Against Huntington's Thesis

- **Historically, certain waves of immigrants were incorrectly thought to be opposed to American values.** Benjamin Franklin expressed concerns that German immigrants could not be assimilated into colonial American life because of their culture and history, and Irish-Catholic immigrants were accused of both giving allegiance to the pope and of being anti-republican in political outlook—fears that proved to be unfounded.
- **Bilingualism in the Hispanic community does not indicate the creation of competing sources of social and political identity.** According to an opinion poll coordinated by the *Washington Post* in 2000, a mere 10 percent of second-generation Hispanic immigrants rely on speaking only Spanish, which follows the pattern of English language adoption by previous waves of immigration to the United States.
- **American political culture is more than its Anglo-Protestant core.** A strength of the American experience is its ability to absorb different cultures and values and transform them into one unique political society. It is arguable that it took both the successive waves of immigration and the freeing of the slaves to move the United States toward the realization of the ideals espoused in the Declaration of Independence.

Questions

1. Is this latest wave of immigration truly unique in American history? If so, are core American political values in danger of becoming undermined?
2. Is American political culture more than its core principles and institutions? If so, what other values and institutions add to the United States' claim that it is a true "melting pot?"

Selected Readings

Samuel Huntington. *Who Are We? The Challenges to America's National Identity.* New York: Simon and Schuster, 2004.

Roger Daniels. *Guarding the Golden Door: American Immigration Policy and Immigrants Since 1882.* New York: Hill and Wang, 2004.

tive action programs, which were created in the 1960s to redress decades of overt racial discrimination, continue to be under attack. As discussed in chapter 6, vocal critics of affirmative action believe that these programs give minorities and women unfair advantages in the job market, as well as in access to higher education. Similarly, as more and more women graduated from college and entered the workforce, some men criticized efforts to widen opportunities for women, while many women complained that a glass ceiling barred their advancement to the highest levels in most occupations. Dramatic changes in educational and employment attainment for women, revealed in Table 1.2, also underscore these changes.

Demographics also affect politics and government because an individual's perspective influences how he or she hears debates on various issues. Thus, many African Americans viewed former football great O.J. Simpson's acquittal as vindication for decades of unjust treatment experienced by blacks in the criminal justice system, and the poor and working class viewed corporate collapses quite differently from many wealthy executives.

These cleavages and the emphasis many politicians put on our demographic differences play out in many ways in American politics. Baby Boomers and the elderly object to any changes in Social Security or Medicare, while those in Generation X vote

TABLE 1.2	Men and Women in a Changing Society			
	1970		2003	
	Men	*Women*	*Men*	*Women*
Estimated life expectancy	67	74	74	80
% high school graduates	53	52	45	65
% of BAs awarded	56	43	43	56
% of MAs awarded	60	40	41	59
% of PhDs awarded	87	13	55.1	44.9
% of JDs awarded	95	5	52.7	47.3
Median earnings	$26,760	$14,232	$29,101	$16,614
Single parents	1.2 million	5.6 million	4.4 million	13.1 million

Sources: 1970 data: U.S. Census Bureau, *1996 Statistical Abstract of the United States.* U.S. Department of Commerce, Economics and Statistics Administration, Bureau of the Census. 2003 data: U.S. Census Bureau, *2003 Statistical Abstract of the United States.*

for politicians who support change, if they vote at all. Many policies are targeted at one group or the other, further exacerbating differences—real or imagined—and lawmakers often find themselves the target of many different factions. This diversity can make it difficult to devise coherent policies to "promote the general welfare," as promised in the Constitution.

IDEOLOGY OF THE AMERICAN PUBLIC

political ideology
The coherent set of values and beliefs about the purpose and scope of government held by groups and individuals.

POLITICAL IDEOLOGY IS THE COHERENT SET of values and beliefs about the purpose and scope of government held by groups and individuals. "It is the means by which the basic values held by a party, class, group or individual are articulated."[16] Most Americans espouse liberalism or conservatism, although a growing number call themselves libertarians. Libertarians do not place themselves on the traditional liberal/conservative continuum used by political scientists.

In general, conservatives tend to identify with the Republican Party; liberals usually identify with the Democratic Party. Both parties, in fact, make frequent reference to their own conservative and liberal wings. Thus, many commentators have difficulty identifying ideological differences between liberal Republicans and conservative Democrats. These groups often make up the bulk of those people willing to identify themselves on the political spectrum as moderates, as is illustrated in Figure 1.4. However, in recent years there has been a growing split in ideology between the two groups (see Analyzing Visuals: Popular Vote by County—An Ideological Divide?).

Visual Literacy
Who Are Liberals and Conservatives?

Conservatives

conservative
One thought to believe that a government is best that governs least and that big government can only infringe on individual, personal, and economic rights.

According to William Safire's *New Political Dictionary*, a **conservative** "is a defender of the status quo who, when change becomes necessary in tested institutions or practices, prefers that it come slowly, and in moderation."[17] As shown in Table 1.3, Conservatives tend to believe that a government is best that governs least, and that big government can only infringe on individual, personal, and economic rights. They want less government, especially in terms of regulation of the economy. Conservatives favor local and state action over federal action, and emphasize fiscal responsibility, most notably in the form of balanced budgets. Conservatives are likely to support smaller, less activist governments and believe that domestic problems like homelessness, poverty, and discrimination are better dealt with by the private sector than by the government. They also tend to be more churchgoing and look to government to regulate some aspects of personal behavior such as abortion or same-sex marriage.

TABLE 1.3	Liberal? Conservative? Libertarian? Chart Your Views on These Issues				
				Government Support of:	
	Abortion Rights	*Environmental Regulation*	*Gun Control Laws*	*Poor*	*Domestic Unions*
Conservative	Oppose	Oppose	Oppose	Oppose	Oppose
Liberal	Favor	Favor	Favor	Favor	Favor
Libertarian	Favor	Oppose	Oppose	Oppose	Favor

Analyzing Visuals

POPULAR VOTE BY COUNTY—AN IDEOLOGICAL DIVIDE?

As the 2004 presidential election approached, analysts began to speak of a growing split in ideology that was occurring throughout the United States. After the election, a quick look at a U.S. map showing state-by-state Electoral College results made clear the split between those voters from the Northeast and West Coast and those in the vast expanse of states between these coasts. However, a careful look at a U.S. map showing the popular vote by county brings out several other demographic differences. After studying the map depicted below, answer the following questions: Note the numerous blocks of counties within the noncoastal states that voted for John Kerry rather than for George W. Bush, despite a state Electoral College win for Bush. What demographic factors might account for this trend? In a number of states—for example, Utah, Oklahoma, Nevada, Kansas, and Nebraska—Kerry won very few or no counties. What might account for this result? Do you recognize any other demographic aspects as you view the county map? Now take a look at the Electoral College map shown in chapter 13 of the text. Describe the differences you see between that map and the county-by-county map depicted below.

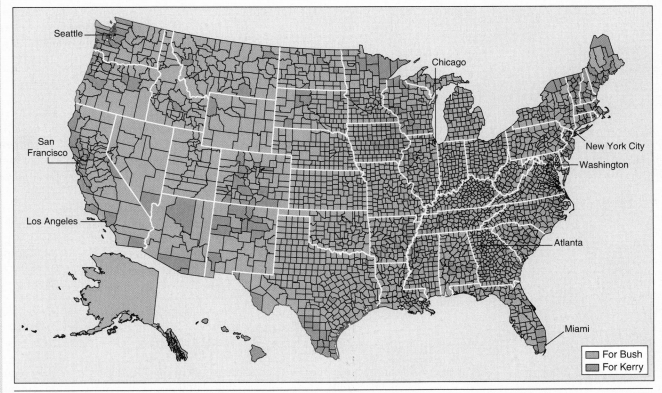

Sources: Associated Press; *Congressional Record;* Census Bureau.

Liberals

Liberalism is a political view held by those who "seek to change the political, economic, or social status quo to foster the development and well-being of the individual."[18] Safire defines a **liberal** as "currently one who believes in more government action to meet individual needs, originally one who resisted government encroachments on individual liberties."[19] Liberals now are considered to favor a big government that plays an active role in the economy. They also stress the need for the government to provide for the poor and homeless, to provide a wide array of other social services, and to take

liberal
One considered to favor extensive governmental involvement in the economy and the provision of social services and to take an activist role in protecting the rights of women, the elderly, minorities, and the environment.

FIGURE 1.4   Adult Self-
Identification as Liberal,
Moderate, or Conservative,
1974–2004. ■

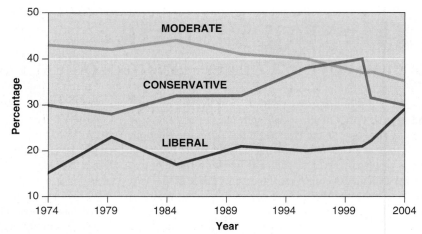

Source: Roper Center at the University of Connecticut, *Public Opinion Online.*

an activist role in protecting the rights of women, the elderly, minorities, gays and lesbians, and the environment. It is a political philosophy that has roots in the American Revolution and eighteenth-century liberalism. Today, many of its supporters refer to it as the "modern revival of classical liberalism."[20]

Libertarians

Libertarianism is a political philosophy based largely on individual freedom and the curtailment of state power. **Libertarians** have long believed in the evils of big government and stress that government should not involve itself in the plight of the people or attempt to remedy any social ills. Basically, libertarians, although a very diverse lot, favor a free market economy and an end to governmental intrusion in the area of personal liberties. Generation X-ers are more libertarian in political philosophy than any other age cohort. In 2004, nearly 600 members of the Libertarian Party held public office—more than the combined total of office holders representing all of the other third parties. Liberals criticize libertarian calls for elimination of all government-sponsored welfare and public works programs; conservatives bemoan libertarian calls for reductions in the defense budget and elimination of federal agencies such as the Central Intelligence Agency and the Federal Bureau of Investigation.

libertarian
One who favors a free market economy and no governmental interference in personal liberties.

Problems with Political Labels

When considering what it means when someone identifies himself or herself as a conservative, liberal, libertarian, or some other political philosophy, it is important to remember that the labels can be quite misleading and do not necessarily allow us to predict political opinions. In a perfect world, liberals would be liberal and conservatives would be conservative. Studies reveal, however, that many people who call themselves conservative actually take fairly liberal positions on many policy issues. In fact, anywhere from 20 percent to 60 percent will take a traditionally conservative position on one issue and a traditionally liberal position on another.[21] People who take conservative stances against "big government," for example, often support increases in spending for the elderly, education, or health care. It is also not unusual to encounter a person who could be considered liberal on social issues such as abortion and civil rights but conservative on economic or pocketbook issues. Moreover, libertarians, for example, often are against any governmental restrictions on abortion (a liberal view) but against any kind of welfare spending (a conservative

Photo courtesy: left, Greg Whitesell/UPI Photo/Landov; right, Roger L. Wollenberg/Landov

■ Representative Tom Delay (R–TX), the House Majority Whip, and Representative Nancy Pelosi (D–CA), the House Minority Leader, are both members of the 109th Congress. In the House they stand at opposite ends of the conservative (Delay) and liberal (Pelosi) spectrum and are two of their parties' most prominent figures.

view). Today, like libertarians, most Americans' positions on specific issues cut across liberal/conservative ideological boundaries to such a degree that new, more varied ideological categories may soon be needed to capture division within American political thought.

CURRENT ATTITUDES TOWARD AMERICAN GOVERNMENT

AMERICANS' VIEWS ABOUT AND EXPECTATIONS OF government and democracy affect the political system at all levels. It has now become part of our political culture to expect negative campaigns, dishonest politicians, and political pundits who make their living bashing politicians and the political process. How Americans view politics, the economy, and their ability to achieve the **American dream**—an American ideal of a happy and successful life to which many aspire, which often includes wealth, a house, a better life for one's children, and, for some, the ability to grow up to be president—also is influenced by their political ideology as well as by their social, economic, educational, and personal circumstances.

Since the early 1990s, the major sources of most individuals' on-the-air news—the four major networks (ABC, CBS, FOX, and NBC) along with CNN and C-SPAN—have been supplemented dramatically as the number of news and quasi-news outlets has grown exponentially. First there were weekly programs such as *Dateline* on the regular networks. Next came FOX News, MSNBC, and CNBC—all competing for similar audiences. During the 2004 election, for example, more people turned to a cable news program than to the regular networks for their political coverage. In addition, the Internet has quickly developed as an instantaneous source of news, as well as rumor, about politics. One online newsletter, the *Drudge Report*, was actually the first to break the story about the sexual relationship between President Bill Clinton and Monica Lewinsky.

As more and more news programs develop, the pressure on each network or news program to be the first with the news—often whether actually verifiable or not—multiplies exponentially, as was illustrated on Election Night 2000 when all of the networks rushed to call states for a particular candidate and to be the first to predict the overall

American dream
An American ideal of a happy, successful life, which often includes wealth, a house, a better life for one's children, and, for some, the ability to grow up to be president.

winner. The competition for news stories, as well as the instantaneous nature of these communications, still often highlights the negative, the sensational, the sound bite, and usually the extremes. It's hard to remain upbeat about America or politics amidst the media's focus on personality and scandal. It's hard to remain positive about the fate of Americans and their families if you listen to talk radio or watch talk news shows that feature guests trying to outshout each other or watch campaign ads that highlight only the negative.

High Expectations

In roughly the first 150 years of our nation's history, the federal government had few responsibilities, and its citizens had few expectations of it beyond national defense, printing money, and collecting tariffs and taxes. The state governments were generally far more powerful than the federal government in matters affecting the everyday lives of Americans (see chapters 3 and 4).

As the nation and its economy grew in size and complexity, the federal government took on more responsibilities, such as regulating some businesses, providing poverty relief, and inspecting food. Then, in response to the Great Depression of the 1930s, President Franklin D. Roosevelt's New Deal government programs proliferated in almost every area of American life, including job creation, income security, and aid to the poor. Since then, many Americans have looked to the government for solutions to all kinds of problems.

Politicians, too, have often contributed to rising public expectations by promising far more than they or government could deliver. Although President George W. Bush vowed to "leave no child behind," the high costs of waging war, a failing economy, and increases in the cost of homeland security left little money to fund that ambitious program to ensure minimal educational standards for all children nationwide.

As voters look to governments to solve a variety of problems from education to terrorism, their expectations are not always met. Unmet expectations have led to cynicism about government and apathy, as evidenced in low voter turnout. It may be that Americans have come to expect too much from the national government and must simply readjust their expectations. Still, as revealed in Table 1.4, after many years of more positive views toward a variety of governmental and nongovernmental institutions, Americans' confidence in most of these institutions fell quite sharply in recent years. And, as revealed in Politics Now: Deepening Distrust of the United States, views about America from abroad aren't too favorable, either.

Comparative

Comparing Political
Landscapes

A Missing Appreciation of the Good

During the Revolutionary period, average citizens were passionate about politics because the stakes—the very survival of the new nation—were so high. Until September 11, 2001, the stakes weren't readily apparent to many people. Today, however, if you don't have faith in America, its institutions, or symbols (and Table 1.4 shows that many of us don't), it becomes even easier to blame the government for all kinds of woes—personal as well as societal—or to fail to credit governments for the things they do well. Many Americans, for example, enjoy a remarkably high standard of living, and much of it is due to governmental programs and protections. (See Table 1.5 for quality of life measures.)

Even in the short time between when you get up in the morning and when you leave for classes or work, the government—or its rulings or regulations—pervades your life. The national or state governments, for example, set the standards for whether you wake up on Eastern, Central, Mountain, or Pacific Standard Time. The national government regulates the airwaves and

TABLE 1.4	Faith in Institutions				
Percentage of Americans Declaring They Had a "Great Deal" of Confidence in the Institution					
	1966	1975	1986	1996	2004
Congress	42%	13%	16%	8%	8%
Executive branch	41	13	21	10	25
The press	29	26	18	11	9
Business & industry	55	19	24	23	19
Medicine	73	51	46	45	19

Sources: *Newsweek* (January 8, 1996): 32; *Public Perspective* 8 (February/March 1994): 4. Data for 2004: *Public Opinion Online*.

Politics Now

DEEPENING DISAPPROVAL OF U.S. INVOLVEMENT IN IRAQ

Just as Americans' confidence in the institutions of government has fallen, so has global public opinion toward the United States. Although many citizens throughout the world stood solidly with the United States in the aftermath of the September 11, 2001, terrorist attacks, the actions of the United States in Iraq, as well as concerns about globalization, have made Americans and America the target of considerable wrath, even among citizens of normally strong allies. The Spanish electorate's stunning election within days after a terrorist attack of an anti–Iraq War prime minister who pledged to withdraw Spain's troops from Iraq underscores this shift in support for American foreign policy.

Although 67 percent of Americans polled in one 2004 survey expressed their belief that "the U.S.-led war on terrorism [was] a sincere effort to reduce international terrorism," most citizens of other nations did not agree, as is revealed in the figure shown here. Similarly, in Morocco,

Jordan, and Pakistan, George W. Bush's unfavorable ratings are higher than Osama bin Laden's! The majority of those polled in Morocco and Jordan even believe that suicide bombings carried out against Americans in Iraq are justified. Said former Secretary of State Madeleine Albright, "the broad mistrust of American leadership will be difficult to reverse."[a]

Surveys also find that most Western Europeans hold an unfavorable view of President George W. Bush and American foreign policy. Can you think of other reasons why the citizens of other nations distrust the United States? Are these concerns well founded? What might be the consequences of this mistrust of the United States when coupled with Americans' distrust of many political institutions in general?

[a] Quoted in Susan Page, "Survey Tracks Deepening Distrust Toward U.S.," *USA Today* (March 17, 2004): 7A.

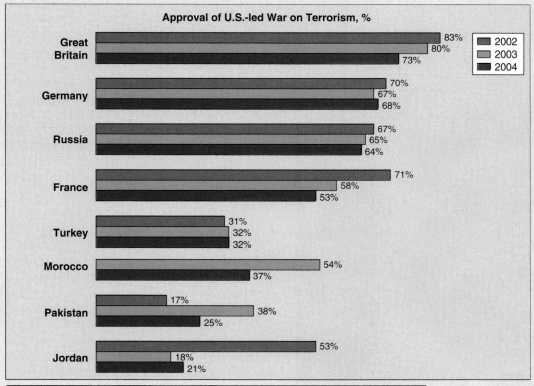

Approval of U.S.-led War on Terrorism, %

Country	2002	2003	2004
Great Britain	83%	80%	73%
Germany	70%	67%	68%
Russia	67%	65%	64%
France	71%	58%	53%
Turkey	31%	32%	32%
Morocco		54%	37%
Pakistan	17%	38%	25%
Jordan	53%	18%	21%

Source: A Year After Iraq War, Pew Global Attitudes Project, March 16, 2004.

licenses the radio or television broadcasts you might listen to or glance at as you eat and get dressed. States, too, regulate and tax telecommunications. Whether the water you use as you brush your teeth contains fluoride is a state or local governmental issue. The federal Food and Drug Administration inspects your breakfast meat and sets standards for the advertising on your cereal box, orange juice carton, and other food packaging. States set standards for food

TABLE 1.5 How Are Americans Really Doing?			
	1945	1970	2003
Life expectancy	65.9	70.8	75.4
Per capita income (1999 constant dollars)	$6,367	$12,816	$21,181
Adults who are high school grads	25%[a]	52.3%	84.1%
Adults who are college grads	5%[a]	10.7%	25.6%
Households with phones	46%	87%	94.2%
Households with cable TV	0%	4%	67.5%
Women in labor force	29%	38%	60%
Own their own home	46%	63%	66.9%
Below poverty rate	39.7%[b]	12.6%	11.8%

[a]1940 figure.   [b]1949 figure.

Source: U.S. Census Bureau, 2003 Statistical Abstract of the United States.

labeling. Are they really "lite," "high in fiber," or "fresh squeezed"? Usually, one or more levels of government are authorized to decide these matters.

Although all governments have problems, it is important to stress the good they can do. In the aftermath of the Great Depression in the United States, for example, the government created the Social Security program, which dramatically decreased poverty among the elderly. Our contract laws and judicial system provide an efficient framework for business, assuring people that they have a recourse in the courts should someone fail to deliver as promised. Government-guaranteed student loan programs make it possible for many students to attend college. Even something as seemingly mundane as our uniform bankruptcy laws help protect both a business enterprise and its creditors if the enterprise collapses.

Mistrust of Politicians

It's not difficult to see why Americans might be distrustful of politicians. In August 1998, after President Bill Clinton announced to the American public that he had misled them concerning his relationship with Monica Lewinsky, 45 percent said they were disgusted, 33 percent were angry, but only 18 percent were surprised, according to a poll conducted by the *Washington Post*.[22]

President Bill Clinton wasn't the only politician to incur the public's distrust. One 1998 poll conducted by the Pew Charitable Trusts found that 40 percent of those polled thought that most politicians were "crooks."[23] These perceptions are reinforced when politicians such as James McGreevey, the Democratic governor of New Jersey, are forced to resign under the threat of imminent corruption charges. Most politicians, however, are hard working and pride themselves on being able to deliver programs and services to the residents of their districts.

■ New Jersey Governor James McGreevey, shown here with his wife, as rumors of corruption surfaced he announced his homosexuality and his resignation from the governorship.

Photo courtesy: Daniel Hulshizer/AP/Wide World Photos

Voter Apathy

"Campaigns are the conversation of democracy," an observer once said.[24] But, a Gallup poll conducted after the 1988 presidential contest between George Bush and Michael Dukakis found that 30 percent of those who voted would have preferred to check off a "no confidence in either" box had they been given the choice.

Americans, unlike voters in most other societies, get an opportunity to vote on a host of candidates and issues, but some say those choices may just be too numbing. Responsible voters may simply opt not to go to the polls, fearing that they lack sufficient information of the vast array of candidates and issues facing them.

A Census Bureau report examining the reasons given by the millions of eligible voters who stayed home from the polls on Election Day in 2002 showed that being too busy was the single biggest reason Americans gave for not voting. The head of the Committee for the Study of the American Electorate thinks that time is just an excuse.[25] Instead, he believes many Americans don't vote because they lack real choices. Why vote, if your vote won't make much difference? In fact, Ralph Nader tried to run as an alternative to the two major parties in 2000 and 2004, arguing that there was little difference between Republicans and Democrats.

Some commentators have noted that nonvoting may even be a sign of contentment. If things are good, or you perceive that there is no need for change, why vote?

Redefining Our Expectations

Just as it is important to recognize that governments serve many important purposes, it is also important to recognize that government and politics are not static. Politics, moreover, involves conflicts over different and sometimes opposing ideologies, and these ideologies are very much influenced by one's racial, economic, and historical experiences. These divisions are real and affect the political process at all levels. It is clear to most Americans today that politics and government no longer can be counted on to cure all of America's ills. Government, however, will always play a major role. True political leaders will need to help Americans come to terms with America as it is today—not as it was in the past—real or imaginary. Perhaps a discussion on how "community" is necessary for everybody to get along (and necessary for democracy) is in order. Some democratic theorists suggest that the citizen-activist must be ultimately responsible for the resolution of these divisions.

The current frustration and dissatisfaction with politics and government may be just another phase, as the changing American body politic seeks to redefine its ideas about and expectations of government. This process is one that is likely to define politics well into the future, but the individualistic nature of the American system will have long-lasting consequences on how that redefinition can be accomplished. Americans want less government, but as they get older, they don't want less Social Security. They want lower taxes and better roads, but they don't want to pay for toll roads. They want better education for their children but lower expenditures on schools. They want greater security at airports but low fares and quick boarding. Some clearly want less for others but not themselves, a demand that puts politicians in the position of nearly always disappointing voters. This inability to please voters and find a middle ground undoubtedly led to the unprecedented number of members of Congress who have retired in recent years.

Politicians, as well as their constituents, are looking for ways to redefine the role of government, much in the same way that the Framers did when they met in Philadelphia to forge a solution between Americans' quest for liberty and freedom tempered by order and governmental authority. While citizens charge that it is still government as usual, a change is taking place in Washington, D.C. Sacrosanct programs such as Social Security and welfare continually are being reexamined, and some powers and responsibilities are slowly being returned to the states. Thus, the times may be different, but the questions about government and its role in our lives remain the same.

Although national crises such as the Civil War, the Great Depression, Watergate, and the 9/11 terrorist attacks created major turmoil, they demonstrated that our system can survive and even change in the face of enormous political, societal, and institutional pressures. Often, these crises have produced considerable reforms. The Civil War led

Photo courtesy: Reuters/Jamal Wilson/Archive Photos

■ Doris "Granny D" Haddock walked 3,200 miles across America to agitate for campaign finance reform in 2000. In 2004, Haddock, along with two friends, drove across the United States in a brightly painted camper. This time, Granny D was trying to motivate single women to vote. Although they make up 46 percent of all women eligible to vote, historically, unmarried women vote in fewer numbers than their married sisters. Underscoring her commitment, also in 2004, she ran unsuccessfully for the U.S. Senate from New Hampshire.

to the dismantling of the slavery system and to the passage of the Thirteenth, Fourteenth, and Fifteenth Amendments (see chapter 6), which planted the seeds of recognition of African Americans as American citizens. The Great Depression led to the New Deal and the creation of a government more actively involved in economic and social regulation. In the 1970s, the Watergate scandal and resignation of President Richard M. Nixon resulted in stricter ethics laws that have led to the resignation or removal of many unethical elected officials. Post 9/11, Americans seem more willing to accept limits on civil liberties to battle terrorism. At the same time, they are more aware of the nation's interdependence with the rest of the world. President George W. Bush even took the lead in an effort to export American democracy to the world while also educating the American public that these actions are never easy and without huge personal and economic costs.

SUMMARY

IN THIS CHAPTER, we have made the following points:

1. **Government: What It Is and Why We Need It**
Governments, which are made up of individuals and institutions, are the vehicles through which policies are made and affairs of state are conducted. We need governments to maintain order because governments alone can use force legitimately. Governments have many functions. In the U.S. context, most are included in the Preamble to the Constitution. Governments take many forms depending on the number who rule as well as whose interests are represented.

2. **Roots of American Government: Where Did the Ideas Come From?**
The American political system is based on several principles that have their roots in classical Greek ideas. The ideas of social contract theorists John Locke and Thomas Hobbes, who held the belief that people are free and equal by God-given right, have continuing implications for our ideas of the proper role of government in our indirect democracy.

3. **American Political Culture and the Characteristics of American Democracy**
Key characteristics of the political culture are personal liberty, equality, popular consent and majority rule, popular sovereignty, civil society, and individualism.

4. **Changing Characteristics of the American People**
Several characteristics of the American electorate can help us understand how the system continues to evolve and change. Chief among these are changes in size, population, and demographics.

5. **Ideology of the American Public**
Most Americans identify themselves on a traditional conservative-to-liberal continuum, with most believing themselves to be moderates. Libertarians often hold liberal views on many issues and conservative views on others.

6. **Current Attitudes Toward American Government**
Americans have high and often unrealistic expectations of government. At the same time, they often fail to appreciate how much their government actually does for them. Some of this failure may be due to Americans' general mistrust of politicians, which may explain some of the apathy evidenced in the electorate.

KEY TERMS

American dream, p. 25
citizen, p. 5
civil society, p. 13
conservative, p. 22
democracy, p. 9
direct democracy, p. 12
government, p. 5
indirect (representative) democracy, p. 12
liberal, p. 23
libertarian, p. 24
majority rule, p. 13
monarchy, p. 8
natural law, p. 13
oligarchy, p. 8
personal liberty, p. 12
political culture, p. 12
political ideology, p. 22
politics, p. 5
popular consent, p. 13
popular sovereignty, p. 13
republic, p. 12
social contract, p. 9
social contract theory, p. 9
totalitarianism, p. 8

SELECTED READINGS

Almond, Gabriel A., and Sidney Verba. *Civic Culture: Political Attitudes and Democracy in Five Nations*. Princeton, NJ: Princeton University Press, 1963.

Craig, Stephen C., and Stephen Earl Bennett, eds. *After the Boom: The Politics of Generation X*. Lanham, MD: Rowman and Littlefield, 1997.

Dahl, Robert A. *Polyarchy: Participation and Opposition*. New Haven, CT: Yale University Press, 1971.

Elshtain, Jean Bethke. *Democracy on Trial*. New York: Basic Books, 1995.

Glendon, Mary Ann. *Rights Talk: The Impoverishment of Political Discourse*. New York: Free Press, 1991.

Grossman, Lawrence K. *The Electronic Republic: Reshaping Democracy in the Information Age*. New York: Viking, 1995.

Hobbes, Thomas. *Leviathan*. Richard Tuck, ed. New York: Cambridge University Press, 1996.

Hochschild, Jennifer L. *Facing Up to the American Dream: Race, Class, and the Soul of the Nation*. Princeton, NJ: Princeton University Press, 1995.

Hunter, James Davison. *Culture Wars: The Struggle to Define America*. New York: Basic Books, 1991.

Jamieson, Kathleen Hall. *Dirty Politics: Deception, Distraction, and Democracy*. New York: Oxford University Press, 1992.

Locke, John. *Two Treatises of Government*. Peter Lasleti, ed. New York: Cambridge University Press, 1988.

Nye, Joseph S., Jr. *The Paradox of American Power: Why the World's Superpower Can't Go It Alone*. New York: Oxford University Press, 2002.

Putnam, Robert D. *Bowling Alone: Collapse and Revival of the American Community*. New York: Simon and Schuster, 2000.

Skocpol, Theda, and Morris Fiorina, eds. *Civic Engagement in American Democracy*. Washington, DC: Brookings Institution Press, 1999.

Verba, Sidney, Kay Schlozman, and Henry Brady. *Voice and Equality: Civic Volunteerism in American Politics*. Cambridge, MA: Harvard University Press, 1995.

Zakaria, Fareed. *The Future of Freedom: Illiberal Democracy at Home and Abroad*. New York: Norton, 2003.

WEB EXPLORATIONS

To connect with others who are interested in politics, see
http://www.pbs.org/news/news_government.html

For more on Aristotle and natural law, see
http://www.perseus.tufts.edu/cgi-bin/ptext?doc=Perseus%3Aabo%3Atlg%2C0086%2C035&query=1252a

For more on Thomas Hobbes and John Locke, see
http://www.iep.utm.edu/h/hobmoral.htm and
http://www.utm.edu/research/iep/l/locke.htm

To get a minute by minute update on U.S. population, see
http://www.census.gov/

For more detail on population projections, see
http://www.census.gov/population/www/projections/natsum.html

To learn more about Generation Y, see
http://www.cato.org/research/articles/firey-011203.html

For more information on families and household composition, see
http://www.census.gov/population/socdemo/hh-fam/98ppla.txt

For more information on conservatives, see
http://www.conservative.org/

For more information on liberals, see
http://www.turnleft.com/

For more information on libertarians, see
http://www.lp.org/ and
http://www.cato.org/

To find out your ideological stance, go to
http://people-press.org/fit/

For more information on the American electorate, see
http://www.census.gov/population/www/socdemo/voting/p20-542.html

Photo courtesy: Joseph Sohm; Visions of America/Corbis

The Constitution

AT AGE EIGHTEEN, all American citizens are eligible to vote in state and national elections. This has not always been the case. It took an amendment to the U.S. Constitution—one of only seventeen that have been added since the Bill of Rights was ratified in 1791—to guarantee the franchise to those under twenty-one years of age.

In 1942, during World War II, Representative Jennings Randolph (D–WV) proposed that the voting age be lowered to eighteen, believing that since young men were old enough to be drafted to fight and die for their country, they also should be allowed to vote. He continued to reintroduce his proposal during every session of Congress, and in 1954 President Dwight D. Eisenhower endorsed the idea in his State of the Union message. Presidents Lyndon B. Johnson and Richard M. Nixon—men who had also called upon the nation's young men to fight on foreign shores—echoed his appeal.[1]

During the 1960s, the campaign to lower the voting age took on a new sense of urgency as hundreds of thousands of young men were drafted to fight in Vietnam and thousands of men and women were killed in action. "Old Enough to Fight, Old Enough to Vote," was one popular slogan of the day. By 1970, four states—who under the U.S. Constitution are allowed to set the eligibility requirements for their voters—had lowered their voting ages to eighteen. Later that year, Congress passed legislation lowering the voting age in national, state, and local elections to eighteen.

The state of Oregon, however, challenged the constitutionality of the law in court, arguing that Congress had not been given the authority to establish a uniform voting age in state and local government under the Constitution. The U.S. Supreme Court agreed.[2] The decision from the sharply divided Court meant that those under age twenty-one could vote in national elections but that the states were free to prohibit them from voting in state and local elections. The decision presented the states with a logistical nightmare. States setting the voting age at twenty-one would be forced to keep two sets of registration books: one for voters twenty-one and over, and one for voters under twenty-one.

Jennings Randolph, by then a senator from West Virginia, reintroduced his proposed amendment to lower the national voting age to eighteen.[3] Within three months of the Supreme Court's decision, Congress sent the proposed Twenty-Sixth Amendment to the states for their ratification. The required three-fourths of the states ratified the amendment within three months—making its adoption on June 30, 1971, the quickest in the history of the constitutional amending process.

However, young people never have voted in large numbers. In spite of issues of concern to those under the age of twenty-five, including a possible draft, Internet privacy, reproductive rights, credit card and cell phone rules and regulations, rising college tuitions, and the continuance of student loan programs, until 2004 voter turnout among those age eighteen to twenty-four continued to decline. Massive voter registration drives and many voter awareness campaigns by groups including Rock the Vote and the HipHopAction Network, however, produced record numbers of young voters in 2004.

THE CONSTITUTION INTENTIONALLY WAS WRITTEN to forestall the need for amendment, and the process by which it could be changed or amended was made time consuming and difficult. Over the years, thousands of amendments—including those to prohibit child labor, provide equal rights for women, grant statehood to the District of Columbia, balance the federal budget, and ban flag burning—have been debated or sent to the states for their approval, only to die slow deaths. Only twenty-seven amendments have successfully made their way into the Constitution. What the Framers came up with in Philadelphia has continued to work, in spite of increasing demands on and dissatisfaction with our national government. Perhaps Americans are happier with the system of government created by the Framers than they realize.

The ideas that went into the making of the Constitution and the ways in which it has evolved to address the problems of a growing and ever changing nation are at the core of our discussion in this chapter.

- First, we will examine *the origins of a new nation* and the circumstances surrounding the Declaration of Independence and the break with Great Britain.
- Second, we will discuss *the first attempt at American government* created by the *Articles of Confederation*.
- Third, we will examine the circumstances surrounding *writing a Constitution* in Philadelphia.
- Fourth, we will review the results of the Framers' efforts—*the U.S. Constitution*.
- Fifth, we will present *the drive for ratification* of the new government.
- Finally, we will address *methods of amending the Constitution*.

THE ORIGINS OF A NEW NATION

STARTING IN THE EARLY SEVENTEENTH CENTURY, colonists came to the New World for a variety of reasons. Often, as detailed in chapter 1, it was to escape religious persecution. Others came seeking a new start on a continent where land was plentiful. The independence and diversity of the settlers in the New World made the question of how best to rule the new colonies a tricky one. More than merely an ocean separated England from the colonies; the colonists were independent people, and it soon became clear that the Crown could not govern its subjects in the colonies with the same close rein used at home. King James I thus allowed some local participation in decision making through arrangements such as the first elected colonial assembly, the Virginia House of Burgesses, and the elected General Court that governed the Massachusetts Bay colony after 1629. Almost all the colonists agreed that the king ruled by divine right, but English monarchs allowed the colonists significant liberties in terms of self-government, religious practices, and economic organization. For 140 years, this system worked fairly well.[4]

By the early 1760s, however, a century and a half of physical separation, development of colonial industry, and the relative self-governance of the colonies led to weakening ties with—and loyalties to—the Crown. By this time, each of the thirteen colonies had drafted its own written constitution, which provided the fundamental rules or laws for each colony. Moreover, many of the most oppressive British traditions—feudalism, a rigid class system, and the absolute authority of the king—were absent in the New World. Land was abundant. The guild and craft systems that severely limited entry into many skilled professions in England did not exist in the colonies. Although the role of religion was central to the lives of most colonists, there was no single state church, and the British practice of compulsory tithing (giving a fixed percentage of one's earnings to the state-sanctioned and -supported church) was nonexistent.

Trade and Taxation

Mercantilism, an economic theory designed to increase a nation's wealth through the development of commercial industry and a favorable balance of trade, justified Britain's maintenance of strict import/export controls on the colonies. After 1650, for example, Parliament passed a series of navigation acts to prevent its chief rival, Holland, from trading with the English colonies. From 1650 until well into the 1700s, England tried to regulate colonial imports and exports, believing that it was critical to export more goods than it imported as a way of increasing the gold and silver in its treasury. These policies, however, were difficult to enforce and were widely ignored by the colonists, who saw little self-benefit in them. Thus, for years, an unwritten agreement existed. The colonists relinquished to the Crown and the British Parliament the authority to regulate trade and conduct international affairs, but they retained the right to levy their own taxes.

> **mercantilism**
> An economic theory designed to increase a nation's wealth through the development of commercial industry and a favorable balance of trade.

This fragile agreement was soon put to the test. The French and Indian War, fought from 1756 to 1763 on the western frontier of the colonies and in Canada, was part of a global war initiated by the British. This American phase of the Seven Years' War was fought between England and France with its Indian allies. In North America, its immediate cause was the rival claims of those two European nations for the lands between the Allegheny Mountains and the Mississippi River. The Treaty of Paris (signed in 1763) signaled the end of the war. The colonists expected that with the Indian problem on the western frontier now under control, westward migration and settlement could begin in earnest. In 1763, they were shocked when the Crown decreed that there was to be no further westward movement by British subjects. Parliament believed that expansion into Indian territory would lead to new expenditures for the defense of the settlers, draining the British treasury, which had yet to recover from the high cost of waging the war.

To raise money to pay for the war as well as the expenses of administering the colonies, Parliament enacted the Sugar Act in 1764, which placed taxes on sugar, wine, coffee, and other products commonly exported to the colonies. A postwar colonial depression heightened resentment of the tax. Major protest, however, failed to materialize until

Photo courtesy: Painting by John Singleton Copley. Courtesy, Museum of Fine Arts, Boston. Reproduced with permission. © 2001, Museum of Fine Arts, Boston. All rights reserved.

■ Today, Samuel Adams (1722–1803) is well known for the beer that bears his name. His original claim to fame was as a leader against the British and loyalist oppressors (although he did bankrupt his family's brewery business). As a member of the Massachusetts legislature, he advocated defiance of the Stamp Act. With the passage of the Townshend Acts in 1767, he organized a letter-writing campaign urging other colonies to join in resistance. Later, in 1772, he founded the Committees of Correspondence to unite the colonies.

Stamp Act Congress
Meeting of representatives of nine of the thirteen colonies held in New York City in 1765, during which representatives drafted a document to send to the king listing how their rights had been violated.

imposition of the Stamp Act by the British Parliament in 1765. This law required that all paper items bought and sold in the colonies carry a stamp mandated by the Crown. The tax itself was not offensive to the colonists. However, they feared this act would establish a precedent for the British Parliament not only to regulate commerce in the colonies, but also to raise revenues from the colonists without the approval of the colonial governments. Around the colonies, the political cry "no taxation without representation" became prominent. To add insult to injury, in 1765, Parliament passed the Quartering Act, which required the colonists to furnish barracks or provide living quarters within their own homes for British troops.

Most colonists, especially those in New England, where these acts hit merchants hardest, were outraged. Men throughout the colonies organized the Sons of Liberty, under the leadership of Samuel Adams and Patrick Henry. Women formed the Daughters of Liberty. Protests against the Stamp Act were violent and loud. Riots, often led by the Sons of Liberty, broke out. They were especially violent in Boston, where the colonial governor's home was burned by an angry mob, and British stamp agents charged with collecting the tax were threatened. A boycott of goods needing the stamps as well as British imports also was organized.

First Steps Toward Independence

In 1765, nine of the thirteen colonies sent representatives to a meeting in New York City, where a detailed list of Crown violations of the colonists' fundamental rights was drafted. Known as the **Stamp Act Congress,** this gathering was the first official meeting of the colonies and the first step toward a unified nation. Attendees defined what they thought to be the proper relationship between colonial governments and the British Parliament; they ardently believed Parliament had no authority to tax them without representation in that body. In contrast, the British believed that direct representation of the colonists was impractical and that members of Parliament represented the best interests of all the English, including the colonists.

The Stamp Act Congress and its petitions to the Crown did little to stop the onslaught of taxing measures. Parliament did, however, repeal the Stamp Act and revise the Sugar Act in 1766, largely because of the uproar made by British merchants who were losing large sums of money as a result of the boycotts. Rather than appeasing the colonists, however, these actions emboldened them to increase their resistance. In 1767, Parliament enacted the Townshend Acts, which imposed duties on all kinds of colonial imports, including tea. Response from the Sons and Daughters of Liberty was immediate. Another boycott was announced, and almost all colonists gave up their favorite drink in a united show of resistance to the tax and British authority.[5] Tensions continued to run high, especially after the British sent 4,000 troops to Boston. On

March 5, 1770, English troops opened fire on a mob that included disgruntled dock workers, whose jobs had been taken by British soldiers, and members of the Sons of Liberty, who were taunting the soldiers in front of the Boston Customs House. Five colonists were killed in what became known as the Boston Massacre. Following this confrontation, all duties except those on tea were lifted. The tea tax, however, continued to be a symbolic irritant. In 1772, at the suggestion of Samuel Adams, Boston and other towns around Massachusetts set up **Committees of Correspondence** to articulate ideas and keep communications open around the colony. By 1774, twelve colonies had formed committees to maintain a flow of information among like-minded colonists.

Meanwhile, despite dissent in England over the treatment of the colonies, Parliament passed another tea tax designed to shore up the sagging sales of the East India Company, a British exporter of tea. The colonists' boycott had left that British trading house with more than 18 million pounds of tea in its warehouses. To rescue British merchants from disaster, in 1773 Parliament passed the Tea Act, granting a monopoly to the financially strapped East India Company to sell the tea imported from Britain. The company was allowed to funnel business to American merchants loyal to the Crown, thereby undercutting colonial merchants, who could sell only tea imported from other nations. The effect was to drive down the price of tea and to hurt colonial merchants, who were forced to buy tea at the higher prices from other sources.

When the next shipment of tea arrived in Boston from Great Britain, the colonists responded by throwing the Boston Tea Party. Similar tea parties were held in other colonies. When the news of these actions reached King George, he flew into a rage against the actions of his disloyal subjects. "The die is now cast," the king told his prime minister. "The colonies must either submit or triumph."

King George's first act of retaliation was to persuade Parliament to pass the Coercive Acts in 1774. Known in the colonies as the Intolerable Acts, they contained a key provision calling for a total blockade of Boston Harbor until restitution was made for the tea. Another provision reinforced the Quartering Act. It gave royal governors the authority to house British soldiers in the homes of private citizens, allowing Britain to send an additional 4,000 soldiers to patrol Boston.

Committees of Correspondence
Organizations in each of the American colonies created to keep colonists abreast of developments with the British; served as powerful molders of public opinion against the British.

Photo courtesy: Bettmann/Corbis

■ To hurt American merchants loyal to the crown, colonists threw a "Boston Tea Party" on December 16, 1773.

■ Paul Revere's engraving of the Boston Massacre was potent propaganda. Five men were killed, not seven, as the legend states, and the rioters in front of the State House (left) were scarcely as docile as Revere portrayed them.

Photo courtesy: Collection of the New York Historical Society, negative no. 29405

The First Continental Congress

The British could never have guessed how the cumulative impact of these actions would unite the colonists. Samuel Adams's Committees of Correspondence spread the word, and food and money were sent to the people of Boston from all over the thirteen colonies. The tax itself was no longer the key issue; now the extent of British authority over the colonies was the far more important question. At the request of the colonial assemblies of Massachusetts and Virginia, all but Georgia's colonial assembly agreed to select a group of delegates to attend a continental congress authorized to communicate with the king on behalf of the now-united colonies.

First Continental Congress
Meeting held in Philadelphia from September 5 to October 26, 1774, in which fifty-six delegates (from every colony except Georgia) adopted a resolution in opposition to the Coercive Acts.

The **First Continental Congress** met in Philadelphia from September 5 to October 26, 1774. It was made up of fifty-six delegates from Connecticut, Delaware, Maryland, Massachusetts, New Hampshire, New Jersey, North Carolina, Pennsylvania, South Carolina, Rhode Island, and Virginia. Only Georgia refused to send any delegates. The colonists had yet to think of breaking with Great Britain; at this point, they simply wanted to iron out their differences with the king. By October, they had agreed on a series of resolutions to oppose the Coercive Acts and to establish a formal organization to boycott British goods. The Congress also drafted a Declaration of Rights and Resolves, which called for colonial rights of petition and assembly, trial by peers, freedom from a standing army, and the selection of representative councils to levy taxes. The Congress further agreed that if the king did not capitulate to their demands, they would meet again in Philadelphia in May 1775.

The Second Continental Congress

King George refused to yield, tensions continued to rise, and a **Second Continental Congress** was deemed necessary. Before it could meet, fighting broke out early in the morning of April 19, 1775, at Lexington and Concord, Massachusetts, with what Ralph Waldo Emerson called "the shot heard round the world." Eight colonial soldiers, called Minutemen, were killed, and 16,000 British troops besieged Boston.

When the Second Continental Congress convened in Philadelphia on May 10, 1775, delegates were united by their increased hostility to Great Britain. In a final attempt to avert conflict, the Second Continental Congress adopted the Olive Branch Petition on July 5, 1775, asking the king to end hostilities. King George rejected the petition and sent an additional 20,000 troops to quell the rebellion. As a precautionary measure, the Congress already had appointed George Washington of Virginia as commander in chief of the Continental Army. The selection of a southern leader was a strategic decision, because up to that time British oppression largely was felt in the Northeast. In fact, the war essentially had begun with the shots fired at Lexington and Concord in April 1775.

In January 1776, Thomas Paine, with the support and encouragement of Benjamin Franklin, issued (at first anonymously) *Common Sense*, a pamphlet forcefully arguing for independence from Great Britain. In frank, easy-to-understand language, Paine denounced the corrupt British monarchy and offered reasons to break with Great Britain. "The blood of the slain, the weeping voice of nature cries 'Tis Time to Part,'" wrote Paine. *Common Sense*, widely read throughout the colonies, was instrumental in changing minds in a very short time. In its first three months of publication, the forty-seven-page *Common Sense* sold 120,000 copies, the equivalent of almost 22 million books, given the current U.S. population. One copy of *Common Sense* was in distribution for every thirteen people in the colonies—a truly astonishing number, given the low literacy rate.

Common Sense galvanized the American public against reconciliation with England. On May 15, 1776, Virginia became the first colony to call for independence, instructing one of its delegates to the Second Continental Congress to introduce a resolution to that effect. On June 7, 1776, Richard Henry Lee of Virginia rose to move "that these United Colonies are, and of right ought to be, free and independent States, and that all connection between them and the State of Great Britain is, and ought to be, dissolved." His three-part resolution—which called for independence, the formation of foreign alliances, and preparation of a plan of **confederation**—triggered hot debate among the delegates. A proclamation of independence from Great Britain was treason, a crime punishable by death. Although six of the thirteen colonies had already instructed their delegates to vote for independence, the Second Continental Congress was suspended to allow its delegates to return home to their respective colonial legislatures for final instructions. Independence was not a move to be taken lightly.

Photo courtesy: Bettmann/Corbis

■ After the success of *Common Sense*, Thomas Paine wrote a series of essays collectively entitled *The Crisis* to arouse colonists' support for the Revolutionary War. The first *Crisis* papers contain the famous words "These are the times that try men's souls."

Second Continental Congress
Meeting that convened in Philadelphia on May 10, 1775, at which it was decided that an army should be raised and George Washington of Virginia was named commander in chief.

confederation
Type of government where the national government derives its powers from the states; a league of independent states.

The Declaration of Independence

Declaration of Independence
Document drafted by Thomas Jefferson in 1776 that proclaimed the right of the American colonies to separate from Great Britain.

Committees were set up to consider each point of Richard Henry Lee's proposal. A committee of five was selected to begin work on a **Declaration of Independence.** The Congress selected Benjamin Franklin of Pennsylvania, John Adams of Massachusetts, Robert Livingston of New York, and Roger Sherman of Connecticut as members of the committee. Adams lobbied hard for a Southerner to add balance. Thus, owing to his southern origin as well as his "peculiar felicity of expression," Thomas Jefferson of Virginia was selected as chair.

On July 2, 1776, twelve of the thirteen colonies (with New York abstaining) voted for independence. Two days later, the Second Continental Congress voted to adopt the Declaration of Independence penned by Thomas Jefferson. On July 9, 1776, the Declaration, now with the approval of New York, was read aloud in Philadelphia.[6]

In simple but eloquent language, Jefferson set out the reasons for the colonies' separation from Great Britain. Most of his stirring rhetoric drew heavily on the works of seventeenth- and eighteenth-century political philosophers, particularly the English philosopher John Locke (see chapter 1), who had written South Carolina's first constitution, a colonial charter drawn up in 1663 when South Carolina was formed by King Charles II and mercantile houses in England. In fact, many of the words in the opening of the Declaration of Independence closely resemble passages from Locke's *Two Treatises of Government.*

Locke was a proponent of social contract theory, a philosophy of government that held that governments exist based on the consent of the governed. According to Locke, people leave the state of nature and agree to set up a government largely for the protection of property. In colonial times, property did not mean just land. Locke's notion of property rights included life, liberty, and material possessions. Furthermore, argued Locke, individuals who give their consent to be governed have the right to resist or remove rulers who deviate from those purposes. Such a government exists for the good of its subjects and not for the benefit of those who govern. Thus, rebellion was the ultimate sanction against a government that violated the rights of its citizens.

■ The author of the Declaration of Independence, Thomas Jefferson (1743–1826) was a philosopher, farmer, inventor, and diplomat. He also served as the third president of the United States. Although Jefferson considered liberty an unalienable right of humanity, he owned slaves his entire life. In 1998, DNA evidence combined with historical documentation convinced many scholars and members of the public that Jefferson had fathered at least one child, Eston Hemings, by his slave Sally Hemings. Here, descendants of that union celebrate those findings.

Photo courtesy: Richmond Times-Dispatch, Bob Brown/AP/Wide World Photos

It is easy to see the colonists' debt to John Locke. In ringing language, the Declaration of Independence proclaims:

> We hold these truths to be self-evident, that all men are created equal, that they are endowed by their Creator with certain unalienable Rights, that among these are Life, Liberty and the pursuit of Happiness.

Jefferson and others in attendance at the Second Continental Congress wanted to have a document that would stand for all time, justifying their break with the Crown and clarifying their notions of the proper form of government. So, Jefferson continued:

> That to secure these rights, Governments are instituted among Men, deriving their just powers from the consent of the governed. That whenever any Form of Government becomes destructive of these ends, it is the Right of the People to alter or abolish it, and to institute new Government, laying its foundation on such Principles and organizing its Powers in such form, as to them shall seem most likely to effect their Safety and Happiness.

After this stirring preamble, the Declaration went on to enumerate the wrongs that the colonists had suffered under British rule. All pertained to the denial of personal rights and liberties, many of which would later be guaranteed by the U.S. Constitution through the Bill of Rights.

After the Declaration was signed and transmitted to the king, the Revolutionary War was fought with a greater vengeance. At a September 1776 peace conference on Staten Island (New York), British General William Howe demanded revocation of the Declaration of Independence. Washington's Continental Army refused, and the war raged on while the Continental Congress attempted to fashion a new united government.

THE FIRST ATTEMPT AT GOVERNMENT: THE ARTICLES OF CONFEDERATION

AS NOTED EARLIER, the British had no written constitution. The delegates to the Second Continental Congress were attempting to codify arrangements that had never before been put into legal terminology. To make things more complicated, the delegates had to arrive at these decisions in a wartime atmosphere. Nevertheless, in late 1777, the **Articles of Confederation,** creating a loose "league of friendship" between the thirteen sovereign or independent states, were passed by the Congress and presented to the states for their ratification.

Articles of Confederation
The compact among the thirteen original states that was the basis of their government. Written in 1776, the Articles were not ratified by all the states until 1781.

The Articles created a type of government called a confederation or confederacy. Unlike Great Britain's unitary system of government, wherein all of the powers of the government reside in the national government, the national government in a confederation derives all of its powers directly from the states. Thus, the national government in a confederacy is weaker than the sum of its parts, and the states often consider themselves independent nation-states linked together only for limited purposes such as national defense. So, the Articles of Confederation proposed the following:

- A national government with a Congress empowered to make peace, coin money, appoint officers for an army, control the post office, and negotiate with Indian tribes.
- Each state's retention of its independence and sovereignty, or ultimate authority, to govern within its territories.
- One vote in the Continental Congress for each state, regardless of size.
- The vote of nine states to pass any measure (a unanimous vote for any amendment).
- The selection and payment of delegates to the Congress by their respective state legislatures.

The Articles, finally ratified by all thirteen states in March 1781, fashioned a government that reflected the political philosophy of the times.[7] Although it had its flaws, the government under the Articles of Confederation saw the nation through the Revolutionary War. However, once the British surrendered in 1781, and the new nation found itself no longer united by the war effort, the government quickly fell into chaos.

Problems Under the Articles of Confederation

In today's America, we ship goods, travel by car and airplane across state lines, make interstate phone calls, and more. Over 250 years ago, Americans had great loyalties to their states and often did not even think of themselves as Americans. This lack of national sentiment or loyalty in the absence of a war to unite the citizenry fostered a reluctance to give any power to the national government. By 1784, just one year after the Revolutionary Army was disbanded, governing the new nation under the Articles of Confederation proved unworkable.[8] In fact, historians refer to the chaotic period from 1781 to 1789 when the former colonies were governed under the Articles of Confederation as the "critical period." Congress rarely could assemble the required quorum of nine states to conduct business. Even when it did meet, there was little agreement among the states on any policies. To raise revenue to pay off war debts and run the government, various land, poll, and liquor taxes were proposed. But, since Congress had no specific power to tax, all these proposals were rejected. At one point, Congress was even driven out of Philadelphia (then the capital of the new national government) by its own unpaid army.

Although the national government could coin money, it had no resources to back up the value of its currency. Continental dollars were worth little, and trade between states became chaotic as some states began to coin their own money. Another weakness was that the Articles of Confederation did not allow Congress to regulate commerce among the states and with foreign nations. As a result, individual states attempted to enter into agreements with other countries, and foreign nations were suspicious of trade agreements made with the Congress of the Confederation. In 1785, for example, Massachusetts banned the export of goods in British ships, and Pennsylvania levied heavy duties on ships of nations that had no treaties with the U.S. government.

Fearful of a chief executive who would rule tyrannically, the draftees of the Articles made no provision for an executive branch of government that would be responsible for executing, or implementing, laws passed by the legislative branch. Instead, the president was merely the presiding officer at meetings. John Hanson, a former member of the Maryland House of Delegates and of the First Continental Congress, was the first person to preside over the Congress of the Confederation. Therefore, he is often referred to as the first president of the United States.

The Articles of Confederation, moreover, had no provision for a judicial system to handle the growing number of economic conflicts and boundary disputes among the individual states. Several states claimed the same lands to the west, and Pennsylvania and Virginia went to war with each other.

The Articles' greatest weakness, however, was the lack of a strong central government. Although states had operated independently before the war, during the war they acceded to the national government's authority to wage armed conflict. Once the war was over, however, each state resumed its sovereign status and was unwilling to give up rights, such as the power to tax, to an untested national government. Consequently, the government was unable to force the states to abide by the provisions of the Treaty of Paris, signed in 1783, which officially ended the war. For example, states passed laws to allow debtors who owed money to Great Britain to postpone payment. States also opted not to restore property to citizens who had remained loyal to Britain during the war. Both actions were in violation of the treaty.

The crumbling economy was made worse by a series of bad harvests that failed to produce cash crops, thus making it difficult for farmers to get out of debt quickly.

George Washington and Alexander Hamilton, both interested in the questions of trade and frontier expansion, soon saw the need for a stronger national government with the authority to act to solve some of these problems. They were not alone. In 1785 and 1786, some state governments began to discuss ways to strengthen the national government. Finally, several states joined together to call for a convention in Philadelphia in 1787.

Shays's Rebellion

Before the Constitutional Convention could take place, however, new unrest broke out in America. In 1780, Massachusetts adopted a constitution that appeared to favor the interests of the wealthy. Property-owning requirements barred the lower and middle classes from voting and office holding. And, as the economy of Massachusetts worsened, banks foreclosed on the farms of many Massachusetts Continental Army veterans who were waiting for promised bonuses that the national government had no funds to pay. The last straw came in 1786, when the Massachusetts legislature enacted a new law requiring the payment of all debts in cash. Frustration and outrage at the new law caused Daniel Shays, a former Revolutionary War army captain, and 1,500 armed, disgruntled farmers to march to Springfield, Massachusetts. This group forcibly restrained the state court located there from foreclosing on the mortgages on their farms.

The Congress immediately authorized the secretary of war to call for a new national militia. A $530,000 appropriation was made for this purpose, but every state except Virginia refused Congress's request for money. The governor of Massachusetts then tried to raise a state militia, but because of the poor economy, the state treasury lacked the necessary funds to support his action. Frantic attempts to collect private financial support were made, and a militia finally was assembled. By February 4, 1787, this privately paid force put a stop to what was called **Shays's Rebellion.** The failure of the Congress to muster an army to put down the rebellion provided a dramatic example of the weaknesses inherent in the Articles of Confederation and shocked the nation's leaders into recognizing the new government's overwhelming inadequacies.

Photo courtesy: Bettmann/Corbis

■ With Daniel Shays in the lead, a group of farmers and Revolutionary War veterans marched on the courthouse in Springfield, Massachusetts, to stop the state court from foreclosing on farmers' mortgages.

Shays's Rebellion
A 1786 rebellion in which an army of 1,500 disgruntled and angry farmers led by Daniel Shays marched to Springfield, Massachusetts, and forcibly restrained the state court from foreclosing mortgages on their farms.

THE MIRACLE AT PHILADELPHIA: WRITING A CONSTITUTION

ON FEBRUARY 21, 1787, in the throes of economic turmoil and with domestic tranquility gone haywire, the Congress passed an official resolution. It called for a Constitutional Convention in Philadelphia for "the sole and express purpose of revising the Articles of Confederation."

However, many delegates that gathered in sweltering Philadelphia on May 25, 1787, were prepared to take potentially treasonous steps to preserve the union. For example, on the first day the convention was in session, Edmund Randolph and James Madison of Virginia proposed fifteen resolutions creating an entirely new government (later known as the Virginia Plan). Their enthusiasm, however, was not universal. Many delegates, including William Paterson of New Jersey, considered these resolutions to

Photo courtesy: William Thomas Cain/Getty Images

■ July 4th celebration at Independence Hall in Philadelphia, Pennsylvania, where the Declaration was first read aloud.

constitution
A document establishing the structure, functions, and limitations of a government.

be in violation of the convention's charter, and proposed the New Jersey Plan, which took greater steps to preserve the Articles.

These proposals met heated debate on the convention's floor. Eventually the Virginia Plan triumphed following a declaration from Randolph that, "When the salvation of the Republic is at stake, it would be treason not to propose what we found necessary."

Though the basic structure of the new government was established, the work of the Constitutional Convention was not complete. These differences were resolved through a series of compromises, and less than one hundred days after the meeting convened, the Framers created a new government to submit to the electorate for its approval.

The Characteristics and Motives of the Framers

Fifty-five of the seventy-four delegates ultimately chosen by their state legislatures to attend the Constitutional Convention labored long and hard that hot summer. Owing to the high stakes of their action, all of the convention's work was conducted behind closed doors. George Washington of Virginia, who was unanimously elected the convention's presiding officer, cautioned delegates not to reveal details of the convention even to their family members. Further, the delegates agreed to accompany Benjamin Franklin of Pennsylvania to all of his meals. They feared that the normally gregarious gentleman might get carried away with the mood or by liquor and inadvertently let news of the proceedings slip from his tongue.

All of the delegates to the Constitutional Convention were men; hence, they often are referred to as the "Founding Fathers." Most of them, however, were quite young; many were in their twenties and thirties, and only one—Franklin, at eighty-one—was quite old. Several owned slaves. (See Analyzing Visuals: Who Were the Framers?) Here, we generally refer to the delegates as the Framers, because their work provided the framework for our new government. The Framers brought with them a vast amount of political, educational, legal, and business experience. It is clear that they were an exceptional lot who ultimately produced a brilliant **constitution,** or document establishing the structure, functions, and limitations of a government.

However, debate about the Framers' motives filled the air during the ratification struggle and has provided grist for the mill of historians and political scientists over the years. In his *Economic Interpretation of the Constitution of the United States* (1913), Charles A. Beard argued that the 1780s were a critical period not for the nation as a whole, but rather for businessmen who feared that a weak, decentralized government could harm their economic interests.[9] Beard argued that the merchants wanted a strong national government to promote industry and trade, to protect private property, and most importantly, to ensure payment of the public debt—much of which was owed to them. Therefore, according to Beard, the Constitution represents "an economic document drawn with superb skill by men whose property interests were immediately at stake."[10]

By the 1950s, this view had fallen into disfavor when other historians were unable to find direct links between wealth and the Framers' motives for establishing the Constitution and others faulted Beard's failure to consider the impact of religion and individual views about government.[11] In the 1960s, however, another group of historians began to argue that social and economic factors were, in fact, important motives for supporting the Constitution. In *The Anti-Federalists* (1961), Jackson Turner Main posited that while the Constitution's supporters might not have been the united group of creditors suggested by Beard, they were wealthier, came from higher social strata, and had greater concern for maintaining the prevailing social order than the general

Analyzing Visuals

WHO WERE THE FRAMERS?

Who were the Framers of the U.S. Constitution? Of the fifty-five delegates who attended some portion of the Philadelphia meetings, seventeen were slaveholders who owned approximately 1,400 slaves. (George Washington, George Mason, and John Rutledge held the greatest number of slaves at the time of the convention.) In terms of education, thirty-one went to college; twenty-four did not. Most of those who did not attend college were trained as business, legal, and printing apprentices. Seven delegates signed both the U.S. Constitution and the Declaration of Independence. After studying the graph and the material on writing and signing the Constitution in this chapter, answer the follow-

ing critical thinking questions: What is the relationship, if any, between the number of a state's delegates who served in the Continental Congresses and the number of the state's signers of the Constitution? What is the relationship, if any, between a state's population (shown in parentheses in the graph) and the number of the state's signers of the U.S. Constitution? What does that suggest about the conflict between the large states and small states? What is the relationship, if any, between the number of a state's delegates who were slaveholders and the number of the state's signers of the U.S. Constitution? What does that suggest about the conflicts over slavery at the convention?

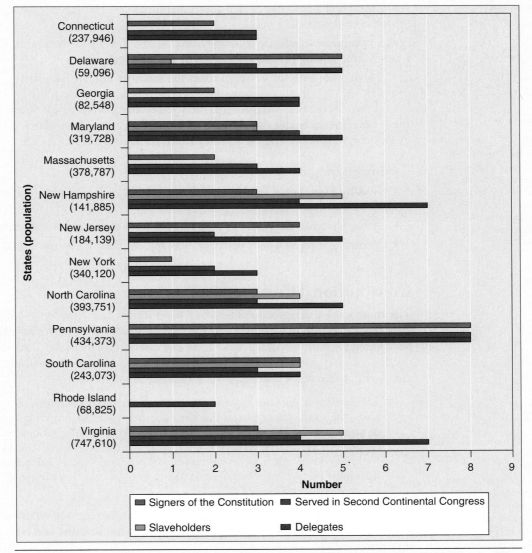

Sources: Clinton Rossiter, *The Grand Convention* (New York: Macmillan, 1966); National Archives and Records Administration, "The Founding Fathers: A Brief Overview," http://www.archives.gov/exhibit_hall/charters_of_freedom/constitution/founding_fathers_overview.html.

public.[12] In 1969, Gordon S. Wood's *The Creation of the American Republic* resurrected this debate. Wood deemphasized economics to argue that major social divisions explained different groups' support for (or opposition to) the new Constitution. He concluded that the Framers were representatives of a class that favored order and stability over some of the more radical ideas that had inspired the American Revolutionary War and the break with Britain.[13]

The Virginia and New Jersey Plans

The less populous states were concerned with being lost in any new system of government where states were not treated as equals regardless of population. It is not surprising that a large state and then a small one, Virginia and New Jersey, respectively weighed in with ideas about how the new government should operate.

The **Virginia Plan** called for a national system based heavily on the European nation-state model, wherein the national government derives its powers from the people and not from the member states.

Its key features included:

■ Creation of a powerful central government with three branches—the legislative, executive, and judicial.

■ A two-house legislature with one house elected directly by the people, the other chosen from among persons nominated by the state legislatures.

■ A legislature with the power to select the executive and the judiciary.

In general, smaller states such as New Jersey and Connecticut felt comfortable with the arrangements under the Articles of Confederation. These states offered another model of government, the **New Jersey Plan.** Its key features included:

■ Strengthening the Articles, not replacing them.

■ Creating a one-house legislature with one vote for each state with representatives chosen by state legislatures.

■ Giving Congress the power to raise revenue from duties and postal service.

■ Creating a Supreme Court with members appointed for life by the executive officers.

Constitutional Compromises

The most serious disagreement between the Virginia and New Jersey plans concerned state representation in Congress and the North/South division over how slaves were to be counted for purposes of representation and taxation. When a deadlock loomed, Connecticut offered its own compromise. Each state would have an equal vote in the Senate. Again, there was a stalemate. As Benjamin Franklin put it:

> The diversity of opinions turns on two points. If a proportional representation takes place, the small states contend that their liberties will be in danger. If an equality of votes is to be put in its place, large states say that their money will be in danger. . . . When a broad table is to be made and the edges of a plank do not fit, the artist takes a little from both sides and makes a good joint. In like manner, both sides must part with some of their demands, in order that they both join in some accommodating position.[14]

A committee to work out an agreement soon reported back what became known as the **Great Compromise.** Taking ideas from both the Virginia and New Jersey plans, it recommended:

Virginia Plan
The first general plan for the Constitution, proposed by James Madison. Its key points were a bicameral legislature, an executive chosen by the legislature, and a judiciary also named by the legislature.

New Jersey Plan
A framework for the Constitution proposed by a group of small states; its key points were a one-house legislature with one vote for each state, the establishment of the acts of Congress as the "supreme law" of the land, and a supreme judiciary with limited power.

Great Compromise
A decision made during the Constitutional Convention to give each state the same number of representatives in the Senate regardless of size; representation in the House was determined by population.

- In one house of the legislature (later called the House of Representatives), there would be fifty-six representatives—one representative for every 30,000 inhabitants. Representatives would be elected directly by the people.

- That house should have the power to originate all bills for raising and spending money.

- In the second house of the legislature (later called the Senate), each state should have an equal vote, and representatives would be selected by the state legislatures.

- In dividing power between the national and state governments, national power would be supreme.[15]

The Great Compromise ultimately met with the approval of all states in attendance. The smaller states were pleased because they got equal representation in the Senate; the larger states were satisfied with the proportional representation in the House of Representatives. The small states then would dominate the Senate while the large states, such as Virginia and Pennsylvania, would control the House. But, because both houses had to pass any legislation, neither body could dominate the other.

The Great Compromise dealt with one major concern of the Framers—how best to treat the differences in large and small states—but other problems stemming largely from regional differences remained. Slavery was one of the thorniest. Southerners feared that the new national government would interfere with its lucrative cotton trade as well as slavery. Thus, when a tax on the importation of slaves was proposed, the convention turned to the larger question of slavery, which divided the northern and southern states. Consequently, in exchange for northern support of continuing the slave trade for twenty more years and for a twenty-year ban on taxing exports to protect the cotton trade, Southerners consented to a provision requiring only a majority vote on navigation laws, the national government was given the authority to regulate foreign commerce, and the Senate was required to cast a two-thirds vote to pass treaties. The southern states, which made up more than one-third of the new nation at that time, would be able to check the Senate's power. The delegates from these states also believed that there would be enough slaves in the United States by 1808 to supply the labor needed for southern agriculture.

Another sticking point concerning slavery remained: how to determine state population for purposes of representation in the House of Representatives. Slaves could not vote, but the southern states wanted them included for purposes of determining population. After considerable dissension, it was decided that population for purposes of representation and the apportionment of direct taxes would be calculated by adding the "whole Number of Free Persons" to "three-fifths of all other Persons." "All other Persons" was the delegates' tactful way of referring to slaves. Known as the **Three-Fifths Compromise,** this highly political deal assured that the South would hold 47 percent of the House—enough to prevent attacks on slavery but not so much as to foster the spread of slavery northward.

Three-Fifths Compromise
Agreement reached at the Constitutional Convention stipulating that each slave was to be counted as three-fifths of a person for purposes of determining population for representation in the U.S. House of Representatives.

Unfinished Business Affecting the Executive Branch

The Framers next turned to fashioning an executive branch. While they agreed on the idea of a one-person executive, they could not settle on the length of the term of office, nor on how the chief executive should be selected. With Shays's Rebellion still fresh in their minds, the delegates feared putting too much power, including selection of a president, into the hands of the lower classes. At the same time, representatives from the smaller states feared that the selection of the chief executive by the legislature would put additional power into the hands of the large states.

Amid these fears, the Committee on Unfinished Portions, whose sole responsibility was to iron out problems and disagreements concerning the office of chief executive, conducted its work. The committee recommended that the presidential term of office be fixed at four years instead of seven, as had earlier been proposed. By choosing not to mention a period of time within which the chief executive would be eligible for reelection, they made it possible for a president to serve more than one term.

The Framers also created the Electoral College and drafted rules concerning removal of a sitting president. The Electoral College system gave individual states a key role, because each state would select electors equal to the number of representatives it had in the House and Senate. It was a vague compromise that removed election of the president and vice president from both the Congress and the people and put it in the hands of electors whose method of selection would be left to the states. As Alexander Hamilton noted in *Federalist No. 68*, the Electoral College was fashioned to avoid the "tumult and disorder" that the Framers feared could result if the masses were allowed to vote directly for president. Instead, the selection of the president was left to a small number of men (the Electoral College) who "possess[ed] the information and discernment requisite" to decide, in Hamilton's words, the "complicated" business of selecting the president. (For details about the Electoral College, see chapter 13.)

In drafting the new Constitution, the Framers also were careful to include a provision for removal of the chief executive. The House of Representatives was given the sole responsibility of investigating and charging a president or vice president with "Treason, Bribery, or other high Crimes and Misdemeanors." A majority vote then would result in issuing articles of impeachment against the president or vice president. In turn, the Senate was given sole responsibility to try the president or vice president on the charges issued by the House. A two-thirds vote of the Senate was required to convict and remove the president or the vice president from office. The chief justice of the United States was to preside over the Senate proceedings in place of the vice president (that body's usual leader) to prevent any conflict of interest on the vice president's part (see chapter 7).

THE U.S. CONSTITUTION

AFTER THE COMPROMISE ON THE PRESIDENCY, work proceeded quickly on the remaining resolutions of the Constitution. The Preamble to the Constitution, the last section to be drafted, contains exceptionally powerful language that forms the bedrock of American political tradition. Its opening line, "We the People of the United States," boldly proclaimed that a loose confederation of independent states no longer existed. Instead, there was but one American people and nation. The original version of the Preamble opened with:

> We the people of the States of New Hampshire, Massachusetts, Rhode Island and the Providence Plantations, Connecticut, New Jersey, New York, Pennsylvania, Delaware, Maryland, Virginia, North Carolina, South Carolina and Georgia, do ordain, declare and establish the following Constitution for the government of ourselves and our Posterity.

Substituting the simple phrase "We the People" ended, at least for the time being, the question of whence the government derived its power: it came directly from the people, not from the states. The next phrase of the Constitution explained the need for the new outline of government: "in Order to form a more perfect Union" indirectly acknowledged the weaknesses of the Articles of Confederation in governing a growing nation. Next, the optimistic goals of the Framers for the new nation were set out: to "establish Justice, insure domestic Tranquility, provide for the common defence, promote the general Welfare, and secure the Blessings of Liberty to ourselves and our Posterity"; followed by the formal creation of a new government: "do ordain and establish this Constitution for the United States of America."

On September 17, 1787, the Constitution was approved by the delegates from all twelve states in attendance. While the completed document did not satisfy all the delegates, of the forty-one in attendance, thirty-nine ultimately signed it. The sentiments uttered by Benjamin Franklin probably well reflected those of many others: "Thus, I consent, Sir, to this Constitution because I expect no better, and because I am not sure that it is not the best."[16]

The Basic Principles of the Constitution

The ideas of political philosophers, especially two political philosophers, the French Montesquieu (1689–1755) and the English John Locke, heavily influenced the shape and nature of the government proposed by the Framers. Montesquieu, who actually drew many of his ideas about government from the works of Greek political philosopher Aristotle, was heavily quoted during the Constitutional Convention.

The proposed structure of the new national government owed much to the writings of Montesquieu, who advocated distinct functions for each branch of government, called **separation of powers,** with a system of **checks and balances** between each branch. The Constitution's concern with the distribution of power between states and the national government also reveals the heavy influence of political philosophers, as well as the colonists' experience under the Articles of Confederation.[17]

Federalism.
The question before and during the convention was how much power states would give up to the national government. Given the nation's experiences under the Articles of Confederation, the Framers believed that a strong national government was necessary for the new nation's survival. However, they were reluctant to create a powerful government after the model of Britain, the country from which they had just won their independence. Its unitary system was not even considered by the colonists. Instead, they employed a system (now known as the **federal system**) that divides the power of government between a strong national government and the individual states. This system, as the Supreme Court reaffirmed in 1995 in considering the constitutionality of state-imposed term limits on federal office holding, was based on the principle that the federal, or national, government derived its power from the citizens, not the states, as the national government had done under the Articles of Confederation.[18]

Opponents of this system feared that a strong national government would infringe on their liberty. But, supporters of a federal system, such as James Madison, argued that a strong national government with distinct state governments could, if properly directed by constitutional arrangements, actually be a source of expanded liberties and national unity. The Framers viewed the division of governmental authority between the national government and the states as a means of checking power with power, and providing the people with double security against governmental tyranny. Later, the passage of the Tenth Amendment, which stated that powers not given to the national government were reserved by the states or the people, further clarified the federal structure (see chapter 3).

Separation of Powers.
Madison and many of the Framers clearly feared putting too much power into the hands of any one individual or branch of government. Madison's famous words, "Ambition must be made to counteract ambition," were widely believed at the Philadelphia convention.

Separation of powers is simply a way of parceling out power among the three branches of government. Its three key features are:

1. Three distinct branches of government: the legislative, the executive, and the judicial.
2. Three separately staffed branches of government to exercise these functions.
3. Constitutional equality and independence of each branch.

separation of powers
A way of dividing power among three branches of government in which members of the House of Representatives, members of the Senate, the president, and the federal courts are selected by and responsible to different constituencies.

checks and balances
A governmental structure that gives each of the three branches of government some degree of oversight and control over the actions of the others.

federal system
Plan of government created in the U.S. Constitution in which power is divided between the national government and the state governments and in which independent states are bound together under one national government.

FIGURE 2.1   Separation of Powers and Checks and Balances Illustrated. ■

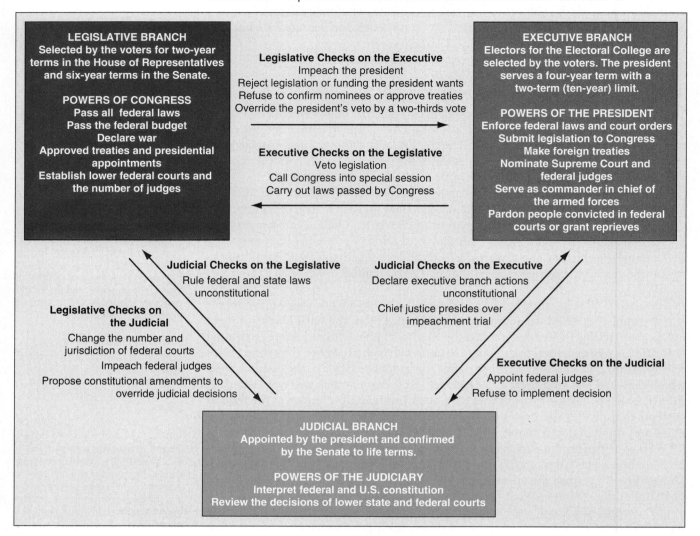

As illustrated in Figure 2.1, the Framers were careful to create a system in which law-making, law-enforcing, and law-interpreting functions were assigned to independent branches of government. On the national level (and in most states), only the legislature has the authority to make laws; the chief executive enforces laws; and the judiciary interprets them. Moreover, initially, members of the House of Representatives, members of the Senate, the president, and members of the federal courts were selected by and were therefore responsible to different constituencies. Madison believed that the scheme devised by the Framers would divide the offices of the new government and their methods of selection among many individuals, providing each office holder with the "necessary means and personal motives to resist encroachment" on his or her power. The Constitution originally placed the selection of senators directly with state legislators, making them more accountable to the states. The Seventeenth Amendment, ratified in 1913, however, called for direct election of senators by the voters, making them directly accountable to the people, thereby making the system more democratic.

The Framers could not have foreseen the intermingling of governmental functions that has since evolved. Locke, in fact, cautioned against giving a legislature the ability to delegate its powers. In Article I of the Constitution, the legislative power is vested in the Congress. But, the president is also given legislative powers via his ability to veto legislation, although his veto can be overridden by a two-thirds vote in Congress. Judicial interpretation, including judicial review, a process cemented by the 1803 decision in *Marbury* v. *Madison*, then helps to clarify the implementation of legislation enacted through this process.

So, instead of a pure system of separation of powers, a symbiotic, or interdependent, relationship among the three branches of government has existed from the beginning. Or, as one scholar has explained, there are "separated institutions sharing powers."[19] While Congress still is entrusted with making the laws, the president, as a single person who can easily capture the attention of the media and the electorate, retains tremendous power in setting the agenda and proposing legislation. And, although the Supreme Court's major function is to interpret the law, its involvement in areas such as the 2000 presidential election, criminal procedure, abortion, and other issues has led many to charge that it has surpassed its constitutional authority and become, in effect, a law-making body.

Checks and Balances.   The separation of powers among the three branches of the national government is not complete. According to Montesquieu and the Framers, the powers of each branch (as well as the two houses of the national legislature and between the states and the national government) could be used to check the powers of the other two branches of government. The power of each branch of government is checked, or limited, and balanced because the legislative, executive, and judicial branches share some authority and no branch has exclusive domain over any single activity. The creation of this system allowed the Framers to minimize the threat of tyranny from any one branch. Thus, for almost every power granted to one branch, an equal control was established in the other two branches. The Congress could check the power of the president, the Supreme Court, and so on, carefully creating balance among the three branches. For example, although the president, as the commander in chief, has the power to deploy American troops, as George W. Bush did to Iraq in 2003, he needed authorization from the Congress to keep the troops in the Middle East for longer than ninety days. Similarly, to pay for this mission, the president had to ask Congress to appropriate funds, which it did in the form of an initial $87 billion supplemental appropriations bill and additional funds.

Visual Literacy
The American System of Checks and Balances

The Articles of the Constitution

The document finally signed by the Framers condensed numerous resolutions into a Preamble and seven separate articles. The first three articles established the three branches of government, defined their internal operations, and clarified their relationships with one another. All branches of government were technically considered equal, yet some initially appeared more equal than others. The order of the articles, and the detail contained in the first three, reflects the Framers' concern that these branches of government might abuse their powers. The four remaining articles define the relationships among the states, declare national law to be supreme, and set out methods of amending the Constitution.

Article I: The Legislative Branch.   Article I vests all legislative powers in the Congress and establishes a bicameral legislature, consisting of the Senate and the House of Representatives. It also sets out the qualifications for holding office in each house, the terms of office, the methods of selection of representatives and senators, and the system of apportionment among the states to determine membership in the House of Representatives. Article I, section 2, specifies that an "enumeration" of the citizenry must take place every ten years in a manner to be directed by the U.S. Congress.

The "Equal Opportunity to Govern" Amendment

> **Overview:** Article II, section 1, clause 5, of the U.S. Constitution declares: "No person except a natural-born citizen, or a citizen of the United States at the time of the Adoption of this Constitution, shall be eligible to the Office of President." Why would the Founders put such a restriction on the qualifications for president of the United States? In a letter to Washington, John Jay argued that the duty of commander in chief was too important to be given to a foreign-born person—the potential for conflict of interest, danger, and appearance of impropriety in matters of war and foreign policy should not be left to chance. Charles Pinckney, a South Carolina delegate to the Constitutional Convention, expressed concern that foreign governments would use whatever means necessary to influence international events, and he cited the example of Russia, Prussia, and Austria manipulating the election of Stanislaus II to the Polish throne—only to divide Polish lands among themselves. Furthermore, Pinckney contended that the clause would ensure the "experience" of American politics and principles and guarantee "attachment to the country" so as to further eliminate the potential for mischief and foreign intrigue.

The recent election of Austrian-born Arnold Schwarzenegger and of Canadian-born Jennifer Granholm to the governorships of California and Michigan, respectively, has reopened the debate concerning the citizenship requirement for president. Why shouldn't naturalized citizens be eligible for president? Many naturalized citizens have performed great service to their adopted country; both Henry Kissinger (born in Germany) and Madeleine Albright (born in Czechoslovakia) performed admirably as secretary of state, and over 700 foreign-born Congressional Medal of Honor recipients have demonstrated patriotism and the willingness to die for the country they embraced. With these viewpoints in mind, in July 2003, Senator Orrin Hatch introduced the Equal Opportunity to Govern Amendment to strike the natural-born-citizen clause from the Constitution. The proposed amendment takes into account the Framers' fear of foreign intervention and of divided loyalty by placing a lengthy citizenship requirement—twenty years—before naturalized citizens become eligible to run for presidential office.

Is it just that a nation whose fundamental principle is equality of citizens has a constitutional clause that denies some citizens the presidency? Doesn't the Constitution allow the means to adapt to changes in history and social mores, and further to realize the principle of equality of citizens? On the other hand, shouldn't a president be above the appearance of suspicion and divided loyalty? Doesn't the clause help prevent corruption from foreign sources?

Arguments for the Equal Opportunity to Govern Amendment

- **The United States is in part built by its immigrant population and they should have a share in all political offices.** America is a nation of immigrants and many of the original Founders were foreign born, notably Alexander Hamilton, who helped shaped Washington's administration and the executive branch. The Constitution allows for naturalized citizens to attain other high

---

enumerated powers
Seventeen specific powers granted to Congress under Article I, section 8, of the U.S. Constitution; these powers include taxation, coinage of money, regulation of commerce, and the authority to provide for a national defense.

necessary and proper clause
The final paragraph of Article I, section 8, of the U.S. Constitution, which gives Congress the authority to pass all laws "necessary and proper" to carry out the enumerated powers specified in the Constitution; also called the elastic clause.

One of the most important sections of Article I is section 8. It carefully lists the powers the Framers wished the new Congress to possess. These specified or **enumerated powers** contain many key provisions that had been denied to the Continental Congress under the Articles of Confederation. For example, one of the major weaknesses of the Articles was Congress's lack of authority to deal with trade wars. The Constitution remedied this problem by authorizing Congress to "regulate Commerce with foreign Nations, and among the several States." Congress was also given the authority to coin money.

Today, Congress often enacts legislation that no specific clause of Article I, section 8, appears to authorize. Laws dealing with subjects such as the environment, welfare, education, and communication are often justified by reference to a particular power plus the necessary and proper clause. After careful enumeration of seventeen powers of Congress in Article I, section 8, a final, general clause authorizing Congress to "make all Laws which shall be necessary and proper for carrying into Execution the foregoing Powers" was added to Article I. Often referred to as the elastic clause, the **necessary and proper clause** has been a source of tremendous congressional activity never anticipated by the Framers, as definitions of "necessary" and "proper" have been stretched to political office such as speaker of the House, senator, or Supreme Court justice; why should naturalized citizens be denied the presidency?

- **The natural-born-citizen clause has outlived its usefulness.** The Constitution has proved to be durable and the problems that existed in 1787 either have changed or do not exist in the twenty-first century. The amendment process was created to allow for historical and political change, and ratification of the Equal Opportunity to Govern Amendment will increase the talent pool for presidential nominees, thus increasing the quality and choice of presidential aspirants for the American people.
- **The natural-born-citizen clause is discriminatory.** The clause is un-American in that it denies equality of opportunity for all American citizens. Naturalized citizens serve in the military, pay taxes, run for local, state, and federal office, endure the same national hardships and crises, and add to the overall quality of American life; thus, naturalized citizens should have the same rights and privileges as the native born.

Arguments Against the Equal Opportunity to Govern Amendment

- **Foreign governments still attempt to have undue influence in American politics.** The Framers were correct in assuming foreign governments attempt to manipulate American politics. For example, in 1999, the Democratic National Committee returned over $600,000 in campaign contributions to Chinese nationals attempting to gain influence with the Clinton administration. The clause was meant to be another institutional safeguard against presidential corruption.

- **Running for president is not a right.** The Office of the President is an institution designed for republican purposes. The Founders strongly believed foreign influence within the U.S. government must be restricted (the language was unanimously adopted by the Constitutional Convention) and thus they did not grant a right to run for presidential office.
- **There is no public movement or outcry to remove this clause from the Constitution.** Many constitutional scholars argue the Constitution should be amended only for pressing reasons, and amendments should be construed with a view to the well-being of future generations. Foreign policy and events are too fluid and too volatile to risk undermining the president's foreign policy and commander-in-chief authority. Until the American people determine otherwise, the clause should remain.

Questions

1. Is the natural-born clause discriminatory? Does it truly deny equality of citizenship and opportunity? If so, shouldn't the Constitution be amended to realize the principle of equality of citizens?
2. Were the Framers wise in their analysis of foreign influence on American politics? Did they create a true institutional barrier to help prevent corruption by foreign governments?

Selected Reading

Akhil Amar. *America's Constitution: A Guided Tour.* New York: Random House, 2004.

---

accommodate changing needs and times. The clause is the basis for the **implied powers** that Congress uses to execute its other powers. Congress's enumerated power to regulate commerce has been linked with the necessary and proper clause in a variety of Supreme Court cases. As a result, laws banning prostitution where travel across state lines is involved, regulating trains and planes, establishing federal minimum-wage and maximum-hour laws, and mandating drug testing for certain workers have passed constitutional muster.

implied powers
Powers derived from the enumerated powers and the necessary and proper clause. These powers are not stated specifically but are considered to be reasonably implied through the exercise of delegated powers.

Article II: The Executive Branch. Article II vests the executive power, that is, the authority to execute the laws of the nation, in a president of the United States. Section 1 sets the president's term of office at four years and explains the Electoral College. It also states the qualifications for office and describes a mechanism to replace the president in case of death, disability, or removal.

The powers and duties of the president are set out in section 3. Among the most important of these are the president's role as commander in chief of the armed forces, the authority to make treaties with the consent of the Senate, and the authority to

■ President George W. Bush delivers the State of the Union Address to Congress as millions across the nation watch in their homes. Behind him are the vice president and the speaker of the House.

Photo courtesy: © Dennis Brack

"appoint Ambassadors, other public Ministers and Consuls, the Judges of the supreme Court, and all other Officers of the United States." Other sections of Article II instruct the president to report directly to Congress "from time to time," in what has come to be known as the State of the Union Address, and to "take Care that the Laws be faithfully executed." Section 4 provides the mechanism for removal of the president, vice president, and other officers of the United States for "Treason, Bribery, or other high Crimes and Misdemeanors" (see chapter 8).

Article III: The Judicial Branch.   Article III establishes a Supreme Court and defines its jurisdiction. During the Philadelphia meeting, the small and large states differed significantly as to the desirability of an independent judiciary and on the role of state courts in the national court system. The smaller states feared that a strong unelected judiciary would trample on their liberties. In compromise, Congress was permitted, but not required, to establish lower national courts. Thus, state courts and the national court system would exist side by side with distinct areas of authority. Federal courts were given authority to decide cases arising under federal law. The Supreme Court was also given the power to settle disputes between states, or between a state and the national government. Ultimately, it was up to the Supreme Court to determine what provisions of the Constitution actually meant.

Although some delegates to the convention urged that the president be allowed to remove federal judges, ultimately judges were given appointments for life, presuming "good behavior." And, like the president's, their salaries cannot be lowered while they hold office. This provision was adopted to ensure that the legislature did not attempt to punish the Supreme Court or any other judges for unpopular decisions.

Articles IV Through VII.   The remainder of the articles in the Constitution attempted to anticipate problems that might occur in the operation of the new national

WRITING A CONSTITUTION: HOW DO WE COMPARE?

There is no such thing as a one-size-fits-all constitution. National constitutions frequently are products of political crises. The U.S. Constitution was written following the Revolutionary War and the failure of the Articles of Confederation to provide a workable governing structure. South Africa wrote its 1996 constitution after the struggle to end apartheid. Russia wrote its 1993 constitution following the breakup of the Soviet Union and the fall of communism. In the Middle East, Iran created a new constitution in 1979 after the shah was forced from power. Following the end of Saddam Hussein's regime, Iraq began to put a new constitution in place. In August 2004, more than 1,100 Iraqis met at a conference to select an interim national assembly to take the next step toward full democratization.

The content of these constitutions reflects not only the struggles of the moment but also the country's historical experiences and the influence of ideas about the meaning of good government and the proper relationship between those in power and those whom they rule. These influences often can pull constitutions into different directions requiring political compromises and creating lengthy and complex documents. The Russian Constitution of 1993 contained 146 articles; as of 2002, the Mexican Constitution had 123 articles.

In spite of these variations, four important features are common to all constitutions. First, most contain a preamble that sets forward the principles on which the government is to operate. Although this section often contains a great deal of flowery rhetoric, it also tells us much about the country. The Soviet constitution of 1917 proclaimed in its preamble: "The Great Socialist October Revolution, carried out by the workers and peasants of Russia under the leadership of the Communist Party headed by V. I. Lenin, overturned the power of the capitalists and landowners, broke the chains of oppression, and established the dictatorship of the proletariat." Nigeria, a country that has experienced much ethnic strife and a bloody civil war, begins its most recent constitution with the words "we the people . . . [have] solemnly resolved: to live in unity and harmony as one indivisible and indissoluble Sovereign Nation under God dedicated to the promotion of inter-African solidarity."

Second, constitutions specify the organization of the government. Whereas the United States has a system of checks and balances among the president, Congress, and the courts, the French and Russian constitutions created strong presidents whose powers exceed those of the other two branches.

Third, constitutions specify individual rights. The U.S. Constitution does this through its Bill of Rights and other amendments. In some cases, references may also be added to government obligations to citizens. Brazil's 1988 constitution pledged the government would ensure citizens the rights to work and to receive medical care.

Fourth, constitutions provide a means for making amendments. In general terms we can distinguish between rigid constitutional frameworks that are difficult to change and flexible ones. Each has its advantages. Rigid frameworks provide predictability and ensure that if an extremist group achieves power it cannot easily change the rules. Flexible frameworks allow constitutions to remain relevant to the changing requirements of governing societies and the changing definitions of human rights. In Canada, both houses of the parliament have to approve an amendment, as do two-thirds of the provinces containing at least one-half the population of the country. In Japan, a two-thirds majority in both houses of the parliament must approve an amendment, and then a majority of the population must do so in a referendum.

Lastly, we should note that not all constitutions are written. In Great Britain the constitution is collectively made up of key documents such as the Magna Carta and acts of Parliament. Israeli leaders tried to write a constitution in 1949 shortly after its independence but gave up because of deep conflicts between religious and secular groups. Like Great Britain, Israel's constitution is a series of basic laws. Saudi Arabia's constitution, too, is not a written one but is, instead, a series of royal decrees.

Questions

1. If you were writing a constitution today, what would be the most important influences on your decisions about what you will include?
2. How important is it that constitutions be written?

government as well as its relations to the states. Article IV begins with what is called the full faith and credit clause, which mandates that states honor the laws and judicial proceedings of the other states. Article IV also includes the mechanisms for admitting new states to the union.

Article V (discussed in greater detail on p. 61) specifies how amendments can be added to the Constitution. The Bill of Rights, which added ten amendments to the

Comparative
Comparing Constitutions

supremacy clause
Portion of Article VI of the U.S. Constitution mandating that national law is supreme to (that is, supersedes) all other laws passed by the states or by any other subdivision of government.

Constitution in 1791, was one of the first items of business when the First Congress met in 1789. Since then, only seventeen additional amendments have been ratified.

Article VI contains the supremacy clause, which asserts the basic primacy of the Constitution and national law over state laws and constitutions. The **supremacy clause** provides that the "Constitution, and the laws of the United States" as well as all treaties are to be the supreme law of the land. All national and state officers and judges are bound by national law and take oaths to support the federal Constitution above any state law or constitution. Because of the supremacy clause, any legitimate exercise of national power supersedes any state laws or action, in a process that is called preemption. Without the supremacy clause and the federal court's ability to invoke it, the national government would have little actual enforceable power; thus, many commentators call the supremacy clause the linchpin of the entire federal system.

Mindful of the potential problems that could occur if church and state were too enmeshed, Article VI also specifies that no religious test shall be required for holding any office. This mandate strengthens the separation of church and state guarantee that was quickly added to the Constitution when the First Amendment was ratified.

The seventh and final article of the Constitution concerns the procedures for ratification of the new Constitution: nine of the thirteen states would have to agree to, or ratify, its new provisions before it would become the supreme law of the land.

THE DRIVE FOR RATIFICATION

WHILE DELEGATES TO THE CONSTITUTIONAL CONVENTION labored in Philadelphia, the Congress of the Confederation continued to govern the former colonies under the Articles of Confederation. The day after the Constitution was signed, William Jackson, the secretary of the Constitutional Convention, left for New York City, by then the nation's capital, to deliver the official copy of the document to the Congress. He also took with him a resolution of the delegates calling upon each of the states to vote on the new Constitution. Anticipating resistance from the representatives in the state legislatures, however, the Framers required the states to call special ratifying conventions to consider the proposed Constitution.

Jackson carried a letter from General George Washington with the proposed Constitution. In a few eloquent words, Washington summed up the sentiments of the Framers and the spirit of compromise that had permeated the long weeks in Philadelphia:

> That it will meet the full and entire approbation of every state is not perhaps to be expected, but each [state] will doubtless consider, that had her interest alone been consulted, the consequences might have been particularly disagreeable or injurious to others; that it is liable to as few exceptions as could reasonably have been expected, we hope and believe; that it may promote lasting welfare of that country so dear to us all, and secure her freedom and happiness is our ardent wish.[20]

The Second Continental Congress immediately accepted the work of the convention and forwarded the proposed Constitution to the states for their vote. It was by no means certain, however, that the new Constitution would be adopted. From the fall of 1787 to the summer of 1788, the proposed Constitution was debated hotly around the nation. State politicians understandably feared a strong central government. Farmers and other working-class people were fearful of a distant national government. Those who had accrued substantial debts during the economic chaos following the Revolutionary War feared that a new government with a new financial policy would plunge them into even greater debt. The public in general was very leery of taxes—these were the same people who had revolted against the king's taxes. At the heart of many of their concerns was an underlying fear of the massive changes that would be brought about by a new system. Favoring the Constitution were wealthy merchants, lawyers, bankers, and those who believed that the new nation could not continue to exist under the Articles of Confederation. For them, it all boiled down to one simple question offered by James Madison: "Whether or not the Union shall or shall not be continued."

Federalists Versus Anti-Federalists

Almost as soon as the ink was dry on the last signature to the Constitution, those who favored the new strong national government chose to call themselves **Federalists.** They were well aware that many still generally opposed the notion of a strong national government. Thus, they did not want to risk being labeled nationalists, so they tried to get the upper hand in the debate by nicknaming their opponents **Anti-Federalists.** Those put in the latter category insisted that they were instead Federal Republicans, who believed in a federal system. As noted in Table 2.1, Anti-Federalists argued that they simply wanted to protect state governments from the tyranny of a too powerful national government.[21]

Federalists and Anti-Federalists participated in the mass meetings that were held in state legislatures to discuss the pros and cons of the new plan. Tempers ran high at public meetings, where differences between the opposing groups were highlighted. Fervent debates were published in newspapers, which played a powerful role in the adoption process. The entire Constitution, in fact, was printed in the *Pennsylvania Packet* just two days after the convention's end. Other major papers quickly followed suit. Soon, opinion pieces on both sides of the adoption issue began to appear around the nation, often written under pseudonyms such as "Caesar" or "Constant Reader," as was the custom of the day.

The Federalist Papers

One name stood out from all the rest: "Publius" (Latin for "the people"). Between October 1787 and May 1788, eighty-five articles written under that pen name routinely appeared in newspapers in New York, a state where ratification was in doubt. Most were written by Alexander Hamilton and James Madison. Hamilton, a young, fiery New Yorker born in the British West Indies, wrote fifty-one; Madison, a Virginian who later served as the fourth president, wrote twenty-six; and jointly they penned another three. John Jay, also of New York, and later the first chief justice of the United States, wrote five of the pieces. These eighty-five essays became known as *The Federalist Papers.*

Federalists
Those who favored a stronger national government and supported the proposed U.S. Constitution; later became the first U.S. political party.

Anti-Federalists
Those who favored strong state governments and a weak national government; opposed the ratification of the U.S. Constitution.

The Federalist Papers
A series of eighty-five political papers written by John Jay, Alexander Hamilton, and James Madison in support of ratification of the U.S. Constitution.

TABLE 2.1 Federalists and Anti-Federalists Compared		
	Federalists	*Anti-Federalists*
Who were they?	Property owners, landed rich, merchants of Northeast and Middle Atlantic states.	Small farmers, shopkeepers, laborers.
Political philosophy	Elitist: saw themselves and those of their class as most fit to govern (others were to be governed).	Believed in the decency of the common man and in participatory democracy; viewed elites as corrupt; sought greater protection of individual rights.
Type of government favored	Powerful central government; two-house legislature; upper house (six-year term) further removed from the people, whom they distrusted.	Wanted stronger state governments (closer to the people) at the expense of the powers of the national government; sought smaller electoral districts, frequent elections, referendum and recall, and a large unicameral legislature to provide for greater class and occupational representation.
Alliances	Pro-British, Anti-French	Anti-British, Pro-French

Photos courtesy: left, The Metropolitan Museum of Art, Gift of Henry G. Marquand; 1881 (81.11) copyright © 1987 The Metropolitan Museum af Art; center, Colonial Williamsburg Foundation; right, Bettmann/Corbis.

■ Alexander Hamilton (left), James Madison (center), and John Jay (right) were important early Federalist leaders. Jay wrote five of *The Federalist Papers* and Madison and Hamilton wrote the rest. Madison served in the House of Representatives (1789–1797) and as secretary of state in the Jefferson administration (1801–1808). In 1808, he was elected fourth president of the United States and served two terms (1809–1817). Hamilton became the first secretary of the treasury (1789–1795). He was killed in 1804 in a duel with Vice President Aaron Burr, who was angered by Hamilton's negative comments about his character. Jay became the first chief justice of the United States (1789–1795) and negotiated the Jay Treaty with Great Britain in 1794. He then served as governor of New York from 1795 to 1801.

Today, *The Federalist Papers* are considered masterful explanations of the Framers' intentions as they drafted the new Constitution. At the time, although they were reprinted widely, they were far too theoretical to have much impact on those who would ultimately vote on the proposed Constitution. Dry and scholarly, they lacked the fervor of much of the political rhetoric that was then in use. *The Federalist Papers* did, however, highlight the reasons for the structure of the new government and its benefits. According to *Federalist No. 10*, for example, the new Constitution was called "a republican remedy for the disease incident to republican government." These musings of Madison, Hamilton, and Jay continue to be the clearest articulation of the political theories and philosophies that lie at the heart of our Constitution.

Forced on the defensive, the Anti-Federalists responded to *The Federalist Papers* with their own series of letters written by Anti-Federalists adopting the pen names of "Brutus" and "Cato," two ancient Romans famous for their intolerance of tyranny. These letters (actually essays) undertook a line-by-line critique of the Constitution.

Anti-Federalists argued that a strong central government would render the states powerless.[22] They stressed the strengths the government had been granted under the Articles of Confederation, and argued that the Articles, not the proposed Constitution, created a true federal system. Moreover, they argued that the strong national government would tax heavily, that the Supreme Court would overwhelm the states by invalidating state laws, and that the president eventually would have too much power, as commander in chief of a large and powerful army.[23]

In particular, the Anti-Federalists feared the power of the national government to run roughshod over the liberties of the people. They proposed that the taxing power of Congress be limited, that the executive be curbed by a council, that the military consist of state militias rather than a national force, and that the jurisdiction of the Supreme Court be limited to prevent it from reviewing and potentially overturning the decisions of state courts. But, their most effective argument concerned the absence of a bill of rights in the Constitution. James Madison answered these criticisms in *Federalist Nos. 10* and *51*. (The texts of these two essays are printed in Appendices III and IV.) In *Federalist No. 10*, Madison pointed out that the voters would not always succeed in electing "enlightened statesmen" as their representatives. The greatest threat to individual liberties would therefore come from factions within the government, who might place narrow interests above broader national interests and the rights of citizens. While recognizing that no form of government could protect the country from unscrupulous politicians, Madison argued that the organization of the new government would minimize the effects of political factions. The great advantage of a federal system, Madison maintained, was that it created the "happy combination" of a national government too large to be controlled by any single faction, and several state governments that would be smaller and more responsive to local needs. Moreover, he argued in *Federalist No. 51* that the proposed federal government's separation of powers would prohibit any one branch from either dominating the national government or violating the rights of citizens.

Ratifying the Constitution

Debate continued in the thirteen states as votes were taken from December 1787 to June 1788, in accordance with the ratifying process laid out in Article VII of the proposed Constitution. Three states acted quickly to ratify the new Constitution. Two small states, Delaware and New Jersey, voted to ratify before the large states could rethink the notion of equal representation of the states in the Senate. Pennsylvania, where Federalists were well organized, was also one of the first three states to ratify. Massachusetts assented to the new government but tempered its support by calling for an immediate addition of amendments, including one protecting personal rights. New Hampshire became the crucial ninth state to ratify on June 21, 1788. This action completed the ratification process outlined in Article VII of the Constitution and marked the beginning of a new nation. But, New York and Virginia, which at that time accounted for more than 40 percent of the new nation's population, had not yet ratified the Constitution. Thus, the practical future of the new nation remained in doubt.

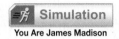
Simulation
You Are James Madison

Hamilton in New York and Madison in Virginia worked feverishly to convince delegates to their state conventions to vote for the new government. In New York, sentiment against the Constitution was high. In Albany, fighting resulting in injuries and death broke out over ratification. When news of Virginia's acceptance of the Constitution reached the New York convention, Hamilton finally was able to convince a majority of those present to follow suit by a narrow margin of three votes. Both states also recommended the addition of a series of structural amendments and a bill of rights.

North Carolina and Rhode Island continued to hold out against ratification. Both had recently printed new currencies and feared that values would plummet in a federal system where the Congress was authorized to coin money. On August 2, 1788, North Carolina became the first state to reject the Constitution on the grounds that no Anti-Federalist amendments were included. Soon after, in September 1789, owing much to the Anti-Federalist pressure for additional protections from the national government, Congress submitted the **Bill of Rights** to the states for their ratification. North Carolina then ratified the Constitution by a vote of 194–77. Rhode Island, the only state that had not sent representatives to Philadelphia, remained out of the new nation until 1790. Finally, under threats from its largest cities to secede from the state, the legislature called a convention that ratified the Constitution by only two votes (34–32)—one year after George Washington became the first president of the United States.

Bill of Rights
The first ten amendments to the U.S. Constitution.

Amending the Constitution: The Bill of Rights

Once the Constitution was ratified, elections were held. When Congress convened, it immediately sent a set of amendments to the states for their ratification. An amendment authorizing the enlargement of the House of Representatives and another to prevent members of the House from raising their own salaries failed to garner favorable votes in the necessary three-fourths of the states. (See On Campus: A Student's Revenge: The Twenty-Seventh [Madison] Amendment.) The remaining ten amendments, known as the Bill of Rights, were ratified by 1791 in accordance with the procedures set out in the Constitution. Sought by Anti-Federalists as a protection for individual liberties, they offered numerous specific limitations on the national govern-

Timeline
The History of Constitutional Amendments

A STUDENT'S REVENGE: THE TWENTY-SEVENTH (MADISON) AMENDMENT

On June 8, 1789, in a speech before the House of Representatives, James Madison stated:

> there is a seeming impropriety in leaving any set of men without controul to put their hand into the public coffers, to take out money to put into their pockets. . . . I have gone therefore so far as to fix it, that no law, varying the compensation, shall operate until there is a change in the legislation.

When Madison proposed that any salary increase for members of Congress could not take effect until the next session of Congress, he had no way of knowing that more than two centuries would pass before his plan, now known as the Twenty-Seventh Amendment, would become an official part of the Constitution. In fact, Madison deemed it worthy of addition only because the conventions of three states (Virginia, New York, and North Carolina) demanded that it be included.

By 1791, when the Bill of Rights was added to the Constitution, only six states had ratified Madison's amendment, and it seemed destined to fade into obscurity. In 1982, however, Gregory Watson, a sophomore majoring in economics at the University of Texas–Austin, discovered the unratified compensation amendment while looking for a paper topic for an American government class. Intrigued, Watson wrote a paper arguing that the proposed amendment was still viable because it had no internal time limit and, therefore, should still be ratified. Watson received a C on the paper.

Despite his grade, Watson began a ten-year, $6,000 self-financed crusade to renew interest in the compensation amendment. Watson and his allies reasoned that the amendment should be revived because of the public's growing anger with the fact that members of Congress had sought to raise their salaries without going on the record as having done so. Watson's perseverance paid off.

Photo courtesy: Ziggy Kaluzny/People Magazine Syndication

Gregory Watson with a document that contains the first ten amendments to the Constitution, as well as the compensation amendment ("Article the second: No law varying the compensation for services of the Senators and Representatives shall take effect until an election of Representatives shall have intervened"), which finally was ratified in 1992 as the Twenty-Seventh Amendment.

On May 7, 1992, the amendment was ratified by the requisite thirty-eight states. On May 18, the United States Archivist certified that the amendment was part of the Constitution, a decision that was overwhelmingly confirmed by the House of Representatives on May 19 and by the Senate on May 20. At the same time that the Senate approved the Twenty-Seventh Amendment, it also took action to ensure that a similar situation would never occur by declaring dead four other amendments.

Source: Fordham Law Review (December 1992): 497–539; and Anne Marie Kilday, "Amendment Expert Agrees with Congressional Pay Ruling," Dallas Morning News (February 14, 1993): 13A.

ment's ability to interfere with a wide variety of personal liberties, some of which were already guaranteed by many state constitutions (see chapters 5 and 6).

The Bill of Rights includes numerous specific protections of personal rights. Freedom of expression, speech, press, religion, and assembly are guaranteed by the First Amendment. The Bill of Rights also contains numerous safeguards for those accused of crimes.

Two of the amendments of the Bill of Rights were reactions to British rule—the right to bear arms (Second Amendment) and the right not to have soldiers quartered in private homes (Third Amendment). More general rights are also included in the Bill of Rights. The Ninth Amendment notes that these enumerated rights are not inclusive, meaning they are not the only rights to be enjoyed by the people, and the Tenth Amendment states that powers not given to the national government are reserved by the states or the people.

METHODS OF AMENDING THE CONSTITUTION

THE FRAMERS DID NOT WANT to fashion a government that could be too influenced by the whims of the people. Therefore, they made the formal amendment process a slow one to ensure that the Constitution was not impulsively amended. In keeping with this intent, only seventeen amendments have been added since the addition of the Bill of Rights. However, informal amendments, prompted by judicial interpretation and cultural and social change, have had a tremendous impact on the Constitution.

Formal Methods of Amending the Constitution

Article V of the Constitution creates a two-stage amendment process: proposal and ratification.[24] The Constitution specifies two ways to accomplish each stage. As illustrated in Figure 2.2, amendments to the Constitution can be proposed by: (1) a vote of two-thirds of the members in both houses of Congress; or, (2) a vote of two-thirds of the state legislatures specifically requesting Congress to call a national convention to propose amendments.

The second method has never been used. Historically, it has served as a fairly effective threat, forcing Congress to consider amendments that might otherwise never have been debated. In the 1980s, for example, several states called on Congress to enact a balanced budget amendment. To forestall the need for a special constitutional convention, in 1985, Congress enacted the Gramm-Rudman-Hollings Act, which called for a balanced budget by the 1991 fiscal year. But, Congress could not meet that target. The act was amended repeatedly until 1993, when Congress postponed the call for a balanced budget, the need for which faded in light of surpluses that occurred during the Clinton administration. The act also was ruled unconstitutional by a three-judge district court that declared the law violated separation of powers principles.

The ratification process is fairly straightforward. When Congress votes to propose an amendment, the Constitution specifies that the ratification process must occur in one of two ways: (1) a favorable vote in three-fourths of the state legislatures; or, (2) a favorable vote in specially called ratifying conventions in three-fourths of the states.

The Constitution itself was ratified by the favorable vote of nine states in specially called ratifying conventions. The Framers feared that the power of special interests in state legislatures would prevent a positive vote on the new Constitution. Since ratification of the Constitution, however, only one ratifying convention has been called. The Eighteenth Amendment, which caused the Prohibition era by outlawing nationwide the sale of alcoholic beverages, was ratified by the first method—a vote in state legislatures. Millions

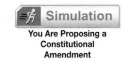

You Are Proposing a Constitutional Amendment

FIGURE 2.2   Methods of Amending the Consitution. ■

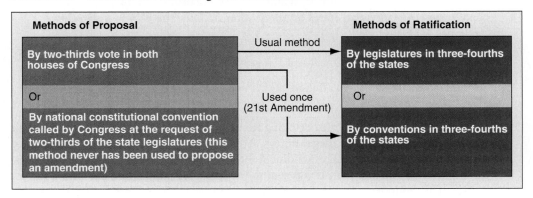

The Living Constitution

The Congress, whenever two thirds of both houses shall deem it necessary, shall propose amendments to this Constitution, or, on the application of the legislatures of two thirds of the several states, shall call a convention for proposing amendments, which, in either case, shall be valid to all intents and purposes, as part of this Constitution, when ratified by the legislatures of three fourths of the several states, or by conventions in three fourths thereof, as the one or the other mode of ratification may be proposed by the Congress.

—Article V

With this article, the Framers acknowledged the potential need to change or amend the Constitution. This article provides for two methods to propose amendments: by a two-thirds vote of both houses of Congress or by a two-thirds vote of the state legislatures. It also specifies two alternative methods of ratification of proposed amendments: by a three-quarters vote of the state legislatures, or by a similar vote in state ratifying conventions.

During the Constitutional Convention in Philadelphia, the Framers were divided as to how frequently or how easily the Constitution was to be amended. The original suggestion was to allow the document to be amended "when soever it shall seem necessary." The Committee on Detail wanted to entrust this authority to the state legislatures; however, others feared that it would give states too much power. James Madison alleviated these fears by suggesting that both Congress and the states have a role in the process.

In the late 1960s and early 1970s, leaders of the new women's rights movement sought an equal rights amendment to the Constitution. Their efforts were rewarded when the ERA was approved in the House and Senate by overwhelming majorities in 1971 and then sent out to the states for their approval. In spite of tremendous lobbying, a strong anti-ERA movement emerged and the amendment failed to gain approval in three-quarters of the state legislatures. While it is not unusual to have over 100 potential amendments introduced in each session of Congress, some to ban same-sex marriage, stop flag burning, and allow naturalized citizens to become president are those most often mentioned of late.

The failed battles for the ERA as well as other amendments, including one to prohibit child labor and another to grant statehood to the District of Columbia, underscore how difficult it is to amend the Constitution. Thus, unlike the constitutions of individual states or many other nations, the U.S. Constitution rarely has been amended.

broke the law, others died from drinking homemade liquor, and still others made their fortunes selling bootleg or illegal liquor. After a decade of these problems, Congress decided to act. An additional amendment—the Twenty-First—was proposed to repeal the Eighteenth Amendment. It was sent to the states for ratification, but with a call for ratifying conventions, not a vote in the state legislatures.[25] Members of Congress correctly predicted that the move to repeal the Eighteenth Amendment would encounter opposition in the statehouses, which were largely controlled by conservative rural interests. Thus, Congress's decision to use the convention method led to quick approval of the Twenty-First Amendment.

The intensity of efforts to amend the Constitution has varied considerably, depending on the nature of the change proposed. Whereas the Twenty-First Amendment took only ten months to ratify, an equal rights amendment (ERA) was introduced in every session of Congress from 1923 until 1972, when Congress finally voted favorably for it. Even then, years of lobbying by women's groups were insufficient to garner necessary state support. By 1982, the congressionally mandated date for ratification, only thirty-five states—three short of the number required—had voted favorably on the amendment.[26]

Congress also has made several attempts to pass an amendment to ban flag burning, prompted by a Supreme Court decision protecting such actions as free speech. Many were outraged by the Court's 5–4 decision in *Texas* v. *Johnson* (1989) but have been unable to muster the two-thirds vote necessary to send the proposed amendment to the states.[27] More recently, senators have proposed a variety of constitutional amendments ranging from one protecting victims' rights to others balancing the federal budget and banning same-sex marriages. If the history of the failed ERA is any indication, chances are slim that either amendment will be ratified quickly.

Informal Methods of Amending the Constitution

The formal amendment process is not the only way that the Constitution has been changed over time. Judicial interpretation and cultural and social change also have had a major impact on the way the Constitution has evolved.

Photo courtesy: Hulton Archive/Getty Images

■ For all its moral foundation in groups such as the Women's Christian Temperance Union (WCTU), whose members invaded bars to protest the sale of alcoholic beverages, the Eighteenth (Prohibition) Amendment was a disaster. Among its side effects was the rise of powerful crime organizations responsible for illegal sales of alcoholic beverages. Once proposed, it took only ten months to ratify the Twenty-First Amendment, which repealed the Prohibition Amendment.

Judicial Interpretation. As early as 1803, under the leadership of Chief Justice John Marshall, the Supreme Court declared in *Marbury* v. *Madison* that the federal courts had the power to nullify acts of the nation's government when they were found to be in conflict with the Constitution.[28] Over the years, this check on the other branches of government and on the states has increased the authority of the Court and significantly has altered the meaning of various provisions of the Constitution, a fact that prompted Woodrow Wilson to call the Supreme Court "a constitutional convention in continuous session." (More detail on the Supreme Court's role in interpreting the Constitution is found in chapters 5, 6, and 10 especially, as well as in other chapters in this book.)

Today, some analysts argue that the original intent of the Framers, as evidenced in *The Federalist Papers*, as well as in private notes taken by James Madison at the Constitutional Convention, should govern judicial interpretation of the Constitution.[29] Others argue that the Framers knew that a changing society needed an elastic, flexible document that could conform to the ages.[30] In all likelihood, the vagueness of the document was purposeful. Those in attendance in Philadelphia recognized that they could not agree on everything and that it was wiser to leave interpretation to those who would follow them.

POLITICS AND AMENDING THE CONSTITUTION

"The union of a man and a woman is the most enduring human institution, honored and encouraged in all cultures and by every religious faith." So spoke President George W. Bush in announcing his initial support of congressional action to amend the Constitution to ban same-sex marriages. He did not endorse a specific amendment but instead called upon Congress to endorse an amendment in the wake of the specter of the thousands of same-sex marriages that were conducted in San Francisco, California (and later ruled invalid by that state's Supreme Court).

Members of the House and Senate took up the president's call. In May 2003, Representative Marilyn Musgrave (R–CO) and five co-sponsors introduced a resolution to amend the Constitution to define marriage as a union between a man and a woman. A companion resolution was introduced in the Senate on November 2003 by Senator Wayne Allard (R–CO). Neither action went anywhere. Some states, however, were not so reticent. In 2004, eleven states had varying forms of state constitutional amendment provisions on their ballots.

Although neither presidential candidate supported same-sex marriage, it became a major factor in the 2004 campaign as the press highlighted the state efforts and the May 2004 actions of the Massachusetts Supreme Court (and the home state of Senator John Kerry) that legalized same-sex marriages in that commonwealth. In 1996, Congress had overwhelmingly passed the federal Defense of Marriage Act. It prevents federal recognition of same-sex marriage and allows states not to recognize same-sex marriages or legal unions from other states, such as Massachusetts or Vermont. In spite of that act, President Bush and many others continued to claim that a constitutional amendment was necessary because there was "no assurance that the Defense of Marriage Act will not be struck down by activist courts."[a] Of particular concern was the fact that the Constitution's full faith and credit clause requires states to honor legal contracts made in other states.

Nationwide campaigns to pass as well as to defeat the amendments were waged by a variety of interest groups, including the Human Rights Campaign (HRC), the largest gay rights group in the United States. But, as it was fighting these state amendments, the Republican leadership in the House and Senate decided to resurrect the proposed amendment to force lawmakers, especially members of the House who were all up for re-election, as well as John Kerry and John Edwards in the Senate, to go on record as for or against the proposed federal constitutional amendment.

The 2003 resolution calling for a constitutional amendment introduced by Musgrave and Allard had read:

> Marriage in the United States shall consist only of the union of a man and a woman. Neither this Constitution nor the Constitution of any state, **nor state or federal law,** shall be construed to require that marital status or the legal incidents thereof be conferred upon **unmarried couples or groups.**

When the new Federal Marriage Amendment was introduced in September 2004, it was modified slightly to read:

> Marriage in the United States shall consist only of the union of a man and a woman. Neither this Constitution nor the Constitution of any **State,** shall be construed to require that marriage or the legal incidents thereof be conferred upon **any union other that the union of a man and a woman.**

In the Senate, the amendment was killed for the 108th session in July when a procedural vote to get the resolution to the floor failed on a 48–50 vote—12 votes shy of the 60 votes required by Senate rules. (Note: 67 votes are necessary for a constitutional amendment to be approved by the Senate.) Six Republicans and one Independent voted with 43 Democrats to kill the amendment. The White House issued a statement noting the president's "disappointment" and urged the House to take up the measure, which it did a few days later. The resolution did come to a floor vote there, but the 227–186 vote tally failed to reach the two-thirds required.

Although the move for an amendment failed, its backers were heartened by what happened in the states. Efforts to highlight the need for a federal amendment bolstered ballot measures in key swing states, especially Ohio and Michigan. Studies conducted after the election concluded that focus on same-sex marriage and moral values drew some African American voters who generally opposed same-sex marriage to the polls—diminishing traditional Democratic Party strength and energizing in all eleven states the Republican Party's conservative base. All of the eleven state bans on same-sex marriage passed by significant majorities, which harbingers well for state support of a constitutional amendment should it be sent to the states for their ratification.

In addition, in December 2004, the U.S. Supreme Court rejected an appeal of the Massachusetts Supreme Court's legalization of same-sex marriage, which may provide additional fodder for members of Congress to step up efforts to pass the amendment.

Questions

1. Senator Allard changed the language of his amendment when some Republicans voiced objections that it would prevent states from legalizing civil unions, which provide many legal protections for heterosexual as well as same-sex couples. How do you think the language change might affect the eventual ratification of such an amendment?
2. Historically, issues about marriage have been left to the states. How appropriate do you think it is to alter the Constitution to take authority over marriage away from the states? Can you think of other instances in which authority has been taken away from the states?

[a]CNN.com, "Bush Calls for Ban on Same-Sex Marriages," cnn.allpolitics/02/24/elec04.prez.bush.marriage
[b]Human Rights Campaign, "HRC: Changing the Constitution Can't Be Concealed with Tweaks and Maneuvering," March 2004 press release.

Analyzing Visuals

WHY DID THE FRAMERS WRITE THE CONSTITUTION AS THEY DID?

The U.S. Constitution contains many phrases that are open to several interpretations. There are also omissions that raise questions about the democratic nature of the Constitution. The lingering question of how to interpret the Constitution still sparks debates among scholars and citizens. In the cartoon below, Garry Trudeau depicts a conversation between two Framers of the Constitution.

Analyze the cartoon by answering the following questions: Who were Pinckney and Rutledge, mentioned in the first frame? To what does the representation compromise refer? Which position on the interpretation of the Constitution does the cartoonist appear to take? Which effect is the cartoonist trying to achieve: exaggeration, irony, or juxtaposition? Does the cartoon achieve its desired effect?

DOONESBURY

Garry Trudeau

Photo courtesy: Doonesbury © G. B. Trudeau. Reprinted with permission of Universal Press Syndicate. All rights reserved.

Recently, law professor Mark V. Tushnet has offered a particularly stinging criticism of judicial review and our reliance on the courts to interpret the law. He believes that, under our present system, Americans are unwilling to enforce the provisions of the Constitution because they believe this is the sole province of the court system. If we were to eliminate the deference given to court decisions, Tushnet argues, citizens would be compelled to become involved in enforcing their Constitution, thereby creating a system of populist constitutional law, and a more representative government.[31]

Social and Cultural Change. Even the most far-sighted of those in attendance at the Constitutional Convention could not have anticipated the vast changes that have occurred in the United States. For example, although many were uncomfortable with the Three-Fifths Compromise and others hoped for the abolition of slavery, none could have imagined the status of African Americans today, or that Colin Powell or Condoleezza Rice would serve as the U.S. secretary of state. Likewise, few of the Framers could have anticipated the diverse roles that women would play in American society. The Constitution often has evolved to accommodate such social and cultural changes. Thus, although there is no specific amendment guaranteeing women equal protection of the law, the federal courts have interpreted the Constitution to prohibit many forms of gender discrimination, thereby recognizing cultural and societal change.

Social change has also caused changes in the way institutions of government act. As problems such as the Great Depression appeared national in scope, Congress took on more and more power at the expense of the states to solve the economic and social crisis. In fact, Yale law professor Bruce Ackerman argues that on certain occasions, extraordinary times call for extraordinary measures such as the New Deal that, in effect, amend the Constitution. Thus, congressional passage (and the Supreme Court's eventual acceptance) of sweeping New Deal legislation that altered the balance of power between the national government and the states truly changed the Constitution without benefit of amendment.[32] Today, however, Congress is moving to return much of that power to the states. The actions of the 104th and 105th Congresses (1995–1999), in particular, to return powers and responsibilities to the states may be viewed as an informal attempt not necessarily to amend the Constitution but to return the balance of power between the national and state government to that which the Framers intended.

Advances in technology also have brought about constitutional change. Wiretapping and other forms of electronic surveillance, for example, now are regulated by the First and Fourth Amendments. Similarly, HIV testing must be balanced against constitutional protections, and all kinds of new constitutional questions are posed in the wake of congressional efforts to regulate what kinds of information can be disseminated on the Internet. Still, in spite of these massive changes, the Constitution survives, changed and ever changing after more than 200 years.

SUMMARY

THE U.S. CONSTITUTION has proven to be a remarkably enduring document. In explaining how and why the Constitution came into being, this chapter has covered the following points:

1. **The Origins of a New Nation**

   While settlers came to the New World for a variety of reasons, most remained loyal to Great Britain and considered themselves subjects of the king. Over the years, as new generations of Americans were born on colonial soil, those ties weakened. A series of taxes levied by the Crown ultimately led the colonists to convene a Continental Congress and to declare their independence.

2. **The First Attempt at Government: The Articles of Confederation**

   The Articles of Confederation (1781) created a loose league of friendship between the new national government and the states. Numerous weaknesses in the new government became apparent by 1784. Among the major flaws were Congress's inability to tax or regulate commerce, the absence of an executive to administer the government, the lack of a strong central government, and no judiciary.

3. **The Miracle at Philadelphia: Writing a Constitution**

   When the weaknesses under the Articles of Confederation became apparent, the states called for a meeting to reform them. The Constitutional Convention (1787) quickly threw out the Articles of Confederation and fashioned a new, more workable form of government. The Constitution was the result of a series of compromises, including those over representation, over issues involving large and small states, and over how to determine population. Compromises were also made about how members of each branch of government were to be selected. The Electoral College was created to give states a key role in the selection of the president.

4. **The U.S. Constitution**

   The proposed U.S. Constitution created a federal system that drew heavily on Montesquieu's ideas about separation of powers. These ideas concerned a way of parceling out power among the three branches of government, and checks and balances to prevent any one branch from having too much power.

5. **The Drive for Ratification**

   The drive for ratification became a fierce fight between Federalists and Anti-Federalists. Federalists lobbied for the strong national government created by the Constitution; Anti-Federalists favored greater state power.

6. **Methods of Amending the Constitution**

   The Framers did not want to fashion a government that could respond to the whims of the people. Therefore, they designed a deliberate two-stage formal amendment process that required approval on the federal and state levels; this process has rarely been used. However, informal amendments, prompted by judicial interpretation and by cultural and social change, have had a tremendous impact on the Constitution.

KEY TERMS

SELECTED READINGS

Ackerman, Bruce. *We the People.* Cambridge, MA: Belknap Press, 1991.

Bailyn, Bernard. *The Ideological Origins of the American Revolution.* Cambridge, MA: Belknap Press, 1967.

Beard, Charles A. *An Economic Interpretation of the Constitution of the United States,* reissue ed. New York: Free Press, 1996.

Bernstein, Richard B., with Jerome Agel. *Amending America,* reissue ed. Lawrence: University Press of Kansas, 1995.

Bowen, Catherine Drinker. *Miracle at Philadelphia.* Boston: Little, Brown, 1986.

Brinkley, Alan, Nelson W. Polsby, and Kathleen M. Sullivan. *New Federalist Papers: Essays in Defense of the Constitution.* New York: Norton, 1997.

Dahl, Robert A. *How Democratic Is the American Constitution?* New Haven, CT: Yale University Press, 2002.

Hamilton, Alexander, James Madison, and John Jay. *The Federalist Papers.* New York: Bantam Books, 1989 (first published in 1788).

Ketchman, Ralph, ed. *The Anti-Federalist Papers and the Constitutional Convention Debated.* New York: Mentor Books, 1996.

Kyvig, David E. *Explicit and Authentic Acts: Amending the U.S. Constitution, 1776–1995.* Lawrence: University Press of Kansas, 1996.

Levy, Leonard W., ed. *Essays on the Making of the Constitution,* 2nd ed. New York: Oxford University Press, 1987.

Main, Jackson Turner. *The Social Structure of Revolutionary America.* Princeton, NJ: Princeton University Press, 1965.

Rossiter, Clinton. *1787: Grand Convention,* reissue ed. New York: Norton, 1987.

Simon, James F. *What Kind of Nation: Thomas Jefferson, John Marshall, and the Epic Struggle to Create a United States.* New York: Simon and Schuster, 2003.

Stoner, James R., Jr. *Common Law and Liberal Theory.* Lawrence: University Press of Kansas, 1992.

Storing, Herbert J. *What the Anti-Federalists Were For.* Chicago: University of Chicago Press, 1981.

Sunstein, Cass R. *Designing Democracy: What Constitutions Do.* New York: Oxford University Press, 2001.

Vile, John R. *Encyclopedia of Constitutional Amendments, and Amending Issues, 1789–1995.* Santa Barbara, CA: ABC-CLIO, 1996.

Wood, Gordon S. *The Creation of the American Republic, 1776–1787,* reissue ed. New York: Norton, 1993.

WEB EXPLORATIONS

For more information on the work of the Continental Congress, see
http://lcweb2.loc.gov/ammem/bdsds/intro01.html

For a full text of the Articles of Confederation, see
http://www.usconstitution.net/articles.html

For demographic background on the Framers, see
http://www.usconstitution.net/constframedata.html

To compare *The Federalist Papers* with *The Anti-Federalist Papers,* see
http://www.law.emory.edu/FEDERAL/federalist/ and
http://wepin.com/articles/afp/index.htm

For the text of these failed amendments to the U.S. Constitution, see
http://www.usconstitution.net/constamfail.html

The Constitution of the United States of America

We the People of the United States, in Order to form a more perfect Union, establish Justice, insure domestic Tranquility, provide for the common defence, promote the general Welfare, and secure the Blessings of Liberty to ourselves and our Posterity, do ordain and establish this Constitution for the United States of America.

ARTICLE I
Section 1.

All legislative Powers herein granted shall be vested in a Congress of the United States, which shall consist of a Senate and House of Representatives.

Article I is the longest and most detailed of any of the articles, sections, or amendments that make up the United States Constitution. By *enumerating* the powers of Congress, the Framers attached limits to the enormous authority they had vested in the legislative branch. At the same time, the allocation of certain powers to Congress ensured that the legislative branch would maintain control over certain vital areas of public policy and that it would be protected from incursions by the executive and judicial branches. Moreover, by clearly vesting Congress with certain powers (for example, the power to regulate interstate commerce), Article I established a water's edge for the exercise of state power in what were now national affairs.

Originally, Article I also contained restrictions limiting the amendment of several of its provisions, a feature found nowhere else in the Constitution. Section 4 prohibited Congress from making any law banning the importation of slaves until 1808, and section 9 prohibited Congress from levying an income tax on the general population. Neither section is operative any longer. Section 4 expired on its own, and section 9 was modified by passage of the Sixteenth Amendment, which established the income tax (see page 88).

Despite the great care the Framers took to limit the exercise of congressional authority to those powers enumerated in Article I, the power of Congress has grown tremendously since the nation's founding. Under Chief Justice John Marshall (1801–1835), the U.S. Supreme Court interpreted the Constitution to favor the power of the national government over the states and to permit Congress to exercise both its *enumerated* (the power to regulate interstate commerce) and *implied* (the necessary and proper clause) powers in broad fashion. With only the occasional exception, the Court has never really challenged the legislative power vested in Congress to engage numerous areas of public policy that some constitutional scholars (and politicians and voters) believe are the province of the states. Perhaps the only area in which legislative power has diminished over the years has been the war-making power granted to Congress, something that lawmakers, for all their occasional criticism of presidential conduct of foreign policy, have ceded to the executive branch rather willingly.

Section 2.

The House of Representatives shall be composed of Members chosen every second Year by the People of the several States, and the Electors in each State shall have the Qualifications requisite for Electors of the most numerous Branch of the State Legislature.

No person shall be a Representative who shall not have attained to the Age of twenty five Years, and been seven Years a Citizen of the United States, and who shall not, when elected, be an Inhabitant of that State in which he shall be chosen.

The qualifications clause, which sets out the age and residency requirements for individuals who wish to run for the House of Representatives, became the centerpiece of a national debate that emerged during the late 1980s and early 1990s over term limits for members of Congress. In *U.S. Term Limits* v. *Thornton* (1995), the Supreme Court ruled that section 2, clause 2, did not specify any other qualification to serve in the House other than age and residency (as did section 3, clause 3, to run for the Senate). Thus, no state could restrict an individual's right to run for Congress. The Court ruled that any modification to the qualifications clause would have to come through a constitutional amendment.

Representatives and direct Taxes shall be apportioned among the several States which may be included within this Union, according to their respective Numbers which shall be determined by adding to the whole Number of free Persons, including those bound to Service for a Term of Years, and excluding Indians not taxed, three fifths of all other Persons. The actual Enumeration shall be made within three Years after the first Meeting of the Congress of the United States, and within every subsequent Term ten Years, in such Manner as they shall by Law direct. The Number of Representatives shall not exceed one for every thirty Thousand, but each State shall have at Least one Representative; and until such enumerations shall be made, the State of New Hampshire shall be entitled to chuse three, Massachusetts eight, Rhode-Island and Providence Plantations one, Connecticut five, New-York six, New Jersey four, Pennsylvania eight, Delaware one, Maryland six, Virginia ten, North Carolina five, South Carolina five, and Georgia three.

Under the Articles of Confederation, "direct" taxes (such as taxes on property) were apportioned based on land value, not population. This encouraged states to diminish the value of their land in order to reduce their tax burden. Prior to the Constitutional Convention of 1787, several prominent delegates met to discuss—and ultimately propose—changing the method for direct taxation from land value to the population of each state. A major sticking point among the delegates on this issue was how to count slaves for taxation purposes. Southern states wanted to diminish the value of slaves for tax purposes, while northern states wanted to count slaves as closer to a full person. On the other hand, southern states wanted to count slaves as "whole persons" for purposes of representation to increase their power in the House of Representatives, but northern states rejected this proposal. Ultimately, the delegates settled on the "Three-Fifths Compromise," which treated each slave as three-fifths of a person for tax and representation purposes.

At the beginning, the Three-Fifths Compromise enhanced southern power in the House. In 1790, when the 1st Congress convened, the South held 45 percent of the seats, despite a significantly smaller free population than the North. Over time, however, the South saw its power in the House diminish. By the 1830s, the South held just over 30 percent of House seats, which gave it just enough power to thwart northern initiatives on slavery questions and territorial issues, but not enough power to defeat the growing power of the North to control commercial and economic policy. This standoff between the North and South led to such events as South Carolina Senator John C. Calhoun's doctrine of nullification and secession, which argued that a state could nullify any federal law not consistent with regional or state interests. By the 1850s, the Three-Fifths Compromise had made the South dependent on expanding the number of slaveholding territories eligible for admission to the union and a judicial system sympathetic to slaveholding interests. The Three-Fifths Compromise was repealed by section 2 of the Fourteenth Amendment (see page 87).

When vacancies happen in the Representation from any State, the Executive Authority thereof shall issue Writs of Election to fill such Vacancies.

This clause permits the governor of a state to call an election to replace any member of the House of Representatives who is unable to complete a term of office due to death, resignation, or removal from the House. In some cases, a governor will appoint a successor to fill out a term; in other cases, the governor will call a special election. A governor's decision is shaped less by constitutional guidelines and more by partisan interests. For example, a Democratic governor might choose to appoint a Democratic successor if he or she believes that a Republican candidate might have an advantage in a special election.

The House of Representatives shall chuse their speaker and other Officers; and shall have the sole Power of Impeachment.

Clause 5 establishes the only officer of the House of Representatives—the speaker. The remaining offices (party leaders, whips, and so on) are created by the House.

The House also has the sole power of impeachment against members of the executive and judicial branches. The House, like the Senate, is responsible for disciplining its own members. In *Nixon v. U.S.* (1993), the Supreme Court ruled that government officials who are the subject of impeachment proceedings may not challenge them in court. The Court ruled that the sole power given to the House over impeachment precludes judicial intervention.

Section 3.

The Senate of the United States shall be composed of two Senators from each State chosen by the Legislature thereof, for six Years; and each Senator shall have one Vote.

The provision of this clause establishing the election of senators by state legislatures was repealed by the Seventeenth Amendment (see page 88).

Immediately after they shall be assembled in Consequence of the first Election, they shall be divided as equally as may be into three Classes. The Seats of the Senators of the first Class shall be vacated at the Expiration of the second year, of the second Class at the Expiration of the fourth Year, and of the third Class at the Expiration of the sixth Year, so that one third may be chosen every second Year and if Vacancies happen by Resignation, or otherwise, during the Recess of the Legislature of any State, the Executive thereof may make temporary Appointments until the next Meeting of the Legislature, which shall then fill such Vacancies.

Vacancies for senators are handled the same way as vacancies for representatives—through appointment or special election. The Seventeenth Amendment modified the language authorizing the state legislature to choose a replacement for a vacant Senate position.

No Person shall be a Senator who shall not have attained to the Age of thirty Years, and been nine Years a Citizen of the United States, and who shall not, when elected, be an Inhabitant of that State for which he shall be chosen.

The Vice President of the United States shall be President of the Senate, but shall have no Vote, unless they be equally divided.

Clause 4 gives the vice president the authority to vote to break a tie in the Senate. This is the only constitutional duty the Constitution specifies for the vice president. As president of the Senate, the vice president also presides over procedural matters of that body, although this is not a responsibility that vice presidents have really ever shouldered.

The Senate shall chuse their other Officers, and also a President pro tempore, in the Absence of the Vice President, or when he shall exercise the Office of President of the United States.

Clause 5 creates the position of *president pro tempore* (the president of the time), the only Senate office established by the Constitution to handle the duties of the vice president set out in section 3, clause 4.

The Senate shall have the sole Power to try all Impeachments. When sitting for that Purpose, they shall be on Oath or Affirmation. When the President of the United States is tried, the Chief Justice shall preside: And no Person shall be convicted without the Concurrence of two thirds of the Members present.

Judgment in Cases of Impeachment shall not extend further than to removal from Office, and disqualification to hold and enjoy any Office of honor, Trust or Profit under the United States; but the Party convicted shall nevertheless be liable and subject to Indictment, Trial, Judgment and Punishment, according to law.

Just as the House of Representatives has the sole power to bring impeachment against executive and judicial branch officials, the Senate has the sole power to try all impeachments. Unless the president is facing trial in the Senate, the vice president serves as the presiding officer. In 1998, President Bill Clinton was tried on two articles of impeachment (four were brought against him in the House) and found not guilty on each count. The presiding officer in President Clinton's impeachment trial was Chief Justice William H. Rehnquist.

A conviction results in the removal of an official from office. It does not prohibit subsequent civil or criminal action against that individual. Nor does it prohibit an impeached and convicted official from returning to federal office. In 1989, Alcee Hastings, a trial judge with ten years experience on the U.S. District Court for the Southern District of Florida, was convicted on impeachment charges and removed from office. In 1992, he ran successfully for the 23rd District seat of the U.S. House of Representatives, where he continues to serve as of this writing.

Section 4.

The Times, Places and Manner of holding Elections for Senators and Representatives, shall be prescribed in each State by the Legislature thereof; but the Congress may at any time by Law make or alter such Regulations, except as to the Places of chusing Senators.

The Congress shall assemble at least once in every Year, and such Meeting shall be on the first Monday in December, unless they shall by Law appoint a different Day.

Section 4 authorizes the states to establish the rules governing elections for members of Congress, but Congress has never hesitated to exercise its law-making power in this area when it has believed that improvements were necessary to improve the electoral process. The first such action did not come until 1842, when Congress passed legislation making elections to the House based on single-member districts, not from the general population. By the turn of the twentieth century, Congress had passed legislation establishing additional criteria such as the rough equality of population among districts and territorial compactness and contiguity. Article I, section 4, is one of the three main areas from which Congress derives the power to regulate the electoral process. The other two are the necessary and proper clause of Article I, section 8, clause 3, and section 2 of the Fifteenth Amendment.

Section 5.

Each House shall be the Judge of the Elections, Returns and Qualifications of its own Members, and a Majority of each shall constitute a Quorum to do business; but a smaller Number may adjourn from day to day, and may be authorized to compel the Attendance of absent Members, in such Manner, and under such Penalties as each House may provide.

Each House may determine the Rules of its Proceedings, punish its Members for disorderly Behaviour, and with the Concurrence of two thirds, expel a Member.

Clause 2 gives power to the House and Senate to establish the rules and decorum for each chamber. Expulsion from either the House or the Senate does not preclude a member from running for congressional office again or serving in any other official capacity. In *Powell* v. *McCormack* (1969), the Supreme Court ruled that the House's decision to exclude an individual from the

Authority over all Places purchased by the Consent of the Legislature of the State in which the Same shall be for the Erection of Forts, Magazines, Arsenals, dock-Yards, and other needful Buildings;—And

Article I, section 8, clause 1, is, in many ways, the engine of congressional power. First, clause 1 gives Congress the power to tax and spend, a power the Supreme Court has interpreted as "exhaustive" and "reaching every subject." Second, in giving Congress the power to provide for the common defense and general welfare, it offers no specific constraint on what Congress may spend public funds for and how much it may spend. Third, section 8 gives Congress complete authority in numerous areas of policy that affect Americans at home and abroad on a massive scale. These powers include the power to regulate interstate commerce (which Congress has relied on to establish federal civil rights law), to make war (a power that Congress, since the end of World War II in 1945, has increasingly deferred to the president), and to establish the federal judicial system.

Clause 1 is often cited by constitutional scholars as an example of how the Constitution constrains legislative power by limiting the powers that Congress may exercise. To a certain extent, this is true. But it is also true that the Court has granted Congress extensive power to legislate in certain areas that bear only a tangential relationship to the specific language of some of the provisions of clause 1. For example, in *Katzenbach* v. *McClung* (1964), the Court turned back a challenge to the constitutionality of the Civil Rights Act of 1964, which Congress had passed under its authority to regulate interstate commerce. The Court ruled that racial discrimination had an adverse effect on the free flow of commerce.

Clause 2 establishes the seat of the federal government—first New York City, now Washington, D.C. The clause also makes Congress the legislative body of the nation's capital, a power that extends to other federal bodies, such as forts, military bases, and other places where federal buildings are located.

To make all Laws which shall be necessary and proper for carrying into Execution the foregoing Powers, and all other Powers vested by this Constitution in the Government of the United States, or in any Department or Officer thereof.

Better known as the necessary and proper clause, this provision of Article I was one of the most contested points between Federalists and Anti-Federalists during the ratification debates over the Constitution. Anti-Federalists feared that the language was too broad and all-encompassing, and, if interpreted by a Supreme Court sympathetic to the nationalist ambitions of the Federalist Party, would give Congress limitless power to exercise legislative authority over state and local matters. In *McCulloch* v. *Maryland* (1819), Chief Justice John Marshall offered what constitutional scholars believe remains the definitive interpretation of the necessary and proper clause. While *McCulloch* certainly did cement the power of Congress in the federal system, the expansive definition given the necessary and proper clause by the Court is also testament to the flexible nature of the Constitution, and why so few amendments have been added to the original document.

Section 9.

The Migration or Importation of such Persons as any of the States now existing shall think proper to admit, shall not be prohibited by the Congress prior to the Year one thousand eight hundred and eight, but a Tax or duty may be imposed on such Importation, not exceeding ten dollars for each Person.

Like the other provisions of the Constitution that refer to slavery, such as the Three-Fifths Compromise, section 9 creates policy governing the institution without ever mentioning the word. The importation clause was a compromise between slave traders, who wanted to continue the practice, and opponents of slavery, who needed southern support to ratify the Constitution. In 1808, Congress passed legislation banning the importation of slaves; until then, Congress used its power to tax slaves brought to the United States.

The Privilege of the Writ of Habeas Corpus shall not be suspended, unless when in Cases of Rebellion or Invasion the public Safety may require it.

Clause 2 is the only place where the writ of *habeas corpus*—the "Great Writ," as it was known to the Framers—is mentioned in the Constitution. Only the federal government is bound by clause 2. The writ may only be suspended in times of crisis and rebellion, and then it is Congress that has the power, not the president.

No Bill of Attainder or ex post facto Law shall be passed.

A bill of attainder is a legislative act punishing a person with "pains and penalties" without the benefit of a hearing or trial. The fundamental purpose of the ban on bills of attainder is to prevent trial by legislature and other arbitrary punishments for persons vulnerable to extra-judicial proceedings. An *ex post facto law* is one passed making a previously committed civil or criminal action subject to penalty. In Calder v. Bull (1798), the Court ruled that the ban on *ex post facto* laws applied only to penal and criminal actions.

A similar restriction on the states is found in Article I, section 10, clause 1.

No Capitation, or other direct, Tax shall be laid, unless in Proportion to the Census or Enumeration herein before directed to be taken.

This clause, which originally prohibited Congress from levying an income tax, was modified by the Sixteenth Amendment, passed in 1913 (see page 88).

No Tax or Duty shall be laid on Articles exported from any State.

Clause 5 prohibits Congress from levying a tax on any good or article exported from a state to a foreign country or to another state. Many southern states feared that northern members of Congress would attempt to weaken the South's slave-based economy by taxing exports. This clause prohibited such action. Congress may prohibit the shipment of certain items from one state to another—beer and wine, for example—and to other countries.

No Preference shall be given by any Regulation of Commerce or Revenue to the Ports of one State over those of another: nor shall Vessels bound to, or from, one State, be obliged to enter, clear, or pay Duties in another.

Congress is prohibited from making laws regulating trade that favor one state over another. Clause 6 also prohibits Congress from establishing preferences for certain ports or trade centers over others, although it may, under its power to regulate interstate commerce, pass laws that incidentally benefit certain states or maritime outlets. The Supreme Court has ruled that states are not bound by the limitations on Congress expressed in this clause.

No money shall be drawn from the Treasury, but in Consequence of Appropriations made by Law; and a regular Statement and Account of the Receipts and Expenditures of all public Money shall be published from time to time.

Clause 7 serves two fundamental purposes. First, the clause prohibits any governmental body receiving federal funds from spending those funds without the approval of Congress. Once Congress has determined that federal funds are to be spent in a certain way, the executive branch may not exercise any discretion over that decision. Second, by restricting executive control of spending power, the clause firmly reinforces congressional authority over revenue and spending, a key feature of the separation of powers.

No Title of Nobility shall be granted by the United States: And no Person holding any Office of Profit or Trust under them, shall, without the Consent of the Congress, accept of any present, Emolument, Office, or Title, of any kind whatever, from any King, Prince, or foreign State.

This provision is among the first school-taught lessons about the Constitution. To reinforce the commitment to representative democracy, the Framers prohibited a title of nobility from being conferred on any public official. This clause also prohibits any government official from accepting compensation, gifts, or similar benefits from any foreign government for services rendered without the consent of Congress.

Section 10.

No state shall enter into any Treaty, Alliance, or Confederation; grant Letters of Marque and Reprisal; coin Money; emit Bills of Credit; make any Thing but gold and silver Coin a Tender in Payment of Debts; pass any Bill of Attainder, ex post facto Law, or Law impairing the Obligation of Contracts, or grant any Title of Nobility.

This clause denies several powers to the states that were once permissible under the Articles of Confederation, and it emphasizes the Framers' commitment under the Constitution to a strong national government with Congress as the centrifugal force. During the Civil War, the Union relied on this clause in support of its view that the Confederate states had no legal existence but instead were merely "states in rebellion" against the United States.

The restrictions on states passing either bills of attainder or *ex post facto* laws have come into play at various points in American history. During Reconstruction, several states enacted legislation prohibiting any individual who aided the Confederacy from entering certain professions or enjoying other benefits available to citizens who remained loyal to the Union. The Supreme Court struck down these laws on the grounds that they violated this clause.

The provision prohibiting states from passing any law "impairing the Obligation of Contracts," better known as the contract clause, has been the subject of considerable litigation before the Supreme Court. The contract clause was intended to bar the states from interfering in private contracts between consensual parties and was considered an important limit on the power of states to restrict the fledgling national economic order of the early republic. Early on, the Court considered many laws that restricted the terms set out in private contracts as unconstitutional. But as the United States became a more industrial society, and as citizen demands grew for government regulation of the economy, the environment, and social welfare benefits, the Court softened its position on the contract clause to permit states to make laws that served a reasonable public interest. A key case involving the contract clause is *Home Building and Loan Association* v. *Blaisdell* (1934). In *Blaisdell*, the Court ruled that a Depression-era law passed by the Minnesota legislature forgiving mortgage payments by homeowners to banks did not violate the contract clause.

No State shall, without the Consent of the Congress, lay any Imposts or Duties on Imports or Exports, except what may be absolutely necessary for executing its inspection Laws: and the net Produce of all Duties and Imposts, laid by any State on Imports or Exports, shall be for the Use of the Treasury of the United States, and all such Laws shall be subject to the Revision and Controul of the Congress.

No state may tax goods leaving or entering a state, although it may charge reasonable fees for inspections considered necessary to the public interest. The restriction on import and export taxes applies only to those goods entering from or leaving for a foreign country.

No State shall, without the Consent of Congress, lay any Duty of Tonnage, keep Troops, or Ships of War in time of Peace, enter into any Agreement or Compact with another State, or with a foreign Power, or engage in War, unless actually invaded, or in such imminent Danger as will not admit of delay.

Clause 3 cements the power of Congress to control acts of war and make treaties with foreign countries. The Framers wanted to correct any perception to the contrary gained from the Articles of Confederation that states were free to act independently of the national government on negotiated matters with foreign countries. They also wanted to ensure that any state that entered into a compact with another state—something this clause does not prohibit—must receive permission from Congress.

ARTICLE II

Section 1.

The executive Power shall be vested in a President of the United States of America. He shall hold his Office during the Term of four Years, and, together with the Vice President, chosen for the same Term, be elected as follows.

In *Federalist No. 70*, Alexander Hamilton argued for an "energetic executive" branch headed by a single, elected president not necessarily beholden to the majority party in Congress. Hamilton believed that a nationally elected president would not be bound by the narrow, parochial interests that drove legislative law-making. The president would possess both the veto power over Congress and a platform from which to articulate a national vision in both domestic and foreign affairs.

Hamilton believed that the constitutional boundaries placed on executive power through the separation of powers and the fact that the president was accountable to a national electorate constrained any possibility that the office would come to resemble the monarchies of Europe. However, most presidential scholars agree that the modern presidency has grown in power precisely because of the general nature of the enabling powers of Article II.

Each State shall appoint, in such Manner as the Legislature thereof may direct, a Number of Electors, equal to the whole Number of Senators and Representatives to which the State may be entitled in the Congress; but no Senator or Representative, or Person holding an Office of Trust of Profit under the United States, shall be appointed an Elector.

Clause 2 established the Electoral College and set the number of electors from each state at the total of senators and representatives serving in Congress.

The Electors shall meet in their respective States, and vote by Ballot for two Persons, of whom one at least shall not be an Inhabitant of the same State with themselves. And they shall make a List of all the Persons voted for, and, of the Number of Votes for each; which List they shall sign and certify, and transmit sealed to the Seat of the Government of the United States, directed to the President of the Senate. The President of the Senate shall, in the Presence of the Senate and House of Representatives, open all the Certificates, and the Votes shall then be counted. The Person having the greatest Number of Votes shall be the President, if such Number be a Majority of the whole Number of Electors appointed; and if there be more than one who have such Majority, and have an equal Number of Votes, then the House of Representatives shall immediately chuse by Ballot one of them for President; and if no Person have a Majority, then from the five highest on the List the said House shall in like Manner chuse the President. But in chusing the President, the Votes shall be taken by States, the Representation from each State having one Vote; A quorum for this Purpose shall consist of a Member or Members from two thirds of the States, and a Majority of all the States shall be necessary to a Choice. In every Case, after the Choice of the President, the Person having the greatest Number of Votes of the Electors shall be the Vice President. But if there should remain two or more who have equal Votes, the Senate shall chuse from them by Ballot the Vice President.

This provision of section 1 described the rules for calling the Electoral College to vote for president and vice president. Originally, the electors did not vote separately for president and vice president. After the 1800 election, which saw Thomas Jefferson and Aaron Burr receive the identical number of electoral votes even though it was clear that Jefferson was the presidential candidate and Burr the vice presidential candidate, the nation ratified the Twelfth Amendment (see page 85).

The Twelfth Amendment did not resolve what many constitutional scholars today believe are the inadequacies of the Electoral College system. In 1824, the presidential election ended in a four-way tie, and the House of Representatives elected second-place finisher John Quincy Adams. In 1876, Benjamin Harrison lost the popular vote but won the presidency after recounts awarded him an Electoral College majority. But perhaps the most controversial election of all came in 2000, when George W. Bush, who lost the popular contest to Al Gore by approximately 500,000 votes, was named the presidential victor after a

six-week court battle over the vote count in Florida. After the Supreme Court ruled against the position of Al Gore that a recount of the Florida popular vote should continue until all votes had been counted, an outcome that would have left the nation without a president-elect for several more weeks, Bush was awarded Florida's electoral votes, which gave him 271, just one more than he needed to win the office. Outraged Democrats pledged to mount a case for Electoral College reform, but, as was so often the case before, nothing happened.

The Congress may determine the Time of chusing the Electors, and the Day on which they shall give their Votes; which Day shall be the same throughout the United States.

No Person except a natural born Citizen, or a Citizen of the United States, at the time of the Adoption of this Constitution, shall be eligible to the Office of President; neither shall any Person be eligible to that Office who shall not have attained to the Age of thirty five Years, and been fourteen Years a Resident within the United States.

This provision of Article II is referred to as the presidential eligibility clause. In addition to setting out the age and resident requirements of presidential aspirants, this clause defines who may *not* run for president—any foreign-born individual who has nonetheless obtained United States citizenship. For example, Michigan Governor Jennifer Granholm, who has lived in the United States since she was four years old, may not run for president because she was born in Canada. The same is true for California Governor Arnold Schwarzenegger, who was born in Austria but has lived in the United States his entire adult life. Judicial interpretation of the presidential eligibility clause has not resolved the question of whether children born to U.S. citizens are eligible to run for president if they meet the residency requirements.

In Case of the Removal of the President from Office, or of his Death, Resignation, or Inability to discharge the Powers and Duties of the said Office, the Same shall devolve on the Vice President, and the Congress may by Law provide for the Case of Removal, Death, Resignation or Inability, both of the President and Vice President, declaring what Officer shall then act as President, and such Officer shall act accordingly, until the Disability be removed, or a President shall be elected.

This presidential succession clause has been modified by the Twenty-Fifth Amendment (see page 92).

The President shall, at stated Times, receive for his Services, a Compensation, which shall neither be encreased nor diminished during the Period for which he shall have been elected, and he shall not receive within that Period any other Emolument from the United States, or any of them.

Presidential compensation, like compensation for members of Congress, may not be increased for the current occupant of the office. The president is not eligible for any other public compensation during time in office. However, the president may continue to receive income such as interest on investments or book royalties.

Before he enter on the Execution of his Office, he shall take the following Oath or Affirmation:—"I do solemnly swear (or affirm) that I will faithfully execute the Office of President of the United States, and will to the best of my Ability, preserve, protect and defend the Constitution of the United States."

Since George Washington's inaugural in 1789, each president has added the phrase "so help me God" to the end of the presidential oath. Although Abraham Lincoln cited the oath to justify his suspension of the writ of *habeas corpus* during the Civil War, no other president has relied on the oath to justify action that stretched the boundaries of executive power. Presidents taking extraordinary action either at home or abroad have relied on either the commander-in-chief clause of section 2, clause 1, or the provision of section 3 authorizing the president to "faithfully execut[e]" the laws of the United States.

Section 2.

The President shall be Commander in Chief of the Army and Navy of the United States, and of the Militia of the several States, when called into the actual Service of the United States; he may require the Opinion, in writing, of the principal Officer in each of the executive Departments, upon any Subject relating to the Duties of their respective Offices, and he shall have Power to grant Reprieves and Pardons for Offences against the United States, except in Cases of Impeachment.

Section 2, clause 1, establishes the president as commander in chief of the Army and Navy of the United States. In modern times, that authority has extended to the Air Force, the Marines, and all other branches of the armed forces operating under the command of the United States, including state militias, reserve units, and national guards. Article I provides that Congress, and not the president, has the power to declare war. But since World War II, no American president has received or requested a declaration of war to commit the armed forces to military conflicts, including those clearly acknowledged as large-scale war (Korea, Vietnam, the 1991 Persian Gulf War, Afghanistan, and the Iraq War). For these conflicts, the president received congressional *authorization* to use force, but not an Article I declaration.

Clause 1 also implicitly creates the Cabinet by authorizing the president to request the opinion "in writing" of the principal officers of the executive branch. The power to create Cabinet-level offices resides with Congress, not the president.

Presidential power to pardon is broad and limited only in cases of impeachment. Perhaps the most controversial pardon in American political history was President Gerald R. Ford's decision to pardon former President Richard M. Nixon, who resigned his office on August 8, 1974, after news reports and congressional inquiries strongly implicated him in the Watergate scandal. A real possibility existed that President Nixon could be tried on criminal charges as the result of his alleged activities during the Watergate scandal.

He shall have Power, by and with the Advice and Consent of the Senate, to make Treaties, provided two thirds of the Senators present concur; and he shall nominate, and by and with the Advice and Consent of the Senate, shall appoint Ambassadors, other public Ministers and Consuls, Judges of the supreme Court, and all other Officers of the United States, whose Appointments are not herein otherwise provided for, and which shall be established by Law: but the Congress may by Law vest the Appointment of such inferior Officers, as they think proper, in the President alone, in the Courts of Law, or in the Heads of Departments.

The President shall have Power to fill up all Vacancies that may happen during the Recess of the Senate, by granting Commissions which shall expire at the End of their next Session.

Clause 2 describes several powers the president may exercise in conjunction with the advice and consent of the Senate. These powers include the power, upon the approval of two-thirds of the Senate, to make treaties with foreign countries. But the Constitution is silent on the question of whether a president (or Congress) may terminate a treaty by refusing to honor it or simply repealing it outright. When President Jimmy Carter terminated a treaty with China over the objection of Congress, several members sought a judicial resolution of the action; the Court, however, did not decide the case on the merits and offered no resolution on the matter.

The president does not require a two-thirds majority for approval of appointments to the federal judiciary, foreign ambassadorships, Cabinet-level positions, high-ranking positions in non-Cabinet agencies, and high-level military offices. But the fact that the Senate must approve presidential appointments in these areas provides Congress (senators often listen to the constituents of House members on controversial choices) with an important check on presidential power to shape the contours of the executive branch.

The final provision of clause 2 permits Congress to determine whether Senate approval is necessary for lower-level appointments to executive branch or military positions.

A more controversial power related to presidential appointment power is the power of the president to *remove* officials from public office. The first real confrontation over presidential removal power came after Congress passed the Tenure in Office Act of 1867, a measure intended to prevent President Andrew Johnson from removing officials who had been approved by the Senate. In 1887, Congress repealed the law and returned removal power to the president. In 1926, the Supreme Court finally settled the question of presidential removal power when it ruled in *Myers* v. *U.S.* that the president had the sole power to remove officials from executive-branch positions. But the Court later ruled in *Humphrey's Executor* v. *U.S.* (1935) that presidential removal power did not extend to positions that were "quasi-legislative" or "quasi-judicial."

Section 3.

He shall from time to time give to the Congress Information of the State of the Union, and recommend to their Consideration such Measures as he shall judge necessary and expedient; he may, on extraordinary Occasions, convene both Houses, or either of them, and in Case of Disagreement between them, with Respect to the Time of Adjournment, he may adjourn them to such Time as he shall think proper; he shall receive Ambassadors and other public Ministers; he shall take Care that the Laws be faithfully executed, and shall Commission all the Officers of the United States.

The president is required to deliver a State of the Union message to Congress each year. The nation's first two presidents, George Washington and John Adams, delivered their addresses in person. But the nation's third president, Thomas Jefferson, believed that the practice too closely resembled the Speech from the Throne delivered by British royalty. Instead, Jefferson prepared remarks for recitation before Congress by an assistant or clerk of Congress. Every American president after Jefferson followed suit until Woodrow Wilson renewed the original practice after his first year in office. Now, the State of the Union Address is a major media event, although it is less an assessment of the nation's health and happiness and more a presidential wish-list for policy initiatives and the touting of partisan accomplishments.

The final provision of section 3 authorizing the president to faithfully execute the laws of the United States has proven controversial over the years. Presidents have cited this broad language to justify such far-reaching action as the suspension of the writ of *habeas corpus,* as President Abraham Lincoln did during the Civil War before being rebuffed by the Supreme Court in *Ex parte McCardle* (1867), and the doctrine of executive privilege, which, as asserted by various presidents, permits the executive branch to withhold sensitive information from the public or the other branches of government for national security reasons. The Court has been of two minds about the doctrine of executive privilege. On the one hand, the Court has said in such cases as *New York Times* v. *U.S.* (1971) and *U.S.* v. *Nixon* (1974) that the president has the power to withhold information to protect vital secrets and the nation's security. On the other hand, the Court has said, in ruling against the assertion of executive privilege in these two cases, that only an exceptional and demonstrated case can justify allowing the president to withhold information.

Section 4.

The President, Vice President and all civil Officers of the United States, shall be removed from Office on Impeachment for, and Conviction of, Treason, Bribery, or other High Crimes and Misdemeanors.

Presidential impeachment, like impeachment of the other described offices in section 4, is the responsibility of the House of Representatives. There is no judicial definition to what constitutes a high crime or misdemeanor. Complicating the matter further is that only the House and Senate are given responsibility over the impeachment process. No federal official subject to impeachment may challenge the action in federal court, as the Supreme Court has ruled that the rules governing impeachment are not actionable in court. Only two presidents, Andrew Johnson in 1868 and Bill Clinton in 1998, have ever been impeached. Neither president was convicted by the Senate of the charges brought against them.

ARTICLE III
Section 1.

The judicial Power of the United States, shall be vested in one supreme Court, and in such inferior Courts as the Congress may from time to time ordain and establish. The Judges, both of the supreme and inferior Courts, shall hold their Offices during good Behaviour, and shall, at stated Times, receive for their Services, a Compensation, which shall not be diminished during their Continuance in Office.

Like the power of Congress and the executive branch under Articles I and II, respectively, of the Constitution, the power of the federal judiciary has developed as the result of constitutional silences and ambiguities. Article III establishes only one federal court, the Supreme Court, and leaves to Congress the power to establish "inferior" courts as it deems necessary. Many students are surprised to learn that the power of judicial review was established by Congress, not the Supreme Court. Although the Court did articulate the power of judicial review in *Marbury* v. *Madison* (1803), that decision only applied to the power of the federal courts to review federal laws. The power of the federal courts to review state laws that allegedly trespassed upon the Constitution was established by the Judiciary Act of 1789. But on the fundamental question of what constitutes the foundation and scope of judicial

power, there is little doubt that the Court, not Congress, has been the foremost exponent of its own authority. Often, the Court has justified its authority to limit the power of the other branches to regulate its affairs by pointing to other provisions of the Constitution, most notably the supremacy clause of Article VI and section 5 of the Fourteenth Amendment, as well as Article III.

Section 2.

The judicial Power shall extend to all Cases, in Law and Equity, arising under this Constitution, the Laws of the United States, and Treaties made, or which shall be made, under their Authority;—to all Cases affecting Ambassadors, other public Ministers and Consuls;—to all Cases of admiralty and maritime Jurisdiction;—to Controversies to which the United States shall be a Party;—to Controversies between two or more States;—between a State and Citizens of another State;—between Citizens of different States;— between Citizens of the same State claiming Lands under Grants of different States,—and between a State, or the Citizens thereof, and foreign States, Citizens or Subjects.

In all Cases affecting Ambassadors, other public Ministers and Consuls, and those in which a State shall be Party, the supreme Court shall have original Jurisdiction. In all the other Cases before mentioned, the supreme Court shall have appellate Jurisdiction, both as to Law and Fact, with such Exceptions, and under such Regulations as the Congress shall make.

The Trial of all Crimes, except in Cases of Impeachment, shall be by Jury; and such Trial shall be held in the State where the said Crimes shall have been committed; but when not committed within any State, the Trial shall be at such Place or Places as the Congress may by Law have directed.

Section 1 invests the judicial power in "one Supreme Court," but it is in section 2 that we find the source of much of the controversy of the exercise of this power since *Marbury* was decided. By extending the judicial power to all "Cases, in Law and Equity, arising under the Constitution, [and] the laws of the United States," section 2 authorizes the Court to both decide matters of law and, if necessary, mandate a remedy commensurate with the degree of a constitutional violation. For example, in *Swann* v. *Charlotte-Mecklenburg Board of Education* (1971), the Court ruled that a lower court, having found that a school system had failed to meet desegregation requirements, had the power to order busing and other remedies to the constitutional violations it found in *Brown* v. *Board of Education* (1954).

Federal judicial power no longer extends to cases involving lawsuits between a state and citizens of another state. This provision was superceded by the Eleventh Amendment.

Section 2 also includes the exceptions and regulations clause. This clause has been used by congressional opponents of some of the Court's more controversial and generally liberal decisions. Although most scholars believe the clause limits the power of Congress to create broad jurisdiction for the courts it creates, others have argued that it permits Congress to strip the federal courts of jurisdiction to hear particular cases. Some opponents of the Court's decisions legalizing abortion, authorizing school busing, and upholding affirmative action have attempted to curb the power of federal courts to rule in such areas by stripping them of jurisdiction in such cases. To date, no president has ever signed such legislation.

Section 3.

Treason against the United States, shall consist only in levying War against them, or in adhering to their Enemies, giving them Aid and Comfort. No Person shall be convicted of Treason unless on the Testimony of two Witnesses to the same overt Act, or on Confession in open Court.

The Congress shall have Power to declare the Punishment of Treason, but no Attainder of Treason shall work Corruption of Blood, or Forfeiture except during the Life of the Person attainted.

Article III defines the only crime mentioned by the Constitution: treason.

ARTICLE IV
Section 1.

Full Faith and Credit shall be given in each State to the public Acts, Records, and judicial Proceedings of every other State. And the Congress may by general Laws prescribe the Manner in which such Acts, Records and Proceedings shall be proved, and the Effect thereof.

The full faith and credit clause rests on principles borrowed from international law that require one country to recognize contracts made in another country absent a compelling public policy reason to the contrary. Here, this principle, referred to in the law as *comity*, applied to the relationship between the states. For example, a driver's license issued in Ohio is good in Montana. The full and faith credit clause also requires a state to recognize public acts and court proceedings of another state. For the most part, interpretation of the full faith and credit clause has not been controversial. That may well change, as advocates of same-sex marriage have suggested that such a marriage performed in one state must be recognized in another state, as is the case with heterosexual marriage. A constitutional challenge to the clause may well center on the public policy exception recognized in other areas of law.

Section 2.

The Citizens of each State shall be entitled to all Privileges and Immunities of Citizens in the several States.

A Person charged in any State with Treason, Felony, or other Crime, who shall flee from Justice, and be found in another State, shall on Demand of the executive Authority of the State from which he fled, be delivered up, to be removed to the State having Jurisdiction of the Crime.

The extradition clause requires that the governor of one state deliver a fugitive from justice to the state from which that fugitive fled. Congress passed the Fugitive Act of 1793 to give definition to this provision, but the federal government has no authority to compel state authorities to extradite a fugitive from one state to another. A state may, however, sue another state in federal court to force the return of a fugitive.

No Person held to Service or Labour in one State under the Laws thereof, escaping into another, shall, in Consequence of any Law or Regulation therein, be discharged from such Service or Labour, but shall be delivered up on Claim of the Party to whom such Service or Labour may be due.

The fugitive slave clause, which required any state, including those outside the slave-holding states of the South, to return escaped slaves to their owners, was repealed in 1865 by the Thirteenth Amendment. Prior to 1865, Congress passed laws in 1793 and 1850 to enforce the clause, leaving states without power to make concurrent laws on the subject, ensuring that the southern states would always have the Constitution on their side to protect slavery.

Section 3.

New States may be admitted by the Congress into this Union; but no new State shall be formed or erected within the Jurisdiction of any other State; nor any State be formed by the Junction of two or more States, or Parts of States, without the Consent of the Legislatures of the States concerned as well as of the Congress.

The Congress shall have Power to dispose of and make all needful Rules and Regulations respecting the Territory or other Property belonging to the United States; and nothing in this Constitution shall be so construed as to Prejudice any Claims of the United States, or of any particular State.

Section 4.

The United States shall guarantee to every State in this Union a Republican Form of Government, and shall protect each of them against Invasion; and on Application of the Legislature, or of the Executive (when the Legislature cannot be convened) against domestic Violence.

ARTICLE V

The Congress, whenever two thirds of both Houses shall deem it necessary, shall propose Amendments to this Constitution, or, on the Application of the Legislatures of two thirds of the several States, shall call a Convention for proposing Amendments, which, in either Case, shall be valid to all Intents and Purposes, as Part of this Constitution, when ratified by the Legislatures of three fourths of the several States, or by Conventions in three fourths thereof, as the one or the other Mode of Ratification may be proposed by the Congress; Provided that no Amendment which may be made prior to the Year One thousand eight hundred and eight shall in any Manner affect the first and fourth Clauses in the Ninth Section of the first Article; and that no State, without its Consent, shall be deprived of its equal Suffrage in the Senate.

Changes to the Articles of Confederation had required the unanimous approval of the states. But, Article V of the U.S. Constitution offers multiple options—none of which require unanimity—for constitutional change. Article V was quite crucial to the ratification of the Constitution. Federalists who supported the Constitution wanted to ensure that any additions or modifications to the nation's charter would require the approval of more than a simple majority of citizens. This is why any amendment coming out of Congress requires two-thirds of the House and Senate for approval. The same is true for the rule requiring three-fourths of the states to ratify an amendment (either through conventions or state legislative action). Anti-Federalists who either opposed the Constitution or had reservations about key sections of it were soothed by the prospect of an amending process that did not require the unanimous approval of the states.

Only twenty-seven amendments since 1789 have been added to the Constitution, the first fifteen of which were added by 1870. Since 1933, when the nation repealed Prohibition by passing the Twenty-First Amendment, the Constitution has been amended only six times. In the modern constitutional era, efforts to amend the Constitution have generally centered on unhappiness with Supreme Court decisions (on school prayer, flag burning, school busing, abortion rights) or state court rulings with national implications (such as same-sex marriage) rather than any structural defect in the original Constitution (unlike woman's suffrage or presidential succession) or a seismic political event (the Civil War). To date, none of these efforts have been successful.

Article VI made the national government responsible for all debts incurred by the Revolutionary War. This ensured that manufacturing and banking interests would be repaid for the losses they sustained during the conflict. But the most important provisions of Article VI by far are contained in its second and third clauses.

Clause 2 took another major step forward for national power and away from the confederate approach to government structure of the Articles of Confederation. By making "this Constitution" and all laws made under its authority the "supreme Law of the Land," Article VI created what constitutional scholars call the supremacy clause. The Supreme Court has invoked the supremacy clause on several occasions to rebut challenges mounted by states to its decisions or acts of Congress. Among the more notable decisions by the Supreme Court that have cited the supremacy clause to mandate compliance with a previous ruling is *Cooper* v. *Aaron* (1958). In *Cooper*, the Court cited the supremacy clause in rejecting the argument of Governor Orval Faubus of Arkansas claiming that local schools were not obligated to follow the *Brown* v. *Board of Education* (1954) ruling. The Court said that *Brown* was the law of the land and, as such, all school boards were required to comply with its requirement to desegregate their schools.

Although most Americans rightly point to the First Amendment as the baseline for the guarantee for religious freedom, clause 3 of Article VI contains an important contribution to this principle—the ban on religious tests or qualifications to hold public office. Holders of public office, no matter how great or small, were required to affirm their allegiance to the Constitution and the laws of the United States, but they could not be required to profess a belief in God or meet any other religious qualification. Numerous states nonetheless ignored this requirement until 1961, when the Supreme Court ruled in *Torcaso* v. *Watkins* that states could not administer religious oaths to holders of public office.

ARTICLE VI

All Debts contracted and Engagements entered into, before the Adoption of this Constitution, shall be as valid against the United States under this Constitution, as under the Confederation.

This Constitution, and the Laws of the United States which shall be made in Pursuance thereof; and all Treaties made, or which shall be made, under the Authority of the United States, shall be the supreme Law of the Land; and the Judges in every State shall be bound thereby, any Thing in the Constitution or Laws of any State to the Contrary notwithstanding.

The Senators and Representatives before mentioned, and the Members of the several State Legislatures, and all executive and judicial Officers, both of the United States and of the several States, shall be bound by Oath or Affirmation, to support this Constitution; but no religious Test shall ever be required as a Qualification to any Office or public Trust under the United States.

ARTICLE VII

The Ratification of the Conventions of nine States, shall be sufficient for the Establishment of this Constitution between the States so ratifying the Same.

Done in Convention by the Unanimous Consent of the States present the Seventeenth Day of September in the Year of our Lord one thousand seven hundred and Eighty seven and of the Independence of the United States of America the Twelfth. IN WITNESS whereof We have hereunto subscribed our Names,

G. WASHINGTON,
Presid't. and deputy from Virginia

Attest
WILLIAM JACKSON,
Secretary

DELAWARE
George Read
Gunning Bedford, Jr.
John Dickinson
Richard Basset
Jacob Broom

MASSACHUSETTS BAY
Nathaniel Gorham
Rufus King

CONNECTICUT
William Samuel Johnson
Roger Sherman

NEW YORK
Alexander Hamilton

NEW JERSEY
William Livingston
David Brearley
William Paterson
Jonathan Dayton

PENNSYLVANIA
Benjamin Franklin
Thomas Mifflin
Robert Morris
George Clymer
Thomas FitzSimons
Jared Ingersoll
James Wilson
Gouverneur Morris

NEW HAMPSHIRE
John Langdon
Nicholas Gilman

MARYLAND
James McHenry
Daniel of St. Thomas
 Jenifer
Daniel Carroll

VIRGINIA
John Blair
James Madison, Jr.

NORTH CAROLINA
William Blount
Richard Dobbs Spaight
Hugh Williamson

SOUTH CAROLINA
John Rutledge
Charles Cotesworth Pinckney
Charles Pinckney
Pierce Butler

GEORGIA
William Few
Abraham Baldwin

Articles in addition to, and amendment of the Constitution of the United States of America, proposed by Congress and ratified by the Legislatures of the several states, pursuant to the Fifth Article of the original Constitution.

(The first ten amendments were passed by Congress on September 25, 1789, and were ratified on December 15, 1791.)

AMENDMENT I

Congress shall make no law respecting an establishment of religion, or prohibiting the free exercise thereof; or abridging the freedom of speech, or of the press; or the right of the people peaceably to assemble, and to petition the Government for a redress of grievances.

For many Americans, the First Amendment represents the core of what the Bill of Rights stands for: limits on government power to limit or compel religious beliefs, the right to hold political opinions and express them, protection for a free press, the right to assemble peaceably, and the right to petition, through protest or the ballot, the government for a redress of political grievances. But it is also important to remember that the First Amendment, like most of the Bill of Rights, did not apply to state governments until the Supreme Court began to apply their substantive guarantees through the Fourteenth Amendment, a process that did not begin until 1925 in *Gitlow* v. *New York*.

Until then, state and local governments often failed to honor the rights and liberties that Congress, and by extension the national government, was expressly forbidden by the Constitution from withholding. For example, southern states, prior to the Civil War, outlawed pro-abolition literature; numerous states continued to collect taxes on behalf of state-sponsored churches and religious education; newspapers were often forbidden from publishing exposes on industry or political leaders because such speech was considered seditious and thus subject to prior restraint; public protests on behalf of unpopular causes were often banned by state breach of peace laws.

The Supreme Court has recognized other important rights implied by the enumerated guarantees of the First Amendment. These include the right to association, even when such association might come in the form of clubs or organizations that discriminate on the basis of race, sex, or religion, and the right to personal privacy, which the Supreme Court held in *Griswold* v. *Connecticut* (1965) was based in part on the right of married couples to make decisions about contraception, a decision protected by one's personal religious and political beliefs.

AMENDMENT II

A well regulated Militia, being necessary to the security of a free State, the right of the people to keep and bear Arms, shall not be infringed.

Few issues in American politics generate as much emotional heat as the extent to which Americans have a right to keep and bear arms. Supporters of broad gun ownership rights, such as the National Rifle Association, argue that the Second Amendment protects an almost absolute individual right to own just about any small arm that can be manufactured, whether for reasons of sport or self-defense. Proponents of gun control, such as The Brady Campaign to Prevent Gun Violence, argue that the amendment creates no such individual right, but refers instead to the Framers' belief—now outdated—that citizen militias had the right to form in order to protect themselves against other states and, if need be, the national government. Under this view, Congress and the states are free to regulate gun ownership and use as they see fit, provided that the national and state governments are within their constitutional orbit of power to do so.

The Supreme Court has not offered much help on the meaning of the Second Amendment. It has handed down only one case truly relying on the amendment, *U.S.* v. *Miller* (1939). There, a unanimous Court upheld a federal law requiring the registration of sawed-off shotguns purchased for personal use. While the Court rejected the position that the Second Amendment established an individual right to keep and bear arms, it did not close the door on individual gun ownership. This remains the constitutional baseline from which legislative battles over gun control legislation continue to be fought.

AMENDMENT III

No Soldier shall, in time of peace be quartered in any house, without the consent of the Owner, nor in time of war, but in a manner to be prescribed by law.

Among the complaints directed at King George III in the Declaration of Independence was the colonial-era practice of quartering large numbers of troops in private homes. The practice of quartering soldiers, along with the forced maintenance of British standing armies in times of peace without the consent of the colonial legislatures, formed a major component of the political grievances directed at the British Crown. The Third Amendment was intended to protect individuals and their property from the abuse common to the practice of quartering soldiers.

The Supreme Court has never ruled on the meaning of the Third Amendment, making it the only provision of the Bill of Rights to escape such attention. But the Court has referred to the Third Amendment as part of the penumbra of constitutional rights forming the basis for the right of personal privacy established in *Griswold* v. *Connecticut* (1965).

AMENDMENT IV

The right of the people to be secure in their persons, houses, papers, and effects, against unreasonable searches and seizures, shall not be violated, and no warrants shall issue, but upon probable cause, supported by Oath or affirmation, and particularly describing the place to be searched, and the persons or things to be seized.

Although the Fourth Amendment is often discussed in tandem with the Fifth, Sixth, and Eighth Amendments—the other major provisions of the Bill of Rights outlining the criminal due process guarantees of citizens—it shares a similar undercurrent that motivated the adoption of the Third Amendment: to eliminate the practice of British officers from using the general writ of assistance to enter private homes, conduct searches, and seize personal property. British officers had not been required to offer a specific reason for a search or justify the taking of particular items. In most cases, the writ of assistance was used to confiscate items considered to have violated the strict British customs laws of the colonial era.

The twin pillars of the Fourth Amendment, the probable cause and warrant requirements, are a direct reflection of the disdain the Framers had for the Revolutionary-era practices of the British. But like the First Amendment, the guarantees of the Fourth Amendment did not apply to state and local law enforcement practices until well after the ratification of the Fourteenth Amendment. Until *Wolf* v. *Colorado* (1949), when the Court ruled that the Fourteenth Amendment made the Fourth Amendment binding on the states, evidence seized in violation of the probable cause or warrant requirements could be used against a criminal suspect. The Court's best-known decision on the Fourth Amendment, *Mapp* v. *Ohio* (1961), which established the exclusionary rule, also marked the high-water point in the rights afforded to criminal suspects challenging an unlawful search. Since the late 1970s, the Court has steadily added exceptions to the Fourth Amendment to permit law enforcement officers to engage in warrantless searches and seizures, provided that such practices meet a threshold of reasonableness in the context of the circumstances under which they are undertaken.

AMENDMENT V

No person shall be held to answer for a capital, or otherwise infamous crime, unless on a presentment or indictment of a Grand Jury, except in cases arising in the land or naval forces, or in the Militia, when in actual service in time of War or public danger; nor shall any person be subject for the same offence to be twice put in jeopardy of life or limb; nor shall be compelled in any criminal case to be a witness against himself, nor be deprived of life, liberty, or property, without due process of law; nor shall private property be taken for public use, without just compensation.

The Fifth Amendment, along with the Sixth Amendment, is the legacy of the Star Chamber tactics that figured prominently in the colonial-era system of British justice. By requiring that no person could be held for a "capital, or otherwise infamous" crime except upon indictment by a grand jury, the Fifth Amendment took an important step toward making the criminal indictment process a public function. Along with the public trial and trial by jury guarantees of the Sixth Amendment, the grand jury provision of the Fifth Amendment established that the government would have to make its case against the accused in public. Also, by guaranteeing that no person could be compelled to testify against himself or herself in a criminal proceeding, the Fifth Amendment highlighted the adversarial nature of the American criminal justice system, a feature that is distinct from its British counterpart. "Pleading the Fifth" is permissible in any criminal, civil, administrative, judicial, or investigatory context. *Miranda* v. *Arizona* (1966), one of the most famous rulings of the Supreme Court, established a right to silence that combined the ban against self-incrimination of the Fifth Amendment with the Sixth Amendment's guarantee of the assistance of counsel. The right to silence, unlike the ban against self-incrimination, extends to any aspect of an interrogation.

The Fifth Amendment also forbids double jeopardy, which prohibits the prosecution of a crime against the same person in the same jurisdiction twice, and prevents the government from taking life, liberty, or property without due process of law. This phrase was reproduced in the Fourteenth Amendment, placing an identical set of constraints on the states. The Court has applied all the guarantees of the Fifth Amendment, with the exception of the grand jury provision, to the states through the due process clause of the Fourteenth Amendment. Some constitutional scholars also consider the due process clause of the Fifth Amendment to embrace an equal protection provision when applied to federal cases.

The final provision of the Fifth Amendment prohibits the government from taking private property for public use without just compensation. Litigation on the takings clause, as some scholars refer to this provision, has generally centered on two major questions. The first is what constitutes a taking, either by the government's decision to seize private property or by regulating it to the point where its value is greatly diminished. The second question centers on what the appropriate level of compensation is for owners who have successfully established a taking.

AMENDMENT VI

In all criminal prosecutions, the accused shall enjoy the right to a speedy and public trial, by an impartial jury of the State and district wherein the crime shall have been committed, which district shall have been previously ascertained by law, and to be informed of the nature and cause of the accusation; to be confronted with the witnesses against him; to have compulsory process for obtaining witnesses in his favor, and to have the assistance of counsel for his defence.

The centerpiece of the constitutional guarantees afforded to individuals facing criminal prosecution, the Sixth Amendment sets out eight specific rights, more than any other provision of the Bill of Rights. As with the Fifth Amendment, the core features of the Sixth Amendment build upon the unfortunate legacy of the Star Chamber practices of colonial-era Britain. The very first provision of the Sixth Amendment mandates that individuals subject to criminal prosecution receive "a speedy and public trial"; it then requires that all such trials take place in public, with the defendant informed of the cause and nature of the accusation against him or her. The common theme underlying these sections of the Sixth Amendment, as well as those requiring witnesses for the prosecution to testify in public, allowing the defendant to produce witnesses on his or her own behalf, and securing the assistance of counsel, is that any citizen threatened with the deprivation of liberty is entitled to have the case made against him or her in public. The Fifth Amendment cleared an important initial hurdle to secret justice by requiring the government to produce evidence that did not rely on confessions and self-incrimination; the Fourth Amendment required that any such evidence must be acquired lawfully

and with the knowledge of a public magistrate. The Sixth Amendment establishes, in principle, the American criminal justice system as one that is open and public.

Since the vast majority of criminal prosecutions in the United States are undertaken by state and local authorities, the parchment promises of the Sixth Amendment did not extend to most Americans until the Supreme Court began incorporating the guarantees of the Bill of Rights to the states through the Fourteenth Amendment. Perhaps the best-known case involving the Sixth Amendment is *Gideon* v. *Wainwright* (1963), which held that all persons accused of a serious crime are entitled to an attorney, even if they cannot afford one, a rule that was soon extended to cover misdemeanors as well. Three years later, the Supreme Court fused the right to counsel rule established in *Gideon* with the Fifth Amendment ban against self-incrimination to create the principles animating *Miranda* v. *Arizona*. For a long time, the Court had never interpreted the Fifth and Sixth Amendments to mean that individuals had rights to criminal due process guarantees if they did not know about them or could not afford them. Decisions such as *Gideon* and *Miranda* offered a clear departure from this position.

The speedy and public trial clauses only require that criminal trials take place in public within a reasonable amount of time after the period of indictment, and that juries in such cases are unbiased. Americans also often cite the Sixth Amendment as entitling them to a trial by a "jury of one's peers." This is true to the extent individuals are entitled to a trial in the jurisdiction where the crime is alleged to have been committed. It does not mean, however, that they are entitled to a trial by persons of a similar age or background, for example.

AMENDMENT VII

In Suits at common law, where the value in controversy shall exceed twenty dollars, the right of trial by jury shall be preserved, and no fact tried by a jury, shall be otherwise re-examined in any Court of the United States, than according to the rules of the common law.

One feature of the British courts that the Framers sought to preserve in the American civil law system was the distinction between courts of *common law* and courts of *equity*. Common law courts heard cases involving strict legal rules, while equity courts based their decisions on principles of fairness and totality of circumstances. Common law courts featured juries, who were authorized to return verdicts entitling plaintiffs to financial compensation for losses incurred, whereas equity courts relied upon judges to make determinations about appropriate relief for successful parties. Relief in equity courts did not consist of monetary awards, but injunctions, cease-and-desist orders, and so on. The Seventh Amendment carried over this British feature into the Constitution.

In 1938, Congress amended the Federal Rules of Civil Procedure to combine the function of civil common law and equity courts. In cases involving both legal and equitable claims, a federal judge must first decide the issue of law before moving to the equitable relief, or remedy, component of the trial. Judges are permitted to instruct juries on matters of law and fact, and may emphasize certain facts or legal issues to the jury in their instructions to the jury. But the jury alone decides guilt or innocence. In some extraordinary cases, a judge may overturn the verdict of a jury. This happens only when a judge believes the jury has disregarded completely the facts and evidence before it in reaching a verdict.

Congress has also changed the $20 threshold for the right to a trial by jury. The amount is now $75,000. Finally, the Seventh Amendment has never been incorporated to the states through the Fourteenth Amendment.

AMENDMENT VIII

Excessive bail shall not be required, nor excessive fines imposed, nor cruel and unusual punishments inflicted.

For an amendment of so few words, the Eighth Amendment has generated an enormous volume of commentary and litigation since its ratification. This should not be surprising, as the three major provisions of the amendment deal with some of the most sensitive and emotionally charged issues involving the rights of criminal defendants.

The origin of the excessive bail clause stems from the reforms to the British system instituted by the 1689 English Bill of Rights. Having had limited success in preventing law enforcement officials from detaining suspects by imposing outrageous bail requirements, Britain amended previous laws to say that "excessive bail ought not to be required." Much like the British model, the Eighth Amendment does not state what an "excessive bail" is or the particular criminal offense that warrants a high bail amount. The Supreme Court has offered two fundamental rules on the excessive bail clause. First, a judge has the discretion to decide if a criminal offense is sufficiently serious to justify high bail. Second, a judge has the power, under *U.S.* v. *Salerno* (1987), to deny a criminal defendant bail as a "preventative measure." In both such cases, a judge's action must be considered proportionate to the nature of the criminal offense for which an individual stands accused.

Like the excessive bail clause, the excessive fines clause is rooted in the English Bill of Rights. The clause applies only to criminal proceedings, not civil litigation. For example, a tobacco company cannot appeal what it believes is an excessive jury award under this clause. An indigent criminal defendant, however, can challenge a fine levied in connection with a criminal conviction.

The most controversial section of the Eighth Amendment is the clause forbidding cruel and unusual punishments. The absence of such a guarantee from the Constitution was a major impetus for the adoption of the Bill of Rights. While most historians agree that the Framers wanted to prohibit barbaric forms of punishment, including torture, as well as arbitrary and disproportionate penalties, there is little consensus on what specific punishments met this definition. By the late 1800s, the Supreme Court had ruled that such punishments as public burnings, disembowelment, and drawing and quartering crossed the Eighth Amendment barrier. In *Weems* v. *U.S.* (1910), the Court went the additional of step of concluding that any punishment considered "excessive" would violate the cruel and unusual punishment clause. And, in *Solem* v. *Helm* (1983), the Court developed a "proportionality" standard that required punishments, even simple incarceration, to bear a rational relationship to the offense.

The Court has never ruled, however, that the death penalty per se violates the Eighth Amendment. It has developed certain rules and exceptions governing the application of the death penalty, such as requiring a criminal defendant actually to have killed, or attempted to have killed, a victim. It has also ruled that the mentally retarded, as a class, are exempt from the death penalty. But it has also issued highly controversial decisions concluding, for example, that neither racial disparities in the application of capital punishment nor juvenile status at the time the offense was committed violate the Eighth Amendment. Absent a four-year ban on the practice between 1972 and 1976, the death penalty has always been an available punishment in the American criminal justice system.

AMENDMENT IX

The enumeration in the Constitution, of certain rights, shall not be construed to deny or disparage others retained by the people.

A major point of contention between the Federalists and Anti-Federalists was the need for a bill of rights. In *Federalist No. 84*, Alexander Hamilton argued that a bill of rights was unnecessary, as there was no need to place limits on the power of government to do things that it was not authorized by the Constitution to do. Hamilton also argued that it would be impossible to list all the rights "retained by the people." Protecting some rights but not others would suggest that Americans had surrendered certain rights to their government when, in Hamilton's view, the Constitution did nothing of the sort.

Given his well-deserved reputation for unbridled national power, Hamilton's views have often been dismissed as a cynical ploy to sidestep any meaningful discussion of the Bill of Rights and speed along the ratification process. But James Madison, along with Thomas Jefferson, held a much deeper belief in the need for a bill of rights. Madison also believed that the enumeration of certain rights and liberties in the Constitution should not be understood to deny others that exist as a condition of citizenship in a free society. Madison, the primary author of the Bill of Rights, included the Ninth Amendment to underscore this belief.

The Supreme Court has never offered a clear and definitive interpretation of the Ninth Amendment, primarily because it has been wary of giving such general language any substantive definition. The amendment has been cited in such decisions as *Griswold* v. *Connecticut* (1965) and *Richmond Newspapers* v. *Virginia* (1980) along with other constitutional amendments to bolster the case on behalf of an asserted constitutional right. The difficulty in constructing a specific meaning for the Ninth Amendment can be illustrated by the fact that both supporters and opponents of legal abortion have cited it to defend the feasibility of their respective positions.

AMENDMENT X

The powers not delegated to the United States by the Constitution, nor prohibited by it to the States, are reserved to the States respectively, or to the people.

The Tenth Amendment generated little controversy during the ratification process over the Bill of Rights. As the Supreme Court later ruled in *U.S.* v. *Darby* (1941), the Tenth Amendment states a truism about the relationship between the boundaries of national and state power—that the states retain those powers not specifically set out in the Constitution as belonging to the national government. There is little in the history in the debate over the Tenth Amendment to suggest that its language is anything other than declaratory. Indeed, the refusal of the 1st Congress to insert the word "expressly" before "delegated" strongly suggests that James Madison, who offered the most thorough explanation of the amendment during the floor debates, intended to leave room for this relationship to evolve as future events made necessary.

The earliest political and constitutional developments involving the Tenth Amendment tilted the balance of power firmly in favor of national power. Alexander Hamilton's vision for a national bank to consolidate the nation's currency and trading position was realized in *McCullough* v. *Maryland* (1819), in which the Court held that Article I granted Congress broad power to make all laws "necessary and proper" to the exercise of its legislative power. By no means, however, did *McCullough* settle the argument over the power reserved to the states. Led by Chief Justice Roger Taney, the Court handed down several decisions in the three decades leading up to the Civil War that offered substantial protection to the southern states on the matters closest to their hearts: slavery and economic sovereignty. From the period after the Civil War until the New Deal, the Court continued to shield states from congressional legislation designed to regulate the economy and promote social and political reform. After the constitutional revolution of 1937, when the Court threw its support behind the New Deal, Congress received a blank constitutional check to engage in the regulatory action that featured an unprecedented level of federal intervention in economic and social matters once the purview of the states, one that would last almost sixty years.

Beginning in *New York* v. *U.S.* (1992), however, the Court, in striking down a key provision of a federal environmental law, began to revisit the New Deal assumptions that underlay its modern interpretation of the Tenth Amendment. A few years later, in *U.S.* v. *Lopez* (1995), it invalidated a federal gun control law on the ground that Congress lacked authority under the commerce clause to regulate gun possession. And, in *U.S.* v. *Printz* (1997), the Tenth Amendment explicitly was cited to strike down an important section of the Brady Bill, a congressional law that required states to conduct background checks on prospective gun buyers. Although the Court has not returned to the dual federalism posture on the Tenth Amendment that it built from the years between the Taney Court and the triumph of the New Deal, these decisions make clear that the constitutional status of the states as actors in the federal system has been dramatically strengthened.

AMENDMENT XI *(Ratified on February 7, 1795)*

The Judicial power of the United States shall not be construed to extend to any suit in law or equity, commenced or prosecuted against one of the United States by Citizens of another State, or by Citizens or Subjects of any Foreign State.

The Eleventh Amendment was prompted by one the earliest notable decisions of the Supreme Court, *Chisolm* v. *Georgia* (1793). In *Chisolm*, the Court held that Article III and the enforcement provision of the Judiciary Act of 1789 permitted a citizen of one state to bring suit against another state in federal court. Almost immediately after *Chisolm*, the Eleventh Amendment was introduced and promptly ratified, as the states saw this decision as a threat to their sovereignty under the new Constitution. The amendment was passed in less than a year, which, by the standards of the era, was remarkably fast.

The Eleventh Amendment nullified the result in *Chisolm* but did not completely bar a citizen from bringing suit against a state in federal court. Citizens may bring lawsuits against state officials in federal court if they can satisfy the requirement that their rights under federal constitutional or statutory law have been violated. The Eleventh Amendment has not been extensively litigated in modern times, but the extent to which states are immune under federal law from citizen lawsuits has reemerged as an important constitutional question in recent years. For example, the Court has said in several cases that the doctrine of sovereign immunity prevents citizens from suing state agencies under the Americans with Disabilities Act of 1990. But as recently as 2003, the Court, in *Nevada* v. *Hibbs*, ruled that the Family and Medical Leave Act of 1993 did not immunize state government agencies against lawsuits brought by former state employees. States are also free to waive their immunity and consent to a lawsuit.

AMENDMENT XII *(Ratified on June 15, 1804)*

The Electors shall meet in their respective states, and vote by ballot for President and Vice-President, one of whom, at least, shall not be an inhabitant of the same state with themselves; they shall name in their ballots the person voted for as President, and in distinct ballots the person voted for as Vice-President, and they shall make distinct lists of all persons voted for as President, and of all persons voted for as Vice-President, and of the number of votes for each, which lists they shall sign and certify, and transmit sealed to the seat of the government of the United States, directed to the President of the Senate;—The President of the Senate shall, in the presence of the Senate and House of Representatives, open all the certificates and the votes shall then be counted;—The person having the greatest number of votes for President, shall be the President, if such number be a majority of the whole number of Electors appointed; and if no person have such majority; then from the persons having the highest numbers not exceeding three on the list of those voted for as President, the House of Representatives shall choose immediately, by ballot, the President. But in choosing the President, the votes shall be taken by states, the representation from each state having one vote; a quorum for this purpose shall consist of a member or members from two-thirds of the states, and a majority of all the states shall be necessary to a choice. And if the House of Representatives shall not choose a President whenever the right of choice shall devolve upon them, before the fourth day of March next following, then the Vice-President shall act as President, as in the case of the death or other constitutional disability of the President.—The person having the greatest number of votes as Vice-President, shall be the Vice-President, if such number be a majority of the whole number of Electors appointed, and if no person have a majority, then from the two highest numbers on the list, the Senate shall choose the Vice-President; a quorum for the purpose shall consist of two-thirds of the whole number of Senators, and a majority of the whole number shall be necessary to a choice. But no person constitutionally ineligible to the office of President shall be eligible to that of Vice-President of the United States.

The Twelfth Amendment was added to the Constitution after the 1800 presidential election was thrown into the House of Representatives. Thomas Jefferson and Aaron Burr, running on the Democratic-Republican Party ticket, each received seventy-three electoral votes for president, even though everyone knew that Jefferson was the presidential candidate and Burr the vice presidential candidate. This was possible because Article II, section 1, did not require electors to vote for president and vice president separately. The Twelfth Amendment remedied this deficiency by requiring electors to cast their votes for president and vice president separately.

Whether it intended to or not, the Twelfth Amendment took a major step toward institutionalizing the party system in the United States. The 1796 election yielded a president and vice president from different parties, a clear indication that partisan differences were emerging in a distinct form. The 1800 election simply highlighted the problem further. By requiring electors to make their presidential and vice presidential choices separately, the Twelfth Amendment conceded that a party system in American politics had indeed evolved, an inevitable but nonetheless disappointing development to the architects of the original constitutional vision.

AMENDMENT XIII
(Ratified on December 6, 1865)

Section 1.

Neither slavery nor involuntary servitude, except as a punishment for crime whereof the party shall have been duly convicted, shall exist within the United States, or any place subject to their jurisdiction.

Section 2.

Congress shall have power to enforce this article by appropriate legislation.

The Thirteenth, Fourteenth, and Fifteenth Amendments are known collectively as the Civil War Amendments.

In anticipation of a Union victory, the Thirteenth Amendment was passed by Congress and sent to the states for ratification before the end of the Civil War. The amendment not only formally abolished slavery and involuntary servitude; it also served as the constitutional foundation for the nation's first major civil rights legislation, the Civil Rights Act of 1866. This law extended numerous rights to African Americans previously held in servitude as well as those having "free" status during the Civil War, including the right to purchase, rent, and sell personal property, to bring suit in federal court, to enter into contracts, and to receive the full and equal benefit of all laws "enjoyed by white citizens." The Thirteenth Amendment overturned the pre–Civil War decision of the Supreme Court in *Dred Scott* v. *Sandford* (1857), which held that slaves were not people entitled to constitutional rights, but property subject to the civil law binding them to their masters.

In modern times, the Court has ruled that the Thirteenth Amendment prohibits any action that recognizes a "badge" or "condition" of slavery, such as housing discrimination and certain forms of employment discrimination. The Department of Justice also has used the Thirteenth Amendment to file lawsuits against manufacturing sweatshops and other criminal enterprises in which persons are forced to work without compensation.

AMENDMENT XIV
(Ratified on July 9, 1868)

Section 1.

All persons born or naturalized in the United States, and subject to the jurisdiction thereof, are citizens of the United States and of the State wherein they reside. No State shall make or enforce any law which shall abridge the privileges or immunities of citizens of the United States; nor shall any State deprive any person of life, liberty, or property, without due process of law; nor deny to any person within its jurisdiction the equal protection of the laws.

Many constitutional scholars believe the Fourteenth Amendment is the most important addition to the Constitution since the Bill of Rights was ratified in 1791. In addition to serving as a cornerstone of Reconstruction policy, section 1 eliminated the distinction between the rights and liberties of Americans as citizens of their respective states and those to which they were entitled under the Bill of Rights as citizens of the United States. The Republican leadership that drafted and steered the Fourteenth Amendment to passage left no doubt that the three major provisions of section 1, which placed express limits on state power to abridge rights and liberties protected as a condition of national citizenship, were intended to make the Bill of Rights binding upon the states, thus overruling *Barron* v. *Baltimore* (1833). Although the Supreme Court has never endorsed this view, the selective incorporation of the Bill of Rights to the states during the twentieth century through the Fourteenth Amendment ultimately made the Reconstruction-era vision of the Republicans a reality. The former Confederate states were required to ratify the Fourteenth Amendment to qualify for readmission into the Union.

Section 2.

Representatives shall be apportioned among the several States according to their respective numbers, counting the whole number of persons in each State, excluding Indians not taxed. But when the right to vote at any election for the choice of electors for President and Vice President of the United States, Representatives in Congress, the Executive and Judicial officers of a State, or the members of the Legislature thereof, is denied to any of the male inhabitants of such State, being twenty-one years of age, and citizens of the United States, or in any way abridged, except for participation in rebellion, or other crime, the basis of representation therein shall be reduced in the proportion which the number of such male citizens shall bear to the whole number of male citizens twenty-one years of age in such State.

Section 2 established two major changes to the Constitution. First, by stating that representatives from each state would be apportioned based on the number of "whole" persons in each state, section 2 modified theThree-Fifths Compromise of Article 1, section 2, clause 3, of the original Constitution. Note, however, that section 2 still called for the exclusion of Indians "not taxed" from the apportionment criteria. Second, section 2, for the first time anywhere in the Constitution, mentions that only "male" inhabitants of the states age twenty-one or older would be counted toward representation in the House of Representatives and eligible to vote. The Military Reconstruction Act of 1867 had

strengthened Republican power in the southern states by stripping former Confederates of the right to vote, a law that, in conjunction with the gradual addition of blacks to the voting rolls, made enactment of the Fourteenth Amendment possible. Section 2 further solidified the Republican presence in the South by eliminating from apportionment counts any person that participated in the rebellion against the Union.

Section 3.

No person shall be a Senator or Representative in Congress, or elector of President and Vice President, or hold any office, civil or military, under the United States, or under any State, who, having previously taken an oath, as a member of Congress, or as an officer of the United States, or as a member of any State legislature, or as an executive or judicial officer of any State, to support the Constitution of the United States, shall have engaged in insurrection or rebellion against the same, or given aid or comfort to the enemies thereof. But Congress may by a vote of two-thirds of each House, remove such disability.

Section 3 also reflected the power of the Reconstruction-era Republicans over the South. By eliminating the eligibility of former Confederates for public office or to serve as an elector for president or vice president, the Republicans strengthened their presence in Congress and throughout national politics. This measure also allowed African Americans to run for and hold office in the South, which they were doing by 1870, the same year the Fifteenth Amendment was ratified.

In December 1868, five months after the ratification of the Fourteenth Amendment, President Andrew Johnson declared universal amnesty for all former Confederates. This measure had the effect of returning white politicians and by extension the Democratic Party to power in the South. Republican concern over this development was a major force behind the adoption of the Fifteenth Amendment, which was viewed as an instrument to protect Republican political power by securing black enfranchisement. However, Republican president Ulysses S. Grant, who defeated Johnson in 1868, pardoned all but a few hundred remaining Confederate sympathizers by signing the Amnesty Act of 1872. Decisions such as these began the gradual undoing of Republican commitment to black civil rights in the South.

Section 4.

The validity of the public debt of the United States, authorized by law, including debts incurred for payment of pensions and bounties for services in suppressing insurrection or rebellion, shall not be questioned. But neither the United States nor any State shall assume or pay any debt or obligation incurred in aid of insurrection or rebellion against the United States, or any claim for the loss or emancipation of any slave, but all such debts, obligations and claims shall be held illegal and void.

Section 4 repudiated the South's desire to have Congress forgive the Confederacy's war debts. It also rejected any claim that former slaveholders had to be compensated for the loss of their slaves.

Section 5.

The Congress shall have power to enforce, by appropriate legislation, the provisions of this article.

By giving Congress the power to enforce the provisions of the Fourteenth Amendment, section 5 reiterated the post–Civil War emphasis on national citizenship and the limit on state power to deny individuals their constitutional rights. Section 5 also extended congressional law-making power beyond those areas outlined in Article I. But the Court has taken a mixed view of the scope of congressional power to enforce the Fourteenth Amendment. In *Katzenbach* v. *Morgan* (1966), for example, the Supreme Court offered a broad ruling on the section 5 power of Congress. It held that Congress could enact laws establishing rights beyond what the Court said the Constitution required, as long as such laws were designed to establish a remedial constitutional right or protect citizens from a potential constitutional violation. In other cases, such as *City of Boerne* v. *Flores* (1997) and *U.S.* v. *Morrison* (2000), the Court ruled that Congress may not intrude upon the authority of the judicial branch to define the meaning of the Constitution or intrude on the power of the states to make laws within their own domain.

AMENDMENT XV
(Ratified on February 3, 1870)

Section 1.

The right of citizens of the United States to vote shall not be denied or abridged by the United States or by any State on account of race, color, or previous condition of servitude.

Section 2.

The Congress shall have power to enforce this article by appropriate legislation.

The Fifteenth Amendment was the most controversial of the Civil War Amendments, both for what it did and did not do. Although the adoption of the Thirteenth and Fourteenth Amendments made clear that blacks could not be returned to their pre–Civil War slavery, enthusiasm for a constitutional right of black suffrage, even among the northern states, was another matter. On the one hand, the extension of voting rights to blacks was the most dramatic outcome of the Civil War. The former Confederate states had to ratify the Fifteenth Amendment as a condition for readmission into the Union. On the other hand, the rejection of proposed language forbidding discrimination on the basis of property ownership, education, or religious belief gave states the power to regulate the vote as they wished. And, with the collapse of Reconstruction after the

1876 election, southern states implemented laws created by this opening with full force, successfully crippling black voter registration for generations to come in the region where most African Americans lived. Full enfranchisement for African Americans would not arrive until the passage of the Voting Rights Act of 1965, almost one hundred years after the ratification of the Fifteenth Amendment.

The Fifteenth Amendment also divided woman's rights organizations that had campaigned on behalf of abolition and black enfranchisement. Feminists such as Elizabeth Cady Stanton and Susan B. Anthony were furious over the exclusion of women from the Fifteenth Amendment and opposed its ratification, while others, such as Lucy Stone, were willing to support black voting rights at the expense of woman's suffrage, leaving that battle for another day. The Supreme Court sided with those who opposed female enfranchisement, ruling in *Minor* v. *Happersett* (1875) that the Fourteenth Amendment did not recognize among the privileges and immunities of American citizenship a constitutional right to vote.

AMENDMENT XVI
(Ratified on February 3, 1913)

The Congress shall have power to lay and collect taxes on incomes, from whatever source derived, without apportionment among the several States, and without regard to any census or enumeration.

The Sixteenth Amendment was a response to the Supreme Court's sharply divided ruling in *Pollock* v. *Farmers' Loan & Trust Co.* (1895), which struck down the Income Tax Act of 1894 as unconstitutional. The Court, by a 5–4 margin, held that the law violated Article I, section 9, which prevented Congress from enacting a direct tax (on individuals) unless in proportion to the U.S. Census. In some ways, this was a curious holding, since the Court had permitted Congress to enact a direct tax on individuals during the Civil War. Between the *Pollock* decision and the enactment of the Sixteenth Amendment, the Court approved of taxes levied on corporations, as such taxes were not really taxes but "excises" levied on "incidents of ownership."

Anti-tax groups have claimed the Sixteenth Amendment was never properly ratified and is thus unconstitutional. The federal courts have rejected that view and have sanctioned and fined individuals who have brought such frivolous challenges to court.

AMENDMENT XVII
(Ratified on April 8, 1913)

The Senate of the United States shall be composed of two Senators from each State, elected by the people thereof, for six years; and each Senator shall have one vote. The electors in each State shall have the qualifications requisite for electors of the most numerous branch of the State legislatures.

When vacancies happen in the representation of any State in the Senate, the executive authority of such State shall issue writs of election to fill such vacancies: Provided, That the legislature of any State may empower the executive thereof to make temporary appointments until the people fill the vacancies by election as the legislature may direct.

This amendment shall not be so construed as to affect the election or term of any Senator chosen before it becomes valid as part of the Constitution.

The Seventeenth Amendment repealed the language in Article I, section 3, of the original Constitution, which called for the election of U.S. senators by state legislatures. This method had its roots in the selection of delegates to the Constitutional Convention, who were chosen by the state legislatures. It was also the preferred method of the Framers, who believed that having state legislatures elect senators would strengthen the relationship between the states and the national government, and also contribute to the stability of Congress by removing popular electoral pressure from the upper chamber.

Dissatisfaction set in with this method during the period leading up to the Civil War, especially by the 1850s. Indiana, for example, deeply divided between Union supporters in the northern part of the state and Confederate sympathizers in the southern part, could not agree on the selection of senators and was without representation for two years. After the Civil War, numerous Senate elections were tainted by corruption, and many more resulted in ties that prevented seating senators in a timely fashion. In 1899, Delaware's election was so mired in controversy that it did not have representation in the Senate for four years.

The ratification of the Seventeenth Amendment was the result of almost two decades of persistent efforts at reform. By 1912, twenty-nine states had changes their election laws to require the popular election of senators. In the years before that, constitutional amendments were introduced on a regular basis calling for the popular election of senators. Although many powerful legislators entrenched in the Senate resisted such change, the tide of reform, now aided by journalists and scholars sympathetic to the cause, proved too powerful to withstand. One year after the Seventeenth Amendment was sent to the states for ratification all members of the Senate were elected by the popular vote.

AMENDMENT XVIII
(Ratified on January 16, 1919)

Section 1.

After one year from the ratification of this article the manufacture, sale, or transportation of intoxicating liquors within, the importation thereof into, or the exportation thereof from the United States and all territory subject to the jurisdiction thereof for beverage purposes is hereby prohibited.

Section 2.

The Congress and the several States shall have concurrent power to enforce this article by appropriate legislation.

Section 3.

This article shall be inoperative unless it shall have been ratified as an amendment to the Constitution by the legislatures of the several States, as provided in the Constitution, within seven years from the date of the submission hereof to the States by the Congress.

The Eighteenth Amendment was the end result of a crusade against the consumption of alcoholic beverages than began during the early nineteenth century. A combination of Christian organizations emboldened by the second Great Awakening and women's groups, who believed alcohol contributed greatly to domestic violence and poverty, campaigned to abolish manufacture, sale, and use of alcoholic beverages in the United States. Their campaign was moderately successful in the pre–Civil War era. By 1855, thirteen states had banned the sale of "intoxicating" beverages. By the end of the Civil War, however, ten states had repealed their prohibition laws.

Another wave of anti-alcohol campaigning soon emerged, however, as the Women's Christian Temperance Union, founded in 1874 and 250,000 strong by 1911, and the Anti-Saloon League, founded in 1913, pressed the case for Prohibition. Among the arguments offered by supporters of Prohibition were that the cereal grains used in the manufacture of beer and liquor diverted valuable resources from food supplies and that the malaise of drunkenness sapped the strength of manufacturing production at home and the conduct of America's soldiers in World War I. Underneath the formal case for Prohibition was a considerable anti-immigrant sentiment, as many Prohibitionists considered the waves of Italian, Irish, Poles, and German immigrants unduly dependent on alcohol.

In 1919, Congress passed the Eighteenth Amendment over President Woodrow Wilson's veto. That same year, Congress passed the Volstead Act, which implemented Prohibition and authorized law enforcement to target illegal shipments of alcohol into the United States (mostly from Canada, which, ironically, also mandated Prohibition in most of its provinces during this time) as well as alcoholic beverages illegally manufactured in the United States. Evidence remains inconclusive over just how successful the Eighteenth Amendment was in reducing alcohol consumption in the United States. More certain was the billion-dollar windfall that Prohibition created for organized crime, as well as small-time smugglers and bootleggers.

AMENDMENT XIX
(Ratified on August 18, 1920)

The right of citizens of the United States to vote shall not be denied or abridged by the United States or by any State on account of sex.

Congress shall have power to enforce this article by appropriate legislation.

The two major woman's rights organizations of the nineteenth century most active in the battle for female enfranchisement were the National Woman Suffrage Association and the American Woman Suffrage Association. The NWSA campaigned for a constitutional amendment modeled on the Fifteenth Amendment, which had secured African American voting rights, while the AWSA preferred to pursue women's voting rights through state-level legislative initiatives. In 1890, the two organizations combined to form the National American Woman Suffrage Association. By 1919, the NAWSA, the newer, more radical national woman's party, and other activists had secured congressional passage of the Nineteenth Amendment by a broad margin. It was ratified by the states just over a year later.

The Nineteenth Amendment, however, did not free black women from the voting restrictions that southern states placed in the way of African Americans. They and other minorities were not protected from such restrictions until the passage of the Voting Rights of 1965.

AMENDMENT XX
(Ratified on February 6, 1933)

Section 1.

The terms of the President and Vice President shall end at noon on the 20th day of January, and the terms of Senators and Representatives at noon on the 3d day of January, of the years in which such terms would have ended if this article had not been ratified; and the terms of their successors shall then begin.

Section 2.

The Congress shall assemble at least once in every year, and such meeting shall begin at noon on the 3d day of January, unless they shall by law appoint a different day.

Section 3.

If, at the time fixed for the beginning of the term of the President, the President elect shall have died, the Vice President elect shall become President. If a President shall not have been chosen before the time fixed for the beginning of his term, or if the President elect shall have failed to qualify, then the Vice President elect shall act as President until a President shall have qualified; and the Congress may by law provide for the case wherein neither a President elect nor a Vice President elect shall have qualified, declaring who shall then act as President, or the manner in which one who is to act shall be selected, and such person shall act accordingly until a President or Vice President shall have qualified.

Section 4.

The Congress may by law provide for the case of the death of any of the persons from whom the House of Representatives may choose a President whenever the rights of choice shall have devolved upon them, and for the case of the death of any of the persons from whom the Senate may choose a Vice President whenever the right of choice shall have devolved upon them.

Section 5.

Sections 1 and 2 shall take effect on the 15th day of October following the ratification of this article.

Section 6.

This article shall be inoperative unless it shall have been ratified as an amendment to the Constitution by the legislatures of three-fourths of the several States within seven years from the date of its submission.

The Twentieth Amendment is often called the lame duck amendment because its fundamental purpose was to shorten the time between the November elections, particularly in a presidential election year, and the starting date of the new presidential term and the commencement of the new congressional session. The amendment modified section 1 of the Twelfth Amendment by moving the beginning of the annual legislative session from March 4 to January 3. This change meant that the newly elected Congress would decide any presidential election thrown into the House of Representatives. It also eliminated the possibility that the nation would have to endure two additional months without a chief executive.

The Twentieth Amendment also modified Article I of the Constitution by placing a fixed time—noon—to begin the congressional session.

AMENDMENT XXI
(Ratified on December 5, 1933)

Section 1.

The eighteenth article of amendment to the Constitution of the United States is hereby repealed.

Section 2.

The transportation or importation into any State, Territory, or possession of the United States for delivery or use therein of intoxicating liquors, in violation of the laws thereof, is hereby prohibited.

Section 3.

This article shall be inoperative unless it shall have been ratified as an amendment to the Constitution by conventions in the several States, as provided in the Constitution, within seven years from the date of the submission hereof to the States by the Congress.

The Twenty-First Amendment repealed the Eighteenth Amendment, which was the first and last time that a constitutional amendment has been repealed. The Twenty-First Amendment is also the only amendment to the

Constitution approved by state ratifying conventions rather than a popular vote.

By the late 1920s, Americans had tired of Prohibition, and the arrival of the Great Depression in 1929 did nothing to lift their spirits. Few public officials, well aware of the extensive criminal enterprises that had grown up around Prohibition and had made a mockery of the practice, attempted to defend Prohibition as a success. Indeed, Franklin D. Roosevelt, in his initial bid for the presidency in 1932, made the repeal of Prohibition a campaign promise. In January 1933, Congress amended the Volstead Act to permit the sale of alcoholic beverages with an alcohol content of 3.2 percent. The ratification of the Twenty-First Amendment in December returned absolute control of the regulation of alcohol to the states. States are now free to regulate alcohol as they see fit. They may, for example, limit the quantity and type of alcohol sold to consumers, or ban alcohol sales completely. The Supreme Court, in *South Carolina* v. *Dole* (1984), ruled that Congress may require the states to set a certain age for the consumption of alcohol in return for participation in a federal program without violating the Twenty-First Amendment.

that had operated in principle. Theodore Roosevelt, having ascended to the presidency after the assassination of William McKinley in 1901, was elected to his second term in 1904. He then sat out a term, and then ran against Woodrow Wilson in the 1912 election and lost.

The first president to serve more than two terms was Franklin D. Roosevelt, and it was his success that inspired the enactment of the Twenty-Second Amendment. In 1946, Republicans took control of Congress for the first time in sixteen years and were determined to guard against such future Democratic dynasties. A year later, Congress, in one of the most party-line votes in the history of the amending process, approved the Twenty-Second Amendment. Every Republican member of the House and Senate who voted on the amendment voted for it. The remaining votes came almost exclusively from southern Democrats, whose relationship with Roosevelt was never more than a marriage of convenience. Ironically, some Republicans began to call for the repeal of the Twenty-Second Amendment toward the end of popular Republican Dwight D. Eisenhower's second term in 1956. A similar movement emerged in the late 1980s toward the end of Republican Ronald Reagan's second term. The American public at large, however, has shown little enthusiasm for repealing the Twenty-Second Amendment.

AMENDMENT XXII
(Ratified on February 27, 1951)

Section 1.

No person shall be elected to the office of the President more than twice, and no person who has held the office of President, or acted as President, for more than two years of a term to which some other person was elected President shall be elected to the office of the President more than once. But this Article shall not apply to any person holding the office of President when this Article was proposed by the Congress, and shall not prevent any person who may be holding the office of President, or acting as President, during the term within which this Article becomes operative from holding the office of President or acting as President during the remainder of such term.

Section 2.

This article shall be inoperative unless it shall have been ratified as an amendment to the Constitution by the legislatures of three-fourths of the several States within seven years from the date of its submission to the States by the Congress.

Thomas Jefferson, who served as the third president of the United States, was the first person of public stature to suggest a constitutional provision limiting presidential terms. "If some termination to the services of the chief Magistrate be not fixed by the Constitution," said Jefferson, "or supplied by practice, his office, nominally four years, will in fact become for life." Until Ulysses S. Grant's unsuccessful attempt to secure his party's nomination to a third term, no other president attempted to extend the two-term limit

AMENDMENT XXIII
(Ratified on March 29, 1961)

Section 1.

The District constituting the seat of Government of the United States shall appoint in such manner as the Congress may direct:

A number of electors of President and Vice President equal to the whole number of Senators and Representatives in Congress to which the District would be entitled if it were a State, but in no event more than the least populous State; they shall be in addition to those appointed by the States, but they shall be considered, for the purposes of the election of President and Vice President, to be electors appointed by a State; and they shall meet in the District and perform such duties as provided by the twelfth article of amendment.

Section 2.

The Congress shall have power to enforce this article by appropriate legislation.

Article II, section 2, of the Constitution limits participation in presidential elections to citizens who reside in the states. The Twenty-Third Amendment amended this provision to include residents of the District of Columbia. Since the District was envisioned as the seat of the national government with a transient population, the Constitution afforded no right of representation to its residents in Congress. By the time the Twenty-Third Amendment was ratified, the District had a greater population than twelve states.

In 1978, Congress introduced a constitutional amendment to give the District of Columbia representation in the House and the Senate. By 1985, the ratification period for the amendment expired without the necessary three-fourths approval from the states.

AMENDMENT XXIV
(Ratified on January 23, 1964)

Section 1.

The right of citizens of the United States to vote in any primary or other election for President or Vice President, for electors for President or Vice President, or for Senator or Representative in Congress, shall not be denied or abridged by the United States or any State by reason of failure to pay any poll tax or other tax.

Section 2.

The Congress shall have power to enforce this article by appropriate legislation.

The Twenty-Fourth Amendment continued the work of the Fifteenth Amendment. By abolishing the poll tax, the amendment eliminated one of the most popular tools used by voting registrars to prevent most African Americans and other minorities from taking part in the electoral process. Property ownership and literacy tests as conditions of the franchise extended back to the colonial era and were not particular to any region of the United States. But the poll tax was a southern invention, coming after the enactment of the Fifteenth Amendment. By the fall of Reconstruction in 1877, eleven southern states had enacted poll tax laws. The poll tax was disproportionately enforced against poor African American voters and, in some cases, poor whites.

Congress had begun to debate a constitutional amendment to abolish the poll tax as far back as 1939, but it took the momentum of the civil rights movement to move this process forward. Shortly after the ratification of the Twenty-Fourth Amendment, Congress enacted the Civil Rights Act of 1964, the most sweeping and effective federal civil rights law to date. By the time of ratification of the Twenty-Fourth Amendment, only five states had poll taxes on their books. Spurred on by the spirit of the times, Congress enacted the Voting Rights Act of 1965, which enforced the poll tax ban of the Twenty-Fourth Amendment and also abolished literacy tests, property qualifications, and other obstacles to voter registration. In 1966, in *Harper v. Board of Elections*, the Supreme Court rejected a constitutional challenge to the historic voting rights law.

AMENDMENT XXV
(Ratified on February 10, 1967)

Section 1.

In case of the removal of the President from office or of his death or resignation, the Vice President shall become President.

Section 2.

Whenever there is a vacancy in the office of the Vice President, the President shall nominate a Vice President who shall take office upon confirmation by a majority vote of both Houses of Congress.

Section 3.

Whenever the President transmits to the President pro tempore of the Senate and the Speaker of the House of Representatives his written declaration that he is unable to discharge the powers and duties of his office, and until he transmits to them a written declaration to the contrary, such powers and duties shall be discharged by the Vice President as Acting President.

Section 4.

Whenever the Vice President and a majority of either the principal officers of the executive departments or of such other body as Congress may by law provide, transmit to the President pro tempore of the Senate and the Speaker of the House of Representatives their written declaration that the President is unable to discharge the powers and duties of his office, the Vice President shall immediately assume the powers and duties of the office as Acting President.

Thereafter, when the President transmits to the President pro tempore of the Senate and the Speaker of the House of Representatives his written declaration that no inability exists, he shall resume the powers and duties of his office unless the Vice President and a majority of either the principal officers of the executive department or of such other body as Congress may by law provide, transmit within four days to the President pro tempore of the Senate and the Speaker of the House of Representatives their written declaration that the President is unable to discharge the powers and duties of his office. Thereupon Congress shall decide the issue, assembling within forty-eight hours for that purpose if not in session. If the Congress, within twenty-one days after receipt of the latter written declaration, or, if Congress is not in session, within twenty-one days after Congress is required to assemble, determines by two-thirds vote of both Houses that the President is unable to discharge the powers and duties of his office, the Vice President shall continue to discharge the same as Acting President; otherwise, the President shall resume the powers and duties of his office.

Several tragedies to the men who occupied the offices of president and vice president and the lack of constitutional clarity about the path of succession in event of presidential and vice presidential disability spurred the enactment of the Twenty-Fifth Amendment.

Whether the vice president was merely an acting president or assumed the permanent powers of the office for the remainder of the term upon the death of a president was answered in 1841 when John Tyler became president upon the death of William Henry Harrison, who died only a month after his inauguration. Seven more presidents died in office before the enactment of the Twenty-Fifth Amendment, and in each case the vice president assumed the presidency without controversy. What this amendment answered that the original Constitution did not was the method of vice presidential succession. The vice presidency often went unfilled for months at a time as the result of constitutional ambiguity. Since the enactment of the amendment, there have been two occasions when the president appointed a vice president. Both took place during the second term of President Richard Nixon. For the first time in United States history, the nation witnessed a presidential term served out by two men, President Gerald R. Ford and Vice President Nelson A. Rockefeller, neither of whom had been elected to the position.

The Twenty-Fifth Amendment also settled the path of succession in the event of presidential disability. This provision of the amendment was prompted by the memories of James Garfield lying in a coma for eighty days after being struck by an assassin's bullet and Woodrow Wilson's bedridden state for the last eighteen months of his term after a stroke. The first president to invoke the disability provision of the Twenty-Fifth Amendment was Ronald Reagan, who made Vice President George Bush acting president for the eight hours while he underwent surgery. The only other time a president invoked this provision came in 2002, when George W. Bush underwent minor surgery and transferred the powers of his office to Vice President Dick Cheney.

The provision authorizing the vice president, in consultation with Congress and members of the Cabinet, to declare the president disabled has never been invoked.

AMENDMENT XXVI
(Ratified on July 1, 1971)

Section 1.

The right of citizens of the United States, who are eighteen years of age or older, to vote shall not be denied or abridged by the United States or by any State on account of age.

Section 2.

The Congress shall have power to enforce this article by appropriate legislation.

The Twenty-Sixth Amendment was a direct response to the unpopularity of the Vietnam War and was spurred by calls to lower the voting age to eighteen so that draft-eligible men could voice their opinion on the war through the ballot box. In 1970, Congress had amended the Voting Rights Act of 1965 to lower the voting age to eighteen in all national, state, and local elections. Many states resisted compliance, claiming that Congress, while having the power to establish the voting age in national elections, had no such authority in state and local elections. In *Oregon* v. *Mitchell* (1970), the Supreme Court agreed with that view. Congress responded by drafting the Twenty-Sixth Amendment, and the states ratified it quickly and without controversy.

AMENDMENT XXVII
(Ratified on May 7, 1992)

No law, varying the compensation for the services of the Senators and Representatives shall take effect until an election of Representatives shall have intervened.

The Twenty-Seventh Amendment was originally introduced in 1789 during the 1st Congress as one of the original twelve amendments to the Constitution. Only six of the necessary eleven (of thirteen) states had ratified the amendment by 1791. As more states came into the union, the prospect of the amendment's passage only dwindled. No additional state ratified the amendment until 1873, when Ohio approved its addition to the Constitution.

Sometime in the early 1980s, a University of Texas student discovered the amendment and launched an intensive effort to bring it to the public's attention for ratification. The amendment's core purpose, preventing members of Congress from raising their salaries during the terms in which they served, meshed well with another grassroots movement that began during this time, the campaign to impose term limits on members of the House and Senate. Nothing in the nation's constitutional or statutory law prohibited the resurrection of the Twenty-Seventh Amendment for voter approval. In 1939, the Supreme Court had ruled in *Coleman* v. *Miller* that amendments could remain indefinitely before the public unless Congress had set a specific time limit on the ratification process. By 1992, the amendment had received the necessary three-fourths approval of the states, making it the last successful effort to amend the Constitution. The Twenty-Seventh Amendment has not, however, barred Congress from increasing its compensation through annual cost-of-living-adjustments.

Photo courtesy: Joe Cavaretta/AP/Wide World Photos

Federalism

IN 2003, RECALLED THE REPUBLICAN GOVERNOR of Nevada, Kenny Guinn (pictured to the left), the state was "like a casino gambler digging into his life savings just to stay in the game."[1] Like many other states, Nevada had built up significant "rainy day funds" during the budget surplus years of the 1990s, only to see them dwindle in the early 2000s. Nevada had to use $135 million of its $136 million fund to keep its budget balanced. Other states, too, had to raid the piggy bank. Across the nation, in a failing economy, state expenses rose sharply for post–September 11, 2001, security measures and to meet increased demands for state services as unemployment went up, along with the cost of providing health care for the states' poor and aged.

States took a variety of approaches to solving their budget woes. Many enacted new taxes and fees from increased car registration rates to costs for recording deeds as home sales and refinancings skyrocketed when mortgage interest rates fell. Tuition rates and fees at many state colleges and universities rose significantly—some by as much as 25 percent! Cities and other local governments similarly looked for new ways to raise revenue, from increased parking fines to better enforcement of traffic laws, to higher fines for overdue library books.

Still, "After three years during which state revenues proved exceedingly dismal, the picture [was] notably—but cautiously—brighter at the end of fiscal 2004," found a report from the National Association of State Budget officers. But, noted its executive director, "the picture is far from rosy. If the states were patients, you could say they are out of intensive care, but they're not out of the hospital yet."[2]

The woes that many states experienced in 2000, and dramatically after 9/11, vividly illustrate the interrelated nature of the state and national governments in our federal system. In 2003, when two-thirds of the states faced serious budget shortfalls, they pressured Congress to rescue them, which resulted in $20 billion in emergency aid. For states like Nevada, "The $67 million we got from Congress . . . was a nice little shot in the arm," said its budget administrator.[3]

Some of those dollars went to fund programs mandated by the national government. The federal No Child Left Behind Act creates nationwide educational priorities, for example, but it also requires states to spend billions on standardized testing.[4] The nationally mandated Medicaid program establishes health cover-age for the poor, but it also requires states to spend more than 20 percent of their budgets on Medicaid.[5]

In theory, this kind of federal/state relationship, which attempts to shrink the size of the federal government and return power to state agencies, should create programs that are more tailored to the needs of citizens. Proponents of what is known as the "devolution revolution" argue that state and local governments are closer to their citizens and more able to meet the needs of the region.

FROM ITS VERY BEGINNING, the challenge for the United States of America was to preserve the traditional independence and rights of the states while establishing an effective national government. In *Federalist No. 51*, James Madison highlighted the unique structure of governmental powers created by the Framers: "The power surrendered by the people is first divided between two distinct governments, and then . . . subdivided among distinct and separate departments. Hence, a double security arises to the rights of the people."

The Framers, fearing tyranny, divided powers between the state and the national governments. At each level, moreover, powers were divided among executive, legislative, and judicial branches. The people are the ultimate power from which both the national government and the state governments derive their power.

Although most of the delegates to the Constitutional Convention favored a strong federal government, they knew that some compromise about the distribution of powers would be necessary. Some of the Framers wanted to continue with the confederate form of government defined in the Articles of Confederation; others wanted a more centralized system, similar to that of Great Britain. Their solution was to create the world's first federal system, in which the thirteen sovereign or independent states were bound together under one national government.

Today, the Constitution ultimately binds more than 87,000 different state and local governments, although the word "federal" never appears in that document (see Figure 3.1). The Constitution lays out the duties, obligations, and powers of the states. Throughout history, however, the system and the rules that guide it have been continually stretched, reshaped, and reinterpreted by crises, historical evolution, public expectations, and judicial interpretation. All these forces have had tremendous influence on who makes policy decisions and how these decisions get made, as is underscored in our opening vignette.

Issues involving the distribution of power between the national government and the states affect you on a daily basis. You do not, for example, need a passport to go from Texas to Oklahoma. There is but one national currency and a national minimum wage. But, many differences exist among the laws of the various states. The age at which you may marry is a state issue, as are laws governing divorce, child custody, and most criminal laws, including how—or if—the death penalty is implemented. Although some policies or programs are under the authority of the state or local government, others, such as air traffic regulation, are solely within the province of the national gov-

FIGURE 3.1   Number of Governments in the United
              States. ■

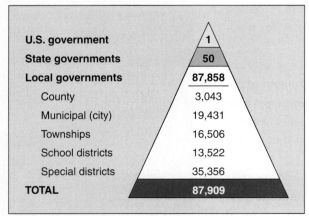

U.S. government	1
State governments	50
Local governments	87,858
County	3,043
Municipal (city)	19,431
Townships	16,506
School districts	13,522
Special districts	35,356
TOTAL	87,909

Source: U.S. Census Bureau, http://www.census.gov/govs/www/gid.html.

ernment.[6] In many areas, however, the national and state governments work together cooperatively in a system of shared powers. At times, the national government cooperates with or supports programs only if the states meet certain conditions. To receive federal funds for the construction and maintenance of highways, for example, states must follow federal rules about the kinds of roads they build.

To understand the current relationship between the states and the federal government and to better grasp some of the issues that arise from this constantly changing relationship, in this chapter, we will examine the following topics:

- First, we will look at *the roots of the federal system* and *governmental powers under the Constitution* created by the Framers.

- Second, we will explore the relationship between *federalism and the Marshall Court.*

- Third, we will examine the development of *dual federalism* before and after the *Civil War.*

- Fourth, we will analyze *cooperative federalism and the growth of national government.*

- Finally, we will discuss *new federalism,* the movement toward *returning power to the states.*

THE ROOTS OF THE FEDERAL SYSTEM: GOVERNMENTAL POWERS UNDER THE CONSTITUTION

AS DISCUSSED IN CHAPTER 2, the Framers of the Constitution were the first to adopt a **federal system** of government. This system of government, where the national government and state governments derive all authority from the people, was designed to remedy many of the problems experienced by the Framers under the Articles of Confederation. Under the Articles, the United States was governed by a confederation government, where the national government derived all of its powers from the states. This led to a weak national government that was often unable to respond to even small crises, such as Shays's Rebellion.

The new system of government also had to be different from the **unitary system** found in Great Britain, where the local and regional governments derived all their power from a strong national government. (Figure 3.2 illustrates these different forms of government.) Having been under the rule of English kings, whom they considered tyrants, the Framers feared centralizing power in one government or institution. Therefore, they made both the state and the federal government accountable to the people at large. While the governments shared some powers, such as the ability to tax, each government was supreme in some spheres, as depicted in Figure 3.3 and described in the following section.

The federal system as conceived by the Framers has proven tremendously effective. Since the creation of the U.S. system, many other nations including Canada (1867), Mexico (1917), and Russia (1993) have adopted federal systems in their constitutions. (See Global Perspective: Federalism Around the World.)

National Powers Under the Constitution

Chief among the exclusive powers of the national government are the authorities to coin money, conduct foreign relations, provide for an army and navy, declare war, and establish a national court system. All of these powers set out in Article I, section 8, of the Constitution are called **enumerated powers.** Article I, section 8, also contains the

federal system
System of government where the national government and state governments derive all authority from the people.

unitary system
System of government where the local and regional governments derive all authority from a strong national government.

Comparative
Comparing Federal and Unitary Systems

enumerated powers
Seventeen specific powers granted to Congress under Article I, section 8, of the U.S. Constitution; these powers include taxation, coinage of money, regulation of commerce, and the authority to provide for a national defense.

FIGURE 3.2   The Federal,
Confederation, and Unitary
Systems of Government
The source of governmental author-
ity and power differs dramatically in
various systems of government. ■

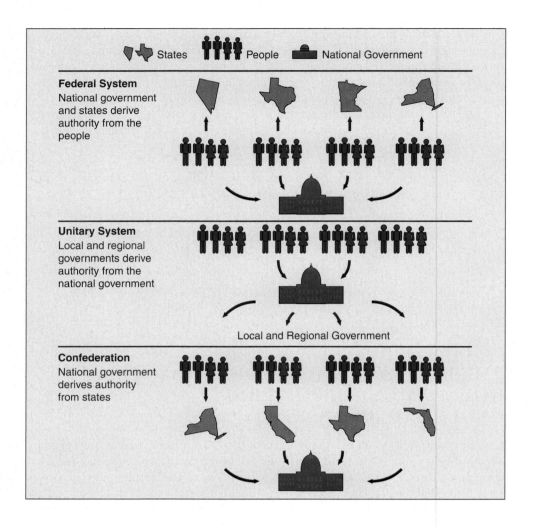

necessary and proper clause
The final paragraph of Article I, section 8, of the U.S. Constitution,
which gives Congress the authority
to pass all laws "necessary and
proper" to carry out the enumerated
powers specified in the Constitution;
also called the elastic clause.

necessary and proper clause, which gives Congress the authority to enact any laws
"necessary and proper" for carrying out any of its enumerated powers. These powers
derived from enumerated powers and the necessary and proper clause are known as
implied powers.

The federal government's right to tax was also clearly set out in the new Constitution. The Framers wanted to avoid the financial problems that the national government
experienced under the Articles of Confederation. If the national government was to be
strong, its power to raise revenue had to be unquestionable. Although the new national
government had no power under the Constitution to levy a national income tax, that
was changed by the passage of the Sixteenth Amendment in 1913. Eventually, as discussed later in this chapter, this new taxing power became a powerful catalyst for further expansion of the national government.

Article VI of the federal Constitution underscores the notion that the national government is to be supreme in situations of conflict between state and national law. It
declares that the U.S. Constitution, the laws of the United States, and its treaties are to
be "the supreme Law of the Land; and the Judges in every State shall be bound thereby."

In spite of this explicit language, the meaning of what is called the **supremacy
clause** has been subject to continuous judicial interpretation. In 1920, for example,
Missouri sought to prevent a U.S. game warden from enforcing the Migratory Bird
Treaty Act of 1918, which prohibited the killing or capturing of many species of birds
as they made their annual migration across the international border from Canada to

supremacy clause
Portion of Article VI of the U.S.
Constitution mandating that
national law is supreme to (that is,
supersedes) all other laws passed by
the states or by any other subdivision
of government.

Global Perspective

FEDERALISM AROUND THE WORLD

One of the most fundamental decisions that constitutional framers must make involves choosing between a unitary and a federal framework for organizing political power. In a federal system, such as exists in the United States, political power is firmly divided between the national government and states. In India's federal system, for example, states have jurisdiction over public health, education, agriculture, forests, and fisheries. In a unitary system, all political power rests with the national government. It may delegate the power to make or implement policies to lesser governmental units such as states, provinces, or cities, but those decisions reside with the national government alone. Thus, a ministry (department) of education in a unitary system has the power to set the curriculum for all children in the country regardless of where they live. There may be a national police force and only one court system with judges appointed by the central government. Great Britain and France are the best-known unitary states. A major political controversy currently underway in France is the decision by the central government to forbid schoolchildren from wearing head coverings in school. Many Muslims residing in France see this as an affront to their culture, but French authorities view the policy as consistent with the principles of a secular state and an affirmation of the primacy of French culture.

Around the world there are far more unitary political systems than federal ones. A survey of one hundred constitutions in 2000 found that only twenty were federal states (see the figure). What is immediately obvious is that many of these states are among the world's largest states. Russia has a population of 145 million and is divided into 89 components. Brazil has a population of 177 million and has 26 states and a capital territory. Nigeria has a population of 133 million and is divided into 36 states and a capital area. India has a population of 1.05 billion and contains 25 states.

Both systems of governments have their backers. Advocates of federalism assert that it promotes and protects regional/ethnic uniqueness, allows citizens choice, brings citizens closer to their governments, and promotes experimentation. Critics of federalism and those who advocate a unitary system maintain that federalism creates a slow and cumbersome decision-making process, it denies equal treatment to all citizens, and states lack the financial resources to address many of today's problems. The United States' immediate neighbors, Canada and Mexico, are fed-

erations illustrating both sides of the debate. Quebec, a predominately French-speaking province in Canada, relies heavily upon federalism to maintain its identity. In Mexico, economic problems and the long history of one-party rule have led to increased centralization of power in the national government.

Both federal and unitary political systems around the world have begun to incorporate elements of the other in order to deal effectively with contemporary issues. Unitary systems have undertaken policies to grant subnational regions within their respective countries more autonomy. In Great Britain, this process has focused on Scotland and Wales. Spain, which has long confronted strong regional-nationalist sentiment in northern Spain from the Basques and Catalans, has moved to grant increased powers to regional governments and has given them some power over language rights, taxation policy, and other local matters, along with a regional parliament. Federal systems have moved in the opposite direction, incorporating features that promote centralization and uniformity. In Germany, for example, civil service rules are the same in all land (state) governments, and the constitution requires that there be a "unity of living standards" throughout the country.

Questions

1. Which do you think is better suited for solving problems in today's world, a unitary or federal system? Why?
2. Which aspects of the American federal system would you most recommend to a country considering rewriting their constitution? Which feature would you least recommend to them?

Source: Robert Maddex, *Constitutions of the World*, 2nd ed. (Washington, DC: Congressional Quarterly Press, 2000).

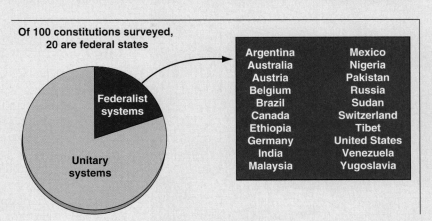

Of 100 constitutions surveyed, 20 are federal states

Federalist systems

Unitary systems

Argentina	Mexico
Australia	Nigeria
Austria	Pakistan
Belgium	Russia
Brazil	Sudan
Canada	Switzerland
Ethiopia	Tibet
Germany	United States
India	Venezuela
Malaysia	Yugoslavia

Photo courtesy: Judy Gelles/Stock Boston, Inc.

■ Here, in an example of concurrent state and national power, birds are protected by both governments.

privileges and immunities clause
Part of Article IV of the Constitution guaranteeing that the citizens of each state are afforded the same rights as citizens of all other states.

Tenth Amendment
The final part of the Bill of Rights that defines the basic principle of American federalism in stating: "The powers not delegated to the United States by the Constitution, nor prohibited by it to the States, are reserved to the States respectively, or to the people."

reserve (or police) powers
Powers reserved to the states by the Tenth Amendment that lie at the foundation of a state's right to legislate for the public health and welfare of its citizens.

concurrent powers
Authority possessed by both the state and national governments that may be exercised concurrently as long as that power is not exclusively within the scope of national power or in conflict with national law.

parts of the United States.[7] Missouri argued that the Tenth Amendment, which reserved a state's powers to legislate for the general welfare of its citizens, allowed Missouri to regulate hunting. But, the Court ruled that since the treaty was legal, it must be considered the supreme law of the land. (See also *McCulloch* v. *Maryland* [1819].)

State Powers Under the Constitution

Because states had all the power at the time the Constitution was written, the Framers felt no need, as they did for the new national government, to list and restate the powers of the states. Article I, however, allows states to set the "Times, Places, and Manner, for holding elections for senators and representatives." This article also guarantees each state two members in the Senate and prevents Congress from limiting the slave trade before 1808. Article II requires that each state appoint electors to vote for president, and Article IV contains the **privileges and immunities clause,** guaranteeing that the citizens of each state are afforded the same rights as citizens of all other states. In addition, Article IV provides each state a "Republican Form of Government," meaning one that represents the citizens of the state. It also assures that the national government will protect the states against foreign attacks and domestic rebellion.

It was not until the **Tenth Amendment,** the final part of the Bill of Rights, that the states' powers were described in greater detail: "The powers not delegated to the United States by the Constitution, nor prohibited by it to the States, are reserved to the States respectively, or to the people" (see The Living Constitution: Tenth Amendment). These powers, often called the states' **reserve** or **police powers,** include the ability to legislate for the public health, safety, and morals of their citizens. Today, the states' rights to legislate under their police powers are used as the rationale for many states' restrictions on abortion, including twenty-four-hour waiting requirements and provisions requiring minors to obtain parental consent. Police powers are also the basis for state criminal laws, the reason some states have the death penalty and others do not. So long as the U.S. Supreme Court continues to find that the death penalty does not violate the U.S. Constitution, the states may impose it, be it by lethal injection, gas chamber, or the electric chair.

Concurrent and Denied Powers Under the Constitution

As revealed in Figure 3.3, national and state powers overlap. The area where the systems overlap represents **concurrent powers**—powers shared by the national and state governments. States already had the power to tax; the Constitution extended this power to the national government as well. Other important concurrent powers include the right to borrow money, establish courts, and make and enforce laws necessary to carry out these powers.

Article I denies certain powers to the national and state governments. In keeping with the Framers' desire to forge a national economy, states are prohibited from entering treaties, coining money, or impairing obligation of contracts. States also are prohibited from entering into compacts with other states without express congressional

FIGURE 3.3   The Distribution of Governmental Power in the Federal System. ■

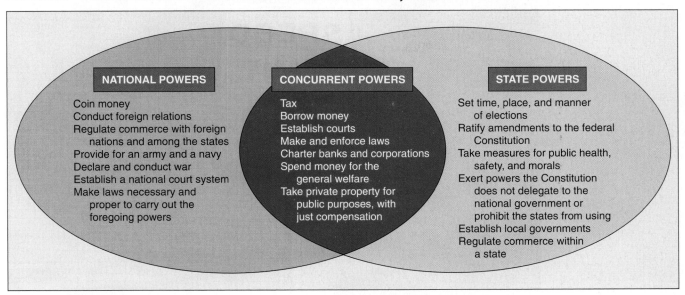

NATIONAL POWERS

Coin money
Conduct foreign relations
Regulate commerce with foreign
   nations and among the states
Provide for an army and a navy
Declare and conduct war
Establish a national court system
Make laws necessary and
   proper to carry out the
   foregoing powers

CONCURRENT POWERS

Tax
Borrow money
Establish courts
Make and enforce laws
Charter banks and corporations
Spend money for the
   general welfare
Take private property for
   public purposes, with
   just compensation

STATE POWERS

Set time, place, and manner
   of elections
Ratify amendments to the federal
   Constitution
Take measures for public health,
   safety, and morals
Exert powers the Constitution
   does not delegate to the
   national government or
   prohibit the states from using
Establish local governments
Regulate commerce within
   a state

approval. In a similar vein, Congress is barred from favoring one state over another in regulating commerce, and it cannot lay duties on items exported from any state.

Both the national and state governments are denied the authority to take arbitrary actions affecting constitutional rights and liberties. Neither national nor state governments may pass a **bill of attainder,** a law declaring an act illegal without a judicial trial. The Constitution also bars the national and state governments from passing *ex post facto* **laws,** laws that make an act punishable as a crime even if the action was legal at the time it was committed. (For more on civil rights and liberties, see chapters 5 and 6.)

Relations Among the States

In addition to delineating the relationship of the states with the national government, the Constitution provides a mechanism for resolving interstate disputes and facilitating relations among states. To avoid any sense of favoritism, it provides that disputes between states be settled directly by the U.S. Supreme Court under its original jurisdiction as mandated by Article III of the Constitution (see chapter 10). Moreover, Article IV requires that each state give "Full Faith and Credit...to the public Acts, Records and judicial Proceedings of every other State." The **full faith and credit clause** ensures that judicial decrees and contracts made in one state will be binding and enforceable in another, thereby facilitating trade and other commercial relationships.

In 1997, the Supreme Court ruled that the full faith and credit clause mandates that state courts always must honor the judgments of other state courts, even if to do so is against state public policy or existing state laws. Failure to do so would allow a single state to "rule the world," said Supreme Court Associate Justice Ruth Bader Ginsburg during oral argument.[8] The Violence Against Women Act, for example, specifically requires states to give full faith and credit to protective orders issued by other states.[9]

bill of attainder
A law declaring an act illegal without a judicial trial.

ex post facto **law**
Law passed after the fact, thereby making previously legal activity illegal and subject to current penalty; prohibited by the U.S. Constitution.

full faith and credit clause
Portion of Article IV of the Constitution that ensures judicial decrees and contracts made in one state will be binding and enforceable in any other state.

Photo courtesy: K.M. Cannon, Nevada Appeal/AP/Wide World Photos

■ Interstate speed limits are federalism issues. The National Highway System Designation Act of 1995 allows states to set their own speed limits, reversing an earlier national law that set 55 mph as a national standard. Top state speeds now range from 55 to 75 mph.

Article IV also requires states to extradite, or return, criminals to states where they have been convicted or are to stand trial. For example, Timothy Reed, an Indian-rights activist, spent five years in New Mexico fighting extradition to Ohio.[10] In 1998, the New Mexico Supreme Court ordered him released from custody in spite of an order from the New Mexico governor ordering his extradition to Ohio. The U.S. Supreme Court found that the Supreme Court of New Mexico went beyond its authority and that Reed should be returned to Ohio.[11]

As noted above, the U.S. Constitution gives the Supreme Court the final authority to decide controversies between the states. New York and New Jersey, for example, ended up before the Supreme Court arguing over the title to Ellis Island, based on the 1834 agreement between the two states that set the boundary lines between them as the middle of the Hudson River. New York got authority over the island, where over 12 million immigrants were processed between 1892 and 1954, but New Jersey retained rights to the submerged lands on its side. Ultimately, the Supreme Court ruled that New Jersey was entitled to all of the new lands that were created when the U.S. government filled in the island's natural shoreline; New York, however, still retained title and thus bragging rights to the museum dedicated to chronicling the history of U.S. immigration.[12]

To facilitate relations among states, Article 1, section 10, clause 3, of the U.S. Constitution sets the legal foundation for interstate cooperation in the form of **interstate compacts,** contracts between states that carry the force of law. It reads, "No State shall, without the consent of Congress . . . enter into any Agreement or Compact with

interstate compacts
Contracts between states that carry the force of law; generally now used as a tool to address multistate policy concerns.

The Living Constitution

The Powers not delegated to the United States by the Constitution, nor prohibited by it to the States, are reserved to the states respectively, or to the people.

—Tenth Amendment

This amendment to the Constitution—a simple affirmation that any powers not specifically given to the national government are left to the province of the states or to the citizenry—was actually unnecessary and added nothing to the original document. During the ratification debates, however, Anti-Federalists continued to be concerned that the national government would claim powers not intended for it at the expense of the states. Still, during the debates over this amendment, both houses of Congress rejected efforts to insert the word "expressly" before the word delegated. Thus, it was clear that the amendment was not intended to be the yardstick by which to measure the powers of the national government. This was reinforced by comments made by James Madison during the debate that took place over Alexander Hamilton's efforts to establish a national bank. "Interference with the power of the States was no constitutional criterion of the power of Congress."

By the end of the New Deal, the Supreme Court had come to interpret the Tenth Amendment to allow Congress, pursuant to its authority under the commerce clause, to legislate in a wide array of areas that the states might never have foreseen when they ratified the amendment. In fact, until the 1970s, Congress's ability to legislate to regulate commerce appeared to trump any actions of the states. Since the mid-1970s, however, the Court has been very closely divided about how much authority must be reserved to the states vis-à-vis their authority to regulate commerce, especially when it involves regulation of activities of states as sovereign entities. The Court now requires Congress to attach statements of clear intention to tread on state powers. It is then up to the Court to determine if Congress has claimed powers beyond its authority under the Constitution.

another state." Before 1920, interstate compacts were largely bistate compacts that addressed boundary disputes or acted to help two states accomplish some objective.

More than 200 interstate compacts exist today. While some deal with rudimentary items such as state boundaries, others help states carry out their policy objectives, and they play an important role in helping states carry out their functions. Although several bistate compacts still exist, other compacts have as many as fifty signatories.[13] The Drivers License Compact, for example, was signed by all fifty states to facilitate nationwide recognition of licenses issued in the respective states.

States today find that interstate compacts help them maintain state control because compacts with other states allow for sharing resources, expertise, and responses that often are available more quickly than those from the federal government. The Emergency Management Assistance Compact, for example, allows states to cooperate and to share resources in the event of natural and man-made disasters. On 9/11, assistance to New

TABLE 3.1 Compacts by the Numbers	
Interstate compacts with 25 or more members	13
Least compact memberships by a state (HI & WI)	14
Most compact memberships by a state (NH & VA)	42
Average compact memberships by a state	27
Compacts developed prior to 1920	36
Compacts developed since 1920	150+
Interstate compacts currently in operation	200+

Source: John Mountjoy, "Interstate Cooperation: Interstate Compacts Make a Comeback," *Council of State Governments* (Spring 2001): Available online at http://www.csg.org.

York and Virginia came from a host of states surrounding the areas of terrorist attacks. (For more on compacts, see Table 3.1.)

Relations Within the States: Local Government

The Constitution gives local governments, including counties, municipalities, townships, and school districts, no independent standing. Thus, their authority is not granted directly by the people, but through state governments, which establish or charter administrative subdivisions to execute the duties of the state government on a smaller scale. For more information on the relationship between state and local governments, see chapter 4.

FEDERALISM AND THE MARSHALL COURT

THE NATURE OF FEDERALISM and its allocation of power between the national government and the states have changed dramatically over the past two hundred years, and this change is largely due to the rulings of the U.S. Supreme Court. The debate continues today, too, as many Americans, frustrated with the national government's performance on a number of issues, look for a return of more power to the states. Because the distribution of power between the national and state governments is not clearly delineated in the Constitution, over the years the U.S. Supreme Court has played a major role in defining the nature of the federal system.

The first few years that the Supreme Court sat, it handled few major cases. As described in chapter 10, the Supreme Court was viewed as weak, and many men declined the honor of serving as a Supreme Court justice. The appointment of John Marshall as chief justice of the United States, however, changed all of this. In a series of decisions, he and his associates carved out an important role for the Court, especially in defining the nature of the federal/state relationship. Two rulings in the early 1800s, *McCulloch* v. *Maryland* (1819) and *Gibbons* v. *Ogden* (1824), had a major impact on the balance of power between the national government and the states.

Federalism and the Supreme Court

McCulloch v. *Maryland* (1819)
The Supreme Court upheld the power of the national government and denied the right of a state to tax the bank. The Court's broad interpretation of the necessary and proper clause paved the way for later rulings upholding expansive federal powers.

McCulloch v. *Maryland* (1819)

McCulloch v. *Maryland* (1819) was the first major Supreme Court decision of the Marshall Court to define the relationship between the national and state governments. In 1816, Congress chartered the Second Bank of the United States. (The charter of the First Bank had been allowed to expire.) In 1818, the Maryland state legislature levied a tax requiring all banks not chartered by Maryland (that is, the Second Bank of the United States) to: (1) buy stamped paper from the state on which the Second Bank's notes were to be issued; (2) pay the state $15,000 a year; or, (3) go out of business. James McCulloch, the head cashier of the Baltimore branch of the Bank of the United States, refused to pay the tax, and Maryland brought suit against him. After losing in a Maryland state court, McCulloch appealed his conviction to the U.S. Supreme Court by order of the U.S. secretary of the treasury. In a unanimous opinion, the Court answered the two central questions that had been put to it: Did Congress have the authority to charter a bank? If it did, could a state tax it?

Chief Justice John Marshall's answer to the first question—whether Congress had the right to establish a bank or another type of corporation, given that the Constitution does not explicitly mention such a power—continues to stand as the classic exposition of the doctrine of implied powers and as a reaffirmation of the propriety of a strong national government. Although the word "bank" cannot be found in the Constitution, the Constitution enumerates powers that give Congress the authority to levy and collect taxes, issue a currency, and borrow funds. From these enumerated powers, Marshall found, it was reasonable to imply that Congress had the power to charter a bank, which could be considered "necessary and proper" to the exercise of its aforementioned enumerated powers.

Marshall next addressed the question of whether a federal bank could be taxed by any state government. To Marshall, this was not a difficult question. The national government was dependent on the people, not the states, for its powers. In addition, Marshall noted, the Constitution specifically calls for the national law to be supreme. "The power to tax involves the power to destroy," wrote Marshall.[14] Thus, the state tax violated the supremacy clause, because individual states cannot interfere with the operations of the national government, whose laws are supreme.

The Court's decision in *McCulloch* has far-reaching consequences even today. The necessary and proper clause is used to justify federal action in many areas, including education, health, and welfare. Furthermore, had Marshall allowed the state of Maryland to tax the Second Bank, it is possible that states could have attempted to tax all federal agencies located within their boundaries, a costly proposition that could have driven the federal government into insurmountable debt.

Gibbons v. *Ogden* (1824)

Shortly after *McCulloch*, the Marshall Court had another opportunity to rule in favor of a broad interpretation of the scope of national power. ***Gibbons* v. *Ogden*** (1824) involved a dispute that arose after the New York State legislature granted to Robert Fulton the exclusive right to operate steamboats on the Hudson River. Simultaneously, Congress licensed a ship to sail on the same waters. By the time the case reached the Supreme Court, it was complicated both factually and procedurally. Suffice it to say that both New York and New Jersey wanted to control shipping on the lower Hudson River. But, *Gibbons* actually addressed one simple, very important question: what was the scope of Congress's authority under the commerce clause? The states argued that "commerce," as mentioned in Article I, should be interpreted narrowly to include only direct dealings in products. In *Gibbons*, however, the Supreme Court ruled that Congress's power to regulate interstate commerce included the power to regulate commercial activity as well, and that the commerce power had no limits except those specifically found in the Constitution. Thus, New York had no constitutional authority to grant a monopoly to a single steamboat operator, an act that interfered with interstate commerce.[15] Like the necessary and proper clause, today, the commerce clause is used to justify a great deal of federal legislation, including regulation of highways, the stock market, and even segregation.

Gibbons v. *Ogden* (1824)
The Supreme Court upheld broad congressional power to regulate interstate commerce. The Court's broad interpretation of the Constitution's commerce clause paved the way for later rulings upholding expansive federal powers.

DUAL FEDERALISM: THE TANEY COURT, SLAVERY, AND THE CIVIL WAR

IN SPITE OF NATIONALIST Marshall Court decisions such as *McCulloch* and *Gibbons*, strong debate continued in the United States over national versus state power. It was under the leadership of Chief Justice Marshall's successor, Roger B. Taney (1835–1863), that the Supreme Court articulated the notions of concurrent power and **dual federalism.** Dual federalism posits that having separated and equally powerful state and national governments is the best arrangement. Adherents of this theory typically believe that the national government should not exceed its constitutionally enumerated powers, and, as stated in the Tenth Amendment, all other powers are, and should be, reserved to the states or the people.

dual federalism
The belief that having separate and equally powerful levels of government is the best arrangement.

Dred Scott: Slavery and the Supreme Court

Photo courtesy: Missouri Historical Society

DRED SCOTT, BORN INTO SLAVERY around 1795, became the named plaintiff in a case that was to have major ramifications on the nature of the federal system. In 1833, Scott was sold by his original owners, the Blow family, to Dr. Emerson in St. Louis, Missouri. The next year he was taken to Illinois and later to the Wisconsin Territory, returning to St. Louis in 1838.[a]

When Emerson died in 1843, Scott tried to buy his freedom. Before he could, however, he was transferred to Emerson's widow, who moved to New York, leaving Scott in the custody of his first owners, the Blows. Some of the Blows (Henry Blow later founded the anti-slavery Free Soil Party) and other abolitionists gave money to support a test case seeking Scott's freedom: They believed that his residence in Illinois and later in the Wisconsin Territory, which both prohibited slavery, made him a free man.

After many delays, the U.S. Supreme Court ruled 7–2 that Scott was not a citizen of the United States. "Slaves," said the Court, "were never thought of or spoken of except as property." Chief Justice Roger B. Taney tried to fashion a broad ruling to settle the slavery question. Writing for the majority in *Dred Scott* v. *Sandford* (1857), he concluded that Congress lacked the constitutional authority to bar slavery in the territories. The decision narrowed the scope of national power while it enhanced that of the states. Moreover, for the first time since *Marbury* v. *Madison* (1803), the Court found an act of Congress, the Missouri Compromise, unconstitutional. And, by limiting what the national government could do concerning slavery, it in all likelihood quickened the march toward the Civil War.

Dred Scott was given his freedom later in 1857, when the Emersons permanently returned him to the anti-slavery Blows. He died of tuberculosis one year later.

---

[a] Don E. Ferenbacher, "The Dred Scott Case," in John A. Garraty, ed., *Quarrels That Have Shaped the Constitution* (New York: Harper and Row, 1964), ch. 6.

Dred Scott and the Advent of Civil War

During the Taney court era, the comfortable role of the Supreme Court as the arbiter of competing national and state interests became troublesome when the justices were called upon to deal with the controversial issue of slavery. In cases such as *Dred Scott* v. *Sandford* (1857), the Court tried to manage the slavery issue by resolving questions of ownership, the status of fugitive slaves, and slavery in the new territories.[16] These cases generally were settled in favor of slavery and states' rights within the framework of dual federalism. In *Dred Scott*, for example, the Taney Court, in declaring the Missouri Compromise unconstitutional, ruled that Congress lacked the authority to ban slavery in the territories (see Roots of Government: Dred Scott: Slavery and the Supreme Court.) This decision seemed to rule out any nationally legislated solution to the slavery question, leaving the problem in the hands of the state legislatures and the people, who did not have the power to impose their will on other states.

The Civil War, Its Aftermath, and the Continuation of Dual Federalism

The Civil War (1861–1865) forever changed the nature of federalism. In the aftermath of the war, the national government grew in size and powers. It also attempted to impose its will on the state governments through the Thirteenth, Fourteenth, and Fifteenth Amendments. These three amendments, known collectively as the Civil War Amendments, prohibited slavery and granted civil and political rights (including the franchise for males) to African Americans.

The U.S. Supreme Court, however, continued to adhere to its belief in the concept of dual federalism. Therefore, in spite of the growth of the national government's powers, the importance of the state governments' powers was not diminished until 1933, when the next major change in the federal system occurred. Generally, the Court upheld any laws passed under the states' police powers, which allow states to pass laws to protect the general welfare of their citizens. These laws included those affecting commerce, labor relations, and manufacturing. After the Court's decision in *Plessy* v. *Ferguson* (1896), in which the Court ruled that state maintenance of "separate but equal" facilities for blacks and whites was constitutional, most civil rights and voting cases also became state matters, in spite of the Civil War Amendments.[17]

The Court also developed legal doctrine in a series of cases that reinforced the national government's ability to regulate commerce. By the 1930s, these two somewhat contradictory approaches led to confusion: States, for example, could not tax gasoline used by federal vehicles,[18] and the national government could not tax the sale of motorcycles to the city police department.[19] In this period, the Court, however, did recognize the need for national control over new technological developments, such as the telegraph.[20] And, beginning in the 1880s, the Court allowed Congress to regulate many aspects of economic relationships, such as monopolies, an area of regulation formerly thought to be in the exclusive realm of the states. Passage of laws such as the Interstate Commerce Act in 1887 and the Sherman Anti-Trust Act in 1890 allowed Congress to establish itself as an important player in the growing national economy.

Despite finding that most of these federal laws were constitutional, the Supreme Court did not enlarge the scope of national power consistently. In 1895, for example, the United States filed suit against four sugar refiners, alleging that their sale would give their buyer control of 98 percent of the U.S. sugar-refining business. The Supreme Court ruled that congressional efforts to control monopolies (through passage of the Sherman Anti-Trust Act) did not give Congress the authority to prevent the sale of these sugar-refining businesses, because manufacturing was not commerce. Therefore, the companies and their actions were beyond the scope of Congress's authority to regulate.[21]

Setting the Stage for a Stronger National Government

In 1895, the U.S. Supreme Court found a congressional effort to tax personal incomes unconstitutional, although an earlier Court had found a similar tax levied during the Civil War constitutional.[22] Thus, Congress and the state legislatures were moved to ratify the **Sixteenth Amendment.** The Sixteenth Amendment gave Congress the power to levy and collect taxes on incomes without apportioning them among the states. The revenues taken in by the federal government through taxation of personal income "removed a major constraint on the federal government by giving it access to almost unlimited revenues."[23] If money is power, the income tax and the revenues it generated greatly enhanced the power of the federal government and its ability to enter policy areas where it formerly had few funds to spend.

Sixteenth Amendment
Authorized Congress to enact a national income tax.

The **Seventeenth Amendment,** ratified in 1913, similarly enhanced the power of the national government at the expense of the states. This amendment terminated the state legislatures' election of senators and put their election in the hands of the people. With senators no longer directly accountable to the state legislators who elected them, states lost their principal protectors in Congress. Coupled with the Sixteenth Amendment, this amendment paved the way for a drastic change in the relationship between national and state governments in the United States.

Seventeenth Amendment
Made senators directly elected by the people; removed their selection from state legislatures.

COOPERATIVE FEDERALISM: THE NEW DEAL AND THE GROWTH OF NATIONAL GOVERNMENT

THE ERA OF DUAL FEDERALISM came to an abrupt end in the 1930s. While the ratification of the Sixteenth and Seventeenth Amendments set the stage for expanded national government, the catalyst for dual federalism's demise was a series of economic events that ended in the cataclysm of the Great Depression:

- In 1921, the nation experienced a severe slump in agricultural prices.
- In 1926, the construction industry went into decline.
- In the summer of 1929, inventories of consumer goods and automobiles were at an all-time high.
- Throughout the 1920s, bank failures were common.
- On October 29, 1929, stock prices, which had risen steadily since 1926, crashed, taking with them the entire national economy.

Despite the severity of these indicators, Presidents Calvin Coolidge and Herbert Hoover took little action, believing that the national depression was an amalgamation of state economic crises that should be dealt with by state and local governments. However, by 1933, the situation could no longer be ignored.

The New Deal

Rampant unemployment (historians estimate it was as high as 40–50 percent) was the hallmark of the Great Depression. In 1933, to combat severe problems facing the nation, newly elected President Franklin D. Roosevelt (FDR) proposed a variety of innovative programs under the rubric of "the New Deal" and ushered in a new era in American politics. FDR used the full power of the office of the president as well as his highly effective communication skills to sell the American public and Congress on a whole new ideology of government. Not only were the scope and role of national government remarkably altered, but so was the relationship between each state and the national government.

The New Deal period (1933–1939) was characterized by intense government activity on the national level. It was clear to most politicians that to find national solutions to the Depression, which was affecting the citizens of every state in the union, the national government would have to exercise tremendous authority.

In the first few weeks of the legislative session after FDR's inauguration, Congress and the president acted quickly to bolster confidence in the national government. Congress passed a series of acts creating new agencies and programs proposed by the president. These new agencies, often known by their initials, created what many termed an alphabetocracy. Among the more significant programs were the Federal Housing Administration (FHA), which provided federal financing for new home construction; the Civilian Conservation Corps (CCC), a work relief program for farmers and home owners; and the Agricultural Adjustment Administration (AAA) and the National Recovery Administration (NRA), which imposed restrictions on production in agriculture and many industries.

These programs tremendously enlarged the scope of the national government. Those who feared this unprecedented use of national power quickly challenged the constitutionality of New Deal programs in court. And, at least initially, the Supreme Court often agreed with them.

■ One of the hallmarks of the New Deal and FDR's presidency was the national government's new involvement of cities in the federal system. Here, New York City Mayor Fiorello La Guardia (for whom one New York airport is named) is commissioned by FDR as the director of civil defense.

Photo courtesy: AP/Wide World Photos

Through the mid-1930s, the Supreme Court continued to rule that certain aspects of the New Deal went beyond the authority of Congress to regulate commerce. The Court's *laissez-faire,* or hands-off, attitude toward the economy was reflected in a series of decisions ruling various aspects of New Deal programs unconstitutional.

FDR and the Congress were outraged. FDR's frustration with the Court prompted him to suggest what ultimately was nicknamed his "Court-packing plan." Knowing that he could do little to change the minds of those already on the Court, FDR suggested enlarging its size from nine to thirteen justices. This would have given him the opportunity to pack the Court with a majority of justices predisposed toward the constitutional validity of the New Deal.

Even though Roosevelt was popular, the Court-packing plan was not. Congress and the public were outraged that he even suggested tampering with an institution of government. Nevertheless, the Court appeared to respond to this threat. In 1937, it reversed its series of anti–New Deal decisions, concluding that Congress (and therefore the national government) had the authority to legislate in any area so long as what was regulated affected commerce in any way. Congress then used this newly recognized power to legislate in a wide array of areas, including maximum hour and minimum wage laws, and regulation of child labor. Moreover, the Court also upheld the constitutionality of the bulk of the massive New Deal relief programs, such as the National Labor Relations Act of 1935, which authorized collective bargaining between unions and employees in *NLRB* v. *Jones and Laughlin Steel Co.* (1937);[24] the Fair Labor Standards Act of 1938, which prohibited the interstate shipment of goods made by employees earning less than the federally mandated minimum wage;[25] and the Agricultural Adjustment Act of 1938, which provided crop subsidies to farmers.[26]

Photo courtesy: Hulton Archive/Getty Images

■ This cartoon pokes fun at FDR (with his aide, Harold Ickes) and their unpopular plan to expand the size of the Supreme Court to allow FDR to add justices to undo the majority's anti–New Deal position.

The New Deal programs forced all levels of government to work cooperatively with one another. Indeed, local governments—mainly in big cities—became a third partner in the federal system, as FDR relied on big-city Democratic political machines to turn out voters to support his programs. For the first time in U.S. history, in essence, cities were embraced as equal partners in an intergovernmental system and became players in the national political arena because many in the national legislature wanted to bypass state legislatures, where urban interests usually were underrepresented significantly.

The Changing Nature of Federalism: From Layer Cake to Marble Cake

Before the Depression and the New Deal, most political scientists likened the federal system to a layer cake: each level or layer of government—national, state, and local—had clearly defined powers and responsibilities. After the New Deal, however, the nature of the federal system changed. Government now looked something like a marble cake:

> Wherever you slice through it you reveal an inseparable mixture of differently colored ingredients. . . . Vertical and diagonal lines almost obliterate the horizontal ones, and in some places there are unexpected whirls and an imperceptible merging of colors, so that it is difficult to tell where one ends and the other begins.[27]

Analyzing Visuals

DOMESTIC GRANT-IN-AID OUTLAYS, 1940–2008

The table below provides data on grants-in-aid from the national government to state and local governments between 1940 and 2008. Study the data provided in the table and answer the following critical thinking questions: If the amounts were indicated in constant dollars rather than in current dollars, would the figures change significantly? According to the table, which decades experienced a significant increase in domestic grants-in-aid in terms of total dollars, percentage of domestic programs, percentage of state and local expenditures, and percentage of the gross domestic product? How do those increases relate to the various interpretations of federalism (including cooperative federalism and new federalism)? What do you think explains the variations in grants-in-aid over time? See Analyzing Visuals: A Brief Guide for additional guidance in analyzing tables.

		Federal Grants as a Percentage of Federal Outlays			
Year	Total Gross Domestic Grants-in-Aid (billions)	Total	Domestic Programs[a]	State and Local Expenditures	Product
1940	$0.9	9.2	n/a	n/a	0.9
1950	2.3	5.3	n/a	n/a	0.8
1960	7.0	7.6	18.0	19.0	1.4
1970	24.1	12.3	23.0	24.0	2.4
1980	91.4	15.5	22.0	31.0	3.4
1990	135.3	10.8	17.0	21.0	2.4
1995	225.0	14.8	22.0	25.0	3.1
2000	284.7	15.9	22.7	n/a[b]	2.9
2005	422.4	18.0	24.6	n/a[b]	3.6
2008	482.3	17.8	n/a	n/a[b]	3.5

Note: Amounts are in current dollars. Fiscal years.

Includes off-budget outlays; all grants are on-budget.

[a] Excludes outlays for national defense and net interest.
[b] Data no longer provided by federal government in this form.

Source: Office of Management and Budget, Historical Tables, Budget of the United States Government, Fiscal Year 2004. January 2003. Accessed December 8, 2004, http://www.whitehouse.gov/omb/budget/fy2004/hist.html.

The metaphor of marble cake federalism refers to what political scientists call **cooperative federalism,** a term that describes the intertwined relationship among the national, state, and local governments that began with the New Deal. States began to take a secondary, albeit important, cooperative role in the scheme of governance, as did many cities. Nowhere is this shift in power from the states to the national government clearer than in the growth of federal grant programs that began in earnest during the New Deal. Between the New Deal and the 1990s, the tremendous growth in these programs, and in federal government spending in general, changed the nature and discussion of federalism from "How much power should the national government have?" to "How much say in the policies of the states can the national government buy?" (See Analyzing Visuals: Domestic Grant-in-Aid Outlays, 1940–2005.) During the 1970s energy crisis, the national government initially imposed a national 55 mph speed limit on the states, for example. Subsequent efforts forced states to adopt minimum-age drink restrictions in order to obtain federal transportation funds. (See Politics Now: Alcohol Policies.)

cooperative federalism
The relationship between the national and state governments that began with the New Deal.

Federal Grants and National Efforts to Influence the States

As early as 1790, Congress appropriated funds for the states to pay debts incurred during the Revolutionary War. But, it wasn't until the Civil War that Congress enacted its

ALCOHOL POLICIES

At the end of its 2003–2004 session, the U.S. Supreme Court agreed to take up the question of the constitutionality of state laws that prohibit or otherwise restrict the interstate shipment of wine to consumers. The wine controversy involves the scope of Congress's authority under the commerce clause versus the Twenty-First Amendment, which ended Prohibition and gave the states considerable power to regulate the sale and transportation of alcoholic beverages. As the Court said in granting review, the question was a simple one: "Does a State's regulatory scheme that permits in-state wineries directly to ship alcohol to consumers but restricts the ability of out-of-state wineries to do so violate the dormant commerce clause in light of Sec. 2 of the Twenty-First Amendment?"[a]

The stakes are considerable for vintners who, with the growth of e-commerce, now often get orders from potential out-of-state buyers. States are concerned about the loss of tax revenues, and wholesalers fear a loss of sales to consumers. But, this issue again puts the state and national governments potentially at odds as they often have been since the Twenty-First Amendment allowed states to regulate alcohol.

In 1982, for example, at the highly emotional urging of Mothers Against Drunk Drivers, Congress passed the Sur-

face Transportation Act, which withheld 5 percent of federal highway funds from states that failed to pass legislation prohibiting persons under the age of twenty-one from drinking alcoholic beverages. (Eventually states were fined 10 percent.) In other words: no increased drinking age, fewer federal dollars for roads.

Later, in 1999, Congress passed more carrot and stick legislation to pressure states to adopt uniform measures to lower the blood alcohol levels that they considered legal indication of drunkenness. In 2003, Congress again acted, this time penalizing the few states that had yet to lower their limits to 0.08 by withholding 2 percent of their annual highway funds per year.

1. Should drunk driving laws be left to the states or to the national government? Is the national government's carrot and stick approach a basic violation of the principles of federalism?
2. Should states be able to regulate the sale and distribution of liquor across state lines?

---

[a] Tony Mauro, "Wine and Beef Cases on High Court Menu," *Legal Times* (May 25, 2004).

---

first true federal grant program, which allocated federal funds to the states for a specific purpose.

Most commentators believe the start of this redistribution of funds began with the Morrill Land Grant Act of 1862, which gave each state 30,000 acres of public land for each representative in Congress. Income from the sale of these lands was to be earmarked for the establishment and support of agricultural and mechanical arts colleges. Sixty-nine land-grant colleges— including Texas A&M University, the University of Georgia, and Michigan State University—were founded or significantly assisted, making this grant program the single most important piece of education legislation passed in the United States up to that time.

As we have seen, Franklin D. Roosevelt's New Deal program increased the flow of federal dollars to the states with the infusion of massive federal dollars for a variety of public works programs, including building and road construction. In the boom times of World War II, even more new federal programs were introduced. By the 1950s and 1960s, federal grant-in-aid programs were well entrenched. They often defined federal/state relationships and made the national government a major player in domestic policy. Until the 1960s, however, most federal grant programs were constructed in cooperation with the states and were designed to assist the states in the furtherance of their traditional responsibilities to protect the health, welfare, and safety of their citizens. Most of these programs were **categorical grants,** ones for which Congress appropriates funds for specific purposes. Categorical grants allocate federal dollars by a precise formula and are subject to detailed conditions imposed by the national government, often on a matching basis; that is, states must contribute money to match federal funds, although the national government may pay as much as 90 percent of the total.

categorical grant
Grant for which Congress appropriates funds for a specific purpose.

By the early 1960s, as concern about the poor and minorities rose, and as states (especially in the South) were blamed for perpetuating discrimination, those in power in the national government saw grants as a way to force states to behave in ways desired by the national government.[28] If the states would not cooperate with the national government to further its goals, it would withhold funds.

In 1964, the Democratic administration of President Lyndon B. Johnson (LBJ) launched its "Great Society" program, which included what LBJ called a "War on Poverty." The Great Society program was a broad attempt to combat poverty and discrimination. In a frenzy of activity in Washington not seen since the New Deal, federal funds were channeled to states, to local governments, and even directly to citizen action groups in an effort to alleviate social ills that the states had been unable or unwilling to remedy. There was money for urban renewal, education, and poverty programs, including Head Start and job training. The move to fund local groups directly was made by the most liberal members of Congress to bypass not only conservative state legislatures, but also conservative mayors and councils in cities such as Chicago, who were perceived as disinclined to help their poor, often African American, constituencies. Thus, these programs often pitted governors and mayors against community activists, who became key players in the distribution of federal dollars.

These new grants altered the fragile federal/state balance of power that had been at the core of many older federal grant programs. During the Johnson administration, the national government began to use federal grants as a way to further what federal (and not state) officials perceived to be national needs. Grants based on what states wanted or believed they needed began to decline, while grants based on what the national government wanted states to do to foster national goals increased dramatically. Soon, states routinely asked Washington for help. From pollution to economic development and law enforcement, creating a federal grant seemed like the perfect solution to every problem.[29]

Not all federal programs mandating state or local action came with federal money, however. And, while presidents Richard M. Nixon, Gerald Ford, and Jimmy Carter voiced their opposition to big government, their efforts to rein it in were largely unsuccessful.

NEW FEDERALISM: RETURNING POWER TO THE STATES

IN 1980, former California Governor Ronald Reagan was elected president, pledging to advance what he called a **New Federalism** and a return of power to the states. This policy set the tone for the federal/state relationship that was maintained from the 1980s until 2001. Presidents and Congresses, both Republican and Democrat, took steps to shrink the size of the federal government in favor of programs administered by state governments. President Bill Clinton lauded the demise of big government. And, on the campaign trail in 2000, George W. Bush also seemed committed to this devolution. A struggling economy and the events of 9/11, however, have led to substantial growth in the power and scope of the federal government.

New Federalism
Federal/state relationship proposed by Reagan administration during the 1980s; hallmark is returning administrative powers to the state governments.

The Reagan Revolution

The Republican Reagan Revolution had at its heart strong views about the role of states in the federal system. While many Democrats and liberal interest groups argued that grants-in-aid were an effective way to raise the level of services provided to the poor, others, including Reagan, attacked them as imposing national priorities on the states. Policy decisions were made at the national level. The states, always in search of funds, were forced to follow the priorities of the national government. States found it very hard to resist the lure of grants, even though many were contingent on some sort of state investment of matching or proportional funds.

Shortly after taking office, Reagan proposed massive cuts in federal domestic programs and drastic income tax cuts. The Reagan administration's budget and its policies dramatically altered the relationships among federal, state, and local governments. For the first time in thirty years, federal aid to state and local governments declined.[30] Reagan persuaded Congress to consolidate many categorical grants (for specific programs that often require matching funds) into far fewer, less restrictive **block grants**—broad grants to states for specific activities such as secondary education or health services, with few strings attached. He also ended general revenue sharing, which had provided significant unrestricted funds to the states.

By the end of the presidencies of Ronald Reagan and George Bush in 1993, most block grants fell into one of four categories: health, income security, education, or transportation. Yet, many politicians, including most state governors, urged the consolidation of even more programs into block grants. Calls to reform the welfare system, particularly to allow more latitude to the states in an effort to get back to the Hamiltonian notion of states as laboratories of experiment, seemed popular with citizens and governments alike. New Federalism had taken hold.

The Devolution Revolution

In 1992, Bill Clinton was elected president—the first Democrat in twelve years. Although Clinton was a former governor, he was more predisposed to federal programs than his Republican predecessors. In 1994, however, Republicans won a majority in both houses of Congress, and every Republican governor who sought reelection was victorious, while some popular Democratic governors, such as Ann Richards of Texas, lost (to George W. Bush). In *Federalist No. 17,* Alexander Hamilton noted that "it will always be far easier for the State government to encroach upon the national authorities than for the national government to encroach upon the State authorities." He was wrong. By 1994, many state governors and the Republican Party were rebelling against the power of the national government.

The Contract with America, proposed by then House Minority Whip Newt Gingrich (R–GA), was a campaign document signed by nearly all Republican candidates (and incumbents) seeking election to the House of Representatives in 1994. In it, Republican candidates pledged to force a national debate on the role of the national government in regard to the states. A top priority was scaling back the federal government, an effort that some commentators called the devolution revolution. Poll after poll, moreover, revealed that many Americans believed the national government had too much power (48 percent) and that they favored their states' assuming many of the powers and functions now exercised by the federal government (59 percent).[31]

Running under a clear set of priorities contained in the Contract, Republican candidates took back the House of Representatives for the first time in more than forty years. A majority of the legislative proposals based on the Contract passed the House of Representatives during the first one hundred days of the 104th Congress. However, very few of the Contract's proposals, including acts requiring a balanced budget and tax reforms, passed the Senate and became law.

On some issues, however, the Republicans were able to achieve their goals. For example, before 1995, **unfunded mandates,** national laws that direct state or local governments to comply with federal rules or regulations (such as clean air or water standards) but contain no federal funding to defray the cost of meeting these requirements, absorbed nearly 30 percent of some local budgets. Columbus, Ohio, for example, faced a $1 billion bill to comply with the federal Clean Water Act and the Safe Drinking Water Act. Republicans in Congress, loyal to the concerns of these governments,

block grant
Broad grant with few strings attached; given to states by the federal government for specified activities, such as secondary education or health services.

unfunded mandates
National laws that direct states or local governments to comply with federal rules or regulations (such as clean air or water standards) but contain no federal funding to defray the cost of meeting these requirements.

secured passage of the Unfunded Mandates Reform Act of 1995. This act prevented Congress from passing costly federal programs without debate on how to fund them and addressed a primary concern for state governments.

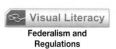
Visual Literacy
Federalism and
Regulations

Another important act passed by the Republican-controlled Congress and signed into law by President Bill Clinton was the Personal Responsibility and Work Opportunity Reconciliation Act of 1996. This legislation replaced the existing welfare program, known as Aid to Families with Dependent Children (AFDC), with a program known as Temporary Assistance for Needy Families (TANF). TANF returned much of the administrative power for welfare programs to the states, and became a hallmark of the devolution revolution.

In the short run, these and other programs, coupled with a growing economy, produced record federal and state budget surpluses. States were in the best fiscal shape they had been in since the 1970s. According to the National Conference of State Legislatures, total state budget surpluses in 1998 exceeded $30 billion. These tax surpluses allowed many states to increase spending, while other states offered their residents steep tax cuts. Mississippi, for example, increased its per capita spending by 42.4 percent, while Alaska opted to reduce taxes by 44.2 percent.[32]

Despite these strong economic conditions, Vice President Al Gore failed to turn the success of the Clinton administration into a Gore presidency in 2000. His opponent, Texas Governor George W. Bush, campaigned on a platform of limited federal government, arguing that state and local governments should have extensive administrative powers over programs such as education and welfare.

Federalism Under the Bush Administration

On the campaign trail, President George W. Bush could not have foreseen the circumstances that would surround much of his presidency. A struggling economy, terrorist attacks on the World Trade Center and the Pentagon, and the rising costs of education and welfare produced state and federal budget deficits that would have been unimaginable only a few years before.

By 2003, many state governments faced budget shortfalls of more than $30 billion. Because state governments, unlike the federal government, are required to balance their budgets, governors and legislators struggled to make ends meet. Some states raised taxes, and others cut services, including school construction and infrastructure repairs. As illustrated in the opening vignette, however, many states made dramatic changes to counter their shrinking coffers. By 2004, thirty-two states, helped by $20 billion in emergency funds from the national government, projected surpluses.[33]

The federal government struggled with a $521 billion budget deficit of its own in 2004, with an optimistic $363 billion projected for 2005. However, most remarkable on the federal level was the tremendous expansion of the size and cost of the post-9/11 government. Bush, who campaigned on the idea of limited federal power, found himself asking Congress to create a huge new Cabinet department, the Department of Homeland Security, and federalizing thousands of airport security personnel. In addition, the No Child Left Behind Act created a host of federal requirements. These requirements have already built frustration among state and local officials, who argue that

■ Michigan Democratic Governor Jennifer Grenholm heads a state hard hit by cuts in some federal programs and the loss of jobs.

Photo courtesy: AP Photo/Jerry S. Mendoza

THE NO CHILD LEFT BEHIND ACT

OVERVIEW: The U.S. Constitution is silent in regard to educating American citizens. According to traditional interpretation of the Constitution, the Ninth and Tenth Amendments give the states and American people rights and powers not expressly mentioned or prohibited by the Constitution. It was the Framers' belief the federal principle would allow for and accommodate diverse opinions regarding life, liberty, and happiness—and it is the responsibility of the individual states to educate citizens accordingly. Historically, the states have assumed this task relatively free from federal interference, but over the last fifty years, declining educational attainment, coupled with the inability of the states to address this problem, has put education policy at the forefront of domestic policy debate. To correct this problem, the No Child Left Behind Act (NCLB) was signed into law in January 2002. NCLB was a controversial piece of legislation giving the national government substantial authority over state educational establishments; several years after enactment, NCLB is still controversial.

Though many educators and politicians agree on the goals set by the No Child Left Behind Act (NCLB)—higher educational standards, greater school accountability, ensuring qualified teachers, closing the gap in student achievement—NCLB is criticized by the two major political parties, even though significant congressional majorities of both parties voted for the act. Republicans complain that NCLB impermissibly allows federal intrusion into the educational rights of states, and Democrats worry that the federal government is not providing enough funding to meet NCLB's strict guidelines. Nevertheless, in practice, both parties seem to have switched ideological positions in regard

to the federal government's role. Though the Republicans in 1996 advocated eliminating the Department of Education and reducing education expenditures, the Bush administration has significantly increased education funding; conversely, Democrats, who have traditionally advocated an increased federal role in education, now advocate states' rights (though with increased federal spending as well). Though it is too soon to determine the act's effectiveness, and though there is dramatic new federal involvement in education policy, NCLB is supported by a considerable majority of the American people of all demographics.

In the Information Age, it is imperative that all citizens have the requisite skills to survive and thrive in the new economy. With this in mind, what is the best way to ensure that all can realize their vision of life, liberty, and happiness? What is the best way to ensure a quality education for all Americans? Where does proper authority to educate children lie? How can the federal government determine the best way to educate children in a nation in which there are numerous ethnicities, religions, and cultures, all having differing views on what constitutes education? However, since the federal government in part funds state educational establishments, shouldn't it have a say in how its funds are spent? Since American education achievement lags behind education in other advanced modern democracies, shouldn't school systems and teachers be held accountable, and if so, what is the best way to address this problem?

Arguments for the No Child Left Behind Act

- **NCLB gives state and local school districts the flexibility to meet its requirements.** The law gives states the

administering the schools, from class size to accountability testing, should be their responsibility.[34]

This trend of **preemption,** or allowing the national government to override state or local actions in certain areas, is not new. The phenomenal growth of preemption statutes, laws that allow the federal government to assume partial or full responsibility for state and local governmental functions, began in 1965 during the Johnson administration. Since then, Congress routinely used its authority under the commerce clause to preempt state laws. However, until recently, preemption statutes were generally supported by Democrats in Congress and the White House, not Republicans. The Bush

preemption
A concept derived from the Constitution's supremacy clause that allows the national government to override or preempt state or local actions in certain areas.

liberty to define standards and the means to meet and measure them. As long as NCLB guidelines are met, the states are generally free to innovate, educate, and test according to their needs.

- **NCLB is not an unfunded mandate.** The General Accounting Office has ruled that NCLB does not meet the description of an unfunded mandate as defined by the 1995 Unfunded Mandates Reform Act, primarily because state school systems have the option of accepting or rejecting NCLB funding. Federal spending accounts for only 8 percent of all educational expenditures in the United States.

- **NCLB represents federal responsiveness to the needs of parents with children in public schools.** Not only have the states failed to meet the guidelines set forth by various federal policy initiatives, but they have failed the expectations of parents as well. For example, Goals 2000 (1994) mandated a 90 percent high school graduation rate by 2000 and a number one rank in math and science for American students internationally. By 2000, the graduation rate was only 75 percent and American students ranked not first but nineteenth in math and eighteenth in science.

Arguments Against the No Child Left Behind Act

- **NCLB requirements force school districts to teach to the test.** Rather than teaching analytical and creative thinking, the testing requirements force school districts to have students cram for the exam, thus undermining the primary goal of a true education.

- **NCLB does not distinguish between disabled and non-English-speaking students and able students proficient in English.** A primary problem with NCLB is that it combines all students, regardless of their language level or other core educational proficiencies. This is an unfair burden on educators in school systems with a disproportionate number of disabled or non-English-speaking students, as NCLB's punitive sections assume an able, English-speaking student body.

- **NCLB should be considered an impermissible intrusion on the prerogatives of state educational establishments.** A primary concern of the Framers was excessive federal control over state policy. NCLB erodes the line separating federal and state authority. If school systems are not addressing the concerns of parents and educational problems, it is the proper duty of the states to address these issues.

Questions

1. Does NCLB place too many guidelines on state educational establishments? If so, what is the best way to ensure higher standards and school accountability?

2. Does NCLB give the federal government too much authority over a policy domain that has traditionally belonged to the states? Since school districts reflect local mores and attitudes, are students best educated based on local guidelines?

Selected Readings

Robert D. Barr. *Saving Our Students, Saving Our Schools: 50 Proven Strategies for Revitalizing At-Risk Students and Low Performing Schools.* Iri/Skylight Training and Publishing, 2003

Ken Goodman et al. *Saving Our Schools: The Case for Public Education.* RDR Books, 2004.

administration's use of these laws, therefore, reflects a new era in preemption. (See Join the Debate: The No Child Left Behind Act.)

The Supreme Court: A Return to States' Rights?

The role of the Supreme Court in determining the parameters of federalism cannot be underestimated. Although Congress passed sweeping New Deal legislation, it was not until the Supreme Court finally reversed itself and found those programs constitutional that any real change occurred in the federal/state relationship. From the New Deal until

TABLE 3.2   Major Federalism Cases Indicating the Supreme Court's General Devolution of Power Back to the States

Case	Year	Vote	Issue/Question	Decision
Webster v. Reproductive Health Services	1989	5–4	Are several state abortion restrictions constitutional?	Yes. In upholding most of the restrictions, the Court invited the states to begin to enact new state restrictions.
New York v. Smith	1992	6–3	Does the Low-Level Waste Act, which requires states to dispose of radioactive waste within their borders, violate the Tenth Amendment?	Yes. The section of the act that requires the states to take legal ownership of waste is unconstitutional because it forces states into the service of the federal government.
U.S. v. Lopez	1995	5–4	Does Congress have the authority to regulate guns within 1,000 feet of a public school?	No. Only states have this authority; no connection to commerce found.
Seminole Tribe v. Florida	1996	5–4	Can Congress impose a duty on the states to negotiate with Indian tribes?	No. Federal courts have no jurisdiction over an Indian tribe's suit to force a state to comply with the Indian Gaming Regulations Act, thus upholding the state's sovereign immunity (immunity from a lawsuit).
Boerne v. Flores	1997	5–4	Is the federal Religious Freedom Restoration Act and its application of local zoning ordinances to a church constitutional?	No. Sections of the act are beyond the power of Congress to force on the states.
Printz v. U.S.	1997	5–4	Can Congress temporarily require local law enforcement officials to conduct background checks on handgun purchasers?	No. Congress lacks the authority to compel state officers to execute federal laws.
Florida Prepaid v. College Savings Bank	1999	5–4	Can Congress change patent laws to affect state sovereign immunity?	No. Congress lacks authority under the commerce clause and the patent clause to eliminate sovereign immunity.
Alden v. Maine	1999	5–4	Can Congress void state immunity from lawsuit in state courts?	No. Congress lacks the authority to eliminate a state's immunity in its own courts.
U.S. v. Morrison	2000	5–4	Does Congress have the authority to provide a federal remedy for victims of gender-motivated violence under the commerce clause of the Fourteenth Amendment?	No. Portions of Violence Against Women Act were found unconstitutional.

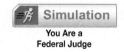

Simulation
You Are a Federal Judge

the 1980s, the Supreme Court's impact on the federal system was generally to expand the national government's authority at the expense of the states.

Beginning in the late 1980s, however, the Court's willingness to allow Congress to regulate in a variety of areas waned. Once Ronald Reagan was elected president, he attempted to appoint new justices committed to the notion of states rights and to rolling back federal intervention in matters that many Republicans believed properly resided within the province of the states and not Congress or the federal courts.

Mario M. Cuomo, a former Democratic New York governor, has referred to the decisions of what he called the Reagan-Bush Court as creating "a kind of new judicial federalism." According to Cuomo, this new federalism could be characterized by the Court's withdrawal of "rights and emphases previously thought to be national."[35] Illustrative of this trend are the Supreme Court's decisions in *Webster* v. *Reproductive Health Services* (1989)[36] and *Planned Parenthood of Southeastern Pennsylvania* v. *Casey* (1992).[37] In *Webster*, the Court first gave new latitude—and even encouragement—to the states to fashion more restrictive abortion laws, as underscored in Table 3.2. Since *Webster*, most states have enacted new restrictions on abortion, with spousal or parental con-

Analyzing Visuals

STATE-BY-STATE REPORT CARD ON ACCESS TO ABORTION

A liberal interest group, NARAL Pro-Choice America rates each state and the District of Columbia in fourteen categories related to abortion access, including bans on partial birth abortion procedures and counseling, clinic violence, the length of waiting periods, access for minors, and public funding, which it then translates into grades. NARAL gives an A only to states it evaluates as pro-choice on every issue on its agenda. After studying the map, answer the following critical thinking questions: What do the states that receive A's have in common? How might factors such as political culture, geography, and social characteristics of the population influence a state's laws concerning abortion? If a group that opposes abortion, such as the National Right to Life Committee, were to grade the states, would its ratings include the same categories or factors? Explain your answer. See Analyzing Visuals: A Brief Guide for additional guidance in analyzing maps.

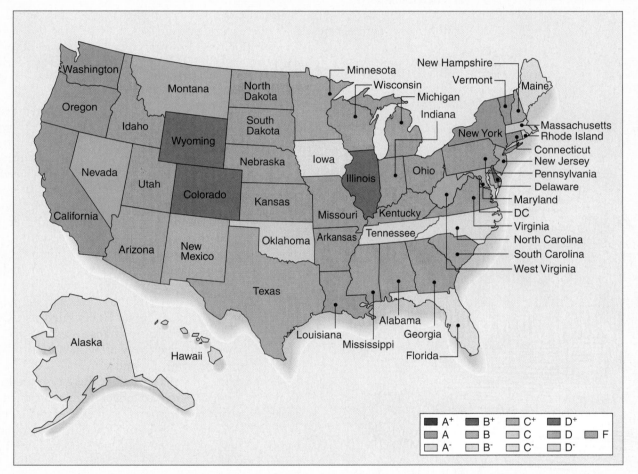

Source: NARAL Pro-Choice America/NARAL Foundation, "Who Decides? A State-by-State Review of Abortion and Reproductive Rights," 2004. Accessed July 1, 2004, http://www.naral.org/yourstate/whodecides/index.cfm. Reprinted by permission.

sent, informed consent or waiting periods, or bans on late-term or partial birth abortions being the most common. (See Analyzing Visuals: State-by-State Report Card on Access to Abortion.) The Court consistently has upheld the authority of the individual states to limit a minor's access to abortion through imposition of parental consent or notification laws. And, it also consistently has declined to review most other restrictions, including twenty-four-hour waiting period requirements. In 2000, however, a badly divided 5–4 Court struck down a Nebraska ban on partial birth abortions (as discussed in chapter 5).[38]

The addition of two justices by President Bill Clinton did little to stem the course of a Court bent on rebalancing the nature of the federal system. Since 1989, the Supreme Court has decided several major cases dealing with the nature of the federal system. Most of these have been 5–4 decisions and most have been decided against increased congressional power or in a manner to provide the states with greater authority over a variety of issues and policies. In *U.S.* v. *Lopez* (1995), for example, which involved the conviction of a student charged with carrying a concealed handgun onto school property, a five-person majority of the Court ruled that Congress lacked constitutional authority under the commerce clause to regulate guns within 1,000 feet of a school.[39] The majority concluded that local gun control in the schools was a state, not a federal, matter.

One year later, again a badly divided Court ruled that Congress lacked the authority to require states to negotiate with Indian tribes about gaming.[40] The U.S. Constitution specifically gives Congress the right to deal with Indian tribes, but the Court found that Florida's **sovereign immunity** protected the state from this kind of congressional directive about how to conduct its business. In 1997, the Court decided two more major cases dealing with the scope of Congress's authority to regulate in areas historically left to the province of the states: zoning and local law enforcement. In one, a majority of the Court ruled that sections of the Religious Freedom Restoration Act were unconstitutional because Congress lacked the authority to meddle in local zoning regulations, even if a church was involved.[41] Another 5–4 majority ruled that Congress lacked the authority to require local law enforcement officials to conduct background checks on handgun purchasers until the federal government was able to implement a national system.[42] In 1999, in another case involving sovereign immunity, a slim majority of the Supreme Court ruled that Congress lacked the authority to change patent laws in a manner that would negatively affect a state's right to assert its immunity from lawsuits.[43]

The combined impact of all of these cases makes it clear that the Court will no longer countenance federal excursions into powers reserved to the states. As the power of Congress to legislate in a wide array of areas has been limited, the hands of the states have been strengthened.

In 2000, the Supreme Court's decision to stay a ruling of the Florida State Supreme Court ordering a manual recount of ballots surprised many observers, given the majority of the Court's reluctance over the last decade to interfere in areas historically left to the states. The Court's 5–4 decision in *Bush* v. *Gore* (2000), which followed fairly observable liberal/conservative lines, was surprising in that justices normally opposed to federal intervention in state matters found that the Florida

sovereign immunity
The right of a state to be free from lawsuit unless it gives permission to the suit. Under the Eleventh Amendment, all states are considered sovereign.

■ The conservative Rehnquist Court usually defers to state courts as well as judgments of the state legislatures.

Photo courtesy: © 2000 by Herblock in the Washington Post

"I GUESS I JUST HADN'T NOTICED IT BEFORE"

©2000 HERBLOCK

LEGISLATING AGAINST VIOLENCE AGAINST WOMEN: A CASUALTY OF THE DEVOLUTION REVOLUTION?

As originally enacted in 1994, the Violence Against Women Act (VAWA) allowed women to file civil lawsuits in federal court if they could prove that they were the victims of rape, domestic violence, or other crimes motivated by gender. VAWA was widely praised as an effective mechanism to combat domestic violence. In its first five years, $1.6 million was allocated for states and local governments to pay for a variety of programs, including a national toll-free hotline for victims of violence that averages 13,000 calls per month, funding for special police sex crime units, and civil and legal assistance for women in need of restraining orders.[a] It also provided money to promote awareness of campus rape and domestic violence and to enhance reporting of crimes such as what is often termed date rape.

Most of the early publicity surrounding VAWA stemmed from a challenge to one of its provisions. The suit brought by Christy Brzonkala was the first brought under the act's civil damages provision. While she was a student at Virginia Polytechnic Institute, Brzonkala alleged that two football players there raped her. After the university took no action against the students, she sued the school and the students. No criminal charges were ever filed in her case. The conservative federal appeals court in Richmond, Virginia—in contrast to contrary rulings in seventeen other courts—ruled that Congress had overstepped its authority because the alleged crimes were "within the exclusive purview of the states."[b] The Clinton administration and the National Organization for Women Legal Defense and Education Fund (now called Legal Momentum) appealed that decision to the Supreme Court on her behalf.

Photo courtesy: Cindy Pinkston, January 1996

Christy Brzonkala, the petitioner in U.S. v. Morrison.

In 2000, five justices of the Supreme Court, including Justice Sandra Day O'Connor, ruled that Congress had no authority under the commerce clause to provide a federal remedy to victims of gender-motivated violence, a decision viewed as greatly reining in congressional power.[c] Thus, today, students abused on campus no longer have this federal remedy as the Court devolves more power to the states.

---

[a] Juliet Eilperin, "Reauthorization of Domestic Violence Act Is at Risk," *Washington Post* (September 13, 2000): A6.

[b] Tony Mauro, "Court Will Review Laws of Protection," *USA Today* (September 29, 1999): 4A.

[c] *U.S.* v. *Morrison*, 529 U.S. 598 (2000).

Supreme Court, which purportedly based its decisions solely on its interpretation of Florida law, violated federal law and the U.S. Constitution.[44] Thus, the conservative, historically pro–states' rights justices in the majority used federal law to justify their decision.

During the 2002–2003 term, however, the Court took an unexpected turn in its federalism devolution revolution.[45] In a case opening states to lawsuits for alleged violations of the federal Family and Medical Leave Act (FMLA), writing for a six-person majority, Chief Justice William H. Rehnquist rejected Nevada's claim that it was immune from suit under FMLA. Rehnquist noted that the law was an appropriate exercise of Congress's power to combat sex-role stereotypes about the domestic responsibilities of female workers and "thereby dismantle persisting gender-based barriers that women faced in the workplace."[46]

Participation

Is Federalism Dead and Should It Be?

SUMMARY

THE INADEQUACIES of the confederate form of government created by the Articles of Confederation led the Framers to create a federal system of government that divided power between the national and state governments, with each ultimately responsible to the people. In describing the evolution of this system throughout American history, we have made the following points:

1. **The Roots of the Federal System: Governmental Powers Under the Constitution**
   The national and state governments have both enumerated and implied powers under the Constitution. The national and state governments share some concurrent powers. Other powers are expressly denied to both governments, although the national government is ultimately declared supreme. The Constitution also lays the groundwork for the Supreme Court to be the arbiter in disagreements between states.

2. **Federalism and the Marshall Court**
   Over the years, the powers of the national government have increased tremendously at the expense of the states. Early on, the Supreme Court played a key role in defining the relationship and powers of the national government through its broad interpretations of the supremacy and commerce clauses.

3. **Dual Federalism: The Taney Court, Slavery, and the Civil War**
   For many years, dual federalism, as articulated by the Taney Court, tended to limit the national government's authority in areas such as slavery and civil rights, and was the norm in relations between the national and state governments. However, the beginnings of a departure from this view became evident with the ratification of the Sixteenth and Seventeenth Amendments in 1913.

4. **Cooperative Federalism: The New Deal and the Growth of National Government**
   The notion of a limited federal government ultimately fell by the wayside in the wake of the Great Depression and Franklin D. Roosevelt's New Deal. This growth in the size and role of the federal government escalated during the Lyndon B. Johnson administration and into the mid to late 1970s. Federal grants became popular solutions for a host of state and local problems.

5. **New Federalism: Returning Power to the States**
   After his election in 1980, Ronald Reagan tried to shrink the size and powers of the federal government through what he termed New Federalism. This trend continued through the 1990s, most notably through a campaign document known as the Contract with America. Initially, the George W. Bush administration seemed committed to this devolution, but a struggling economy and the events of 9/11 led to substantial growth in the size of the federal government.

KEY TERMS

bill of attainder, p. 101
block grant, p. 114
categorical grant, p. 112
concurrent powers, p. 100
confederation, p. 97
cooperative federalism, p. 111
dual federalism, p. 105
enumerated powers, p. 97
ex post facto law, p. 101
federal system, p. 97
full faith and credit clause, p. 101
Gibbons v. *Ogden* (1824), p. 103
implied powers, p. 98
interstate compacts, p. 102
McCulloch v. *Maryland* (1819), p. 104
necessary and proper clause, p. 98
New Federalism, p. 112
preemption, p. 116
privileges and immunities clause, p. 100
reserve (or police) powers, p. 100
Seventeenth Amendment, p. 107
Sixteenth Amendment, p. 107
sovereign immunity, p. 120
supremacy clause, p. 98
Tenth Amendment, p. 100
unfunded mandates, p. 114
unitary system, p. 97

SELECTED READINGS

Bowman, Ann O'M., and Richard C. Kearney. *State and Local Government,* 5th ed. Boston: Houghton Mifflin, 2001.

Conlan, Timothy J. *From New Federalism to Devolution: Twenty-Five Years of Intergovernmental Reform.* Washington, DC: Brookings Institution, 1998.

Derthick, Martha. *The Influence of Federal Grants.* Cambridge, MA: Harvard University Press, 1970.

Elazar, Daniel J., and John Kincaid, eds. *The Covenant Connection: From Federal Theology to Modern Federalism.* Lexington, MA: Lexington Books, 2000.

Finegold, Kenneth, and Theda Skocpol. *State and Party in America's New Deal.* Madison: University of Wisconsin Press, 1995.

Grodzins, Morton. *The American System: A View of Government in the United States.* Chicago: Rand McNally, 1966.

Kincaid, John. *The Encyclopedia of American Federalism.* Washington, DC: CQ Press, 2005.

McCabe, Neil Colman, ed. *Comparative Federalism in the Devolution Era.* Lanham, MD: Rowman and Littlefield, 2003.

Nagel, Robert F. *The Implosion of American Federalism.* New York: Oxford University Press, 2002.

Walker, David B. *The Rebirth of Federalism: Slouching Toward Washington,* 2nd ed. New York: Seven Bridges Press, 1999.

Zimmerman, Joseph F. *Interstate Cooperation: Compacts and Administrative Agreements.* New York: Praeger, 2002.

WEB EXPLORATIONS

For a directory of federalism links, see
http://xxx.infidels.org/~nap/index.federalism.html

For more on your state and local governments, see
http://www.statelocalgov.net/

For scholarly works on federalism, see
http://www.temple.edu/federalism and
http://www.cato.org/pubs/journal/cj14n1-7.html and
http://www.urban.org/Template.cfm?NavMenuID=24&template=/
TaggedContent/ViewPublication.cfm&PublicationID=5874

For perspectives on the federal system, see
http://www.usembassy.beusa/usapolitical.htm

For more information on interstate compacts, see
http://ssl.csg.org/compactlaws/comlistlinks.html

For the full text of *McCulloch* v. *Maryland* (1819), see
http://www.landmarkcases.org/mcculloch/home.html

For the full text of *Gibbons* v. *Ogden* (1824), see
http://www.landmarkcases.org/gibbons/legacy.html

For more information on the Great Depression, see
http://newdeal.feri.org/

For more on the devolution revolution, see
http://www.brookings.edu/comm/policybriefs/pb03.htm

To analyze where your state stands relative to other states, see
http://www.taxfoundation.org/statefinance.html

For more information on state abortion restrictions, see
http://www.naral.org/

For more about local gun control initiatives, see
http://www.guncite.com/

Photo courtesy: Damian Dovarganes/AP/Wide World Photos

State and Local Government

4

IN NOVEMBER 2002, California voters narrowly reelected their Democratic governor, Gray Davis. Davis was not especially popular, but his Republican opponent that year was viewed even more negatively, and voters chose to retain Davis for another four years. Eleven months later, however, Davis was booted out of office. Californians were exercising a rarely used mechanism in their state constitution that gives them the opportunity to petition for a vote on whether to recall one of their elected officials. Why had they used this against Davis?

When the extent of the state's budget shortfall—estimated to be $38.5 billion—was announced a few months after Davis's 2002 reelection victory, and Davis indicated he would support some tax increases in order to meet part of the budget shortfall, Californians began circulating petitions to oust their governor. Davis argued that the national economic crisis was responsible for the state's budget mess, and he blamed intransigent Republicans in the state legislature for their unwillingness to compromise on emergency measures. But, Davis had alienated many in his first term by his messy handling of an electricity shortage in the state, leading to blackouts and exorbitant contracts with several energy suppliers. His nonstop fundraising during his first four years had also raised eyebrows, with many noting how Davis rewarded his financial supporters with lucrative state contracts or pay increases—such as a healthy raise for the state prison guards whose union contributed generously to his campaign. The release of the state's projected budget shortfall in early 2003 suggested massive program cuts and higher taxes, and voters were fed up. According to one reporter, "Californians want a target for their fiscal pain and frustration, and Davis has become the state insignia for economic ineptitude."[1] Another observer remarked about Davis, "Everybody hates him."[2]

Financed heavily by a Republican member of Congress from southern California who wanted to become governor himself, the recall petition drive obtained the required number of signatures by the summer of 2003, and a media circus set in. The recall election was scheduled for October, and the ballot would have two parts. Part one would be a simple question: should Governor Gray Davis be recalled? The second part of the question was an open election as to who would replace Davis if the "Yes" vote prevailed on part one. Over 130 candidates made their way onto this ballot, including a handful of leading political figures, a porn star, a former child actor, dozens of celebrity wannabes, several earnest citizens, and former bodybuilder and movie action hero Arnold Schwarzenegger. For a while, it looked to much of the world as though Californians had gone crazy. But, when the official recall campaign entered its final month, it was clear that most voters would vote "Yes" on recalling Davis. In the words of one voter: "I never thought in a million years that I'd be for a recall, but it does send a message loud and clear—that we the people can do something."[3] The well-known Schwarzenegger, a moderate Republican, ran an upbeat campaign, his speeches peppered with his famous movie catchphrases, such as "Hasta la vista, baby!" and "I'll be back!" He did not give many hints as to what he would do as governor, but voters were ready for a change, and no other candidate could match his appeal. In the election, over 55 percent of the voters chose to recall Davis, and Schwarzenegger easily won the vote to replace him. Californians had participated in a rare display of direct democracy and changed their state's governor between regular elections.

THE RELATIONSHIPS AMONG THE VARIOUS GOVERNMENTS in our country are dynamic. The legal authority, the financial resources, and the political will of federal, state, and municipal governments are constantly changing. On the one hand, this provides groups and individuals with many points of access to government. On the other hand, the multiple, changing jurisdictions that govern our society can be a challenging puzzle. Californians who move to other parts of the country, for example, will find that most states do not have a recall provision, nor does the U.S. Constitution.

This chapter will present the basic patterns and principles of state and local governance so that you might readily understand how public policies in your community are made and applied.

- First, we will review *the evolution of state and local governments.*
- Second, we will describe the major institutions of *state governments,* including trends in state elections.
- Third, we will examine the different types of *local governments* and explain the bases for their authority as well as the special traits of their institutions.
- Fourth, we will identify the nature of *grassroots power and politics.*
- Fifth, we will discuss federal and state government *relations with Indian nations.*
- Finally, we will explain the budgeting process for *state and local finances.*

THE EVOLUTION OF STATE AND LOCAL GOVERNMENTS

AS POINTED OUT IN CHAPTER 3, the basic, original unit of government in this country was the state. The thirteen colonial governments became thirteen state governments, and their constitutions preceded the U.S. Constitution. The states initially were loosely tied together in the Articles of Confederation but then formed a closer union and more powerful national government.

State governments, likewise, determined the existence of local governments. As we will later discuss in more detail, in some cases—such as counties and, for most states, school districts—state laws *create* local governments. In others, such as towns and cities, states *recognize* and *authorize* local governments in response to petitions from citizens.

In other words, governance in the United States is not built from the bottom. Local communities do not form states, which then form the United States. Instead, states are the basic units, which on the one hand establish local governments and on the other hand are the building blocks of the federal government.

In the past, state and local governments were primarily part-time governments. Initially, almost all state and local elected officials were part-time. Except for governors and a handful of big-city mayors, people in office were farmers, teachers, lawyers, and shop owners who did public service during their spare time. This was true as well for many judges and local government bureaucrats.

As the responsibilities and challenges of government grew, more state and local officials became full-time. Increases in the need for urban services led to more full-time local governments. Despite this trend, states with high levels of urbanization did not always have governments that responded to the specific needs of urban populations. The boundaries of districts from which state legislators got elected did not change in response to population shifts in the post–Civil War period. As a result, state legislatures did not represent the character of their respective states. One legislator from a rural area might represent 50,000 people, whereas a legislator from an urban setting might represent as many as 500,000 constituents. Such a pattern led to low priority for urban needs.

This kind of misrepresentation remained in place until the 1960s. The ruling by the U.S. Supreme Court in *Baker* v. *Carr* (1962) became a watershed in the evolution of state and local governments. The Court applied the Fourteenth Amendment of the U.S. Constitution and decreed that equal protection and the **one-person, one-vote** principles required that there be the same number of people in each of the legislative districts within a single state. As a result, state legislatures became more representative, and the agendas of state governments became much more relevant to the needs of all constituents than they had been.

The 1960s and 1970s were a period in which the federal government added both to the responsibilities and to the efficiency of state and local governments. Federal programs to combat poverty, revitalize urban areas, and protect the environment were designed to be administered by state and local officials rather than federal agencies. With these programs came federal assistance and sometimes mandates to improve the capacities of subnational governments.

Since the 1970s, some trends in federalism have enhanced the importance of state and local governments. Conscious efforts since the Nixon administration were made to reverse the aggregation of power and authority in Washington, D.C. In part, this was philosophical, but it was also necessary. During the Reagan administration, the debt of the federal government more than tripled, and the flow of federal money and mandates that fueled much of the growth of state and local governments was reduced.

But, as noted in chapter 3, not all recent developments have enhanced the powers of state and local governments. In 2002, President George W. Bush signed a law that allows the federal government to force state and local authorities to turn over public schools to private businesses to manage if the schools are considered failing. In response to the terrorist attacks of September 11, 2001, the federal government expanded its role in domestic security, traditionally the responsibility of state and local police and public health officials.

Despite the conflicting messages, it is still clear that state and local governments have roles and responsibilities of increasing importance. For the most part, the political leaders of these jurisdictions relish these developments. Some states and cities, for

one-person, one-vote
The principle that each legislative district within a state should have the same number of eligible voters so that representation is equitably based on population.

Photo courtesy: Gilles Peress/Magnum Photos

■ The heroic work of New York City firefighters and rescue workers in response to the 9/11 terrorist attacks was a vivid reminder of the importance of state and local governments. We depend heavily on state and local agencies for our safety and for services that affect our daily living.

example, are taking bold initiatives and even establishing direct ties with other countries in order to spur economic growth.[4] Others, especially in smaller and medium-sized communities, are overwhelmed with all there is to do.

STATE GOVERNMENTS

STATE GOVERNMENTS HAVE PRIMARY RESPONSIBILITY for education, public health, transportation, economic development, and criminal justice. The state is also the unit of government that licenses and regulates various professions, such as doctors, lawyers, barbers, and architects. More recently, state governments have been active in welfare and the environment, in part as agents administering federal policies and programs and in part on their own.

State Constitutions

state constitution
The document that describes the basic policies, procedures, and institutions of the government of a specific state, much as the U.S. Constitution does for the federal government.

Whereas a major goal of the writers of the U.S. Constitution in 1787 was to *empower* the national government, the authors of the original **state constitutions** wanted to *limit* government. The Constitutional Convention in Philadelphia was convened, as you recall from chapter 2, because of the perception that the national government under the Articles of Confederation was not strong enough. The debates were primarily over how strong the national, or federal, government should be.

In contrast, the assumption of the authors of the first thirteen state constitutions, based on their backgrounds in the philosophy and experiences of monarchical rule, was that government was all powerful, and so the question was how to limit it. The state constitutions were written and adopted before the Constitutional Convention and included provisions that government may not interfere with basic indi-

The Living Constitution

The Judicial Power of the United States shall not be construed to extend to any suit in law or equity, commenced or prosecuted against one of the United States by Citizens of another State, or by Citizens or Subjects of any foreign State.

— Eleventh Amendment

The Eleventh Amendment to the Constitution has been interpreted to grant the several states *sovereign immunity;* that is, a state cannot be sued in federal or state court without its consent. This amendment further defines the distribution of authority between federal and state governments, and it has been construed to give the states protection from the encroachment of federal power.

The Eleventh Amendment was a response to the angry public outcry regarding the Supreme Court's decision in *Chisholm* v. *Georgia*—a decision in which the Court held that the Judiciary Act of 1789 gave it original jurisdiction in cases regarding suits between states and citizens of other states. The *Chisholm* decision was not only widely regarded as being an untenable intrusion on state authority, but it was also considered a confirmation of Anti-Federalist fears that such a reading of Article III would "prove most pernicious and destructive" to states' rights.

The amendment was proposed at the very first meeting of Congress following the *Chisholm* decision in March 1794, and it was consequently ratified with "vehement speed" by February 1795. Interpretation of the Eleventh Amendment has subsequently been subject to inconsistent and obscure construction, and it has been a source of considerable dispute for constitutional scholars. Beginning with the New Deal however, the federal government began to use the commerce clause to considerably expand its authority; the result was the increasing centralization and importance of the national government at the expense of substantial state power.

The Eleventh Amendment has received mounting scrutiny over the last decade because of the Rehnquist Court's use of the amendment to return numerous powers to the states, and thus to alter fundamentally the relationship the states have had with the federal government for over half a century. The trend of the current Court is to reestablish traditional state sovereignty as part of its quest to restore the constitutional principle of federalism.

vidual liberties. Although these provisions were integral parts of each of the state constitutions, they were added to the federal constitution as the first ten amendments: the Bill of Rights.

The first state constitutions provided for the major institutions of government, such as executives (the governors), legislatures, and courts, with an emphasis on limiting the authority of each institution.[5] These constitutions did not, however, fully embrace the principle of checks and balances that is found in the U.S. Constitution. The office of governor was particularly weak. Not surprisingly, the most powerful institution was the

Participation

Explore Your State
Constitution

GRADUATED DRIVER LICENSING

Once upon a time, young adults who were sixteen years old and could pass the required tests could get a driver's license. Now all but thirteen states have Graduated Driver Licensing (GDL) programs that put restrictions on those licenses. Specific provisions vary among the states, but generally new drivers may not drive unsupervised by an older adult for the first thirty to fifty hours after receiving their license, and even after that they may not drive unsupervised between 10 p.m. and 5 a.m. In ten states, teenagers who drive may not have more than two passengers, and in another eight states, they may not have anyone (other than family members) younger than twenty years old in the car with them.[a]

State legislatures responded to parents, insurance companies, and the federal Department of Transportation's National Highway Traffic Safety Administration in passing GDL programs. Car crashes are the leading killer of teenagers. This age group has the highest accident rate of any cohort, and sixteen-year-olds crash more than twice as often as eighteen- and nineteen-year-olds. After North Carolina adopted GDL, it saw a 26 percent drop in crashes involving sixteen-year-olds. Michigan noted a 31 percent decrease, and in Kentucky it was 32 percent.[b] These are impressive records.

But, placing restrictions on novice drivers has also met opposition. Opponents argue that it is not fair for all sixteen-year-olds to have limits because some are bad drivers. Some families need help from their new drivers, and the GDL rules limit young drivers' abilities to share driving responsibilities without supervision. Those in rural areas, often without access to public transportation, have been particularly unhappy with GDL legislation. In some states, the restrictions are stricter than what many states use as punishments for those convicted of drunk driving.

Despite these arguments, legislators in thirty-seven states have placed conditions on young drivers. Law-makers in the remaining states are considering adopting GDL programs. Frequently a legislator proposes GDL in response to a specific tragedy involving a new driver. The tragedy sets the agenda. Then, the pressure of the federal government and local advocates, armed with data about the reduction in accidents where there are GDL laws, generates the support to enact the law.

---

[a] "U.S. Licensing Systems for Young Drivers: Laws as of June 2002," Insurance Institute for Highway Safety (Arlington, VA).

[b] State Legislative Fact Sheets, http://www.nhtsa.dot.gov/people/outreach/stateleg/graddriverlic.htm.

---

legislature. In fact, initially only South Carolina, New York, and Massachusetts gave their governors the authority to veto legislation.

The first state constitutions set the pattern for what was to come. In one of its last actions, the national congress under the Articles of Confederation passed the Northwest Ordinance of 1787, which addressed how new states might join the union. Lawmakers were responding primarily to settlers in what is now Ohio but extended coverage to the territory that includes Wisconsin, Illinois, Michigan, and Indiana—which the people in the original states considered the "northwest." The basic blueprint included in the ordinance was that a territory might successfully petition for statehood if it had at least 60,000 free inhabitants (slaves and American Indians did not count) and a constitution that was both similar to the documents of existing states and compatible with the national constitution. The first white settlers in the territory covered by the Northwest Ordinance were originally from New York and Massachusetts, with some individuals and families direct from Europe. Not surprisingly, the initial constitutions of these states were almost identical to those of New York and Massachusetts.[6]

The Civil War had a profound impact on the constitutions of southern states. Southern states adopted new constitutions when they seceded and formed the Confederacy. After the Civil War, they had to adopt new constitutions acceptable to the Congress in Washington, D.C. These constitutions typically provided former slaves with considerable power and disenfranchised those who had been active in the Confederacy. These were not realistic constitutions. They divorced political power from economic wealth and social status, formal authority from informal influence. White communities simply ignored government and ruled themselves informally as much as possible. After less than ten years of this, whites reasserted political control and rewrote state constitutions.

The new documents reflected white distrust of government control and provided for a narrow scope of authority for state governments. Governors could serve for only two-year terms. Legislatures could meet for only short periods of time and in some cases only once every other year. Law enforcement authority, both police and justices of the peace, rested squarely in local community power structures.

Western states entered the union with constitutions that also envisioned weak governments. Here the central concern was to avoid the development of political machines. In large cities in the Northeast and Midwest, machines based on bloc voting by new immigrants wrested political control from traditional elites. New states in the West sought to keep machine politics from ever getting started in the first place.

The most effective national anti-machine effort was the **Progressive movement,** led by such figures as Woodrow Wilson, Theodore Roosevelt, Robert M. La Follette, and Hiram Johnson, who advocated changes that involved direct voter participation and bypassed traditional institutions.[7] These reforms included the use of primaries for nominating candidates instead of closed party processes, the initiative for allowing voters to enact laws directly rather than go through legislatures and governors, and the recall for constituents to remove officials from office in the middle of their term (such as the 2003 recall of California's governor, discussed in the chapter opening vignette). Progressives succeeded in getting their proposals adopted as statutes in existing states and in the constitutions of new states emerging from western territories.

Though weak state government institutions may have been a reasonable response to earlier concerns, the trend since the 1960s, throughout the United States, has been to amend state constitutions in order to enhance the ability of governors, legislatures, and courts to address problems. In the 1970s alone, over 300 amendments to state constitutions were adopted. Most were to lengthen the terms of governors and provide chief executives with more authority over spending and administration, to streamline courts, and to make legislatures professional and full-time.[8]

Constitutional changes have also reflected some ambivalence. While there has been widespread recognition that state governments must be more capable, there is also concern about what that might mean in taxes and in the entrenchment of power. Thus, reforms have included severe restrictions on the ability of state and local governments to raise taxes and limits on how long legislators in some states might serve. Historic distrust of government continues.

Compared with the U.S. Constitution, state constitutions are relatively easy to amend. Every state allows for the convening of a constitutional convention, and over 200 have been held. Also, every state has a process whereby the legislature can pass an amendment to the constitution, usually by a two-thirds or three-fourths vote, and then submit the change to the voters for their approval in a referendum. Seventeen states, mostly in the West, allow for amendments simply by getting the proposal on a statewide ballot, without involvement of the legislature or governor.

An implication of the relatively simple amendment processes is frequent changes. All but nineteen states have adopted wholly new constitutions since they were first admitted, and almost 6,000 specific amendments have been adopted. Another effect of the process is that state constitutions tend to be longer than the U.S. Constitution and include provisions that more appropriately should be statutes or administrative rules. The California constitution, for example, not only establishes state government institutions and protects individual rights but also defines how long a wrestling match may be. Arkansas includes in its constitution what colors should be used for copies of registration documents.

Progressive movement
Advocated measures to destroy political machines and instead have direct participation by voters in the nomination of candidates and the establishment of public policy.

Explaining Differences in
State Laws

■ Wisconsin's Robert M. La Follette, a Republican, championed Progressive reforms both as governor from 1901 to 1906 and as a U.S. senator for nearly twenty years.

Photo courtesy: Wisconsin Historical Society

Governors

governor
Chief elected executive in state government.

Governors have always been the most visible elected officials in state governments. Initially, that visibility supported the ceremonial role of governors as their primary function. Now that visibility serves governors as they set the agenda and provide leadership for others in state governments. (See Figure 4.1.)

The most important role that current governors play is in identifying the most pressing problems facing their respective states and proposing solutions to those problems. Governors first establish agendas when they campaign for office. After inauguration, the most effective way for the chief executive to initiate policy changes is when submitting the budget for legislative approval.

Budgets are critical to the business of state governments. The ways in which money is raised and spent say a lot about the priorities of decision makers. Until the 1920s, state legislatures commonly compiled and passed budgets and then submitted them for gubernatorial approval or veto. As part of the efforts since the 1960s to strengthen the effectiveness of state governments, governors were, like presidents, given the major responsibility for starting the budget process. Now nearly all states have their governors propose budgets.

package or general veto
The authority of a chief executive to void an entire bill that has been passed by the legislature. This veto applies to all bills, whether or not they have taxing or spending components, and the legislature may override this veto, usually with a two-thirds majority of each chamber.

line-item veto
The authority of a chief executive to delete part of a bill passed by the legislature that involves taxing or spending. The legislature may override a veto, usually with a two-thirds majority of each chamber.

The role of governor as budget initiator is especially important when coupled with the governor's veto authority and executive responsibilities. Like presidents, governors also have **package** or **general veto** authority, which is the power to reject a bill in its entirety. In addition, governors in all but seven states may exercise a **line-item veto** on bills that involve spending or taxing. A line-item veto strikes only part of a bill that has been passed by the legislature. It allows a chief executive to delete a particular program or expenditure from a

FIGURE 4.1   Party of State Governors, 2005
Republicans control a majority of the governorships, including those of the four most populous states. ■

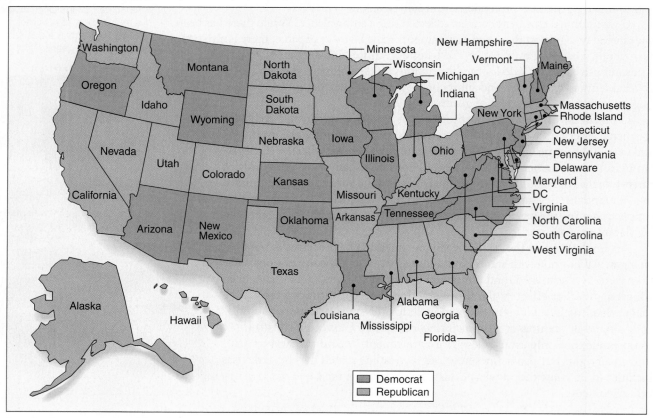

Source: http://www.ncsl.org/statevote2002/govParty_post2002.htm, and updates by the authors.

budget bill and let the remaining provisions become law. The intent of this authority is to enable governors to revise the work of legislators in order to produce a balanced budget.

When Tommy Thompson, U.S. Secretary of Health and Human Services from 2001 to 2004, was governor of Wisconsin, he was the most extensive and creative user of the line-item veto. He reversed the intent of legislation by vetoing the word "not" in a sentence and created entirely new laws by eliminating specific letters and numerals to make new words and numbers. Voters in Wisconsin were so upset with this free use of the veto pen that in 1993 they passed the "Vanna White amendment" to the state constitution, prohibiting the governor from striking letters within words and numerals within numbers. Not to be outmaneuvered, Governor Thompson then used his veto authority to actually *insert* new words and numbers in bills that had passed the legislature. The Wisconsin state supreme court, in 1995, upheld this interpretation of veto, as long as the net effect of the vetoes was not to increase spending.

While the Wisconsin case is extreme, it illustrates the significant power that veto authority can provide. Legislators can override vetoes, usually with a two-thirds vote in each of the chambers, but this rarely happens. Only 6 percent of gubernatorial vetoes are overturned.[9]

The executive responsibilities of governors provide an opportunity to affect public policies after laws have been passed. Agencies are responsible for implementing the laws. That may mean improving a road, enforcing a regulation, or providing a service. The speed and care with which implementation occurs are often under the influence of the governor.[10] Likewise, governors can affect the many details and interpretations that must be decided. State statutes require drivers of vehicles to have a license, but they typically let an agency decide exactly what one must do to get a license, where one can take the tests, and what happens if someone fails a test. Governors can influence these decisions primarily through appointing the heads of state administrative agencies.

One of the methods of limiting gubernatorial power is to curtail appointment authority.[11] Unlike the federal government, for example, states have some major agencies headed by individuals who are elected rather than appointed by the chief executive. Forty-three states, for example, elect their attorney general, a position that is part of the president's Cabinet. The positions of secretary of state, treasurer, and auditor are also usually filled by elected rather than appointed officials. Some states elect their head of education, agriculture, or labor. The movement throughout states to strengthen the institutions of their governments has included increasing the number of senior positions that are filled by gubernatorial appointments so that governors, like heads of major corporations, can assemble their own policy and management teams.

Another position that is filled by presidential appointment in the federal government, but in most cases is elected in state governments, is judge. The structure of state courts and how judges are selected will be discussed later in the chapter. This is one more example of approaches that have been taken to restrict the authority of governors.

Nonetheless, governors are major actors in the judicial system. With the legislature, they define what is a crime within a state and attach penalties that should be meted out to those convicted of committing crimes. Once someone has been convicted, they will be institutionalized or supervised by an agency that is, in every state, headed by a gubernatorial appointment. Moreover, governors have authority to grant a **pardon** to someone who has been convicted, thereby eliminating all penalties and wiping the court action from an individual's record. Governors may also **commute** all or part of a sentence, which leaves the conviction on record even though the penalty is reduced. In addition, governors grant **parole** to prisoners who have served part of their terms. Typically, governors are advised by a parole board on whether or not to grant a parole.

Finally, under the U.S. Constitution, governors have the discretion to **extradite** individuals. This means that a governor may decide to send someone, against his or her will, to another state to face criminal charges. When Mario Cuomo, who opposed the death penalty, was governor of New York, he refused to extradite someone to a state that used capital punishment. That refusal became an issue in Governor Cuomo's

pardon
The authority of a governor to cancel someone's conviction of a crime by a court and to eliminate all sanctions and punishments resulting from the conviction.

commute
The action of a governor to cancel all or part of the sentence of someone convicted of a crime, while keeping the conviction on the record.

parole
The authority of a governor to release a prisoner before his or her full sentence has been completed and to specify conditions that must be met as part of the release.

extradite
To send someone against his or her will to another state to face criminal charges.

unsuccessful bid for reelection in 1994. The newly elected governor, George Pataki, ordered the extradition shortly after he was inaugurated. In fact, with the support of Governor Pataki, New York adopted the death penalty.

Gubernatorial participation in the judicial process has led to some of the most colorful controversies in state politics. James E. Ferguson, as governor of Texas, granted 2,253 pardons between 1915 and 1917. His successor, William P. Hobby, granted 1,518 during the next two years, and then Governor Miriam "Ma" Ferguson outdid her husband by issuing almost 3,800 during her term. Texans were used to shady wheeling and dealing in politics, but this volume of pardons seemed a bit excessive. The Texas constitution was amended to remove authority to grant pardons and paroles from the governor; this power was placed in the hands of a board. Governors of the Lone Star State now have the lowest amount of authority among the fifty state chief executives to check actions of the judiciary.[12]

The general trend since the 1960s has been an increase rather than decrease in the power and authority of governors.[13] Given the historic desire to have weak chief executives, some of the enhancement of gubernatorial powers has come at the cost of the prerogatives of other institutions. This is particularly the case with veto authority and the role in the budgetary process.

State Legislatures

The principles of representative democracy are embodied primarily in the legislature. Legislatures, as mentioned above, were initially established to be the most powerful of the institutions of state government. In over half of the original states, legislatures began without the check of a gubernatorial veto. Until the twentieth century, most state legislatures were responsible for executive chores such as formulating a budget and making administrative appointments.

These tasks were, even more than was envisioned for the U.S. Congress, to be done by "citizen legislators" as a part-time responsibility. The image was that individuals would convene in the state capitol for short periods of time to conduct the state's business. State constitutions and statutes specified the part-time operation of the legislature and provided only limited compensation for those who served.

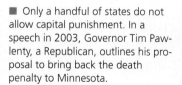

■ Only a handful of states do not allow capital punishment. In a speech in 2003, Governor Tim Pawlenty, a Republican, outlines his proposal to bring back the death penalty to Minnesota.

Photo courtesy: Nathan Berndt/Getty Images

As mentioned earlier, the one-person, one-vote ruling of the U.S. Supreme Court in *Baker* v. *Carr* (1962) marked a turning point in the history of state legislatures, and state governments generally. Once legislatures more accurately represented their states, agendas became more relevant and policies were more appropriate.[14] State legislatures not only became more representative; they became more professional. Legislators worked more days—some of them full-time. In 1960, only eighteen state legislatures met annually. As of 2005, forty-three met every year and only seven every other year. Moreover, the floor sessions were longer, and between sessions legislators and their staff increasingly did committee work and conducted special studies.[15] In 2004, California's newly elected Governor Arnold Schwarzenegger criticized the full-time role of state legislators, arguing that this made legislators think they had to enact more laws: "Spending so much time in Sacramento, without anything to do, then out of that comes strange bills."[16]

All states except Nebraska have two legislative houses. One, the senate, typically has fewer members than the other, usually called the "house" or the "assembly." The most common ratio between the two chambers is 1:3. In fourteen states the ratio is 1:2, and in New Hampshire it is 1:16. Another difference between the two bodies in thirty-four of the states is that senators serve four-year terms, whereas representatives in the larger house serve two-year terms. In eleven states, everyone in both houses serves two-year terms, and in the remaining, including Nebraska, everyone serves for four years.

Although it has been common to have limits on how many terms someone may serve as governor, **term limits** for legislators is a development of the 1980s and 1990s. By 2004, sixteen states had laws in effect limiting the number of years one might be a state legislator. Depending on the state, limits vary between six and twelve years. (See Table 4.1.)

Proponents of term limits included minority party leaders who calculated—sometimes in error—that they stood a better chance of gaining seats if incumbents had to leave after a certain period of time. Others saw term limits as a means of achieving the ideal of citizen legislator. Supporters of term limits embraced the concept of having people serve as a legislator in addition to whatever else they did in life, as opposed to pursuing a career as an elected official.[17]

term limits
Restrictions that exist in some states about how long an individual may serve in state or local elected offices.

TABLE 4.1	States with Term Limits for State Legislators			
	HOUSE		*SENATE*	
	Effective Date	*Limit (years)*	*Effective Date*	*Limit (years)*
Maine	1996	8	1996	8
California	1996	6	1998	8
Colorado	1998	8	1998	8
Arkansas	1998	6	2000	8
Michigan	1998	6	2002	8
Florida	2000	8	2000	8
Ohio	2000	8	2000	8
South Dakota	2000	8	2000	8
Montana	2000	8	2000	8
Arizona	2000	8	2000	8
Missouri[a]	2002	8	2002	8
Oklahoma	2004	12	2004	12
Wyoming	2006	12	2006	12
Louisiana	2007	12	2007	12
Nebraska	n/a	n/a	2008	8
Nevada	2010	12	2010	12

[a]Because of special elections, term limits were effective in 1998 for one senator and in 2001 for five House members.

Source: http://www.ncsl.org/programs/legman/about/states.htm, accessed April 19, 2004.

Join the Debate

TERM LIMITS AT THE STATE AND LOCAL LEVEL

OVERVIEW: According to the principle of federalism, state and local governments are understood to best represent the desires and address the needs of individual citizens. The closeness of local and state government to the daily lives of individuals was assumed to foster a type of intimacy between representatives and their constituents. After all, isn't it reasonable that citizens should have knowledge of and relatively easy access to those elected officials who affect the law and policies guiding our everyday actions and locales? Elected officials help make policy and law regarding such concerns as whether one may smoke in local restaurants and taverns, whether one may use a cell phone while driving, and whether property immediately adjacent to a major historical landmark such as Valley Forge is opened to commercial and residential development. Since state and local governments have a significant impact on how we live, shouldn't voters have the right to determine how long elected officials remain in office?

The term limits movement gained strength in the late 1980s as a response to the public's frustration with career politicians. Concerned about incumbency rates that in some cases exceeded 90 percent, a significant number of voters determined that term limits would be a way to compel an elected official to govern with an eye toward the well-being of his or her constituents, rather than governing with a view to a political career in the same office. Advocates of term limits argue that by having a stable turnover of elected officials, a continual stream of fresh ideas and new talent will be introduced into the political process, and American democracy will as a result benefit from active and innovative elected officials. Furthermore, advocates argue, democratic choice will be enhanced, since the frequent opening of electoral office will offer voters truly contested elections rather than an incumbent who uses institutional power and prerogatives to deter potential challengers to his or her office. Advocates say that elected officials oppose term limits because they threaten the entrenched power of incumbents.

Those opposed to this movement argue that term limits actually deprive voters of choice, since term limits will force good, qualified officials out of office. This exodus then deprives constituents of the choice to reelect those officials who have not only demonstrated skill and competency in office, but have also earned the electorate's trust and esteem. Opponents argue that term limits prevent the development of an expert and experienced political class that can maintain governmental continuity and guide law and policy over the long term. Should voters become unhappy with an elected official's performance or conduct in office, voters can always remove the official or vote against him or her in the next election.

Current research is inconclusive in regard to the effects of term limits given that it has been only a few years since the first term-limited officials have retired from office, and it will be several more years until data are available to draw solid inferences on the effects of the term-limits movement.

Arguments for Term Limits

- **Term limits help prevent a state's political institutions and policies from becoming stagnant.** Term limits statutes increase electoral competition by giving more capable and concerned citizens the chance to seek office. Talented citizens would thus be encouraged to run for office because more elective offices would become available as incumbents retired. Also, there is an increased likelihood that freshman officials would have an immediate impact on politics and policy because of the

State legislatures are still primarily part-time, citizen bodies.[18] Every election puts new members in about one-fourth of the seats. Only a handful of legislators in each state envision careers as state lawmakers. Those with long-term political aspirations tend to view service in a state chamber as a step on a journey to some other office, in the state capital or in Washington, D.C. For some, their goal is to don a black robe and preside in a courtroom.

State Courts

Almost everyone is in a courtroom at some point. It may be as a judge, a juror, an attorney, a court officer, or a litigant. It may also be for some administrative function such decreased control of incumbents over committees and other law- and policy-making institutions.

- **Term limits call truly public-spirited citizens to elective office.** Political office may no longer be seen as a career move but as a chance for those with other livelihoods to exercise public-spiritedness and discharge public duties. Office-seekers can make political, legislative, and policy considerations based on what they believe is best for their constituents and districts; moreover, the effects of interest group activity and lobbyists will be diminished, since elected officials will no longer depend on long-term relationships with these groups for campaign-finance and career considerations.

- **Voters overwhelmingly support term limits for elected officials.** Between 1990 and 2000, voters by overwhelming margins (on average 68%) passed term limits on elective offices in nineteen states. According to the Cato Institute, the term limits movement is "one of the most successful grassroots political efforts in U.S. history" — it has subjected over 17,000 local politicians in over 3,000 localities to term limits. Much like the Progressive movement's reforms, the term-limit movement is an attempt by citizens to force elected officials to focus on governance rather than reelection and political careers.

Arguments Against Term Limits

- **Term limits reduce professionalism in government.** Imposing term limits will reduce the numbers of experienced legislators. Long-term tenure in elected office allows law and policy makers to gain experience and deep knowledge of their governmental and political institutions, and this knowledge and experience allow them to govern effectively and efficiently. Continual turnover of elected officials introduces instability and the loss of long-term cohesiveness into legislative bodies, since elected officials are primarily compelled to leave office just as they gain requisite experience.

- **Term limits enhance the influence of lobbyists and staffs.** Career politicians know where to go and whom to trust for policy and legislative information. Newly elected officials need information in order to govern well, and they may become too dependent on information and advice from career staffs, lobbyists, and interest groups in order to make informed decisions. Staffs and interest groups are likely to provide information that puts their particular policy preference in a favorable light.

- **Citizens should have the right to determine how long elected officials remain in office.** Term limits impose an infringement on the liberties of both voters and office holders. Voters lose the freedom to vote for whom they wish, and office holders lose the freedom to remain in office to ensure the well-being of their constituents and districts over the long term. The voters themselves enforce term limits when they vote not to return corrupt or incompetent elected officials back to office. The American people are wise enough to vote their interests.

Questions

1. Who do you think has the better argument—those who advocate or those who oppose term limits? Why?
2. Is a professional political class necessary for good policy? Or does "new blood" in elected office bring about desired policy change?

Selected Readings

Gideon Doron and Michael Harris. *Term Limits*. Lexington Books, 2001.

Thad Kousser. *Term Limits and the Dismantling of State Legislative Professionalism*. Cambridge University Press, 2004.

as an adoption, a name change, or the implementation of a will. Few of us will ever be in a federal court; almost all of us will be in a state court (except people who live in Washington, D.C., where *all* courts are federal courts).

The primary function of courts is to settle disputes, and most disputes are matters of state, not federal, laws. For the most part, criminal behavior is defined by state legislatures. Family law, dealing with marriage, divorce, adoption, child custody, and the like, is found in state statutes. Contracts, liability, land use, and much that is fundamental to everyday business activity and economic development also are part of state governance.

A common misunderstanding is that the courts in the United States are all part of a single system, with the U.S. Supreme Court at the head. In fact, state and federal courts are separate, with their own rules, procedures, and routes for appeal. The only time state and federal courts converge is when a case involves a claim that a state law or practice violates a federal law or the Constitution or a state court judge has interpreted the Constitution. (See chapter 10 for more on the judiciary.)

Sometimes federal and state laws are directly related. If there is a contradiction between the two, then federal law prevails. A state statute that allowed or encouraged racial discrimination, for example, would directly conflict with the 1964 federal Civil Rights Act. Through a rule known as **inclusion,** state courts would be obliged to enforce the federal law.

Since the 1970s, the U.S. Supreme Court has generally taken the position that, especially with regard to individual rights protected in the Constitution, state courts should be encouraged to regard the federal government as setting minimums.[19] If state constitutions and laws provide additional protections or benefits, then state courts should enforce those standards.

Like other state government institutions, courts have modernized in the past few decades. Many states reorganized their court systems in the 1970s to follow a model that relied on full-time, qualified judges and simplified appeal routes, which enabled state supreme courts to have a manageable workload. Figure 4.2 illustrates the court structure that is now common among the states.

Most court cases in urban areas begin in a court that specializes in issues such as family disputes, traffic, small claims (less than $500 or $1,000), or probate (wills) or in a general jurisdiction municipal court. Small towns and rural areas usually do not have specialized courts. If they do, the position of judge is part-time. Cases here start in county-level courts that deal with the full array of disputes.

Specialized courts do not use juries. A single judge hears the case and decides the case. Other courts at this level do have juries if requested by the litigants (parties in a case). A major responsibility of the judges and juries that deliberate on cases when they are originated is to evaluate the credibility of the witnesses and evidence. When cases are heard on appeal, the only individuals making presentations are attorneys.

Appellate courts have panels of judges. There are no juries in these courtrooms. An important feature of the court reorganizations of the 1970s is that a court of appeals exists between the circuit or county courts and the state supreme court. This court is to cover part of the state and is supposed to accept all appeals. In part, this appellate level is to allow supreme courts to decide whether or not they will hear a case. The basic principle is that all litigants should have at least one opportunity to appeal a decision. If the

inclusion
The principle that state courts will apply federal laws when those laws directly conflict with the laws of a state.

FIGURE 4.2 State Court Structure

Most state courts have the basic organization shown here. ■

	Jury or Bench Trials	Jurisdiction	Judges
STATE SUPREME COURT	Bench only	Appeal (limited)	Panel of judges, elected/appointed for fixed term
APPEALS COURTS	Bench only	Appeal (readily granted)	Panel of judges, elected/appointed for fixed term
CIRCUIT OR COUNTY COURTS	Jury and bench	Original and appeal	One judge per court, elected/appointed for fixed term
MUNICIPAL AND SPECIAL COURTS	Jury and bench	Original	One judge per court, elected/appointed for fixed term

state supreme court is the only place where an appeal can be lodged, that court is almost inevitably going to have too heavy a caseload and unreasonable backlogs will develop.

Most state judges are elected to the bench for a specific term. This differs from the federal government, where the president appoints judges for indefinite terms. Only six states use gubernatorial appointments. The first states had their legislatures elect judges, and that is still the case in Connecticut, Rhode Island, South Carolina, Vermont, and Virginia. As Table 4.2 shows, in sixteen states, voters elect judges and use party identification. In their efforts to limit and even destroy political machines, Progressives at the turn of the twentieth century advocated electing judges without party labels. Today, sixteen states use nonpartisan elections for selecting their judges. The remaining states went a step further and allowed for the election of judges but only after screening for qualifications. This process is referred to as the **Missouri** (or Merit) **Plan.** The governor selects someone from a list prepared by an independent panel and appoints him or her as a judge for a specific term of years. If a judge wishes to serve for an additional term, he or she must receive approval from the voters, who express themselves on a "yes/no" ballot. If a majority of voters cast a "no" ballot, the process starts all over. Five states (California, Kansas, Missouri, Oklahoma, and Tennessee) use the Missouri Plan for some judicial positions and nonpartisan elections for the others.

Missouri (Merit) Plan
A method of selecting judges in which a governor must appoint someone from a list provided by an independent panel. Judges are then kept in office if they get a majority of "yes" votes in general elections.

Elections and Political Parties

Elections are the vehicle for determining who will fill major state government positions and who will direct the institutions of state government. Almost all contests for state government posts are partisan. The major exceptions are judicial elections in many states, as noted above, and the senate in Nebraska's unicameral legislature. Although party labels are not used and political parties are not formally participants in nonpartisan races, the party identity of some candidates may be known and may have some influence.

Political parties have different histories and roles in the various states. The chart in Analyzing Visuals: Patterns of Party Competition in State Legislatures shows the trends in the member of state legislative seats won by Republicans and Democrats. Most states have experienced significant competition between Republicans and Democrats since the Civil War. These states often have party control split between the two houses of the legislature and the governor's office or have frequent changes in party control of state government. This pattern has applied to southern states only once since the 1990s.

Since 1994, the Republicans have made gains in state elections. One of the reasons for Republican success is that voters in the South who had been voting for conservative Democrats began voting for conservative Republicans. Southerners have supported Republican presidential candidates since the Democratic Party began asserting leadership for civil rights following World War II. Alignment with Republicans in contests for state and congressional positions has been a more gradual process, but the 2002 elections continued that trend. In short, Southerners no longer represent a significant minority within the national Democratic Party but instead are part of the majority within the Republican Party—nationally and regionally.

Republicans currently hold a majority of the nation's governorships, with Arnold Schwarzenegger's victory in California's recall election in 2003 giving them executive control of the nation's four most populous states. (See Figure 4.1.) Sonny

TABLE 4.2	Judicial Selection Patterns
Partisan Election	**Nonpartisan Election**
Alabama	Arizona
Indiana	Arkansas
Illinois	California
Kansas	Florida
Louisiana	Georgia
Mississippi	Idaho
Missouri	Kentucky
New Mexico	Michigan
New York	Minnesota
North Carolina	Montana
Pennsylvania	Nevada
Tennessee	North Dakota
Texas	Ohio
West Virginia	Oregon
	Oklahoma
	South Dakota
	Washington
	Wisconsin
Election by Legislature	**Appointment by Governor**
Connecticut	Delaware
Rhode Island	Hawaii
South Carolina	Maryland
Vermont	Massachusetts
Virginia	New Hampshire
	New Jersey

Missouri (Merit) Plan		
Alaska	Iowa	Oklahoma
California	Kansas	Tennessee
Colorado	Missouri	Utah
Indiana	Nebraska	Wyoming

Source: The Book of the States, 2000–2001, 137–39. ©2000, Council of State Governments, with updates. Reprinted with permission.

Analyzing Visuals

PATTERNS OF PARTY COMPETITION IN STATE LEGISLATURES

This graph presents the trends of Republican and Democratic Party success in winning seats in state legislatures. Until the 1960s, the Democratic Party dominated the legislatures of southern states and the Republican Party did best outside that region. Based on the information presented in the graph and the chapter discussion on the parties in state legislatures, answer the following critical thinking questions: What trends do you see in the regional patterns of party competition? Do the regional trends allow you to make a summary statement about the national picture of parties in state legislatures? What major movement nationally led to the decline of Democratic dominance in southern states? What major national event contributed to a surge in Democratic strength in the mid-1970s? How would you explain the even competitiveness of the Republicans and Democrats since the mid-1990s?

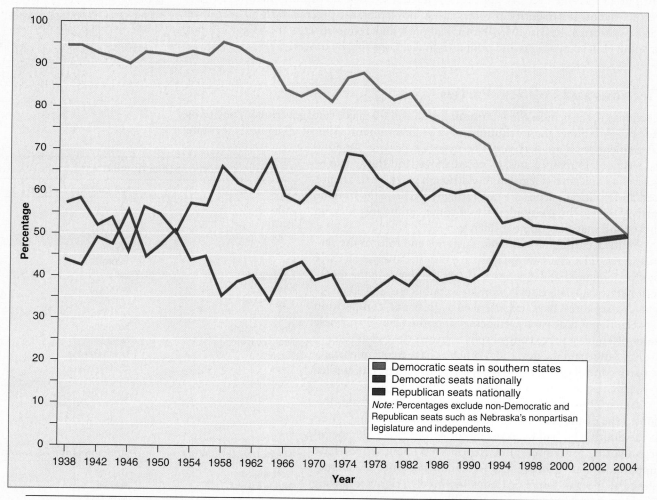

Democratic seats in southern states
Democratic seats nationally
Republican seats nationally
Note: Percentages exclude non-Democratic and Republican seats such as Nebraska's nonpartisan legislature and independents.

Source: National Conference of State Legislatures, http://www.ncsl.org/statevote/legpartycontrol_post2004.htm. Updated by the authors.

Perdue, a Republican, won the gubernatorial race in Georgia in 2002, the last southern state that had elected only Democratic governors since the Reconstruction era after the Civil War. That same year, GOP candidates also defeated Democratic incumbent governors in Alabama and South Carolina. Still, Democrats in 2002 recaptured the governorships in several states, including Illinois, Pennsylvania, Michigan, and Wisconsin, all of which had been under Republican executives for eight years or more. Republicans took over the governorships of Mississippi and Kentucky in 2003, while a Democrat won the Louisiana governorship that November. In the 2004 elections, Missouri and Indiana replaced Democratic governors with Republicans, and New Hampshire and Montana replaced Republicans with Democrats.

It is easy to exaggerate the importance of partisanship in state politics. A few normally Republican states—Wyoming and Kansas, for example—currently have Democratic governors, while some normally Democratic states—such as Massachusetts, Maryland, and Hawaii—have Republican governors. Whether at the state or the national level, the differences between Republicans and Democrats are important but not always drastic. While party labels and organizations matter, campaigns are primarily centered on individual candidates. Voters often have an opportunity to meet face to face with those contending for state government offices. A common strategy of candidates is to downplay their party identification, both to emphasize their strengths as individuals and to appeal to independent voters. After the election, party labels are important in determining who is in the majority in the legislature and therefore who will control committees and who will preside. That affects the agenda and the dynamics of policy making, but even here parties typically lack the homogeneity and the discipline to determine outcomes.

Elections since the 1960s have led increasingly to ethnic and racial diversity among state and local officials. It is now common for African Americans, Latinos, and women to be mayors, including in some of the largest cities. In 2002, 22 percent of the 7,424 state legislators were women. This percentage was the lowest in the southern states, and the range nationally was from 8 percent in Alabama to 39 percent in Washington State. Also in 2002, ten women succeeded in becoming their party's candidate for governor in the general election, and four of them ultimately won. As of 2005, seven states had women governors.

Photo courtesy: Daily Star, Kari Wheeler/AP/Wide World Photos

■ In a close election against a Republican opponent who was an a Native American, Kathleen Blanco was elected governor of Louisiana in November 2003. Blanco, a Democrat, is the state's first woman governor.

Direct Democracy

Ballots almost always include state and local referenda and initiative questions, as well as the names of candidates. (There is no provision for a national referendum or initiative.) As mentioned earlier, a Progressive reform meant to weaken parties was to provide opportunities for voters to legislate directly and not have to go through state legislatures and governors.[20] That process, known as the **direct initiative,** is available in eighteen states, most of them in the West. (See Table 4.3.) Citizens in these states have been able to enact laws as wide ranging as legalizing physician assisted suicide, limiting property taxes, building mass transit systems, protecting endangered species, and establishing prison terms for certain criminal behaviors.

A disadvantage of the direct initiative is the possibility that a law may be passed solely because of public opinion, which might be shaped largely by thirty-second television commercials and short slogans. Unlike the process when a legislative body debates a measure, there is no easy opportunity for making amendments to successful initiatives.

Sometimes initiatives are passed and then set aside by courts because they violate the state or federal constitution or because the federal government preempts the state. When California, for example, passed Proposition 187 in 1994 denying most public services to unregistered immigrants, federal courts kept the state from implementing the law because it trespassed on federal immigration policy and violated the U.S. Constitution.

Debate, deliberation, and amendment are included in the **indirect initiative.** In this process, legislatures first consider the issue and then pass a bill that will become law if approved by the voters. The governor plays no role. Of the eleven states that have the indirect initiative, five also have the direct initiative.

direct initiative
A process in which voters can place a proposal on a ballot and enact it into law without involving the legislature or the governor.

The Initiative and Referendum

indirect initiative
A process in which the legislature places a proposal on a ballot and allows voters to enact it into law, without involving the governor or further action by the legislature.

TABLE 4.3	Authority for the Initiative and Popular Referendum		
State	Direct Initiative	Indirect Initiative	Popular Referendum
Alaska		X	X
Arizona		X	X
Arkansas	X		X
California	X		X
Colorado	X		
Florida	X		
Idaho	X		X
Illinois	X		
Kentucky			X
Maine		X	X
Maryland			X
Massachusetts		X	X
Michigan	X	X	X
Mississippi		X	
Missouri	X		X
Montana	X		X
Nebraska	X		X
Nevada	X	X	X
New Mexico			X
North Dakota	X		X
Ohio	X	X	X
Oklahoma	X		X
Oregon	X		X
South Dakota	X		X
Utah	X	X	X
Washington	X	X	X
Wyoming		X	X

Source: Based on The Book of the States, 2001–2002, 211. ©2001 Council of State Governments; and Fact Sheet: Information on the Statewide Initiative Process in the United States, Initiative and Referendum Institute at the University of Southern California.

Voters in twenty-three states have the opportunity to veto some bills. In these states, voters may circulate a petition objecting to a particular law passed in a recent session of the legislature. If enough signatures are collected, then an item appears on the next statewide ballot, giving the electorate the chance to object and therefore veto the legislation. This is known as a **direct** or **popular referendum**.

All state and local legislative bodies may place an **advisory referendum** on a ballot. As the name implies, this is a device to take the pulse of the voters on a particular issue and has no binding effect. In addition, voter approval is required in a referendum to amend constitutions and, in some cases, to allow a governmental unit to borrow money through issuing bonds.

Finally, eighteen states provide for some form of **recall** election. As discussed in regard to the California recall at the beginning of this chapter, voters in these states have the power to petition for an election to remove an officeholder before the next scheduled election. Although not often used, judges, state legislators, and other officeholders are occasionally the subject of a recall campaign. Unlike California, most states that allow a recall require a higher threshold of voters to petition for such an election, and some of those allow for a recall only if certain criminal or immoral behavior has been committed by the elected official.[21]

direct (popular) referendum
A process in which voters can veto a bill recently passed in the legislature by placing the issue on a ballot and expressing disapproval.

advisory referendum
A process in which voters cast nonbinding ballots on an issue or proposal.

recall
A process in which voters can petition for a vote to remove officeholders between elections.

LOCAL GOVERNMENTS

THE INSTITUTIONS AND POLITICS of local governance are even more individualized than those of state governments. In part this is because officials are friends, neighbors, and acquaintances living in the communities they serve. Except in large cities, most elected officials fulfill their responsibilities on a part-time basis. The personal nature of local governance is also due to the immediacy of the issues. The responsibilities of local governments include public health and safety in their communities, education of children in the area, jobs and economic vitality, zoning land for particular uses, and assistance to those in need. Local government policies and activities are the stuff of everyday living.

Charters

Romantic notions of democracy in America regard local governments as the building blocks of governance by the people. Alexis de Tocqueville, the critic credited with capturing the essence of early America, described government in the new country as a series of social contracts starting at the grass roots. He said, "the township was organized before the county, the county before the state, the state before the union."[22] It sounds good, but it's wrong.

Photo courtesy: Dob Daemmrich/Stock Boston, Inc.

■ Responsibilities of local governments are wide ranging—from collecting the garbage in Minneapolis and filling potholes in Buffalo to patrolling the beach at Corpus Christi on spring break (shown here).

A more accurate description comes from Judge John F. Dillon. In an 1868 ruling, known as **Dillon's Rule,** Dillon proclaimed: "The true view is this: Municipal corporations owe their origins to and derive their power and rights wholly from the [state] legislature. It breathes into them the breath without which they cannot exist. As it creates, so it may destroy. If it may destroy, it may abridge and control."[23] Dillon's Rule applies to all types of local governments.

There are many categories of local governments. Some of these are created in a somewhat arbitrary way by state governments. Counties and school districts are good examples. State statutes establish the authority for these jurisdictions, set the boundaries, and determine what these governments may and may not do and how they can generate funds.

Local governments must have a **charter** that is acceptable to the state legislature, much as states must have a constitution acceptable to Congress. Charters describe the institutions of government, the processes used to make legally binding decisions, and the scope of issues and services that fall within the jurisdiction of the governmental body being chartered. There are five basic types of charters:

1. **Special Charters.** Historically, as urban areas emerged, each one developed and sought approval for its own charter. To avoid inconsistencies, most state constitutions now prohibit the granting of special charters.

2. **General Charters.** Some states use a standard charter for all jurisdictions, regardless of size or circumstance.

3. **Classified Charters.** This approach classifies cities according to population and then has a standard charter for each classification.

4. **Optional Charters.** A more recent development is for the state to provide several acceptable charters and then let voters in a community choose from these.

5. **Home Rule Charters.** Increasingly, states are specifying the major requirements that a charter must meet and then allowing communities to draft and amend their own charters. State government must still approve the final product.

An important feature of home rule is that the local government is authorized to legislate on any issue that does not conflict with existing state or federal laws. Other approaches list the subjects that a town or city may address.

Dillon's Rule

A court ruling that local governments do not have any inherent sovereignty but instead must be authorized by state government.

charter

A document that, like a constitution, specifies the basic policies, procedures, and institutions of a municipality.

COLLEGE TOWNS AND BINGE DRINKING

Local governments in communities with a college campus confront the challenge of binge drinking among students. Some may argue that students are just having fun and that bar owners are simply running a business. But, what might be regarded as individual choice and private socializing can have public consequences. City officials face pressure from their constituents to curb disruptive and illegal behavior from college students.

According to a study by the Harvard School of Public Health, 44 percent of U.S. college students engage in binge drinking.[a] Binge drinking is defined for men as having at least five drinks in a row, and for women, at least four drinks—a drink equals a twelve-ounce bottle of beer or wine cooler, a four-ounce glass of wine, or a shot of liquor, either by itself or in a mixed drink. A frequent binge drinker is someone who engages in this behavior at least three times in two weeks.

The Harvard study found that 50 percent of male college students and 39 percent of female students acknowledged that they were binge drinkers. Seventy-three percent of the men and 68 percent of the women said that the reason they drank alcoholic beverages was to get intoxicated.

There are no significant differences in the ages or classes of students and the pattern of binge drinking. Some binge drinkers are not yet twenty-one years old and therefore are breaking the law. Binge drinking, regardless of the legal drinking age, is associated with rowdiness, vandalism, fights, and sexual assault. The Harvard study demonstrated that binge drinkers are more likely than other students to miss class, get behind in school work, have unplanned sexual activity, engage in unprotected sex, damage property, and be hurt or injured.

Local and state governments are responsible for issuing licenses to sell alcoholic beverages. Inevitably, they must balance the pressure from bars and restaurants to do business freely and the need to ensure that alcohol is sold and consumed responsibly. An issue for local governments as well as for universities is that laws are broken when underage students drink and when binge drinking leads to assault and vandalism. Also, neighbors in campus areas want quieter, safer nights on the weekend. More central is the concern for health and safety—of the drinkers as well as of those around them.

An initial and obvious response of local governments has been to enhance policing focused on illegal drinking and unlawful behaviors related to the consumption of alcohol. Cities have revoked liquor licenses from businesses that make little effort to ensure that they are not serving underage drinkers. More innovative and proactive measures have included working with bar owners as well as fraternities and sororities to make sure that alcohol is not served to those who show signs of having had enough, educating students about the effects of binge drinking, eliminating sponsorship of events and programs by the alcohol industry, and sponsoring nonalcoholic alternatives for socializing and having fun. A few universities have sought to keep bars from having special deals during a "happy hour," since offering cheaper drinks in a relatively limited amount of time can encourage binge drinking from patrons trying to "get their money's worth." Some bar owners object strongly that these policing efforts interfere with their businesses.

Universities, health officials, police, and city governments all agree that binge drinking by college students is a serious problem. Attempts to curb the problem, however, have met with only limited success. Local government policies and university programs have not fared well as they confront business and individual choice.

---

[a] Henry Wechsler, George W. Dowdall, Andrea Davenport, and William DeJong, "College Alcohol Study," http://www.hsph.harvard.edu/cas/.

Types of Local Governments

There are about 87,000 local governments in the United States. The four major categories are as follows.

county
A geographic district created within a state with a government that has general responsibilities for land, welfare, environment, and, where appropriate, rural service policies.

1. **Counties.** Every state has **counties,** although in Louisiana they are called parishes, and in Alaska, boroughs. With few exceptions, counties have very broad responsibilities and are used by state governments as basic administrative units for welfare and environmental programs, courts, and the registration of land, births, and deaths. County and city boundaries may and do overlap, although state actions have merged city and county in New York, San Francisco, Denver, St. Louis, Nashville, and Honolulu.

2. **Towns.** In the first states and in the Midwest, "town" refers to a form of government in which everyone in a community is invited to an annual meeting to elect

officers, adopt ordinances, and pass a budget. Another use of this term is simply to refer to a medium-sized city. (See Global Perspective: Cities in the World.)

3. **Municipalities.** Villages, towns, and cities are established as **municipalities** and authorized by state governments as people congregate and form communities. Some of the most intense struggles among governments within the United States are over the boundaries, scope of authority, and sources of revenue for municipal governments.

4. **Special Districts. Special districts** are the most numerous form of government. A special district is restricted to a particular policy or service area. School districts are the most common form of special district. Others exist for library service, sewerage, water, and parks. Special districts are governed through a variety of structures. Some have elected heads, and others, appointed. Some of these jurisdictions levy a fee to generate their revenues, whereas others depend on appropriations from a state, city, or county. A reason for the recent proliferation of special districts is to avoid restrictions on funds faced by municipalities, schools, or other jurisdictions. The creation of a special park district, for example, may enable the park to have its own budget and sources of funding and relieve a city or county treasury.

The reasons that a particular municipality or special district was established may be sound, but having multiple governments serving the same community and controlling the same area can create confusion. The challenge is to bridge the separation between cities, school districts, counties, and state agencies to effectively address an issue. A specific response to youth violence, for example, may be to provide a youth center or skateboard rink for young people in a community so they can hang out in a safe and healthy setting. Such a project poses questions about which jurisdictions will provide funding and ensure staffing. Land may have to be rezoned and building permits acquired. Will a park district be involved? Will schools count on this facility for after-school programming? What will be the role and approach of the police department? Who will be in charge?

municipality
A government with general responsibilities, such as a city, town, or village government, that is created in response to the emergence of relatively densely populated areas.

special district
A local government that is responsible for a particular function, such as K–12 education, water, sewerage, or parks.

Photo courtesy: Keven Jacobus/The Image Works

■ One type of informal local government body is the neighborhood association. Whether such associations succeed in communicating clearly and resolving their problems is an open question.

CITIES IN THE WORLD

For many Americans, the cornerstone of government in the United States is local government. It is *their* government, the one with which they are most immediately in touch. It is here that such problems as fighting poverty, keeping the environment clean, providing affordable housing, running a cost-efficient transportation system, and offering high-quality educational opportunities take on a very personal character. According to the 2000 Census, to 79 percent of Americans, local government means urban government.

We are not alone in this view of local government: in fact, only two of the world's ten most populous urban areas are in the United States. The trend toward greater urbanization is one of the most significant global population trends. By 2015 it is estimated that for the first time in human history the majority of the world's population will live in urban centers. By 2025 it is estimated that two-thirds of the population of the developing world will live in urban areas, and that very soon twenty-seven of the world's thirty-three megacities (those with a population of over 8 million) will be found in these developing countries.

The problems the world's cities face are both immense and varied. Consider Lagos, Nigeria. Its urban-area population is around 13 million. In some parts of the city, the population density reaches 200,000 people per square kilometer. In 1995, only 80,000 residents out of 10 million had direct connections to clean water. Sewage is largely disposed of in open ditches. Lagos is also considered one of Nigeria's HIV/AIDS hotspots, with somewhere between 8 and 21 percent of its population being infected with the disease. Complicating the task of addressing these problems is the fact that over twenty different governing bodies operate in Lagos.

Or, consider Shanghai, China, whose urban area is home to 12 million people. Its population is one of the most skilled in China, enjoying a high standard of living in which virtually all permanent residences possess piped water and electricity. But all is not well. Twelve percent of the population is older than sixty-five, and average life expectancy is now seventy-seven. This large aging population places a huge burden on younger citizens to provide for them through high taxes. Moreover, Shanghai also has a large "floating population" that lives in slums and does not share in the city's wealth. Estimates place the number of new immigrants arriving in Shanghai each year at between 500,000 and 1 million.

Local government leaders recognize that they cannot meet the challenges before them by acting alone. In the United States, part of the answer lies with the National League of Cities, whose members range in size from New York City to Bee Cave, Texas. Cities around the world have also begun to partner. One notable organization is the International Council for Local Environmental Initiatives (ICLEI), made up of over 400 local governments around the world with a total population of nearly 300 million. U.S. member cities include: Atlanta, Georgia; Chattanooga, Tennessee; Honolulu, Hawaii; Miami-Dade County, Florida; Muncie, Indiana; New York, New York; Newark, New Jersey; and Tucson, Arizona.

One of the major initiatives undertaken by the ICLEI is Local Agenda 21, which pledges members to embrace sustainable development as a strategy for meeting the challenges of urbanization. Sustainable development holds that in using our natural resources, we must balance the needs of today against the needs of future generations. In Africa, for example, thirty-one cities have signed on to participate in the African Sustainable Cities Network. It is designed to help local governments in Africa to involve citizens in environmental planning. In the United States, the key ICLEI document is Communities 21, which pledges cities to work to protect the environment while improving the quality of life and increasing prosperity. Among those participating are Seattle, Washington, and Santa Monica, California.

Questions

1. When you think about local government in your home town, how do its problems compare to those noted here? How capable is it of solving them?
2. Which is a more important partner for cities in solving their problems: state governments, or Washington, D.C.? Why?

World's Ten Largest Urban Areas in 2003		
City	*Country*	*Population (in millions)*
Tokyo	Japan	31.1
Mexico City	Mexico	21.2
New York	United States	21.2
Seoul	South Korea	20.0
Sao Paulo	Brazil	18.8
Jakarta	Indonesia	17.9
Osaka	Japan	17.6
Delhi	India	17.0
Mumbai (Bombay)	India	17.0
Los Angeles	United States	16.4

Comparing State and Local Governments

Formal and informal arrangements among local governments exist that allow them to cooperate and coordinate their work in a single area. Miami and Dade County in Florida have been an early and visible example. The two jurisdictions have merged their public health services, jointly administer parks, operate a unified mass transit system, and together plan for development and land use. Saint Paul and Minneapolis in Minnesota have also pioneered cooperative arrangements. The establishment of the 911 emergency service can be a catalyst for cooperation by various police, fire, and paramedical agencies in a metropolitan area. Still, there continues to be conflict between governments on occasion and often a failure to even communicate. Local officials and citizens alike find the legacies of past actions creating local governments a serious challenge.

Executives and Legislatures

Except for the traditional New England **town meeting,** where anyone who attends may vote on policy and management issues, local governments have some or all of the following decision-making offices:

- Elected executive, such as a mayor, village president, or county executive.
- Elected council or commission, such as a city council, school board, or county board.
- Appointed manager, such as a city manager or school superintendent.

Local government institutions are not necessarily bound to the principles of separation of powers or checks and balances that the U.S. Constitution requires of the federal government and most state constitutions require of their governments. School boards, for example, commonly have legislative, executive, and judicial authority. School board members are, with few exceptions, part-time officials, so they hire superintendents and rely heavily on them for day-to-day management and for new policy ideas. It is the school board, however, that makes the policies regarding instruction and facilities. The board also does the hiring and contracting to implement those policies. Similarly, the school board sets student conduct rules, determines if a student should be expelled, and then hears appeals from those who are disciplined.

The patterns of executive and legislative institutions in local government have their roots in some of the most profound events in our history. The influx of immigrants into urban areas in the North after the Civil War prompted the growth of **political machines.**[24] New immigrants needed help getting settled. They naturally got much of that help from ethnic neighborhoods, where, for example, a family from Poland would find people who spoke Polish, restaurants with Polish food, and stores and churches with links to the old country. Politicians dealt with these ethnic neighborhoods. If the neighborhood voted to help provide victory for particular candidates for **mayor** and **city council,** then city jobs and services would be provided. Political machines were built on these quid pro quo arrangements. The bosses of those machines were either the elected officials or people who controlled the elected officials.

As part of their efforts to destroy the political machines, Progressives sought reforms that minimized the politics in local government institutions.[25] Progressives favored local governments headed by professional **managers** instead of elected executives. Managers would be appointed by councils, the members of which were elected on a nonpartisan ballot, thus removing the role of parties.

As another way of sapping the strength of ethnic bloc voting, Progressive reformers advocated that council members be elected from the city at large rather than from neighborhood districts. The choice between **district-based elections** and **at-large elections** now, however, raises concerns about discrimination against Latinos and African Americans. At-large elections may keep minority representatives from being elected. On the other hand, a city could be divided into districts that might have an ethnic group constitute a majority within a district. The at-large elections, in short, have the same minimizing effect on these ethnic groups that was intended by Progressives on white ethnic groups.

Photo courtesy: Annie McCormick/Reuters/Corbis

■ Philadelphia's Mayor John F. Street, a Democrat, won reelection to a second term in 2003.

town meeting
Form of local government in which all eligible voters are invited to attend a meeting at which budgets and ordinances are proposed and voted on.

political machine
An organization designed to solicit votes from certain neighborhoods or communities for a particular political party in return for services and jobs if that party wins.

mayor
Chief elected executive of a city.

city council
The legislature in a city government.

manager
A professional executive hired by a city council or county board to manage daily operations and to recommend policy changes.

district-based election
Election in which candidates run for an office that represents only the voters of a specific district within the jurisdiction.

at-large election
Election in which candidates for office must compete throughout the jurisdiction as a whole.

Photo courtesy: © Bettmann/CORBIS 2003

■ In the aftermath of the devastating 1900 hurricane in Galveston, Texas, the commission form of city government came into being. Although abandoned by Galveston, the model spread quickly, and by 1917 almost 500 cities had adopted the commission form of government.

commission
Form of local government in which several officials are elected to top positions that have both legislative and executive responsibilities.

public corporation (authority)
Government organization established to provide a particular service or run a particular facility that is independent of other city or state agencies and is to be operated like a business. Examples include a port authority or a mass transit system.

Progressives argued that the **commission** form of government was an acceptable alternative to mayors and boss politics. The commission evolved as a response to a hurricane in 1900 that killed almost 10,000 people in southern Texas. After the disaster, a group of prominent business leaders in Galveston formed a task force, with each member of the force assuming responsibility for a specific area, such as housing, public safety, and finance. Task force members essentially assumed the roles of both legislators making policy and managers implementing policy. The citizens of Galveston were so impressed with how well this worked that they amended their charter to replace the mayor and city council with a commission, elected at-large and on a nonpartisan basis. The model spread quickly, and by 1917 almost 500 cities had adopted the commission form of government.

As Table 4.4 indicates, half of all U.S. cities have an elected mayor and a council. Mayors differ in how much authority they have. Some are strong and have the power to veto city council action, appoint agency heads, and initiate as well as execute budgets. The charters of other cities do not provide mayors with these formal powers. Except for the largest cities, mayors serve on a part-time basis.

Slightly more than one-third of the municipalities have the Progressive model of government, with an appointed, professional manager and an elected city council. This is the most common pattern among medium-sized cities, whereas the very large and the very small have mayors and councils. Some jurisdictions have both mayors and managers.

Only 2 percent of U.S. cities use the commission form of government. Tulsa, Oklahoma, and Portland, Oregon, are the largest cities run by commissions. Galveston, however, is one of the cities that has abandoned this structure.

Over 1,800 of the almost 3,000 county governments are run by boards or councils that are elected from geographic districts and without any executive. Committees of the county board manage personnel, finance, roads, parks, social services, and the like. Almost 400 counties elect an executive as well as a board, and thus follow the mayor-council model. Almost 800 hire a professional manager.

School districts, with very few exceptions, follow the council-manager model. Other special districts have boards, sometimes called **public corporations** or **authorities,** that are elected or appointed by elected officials. If the district is responsible for services such as water, sewerage, or mass transit, the board is likely to hire and then supervise a manager.

TABLE 4.4	Major Forms of Municipal Government					
Form of Government	1984	1988	1992	1996	1998	2002
Council–Manager	3,387 (48.5%)	3,232	2,760	2,441	2,356	2,290 (34.7%)
Mayor–Council	3,011 (43.1%)	2,943	3,319	3,635	3,686	3,686 (55.8%)
Commission	143 (2.0%)	146	154	168	173	176 (2.7%)
Town Meeting	337 (4.8%)	333	365	363	369	370 (5.6%)
Representative Town Meeting	63 (.9%)	65	70	79	82	81 (1.2%)
Total[a]	6,981	6,719	6,668	6,686	6,666	6,603 (100%)

[a]Totals for U.S. local governments represent only those municipalities with populations of 2,500 and greater. There are close to 30,000 local governments with populations under 2,500.

Source: Statistics from "Inside the Year Book: Cumulative Distributions of U.S. Municipalities," *The Municipal Year Books* 1984–2002, International City/County Management Association (ICMA), Washington, DC.

GRASSROOTS POWER AND POLITICS

POLITICAL PARTICIPATION IN STATE AND, especially, local politics is both more personal and more issue-oriented than at the national level. Much of what happens is outside the framework of political parties. Elections for some state and local government offices, in fact, are **nonpartisan elections,** which means parties do not nominate candidates and ballots do not include any party identification of those running for office. Access and approaches are usually direct. School board members receive phone calls at their homes. Members of the city council and county board bump into constituents while shopping for groceries or cheering their children in youth sports. The concerns that are communicated tend to be specific and neither partisan nor ideological: a particular grade school teacher is unfair and ineffective; playground equipment is unsafe; it seems to be taking forever for the city to issue a building permit so that you can get started on a remodeling project.

In this setting, local news media invariably play a key role. The major newspaper in the state and what might be the only newspaper in a community can shape the agendas of government bodies and the images of government officials. The mere fact that a problem is covered makes it an issue. If gang or cult activity is just a group of kids acting weird and dressing the same way, public officials might ignore it. News coverage of this or certainly of a violent incident, on the other hand, assures attention. Then the question is how the media define the issue—as an isolated and unusual event or as a signal that certain needs are not being met?

The most powerful and influential people in a state or community are not necessarily those who hold offices in government. While there is always a distinction between formal and informal power, the face-to-face character of governance at the grassroots level almost invites informal ties and influence. The part-time officials in particular have a more ambiguous identity than do full-time government officials.

In small to medium-sized communities, it is common for a single family or a traditional elite to be the major decision maker, whether or not one of their members has a formal governmental position.[26] Another frequent pattern is where the owners or managers of the major business in town dominate public decision making. If you want to advocate for some improvements in a local park, a curriculum change in the schools, or a different set of priorities for the police department, it may be more important to get the support of a few key community leaders than the sympathy of the village president or the head of the school board. A newcomer interested in starting a business in a town likewise would be well advised to identify and court the informal elite and not just focus on those who hold a formal office.

Ad hoc, issue-specific organizations are prevalent in state and local governments.[27] Individuals opposed to the plans of a state department of transportation to expand a stretch of highway from two to four lanes will organize, raise funds, and lobby hard to stop the project. Once the project is stopped or completed, that organization will go out of existence. Likewise, neighbors will organize to support or oppose specific development projects or to press for revitalization assistance, and then they will disband once the decision is made. The sporadic but intense activity focused on specific local or regional concerns is an important supplement to the ongoing work of parties and interest groups in state and local governments. A full understanding of what happens at the grass roots requires an appreciation of ad hoc, issue-specific politics as well as the institutions and processes through which state and local governments make and implement public policies.

nonpartisan election
A contest in which candidates run without formal identification or association with a political party.

You Are a Restaurant Owner

RELATIONS WITH INDIAN NATIONS

TREATIES BETWEEN THE FEDERAL GOVERNMENT and American Indian nations directly affect thirty-four states. Most of these states are west of the Mississippi River,

domestic dependent nation
A type of sovereignty that makes an Indian tribe in the United States outside the authority of state governments but reliant on the federal government for the definition of tribal authority.

trust relationship
The legal obligation of the United States federal government to protect the interests of Indian tribes.

but New York, Michigan, Florida, Connecticut, and Wisconsin are also included. Although the treaties were signed by both the United States and an American Indian tribal nation, invariably the tribal leaders signed because of actual or threatened military defeat. The legal status of the various tribes in the United States is that of a **domestic dependent nation,** by which they retain their individual identity and sovereignty but must rely on the U.S. federal government for the interpretation and application of treaty provisions. Under the formal **trust relationship** between the United States and the Indian nations, the federal government is legally and morally obligated to protect Indian interests. State and local governments are clearly affected by federal–tribal relations but have little influence and virtually no legal authority over these relations.

The policy approach of the federal government toward Indians has varied widely (see Table 4.5). From 1830 to 1871, a major goal was to move all Indians to land west of the Mississippi. The policy between 1871 and 1934 was to assimilate Indians into the white culture of the United States. From 1934 until 1953 and then again from 1973 to today, the formal policy was to respect tribal customs, strengthen tribal governments, and promote economic self-determination. Between 1953 and 1973, the federal government terminated the legal status of various tribes, ended services to them, and refused to recognize their treaty rights. This generated protests and led to a resumption of the general policy begun in 1934.[28] While some would argue that the federal government has not been serious or effective enough in supporting treaty rights and self-determination, the current policy received new emphasis with the inclusion of tribes in the devolution of responsibilities from Washington to states and local communities.

States are not parties to the treaties between the United States and American Indian nations and have no direct legal authority over tribes. The federal government has in several specific areas granted some powers to states. The Indian Gaming Regulatory Act of 1988, for example, gives state governments limited authority to negotiate agreements, called **compacts,** with tribes who wish to have casino gambling. Also, in 1953, Congress passed Public Law 280, which allows some states to pursue Indians suspected of criminal behavior even if they are on reservation land.

compact
A formal, legal agreement between a state and a tribe.

For the most part, however, federal–tribal relations provide given constraints and opportunities as states and communities engage in planning and problem solving. The two most important features of federal–tribal relations for state and local governments are land rights and treaty provisions for hunting, fishing, and gathering. Tribes have **reservation land** and **trust land,** neither of which is subject to taxation or regulation by state or local governments. The reservation land was designated in a treaty. Tribes can acquire trust land by purchasing or otherwise securing ownership of a parcel and then seeking to have it placed in trust status by the secretary of the Department of the Interior. Since a tribe can get trust land at any time and any place, there is the potential for disruption of a community's development plans or tax base and an obvious challenge to cordial, working relationships between tribes, the federal government, and state or local government.

reservation land
Land designated in a treaty that is under the authority of an Indian nation and is exempt from most state laws and taxes.

trust land
Land owned by an Indian nation and designated by the federal Bureau of Indian Affairs as exempt from most state laws and taxes.

Hunting, fishing, and gathering activities have important cultural and religious significance for many American Indian nations. Treaty provisions giving rights to tribes to hunt, fish, and gather wild rice or berries on their own land and on public lands and

TABLE 4.5	Federal Policies Toward Indian Nations
Up to 1830	Mix conquest and coexistence. Make treaties.
1830–1871	Force all tribes west of Mississippi. Make treaties.
1871–1934	Assimilate Indians into white culture.
1934–1953	Respect tribal customs and government. Encourage economic self-determination.
1953–1973	Terminate legal status of tribes. Ignore treaty provisions.
1973 to present	Recognize tribes and treaty rights. Encourage constitutions and self-determination.

waterways in land they once owned are key to tribal identity and dignity. These treaty rights supersede regulations enacted for environmental and recreational purposes. Non-Indian anglers and hunters sometimes protest that Indians have special privileges. Environmental planners worry about the potential implications of unregulated Indian activity. In 1999, for example, the Makah tribe in the Northwest celebrated the successful capture and killing of a whale. While the tribe applauded the preservation of an important cultural tradition, wildlife advocates bemoaned the treaty rights that allowed this destruction of a valued animal.

Since Congress passed the Indian Self-Determination and Education Assistance Act in 1975, the federal government has been trying to strengthen tribal governments by encouraging the adoption of constitutions. The Bureau of Indian Affairs offers assistance in writing the constitutions, and other federal agencies, such as the Environmental Protection Agency, are willing to devolve some of their authority for regulating water and air pollution to tribes that have constitutions.

While a tribe may include some traditional patterns of governance in their constitution, the basic concept of a constitution is alien to Indian tribes. The documents read very much like state constitutions, with preambles that espouse principles of democracy and clauses that provide for a familiar separation of powers among executive, legislative, and judicial branches. Not surprisingly, some nations struggle with the mandates of their constitutions and the informal but real power of traditional rule by elders.

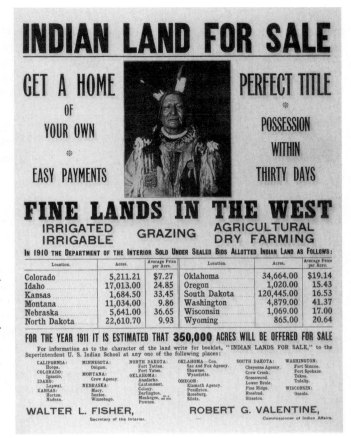

Photo courtesy: Library of Congress

■ An advertisement from the Department of the Interior (c. 1911) luring individuals to purchase land designated as surplus after tribal allotments were made to Indians.

STATE AND LOCAL FINANCES

STATE, TRIBAL, AND LOCAL GOVERNMENTS MUST, of course, have money. Getting that money is one of the most challenging and thankless tasks of public officials. Unlike the federal government, state and local governments must balance their budgets. Unlike private businesses, state and local governments may not spend less money than they have. Whereas the goal of a private business is to have significantly more income than expenses, a governor, mayor, or other local public executive would be criticized for taxing too heavily if something akin to profits appeared on the books.

The budgeting process involves making projections of expenses and revenues. State and local officials face some special uncertainties when they make these guesses. One important factor is the health of the economy. If one is taxing sales or income, those will vary with levels of employment and economic growth. Moreover, the public sector faces double jeopardy when the economy declines. Revenues go down as sales and incomes decline, and at the same time expenses go up as more families and individuals qualify for assistance during harsh times.

Another important factor affecting state and local government budgets is the level of funding that governments give to one another. States have been getting about one-fourth of their funds from Washington, D.C. That level has varied over time and, especially with federal deficit spending, is likely to decline. The amount of the decline will depend as much on political dynamics as it will on the health of the national economy. Local governments do not receive as much, but water and sewerage districts have been getting about 15 percent of their funds from the federal government. Local governments

You Are Director of Economic Development for the City of Baltimore, Maryland

depend heavily on aid from state governments. The pattern varies from one state to another, but on average, school districts get slightly over half of their funds from state governments, counties get almost one-third, and cities about 20 percent.[29]

Not only is federal funding for state and local governments generally declining, but Congress and the president frequently require communities to spend their money for national programs and concerns. The National Governors Association, for example, estimated that states will spend up to $4 billion a year to enhance security at airports, power plants, water sources, and vital infrastructure in the aftermath of the 9/11 terrorist attacks.[30] The federal government will reimburse state and local jurisdictions for less than one-third of their costs. Almost 75 percent of the states had to make major adjustments in their budgets in 2002, in part because of unexpected domestic security expenses and in part because of a national economic downturn.

Different governments depend on different types of taxes and fees. Figure 4.3 presents the pattern of funding for state and local governments. Unlike the federal government, which relies primarily on the income tax, state governments rely almost equally on income taxes and sales taxes. States differ among themselves, of course. Alaska, Delaware, Montana, New Hampshire, and Oregon have no sales tax, whereas some of the southern states have a double-digit sales tax. Alaska, Florida, Nevada, New Hampshire, South Dakota, Tennessee, Texas, Washington, and Wyoming do not tax personal incomes. Tax rates differ among those states that do have an income tax, but the levels are generally less than 10 percent.

Each of the thirty-nine states with budget deficits in 2002 reduced spending, but only seven balanced their books by raising taxes. Tax increases pose risks for officials seeking reelection. More popular ways of getting needed revenues included using "rainy day funds" established in years when there were surpluses, and selling to investors the rights to funds that states were to receive in a legal settlement with tobacco companies.

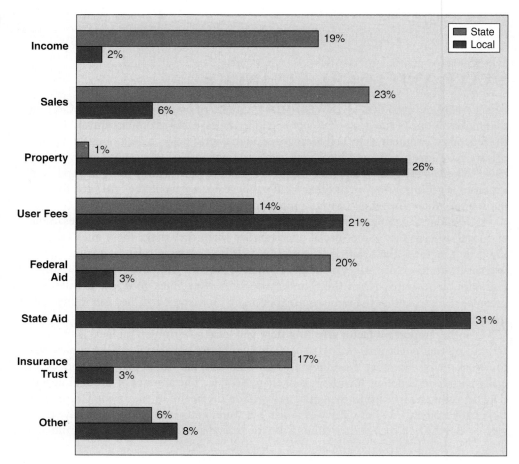

FIGURE 4.3   State and Local Government Revenues (percentage of total revenues). ∎

Analyzing Visuals

STATE AND LOCAL TAX BURDENS

In order to pay for the services they provide, state and local governments rely on a variety of taxes. The major source of revenue for cities, towns, villages, school districts, and counties is a tax on the value of property owned by individuals and businesses. Some local governments also use a tax on the sale of goods and services. States get most of their money by taxing income, sales, and cigarettes. Individual states vary widely in what they tax. Some have no income tax and a very high sales tax, whereas others have a relatively high income tax and a low sales tax.

The visual presents a sample breakdown of expenses and taxes for three households with different levels of income. This allows you to analyze the impact that each of the major types of taxes has on families. Based on the information presented in the graph and the chapter discussion on taxes, answer the following critical thinking questions: Who is most likely to press for lower income taxes? If everyone pays a 5 percent sales tax on food, clothing, and entertainment, whose sales tax is the largest proportion of their total income? If everyone pays $10 in taxes for every $1,000 of value of their property, is the tax progressive or regressive? Is the cigarette tax fair?

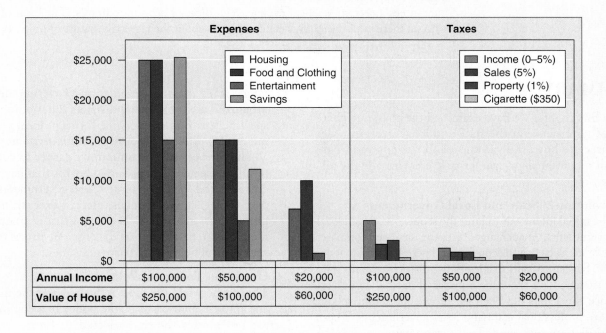

Investors paid states at the rate of $1 immediately in order to get $5 over 25 years. By the fall of 2003, most states had made tough adjustments to balance their budgets, typically opting for program cuts and fee increases rather than tax increases.[31] But the fear of severe damage to education, health care, and public safety led the Republican-dominated Virginia legislature to reverse course in the spring of 2004 and support a series of tax increases proposed by the Democratic governor, Mark Warner.[32]

Local governments rely primarily on property taxes, have little from levies on sales, and receive virtually nothing from income. Schools, in particular, depend on property taxes for funding. Both local and state governments levy user fees, such as admission to parks, licenses for hunting and fishing, tuition for public universities, and charges based on water use. States, more than local governments, administer retirement systems and insurance programs for public employees. Income from the investment of retirement funds is listed but is not generally available for any use other than paying retirement benefits. Similarly, user fees are typically placed in **segregated funds,** which means they can only be used to provide the service for which the fee was charged. Tuition must, in other words, be used by the university and cannot pay for prison costs or maintaining highways.

segregated funds
Money that comes in from a certain tax or fee and then is restricted to a specific use, such as a gasoline tax that is used for road maintenance.

Most people accept user fees as the fairest type of taxation. The problem is that the income is both limited and segregated. In general, taxes can be evaluated according to how much money they can raise, whether the revenue is certain, and who bears the burden. See Analyzing Visuals: State and Local Tax Burdens for examples of the impact of different taxes on households with varying levels of income. Income taxes generate large sums of money, although the amount of money generated will fluctuate according to economic conditions and levels of employment. Of all the taxes, those based on income are the most **progressive taxes,** which means that they are based on the ability to pay.

Sales taxes also generate lots of money, and they vary with how well the economy is doing. These are not based on earnings, but on purchases. Since those with a low income must spend virtually all that they earn in order to live, sales taxes are **regressive taxes.** To counter the regressive nature of sales taxes, some states exempt food, medicine, clothing, and other necessities.

Property taxes vary with the value of one's property, not one's current income or spending. Thus, farmers and those with a fixed income, such as retired persons, may bear more of a burden than their current wealth suggests they should carry. The property tax can be a good revenue earner and is stable, since a jurisdiction can set a tax rate that virtually guarantees a certain level of revenue, regardless of economic trends. The local officials who set these rates invariably hear complaints about the regressive nature of property taxes.

progressive tax
The tax level increases with the wealth or ability of an individual or business to pay.

regressive tax
The tax level increases as the wealth or ability of an individual or business to pay decreases.

SUMMARY

In this chapter we have examined the changing character of governance at the state and local levels in order to appreciate both the variation and the common patterns in subnational governments. We have made the following points:

1. **Evolution of State and Local Governments**
   The initial intent was to limit the scope of state and local governments. That changed with the increased complexity of our society and economy and with the ruling of the U.S. Supreme Court that legislative districts within a state must each have the same number of people. The trend since the 1960s has been for more representative and more professional state and local governments. These jurisdictions and the federal government are forming partnerships with each other and with the private sector to address issues and provide services.

2. **State Governments**
   State governments have traditionally had primary responsibility for criminal justice, education, public health, and economic development. Recently, state officials have assumed a larger role in welfare and environmental policy. State constitutions, which reflect major historical developments in American society, provide the basic framework of institutions and values in which state governments fulfill their roles. Since the 1960s, these governments have dramatically become more competent, professional, and accessible to the general public.

3. **Local Governments**
   Local governance in the United States is conducted by a varied collection of over 87,000 units, most of which are run by part-time officials. These governments range from general jurisdictions covering densely urbanized areas to special districts functioning for a specific, narrow purpose. The forms of local governments also differ. There are town meetings in which all eligible voters in a community gather to conduct business, elected and appointed boards that have both executive and legislative powers, and governments with distinct legislative councils, elected executives, and professional managers. Local politics is frequently nonpartisan, thanks in part to conscious efforts to prevent control by political party machines.

4. **Grassroots Power and Politics**
   Those who wield the most influence over the making and implementation of public policy in a community are not always the ones elected to formal offices. Sometimes power is in the hands of a family, a small number of individuals, or the local media. Whether or not those who are most powerful are the ones in government offices, governance at the grass roots is face to face, between neighbors, friends, and former high school classmates.

5. **Relations with Indian Nations**
   American Indian nations obviously affect and are affected by state and local governments. But, due to treaty rights and the domestic dependent sovereignty of the tribes, the Indian nations have a special relationship with the federal government. Tribes have important protections from the potential vagaries of state and local governments. Conversely, the special status of the tribes poses challenges to coherent and consistent policies in a community. Currently, the federal government is encouraging tribal governments to move to self-determination economically and politi-

cally and to enter into agreements with state and local governments on financial and policy matters.

6. State and Local Finances
Funding government is complex. Revenues are hard to project because governments tax personal and business incomes, sales, and property value—none of which governments can control. State, local, and tribal governments also rely heavily on money given to them by other jurisdictions, including the federal government. The challenge is, given these uncertainties and the general hostility toward taxes, to budget for required services and popular programs.

KEY TERMS

advisory referendum, p. 142
at-large election, p. 147
charter, p. 143
city council, p. 147
commission, p. 148
commute, p. 133
compact, p. 150
county, p. 144
Dillon's Rule, p. 143
direct initiative, p. 141
direct (popular) referendum, p. 142
district-based election, p. 147
domestic dependent nation, p. 150
extradite, p. 133
governor, p. 132
inclusion, p. 138
indirect initiative, p. 141
line-item veto, p. 132
manager, p. 147
mayor, p. 147
Missouri (Merit) Plan, p. 139
municipality, p. 145
nonpartisan election, p. 149
one-person, one-vote, p. 127
package or general veto, p. 132
pardon, p. 133
parole, p. 133
political machine, p. 147
Progressive movement, p. 131
progressive tax, p. 154
public corporation (authority) p. 148
recall, p. 142
regressive tax, p. 154
reservation land, p. 150
segregated funds, p. 153
special district, p. 145
state constitution, p. 128
term limits, p. 135
town meeting p. 147

trust land, p. 150
trust relationship, p. 150

SELECTED READINGS

Banfield, Edward C. *The Unheavenly City*. Boston: Little, Brown, 1970.
Benjamin, Gerald, and Michael J. Malbin, eds. *Limiting Legislative Terms*. Washington, DC: CQ Press, 1992.
Burns, Nancy E. *The Formation of American Local Governments: Private Values in Public Institutions*. New York: Oxford University Press, 1994.
Council of State Governments. *The Book of the States*. Lexington, KY: Council of State Governments, annual.
Crenson, Matthew A. *Neighborhood Politics*. Cambridge, MA: Harvard University Press, 1983.
Cronin, Thomas E. *Direct Democracy: The Politics of Initiative, Referendum, and Recall*. Cambridge, MA: Harvard University Press, 1999.
Dahl, Robert A. *Who Governs? Democracy and Power in an American City*. New Haven, CT: Yale University Press, 1961.
Erie, Steven P. *Rainbow's End: Irish Americans and the Dilemmas of Urban Machine Politics, 1840–1985*. Berkeley: University of California Press, 1988.
Erikson, Robert S., Gerald C. Wright, and John P. McIver. *Statehouse Democracy: Public Opinion and Policy in the American States*. Cambridge, UK: Cambridge University Press, 1993.
Gerston, Larry N., and Terry Christensen. *Recall: California's Political Earthquake*. Armonk, NY: M. E. Sharpe, 2004.
Harrigan, John J., and David C. Nice. *Politics and Policy in States and Communities*, 8th ed. New York: Longman, 2004.
International City/County Management Association. *The Municipal Year Book*. Washington, DC: ICMA, annual.
Jewell, Malcolm E., and Marcia Lynn Whicker. *Legislative Leadership in the American States*. Ann Arbor: University of Michigan Press, 1994.
Renzulli, Diane. *Capitol Offenders: How Private Interests Govern Our States*. Washington, DC: Public Integrity Books, 2000.
Stone, Clarence N. *Regime Politics: Governing Atlanta, 1946–1988*. Lawrence: University Press of Kansas, 1989.
Woliver, Laura R. *From Outrage to Action: The Politics of Grass-Roots Dissent*. Urbana: University of Illinois Press, 1993.

WEB EXPLORATIONS

To find statistics on any branch of government in the fifty states, see the Council of State Governments at
http://www.csg.org/csg/default
To learn about issues that governors nationwide deem most important, see the National Governor's Association at
http://www/ngaorg/
To learn about the policy issues being addressed in your state legislature, see the National Conference of State Legislatures at
http://ncsl.org/
To understand how campaigns are financed in state governments, see the International City/County Management Association at,
http://followthemoney.org/
To learn more about the issues currently of concern to local government, see http://www.1.icma.org/main/sc.asp?t=0
To learn more about American Indian nations and specific tribes, see the National Institute of Money In State Politics at
http://www.nativeweb.org

Photo courtesy: Bebeto Matthews/AP/Wide World Photos

Civil Liberties

ON FEBRUARY 15, 2003, more than 100,000 demonstrators gathered outside the United Nations (UN) headquarters in New York City to protest the impending U.S.-led war with Iraq. The event was attended by citizens from across the country, including a number of celebrities, from actress Susan Sarandon to activists such as Archbishop Desmond Tutu and Martin Luther King III. However, many of the anti-war demonstrators also protested the barricades that police had set up at the UN's Dag Hammarskjöld Plaza and adjacent streets, which prevented them from moving about freely.

New York City officials argued that the barricades were erected for safety and security reasons. However, protesters, backed by the New York Civil Liberties Union, claimed that the limitations infringed upon their First Amendment right to peaceably assemble. Further, citing the civil rights era march from Selma to Montgomery, Alabama, they argued that a marching protest would have had greater impact than any stationary protest.[1]

Alleged prohibitions on Americans' right to peaceably assemble were not confined to New York City. In St. Louis, students were arrested for carrying protest signs outside a designated "protest zone" at a speech given by President George W. Bush. On college campuses across the nation, students wishing to express opposition to the Iraq War were confined to "free speech zones."[2]

During the war on terrorism and Operation Iraqi Freedom, as in previous times of war, balancing civil liberties with national security has been a difficult and contentious process. President Bush, as evidenced by the USA Patriot Act and its progeny, has indicated that he believes it is necessary to suspend some civil liberties normally enjoyed by citizens. Others, including the American Civil Liberties Union and its affiliates, charge that in a time of war, the United States should be a model of civil liberties protections for the nations we fight against, many of which practice massive civil liberties abuses. The atrocities committed by some members of the U.S. military as well as U.S. contractors on Iraqi prisoners as well as those at Guantanamo Bay, Cuba serve to highlight civil liberties abuses, even though prisoners never enjoy the full range of rights guaranteed to U.S. citizens.

CHAPTER OUTLINE

- The First Constitutional Amendments: The Bill of Rights

- First Amendment Guarantees: Freedom of Religion

- First Amendment Guarantees: Freedom of Speech, Press, and Assembly

- The Second Amendment: The Right to Keep and Bear Arms

- The Rights of Criminal Defendants

- The Right to Privacy

civil liberties
The personal guarantees and freedoms that the federal government cannot abridge by law, constitution, or judicial interpretation.

civil rights
The goverment-protected rights of individuals against arbitrary or discriminatory treatment.

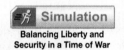

Simulation

Balancing Liberty and Security in a Time of War

WHEN THE BILL OF RIGHTS, which contains many of the most important protections of individual liberties, was written, its drafters were not thinking about issues such as abortion, gay rights, physician assisted suicide, or any of the other personal liberties discussed in this chapter. As a result, the Constitution is nonabsolute in the nature of most **civil liberties,** personal guarantees and freedoms that the government cannot abridge, either by law or by judicial interpretation. Civil liberties guarantees place limitations on the power of the government to restrain or dictate how individuals act. Thus, when we discuss civil liberties such as those found in the Bill of Rights, we are concerned with limits on what governments can and cannot do. **Civil rights,** in contrast, are the goverment-protected rights of individuals against arbitrary or discriminatory treatment. (Civil rights are discussed in chapter 6.)

Questions of civil liberties often present complex problems. As illustrated in the opening vignette, we must decide as a society how much infringement on our personal liberties we want to give the police. We must also consider if we want to have different rules for searching our homes, classrooms, lockers, dorm rooms, and cars. And, do we want to give the Federal Bureau of Investigation (FBI) the right to tap the phones of suspected terrorists or to hold them in jail without access to a lawyer without probable cause? Moreover, in an era of a war on terrorism, it is important to consider what liberties should be accorded to those suspected of terrorist activity.

Civil liberties cases often fall to the judiciary, who must balance the competing interests of the government and the people. Thus, in many of the cases discussed in this chapter, there is a conflict between an individual or group of individuals seeking to exercise what they believe to be a liberty, and the government, be it local, state, or national, seeking to control the exercise of that liberty in an attempt to keep order and preserve the rights (and safety) of others. In other cases, two liberties are in conflict, such as a physician's and her patients' rights to easy access to a medical clinic versus a pro-life advocate's liberty to picket that clinic.

In the wake of September 11, 2001, Americans' perceptions about civil liberties and what they are willing to allow the government to do experienced a sea change. The federal government was given unprecedented authority to curtail civil liberties on a scope never before seen. When any political commentators or civil libertarians voiced concerns about the USA Patriot Act and its consequences—the ability to do so being a hallmark of a free society—not only were their voices drowned out by many politicians and other pundits but their patriotism was attacked as well.

Moreover, during the 2001–2002 term of the Supreme Court of the United States, the justices were forced from their chambers for the first time since they moved into the Supreme Court building in 1935. Threats of airborne anthrax closed the Court and several Senate buildings. While the nation was worrying about terrorist attacks from abroad or from within, a quiet revolution in civil liberties continued apace. The five conservative and four moderate Supreme Court justices—who served together from 1994 through the 2004 term, longer than any other group of justices since 1820—proceeded to make major changes in long-standing practices in a wide range of civil liberties issues.[3] Similarly, the Bush administration continued to advocate new restrictions on civil liberties. Many of the Court's recent decisions, as well as actions of the Bush administration, are discussed in this chapter as we explore the various dimensions of civil liberties guarantees contained in the U.S. Constitution and the Bill of Rights.

- First, we will discuss *the Bill of Rights,* the reasons for its addition to the Constitution, and its eventual application to the states via the incorporation doctrine.
- Second, we will survey the meaning of one of *the First Amendment guarantees: freedom of religion.*

- Third, we will discuss the meanings of other *First Amendment guarantees: freedom of speech, press, and assembly.*

- Fourth, we will discuss *the second Amendment* and *the right to keep and bear arms.*

- Fifth, we will analyze the reasons for many of *the rights of criminal defendants* found in the Bill of Rights and how those rights have been expanded and contracted by the U.S. Supreme Court.

- Finally, we will discuss the meaning of *the right to privacy* and how that concept has been interpreted by the Court.

THE FIRST CONSTITUTIONAL AMENDMENTS: THE BILL OF RIGHTS

IN 1787, MOST STATE CONSTITUTIONS explicitly protected a variety of personal liberties such as speech, religion, freedom from unreasonable searches and seizures, and trial by jury, among others. It was clear that in the new federal system, the new Constitution would redistribute power between the national government and the states. Without an explicit guarantee of specific civil liberties, could the national government be trusted to uphold the freedoms already granted to citizens by their states?

As discussed in chapter 2, recognition of the increased power that would be held by the new national government led Anti-Federalists to stress the need for a bill of rights. Anti-Federalists and many others were confident that they could control the actions of their own state legislators, but they didn't trust the national government to be so protective of their civil liberties.

Photo courtesy: UPI IMAGES/Landov

■ Radio personality Howard Stern was suspended by Clear Channel Communications in February, 2004 for "vulgar, offensive, and insulting" content on his syndicated morning show. Stern and critics of the George W. Bush Administration later speculated that his suspension and subsequent firing were actually the result of his recent, anti-Bush rhetoric.

The notion of adding a bill of rights to the Constitution was not a popular one at the Constitutional Convention. When George Mason of Virginia proposed that such a bill be added to the preface of the proposed Constitution, his resolution was defeated unanimously.[4] In the subsequent ratification debates, Federalists argued that a bill of rights was unnecessary. Not only did most state constitutions already contain those protections, but Federalists believed it was foolhardy to list things that the national government had no power to do.

Some Federalists, however, supported the idea. After the Philadelphia convention, for example, James Madison conducted a lively correspondence about the need for a national bill of rights with Thomas Jefferson. Jefferson was far quicker to support such guarantees than was Madison, who continued to doubt their utility. He believed that a list of protected rights might suggest that those not enumerated were not protected. Politics soon intervened, however, when Madison found himself in a close race against James Monroe for a seat in the House of Representatives in the First Congress. The district was largely Anti-Federalist. So, in an act of political expediency, Madison issued a new series of public letters similar to *The Federalist Papers* in which he vowed to support a bill of rights.

Once elected to the House, Madison made good on his promise and became the prime author of the Bill of Rights. Still, he considered Congress to have far more important matters to handle and viewed his work on the Bill of Rights "a nauseous project."[5]

The insistence of Anti-Federalists on a bill of rights, the fact that some states conditioned their ratification of the Constitution on the addition of these guarantees, and the disagreement among Federalists about writing specific liberty guarantees into the Constitution led to prompt congressional action to put an end to further controversy. This was a time when national stability and support for the new government particularly were needed. Thus, in 1789, Congress sent the proposed Bill of Rights to the states for ratification, which occurred in 1791.

The **Bill of Rights,** the first ten amendments to the Constitution, contains numerous specific guarantees, including those of free speech, press, and religion (for the full text, see the annotated Constitution that begins on page 68). The Ninth and Tenth Amendments, in particular, highlight Anti-Federalist fears of a too-powerful national government. The **Ninth Amendment,** strongly favored by Madison, makes it clear that this special listing of rights does not mean that others don't exist. The Tenth Amendment reiterates that powers not delegated to the national government are reserved to the states or to the people.

Bill of Rights
The first ten amendments to the U.S. Constitution, which largely guarantee specific rights and liberties.

Ninth Amendment
Part of the Bill of Rights that reads "The enumeration in the Constitution, of certain rights, shall not be construed to deny or disparage others retained by the people."

due process clause
Clause contained in the Fifth and Fourteenth Amendments. Over the years, it has been construed to guarantee to individuals a variety of rights ranging from economic liberty to criminal procedural rights to protection from arbitrary governmental action.

The Incorporation Doctrine: The Bill of Rights Made Applicable to the States

The Bill of Rights was intended to limit the powers of the national government to infringe on the rights and liberties of the citizenry. In *Barron* v. *Baltimore* (1833), the Supreme Court ruled that the national Bill of Rights limited only the actions of the U.S. government and not those of the states.[6] In 1868, however, the Fourteenth Amendment was added to the U.S. Constitution. Its language suggested the possibility that some or even all of the protections guaranteed in the Bill of Rights might be interpreted to prevent state infringement of those rights. Section 1 of the Fourteenth Amendment reads: "No State shall...deprive any person of life, liberty, or property, without due process of law." Questions about the scope of "liberty" as well as the meaning of "due process of law" continue even today to engage legal scholars and jurists.

Until nearly the turn of the century, the Supreme Court steadfastly rejected numerous arguments urging it to interpret the **due process clause** found in the Fourteenth

The Living Constitution

The enumeration in the Constitution, of certain rights, shall not be construed to deny or disparage others retained by the people.

—Ninth Amendment

This amendment simply reiterates the belief of many Federalists who believed that it would be impossible to enumerate every fundamental liberty and right. To assuage the concerns of Anti-Federalists, the Ninth Amendment underscores that rights not enumerated are retained by the people.

James Madison, in particular, feared that the enumeration of so many rights and liberties in the first eight amendments to the Constitution would result in the denial of rights that were not enumerated. So, he drafted this amendment to clarify a rule about how the Constitution and Bill of Rights were to be construed.

Until 1965, the Ninth Amendment was rarely mentioned by the Court. In that year, however, it was used for the first time by the Court as a positive affirmation of a particular liberty—marital privacy. Although privacy is not mentioned in the Constitution, it was—according to the Court—one of those fundamental freedoms that the drafters of the Bill of Rights implied as retained. Since 1965, the Court has ruled in favor of a host of fundamental liberties guaranteed by the Ninth Amendment, often in combination with other specific guarantees, including the right to have an abortion.

Amendment as making various provisions contained in the Bill of Rights applicable to the states. In 1897, however, the Court began to increase its jurisdiction over the states.[7] It began to hold states to a **substantive due process** standard whereby states had the legal burden to prove that their laws were a valid exercise of their power to regulate the health, welfare, or public morals of their citizens. Interferences with state power, however, were rare. As a consequence, states continued to pass sedition laws (laws that made it illegal to speak or write any political criticism that threatened to diminish respect for the government, its laws, or public officials), anticipating that the Supreme Court would uphold their constitutionality. These expectations changed dramatically in 1925. Benjamin Gitlow, a member of the Socialist Party, was convicted of violating a New York law that prohibited the advocacy of the violent overthrow of the government. Gitlow had printed 16,000 copies of a manifesto in which he urged workers to rise up to overthrow the U.S. government. Although Gitlow's conviction was upheld, in *Gitlow* v. *New York* (1925), the Supreme Court noted that the states were not completely free to limit forms of political expression:

> For present purposes we may and do assume that freedom of speech and of the press—which are protected by the First Amendment from abridgement by Congress—are among the *fundamental personal rights and "liberties"* protected by the due process clause of the Fourteenth Amendment from impairment by the states [emphasis added].[8]

substantive due process
Judicial interpretation of the Fifth and Fourteenth Amendments' due process clause that protects citizens from arbitrary or unjust laws.

Photo courtesy: AP/Wide World Photos

■ Until *Gitlow* v. *New York* (1925), involving Benjamin Gitlow, the executive secretary of the Socialist Party, it generally was thought that the Fourteenth Amendment did not apply the protections of the Bill of Rights to the states. Here Gitlow, right, is shown testifying before a congressional committee, which was investigating un-American activities.

Gitlow, with its finding that states could not abridge free speech protections, was the first step in the slow development of what is called the **incorporation doctrine.** After *Gitlow*, it took the Court six more years to incorporate another First Amendment freedom—that of the press. *Near* v. *Minnesota* (1931) was the first case in which the Supreme Court found that a state law violated freedom of the press as protected by the First Amendment. Jay Near, the publisher of a weekly Minneapolis newspaper, regularly attacked a variety of groups—African Americans, Catholics, Jews, and labor union leaders. Few escaped his hatred. Near's paper was shut down under the authority of a state criminal libel law banning "malicious, scandalous, or defamatory" publications. Near appealed the closing of his paper, and the Supreme Court ruled that "The fact that the liberty of the press may be abused by miscreant purveyors of scandal does not make any the less necessary the immunity of the press from previous restraint."[9]

incorporation doctrine
An interpretation of the Constitution that holds that the due process clause of the Fourteenth Amendment requires that state and local governments also guarantee those rights.

selective incorporation
A judicial doctrine whereby most but not all of the protections found in the Bill of Rights are made applicable to the states via the Fourteenth Amendment.

fundamental freedoms
Those rights defined by the Court to be essential to order, liberty, and justice.

Selective Incorporation and Fundamental Freedoms

Not all the specific guarantees in the Bill of Rights have been made applicable to the states through the due process clause of the Fourteenth Amendment, as revealed in Table 5.1. Instead, the Court has used the process of **selective incorporation** to limit the rights of states by protecting against abridgement of **fundamental freedoms,** those liberties defined by the Court as essential to order, liberty, and justice. Fundamental freedoms are subject to the Court's most rigorous strict scrutiny review.

Selective incorporation requires the states to respect freedoms of press, speech, and assembly, among other rights. Other guarantees contained in the Second, Third, and Seventh Amendments, such as the right to bear arms, have not been incorporated because the Court has yet to consider them sufficiently fundamental to national notions of liberty and justice.

The rationale for selective incorporation was set out by the Court in *Palko* v. *Connecticut* (1937).[10] Frank Palko was charged with first-degree murder for killing two Connecticut police officers, found guilty of a lesser charge of second-degree murder, and sentenced to life imprisonment. Connecticut appealed. Palko was retried, found guilty of first-degree murder, and sentenced to death. Palko then appealed his second conviction, arguing that it violated the Fifth Amendment's prohibition against double jeopardy because the Fifth Amendment had been made applicable to the states by the due process clause of the Fourteenth Amendment.

The Supreme Court upheld Palko's second conviction and the death sentence. They also chose not to bind states to the Fifth Amendment's double jeopardy clause and concluded that protection from being tried twice (double jeopardy) was not a fundamental freedom. Palko died in Connecticut's gas chamber one year later.

TABLE 5.1 The Selective Incorporation of the Bill of Rights

Amendment	Right	Date	Case Incorporated
I	Speech	1925	*Gitlow* v. *New York*
	Press	1931	*Near* v. *Minnesota*
	Assembly	1937	*DeJonge* v. *Oregon*
	Religion	1940	*Cantwell* v. *Connecticut*
II	Bear arms		Not incorporated (A test has not been presented to the Court in recent history.)
III	No quartering of soldiers		Not incorporated (The quartering problem has not recurred since colonial times.)
IV	No unreasonable searches or seizures	1949	*Wolf* v. *Colorado*
	Exclusionary rule	1961	*Mapp* v. *Ohio*
V	Just compensation	1897	*Chicago, B&C RR Co.* v. *Chicago*
	Self-incrimination	1964	*Malloy* v. *Hogan*
	Double jeopardy	1969	*Benton* v. *Maryland* (overruled *Palko* v. *Connecticut*)
	Grand jury indictment		Not incorporated (The trend in state criminal cases is away from grand juries.)
VI	Public trial	1948	*In re Oliver*
	Right to counsel	1963	*Gideon* v. *Wainwright*
	Confrontation	1965	*Pointer* v. *Texas*
	Impartial trial	1966	*Parker* v. *Gladden*
	Speedy trial	1967	*Klopfer* v. *North Carolina*
	Compulsory trial	1967	*Washington* v. *Texas*
	Criminal jury trial	1968	*Duncan* v. *Louisiana*
VII	Civil jury trial		Not incorporated (Chief Justice Warren Burger wanted to abolish these trials.)
VIII	No cruel and unusual punishment	1962	*Robinson* v. *California*
	No excessive fines or bail		Not incorporated

FIRST AMENDMENT GUARANTEES: FREEDOM OF RELIGION

MANY OF THE FRAMERS were religious men, but they knew what evils could arise if the new nation was not founded with religious freedom as one of its core ideals. Although many colonists had fled Europe to escape religious persecution, most colonies actively persecuted those who did not belong to their predominant religious groups. Nevertheless, in 1774, the colonists uniformly were outraged when the British Parliament passed a law establishing Anglicanism and Roman Catholicism as official religions in the colonies. The First Continental Congress immediately sent a letter of protest announcing its "astonishment that a British Parliament should ever consent to establish . . . a religion [Catholicism] that has deluged [England] in blood and dispersed bigotry, persecution, murder and rebellion through every part of the world."[11]

The Framers' distaste for a national church or religion was reflected in the Constitution. Article VI, for example, provides that "no religious Test shall ever be required as a Qualification to any Office or Public Trust under the United States." This simple statement, however, did not completely reassure those who feared the new Constitution

First Amendment

Part of the Bill of Rights that imposes a number of restrictions on the federal government with respect to the civil liberties of the people, including freedom of religion, speech, press, assembly, and petition.

establishment clause

The first clause in the First Amendment; it prohibits the national government from establishing a national religion.

free exercise clause

The second clause of the First Amendment; it prohibits the U.S. government from interfering with a citizen's right to practice his or her religion.

would curtail individual liberty. Thus, the First Amendment to the Constitution soon was ratified to allay those fears.

The **First Amendment** to the Constitution begins, "Congress shall make no law respecting an establishment of religion, or prohibiting the free exercise thereof." This statement sets the boundaries of governmental action. The **establishment clause** ("Congress shall make no law respecting an establishment of religion") directs the national government not to involve itself in religion. It creates, in Thomas Jefferson's words, a "wall of separation" between church and state. The **free exercise clause** ("or prohibiting the free exercise thereof") guarantees citizens that the national government will not interfere with their practice of religion. These guarantees, however, are not absolute. In the mid-1800s, Mormons traditionally practiced and preached polygamy, the taking of multiple wives. In 1879, when the Supreme Court was first called on to interpret the free exercise clause, it upheld the conviction of a Mormon under a federal law barring polygamy. The Court reasoned that to do otherwise would provide constitutional protections to a full range of religious beliefs, including those as extreme as human sacrifice. "Laws are made for the government of actions," noted the Court, "and while they cannot interfere with mere religious belief and opinions, they may with practices."[12] Later, in 1940, the Supreme Court observed that the First Amendment "embraces two concepts—freedom to believe and freedom to act. The first is absolute, but in the nature of things, the second cannot be. Conduct remains subject to regulation of society."[13]

The Establishment Clause

Over the years, the Court has been divided over how to interpret the establishment clause. Does this clause erect a total wall between church and state, or is some governmental accommodation of religion allowed? While the Supreme Court has upheld the constitutionality of many kinds of church/state entanglements such as public funding to provide sign language interpreters for deaf students in religious schools,[14] the Court has held fast to the rule of strict separation between church and state when issues of prayer in school are involved. In *Engel* v. *Vitale* (1962), the Court first ruled that the recitation in public school classrooms of a twenty-two-word nondenominational prayer drafted by the New Hyde Park, New York, school board was unconstitutional.[15] In 1992, the Court continued its unwillingness to allow organized prayer in public schools by finding unconstitutional the saying of prayer at a middle school graduation.[16] In 2000, the Court ruled that student-led, student-initiated prayer at high school football games violated the establishment clause. But, in 2001, it refused to hear a challenge to a Virginia law that requires students to observe a moment of silence at the start of each school day.[17]

Similarly, in 2004, the Court refused to decide whether the recitation of the pledge of allegiance in a public school classroom was unconstitutional. In that case, it ruled that a noncustodial father lacked the necessary standing to advance the claim that the pledge's phrase "under God" advanced religion.[18]

The Court has gone back and forth in its effort to come up with a workable way to deal with church/state questions. In 1971, in *Lemon* v. *Kurtzman,* the Court tried to carve out a three-part test for laws dealing with religious establishment issues. According to the *Lemon* test, a practice or policy was constitutional if it: (1) had a secular purpose; (2) neither advanced nor inhibited religion; and, (3) did not foster an excessive government entanglement with religion.[19] But, since the early 1980s, the Supreme Court often has sidestepped the *Lemon* test altogether, and has appeared more willing to lower the wall between church and state so long as school prayer is not involved.[20] In 1981, for example, the Court ruled unconstitutional a Missouri law prohibiting the use of state university buildings and grounds for "purposes of religious worship." The law had been used to ban religious groups from using school facilities.[21]

This decision was taken by many members of Congress as a sign that this principle could be extended to secondary and even primary schools. In 1984, Congress passed

THE AMERICAN CIVIL LIBERTIES UNION

THE AMERICAN CIVIL LIBERTIES UNION (ACLU) was created in 1920 by a group that had tried to defend the civil liberties of those who were conscientious objectors to World War I. As the nation's oldest, largest, and premier nonpartisan civil liberties organization, the ACLU works in three major areas of the law: freedom of speech and religion, due process, and equality before the law. It lobbies for legislation affecting these areas and litigates to maintain these rights and liberties.

Over time, the national ACLU or one of its state affiliates (as was the case in our opening vignette) has been involved in one way or another in almost every major civil liberties case discussed in this chapter. It was at the fore of the sedition cases brought in the wake of World War I and was involved in the famous *Scopes* case in 1925, which challenged a Tennessee law that made it a crime to teach evolution. It has represented flag burners, Nazis, and skinheads in its zealous and often unpopular defense of the Bill of Rights.

In addition to filing lawsuits challenging governmental actions that it believes do not uphold the many protections contained in the Bill of Rights, the ACLU also lobbies vigorously at the national and state levels against legislation it believes could negatively restrict civil liberties. In 2003, for example, the ACLU urged state and local governments to pass resolutions designed to prevent citizens from being subject to some of the most controversial provisions of the USA Patriot Act. Portions of that act, including those authorizing racial and ethnic profiling and unauthorized access to Americans' public records, were called "repressive" by the ACLU.[a] The group urged state and local governments to enact provisions invalidating the act. To date, over 295 municipalities and counties, including Seattle, San Francisco, Detroit, and Denver, have adopted resolutions.[b] Alaska, Hawaii, Vermont, and Maine also have enacted a variety of statewide laws.

---

[a] "A Fight for Freedoms," *San Francisco Chronicle* (December 17, 2002): A24.

[b] Michelle K. Massie, "Pittsburgh City Council to Vote on Patriot Act Resolution," *Pittsburgh Post Gazette* (April 25, 2004): C3.

---

the Equal Access Act, which bars public schools from discriminating against groups of students on the basis of "religious, political, philosophical or other content of the speech at such meetings." The constitutionality of this law was upheld in 1990 when the Court ruled that a school board's refusal to allow a Christian Bible club to meet in a public high school classroom during a twice-weekly "activity period" violated the act. According to the decision, the primary effect of the act was neither to advance religion nor to excessively entangle government and religion—even though religious meetings would be held on school grounds with a faculty sponsor. The important factor seemed to be that the students had free choice in their selection of activities, including numerous nonreligious options from which to choose.[22] In 1993, the Court also ruled that religious groups must be allowed to use public schools after hours if that access is also given to other community groups.[23]

In 1995, the Court signaled that it was willing to lower the wall even further. In a case involving the University of Virginia, a 5–4 majority held that the university violated the free speech rights of a fundamentalist Christian group when it refused to fund the groups' student magazine. The importance of this decision was highlighted by Justice David Souter, who noted in dissent: "The Court today, for the first time, approves direct funding of core religious activities by an arm of the state."[24] And, it continues to do so. In 1997, in *Agostini* v. *Felton*, the Supreme Court approved of a New York program that sent public school teachers into parochial schools during school hours to provide remedial education to disadvantaged students. The Court concluded that this was not an excessive entanglement of church and state and therefore was not a violation of the establishment clause.[25]

For more than a quarter century, the Supreme Court basically allowed "books only" as an aid to religious schools, noting that the books go to children, not to the schools themselves. In 2000, however, the Court voted 6–3 to uphold the constitutionality of a federal aid provision that allowed the government to lend books and computers to religious schools.[26] And, in 2002, by a bitterly divided 5–4 vote, the Supreme Court in *Zelman* v. *Simmons-Harris* concluded that governments can give money to parents to allow them to send their children to private or religious schools.[27] The majority opinion, written by Chief Justice William H. Rehnquist, concluded that Cleveland's school voucher program gives families freedom of choice to send their children to the school of their choice. He concluded that the voucher system was neutral toward religion and, thus, was not an official sponsorship of religion prohibited by the establishment clause. In dissent, Justice David Souter called the opinion a "potentially tragic" error that "would force citizens to subsidize faiths they do not even share even as it corrupts religion by making it dependent on government."[28] Basically, building on a line of cases that many argue further erode the wall between church and state, the Court now appears willing to support programs so long as they provide aid to religious and nonreligious schools alike, and the money goes to persons who exercise free choice over how it is used.

The Free Exercise Clause

The free exercise clause of the First Amendment proclaims that "Congress shall make no law . . . prohibiting the free exercise [of religion]." Although the free exercise clause of the First Amendment guarantees individuals the right to be free from governmental interference in the exercise of their religion, this guarantee, like other First Amendment freedoms, is not absolute. When secular law comes into conflict with religious law, the right to exercise one's religious beliefs is often denied—especially if the religious beliefs in question are held by a minority or by an unpopular or "suspicious" religious group. State statutes barring the use of certain illegal drugs, snake handling, and polygamy—all practices of particular religious sects—have been upheld as constitutional when states have shown compelling reasons to regulate these practices. Nonetheless, the Court has made it clear that the free exercise clause requires that a state or the national government remain neutral toward religion.

Many critics of rigid enforcement of such neutrality argue that the government should do what it can to accommodate the religious diversity in our nation. Nevertheless, the Court has interpreted the Constitution to mean that governmental interests can outweigh free exercise rights. In 1990, for example, the Supreme Court ruled that the free exercise clause allowed Oregon to ban the use of sacramental peyote (an illegal hallucinogenic drug) in some Native American tribes' traditional religious services. The focus of the case turned on what standard of review the Court should use. Should the Court use the compelling state interest test? In upholding the state's right to deny unemployment compensation to two workers who had been fired by a private drug rehabilitation clinic because they had ingested an illegal substance, a majority of the Court held that the state did not need to show a compelling interest to limit the free exercise of religion.[29] This decision prompted a dramatic outcry. Congressional response was passage of the Religious Freedom Restoration Act, which reinstated strict scrutiny, requiring states to show a compelling rationale for their activities as the required judicial standard of review. The act would make it harder for states to interfere with how citizens practice their religion. In 1997, however, the Supreme Court ruled that the act was unconstitutional.[30]

In contrast, in 1993, the Supreme Court ruled that members of the Santería Church, an Afro-Cuban religion, had the right to sacrifice animals during religious services. In upholding that practice, the Court ruled that a city ordinance banning such practices was unconstitutionally aimed at the group, thereby denying its members the right to free exercise of their religion.[31]

Although conflicts between religious beliefs and the government are often difficult to settle, the Court has attempted to walk the fine line between the free exercise and establishment clauses. In the area of free exercise, the Court often has had to confront questions of "What is a god?" and "What is a religious faith?"—questions that theologians have grappled with for centuries. In 1965, for example, in a case involving three

■ Rev. Daniel Coughlin, the current House chaplain, is shown here. The chaplain is a powerful reminder that, despite the concerns of some Americans, religion and religious traditions permeate the government. The responsibilities of the House and Senate chaplains include delivering the morning invocation, providing spiritual counsel for members and their families, and holding Bible study groups.

men who were denied conscientious objector deferments during the Vietnam War because they did not subscribe to "traditional" organized religions, the Court ruled unanimously that belief in a supreme being was not essential for recognition as a conscientious objector.[32] Thus, the men were entitled to the deferments because their views paralleled those who objected to war and who belonged to traditional religions. In contrast, despite the Court's having ruled that Catholic, Protestant, Jewish, and Buddhist prison inmates must be allowed to hold religious services,[33] the Court ruled that Islamic prisoners can be denied the same right for security reasons.[34]

FIRST AMENDMENT GUARANTEES: FREEDOM OF SPEECH, PRESS, AND ASSEMBLY

TODAY, SOME MEMBERS OF CONGRESS criticize the movie industry and reality television shows including *Survivor* and *The Bachelor* for pandering to the least common denominator of society. Other groups criticize popular performers such as Eminem for lyrics that promote violence in general, and against women in particular. Janet Jackson's "wardrobe malfunction" as well as Kid Rock's antics at the 2004 Super Bowl, however, launched renewed calls for increased restrictions, the imposition of significant fines on broadcasters, and greater regulation of the airwaves. Today, many civil libertarians believe that the rights to speak, print, and assemble freely are being seriously threatened.[35] (For more details on content regulation, see chapter 15.)

Freedom of Speech and the Press

A democracy depends on a free exchange of ideas, and the First Amendment shows that the Framers were well aware of this fact. Historically, one of the most volatile areas

Comparative
Comparing Civil
Liberties

prior restraint
Constitutional doctrine that prevents the government from prohibiting speech or publication before the fact; generally held to be in violation of the First Amendment.

Timeline
Civil Liberties and
National Security

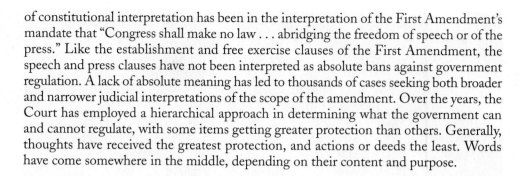

of constitutional interpretation has been in the interpretation of the First Amendment's mandate that "Congress shall make no law . . . abridging the freedom of speech or of the press." Like the establishment and free exercise clauses of the First Amendment, the speech and press clauses have not been interpreted as absolute bans against government regulation. A lack of absolute meaning has led to thousands of cases seeking both broader and narrower judicial interpretations of the scope of the amendment. Over the years, the Court has employed a hierarchical approach in determining what the government can and cannot regulate, with some items getting greater protection than others. Generally, thoughts have received the greatest protection, and actions or deeds the least. Words have come somewhere in the middle, depending on their content and purpose.

The Alien and Sedition Acts.   When the First Amendment was ratified in 1791, it was considered only to protect against **prior restraint** of speech or expression, or to guard against the prohibition of speech or publication before the fact. However, in 1798, the Federalist Congress enacted the Alien and Sedition Acts, which were designed to ban any criticism of the Federalist government by the growing numbers of Democratic-Republicans. These acts made the publication of "any false, scandalous writing against the government of the United States" a criminal offense. Although the law clearly ran in the face of the First Amendment's ban on prior restraint, partisan Federalist judges imposed fines and jail terms on at least ten Democratic-Republican newspaper editors. The acts became a major issue in the 1800 presidential election campaign, which led to the election of Thomas Jefferson, a vocal opponent of the acts. He quickly pardoned all who had been convicted under their provisions and the Democratic-Republican Congress allowed the acts to expire before the Federalist-controlled Supreme Court had an opportunity to rule on the constitutionality of these serious infringements of the First Amendment.

Slavery, the Civil War, and Rights Curtailments.   After the public outcry over the Alien and Sedition Acts, the national government largely got out of the business of regulating speech. But, in its place, the states, which were not yet bound by the Bill of Rights, began to prosecute those who published articles critical of governmental policies. In the 1830s, at the urgings of abolitionists (those who sought an end to slavery), the publication or dissemination of any positive information about slavery became a punishable offense in the North. In the opposite vein, in the South, supporters of slavery enacted laws to prohibit publication of any anti-slavery sentiments. Southern postmasters refused to deliver northern abolitionist papers, a step that amounted to censorship of the mail.

During the Civil War, President Abraham Lincoln effectively suspended the free press provision of the First Amendment (as well as many other sections of the Constitution). He went so far as to order the arrest of the editors of two New York papers who were critical of him. Far from protesting against these blatant violations of the First Amendment, Congress acceded to them. In one instance, William McCardle, a Mississippi newspaper editor who had written in opposition to Lincoln and the Union occupation, was jailed by a military court without having any charges brought against him. He appealed his detainment to the U.S. Supreme Court, arguing that he was being held unlawfully. Congress, fearing that a victory for McCardle would hurt Lincoln's national standing and prompt other similarly treated Confederate editors to follow his lead, enacted legislation prohibiting the Supreme Court from issuing a judgment in any cases involving convictions for publishing statements critical of the United States. Because Article II of the Constitution gives Congress the power to determine the jurisdiction of the Court, the Court was forced to conclude in *Ex parte McCardle* (1869) that it had no authority to rule in the matter.[36]

After the Civil War, states also began to prosecute individuals for seditious speech if they uttered or printed statements critical of the government. Between 1890 and 1900, for example, there were more than one hundred state prosecutions for sedition.[37]

FREEDOM OF THE PRESS (BY REGION)

Americans are quite correctly proud of the independent voice exercised by the U.S. press. But, how do press freedoms in the United States compare with those found in other countries? And, just how free is the American press? Global comparisons can be made along three dimensions. First is the legal environment: what rules and regulations govern media content? Second is the political environment: how much political control is exercised over the content of the news media? Third is the economic environment: who owns the media and how are media outlets financed?

Using these three factors, Freedom House, a nonprofit organization that serves as a watchdog on the relationship between the media and government, issues a report each year on the degree of print, broadcast, and Internet freedom in every country in the world. In 2003, it concluded that the United States was tied for 15th place, along with Monaco and Andorra. Denmark, Iceland, and Sweden were tied for 1st. Closer to home, Canada tied for 23rd place and Mexico for 80th. This ranking placed Canada in the free category, which indicates no significant restrictions on the press, and Mexico in the partly free category, which means some media restrictions exist.

Other countries in the partly free category included Bolivia, where government and opposition supporters threatened and physically harassed journalists, and Romania, where the government engaged in legal harassment of independent media outlets. Russia, tied for 147th, was judged not to have a free press. The government had nearly complete control of the broadcast media—it passed laws and used financial pressure to restrict critical coverage of its policies. These restrictions were particularly true with respect to its handling of the long and bloody war in the break-away province of Chechnya, which has been described as Russia's Vietnam. Morocco was also judged to be not free because of its use of anti-terrorism legislation to limit and punish speech offenses. Iraq continued to be labeled as not having a free press even after the fall of Saddam Hussein due to the widespread violence in the country that claimed the lives of several journalists and the imposition of ambiguous rules governing the media. It tied for 142nd place.

The five countries with the least free press were Libya, Myanmar (Burma), Turkmenistan, Cuba, and North Korea (which came in last, at 193rd). Overall, 73 countries (38 percent) were judged to have a free press, 49 had a partly free

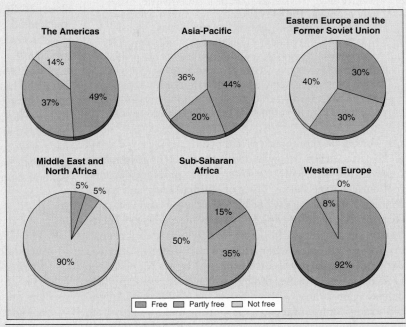

Source: Freedom House, "Global Press Freedoms Deteriorate," and "Freedom of the Press 2003: Table of Global Press Freedom Rankings," both at www.freedomhouse.org/media.

press (25 percent), and 71 (37 percent) did not have a free press. If the populations of the countries in these three categories were combined, we would find that in 2003, only 17 percent of the world's population enjoyed a free press. As the charts above indicate, there was considerable variation among different parts of the world. Only in West Europe do more than 50 percent of the countries have a free press. The Americas (North and South America) just miss reaching this level. Asia-Pacific (those countries in Asia that are in the Pacific Ocean or border it) has the next highest percentage of countries with a free press.

In general, 2003 was not a particularly good year for freedom of the press. Ten states went down in their ranking and only two—Sierra Leone and Kenya—showed improvement, moving from not free to partly free. As a result of these shifts, 5 percent fewer people enjoyed a free press and 5 percent more lived in countries with no free press at all.

Questions

1. What factors would you look at in judging whether a country had a free press?
2. Are economic, political, or cultural factors most important in making the press free?

THE USA PATRIOT ACT

OVERVIEW: The Declaration of Independence forcefully espouses the principles that all individuals have "certain unalienable rights, that among these are Life, Liberty and the pursuit of Happiness," and that it is government's purpose to guarantee the secure enjoyment of these rights. To assure these liberties, government must necessarily use legitimate police force to ensure safety within its borders, and it must use military force to defend the state from outside aggression.

A considerable problem for democratic peoples in free and open societies is how to define the limits of government intervention in the private sphere. This problem becomes particularly acute during times of national crisis and armed conflict. Establishing the line between the government's constitutional duty to "provide for the common defence" and to "secure the blessings of liberty" is complicated. It becomes even more complex when those who threaten America's national security use the freedom and rights found in the United States as a means through which to wage war. To help defend against those wishing to use the openness of American society for harmful ends, the Uniting and Strengthening America by Providing Appropriate Tools Required to Intercept and Obstruct Terrorism Act of 2001, otherwise known as the USA Patriot Act, was signed into law on October 26, 2001, in response to the terrorist attacks on New York City and the Pentagon on September 11, 2001.

The events of 9/11 have thrust the question concerning the balance between liberty and security to the forefront of national discussion, and questions abound regarding the wisdom or folly of the USA Patriot Act. Will the act help defend the United States against terrorist activity, or will it allow the government to abuse its power in the name of national security? Isn't it necessary that government narrow the scope of civil rights and liberties in times of national distress, as has been the case throughout most of American history—for example, when Abraham Lincoln suspended habeas corpus in his effort to preserve the United States? Or, conversely, hasn't American history also demonstrated that injustices have been committed in the name of national security—for example, the U.S. government's internment of Japanese American citizens during World War II?

Arguments for the USA Patriot Act

- **The USA Patriot Act allows the government to use new technologies to address new threats.** Those engaged in terrorist activities today use sophisticated technologies. The USA Patriot Act allows the government to wage the war on terrorism by using the same and superior technologies to find and prosecute those engaged in terrorism and to help reduce the threat of terrorist attacks.
- **The USA Patriot Act dismantles the wall of legal and regulatory policies erected to limit sharply the sharing of information between intelligence, national security, and law enforcement communities.** Prior policy essentially prohibited various government agencies from communicating and coordinating domestic and national

clear and present danger test
Test articulated by the Supreme Court in *Schenck* v. *U.S.* (1919) to draw the line between protected and unprotected speech; the Court looks to see "whether the words used" could "create a clear and present danger that they will bring about substantive evils" that Congress seeks "to prevent."

Moreover, by the dawn of the twentieth century, public opinion in the United States had grown increasingly hostile toward the commentary of Socialists and Communists who attempted to appeal to the growing immigrant population. Groups espousing socialism and communism became the targets of state laws curtailing speech and the written word. By the end of World War I, over thirty states had passed laws to punish seditious speech, and more than 1,900 individuals and over one hundred newspapers were prosecuted for violations.[38] In 1925, however, states' authority to regulate speech was severely restricted by the Court's decision in *Gitlow* v. *New York*. (For more on *Gitlow*, see p. 161.)

World War I and Anti-Governmental Speech. The next major national efforts to restrict freedom of speech and the press did not occur until Congress passed the Espionage Act in 1917. Nearly 2,000 Americans were convicted of violating its various provisions, especially those that made it illegal to urge resistance to the draft or to prohibit the distribution of anti-war leaflets. In *Schenck* v. *U.S.* (1919), the Supreme Court upheld this act, ruling that Congress had a right to restrict speech "of such a nature as to create a clear and present danger that will bring about the substantive evils that Congress has a right to prevent."[39] Under this test, known as the **clear and present danger test,** the circumstances surrounding an incident are important. Under *Schenck*, anti-war leaflets, for example, may be permissible during peacetime, but during World War I they were considered to pose too much of a danger to be permissible.

security activities, thus restricting the flow of valuable information that could prevent terrorist attacks. Now, government agencies can coordinate surveillance activities across domestic and national security policy domains.

- **The USA Patriot Act allows government agencies to use the procedures and tools already available to investigate organized and drug crime.** The USA Patriot Act uses techniques already approved by the courts in investigating such crimes as wire fraud, money laundering, and drug trafficking. These techniques include roving wire taps and judicially approved search warrants, notice of which may be delayed in certain narrow circumstances.

Arguments Against the USA Patriot Act

- **Certain provisions of the USA Patriot Act may violate an individual's right to privacy.** For example, section 216 allows law enforcement officials to get a warrant to track which Web sites a person visits and to collect certain information in regard to an individual's e-mail activity. There need not be any suspicion of criminal activity—all law enforcement authorities need do is to certify that the potential information is relevant to an ongoing criminal investigation.
- **The USA Patriot Act violates the civil rights and liberties of legal immigrants.** The act permits the indefinite detention of immigrants and other noncitizens. The Attorney General may detain immigrants merely upon "reasonable grounds" that one is involved in terrorism or engaged in activity that poses a danger to national security, and this detention may be indefinite

until determination is made that such an individual threatens national security.

- **Safeguards to prevent direct government surveillance of citizens have been reduced.** The Patriot Act repeals certain precautions in regard to the sharing of information between domestic law enforcement agencies and the intelligence community. These safeguards were put in place during the Cold War after the revelation that the Central Intelligence Agency (CIA) and the Federal Bureau of Investigation (FBI) had been conducting joint investigations on American citizens during the McCarthy era and civil rights movement—including surveillance of Martin Luther King Jr.—for political purposes.

Questions

1. Does the USA Patriot Act balance liberty with security? If so, how does it strike that balance? If not, what do you think could be done to redress the imbalance?
2. Is the USA Patriot Act a necessary law? If so, what, in your view, can be done to rectify its flaws? If not, what should be done to ensure the security of the United States against terrorist activity?

Selected Readings

Nat Hentoff. *The War on the Bill of Rights—and the Gathering Resistance.* Seven Stories Press, 2003.

Stephen M. Duncan. *War of a Different Kind: Military Force and America's Search for Homeland Security.* Annapolis, MD: United States Naval Institute, 2004.

For decades, the Supreme Court wrestled with what constituted a danger. Finally, in *Brandenburg* v. *Ohio* (1969), the Court fashioned a new test for deciding whether certain kinds of speech could be regulated by the government: the **direct incitement test.** Now, the government could punish the advocacy of illegal action only if "such advocacy is directed to inciting or producing imminent lawless action and is likely to incite or produce such action."[40] The requirement of "imminent lawless action" makes it more difficult for the government to punish speech and publication and is consistent with the Framers' notion of the special role played by these elements in a democratic society.

direct incitement test
A test articulated by the Supreme Court in *Brandenburg* v. *Ohio* (1969) that holds that advocacy of illegal action is protected by the First Amendment unless imminent lawless action is intended and likely to occur.

Protected Speech and Publications

As discussed, the Supreme Court refuses to uphold the constitutionality of legislation that amounts to prior restraint of the press. Other types of speech and publication are also protected by the Court, including symbolic speech and hate speech.

Prior Restraint.   With only a few exceptions, the Court has made it clear that it will not tolerate prior restraint of speech. For example, in *New York Times Co.* v. *Sullivan* (1971) (also called the Pentagon Papers case), the Supreme Court ruled that the U.S. government could not block the publication of secret Department of Defense documents illegally furnished to the *Times* by anti-war activists.[41] In 1976, the Supreme

Court went even further, noting in *Nebraska Press Association* v. *Stuart* (1976) that any attempt by the government to prevent expression carried "'a heavy presumption' against its constitutionality."[42] In this case, a trial court issued a gag order barring the press from reporting the lurid details of a crime. In balancing the defendant's constitutional right to a fair trial against the press's right to cover a story, the Nebraska trial judge concluded that the defendant's right carried greater weight. The Supreme Court disagreed, holding the press's right to cover the trial paramount. Still, judges are often allowed to issue gag orders affecting parties to a lawsuit or to limit press coverage of a case.

Symbolic Speech.   In addition to the general protection accorded to pure speech, the Supreme Court has extended the reach of the First Amendment to **symbolic speech,** a means of expression that includes symbols or signs. In the words of Justice John Marshall Harlan, these kinds of speech are part of the "free trade in ideas."[43] For more on symbolic speech, see On Campus: Political Speech and Mandatory Student Fees.

symbolic speech
Symbols, signs, and other methods of expression generally also considered to be protected by the First Amendment.

The Supreme Court first acknowledged that symbolic speech was entitled to First Amendment protection in *Stromberg* v. *California* (1931).[44] There, the Court overturned a communist youth camp director's conviction under a state statute prohibiting the display of a red flag, a symbol of opposition to the U.S. government. In a similar vein, the right of high school students to wear black armbands to protest the Vietnam War was upheld in *Tinker* v. *Des Moines Independent Community School District* (1969).[45]

Burning the American flag also has been held a form of protected symbolic speech. In 1989, a sharply divided Supreme Court (5–4) reversed the conviction of Gregory Johnson, who had been found guilty of setting fire to an American flag during the 1984 Republican National Convention in Dallas.[46] There was a major public outcry against the Court. President George Bush and numerous members of Congress called for a constitutional amendment banning flag burning. Others, including Justice William J. Brennan Jr., noted that if it had not been for acts similar to Johnson's, the United States would never have been created nor would a First Amendment guaranteeing the right of political protest exist.

Unable to pass a constitutional amendment, Congress passed the Federal Flag Protection Act of 1989, which authorized federal prosecution of anyone who intentionally desecrated a national flag. Johnson and his colleagues burned another flag and were again convicted. Their conviction was overturned by a 5–4 vote of the Supreme Court. The majority concluded that this federal law "suffered from the same fundamental flaw" as had the earlier Texas state law.[47] Since that decision, Congress has tried several times unsuccessfully to pass a constitutional amendment to ban flag burning.

Hate Speech, Unpopular Speech, and Speech Zones.   "As a thumbnail summary of the last two or three decades of speech issues in the Supreme Court," wrote eminent First Amendment scholar Harry Kalven Jr. in 1966, "we may come to see the Negro as winning back for us the freedoms the Communists seemed to have lost for us."[48] Still, says noted African American scholar Henry Louis Gates Jr., Kalven would be shocked to see the stance that some blacks now take toward the First Amendment, which once protected protests, rallies, and agitation in the 1960s: "The byword among many black activists and black intellectuals is no longer the political imperative to protect free speech; it is the moral imperative to suppress 'hate speech.'"[49]

In the 1990s, a particularly thorny First Amendment area emerged as cities and universities attempted to prohibit what they viewed as offensive hate speech. In *R.A.V.* v. *City of St. Paul* (1992), a St. Paul, Minnesota, ordinance that made it a crime to engage in speech or action

Photo courtesy: Dana Summers/© Tribune Media Services, Inc. All rights reserved. Reprinted with permission.

Political Speech and Mandatory Student Fees

In March 2000, the U.S. Supreme Court ruled unanimously in *Board of Regents* v. *Southworth* that public universities could charge students a mandatory activity fee that could be used to facilitate extracurricular student political speech as long as the programs are neutral in their application.[a]

Scott Southworth, while a law student at the University of Wisconsin, believed that the university's mandatory fee was a violation of his First Amendment right to free speech. He, along with several other law students, objected that their fees went to fund liberal groups. They particularly objected to the support of eighteen of the 125 various groups on campus that benefited from the mandatory activity fee, including the Lesbian, Gay, Bisexual, and Transgender Center, the International Socialist Organization, and the campus women's center.[b]

In ruling against Southworth and for the university, the Court underscored the importance of universities being a forum for the free exchange of political and ideological ideas and perspectives. The *Southworth* case performed that function on the Wisconsin campus even before it was argued before the Supreme Court. A student-led effort called the Southworth Project, for which over a dozen law and journalism students each earned two credits, was begun to make sure that the case was reported on campus in an accurate and sophisticated way. The Southworth Project, said a political science professor, gave "a tremendous boost to the visibility and the thinking process about the case."[c] In essence, the case made the Constitution and what it means come alive on the Wisconsin campus as students pondered

Photo courtesy: Tim Dillon © USA Today. Reprinted with permission.

Colleen Jungbluth, front, and other Wisconsin students as they awaited a ruling on their First Amendment lawsuit.

the effects of First Amendment protections on their ability to learn in a university atmosphere.

[a] *Board of Regents* v. *Southworth*, 529 U.S. 217 (2000).

[b] "U.S. Court Upholds Student Fees Going to Controversial Groups," *Toronto Star* (March 23, 2000): NEXIS.

[c] Mary Beth Marklein, "Fee Fight Proves a Learning Experience," *USA Today* (November 30, 1999): 8D.

likely to arouse "anger," "alarm," or "resentment" on the basis of race, color, creed, religion, or gender was at issue. The Court ruled 5–4 that a white teenager who burned a cross on a black family's front lawn, thereby committing a hate crime under the ordinance, could not be charged under that law because the First Amendment prevents governments from "silencing speech on the basis of its content."[50] In 2003, the Court narrowed this definition, ruling that state governments could constitutionally restrict cross burning when it occurred with the intent of racial intimidation.[51]

Two-thirds of colleges and universities have banned a variety of forms of speech or conduct that creates or fosters an intimidating, hostile, or offensive environment on campus. To prevent disruption of university activities, some universities have also created free speech zones that restrict the time, place, or manner of speech. Critics, including the ACLU, charge that free speech zones imply that speech can be limited on other parts of the campus, which they see as a violation of the First Amendment. They have filed a number of suits in district court, but to date none of these cases has reached the Supreme Court.

Unprotected Speech and Publications

Although the Supreme Court has allowed few governmental bans on most types of speech, some forms of expression are not protected. In 1942, the Supreme Court set out the rationale by which it would distinguish between protected and unprotected speech. According to the Court, libel, fighting words, obscenity, and lewdness are not protected by the First

173

Amendment because "such expressions are no essential part of any exposition of ideals, and are of such slight social value as a step to truth that any benefit that may be derived from them is clearly outweighed by the social interest in order and morality."[52]

libel
False written statements or written statements tending to call someone's reputation into disrepute.

slander
Untrue spoken statements that defame the character of a person.

New York Times Co. v. Sullivan (1964)
The Supreme Court concluded that "actual malice" must be proved to support a finding of libel against a public figure.

Libel and Slander.   Libel is a written statement that defames the character of a person. If the statement is spoken, it is **slander.** In many nations—such as Great Britain, for example—it is relatively easy to sue someone for libel. In the United States, however, the standards of proof are much more difficult. A person who believes that he or she has been a victim of libel must show that the statements made were untrue. Truth is an absolute defense against the charge of libel, no matter how painful or embarrassing the revelations.

It is often more difficult for individuals the Supreme Court considers "public persons or public officials" to sue for libel or slander. *New York Times Co. v. Sullivan* (1964) was the first major libel case considered by the Supreme Court.[53] An Alabama state court found the *Times* guilty of libel for printing a full-page advertisement accusing Alabama officials of physically abusing African Americans during various civil rights protests. (The ad was paid for by civil rights activists, including former First Lady Eleanor Roosevelt.) The Supreme Court overturned the conviction and established that a finding of libel against a public official could stand only if there was a showing of "actual malice," or a knowing disregard for the truth. Proof that the statements were false or negligent was not sufficient to prove actual malice.

In reality, the concept of actual malice can be difficult and confusing. In 1991, the Court directed lower courts to use the phrases "knowledge of falsity" and "reckless disregard of the truth" when giving instructions to juries in libel cases.[54] The actual malice standard also makes it difficult for public officials or persons to win libel cases. Still, many prominent people file libel suits each year; most are settled out of court. For example, actor Tom Cruise dropped his $200 million libel suit against a publisher who claimed he had a videotape of Cruise engaged in a homosexual act when a Los Angeles judge entered a statement that Cruise was not gay into the court record.[55]

fighting words
Words that, "by their very utterance inflict injury or tend to incite an immediate breach of peace." Fighting words are not subject to the restrictions of the First Amendment.

Fighting Words.   In the 1942 case of *Chaplinsky* v. *New Hampshire*, the Court stated that **fighting words, or words that, "by their very utterance inflict injury or tend or incite an immediate breach of peace" are not subject to the restrictions of the First Amendment.[56] Fighting words, which include "profanity, obscenity, and threats," are therefore able to be regulated by the federal and state governments.

These words do not necessarily have to be spoken; fighting words can also come in the form of symbolic expression. For example, in 1968, a California man named Paul Cohen wore a jacket that said "Fuck the Draft. Stop the War" into a Los Angeles county courthouse. He was arrested and charged with disturbing the peace and engaging in offensive conduct. The trial court convicted Cohen, and this conviction was upheld by a state appellate court. However, when the case reached the Supreme Court in 1971, the Court reversed the lower courts' decisions and ruled that forbidding the use of certain words amounted to little more than censorship of ideas.[57]

In 2004, as the presiding officer of the Senate, Vice President Dick Cheney caused quite a stir after he swore at Senator Patrick Leahy (D–VT). Cheney was frustrated by Leahy's actions as ranking minority member on the Judiciary Committee. Senate Democrats kept several Bush judicial nominations from reaching the floor; Cheney's use of an expletive—although not a fighting word—was widely discussed.

**Obscenity.   Through 1957, U.S. courts often based their opinions of what was obscene on an English common-law test that had been set out in 1868: "Whether the tendency of the matter charged as obscenity is to deprive and corrupt those whose minds are open to such immoral influences and into whose hands a publication of this sort might fall."[58] In *Roth* v. *U.S.* (1957), however, the Court abandoned this approach and held that, to be considered obscene, the material in question had to be "utterly without redeeming social importance," and articulated a new test for obscenity: "whether to the average person, applying contemporary community standards, the dominant theme of the material taken as a whole appeals to the prurient interests."[59]

■ Obscenity has been a popular topic of conversation in recent years. For example, in 2004, Vice President Dick Cheney (below) received attention in the media for cursing at Senator Patrick Leahy (at left). The inappropriate language was the result of an argument about Cheney's ties to Haliburton, Inc., a Texas energy firm that has received several contracts for rebuilding efforts in Iraq.

Photo courtesy: left, Mark Wilson/Getty Images; right, Reuters/Corbis

In many ways, the *Roth* test brought with it as many problems as it attempted to solve. Throughout the 1950s and 1960s, "prurient" remained hard to define, as the Supreme Court struggled to find a standard for judging actions or words. Moreover, it was very difficult to prove that a book or movie was "*utterly* without redeeming social value." In general, even some hardcore pornography passed muster under the *Roth* test, prompting some to argue that the Court fostered the increase in the number of sexually oriented publications designed to appeal to those living during the sexual revolution.

Richard M. Nixon made the growth in pornography a major issue when he ran for president in 1968. Nixon pledged to appoint to federal judgeships only those who would uphold law and order and stop coddling criminals and purveyors of porn. Once elected president, Nixon made four appointments to the Supreme Court, including Chief Justice Warren Burger, who wrote the opinion in *Miller v. California* (1973). There, the Court set out a test that redefined obscenity. To make it easier for states to regulate obscene materials, the justices concluded that lower courts must ask "whether the work depicts or describes, in a patently offensive way, sexual conduct specifically defined by state law." The courts also were to determine "whether the work, taken as a whole, lacks serious literary, artistic, political, or scientific value." And, in place of the contemporary community standards gauge used in *Roth*, the Court defined community standards to refer to the locality in question, under the rationale that what is acceptable in New York City might not be acceptable in Maine or Mississippi.[60]

Time and contexts clearly have altered the Court's and, indeed, much of America's perceptions of what works are obscene. But, the Supreme Court has allowed communities great leeway in drafting statutes to deal with obscenity and, even more important, other forms of questionable expression. In 1991, for example, the Court voted 5–4 to allow Indiana to ban totally nude erotic dancing, concluding that the statute furthered a substantial governmental interest, and therefore was not in violation of the First Amendment.[61]

Congress and Obscenity.   While lawmakers have been fairly effective in restricting the sale and distribution of obscene materials, Congress has been particularly concerned with two obscenity and pornography issues: (1) federal funding for the arts; and, (2) the distribution of obscenity and pornography on the Internet.

Visual Literacy

What Speech Is
Protected by the
Constitution?

In 1990, concern over the use of federal dollars by the National Endowment for the Arts (NEA) for works with controversial religious or sexual themes led to passage of legislation requiring the NEA to "[take] into consideration general standards of decency and respect for the diverse beliefs and values of the American public" when it makes annual awards. Several performance artists believed that Congress could not regulate the content of speech solely because it could be offensive; they challenged the statute in federal court. In 1998, the Supreme Court upheld the legislation, ruling that, because decency was only one of the criteria in making funding decisions, the act did not violate the First Amendment.[62]

Monitoring the Internet has proven more difficult for Congress. In 1996, it passed the Communications Decency Act, which prohibited the transmission of obscene materials over the Internet to anyone under age eighteen. In 1997, the Supreme Court ruled in *Reno* v. *American Civil Liberties Union* that the act violated the First Amendment because it was too vague and overbroad.[63] In reaction to the decision, Congress passed the Child Online Protection Act (COPA) in 1998. The new law broadened the definition of pornography to include any "visual depiction that is, or appears to be, a minor engaging in sexually explicit conduct." The act also redefined "visual depiction" to include computer-generated images, shifting the focus of the law from the children who were involved in pornography to protection of children who could see the images via the Internet.[64] The act targeted material "harmful to minors" but applied only to World Wide Web sites, not chat rooms or e-mail. It also targeted only materials used for "commercial purposes."

The ACLU and online publishers immediately challenged the constitutionality of the act, and a U.S. court of appeals in Philadelphia ruled the law was unconstitutional because of its reliance on "community standards" as articulated in *Miller*, which are not enforceable on the Internet. While this case was on appeal to the Supreme Court, Congress enacted the Children's Internet Protection Act, which prohibited public libraries receiving federal funds from allowing minors access to the Web without anti-pornography filters. Meanwhile, in *Ashcroft* v. *Free Speech Coalition* (2002), the Court ruled that Congress had gone too far in a laudable effort to stamp out child pornography.[65] Six justices agreed that the law was too vague because "communities with a narrow view of what words and images are suitable for children might be able to censor Internet content, putting it out of reach of the entire country."[66]

Congressional reaction was immediate. Within two weeks of the Court's decision, lawmakers were drafting more specific legislation to meet the Court's reservations. New regulations were enacted in 2003 as part of an anti-crime bill. In this legislation, Congress further limited the kinds of cyber pornography subject to regulation and allowed those accused of creating and marketing such pornography to "escape conviction if they could show they did not use actual children to produce sexually explicit images."[67] In 2004, the Supreme Court struck down as unconstitutional Congress's latest effort to limit cyberporn. The Court also continued to block enforcement of COPA.[68]

Freedoms of Assembly and Petition

"Peaceful assembly for lawful discussion cannot be made a crime," Chief Justice Charles Evans Hughes wrote in the 1937 case of *DeJonge* v. *Oregon,* which incorporated the First Amendment's freedom of assembly clause.[69] Despite this clear declaration, and an even more ringing declaration in the First Amendment, the fundamental freedoms of assembly and petition have been among the most controversial, especially in times of war. As with other First Amendment freedoms, the Supreme Court often has become the arbiter between the freedom of the people to express dissent and government's authority to limit controversy in the name of national security.

Because the freedom to assemble is hinged on peaceful conduct, the freedoms of assembly and petition are related directly to the freedoms of speech and of the press. If the words or actions taken at any event cross the line of constitutionality, the event itself may constitutionally no longer be protected. Absent that protection, leaders and attendees may be subject to governmental regulation and even criminal charges or civil fines.

THE SECOND AMENDMENT: THE RIGHT TO KEEP AND BEAR ARMS

DURING COLONIAL TIMES, the colonists' distrust of standing armies was evident. Most colonies required all white men to keep and bear arms, and all white men in whole sections of the colonies were deputized to defend their settlements against Indians and other European powers. These local militias were viewed as the best way to keep order and protect liberty.

The Second Amendment was added to the Constitution to ensure that Congress could not pass laws to disarm state militias. This amendment appeased Anti-Federalists, who feared that the new Constitution would cause them to lose the right to "keep and bear arms" as well as an unstated right—the right to revolt against governmental tyranny.

Through the early 1920s, few state statutes were passed to regulate firearms (and generally these laws dealt with the possession of firearms by slaves). The Supreme Court's decision in *Barron* v. *Baltimore* (1833), which refused to incorporate the Bill of Rights to the state governments, prevented federal review of those state laws.[70] Moreover, in *Dred Scott* v. *Sandford* (1857) (see chapter 3), Chief Justice Roger B. Taney listed the right to own and carry arms as a basic right of citizenship.[71]

In 1934, Congress passed the National Firearms Act in response to the increase in organized crime that occurred in the 1920s and 1930s as a result of Prohibition. The act imposed taxes on automatic weapons (such as machine guns) and sawed-off shotguns. In *U.S.* v. *Miller* (1939), a unanimous Court upheld the constitutionality of the act, stating that the Second Amendment was intended to protect a citizen's right to own ordinary militia weapons and not unregistered sawed-off shotguns, which were at issue.[72] *Miller* was the last time the Supreme Court directly addressed the Second Amendment. In *Quilici* v. *Village of Morton Grove* (1983), the Supreme Court refused to review a lower court's ruling upholding the constitutionality of a local ordinance banning handguns against a Second Amendment challenge.[73]

In the aftermath of the assassination attempt on President Ronald Reagan in 1981, many lawmakers called for passage of gun control legislation. At the forefront of that effort was Sarah Brady, the wife of James Brady, the presidential press secretary who was badly wounded and left partially disabled by John Hinckley Jr., President Reagan's assailant. In 1993, her efforts helped to win passage of the Brady

Photo courtesy: Marcy Nighswander/AP/Wide World Photos

■ President Bill Clinton signs the Brady Bill into law flanked by Vice President Al Gore, Attorney General Janet Reno, and James and Sarah Brady and their children.

Bill, which imposed a federal mandatory five-day waiting period on the purchase of handguns.

In 1994, in spite of extensive lobbying by the powerful National Rifle Association (NRA), Congress passed and President Bill Clinton signed the $30.2 billion Violent Crime Control and Law Enforcement Act. In addition to providing money to states for new prisons and law enforcement officers, the act banned the manufacture, sale, transport, or possession of nineteen different kinds of semi-automatic assault weapons.

In 1997, the U.S. Supreme Court ruled 5–4 that the section of the Brady Bill requiring state officials to conduct background checks of prospective handgun owners violated principles of state sovereignty.[74] The background check provision, while important, is not critical to the overall goals of the Brady Bill because a federal record-checking system went into effect in late 1998.

More important to the Brady Bill was the ban on assault weapons. This provision, which prohibited Americans from owning many of the most violent types of guns, carried a ten-year time limit. It expired just before the 2004 presidential and congressional elections. However, neither President Bush nor the Republican-controlled Congress made any serious steps toward renewal, causing many to charge that the move was political and prompted by anti-gun-control interests such as the National Rifle Association, who were major players in the Republican electoral efforts.

Participation

Gun Rights and Gun Control

THE RIGHTS OF CRIMINAL DEFENDANTS

THE FOURTH, FIFTH, SIXTH, AND EIGHTH Amendments supplement constitutional guarantees against writs of *habeas corpus*, *ex post facto* laws, and bills of attainder by providing a variety of procedural guarantees (often called **due process rights**) for those accused of crimes. Particular amendments, as well as other portions of the Constitution, specifically provide procedural guarantees to protect individuals accused of crimes at all stages of the criminal justice process. As is the case with the First Amendment, many of these rights have been interpreted by the Supreme Court to apply to the states. In interpreting the amendments dealing with what are frequently termed "criminal rights," the courts have to grapple not only with the meaning of the amendments but also with how their protections are to be implemented.

Over the years, many individuals criticized liberal Warren Court decisions of the 1950s and 1960s, arguing that its rulings gave criminals more liberties than their victims. The Warren Court made several provisions of the Bill of Rights dealing with the liberties of criminal defendants applicable to the states through the Fourteenth Amendment. It is important to remember that most procedural guarantees apply to individuals charged with crimes—that is, they apply before the individuals have been tried. These liberties were designed to protect those wrongfully accused, although, of course, they often have helped the guilty. But, as Justice William O. Douglas once noted, "Respecting the dignity even of the least worthy citizen . . . raises the stature of all of us."[75]

Many commentators continue to argue, however, that only the guilty are helped by the American system and that criminals should not go unpunished because of simple police error. The dilemma of balancing the liberties of the individual against those of society permeates the entire debate, as well as judicial interpretations of the liberties of criminal defendants.

due process rights
Procedural guarantees provided by the Fourth, Fifth, Sixth, and Eighth Amendments for those accused of crimes.

The Fourth Amendment and Searches and Seizures

The **Fourth Amendment** to the Constitution protects people from unreasonable searches by the federal government. Moreover, in some detail, it sets out what may not be searched unless a warrant is issued, underscoring the Framers' concern with possible government abuses.

Fourth Amendment
Part of the Bill of Rights that reads: "The right of the people to be secure in their persons, houses, papers, and effects, against unreasonable searches and seizures, shall not be violated, and no Warrants shall issue, but upon probable cause, supported by Oath or affirmation, and particularly describing the place to be searched, and the persons or things to be seized."

The right of the people to be secure in their persons, houses, papers, and effects, against unreasonable searches and seizures, shall not be violated, and no Warrants shall issue, but upon probable cause, supported by Oath or affirmation, and particularly describing the place to be searched, and the persons or things to be seized.

The purpose of this amendment was to deny the national government the authority to make general searches. The English Parliament often had issued general writs of assistance that allowed such searches. These general warrants were used against religious and political dissenters, a practice the Framers wanted banned. But, still, the language that they chose left numerous questions to be answered, including the definition of an unreasonable search.

Over the years, in a number of decisions, the Supreme Court has interpreted the Fourth Amendment to allow the police to search: (1) the person arrested; (2) things in plain view of the accused person; and, (3) places or things that the arrested person could touch or reach or are otherwise in the arrestee's immediate control. In 1995, the Court also resolved a decades-old constitutional dispute by ruling unanimously that police must knock and announce their presence before entering a house or apartment to execute a search. But, said the Court, there may be reasonable exceptions to the rule to account for the likelihood of violence or the imminent destruction of evidence.[76]

Warrantless searches often occur if police suspect that someone is committing or is about to commit a crime. In these situations, police may stop and frisk the individual under suspicion. In 1989, the Court ruled that there need be only a "reasonable suspicion" for stopping a suspect—a much lower standard than probable cause.[77] Thus, a suspected drug courier may be stopped for brief questioning but only a frisk search (for weapons) is permitted. A person's answers to the questions may shift reasonable suspicion to probable cause, thus permitting the officer to search further. But, except at borders between the United States and Mexico and Canada (or international airports within U.S. borders), a search requires probable cause.

The Court also ruled in 2001 on a California policy that required individuals, as a condition of their probation, to consent to warrantless searches of their person, property, homes, or vehicles, thus limiting a probationer's Fourth Amendment protections against unreasonable searches and seizures.[78] The Court did not give blanket approval to searches; instead, a unanimous Court said that a probation officer must have a reasonable suspicion of wrongdoing—a lesser standard than probable cause afforded to most citizens.

Searches can also be made without a warrant if consent is obtained, and the Court has ruled that consent can be given by a variety of persons. It has ruled, for example, that police can search a bedroom occupied by two persons as long as they have the consent of one of them.[79]

Simulation
You Are a Police Officer

In situations where no arrest occurs, police must obtain search warrants from a "neutral and detached magistrate" prior to conducting more extensive searches of houses, cars, offices, or any other place where an individual would reasonably have some expectation of privacy.[80] Police cannot get search warrants, for example, to require you to undergo surgery to remove a bullet that might be used to incriminate you, since your expectation of bodily privacy outweighs the need for evidence.[81] But, courts do not require search warrants in possible drunk driving situations. Thus, the police in some states can require you to take a Breathalyzer test to determine whether you have been drinking in excess of legal limits.[82]

Homes, too, are presumed to be private. Firefighters can enter your home to fight a fire without a warrant. But, if they decide to investigate the cause of the fire, they must obtain a warrant before their reentry.[83] In contrast, under the open fields doctrine first articulated by the Supreme Court in 1924, if you own a field, and even if you post "No Trespassing" signs, the police can search your field without a warrant to see if you are illegally growing marijuana, because you cannot reasonably expect privacy in an open field.[84]

In 2001, in a decision that surprised many commentators, by a vote of 5–4, the Supreme Court ruled that drug evidence obtained by using a thermal imager (without a warrant) on a public street to locate the defendant's marijuana hothouse was obtained in violation of the Fourth Amendment.[85] In contrast, the use of low-flying aircraft and helicopters to detect marijuana fields or binoculars to look in a yard have been upheld because officers simply were using their eyesight, not a new technological tool such as the thermal imager.[86]

**Privacy and Rights
of the Accused**

Cars have proven problematic for police and the courts because of their mobile nature. As noted by Chief Justice William H. Taft as early as 1925, "the vehicle can quickly be moved out of the locality or jurisdiction in which the warrant must be sought."[87] Over the years, the Court has become increasingly lenient about the scope of automobile searches.

In 2002, an unusually unanimous Court ruled that when evaluating if a border patrol officer acted lawfully in stopping a suspicious minivan, the totality of the circumstances had to be considered. Wrote Chief Justice William H. Rehnquist, the "balance between the public interest and the individual's right to personal security," tilts in favor of a "standard less than probable cause in brief investigatory stops." This ruling gave law enforcement officers more leeway to pull over suspicious motorists.[88]

Drug Testing.   Testing for drugs is an especially thorny search and seizure issue. If the government can require you to take a Breathalyzer test, can it require you to be tested for drugs? In the wake of growing public concern over drug use, in 1986, President Ronald Reagan signed an executive order requiring many federal employees to undergo drug tests. In 1997, Congress passed a similar law authorizing random drug searches of all congressional employees.

While many private employers and professional athletic organizations routinely require drug tests upon application or as a condition of employment, governmental requirements present constitutional questions about the scope of permissible searches and seizures. In 1989, the Supreme Court ruled that mandatory drug and alcohol testing of employees involved in accidents was constitutional.[89] In 1995, the Court upheld the constitutionally of random drug testing of public high school athletes.[90] And, in 2002, the Court upheld the constitutionality of a Tecumseh, Oklahoma, policy that required mandatory drug testing of high school students participating in any extracurricular activities. Thus, prospective band, choir, debate, or drama club members were subject to the same kind of random drug testing undergone by athletes. Two students who wanted to participate on an academic team sued, arguing that the policy violated their Fourth Amendment right to be free from unreasonable searches and seizures. The Supreme Court disagreed, saying that the school policy was reasonable in furtherance of the school's interest in the prevention and detection of drug abuse. Relying on its rationale in its earlier opinion allowing for the testing of athletes, the Court went on to say that findings of individual suspicion were not necessary for the search of any one student to be reasonable.[91]

Another question has arisen concerning the constitutionality of compulsory drug testing for pregnant women. In 2001, in a 6–3 decision, the Court ruled that the testing of women for cocaine usage and subsequent reporting of positive tests to law enforcement officials was unconstitutional. When pregnant women in South Carolina sought medical care for their pregnancies, they were not told that their urine tests were also tested for cocaine. Thus, some women were arrested after they unknowingly were screened for illegal drug use and then tested positive. The majority of the Court found that the immediate purpose of the drug test was to generate evidence for law enforcement officials and not to give medical treatment to the women. Thus, the women's right to privacy was violated unless they specifically consented to the tests.[92]

In *Chandler* v. *Miller* (1997), the U.S. Supreme Court refused to allow Georgia to require all candidates for state office to pass a urinalysis drug test thirty days before qualifying for nomination or election, concluding that its law violated the search and seizure clause.[93] In general, all employers can require pre-employment drug screening. However, because governments are unconditionally bound by the lawful search provisions of the Fourth Amendment, public employees enjoy more protection in the area of drug testing than do employees of private enterprises.[94]

The Fifth Amendment and Self-Incrimination

The **Fifth Amendment** provides that "No person shall be . . . compelled in any criminal case to be a witness against himself." "Taking the Fifth" is shorthand for exercis-

Fifth Amendment
Part of the Bill of Rights that imposes a number of restrictions on the federal government with respect to the rights of persons suspected of committing a crime. It provides for indictment by a grand jury and protection against self-incrimination, and prevents the national government from denying a person life, liberty, or property without the due process of law. It also prevents the national government from taking property without fair compensation.

ing one's constitutional right not to self-incriminate. The Supreme Court has interpreted this guarantee to be "as broad as the mischief against which it seeks to guard," finding that criminal defendants do not have to take the stand at trial to answer questions, nor can a judge make mention of their failure to do so as evidence of guilt.[95] Moreover, lawyers cannot imply that a defendant who refuses to take the stand must be guilty or have something to hide.

This right not to incriminate oneself also means that prosecutors cannot use as evidence in a trial any of a defendant's statements or confessions that were not made voluntarily. As is the case in many areas of the law, however, judicial interpretation of the term voluntary has changed over time.

In earlier times, it was not unusual for police to beat defendants to obtain their confessions. In 1936, however, the Supreme Court ruled that convictions for murder based solely on confessions given after physical beatings were unconstitutional.[96] Police then began to resort to other measures to force confessions. Defendants, for example, were given the third degree—questioned for hours on end with no sleep or food, or threatened with physical violence until they were mentally beaten into giving confessions. In other situations, family members were threatened. In one case a young mother accused of marijuana possession was told that her welfare benefits would be terminated and her children taken away from her if she failed to talk.[97]

Miranda v. *Arizona* **(1966)** was the Supreme Court's response to these creative efforts to obtain confessions that were not truly voluntary. On March 3, 1963, an eighteen-year-old girl was kidnapped and raped on the outskirts of Phoenix, Arizona. Ten days later police arrested Ernesto Miranda, a poor, mentally disturbed man with a ninth-grade education. In a police-station lineup, the victim identified Miranda as her attacker. Police then took Miranda to a separate room and questioned him for two hours. At first he denied guilt. Eventually, however, he confessed to the crime and wrote and signed a brief statement describing the crime and admitting his guilt. At no time was he told that he did not have to answer any questions or that he could be represented by an attorney.

After Miranda's conviction, his case was appealed on the grounds that his Fifth Amendment right not to incriminate himself had been violated because his confession had been coerced. Writing for the Court, Chief Justice Earl Warren, himself a former district attorney and a former California state attorney general, noted that because police have a tremendous advantage in any interrogation situation, criminal suspects must be given greater protection. A confession obtained in the manner of Miranda's was not truly voluntary; thus, it was inadmissible at trial.

To provide guidelines for police to implement *Miranda,* the Court mandated that: "Prior to any questioning, the person must be warned that he has a right to remain silent, that any statements he does make may be used as evidence against him, and that he has a right to the presence of an attorney, either retained or appointed." In response to this mandate from the Court, police routinely began to read suspects what are now called their *Miranda* **rights,** a practice you undoubtedly have seen repeated over and over in movies and TV police dramas.

Although the Burger Court did not enforce the reading of *Miranda* rights as vehemently as had the Warren Court, Chief Justice Warren Burger, Warren's successor, acknowledged that they had become an integral part of established police procedures.[98] The Rehnquist Court, however, has been more tolerant of the use of coerced confessions and has employed a much more flexible standard to allow their admissibility. In 1991, for example, it ruled that the use of a coerced confession in a criminal trial does not automatically invalidate a conviction if its admission is deemed a "harmless error," that is, if the other evidence is sufficient to convict.[99]

But, in 2000, in an opinion written by Chief Justice William H. Rehnquist, the Court reaffirmed the central holding of *Miranda,* ruling that defendants must be read *Miranda* warnings. The Court went on to say that, despite an act of Congress that stipulated that voluntary statements made during police interrogations were admissible at trial, without *Miranda* warnings, no admissions could be trusted to be truly voluntary.[100]

Photo courtesy: Paul S. Howell/Getty Images

■ Even though Ernesto Miranda's confession was not admitted as evidence at his retrial, his ex-girlfriend's testimony and that of the victim were enough to convince the jury of his guilt. He served nine years in prison before he was released on parole. After his release, he routinely sold autographed cards inscribed with what are called the *Miranda* rights now read to all suspects. In 1976, four years after his release, Miranda was stabbed to death in Phoenix in a bar fight during a card game. Two *Miranda* cards were found on his body, and the person who killed him was read his *Miranda* rights upon his arrest.

Miranda v. *Arizona* (1966)
A landmark Supreme Court ruling that held the Fifth Amendment requires that individuals arrested for a crime must be advised of their right to remain silent and to have counsel present.

Miranda rights
Statements that must be made by the police informing a suspect of his or her constitutional rights protected by the Fifth Amendment, including the right to an attorney provided by the court if the suspect cannot afford one.

The Fourth and Fifth Amendments and the Exclusionary Rule

exclusionary rule
Judicially created rule that prohibits police from using illegally seized evidence at trial.

In *Weeks* v. *U.S.* (1914), the U.S. Supreme Court adopted the **exclusionary rule,** which bars the use of illegally seized evidence at trial. Thus, although the Fourth and Fifth Amendments do not prohibit the use of evidence obtained in violation of their provisions, the exclusionary rule is a judicially created remedy to deter constitutional violations. In *Weeks,* for example, the Court reasoned that allowing police and prosecutors to use the "fruits of a poisonous tree" (a tainted search) would only encourage that activity.[101]

In balancing the need to deter police misconduct against the possibility that guilty individuals could go free, the Warren Court decided that deterring police misconduct was most important. In *Mapp* v. *Ohio* (1961), the Warren Court ruled that "all evidence obtained by searches and seizures in violation of the Constitution, is inadmissible in a state court."[102] This historic and controversial case put law enforcement officers on notice that if they found evidence in violation of any constitutional rights, those efforts would be for naught because the tainted evidence could not be used in federal or state trials. In contrast, the Burger and Rehnquist Courts and, more recently, Congress gradually have chipped away at the exclusionary rule.

In 1976, the Court noted that the exclusionary rule "deflects the truth-finding process and often frees the guilty."[103] Since then, the Court has carved out a variety of limited "good faith exceptions" to the exclusionary rule, allowing the use of tainted evidence in a variety of situations, especially when police have a search warrant and, in good faith, conduct the search on the assumption that the warrant is valid—though it is subsequently found invalid. Since the purpose of the exclusionary rule is to deter police misconduct, and in this situation there is no police misconduct, the courts have permitted the introduction at trial of the seized evidence. Another exception to the exclusionary rule is "inevitable discovery." Evidence illegally seized may be introduced if it would have been discovered anyway in the course of continuing investigation.

The Sixth Amendment and the Right to Counsel

Sixth Amendment
Part of the Bill of Rights that sets out the basic requirements of procedural due process for federal courts to follow in criminal trials. These include speedy and public trials, impartial juries, trials in the state where crime was committed, notice of the charges, the right to confront and obtain favorable witnesses, and the right to counsel.

The **Sixth Amendment** guarantees to an accused person "the Assistance of Counsel in his defense." In the past, this provision meant only that an individual could hire an attorney to represent him or her in court. Since most criminal defendants are too poor to hire private lawyers, this provision was of little assistance to many who found themselves on trial. Recognizing this, Congress required federal courts to provide an attorney for defendants who could not to afford one. This was first required in capital cases (where the death penalty is a possibility); eventually, attorneys were provided to the poor in all federal criminal cases.[104] Similarly, in 1932, the Supreme Court directed states to furnish lawyers to defendants in capital cases.[105] It also began to expand the right to counsel to other state offenses but did so in a piecemeal fashion that gave the states little direction. Given the high cost of providing legal counsel, this ambiguity often made it cost-effective for the states not to provide counsel at all.

These ambiguities came to an end with the Court's decision in *Gideon* v. *Wainwright* (1963).[106] Clarence Earl Gideon, a fifty-one-year-old drifter, was charged with breaking into a Panama City, Florida, pool hall and stealing beer, wine, and some change from a vending machine. At his trial, he asked the judge to appoint a lawyer for him because he was too poor to hire one himself. The judge refused, and Gideon was convicted and given a five-year prison term for petty larceny. The case against Gideon had not been strong, but as a layperson unfamiliar with the law and with trial practice and procedure, he was unable to point out its weaknesses.

The apparent inequities in the system that had resulted in Gideon's conviction continued to bother him. Eventually, he borrowed some paper from a prison guard, consulted books in the prison library, and then drafted and mailed a petition to the U.S. Supreme Court asking it to overrule his conviction.

In a unanimous decision, the Supreme Court agreed with Gideon and his court-appointed lawyer, Abe Fortas, a future associate justice of the Supreme Court. Writing for the Court, Justice Hugo Black explained that "lawyers in criminal courts are necessities, not luxuries." Therefore, the Court concluded, the state must provide an attorney to indigent defendants in felony cases. Underscoring the Court's point, Gideon was acquitted when he was retried with a lawyer to argue his case.

In 1972, the Burger Court expanded the *Gideon* rule, holding that "even in prosecutions for offenses less serious than felonies, a fair trial may require the presence of a lawyer."[107] Seven years later, the Court clarified its decision by holding that defendants charged with offenses where imprisonment is a possibility but not actually imposed do not have a Sixth Amendment right to counsel.[108] Thirty years later, the Rehnquist Court expanded *Gideon* even further by revisiting the "actual imprisonment" standard announced in the 1972 and 1979 cases. In 2002, a 5–4 majority held that if a defendant received a suspended sentence and probation for a minor crime but could be sentenced in future if he or she violated the conditions of probation, then the defendant must be provided with a lawyer.[109]

The Sixth Amendment and Jury Trials

The Sixth Amendment (and, to a lesser extent, Article III of the Constitution) provides that a person accused of a crime shall enjoy the right to a speedy and public trial by an impartial jury—that is, a trial in which a group of the accused's peers act as a fact-finding, deliberative body to determine guilt or innocence. It also provides defendants the right to confront witnesses against them. The Supreme Court has held that jury trials must be available if a prison sentence of six or more months is possible.

Impartiality is a requirement of jury trials that has undergone significant change, with the method of selecting jurors being the most frequently challenged part of the process. Although potential individual jurors who have prejudged a case are not eligible to serve, no groups can be systematically excluded from serving. In 1880, for example, the Supreme Court ruled that African Americans could not be excluded from state jury pools (lists of those eligible to serve).[110] And, in 1975, the Court ruled that to bar women from jury service violated the mandate that juries be a "fair cross section" of the community.[111]

In 1986, the Court expanded the requirement that juries reflect a fair cross section of the community. Historically, lawyers had used peremptory challenges (those for which no cause needs to be given) to exclude African Americans from juries, especially when African Americans were criminal defendants. In *Boston* v. *Kentucky* (1986), the Court ruled that the use of peremptory challenges specifically to exclude African American jurors violated the equal protection clause of the Fourteenth Amendment.[112]

■ When Clarence Earl Gideon wrote out his petition for a writ of certiorari to the Supreme Court (asking the Court, in its discretion, to hear his case), he had no way of knowing that his case would lead to the landmark ruling on the right to counsel, *Gideon* v. *Wainwright* (1963). Nor did he know that Chief Justice Earl Warren actually had instructed his law clerks to be on the lookout for a habeas corpus petition (literally, "you have the body," which argues that the person in jail is there in violation of some statutory or constitutional right) that could be used to guarantee the assistance of counsel for defendants in criminal cases.

Photo courtesy: Supreme Court Historical Society

CIVIL LIBERTIES IN TIMES OF WAR

In *Federalist No. 47*, James Madison warned against unchecked executive power, which had "affected to render the Military independent of and superior to the Civil Power" and had "deprive[ed them], in many Cases of the Benefits of Trial by Jury." Anxiety about tyranny prompted the Framers to place freedom from arbitrary detention at the core of liberty interests protected by the U.S. Constitution.[a] Still, in the wake of the 9/11 terrorist attacks, Congress passed the Authorization for Use of Military Force, giving the president power to "use all necessary appropriate force" against "nations, organizations, or persons" that he deemed to have "Planned, authorized, committed or aided" in the completion of those attacks.

The president then sent U.S. troops to Afghanistan to subdue al Qaeda and to quell the supporting Taliban regime. Soon thereafter, members of the U.S.-supported Afghani Northern Alliance captured, among others, two U.S. citizens in Afghanistan, John Walker Lindh and Yaser Hamdi, who were then handed over to U.S. forces.

The executive branch made the decision to prosecute Lindh for "assisting the Taliban government in opposing the warlords of the Northern Alliance." He was returned to the United States, and a ten-count indictment charged him with conspiring with al-Qaeda to kill U.S. nationals. His confession allegedly was made after he was shackled, naked, and denied food, water, and treatment for an injury. Additionally, he was questioned without a lawyer although his parents had requested that one be appointed for him. Eventually, Lindh agreed to cooperate with government investigators, pled to one count of "supplying services as a foot soldier," and was sentenced to up to twenty years in prison.

In sharp contrast, Hamdi, who although a U.S. citizen had spent much of his life in Saudi Arabia, was sent to a U.S. detention facility at Guantanamo Bay, Cuba, where he was held with no access to the outside world or to an attorney. From there, he was sent to a U.S. military base in Virginia and then to a naval brig in South Carolina. The Department of Justice declined to bring any charges against Hamdi and instead designated him an "enemy combatant."

In July 2002, Hamdi's father filed suit on his son's behalf, seeking a review of the legality of his son's detention. His habeas corpus petition alleged that the government was holding his son in violation of the Fifth and Fourteenth Amendments. A federal judge ordered the United States to allow an attorney to meet with Hamdi in private. While this decision was being appealed, Hamdi was held in solitary confinement with no access to his lawyer. The case finally ended up before the U.S. Supreme Court, where Hamdi, yet to be charged with a crime, argued that his basic civil liberties as an American citizen were being denied. The U.S. government countered that by designating Hamdi an enemy combatant, it was justified holding him in the United States indefinitely—without

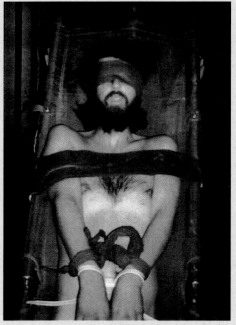

Photo courtesy: AFP/CORBIS

In this photo, John Walker Lindh is shown in shackles after he was captured in Afghanistan.

formal charges or proceedings—until it decided that access to counsel or other actions were warranted.

In June 2004, the U.S. Supreme Court ruled that "a state of war is not a blank check for the president" to deny basic civil liberties to U.S. citizens held in captivity. The Court went on to say that citizens must be apprised of the charges against them and allowed access to lawyers.[b] Although the Court affirmed the right of the president to detain citizens as enemy combatants, it reiterated that such prisoners must be given the right to challenge their captivity before a neutral fact-finder.

Hamdi was released in October 2004, but as a condition of his release he had to renounce his U.S. citizenship and return to Saudi Arabia. This agreement meant that he was never formally charged or brought to trial. Other U.S. citizens still held as enemy combatants are challenging their detainments in federal courts.

Questions

1. How can the government protect citizens in times of terrorist threats without denying citizens constitutionally guaranteed civil liberties?
2. Should the government be allowed to hold indefinitely noncitizens suspected of being or aiding terrorists? Why, or why not?

[1]Lawyers Committee for Human Rights, "Assessing the New Normal: Liberty and Security for the Post September 11 United States," September 2003, 49–50.

[2]*Hamdi et al.* v. *Rumsfeld*, No. 03-6696 (decided June 28, 2004).

In 1994, the Supreme Court answered the major remaining unanswered question about jury selection: can lawyers exclude women from juries through their use of peremptory challenges? This question came up frequently because in rape trials and sex discrimination cases, one side or another often considers it advantageous to select jurors on the basis of their sex. The Supreme Court ruled that the equal protection clause prohibits discrimination in jury selection on the basis of gender. Thus, lawyers cannot strike all potential male jurors based on the belief that males might be more sympathetic to the arguments of a man charged in a paternity suit, a rape trial, or a domestic violence suit, for example.

The right to confront witnesses at trial also is protected by the Sixth Amendment. In 1990, however, the Supreme Court ruled that this right was not absolute. In *Maryland* v. *Craig* (1990), the Court ruled that constitutionally the testimony of a six-year-old alleged child abuse victim via one-way closed circuit television was permissible. The clause's central purpose, said the Court, was to ensure the reliability of testimony by subjecting it to rigorous examination in an adversarial proceeding.[113] In this case, the child was questioned out of the presence of the defendant, who was in communication with his defense and prosecuting attorneys. The defendant, along with the judge and jury, watched the testimony.

The Eighth Amendment and Cruel and Unusual Punishment

The **Eighth Amendment** prohibits "cruel and unusual punishments," a concept rooted in the English common-law tradition. Interestingly, today, the United States is the only Western nation to put people to death for committing crimes. Not surprisingly, there are tremendous regional differences in the imposition of the death penalty, with the South leading in the number of men and women executed each year.

In the 1500s, religious heretics and those critical of the English Crown were subjected to torture to extract confessions, and then were condemned to an equally hideous death by the rack, disembowelment, or other barbarous means. The English Bill of Rights, written in 1687, safeguarded against "cruel and unusual punishments" as a result of public outrage against those practices. The same language found its way into the U.S. Bill of Rights. Prior to the 1960s, however, little judicial attention was paid to the meaning of that phrase, especially in the context of the death penalty.

The death penalty was in use in all of the colonies at the time the U.S. Constitution was adopted, and its constitutionality went unquestioned. In fact, in two separate cases in the late 1800s, the Supreme Court ruled that deaths by public shooting[114] and electrocution were not "cruel and unusual" forms of punishment in the same category as "punishments which inflict torture, such as the rack, the thumbscrew, the iron boot, the stretching of limbs and the like."[115]

In the 1960s, the NAACP Legal Defense Fund (LDF), believing that the death penalty was applied more frequently to African Americans than to members of other groups, orchestrated a carefully designed legal attack on its constitutionality.[116] Public opinion polls revealed that in 1971, on the eve of the LDF's first major death sentence case to reach the Supreme Court, public support for the death penalty had fallen to below 50 percent. With the timing just right, in *Furman* v. *Georgia* (1972), the Supreme Court effectively put an end to capital punishment, at least in the short run.[117] The Court ruled that because the death penalty often was imposed in an arbitrary manner, it constituted cruel and unusual punishment in violation of the Eighth and Fourteenth Amendments. Following *Furman*, several state legislatures enacted new laws designed to meet the Court's objections to the arbitrary nature of the sentence. In 1976, in *Gregg* v. *Georgia*, Georgia's rewritten death penalty statute was ruled constitutional by the Supreme Court in a 7–2 decision.[118]

Eighth Amendment
Part of the Bill of Rights that states: "Excessive bail shall not be required, nor excessive fines imposed, nor cruel and unusual punishments inflicted."

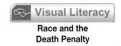
Race and the
Death Penalty

Photo courtesy: Frank Polich/Reuters/Landov

■ Amid questions about the fallibility of America's capital punishment system, Illinois Governor George Ryan commuted the sentences of 167 death row inmates two days before leaving office in 2003. He had earlier declared a moratorium on execution in Illinois.

This ruling did not deter the LDF from continuing to bring death penalty cases before the court. In *McCleskey* v. *Kemp* (1987), a 5–4 Court ruled that imposition of the death penalty—even when it appeared to discriminate against African Americans—did not violate the equal protection clause.[119] Despite the testimony of social scientists and evidence that Georgia was eleven times more likely to seek the death penalty against a black defendant, the Court upheld Warren McCleskey's death sentence. It noted that even if statistics show clear discrimination, there must be a showing of racial discrimination in the case at hand. Five justices concluded that there was no evidence of specific discrimination proved against McCleskey at his trial. Within hours of that defeat, McCleskey's lawyers filed a new appeal, arguing that the informant who gave the only testimony against McCleskey at trial had been placed in McCleskey's cell illegally.

Four years later, McCleskey's death sentence challenge again produced an equally important ruling on the death penalty and criminal procedure from the U.S. Supreme Court. In the second *McCleskey* case, *McCleskey* v. *Zant* (1991), the Court found that the issue of the informant should have been raised during the first appeal, in spite of the fact that McCleskey's lawyers initially were told by the state that the witness was not an informer. *McCleskey* v. *Zant* produced new standards designed to make it much more difficult for death-row inmates to file repeated appeals.[120] Ironically, the informant against McCleskey was freed the night before McCleskey was electrocuted. Justice Lewis Powell, one of those in the five-person majority, later said (after his retirement) that he regretted his vote and should have voted the other way.

The Supreme Court has exempted two key classes of people from the death penalty: those under the age of fifteen and those who are mentally retarded. In 2002, the Court ruled that mentally retarded convicts could not be executed.[121] This 6–3 decision reversed what had been the Court's position on executing the retarded since 1989, a thirteen-year period when several retarded men were executed. Because many states have different standards for assessing retardation, it threw into chaos the laws of twenty states that permit these executions, including Texas, where the governor recently had vetoed legislation banning execution of the retarded. And, the opinion represented a rare win in the Supreme Court for death penalty opponents, who have been faring far better in the individual states. In fact, the Court's majority opinion took special note of the fact that eighteen of the thirty-eight states with the death penalty did not allow the execution of the retarded.[122]

At the state level, a move to at least stay executions took on momentum in March 2000 when Governor George Ryan (R–IL) ordered a moratorium on all executions. Ryan, a death penalty proponent, became disturbed by new evidence collected as a class project by Northwestern University students. The students unearthed information that led to the release of thirteen men on the state's death row. The specter of allowing death sentences to continue in light of evidence showing so many men were wrongly convicted prompted Ryan's much publicized action. Soon thereafter, the Democratic governor of Maryland followed suit after receiving evidence that blacks were much more likely to be sentenced to death than whites; however, the Republican governor who succeeded him lifted the stay. Some states, such as Ohio, have made offers of free DNA testing to those sitting on death row.

Over the past thirteen years, over a hundred persons have been released from death row after DNA tests proved they did not commit the crimes for which they were convicted.[123] In New York, twenty individuals on death row were later found innocent with proof derived from evidence other than DNA.[124] In addition, before leaving office in January 2003, Illinois Governor Ryan commuted the sentences of 167 death row inmates, giving them life in prison instead of death. Ryan also pardoned another four men who had given coerced confessions. This action constituted the single largest anti–death penalty action since the Court's decision in *Gregg,* and it spurred national conversation on the death penalty, which, in recent polls, has seen its lowest levels of support since 1978.

THE RIGHT TO PRIVACY

TO THIS POINT, we have discussed rights and freedoms that have been derived fairly directly from specific guarantees contained in the Bill of Rights. However, the Supreme Court also has given protection to rights not enumerated specifically in the Constitution or Bill of Rights.

Although the Constitution is silent about the **right to privacy,** the Bill of Rights contains many indications that the Framers expected that some areas of life were off limits to governmental regulation. The liberty to practice one's religion guaranteed in the First Amendment implies the right to exercise private, personal beliefs. The guarantee against unreasonable searches and seizures contained in the Fourth Amendment similarly implies that persons are to be secure in their homes and should not fear that police will show up at their doorsteps without cause. As early as 1928, Justice Louis

right to privacy
The right to be let alone; a judicially created doctrine encompassing an individual's decision to use birth control or secure an abortion.

Photo courtesy: Bettmann/Corbis

■ In this 1965 photo, Estelle Griswold (left), executive director of the Planned Parenthood League of Connecticut, and Cornelia Jahncke, its president, celebrate the Supreme Court's ruling in *Griswold* v. *Connecticut.*

Brandeis hailed privacy as "the right to be left alone—the most comprehensive of rights and the right most valued by civilized men."[125] It was not until 1965, however, that the Court attempted to explain the origins of this right.

Birth Control

Today, most Americans take access to many forms of birth control as a matter of course. Condoms are sold in the grocery store, and some television stations air ads for them. Easy access to birth control, however, wasn't always the case. Many states often barred the sale of contraceptives to minors, prohibited the display of contraceptives, or even banned their sale altogether. One of the last states to do away with these kinds of laws was Connecticut. It outlawed the sale of all forms of birth control and even prohibited physicians from discussing it with their married patients until the Supreme Court ruled its restrictive laws unconstitutional.

Griswold v. *Connecticut* (1965) involved a challenge to the constitutionality of an 1879 Connecticut law prohibiting the dissemination of information about and/or the sale of contraceptives.[126] In *Griswold,* seven justices decided that various portions of the Bill of Rights, including the First, Third, Fourth, Ninth, and Fourteenth Amendments, cast what the Court called "penumbras" (unstated liberties on the fringes or in the shadow of more explicitly stated rights), thereby creating zones of privacy, including a married couple's right to plan a family. Thus, the Connecticut statute was ruled unconstitutional because it violated marital privacy, a right the Court concluded could be read into the U.S. Constitution through interpreting several amendments.

Later, the Court expanded the right of privacy to include the right of unmarried individuals to have access to contraceptives. "If the right of privacy means anything," wrote Justice William J. Brennan Jr., "it is the right of the individual, married or single, to be free from unwarranted governmental intrusion into matters so fundamentally affecting a person as the decision to bear or beget a child."[127] Contraceptive rights, however, are often limited for those under age eighteen by state or federal policy. This right to privacy was to be the basis for later decisions from the Court, including the right to secure an abortion.

Abortion

In the early 1960s, two birth-related tragedies occurred. Severely deformed babies were born to European women who had been given the drug thalidomide while pregnant, and, in the United States, a nationwide measles epidemic resulted in the birth of more babies with severe problems. The increasing medical safety of abortions and the growing women's rights movement combined with these tragedies to put pressure on the legal and medical establishments to support laws that would guarantee a woman's access to a safe and legal abortion.

By the late 1960s, fourteen states had voted to liberalize their abortion policies, and four states decriminalized abortion in the early stages of pregnancy. But, many women's rights activists wanted more. They argued that the decision to carry a pregnancy to term was a woman's fundamental constitutional right. In 1973, in one of the most controversial decisions ever handed down, seven members of the Court agreed with this position.

The woman whose case became the catalyst for pro-choice and anti-abortion groups was Norma McCorvey, an itinerant circus worker. The mother of a toddler she was unable to care for, McCorvey could not leave another child in her mother's care. So, she decided to terminate her second pregnancy. She was unable to secure a legal abortion and was frightened by the conditions she found when she sought an illegal, back-alley abortion. McCorvey turned to two young Texas lawyers who were looking for a plaintiff to bring a lawsuit to challenge Texas's restrictive statute. The Texas law allowed abortions only when they were necessary to save the life of the mother. McCorvey, who was unable to obtain a legal abortion, later gave birth and put the baby up for adoption. Nevertheless, she allowed her lawyers to proceed with the case using her as their plaintiff. They used the pseudonym Jane Roe for McCorvey as they challenged the Texas law as enforced by Henry Wade, the district attorney for Dallas County, Texas.

When the case finally came before the Supreme Court, Justice Harry A. Blackmun, a former lawyer at the Mayo Clinic, relied heavily on medical evidence to rule that the Texas law violated a woman's constitutionally guaranteed right to privacy, which he argued included her decision to terminate a pregnancy. Writing for the majority in *Roe v. Wade* **(1973),** Blackmun divided pregnancy into three stages. In the first trimester, a woman's right to privacy gave her an absolute right (in consultation with her physician), free from state interference, to terminate her pregnancy. In the second trimester, the state's interest in the health of the mother gave it the right to regulate abortions—but only to protect the woman's health. Only in the third trimester—when the fetus becomes potentially viable—did the Court find that the state's interest in potential life outweighed a woman's privacy interests. Even in the third trimester, however, abortions to save the life or health of the mother were to be legal.[128]

Roe v. *Wade* unleashed a torrent of political controversy. Anti-abortion groups, caught off guard, scrambled to recoup their losses in Congress. Representative Henry Hyde (R–IL) persuaded Congress to ban the use of Medicaid funds for abortions for poor women, and the constitutionality of the Hyde Amendment was upheld by the Supreme Court in 1977 and again in 1980.[129] The issue also polarized both major political parties.

From the 1970s through the present, the right to an abortion and its constitutional underpinnings in the right to privacy have been under attack by well-organized anti-abortion groups. The administrations of Ronald Reagan and George Bush were strong advocates of the anti-abortion position, regularly urging the Court to overrule *Roe.* They came close to victory in *Webster* v. *Reproductive Health Services* (1989).[130] In *Webster,* the Court upheld state-required fetal viability tests in the second trimester, even though these tests would increase the cost of an abortion considerably. The Court also upheld Missouri's refusal to allow abortions to be performed in state-supported hospitals or by state-funded doctors or nurses. Perhaps most noteworthy, however, was that four justices seemed willing to overrule *Roe* v. *Wade* and that Justice Antonin Scalia publicly rebuked his colleague, Justice Sandra Day O'Connor, then the only woman on the Court, for failing to provide the critical fifth vote to overrule *Roe.*

After *Webster,* states began to enact more restrictive legislation. In *Planned Parenthood of Southeastern Pennsylvania* v. *Casey* (1992), the most important abortion case since *Roe,* Justices O'Connor, Anthony Kennedy, and David Souter, in a jointly authored opinion, wrote that Pennsylvania could limit abortions so long as its regulations did not pose "an undue burden" on pregnant women.[131] The narrowly supported standard, by which the Court upheld a twenty-four-hour waiting period and parental consent requirements, did not overrule *Roe,* but clearly limited its scope by abolishing its trimester approach and substituting the undue burden standard.

Photo courtesy: LM Otero/AP/Wide World Photos

■ A once very popular anti-abortion group, Operation Rescue, staged large scale protests in front of abortion clinics across the nation gaining a surprising new member—Norma McCorvey, the "Jane Roe" of *Roe* v. *Wade* (1973). In 1995, she announced that she had become pro-life.

***Roe* v. *Wade* (1973)**
The Supreme Court found that a woman's right to an abortion was protected by the right to privacy that could be implied from specific guarantees found in the Bill of Rights applied to the states through the Fourteenth Amendment.

Analyzing Visuals

PARTIAL BIRTH ABORTION BAN

In the photograph, as members of Congress look on, President George W. Bush signs the Partial Birth Abortion Ban Act of 2003 at the Ronald Reagan Building and International Trade Center in Washington, D.C. Standing behind the president are, from left, Speaker of the House Dennis Hastert (R–IL), Senator Orrin Hatch (R–UT), Representative James Sensenbrenner (R–WI), Senator Rick Santorum (R–PA), Representative James Oberstar (D–MN), and Senator Mike DeWine (R–OH). After examining the photograph, answer the following critical thinking questions: Do you think that the photographer is making any specific statement about the civil liberties of American women? Are the members of Congress viewing the signing representative of Congress as a whole? Of the general U.S. public?

Photo courtesy: Pablo Martinez Monsivais/AP/Wide World Photos

In 1993, newly elected pro-choice President Bill Clinton ended bans on fetal tissue research, abortions at military hospitals, and federal financing for overseas population control programs, and he lifted the gag rule, a federal regulation enacted in 1987 that barred public health clinics receiving federal dollars from discussing abortion (policies later reversed by George W. Bush).[132] Clinton also ended the ban on testing of RU-486, the so-called French abortion pill, which ultimately was made available in the United States to women with a doctor's prescription late in 2000.

President Clinton used the occasion of his first appointment to the U.S. Supreme Court to select a longtime supporter of abortion rights, Ruth Bader Ginsburg, to replace Justice Byron White, one of the original dissenters in *Roe*. Most commentators believe that this was an important first step in shifting the Court away from any further curtailment of abortion rights, as was the later appointment of Justice Stephen Breyer in 1994.

While President Clinton was attempting to shore up abortion rights through judicial appointments, Republican Congresses made repeated attempts to restrict abortion rights. In March 1996 and again in 1998, Congress passed and sent to President Clinton a bill to ban—for the first time—a specific procedure used in late-term abortions.[133] The president vetoed the Partial Birth Abortion Act over the objections of many of its supporters, including the National Right to Life Committee. Many state legislatures, however, passed their own versions of the act. In 2000, the Supreme Court, however, ruled 5–4 in *Stenberg* v. *Carhart* that a Nebraska partial birth abortion statute was unconstitutionally vague and therefore unenforceable, calling into question the laws of twenty-nine other states with their own bans on late-term procedures.[134] At the same time, it ruled that a Colorado law that prohibited protestors from coming within eight feet of women entering clinics was constitutional.[135] This bubble law was designed to create an eight-foot buffer zone around women as they walked through protesters into a clinic.

By October 2003, however, Republican control of the White House and both houses of Congress facilitated passage of the federal Partial Birth Abortion Ban Act. Pro-choice groups such as Planned Parenthood, the Center for Reproductive Rights, and the American Civil Liberties Union immediately filed lawsuits challenging the constitutionality of this law. At this writing, three federal district courts have ruled it unconstitutional.

Homosexuality

It was not until 2003 that the U.S. Supreme Court ruled that an individual's constitutional right to privacy, which provided the basis for the *Griswold* (contraceptives) and *Roe* (abortion) decisions, prevented the state of Texas from criminalizing private sexual behavior. This monumental decision invalidated the laws of fourteen states, as revealed in Analyzing Visuals: State Sodomy Laws.

In *Lawrence* v. *Texas* (2003), six members of the Court overruled a 1986 decision[136] and found that the Texas law was unconstitutional; five justices found it to violate fundamental privacy rights. Justice Sandra Day O'Connor agreed that the law was unconstitutional, but concluded that it was an equal protection violation. (See chapter 6 for a detailed discussion of the equal protection clause of the Fourteenth Amendment.) Although Justice Antonin Scalia issued a stinging dissent, charging that "the Court has largely signed on to the so-called homosexual agenda," the majority of the Court was unswayed.[137]

Just three years before, the Court upheld a challenge to the Boy Scouts' refusal to allow a gay man to become a scoutmaster.[138] There, the majority of the Court found that a private club's First Amendment right to freedom of association allowed it to use its own moral code to select troop leaders. While the public largely supported the Boy Scouts decision, it also approved of the Court's resolution of the challenge to the Texas sodomy law.[139] A poll taken just before the 2003 ruling showed that the public disagreed with the Court's 1986 decision by a margin of 57 to 38 percent.[140]

Analyzing Visuals

STATE SODOMY LAWS

Before the Supreme Court's decision in *Lawrence v. Texas* (2003), fourteen states still had some sort of sodomy law on their books. The Court's decision effectively invalidated these laws. After studying the U.S. map and its depiction of individual state laws, answer the following critical thinking questions: Which states had laws that apply only to homosexuals? What was the legal position of the majority of states? How might the states' positions have influenced the Court's decision?

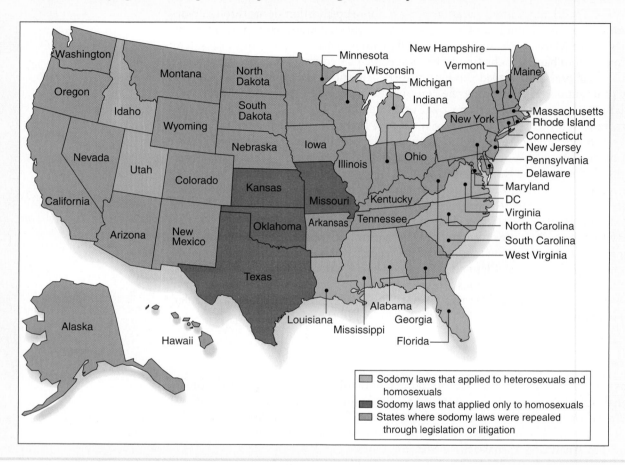

Sodomy laws that applied to heterosexuals and homosexuals

Sodomy laws that applied only to homosexuals

States where sodomy laws were repealed through legislation or litigation

The Right to Die

In 1990, the Supreme Court ruled 5–4 that parents could not withdraw a feeding tube from their comatose daughter after her doctors testified that she could live for many more years if the tube remained in place. Writing for the majority, Chief Justice William H. Rehnquist rejected any attempts to expand the right of privacy into this thorny area of social policy. The Court did note, however, that individuals could terminate medical treatment if they were able to express, or had done so in writing via a living will, their desire to have medical treatment terminated in the event they became incompetent.[141]

In 1997, the U.S. Supreme Court ruled unanimously that terminally ill persons do not have a constitutional right to physician assisted suicide. The Court's action upheld the laws of New York and Washington State that make it a crime for doctors to give life-ending drugs to mentally competent but terminally ill patients who wish to die.[142] But, Oregon enacted a right-to-die or assisted suicide law approved by Oregon voters that allows physicians to prescribe drugs to terminally ill patients. In November 2001, however, Attorney General John Ashcroft issued a legal opinion determining that assisted suicide is not "a legitimate medical purpose," thereby putting physicians who follow their state law in jeopardy of federal prosecution.[143] His memo also called for the revocation of the physicians' drug prescription licenses, putting the state and the national government in conflict in an area that Republicans historically have argued is the province of state authority. Oregon officials immediately (and successfully) sought a court order blocking Ashcroft's attempt to interfere with implementation of Oregon law.[144] Later, a federal judge ruled that Ashcroft had overstepped his authority on every point.[145]

SUMMARY

1. **The First Constitutional Amendments: The Bill of Rights**

   Most of the Framers originally opposed the Bill of Rights. Anti-Federalists, however, continued to stress the need for a bill of rights during the drive for ratification of the Constitution, and some states tried to make their ratification contingent on the addition of a bill of rights. Thus, during its first session, Congress sent the first ten amendments to the Constitution, the Bill of Rights, to the states for their ratification. Later, the addition of the Fourteenth Amendment allowed the Supreme Court to apply some of the amendments to the states through a process called selective incorporation.

2. **First Amendment Guarantees: Freedom of Religion**

   The First Amendment guarantees freedom of religion. The establishment clause, which prohibits the national government from establishing a religion, does not, according to Supreme Court interpretation, create an absolute wall between church and state. While the national and state governments may generally not give direct aid to religious groups, many forms of aid, especially many that benefit children, have been held to be constitutionally permissible. In contrast, the Court has generally barred organized prayer in public schools. The Court largely has adopted an accommodationist approach when interpreting the free exercise clause by allowing some governmental regulation of religious practices.

3. **First Amendment Guarantees: Freedom of Speech, Press, and Assembly**

   Historically, one of the most volatile areas of constitutional interpretation has been in the interpretation of the First Amendment's mandate that "Congress shall make no law . . . abridging the freedom of speech or of the press." Like the establishment and free exercise clauses of the First Amendment, the speech and press clauses have not been interpreted as absolute bans against government regulation.

   Some areas of speech and publication are unconditionally protected by the First Amendment. Among these are prior restraint, symbolic speech, and hate speech. Other areas of speech and publication, however, are unprotected by the First Amendment. These include libel, fighting words, and obscenity and pornography.

   The freedoms of peaceable assembly and petition are directly related to the freedoms of speech and of the press. As with other First Amendment rights, the Supreme Court has often become the arbiter between the right of the people to express dissent and government's right to limit controversy in the name of security.

4. **The Second Amendment: The Right to Keep and Bear Arms**

   Initially, the right to bear arms was envisioned as one dealing with state militias. Over the years, states and Congress have enacted various gun ownership restrictions with little Supreme Court interpretation as a guide to their ultimate constitutionality.

5. The Rights of Criminal Defendants

The Fourth, Fifth, Sixth, and Eighth Amendments provide a variety of procedural guarantees to individuals accused of crimes. In particular, the Fourth Amendment prohibits unreasonable searches and seizures, and the Court has generally refused to allow evidence seized in violation of this safeguard to be used at trial.

Among other rights, the Fifth Amendment guarantees that "no person shall be compelled to be a witness against himself." The Supreme Court has interpreted this provision to require that the government inform the accused of his or her right to remain silent. This provision has also been interpreted to require that illegally obtained confessions must be excluded at trial.

The Sixth Amendment's guarantee of "assistance of counsel" has been interpreted by the Supreme Court to require that the government provide counsel to defendants unable to pay for it in cases where prison sentences may be imposed. The Sixth Amendment also requires an impartial jury, although the meaning of impartial continues to evolve through judicial interpretation.

The Eighth Amendment's ban against "cruel and unusual punishments" has been held not to bar imposition of the death penalty.

6. The Right to Privacy

The right to privacy is a judicially created right carved from the penumbras (unstated liberties implied by more explicitly stated rights) of several amendments, including the First, Third, Fourth, Ninth, and Fourteenth Amendments. Statutes limiting access to birth control or abortion or banning homosexual acts have been ruled unconstitutional violations of the right to privacy. The Court, however, has not extended privacy rights to include the right to die.

KEY TERMS

SELECTED READINGS

Abernathy, M. Glenn, and Barbara A. Perry, *Civil Liberties Under the Constitution*, 6th ed. Columbia: University of South Carolina Press, 1993.

Cole, David, and James X. Dempsey. *Terrorism and the Constitution: Sacrificing Civil Liberties in the Name of National Security*, 2nd ed. Washington, DC: First Amendment Foundation, 2002.

Etzoni, Amitai, and Jason H. Mason. *Rights vs. Public Safety after 9/11: America in an Age of Terrorism*. Lanham, MD: Rowman and Littlefield, 2003.

Fiss, Owen M. *The Irony of Free Speech*. Cambridge, MA: Harvard University Press, 1996.

Friendly, Fred W. *Minnesota Rag: Corruption, Yellow Journalism, and the Case that Saved Freedom of the Press*, reissue ed. Minneapolis: University of Minnesota Press, 2003.

Gates, Henry Louis, Jr., ed. *Speaking of Race, Speaking of Sex: Hate Speech, Civil Rights, and Civil Liberties*. New York: New York University Press, 1995.

Greenawalt, Kent. *Fighting Words: Individuals, Communities, and Liberties of Speech*. Princeton, NJ: Princeton University Press, 1995.

Ivers, Gregg, and Kevin T. McGuire, eds. *Creating Constitutional Change*. Charlottesville: University of Virginia Press, 2004.

Kalven, Harry, Jr. *A Worthy Tradition: Freedom of Speech in America*. New York: Harper and Row, 1988.

Lewis, Anthony. *Gideon's Trumpet*, reissue ed. New York: Vintage Books, 1989.

Lewis, Anthony. *Make No Law: The Sullivan Case and the First Amendment*, reprint ed. New York: Random House, 1991.

Manwaring, David R. *Render unto Caesar: The Flag Salute Controversy*. Chicago: University of Chicago Press, 1962.

O'Brien, David M. *Constitutional Law and Politics*. Vol. 2, *Civil Rights and Civil Liberties*, 5th ed. New York: Norton, 2002.

O'Connor, Karen. *No Neutral Ground: Abortion Politics in an Age of Absolutes.* Boulder, CO: Westview, 1996.

Regan, Priscilla M. *Legislating Privacy: Technology, Social Values, and Public Policy.* Chapel Hill: University of North Carolina Press, 1995.

Weddington, Sarah. *A Question of Choice.* New York: Grosset/Putnam, 1993.

WEB EXPLORATIONS

To view an original copy of the Bill of Rights, see
http://www.archives.gov/national_archives_experience/charters/bill_of_rights.html

For groups with opposing views on how the First Amendment should be interpreted, see
http://www.au.org/
http://www.pfaw.org/
http://www.aclj.org/

For more information on the *Agostini* v. *Felton* case see
http://supct.law.cornell.edu:8080/supct/html/96-552.ZD.html

For more information on the National Endowment for the Arts, see
http://www.arts.endow.gov/

For more information on *Chandler* v. *Miller*, see
http://supct.law.cornell.edu/supct/html/96-126.ZS.html

For other privacy issues, see
http://www.epic.org/ and
http://www.privacy.org/

To compare the different sides of the abortion debate, go to FLITE: Federal Legal Information Through Electronics at
http://www.fedworld.gov/supcourt/
and Roe in a Nutshell at
http://hometown.aol.com/abtrbng/roeins.htm

For more on gay rights and recent court cases, see
http://www.infoplease.com/ipa/A0194028.html

To learn more about the right to die movement, see
http://www.hemlock.org/home.jsp

Photo courtesy: Chrystie Sherman/AP/Wide World Photos

Civil Rights

THERE IS NO QUESTION that in the 1980s, crime in the United States, and in particular New York City, was out of control and Americans demanded that their governments do something about it. Governments at all levels responded with more police and more prisons. But, now that crime is on the wane and no longer even on Americans' list of top ten concerns, ordinary citizens are asking the question that troubled John Locke and Thomas Hobbes over three centuries ago: how much liberty should you give up to the government in return for safety? Case after case makes it clear that people of color, whether native or foreign born, are subject to civil rights deprivations at far higher rates than other identifiable groups. On February 4, 1999, for example, Amadou Diallo, a twenty-two-year-old unarmed African immigrant, stood in the vestibule of his apartment building in the Bronx, New York. Four white plainclothes police officers, who were patrolling the neighborhood in an unmarked car, opened fire on him, eventually firing forty-one shots. He died at the scene.[1] There were no witnesses. The four officers, who eventually were charged with second-degree murder, were members of New York City's Street Crimes Unit. This unit was created in the early 1990s by then-Mayor Rudy Giuliani to help lower the crime rate. Known to have targeted blacks, members of the unit admitted to stopping and searching as many as 225,000 citizens since its establishment.[2]

Members of New York City's frightened minority community, African Americans and new immigrants alike, along with liberal activists and everyday citizens, turned their anger on city police and the mayor, who they believed had used overly aggressive, and often racially biased, techniques to reduce crime. In the months after the shooting, citizens from all walks of life, from future Democratic presidential candidate Al Sharpton and actress Susan Sarandon to street cleaners, protested at City Hall, and even marched from the federal courthouse over the Brooklyn Bridge and into Manhattan in a procession reminiscent of many 1960s civil rights marches. Over 1,500 protesters were arrested at one demonstration, the largest New York City had seen in twenty-five years.[3] Eventually, all four police officers charged with Diallo's killing were acquitted at trial.

CHAPTER OUTLINE

- Slavery, Abolition, and Winning the Right to Vote, 1800–1890

- The Push for Equality, 1890–1954

- The Civil Rights Movement

- The Women's Rights Movement

- Other Groups Mobilize for Rights

- Continuing Controversies in Civil Rights

THE DECLARATION OF INDEPENDENCE, written in 1776, boldly proclaims: "We hold these truths to be self-evident, that all men are created equal, that they are endowed by their Creator with certain unalienable rights." The Constitution, written eleven years later, is silent on the concept of equality. Only through constitutional amendment and Supreme Court definition and redefinition of the rights contained in the Constitution have Americans come close to attaining equal rights. Even so, as our opening vignette highlights, some citizens have yet to experience full equality and the full enjoyment of civil rights many Americans take for granted.

civil rights

Refers to the government-protected rights of individuals against arbitrary or discriminatory treatment by governments or individuals based on categories such as race, sex, national origin, age, religion, or sexual orientation.

The term **civil rights** refers to the goverment-protected rights of individuals against arbitrary or discriminatory treatment by governments or individuals based on categories such as race, sex, national origin, age, religion, or sexual orientation. The Framers considered some civil rights issues. But, as James Madison reflected in *Federalist No. 42*, one entire class of citizens—slaves—were treated in the new Constitution more as property than as people. Delegates to the Constitutional Convention put political expediency before the immorality of slavery and basic civil rights. Moreover, the Constitution considered white women full citizens for purposes of determining state population, but voting qualifications were left to the states, and none allowed women to vote at the time the Constitution was ratified.

Since the Constitution was written, concepts of civil rights have changed dramatically. The addition of the Fourteenth Amendment, one of three Civil War Amendments ratified from 1865 to 1870, introduced the notion of equality into the Constitution by specifying that states could not deny "any person within its jurisdiction equal protection of the laws." Throughout history, the Fourteenth Amendment's equal protection guarantees have been the linchpin of efforts to expand upon the original intent of the amendment to allow its provisions to protect a variety of other groups from discrimination.

The Fourteenth Amendment has generated more litigation to determine and specify its meaning than any other provision of the Constitution. Within a few years of its ratification, women—and later, African Americans and other minorities and disadvantaged groups—took to the courts to seek expanded civil rights in all walks of life. But, the struggle to augment rights was not limited to the courts. Public protest, civil disobedience, legislative lobbying, and appeals to public opinion all have been part of the arsenal of those seeking equality. The Diallo case incorporates all of those actions. Ordinary citizens and celebrities took to the streets, legislators held hearings, police officers were put on trial, and the media reported it all.

Since passage of the Civil War Amendments (1865–1870), there has been a fairly consistent pattern of the expansion of civil rights to more and more groups. In this chapter, we will explore how notions of equality and civil rights have changed in this country as well as current debates over the scope and methods as it seeks to ensure equal rights for all its citizens. To do so, we will discuss slavery, its abolition, and the achievement of voting rights for African Americans and women by examining the evolution of African American rights and women's rights in tandem. To appreciate how each group has drawn ideas, support, and success from the other, throughout this chapter we will consider their parallel developments as well as those of other historically disadvantaged political groups, including Hispanics (now the largest minority group in the United States), Native Americans, the gay and lesbian community, and those with disabilities.

- First, we will discuss *slavery, abolition, and winning the right to vote,* from *1800 to 1890.*

- Second, we will examine African Americans' and women's next *push for equality* from *1890 to 1954,* using two of the Supreme Court's most famous decisions, *Plessy* v. *Ferguson* (1896) and *Brown* v. *Board of Education* (1954), as bookends for our discussion.

- Third, we will analyze *the civil rights movement* and the Civil Rights Act of 1964 and its effects, including its facilitation.
- Fourth, we will discuss the development of a new *women's rights movement* and its push for an equal rights amendment to the U.S. Constitution.
- Fifth, we will present the efforts of *other groups,* including Hispanic Americans, Native Americans, gays and lesbians, and Americans with disabilities, to *mobilize for rights* using methods often modeled after the actions of African Americans and women.
- Finally, we will explore *other continuing controversies in civil rights,* including affirmative action.

SLAVERY, ABOLITION, AND WINNING THE RIGHT TO VOTE, 1800–1890

TODAY, WE TAKE THE RIGHTS of women and blacks to vote for granted. Since 1980, women have outvoted men at the polls in presidential elections; in the 1990s, in fact, African Americans and women became the core of the Democratic Party. But, it wasn't always this way. The period from 1800 to 1890 was one of tremendous change and upheaval in America. Despite the Civil War and the freeing of the slaves, the promise of equality guaranteed to African Americans by the Civil War Amendments failed to become a reality. Women's rights activists also began to make claims for equality, often using the arguments enunciated for the abolition of slavery, but they too fell far short of their goals.

Slavery and Congress

Congress banned the slave trade in 1808, after the expiration of the twenty-year period specified by the Constitution. In 1820, blacks made up 25 percent of the U.S. population and were in the majority in some southern states. By 1840, that figure had fallen to 20 percent. After the introduction of the cotton gin (a machine invented in 1793 that separated seeds from cotton very quickly), the South became even more dependent on agriculture and cheap slave labor as its economic base. At the same time, technological advances were turning the northern states into an increasingly industrialized region, which deepened the cultural and political differences and animosity between the North and the South.

As the nation grew westward in the early 1800s, conflicts between northern and southern states intensified over the admission of new states to the union with free or slave status. The first major crisis occurred in 1820, when Missouri applied for admission to the union as a slave state—that is, one in which slavery would be legal. Missouri's admission would have weighted the Senate in favor of slavery and therefore was opposed by northern senators. To resolve this conflict, Congress passed the Missouri Compromise of 1820. The Compromise prohibited slavery north of the geographical boundary at 36 degrees latitude. This act allowed Missouri to be admitted to the union as a slave state, and to maintain the balance of slave and free states, Maine was carved out of a portion of Massachusetts.

The First Civil Rights Movements: Abolition and Women's Rights

The Missouri Compromise solidified the South in its determination to keep slavery legal, but it also fueled the fervor of those who opposed slavery. William Lloyd Garrison, a

Photo courtesy: Library of Congress

■ Frederick Douglass (1817–1895) was born into slavery but learned how to read and write. Once he escaped to the North (where 250,000 free blacks lived), he became a well-known orator and journalist. In 1847, he started a newspaper, *The North Star*, in Rochester, New York. The paper quickly became a powerful voice against slavery, and he urged President Abraham Lincoln to emancipate the slaves. Douglass was also a firm believer in woman's suffrage.

■ This is the announcement that was placed in local newspapers about the upcoming 1848 Seneca Falls Women's Convention.

Photo courtesy: Library of Congress

THE FIRST CONVENTION

EVER CALLED TO DISCUSS THE

Civil and Political Rights of Women,

SENECA FALLS, N. Y., JULY 19, 20, 1848.

———

WOMAN'S RIGHTS CONVENTION.

———

A Convention to discuss the social, civil, and religious condition and rights of woman will be held in the Wesleyan Chapel, at Seneca Falls, N. Y., on Wednesday and Thursday, the 19th and 20th of July current; commencing at 10 o'clock A. M. During the first day the meeting will be exclusively for women, who are earnestly invited to attend. The public generally are invited to be present on the second day, when Lucretia Mott, of Philadelphia, and other ladies and gentlemen, will address the Convention.*

---

* This call was published in the *Seneca County Courier*, July 14, 1848, without any signatures. The movers of this Convention, who drafted the call, the declaration and resolutions were Elizabeth Cady Stanton, Lucretia Mott, Martha C. Wright, Mary Ann McClintock, and Jane C. Hunt.

white New Englander, galvanized the abolitionist movement in the early 1830s. Garrison, a newspaper editor, founded the American Anti-Slavery Society in 1833; by 1838, it had more than 250,000 members. Given the U.S. population today, the National Association for the Advancement of Colored People (NAACP) would need 3.8 million members to have the same kind of overall proportional membership. (In 2004, NAACP membership exceeded 500,000.)

Slavery was not the only practice that people began to question in the decades following the Missouri Compromise. In 1840, for example, Garrison and Frederick Douglass, a well-known black abolitionist writer, left the Anti-Slavery Society when it refused to accept their demand that women be allowed to participate equally in all its activities. Custom dictated that women not speak out in public, and most laws made women second-class citizens. In most states, for example, women could not divorce their husbands or keep their own wages and inheritances. And, of course, they could not vote.

Elizabeth Cady Stanton and Lucretia Mott, who were to found the first women's rights movement, attended the 1840 meeting of the World Anti-Slavery Society in London with their husbands. After their long journey, they were not allowed to participate in the convention because they were women. As they sat in the balcony, apart from the male delegates, they paused to compare their status to that of the slaves they sought to free. They concluded that women were not much better off than slaves, and they resolved to meet to address these issues. In 1848, they finally sent out a call for the first women's rights convention. Three hundred women and men, including Frederick Douglass, attended the first meeting for women's rights, which was held in Seneca Falls, New York.

The Seneca Falls Convention in 1848 attracted people from all over New York State and other states as well who believed that men and women should be able to enjoy all rights of citizenship equally. It passed resolutions calling for the abolition of legal, economic, and social discrimination against women. All of the resolutions reflected the attendees' dissatisfaction with contemporary moral codes, divorce and criminal laws, and the limited opportunities for women in education, the church, medicine, law, and politics. Ironically, only the call for woman suffrage failed to win unanimous approval. Most who attended the Seneca Falls meeting continued to press for women's rights along with the abolition of slavery.

The 1850s: The Calm Before the Storm

By 1850, much was changing in America: the Gold Rush had spurred westward migration, cities grew as people were lured from their farms, railroads and the telegraph increased mobility and communication, and immigrants flooded into the United States. The woman's movement gained momentum, and slavery continued to tear the nation apart. Harriet Beecher Stowe's *Uncle Tom's Cabin*, a novel that depicted the evils of slavery, further inflamed the country. *Uncle Tom's Cabin* sold more than 300,000 copies in 1852. Equivalent sales today would top 4 million copies.

The tremendous national reaction to Stowe's work, which later prompted President Abraham Lincoln to call Stowe "the little woman who started the big war," had not yet faded when a new controversy over the Missouri Compromise of 1820 became the lightning rod for the first major civil rights case to be addressed by the U.S. Supreme Court. As discussed in chapter 3, in *Dred Scott* v. *Sandford* (1857), the Court bluntly had ruled that the Missouri Compromise, which prohibited slavery north of a set geographical boundary, was unconstitutional. Furthermore, the Court went on to add that slaves were not U.S. citizens, and as a consequence, slaves could not bring suits in federal court.

The Civil War and Its Aftermath: Civil Rights Laws and Constitutional Amendments

The Civil War had many causes, but slavery was clearly a key issue. During the war (1861–1865), abolitionists continued to press for an end to slavery. They were rewarded when President Abraham Lincoln issued the Emancipation Proclamation, which provided that all slaves in states still in active rebellion against the United States would be freed automatically on January 1, 1863. Designed as a measure to gain favor for the war in the North, the Emancipation Proclamation did not free all slaves—it freed only those who lived in the Confederacy, which was made up of states that had seceded from the union. Complete abolition of slavery did not occur until congressional passage and ultimate ratification of the Thirteenth Amendment in 1865.

The Civil War Amendments.   The **Thirteenth Amendment** was the first of the three Civil War Amendments. It banned all forms of "slavery [and] involuntary servitude." Although southern states were required to ratify the Thirteenth Amendment as a condition of their readmission to the Union after the war, most of the former Confederate states quickly passed laws that were designed to restrict opportunities for newly freed slaves. These **Black Codes** prohibited African Americans from voting, sitting on juries, or even appearing in public places. Although Black Codes differed from state to state, all empowered local law-enforcement officials to arrest unemployed blacks, fine them for vagrancy, and hire them out to employers to satisfy their fines. Some state codes went so far as to require African Americans to work on plantations or to be domestics. The Black Codes laid the groundwork for Jim Crow laws, which later would institute segregation in all walks of life in the South.

An outraged Congress enacted the Civil Rights Act of 1866 to invalidate some state Black Codes. President Andrew Johnson vetoed the legislation, but—for the first time in history—Congress overrode a presidential veto. The Civil Rights Act formally made African Americans citizens of the United States and gave the Congress and the federal courts the power to intervene when states attempted to restrict the citizenship rights of male African Americans in matters such as voting. Congress reasoned that African Americans were unlikely to fare well if they had to file discrimination complaints in state courts, where most judges were elected. Passage of a federal law allowed African Americans to challenge discriminatory state practices in the federal courts, where judges were appointed for life by the president.

Because controversy remained over the constitutionality of the act (since the Constitution gives states the right to determine qualifications of voters), the **Fourteenth Amendment** was proposed simultaneously with the Civil Rights Act to guarantee, among other things, citizenship to all freed slaves. Other key provisions of the Fourteenth Amendment barred states from abridging "the privileges or immunities of citizenship" or depriving "any person of life, liberty, or property without due process of law," or "deny any person within its jurisdiction the equal protection of the laws."

Unlike the Thirteenth Amendment, which had near-unanimous support in the North, the Fourteenth Amendment was opposed by many women because it failed to guarantee suffrage for women. During the Civil War, woman's rights activists put aside their claims for expanded rights for women, most notably the right to vote, and threw their energies into the war effort. They were convinced that once slaves were freed and given the right to vote, women similarly would be rewarded with the franchise. They were wrong.

In early 1869, after ratification of the Fourteenth Amendment (which specifically added the word "male" to the Constitution for the first time), woman's rights activists met in Washington, D.C., to argue against passage of any new amendment that would extend suffrage to black males and not to women. The convention resolved that "a man's government is worse than a white man's government, because, in proportion as you increase the tyrants, you make the condition of the disenfranchised class more hopeless and degraded."

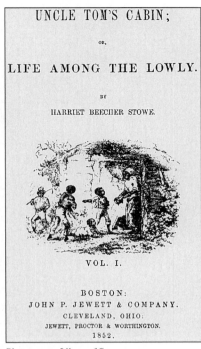

UNCLE TOM'S CABIN;

OR,

LIFE AMONG THE LOWLY.

BY

HARRIET BEECHER STOWE.

VOL. I.

BOSTON:
JOHN P. JEWETT & COMPANY.
CLEVELAND, OHIO:
JEWETT, PROCTOR & WORTHINGTON.
1852.

Photo courtesy: Library of Congress

■ The original title page of *Uncle Tom's Cabin, or Life Among the Lowly*, by Harriet Beecher Stowe.

Thirteenth Amendment
One of the three Civil War Amendments; specifically bans slavery in the United States.

Black Codes
Laws denying most legal rights to newly freed slaves; passed by southern states following the Civil War.

Fourteenth Amendment
One of the three Civil War Amendments; guarantees equal protection and due process of the laws to all U.S. citizens.

The Living Constitution

Neither slavery nor involuntary servitude, except as a punishment for crime whereof the party shall have been duly convicted, shall exist within the United States, or any place subject to their jurisdiction.
—Thirteenth Amendment, Section 1

This amendment, the first of three Civil War Amendments, abolished slavery throughout the United States and its territories. It also prohibited involuntary servitude.

Based on his war power's authority, in 1863, President Abraham Lincoln issued the Emancipation Proclamation abolishing slavery in the states that were in rebellion against the United States. Because Congress was considered to lack the constitutional authority to abolish slavery, after one unsuccessful attempt to garner the two-thirds vote necessary, the proposed Thirteenth Amendment was forwarded to the states on February 1, 1865. The text of the amendment reproduced the words of the Northwest Ordinance of 1787; with its adoption, said one of its sponsors, it relieved Congress "of sectional strifes." Initially, some doubted if any groups other than newly freed African slaves were protected by the provisions of the amendment. Soon, however, the Supreme Court went on to clarify this question by noting: "If Mexican peonage or the Chinese coolie labor system shall develop slavery of the Mexican or Chinese race within our territory, this amendment may safely be trusted to make it void."

In the early 1990s, the Supreme Court was called on several times to construe section 1 of the amendment, especially in regard to involuntary servitude. Thus, provisions of an Alabama law that called for criminal sanctions and jail time for defaulting sharecroppers were considered unconstitutional and Congress enacted a law banning this kind of peonage. More recently, however, the Court has found compulsory high school community service programs not to violate the ban on involuntary servitude. The Court and a host of lower federal and state courts, however, have upheld criminal convictions of those who, for example, psychologically coerced mentally retarded farm laborers into service or who lured foreign workers to the United States with promises of jobs and then forced them to work long hours at little or no pay. Human trafficking, in fact, has been targeted as an especially onerous form of involuntary servitude. The U.S. Department of Justice has undertaken hundreds of investigations in an attempt to end this system.

Fifteenth Amendment
One of the three Civil War Amendments; specifically enfranchised newly freed male slaves.

In spite of these arguments, the **Fifteenth Amendment** was passed by Congress in early 1869. It guaranteed the "right of citizens" to vote regardless of their "race, color or previous condition of servitude." Sex was not mentioned.

Woman's rights activists were shocked. Abolitionists' continued support of the Fifteenth Amendment, which was ratified by the states in 1870, prompted many woman's rights supporters to leave the abolition movement and to work solely for the cause of women's rights. Twice burned, Susan B. Anthony and Elizabeth Cady Stanton decided to form their own group, the National Woman Suffrage Association (NWSA), to achieve that goal. (Another, more conservative group, the American Woman Suffrage

Association, also was formed.) In spite of the NWSA's opposition, however, the Fifteenth Amendment was ratified by the states in 1870.

Civil Rights, Congress, and the Supreme Court

Continued southern resistance to African American equality led Congress to pass the Civil Rights Act of 1875, designed to grant equal access to public accommodations such as theaters, restaurants, and transportation. The act also prohibited the exclusion of African Americans from jury service. By 1877, however, national interest in the legal condition of African Americans waned. Most white Southerners and even some Northerners never had believed in true equality for "freedmen," as former slaves were called. Any rights that freedmen received had been contingent on federal enforcement. Federal occupation of the South ended in 1877. National troops were no longer available to guard polling places and to prevent whites from excluding black voters, and southern states quickly moved to limit African Americans' access to the ballot. Other forms of discrimination also were allowed by judicial decisions upholding **Jim Crow laws,** which required segregation in public schools and facilities including railroads, restaurants, and theaters. Some Jim Crow laws, specifically known as miscegenation laws, barred interracial marriage.

All these laws, at first glance, appeared to conflict with the Civil Rights Act of 1875. In 1883, however, a series of cases decided by the Supreme Court severely damaged the vitality of the 1875 act. The ***Civil Rights Cases*** (1883) were five separate cases involving the convictions of private individuals found to have violated the Civil Rights Act by refusing to extend accommodations to African Americans in theaters, a hotel, and a railroad.[4] In deciding these cases, the Supreme Court ruled that Congress could prohibit only state or governmental action and not private acts of discrimination. The Court thus seriously limited the scope of the Civil Rights Act by concluding that Congress had no authority to prohibit private discrimination in public accommodations.

The Court's opinion in the *Civil Rights Cases* provided a moral reinforcement for the Jim Crow system. Southern states viewed the Court's ruling as an invitation to gut the reach and intent of the Thirteenth, Fourteenth, and Fifteenth Amendments.

In devising ways to make certain that African Americans did not vote, Southerners had to avoid the intent of the Fifteenth Amendment. This amendment did not

The Struggle for Equal Protection

Jim Crow laws
Laws enacted by southern states that discriminated against blacks by creating "whites only" schools, theaters, hotels, and other public accommodations.

Civil Rights Cases (1883)
Name attached to five cases brought under the Civil Rights Act of 1875. In 1883, the Supreme Court decided that discrimination in a variety of public accommodations, including theaters, hotels, and railroads, could not be prohibited by the act because it was private, not state, discrimination.

Photo courtesy: Bettmann/CORBIS

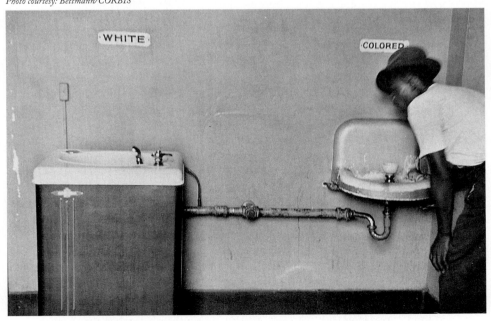

■ Throughout the South, examples of Jim Crow laws abounded. One such law required separate public drinking fountains, shown here. Notice the obvious difference in quality.

guarantee suffrage; it simply said that states could not deny anyone the right to vote on account of race or color. To exclude African Americans in a seemingly racially neutral way, southern states used three devices before the 1890s: (1) poll taxes (small taxes on the right to vote that often came due when poor African American sharecroppers had the least amount of money on hand); (2) some form of property-owning qualifications; and, (3) "literacy" or "understanding" tests, which allowed local voter registration officials to administer difficult reading-comprehension tests to potential voters whom they did not know.

These voting restrictions had an immediate impact. By the late 1890s, black voting fell by 62 percent from the Reconstruction period, while white voting fell by only 26 percent. To make certain that these laws did not further reduce the numbers of poor or uneducated white voters, many southern states added a **grandfather clause** to their voting qualification provisions, granting voting privileges to those who failed to pass a wealth or literacy test only if their grandfathers had voted before Reconstruction. Grandfather clauses effectively denied the descendents of slaves the right to vote.

While African Americans continued to face wide-ranging racism on all fronts, women also confronted discrimination. During this period, married women, by law, could not be recognized as legal entities. Women often were treated in the same category as juveniles and imbeciles, and in many states they were not entitled to wages, inheritances, or custody of their children.

grandfather clause
Voting qualification provision in many southern states that allowed only those whose grandfathers had voted before Reconstruction to vote unless they passed a wealth or literacy test.

THE PUSH FOR EQUALITY, 1890–1954

THE PROGRESSIVE ERA (1890–1920) was characterized by a concerted effort to reform political, economic, and social affairs. Evils such as child labor, the concentration of economic power in the hands of a few industrialists, limited suffrage, political corruption, business monopolies, and prejudice against African Americans all were targets of progressive reform efforts. Distress over the legal inferiority of African Americans was aggravated by the U.S. Supreme Court's decision in **Plessy v. Ferguson (1896),** a case that some commentators point to as the Court's darkest hour.[5]

In 1892, a group of African Americans in Louisiana decided to test the constitutionality of a Louisiana law mandating racial segregation on all public trains. They convinced Homer Plessy, a man of seven-eighths Caucasian and one-eighth African descent, to board a train in New Orleans and proceed to the "whites only" car.[6] He was arrested when he refused to take a seat in the car reserved for African Americans as required by state law. Plessy challenged the law, arguing that the Fourteenth Amendment prohibited racial segregation.

The Supreme Court disagreed. After analyzing the history of African Americans in the United States, the majority concluded that the Louisiana law was constitutional. The justices based their decision on their belief that separate facilities for blacks and whites provided equal protection of the laws. After all, they reasoned, African Americans were not prevented from riding the train; the Louisiana statute required only that the races travel separately. Justice John Marshall Harlan was the lone dissenter. He argued that "the Constitution is colorblind" and that it was senseless to hold constitutional a law "which, practically, puts the badge of servitude and degradation upon a large class of our fellow citizens."

Not surprisingly, the separate-but-equal doctrine enunciated in *Plessy* v. *Ferguson* soon came to mean only separate, as new legal avenues to discriminate against African Americans were enacted into law throughout the South. The Jim Crow system soon expanded and became a way of life and a rigid social code in the American South. Journalist Juan Williams notes in *Eyes on the Prize:*

Plessy v. *Ferguson* (1896)
Plessy challenged a Louisiana statute requiring that railroads provide separate accommodations for blacks and whites. The Court found that separate but equal accommodations did not violate the equal protection clause of the Fourteenth Amendment.

> There were Jim Crow schools, Jim Crow restaurants, Jim Crow water fountains, and Jim Crow customs—blacks were expected to tip their hats when they walked

past whites, but whites did not have to remove their hats even when they entered a black family's home. Whites were to be called "sir" and "ma'am" by blacks, who in turn were called by their first names by whites. People with white skin were to be given a wide berth on the sidewalk; blacks were expected to step aside meekly.[7]

By 1900, equality for African Americans was far from the promise first offered by the Civil War Amendments. Again and again, the Supreme Court nullified the intent of the amendments and sanctioned racial segregation while the states avidly followed its lead.[8]

The Founding of the National Association for the Advancement of Colored People

In 1909, a handful of individuals active in a variety of progressive causes, including woman suffrage and the fight for better working conditions for women and children, met to discuss the idea of a group devoted to the problems of the Negro. Major race riots recently had occurred in several American cities, and progressive reformers were concerned about these outbreaks of violence and the possibility of others. Oswald Garrison Villard, the influential publisher of the *New York Evening Post*—and the grandson of William Lloyd Garrison—called a conference to discuss the problem. This group soon evolved into the National Association for the Advancement of Colored People (NAACP). Along with Villard, its first leaders included W. E. B. DuBois, a founder of the Niagara Movement, a group of educated African Americans who took their name from their first meeting place in Niagara Falls, Ontario, Canada.

Photo courtesy: Photographs and Prints Division, Schomburg Center for Research in Black Culture, New York Public Library, Astor, Lenox, and Tilden Foundations

■ W. E. B. DuBois (second from right in the second row, facing left) is pictured with the original leaders of the Niagara Movement. This 1905 photo was taken on the Canadian side of Niagara Falls. The Niagara reformers met in Canada because no hotel on the U.S. side would accommodate them. At the meeting, a list of injustices suffered by African Americans was detailed.

Key Women's Groups

The struggle for women's rights was revitalized in 1890 when the National and American Woman Suffrage Associations merged. The new organization, the National American Woman Suffrage Association (NAWSA), was headed by Susan B. Anthony. Unlike NWSA, which had sought a wide variety of expanded rights for women, this new association was devoted largely to securing woman suffrage. Its task was greatly facilitated by the proliferation of women's groups that emerged during the Progressive era. In addition to the rapidly growing temperance movement—the move to ban the sale of alcohol, which many women blamed for a variety of social ills—women's groups were created to seek protective legislation in the form of maximum hour or minimum wage laws for women and to work for improved sanitation, public morals, education, and the like. Other organizations that were part of what was called the club movement were created to provide increased cultural and literary experiences for middle-class women. With increased industrialization, for the first time some women found that they had the opportunity to pursue activities other than those centered on the home.

One of the most active groups lobbying on behalf of women during this period was the National Consumers' League (NCL), which successfully lobbied for Oregon legislation limiting women to eight hours of work a day. Curt Muller was then charged and convicted of employing women more than eight hours a day in his small laundry. When he

Photo courtesy: Supreme Court Historical Society/Mrs. Neill Whisnant and Portland, Oregon, Chamber of Commerce

■ In 1908, the U.S. Supreme Court ruled that Oregon's law barring women from working more than eight hours a day in laundries was constitutional. Thus, the conviction of Curt Muller (with arms folded), who owned the laundry where women worked twelve- and fourteen-hour days, was upheld. Ironically, one of the major goals of the later women's movement was to remove this kind of protective legislation.

suffrage movement
The drive for voting rights for women that took place in the United States from 1890 to 1920.

Nineteenth Amendment
Amendment to the Constitution that guaranteed women the right to vote.

appealed his conviction to the U.S. Supreme Court, the NCL sought permission from the state to conduct the defense of the statute.

At the urging of NCL attorney and future U.S. Supreme Court Justice Louis Brandeis, NCL members amassed an impressive array of sociological and medical data that were incorporated into what became known as the Brandeis brief. This contained only three pages of legal argument. More than a hundred pages were devoted to nonlegal, sociological data that were used to convince the Court that Oregon's statute was constitutional. In agreeing with the NCL in *Muller* v. *Oregon* (1908), the Court relied heavily on these data to document women's unique status as mothers to justify their differential legal treatment.[9]

Women seeking the vote used reasoning reflecting the Court's opinion in *Muller*. Discarding earlier notions of full equality, NAWSA based its claim to the right to vote largely on the fact that women, as mothers, should be enfranchised. Furthermore, although many members of the suffrage movement were NAACP members, the new women's movement—called the **suffrage movement** because of its focus on the vote alone and not on broader issues of women's rights—took on racist overtones. Suffragists argued that if undereducated African Americans could vote, why couldn't women? Some NAWSA members even argued that "the enfranchisement of women would ensure immediate and durable white supremacy."

Diverse attitudes clearly were present in the growing suffrage movement, which often tried to be all things to all people. Its roots in the Progressive movement gave it an exceptionally broad base that transformed NAWSA from a small organization of just over 10,000 members in the early 1890s to a true social movement of more than 2 million members in 1917. By 1920, a coalition of women's groups, led by NAWSA and the newer, more radical National Woman's Party, was able to secure ratification of the **Nineteenth Amendment** to the Constitution. It guaranteed all women the right to vote—fifty years after African American males were enfranchised by the Fifteenth Amendment.

After passage of the suffrage amendment in 1920, the fragile alliance of diverse women's groups that had come together to fight for the vote quickly disintegrated. Women returned to their home groups, such as the NCL or the Women's Christian Temperance Union, to pursue their individualized goals. In fact, after the tumult of the suffrage movement, widespread organized activity on behalf of women's rights did not reemerge until the 1960s. In the meantime, however, the NAACP continued to fight racism and racial segregation. In fact, its activities and those of others in the civil rights movement would later give impetus to a new women's movement.

Litigating for Equality

During the 1930s, leaders of the NAACP began to sense that the time was right to launch a full-scale challenge in the federal courts to the constitutionality of *Plessy*'s separate-but-equal doctrine. Clearly, the separate-but-equal doctrine and the proliferation of Jim Crow laws were a bar to any hope of full equality for African Americans. Traditional legislative channels were unlikely to work, given blacks' limited or nonexistent political power. Thus, the federal courts and a long-range litigation strategy were the NAACP's only hopes. The NAACP mapped out a long-range strategy that would first target segregation in professional and graduate education.

Test Cases.   The NAACP opted first to challenge the constitutionality of Jim Crow law schools. In 1935, all southern states maintained fully segregated elementary and secondary schools. Colleges and universities also were segregated, but most states did not provide for postgraduate education for African Americans. NAACP lawyers chose to target law schools because they were institutions that judges could well understand, and integration there would prove less threatening to most whites.

Lloyd Gaines, a graduate of Missouri's all-black Lincoln University, sought admission to the all-white University of Missouri Law School in 1936. He was immediately rejected. In the separate-but-equal spirit, the state offered to build a law school at Lincoln (although no funds were allocated for the project) or, if he didn't want to wait, to pay his tuition at an out-of-state law school. Gaines rejected the offer, sued, lost in the lower courts, and appealed to the U.S. Supreme Court.

Gaines's case was filed at an auspicious time. As discussed in chapter 3, a constitutional revolution of sorts occurred in Supreme Court decision making in 1937. Before this time, the Court was most receptive to and interested in the protection of economic liberties. In 1937, however, the Court reversed itself in a series of cases and began to place individual freedoms and personal liberties on a more protected footing. Thus, in 1938, Gaines's lawyers pleaded his appeal to a far more sympathetic Supreme Court. NAACP attorneys argued that the creation of a separate law school of a lesser caliber than that of the University of Missouri would not and could not afford Gaines an equal education. The justices agreed and ruled that Missouri had failed to meet the separate-but-equal requirements of *Plessy*. The Court ordered Missouri either to admit Gaines to the school or to set up a law school for him.[10]

Recognizing the importance of the Court's ruling, in 1939 the NAACP created a separate, tax-exempt legal defense fund to devise a strategy that would build on the

Photo courtesy: Library of Congress

■ Suffragists demonstrating for the franchise. Parades like this one took place in cities all over the United States.

Missouri case and bring about equal educational opportunities for all African American children. The first head of the NAACP Legal Defense and Educational Fund, commonly referred to as the LDF, was Thurgood Marshall, who later became the first African American to serve on the U.S. Supreme Court. Sensing that the Court would be more amenable to the NAACP's broader goals if it were first forced to address a variety of less threatening claims to educational opportunity, Marshall and the LDF brought a series of carefully crafted test cases to the Court.

The first case involved H. M. Sweatt, a forty-six-year-old African American mail carrier, who applied for admission to the all-white University of Texas Law School in 1946. Rejected on racial grounds, Sweatt sued. The judge gave the state six months to establish a law school or to admit Sweatt to the university. The university then rented a few rooms in downtown Houston and hired two local African American attorneys to be part-time faculty members. (At that time, there was only one full-time African American law school professor in the United States.) The state legislature saw the handwriting on the wall and authorized $3 million for the creation of the Texas State University for Negroes. One hundred thousand dollars of that money was to be for a new law school in Austin across the street from the state capitol building. It consisted of three small basement rooms, a library of more than 10,000 books, access to the state law library, and three part-time first-year instructors as the faculty. Sweatt declined the opportunity to obtain an education there and instead chose to continue his legal challenge.

While working on the Texas case, the LDF also decided to pursue a case involving George McLaurin, a retired university professor who had been denied admission to the doctoral education program at the University of Oklahoma. Marshall reasoned that McLaurin, at age sixty-eight, would be immune from the charges that African Americans wanted integration in order to intermarry with whites. After a lower court ordered McLaurin's admission, the university reserved a dingy alcove in the cafeteria for him to eat in during off-hours, and he was given his own table in the library behind a shelf of newspapers. In what surely "was Oklahoma's most inventive contribution to legalized bigotry since the adoption of the 'grandfather clause,' " McLaurin was forced to sit outside classrooms while lectures and seminars were conducted inside.[11]

The Supreme Court handled these two cases together.[12] The eleven southern states filed an *amicus curiae* (friend of the court) brief, in which they argued that *Plessy* should govern both cases. The LDF received assistance, however, from an unexpected source—the U.S. government. In a dramatic departure from the past, the administration of President Harry S Truman filed a friend of the court brief urging the Court to overrule *Plessy*. Earlier, Truman had issued an executive order desegregating the military.

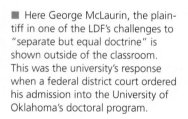

■ Here George McLaurin, the plaintiff in one of the LDF's challenges to "separate but equal doctrine" is shown outside of the classroom. This was the university's response when a federal district court ordered his admission into the University of Oklahoma's doctoral program.

Photo courtesy: Bettmann/Corbis

Since the late 1870s, the U.S. government never had sided against the southern states in a civil rights matter and never had submitted an *amicus* brief supporting the rights of African American citizens. President Truman believed that because many African Americans had fought and died for their country in World War II, this kind of executive action was proper. The Court traditionally gives great weight to briefs from the U.S. government. The Court, however, did not overrule *Plessy*, but the justices found that the measures taken by the states in each case failed to live up to the strictures of the separate-but-equal doctrine. The Court unanimously ruled that the remedies to each situation were inadequate to afford a sound education. In the *Sweatt* case, for example, the Court declared that the "qualities which are incapable of objective measurement but which make for greatness in a law school . . . includ[ing] the reputation of the faculty, experience of the administration, position and influence of the alumni, standing in the community, traditions and prestige" made it impossible for the state to provide an equal education in a segregated setting.[13]

In 1950, after these decisions were handed down, the LDF concluded that the time had come to launch a full-scale attack on the separate-but-equal doctrine. The decisions of the Court were encouraging, and the position of the U.S. government and the population in general appeared to be more receptive to an outright overruling of *Plessy*.

Brown v. Board of Education.   ***Brown v. Board of Education*** (1954) actually was four cases brought from different areas of the South and border states involving public elementary or high school systems that mandated separate schools for blacks and whites.[14] In *Brown*, LDF lawyers, again led by Thurgood Marshall, argued that *Plessy*'s separate-but-equal doctrine was unconstitutional under the **equal protection clause** of the Fourteenth Amendment, and that if the Court was still reluctant to overrule *Plessy*, the only way to equalize the schools was to integrate them. A major component of the LDF's strategy was to prove that the intellectual, psychological, and financial damage that befell African Americans as a result of segregation precluded any court from finding that equality was served by the separate-but-equal policy.

In *Brown*, the LDF presented the Supreme Court with evidence of the harmful consequences of state-imposed racial discrimination. To buttress its claims, the LDF introduced the now-famous doll study, conducted by Kenneth Clark, a prominent African American sociologist who had long studied the negative effects of segregation on African American children. His research revealed that black children not only preferred white dolls when shown black dolls and white dolls, but that most liked the white doll better, many adding that the black doll looked "bad." This information was used to illustrate the negative impact of racial segregation and bias on an African American child's self-image.

The LDF's legal briefs were supported by important *amicus curiae* briefs submitted by the U.S. government, major civil rights groups, labor unions, and religious groups decrying racial segregation. On May 17, 1954, Chief Justice Earl Warren delivered the fourth opinion of the day, *Brown v. Board of Education*. Writing for the Court, Warren stated:

> To separate [some school children] from others . . . solely because of their race generates a feeling of inferiority as to their status in the community that may affect their hearts and minds in a way very unlikely ever to be undone. We conclude, unanimously, that in the field of public education the doctrine of "separate but equal" has no place.

There can be no doubt that *Brown* was the most important civil rights case decided in the twentieth century.[15] It immediately evoked an uproar that shook the nation. Some segregationists called the day the decision was handed down Black Monday. The governor of South Carolina denounced the decision, saying, "Ending segregation would mark the beginning of the end of civilization in the South as we know it."[16] The LDF lawyers who had argued these cases and those cases leading to *Brown*, however, were jubilant.

Remarkable changes had occurred in the civil rights of Americans since 1890. Women had won the right to vote, and after a long and arduous trail of litigation in the federal courts, the Supreme Court had finally overturned its most racist decision of the era, *Plessy v. Ferguson*. The Court boldly proclaimed that separate but equal (at least in education) would no longer pass constitutional muster. The question then became how *Brown* would be interpreted and implemented. Could it be used to invalidate other Jim Crow laws and practices? Would African Americans ever be truly equal under the law?

THE CIVIL RIGHTS MOVEMENT

OUR NOTION OF CIVIL RIGHTS has changed profoundly since the *Brown* decision in 1954. *Brown* served as a catalyst for change, sparking the development of the modern civil rights movement. Women's work in that movement and the student protest move-

Brown v. Board of Education (1954)
U.S. Supreme Court decision holding that school segregation is inherently unconstitutional because it violates the Fourteenth Amendment's guarantee of equal protection; marked the end of legal segregation in the United States.

equal protection clause
Section of the Fourteenth Amendment that guarantees that all citizens receive "equal protection of the laws."

BROWN V. *BOARD OF EDUCATION* AFTER FIFTY YEARS

> **OVERVIEW:** It is difficult to overstate the impact of the Supreme Court decision in *Brown* v. *Board of Education* (1954) on American life. The *Brown* decision was instrumental in making civil rights the highest priority on the domestic policy agenda during the 1950s and 1960s, and it held out the promise of educational equality for all Americans. The Court in *Brown* held "education is perhaps the most important function of state and local governments," and that "In these days, it is doubtful . . . any child may reasonably be expected to succeed in life if he is denied the opportunity of an education"—which the Court believed is a right that "must be made available to all on equal terms." In order for American society to attain justice, the Court understood segregation had to end and that equal educational opportunity is the key through which all Americans are given the tools to survive and thrive in contemporary society.

After five decades, the results of the *Brown* decision have been mixed. The objective of *Brown* was to create equal educational opportunity; however, there is no constitutional mandate for such a prospect. The Constitution does not speak to education, so that right is given to the states to determine, and it follows that with vast discrepancies in wealth and resources between the states, educational establishments will be unequal as well. This problem is exacerbated when fewer funds are allocated to substandard school districts with significant minority populations. Additionally, many members of the middle class, predominately white, have been abandoning the inner cities, leaving poorer, minority populations in underfunded school districts, thus engendering *de facto* segregation. The disparities in education reflect disparities in housing patterns, a problem which is outside the authority of school administrators. Segregation is seen even in integrated schools when a disproportionate number of white and Asian Americans are found in advanced placement classes and a disproportionate number of black and Hispanic Americans are found in remedial and special-needs classes.

A principal effect of *Brown* was to highlight the disparity between the education of majority and minority America. Fifty years later, however, it seems educational segregation may still be the rule rather than the exception. What is the best way to ensure equal educational opportunity for all Americans? Does a diverse classroom necessarily mean a quality education for all? If so, what is the best way to achieve this standard, and if not, what other policy alternatives are available? The 2000 National Assessment of Education Progress (NAEP) shows vast disparities in educational achievement between white and black America. Is segregation the problem, or are there other significant factors as well? What is the best way to ensure a level playing field in the education policy domain?

Arguments for the Effectiveness of *Brown*

- ***Brown* has reframed the way Americans view educational integration.** The Court held in *Brown* that education is "necessary for good citizenship" and the only way to make American society more just is to provide all citizens the opportunity for a quality education in order for all to realize their ideal of the American Dream. Americans now understand that an equal education for all is necessary to improve the lives of individuals and to realize fundamental American political principles.

ment that arose in reaction to the U.S. government's involvement in Vietnam gave women the experience needed to form their own organizations to press for full equality. As African Americans and women became more and more successful, they served as models for other groups who sought equality—Hispanic Americans, Native Americans, homosexuals, the disabled, and others.

School Desegregation After *Brown*

One year after *Brown*, in a case referred to as *Brown* v. *Board of Education II* (1955), the Court ruled that racially segregated systems must be dismantled "with all deliberate speed."[17] To facilitate implementation, the Court placed enforcement of *Brown* in the hands of appointed federal district court judges, who were considered more immune to local political pressures than were elected state court judges.

The NAACP and its LDF continued to resort to the courts to see that *Brown* was implemented, while the South entered into a near conspiracy to avoid the mandates of *Brown II*. In Arkansas, for example, Governor Orval Faubus, who was facing a reelection bid, announced that he would not "be a party to any attempt to force acceptance of change to which people are overwhelmingly opposed."[18] The day before school was to begin, he

- **Brown signaled the end of racial segregation and helped usher in the civil rights movement.** *Brown* was instrumental in creating the social context for the Civil Rights Acts of 1957, 1960, and 1964 and the Voting Rights Act of 1965. Though there is work yet to be done, the sum total of this legislation was to help further and partially realize the goals of social equality and equality before the law.
- **Brown set the model for other social justice movements in the United States.** The legal approach by NAACP LDF lawyers has set the standard for other groups pursuing legal and social equality and inclusion. Supporters of women's rights, Hispanic and Native American rights, gay rights, and rights of the disabled rights may be said to owe a debt of gratitude to the constitutional interpretation and legal strategies offered by the legal team that argued for *Brown* and the U.S. Supreme Court.

Arguments Against the Effectiveness of *Brown*

- **Fifty years later, there are still vast disparities in educational attainment between minority and white students.** According to the NAEP, 63 percent of black, inner-city fourth-graders are unable to attain basic proficiency in reading. And, according to black educator Walter Williams, the average black high school graduate has achieved the educational equivalent of a seventh- or eighth-grade mastery of basic subjects and is thus ill prepared to enter the job market or a university.
- **The goal of *Brown* has yet to be fully realized; instead of educational and social integration, segregation between the races is still a significant problem.** In 2004, approximately 70 percent of African American children attend public schools where greater than 50 percent of the student population is black—in Washington, D.C.,

the student population is 85 percent black. One effect of the *Brown* decision is "white flight"—the movement of the white middle class out of the inner cities to the suburbs and surrounding country.
- **The *Brown* decision does not address other problems that affect educational attainment.** *Brown* does not address other factors understood to affect social and educational achievement. For example, *Brown* does not address issues such as the effect of high rates of illegitimacy in black communities on educational attainment. In a controversial speech to the NAACP, comedian Bill Cosby took black parents to task for not tending to the education of their children; after all, it is not funding or segregation keeping children from spending time doing their homework, from skipping school, and from reading.

Questions

1. Is integration in educational institutions the solution for academic achievement, or are there other, more significant solutions to help close the learning gap?
2. Will an attempt to realize educational equality across the states violate states' rights and the principle of federalism? What is the best way to ensure this equality?

Selected Readings

Robert Cottrol et al. *Brown v. Board of Education: Caste, Culture and the Constitution.* Lawrence: University Press of Kansas, 2003.

Charles J. Ogletree. *All Deliberate Speed: Reflections on the First Half-Century of Brown v. Board of Education.* New York: Norton, 2004.

announced that National Guardsmen would surround Little Rock's Central High School to prevent African American students from entering. While the federal courts in Arkansas continued to order the admission of African American children, the governor remained adamant. Finally, President Dwight D. Eisenhower sent federal troops to Little Rock to protect the rights of the nine students attending Central High.

In reaction to the governor's outrageous conduct, the Court broke with tradition and issued a unanimous decision in *Cooper* v. *Aaron* (1958), which was filed by the Little Rock School Board asking the federal district court for a two-and-one-half-year delay in implementation of its desegregation plans. Each justice signed the opinion individually, underscoring his individual support for the notion that "no state legislator or executive or judicial officer can war against the Constitution without violating his undertaking to support it."[19] The state's actions thus were ruled unconstitutional and its "evasive schemes" illegal.

A New Move for African American Rights

In 1955, soon after *Brown II*, the civil rights movement took another step forward—this time in Montgomery, Alabama. Rosa Parks, the local NAACP's Youth Council adviser, decided to challenge the constitutionality of the segregated bus system. First, Parks and

Photo courtesy: Carl Iwasaki/TimePix

■ On September 25, 1957, troops escorted nine African American children to Central High School in Little Rock, Arkansas. A federal court had ordered the school's desegregation in response to *Brown v. Board of Education* (1954), but Arkansas Governor Orval Faubus fought the ruling. President Dwight D. Eisenhower used the National Guard to provide continuing protection for the students.

other NAACP officials began to raise money for litigation and made speeches around town to garner public support. Then, on December 1, 1955, Rosa Parks made history when she refused to leave her seat on a bus to move to the back to make room for a white male passenger. She was arrested for violating an Alabama law banning integration of public facilities, including buses. After she was freed on bond, Parks and the NAACP decided to enlist city clergy to help her cause. At the same time, they distributed 35,000 handbills calling for African Americans to boycott the Montgomery bus system on the day of Parks's trial. Black ministers used Sunday services to urge their members to support the boycott. On Monday morning, African Americans walked, carpooled, or used black-owned taxicabs. That night, local ministers decided that the boycott should be continued. A new, twenty-six-year-old minister, Martin Luther King Jr., was selected to lead the newly formed Montgomery Improvement Association.

As the boycott dragged on, Montgomery officials and local business owners began to harass the city's African American citizens. The residents held out, despite suffering personal hardship for their actions, ranging from harassment to bankruptcy to job loss. In 1956, a federal court ruled that the segregated bus system violated the equal protection clause of the Fourteenth Amendment. After a year of walking, black Montgomery residents ended their protest when city buses were ordered to integrate. The first effort at nonviolent protest had been successful. Organized boycotts and other forms of nonviolent protest, including sit-ins at segregated restaurants and bus stations, were to follow.

Formation of New Groups

The recognition and respect that Martin Luther King Jr. earned within the African American community helped him to launch the Southern Christian Leadership Conference (SCLC) in 1957, soon after the end of the Montgomery bus boycott. Unlike the NAACP, which had northern origins and had come to rely largely on litigation as a means of achieving expanded equality, the SCLC had a southern base and was rooted more closely in black religious culture. The SCLC's philosophy reflected King's growing belief in the importance of nonviolent protest and civil disobedience.

On February 1, 1960, students at the all-black North Carolina Agricultural and Technical College participated in the first sit-in. Black students marched to a local lunch counter, sat down, and ordered cups of coffee. They were refused service and sat at the counter until police arrived. When the students refused to leave, they were arrested and jailed. Soon thereafter, African American college students around the South did the same. Their actions were the subject of extensive national media attention.

Over spring break 1960, with the assistance of an $800 grant from the SCLC, 200 student delegates—black and white—met at Shaw University in North Carolina to consider recent sit-in actions and to plan for the future. Later that year, the Student Nonviolent Coordinating Committee (SNCC) was formed.

Whereas the SCLC generally worked with church leaders in a community, SNCC was much more of a grassroots organization. Always perceived as more radical than the SCLC, SNCC tended to focus its organizing activities on the young, both black and white.

In addition to joining the sit-in bandwagon, SNCC also came to lead what were called freedom rides, designed to focus attention on segregated public accommodations. Bands of college students and other civil rights activists traveled by bus throughout the South in an effort to force bus stations to desegregate. Often these protesters were met by angry mobs of segregationists and brutal violence, as local police chose not to defend protesters' basic constitutional rights to free speech and peaceful assembly. African Americans were not the only ones to participate in freedom rides; increasingly, white college students from the North began to play an important role in SNCC.

While SNCC continued to sponsor sit-ins and freedom rides, in 1963, Martin Luther King Jr. launched a series of massive nonviolent demonstrations in Birmingham, Alabama, long considered a major stronghold of segregation. Thousands of blacks and whites marched to Birmingham in a show of solidarity. Peaceful marchers were met there by the Birmingham police commissioner, who ordered his officers to use dogs, clubs, and fire hoses on the marchers. Americans across the nation were horrified as they witnessed on television the brutality and abuse heaped on the protesters. As the marchers hoped, these shocking scenes helped convince President John F. Kennedy to propose important civil rights legislation.

The Civil Rights Act of 1964

Both the SCLC and SNCC sought full implementation of Supreme Court decisions dealing with race and an end to racial segregation and discrimination. The cumulative effect of collective actions including sit-ins, boycotts, marches, and freedom rides—as well as the tragic bombings and deaths inflicted in retaliation—led Congress to pass the first major piece of civil rights legislation since the post–Civil War era, the Civil Rights Act of 1964. Several events led to the consideration of this legislation.

In 1963, President John F. Kennedy requested that Congress pass a law banning discrimination in public accommodations. Seizing the moment, Martin Luther King Jr. called for a monumental march on Washington, D.C., to demonstrate widespread support for far-ranging anti-discrimination legislation. It was clear that national laws outlawing discrimination were the only answer: southern legislators would never vote to repeal Jim Crow laws. The March on Washington for Jobs and Freedom was held in August 1963, only a few months after the Birmingham demonstrations. More than 250,000 people heard King deliver his famous "I Have a Dream" speech from the Lincoln Memorial. Before Congress had the opportunity to vote on any legislation, however, John F. Kennedy was assassinated on November 22, 1963, in Dallas, Texas.

When Vice President Lyndon B. Johnson, a southern-born, former Senate majority leader, succeeded Kennedy as president, he put civil rights reform at the top of his legislative priority list, and civil rights activists gained a critical ally. Thus, through the 1960s, the movement subtly changed in focus from peaceful protest and litigation to legislative lobbying. Its focus broadened from integration of school and public facilities and voting rights to issues of housing, jobs, and equal opportunity.

The push for civil rights legislation in the halls of Congress was helped by changes in public opinion. Between 1959 and 1965, southern attitudes toward integrated schools changed enormously. The proportion of Southerners who responded that they would not mind their child's attendance at a racially balanced school doubled.

Analyzing Visuals

POLICE CONFRONT CIVIL RIGHTS DEMONSTRATORS IN BIRMINGHAM

Civil rights demonstrators in the 1960s sought national attention for their cause, and photos in the print media were a powerful tool in swaying public opinion. In the May 1963 photograph by Charles Moore reprinted here, dogs controlled by police officers in Birmingham, Alabama, attack civil rights demonstrators. This photograph first appeared in the May 17, 1963, issue of the very popular *Life* magazine as part of an eleven-page spread of Moore's photographs of the demonstration in Birmingham. The photo was reprinted often and even frequently mentioned on the floor of Congress during debates on the Civil Rights Act of 1964. After examining the photograph, answer the following critical thinking questions: What do you observe about the scene and the various people shown in the photograph? What do you notice about the man who is being attacked by the dogs? The other demonstrators? The police? What emotions does the picture evoke? Why do you think this image was an effective tool in the struggle for civil rights?

Photo courtesy: Charles Moore/Black Star

In spite of strong presidential support and the sway of public opinion, the Civil Rights Act of 1964 did not sail through Congress. Southern senators, led by South Carolina's Strom Thurmond, a Democrat who later switched to the Republican Party, conducted the longest filibuster in the history of the Senate. For eight weeks, Thurmond led the effort to hold up voting on the civil rights bill until cloture (see chapter 7) was invoked and the filibuster ended. Once passed, the **Civil Rights Act of 1964:**

Civil Rights Act of 1964
Legislation passed by Congress to outlaw segregation in public facilities and racial discrimination in employment, education, and voting; created the Equal Employment Opportunity Commission.

- Outlawed arbitrary discrimination in voter registration and expedited voting rights lawsuits.
- Barred discrimination in public accommodations engaged in interstate commerce.
- Authorized the Department of Justice to initiate lawsuits to desegregate public facilities and schools.

Photo courtesy: DALMAS/SIPA Press

■ Civil rights marchers at the historic gathering on the Mall in Washington, D.C., in August 1963, where Martin Luther King Jr. delivered his famous "I Have a Dream" speech. King was later gunned down at age thirty-nine in Memphis, Tennessee.

- Provided for the withholding of federal funds from discriminatory state and local programs.
- Prohibited discrimination in employment on grounds of race, color, religion, national origin, or sex.
- Created the Equal Employment Opportunity Commission (EEOC) to monitor and enforce the bans on employment discrimination.

As challenges were made to the Civil Rights Act of 1964, other changes continued to sweep the United States. African Americans in the North, who believed that their brothers and sisters in the South were making progress against discrimination, found themselves frustrated. Northern blacks were experiencing high unemployment, poverty, discrimination, and little political clout. Some, including Black Muslim leader Malcolm X, even argued that, to survive, African Americans must separate themselves from white culture in every way. These increased tensions resulted in riots in many major cities from 1964 to 1968, when many African Americans in the North took to the streets, burning and looting to vent their rage. The assassination of Martin Luther King Jr. in 1968 triggered a new epidemic of race riots.

The Impact of the Civil Rights Act of 1964

Many Southerners were adamant in their belief that the Civil Rights Act of 1964 was unconstitutional because it went beyond the scope of Congress's authority to legislate under the Constitution, and lawsuits were quickly brought to challenge the act. The Supreme Court upheld its constitutionality when it found that Congress was within the legitimate scope of its commerce power as outlined in Article I.[20]

Education.   One of the key provisions of the Civil Rights Act of 1964 authorized the Department of Justice to bring actions against school districts that failed to comply with *Brown* v. *Board of Education*. By 1964, a full decade after *Brown*, fewer than 1 percent of African American children in the South attended integrated schools.

In *Swann* v. *Charlotte-Mecklenburg School District* (1971), the Supreme Court ruled that all vestiges of state-imposed segregation, called ***de jure* discrimination,** or discrimination by law, must be eliminated at once. The Court also ruled that lower federal courts had the authority to fashion a wide variety of remedies including busing, racial quotas, and the pairing of schools to end dual, segregated school systems.[21]

In *Swann*, the Court was careful to distinguish *de jure* from ***de facto* discrimination,** which is unintentional discrimination often attributable to housing patterns or private acts. The Court noted that its approval of busing was a remedy for intentional, government imposed or sanctioned discrimination only.

Over the years, forced, judicially imposed busing found less and less favor with the Supreme Court, even in situations where *de jure* discrimination had existed. In 1992, the Supreme Court ruled that in a situation where all-black schools still existed despite a 1969 court order to dismantle the *de jure* system, so long as the segregation was not a result of the school board's actions, the school district's actions could be removed from court supervision. In 1995, the Court ruled 5–4 that city school boards can use plans to attract white suburban students to mostly minority urban schools only if both city and suburban schools still show the effects of segregation, thus reversing a lower court desegregation order.[22] Today, the trend is toward dismantling court-ordered desegregation plans, although school districts still are under orders not to discriminate. Still, especially in the North, school segregation has increased steadily over the past fifteen years.[23]

Employment.   Title VII of the Civil Rights Act of 1964 prohibits employers from discriminating against employees for a variety of reasons, including race, sex, age, and national origin. (In 1978, the act was amended to prohibit discrimination based on pregnancy.) In 1971, in one of the first major cases decided under the act, the Supreme Court ruled that employers could be found liable for discrimination if the effect of their employment practices was to exclude African Americans from certain positions.[24] African American employees were allowed to use statistical evidence to show that they had been excluded from all but one department of the Duke Power Company, because it required employees to have a high school education or pass a special test to be eligible for promotion.

The Supreme Court ruled that although the tests did not appear to discriminate against African Americans, their effects—that there were no African American employees in any other departments—were sufficient to shift to the employer the burden of proving that no discrimination occurred. Thus, the Duke Power Company would have to prove that the tests were a business necessity that had a "demonstrable relationship to successful performance" of a particular job.

Photo courtesy: © Bettmann/Corbis

■ In the late 1960s, court-ordered busing to achieve racial integration frequently required police escorts.

***de jure* discrimination**
Racial segregation that is a direct result of law or official policy.

***de facto* discrimination**
Racial discrimination that results from practice (such as housing patterns or other social factors) rather than the law.

The notion of "business necessity," as set out in the Civil Rights Act of 1964 and interpreted by the federal courts, was especially important for women. Women long had been kept out of many occupations on the strength of the belief that customers preferred to deal with male personnel. Conversely, males were barred from flight-attendant positions because the airlines believed that passengers preferred to be served by young, attractive women. Similarly, many large factories, manufacturing establishments, and police and fire departments refused to hire women by subjecting them to arbitrary height and weight requirements, which also disproportionately affected Hispanics. Like the tests declared illegal by the Court, these requirements often could not be shown to be related to job performance and were eventually ruled illegal by the federal courts.

THE WOMEN'S RIGHTS MOVEMENT

JUST AS IN THE ABOLITION MOVEMENT in the 1800s, women from all walks of life also participated in the civil rights movement. Women were important members of new groups such as SNCC and the SCLC as well as more traditional groups such as the NAACP, yet they often found themselves treated as second-class citizens. At one point during a SNCC national meeting, its chair openly proclaimed: "The only position for women in the SNCC is prone."[25] Statements and attitudes like these led some women to found early women's liberation groups that were generally quite radical but small in membership.

Litigation for Equal Rights

As discussed earlier, initial efforts to convince the Supreme Court to declare women enfranchised under the equal protection clause of the Fourteenth Amendment were uniformly unsuccessful. The paternalistic attitudes of the Supreme Court, and perhaps society as well, continued well into the 1970s. As late as 1961, Florida required women who wished to serve on juries to travel to the county courthouse and register for that duty. In contrast, all men who were registered voters automatically were eligible to serve. When Gwendolyn Hoyt was convicted of bludgeoning her adulterous husband to death with a baseball bat, she appealed her conviction, claiming that the exclusion of women from her jury prejudiced her case. She believed that female jurors—her peers—would have been more sympathetic to her and the emotional turmoil that led to her attack on her husband and her claim of temporary insanity. She therefore argued that her trial by an all-male jury violated her rights as guaranteed by the Fourteenth Amendment.

In rejecting her contention, Justice John Harlan (the grandson of the lone dissenting justice in *Plessy*) wrote in *Hoyt* v. *Florida* (1961): "Despite the enlightened emancipation of women from the restrictions and protections of bygone years, and their entry into many parts of community life formerly considered to be reserved to men, a woman is still regarded as the center of home and family life."[26]

These kinds of attitudes and decisions (*Hoyt* was unanimously reversed in 1975) were not sufficient to forge a new movement for women's rights. Shortly after *Hoyt*, however, three events occurred to move women to action. In 1961, soon after his election, President John F. Kennedy created the President's Commission on the Status of Women. The commission's report, *American Women*, released in 1963, documented pervasive discrimination against women in all walks of life. In addition, the civil rights movement and the publication of Betty Friedan's *The Feminine Mystique* (1963), which led some women to question their lives and status in society, added to their dawning recognition that something was wrong.[27] Soon after, the Civil Rights Act of 1964 prohibited discrimination based not only on race but also on sex. Ironically, that provision had been added to Title VII of the Civil Rights Act by southern Democrats. These senators saw a prohibition against sex discrimination in employment as a joke, and viewed its addition as a means to discredit the entire act and ensure its defeat. Thus, it was added at the last minute and female members of Congress seized the opportunity to garner support for the measure.

Equal Employment Opportunity Commission

Federal agency created to enforce the Civil Rights Act of 1964, which forbids discrimination on the basis of race, creed, national origin, religion, or sex in hiring, promotion, or firing.

In 1966, after the **Equal Employment Opportunity Commission** failed to enforce the law as it applied to sex discrimination, female activists formed the National Organization for Women (NOW). From its inception, NOW was modeled closely on the NAACP. Women in NOW were similar to the founders of the NAACP; they wanted to work within the system to prevent discrimination. Initially, most of this activity was geared toward two goals: achievement of equality either by passage of an equal rights amendment to the Constitution, or by judicial decision.

Not all women agreed with the notion of full equality for women. Members of the National Consumers' League, for example, feared that an equal rights amendment would invalidate protective legislation of the kind specifically ruled constitutional in *Muller* v. *Oregon* (1908). Nevertheless, from 1923 to 1972, a proposal for an equal rights amendment was made in every session of every Congress. Every president since Harry S Truman backed it, and by 1972 public opinion favored its ratification.

Equal Rights Amendment

Proposed amendment that would bar discrimination against women by federal or state governments.

Finally, in 1972, in response to pressure from NOW, the National Women's Political Caucus, and a wide variety of other feminist groups, Congress voted in favor of the **Equal Rights Amendment** (ERA) by overwhelming majorities (84–8 in the Senate; 354–24 in the House). The amendment provided that:

> Equality of rights under the law shall not be denied or abridged by the United States or by any state on account of sex.
>
> The Congress shall have the power to enforce, by appropriate legislation, the provisions of this article.

Within a year, twenty-two states ratified the amendment, most by overwhelming margins. But, the tide soon turned. In *Roe* v. *Wade* (1973), the Supreme Court decided that women had a constitutionally protected right to privacy that included the right to terminate a pregnancy. Almost overnight, *Roe* gave the ERA's opponents political fuel. Although privacy rights and the ERA have nothing to do with each other, opponents effectively persuaded many people in states that had yet to ratify the amendment that the two were linked. They also claimed that the ERA and feminists were anti-family and that the ERA would force women out of their homes and into the workforce because husbands would no longer be responsible for their wives' support.

These arguments and the amendment's potential to make women eligible for the military draft brought the ratification effort to a near standstill. In 1974 and 1975, the amendment only squeaked through the Montana and North Dakota legislatures, and two states—Nebraska and Tennessee—voted to rescind their earlier ratifications. By 1978, one year before the deadline for ratification was to expire, thirty-five states had voted for the amendment—three short of the three-fourths necessary for ratification. Efforts in key states such as Illinois and Florida failed as opposition to the ERA intensified. Faced with the prospect of defeat, ERA supporters heavily lobbied Congress to extend the deadline for ratification. Congress extended the ratification period by three years, but to no avail. No additional states ratified the amendment and three more rescinded their votes.

What began as a simple correction to the Constitution turned into a highly controversial proposed change. Even though large numbers of the public favored the ERA, opponents needed to stall ratification in only thirteen states while supporters had to convince legislators in thirty-eight. The success that women's rights activists were having in the courts was hurting the effort. When women first sought the ERA in the late 1960s, the Supreme Court had yet to rule that women were protected by the Fourteenth Amendment's equal protection clause from any kind of discrimination, thus clearly showing the need for an amendment. But, as the Court widened its interpretation of the Constitution to protect women from some sorts of discrimination, in the eyes of many, the need for a new amendment became less urgent. The proposed amendment died without being ratified on June 30, 1982.

While several women's groups worked toward passage of the ERA, NOW and several other groups, including the American Civil Liberties Union (ACLU), formed litigating arms to pressure the courts. But, women faced an immediate roadblock in the Supreme Court's interpretation of the equal protection clause of the Fourteenth Amendment.

The Equal Protection Clause and Constitutional Standards of Review

The Fourteenth Amendment protects all U.S. citizens from state action that violates equal protection of the laws. Most laws, however, are subject to what is called the rational basis or minimum rationality test. This lowest level of scrutiny means that governments must allege a rational foundation for any distinctions they make. Early on, however, the Supreme Court decided that certain freedoms were entitled to a heightened standard of review. As early as 1937, the Supreme Court recognized that certain freedoms were so fundamental that a very heavy burden would be placed on any government that sought to restrict those rights. As discussed in chapter 5, when fundamental freedoms such as those guaranteed by the First Amendment or **suspect classifications** such as race are involved, the Court uses a heightened standard of review called **strict scrutiny** to determine the constitutional validity of the challenged practices, as detailed in Table 6.1. Beginning with *Korematsu* v. *U.S.* (1944), which involved a constitutional challenge to the internment of Japanese Americans as security risks during World War II, Justice Hugo Black noted that "all legal restrictions which curtail the civic rights of a single racial group are immediately suspect," and should be given "the most rigid scrutiny."[28] In *Brown* v. *Board of Education* (1954), the Supreme Court again used the strict scrutiny standard to evaluate the constitutionality of race-based distinctions. In legal terms, this means that if a statute or governmental practice makes a classification based on race, the statute is presumed to be unconstitutional unless the state can provide "compelling affirmative justifications": that is, unless the state can prove the law in question is necessary to accomplish a permissible goal and that it is the least restrictive means through which that goal can be accomplished. (In *Korematsu,* however, the Court concluded that the national risks posed by Japanese Americans were sufficient enough to justify their internment.)

During the 1960s and into the 1970s, the Court routinely struck down as unconstitutional practices and statutes that discriminated on the basis of race. "Whites-only" public parks and recreational facilities, tax-exempt status for private schools that discriminated, and statutes prohibiting racial intermarriage were declared unconstitutional. In contrast, the Court refused even to consider the fact that the equal protection clause might apply to discrimination against women. Finally, in a case argued in 1971 by Ruth Bader Ginsburg (now an associate justice of the Supreme Court) as director of the Women's Rights Project of the ACLU, the Supreme Court ruled that an Idaho law granting a male parent automatic preference over a female parent as the administrator of their deceased child's estate violated the equal protection clause of the Fourteenth Amendment. *Reed* v. *Reed* (1971), the Idaho case, turned the tide in terms of constitutional litigation. Although the Court did not rule that sex was a suspect classification, it concluded that the equal protection clause of the Fourteenth Amendment prohibited unreasonable classifications based on sex.[29]

In 1976, the Court ruled that sex-discrimination complaints would be judged by a new, judicially created intermediate standard of review a step below strict scrutiny.[30] In *Craig* v. *Boren* (1976), the Court carved out a new test to be used in examining claims of sex discrimination: "to withstand constitutional challenge, . . . classifications by gender must serve important governmental objectives and must be substantially related to

suspect classification
Category or class, such as race, that triggers the highest standard of scrutiny from the Supreme Court.

strict scrutiny
A heightened standard of review used by the Supreme Court to determine the constitutional validity of a challenged practice.

TABLE 6.1   The Equal Protection Clause and Standards of Review Used by the Supreme Court to Determine Whether It Has Been Violated

Type of Classification (What kind of statutory classification is at issue?)	Standard of Review (What standard of review will be used?)	Test (What does the Court ask?)	Example (How does the Court apply the test?)
Fundamental freedoms (including religion, assembly, press, privacy). Suspect classifications (including race, alienage, and national origin)	Strict scrutiny or heightened standard	Is classification necessary to the accomplishment of a permissible state goal? Is it the least restrictive way to reach that goal?	*Brown* v. *Board of Education* (1954): Racial segregation not necessary to accomplish the state goal of educating its students.
Gender	Intermediate standard	Does the classification serve an important governmental objective, and is it substantially related to those ends?	*Craig* v. *Boren* (1976): Keeping drunk drivers off the roads may be an important governmental objective, but allowing eighteen- to twenty-one-year-old women to drink alcoholic beverages while prohibiting men of the same age from drinking is not substantially related to that goal.
Others (including age, wealth, and mental retardation)	Minimum rationality standard	Is there any rational foundation for the discrimination?	*City of Cleburne* v. *Cleburne Living Center* (1985): Zoning restrictions against group homes for the retarded have rational basis.

achievement of those objectives." According to the Court, an intermediate standard of review was created within what previously was a two-tier distinction—strict scrutiny and rational basis.

Men, too, can use the Fourteenth Amendment to fight gender-based discrimination. Since 1976, the Court has applied the intermediate standard of constitutional review to most claims that it has heard involving gender. Thus, the following kinds of practices have been found to violate the Fourteenth Amendment:

- Single-sex public nursing schools.[31]
- Laws that consider males adults at twenty-one years but females at eighteen years.[32]
- Laws that allow women but not men to receive alimony.[33]
- State prosecutors' use of peremptory challenges to reject men or women to create more sympathetic juries.[34]
- Virginia's maintenance of an all-male military college, the Virginia Military Institute.[35]
- Different requirements for a child's acquisition of citizenship based on whether the citizen parent is a mother or a father.[36]

In contrast, the Court has upheld the following governmental practices and laws:

- Draft registration provisions for males only.[37]
- State statutory rape laws that apply only to female victims.[38]

The level of review used by the Court is crucial. Clearly, a statute excluding African Americans from draft registration would be unconstitutional. But, because gender is not subject to the same higher standard of review that is used in racial discrimination cases, the exclusion of women from the requirements of the Military Selective Service Act was ruled permissible because the government policy was considered to serve "important governmental objectives."[39]

This history has perhaps clarified why women's rights activists continue to argue that until the passage of an equal rights amendment, women will never enjoy the same rights as men. An amendment would automatically raise the level of scrutiny that the Court applies to gender-based claims, although there are clear indications that the women justices on the Court are inclined toward requiring states to show "exceedingly persuasive justifications" for their actions.[40]

In 1963, Congress passed the Equal Pay Act that requires employers to pay women and men equal pay for equal work. Women have won important victories under the act, but a large wage gap between men and women and men continues to exist, as underscored in Figure 6.1. In spite of the fact that the Equal Pay Act is forty years old, women in 2002 earned 77 percent of what men earned. In fact, a study done by the AFL-CIO shows that this discrimination will cost a twenty-one-year-old female college graduate more than one million dollars over her career.[41]

Statutory Remedies for Sex Discrimination

In part because of the limits of the intermediate standard of review and the fact that the equal protection clause applies only to *governmental* discrimination, women's rights activists began to bombard the courts with sex-discrimination cases. Other cases have been filed under Title VII of the Civil Rights Act, which prohibits discrimination by private (and, after 1972, public) employers. Key victories under Title VII include:

- Consideration of sexual harassment as sex discrimination.[42]
- Inclusion of law firms, which many argued were private partnerships, in the coverage of the act.[43]
- A broad definition of what can be considered sexual harassment, which includes same-sex harassment.[44]
- Allowance of voluntary affirmative action programs to redress historical discrimination against women.[45]

Other victories have come under **Title IX** of the Education Amendments of 1972, which bars educational institutions receiving federal funds from discriminating against

Photo courtesy: Office of the Democratic Leader Nancy Pelosi

■ Nancy Pelosi, the Minority House Leader, pays a tribute to the portrait of Congresswoman Mary Norton (NJ), the first Democratic woman elected to the U.S. House of Representatives. Congresswoman Norton served from 1925–1951 and sought to establish rights for "blue and pink collar" workers. Her strenuous efforts to enforce fair pay and decent working conditions made a crucial impact on our government.

Title IX
Provision of the Educational Amendments of 1972 that bars educational institutions receiving federal funds from discriminating against female students.

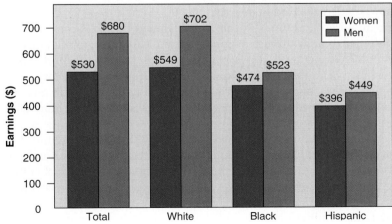

Source: National Committee on Pay Equity.

FIGURE 6.1 The Wage Gap, 2002
The Equal Pay Act was passed in 1963; still women's wages continue to fall short of men's although the gap is closing among all women with the exception of Hispanic women. What factors might account for these glaring inequities? ■

female students. Holding school boards or districts responsible for sexual harassment of students by teachers, for example, was ruled actionable under Title IX by the U.S. Supreme Court.[46]

Title IX, which parallels Title VII, greatly expanded the opportunities for women in elementary, secondary, and postsecondary institutions. It bars educational institutions receiving federal funds from discriminating against female students. Since women's groups, like the NAACP before them, saw eradication of educational discrimination as key to improving other facets of women's lives, they lobbied for it heavily. Most of today's college students did not go through school being excluded from home economics or shop classes because of their sex. Nor, probably, did many attend schools that had no team sports for females. Yet, this was commonly the case in the United States prior to passage of Title IX.[46] Still, sport facilities, access to premium playing times, and quality equipment remain unequal in many high schools and colleges. (See chapter 9 for more on Title IX.)

OTHER GROUPS MOBILIZE FOR RIGHTS

AFRICAN AMERICANS AND WOMEN are not the only groups that have suffered unequal treatment under the law. Denial of civil rights has led many other disadvantaged groups to mobilize. Their efforts have many parallels to the efforts made by African Americans and women. In the wake of the successes of those two groups, and sometimes even before, other traditionally disenfranchised groups organized to gain full equality. Many of them also recognized that litigation and the use of test-case strategies would be key to further civil rights gains. Others have opted for more direct, traditional action. Hispanics were the next group to follow blacks and women in their quest to end discrimination, especially through the courts.

Hispanic Americans

As noted in chapter 1, Hispanic Americans now are the largest minority group in the United States. Until the 1920s, most Hispanics lived in the southwestern United States. In the decades that followed, large numbers of immigrants from Mexico and Puerto Rico came to the United States. These new Mexicans, who quickly became a source of cheap labor, also tended to settle in the Southwest, where they most frequently were employed as migratory farm workers. In contrast, Puerto Ricans mainly moved to New York City. Both groups tended to live in their own neighborhoods, where life was centered around the Roman Catholic Church and the customs of their homeland. Both groups, however, largely lived in poverty.

By the mid-1970s, as the Mexican American and Puerto Rican American populations continued to grow through immigration and childbirth, immigrants from Cuba and several other island and Latin American nations came to the United States seeking a better life. Their problems, however, were often confounded by their need to learn a new language. This language barrier has continued to depress voter registration and voter turnout while contributing to the continued poverty and discrimination suffered by Hispanics.

The earliest push for greater Hispanic rights occurred in the mid-1960s, well before the next major influx of Hispanics to the United States.[48] This new movement included many tactics drawn from the African American civil rights movement, including sit-ins, boycotts, marches, and other activities designed to attract publicity to their cause.[49] Like blacks, women, and Native Americans, Hispanic Americans have some radical militant groups, but the movement has been dominated by more conventional organizations. For example, in 1965, Cesar Chavez organized migrant

HELPING OTHERS TO ACHIEVE THEIR CIVIL RIGHTS

Throughout campuses across the nation, students as well as recent graduates are reaching out to help those who, because they cannot speak English, are far less likely to take advantage of a wide array of local, state, and national programs to assist them in fully participating in the political system.

On some campuses, students (and even some faculty and staff) volunteer to assist campus workers who cannot speak English. At Brandeis University, for example, university workers, many of them immigrants in low-paying kitchen, cleaning, or maintenance positions, are paired with students who help them one on one to learn to read and write English. This student-run program, like many others, is "about more than literacy: It's knocking down barriers, a language gap, and the often rigid class and educational divide between students and workers."[a]

In another program, recent college graduates are making two-year commitments to Teach for America. Teach for America participants attend intensive summer institutes to prepare them for the classroom setting, and they are mentored throughout the year in order to be certified as classroom teachers in an expedited fashion. Teach for America participants generally are placed in low-income schools with grave teacher shortages. A program similar to Teach for America was at the core of former Secretary of Education Rod Paige's success in the Houston school system, where he served as superintendent. President George W. Bush was so impressed that he appointed Paige his first secretary of education and directed him to launch the program on a national basis.

Although these new teachers earn what their traditional counterparts make, they are usually recent graduates who might have been more likely to enter higher-paying professions. Lower-performing, often minority schools now profit from getting the services of high-quality teachers.

Nearly every study of political participation has noted the importance of education as a predictor of voting. With the kinds of knowledge that both of these programs are imparting to their target audiences, college students are significantly advancing the ability of others to demand full civil rights from their government.

---

[a] Peter Schworm, "Breaking Barriers: At Brandeis, Students and Workers Connect Through ESL Breaking Language, Social Barriers," *Boston Globe* (April 11, 2002): B8

---

workers into the United Farm Workers Union and led them in their strike against growers in California. This strike was eventually coupled with a national boycott of several farm products. Other, more conventional groups have tried to use other unions as well as even the Roman Catholic Church as mechanisms to mobilize Hispanics for greater rights.

Hispanics also have relied heavily on litigation. Key groups are the Mexican American Legal Defense and Educational Fund (MALDEF) and the Puerto Rican Legal Defense and Educational Fund. MALDEF was founded in 1968 after members of the League of United Latin American Citizens (LULAC), the nation's largest and oldest Hispanic organization, met with NAACP LDF leaders and, with their assistance, secured a $2.2-million start-up grant from the Ford Foundation. It was created to bring test cases to force school districts to allocate more funds to schools with predominantly low-income minority populations, to implement bilingual education programs, to force employers to hire Hispanics, and to challenge election rules and apportionment plans that undercount or dilute Hispanic voting power.

MALDEF lawyers quickly moved to bring major test cases to the U.S. Supreme Court, both to enhance the visibility of their cause and to win cases. MALDEF has been successful in its efforts to expand voting rights and opportunities to Hispanic Americans. In 1973, for example, it won a major victory when the Supreme Court ruled that multimember electoral districts (in which more than one person represents a single district) in Texas discriminated against African Americans and Hispanic Americans.[50] In multimember systems, legislatures generally add members to larger districts instead of drawing smaller districts in which a minority candidate could get a majority of the votes necessary to win.

While enjoying greater access to elective office, Hispanics still suffer discrimination. Language barriers and substandard educational opportunities continue to plague their progress. In 1973, the U.S. Supreme Court refused to find that a Texas law under which the state appropriated a set dollar amount to each school district per pupil, while allowing wealthier districts to enrich educational programs from other funds, violated the equal protection clause of the Fourteenth Amendment.[51] The lower courts had found that wealth was a suspect classification entitled to strict scrutiny. Using that test, the lower courts had found the Texas plan discriminatory. In contrast, a divided Supreme Court concluded that education was not a fundamental freedom (see chapter 5), and that a charge of discrimination based on wealth would be examined only under a minimal standard of review (the rational basis test).[52]

Throughout the 1970s and 1980s, inter-school-district inequalities persisted, and they frequently had their greatest impact on poor Hispanic children. Recognizing that the increasingly conservative federal courts (see chapter 10) offered no recourse, in 1984, MALDEF filed suit in state court alleging that the Texas school finance policy violated the Texas constitution. In 1989, it won a case in which a state district judge elected by the voters of only a single county declared the state's entire method of financing public schools to be unconstitutional under the state constitution.[53] In 2004, it entered into a settlement with the state of California in a case brought four years earlier to address, in MALDEF's words, "the shocking inequities facing public school children across the state."[54] Its leaders objected to shorter school calendars for schools where enrollment was predominantly Hispanic and other poor sudents.

MALDEF continues to litigate in a wide range of areas of concern to Hispanics. High on its agenda today are affirmative action, the admission of Hispanic students to state colleges and universities, health care for undocumented immigrants, and challenging unfair redistricting practices that make it more difficult to elect Hispanic legislators. It litigates to replace at-large electoral systems with single-district elections to ensure the election of more Hispanics, as well as challenging many state redistricting plans to ensure that Hispanics are adequately represented. Its highly successful Census 2000 educational outreach campaign, moreover, sought to decrease undercounting of Hispanics.

MALDEF also continues to be at the fore of legislative lobbying for expanded rights. Since 2002, it has worked to oppose restrictions concerning driver's license requirements for undocumented immigrants, to gain greater rights for Hispanic workers, and to ensure that redistricting plans do not silence Hispanic voters. It won a victory on this issue in California in 2004. MALDEF also focuses on the rights of Hispanic workers and the effects of legislative redistricting on the voting strength of Hispanics.

Native Americans

Native Americans are the first true Americans, and their status under U.S. law is unique. Under the U.S. Constitution, Indian tribes are considered distinct governments, a situation that has affected Native Americans' treatment by the Supreme Court in contrast to other groups of ethnic minorities. And, minority is a term that accurately describes American Indians. It is estimated that there were as many as 10 million Indians in the

Photo courtesy: George Rodriguez

■ Vice President of Litigation for the Mexican American Legal Defense and Education Fund, Tom Saenz, defends the rights of "Day Laborers," people who are employed and get paid on a daily or short-term basis, to work within a safe environment and receive a living wage for a day's work.

RECLAIMING RIGHTS: INDIANS USE DIVERSE WAYS TO REVERSE THE ECONOMIC ADVERSITY OF DISCRIMINATION

Although the U.S. government formally recognizes 107 Indian tribes within California, only fifteen of these owned casinos in 2004. But in the five years that those casinos have been allowed to operate, they have brought in over $5 billion and are expected to increase that amount exponentially in the near future.[a] One tribe, the United Auburn Indian Community, located east of Sacramento, provides an excellent example of how gaming can affect tribal members. And, events similar to those in California are happening within Indian tribes all over the United States, especially where Indians were forced onto reservations.

Under the U.S. Constitution, Indian tribes on tribal lands are treated as foreign nations and are therefore not subject to the laws of the states or the U.S. government—which generally, until recently, have prohibited gambling in most states. In return for settlements of longtime land disputes, in the 1990s many states entered into agreements with tribes, allowing them to build gambling casinos on their reservations in exchange for a portion of the profits. Most tribes have entered into agreements with states to allow them to permit them to operate slot machines. Connecticut in 2003, for example, earned more than $400 million in this kind of revenue-sharing agreement.

In California, the United Auburn Indian Community spent $125 million to build the Thunder Valley Casino in 2003 and is expected to earn $300 million in its first year of operations. According to the *Los Angeles Times*, just a year earlier not one of the 250 members of the tribe had ever attended college. Members of the tribe lived in slum conditions, nearly 80 percent did not know how to write a check, and many were unable to afford basic amenities such as running water and kitchen appliances.[b] Some were homeless. Now, the tribe has financial consultants to help its members. All get free medical, dental, and vision care. Special education and tutoring programs are helping the tribe's ninety-three children and their parents become more educated, as well as adjusted to the tremendous changes in their economic status.

All over the nation, tribes are using the money earned from casinos to diversify. Many tribes also sell tobacco on their reservations and in their casinos and spas (which many casinos have added), where they are free from state taxes.[c]

Tribes are even donating to political campaigns of candidates whom they see as predisposed to policies favorable to tribes. The Agua Caliente Band of Cahuilla Indians, who sought to build a theme park and golf practice ranges, donated $7.5 million to political campaigns in just one year alone. During the California governor recall of 2004, Indian tribes contributed over $11 million to candidates, highlighting their political clout. These large expenditures, Indians claim, are legal, because as sovereign nations they are immune from federal and state campaign finance disclosure laws. This issue in all likelihood will be decided by the U.S. Supreme Court as Indians, long one of the most disadvantaged groups politically in the United States, with the fewest rights, now begin to exercise their political and economic clout.

---

[a] Louis Sahagun, "Tribes Fear Backlash to Prosperity," *Los Angeles Times* (May 3, 2004): B1.

[b] Sahagun, "Tribes Fear Backlash to Prosperity."

[c] Sahagun, "Tribes Fear Backlash to Prosperity."

New World at the time Europeans arrived in the 1400s, with 3 to 4 million living in what is today the United States. By 1900, the number of Indians in the continental United States had plummeted to less than 2 million. Today, there are 2.7 million.

Many commentators would agree that for years Congress and the courts manipulated Indian law to promote the westward expansion of the United States. The Northwest Ordinance of 1787, passed by the Continental Congress, specified that "good faith should always be observed toward the Indians; their lands and property shall never be taken from them without their consent, and their property rights, and liberty, they shall never be invaded or disturbed, unless in just and lawful wars authorized by Congress." These strictures were not followed. Instead, over the years, "American Indian policy has been described as 'genocide-at-law' promoting both land acquisition and cultural extermination."[55] During the eighteenth and nineteenth centuries, the U.S. government isolated Indians on reservations as it confiscated their lands and denied them basic political rights. Indian reservations were administered by the federal government, and Native Americans often lived in squalid conditions.

With passage of the Dawes Act in 1887, however, the government switched policies to promote assimilation over separation. Each Indian family was given land within the reservation; the rest was sold to whites, thus reducing Indian lands from about 140 million acres to about 47 million. Moreover, to encourage Native Americans to assimilate, Indian children were sent to boarding schools off the reservation, and native languages and rituals were banned. Native Americans didn't become U.S. citizens nor were they given the right to vote until 1924.

At least in part because tribes were small and scattered (and the number of Indians declining), Native Americans formed no protest movement in reaction to these drastic policy changes. It was not until the 1960s, at the same time women were beginning to mobilize for greater civil rights, that Indians, too, began to mobilize to act. In the late 1960s, Indians, many trained by the American Indian Law Center at the University of New Mexico, began to file hundreds of test cases in the federal courts involving tribal fishing rights, tribal land claims, and the taxation of tribal profits. The Native American Rights Fund (NARF), founded that same year, became the NAACP LDF of the Indian rights movement.[56]

Like the civil rights and women's rights movements, the movement for Native American rights had a radical as well as a more traditional branch. In 1973, for example, national attention was drawn to the plight of Indians when members of the radical American Indian movement took over Wounded Knee, South Dakota, the site of the massacre of 150 Indians by the U.S. Army in 1890. Just two years before the protest, the treatment of Indians had been highlighted in the best-selling *Bury My Heart at Wounded Knee*, which in many ways served to mobilize public opinion against the oppression of Native Americans in the same way *Uncle Tom's Cabin* had against slavery.[57]

Native Americans have won some very important victories concerning hunting, fishing, and land rights. Native American tribes all over America have sued to reclaim lands they say were stolen from them by the United States, often more than 200 years ago. Today, these land rights allow Native Americans to play host to a number of casinos across the country, a phenomenon that is explored in Politics Now: Reclaiming Rights.

One of the largest Indian land claims was filed in 1972 on behalf of the Passamaquoddy and the Penobscot tribes, which were seeking return of 12.5 million acres in Maine—about two-thirds of the entire state—and $25 billion in damages. The suit was filed by the Native American Rights Fund and the Indian Service Unit of a legal services office that was funded by the now defunct U.S. Office of Economic Opportunity. It took intervention from the White House before a settlement was reached in 1980, giving each tribe over $40 million.

Native Americans also are litigating to gain access to their sacred places. All over the nation, they have filed lawsuits to stop the building of roads and new construction on ancient burial grounds or other sacred spots. "We are in a battle for the survival of our very way of life," said one tribal leader. "The land is gone. All we've got left is our religion."[58]

Native Americans have not fared particularly well in areas such as religious freedom, especially where tribal practices come into conflict with state law. As noted in chapter 5, the Supreme Court used the rational basis test to rule that a state could infringe on religious exercise (use of peyote as a sacrament in religious ceremonies) by a neutral law, and limited Indian access to religious sites during timber harvesting.[59] Congress attempted to restore some of those rights through passage of the Religious Freedom Restoration Act. The law, however, was later ruled unconstitutional by the Supreme Court.[60]

Native Americans continue to fight the negative stereotypes that plague their progress. Indians contend, for example, that the popular names of thousands of high school, college, and professional sports teams are degrading. This charge has caused some school districts and universities to change the names of their sports teams. Professional teams such as the Atlanta Braves, Cleveland Indians, and Washington Redskins also are under attack. Even the U.S. Commission on Civil Rights has weighed in on the matter, requesting an end to Indian names, mascots, and logos.

While efforts to pressure teams to change their names wage on, Indian tribes have found themselves locked in a controversy with the Department of the Interior over its handling of Indian trust funds, which are to be paid out to Indians for the use of their lands. In 1996, several Indian tribes filed suit to force the federal government to account for the billions of dollars it has collected over the years for its leasing of Indian land, which it took from the Indians and held in trust since the late nineteenth century, and to force reform of the system.[61] As the result of years of mismanagement, the trust, administered by the Department of the Interior, has no records of monies taken in or how they were disbursed. The ongoing class action lawsuit includes 500,000 Indians, who claim that they are owed more than $10 billion. The trial judge found massive mismanagement of the funds, which generate up to $500 million a year, and at one time threatened to hold Secretary of the Interior Gail Norton in contempt. Although this case has been largely deadlocked for the past five years, in early 2004, a mediator was appointed to help bring greater resolution to the conflict.[62]

Gays and Lesbians

Until very recently, gays and lesbians have had an even harder time than other groups in achieving full rights.[63] However, gays and lesbians have, on average, far higher household incomes and educational levels than these other groups, and they are beginning to convert these advantages into political clout at the ballot box and through changes in public opinion. As discussed in chapter 5, like African Americans and women early in their quests for greater civil rights, gays and lesbians initially did not fare well in the Supreme Court. In the late 1970s, the Lambda Legal Defense and Education Fund, the Lesbian Rights Project, and Gay and Lesbian Advocates and Defenders were founded by gay and lesbian activists dedicated to ending legal restrictions on the civil rights of homosexuals.[64] Although these groups have won important legal victories concerning HIV/AIDS discrimination, insurance policy survivor benefits, and even some employment issues, they generally were not as successful as other historically disadvantaged groups.[65]

In 1993, for example, President Bill Clinton tried to get an absolute ban on discrimination against homosexuals in the armed services, who were subject to immediate discharge if their sexual orientation was discovered. Military leaders and then-Senator Sam Nunn (D–GA), as chair of the Senate Armed Services Committee, led the effort against Clinton's proposal. Eventually, Clinton and Senate leaders compromised on what was called the "Don't Ask, Don't Tell" policy. It stipulated that gays and lesbians would no longer be asked if they were homosexual, but they were barred from revealing their sexual orientation (under threat of discharge from the service).[66]

Participation
Civil Rights and
Gay Adoption

However, the public's views toward homosexuality were clearly beginning to change, as signaled by the Court's 1996 decision in *Romer* v. *Evans*.[67] In this case, the Court ruled that an amendment to the Colorado constitution that denied homosexuals the right to seek protection from discrimination was unconstitutional under the equal protection clause of the Fourteenth Amendment.

In 2000, Vermont became the first state to recognize civil unions, marking another landmark in the struggle for equal rights for homosexuals. However, it was the Supreme Court's decision in *Lawrence* v. *Texas* (2003) that really put homosexual rights on the public agenda. In this case, the Court reversed an earlier ruling by finding a Texas statute that banned sodomy to be unconstitutional. Writing for the majority, Justice Anthony Kennedy stated, "[homosexuals'] right to liberty under the due process clause gives them the full right to engage in their conduct without intervention of the government."[68]

Photo courtesy: Jason R. Davis/AP/Wide World Photos

■ George Lane, the appellant in the 2004 Supreme Court case of *Tennessee v. Lane,* involving the scope of the Americans with Disabilities Act, crawled up two flights of stairs to get to a court hearing on a misdemeanor charge.

Following the Court's ruling in *Lawrence,* many Americans were quick to call for additional rights for homosexuals. Many corporations also responded to this amplified call for equal rights. For example, Wal-Mart announced it would ban job discrimination based on sexual orientation. In addition, editorial pages across the country praised the Court's ruling, arguing that the national view toward homosexuality had changed.[69] In November 2003, the Massachusetts Supreme Court further agreed when it ruled that denying homosexuals the right to civil marriage was unconstitutional. The U.S. Supreme Court later refused to hear an appeal of this case.

Still, in 2004, many conservative groups and Republican politicians made same-sex marriage an issue. Referendums or amendments prohibiting same-sex marriage were placed on eleven state ballots and all were passed overwhelmingly by voters.

Disabled Americans

Disabled Americans also have lobbied hard for anti-discrimination legislation as well as equal protection under the Constitution. In the aftermath of World War II, many veterans returned to a nation unequipped to handle their disabilities. The Korean and Vietnam Wars made the problems of disabled veterans all the more clear. These disabled veterans saw the successes of African Americans, women, and other minorities, and they too began to lobby for greater protection against discrimination.[70] In 1990, in coalition with other disabled people, veterans finally were able to convince Congress to pass the Americans with Disabilities Act (ADA). The statute defines a disabled person as someone with a physical or mental impairment that limits one or more "life activities," or who has a record of such impairment. It thus extends the protections of the Civil Rights Act of 1964 to all of those with physical or mental disabilities. It guarantees access to public facilities, employment, and communication services. It also requires employers to acquire or modify work equipment, adjust work schedules, and make existing facilities accessible. Thus, for example, buildings must be accessible to those in wheelchairs, and telecommunications devices must be provided for deaf employees.

In 1999, the U.S. Supreme Court issued a series of four decisions redefining and significantly limiting the scope of the ADA. The cumulative impact of these decisions was to limit dramatically the number of people who can claim coverage under the act. Moreover, these cases "could profoundly affect individuals with a range of impairments—from diabetes and hypertension to severe nearsightedness and hearing loss—who are able to function in society with the help of medicines or aids but whose impairments may still make employers consider them ineligible for certain jobs."[71] Thus, pilots who need glasses to correct their vision cannot claim discrimination when employers fail to hire them because of their correctable vision.[72] In 2004, however, the Court ruled 5–4 that disabled persons could sue states that failed to make reasonable accommodations to assure that courthouses are handicapped accessible.[73]

Simply changing the law, although often an important first step in achieving civil rights, is not the end of the process. Attitudes must also change. As history has shown, that can be a very long process and will be longer given the Court's decisions.

You Are the Mayor

CONTINUING CONTROVERSIES IN CIVIL RIGHTS

SINCE PASSAGE OF MAJOR CIVIL RIGHTS legislation in the 1960s and the Supreme Court's continued interest in upholding the civil rights of many groups, African Americans, women, Hispanics, Native Americans, gays and lesbians, and the disabled have come much closer to the attainment of equal rights. Yet, all of these groups still remain far from enjoying full equality under the Constitution in all walks of life. Private discrimination that cannot be legislated against is one major continuing source of discrimination. Gender equality, for example, has increased but a 2003 poll shows that 12 percent of Americans still would not vote for a woman for president.[74] More strikingly, in response to suggestions that an amendment be added to the Constitution to ban same-sex marriages, 55 percent of those polled in July 2004 favored this type of legislation.

Today, while most Americans agree that discrimination is wrong, most whites believe that affirmative action programs, which were designed in the late 1960s and early 1970s to remedy vestiges of discrimination against African Americans in particular, are no longer needed. White men are particularly opposed to principles of affirmative action, believing that qualified minorities should not receive preference over equally qualified white men.

Affirmative Action

How did affirmative action come to be such a controversial issue? More than fifty years after *Brown* v. *Board of Education* (1954), the civil rights debate centers on the question of equality of opportunity versus equality of results. Most civil rights and women's rights organizations argue that the lingering and pervasive burdens of racism and sexism can be overcome only by taking race or gender into account in fashioning remedies for discrimination. They argue that the Constitution is not and should not be blind to color or sex. Therefore, busing should be used to integrate schools, and women should be given child-care assistance to allow them to compete equally in the marketplace.

The counter-argument holds that if it was once wrong to use labels to discriminate against a group, it should be wrong to use those same labels to help a group. Laws should be neutral, or color-blind. According to this view, quotas and other forms of **affirmative action,** policies designed to give special attention or compensatory treatment to members of a previously disadvantaged group, should be illegal. As early as 1871, Frederick Douglass ridiculed the idea of racial quotas, arguing that they would promote "an image of blacks as privileged wards of the state." They were "absurd as a matter of practice" because some could use them to argue that blacks "should constitute one-eighth of the poets, statesmen, scholars, authors and philosophers."

The debate over affirmative action and equality of opportunity became particularly intense during the presidential administration of Ronald Reagan, in the wake of two court cases that were generally decided in favor of affirmative action shortly before Reagan's election. In 1978, the Supreme Court for the first time fully addressed the issue of affirmative action. Alan Bakke, a thirty-one-year-old paramedic, sought admission to several medical schools and was rejected because of his age. The next year, he applied to the University of California at Davis and was placed on its waiting list. The Davis Medical School maintained two separate admission committees—one for white students

affirmative action
Policies designed to give special attention or compensatory treatment to members of a previously disadvantaged group.

and another for minority students. Bakke was not admitted to the school, although his grades and standardized test scores were higher than those of all of the African American students admitted to the school. In *Regents of the University of California* v. *Bakke* (1978), a sharply divided Court concluded that Bakke's rejection had been illegal because the use of strict quotas was inappropriate.[75] The medical school, however, was free to "take race into account."

Bakke was quickly followed by a 1979 case in which the Court ruled that a factory and a union could voluntarily adopt a quota system in selecting black workers over more senior white workers for a training program. These kinds of programs outraged blue-collar Americans who traditionally had voted for the Democratic Party. In 1980, they abandoned the party in droves to support Ronald Reagan, an ardent foe of affirmative action.

For a while, in spite of the addition of Reagan-appointed Justice Sandra Day O'Connor to the Court, the Court continued to uphold affirmative action plans, especially when there was clear-cut evidence of prior discrimination. In 1987, for example, the Court for the first time ruled that a public employer could use a voluntary plan to promote women even if there was no judicial finding or prior discrimination.[76]

In all these affirmative action cases, the Reagan administration strongly urged the Court to invalidate the plans in question, but to no avail. With changes on the Court, however, including the 1986 elevation to chief justice of William H. Rehnquist, a strong opponent of affirmative action, the continued efforts of the Reagan administration finally began to pay off as the Court heard a new series of cases signaling an end to the advances in civil rights law. In a three-month period in 1989, the Supreme Court handed down five civil rights decisions limiting affirmative action programs and making it harder to prove employment discrimination.

The Legislative Response.   In February 1990, congressional and civil rights leaders unveiled legislation designed to overrule the Court's rulings, which, according to the bill's sponsor, "were an abrupt and unfortunate departure from its historic vigilance in protecting the rights of minorities."[77] The bill passed both houses of Congress but was vetoed by President Reagan's successor, George Bush, and Congress failed to override the veto. In late 1991, however, Congress and the White House reached a compromise on a weaker version of the civil rights bill, which was passed by overwhelming majorities in both houses of Congress. The Civil Rights Act of 1991 overruled the five Supreme Court rulings noted above, but it specifically prohibited the use of quotas.

The Supreme Court, however, has not stayed silent on the issue. In 1995, the Court ruled that Congress, like the states, must show that affirmative action programs meet the strict scrutiny test outlined in Table 6.1.[78] In 1996, the 5th U.S. Circuit Court of Appeals also ruled that the University of Texas Law School's affirmative action admissions program was unconstitutional, throwing the college and university admissions programs in Texas, Oklahoma, and Mississippi into turmoil. Later that year, the U.S. Supreme Court refused to hear the case, thereby allowing the Court of Appeals decision to stand.[79]

By 2002, the U.S. Supreme Court once again found the affirmative action issue ripe for review. In *Grutter* v. *Bollinger* (2003), the Court voted to uphold the constitutionality of the University of Michigan's law school admissions policy, which gave preference to minority applicants.[80] However, in a companion case, the Court struck down Michigan's undergraduate point system, which gave minority applicants twenty automatic points simply because they were minorities.[81]

Taken together, these cases set the stage for a new era in affirmative action in the United States. Although the use of strict quotas and automatic points is not constitutional, the Court clearly believes that there is a place for some preferential treatment, at least until greater racial and ethnic parity is achieved. However, as Justice Sandra Day O'Connor noted in *Grutter*, "a program must remain flexible enough to ensure that each

Analyzing Visuals

AMERICANS VIEW AFFIRMATIVE ACTION

The following Gallup Poll, taken just before the Supreme Court handed down two major affirmative action cases involving the University of Michigan, between June 12 and June 18, 2003, queried non-Hispanic whites, blacks, and Hispanics about their opinions regarding affirmative action. Questions regarded not only affirmative action in general, but also affirmative action as it relates to student admissions to a college or university. After studying the charts and reading the material in this chapter on affirmative action,

answer the following critical thinking questions: Which group of those who were polled was most supportive of affirmative action? Which was the least supportive? Why do you think the opinions differed so greatly in regard to the question about two equally qualified students applying to a college or university? Is the "ALL" category a fair reflection of American views about affirmative action? Why or why not? How do the results of the poll compare to the Supreme Court's decision?

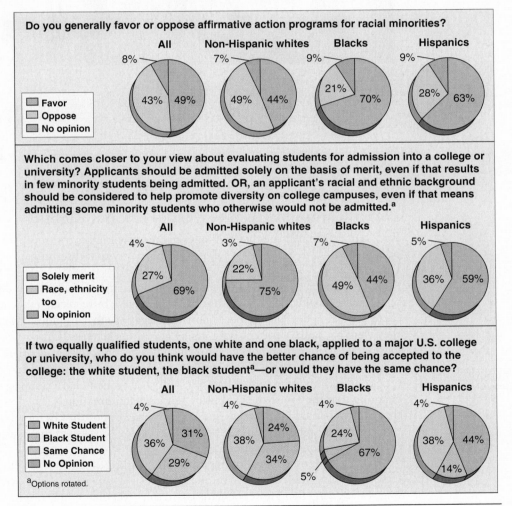

Note: N = 1,385 adults nationwide (MoE +/- 3), including, with oversamples, 821 non-Hispanic whites (MoE +/- 4), 241 blacks (MoE +/- 7), and 266 Hispanics (MoE +/- 7). Interviewing was June 12–15,2003, for non-Hispanic whites, and June 12–18,2003, for blacks and Hispanics.

Source: Gallup Poll, http:www.pollingreport.com.race.htm.

■ 1.6 million female Wal-Mart employees are presently engaged in a class action lawsuit, *Dukes* v. *Wal-Mart Stores, Inc.,* that accuses the retail giant of gender discrimination in wages and promotions. Wal-Mart's lawyers tried to argue against class action status by saying that a class composed of current and former women employees would be too large for one case to handle, but the judge emphatically disagreed. *Dukes* v. *Wal-Mart* is thus far the largest employment discrimination case in U.S. history.

Photo courtesy: William Thomas Cain/Getty Images

Comparing Civil Rights

applicant is evaluated as an individual and not in a way that makes an applicant's race or ethnicity the defining feature of his or her application."[82]

Other Continuing Controversies in Civil Rights

Race is not the only issue that continues to breed civil rights controversies. Recent developments with two corporations illustrate the reality that discrimination persists in the United States.

Beginning in the mid-1990s, many gay rights activists charged that the Cracker Barrel restaurant chain discriminated against homosexuals by requiring that employees exhibit "heterosexual values" on the job. Following allegations that employees were fired because they were gay and a series of boycotts by gay rights activists, Cracker Barrel adopted a new anti-discrimination policy that included protections for sexual orientation.[83]

More recently, the nation's largest employer, Wal-Mart, has been embroiled in a series of discrimination suits. First, six California women filed a claim against the chain, charging that they were the victims of gender discrimination.[84] These women asserted that they were paid lower wages and offered fewer opportunities for advancement than their male colleagues. In June 2004, a federal judge broadened their suit to include 1.6 million women in a class action lawsuit.

In addition, nine illegal immigrants who worked as janitors at Wal-Marts in New Jersey are suing the company for discriminating against them by paying them lower wages and giving them fewer benefits based solely on their ethnic origin. Another group of Wal-Mart employees from twenty-one states are also suing the corporation, claiming that executives knowingly conspired to hire illegal immigrants and, in doing so, violated the workers' civil rights by refusing to pay Social Security and other wage compensation benefits.[85] These suits are representative of a growing trend in discrimination suits filed by immigrants who believe they have been persecuted or disadvantaged following changes in security and immigration law after 9/11.

Global Perspective

WOMEN IN PARLIAMENT

As we have seen in this chapter, the extension of political rights to individuals in a society is often marked by controversy and may occur in stages. In the United States, for example, women were allowed to stand for election in 1788, but not until 1920 and the ratification of the Nineteenth Amendment did they obtain the right to vote. In Canada and Mexico, a reverse process took place. Women received the right to vote with certain restrictions in 1918 and then obtained the right to stand for elected office in 1920, again with certain restrictions. In Mexico, women obtained the right to vote in 1947 and the right to stand for office in 1953. The right of women to stand for election and to vote is not yet universal. In Kuwait, women can do neither. In the United Arab Emirates, the parliament is appointed and neither men nor women have the right to vote or to stand for election.

There can be a significant difference in the right to stand for election and the ability to get elected. If we add up all the members of parliament around the world and break their membership down by gender, we find that as of May 2004 women held 15.4 percent of the seats. The percentage is highest in the Nordic countries (Sweden, Norway, Finland, and Iceland) at 39.7 percent and lowest in the Arab world at 6.4 percent. In the Americas, it averages 18.5 percent.

A closer look reveals that, based on election results from 2002, 14.3 percent of the members of the lower branch of legislatures are women (62 out of 435) and 13 percent of senators are women (13 out of 100). These figures place the United States in a tie for 59th place, with Andorra, in a global ranking of women in parliaments. The table provides us with a picture of how the United States compares with other countries.

Percentage of Women in Lower Houses of Parliament, 2004

Rank	Country	Election year	Seats	Women	% Women	Rank	Country	Election year	Seats	Women	% Women
1	Rwanda	2003	80	39	48.8	48	United Kingdom	2001	659	118	17.9
2	Sweden	2002	349	158	45.3	50	Suriname	2000	51	9	17.6
3	Denmark	2001	179	68	38.0	60	Equatorial Guinea	2004	100	14	14.0
4	Finland	2003	200	75	37.5	75	Lithuania	2000	141	15	10.6
5	Netherlands	2003	150	55	36.7	100	Maldives	1999	50	3	6.0
10	Argentina	2001	256	87	34.0	110	Turkey	2002	550	24	4.4
15	Mozambique	1999	250	75	30.0	115	Iran	2004	290	9	3.1
20	Namibia	1999	72	19	26.4	123	Bahrain	2002	40	0	0.0
25	Switzerland	2003	200	50	25.0	123	Kuwait	2003	65	0	0.0
29	Mexico	2003	500	113	22.6	123	Saudi Arabia	2001	120	0	0.0
30	Eritrea	1994	150	33	22.0						

Source: Interparliamentary Union. www.piu.org/wmn-e/classif.htm

Questions:

1. What might be some of the reasons for the lower numbers of women in parliaments around the world?

2. What can be done to increase the number of women elected to public office?

SUMMARY

WHILE THE FRAMERS AND OTHER AMERICANS basked in the glory of the newly adopted Constitution and Bill of Rights, their protections did not extend to all Americans. In this chapter, we have shown how rights have been expanded to ever-increasing segments of the population. To that end, we have made the following points:

1. Slavery, Abolition, and Winning the Right to Vote, 1800–1890

When the Framers tried to compromise on the issue of slavery, they only postponed dealing with a volatile question that was later to rip the nation apart. Ultimately, the Civil War was fought to end slavery. Among its results were the triumph of the abolitionist position and adoption of the Thirteenth, Fourteenth, and Fifteenth Amendments. During this period, women also sought expanded rights, especially the right to vote, but to no avail.

2. The Push for Equality, 1890–1954

Although the Civil War Amendments were added to the Constitution, the Supreme Court limited their application. As Jim Crow laws were passed throughout the South, the NAACP was founded in the early 1900s to press for equal rights for African Americans. Women's groups also were active during this period, successfully lobbying for passage of the Nineteenth Amendment, which assured them the right to vote. Women's groups such as the National Consumers' League (NCL), for example, began to view litigation as a means to its ends, as it was forced to go to court to argue for the constitutionality of legislation protecting women workers.

3. The Civil Rights Movement

In 1954, the U.S. Supreme Court ruled in *Brown* v. *Board of Education* that state-segregated school systems were unconstitutional. This victory empowered African Americans as they sought an end to other forms of pervasive discrimination. Bus boycotts, sit-ins, freedom rides, pressure for voting rights, and massive nonviolent demonstrations became common tactics. This activity culminated in the passage of the Civil Rights Act of 1964, which gave African Americans another weapon in their legal arsenal.

4. The Women's Rights Movement

After passage of the Civil Rights Act, a new women's rights movement arose. Several women's rights groups were created, and while some sought a constitutional amendment, others attempted to litigate under the equal protection clause. Over the years, the Supreme Court developed different tests to determine the constitutionality of various forms of discrimination. In general, strict scrutiny, the most stringent standard, was applied to race-based claims. An intermediate standard of review was developed to assess the constitutionality of sex discrimination claims.

5. Other Groups Mobilize for Rights

Building on the successes of African Americans and women, other groups, including Hispanic Americans, Native Americans, gays and lesbians, and the disabled, organized to litigate for expanded civil rights as well as to lobby for antidiscrimination laws.

6. Continuing Controversies in Civil Rights

None of the groups discussed in this chapter has yet to reach full equality. One policy, affirmative action, which was designed to remedy education and employment discrimination, continues to be very controversial. And, gays, women, and immigrants continue to use the courts to seek remedies for costly employment discrimination.

KEY TERMS

affirmative action, p. 229
Black Codes, p. 201
Brown v. *Board of Education* (1954), p. 209
civil rights, p. 198
Civil Rights Act of 1964, p. 215
Civil Rights Cases (1883), p. 203
de facto discrimination, p. 216
de jure discrimination, p. 216
Equal Employment Opportunity Commission, p. 218
equal protection clause, p. 209
Equal Rights Amendment, p. 218
Fifteenth Amendment, p. 202
Fourteenth Amendment, p. 201
grandfather clause, p. 204
Jim Crow laws, p. 203
Nineteenth Amendment, p. 206
Plessy v. *Ferguson* (1896), p. 204
strict scrutiny, p. 219
suffrage movement, p. 206
suspect classification, p. 219
Thirteenth Amendment, p. 201
Title IX, p. 221

SELECTED READINGS

Bacchi, Carol Lee. *The Politics of Affirmative Action: 'Women,' Equality and Category Politics.* Thousand Oaks, CA: Sage, 1996.

Eastland, Terry. *Ending Affirmative Action: The Case for Colorblind Justice.* New York: Basic Books, 1997.

Freeman, Jo. *The Politics of Women's Liberation.* New York: Backinprint.com, 2000.

Guinier, Lani. *Who's Qualified?* Boston: Beacon Press, 2001.

Kluger, Richard. *Simple Justice,* reprint ed. New York: Vintage, 2004.

Mansbridge, Jane J. *Why We Lost the ERA.* Chicago: University of Chicago Press, 1986.

McClain, Paula D., and Joseph Stewart Jr. *"Can We All Get Along?" Racial and Ethnic Minorities in American Politics,* 3rd ed. Boulder, CO: Westview, 2001.

McGlen, Nancy E., et al. *Women, Politics, and American Society,* 4th ed. New York: Longman, 2004.

Nobles, Melissa. *Shades of Citizenship: Race and the Census in Modern America.* Palo Alto, CA: Stanford University Press, 2000.

Reed, Adolph, Jr. *Without Justice for All: The New Liberalism and Our Retreat from Racial Equity.* Boulder, CO: Westview, 1999.

Rodriguez, Clara E. *Changing Race: Latinos, the Census, and the History of Ethnicity in the United States.* New York: New York University Press, 2000.

Rosales, Francisco A., and Arturo Rosales, eds. *Chicano! The History of the Mexican American Civil Rights Movement.* Houston, TX: Arte Publico, 1996.

Verba, Sidney, and Gary R. Orren. *Equality in America: The View from the Top*. Cambridge, MA: Harvard University Press, 1985.

Williams, Juan. *Eyes on the Prize: America's Civil Rights Years, 1954–1965*. New York: Penguin, 1987.

Wilson, William Julius. *The Bridge over the Racial Divide: Rising Inequality and Coalition Politics*. Berkeley: University of California Press, 1999.

WEB EXPLORATIONS

For more on civil rights generally, see
http://www.civilrightsproject.harvard.edu/

For more on abolition, the American Anti-Slavery Society, and its leaders, see http://www.loc.gov/exhibits/african/afam005.html

For more about the history of Jim Crow in the South, see
http://www.jimcrowhistory.org/

To read the full text of *Brown* v. *Board of Education* (1954), see
http://caselaw.lp.findlaw.com/cgi-bin/getcase.pl?court=US&vol=347&invol=483

For more about the Montgomery bus boycott and Dr. Martin Luther King Jr., see
http://www.stanford.edu/group/King/about_king/encyclopedia/bus_boycott.html

For more about NOW and the EEOC, see
http://www.now.org
http://www.eeoc.gov/

For more about the Equal Rights Amendment, see
http://www.equalrightsamendment.org/

For more about the ACLU Women's Rights Project, see
http://www.aclu.org/WomensRights/WomensRightsMain.cfm

To learn more about MALDEF, see
http://www.maldef.org/

For more about the Native American Rights Fund, see
http://www.narf.org/

For more about gay and lesbian rights groups, see
http://www.glaad.org/

For more about disability advocacy groups, see
http://www.aapd-dc.org/

Photo courtesy: Larry Downing/Reuters/Corbis

Congress

ON FEBRUARY 6, 2002, REPRESENTATIVE NANCY PELOSI (D–CA) broke through a glass ceiling when she was sworn in as the Democratic House whip, becoming the first woman in history to win an elected position in the formal House leadership.[1] The whip position has long been viewed as a stepping stone to becoming the speaker of the House. House Speakers Tip O'Neill (D–MA) and Newt Gingrich (R–GA) were both former whips. As whip, it was Pelosi's responsibility to convince Democratic members of the House to vote together on the full range of bills before the 107th Congress.

First elected to Congress from California in 1986, Pelosi quickly made her mark as an advocate for human rights in China and as an effective fundraiser. Her fund-raising skills and years of experience in the House, in fact, helped her win the hotly contested race for the whip position. As part of the House leadership, she became the first woman to attend critical White House meetings, where, said Pelosi, "Susan B. Anthony and others are with me."[2]

Although the president's party traditionally loses seats in midterm elections, in 2002 House Republicans actually increased their majority. Critics charged that the Democrats lacked a consistent message. Therefore, soon after the election results were in, House Minority Leader Richard Gephardt (D–MO) resigned from his position, leaving Pelosi in line to succeed him. Representative Harold Ford (D–TN), one of the youngest members of the House, threw his hat into the ring to oppose Pelosi's campaign for the leader's position. Ford, a moderate, charged that Pelosi, who already was being referred to by conservatives as a "San Francisco liberal," was simply too liberal to lead the Democrats back to political viability in the 2004 elections. A majority of the members of the Democratic House Caucus, however, did not appear fazed by these charges; Pelosi was elected minority leader by an overwhelming majority of the caucus members. Steny Hoyer (D–MD), who initially had run against Pelosi for the whip position in the 107th Congress, was elected Democratic whip in the 108th Congress.

The election of Pelosi as Democratic leader sharply alters the look of power in the House of Representatives. As the leader of all House Democrats, Pelosi automatically is accorded tremendous respect, as well as media attention as the face of Democrats in the House. Thus, more than 150 years after

CHAPTER OUTLINE

women first sought the right to vote, a woman member of Congress now leads one party in the House of Representatives. The representation of women in Congress has also come a long way since 1917, when Jeanette Rankin (R–MT) became the first woman elected to Congress. Women currently make up over 50 percent of the population but only 15 percent of the members of Congress.[3]

THE FRAMERS' ORIGINAL CONCEPTION of the representational function of Congress was much narrower than it is today. Instead of regarding members of Congress as representatives of the people, those in attendance at the Constitutional Convention were extremely concerned with creating a legislative body that would be able to make laws to govern the new nation. Over time, Congress has attempted to maintain the role of a law- and policy-making institution, but changes in the demands made on the national government have allowed the executive and judicial branches to gain powers at the expense of the legislative. Moreover, although the Congress as a branch of government has experienced a decline in its authority, the power and the importance of individual members have grown. Thus, the public doesn't think much about Congress itself, but somewhat ironically, citizens hold their own elected representatives in high esteem.

The dual roles that Congress plays contribute to this divide in public opinion. Members of Congress must combine and balance the roles of lawmaker and policy maker with being a representative of their district, their state, their party, and sometimes their race, ethnicity, or gender. Not surprisingly, this balancing act often results in role conflict.

In this chapter, we will analyze the powers of Congress and the competing roles members of Congress play as they represent the interests of their constituents, make laws, and oversee the actions of the other two branches of government. We will also see that, as these functions have changed throughout U.S. history, so has Congress itself.

- First, we will examine what *the Constitution* has to say about Congress—*the legislative branch of government*.

- Second, we will describe *how Congress is organized*. We will compare the two chambers and how their differences affect the course of legislation.

- Third, we will look at *the members of Congress*, including how members get elected, and how they spend their days.

- Fourth, we will examine the various factors that influence *how members* of Congress *make decisions*.

- Fifth, we will outline *the law-making function of Congress*.

- Sixth, we will discuss the ever changing relationship between *Congress and the president*.

- Finally, we will review the relationship between *Congress and the judiciary*.

THE CONSTITUTION AND THE LEGISLATIVE BRANCH OF GOVERNMENT

ARTICLE I OF THE CONSTITUTION describes the structure of the legislative branch of government we know today. As discussed in chapter 2, the Great Compromise at the Constitutional Convention resulted in the creation of an upper house, the Senate, and a lower house, the House of Representatives. Any two-house legislature, such as the one created by the Framers, is called a **bicameral legislature**. Each state is represented in the Senate by two senators, regardless of the state's population. The number of representatives each state sends to the House of Representatives, in contrast, is determined by that state's population.

bicameral legislature
A legislature divided into two houses; the U.S. Congress and the state legislatures are bicameral except Nebraska, which is unicameral.

The U.S. Constitution sets out the formal, or legal, requirements for membership in the House and Senate. As agreed at the Constitutional Convention, House members are to be at least twenty-five years of age; senators, thirty. Members of the House are required to have resided in the United States for at least seven years; those elected to the Senate, nine. Both representatives and senators must be legal residents of the states from which they are elected.

Senators are elected for six-year terms, and originally they were elected by state legislatures because the Framers intended for senators to represent their states' interests in the Senate. State legislators lost this influence over the Senate with the ratification of the Seventeenth Amendment in 1913, which provides for the direct election of senators by voters. Then, as now, one-third of all senators are up for reelection every two years.

Members of the House of Representatives are elected to two-year terms by a vote of the eligible electorate in each congressional district. The Framers expected that the House would be more responsible to the people because they were elected directly by them and more responsive to the people because they were up for reelection every two years.

Apportionment and Redistricting

The U.S. Constitution requires that a census, which entails the counting of all Americans, be conducted every ten years. Until the first census could be taken, the Constitution fixed the number of representatives in the House of Representatives at sixty-five. In 1790, then, one member represented 30,000 people. As the population of the new nation grew and states were added to the union, the House became larger and larger. In 1910, it expanded to 435 members, and in 1929, its size was fixed at that number by statute. When Alaska and Hawaii became states in the 1950s, the number of seats was increased to 437. The number reverted back to 435 in 1963. In 2004, Congress began to consider a plan to increase that number temporarily to 437. Under the plan, the Democratic District of Columbia would get one permanent voting representative. Utah, a largely Republican state, would get one extra representative, having fallen short by fewer than 90 residents of getting one after the 2000 Census.

Each state is allotted its share of these 435 representatives based on its population. After each U.S. Census, the number of seats allotted to each state is adjusted by a constitutionally mandated process called **apportionment.** After seats are apportioned, congressional districts must be redrawn by state legislatures to reflect population shifts to ensure that each member in Congress represents approximately the same number of residents. This process of redrawing congressional districts to reflect increases or decreases in the number of seats allotted to a state, as well as population shifts within a state, is called **redistricting.** The effects of redistricting are discussed in chapter 13.

apportionment
The proportional process of allotting congressional seats to each state following the decennial census.

redistricting
The redrawing of congressional districts to reflect increases or decreases in seats allotted to the states, as well as population shifts within a state.

Constitutional Powers of Congress

The Constitution specifically gives Congress its most important power: the authority to make laws. (See Table 7.1.) Both houses share this law-making power. For example, no **bill** (proposed law) can become law without the consent of both houses. Examples of other constitutionally shared powers include the power to declare war, raise an army and navy, coin money, regulate commerce, establish the federal courts and their jurisdiction, establish rules of immigration and naturalization, and "make all Laws which shall be necessary and proper for carrying into Execution the foregoing Powers." As interpreted by the U.S. Supreme Court, the necessary and proper clause, found at the end of Article I, section 8, when coupled with one or more of the specific powers enumerated in Article I, section 8, has allowed Congress to increase the scope of its authority, often at the expense of the states and into areas not necessarily envisioned by the Framers.

Congress alone is given formal law-making powers in the Constitution. But, it is important to remember that presidents issue proclamations and executive orders with the force of law (see chapter 8), bureaucrats issue quasi-legislative rules (see chapter 9),

bill
A proposed law.

The Living Constitution

The Congress shall have Power…To establish an uniform Rule of Naturalization.

—Article 1, Section 8, Clause 4

This article reiterates the sovereign power of the nation and places authority to draft laws concerning naturalization in the hands of Congress.

Congress's power over naturalization is exclusive—meaning that no state can bestow U.S. citizenship on anyone. Citizenship is a privilege and Congress may make laws limiting or expanding the criteria. The word *citizen* was not defined constitutionally until ratification in 1868 of the Fourteenth Amendment, which sets forth two kinds of citizenship: by birth and through naturalization. Throughout American history, Congress has imposed a variety of limits on naturalization, originally restricting it to "free, white persons." "Orientals" were excluded from eligibility in 1882. At one time those affiliated with the Communist Party and those who lacked "good moral character" (which was construed to exclude homosexuals, drunkards, gamblers, and adulterers) were deemed unfit for citizenship. Most of these restrictions no longer exist, but they do underscore the power of Congress in this matter.

Congress continues to retain the right to naturalize large classes of individuals, as it did in 2000 when it granted automatic citizenship rights to all minor children adopted abroad as long as both adoptive parents were American citizens. Naturalized citizens, however, do not necessarily enjoy the full rights of citizenship enjoyed by other Americans. Congress at any time, subject only to Supreme Court review, can limit the rights and liberties of naturalized citizens, especially in times of national crisis. In the wake of the September 11, 2001, terrorist attacks, when it was revealed that of the forty-eight al-Qaeda–linked operatives who took part in some sort of terrorist activities against the United States, one-third were lawful permanent residents or naturalized citizens, Congress called for greater screening by the Immigration and Naturalization Service for potential terrorists.

and the Supreme Court and lower federal courts render opinions that generate principles that also have the force of law (see chapter 10).

Reflecting the different constituencies and size of each house of Congress (as well as the Framers' intentions), Article I gives special, exclusive powers to each house in addition to their shared role in law-making. For example, as noted in Table 7.2, the Constitution specifies that all revenue bills must originate in the House of Representatives. Over the years, however, this mandate has been blurred, and it is not unusual to see budget bills being considered simultaneously in both houses, especially since, ultimately, each must approve all bills, whether or not they involve revenues. The House also has the power to impeach: the authority to charge the president, vice president, or other "civil officers," including federal judges, with "Treason, Bribery, or other high Crimes and Misdemeanors." Only the Senate is authorized to conduct trials of **impeachment,** with a two-thirds vote being necessary before a federal official can be removed from office.

impeachment
The power delegated to the House of Representatives in the Constitution to charge the president, vice president, or other "civil officers," including federal judges, with "Treason, Bribery, or other high Crimes and Misdemeanors." This is the first step in the constitutional process of removing such government officials from office.

240

TABLE 7.1 The Powers of Congress

The powers of Congress, found in Article I, section 8, of the Constitution, include the power to:

- Lay and collect taxes and duties
- Borrow money
- Regulate commerce with foreign nations and among the states
- Establish rules for naturalization (that is, the process of becoming a citizen) and bankruptcy
- Coin money, set its value, and fix the standard of weights and measures
- Punish counterfeiting
- Establish a post office and post roads
- Issue patents and copyrights
- Define and punish piracies, felonies on the high seas, and crimes against the law of nations
- Create courts inferior to (that is, below) the Supreme Court
- Declare war
- Raise and support an army and navy and make rules for their governance
- Provide for a militia (reserving to the states the right to appoint militia officers and to train the militia under congressional rules)
- Exercise legislative powers over the seat of government (the District of Columbia) and over places purchased to be federal facilities (forts, arsenals, dockyards, and "other needful buildings")
- "Make all Laws which shall be necessary and proper for carrying into Execution the foregoing Powers, and all other Powers vested by this Constitution in the government of the United States" (Note: This "necessary and proper," or "elastic," clause has been interpreted expansively by the Supreme Court, as explained in chapter 2 and the Annotated Constitution.)

TABLE 7.2 Key Differences Between the House and Senate

Constitutional Differences

House	Senate
Initiates all revenue bills	Offers "advice and consent" on many major presidential appointments
Initiates impeachment procedures and passes articles of impeachment	Tries impeached officials Approves treaties
Two-year terms	Six-year terms (one third up for reelection every two years)
435 members (apportioned by population)	100 members (two from each state)

Differences in Operation

House	Senate
More centralized, more formal; stronger leadership Rules Committee fairly powerful in controlling time and rules of debate (in conjunction with the speaker of the House)	Less centralized, less formal; weaker leadership No rules committee; limits on debate come through unanimous consent or cloture of filibuster
More impersonal	More personal
Power distributed less evenly	Power distributed more evenly
Members are highly specialized	Members are generalists
Emphasizes tax and revenue policy	Emphasizes foreign policy

Changes in the Institution

House	Senate
Power centralized in the speaker's inner circle of advisers	Senate workload increasing and informality breaking down; threat of filibusters more frequent than in the past
House procedures are becoming more efficient	Becoming more difficult to pass legislation
Turnover is relatively high, although those seeking reelection almost always win	Turnover is moderate

The House and Senate share in the impeachment process, but the Senate has the sole authority to approve major presidential appointments, including federal judges, ambassadors, and Cabinet- and sub-Cabinet–level positions. The Senate, too, must approve all presidential treaties by a two-thirds vote. Failure by the president to court the Senate can be costly. At the end of World War I, for example, President Woodrow Wilson worked hard to get other nations to accept the Treaty of Versailles, which contained the charter of the proposed League of Nations. He overestimated his support in the Senate, however. That body refused to ratify the treaty, dealing Wilson and his international stature a severe setback.

HOW CONGRESS IS ORGANIZED

EVERY TWO YEARS, a new Congress is seated. After ascertaining the formal qualifications of new members, the Congress organizes itself as it prepares for the business of the coming session. Among the first items on its agenda are the election of new lead-

FIGURE 7.1   Organizational Structure of the House of Representatives and the Senate in the 109th Congress. ▪

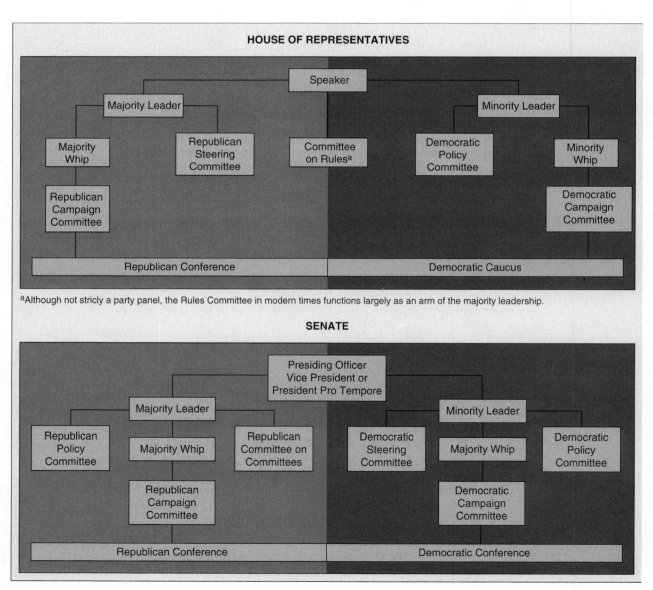

Source: Adapted from Roger H. Davidson and Walter J. Olezek, *Congress and its Members,* 6th ed. Washington, D.C.: CQ Press, 2002.

Roots of Government

LIFE ON THE FLOOR AND IN THE HALLS OF CONGRESS

THROUGHOUT CONGRESS'S FIRST SEVERAL DECADES, partisan, sectional, and state tensions of the day often found their way onto the floors of the U.S. House and Senate. Many members were armed, and during one House debate, thirty members showed their weapons. In 1826, Senator John Randolph of Virginia insulted Secretary of State Henry Clay from the floor of the Senate, referring to Clay as "this being, so brilliant yet so corrupt, which, like a rotten mackerel by moonlight, shined and stunk." Clay immediately challenged Randolph to a duel. Both missed, although Randolph's coat fell victim to a bullet hole. Reacting to public opinion, in 1839, Congress passed a law prohibiting dueling in the District of Columbia.

Nevertheless, dueling continued. A debate in 1851 between representatives from Alabama and North Carolina ended in a duel, but no one was hurt. In 1856, Representative Preston Brooks (D–SC) assaulted Senator Charles Sumner (R–MA) on the floor of the Senate. Brooks claimed he was defending the honor of his region and family. Sumner was disabled and unable to resume his seat in Congress for

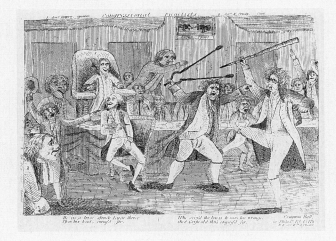

several years. Guns and knives were abundantly evident on the floor of both House and Senate, along with a wide variety of alcoholic beverages.

---

ers and the adoption of rules for conducting its business. As illustrated in Figure 7.1, each house has a hierarchical leadership structure.

The House of Representatives

Even in the first Congress in 1789, the House of Representatives was almost three times larger than the Senate. It is not surprising, then, that from the beginning the House has been organized more tightly, structured more elaborately, and governed by stricter rules. Traditionally, loyalty to the party leadership and voting along party lines has been more common in the House than in the Senate. House leaders also play a key role in moving the business of the House along. Historically, the speaker of the House, the majority and minority leaders, and the Republican and Democratic House whips have made up the party leadership that runs Congress. This group now has been expanded to include deputy whips of both parties.

The Speaker of the House. The **speaker of the House** is the only officer of the House of Representatives specifically mentioned in the Constitution. The office, the chamber's most powerful position, is modeled after a similar office in the British Parliament—the speaker was the one who spoke to the king and conveyed the wishes of the House of Commons to the monarch.[4]

The entire House of Representatives elects the speaker at the beginning of each new Congress. Traditionally, the speaker is a member of the **majority party,** the party in each house with the greatest number of members, as are all committee chairs. (The **minority party** is the party in each house with the second most members.) Although typically not the member with the longest service, the speaker generally has served in the House for a long time and in other House leadership positions as an apprenticeship. The current speaker, Dennis Hastert (R–IL), spent twelve years in the House, and his predecessor Newt Gingrich (R–GA) took sixteen years to work his way to the gavel and dais.

The speaker presides over the House of Representatives, oversees House business, and is the official spokesperson for the House, as well as being second in the line of

speaker of the House
The only officer of the House of Representatives specifically mentioned in the Constitution; elected at the beginning of each new Congress by the entire House; traditionally a member of the majority party.

majority party
The political party in each house of Congress with the most members.

minority party
The political party in each house of Congress with the second most members.

243

ETHICS AND THE CONGRESS

OVERVIEW: Article I, section 5, of the U.S. Constitution gives both chambers of Congress the authority to police the activities and conduct of its members. Because of the nature of congressional office, members enjoy certain protections denied to most Americans—for example, members receive heightened protections for speech, as well as protections against arrest for civil violations during legislative sessions. It is not that members are considered above the law; it is simply that the Constitution's framers believed those engaged in law-making, the highest function of representative government, needed additional freedoms and protections to carry out their duties. Nevertheless, the Constitution does not speak to ethical norms or provide guidelines for correct behavior during congressional assemblies. Over time, ethical oversight and procedure has been determined by the leadership of the two major political parties, who have taken on the responsibility for supervising the behavior of party and congressional members.

The past two decades have seen high-profile ethical lapses from members of Congress. Two speakers have resigned in disgrace, another member resigned after conviction for having sex with a minor and soliciting child pornography, one more pleaded guilty to mail fraud, and yet another was removed after being convicted of bribery and racketeering.

When it comes to ethical lapses regarding campaign finance and party politics, the Congress is less than forthright in detailing ethical failures. Investigations of members are usually secret, and congressional rules do not allow outsiders to bring charges of malfeasance. Prior to 1997, both major par-

ties used accusations of corruption to score political points, so much so that many observers believed protocol in the House would degenerate into disorder. In 1997, the parties in the House instituted an ethics truce in an attempt to bring order and decorum to the legislative process. The primary problem is the secret nature of investigating ethical transgressions; this helps foster the public perception that Congress hides its accountability and protects morally suspect members.

The nature of political office is such that the American people hold elected representatives to high ethical standards; after all, law ultimately reflects the prevailing morality of legislative bodies. How can the American public ensure representatives are held accountable for bad behavior? Should outside watchdog groups be allowed to bring charges of corruption and wrongdoing, or is the electoral process an adequate safeguard against political malfeasance? Should Congress create an independent regulatory body to ensure members' compliance to ethical standards, or should the parties themselves be held to stricter accountability for their members' behavior? What can be done to reestablish trust between the American people and their elected officials?

Arguments Supporting Congressional Oversight Authority

- **The Framers gave Congress traditional parliamentary rights.** Supreme Court Justice Joseph Story, in his *Commentaries on the Constitution*, states that common law gives legislators the right to define contempt, or unethical behavior, based on the fact that members of Congress have unique competency in determining matters of leg-

Timeline

The Power of the Speaker of the House

presidential succession. Moreover, the speaker is the House liaison with the president and generally has great political influence within the chamber. The speaker is also expected to smooth the passage of party-backed legislation through the House.

The first powerful speaker was Henry Clay (R–KY) (see Roots of Government: Life on the Floor and in the Halls of Congress). Serving in Congress at a time when turnover was high, he was elected to the position in 1810, his first term in office. He was the speaker of the House for a total of six terms—longer than anyone else in the nineteenth century.

By the late 1800s, the House ceased to have a revolving door and average stays of members increased. With this professionalization of the House came professionalization in the position of speaker. Between 1896 and 1910, a series of speakers initiated changes that brought more power to the office as speakers largely took control of committee assignments and the appointing of committee chairs. Institutional and personal rule reached its height during the 1903–1910 tenure of Speaker of the House Joseph ("Joe") Cannon (R–IL).

Negative reaction to those strong speakers eventually led to a revolt in 1910 and 1911 in the House and to a reduction of the formal powers of the speaker. As a consequence, many speakers between Cannon and Newt Gingrich, who became speaker in 1995, often islative ethics. Thus, Congress is the "proper and exclusive forum" for determining if ethical breaches have occurred.

- **Congress does respond to unethical behavior by its members.** The Congress is responsive to ethical violations by its members. For example, many members of Congress have resigned in disgrace—in 1995 Senator Bob Packwood resigned due to sexual misconduct; in 1990 Representative Barney Frank was reprimanded for fixing parking tickets for a lover, and in 1991 Senator Alan Cranston was formally reprimanded for his role in the Keating Five savings and loan scandal.

- **Voters are competent to unseat unethical members.** Voters force members to pay attention to ethics or risk losing their seats. For example, Representative Gary Condit was not reelected after his relationship with an intern became public, and Representative Dan Rostenkowski was not returned to office amid allegations of fraud and influence peddling.

Arguments Against Congressional Oversight Authority

- **Congress has demonstrated that it cannot be trusted to exercise oversight over its members.** The 1994 Republican Revolution in the House was in part due to the GOP's promise to "clean up Washington" while adhering to strict ethical standards. During the last decade, rules have been flouted and the Congress has slowly relaxed ethical standards; for example, the 108th House relaxed gift rules, giving lobbyists loopholes so they can provide perks—such as dinners, golfing vacations, and tickets to sporting and cultural events—to members as they attempt to gain access.

- **An independent regulatory agency acting as a filter between members and the ethics process can ensure fairness in investigatory procedure.** An independent, unbiased, nonpartisan entity can ensure members are treated impartially. An independent entity can also ensure allegations of ethical misconduct are investigated fairly and then make recommendations for disposition of allegations. This will help limit partisan political maneuvering.

- **Allowing private individuals and watchdog groups to request investigations would improve accountability.** Establishing a formal procedure for investigations initiated by the public can help increase congressional accountability by putting members under the watchful eye of public interest groups. Members would be less likely to engage in misbehavior if they knew their actions were being observed by those outside their party.

Questions

1. What can be done to make members of Congress adhere to ethical guidelines?

2. In 2005, the House considered changing its ethics rule in a move perceived to protect some House leaders. How did public opinion act to stop those changes?

Selected Readings

Martin and Susan Tolchin. *Glass Houses: Congressional Ethics and the Politics of Venom.* Boulder, CO: Westview, 2001.

Dennis Thompson. *Ethics in Congress: From Individual to Institutional Corruption.* Washington, DC: Brookings Institution Press, 1995.

relied on more informal powers that came from their personal ability to persuade members of their party. Gingrich, the first Republican speaker in forty years, convinced fellow Republicans to return important formal powers to the position. These formal changes, along with his personal leadership skills, allowed Gingrich to exercise greater control over the House and its agenda than any other speaker since the days of Cannon.

In time, Gingrich's highly visible role as a revolutionary transformed him into a negative symbol outside of Washington, D.C., and his public popularity plunged. Gingrich's general unpopularity with large segments of the public worked to reinforce Republicans' discontent with Gingrich. The 105th Republican Congress had few legislative successes; members were forced to accept a budget advanced by the Democratic-controlled White House, and Republicans running for office in 1998 lacked the coherent theme that had been so successful for them in 1994. These were but two of many reasons that prompted several members to announce that they would run against Gingrich for the position of speaker. Gingrich, who could read the writing on the wall, opted to resign as speaker (later he resigned altogether from the House) rather than face the prospect that he might not be reelected to the position he had coveted for so long.

Photo courtesy: Ron Sachs/Corbis Sygma

■ House leaders—Majority House Whip Tom DeLay (R–TX) and Speaker of the House Dennis Hastert (R–IL)—talk to reporters after meeting with President George W. Bush at the White House.

After their first choice to replace Gingrich resigned from the House after acknowledging an extramarital affair, Republicans turned to someone largely unknown to the public: a well-liked and respected one-time high school wrestling coach and social studies teacher, Dennis Hastert (R–IL). Since coming into his "accidental speakership," Hastert has shown himself to be a "pragmatic and cautious politician" known for his low-profile leadership style.[5] Until campaign finance reform debates during the 107th Congress, he never "lost a vote on the rule to govern floor debate, a feat not seen in at least a decade."[6]

Other House Leaders.   After the speaker, the next most powerful people in the House are the majority and minority leaders, who are elected in their individual **party caucuses** or **conferences.** The **majority leader** is the second most important person in the House; his or her counterpart on the other side of the aisle (the House is organized so that if you are facing the front of the chamber, Democrats sit on the left side and Republicans on the right side of the center aisle) is the **minority leader.** The majority leader helps

party caucus or conference
A formal gathering of all party members.

majority leader
The elected leader of the party controlling the most seats in the House of Representatives or the Senate; is second in authority to the speaker of the House and in the Senate is regarded as its most powerful member.

minority leader
The elected leader of the party with the second highest number of elected representatives in the House of Representatives or the Senate.

whip
One of several representatives who keep close contact with all members and take nose counts on key votes, prepare summaries of bills, and in general act as communications links within the party.

the speaker schedule proposed legislation for debate on the House floor. In the past, both leaders worked closely with the speaker. In the 108th Congress, however, Republicans rarely consulted Minority Leader Pelosi, prompting her to call for a new code of cooperation, as described in Politics Now: A Minority Bill of Rights?

The Republican and Democratic **whips,** who are elected by party members in caucuses, assist the speaker and majority and minority leaders in their leadership efforts. The position of whip originated in the British House of Commons, where it was named after the "whipper in," the rider who keeps the hounds together in a fox hunt. Party whips—who were first designated in the U.S. House of Representatives in 1899 and in the Senate in 1913—do, as their name suggests, try to whip fellow Democrats or Republicans into line on partisan issues. They try to maintain close contact with all members on important votes, prepare summaries of content and implications of bills, get "nose counts" during debates and votes, and in general get members to toe the party line. Whips and their deputy whips also serve as communications links, distributing word of the party line from leaders to rank-and-file members and alerting leaders to concerns in the ranks. Whips can be extraordinarily effective. In 1998, for example, when President Bill Clinton returned home from his trip to the Middle East amid calls for his impeachment, he was stunned to learn that moderate Republicans whom he had counted on to vote against his impeachment were "dropping like flies." The reason? Then-House Republican Whip Tom DeLay (R–TX) threatened Republicans that they would be denied coveted committee assignments and would even face Republican challengers in the next primary season unless they voted the party line.

The Senate

The Constitution specifies that the presiding officer of the Senate is the vice president of the United States. Because he is not a member of the Senate, he votes only in the case of a tie. In 2001, first Vice President Al Gore and then Vice President Dick

A MINORITY BILL OF RIGHTS?

It is customary for the party in control of the House of Representatives to limit the minority's ability to amend bills as well as shape the debate on proposed legislation. But Democrats, as the minority party after forty years of control, are charging that Republicans are wielding their power in unfair ways that damage the deliberative process of that body. A scholar from the moderate to conservative American Enterprise Institute said that Democrats' complaints have some merit. "Republicans are at a point now where, reveling in the power they have, they are using techniques to jam bills through even when they don't have to . . . simply because they can."[a]

In 2004, in an effort to allow the minority party more input, Democratic Leader Nancy Pelosi proposed a "Minority Bill of Rights," which she pledged to follow if the Democrats regain power. Among its provisions are calls for:

- *Bipartisan administration of the House.* This would provide for regular consultation between the leaders of both parties concerning scheduling, administration, and operation of the House. This would include a guarantee that the minority party would get at least one-third of committee budgets and office space.

In the past, meetings of minority and majority party leaders were routine, as were meetings between committee chairs and ranking members. Speaker Dennis Hastert rarely meets with Pelosi, and only a few committee chairs consult with ranking minority members. The budget and office space condition was followed in the 108th Congress, and Pelosi says it should be mandatory.

- *Regular order for legislation.* This would require that bills be developed following full hearings and open commit-

tee and subcommittee mark-ups, and that members would have at least twenty-four hours to read any bill before it came to a vote. This would also mandate that all floor votes be completed within fifteen minutes.

In the 108th Congress, Republicans delayed floor votes in order to allow the whips and other leaders to convince members to change their votes. For example, the Republicans held up voting on the Medicare prescription drug bill for nearly three hours until well after midnight, to convince Republican dissidents to change their votes after the leadership appeared headed for defeat. On other legislation, the Republican leadership met until one or two o'clock in the morning, then scheduled votes on what it had done for ten o'clock the same morning. This did not allow many rank and file members to be familiar with the legislation they were voting on.

- *Collaboration on final legislation.* In the 108th Congress, the Rules Committee frequently rejected amendments from Democrats. Thus, Pelosi called for regular House-Senate conference committee meetings that would allow minority party members some input into final conference committee legislation.

Questions

1. Do you think these suggestions should be adopted? Why or why not?

2. Can you think of other suggestions to cure the problems Pelosi seeks to address?

[a] Charles Babington, "Pelosi Seeks House Minority 'Bill of Rights,' Hastert Dismisses Democrats' Complaint, Saying GOP Record Is Better Than Foes'," *Washington Post* (June 24, 2004): A23.

Cheney briefly presided over an evenly divided Senate, the first time this had happened since 1881.

The official chair of the Senate is the president pro tempore, or pro tem, who is selected by the majority party and presides over the Senate in the absence of the vice president. The position of pro tem today is primarily an honorific office that generally goes to the most senior senator of the majority party. Once elected, the pro tem stays in that office until there is a change in the majority party in the Senate. Since presiding over the Senate can be a rather perfunctory duty, neither the vice president nor the president pro tempore actually perform the task very often. Instead, the duty of presiding over the Senate rotates among junior members of the chamber, allowing more senior members to attend more important meetings.

The true leader of the Senate is the majority leader, elected to the position by the majority party. Because the Senate is a smaller and more collegial body, operating without many of the more formal House rules concerning debate, the majority leader is not nearly as powerful as the speaker of the House. The Republican and

Democratic whips round out the leadership positions in the Senate and perform functions similar to those of their House counterparts. But, leading and whipping in the Senate can be quite a challenge. Senate rules always have given tremendous power to individual senators; in most cases senators can offer any kind of amendments to legislation on the floor, and an individual senator can bring all work on the floor to a halt indefinitely through a filibuster unless three-fifths of the senators vote to cut him or her off.[7]

Because of the Senate's smaller size, organization and formal rules never have played the same role in the Senate that they do in the House. Through the 1960s, it was a gentlemen's club whose folkways—unwritten rules of behavior—governed its operation. One such folkway, for example, stipulated that political disagreements not become personal criticisms. A senator who disliked another referred to that senator as "the able, learned, and distinguished senator." A member who really couldn't stand another called that senator "my very able, learned, and distinguished colleague."

In the 1960s and 1970s, senators became more and more active on and off the Senate floor in a variety of issues, and extended debates often occurred on the floor without the rigid rules of courtesy that had once been the hallmark of the body. These changes weren't accompanied by giving additional powers to the Senate majority leader, who now often has difficulty controlling "the more active, assertive, and consequently less predictable membership" of the Senate.[8]

The Role of Political Parties in Organizing Congress

The organization of both houses of Congress is closely tied to political parties and their strength in each house. (For the party breakdowns in the 109th Congress, see Figure 7.2.) Parties play a key role in the committee system, an organizational feature of Congress that facilitates its law-making and oversight functions. The committees, controlled by the majority party in each house of Congress, often set the congressional agendas, although under Newt Gingrich's leadership, chairs' power eroded substantially in the House of Representatives as the speaker's power was enhanced.[9]

At the beginning of each new Congress—the 109th Congress, for example, will sit in two sessions, one in 2005 and one in 2006—the members of each party gather in their party caucus or conference. Historically, these caucuses have enjoyed varied powers, but today the party caucuses—now called caucus by House Democrats and conference by House and Senate Republicans and Senate Democrats—have several roles, including nominating or electing party officers, reviewing committee assignments, discussing party policy, imposing party discipline, setting party themes, and coordinating media, including talk radio. Conference and caucus chairs are recognized party leaders who work with other leaders in the House or Senate.[10]

Each caucus or conference has specialized committees that fulfill certain tasks. House Republicans, for example, have a Committee on Committees that makes committee assignments. The Democrats' Steering Committee performs this function. Each party also has a congressional campaign committee to assist members in their reelection bids.

The Committee System

The saying "Congress in session is Congress on exhibition, whilst Congress in its committee rooms is Congress at work" may not be as true today as it was when Woodrow Wilson wrote it in 1885.[11] Still, "The work that takes place in the committee and subcommittee rooms of Capitol Hill is critical to the productivity and effectiveness of Congress."[12] Standing committees are the first and last places to

FIGURE 7.2 The 109th Congress. ■

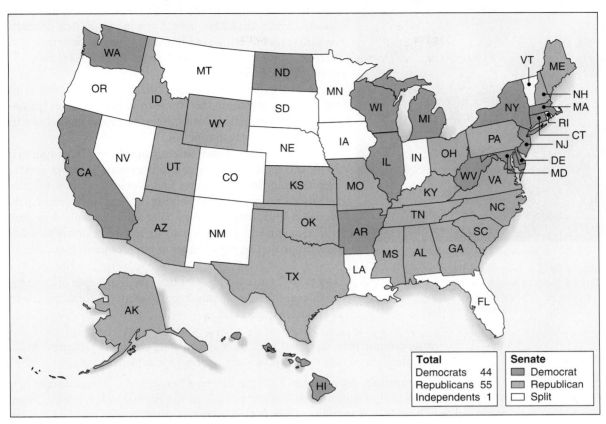

Total
Democrats 44
Republicans 55
Independents 1

Senate
■ Democrat
■ Republican
□ Split

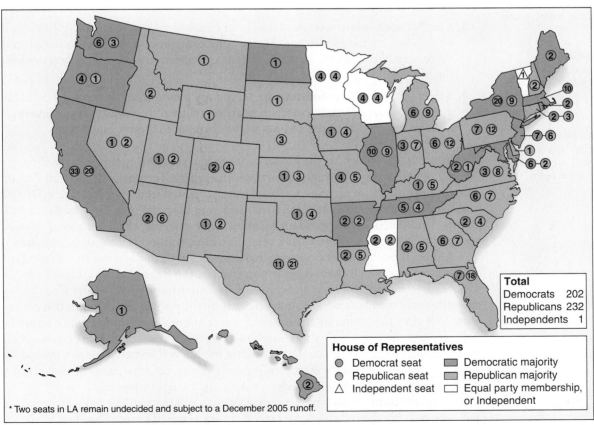

Total
Democrats 202
Republicans 232
Independents 1

House of Representatives
● Democrat seat ■ Democratic majority
● Republican seat ■ Republican majority
△ Independent seat □ Equal party membership, or Independent

* Two seats in LA remain undecided and subject to a December 2005 runoff.

Photo courtesy: Tony Talbot/AP/Wide World Photos

■ Representative Bernie Sanders (I–VT), right, shares a toast of milk with Senator Jim Jeffords (I–VT) at a news conference celebrating the Northeast Dairy Compact. Sanders and Jeffords, the only independents in the 109th Congress, both vote with Democrats.

which most bills go. Usually committee members play key roles in floor debate in the full House or Senate about the merits of bills that have been introduced. When different versions of a bill are passed in the House and Senate, a conference committee with members of both houses meets to iron out the differences.

The organization and specialization of committees are especially important in the House of Representatives because of its size. The establishment of subcommittees allows for even greater specialization.

Congress created an institutionalized committee system in 1816, and more and more committees were added over time. The large number of committees resulted in duplication of duties and jurisdictional battles. When Republicans took control of the House in 1995, they cut several committees and subcommittees and reorganized (and renamed) several committees to lessen duplication and highlight issues of importance to them.[13]

Types of Committees.   There are four types of congressional committees: (1) standing; (2) joint; (3) conference; and, (4) select, or special.[14]

1. **Standing committees,** so called because they continue from one Congress to the next, are the committees to which bills are referred for consideration.

2. **Joint committees** are set up to expedite business between the houses and to help focus public attention on major matters, such as the economy, taxation, or scandals. They include members from both houses of Congress who conduct investigations or special studies.

3. **Conference committees** are special joint committees that reconcile differences in bills passed by the House and Senate. The conference committee is made up of those members from the House and Senate committees that originally considered the bill.

4. **Select (or special) committees** are temporary committees appointed for specific purposes. Generally such committees are established to conduct special investigations or studies and to report back to the chamber that established them.

standing committee
Committee to which proposed bills are referred.

joint committee
Includes members from both houses of Congress; conducts investigations or special studies.

conference committee
Joint committee created to iron out differences between Senate and House versions of a specific piece of legislation.

select (or special) committee
Temporary committee appointed for specific purpose, such as conducting a special investigation or study.

In the 109th Congress, the House has nineteen standing committees, as shown in Table 7.3, each with an average of thirty-one members. Together, these standing committees have a total of eighty-six subcommittees that collectively act as the eyes, ears, and hands of the House. They consider issues roughly parallel to those of the departments represented in the president's Cabinet. For example, there are committees on agriculture, education, the judiciary, veterans affairs, transportation, and commerce.

Although most committees in one house parallel those in the other, the House Rules Committee, for which there is no counterpart in the Senate, plays a key role in the House's law-making process. Indicative of the importance of the Rules Committee, majority party members are appointed directly by the speaker. This committee reviews most bills after they come from a committee and before they go to the full chamber for consideration. Performing a traffic cop function, the Rules Committee gives each bill what is called a rule, which contains the date the bill will come up for debate and the time that will be allotted for discussion, and often specifies what kinds of amendments can be offered. Bills considered under a closed rule cannot be amended.

Standing committees have considerable power. They can kill bills, amend them radically, or hurry them through the process. In the words of former President Woodrow Wilson, once a bill is referred to a committee, it "crosses a parliamentary bridge of sighs to dim dungeons of silence from whence it never will return."[15] Committees report out

TABLE 7.3 Committees of the 109th Congress (with a Subcommittee Example)

Standing Committees

House	Senate
Agriculture	Agriculture, Nutrition, and Forestry
Appropriations	Appropriations
Armed Services	Armed Services
Budget	Banking, Housing, and Urban Affairs
Education and the Workforce	Budget
Energy and Commerce	Commerce, Science, and Transportation
Financial Services	Energy and Natural Resources
Government Reform	Environment and Public Works
House Administration	Finance
International Relations	Foreign Relations
Judiciary	Governmental Affairs
Courts, the Internet, and Intellectual Property	Health, Education, Labor, and Pensions
Immigration, Border Security, and Claims	Judiciary
Commercial and Administrative Law	Judiciary Subcommittees
Crime, Terrorism, and Homeland Security	Immigration, Border Security, and Citizenship
Constitution	Antitrust, Competition Policy, and Consumer
Resources	Rights
Rules	Terrorism, Technology, and Homeland Security
Science	Crime, Corrections, and Victims' Rights
Small Business	The Constitution, Civil Rights, and Property
Standards of Official Conduct	Rights
Transportation and Infrastructure	Rules and Administration
Veterans Affairs	Small Business and Entrepreneurship
Ways and Means	Veterans Affairs

Select, Special, and Other Committees

House	Senate	Joint Committees
Select Intelligence	Special Aging	Economics
Select Homeland Security	Select Ethics	Printing
	Select Intelligence	Taxation
	Indian Affairs	Library

discharge petition
Petition that gives a majority of the House of Representatives the authority to bring an issue to the floor in the face of committee inaction.

to the full House or Senate only a small fraction of the bills assigned to them. Bills can be forced out of a House committee by a **discharge petition** signed by a majority (218) of the House membership.

In the 109th Congress, the Senate has sixteen standing committees ranging in size from fifteen to twenty-nine members. It also has sixty-eight subcommittees, which allows all majority party senators to chair one.

In contrast to the House, whose members hold few committee assignments (an average of 1.8 standing and three subcommittees), senators each serve on an average of three to four committees and seven subcommittees. Whereas the committee system allows House members to become policy or issue specialists, Senate members often are generalists. In the 109th Congress, Senator Kay Bailey Hutchison (R–TX), for example, serves on several committees, including Appropriations; Commerce, Science, and Transportation; Veterans Affairs; and Rules. She serves on even more subcommittees, chairing two of them, and is the vice chair of the Republican Conference.

Senate committees enjoy the same power over framing legislation that House committees do, but the Senate, being an institution more

■ In 2002, Representatives Linda and Loretta Sanchez (both D–CA) became the first sisters to serve together in the U.S. Congress. Since then, they have pushed for women's issues, such as enforcement of Title IX, research for breast cancer, and protections against sexual assault in the military.

Photo courtesy: Office of Representative Loretta Sanchez

Photo courtesy: Hillery Smith Garrison/AP/Wide World Photos

■ Depending on whether or not his party controls the Senate, Robert Byrd (D–VA) has served as president pro tem of the Senate as well as the chair of the powerful Appropriations Committee. Senator Byrd is known as the "Prince of Pork" for his ability to "bring home the bacon" in the form of public works projects to West Virginia.

pork
Legislation that allows representatives to bring home the bacon to their districts in the form of public works programs, military bases, or other programs designed to benefit their districts directly.

■ Democrat Stephanie Herseth listens to the applause of supporters after winning the special election for South Dakota's U.S. House seat in June, 2004. When Herseth got to the Hill, members of the Resources and Veterans Affairs Committee gave up their seats for Herseth believing these appointments would help her November 2004 re-election bid.

open to individual input than the House, gives less deference to the work done in committees. In the Senate, legislation is more likely to be rewritten on the floor, where all senators can participate and add amendments at any time.

Committee Membership.   Many newly elected members of Congress come into the body with their sights on certain committee assignments. Others are more flexible. Many legislators seeking committee assignments inform their party's selection committee of their preferences. They often request assignments based on their own interests or expertise or on a particular committee's ability to help their prospects for reelection. One political scientist has noted that committee assignments are to members what stocks are to investors—they seek to acquire those that will add to the value of their portfolios.[16]

Representatives often seek committee assignments that have access to what is known as **pork,** legislation that allows representatives to bring money and jobs to their districts in the form of public works programs, military bases, or other programs. In the past, a seat on the Armed Services Committee, for example, would allow a member to bring lucrative defense contracts back to his or her district, or to discourage base closings within his or her district or state. In one example from the 2004 appropriations bill, the House approved $2 million to help develop a youth golf program in Florida.[17]

Legislators who bring jobs and new public works programs back to their districts are hard to defeat when up for reelection. But, ironically, these are the programs that attract much of the public criticism directed at the federal government in general and Congress in particular. Thus, it is somewhat paradoxical that pork improves a member's chances for reelection. Senator Robert Byrd (D–WV) is regarded as the Prince of Pork. He even got the U.S. Coast Guard Operations Systems Center built in a landlocked state, West Virginia.

Pork isn't the only motivator for those seeking strategic committee assignments.[18] Some committees, such as Energy and Commerce, facilitate reelection by giving House members influence over decisions that affect large campaign contributors. Other committees, such as Education and the Workforce or Judiciary, attract members eager to work on the policy responsibilities assigned to the committee even if the appointment does them little good at the ballot box. Another motivator for certain committee assignments is the desire to have power and influence within the chamber. The Appropriations and Budget Committees provide that kind of reward for some members, given the monetary impact of the committees. Congress can approve programs, but unless money for them is appropriated in the budget, they are largely symbolic.

In both the House and the Senate, committee membership generally reflects the party distribution within that chamber. For example, at the outset of the 109th Congress, Republicans held a narrow majority of House seats (229) and thus claimed about a 55 percent share of the seats on several committees, including International Relations, Energy and Commerce, and Education and the Workforce. On committees more critical to the operation of the House or to the setting of national policy, the majority often takes a disproportionate share of the slots. Since the Rules Committee regulates access to the floor for legislation approved by other standing committees, control by the majority party is essential for it to manage the flow of legislation. For this reason, no matter how narrow the majority party's margin in the chamber, it makes up more than two-thirds of the Rules Committee membership. In the Senate, during its brief 50–50 split in 2001, the leaders agreed to equal representation on committees, along with equal staffing, office space, and budget.

Photo courtesy: Doug Dreyer/AP/Wide World Photos

THE PARLIAMENT OF THE "UNITED STATES OF EUROPE"

The union of thirteen separate British colonies into the United States and the subsequent expansion into a country of 50 states spanning a continent and beyond is one of the amazing political stories of history. Today, another amazing political story is unfolding. In 1956, six countries in Western Europe—France, Italy, West Germany, Belgium, the Netherlands, and Luxembourg—came together to create the European Common Market. It was an economic union, not a political one, but virtually from the outset some political commentators saw in it the nucleus of a "United States of Europe." Still, for most observers, it was an inconceivable notion that many of the states of Europe, which had fought two long and brutal world wars in the twentieth century and then became the primary battleground for the Cold War, might overcome their differences and voluntarily and peacefully form a single country. Yet, this vision slowly appears to be becoming true.

The process of unification begun in 1956 has passed through several stages. A first expansion in membership occurred in 1973 when Denmark, Ireland, and Great Britain joined the then Common Market. Greece joined in 1981, and Spain and Portugal joined in 1986. In 1994, Austria, Finland, and Sweden became members. Enlargement reached a new milestone in May 2004 when ten new states joined what is today known as the European Union (EU). Even more significant than the number of states that joined (increasing membership from fifteen to twenty-five) or the overnight growth of its population (by 20 percent to 450 million) was the identity of the states that joined. Five of the ten were Eastern European states once ruled by communism: the Czech Republic, Slovenia, Slovakia, Poland, and Hungary. Three states had actually been part of the Soviet Union before it collapsed: Latvia, Estonia, and Lithuania. The other two were Malta and Cyprus. The EU was now truly becoming continental in scope and may continue to grow. Turkey hopes to be admitted in the near future, and another round of expansion is set for 2007.

As with the American experience, adding new states (countries) requires making a series of adjustments in how the EU is governed. One of the most significant changes was adjusting the size of the legislature, the European parliament. It had 140 members when first created in 1958. With this latest expansion, it now has 787 members. The distribution of seats by country is shown in the table.

The United States has a system of checks and balances in which Congress and the president possess separate powers. This is not the case in the EU. The essential power of the EU is "codecision." This means that the EU acts as a partner with the European Commission (made up of representatives appointed by member countries) in making policy. In some cases, such as taxation policy, the parliament only gives an opinion.

Making the European parliament bigger was necessary to ensure that all of the countries belonging to the EU are fairly represented. To reach the goal of bringing the states of Europe together in a democracy, the EU had to answer questions such as the following.

Distribution of Seats in the European Parliment

Country	Seats	Country	Seats
Austria	21	Latvia	9
Belgium	25	Lithuania	13
Cyprus	6	Luxembourg	6
Czech Republic	24	Malta	4
Denmark	16	Netherlands	31
Estonia	6	Poland	54
Finland	16	Portugal	25
France	87	Slovakia	14
Germany	99	Slovenia	7
Greece	25	Spain	64
Hungary	24	Sweden	22
Ireland	15	United Kingdom	87
Italy	87		

- *How are members to be chosen?* The first answer given was that members should be appointed by their national parliaments. Since 1979, members have been directly elected by the people.
- *Who can vote for members to the European parliament?* The voting age in all countries is eighteen. Even if you are not a citizen of the country you are living in, you may still vote in that country for members of the European parliament provided you are considered a resident of that country. Definitions of residence, however, vary greatly. So do rules governing the right of citizens living abroad to submit absentee ballots in their home country.
- *Who can run for a seat in the European parliament?* Age requirements vary from country to country, ranging from a low of eighteen to a high of twenty-five. Luxembourg also has a ten-year residency requirement.
- *When are elections held?* There is no single day for parliamentary elections. In 1999, the most frequent voting day was Sunday, June 13, but in four countries it was June 10 because Thursday is the traditional voting day there.
- *How will the parliament be organized?* Members do not sit as part of country delegations but according to their political affiliation. Among the political groups that can be found in the European parliament are the European People's Party, the Party of European Socialists, the European Liberal Democratic Party, and the Reform Party.
- *How many committees should there be?* There are currently seventeen committees as well as a number of parliamentary delegations.

Questions

1. How does current and past U.S. experience compare to that of the European Union in terms of selecting members of the legislature and organizing the legislative body for work?

2. Would policy making in the United States be improved if Congress and the president worked together as partners, rather than as separate, competing powers? Explain your answer.

Photo courtesy: Luke Frazza/AFP/CORBIS

■ Representative Barney Frank (D–MA) has been in the rare position of having fun while being in the minority party. Says Frank, "I'm a counterpuncher, happiest fighting on the defensive. Besides, I really dislike what the Republicans are doing. I think they are bad for the country and for vulnerable people. I feel, 'Boy, this is a moral opportunity—you've got to fight this.' Also, I'm used to being in a minority. Hey, I'm a left-handed gay Jew. I've never felt, automatically, a member of any majority."

seniority
Time of continuous service on a committee.

Committee Chairs. Committee chairs enjoy tremendous power and prestige. They are authorized to select all subcommittee chairs, call meetings, and recommend majority members to sit on conference committees. Committee chairs may even opt to kill a bill by refusing to schedule hearings on it. They also have a large committee staff at their disposal and are often recipients of favors from lobbyists, who recognize the chair's unique position of power. Personal skill, influence, and expertise are a chair's best allies.

Historically, committee chairs were the majority party members with the longest continuous service on the committee. Committee chairs in the House, unlike the Senate, are no longer selected by **seniority,** or time of continuous service on the committee. Today, the House leadership interviews potential chairs to make certain that candidates demonstrate loyalty to the party. For example, in 2003, Representative Christopher Shays (R–CT), who went against the Republican Party in supporting campaign finance reform, was passed over as chair of the House Resources Committee in

favor of a less senior but more loyal committee member.[19] In 1995 and 1997 respectively, the House and Senate enacted a term limit of six years for all committee chairs. This term limit has forced many longtime committee chairs to step down. However, these chairs often take over another committee. For example, Representative Henry Hyde (R–IL) stepped down as chair of the House Judiciary Committee in favor of a new position as chair of the International Relations Committee.

■ Senate Majority Leader Bill Frist (R–TN), left, talks to House Majority Leader Tom DeLay (R–TX) at the 2003 Congress of Tommorrow retreat that brought House and Senate Republicans together.

Photo courtesy: REUTERS/William Philpott/Corbis

THE MEMBERS OF CONGRESS

TODAY, MANY MEMBERS OF CONGRESS find the job exciting in spite of public criticism of the institution. But, it wasn't always so. Until Washington, D.C., got air-conditioning and drained its swamps, it was a miserable town. Most representatives spent as little time as possible there, viewing the Congress, especially the House, as a stepping stone to other political positions back home. It was only after World War I that House members became congressional careerists who viewed their work in Washington as long term.[20]

Many members of Congress clearly relish their work, although there are indications that the high cost of living in Washington and of maintaining two homes, political scandals, intense media scrutiny, the need to tackle hard issues, and a growth of partisan dissension are taking a toll on many members. Those no longer in the majority, in particular, often don't see their service in Congress as satisfying. Research by political scientists shows that "members voluntarily depart when their electoral, policy, and institutional situations no longer seem desirable."[21] The increasing partisanship of the Congress also plays a role in many retirements. When asked why he was leaving the Senate, Warren Rudman (R–NH) remarked, "It's the whole atmosphere. It's become so partisan, so intense, in many ways it's just hateful."[22]

Former House and Senate members also can make a lot more money in the private sector. Former House Appropriations Chair Robert Livingston built the tenth largest lobbying firm in D.C. in only four years, earning millions each year from clients who understand the access former members retain.[23] Since 1995, 272 former members have registered as lobbyists.[24]

Members must attempt to appease two constituencies—party leaders, colleagues, and lobbyists in Washington, D.C., and constituents at home.[25] Members spend full days at home as well as in D.C. According to one study of House members in non-election years, average representatives made thirty-five trips back home to their districts and spent an average 138 days a year there.[26] Hedrick Smith, a Pulitzer Prize–winning reporter for the *New York Times*, has aptly described a member's days as a "kaleidoscopic jumble: breakfast with reporters, morning staff meetings, simultaneous committee hearings to juggle, back-to-back sessions with lobbyists and constituents, phone calls, briefings, constant buzzers interrupting office work to make quorum calls and votes on the run, afternoon speeches, evening meetings, receptions, fund-raisers, all crammed into four days so they can race home for a weekend gauntlet of campaigning. It's a rat race."[27] Table 7.4 shows a representative day in the life of a member of Congress.

TABLE 7.4 A Day in the Life of a Member of Congress

Typical Member's At-Home Schedule[a]		*Typical Member's Washington Schedule*[b]	
7:30 a.m.	Business group breakfast, 20 leaders of the business community	8:30 a.m.	Breakfast with former member
8:45 a.m.	Hoover Elementary School, 6th grade class assembly	9:30 a.m.	Committee on Science, Space, and Technology hearing on research and development in the 1990s
9:45 a.m.	National Agriculture Day speech, Holiday Inn South	10:00 a.m.	Briefing by FAA officials for members of Congress who represent families of victims of Pan Am Flight #103
10:45 a.m.	Supplemental Food Shelf, pass foodstuffs to needy families	10:00 a.m.	Energy and Commerce Committee mark-up session on Fairness in Broadcasting
12:00 noon	Community College, student/faculty lunch, speech, and Q & A	12:00 noon	Reception/photo opportunity with telecommunications officials
1:00 p.m.	Sunset Terrace Elementary School, assembly 4th, 5th, 6th graders, remarks/Q & A	12:00 noon	House convenes
(Travel Time: 1:45 p.m.–2:45 p.m.)		12:00 noon	Lunch with personal friend at Watergate Hotel
2:45 p.m.	Plainview Day Care facility owner wishes to discuss changes in federal law	1:30 p.m.	Subcommittee on Science Space Applications hearing
4:00 p.m.	Town Hall Meeting, American Legion	1:30 p.m.	Subcommittee on Health and Environment mark-up session on Trauma Care Systems Planning Act
(Travel Time: 5:00 p.m.–5:45 p.m.)		3:00 p.m.	Meeting with officials of the National Alliance for Animal Legislation
5:45 p.m.	PTA meeting, speech, education issues before Congress (also citizen involvement with national associations)	4:30 p.m.	Meeting with delegates from American Jewish Congress on foreign aid bill
6:30 p.m.	Annual Dinner, St. John's Lutheran Church Developmental Activity Center	5:00 p.m.	New York University reception
7:15 p.m.	Association for Children for Enforcement of Support meeting to discuss problems of enforcing child support payments	5:00 p.m.	Briefing by the commissioner of the Bureau of Labor (statistics on the uninsured)
(Travel Time: 8:00 p.m.–8:30 p.m.)		5:30 p.m.	Reception/fundraiser for party whip
8:30 p.m.	Students Against Drunk Driving (SADD) meeting, speech, address drinking age, drunk driving, uniform federal penalties	6:00 p.m.	Reception/fundraiser for fellow member
		6:00 p.m.	"Cajun" reception/fundraiser for Louisiana member
9:30 p.m.	State university class, discuss business issues before Congress	6:00 p.m.	Winetasting reception by New York wine industry
		8:00 p.m.	Back to Capitol Hill for a vote

[a]Craig Shultz, ed., *Setting Course: A Congressional Management Guide* (Washington, DC: American University, 1994), 335.
[b]http://congress.indiana.edu/learn_about/schedule.htm.

STILL THE BEST CONGRESSIONAL TERM-LIMITING DEVICE.

Photo courtesy: Oliphant, © Universal Press Syndicate. Reprinted with permission. All rights reserved.

Running for Office and Staying in Office

Despite the long hours, hard work, and sometimes even abuse that senators and representatives experience, thousands aspire to these jobs every year. Yet, only 535 men and women (plus five nonvoting delegates) actually serve in the U.S. Congress. Membership in one of the two major political parties is almost always a prerequisite for election, because election laws in various states often discriminate against independents (those without party affiliation) and minor-party candidates. As discussed in chapter 14, money is the mother's milk of politics—the ability to raise money often is key to any member's victory, and many members spend nearly all of their free time on the phone dialing for dollars or attending fundraisers.

incumbency
The fact that being in office helps a person stay in office because of a variety of benefits that go with the position.

    Incumbency helps members stay in office once they are elected.[28] It's often very difficult for outsiders to win because they don't have the advantages (enumerated in Table 7.5) enjoyed by incumbents, including name recognition, access to free media, inside track on fund-raising, and a district drawn to favor the incumbent. As illustrated in Analyzing Visuals: Approval Ratings of Congress and Individual Representatives, which compares the way poll respondents feel about their own representatives to how

TABLE 7.5   The Advantages of Incumbency

- Name recognition gained through previous campaigns and repeated visits to the district to make appearances at various public events.
- Credit claimed for bringing federal money into the district in the form of grants and contracts.
- Positive evaluations from constituents earned by doing favors (casework) such as helping cut red tape and tracking down federal aid, and tasks handled by publicly supported professional staff members.
- Distribution of newsletters and other noncampaign materials free through the mails by using the "frank" (an envelope that contains the legislator's signature in place of a stamp).
- Access to media—incumbents are news makers who provide reporters with tips and quotes.
- Greater ease in fund-raising—their high reelection rates make them a good bet for people or groups willing to give campaign contributions in hopes of having access to powerful decision makers.
- Experience in running a campaign, putting together a campaign staff, making speeches, understanding constituent concerns, and connecting with people.
- Superior knowledge about a wide range of issues gained through work on committees, review of legislation, and previous campaigns.
- A record for supp orting locally popular policy positions.
- A district drawn to enhance electability.

Analyzing Visuals

APPROVAL RATINGS OF CONGRESS AND INDIVIDUAL REPRESENTATIVES

For many years, political scientists have noted that approval ratings of Congress as an institution are generally quite low, rarely exceeding 50 percent approval. On the other hand, the public's approval rating of its own member tends to be much higher, usually above 50 percent. The line graph demonstrates the differences between these ratings since 1990. Do the data for approval of Congress and approval of one's own representative follow similar trends over the period covered in the figure? What factors do you think account for the differences in the ratings of Congress and of one's own representative? What are the effects of the differences in these ratings?

Note that the question regarding one's own representative was a slightly different one in 2004 from the earlier question—asking not just about approval but also about reelection. Do you think that this difference in wording affected the rating positively or negatively?

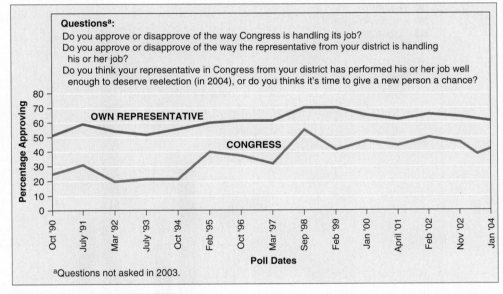

Questions[a]:
Do you approve or disapprove of the way Congress is handling its job?
Do you approve or disapprove of the way the representative from your district is handling his or her job?
Do you think your representative in Congress from your district has performed his or her job well enough to deserve reelection (in 2004), or do you thinks it's time to give a new person a chance?

OWN REPRESENTATIVE

CONGRESS

Percentage Approving (y-axis: 0, 10, 20, 30, 40, 50, 60, 70, 80)

Poll Dates (x-axis: Oct '90, July '91, Mar '92, July '93, Oct '94, Feb '95, Oct '96, Mar '97, Sep '98, Feb '99, Jan '00, April '01, Feb '02, Nov '02, Jan '04)

[a]Questions not asked in 2003.

Source: Data derived from R-Poll, LEXIS/NEXIS.

they feel about Congress as an institution, most Americans approve of their *own* members of Congress while having very low regard for Congress collectively.

It is not surprising, then, that from 1980 to 1990, an average of 95 percent of the incumbents who sought reelection won their primary and general election races.[29] More recent elections saw even higher proportions of incumbents returning to office. One study concluded that unless a member of Congress was involved in a serious scandal, his or her chances of defeat were minimal.[30] In 2004, only seven members seeking reelection lost their races. Four were in Texas, where a redistricting plan forced several incumbents to run against each other.

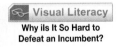

Visual Literacy
Why ils It So Hard to Defeat an Incumbent?

Congressional Demographics

Congress is better educated, richer, more male, and more white than the rest of the United States. In fact, all but three senators are college graduates; 401 representatives share that honor. Over two-thirds of each body also hold advanced degrees.[31] Many members of both Houses have significant inherited wealth, but given their educational attainment, which is far higher than the average American's, it is not surprising to find so many wealthy members of Congress.

Analyzing Visuals

FEMALE AND MINORITY MEMBERS OF CONGRESS

Do you think it makes a difference if members of Congress come from a particular group? The graph you see below makes clear that the numbers of women, African Americans, and Hispanics in Congress have grown enormously during the last forty years. Given the total of 540 (includes five delegates) members serving in the Congress, study the graph and then calculate the percentage of representation in the Congress for each group. Do you think that these numbers are representa-

tive of the nation as a whole? Of your state or local region? The numbers of Asian Pacific Americans and Native Americans in Congress have been so low—presently seven and zero, respectively—that these figures have not been included in the graph. What might this representation, or lack of representation, mean politically to states such as Hawaii, Alaska, Washington, and California, with large numbers of Asian Pacific Americans and Native Americans?

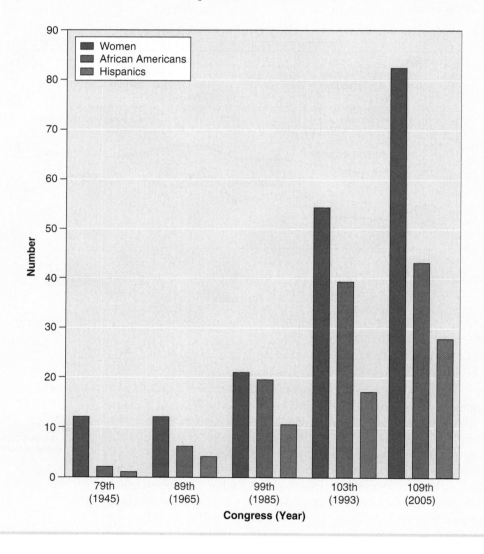

One hundred seventy members of Congress are millionaires. The Senate, in fact, is often called the Millionaires Club, and its members sport names including Rockefeller and Kennedy. In fact, twenty-one senators are worth at least $3.1 million. Twenty-nine members of the House have a net worth over that amount.[32]

The average age of senators is sixty. John Sununu (R–NH) is the youngest senator at forty-one. The average age of House members is fifty-four; Representative Adam Putnam (R–FL) was first elected to the House in 2000 at age twenty-five and continues to be the youngest member of Congress.

As revealed in Analyzing Visuals: Female and Minority Members of Congress, the 1992 elections saw a record number of women, African Americans, and other minorities elected to Congress. By the 109th Congress, the total number of women members increased to eighty-two: sixty-eight in the House and fourteen in the Senate. In 2005, the number of African Americans serving in the House rose from thirty-nine to forty-two. Barack Obama (D–IL), elected to the Senate in 2004, is the first African American to serve there in several years. In the 109th Congress, only twenty-six Hispanics serve in the House—most of them Democrats. Two Hispanics were elected to the Senate in 2004, Ken Salazar (D–CO), and Mel Martinez (R–FL). Also serving in the 109th Congress are two Asian Pacific Islanders in the Senate and five in the House of Representatives.

Occupationally, members of Congress no longer are overwhelmingly lawyers, although lawyers continue to be the largest single occupational group. In the 108th Congress, 275 were former state legislators and 111 were former congressional staffers. The number of veterans in Congress has continued to decline since the end of the Vietnam War.[33]

Theories of Representation

Over the years, political theorists have offered various ideas about how constituents' interests are best represented in any legislative body. Does it make a difference if the members of Congress come from or are members of a particular group? Are they bound to vote the way their constituents expect them to vote even if they personally favor another policy? Your answer to these questions may depend on your view of the representative function of legislators.

British political philosopher Edmund Burke (1729–1797), who also served in the British Parliament, believed that although he was elected from Bristol, it was his duty to represent the interests of the entire nation. He reasoned that elected officials were obliged to vote as they personally thought best. According to Burke, representatives should be **trustees** who listen to the opinions of their constituents and then can be trusted to use their own best judgment to make final decisions.

A second theory of representation holds that representatives are **delegates.** True delegates are representatives who vote the way their constituents would want them to, whether or not those opinions are the representative's. Delegates, therefore, must be ready and willing to vote against their conscience or personal policy preferences if they know how their constituents feel about a particular issue. Not surprisingly, members of Congress and other legislative bodies generally don't fall neatly into either category. It is often unclear how constituents feel about a particular issue, or there may be conflicting opinions within a single constituency. With these difficulties in mind, a third theory of representation holds that **politicos** alternately don the hat of trustee or delegate, depending on the issue. On an issue of great concern to their constituents, representatives most likely will vote as delegates; on other issues, perhaps those that are less visible, representatives will act as trustees and use their own best judgment. Research by political scientists supports this view.[34]

Comparative
Comparing Legislatures

trustee
Role played by elected representatives who listen to constituents' opinions and then use their best judgment to make final decisions.

delegate
Role played by elected representatives who vote the way their constituents would want them to, regardless of their own opinions.

politico
Role played by elected representatives who act as trustees or as delegates, depending on the issue.

How a representative views his or her role—as a trustee, delegate, or politico—may still not answer the question of whether it makes a difference if a representative or senator is male or female, African American, Hispanic, or Caucasian, young or old, gay or straight. Burke's ideas about representation don't even begin to address more practical issues of representation. Can a man, for example, represent the interests of women as well as a woman? Can a rich woman represent the interests of the poor? Are veterans more sensitive to veterans' issues?

Interestingly, one NBC/*Wall Street Journal* poll conducted in 2000 found that a majority of people agreed that it would be "better for society" if "most of the members of Congress were women."[35] Many voters believe that women are not only more interested in, but better suited to deal with, a wide range of domestic issues, such as education and health care.[36] Moreover, women representatives often have played prominent roles in advancing issues of concern to women.[37] One study by the Center for American Women and Politics, for example, found that most women in the 103rd Congress "felt a special responsibility to represent women, particularly to represent their life experiences. . . . They undertook this additional responsibility while first, and foremost, like all members of Congress, representing their own districts." However, research finds that Republican women, especially those elected more recently, "may be willing to downplay their commitment to women's issues in order to make gains on other district and policy priorities that conform more easily to the Republican agenda."[38]

The actions of the lone Native American who served in the Senate until 2005 underscore the representative function that members play in Congress. Senator Ben Nighthorse Campbell (R–CO), for example, not surprisingly served on the Committee on Indian Affairs. Earlier, as a member of the House, he fought successfully for legislation to establish the National Museum of the American Indian on the Mall

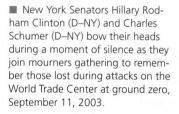

■ New York Senators Hillary Rodham Clinton (D–NY) and Charles Schumer (D–NY) bow their heads during a moment of silence as they join mourners gathering to remember those lost during attacks on the World Trade Center at ground zero, September 11, 2003.

Photo courtesy: Ruth Fremson/Reuters/Landov

in Washington, D.C. New African American and Hispanic senators are expected to be similarly reactive to issues of racial importance.

HOW MEMBERS MAKE DECISIONS

AS A BILL MAKES ITS WAY through the labyrinth of the law-making process described above, members are confronted with the question: "How should I vote?" Members adhere to their own personal beliefs on some matters, but their views often are moderated by other considerations. To avoid making any voting mistakes, members look to a variety of sources for cues.

Photo courtesy: The Register Mail, Mia Algotti/AP/Wide World Photos

■ Democrat Barack Obama (D–IL) on the campaign trail in 2004. Obama is the only African American serving in the Senate.

Party

Members often look to party leaders for indicators of how to vote. Indeed, it is the whips' job in each chamber to reinforce the need for party cohesion, particularly on issues of concern to the party. From 1970 to the mid-1990s, the incidence of party votes in which majorities of the two parties took opposing sides roughly doubled to more than 60 percent of all roll-call votes.[39] When the Republicans took control of Congress in 1995, it became the most partisan year in generations.

Partisanship still reigns supreme in both houses of Congress. In the 107th Congress, for example, there was perfect party unity on all major votes taken in the House.[40] In the 108th Congress, Democratic senators demonstrated unanimity in filibustering several presidential judicial nominations to the U.S. Courts of Appeals. While some charged that this was not evidence of party unity, but instead elected officials taking their direction from major liberal special interest groups, there can be no doubt that in both closely divided houses, party reigns supreme.[41]

With Republicans in control of both houses in recent Congresses, many critics also charge that both parties have pressured their members to take increasingly partisan positions. Surprisingly, in times of **divided government,** when different political parties control the executive and legislative branches, most commentators noted how rancorous law-making could get. Today, with Congress and the presidency controlled by one party, it seems as though things have only gotten worse. An overwhelming number of members of Congress elected as Republicans or Democrats feel a strong obligation to their party. And, if the president is of the same party, the pressure to vote the party line is only increased.

Party loyalty is not the only reason members vote the way they do. Both parties have committees in both houses of Congress that provide extraordinary campaign assistance in the form of funding, political and media consulting, and direct mailing. Members know that if they fail to go along with the party on major votes, they risk losing this critical campaign support. Similarly, both senators and representatives can be assisted in their reelection bids by having the president (if he is of the same party) or highly popular political leaders come to their states or districts to assist them in their electioneering activities.

divided government
The political condition in which different political parties control the White House and Congress.

Constituents

Constituents—the people who live and vote in the home district or state—are always in the member's mind when casting a vote.[42] Studies by political scientists show that

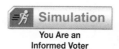

Simulation

You Are an
Informed Voter

members vote in conformity with prevailing opinion in their districts about two-thirds of the time.[43] On average, Congress passes laws that reflect national public opinion at about the same rate.[44] It is rare for a legislator to vote against the wishes of his or her constituency regularly, particularly on issues of welfare rights, domestic policy, or other highly salient issues such as civil rights, abortion, or war. Most constituents often have strong convictions on one or more of these issues. For example, during the 1960s, representatives from southern states could not hope to keep their seats for long if they voted in favor of proposed civil rights legislation. But, gauging how voters feel about any particular issue often is not easy. Because it is virtually impossible to know how the folks back home feel on all issues, a representative's perception of their preferences is important. Even when voters have opinions, legislators may get little guidance if their district is narrowly divided. Abortion is an issue about which many voters feel passionately, but a legislator whose district has roughly equal numbers of pro-choice and pro-life advocates can satisfy only a portion of his or her constituents.

Legislators tend to act on their own preferences as trustees when dealing with topics that have come through the committees on which they serve or with issues that they know about as a result of experience in other contexts, such as their vocation. On items of little concern to people back in the district or for which the legislator has little first-hand knowledge, the tendency is to turn to other sources for voting cues.

Colleagues and Caucuses

logrolling
Vote trading; voting yea to support a colleague's bill in return for a promise of future support.

The range and complexity of issues confronting Congress mean that no one can be up to speed on more than a few topics. When members must vote on bills about which they know very little, they often turn for advice to colleagues who have served on the committee that handled the legislation. On issues that are of little interest to a legislator, **logrolling,** or vote trading, often occurs. Logrolling often takes place on specialized bills targeting money or projects to selected congressional districts. An unaffected member often will exchange a yea vote for the promise of a future yea vote on a similar piece of specialized legislation.

Members may also look to other representatives who share common interests. Special-interest caucuses created around issues, home states, regions, congressional class, or other shared interests facilitate this communication. Prior to 1995, the power of these groups was even more evident, as several caucuses enjoyed formal status within the legislative body and were provided staff, office space, and budgets. Today, however, all caucuses are informal in nature, although some are far more organized than others. The Congressional Women's Caucus, for example, has formal elections of its Republican and Democratic co-chairs and vice chairs, provides staff members detailed to work on issues of common concern to caucus members, and meets regularly to urge its members to support legislation of interest to women.

■ Melvin Watt, (D–NC) discusses his selection as the new chair of the Congressional Black Caucus at a news conference on Capitol Hill in December 2004. Watt succeeds Elijah Cummings (D–MD) at left.

Photo courtesy: Dennis Cook/AP/Wide World Photos

Interest Groups, Lobbyists, and Political Action Committees

A primary function of most lobbyists, whether they work for interest groups, trade associations, or large corporations, is to provide information to supportive or potentially supportive legislators, committees, and their staffs.[45] It is likely, for example, that a representative knows the National Rifle Association's (NRA) position on gun control legislation. What the legislator needs to get from the NRA is information and substantial research on the feasibility and impact of such legislation. How could the states implement such legislation? Is it constitutional? Will it really have an impact on violent crime or crime in schools? Organized interests can win over undecided legislators or confirm the support of their friends by providing information that legislators use to justify the position they have embraced. They also can supply direct campaign contributions, volunteers, and publicity to members seeking reelection.

Pressure groups also use grassroots appeals to pressure legislators by urging their members in a particular state or district to call, write, fax, or e-mail their senators or representatives. Lobbyists can't vote, but voters back home can and do. Lobbyists and the corporate or other interests they represent, however, can contribute to political campaigns and are an important source of campaign contributions. Many have political action committees (PACs) to help support members seeking reelection.

While a link to a legislator's constituents may be the most effective way to influence behavior, it is not the only path of interest-group influence on member decision making.[46] The high cost of campaigning has made members of Congress, especially those without huge personal fortunes, attentive to those who help pay the tab for the high cost of many campaigns. The almost 5,000 PACs organized by interest groups are a major source of most members' campaign funding. When an issue comes up that is of little consequence to his or her constituents, there is, not surprisingly, a tendency to support the positions of those interests who helped pay for the last campaign. After all, who wants to bite the hand that feeds him or her? (Interest groups and PACs are discussed in detail in chapter 16. PACs are also discussed in chapter 14.)

Staff and Support Agencies

Members of Congress rely heavily on members of their staffs for information on pending legislation.[47] Not only do staff members meet regularly with staffers from other offices about proposed legislation or upcoming hearings, but staff members also prepare summaries of bills and brief the representative or senator based on their research and meetings. Especially if a bill is nonideological or one on which the member has no real position, staff members can be very influential. In many cases, lobbyists are just as likely to contact key staffers as they are members.

Congressional committees and subcommittees also have their own dedicated staff to assist committee members. Additional support for members comes from support personnel at the Congressional Budget Office (CBO), the Congressional Research Service (CRS) at the Library of Congress, and the General Accountability Office (GAO) (see Table 7.6).

TABLE 7.6 Congressional Support Agencies		
Congressional Budget Office (CBO)	*Congressional Research Service (CRS)*	*General Accountability Office (GAO)*
The CBO was created in 1974 to evaluate the economic effect of different spending programs and to provide information on the cost of proposed policies. It is responsible for analyzing the president's budget and economic projections. The CBO provides Congress and individual members with a valuable second opinion to use in budget debates.	Created in 1914 as the Legislative Research Service (LRS), CRS is administered by the Library of Congress. It responds to more than a quarter of a million congressional requests for information each year. Its staff conducts nonpartisan studies of public issues, compiles facts on both sides of issues, and conducts major research projects for committees at the request of members. The CRS also prepares summaries of all bills introduced and tracks the progress.	The General Accounting Office (GAO) was established in 1921 as an independent regulatory agency for the purpose of auditing the financial expenditures of the executive branch and federal agencies. Today, the GAO performs four additional functions: it sets government standards for accounting, it provides a variety of legal opinions, it settles claims against the government, and it conducts studies upon congressional request. In 2004, its name was changed to the Government Accountability Office to better reflect its function.

THE LAW-MAKING FUNCTION OF CONGRESS

THE ORGANIZATION OF CONGRESS allows it to fulfill its constitutional responsibilities, chief among which is its law-making function. It is through this power that Congress affects the day-to-day lives of all Americans and sets policy for the future. Proposals for legislation—be they about education, violence against women, trade with China, gun control, or foreign aid—can come from the president, executive agencies, committee staffs, interest groups, or even private individuals. Only members of the House or Senate, however, formally can submit a bill for congressional consideration (although many are initially drafted by lobbyists). Once a bill is introduced by a member of Congress, it usually reaches a dead end. Of the approximately 9,000 or so bills introduced during any session of Congress, fewer than 10 percent are made into law.

It is probably useful to think of Congress as a system of multiple vetoes, which was what the Framers desired. They wanted to disperse power, and as Congress has evolved it has come closer and closer to the Framers' intentions. As a bill goes through Congress, there is a dispersion of power as roadblocks to passage must be surmounted at numerous steps in the process. In addition to realistic roadblocks, caution signs and other opportunities for delay abound. A member who sponsors a bill must get through every obstacle. In contrast, successful opposition means winning at only one of many stages, including: (1) the subcommittee; (2) the House full committee; (3) the House Rules Committee; (4) the House; (5) the Senate subcommittee; (6) the full Senate committee; (7) the Senate; (8) floor leaders in both Houses; (9) the House-Senate conference committee; and, (10) the president.

The story of how a bill becomes a law in the United States can be told in two different ways. The first is the textbook method, which provides a greatly simplified road map of the process to make it easier to understand. We'll review this method first.

How a Bill Becomes a Law: The Textbook Version

A bill must survive three stages before it becomes a law. It must be approved by one or more standing committees and both chambers, and, if House and Senate versions differ, each house must accept a conference report resolving those differences. A bill may be killed during any of these stages, so it is much easier to defeat a bill than it is to get one passed. The House and Senate have parallel processes, and often the same bill is introduced in each chamber at the same time.

Simulation

You Are a Member of Congress

A bill must be introduced by a member of Congress, but, in an attempt to show support for the aims of the bill, it is often sponsored by several other members (called co-sponsors).[48] Once introduced, the bill is sent to the clerk of the chamber, who gives it a number (for example, HR 1 or S 1—indicating House or Senate bill number one for the Congress). The bill is then printed, distributed, and sent to the appropriate committee or committees for consideration.

The first action takes place within the committee, after it is referred there by the speaker. The committee usually refers the bill to one of its subcommittees, which researches the bill and decides whether to hold hearings on it. The subcommittee hearings provide the opportunity for those on both sides of the issue to voice their opinions. Most of these hearings are now open to the public because of 1970s sunshine laws, which require open sessions. After the hearings, the bill is revised in subcommittee, and then the subcommittee votes to approve or defeat the bill. If the subcommittee votes in favor of the bill, it is returned to the full committee, which then either rejects the bill or sends it to the House or Senate floor with a favorable recommendation (see Figure 7.3).

The second stage of action takes place on the House or Senate floor. As previously discussed, in the House, before a bill may be debated on the floor, it must be approved by the Rules Committee and given a rule and a place on the calendar, or schedule. (House budget bills, however, don't go to the Rules Committee.) In the House, the rule given to a bill determines the limits on the floor debate and specifies what types of

FIGURE 7.3 How a Bill Becomes a Law. ■

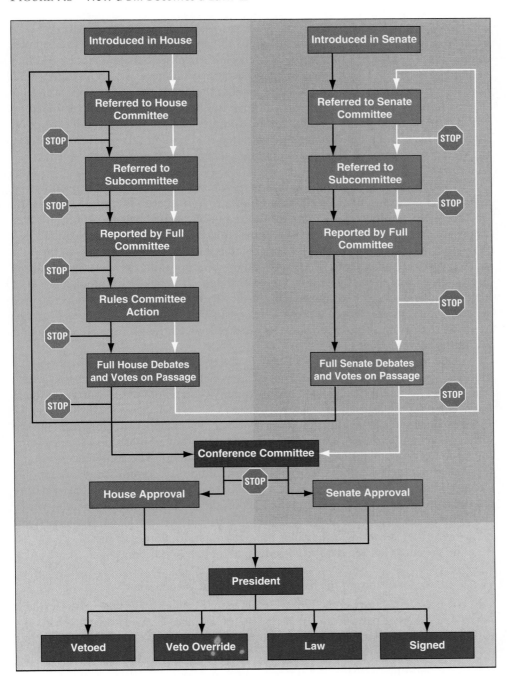

amendments, if any, may be attached to the bill. Once the Rules Committee considers the bill, it is put on the calendar.

When the day arrives for floor debate, the House may choose to form a Committee of the Whole. This procedure allows the House to deliberate with only one hundred members present, to expedite consideration of the bill. On the House floor, the bill is debated, amendments are offered, and a vote ultimately is taken by the full House. If the bill survives, it is sent to the Senate for consideration if it was not considered there simultaneously.

Unlike the House, where debate is necessarily limited given the size of the body, bills may be held up by a hold or a filibuster in the Senate. A **hold** is a tactic by which a senator asks to be informed before a particular bill is brought to the floor. This request

hold
A tactic by which a senator asks to be informed before a particular bill is brought to the floor. This stops the bill from coming to the floor until the hold is removed.

signals the Senate leadership and the sponsors of the bill that a colleague may have objections to the bill and should be consulted before further action is taken.

Holds are powerful tools. In 2002, for example, Senator Joe Biden (D–DE) became so upset with congressional failure to fund Amtrak security (Biden takes Amtrak back and forth to his home in Delaware when the Senate is in session) that he put holds on two Department of Transportation nominees, whom he called "fine, decent, and competent people." This meant that their nominations could not be considered until he removed his hold. In return, the Bush administration retaliated by withholding a third of the funding for a University of Delaware research project on high-speed trains. As the *Washington Post* noted in reporting this story, "Welcome to the wild wacky world of Washington politics, where people sometimes destroy a village to save it."[49]

Filibusters, which allow for unlimited debate on a bill (or on presidential appointments), grew out of the absence of rules to limit speech in the Senate. In contrast to a hold, a filibuster is a more formal and public way of halting action on a bill. There are no rules on the content of a filibuster as long as a senator keeps on talking. A senator may read from a phone book, recite poetry, or read cookbooks in order to delay a vote. Often, a team of senators takes turns speaking to keep the filibuster going in the hope that a bill will be tabled or killed. In 1964, for example, a group of northern liberal senators continued a filibuster for eighty-two days in effort to prevent amendments that would weaken a civil rights bill. Still, filibusters often are more of a threat than an actual event on the Senate floor, although they are once again becoming more frequent.

There is only one way to end a filibuster. Sixteen senators must sign a motion for **cloture.** This motion requires the votes of sixty members to limit debate; after a cloture motion passes the Senate floor, members may spend no more than thirty additional hours debating the legislation at issue.

The third stage of action takes place when the two chambers of Congress approve different versions of the same bill. When this happens, they establish a conference committee to iron out the differences between the two versions. The conference committee, whose members are from the original House and Senate committees, hammers out a compromise, which is returned to each chamber for a final vote. Sometimes the conference committee fails to agree and the bill dies there. No changes or amendments to the compromise version are allowed. If the bill is passed, it is sent to the president, who either signs it or **vetoes** it. If the bill is not passed in both houses, it dies.

The president has ten days to consider a bill. He has four options:

1. The president can sign the bill, at which point it becomes law.

2. The president can veto the bill, which is more likely to occur when the president is of a different party from the majority in Congress; Congress may override the president's veto with a two-thirds vote in each chamber, a very difficult task).

3. The president can wait the full ten days, at the end of which time the bill becomes law without his signature if Congress is still in session.

4. If the Congress adjourns before the ten days are up, the president can choose not to sign the bill, and it is considered pocket vetoed.

A **pocket veto** figuratively allows bills stashed in the president's pocket to die. The only way for a bill then to become law is for it to be reintroduced in the next session and be put through the process all over again. Because Congress sets its own date of adjournment, technically the session could be continued the few extra days necessary to prevent a pocket veto. Extensions are unlikely, however, as sessions are scheduled to adjourn close to the November elections or the December holidays.

filibuster
A formal way of halting action on a bill by means of long speeches or unlimited debate in the Senate.

cloture
Mechanism requiring sixty senators to vote to cut off debate.

veto
Formal constitutional authority of the president to reject bills passed by both houses of the legislative body, thus preventing their becoming law without further congressional activity.

pocket veto
If Congress adjourns during the ten days the president has to consider a bill passed by both houses of Congress, without the president's signature, the bill is considered vetoed.

How a Bill Really Becomes a Law:
The China Trade Act of 2000

For each bill introduced in Congress, enactment is a long shot. A bill's supporters struggle to get from filing in both houses of Congress to the president's signature, and each bill follows a unique course. The progress of the trade legislation described below is probably even quirkier than most bills that actually become law.

Under the Trade Act of 1974, part of a two-decades-old American Cold War policy, the president of the United States was empowered to grant any nation "most favored" trade status, a designation that brings favorable U.S. tariff treatment. By law, however, the president was limited to extending that status to communist countries on a year by year (instead of permanent) basis subject to congressional review. Thus, since passage of that act, China, as a communist nation, could receive this status only a year at a time, even though it provided a huge potential market for U.S. goods. President Bill Clinton and many members of the business community wanted this year by year reauthorization dropped once China was scheduled to join the World Trade Organization. To do that required a new act of Congress. Ironically, the Clinton administration's push for this bill also allied President Clinton with many Republicans who favored opening trade to a nation with billions of new consumers. Many of the Republicans' biggest financial and political supporters would benefit from opening Chinese markets and removing barriers to service providers such as banks and telecommunications companies. In contrast, unions, a traditionally Democratic constituency, feared further loss of jobs to foreign shores.

Legislation to extend what is called permanent normal trade relations (PNTR) was viewed by Clinton as a means of putting "his imprint on foreign policy [as] the president who cemented in place the post-Cold-War experiment of using economic engagement to foster political change among America's neighbors and its potential adversaries."[50] He had begun this effort in 1993 after he pushed through Congress passage of the North American Free Trade Agreement (NAFTA) with Mexico and Canada. Now, as his time in office was coming to an end, he wanted Congress to act to allow him to cement PNTR with China.

As soon as the United States completed a bilateral agreement to make China a member of the World Trade Organization in November 1999 and early 2000, Clinton met with more than one hundred lawmakers individually or in groups, called scores more on the phone, and traveled to the Midwest and California to build support for the proposed legislation, which was necessary to implement this agreement. While Clinton was setting the stage for congressional action, the U.S. Chamber of Commerce and the Business Roundtable launched a $10 million ad campaign—the largest ever for a single legislative issue.[51]

On March 8, 2000, Clinton transmitted the text of legislation he was requesting to Congress. This proposed legislation, called S 2277, was formally introduced in the Senate on March 23 by Senator William Roth Jr. (R–DE). It was then read twice and referred to the Finance Committee. In the House, hearings on the China trade policy were held throughout the spring, even before the Clinton legislation formally was introduced. Anticipating concern from colleagues about China's human rights abuses, labor market issues, and the rule of law, some members proposed that Congress create (under separate legislation) a U.S. Congressional-Executive Commission on China to monitor those issues. HR 4444, the bill that Clinton sought, was introduced formally in the House on May 15, 2000, by Representative Bill Archer (R–TX). It was referred to the House Ways and Means Committee shortly thereafter and a mark-up session was held on May 17. It was reported out of committee on the same day by a vote of 34–4. On May 23, 2000, HR 4444 received a rule from the Rules Committee allowing for three hours of debate. The bill was closed to amendments except motions to recommit, and the House Republican leadership "closed ranks behind the bill," claiming that economic change would foster political change.[52] But, they still had to sell this idea to their colleagues, many of whom balked at extending trade advantages to a communist government with a history of rights violations, including religious persecution and the denial of political rights to many. The rights legislation was designed to assuage those fears.

While the House Committee on International Relations was holding hearings (and even before), the Clinton administration sprang into action. Secretary of Commerce William Daley and several other Cabinet members were sent out to say the same thing over and over again: the bill will mean jobs for Americans and stability in Asia. Republican leaders got Chinese dissidents to say that the bill would improve human rights in China, and televangelist Billy Graham was recruited by the leadership to endorse the measure. At the same time, interest groups on both sides of the debate rushed to convince legislators to support their respective positions. Organized labor, still stinging from its NAFTA loss, was the biggest opponent of the bill. Teamsters and members of the United Auto Workers roamed the halls of Congress, trying to lobby members of the House.[53] Vice President Al Gore, knowing that he would need union support in the upcoming presidential election, broke ranks with the president and said that the bill would only serve to move American jobs to China.

On the other side, lobbyists from large corporations, including Procter & Gamble, and interest groups such as the Business Roundtable, used their cell phones and personal contacts to cajole legislators. "It's like a big wave hitting the shore," said one uncommitted Republican legislator from Staten Island, New York.[54] For the first time, he was lobbied by rank-and-file office workers at the request of their corporate offices, as well as union members. Another member of Congress was contacted by former President George Bush and Secretary of Defense William Cohen, and he received a special defense briefing from the Central Intelligence Agency. The president of the AFL-CIO also personally visited him. All stops were out, and this was the kind of treatment most undecided members received.

House debate on the bill began on May 24, 2000. That morning, House Republican Whip Tom DeLay (R–TX) didn't know if he had enough votes to support the measure to ensure its passage. The bare minimum he needed was 150 Republicans if he was to push the bill over the top.[55] DeLay lined up lots of assistance. Somewhat ironically, Texas Governor George W. Bush and retired General Colin Powell were enlisted to help convince wavering Republicans to support the Democratic president's goals. Powell, in particular, was called on to assuage national security concerns of several conservative representatives. Scores of pro-trade lobbyists spread out over Capitol Hill like locusts looking to light on any wavering legislators. A last-minute amendment to create a twenty-three-member commission to monitor human rights and a second to monitor surges in Chinese imports helped garner the votes of at least twenty more legislators.

Debate then came on a motion from House Democratic Whip David Bonior (D–MI) to recommit the bill to the Ways and Means and International Relations Committees to give them the opportunity to add an amendment to the bill to provide conditions under which withdrawals of normal trade relations with China could occur should China attack or invade Taiwan. This motion failed on a vote of 176–258. As lobbyists stepped up their efforts, their actions and those of the Republican leadership and the Clinton administration bore fruit. Every single uncommitted Republican voted for the bill, joining seventy-three Democrats to grant China permanent normal trade status as the bill passed by a surprisingly large margin of 237–197. "Frankly, they surprised me a bit. Members in the last few hours really turned around and understood how important this was," said DeLay, who earned the nickname "The Hammer" for his efforts to have members vote his way. Stunned labor leaders admitted that they were outgunned. "The business community unleashed an unprecedented campaign that was hard for anyone to match," said the president of the United Auto Workers.[56]

As the bill was transmitted to the Senate, critics sprang into action. Senator Jesse Helms (R–NC), chair of the Foreign Relations Committee and a major critic of the Beijing government, immediately put fellow Republicans on notice that he would not rubber stamp the actions of the House. Although amendments were not allowed in the House, Senate rules that permit amendment were seen as a way of changing the nature of the bill and causing the amended version to go back to the House for a vote. Secretary Daley immediately went to see the Senate majority leader and members of the Senate Finance Committee, which had jurisdiction over the bill, to ask their assistance in fending off amendments.

While hearings on China were being held in the House, the Senate Finance Committee had been considering the bill. Once it passed the House, however, it was reported out of the Senate Finance Committee immediately on May 25. On that day, Senators Fred Thompson (R–TN) and Robert Torricelli (D–NJ) held a press conference to announce that they would offer parallel legislation based on their concerns about Chinese proliferation of weapons of mass destruction to continue a yearly review of China as a condition of open trade with that nation. They viewed the opening of PNTR to China as a national security as well as a trade issue.

The Senate began debating S 2277 on July 26, 2000. The next day, after a filibuster was begun by several opponents of the bill, including Senators Robert Byrd (D–WV), Jesse Helms (R–NC), Barbara Mikulski (D–MD), and Ben Nighthorse Campbell (R–CO), a move to invoke cloture was brought by the majority leader and several others. Cloture then was invoked by a vote of 86–12, well over the sixty votes required. The Senate recessed shortly thereafter. Debate on S 2277 began anew on September 5, after the Labor Day recess. At that time, until the final vote on September 19, 2000, scores of amendments were offered by senators; all failed by various margins. On September 19, 2000, the bill passed without amendment on an 83–15 vote with most senators voting as they had done on the cloture motion. Throughout that period, however, lobbyists kept up their pressure on the committed to make sure that no amendments were added to the bill that would require House reconsideration.

The bill was signed by President Clinton on October 10, 2000, amid considerable fanfare. Throughout the course of this bill becoming law, Clinton used his office in a way reminiscent of Lyndon B. Johnson's cajoling of recalcitrant legislators. One member got a new zip code for a small town and another got a natural gas pipeline for his district.[57] In the end, these kinds of efforts were crucial to House passage of the bill.

China became a member of the World Trade Organization on December 11, 2001. On December 28, 2001, President George W. Bush signed a formal proclamation granting normal trading status to China, ending annual reviews. In 2004, however, the United States and the European Union lodged WTO complaints against China, charging that the state failed to fulfill promises to open its markets to other nations.[58]

CONGRESS AND THE PRESIDENT

THE CONSTITUTION ENVISIONED that the Congress and the president would have discrete powers and that one branch would be able to hold the other in check. Over the years, and especially since the 1930s, the president often has held the upper hand. In times of crisis or simply when it was unable to meet public demands for solutions, Congress willingly has handed over its authority to the chief executive. Even though the chief executive has been granted greater latitude, legislators do, of course, retain ultimate legislative authority to question executive actions and to halt administration activities by cutting off funds. Congress also wields ultimate power over the president, since it can impeach and even remove him from office.

The Shifting Balance of Power

The balance of power between Congress and the executive branch has seesawed over time. The post–Civil War Congress attempted to regain control of the vast executive powers that President Abraham Lincoln, recently slain, had assumed. Angered at the refusal of Lincoln's successor, Andrew Johnson, to go along with its radical "reforms" of the South, Congress passed the Tenure of Office Act, which prevented the president, under the threat of civil penalty, from removing any Cabinet-level appointees of the previous administration. Johnson accepted the challenge and fired Lincoln's secretary of war, who many believed was guilty of heinous war crimes. The House voted to impeach Johnson, but the desertion of a handful of Republican senators prevented him from being removed from office. (The effort fell short by one vote.) Nonetheless, the president's power had been greatly weakened, and the Congress again became the center of power and authority in the federal government.

Beginning in the early 1900s, however, a series of strong presidents acted at the expense of congressional power. Theodore Roosevelt, Franklin D. Roosevelt, and Lyndon B. Johnson, especially, viewed the presidency as carrying with it enormous powers.

Over the years, especially since the presidency of Franklin D. Roosevelt, Congress has ceded to the president a major role in the legislative process. Today, Congress often finds itself responding to executive branch proposals. Critics of Congress point to its slow and unwieldy nature as well as the complexity of national problems as reasons that Congress often doesn't seem to act on its own.

oversight
Congressional review of the activities of an agency, department, or office.

■ Condoleezza Rice testifies before the U.S. Senate Foreign Relations Committee during her confirmation hearing to become Secretary of State. The often heated questioning in January of 2005 was fully televised and created such sparring between Rice and some Democratic senators that it was even parodied in a skit on Saturday Night Live.

Photo courtesy: © Larry Downing/Reuters/Corbis

Congressional Oversight of the Executive Branch

Since the 1960s, Congress has increased its **oversight** of the executive branch.[59] Oversight subcommittees became particularly prominent in the 1970s and 1980s as a means of promoting investigation and program review, to determine if an agency, department, or office is carrying out its responsibilities as intended by Congress.[60] Congressional oversight also includes checking on possible abuses of power by members of the military and governmental officials, including the president.

Key to Congress's performance of its oversight function is its ability to question members of the administration to see if they are enforcing and interpreting the laws as intended by Congress. These committee hearings, now routinely televised, are among Congress's most visible and dramatic actions.

The hearings are not used simply to gather information. Hearings may focus on particular executive branch actions and often signal that Congress believes changes in policy need to be made before an agency next comes before the committee to justify its budget. Hearings also are used to improve program administration. Since most members of House and Senate committees and subcommittees are interested in the issues under their jurisdiction, they often want to help and not hinder policy makers.

Although most top government officials appear before various House and Senate committees regularly to update them on their activities, this is not necessarily the case for those who do not require Senate confirmation, such as, in the George W. Bush administration, National Security Advisor

Condoleezza Rice. Sometimes members of the administration are reluctant to appear before Congress.

Legislators augment their formal oversight of the executive branch by allowing citizens to appeal adverse bureaucratic decisions to agencies, Congress, and even the courts. The Congressional Review Act of 1996 allows Congress to nullify agency regulations by joint resolutions of legislative disapproval. This process, called **congressional review,** is another method of exercising congressional oversight.[61] The act provides Congress with sixty days to disapprove newly announced agency regulations, often passed to implement some congressional action. A regulation is disapproved if the resolution is passed by both chambers and signed by the president, or when Congress overrides a presidential veto of a disapproving resolution. This act was not used until 2001, when Congress reversed Clinton administration ergonomics regulations, which were intended to prevent job-related repetitive stress injuries.

congressional review
A process whereby Congress can nullify agency regulations by a joint resolution of legislative disapproval.

Foreign Affairs Oversight.
The Constitution divides foreign policy powers between the executive and the legislative branches. The president has the power to wage war and negotiate treaties, whereas the Congress has the power to declare war and the Senate has the power to ratify treaties. The executive branch, however, has become preeminent in foreign affairs despite the constitutional division of powers. This supremacy is partly due to a series of crises and the development of nuclear weapons in the twentieth century; both have necessitated quick decision making and secrecy, which are much easier to manage in the executive branch. Congress, with its 535 members, has a more difficult time reaching a consensus and keeping secrets.

After years of playing second fiddle to a series of presidents from Theodore Roosevelt to Richard M. Nixon, a "snoozing Congress" was "aroused" and seized for itself the authority and expertise necessary to go head-to-head with the chief executive.[62] In a delayed response to Lyndon B. Johnson's conduct of the Vietnam War, Congress passed in 1973 the **War Powers Act** over President Nixon's veto. This act requires presidents to obtain congressional approval before committing U.S. forces to a combat zone. It also requires them to notify Congress within forty-eight hours of committing troops to foreign soil. In addition, the president must withdraw troops within sixty days unless Congress votes to declare war. The president also is required to consult with Congress, if at all possible, prior to committing troops.

War Powers Act
Passed by Congress in 1973; the president is limited in the deployment of troops overseas to a sixty-day period in peacetime (which can be extended for an extra thirty days to permit withdrawal) unless Congress explicitly gives its approval for a longer period.

The War Powers Act has been of limited effectiveness in claiming a larger congressional role in international crisis situations. Presidents Gerald Ford, Jimmy Carter, and Ronald Reagan never consulted Congress in advance of committing troops, citing the need for secrecy and swift movement, although each president did notify Congress shortly after the incidents. They contended that the War Powers Act was probably unconstitutional because it limits presidential prerogatives as commander in chief.

In 2001, when Congress passed a joint resolution authorizing the president to use force against terrorists, the resolution included language that met War Powers Act requirements and waived the sixty-day limit on the president's authority to involve U.S. troops abroad. This action prompted two senators who served in Vietnam, John McCain (R–AZ) and John Kerry (D–MA), to express concern over handing the president such open-ended use of military force. These concerns may have been valid, as some critics say President George W. Bush took the congressional resolution as a blank check. Said one high-ranking Department of Justice official, "the president enjoys broad unilateral authority to use force in the war on terrorism—with or without specific congressional authorization."[63]

Confirmation of Presidential Appointments.
The Senate plays a special oversight function through its ability to confirm key members of the executive branch, as well as presidential appointments to the federal courts. As discussed in chapters 9 and

10, although the Senate generally confirms most presidential nominees, it does not always do so. A wise president considers senatorial reaction before nominating potentially controversial individuals to his administration or to the federal courts.

The Impeachment Process.   As discussed earlier, the impeachment process is Congress's ultimate oversight of the U.S. president (as well as of federal court judges). The U.S. Constitution is quite vague about the impeachment process, and much of the debate about it concerns what is an impeachable offense. The Constitution specifies that a president can be impeached for treason, bribery, or other "high crimes and misdemeanors." Most commentators agree that this phrase was meant to mean significant abuses of power. In *Federalist No. 65*, Alexander Hamilton noted his belief that impeachable offenses "are of a nature which may with peculiar propriety be denominated political, as they relate chiefly to injuries done immediately to society itself."

House and Senate rules control how the impeachment process operates (see Table 7.7). Yet, because the process is used so rarely, and under such disparate circumstances, there are few hard and fast rules. Until 1998, the U.S. House of Representatives had voted to impeach only sixteen federal officials—and only one of those was a president, Andrew Johnson. (Of those, seven were convicted and removed from office and three resigned before the process described below was completed.)

Until late 1998, only three resolutions against presidents had resulted in further action: (1) John Tyler, charged with corruption and misconduct in 1843; (2) Andrew Johnson, charged with serious misconduct in 1868; and, (3) Richard M. Nixon, charged with obstruction and the abuse of power in 1974. The House rejected the charges against Tyler; Johnson was acquitted by the Senate by a one-vote margin; and Nixon resigned before the full House voted on the articles of impeachment. Four articles of impeachment against President Bill Clinton were considered in the House in 1998; two of these were sent to the Senate, where the president was found not guilty of the charges contained in both articles.

TABLE 7.7   The Eight Stages of the Impeachment Process

1. **The Resolution.** A resolution, called an inquiry of impeachment, is sent to the House Judiciary Committee. Members also may introduce bills of impeachment, which are referred to the Judiciary Committee.
2. **The Committee Vote.** After the consideration of voluminous evidence, the Judiciary Committee votes on the resolution or bill of impeachment. A positive vote from the committee indicates its belief that there is sufficiently strong evidence for impeachment in the House.
3. **The House Vote.** If the articles of impeachment are recommended by the House Judiciary Committee, the full House votes to approve (or disapprove) a Judiciary Committee decision to conduct full-blown impeachment hearings.
4. **The Hearings.** Extensive evidentiary hearings are held by the House Judiciary Committee concerning the allegations of wrongdoing. Witnesses may be called and the scope of the inquiry may be widened at this time. The committee heard only from the independent counsel in the Clinton case.
5. **The Report.** The committee votes on one or more articles of impeachment. Reports supporting this finding (as well as dissenting views) are forwarded to the House and become the basis for its consideration of specific articles of impeachment.
6. **The House Vote.** The full House votes on each article of impeachment. A simple majority vote on any article is sufficient to send that article to the Senate for its consideration.
7. **The Trial in the Senate.** A trial is conducted on the floor of the Senate with the House Judiciary Committee bringing the case against the president, who is represented by his own private attorneys. The Senate, in essence, acts as the jury, with the chief justice of the United States presiding over the trial.
8. **The Senate Vote.** The full Senate votes on each article of impeachment. If there is a two-thirds vote on any article, the president automatically is removed from office and the vice president assumes the duty of the president. Both articles issued against President Clinton, charging him with lying to a grand jury and encouraging a grand jury witness to lie or mislead, were defeated in the Senate.

CONGRESS AND THE JUDICIARY

As PART OF OUR SYSTEM of checks and balances, the power of judicial review (discussed in chapters 2 and 10) gives the Supreme Court the power to review the constitutionality of acts of Congress. This is a potent power because Congress must ever be mindful to make sure that the laws that it passes are in accord with the U.S. Constitution. That is not to say, however, that Congress always does this. In spite of a recent Supreme Court case that indicated that a Nebraska state law banning partial birth abortion was unconstitutional, the U.S. Congress passed its own version outlawing the procedure despite extensive commentary that it would also be declared unconstitutional. Proponents wanted to get other members on record about their support or lack of support before the 2004 elections so that the issue could be used by Republicans to highlight the votes of Democrats—including John Kerry and John Edwards, who voted against the bill.

Congress exercises its control over the judiciary in a variety of ways. Not only does it have the constitutional authority to establish the size of the Supreme Court, its appellate jurisdiction, and the structure of the federal court system, but the Senate also has the authority to accept or reject presidential nominees to the federal courts (as well as executive branch appointments).

In the case of federal district court appointments, senators often have considerable say in the nomination of judges from their states through **senatorial courtesy,** a process by which presidents generally defer to the senators who represent the state where the vacancy occurs. The judicial nominees of both Presidents Bill Clinton and George W. Bush have encountered a particularly hostile Senate. "Appointments have always been the battleground for policy disputes," says political scientist Calvin MacKenzie. But now, "what's new is the rawness of it—all of the veneer is off."[64] (Nominations to the Supreme Court and lower federal courts are discussed in chapter 10.)

senatorial courtesy
A process by which presidents, when selecting district court judges, defer to the senator in whose state the vacancy occurs.

An equally potentially potent form of congressional oversight of the judicial branch, which involves both the House and the Senate, is the setting of the jurisdiction of the federal courts. Originally, the jurisdiction, or ability of the federal courts to hear cases, was quite limited. Over time, however, as Congress legislated to regulate the economy and even crime, the caseload of the courts skyrocketed. No matter how busy federal judges are, it is ultimately up to the Congress to determine the number of judges on each court.

In 2004, several members of Congress, unhappy with Supreme Court decisions and the Senate's failure to pass a proposed constitutional amendment to ban same-sex marriage, began to push for a bill to prevent federal courts from hearing challenges to the federal Defense of Marriage Act. In the House, the majority leader pledged to promote similar legislation to bar court challenges to the Pledge of Allegiance and other social issues, including abortion. When Congress rears the ugly head of jurisdiction, it is signaling to the federal courts that Congress believes federal judges have gone too far.

SUMMARY

THE SIZE AND SCOPE OF CONGRESS, and the demands put on it, have increased tremendously over the years. In presenting the important role that Congress plays in American politics, we have made the following points:

1. The Constitution and the Legislative Branch of Government

The Constitution created a bicameral legislature with members of each body to be elected differently, and thus to represent different constituencies. Article I of the Constitution sets forth qualifications for office, states age minimums, and specifies how legislators are to be distributed among the states. The Constitution also requires seats in the House of Representatives to be apportioned by population. Thus, after every U.S. Census, district lines must be redrawn to reflect population shifts. The Constitution also provides a vast array of enumerated and implied powers to Congress. Some, such as law-making and oversight, are shared by both houses of Congress; others are not.

2. How Congress Is Organized

Political parties play a major role in the way Congress is organized. The speaker of the House is traditionally a member of the majority party, and members of the majority party chair all committees. Because the House of Representatives is large, the speaker enforces more rigid rules on the House than exist in the Senate. In addition to the party leaders, Congress has a labyrinth of committees and subcommittees that cover the entire range of government policies, often with a confusing tangle of shared responsibilities. Each legislator serves on one or more committees and multiple subcommittees. It is in these environments that many policies are shaped and that members make their primary contributions to solving public problems.

3. The Members of Congress

Members of Congress live in two worlds—in their home districts and in the District of Columbia. They must attempt to appease two constituencies—party leaders, colleagues, and lobbyists in Washington, D.C., and constituents in their home districts. Members, especially those in the House, never stop running for office. Incumbency is an important factor in winning reelection.

4. How Members Make Decisions

A multitude of factors impinge on legislators as they decide policy issues. These include political party, constituents, colleagues and caucuses, staff and support agencies and interest groups, lobbyists, and political action committees.

5. The Law-making Function of Congress

The road to enacting a bill into law is long and strewn with obstacles, and only a small share of the proposals introduced become law. Legislation must be approved by committees in each house and on the floor of each chamber. In addition, most House legislation initially is considered by a subcommittee and must be approved by the Rules Committee before getting to the floor. Legislation that is passed in different forms by the two chambers must be resolved in a conference before going back to each chamber for a vote and then to the president, who can sign the proposal into law, veto it, or allow it to become law without his signature. If Congress adjourns within ten days of passing legislation, that bill will die if the president does not sign it.

6. Congress and the President

Although the Framers intended for Congress and the president to have discrete spheres of authority, over time, power shifted between the two branches, with Congress often appearing to lose power to the benefit of the president. Still, Congress has attempted to oversee the actions of the president and the executive branch through committee hearings where members of the administration testify. Congress also uses congressional review to limit presidential power. Congress also has attempted to rein in presidential power through passage of the War Powers Act, to little practical effect. Congress, through the Senate, also possesses the power to confirm or reject presidential appointments. Its ultimate weapon is the power of impeachment and conviction.

7. Congress and the Judiciary

Congress exercises its control over the judiciary in a variety of ways. Not only does it have the constitutional authority to establish the size of the Supreme Court, its appellate jurisdiction, and the structure of the federal court system, but the Senate also has the authority to accept or reject presidential nominees to the federal courts (as well as executive branch appointments).

KEY TERMS

apportionment, p. 240
bicameral legislature, p. 238
bill, p. 240
cloture, p. 266
conference committee, p. 250
congressional review, p. 271
delegate, p. 260
discharge petition, p. 252
divided government, p. 261
filibuster, p. 266
hold, p. 265
impeachment, p. 241
incumbency, p. 256
joint committee, p. 250
logrolling, p. 262
majority leader, p. 246
majority party, p. 243
minority leader, p. 246
minority party, p. 243
oversight, p. 270
party caucus or conference, p. 246
pocket veto, p. 266
politico, p. 260
pork, p. 252
redistricting, p. 240
select (or special) committee 250
senatorial courtesy, p. 273
seniority, p. 254
speaker of the House, p. 243
standing committee, p. 250
trustee, p. 259
veto, p. 266
War Powers Act, p. 271
whip, p. 246

SELECTED READINGS

Bianco, William T., ed. *Congress on Display, Congress at Work.* Ann Arbor: University of Michigan Press, 2000.

Campbell, Colton C., and Paul S. Herrnson. *War Stories from Capitol Hill.* New York: Pearson, 2003.

Davidson, Roger H., and Walter Oleszek. *Congress and Its Members,* 9th ed. Washington, DC: CQ Press, 2003.

Deering, Christopher J., and Steven S. Smith, *Committees in Congress,* 3rd ed. Washington, DC: CQ Press, 1997.

Dodd, Lawrence C., and Bruce I. Oppenheimer, eds. *Congress Reconsidered,* 7th ed. Washington, DC: CQ Press, 2000.

Fenno, Richard F., Jr. *Going Home: Black Representatives and Their Constituents.* Chicago: University of Chicago Press, 2003.

Fenno, Richard F., Jr. *Home Style: House Members in Their Districts,* reprint ed. New York: Longman, 2002.

Gertzog, Irwin N. *Women and Power on Capitol Hill: Reconstructing the Congressional Women's Caucus.* Boulder, CO: Lynne Rienner, 2004.

Hibbing, John R., and Elizabeth Theiss-Morse. *Congress as Public Enemy: Public Attitudes Toward American Political Institutions.* New York: Cambridge University Press, 1996.

King, David C. *Turf Wars: How Congressional Committees Claim Jurisdiction.* Chicago: University of Chicago Press, 1997.

Mayhew, David R. *Congress: The Electoral Connection.* New Haven, CT: Yale University Press, 1974.

Oleszek, Walter J. *Congressional Procedures and the Policy Process,* 6th ed. Washington, DC: CQ Press, 2004.

Polsby, Nelson W. *How Congress Evolves: Social Bases of Institutional Changes.* New York: Oxford University Press, 2003.

Price, David E. *The Congressional Experience: A View from the Hill,* 2nd ed. Boulder, CO: Westview, 2000.

Rosenthal, Cindy Simon, ed. *Women Transforming Congress.* Norman: University of Oklahoma Press, 2003.

Schickler, Eric. *Disjointed Pluralism: Institutional Innovation and the Development of the U.S. Congress.* Princeton, NJ: Princeton University Press, 2001.

Swers, Michele. *The Difference Women Make: The Policy Impact of Women in Congress.* Chicago: University of Chicago Press, 2002.

Thurber, James A., ed. *Rivals for Power: Congressional Presidential Relations.* Lanham, MD: Rowman and Littlefield, 2001.

WEB EXPLORATIONS

To find out who your representative is and how he or she votes, see
http://www.thomas.loc.gov

To learn more about the legislative branch, see
www.senate.gov/
www.house.gov/

To evaluate your own representative, see
http://scorecard.aclu.org/scorecardmain.html

To learn more about the 109th Congress, see
http://clerk.house.gov/

For more on the offices of the Congress, including the speaker of the House and his activities, see
http://speakernews.house.gov/

To get up-to-date data on House leaders, see
http://tomdelay.house.gov/ and
http://democraticleader.house.gov/

For information on specific committees, see
www.senate.gov/
www.house.gov/

Photo courtesy: Dennis Brack

The Presidency

WHEN RONALD REAGAN DIED on June 5, 2004, many Americans, first in California and then in Washington, D.C., lined up for hours to pay their respects to the man who had been the fortieth president of the United States. Many people were able to see, for the first time in recent memory, the grandeur of a presidential state funeral. Reagan was the first president to lie in state in the Rotunda of the Capitol since Lyndon B. Johnson did in January 1973, and one of only nine American presidents to receive that honor.

The 200 plus years of presidential funerals underscore the esteem with which most Americans accord the office of the president, regardless of its occupant. Just before the first president, George Washington, died, he made it known that he wanted his burial to be a quiet one, "without parade or funeral oration." He also asked that he not be buried for three days; at that time, it was not without precedent to make this kind of request out of fear of being buried alive. Despite these requests, Washington's funeral was a state occasion as hundreds of soldiers, with their rifles held backward, marched to Mount Vernon, Virginia, where he was interred. Across the nation, imitation funerals were held, and the military wore black arm bands for six months.[1] It was during Washington's memorial service that Henry Lee declared that the former president was "first in war, first in peace, and first in the hearts of his countrymen."[2]

When Abraham Lincoln died in 1865 after being wounded by an assassin's bullet, more than a dozen funerals were held for him. Hundreds of thousands of mourners lined the way as the train carrying his open casket traveled the 1,700 miles to Illinois, where he was buried next to the body of his young son, who had died three years earlier. Most president's bodies were transported to their final resting place by train, allowing ordinary Americans the opportunity to pay their respects as the train traveled long distances. When Franklin D. Roosevelt died in Warm Springs, Georgia, his body was transported to Washington, D.C., and then to Hyde Park, New York, where he, like Washington, was buried on his family's estate.

Today, one of the first things a president is asked to do upon taking office is to consider his funeral plans. The military alone has a book 138

pages long devoted to the kind of ceremony and traditions that were so evident in the Reagan funeral: a
horse-drawn caisson; a riderless horse with boots
hung backward in the stirrups to indicate that the
deceased will ride no more; a twenty-one-gun salute;
a flyover by military aircraft. Each president's family,
however, has personalized their private, yet also public opportunity to mourn. The Reagan family, for
example, filed a 300-page plan for the funeral in 1989
and updated it regularly. Former presidents Gerald R.
Ford, Jimmy Carter, and George Bush all have filed
formal plans; Bill Clinton and George W. Bush have
yet to do so.

The Reagan funeral also created a national timeout
from the news of war, and even presidential campaigns
were halted in respect for the deceased president. One
historian commented that the event gave Americans
the opportunity to "rediscover . . . what holds us
together instead of what pulls us apart."³ This is often
the role of presidents . . . in life or in death.

THE AUTHORITY GRANTED TO the president by the U.S. Constitution and
through subsequent congressional legislation makes it a position with awe-
some responsibility. Not only did the Framers not envision such a powerful
role for the president, but they could not have foreseen the skepticism with
which many presidential actions are now greeted in the press, on talk radio, and on the
Internet. Presidents have gone into policy arenas never dreamed of by the Framers.
Imagine, for example, what the Framers might have thought about President Bush's
2004 State of the Union message, which advocated colonizing Mars and addressed
steroid use.

The modern media, used by successful presidents to help advance their agendas,
have brought us closer to our presidents and made them seem more human, a mixed
blessing for those trying to lead. Only two photographs exist of Franklin D. Roosevelt
in a wheelchair—his paralysis was a closely guarded secret. Five decades later, Bill Clinton was asked on national TV what kind of underwear he preferred (briefs). Later, revelations about his conduct with Monica Lewinsky made this exchange seem tame. This
demystifying of the president and the increased mistrust of government make governing a difficult job.

A president relies on more than the formal powers of office to lead the nation: public opinion and public confidence are key components of his ability to get his programs
adopted and his vision of the nation implemented. As political scientist Richard E.
Neustadt has noted, the president's power often rests on his power to persuade.⁴ To persuade, he not only must be able to forge links with members of Congress, but he also
must have the support of the American people and the respect of foreign leaders.

The abilities to persuade and to marshal the informal powers of the presidency have
become more important over time. In fact, the presidency of George W. Bush and the
circumstances that surround it are dramatically different from the presidency of his
father George Bush (1989–1993). America is changing dramatically and so are the
responsibilities of the president and people's expectations of the person who holds that
office. Presidents in the last century battled the Great Depression, fascism, communism, and several wars involving American soldiers. With the Cold War over, until the
war in Iraq, there were few chances for modern presidents to demonstrate their leadership in a time of crisis or threat.

The tension between public expectations about the presidency and the formal
powers of the president permeate our discussion of how the office has evolved from
its humble origins in Article II of the Constitution to its current stature. In this
chapter,

- First, we will examine *the roots of and rules governing the office of president of the United States* and discuss how the Framers created a chief executive officer for the new nation.

- Second, we will discuss *the constitutional powers of the president.*

- Third, we will examine *the development and expansion of presidential power* and a more personalized presidency. How well a president is able to execute the laws often depends strongly on his personality, popularity, and leadership style.

- Fourth, we will discuss the development of what is called *the presidential establishment*. Myriad departments, special assistants, and a staff of advisers help the president but also make it easier for a president to lose touch with the common citizen.

- Fifth, we will focus on *the president as policy maker.*

- Finally, we will examine *presidential leadership and the importance of public opinion*, including the effect that public opinion has on the American presidency as well as the role the president plays in molding public opinion.

THE ROOTS OF AND RULES GOVERNING THE OFFICE OF PRESIDENT OF THE UNITED STATES

THE EARLIEST EXAMPLE OF EXECUTIVE POWER in the colonies was the position of royal governor. These appointees of the king of England governed each colony and normally were entrusted with the "powers of appointment, military command, expenditure, and—within limitations—pardon, as well as with large powers in connection with the powers of law making."[5] Royal governors often found themselves at odds with the colonists and especially with elected colonial legislatures. As representatives of the Crown, the governors were distrusted and disdained by the people, many of whom had fled from Great Britain to escape royal domination. Others, generations removed from England, no longer felt strong ties to the king and his power over them.

When the colonists declared their independence from England in 1776, their distrust of a strong chief executive remained. Most state constitutions reduced the office of governor to a symbolic post elected annually by the legislature. Some states did entrust wider powers to their chief executives. The governor of New York, for example, was elected directly by the people. Perhaps because he then was accountable to the people, he was given the power to pardon, the duty to execute the laws faithfully to the best of his ability, and the power to act as commander in chief of the state militia.

Under the Articles of Confederation, there had been no executive branch of government; the eighteen different men who served as the president of the Continental Congress of the United States of America were president in name only—they had no actual authority or power in the new nation. When the delegates to the Constitutional Convention met in Philadelphia to fashion a new government, there was little dissention about the need for an executive branch to implement the laws made by Congress. Although some delegates suggested there should be multiple executives, eventually the Framers agreed that executive authority should be vested in one person. This agreement was relatively seamless because the Framers were sure that George Washington—whom they had trusted with their lives during the Revolutionary War—would become the first president of the new nation.

The Framers also had no problem in agreeing on a title for the new office. Borrowing from the constitutions of several states, the Framers called the new chief executive the president. How the president was to be chosen and by whom was a major stumbling block. James Wilson of Philadelphia suggested a single, more powerful president, who would be elected by the people and "independent of the legislature." Wilson also suggested giving the executive an absolute veto over the acts of Congress. "Without such a defense," he wrote, "the legislature can at any moment sink it [the executive] into non-existence."[6]

The manner of the president's election haunted the Framers for some time, and their solution to the dilemma—the creation of the Electoral College—is described in detail in chapter 13. We leave the resolution of that issue aside for now and turn instead to details of the issues the Framers resolved quickly.

Presidential Qualifications and Terms of Office

The Constitution requires that the president (and the vice president, whose major function is to succeed the president in the event of his death or disability) be a natural-born citizen of the United States, at least thirty-five years old, and a resident of the United States for at least fourteen years. In the 1700s, it was not uncommon for those engaged in international diplomacy to be out of the country for substantial periods of time, and the Framers wanted to make sure that prospective presidents spent significant time on this country's shores before running for its highest elective office. Most presidents have prior elective experience, too, as revealed in Table 8.1. While there is no constitutional bar to a woman or member of a minority group seeking the presidency, no one other than a white male has been elected to this office.

Although only two of the last five presidents were not reelected to a second term, at one time the length of a president's term was controversial. Four-, seven-, and eleven-year terms with no eligibility for reelection were suggested by various delegates to the Constitutional Convention. The Framers ultimately reached agreement on a four-year term with eligibility for reelection.

The first president, George Washington (1789–1797), sought reelection only once, and a two-term limit for presidents became traditional. Although Ulysses S. Grant unsuccessfully sought a third term, the two terms established by Washington remained the standard for 150 years, avoiding the Framers' much-feared "constitutional monarch," a perpetually reelected tyrant. In the 1930s and 1940s, however, Franklin D. Roosevelt ran successfully in four elections as Americans fought first the Great Depression and then World War II. Despite Roosevelt's popularity, negative reaction to his long tenure in office ultimately led to passage (and ratification in 1951) of the **Twenty-Second Amendment**. It limits presidents to two four-year terms. A vice president who succeeded a president due to death, resignation, or impeachment would be eligible for a total of ten years in office: two years of a president's remaining term and two elected terms.

The Framers paid little attention to the office of vice president beyond the need to have an immediate official stand-in for the president. Initially, for example, the vice president's one and only function was to assume the office of president in the case of the death of the president or some other emergency. After further debate, the delegates made the vice president the presiding officer of the Senate (except in cases of presidential impeachment). They feared that if the Senate's presiding officer were chosen from the Senate itself, one

Twenty-Second Amendment
Adopted in 1951, prevents a president from serving more than two terms, or more than ten years if he came to office via the death or impeachment of his predecessor.

■ The election of Arnold Schwarzenegger as California governor brought forward again the debate about whether presidents must be natural-born citizens. Because the United States is a nation of immigrants, many people argue that all citizens should have the opportunity to become president.

Photo courtesy: Ken James/UPI/Landov

TABLE 8.1 Personal Characteristics of the U.S. Presidents

President	Place of Birth	Higher Education	Occupation	Years in Congress	Years As Governer	Years As Vice President	Age at Becoming President
George Washington	VA	William & Mary	Farmer/surveyor	2	0	0	57
John Adams	MA	Harvard	Farmer/lawyer	5	0	4	61
Thomas Jefferson	VA	William & Mary	Farmer/lawyer	5	3	4	58
James Madison	VA	Princeton	Farmer	15	0	0	58
James Monroe	VA	William & Mary	Farmer/lawyer	7	4	0	59
John Quincy Adams	MA	Harvard	Lawyer	0[a]	0	0	58
Andrew Jackson	SC	None	Lawyer	4	0	0	62
Martin Van Buren	NY	None	Lawyer	8	0	4	55
William H. Harrison	VA	Hampden	Military	0	0	0	68
John Tyler	VA	William & Mary	Lawyer	12	2	0	51
James K. Polk	NC	North Carolina	Lawyer	14	3	0	50
Zachary Taylor	VA	None	Military	0	0	0	65
Millard Fillmore	NY	None	Lawyer	8	0	1	50
Franklin Pierce	NH	Bowdoin	Lawyer	9	0	0	48
James Buchanan	PA	Dickinson	Lawyer	20	0	0	65
Abraham Lincoln	KY	None	Lawyer	2	0	0	52
Andrew Johnson	NC	None	Tailor	14	4	0	57
Ulysses S. Grant	OH	West Point	Military	0	0	0	47
Rutherford B. Hayes	OH	Kenyon	Lawyer	3	6	0	55
James A. Garfield	OH	Williams	Educator/lawyer	18	0	0	50
Chester A. Arthur	VT	Union	Lawyer	0	0	1	51
Grover Cleveland	NJ	None	Lawyer	0	2	0	48
Benjamin Harrison	OH	Miami (Ohio)	Lawyer	6	0	0	56
Grover Cleveland	NJ	None	Lawyer	0	2	0	53
William McKinley	OH	Allegheny	Lawyer	14	4	0	54
Theodore Roosevelt	NY	Harvard	Lawyer/author	0	2	1	43
William H. Taft	OH	Yale	Lawyer	0	0	0	52
Woodrow Wilson	VA	Princeton	Educator	0	2	0	56
Warren G. Harding	OH	Ohio Central	Newspaper editor	6	0	0	56
Calvin Coolidge	VT	Amherst	Lawyer	0	2	3	51
Herbert Hoover	IA	Stanford	Engineer	0	0	0	55
Franklin D. Roosevelt	NY	Columbia	Lawyer	0	4	0	49
Harry S Truman	MO	None	Clerk/store owner	10	0	0	61
Dwight D. Eisenhower	TX	West Point	Military	0	0	0	63
John F. Kennedy	MA	Harvard	Journalist	14	0	0	43
Lyndon B. Johnson	TX	Southwest Texas State Teachers' College	Educator	24	0	3	55
Richard M. Nixon	CA	Whittier/Duke	Lawyer	6	0	8	56
Gerald R. Ford	NE	Michigan/Yale	Lawyer	25	0	2	61
Jimmy Carter	GA	Naval Academy	Farmer/ business owner	0	4	0	52
Ronald Reagan	IL	Eureka	Actor	0	8	0	69
George Bush	MA	Yale	Business owner	4	0	8	64
Bill Clinton	AR	Georgetown/Yale	Lawyer	0	12	0	46
George W. Bush	CT	Yale/Harvard	Business owner	0	6	0	54

[a] Adams served in the U.S. House for six years after leaving the presidency.

Sources: Adapted from Presidential Elections Since 1789, 4th ed. (Washington, DC: CQ Press, 1987), 4; Norman Thomas, Joseph Pika, and Richard Watson, The Politics of the Presidency, 3rd ed. (Washington, DC: CQ Press, 1993), 490; Harold W. Stanley and Richard G. Niemi, eds., Vital Statistics on American Politics 2001–2002 (Washington, DC: CQ Press, 2001).

state would be short a representative. However, the vice president was given the authority to vote in that body in the event of a tie.

During the Constitutional Convention, Benjamin Franklin was a staunch supporter of including a provision allowing for **impeachment,** a process by which to begin to remove an official from office. He noted that "historically, the lack of power to impeach had necessitated recourse to assassination."[7] Not surprisingly, then, he urged the rest of the delegates to formulate a legal mechanism to remove the president and vice president.

impeachment
The power delegated to the House of Representatives in the Constitution to charge the president, vice president, or other "civil officers," including federal judges, with "Treason, Bribery, or other high Crimes and Misdemeanors." This is the first step in the constitutional process of removing such government officials from office.

Photo courtesy: © Alex Webb/Magnum Photos

■ President Richard M. Nixon gives one final salute as he leaves the White House after resigning from office.

executive privilege
An implied presidental power that allows the president to refuse to disclose information regarding confidential conversations or national security to Congress or the judiciary.

***U.S. v. Nixon* (1974)**
Key Supreme Court ruling on power of the president, finding that there is no absolute constitutional executive privilege to allow a president to refuse to comply with a court order to produce information needed in a criminal trial.

The impeachment provision ultimately included in Article II was adopted as a check on the power of the president. As we discussed in detail in chapter 7, each house of Congress was given a role to play in the impeachment process to assure that the chief executive could be removed only for "Treason, Bribery, or other high Crimes and Misdemeanors." The House is empowered to vote to impeach the president by a simple majority vote. The Senate then acts as a court of law and tries the president for the charged offenses. A two-thirds majority vote in the Senate on any count contained in the articles of impeachment is necessary to remove the president from office. Only two presidents, Andrew Johnson and Bill Clinton, were impeached by the House of Representatives. Neither man, however, was removed from office by the Senate. (For more on how the impeachment process works, see Table 7.7: The Eight Stages of the Impeachment Process.)

In 1974, President Richard M. Nixon resigned from office rather than face the certainty of impeachment, trial, and removal from office for his role in covering up details about a break-in at the Democratic Party's national headquarters in the Watergate office complex. What came to be known simply as Watergate also produced a major decision from the Supreme Court on the scope of what is termed **executive privilege**. In ***U.S. v. Nixon* (1974),** the Supreme Court ruled unanimously that there was no overriding executive privilege that sanctioned the president's refusal to comply with a court order to produce information for use in the trial of the Watergate defendants.

Rules of Succession

Through 2005, eight presidents have died in office from illness or assassination. William H. Harrison was the first president to die in office—he caught a cold at his inauguration in 1841 and died one month later. (John Tyler thus became the first vice president to succeed to the presidency.) In 1865, Abraham Lincoln became the first president to be assassinated.

The Framers were aware that a system of orderly transfer of power was necessary; this was the primary reason they created the office of the vice president. To further clarify the order of presidential succession, in 1947, Congress passed the Presidential Succession Act, which lists—in order—those in line (after the vice president) to succeed the president:

1. Speaker of the House of Representatives
2. President pro tempore of the Senate
3. Secretaries of state, treasury, and defense, and other Cabinet heads in order of the creation of their department.

Twenty-Fifth Amendment
Adopted in 1967 to establish procedures for filling vacancies in the office of president and vice president as well as providing for procedures to deal with the disability of a president.

The Succession Act has never been used because there has always been a vice president to take over when a president died in office. The **Twenty-Fifth Amendment,** in fact, was added to the Constitution in 1967 to assure that this will continue to be the case. Should a vacancy occur in the office of the vice president, the Twenty-Fifth Amendment directs the president to appoint a new vice president, subject to the approval (by a simple majority) of both houses of Congress.

The Living Constitution

Whenever there is a vacancy in the office of the Vice President, the President shall nominate a Vice President who shall take office upon confirmation by a majority vote of both Houses of Congress.
—Twenty-Fifth Amendment, Section 2

This clause of the Twenty-Fifth Amendment allows a president to fill a vacancy in the office of vice president by a simple majority of both Houses of Congress. The purpose of this amendment, which also deals with vacancies in the office of the president, was to remedy some structural flaws in Article II. At the time of this amendment's addition to the Constitution in 1965, seven vice presidents had died in office and one had resigned. For over 20 percent of the nation's history there had been no vice president to assume the office of the president in case of his death or infirmity. When John F. Kennedy was assassinated, Vice President Lyndon B. Johnson became president and the office of vice president was vacant. Since Johnson had suffered a heart attack as vice president, members of Congress were anxious to remedy the problems that might occur should there be no vice president.

Richard M. Nixon followed Johnson as president, and ironically, during Nixon's presidency, the office of the vice president became empty twice! First, Nixon's vice president, Spiro T. Agnew, was forced to resign amid allegations of illegal activity as a county executive in Maryland; he was replaced by popular House Minority Leader Gerald R. Ford (R–MI), who had no trouble getting a majority vote in both houses of Congress to confirm his nomination. When Nixon resigned rather than face sure impeachment, Ford became president and selected the former governor of New York, Nelson A. Rockefeller, to be his vice president.

As pointed out in The Living Constitution, the Twenty-Fifth Amendment has been used twice in its relatively short history. In 1973, President Richard M. Nixon selected House Minority Leader Gerald R. Ford (R–MI) to replace Vice President Spiro T. Agnew after Agnew resigned in the wake of charges of bribe taking, corruption, and income tax evasion while an elected official in Maryland. Less than a year later, when Vice President Ford became the thirty-eighth president after Nixon's resignation, he nominated, and the House and Senate approved, former New York Governor Nelson A. Rockefeller to be his vice president. This chain of events set up for the first time in U.S. history a situation in which neither the president nor the vice president had been elected to those positions.

The Twenty-Fifth Amendment also contains a section that allows the vice president and a majority of the Cabinet (or some other body determined by Congress) to deem a president unable to fulfill his duties. It sets up a procedure to allow the vice president to become acting president if the president is incapacitated. The president also voluntarily can relinquish his power. In 1985, following the spirit of the amendment, President Ronald Reagan sent Vice President George Bush a letter that made Bush the acting president during Reagan's eight-hour surgery for colon cancer.

THE CONSTITUTIONAL POWERS OF THE PRESIDENT

THOUGH THE FRAMERS nearly unanimously agreed about the need for a strong central government and a greatly empowered Congress, they did not agree about the proper role of the president or the sweep of his authority. In contrast to Article I's laundry list of enumerated powers for the Congress, Article II details few presidential powers. Perhaps the most important section of Article II is its first sentence: "The executive Power shall be vested in a President of the United States of America." Nonetheless, the sum total of his presidential powers, enumerated below, allows him to become a major player in the policy process.

The Appointment Power

To help the president enforce laws passed by Congress, the Constitution authorizes him to appoint, with the advice and consent of the Senate, "Ambassadors, other public Ministers and Consuls, judges of the supreme Court, and all other Officers of the United States, whose Appointments are not herein otherwise provided for, and which shall be established by Law." Although this section of the Constitution deals only with appointments, behind that language is a powerful policy-making tool. The president has the authority to make more than 6,000 appointments to his administration (of which 1,125 require Senate confirmation),[8] and he technically appoints more than 75,000 military personnel. Many of these appointees are in positions to wield substantial authority over the course and direction of public policy. Although Congress has the authority "to make all laws," through the president's enforcement power—and his chosen assistants—he often can set the policy agenda for the nation. And, especially in the context of his ability to make appointments to the federal courts, his influence can be felt far past his term of office.

It is not surprising, then, that selecting the right people is often one of a president's most important tasks. Presidents look for a blend of loyalty, competence, and integrity. Identifying these qualities in people is a major challenge that every new president faces. Recent presidents, especially Bill Clinton and George W. Bush, have made an effort to create a Cabinet and staff that, in President Clinton's terms, looks "more like America," as is underscored in Table 8.2, which indicates the proportion of women appointed by recent presidents. In fact, of the first five major appointments announced by President George W. Bush during his first term, all but one were women or minorities: retired General Colin Powell (secretary of state), Condoleezza Rice (national security adviser), Texas Supreme Court Justice Alberto Gonzales (White House counsel), and longtime Bush adviser Karen Hughes (counselor to the president)—two blacks, two women, and a Hispanic. President Bush's early second term Cabinet appointments were also historic and included the nomination of Rice as secretary of state and Gonzales as the attorney general.

TABLE 8.2   Presidential Teams (Senior Administrative Positions Requiring Senate Confirmation)

	Total Appointments	Total Women	Percentage Women
Jimmy Carter	1,087	191	17.6%
Ronald Reagan	2,349	277	11.8%
George Bush	1,079	215	19.9%
Bill Clinton	1,257	528	42%
George W. Bush	862[a]	182	21%

[a]As of June 2002.

Sources: "Insiders Say White House Has Its Own Glass Ceiling," *Atlanta Journal and Constitution* (April 10, 1995): A4; and Judi Hasson, "Senate GOP Leader Lott Says He'll Work with Clinton," *USA Today* (December 4, 1996): 8A. Updated by the authors from data available at http://www.appointee.org.

In the past, when a president forwarded a nomination to the Senate for its approval, his selections traditionally were given great respect—especially those for the **Cabinet**, an advisory group selected by the president to help him make decisions and execute the laws. In fact, until the Clinton administration, the vast majority (97 percent) of all presidential nominations were confirmed.[9]

Rejections of presidential nominees as well as onerous delays in their approval can have a major impact on the course of an administration. Rejections leave a president without first choices, affect a president's relationship with the Senate, and affect how the president is perceived by the public. Rejections and delays also have a chilling effect on other potential nominees. George W. Bush's nomination of conservative John Ashcroft as attorney general unleashed a torrent of liberal criticism and protracted hearings. But, in the end, Ashcroft was confirmed on a 58–42 vote. It wasn't until fourteen months into his presidency that one of President Bush's nominees, Charles W. Pickering, Jr. to the U.S. Court of Appeals, was defeated. Even though Republicans controlled the Senate, Democrats launched filibusters to keep some of the president's federal judge nominations from coming to the floor for a vote.

The Power to Convene Congress

The Constitution requires the president to inform the Congress periodically of "the State of the Union," and authorizes the president to convene either or both houses of Congress on "extraordinary Occasions." In *Federalist No. 77*, Hamilton justified the latter by noting that because the Senate and the chief executive enjoy concurrent powers to make treaties, "It might often be necessary to call it together with a view to this object, when it would be unnecessary and improper to convene the House of Representatives." The power to convene Congress was important when Congress did not sit in nearly year-round sessions. Today this power has little more than symbolic significance.

The Power to Make Treaties

The president's power to make treaties with foreign nations is checked by the Constitution's stipulation that all treaties must be approved by at least two-thirds of the members of the Senate. The chief executive can also "receive ambassadors," wording that has been interpreted to allow the president to recognize the very existence of other nations.

Historically, the Senate ratifies about 70 percent of the treaties submitted to it by the president.[10] Only sixteen treaties that have been put to a vote have been rejected, often under highly partisan circumstances. Perhaps the most notable example of the Senate's refusal to ratify a treaty was its defeat of the Treaty of Versailles submitted by President Woodrow Wilson in 1919. The treaty was an agreement among the major nations to end World War I. At Wilson's insistence, it also called for the creation of the League of Nations—a precursor of the United Nations—to foster continued peace and international disarmament. In struggling to gain international acceptance for the League, Wilson had taken American support for granted. This was a dramatic miscalculation. Isolationists, led by Senator Henry Cabot Lodge (R–MA), opposed U.S. participation in the League on the grounds that the League would place the United States in the center of every major international conflict. Proponents countered that, League or no League, the United States had emerged from World War I as a world power and that membership in the League of Nations would enhance its new role. The vote in the Senate for ratification was very close, but the isolationists prevailed—the United States stayed out of the League, and Wilson was devastated.

Cabinet
The formal body of presidential advisers who head the fifteen executive departments. Presidents often add others to this body of formal advisers.

■ When President George W. Bush became frustrated by the Senate's failure to approve Charles W. Pickering's appointment to the bench, the president elevated Pickering with a recess appointment, which sidestepped the confirmation process. Declining to face another Senate vote, Pickering resigned from the U.S. Court of Appeals after serving less than a year.

Photo courtesy: Brooks Kraft/Corbis

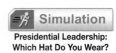

Simulation

Presidential Leadership:
Which Hat Do You Wear?

The Senate also may require substantial amendment of a treaty prior to its consent. When President Jimmy Carter proposed the controversial Panama Canal treaty in 1977 to turn the canal over to Panama, for example, the Senate required several conditions to be ironed out before approving the canal's return. U.S. control of the canal came about because the United States supported Panama's efforts to seek independence from Colombia in 1903. In 1904, under a treaty, the new nation of Panama granted the United States the rights, for a period of one hundred years, to the strip of land through the center of Panama that became the canal. The U.S. Senate's narrow vote to accept the treaty negotiated by the Carter administration remedied a long-standing, contentious issue that was hampering U.S.-Latin American relations.

When trade agreements are at issue, presidents often are forced to be mindful of the wishes of Congress. What is called congressional "fast track" authority protects a president's ability to negotiate trade agreements with confidence that the accords will not be altered by Congress. Trade agreements submitted to Congress under fast track procedures bar amendments and require an up or down vote in Congress within ninety days of introduction.

Presidents often try to get around the constitutional "advice and consent" of the Senate requirement for ratification of treaties and the congressional approval requirement for trade agreements by entering into an **executive agreement,** which allows the president to form secret and highly sensitive arrangements with foreign nations without Senate approval. Presidents have used these agreements since the days of George Washington, and their use has been upheld by the courts. Although executive agreements are not binding on subsequent administrations, since 1900 they have been used far more frequently than treaties, further cementing the role of the president in foreign affairs, as revealed in Table 8.3.

executive agreement
Formal government agreement entered into by the president that does not require the advice and consent of the U.S. Senate.

veto power
The formal, constitutional authority of the president to reject bills passed by both houses of Congress, thus preventing their becoming law without further congressional action.

Veto Power

Presidents can affect the policy process through the **veto power,** the authority to reject any congressional legislation. "Presidential vetoes have been vital to the development of the twentieth-century presidency."[11] The threat of a presidential veto often prompts members of Congress to fashion legislation that they know will receive presidential acquiescence, if not support. Thus, simply threatening to veto legislation often gives a president another way to influence law-making.

During the Constitutional Convention, proponents of a strong executive argued that the president should have an absolute and final veto over acts of Congress. Opponents of this idea, including Benjamin Franklin, countered that in their home states the executive veto "was constantly made use of to extort money" from legislators. James Madison made the most compelling argument for a compromise on the issue:

> Experience has proven a tendency in our governments to throw all power into the legislative vortex. The Executives of the States are in general little more than Ciphers, the legislatures omnipotent. If no effectual check be devised for restraining the instability and encroachments of the latter, a revolution of some kind or other would be inevitable.[12]

In keeping with the system of checks and balances, then, the president was given the veto power, but only as a "qualified negative." Although the president was given the authority to veto any act of Congress (with the exception of

		Number of
Years	Number of Treaties	Executive Agreements
1789–1839	60	27
1839–1889	215	238
1889–1929	382	763
1930–1932	49	41
1933–1944 (F. Roosevelt)	131	369
1945–1952 (Truman)	132	1,324
1953–1960 (Eisenhower)	89	1,834
1961–1963 (Kennedy)	36	813
1964–1968 (L. Johnson)	67	1,083
1969–1974 (Nixon)	93	1,317
1975–1976 (Ford)	26	666
1977–1980 (Carter)	79	1,476
1981–1988 (Reagan)	125	2,840
1989–1992 (Bush)	67	1,350
1993–2000 (Clinton)	209	2,047
2001–2002 (G.W. Bush)	21	262

TABLE 8.3   Treaties and Executive Agreements Concluded by the United States, 1789–2002

Note: Number of treaties includes those concluded during the indicated span of years. Some of these treaties did not receive the consent of the U.S. Senate. Varying definitions of what an executive agreement comprises and their entry-into-force date make the above numbers approximate.

Sources: 1789–1980: *Congressional Quarterly's Guide to Congress,* 291; 1981–2002: Office of the Assistant Legal Adviser for Treaty Affairs. U.S. Department of State.

THE PRESIDENT'S MANY HATS

Photo courtesy: John Bryson/Time Pix

■ Chief law enforcer: National Guard troops sent by President Dwight D. Eisenhower enforce federal court decisions ordering the integration of public schools in Little Rock, Arkansas.

Photo courtesy: Mark Reinstein/The Image Works

■ Leader of the party: Ronald Reagan mobilized conservatives and changed the nature of the Republican Party.

Photo courtesy: Wally McNamee/Folio, Inc.

■ Commander in chief: President George Bush and his wife, Barbara, with troops in the Persian Gulf.

Photo courtesy: Bettmann/Corbis

■ Shaper of domestic policy: President Jimmy Carter announces new energy policies. Here, he wears a sweater to underscore that thermostats in the White House were turned down to save energy.

Photo courtesy: Dirck Halstead/Getty Images

■ Key player in the legislative process. President Bill Clinton proposes legislation to Congress and the nation.

Photo courtesy: Bettmann/CORBIS

■ Chief of state: President John F. Kennedy and his wife, Jacqueline, with the president of France and his wife during the Kennedys' widely publicized 1961 trip to that nation.

joint resolutions that propose constitutional amendments), Congress was given the authority to override an executive veto by a two-thirds vote in each house. The veto is a powerful policy tool because Congress cannot usually muster enough votes to override a veto. Thus, in over 200 years, there have been approximately 2,500 presidential vetoes and only about a hundred have been overridden, as revealed in Table 8.4.

As early as 1873, in his State of the Union message, President Ulysses S. Grant proposed a constitutional amendment to give to presidents a **line-item veto,** a power enjoyed by many governors to disapprove of individual items within a spending bill and not just the bill in its entirety. Over the years, 150 resolutions calling for a line-item veto were introduced in Congress. Presidents from Gerald R. Ford to Bill Clinton supported the concept. Finally, in 1996, Congress enacted legislation that gave the president the authority to veto specific spending provisions within a bill without vetoing the bill in its entirety. This move allowed the president to project his policy priorities into the budget by vetoing any programs inconsistent with his policy goals. It also allowed President Clinton to do away with more outrageous examples of pork (legislators' pet projects that often find their way into a budget). The city of New York soon challenged the line-item veto law when the president used it to stop payment of some congressionally authorized funds to the city. In *Clinton v. City of New York* (1998), the U.S. Supreme Court ruled that the line-item veto was unconstitutional because it gave powers to the president denied him by the U.S. Constitution. Significant alterations of executive/congressional powers, said the Court, require constitutional amendment.[13]

line-item veto

The authority of a chief executive to delete part of a bill passed by the legislature that involves taxing or spending. The legislature may override a veto, usually with a two-thirds majority of each chamber.

TABLE 8.4	Presidential Vetoes			
President	Regular Vetoes	Vetoes Overridden	Pocket Vetoes	Total Vetoes
Washington	2	0	0	2
J. Adams	0	0	0	0
Jefferson	0	0	0	0
Madison	5	0	2	7
Monroe	1	0	0	1
J. Q. Adams	0	0	0	0
Jackson	5	0	7	12
Van Buren	0	0	1	1
W. H. Harrison	0	0	0	0
Tyler	6	1	4	10
Polk	2	0	1	3
Taylor	0	0	0	0
Fillmore	0	0	0	0
Pierce	9	5	0	9
Buchanan	4	0	3	7
Lincoln	2	0	5	7
A. Johnson	21	15	8	29
Grant	45	4	48	93
Hayes	12	1	1	13
Garfield	0	0	0	0
Arthur	4	1	8	12
Cleveland	304	2	110	414
B. Harrison	19	1	25	44
Cleveland	42	5	128	170
McKinley	6	0	36	42
T. Roosevelt	42	1	40	82
Harding	5	0	1	6
Coolidge	20	4	30	50
Hoover	21	3	16	37
F. Roosevelt	372	9	263	635
Truman	180	12	70	250
Eisenhower	73	2	108	181
Kennedy	12	0	9	21
L. Johnson	16	0	14	30
Nixon	26	7	17	432
Ford	48	12	18	66
Carter	13	2	18	31
Reagan	39	9	39	78
Bush	29	1	17	46
Clinton	37	2	1	38
G. W. Bush[a]	0	0	0	0
Total	1,485	107	1,068	2,553

[a]As of January 2005.

Sources: Harold W. Stanley and Richard G. Niemi, eds., *Vital Statistics on American Politics, 2001–2002* (Washington, DC: CQ Press, 2001): 256. Data for Clinton and G. W. Bush from Office of the Clerk, U.S. House of Representatives, http://clerk.house.gov/histHigh/Congressional_History/vetoes.php.

The Power to Preside over the Military as Commander in Chief

One of the most important constitutional executive powers is the president's authority over the military. Article II states that the president is "Commander in Chief of the Army and Navy of the United States." While the Constitution specifically grants Congress the authority to declare war, presidents since Abraham Lincoln have used the commander-in-chief clause in conjunction with the chief executive's duty to "take Care that the Laws be faithfully executed" to wage war (and to broaden various powers).

Modern presidents continually clash with Congress over the ability to commence hostilities. The Vietnam War, in which 58,000 American soldiers were killed and 300,000 were wounded, was conducted (at a cost of $150 billion) without a congressional declaration of war. In fact, acknowledging President Lyndon B. Johnson's claim to war-making authority, in 1964 Congress passed—with only two dissenting votes—the Gulf of Tonkin Resolution, which authorized a massive commitment of U.S. forces in South Vietnam.

During that highly controversial war, Presidents Johnson and then Nixon routinely assured members of

Congress that victory was near. In 1971, however, publication of what were called *The Pentagon Papers* revealed what many people had suspected all along: Lyndon B. Johnson systematically had altered casualty figures and distorted key facts to place the progress of the war in a more positive light. In 1973, Congress passed the **War Powers Act** to limit the president's authority to introduce American troops into hostile foreign lands without congressional approval. President Nixon vetoed the act, but it was overridden by a two-thirds majority in both houses of Congress.

Presidents since Richard M. Nixon have continued to insist that the War Powers Act is an unconstitutional infringement of their executive power. In 2001, President George W. Bush sought, and both houses of Congress approved, a joint resolution authorizing the use of force against "those responsible for the recent [September 11] attacks launched against the United States." This resolution actually gave the president more open-ended authority to wage war than his father had received in 1991 to conduct the Persian Gulf War or President Lyndon B. Johnson had received after the Gulf of Tonkin Resolution in 1964.[14] Later, in October 2002, after President Bush declared Iraq to be a "grave threat to peace," the House (296–133) and Senate (77–23) voted overwhelmingly to allow the president to use force in Iraq "as he determines to be necessary and appropriate," thereby conferring tremendous authority on the president to wage war. (See Join the Debate: The War Powers Act.)

Photo courtesy: Anja Niedringhaus/Pool/Reuters/Corbis

■ In 2003 President George W. Bush surprised American troops in Iraq on Thanksgiving Day.

War Powers Act
Passed by Congress in 1973; the president is limited in the deployment of troops overseas to a sixty-day period in peacetime (which can be extended for an extra thirty days to permit withdrawal) unless Congress explicitly gives its approval for a longer period.

The Pardoning Power

Presidents can exercise a check on judicial power through their constitutional authority to grant reprieves or pardons. A **pardon** is an executive grant releasing an individual from the punishment or legal consequences of a crime before or after conviction, and restores all rights and privileges of citizenship. Presidents exercise complete pardoning power for federal offenses except in cases of impeachment, which cannot be pardoned. President Gerald R. Ford granted the most famous presidential pardon when he pardoned former President Nixon—who had not been formally charged with any crime—"for any offenses against the United States, which he, Richard Nixon, has committed or may have committed while in office." This unilateral, absolute pardon prevented the former president from ever being tried for any crimes he may have committed. It also unleashed a torrent of public criticism against Ford and questions about whether Nixon had discussed the pardon with Ford before Nixon's resignation. Many analysts attribute Ford's defeat in his 1976 bid for the presidency to that pardon.

Even though pardons are generally directed toward a specific individual, presidents have also used them to offer general amnesties. Presidents George Washington, John Adams, James Madison, Abraham Lincoln, Andrew Johnson, Theodore Roosevelt, Harry S Truman, and Jimmy Carter used general pardons to grant amnesty to large classes of individuals for illegal acts. Carter, for example, incurred the wrath of many veterans' groups when he made an offer of unconditional amnesty to approximately 10,000 men who had fled the United States or gone into hiding to avoid being drafted for military service in the Vietnam War.

pardon
An executive grant providing restoration of all rights and privileges of citizenship to a specific individual charged or convicted of a crime.

THE WAR POWERS ACT

OVERVIEW: It is difficult to interpret how the Constitution divides war powers between Congress and the president. Over the course of American history, it is the executive branch that has assumed considerable constitutional discretion in how the United States engages in war and diplomacy. Though the Constitution gives Congress the authority to declare war, "to make rules for the government and regulation of" military forces, and to provide appropriations for the armed services, it is the president's constitutional jurisdiction over the war power that has steadily increased since the nation's founding. For example, President James Madison would not go to war with Great Britain in 1812 without a war declaration from Congress, yet the last six major American conflicts—in Korea, Vietnam, the Persian Gulf, Kosovo, Afghanistan, and Iraq—were conducted without formal declarations of war. And, at times, presidents have withheld information from Congress. During the Vietnam War, President Richard M. Nixon, for example, authorized bombing neutral Cambodia and Laos without notifying Congress.

The War Powers Act of 1973 was an attempt to rein in the war-making authority of the president by demanding, among other things, that the executive notify Congress when committing the U.S. military to hostile action. The War Powers Act requires the president "in every possible instance" to report to Congress within forty-eight hours after deploying the armed forces to combat; implied is the understanding that the information Congress receives is timely and accurate.

The intelligence information that the president and Congress receive is critically important in determining whether to engage in and support armed conflict. The president's constitutional authority as commander in chief gives him access to significant intelligence resources through which to conduct foreign affairs, but sometimes these sources are flawed. President Bill Clinton, for example, ordered the destruction of a chemical plant in Sudan that he believed produced nerve gas but that may have produced less dangerous pharmaceuticals. More recently, President George W. Bush made the case for invading Iraq in part due to the fear that Iraq possessed, after having displayed the will to use, weapons of mass destruction (WMD). WMDs loomed large in the national debate about whether to intervene in Iraq, and the fact that stockpiles are not found raised concerns of many senators who voted to authorize the use of force there.

According to *Federalist No. 3*, the decision to go to war is one of the most solemn a republic can make. Considering the events of September 11, 2001, should a president, in times of crisis, be limited in his ability to defend the United States? Conversely, should there be additional constitutional constraints on the executive's war-making authority in light of the experience of American history? What can be done to ensure that when the United States goes to war, the war is both necessary and just and is conducted with the least amount of casualties and damage to all parties? How can the American people be sure the information that they, the Congress, and the president receive is accurate and timely?

Arguments for the War Powers Act

- **The War Powers Act reflects the will of the American people.** The doctrine of civilian supremacy places ultimate war-making authority with the American people, and the War Powers Resolution reflects the will of the people as expressed through the representative institution of Congress. This support is confirmed by the congressional override of President Richard M. Nixon's veto.
- **The War Powers Act is an attempt by Congress to restore the balance of shared control of the military with the executive.** The act's stated purpose is to "fulfill the intent of the framers . . . and insure that the collective

THE DEVELOPMENT AND EXPANSION OF PRESIDENTIAL POWER

EACH PRESIDENT BRINGS to the position not only a vision of America, but also expectations about how to use presidential authority. Through 2005, the forty-two men who have held the nation's highest office have been a diverse lot. (While there have been forty-three presidents, only forty-two men have held the office: Grover Cleveland served as the twenty-second and twenty-fourth president because he was elected to nonconsecutive terms in 1884 and 1892.) Most presidents find accomplishing their goals much more difficult than they envisioned. After President John F. Kennedy was in office two years, for example, he noted publicly that there were "greater limitations judgment of both the Congress and the President will apply to the introduction of United States Armed Forces into hostilities . . . and to the continued use of such forces." This is an attempt to return to the constitutional principle that waging war is to be shared by both branches of government.

- **The War Powers Act is an additional check on the president's authority as commander in chief.** The act is an attempt to prevent future presidents from engaging in hostilities of questionable importance to U.S. national security and to force deliberation within the government in regard to armed conflict. For example, had Congress known of President Lyndon B. Johnson's use of faulty or intentionally misleading information to increase U.S. military involvement in Vietnam after the Gulf of Tonkin incident, U.S. involvement in Southeast Asia may have taken a different, less costly path in both lives and expenditures.

Arguments Against the War Powers Act

- **International relations can be so volatile that the president must be able to act quickly without hindrance.** Alexander Hamilton argued that the reasons for war are "infinite" and that the United States must have an institution that can react quickly and with force to defend the United States. He found this energy in government in the executive—and the American executive was created to act quickly without relative interference during exceptional times of crisis.
- **The Supreme Court has upheld an expanded interpretation of the president's authority. In** *U.S.* **v.** *Curtiss-Wright* (1936), the Court found that the president and "not Congress has the better opportunity of knowing the conditions which prevail in foreign countries, and especially this is true during times of war. He has his confidential sources of information. . . . Secrecy in respect of information gathered by them may be highly necessary and the premature disclosure of it productive of harmful results." Thus, the Court concluded that the president is uniquely responsible in the area of foreign policy and war making.

- **During times of conflict, it is the president's duty to "preserve, protect and defend" the Constitution, and thus the country it governs, and it is the executive's prerogative to decide the means to do so.** During extraordinary times, the president must take extraordinary means to defend the state without undue interference from Congress. *Federalist No. 8* argues: "It is the nature of war to increase the executive at the expense of the legislative authority" as this is considered a natural shift in power. A historical example is President Abraham Lincoln's use of presidential power during the Civil War and a current example would be the war on terrorism.

Questions

1. Is the War Powers Act unconstitutional? Does Congress have the constitutional right to limit the war-making power of the executive? If so, what implications does this have for U.S. national security?
2. Do the American people have the right and need to specific information and intelligence regarding matters of war and peace? Doesn't the representative principle mean elected officials are charged with making certain decisions without informing the public, especially when that information may be confidential in nature?

Selected Readings

Louis Fisher. *Presidential War Power.* Lawrence: University Press of Kansas, 2004.

John Hart Ely. *War and Responsibility: Constitutional Lessons of Viet Nam and Its Aftermath.* Princeton, NJ: Princeton University Press, 1995.

upon our ability to bring about a favorable result than I had imagined."[15] Similarly, as he was leaving office, President Harry S Truman mused about what surprises awaited his successor, Dwight D. Eisenhower, a former general: "He'll sit here and he'll say, 'Do this! Do that!' And nothing will happen. Poor Ike—it won't be a bit like the army. He'll find it very frustrating."[16]

A president's authority is limited by the formal powers enumerated in Article II of the Constitution and by the Supreme Court's interpretation of those constitutional provisions. How a president wields these powers is affected by the times in which the president serves, his confidantes and advisers, and the president's personality and leadership abilities. The 1950s postwar era of good feelings and economic prosperity presided over by the grandfatherly former war hero Dwight D. Eisenhower, for

TABLE 8.5   The Best and the Worst Presidents

Who was the best president and who was the worst? Many surveys of scholars have been taken over the years to answer this question, and virtually all have ranked Abraham Lincoln the best. A 2000 C-SPAN survey of fifty-eight historians, for example, came up with these results:

Ten Best Presidents	Ten Worst Presidents
1. Lincoln (best)	1. Buchanan (worst)
2. F. Roosevelt	2. A. Johnson
3. Washington	3. Pierce
4. T. Roosevelt	4. Harding
5. Truman	5. W. Harrison
6. Wilson	6. Tyler
7. Jefferson	7. Fillmore
8. Kennedy	8. Hoover
9. Eisenhower	9. Grant
10. L. Johnson (10th best)	10. Arthur (10th worst)

Source: Susan Page, "Putting Presidents in Their Place," *USA Today* (February 21, 2000): 8A.

Participation

Rate the Presidents

inherent powers
Powers of the president that can be derived or inferred from specific powers in the Constitution.

instance, called for a very different leader from the one needed by the Civil War–torn nation governed by Abraham Lincoln. Furthermore, not only do different times call for different kinds of leaders; they also often provide limits, or conversely, wide opportunities, for whoever serves as president at the time. Crises, in particular, trigger expansions of presidential power. The danger to the union posed by the Civil War in the 1860s required a strong leader to take up the reins of government. Because of his leadership during this crisis, Lincoln is generally ranked by historians as the best president (see Table 8.5).

Establishing Presidents' Authority: Washington, Adams, and Jefferson

The first three presidents, and their conceptions of the presidency, continue to have a profound impact on American government. When President George Washington was sworn in on a cold, blustery day in New York City on April 30, 1789, he took over an office and a government that were yet to be created. Eventually, a few hundred postal workers were hired and Washington appointed a small group of Cabinet advisers and clerks. During Washington's two terms, the entire federal budget was only about $40 million, or approximately $10 for every citizen in America. In contrast, in 2004, the federal budget was $2.3 trillion, or $7,900, for every man, woman, and child.

George Washington set several important precedents for future presidents:

- He took every opportunity to establish the primacy of the national government. In 1794, for example, Washington used the militia of four states to put down the Whiskey Rebellion, an uprising of 3,000 western Pennsylvania farmers opposed to the payment of a federal excise tax on liquor. Leading those 1,500 troops was Secretary of the Treasury Alexander Hamilton, whose duty it was to collect federal taxes. Washington's action helped establish the idea of federal supremacy and the authority of the executive branch to collect the taxes levied by Congress.

- Washington began the practice of regular meetings with his advisers (called the Cabinet), thus establishing the Cabinet system.

- He asserted the prominence of the role of the chief executive in the conduct of foreign affairs. He sent envoys to negotiate the Jay Treaty to end continued hostilities with Great Britain. Then, over senatorial objection, he continued to assert his authority first to negotiate treaties and then simply to submit them to the Senate for its approval. Washington made it clear that the Senate's function was limited to approval of treaties and did not include negotiation with foreign powers.

- He claimed the inherent power of the presidency as the basis for proclaiming a policy of strict neutrality when the British and French were at war. Although the Constitution is silent about a president's authority to declare neutrality, Washington's supporters argued that the Constitution granted the president **inherent powers**— that is, powers that can be derived or inferred from what is formally described in the Constitution. Thus, they argued, the president's power to conduct diplomatic relations could be inferred from the Constitution. Since neither Congress nor the Supreme Court later disagreed, this power was presumed added to the list of specific, enumerated presidential powers found in Article II.

Like Washington, the next two presidents, John Adams and Thomas Jefferson, acted in ways that were critical to the development of the presidency as well as to the president's role in the political system. Adams's poor leadership skills, for example, heightened the divisions between Federalists and Anti-Federalists and probably quickened the development of political parties (see chapter 12). Soon thereafter, Jefferson used the party system to cement strong ties with the Congress and expanded the role of the president in the legislative process. Like Washington, he claimed that certain presidential powers were inherent and used those inherent powers to justify his expansion of the size of the nation through the Louisiana Purchase in 1803.

Incremental Expansion of Presidential Powers: 1809–1933

Although the first three presidents made enormous contributions to the office of the chief executive, the very nature of the way government had to function in its formative years caused the balance of power to be heavily weighted in favor of a strong Congress. Americans routinely had close contacts with their representatives in Congress, while to most citizens the president seemed a remote figure. Members of Congress frequently were at home, where they were seen by voters; few citizens ever even gazed on a president.

By the end of Jefferson's first term, it was clear that the Framers' initial fear of an all-powerful, monarchical president was unfounded. The strength of Congress and the relatively weak presidents who came after Jefferson allowed Congress quickly to assert itself as the most powerful branch of government. In fact, with but few exceptions, most presidents from James Madison to Herbert Hoover failed to exercise the powers of the presidency in any significant manner.

Andrew Jackson was the first president to act as a strong national leader, representing more than just a landed, propertied elite. By the time Jackson ran for president in 1828, eleven new states had been added to the union, and the number of white males eligible to vote had increased dramatically as property requirements for voting were removed by nearly all states. The election of Jackson, a Tennessean, as the seventh president signaled the end of an era: he was the first president not to be either a Virginian or an Adams. His election launched the beginning of Jacksonian democracy, a concept that embodied the western, frontier, egalitarian spirit personified by Jackson, the first common man to be elected president. The masses loved him, and legends were built around his down-to-earth image. Jackson, for example, once was asked to give a post-mastership to a soldier who had lost his leg on the battlefield and needed the job to support his family. When told that the man hadn't voted for him, Jackson responded: "If he lost his leg fighting for his country, that is vote enough for me."[17]

Jackson used his image and personal power to buttress the developing party system by rewarding loyal followers of his Democratic Party with presidential appointments. He frequently found himself at odds with Congress and made extensive use of the veto power. His veto of twelve bills surpassed the combined total of nine vetoes used by his six predecessors. Jackson also reasserted the supremacy of the national government (and the presidency) by facing down South Carolina's nullification of a federal tariff law.

Abraham Lincoln's approach to the presidency was similar to Jackson's. Moreover, the unprecedented emergency of the Civil War allowed Lincoln to assume powers that no president before him had claimed. Because Lincoln believed he needed to act quickly for the very survival of the union, he frequently took action without first obtaining the approval of Congress. Among many of Lincoln's legally questionable acts:

- He suspended the writ of *habeas corpus*, which allows those in prison to petition to be released, citing the need to jail persons even suspected of disloyal practices.
- He expanded the size of the U.S. army above congressionally mandated ceilings.
- He ordered a blockade of southern ports, in effect initiating a war without the approval of Congress.
- He closed the U.S. mails to treasonable correspondence.

Lincoln argued that the inherent powers of his office allowed him to circumvent the Constitution in a time of war or national crisis. Since the Constitution conferred on the president the duty to make sure that the laws of the United States are faithfully executed, reasoned Lincoln, the acts enumerated above were constitutional. He simply refused to allow the nation to crumble because of what he viewed as technical requirements of the Constitution.

The Growth of the Modern Presidency

Before the days of instantaneous communication, the nation could afford to allow Congress, with its relatively slow deliberative processes, to make most decisions. Furthermore, decision making might have been left to Congress because its members, and not the president, were closest to the people. As times and technology have changed, however, so have the public's expectations of anyone who becomes president. For example, the breakneck speed with which so many cable news networks as well as their Internet sites report national and international events has intensified the public's expectation that, in a crisis, the president will be the individual to act quickly and decisively on behalf of the entire nation. Congress often is just too slow to respond to fast-changing events—especially in foreign affairs.

In the twentieth and twenty-first centuries, the general trend has been for presidential—as opposed to congressional—decision making to be more and more important. The start of this trend can be traced to the four-term presidency of Franklin D. Roosevelt (FDR), who led the nation through several crises. This growth of presidential power and the growth of the federal government and its programs in general are now criticized by many. To understand the basis for many of the calls for reform of the political system being made today, it is critical to understand how the growth of government and the role of the president occurred.[18]

FDR took office in 1933 in the midst of a major crisis—the Great Depression—during which a substantial portion of the U.S. workforce was unemployed. Noting the sorry state of the national economy in his inaugural address, FDR concluded: "This nation asks for action and action now." To jump-start the American economy, FDR asked Congress for and was given "broad executive powers to wage a war against the emergency, as great as the power that would be given to me if we were in fact invaded by a foreign foe."[19]

Just as Abraham Lincoln had taken bold steps on his inauguration, Roosevelt also acted quickly. He immediately fashioned a plan for national recovery called the **New Deal,** a package of bold and controversial programs designed to invigorate the failing American economy (these are discussed in detail in chapter 3).

New Deal

The name given to the program of "Relief, Recovery, Reform" begun by President Franklin D. Roosevelt in 1933 to bring the United States out of the Great Depression.

■ President Franklin D. Roosevelt delivering one of his famous fireside chats to the American people. Roosevelt projected the voice and image of such a vigorous and active president that no one listening to him or seeing him in the newsreels would have guessed that he used a wheelchair as a result of polio.

Photo courtesy: AP/Wide World Photos

Roosevelt served an unprecedented twelve years in office; he was elected to four terms but died shortly after beginning the last one. During his years in office, the nation went from the economic war of the Great Depression to the real international conflict of World War II. The institution of the presidency changed profoundly and permanently as new federal agencies were created to implement New Deal programs as the executive branch became responsible for implementing a wide variety of new programs.

Not only did FDR create a new bureaucracy to implement his pet programs, but he also personalized the presidency by establishing a new relationship between the president and the people. In his radio addresses, or fireside chats, as he liked to call them, he spoke directly to the public in a relaxed and informal manner about serious issues.

To his successors, FDR left the modern presidency, including a burgeoning federal bureaucracy (see chapter 9), an active and usually leading role in both domestic and foreign policy and legislation, and a nationalized executive office that used technology—first radio and then television—to bring the president closer to the public than ever before.

THE PRESIDENTIAL ESTABLISHMENT

AS THE RESPONSIBILITIES AND SCOPE of presidential authority grew over the years, so did the executive branch, including the number of people working directly for the president in the White House. The vice president and his staff, the Cabinet, the first lady and her staff, the Executive Office of the President, and the White House staff all help the president fulfill his duties as chief executive.

The Vice President

For many years the vice presidency was considered a sure place for a public official to disappear into obscurity. When John Adams wrote to his wife, Abigail, about his position as America's first vice president, he said it was "the most insignificant office that was the invention of man . . . or his imagination conceived."[20]

Historically, presidents chose their vice presidents largely to balance—politically, geographically, or otherwise—the presidential ticket, with little thought given to the possibility that the vice president would become president. Franklin D. Roosevelt, for example, a liberal New Yorker, selected John Nance Garner, a conservative Texan, to be his running mate in 1932. After serving two terms, Garner—who openly disagreed with Roosevelt over many policies, including Roosevelt's decision to seek a third term—unsuccessfully sought the 1940 presidential nomination himself. The Bush/Cheney

Questions Arise About Mr. Cheney's Connection to ENRON

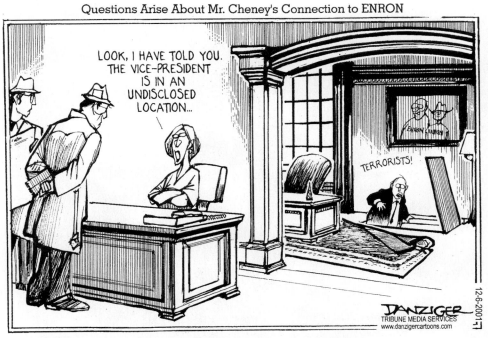

■ Immediately after 9/11, Vice President Dick Cheney was moved to what was called an "undisclosed location." The formerly very visible vice president was no longer around, and in the wake of a Government Accounting Office request for documents about his and the administration's connections to the oil industry, political cartoonists used his being unavailable at an undisclosed location for continued security reasons as an opportunity to poke fun at him.

Photo courtesy: Danziger/© Tribune Media Services, Inc. All Rights Reserved. Reprinted with permission ticket in 2000 showed an effort to balance the ticket in ways different from the past. Most commentators agreed that Dick Cheney was chosen to provide "gravitas"—a sense of national governmental experience, especially in foreign affairs, that Governor Bush neither had nor claimed. Similarly, Senator John Edwards (D–NC) was selected as John Kerry's 2004 running mate to soften Kerry's somewhat aloof demeanor.

How much power a vice president has depends on how much the president is willing to give him. Jimmy Carter was the first president to give his vice president, Walter Mondale, more than ceremonial duties. In fact, Walter Mondale was the first vice president to have an office in the White House. (It wasn't until 1961 that a vice president even had an office in the Executive Office Building next door to the White House!) The Mondale model of an active vice president has now become the norm.

The question still exists, however, as to whether the vice presidency is a stepping stone to the presidency. As the 2000 campaign underscored, the vice president of a very popular president at a time of unprecedented economic prosperity, Al Gore, was unable to translate that good will into election for himself.

The Cabinet

The Cabinet, which has no basis in the Constitution, is an informal institution based on practice and precedent whose membership is determined by tradition and presidential discretion. By custom, this advisory group selected by the president includes the heads of major executive departments. Presidents today also include their vice presidents in Cabinet meetings, as well as any other agency heads or officials to whom they would like to accord Cabinet-level status.

As a body, the Cabinet's major function is to help the president execute the laws and assist him in making decisions. Although the Framers had discussed the idea of some form of national executive council, they did not include a provision for one in the Constitution. They did recognize, however, the need for departments of government and departmental heads.

■ President George W. Bush with Vice President Dick Cheney chats with Secretary of State Colin Powell and National Security Advisor Condoleezza Rice. When Powell resigned after the president's re-election, Rice was appointed and conirmed as the first African American female secretary of state.

Photo courtesy: Mark Wilson/Getty Images

TABLE 8.6   The U.S. Cabinet and Responsibilities of Each Executive Department

Department Head	Department	Date of Creation	Responsibilities
Secretary of State	Department of State	1789	Responsible for the making of foreign policy, including treaty negotiation
Secretary of the Treasury	Department of the Treasury	1789	Responsible for government funds and regulation of alcohol, firearms, and tobacco
Secretary of Defense	Department of Defense	1789, 1947	Created by consolidating the former Departments of War, the Army, the Navy, and the Air Force; responsible for national defense
Attorney General	Department of Justice	1870	Represents U.S. government in all federal courts, investigates and prosecutes violations of federal law
Secretary of the Interior	Department of the Interior	1849	Manages the nation's natural resources, including wildlife and public lands
Secretary of Agriculture	Department of Agriculture	Created 1862; elevated to Cabinet status 1889	Assists the nation's farmers, oversees food-quality programs, administers food stamp and school lunch programs
Secretary of Commerce	Department of Commerce	1903	Aids businesses and conducts the U.S. Census (originally the Department of Commerce and Labor)
Secretary of Labor	Department of Labor	1913	Runs labor programs, keeps labor statistics, aids labor through enforcement of laws
Secretary of Health and Human Services	Department of Health and Human Services	1953	Runs health, welfare, and Social Security programs; created as the Department of Health, Education, and Welfare (lost its education function in 1979)
Secretary of Housing and Urban Development	Department of Housing and Urban Development	1965	Responsible for urban and housing programs
Secretary of Transportation	Department of Transportation	1966	Responsible for mass transportation and highway programs
Secretary of Energy	Department of Energy	1977	Responsible for energy policy and research, including atomic energy
Secretary of Education	Department of Education	1979	Responsible for the federal government's education programs
Secretary of Veterans Affairs	Department of Veterans Affairs	1989	Responsible for programs aiding veterans
Secretary of Homeland Security	Department of Homeland Security	2002	Responsible for all issues pertaining to homeland security

As revealed in Table 8.6, over the years the Cabinet has grown as new departments have accommodated for new pressures on the president to act in areas that initially were not considered within the scope of concern of the national government. As interest groups, in particular, pressured Congress and the president to recognize their demands for services and governmental action, they often were rewarded by the creation of an executive department. Since each was headed by a secretary who automatically became a member of the president's Cabinet, powerful groups including farmers (Agriculture), business people (Commerce), workers (Labor), and teachers (Education) saw the creation of a department as increasing their access to the president.

The size of the president's Cabinet has increased over the years at the same time that most presidents' reliance on their Cabinet secretaries has decreased, although some individual members of a president's Cabinet may be very influential. Former Secretary of Commerce Don Evans, for example, was an old friend of George W. Bush's. Evans served as secretary for Bush's whole first term before resigning. (Chapter 9 provides a more detailed discussion of the Cabinet's role in executing U.S. policy.)

The First Lady

From the time of Martha Washington, first ladies (a term coined during the Civil War) have assisted presidents as informal advisers while making other, more public,

Photo courtesy: Stock Montage, Inc.

■ In 1919, President Woodrow Wilson had what many believed to be a nervous collapse in the summer and a debilitating stroke in the fall that incapacitated him for several months. His wife, Edith Bolling Galt Wilson, refused to admit his advisers to his sickroom, and rumors flew about the "First Lady President," as many suspected it was his wife and not Wilson who was issuing the orders.

significant contributions to American society. Until recently, the only formal national recognition given to first ladies was an exhibit of inaugural ball gowns at the Smithsonian Institution. In 1992, in keeping with increased recognition of the many roles of first ladies, the Smithsonian launched an exhibit that highlighted the personal accomplishments of first ladies. This 1992 exhibit was built around three themes: (1) the political role of the first ladies, including how they were portrayed in the media and perceived by the public; (2) their contributions to society, especially their personal causes; and, (3) still, of course, their inaugural gowns.

Hillary Rodham Clinton was not the first first lady who worked for or with her husband. Abigail Adams was a constant sounding board for her husband, John. An early feminist, as early as 1776 she cautioned him "to Remember the Ladies" in any new code of laws. Edith Bolling Galt Wilson was probably the most powerful first lady. When Woodrow Wilson collapsed and was left partly paralyzed in 1919, she became his surrogate and decided whom and what the stricken president saw. Her detractors dubbed her "Acting First Man."

Eleanor Roosevelt also played a powerful and much criticized role in national affairs. Not only did she write a nationally syndicated daily newspaper column, but she traveled and lectured widely, worked tirelessly on thankless Democratic Party matters, and raised six children. After FDR's death, she shone in her own right as U.S. delegate to the United Nations, where she headed the commission that drafted the covenant on human rights. Later, she headed John F. Kennedy's Commission on the Status of Women. Rosalyn Carter also took an activist role by attending Cabinet meetings and traveling to Latin America as her husband's policy representative.

Initially, Laura Bush, a former librarian, seemed to be following the path of her mother-in-law, former First Lady Barbara Bush. She adopted a behind-the-scenes role and made literacy the focus of her activities. In the aftermath of the tragedy of 9/11, the first lady immediately took on a more public role. She gave the president's weekly radio address, highlighting the status of women in Afghanistan under the oppressive Taliban regime, and then continued to speak out, calling for improvements in the legal status of women. She even went to the United Nations to call for international support for women under the Taliban. She also took to the campaign trail in 2002 and 2004, very effectively fund-raising on behalf of Republican candidates, including her husband.

The Executive Office of the President (EOP)

Executive Office of the President (EOP)
Establishment created in 1939 to help the president oversee the executive branch bureaucracy.

The **Executive Office of the President (EOP)** was established by FDR in 1939 to oversee his New Deal programs. It was created to provide the president with a general staff to help him direct the diverse activities of the executive branch. In fact, it is a mini-bureaucracy of several advisers and offices located in the ornate Executive Office Building next to the White House on Pennsylvania Avenue, as well as in the White House itself, where the president's closest advisers often are located.

The EOP has expanded over time to include several advisory and policy-making agencies and task forces. Over time, the units of the EOP have become the prime policy makers in their fields of expertise as they play key roles in advancing the president's policy preferences. Among the EOP's most important members are the National Security Council, the Council of Economic Advisers, the Office of Management and Budget, the Office of the Vice President, and the U.S. Trade Representative.

The National Security Council (NSC) was established in 1947 to advise the president on American military affairs and foreign policy. The NSC is composed of the president, the vice president, and the secretaries of state and defense. The chair of the

Joint Chiefs of Staff and the director of the Central Intelligence Agency also participate. Others such as the White House chief of staff and the general counsel may attend. The national security adviser runs the staff of the NSC, coordinates information and options, and advises the president.

Although the president appoints the members of each of these bodies, they must perform their tasks in accordance with congressional legislation. As with the Cabinet, depending on who serves in key positions, these mini-agencies may not be truly responsible to the president.

Presidents can give clear indications of their policy preferences by the kinds of offices they include in the EOP. President George W. Bush, for example, not only moved or consolidated several offices when he became president in 2001, but he quickly sought to create a new Office of Faith-Based and Community Initiatives to help him achieve his goal of greater religious involvement in matters of domestic policy.

The White House Staff

Often more directly responsible to the president are the members of the White House staff: the personal assistants to the president, including senior aides, their deputies, assistants with professional duties, and clerical and administrative aides. As personal assistants, these advisers are not subject to Senate confirmation, nor do they have divided loyalties. Their power is derived from their personal relationship to the president, and they have no independent legal authority.

Although presidents organize the White House staff in different ways, they typically have a chief of staff whose job is to facilitate the smooth running of the staff and the executive branch of government. Successful chiefs of staff also have protected the president from mistakes and helped implement policies to obtain the maximum political advantage for the president. Other key White House aides include those who help plan domestic policy, maintain relations with Congress and interest groups, deal with the media, provide economic expertise, and execute political strategies.

As presidents have tried to consolidate power in the White House, and as public demands on the president have grown, the size of the White House staff has increased—from fifty-one in 1943, to 247 in 1953, to a high of 583 in 1972. Since that time, staffs have been trimmed, generally running around 500. During his 1992 presidential campaign, Bill Clinton promised to cut the size of the White House staff and that of the Executive Office of the President, and eventually he reduced the size of his staff by approximately 15 percent. The current White House has fewer than 400 staffers.

Although White House staffers prefer to be located in the White House in spite of its small offices, many staffers are relegated to the old Executive Office Building next door because White House office space is limited. In Washington, the size of the office is not the measure of power that it often is in corporations. Instead, power in the White House goes to those who have the president's ear and the offices closest to the Oval Office.

THE PRESIDENT AS POLICY MAKER

WHEN FDR SENT HIS first legislative package to Congress, he broke the traditional model of law-making.[21] As envisioned by the Framers, it was to be Congress that made the laws. Now FDR was claiming a leadership role for the president in the legislative process. Said the president of this new relationship: "It is the duty of the President to propose and it is the privilege of the Congress to dispose."[22] With those words and the actions that followed, FDR shifted the presidency into a law- and policy-maker role. Now the president and the executive branch not only executed the laws but generally suggested them, too.

Photo courtesy: Bettmann/CORBIS

■ President Lyndon B. Johnson signs the long awaited Civil Rights Act of 1964. Immediately to his right is Senator Edward Brooke (R–MA), the first African American to be popularly elected as a U.S. senator. On his left is Senator Walter Mondale (D–MN), who later served as vice president. Next to Mondale is Thurgood Marshall, who Johnson later appointed to the U.S. Supreme Court, where he became its first African American member.

The President's Role in Proposing and Facilitating Legislation

From FDR's presidency to the Republican-controlled 104th Congress, the public looked routinely to the president to formulate concrete legislative plans to propose to Congress, which subsequently adopted, modified, or rejected his plans for the nation. Then, in 1994, it appeared for a while that the electorate wanted Congress to reassert itself in the legislative process. In fact, the Contract with America was a Republican call for Congress to take the reins of the law-making process. But several Republican Congresses failed to pass many of the items of the contract, and President Bill Clinton's continued forceful presence in the budgetary process made a resurgent role for Congress largely illusory. The same scenario holds true for President George W. Bush.

Modern presidents continue to play a major role in setting the legislative agenda, especially in an era when the House and Senate are narrowly divided along partisan lines. Without working majorities, "merely placing a program before Congress is not enough," as President Lyndon B. Johnson (LBJ) once explained. "Without constant attention from the administration, most legislation moves through the congressional process at the speed of a glacier."[23] Thus, the president's most important power (and often the source of his greatest frustration), in addition to support of the public, is his ability to construct coalitions within Congress that will work for passage of his legislation. FDR and LBJ were among the best presidents at working Congress, but they were helped by Democratic majorities in both houses of Congress.[24]

On the whole, presidents have a hard time getting Congress to pass their programs.[25] Passage is especially difficult if the president presides over a divided government, which occurs when the presidency and Congress are controlled by different political parties (see chapter 7). Recent research by political scientists, however, shows that presidents are much more likely to win on bills central to their announced agendas, such as President George W. Bush's victory on the Iraq war resolution, than to secure passage of legislation proposed by others.[26]

Because presidents generally experience declining support for policies they advocate throughout their terms, it is important that a president propose key plans early in his administration, during the honeymoon period, a time when the goodwill toward the president often allows a president to secure passage of legislation that he would not be able to gain at a later period. Even President Lyndon B. Johnson, who was able to get nearly 60 percent of his programs through Congress, noted: "You've got to give it all you can, that first year . . . before they start worrying about themselves. . . . You can't put anything through when half the Congress is thinking how to beat you."[27]

Presidents can also use **patronage** (jobs, grants, or other special favors that are given as rewards to friends and political allies for their support) and personal rewards to win support. Invitations to the White House and campaign visits to the home districts of members of Congress running for office are two ways to curry favor with legislators, and inattention to key members can prove deadly to a president's legislative program. Former Speaker of the House Tip O'Neill (D–MA) reportedly was quite irritated when the Carter transition team refused O'Neill's request for extra tickets to Jimmy Carter's inaugural. This incident did not exactly get the president off to a good start with the powerful speaker.

Another way a president can bolster support for his legislative package is to call on his political party. As the informal leader of his party, he should be able to use that position to his advantage in Congress, where party loyalty is very important. This strategy works best when the president has carried members of his party into office on his coattails, as was the case in the Johnson and Reagan landslides of 1964 and 1984, respectively. In fact, many scholars regard President Lyndon B. Johnson as the most effective legislative leader.[28] Not only had he served in the House and as Senate majority leader, but he also enjoyed a comfortable Democratic Party majority in Congress, and many Democrats owed their victories to President Johnson's landslide win over his Republican challenger, Senator Barry Goldwater (R–AZ).[29]

patronage
Jobs, grants, or other special favors that are given as rewards to friends and political allies for their support.

Photo courtesy: J. Scott Applewhite/AP/Wide World Photos

■ President Bill Clinton and Vice President Al Gore celebrate the first balanced budget in years, a feat not likely to be repeated soon in light of the federal tax cuts and huge spending increases under the next president, George W. Bush. In January 2005 the White House announced that the federal budget deficit was expected to rise to $427 billion, a figure including a new request from President Bush to help pay for the war in Iraq.

The Budgetary Process and Legislative Implementation

Closely associated with a president's ability to pass legislation is his ability to secure funding for new and existing programs. A president sets national policy and priorities through his budget proposals and his continued insistence on their congressional passage. The budget proposal not only outlines the programs he wants but indicates the importance of each program by the amount of funding requested for each and for its associated agency or department.

Because the Framers gave Congress the power of the purse, Congress had primary responsibility for the budget process until 1930. The economic disaster set off by the stock market crash of 1929, however, gave FDR, once elected in 1932, the opportunity to assert himself in the congressional budgetary process, just as he inserted himself into the legislative process. In 1939, the Bureau of the Budget, which had been created in 1921 to help the president tell Congress how much money it would take to run the executive branch of government, was made part of the newly created Executive Office of the President. In 1970, President Nixon changed its name to the **Office of Management and Budget (OMB)** to clarify its function in the executive branch.

The OMB works exclusively for the president and employs hundreds of budget and policy experts. Key OMB responsibilities include preparing the president's annual budget proposal, designing the president's program, and reviewing the progress, budget, and program proposals of the executive department agencies. It also supplies economic forecasts to the president and conducts detailed analyses of proposed bills and agency rules. OMB reports allow the president to attach price tags to his legislative proposals and defend the presidential budget. The OMB budget is a huge document, and even those who prepare it have a hard time deciphering all of its provisions. Even so, the expertise of the OMB directors often gives them an advantage over members of Congress.

Policy Making Through Regulation

Proposing legislation and using the budget to advance policy priorities are not the only ways that presidents can affect the policy process, especially in times of highly divided government. Executive orders offer the president an opportunity to make policy without legislative approval. Major policy changes have been made when a president has issued an **executive order,** a rule or regulation issued by the president that has the effect of law. While many executive orders are issued to help clarify or implement legislation enacted by Congress, other executive orders have the effect of making new policy. President Harry S Truman ordered an end to segregation in the military through an executive order, and affirmative action was institutionalized as national policy through Executive Order 11246, issued by Lyndon B. Johnson in 1966.

Executive orders have been used since the 1980s to set national policies toward abortion. President Ronald Reagan, for example, used an executive order to stop federal funding of fetal tissue research and to end federal funding of any groups providing abortion counseling. President Bill Clinton immediately rescinded those orders when he became president. One of President George W. Bush's first acts upon taking office was to reverse those Clinton orders.

Like presidents before him, George W. Bush has used executive orders to put his policy stamp on a wide array of important issues. After much soul searching, for example, he signed an executive order limiting federal funding of stem cell research to the sixty or so cell lines currently in the possession of scientific researchers.[30] An executive order also was used to allow military tribunals to try any foreigners captured by U.S. forces in Afghanistan or linked to the terrorist acts of 9/11. One of President George W. Bush's more controversial executive orders eviscerated the 1978 Presidential Records Act. This act was written after the Watergate scandal and "established that the records of presidents belong to the American people."[31] Now, not only do former vice presidents as well as former presi-

Office of Management and Budget (OMB)
The office that prepares the president's annual budget proposal, reviews the budget and programs of the executive departments, supplies economic forecasts, and conducts detailed analyses of proposed bills and agency rules.

executive order
A rule or regulation issued by the president that has the effect of law. All executive orders must be published in the Federal Register.

Timeline

"With the Stroke of a Pen": The Executive Order over Time

THE PRESIDENT AS POLICY MAKER: TURNING THE RECOMMENDATIONS OF THE 9/11 COMMISSION INTO LAW

On July 22, 2004, the bipartisan National Commission on Terrorist Attacks Upon the United States (better known as the 9/11 Commission) released its "Final Report" to the public. The report became an immediate best seller, winning praise for its clarity and vision. In their most ambitious recommendation, the ten members of the commission, led by Chair Thomas H. Kean, a former Republican governor of New Jersey, and Vice Chair Lee Hamilton, a former Democratic member of the House of Representatives from Indiana, called for a complete overhaul of the U.S. intelligence community. Through their recommendations, the commission sought to create greater responsibility, accountability, and unity among the nation's fifteen intelligence agencies—goals that they deemed essential to improving the nation's ability to gather, share, analyze, and act on intelligence information. To carry this message to the nation, the ten commission members also took the unusual step of creating the 9/11 Public Discourse Project and traveled around the country to explain and promote the findings and recommendations of the commission.

President George W. Bush initially opposed the creation of the 9/11 Commission. Nonetheless, Congress created the commission in November 2002. Although the administration generally cooperated with the commission, it also resisted or constrained elements of the commission's investigation. In the end, however, the administration provided critical information to the commission, including direct testimony by President Bush, Vice President Dick Cheney, and then National Security Advisor Condoleezza Rice.

Key figures in both political parties, such as Senators John F. Kerry (D–MA) and John McCain (R–AZ) and House Minority Leader Nancy Pelosi (D–CA) urged Congress and the president to turn all forty-one recommendations in the final report into law as quickly as possible. In late August 2004, President Bush demonstrated his support for the recommendations by signing several executive orders that temporarily would give the director of central intelligence greater authority over all fifteen national intelligence agencies and implement other commission recommendations in anticipation of Congress passing new legislation. In early October, the Senate overwhelmingly passed a reform bill, but the Republican leadership in the House of Representatives believed that they should take more time to review the report and apply their own expertise to craft the reforms.

Several powerful members of the House contested the commission's recommendation to transfer control over the bulk of the $40 billion annual national intelligence budget, particularly that of the National Security Agency, the National Geospatial-Intelligence Agency, and the National

Reconnaissance Office, away from the Department of Defense and House Armed Services Committee, to a new director of national intelligence, who would report directly to the president, and the House Intelligence Committee. Other House Republicans also wanted more restrictions on immigration and expanded powers for law enforcement agencies to counter terrorism. Consequently, Republican leaders had to block a vote on the bill in November 2004 when it could not muster a majority of Republican House members to support the reforms, even after President Bush called Senate leaders to help work out a compromise. If the deadlock continued, the first major piece of legislation endorsed by the president after his reelection would go down to defeat.

After several more weeks of intense discussions, however, President Bush brokered a compromise deal with Republican House leaders in early December 2004 that left control over intelligence-gathering satellites and reconnaissance aircraft in the hands of the Department of Defense . The White House suggested new language regarding Department of Defense control over some intelligence resources, President Bush called on Congress to pass the bill in his weekly radio talk to the nation, while Vice President Cheney phoned several reluctant House Republicans to get their support for the legislation.[a] Finally, on December 7, 2004—the last working day of the 108th session of Congress—the House passed the compromise measure, which the Senate approved the following day and President Bush signed into law. "Some people, including me, were not sure which side of this he [President Bush] was on in the early stages, or whether he might be on both sides of this," noted the senior Democratic member of the House Intelligence Committee, Jane Harmon (D–CA), then "it turned out, in the later weeks, that he and his White House staff were all over this and really helped bring this across the finish line."[b]

Questions

1. Generally, presidents enjoy their greatest success rates right after their election or reelection. Why do you think that passage of this legislation proved so difficult?
2. In legislation directly affecting the structure of the executive branch, as well as lines of authority to the president, how much weight should Congress pay to the president's recommendations?

[a] Charles Babington, "House Approves Intelligence Bill," *Washington Post* (December 8, 2004) A1, A4.

[b] James Kuhnhenn, "House OK's Intelligence Overhaul Bill," *Miami Herald* (December 8, 2004) http://www.miami.com/mld/miamiherald/news/.

Photo courtesy: Michael Okoniewski/Getty Images

■ A campaigning George W. Bush seeks the support of a local Police Benevolent Association.

dents have veto power, but scholars, journalists, and other interested persons must demonstrate a specific "need to know" when requesting presidential or vice presidential documents.[32] For whatever reason the order was issued, it demonstrates how easily presidents may thwart the wishes of Congress and substitute their own policy preferences through executive orders, which require congressional action to make them unenforceable.

PRESIDENTIAL LEADERSHIP AND THE IMPORTANCE OF PUBLIC OPINION

A PRESIDENT'S ABILITY to get his programs adopted or implemented depends on many factors, including his leadership abilities, his personality and powers of persuasion, his ability to mobilize public opinion to support his actions, and the public's perception of his performance.

Presidential Leadership

Leadership is not an easy thing to exercise, and it remains an elusive concept for scholars to identify and measure, but it is important to all presidents seeking support for their programs and policies. Moreover, ideas about the importance of effective leaders have deep roots in our political culture. The leadership abilities of the great presidents—Washington, Jefferson, Lincoln, and FDR—have been extolled over and over again, leading us to fault modern presidents who fail to cloak themselves in the armor of leadership. Americans thus have come to believe that "If presidential leadership works some of the time, why not all of the time?"[33] This attitude, in turn, directly influences what we expect presidents to do and how we evaluate them (see Analyzing Visuals: Barber's Presidential

■ Most pundits as well as the public agree that President George W. Bush grew into his office in the aftermath of 9/11.

Photo courtesy: Rick McKee/Augusta Chronicle

Analyzing Visuals

BARBER'S PRESIDENTIAL PERSONALITIES

Does presidential character, which political scientist James David Barber defines as the "way the president orients himself toward life," seriously affect how a president handles his job? In an approach to analyzing and predicting presidential behavior criticized and rejected by many other political scientists, Barber has suggested that patterns of behavior, many that may be ingrained during childhood, exist and can help explain presidential behavior.

Barber believes that there are four presidential character types, based on energy level (whether the president is active or passive) and the degree of enjoyment a president finds in the job (whether the president has a positive or negative attitude). Barber believes that active and positive presidents are more successful than passive and negative presidents. Active-positive presidents, he argues, generally enjoyed warm and supportive childhood environments and are basically happy individuals open to new life experiences. They approach the presidency with a characteristic zest for life and have a drive to lead and succeed. In contrast, passive-negative presidents find themselves reacting to circumstances, are likely to take directions from others, and fail to make full use of the enormous resources of the executive office.

The table classifies presidents from Taft through George Bush according to Barber's categories. After reviewing the table, answer the following critical thinking questions based on your understanding of the president's

	Active	Passive
Positive	F. Roosevelt	Taft
	Truman	Harding
	Kennedy	Reagan
	Ford	
	Carter[a]	
	Bush	
Negative	Wilson	Coolidge
	Hoover	Eisenhower
	L. Johnson	
	Nixon	

[a]Some scholars think that Carter better fits the active-negative typology.

Source: James David Barber, *The Presidential Character: Predicting Performance in the White House,* 4th ed. (Englewood Cliffs, NJ: Prentice Hall, 1992).

performance in office: Would you consider Jimmy Carter, whom Barber considers an active-positive character type, a successful president? Why might some of the highest-rated presidents have character flaws? What actions or policy failures are associated with the four active-negative presidents? What factors in addition to personality could influence presidential behavior? How would you classify President Bill Clinton? President George W. Bush?

Source: James David Barber, *The Presidential Character: Predicting Performance in the White House,* 4th ed. (Englewood Cliffs, NJ: Prentice Hall, 1992).

Personalities). Research by political scientists shows that presidents can exercise leadership by increasing public attention to particular issues. Analyses of presidential State of the Union Addresses, for example, reveal that mentions of particular policies translate into more Americans mentioning those policies as the most important problems facing the nation.[34]

The presidency often transforms its occupants. There is an old adage that great crises make great presidents. President Franklin D. Roosevelt's handling of the Great Depression solidified his place in American history, as did Abraham Lincoln's handling of the Civil War. Many critics argue that 9/11, transformed George W. Bush's presidency to the degree that commentators refer to the pre- and post-9/11 president.[35] President Bush not only cast himself as the strong leader of the United States but portrayed himself as the worldwide leader in the war against terrorism, transforming himself from the candidate who disavowed interest in or much knowledge of international affairs. His newfound self-confidence was what Americans look for in a time of crisis.

Frequently, the difference between great and mediocre presidents centers on their ability to grasp the importance of leadership style. Truly great presidents, such as Abraham Lincoln and Franklin D. Roosevelt, understood that the White House was a seat of power from which decisions could flow to shape the national destiny. They recognized that their day-to-day activities and how they went about them

Comparative

Comparing Chief
Executives

should be designed to bolster support for their policies and to secure congressional and popular backing that could translate their intuitive judgment into meaningful action. Mediocre presidents, on the other hand, have tended to regard the White House as "a stage for the presentation of performances to the public" or a fitting honor to cap a career.[36]

Presidential Personality and the Power to Persuade

In trying to lead against long odds, a president must not only exercise the constitutional powers of the chief executive but also persuade enough of the country that his actions are the right ones so that he can carry them out without national strife.[37] A president's personality and ability to persuade others are key to amassing greater power and authority. The power to persuade is the president's ability to gain the support of members of Congress, the public, and even foreign leaders, and thus to set the national agenda. Persuasion is key, political scientist Richard E. Neustadt says, because constitutional powers alone don't provide modern presidents with the authority to meet rising public expectations.[38]

Going Public: Mobilizing Public Opinion

On average, President Bill Clinton spoke to the public in a variety of venues about 550 times a year. President Ronald Reagan, often remembered as a master of public relations and the media, averaged 320 appearances a year; the folksy President Harry S Truman, only 88 times a year.[39] What's the difference? The postmodern president has to try to govern amid the din of several competing twenty-four-hour news channels and an Internet news cycle that makes events of an hour ago old news. This rapid change provides presidents with rare opportunities while at the same time representing daunting challenges.

Historically, even before the days of radio and television, presidents tried to reach out to the public to gain support for their programs through what President Theodore Roosevelt called the bully pulpit. The development of commercial air travel and radio, newsreels, television, and communication satellites have made direct communication to larger numbers of voters easier. Presidents, first ladies, and other presidential advisers travel all over the world to expand their views and to build personal support as well as support for administration programs.

Direct, presidential appeals to the electorate like those often made by recent presidents are referred to as "going public."[40] Going public means that a president goes over the heads of members of Congress to gain support from the people, who can then place pressure on their elected officials in Washington.

Like most presidents, Bill Clinton was keenly aware of the importance of maintaining his connection with the public. Beginning with his 1992 campaign, Clinton often appeared on *Larry King Live* on CNN. Even after becoming president, Clinton continued to take his case directly to the people. He launched his health care reform proposals, for example, on a prime-time edition of *Nightline* hosted by Ted Koppel. For an hour and a half, the president took audience questions about his health plan, impressing even those who doubted the plan with his impressive grasp of details. Moreover, at a black-tie dinner honoring radio and television correspondents, Clinton responded to criticisms leveled against him for not holding traditional press conferences by pointing out how clever he was to ignore the traditional press. "You know why I can stiff you on the press conferences? Because Larry King liberated me from you by giving me to the American people directly," quipped Clinton.[41] George W. Bush continued in the Clinton tradition of rarely holding press conferences

■ President George W. Bush with former baseball great Cal Ripken and a former member of the original Girls Professional Baseball League (dramatized in the film *A League of Their Own*) at a T-Ball game on the white house lawn.

Photo courtesy: Karen O'Connor

Global Perspective

IN THE PUBLIC EYE: PRIME MINISTERS AND PRESIDENTS

Many Americans might find the parliamentary system of government strange. Historically, however, new democratic regimes have had two models to choose from: the American presidential system and the British parliamentary system. (The proportion of nations adopting each type is revealed in the figure.) The American system is based on a Constitution that was the product of political creativity and compromise more than two hundred years ago. The U.S. Constitution survives essentially intact, although changes in the way various players interpret its provisions have resulted in dramatic shifts in the balance of power between the legislative and executive branches of government in Washington, D.C., and between the federal government and the states.

In contrast, the British system has no written constitution but is the product of a long series of agreements between the monarchy, feudal lords, the business class, trade unions, and other segments of British society, going back to the thirteenth century. The one principle that has guided British constitutional law for the past two or three centuries is "parliamentary sovereignty"—that is, that the House of Commons (and to an increasingly lesser extent, the House of Lords) governs Britain. The leadership of the House of Commons is determined by the majority party (or coalition of several parties). The British Cabinet is made up of members of Parliament (MPs) who have typically served many terms and have demonstrated their party loyalty. Led by the prime minister, who serves as the head of government, they administer each of the departments in Britain.

Because prime ministers are selected by their respective parties, most of these leaders have considerable experience and moderate temperament (with a few flamboyant exceptions). Their job security depends on making sure their party remains in the majority, and so they tend to work closely with party regulars. Leaders such as John Major of the United Kingdom and John Howard of Australia are typical in their rather cautious approach to public life. Major's predecessor, Margaret Thatcher, however, ended up alienating both the British public and the Conservative Party leadership, which voted her out of her position as head of the party, and thereby removed her as prime minister without a direct election.

Most democratic systems in the developing world have adopted the presidential system. In many instances this is a result of American influence, whereas in others it represents a concession to those who support authoritarianism rather than democracy. The separate election of a president means that his or her political support is dependent not on the legislature, but instead on personal popularity with the masses. The result is that presidential systems often produce more charismatic and independent personalities, such as populist leaders Hugo Chavez, who became the president of Venezuela in 1998, and Lula da Silva, who became the president of Brazil in 2002.

Questions

1. Does the American style of selecting leaders predispose it to picking certain types of presidents? Are they populist and flamboyant? Are they independent from political parties? Are they seasoned and experienced in national leadership?
2. What aspects of the British parliamentary system might be better than those of the U.S. presidential system?

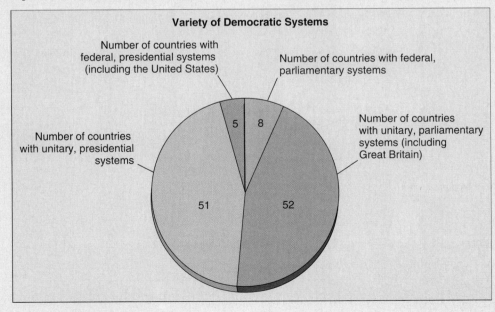

Variety of Democratic Systems

Number of countries with federal, presidential systems (including the United States): 5

Number of countries with federal, parliamentary systems: 8

Number of countries with unitary, presidential systems: 51

Number of countries with unitary, parliamentary systems (including Great Britain): 52

Analyzing Visuals

PRESIDENTIAL APPROVAL RATINGS SINCE 1938

Presidential approval ratings traditionally have followed a cyclical pattern. Presidents generally have enjoyed their highest ratings at the beginning of their terms and experienced lower ratings toward the end. Presidents George Bush, Bill Clinton, and George W. Bush, however, enjoyed popularity surges during the course of their terms. Despite the Monica Lewinsky crisis and the threat of impeachment, Clinton's approval ratings continued to rise in 1998 and 1999. They peaked at 73 percent at the end of 1998—the highest rating of his administration. Clinton left office with

a 66 percent approval rating. Similarly, President George W. Bush got a spectacular and sustained boost after 9/11.

After viewing the line graph of presidential approval scores and reading the related chapter material, answer the following critical thinking questions about presidential approval: What types of events (domestic or international) tend to boost presidential approval? Why do you think that the cyclical pattern of presidential approval exists? What do you think enabled George W. Bush to sustain his high approval rating for a relatively long period after the 9/11 terrorist attacks?

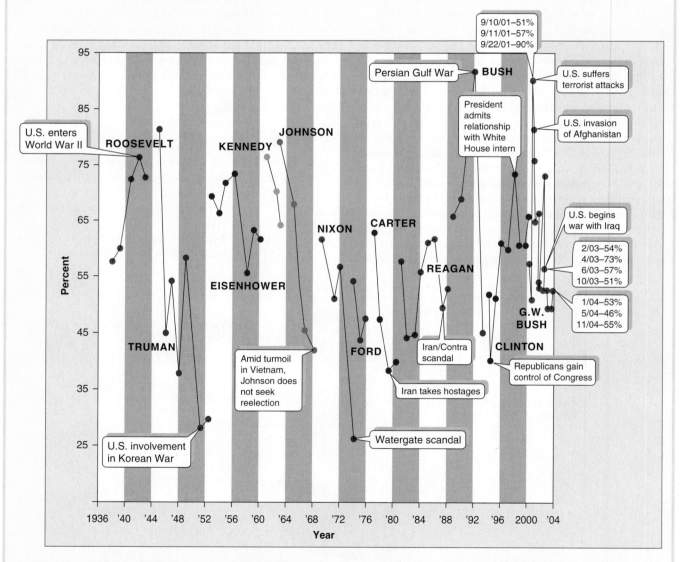

Sources: USA Today (August 14, 2000): 6A. ©2000, USA Today. Reprinted by permission. "President Bush: Job Ratings," and CNN/USA Today/Gallup Poll,. PollingReport.com., 2002,. accessed November 10, 2002, http://www.pollingreport.com/BushJob.htm. Updated by author.

yet trying to go directly to the people. He chose, for example, to give important speeches on the ongoing war in Iraq before receptive audiences, including ones at the National War College and the U.S. Air Force Academy.

The Public's Perception of Presidential Performance

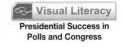

Visual Literacy
Presidential Success in Polls and Congress

Historically, a president has the best chances of convincing Congress to follow his policy lead when his public opinion ratings are high. Presidential popularity, however, generally follows a cyclical pattern. These cycles have been recorded since 1938, when pollsters first began to track presidential popularity.

Typically, as shown in Analyzing Visuals: Presidential Approval Ratings Since 1938, presidents enjoy their highest level of public approval at the beginning of their terms and try to take advantage of this honeymoon period to get their programs passed by Congress as soon as possible. Each action a president takes, however, is divisive—some people will approve, and others will disapprove. Disapproval tends to have a cumulative effect. Inevitably, as a general rule, a president's popularity wanes, although Bill Clinton, who ended with a higher approval rating than any president in recent history, was a notable exception.

Since Lyndon B. Johnson's presidency, only four presidents have left office with approval ratings of more than 50 percent. (See Analyzing Visuals: Presidential Approval Ratings Since 1938.) Many credit this trend to events such as Vietnam, Watergate, the Iran hostage crisis, the Iran-Contra scandal, and the Iraq War, which have made the public increasingly skeptical of presidential performance. Presidents George Bush, Bill Clinton, and George W. Bush, however, experienced increases in their presidential performance scores during the course of their presidencies.

President George Bush's rapid rise in popularity occurred after the major and, perhaps more important, quick victory in the 1991 Persian Gulf War. His popularity, however, plummeted as the good feelings faded and Americans began to feel the pinch of recession. In contrast, President Bill Clinton's approval scores skyrocketed after the 1996 Democratic National Convention. More interestingly, Clinton's high approval ratings continued in the wake of allegations of wrongdoing in the Oval Office, his eventual admission of inappropriate conduct, and through his impeachment proceedings. In fact, when Clinton went to the American public and admitted that he misled them about his relationship with Monica Lewinsky, an ABC poll conducted immediately after his speech showed a 10-point jump in his job approval rating.[42]

Most presidents experience surges in popularity after major international events, but they generally don't last long. Each of the last twelve presidents has experienced at least one "rallying" point based on a foreign event. Before President George W. Bush, rallies lasted an average of ten weeks, with the longest being seven months.[43] These popularity surges allow presidents to make some policy decisions that they believe are for the good of the nation, even though the policies are unpopular with the public.

SUMMARY

BECAUSE THE FRAMERS FEARED a tyrannical monarch, they gave considerable thought to the office of the chief executive. Since ratification of the Constitution, the office has changed considerably—more through practice and need than from changes in the Constitution. In chronicling these changes, we have made the following points:

1. The Roots of and Rules Governing the Office of President of the United States

Distrust of a too powerful leader led the Framers to create an executive office with limited powers. They mandated that a president be at least thirty-five years old, a natural-born citizen, and a resident of the United States for at least fourteen years, and they opted not to limit the president's term of office. To further guard against tyranny, they made provisions for the removal of the president.

2. **The Constitutional Powers of the President**

The Framers gave the president a variety of specific constitutional powers in Article II, including the appointment power, the power to convene Congress, and the power to make treaties. In addition, the president derives considerable power from being commander in chief of the military. The Constitution also gives the president the power to grant pardons and to veto acts of Congress.

3. **The Development and Expansion of Presidential Power**

The development of presidential power has depended on the personal force of those who have held the office. George Washington, in particular, took several actions to establish the primacy of the president in national affairs and as true chief executive of a strong national government. But, with only a few exceptions, subsequent presidents often let Congress dominate in national affairs. With the election of FDR, however, the power of the president increased, and presidential decision making became more important in national and foreign affairs.

4. **The Presidential Establishment**

As the responsibilities of the president have grown, so has the executive branch of government. FDR established the Executive Office of the President to help him govern. Perhaps the most key policy advisers are those closest to the president: the vice president, the White House staff, some members of the Executive Office of the President, and sometimes, the first lady.

5. **The President as Policy Maker**

Since FDR, the public has looked to the president to propose legislation to Congress. Through proposing legislation, advancing budgets, and involvement in the regulatory process, presidents make policy.

6. **Presidential Leadership and the Importance of Public Opinion**

To gain support for his programs or proposed budget, the president uses a variety of skills, including personal leadership, patronage, persuasion, and direct appeals to the public. How the president goes about winning support is determined by his leadership and personal style, affected by his character and his ability to persuade. Since the 1970s, however, the American public has been increasingly skeptical of presidential actions, and few presidents have enjoyed extended periods of the kind of popularity needed to help win support for programmatic change.

KEY TERMS

Cabinet, p. 285
executive agreement, p. 286
Executive Office of the President (EOP), p. 294
executive order, p. 302
executive privilege, p. 282
impeachment, p. 281
inherent powers, p. 292
line-item veto, p. 288
New Deal, p. 294
Office of Management and Budget (OMB), p. 301
pardon, p. 289
patronage, p. 301
Twenty-Fifth Amendment, p. 282
Twenty-Second Amendment, p. 280
U.S. v. Nixon (1974), p. 282
veto power, p. 286
War Powers Act, p. 289

SELECTED READINGS

Barber, James David. *The Presidential Character: Predicting Presidential Performance in the White House,* 4th ed. Englewood Cliffs, NJ: Prentice Hall, 1992.

Campbell, Karlyn Kohr, and Kathleen Hall Jamieson. *Deeds Done in Words: Presidential Rhetoric and the Genres of Governance.* Chicago: University of Chicago Press, 1990.

Cooper, Philip J. *By Order of the President: The Use and Abuse of Executive Direct Action.* Lawrence: University Press of Kansas, 2002.

Dallek, Robert. *Hail to the Chief: The Making and Unmaking of American Presidents.* New York: Oxford University Press, 2001.

Daynes, Byron W., and Glen Sussman. *The American Presidency and the Social Agenda.* Upper Saddle River, NJ: Prentice Hall, 2001.

Edwards, George C., III, and Stephen J. Wayne. *Presidential Leadership: Politics and Policy Making,* 6th ed. New York: Bedford Books, 2002.

Greenstein, Fred I. *The Presidential Difference: Leadership Style from FDR to George W. Bush,* 2nd ed. Princeton, NJ: Princeton University Press, 2004.

Kellerman, Barbara. *The Political Presidency: Practice of Leadership from Kennedy Through Reagan.* New York: Oxford University Press, 1997.

Martin, Janet M. *The American Presidency and Women: Promise, Performance, and Illusion.* College Station: Texas A&M Press, 2003.

Neustadt, Richard E. *Presidential Power and the Modern Presidents.* New York: Free Press, 1991.

Pfiffner, James P. *Modern Presidency.* Belmont, CA: Wadsworth, 2000.

Ragsdale, Lyn. *Vital Statistics on the Presidency: Washington to Clinton.* Washington, DC: CQ Press, 1998.

Rossiter, Clinton. *The American Presidency.* Baltimore, MD: Johns Hopkins University Press, 1987.

Skowronek, Stephen. *The Politics Presidents Make: Leadership from John Adams to Bill Clinton.* Cambridge, MA: Harvard University Press, 1997.

Walcott, Charles E., and Karen Hult. *Governing the White House.* Lawrence: University Press of Kansas, 1995.

Warshaw, Shirley Anne. *The Keys to Power: Managing the Presidency,* 2nd ed. New York: Longman, 2004.

WEB EXPLORATIONS

To learn more about specific presidents, see
http://www.nara.gov/nara/president/address.html

For a chronology of the Clinton impeachment proceedings, see
http://www.washintonpost.com/wp-srv/politics/special/clinton/timeline.htm

For more on the vice president, see
http://www.whitehouse.gov/vicepresident/

To learn more about presidential pardons, go to
http://jurist.law.pitt.edu/pardons0a.htm

For more on the modern White House, see
http://www.whitehouse.gov/

For more on first ladies, see
www.firstladies.org/

To try your hand at balancing the budget, go to
http://www.nathannewman.org/nbs/

For more details on Watergate, see
http://watergate.info/

For more on the White House Project, see
http://www.thewhitehouseproject.org/

Photo courtesy: Charles Dharapak/AP/Wide World Photos

The Executive Branch and the Federal Bureaucracy

FREQUENTLY, CRITICS OF THE BUREAUCRACY ARGUE that the maze of administrative regulations, rules, and procedures makes it difficult for individual citizens to obtain government services, from student loans to drivers' licenses. One bureaucrat might tell you to do X; another one will tell you to do Y—after you have stood in the wrong line for an hour or two. But, it is unusual for a major actor in the bureaucracy not to know what other actors are doing.

However, the major governmental reorganization that occurred in the wake of the September 11, 2001, terrorist attacks has caused a number of conflicts over departmental responsibilities. For example, as a part of the reorganization, Congress authorized the creation of a Department of Homeland Security. Under the Homeland Security Act of 2002, the department alone has the authority to issue threat warnings, with the cooperation of several agencies and the White House. These warnings are usually issued by the department's secretary; during President George W. Bush's first term, this post was filled by former Pennsylvania Governor Tom Ridge.

But, on May 27, 2004, Attorney General John Ashcroft and FBI Director Robert Mueller called a press conference to ask the public's help in capturing seven suspected terrorists within the United States. In that same press conference, they addressed an imminent terrorism threat to the United States. Both men concluded that a terrorist attack on the United States was likely in the next few months. News accounts quickly revealed that Secretary Ridge first heard about Ashcroft's and Mueller's concerns as he watched television along with millions of other Americans. In fact, earlier that day on several morning news shows, Ridge had downplayed any increased risks of terrorist attack.

Lawmakers, whose job it is to oversee the Department of Homeland Security, were irate and said that the comments made by Ashcroft and Mueller undermined efforts of the national government to assure its citizens of their safety. For example, Representative Christopher Cox (R–CA), who chairs the House Committee overseeing the Department of Homeland Security, remarked,

"The reason that Congress created the Department of Homeland Security is that we need to merge the various parts of government responsible for pieces of the war on terrorism into one coordinated effort."[1]

The White House was quick to call a meeting of all of the principals, who then issued a joint statement in an effort to clear the air of conflicting messages. But, to the general public, the issue was not one of conflicting messages. It underscored the common perception that the federal bureaucracy is rife with problems in spite of continued efforts to improve performance and communication that actually have succeeded in some areas.

bureaucracy
A set of complex hierarchical departments, agencies, commissions, and their staffs that exist to help a chief executive officer carry out his or her duties. Bureaucracies may be private organizations of governmental units.

THE FEDERAL BUREAUCRACY often is called the "fourth branch of government" because of the tremendous power that agencies and bureaus can exercise. Politicians often charge that the **bureaucracy,** the thousands of federal government agencies and institutions that implement and administer federal law and federal programs, is too large, too powerful, and too unaccountable to the people or even to elected officials. Many politicians, elected officials, and voters complain that the federal bureaucracy is too wasteful. Nevertheless, few critics discuss the fact that laws and policies also are implemented by state and local bureaucracies and bureaucrats whose numbers are proportionally far larger, and often far less efficient, than those working for the federal government.

Although many Americans are uncomfortable with the large role of the federal government in policy making, current studies show that most users of federal agencies rate quite favorably the agencies and the services they receive. Many of those polled by the Pew Research Center as part of its efforts to assess America's often seemingly conflicting views about the federal government and its services were frustrated by complicated rules and the slowness of a particular agency. Still, a majority gave most agencies overall high marks. Most of those polled drew sharp distinctions between particular agencies and the government as a whole, although the federal government, especially the executive branch, is largely composed of agencies, as we will discuss later in this chapter. For example, 84 percent of physicians and pharmacists rated the Food and Drug Administration favorably, whereas only one-half were positive about the government in general.[2] The survey also found that attitudes toward particular agencies were related to public support for their functions. Thus, the public, which views clean air and water as a national priority, was much more likely to rate the Environmental Protection Agency highly.

Harold D. Lasswell once defined political science as the "study of who gets what, when, and how."[3] It is by studying the bureaucracy that those questions can perhaps best be answered. To allow you to understand the role of the bureaucracy, this chapter explores the following issues:

1. First, we will examine *the executive branch and the development of the federal bureaucracy.*
2. Second, we will examine *the modern bureaucracy* by discussing bureaucrats and the formal organization of the bureaucracy.
3. Third, we will discuss *how the bureaucracy* works.
4. Finally, we will discuss *making agencies accountable.*

THE EXECUTIVE BRANCH AND THE DEVELOPMENT OF THE FEDERAL BUREAUCRACY

IN THE AMERICAN SYSTEM, the bureaucracy can be thought of as the part of the government that makes policy as it links together the three branches of the national government in the federal system. Although Congress makes the laws, it must rely on bureaucrats in the executive branch to enforce and implement them. Commissions such as the Equal Employment Opportunity Commission (EEOC), which is charged with enforcing federal anti-discrimination laws, have the power not only to make rules, but also to settle disputes between parties concerning the enforcement and implementation of those rules. Often, agency determinations are challenged in the courts. Because most administrative agencies that make up part of the bureaucracy enjoy reputations for special expertise in clearly defined policy areas, the federal judiciary routinely defers to bureaucratic administrative decision makers.

German sociologist Max Weber believed bureaucracies were a rational way for complex societies to organize themselves. Model bureaucracies, said Weber, are characterized by certain features, including:

Photo courtesy: NMR © Rob Crandall/The Image Works

1. A chain of command in which authority flows from top to bottom.

2. A division of labor whereby work is apportioned among specialized workers to increase productivity.

3. Clear lines of authority among workers and their superiors.

4. A goal orientation that determines structure, authority, and rules.

5. Impersonality, whereby all employees are treated fairly based on merit and all clients are served equally, without discrimination, according to established rules.

6. Productivity, whereby all work and actions are evaluated according to established rules.[4]

■ The Federal bureaucracy encompasses numerous agencies and institutions. Here, an employee of the Bureau of Engraving and Printing checks new U.S. dollar bills.

Clearly, this Weberian idea is somewhat idealistic, and even the best-run government agencies don't always work this way, but most are trying.

In 2005, the executive branch had approximately 1.8 million civilian employees employed directly by the president or his advisers or in independent agencies or commissions. The Department of Defense had an additional 2 million in the military. The Postal Service, which is a quasi-governmental corporation not part of the executive branch, has more than 800,000 employees (and is second only to Wal-Mart in total number of employees).[5]

In 1789, conditions were quite different. Only three departments existed under the Articles of Confederation: Foreign Affairs, War, and Treasury. George Washington inherited those departments, and soon, the head of each department was called its secretary and Foreign Affairs was renamed the Department of State. To provide the president with legal advice, Congress also created the office of attorney general. From the beginning, individuals appointed as Cabinet secretaries (as well as the attorney general) were subject to approval by the U.S. Senate, but they were removable by the president alone. Even the First Congress realized how important it was that a president be surrounded by those in whom he had complete confidence and trust.

From 1816 to 1861, the size of the federal executive branch and the bureaucracy grew as increased demands were made on existing departments and new departments were created. The Postal Service, for example, which Article I constitutionally authorized the Congress to create, was forced to expand to meet the needs of a growing and westward-expanding population. Andrew Jackson removed the Post Office from the jurisdiction of the Department of the Treasury in 1829 and promoted the postmaster general to Cabinet rank.

The post office quickly became a major source of jobs President Jackson could fill by presidential appointment, as every small town and village in the United States had

Timeline

Evolution of the Federal Bureaucracy

spoils system
The firing of public-office holders of a defeated political party and their replacement with loyalists of the newly elected party.

its own postmaster. In commenting on Jackson's wide use of political positions to reward friends and loyalists, one fellow Jacksonian Democrat commented: "to the victor belongs the spoils." From that statement came the term **spoils system,** which describes an executive's ability to fire public officeholders of the defeated political party and replace them with party loyalists.

The Civil War and the Growth of Government

As discussed in chapter 3, the Civil War (1861–1865) permanently changed the nature of the federal bureaucracy. As the nation geared up for war, thousands of additional employees were added to existing departments. The Civil War also spawned the need for new government agencies. A series of poor harvests and distribution problems led President Abraham Lincoln (who understood that you need well-fed troops to conduct a war) to create the Department of Agriculture in 1862, although it was not given full Cabinet-level status until 1889.

patronage
Jobs, grants, or other special favors that are given as rewards to friends and political allies for their support.

After the Civil War, the need for a strong national government continued unabated. The Pension Office was established in 1866 to pay benefits to the thousands of Union veterans who had fought in the war (more than 127,000 veterans initially were eligible for benefits). Justice was made a department in 1870, and other departments were added through 1900. Agriculture became a full-fledged department and began to play an important role in informing farmers about the latest developments in soil conservation, livestock breeding, and planting techniques. The increase in the types and nature of government services resulted in a parallel rise in the number of federal jobs, as illustrated in Analyzing Visuals: The Ebb and Flow of Federal Employees in the Executive Branch, 1789–2004. Many of the new jobs were used by the president or leaders of the president's political party for **patronage,** that is, jobs, grants, or other special favors given as rewards to friends and political allies for their support. Political patronage often is defended as an essential element of the party system because it provides rewards and inducements for party workers.

Pendleton Act
Reform measure that created the Civil Service Commission to administer a partial merit system. The act classified the federal service by grades, to which appointments were made based on the results of a competitive examination. It made it illegal for federal political appointees to be required to contribute to a particular political party.

From the Spoils System to the Merit System

The spoils system reached a high-water mark during Abraham Lincoln's presidency. By the time James A. Garfield, a former distinguished Civil War officer, was elected president in 1880, many reformers were calling for changes in the patronage system. On his election to office, Garfield, like many presidents before him, was besieged by office seekers. Washington, D.C., had not seen such a demand for political jobs since Abraham Lincoln became the first president elected as a Republican. Garfield's immediate predecessor, Rutherford B. Hayes, had favored the idea of the replacement of the spoils system with a merit system based on test scores and ability. Congress, however, failed to pass the legislation he proposed. Possibly because potential job seekers wanted to secure positions before Congress had the opportunity to act on an overhauled civil service system, thousands pressed Garfield for positions. This siege prompted Garfield to record in his diary: "My day is frittered away with the personal seeking of people when it ought to be given to the great problems which concern the whole country."[6] Garfield resolved to reform the civil service, but his life was cut short by the bullets of an assassin who, ironically, was a frustrated job seeker.

Photo courtesy: Bettmann/CORBIS

■ A political cartoonist's view of how President Andrew Jackson would be immortalized for his use of the spoils system.

Public reaction to Garfield's death and increasing criticism of the spoils system prompted Congress to pass the Civil Service Reform Act in 1883, more commonly known as the **Pendleton Act,** named in honor of its sponsor, Senator George

■ An artist's interpretation of President James A. Garfield's assassination at the hands of an unhappy office seeker.

Photo courtesy: Bettmann/CORBIS

H. Pendleton (D–OH). It established the principle of federal employment on the basis of open, competitive exams and created a bipartisan three-member Civil Service Commission, which operated until 1978. Initially, only about 10 percent of the positions in the federal **civil service system** were covered by the law, but later laws and executive orders extended coverage of the act to over 90 percent of all federal employees. This new system was called the **merit system,** one characteristic of Weber's model bureaucracy.

Regulating the Economy and the Growth of Government in the Twentieth Century

As the nation grew, so did the bureaucracy. In the wake of the tremendous growth of big business (especially railroads), widespread price fixing, and other unfair business practices that occurred after the Civil War, Congress created the Interstate Commerce Commission (ICC). In creating the ICC, Congress was reacting to public outcries over the exorbitant rates charged by railroad companies for hauling freight. It became the first **independent regulatory commission,** an agency outside a major executive department. Independent regulatory commissions such as the ICC, generally concerned with particular aspects of the economy, are created by Congress to be independent of direct presidential authority. Commission members are appointed by the president and hold their jobs for fixed terms, but they are not removable by the president unless they fail to uphold their oaths of office. In 1887, the creation of the ICC also marked a shift in the focus of the bureaucracy from service to regulation. Its creation gave the government—in the shape of the bureaucracy—vast powers over individual and property rights.

When Theodore Roosevelt, a progressive Republican, became president in 1901, the movement toward governmental regulation of the economic sphere was strengthened. The size of the bureaucracy was further increased when, in 1903, Roosevelt

civil service system
The system created by civil service laws by which many appointments to the federal bureaucracy are made.

merit system
The system by which federal civil service jobs are classified into grades or levels, to which appointments are made on the basis of performance on competitive examinations.

independent regulatory commission
An agency created by Congress that is generally concerned with a specific aspect of the economy.

Analyzing Visuals

NUMBER OF FEDERAL EMPLOYEES IN THE EXECUTIVE BRANCH, 1789–2002

The federal government grew slowly until the 1930s, when Franklin D. Roosevelt's New Deal programs were created in response to the high unemployment and weak financial markets of the Great Depression. A more modest spike in the federal workforce occurred in the mid-1960s during Lyndon B. Johnson's Great Society program. Through 2005, seven new executive departments were created: the Department of Housing and Urban Development (1965), the Department of Transportation (1966), the Department of Energy (1977), the Department of Education and the Department of Health and Human Services (1979—created out of the old Department of Health, Education, and Welfare), the Department of Veterans Affairs (1989), and the Department of Homeland Security (2003). It is important to note that while the number of federal employees has gone down, agencies increasingly make use of outside contractors to do their work.

After reviewing the data and balloons in the line graph and reading the material in this chapter on the roots and development of the executive branch and federal bureaucracy, answer the following critical thinking questions: Before the United States' involvement in World War II, what was the principal reason for the growth in the number of federal employees? The rapid decline in federal employees between 1945 and 1950 resulted from the end of World War II, but why do you think the number of federal employees declined after 1970? What do you think caused the increase in federal employees between 1975 and 1990?

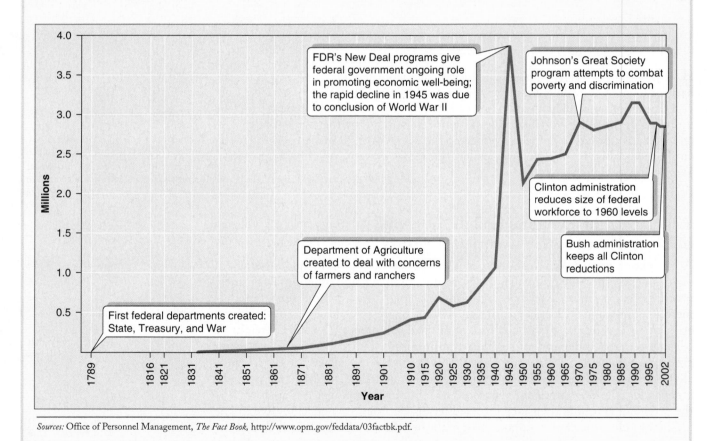

Sources: Office of Personnel Management, *The Fact Book,* http://www.opm.gov/feddata/03factbk.pdf.

asked Congress to establish a Department of Commerce and Labor to oversee employer-employee relations. At the turn of the twentieth century, many workers toiled long hours for low wages in substandard conditions. Many employers refused to recognize the rights of workers to join unions, and many businesses had grown so large and powerful that they could force workers to accept substandard conditions.

In 1913, when it became clear that one agency could not well represent the interests of both employers and employees, President Woodrow Wilson divided the Department of Commerce and Labor, creating two separate departments: Commerce and Labor. One year later, in 1914, Congress created the Federal Trade Commission (FTC). Its function was to protect small businesses and the public from unfair competition, especially from big business. Bureaus within departments also were created to concentrate on a variety of issues.

As discussed in chapter 3, the ratification of the Sixteenth Amendment to the Constitution in 1913 affected the size of government and the possibilities for growth. It gave Congress the authority to implement a federal income tax to supplement the national treasury and provided an infusion of funds to support new federal agencies, services, and governmental programs.

In the wake of the high unemployment and weak financial markets of the Great Depression, President Franklin D. Roosevelt created hundreds of new government agencies to regulate business

Photo courtesy: AP/Wide World Photos

■ During the New Deal, President Franklin D. Roosevelt suggested and Congress enacted the Emergency Relief Appropriation Act, which authorized the Works Progress Administration (WPA) to hire thousands of unemployed workers to complete numerous public work projects.

practices and various aspects of the economy. Roosevelt proposed, and the Congress enacted, far-ranging economic legislation. The desperate mood of the nation supported these moves, as most Americans began to change their ideas about the proper role of government and the provision of governmental services. Formerly, most Americans had believed in a hands-off approach; now they considered it the government's job to get the economy going and get Americans back to work.

During World War II, the federal government continued to grow tremendously to meet the needs of a nation at war. Tax rates were increased to support the war, and they never again fell to prewar levels. After the war, this infusion of new monies and veterans' demands for services led to a variety of new programs and a much bigger government. The G.I. (Government Issue) Bill, for example, provided college loans for returning veterans and reduced mortgage rates to allow them to buy homes. The national government's involvement in these programs not only affected more people but also led to its greater involvement in more regulation. Homes bought with Veterans Housing Authority loans, for example, had to meet certain specifications. With these programs, Americans became increasingly accustomed to the national government's role in entirely new areas such as affordable middle-class housing, which never would have existed without government assistance.

Within two decades after World War II, the civil rights movement and President Lyndon B. Johnson's War on Poverty produced additional growth in the bureaucracy. The Equal Employment Opportunity Commission (EEOC) was created in 1965 (by the Civil Rights Act of 1964). The Departments of Housing and Urban Development (HUD) and Transportation were created in 1965 and 1966, respectively. These expansions of the bureaucracy corresponded to increases in the president's power and his ability to persuade Congress that new agencies would be an effective way to solve pressing social problems. Remember from chapter 8 that most major expansions of bureaucratic and presidential power occurred during times of war, social crisis, or economic emergency, as is underscored by the recent creation of the new, huge Department of Homeland Security.

Government Workers and Political Involvement

As an increasing proportion of the American workforce came to work for the U.S. government as a result of the New Deal recovery programs, many began to fear that the members of the civil service would play major roles not only in implementing public policy but also in electing members of Congress and even the president. Consequently, Congress enacted the Political Activities Act of 1939, commonly known as the **Hatch Act,** named in honor of its main sponsor, Senator Carl Hatch (D–NM). It was designed to prohibit federal employees from becoming directly involved in working for political candidates.

Although presidents as far back as Thomas Jefferson had advocated efforts to limit the opportunities for federal civil servants to influence the votes of others, over the years many criticized the Hatch Act as too extreme. Critics argued that it denied millions of federal employees First Amendment guarantees of freedom of speech and association and discouraged political participation among a group of people who might otherwise be strong political activists. Critics also argued that civil servants should become more involved in campaigns, particularly at the state and local level, to understand better the needs of the citizens they serve.

In 1993, in response to criticisms of the Hatch Act and at the urgings of President Bill Clinton, Congress enacted the **Federal Employees Political Activities Act.** This liberalization of the Hatch Act allows employees to run for public office in nonpartisan elections, contribute money to political organizations, and campaign for or against candidates in partisan elections. They still, however, are prohibited from engaging in political activity while on duty, soliciting contributions from the general public, or running for office in partisan elections. During the signing ceremony, Clinton said the law will "mean more responsive, more satisfied, happier, and more productive federal employees."[7] See Table 9.1 for more specifics about the Federal Employees Political Activities Act .

Some workers, however, didn't even realize that they were federal employees. The Hatch Act, for example, had a surprising effect when a teacher in the Washington, D.C., public schools was fired for running for the D.C. city council, a race he lost in a landslide. Prior to the 1993 amendments, D.C. employees were exempt from the Hatch Act's reach. But, political wrangling led to their being covered in the 1993 amendments. Thus, because D.C. employees are treated as federal workers, they are not exempt from Hatch Act provisions that bar federal workers from running for public office in partisan elections. Initially, the teacher wasn't aware of the prohibition, but he refused to terminate his candidacy even after being notified that it could cost him his job.[8]

Hatch Act
Law enacted in 1939 to prohibit civil servants from taking activist roles in partisan campaigns. This act prohibited federal employees from making political contributions, working for a particular party, or campaigning for a particular candidate.

Federal Employees Political Activities Act
1993 liberalization of the Hatch Act. Federal employees are now allowed to run for office in nonpartisan elections and to contribute money to campaigns in partisan elections.

THE MODERN BUREAUCRACY

CRITICS CONTINUALLY LAMENT that the national government is not run like a business. Private businesses as well as all levels of government have their own bureaucratic structures. But, the national government differs from private business in numerous ways. Governments exist for the public good, not to make money. Businesses are driven by a profit motive; government leaders, but not bureaucrats, are driven by reelection. Businesses get their money from customers; the national government gets its money from taxpayers. Another difference between a bureaucracy and a business is that it is difficult to determine to whom bureaucracies are responsible. Is it the president? Congress? The citizenry? Still, governments can learn much from business, and recent reform efforts have tried to apply business solutions to create a government that works better and costs less.

| TABLE 9.1   The Liberalized Hatch Act |

Here are some examples of permissible and prohibited activities for federal employees under the Hatch Act, as modified by the Federal Employees Political Activities Act of 1993.

Federal Employees

- **May** be candidates for public office in nonpartisan elections
- **May** assist in voter registration drives
- **May** express opinions about candidates and issues
- **May** contribute money to political organizations
- **May** attend political fund-raising functions
- **May** attend and be active at political rallies and meetings
- **May** join and be active members of a political party or club
- **May** sign nominating petitions
- **May** campaign for or against referendum questions, constitutional amendments, and municipal ordinances
- **May** campaign for or against candidates in partisan elections
- **May** make campaign speeches for candidates in partisan elections
- **May** distribute campaign literature in partisan elections
- **May** hold office in political clubs or parties

- **May not** use their official authority or influence to interfere with an election
- **May not** collect political contributions unless both individuals are members of the same federal labor organization or employee organization and the one solicited is not a subordinate employee
- **May not** knowingly solicit or discourage the political activity of any person who has business before the agency
- **May not** engage in political activity while on duty
- **May not** engage in political activity in any government office
- **May not** engage in political activity while wearing an official uniform
- **May not** engage in political activity while using a government vehicle
- **May not** solicit political contributions from the general public
- **May not** be candidates for public office in partisan elections

Source: U.S. Special Counsel's Office.

The different natures of government and business have a tremendous impact on the way the bureaucracy operates. Because all of the incentive in government "is in the direction of not making mistakes," public employees view risks and rewards very differently from their private-sector counterparts.[9] The key to the modern bureaucracy is to understand who bureaucrats are, how the bureaucracy is organized, and how organization and personnel affect each other. It also is key to understand that government cannot be run like a business. An understanding of these facts and factors can help in the search for ways to motivate positive change in the bureaucracy.

Although many Americans bemoan a growing federal bureaucracy, they are actually wrong. Presidents since Calvin Coolidge have tried to control the size of the bureaucracy. His Two Percent Club was created to cut staff, as its name implies, by two percent. Later, President Richard M. Nixon, for example, proposed a plan to combine fifty domestic agencies and seven different departments into four large "super departments."[10] The Clinton administration was also bullish on reform. The President's Task Force on Reinventing Government cut the size of the federal workforce, halved the growing number of federal regulations, and set customer service standards to direct agencies to put the people they serve first. President George W. Bush also put bureaucratic reform as a priority and expanded upon Clinton administration efforts toward a more paperless government. That effort, however, lost some momentum in the aftermath of 9/11, which resulted in the creation of additional federal programs and offices and even a new Department of Homeland Security. Still, the Bush administration has continued, as discussed in chapter 3, to return responsibilities back to state and local governments. As that has happened, however, the size of state and local bureaucracies has grown proportionately. It is important to note that the following discussion pertains only to the federal bureaucracy.

Who Are Bureaucrats?

Federal bureaucrats are career government employees who work in the executive branch in the Cabinet-level departments and independent agencies that comprise more than 2,000 bureaus, divisions, branches, offices, services, and other subunits of the federal government. There are approximately 1.8 million federal workers in the executive branch, a figure that does not include postal workers and uniformed military personnel. Nearly one-third of all civilian employees work in the U.S. Postal Service, as illustrated in Figure 9.1. The remaining federal civilian workers are spread out among the various executive departments and agencies throughout the United States. Most of these federal employees are paid according to what is called the "General Schedule" (GS). They advance within GS grades and into higher GS levels and salaries as their careers progress.

As a result of reforms during the Truman administration that built on the Pendleton Act, most civilian federal governmental employees today are selected by merit standards, which include tests (such as civil service or foreign service exams) and educational criteria. Merit systems protect federal employees from being fired for political reasons. (For a description of how a federal employee can be fired, see Table 9.2.)

At the lower levels of the U.S. Civil Service, most positions are filled by competitive examinations. These usually involve a written test, although the same position in the private sector would not. Mid-level to upper ranges of federal positions do not normally require tests; instead, applicants simply submit a resume, or even apply by phone. Personnel departments then evaluate potential candidates and rank candidates according to how well they fit a particular job opening. Only the names of those deemed "qualified" are then forwarded to the official filling the vacancy. This can be a time-consuming process; it often takes six to nine months before a position can be filled in this manner.

The remaining 10 percent of the federal workforce is made up of persons not covered by the civil service system. These positions generally fall into three categories:

1. Appointive policy-making positions. More than 6,000 people are presidential appointees. Some of these, including Cabinet secretaries, are subject to Senate confirmation. These appointees, in turn, are responsible for appointing thousands of high-level policy-making assistants who form the top of the bureaucratic hierarchy.

2. Independent regulatory commissioners. Although each president gets to appoint as many as one hundred commissioners, they become independent of his direct political influence once they take office.

3. Low-level, nonpolicy patronage positions. At one time, the U.S. Postal Service was the largest source of these government jobs. In 1971, Congress reorganized the Postal Service and removed positions such as local postmaster from the political patronage/rewards pool. Since then, these types of positions generally concern secretarial assistants to policy makers.

More than 15,000 job skills are represented in the federal government, and its workers are perhaps the best trained and most skilled and efficient in the world (see Global Perspective: Who Are the Bureaucrats? Should We Care?). Government employees, whose average age is forty-seven years, with an average length of service at seventeen years, include forest rangers, FBI agents, foreign service officers, computer programmers, security guards, librarians, administrators, engineers, plumbers, lawyers, doctors, postal carriers, and zoologists, among others. The diversity of government jobs mirrors the diversity of jobs in the private sector. The federal workforce, itself, is also diverse. As revealed in Analyzing Visuals: Characteristics and Rank Distribution of Federal Civilian Employees, the federal workforce largely reflects the racial and ethnic composition of the United States as a whole, although the employment of women lags behind that of men. Women still make up more than 60 percent of the lowest GS levels but have raised their proportion of positions in the GS 13–15 ranks from 18 percent in 1990 to over 30 percent in 2002.[11]

There are about 326,000 federal workers in the nation's capital; the rest are located in regional, state, and local offices scattered throughout the country. To enhance effi-

Participation

Who Wants to Be a Bureaucrat?

Comparative

Comparing Bureaucracies

Visual Literacy

The Changing Face of the Federal Bureaucracy

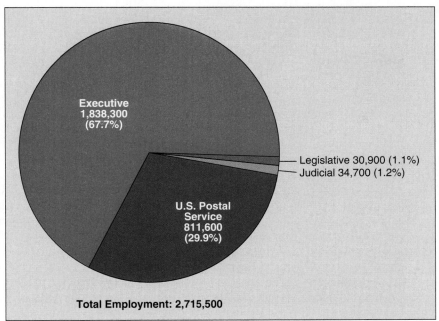

FIGURE 9.1   Distribution of Federal Civilian Employment. ■

Source: Office of Personnel Management, *2003 Fact Book.*

ciency, the United States is broken up into several regions, with most agencies having regional offices in one city in that region. (See Figure 9.2.) The decentralization of the bureaucracy facilitates accessibility to the public. The Social Security Administration, for example, has numerous offices so that its clients can have a place nearby to take their paperwork, questions, and problems. Decentralization also helps distribute jobs and incomes across the country.

The graying of the federal workforce is of concern to many. More than two-thirds of those in the highest nonpolitical positions as well as a large number of mid-level managers are eligible to retire.[12] Many in government hope that the Presidential Management Fellows Program, formerly known as the Presidential Management Intern (PMI) Program, which was begun in 1977 to hire and train future managers and executives, will be enhanced to make up for the shortfall in experienced managers that the federal government is now

TABLE 9.2 How to Fire a Federal Bureaucrat

Removing federal employees for poor performance is very difficult and rare. In 1997, for example, of the federal government's 2.7 million employees, 3,550 were terminated for poor performance. Only 100 were demoted and only 1,257 failed to get a pay raise based on their poor performance.[a] Civil service rules make it easier to fire someone for misconduct than poor performance. Incompetent employees must be given notice by their supervisors and given an opportunity for remedial training.

To fire a member of the competitive civil service, explicit procedures must be followed:

1. At least thirty days' written notice must be given to an employee in advance of firing or demotion for incompetence or misconduct.
2. The written notification must contain a statement of reasons for the action and specific examples of unacceptable performance.
3. The employee has the right to reply both orally and in written form to the charges, and has the right to an attorney.
4. Appeals from any adverse action against the employee can be made to the three-person Merit Systems Protection Board (MSPB), a bipartisan body appointed by the president and confirmed by the Senate.
5. All employees have the right to a hearing and to an attorney in front of the MSPB.
6. All decisions of the MSPB may be appealed by the employee to the U.S. Court of Appeals.

[a] D. Mark Wilson, "Inadequate Remedies for Poorly Performing Federal Workers Would Undermine Airport Security," Heritage Foundation WebMemo 54 (November 8, 2001).

WHO ARE THE BUREAUCRATS? SHOULD WE CARE?

It is tempting to think of the bureaucracy simply as a machine created by political officials to carry out the laws they have passed and the regulations they have established. In looking at bureaucracy as a machine, we tend not to worry about differences among the people who work in the bureaucracy. Civil servants are expected to be neutral, competent, and expert and to drive the machine without regard to their personal values. An important line of thought in the study of bureaucracy, known as the representative bureaucracy perspective, argues, however, that to view bureaucracy as a machine is a mistake. Instead, bureaucracy is about people. First, it is about the people within the bureaucracy. The different ideas people have about what is right and wrong, the appropriate way to behave, and what—if anything—the government owes the people and the people owe the government inevitably influence how civil servants approach their jobs and the types of decisions they make. Second, it is about the people with whom the bureaucracy interacts. Minority groups may not be well served by the bureaucracy if everyone in it comes from groups with values different from theirs. They may not be able to communicate effectively with the bureaucrats or receive a sympathetic hearing from them.

From the representative bureaucracy perspective, it is extremely important to know who these bureaucrats are in terms of their social, economic, and cultural backgrounds. Systematic comparative data of this type are hard to come by. The table below presents information on the background of high-ranking civil servants in Canada and Israel in terms of their social class, level of education, minority status, and gender.

Worldwide, most high ranking civil servants come from middle-class backgrounds. Germany is typical of many West European countries with only 11 percent of its bureaucrats coming from working-class backgrounds. Pakistan is even lower at 2 percent. Almost everywhere, high-ranking civil servants have at least some form of college education. This shared characteristic hides some important differences, however. In the United States, many civil servants graduate from state-supported universities; however, in Great Britain, France, Japan, South Korea, and Greece, to name only a few countries, there has been a long-standing bias for recruiting civil servants from only a few elite universities. Another difference is that some states, such as Great Britain, emphasize a generalist education, and others, such as Germany and Sweden, stress the importance of a professional or technical education.

In most countries, the dominant ethnic group is overrepresented. In the United States, the dominant ethnic group makes up 63 percent of the total civil service numbers. In some countries, specific bureaucratic positions are reserved for people from specific ethnic groups—the practice in Austria, Belgium, and Lebanon. Along with ethnicity, gender is a major dividing line within bureaucracies. Although in many countries over 50 percent of the civil service is made up of women, rarely are many found in the higher civil service ranks. In Australia, only 2 percent of higher civil servants are women; in Finland and Italy, 4 percent.

Questions

1. How important is it that the U.S. bureaucracy looks like the American population?
2. Which of the background characteristics discussed here do you think is most important for creating a representative bureaucracy?

Backgrounds of Civil Servants in Two Democracies (percentages)

	Social Background		Education		Ethnic Group		Gender	
Canada	Upper	44	High School*	2	Dominant	70	Female	47
	Middle	19	College Grad	34	Minority	30	Male	53
	Working	36	Post College	65				
Israel	Upper	18	High School*	49	Dominant	81	Female	52
	Middle	59	College Grad	28	Minority	19	Male	48
	Working	23	Post College	23				

*This category combines those with a high school diploma and some college. In Israel all of these had some college.

Source: B. Guy Peters, *The Politics of Bureaucracy* (New York: Routledge, 2001), pp. 112-125.

facing. Agencies even are contemplating ways to pay the college loans of prospective recruits while at the same time trying to enhance benefits to attract older workers.[13] At the same time the federal government is trying to recruit and retain federal workers, it is also trying to shrink the number of federal employees by using outside contractors. Federal employees are very difficult to fire, as is underscored in Table 9.2, and outside contractors often are cheaper. The Bush administration, for example, concluded that 850,000 federal jobs are essentially commercial in nature and could be performed more cost-effectively by private corporations, and that half should be outsourced as quickly as possible.[14]

Formal Organization

While even experts can't agree on the exact number of separate governmental agencies, commissions, and departments that make up the federal bureaucracy, there are at least 1,149 civilian agencies.[15] A distinctive feature of the executive bureaucracy is its traditional division into areas of specialization. For example, the Occupational Safety and Health Administration (OSHA) handles occupational safety, and the Department of State specializes in foreign affairs. It is not unusual, however, for more than one agency to be involved in a particular issue or for one agency to be involved in myriad issues. In fact, numerous agencies often have authority in the same issue areas, making administration even more difficult.

Agencies fall into four general types: (1) Cabinet departments; (2) government corporations; (3) independent agencies; and, (4) regulatory commissions.

The Cabinet Departments.   The fifteen Cabinet **departments** are major administrative units that have responsibility for conducting a broad area of government operations.

departments
Major administrative units with responsibility for a broad area of government operations. Departmental status usually indicates a permanent national interest in a particular governmental function, such as defense, commerce, or agriculture.

FIGURE 9.2   Federal Agency Regions and City Headquarters. ■

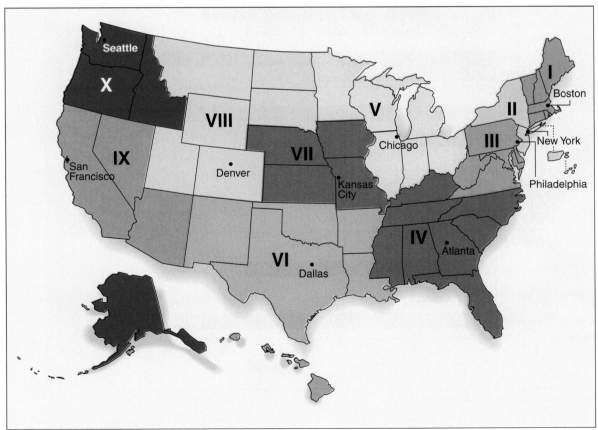

Source: Department of Health and Human Services, http://www.hhs.gov/images/regions.gif.

Analyzing Visuals

CHARACTERISTICS AND RANK DISTRIBUTION OF FEDERAL CIVILIAN EMPLOYEES

The bar graph depicts the percentage of the federal civilian workforce in several categories: gender, gender and rank, race or ethnicity, disability, age, length of service, and union representation. After reviewing the data displayed in the graph, answer the following critical thinking questions: What do you notice about the percentages of males and females in the lowest (GS-01 through GS-04) and the highest (GS-13 through GS-15)

grades? How would you explain the differences in percentages of males and females in those grades? Which racial/ethnic groups are represented in percentages that are greater than their percentages in the population (see the population statistics in the Changes in Racial and Ethnic Distributions section in chapter 1)? What do you think would explain the high percentage of the federal civilian workforce represented by a union?

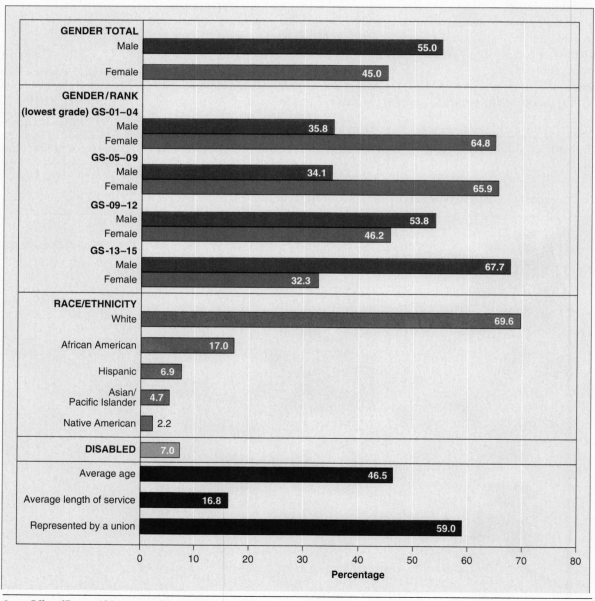

Source: Office of Personnel Management, *2003 Fact Book.*

The Living Constitution

The President. . .may require the Opinion, in writing, of the principle Officer in each of the executive Departments, upon any subject relating to the Duties of their respective Office.

—Article II, Section 2, Clause 1

This clause, along with additional language designating that the president shall be the commander in chief, notes that the heads of departments are to serve as advisers to the president. There is no mention of the Cabinet in the Constitution.

This meager language is all that remains of the Framers' initial efforts to create a council to guide the president. Those in attendance at the Constitutional Convention largely favored the idea of a council, but could not agree on who should be a part of that body. Some actually wanted members from the House and Senate who would rotate into the bureaucracy; most, however, appeared to support the idea of the heads of departments along with the chief justice, who would preside when the president was unavailable. The resulting language above depicts a one-sided arrangement whereby the heads of executive departments must simply answer in writing questions put to them by the president.

The Cabinet of today is totally different from the structure envisioned by the Framers. George Washington was the first to convene a meeting of what he called his Cabinet. Some presidents have used their Cabinets as trusted advisers; others have used them to demonstrate that they are committed to political, racial, ethnic, or gender diversity, and have relied more on White House aides than particular Cabinet members. Who is included in the Cabinet, as well as how it is used, is solely up to the discretion of the sitting president.

Cabinet departments account for about 60 percent of the federal workforce. The vice president, the heads of all of the departments, as well as the heads of the Environmental Protection Agency (EPA), Office of Management and Budget (OMB), Office of National Drug Control Policy, the U.S. Trade Representative, and the president's chief of staff make up his formal Cabinet.

The executive branch departments depicted in Figure 9.3 are headed by Cabinet members called secretaries (except the Department of Justice, which is headed by the attorney general). The secretaries are responsible for establishing their department's general policy and overseeing its operations. As discussed in chapter 8, Cabinet secretaries are responsible directly to the president but are often viewed as having two masters—the president and those affected by their department. Cabinet secretaries also are tied to Congress, from which they get their appropriations and the discretion to implement legislation and make rules and policy.

Although departments vary considerably in size, prestige, and power, they share certain features. Each department covers a broad area of responsibility generally reflected by its name. Each secretary is assisted by one or more deputies or undersecretaries who take part of the administrative burden off the secretary's shoulders, as well as by several assistant secretaries who direct major programs within the department. In addition, each secretary, like the president, has numerous assistants who help with planning, budgeting, personnel,

■ Shortly after the November 2004 elections, Prresident George W. Bush nominates a long-time close aide, White House domestic policy adviser Margaret Spellings, as the next secretary of education. After brief congressional hearings, her appointment was quickly confirmed.

Photo courtesy: © Brooks Kraft/Corbis

FIGURE 9.3   The Executive Branch. ▪

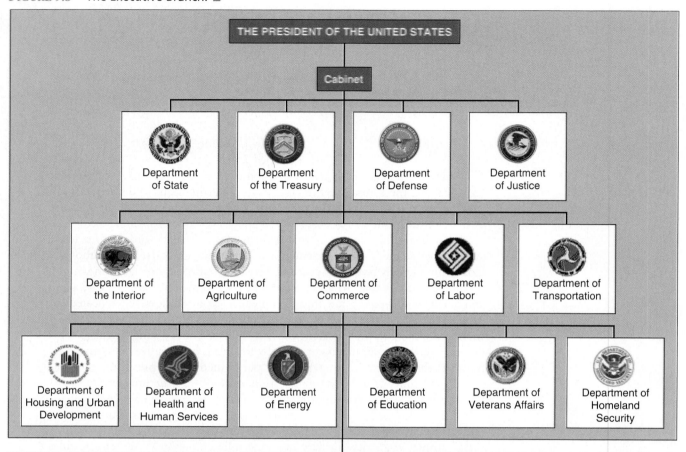

Independent Agencies and Government Corporations

Advisory Council on Historic Preservation
African Development Foundation
American Battle Monuments Commission
Appalachian Regional Commission
Architectural and Transportation
    Barriers Compliance Board
Arctic Research Commission
Armed Forces Retirement Home
Barry M. Goldwater Scholarship and
    Excellence in Education Foundation
Broadcasting Board of Governors
Central Intelligence Agency
Civil Air Patrol Great Lakes Region
Commission on Civil Rights
Commission of Fine Arts
Committee for Purchase from People
    Who Are Blind or Severely Disabled
Commodity Futures Trading Commission
Consumer Product Safety Commission
Corporation for National Service
Defense Nuclear Facilities Safety Board
Delaware River Basin Commission
Environmental Protection Agency
Equal Employment Opportunity Commission
Export-Import Bank of the U.S.
Farm Credit Administration
Federal Communications Commission
Federal Deposit Insurance Corporation
Federal Election Commission
Federal Emergency Management Agency
Federal Energy Regulatory Commission
Federal Housing Finance Board
Federal Labor Relations Authority
Federal Maritime Commission

Federal Mediation and Conciliation Service
Federal Mine Safety and Health Review Commission
Federal Reserve System
Federal Retirement Thrift Investment Board
Federal Trade Commission
General Services Administration
Harry S Truman Scholarship Foundation
Inter-American Foundation
International Boundary and Water Commission,
    United States and Mexico
International Broadcasting Bureau
Interstate Commission on the Potomac River Basin
James Madison Memorial Fellowship Foundation
Japan–United States Friendship Commission
Marine Mammal Commission
Merit Systems Protection Board
National Aeronautics and Space Administration
National Archives and Records Administration
National Capital Planning Commission
National Commission on Libraries and
    Information Science
National Council on Disability
National Credit Union Administration
National Foundation on the Arts
    and the Humanities
National Labor Relations Board
National Mediation Board
National Performance Review
National Railroad Passenger Corporation (Amtrak)
National Science Foundation
National Transportation Safety Board
Nuclear Regulatory Commission
Occupational Safety and Health Review Commission
Office of Government Ethics

Office of Navajo and Hopi Indian Relocation
Office of Personnel Management
Office of Special Counsel
Overseas Private Investment Corporation
Peace Corps
Pension Benefit Guaranty Corporation
Physician Payment Review Commission
Postal Rate Commission
President's Commission on White House
    Fellowships
President's Committee on Employment
    of People with Disabilities
Railroad Retirement Board
Securities and Exchange Commission
Selective Service System
Small Business Administration
Smithsonian Institution
Social Security Administration
Surface Transportation Board
Susquehanna River Basin Commission
Tennesse Valley Authority
Trade Development Agency
U.S. Arms Control and Disarmament Agency
U.S. Chemical Safety and Hazard
    Investigation Board
U.S. Holocaust Memorial Council
U.S. Information Agency
U.S. Institute of Peace
U.S. International Development
    Corporation Agency
U.S. International Trade Commission
U.S. Postal Service
Woodrow Wilson International Center
    for Scholars

legal services, public relations, and their key staff functions. Most departments are subdivided into bureaus, divisions, sections, or other smaller units, and it is at this level that the real work of each agency is done. Most departments are subdivided along functional lines, but the basis for division may be geography, work processes (for example, the new Transportation Security Agency is housed in the Department of Homeland Security), or clientele (such as the Bureau of Indian Affairs in the Department of the Interior).

Departmental status generally signifies a strong permanent national interest to promote a particular function. Moreover, some departments are organized to foster and promote the interests of a given clientele—that is, a specific social or economic group. Such departments are called clientele agencies. The Departments of Agriculture, Education, Energy, Labor, and Veterans Affairs, and the Bureau of Indian Affairs in the Department of the Interior, are examples of clientele agencies or bureaus. The Department of Labor's Women's Bureau is another good example of a clientele agency. Created by Congress in 1920, over time the Women's Bureau helped ease women into the war industry in World War II, played an important role in establishing President Kennedy's Commission on the Status of Women, and worked to get the Equal Pay Act passed in 1963 and the Family and Medical Leave Act in 1993. In early 2002, the Bush administration announced that it planned to eliminate all of the regional offices of the bureau. This action was met with an outcry from women's rights groups and labor unions. When even Secretary of Labor Elaine Chao protested, these plans were dropped for the time being.

Because many of these agencies were created at the urging of well-organized interests to advance their particular objectives, it is not surprising that clientele groups are powerful lobbies with their respective agencies in Washington. The clientele agencies and groups also are active at the regional level, where the agencies devote a substantial part of their resources to program implementation.

Photo courtesy: AP/Wide World Photos

■ Workers install housing for turbines during the 1941 construction of the Tennessee Valley Authority's Cherokee Dam in Tennessee. Today, the TVA continues to provide electricity at reduced rates to millions of Americans living in the Appalachian region.

Government Corporations.

Government corporations are the most recent addition to the bureaucracy. Dating from the early 1930s, they are businesses established by Congress to perform functions that could be provided by private businesses. The corporations are formed when the government chooses to engage in activities that primarily are commercial in nature, produce revenue, and require greater flexibility than Congress generally allows regular departments. Some of the better-known government corporations include Amtrak and the Federal Deposit Insurance Corporation. Unlike other governmental agencies, government corporations charge for their services. For example, the largest government corporation, the U.S. Postal Service—whose functions could be handled by a private corporation, such as the United Parcel Service (UPS)—exists today to ensure delivery of mail throughout the United States at cheaper rates than those a private business might charge. Similarly, the Tennessee Valley Authority (TVA) provides electricity at reduced rates to millions of Americans in the Appalachian region of the Southeast, generally a low-income area that had failed to attract private utility companies to provide service there.

In cases such as the TVA, where the financial incentives for private industry to provide services are minimal, Congress often believes that it must act. In other cases, it steps in to salvage valuable public assets. For example, when passenger rail service in the United States became unprofitable, Congress stepped in to create Amtrak, nationalizing the passenger-train industry to keep passenger trains running.

Independent Executive Agencies.

Independent executive agencies closely resemble Cabinet departments but have narrower areas of responsibility. Generally speaking, independent agencies perform service rather than regulatory functions. The heads of these agencies are appointed by the president and serve, like Cabinet secretaries, at his pleasure.

government corporations
Businesses established by Congress that perform functions that could be provided by private businesses (such as the U.S. Postal Service).

independent executive agencies
Governmental units that closely resemble a Cabinet department but have a narrower area of responsibility (such as the Central Intelligence Agency) and are not part of any Cabinet department.

Independent agencies exist apart from executive departments for practical or symbolic reasons. The National Aeronautics and Space Administration (NASA), for example, could have been placed within the Department of Defense. Such positioning, however, could have conjured up thoughts of a space program dedicated solely to military purposes, rather than to civilian satellite communication or scientific exploration. Similarly, the Environmental Protection Agency (EPA) was created in 1970 to administer federal programs aimed at controlling pollution and protecting the nation's environment. It administers all congressional laws concerning the environment and pollution. Along with the Council on Environmental Quality, a staff agency in the Executive Office of the President, the EPA advises the president on environmental concerns, and its head is considered a member of the president's Cabinet.[16] It also administers programs transferred to it with personnel detailed from the Departments of Agriculture, Energy, Interior, and Health and Human Services, and the Nuclear Regulatory Commission, among other agencies. The expanding national focus on the environment, in fact, has brought about numerous calls to elevate the EPA to Cabinet-level status to reinforce a long-term national commitment to improved air and water and other environmental issues.

You Are the President of Medicorp

Independent Regulatory Commissions.   Independent regulatory commissions are agencies created by Congress to exist outside the major departments to regulate a specific economic activity or interest. Because of the complexity of modern economic issues, Congress sought to create agencies that could develop expertise and provide continuity of policy with respect to economic issues because neither Congress nor the courts have the time or specific talents to do so. Examples include the National Labor Relations Board, the Federal Reserve Board, the Federal Communications Commission, and the Securities and Exchange Commission (SEC).[17]

Older boards and commissions, such as the SEC and the Federal Reserve Board, generally are charged with overseeing a certain industry. Most were created specifically to be free from partisan political pressure. Each is headed by a board composed of five to seven members (always an odd number, to avoid tie votes) who are selected by the president and confirmed by the Senate for fixed, staggered terms to increase the chances of a bipartisan board. Unlike executive department heads, they cannot easily be removed by the president. In 1935, the U.S. Supreme Court ruled that in creating independent commissions, the Congress had intended that they be independent panels of experts as far removed as possible from immediate political pressures.[18]

Newer regulatory boards are more concerned with how the business sector relates to public health and safety. The Occupational Safety and Health Administration (OSHA), for example, promotes job safety. These boards and commissions often lack autonomy and freedom from political pressures; they are generally headed by a single administrator who can be removed by the president. Thus, they are far more susceptible to the political wishes of the president who appoints them.

HOW THE BUREAUCRACY WORKS

WHEN CONGRESS CREATES any kind of department, agency, or commission, it is actually delegating some of its powers listed in Article I, section 8, of the U.S. Constitution. Therefore, the laws creating departments, agencies, corporations, or commissions carefully describe their purpose and give them the authority to make numerous policy decisions, which have the effect of law. Congress recognizes that it does not have the time, expertise, or ability to involve itself in every detail of every program; therefore, it sets general guidelines for agency action and leaves it to the agency to work out the details. How agencies execute congressional wishes is called **implementation,** the process by which a law or policy is put into operation.

Historically, political scientists attempting to study how the bureaucracy made policy investigated what they termed **iron triangles,** a term that was used to refer to the relatively stable relationships and patterns of interaction that occurred among federal

implementation
The process by which a law or policy is put into operation by the bureaucracy.

iron triangles
The relatively stable relationships and patterns of interaction that occur among an agency, interest groups, and congressional committees or subcommittees.

workers in agencies or departments, interest groups, and relevant congressional subcommittees (see Figure 9.4). Today, however, iron triangles no longer dominate most policy processes, although some persist, such as the relationship between the Department of Veterans Affairs, the House Committee on Veterans Affairs, and the American Legion and the Veterans of Foreign Wars, the two largest veterans groups. Both individual veterans and organizations such as these continually lobby or are in contact with the federal employees who are responsible for promulgating rules and implementing policies that affect veterans on a daily basis.

Many political scientists examining external influences on the modern bureaucracy prefer to examine **issue networks.** In general, issue networks, like iron triangles, include agency officials, members of Congress (and committee staffers), and interest group lobbyists. But, they also include lawyers, consultants, academics, public relations specialists, and sometimes even the courts. Unlike iron triangles, issue networks are constantly changing as members with technical expertise or newly interested parties become involved in issue areas.

As a result of the increasing complexity of many policy domains, many alliances have also been created within the bureaucracy. One such example is **interagency councils,** working groups that bring together representatives of several departments and agencies to facilitate the coordination of policy making and implementation. Depending on how well these councils are funded, they can be the prime movers of administration policy in any area where an interagency council exists. The U.S. Interagency Council on the Homeless, for example, was created in 1987 to coordinate the activities of the more than fifty governmental agencies and programs that work to alleviate homelessness.

In areas where there are extraordinarily complex policy problems, recent presidential administrations have created policy coordinating committees (PCCs) to facilitate interaction among agencies and departments at the subcabinet level. These PCCs have gained increasing favor post-9/11. For example, the PCC on Terrorist Financing, which includes representatives from the Departments of Treasury, State, Defense, and Justice, along with the CIA and FBI, conducted a study that recommended to the president that he ask the Saudi government to take action against alleged terrorist financiers.[19] Similarly, in the wake of the 2003 *Columbia* space shuttle disaster, a PPC on space was created to review NASA's evaluation of why the disaster occurred.[20]

FIGURE 9.4   An Iron Triangle. ■

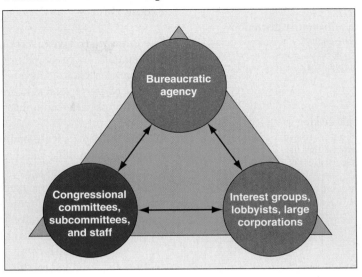

issue networks
The loose and informal relationships that exist among a large number of actors who work in broad policy areas.

interagency councils
Working groups created to facilitate coordination of policy making and implementation across a host of governmental agencies.

■ Mars Exploration project members speak to the press at NASA's Jet Propulsion Laboratory in Pasadena, California, shortly before the Mars landing of the "rover" named Spirit, in January 2004. While on its mission, the Spirit was able to take more than 30,000 photos of the planet.

Making Policy

The end product of all of these decision-making bodies is policy making. Policy making and implementation take place on both informal and formal levels. Practically, many decisions are left to individual government employees on a day-to-day basis. Department of Justice lawyers, for example, make daily decisions about whether or not to prosecute someone. Similarly, street-level Internal Revenue Service agents make many decisions during personal audits. These street-level bureaucrats make policy on two levels. First, they exercise wide discretion in decisions concerning citizens with whom they interact. Second, taken together, their individual actions

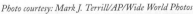
Photo courtesy: Mark J. Terrill/AP/Wide World Photos

add up to agency behavior.[21] Thus, how bureaucrats interpret and how they apply (or choose not to apply) various policies are equally important parts of the policy-making process.

administrative discretion
The ability of bureaucrats to make choices concerning the best way to implement congressional intentions.

Administrative discretion, the ability to make choices concerning the best way to implement congressional or executive intentions, also allows decision makers (whether they are in a Cabinet-level position or at the lowest GS levels) a tremendous amount of leeway. It is exercised through two formal administrative procedures: rule making and administrative adjudication.

rule making
A quasi-legislative administrative process that has the characteristics of a legislative act.

Rule Making.
Rule making is a quasi-legislative administrative process that results in regulations and has the characteristics of a legislative act. **Regulations** are the rules that govern the operation of all government programs and have the force of law. In essence, then, bureaucratic rule makers often act as lawmakers as well as law enforcers when they make rules or draft regulations to implement various congressional statutes. The rule-making process is illustrated in Figure 9.5. Some political scientists say that rule making "is the single most important function performed by agencies of government."[22]

regulations
Rules that govern the operation of a particular government program that have the force of law.

Because regulations often involve political conflict, the 1946 Administrative Procedures Act established rule-making procedures to give everyone the chance to participate in the process. The act requires that: (1) public notice of the time, place, and nature of the rule-making proceedings be provided in the *Federal Register;* (2) interested par-

FIGURE 9.5   How a Regulation Is Made. ∎

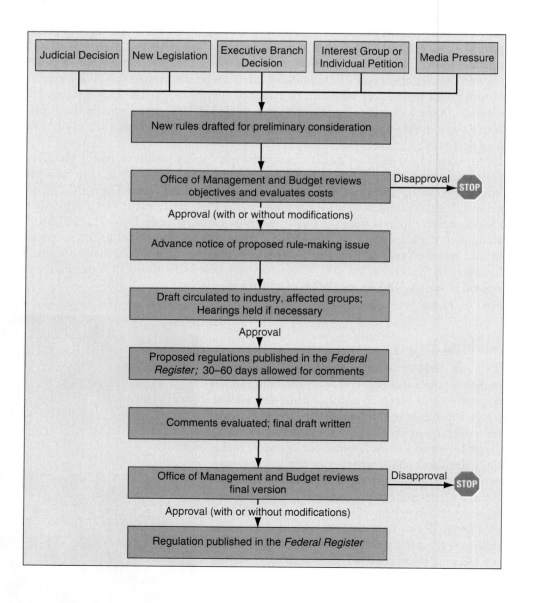

ENFORCING GENDER EQUITY IN COLLEGE ATHLETICS

In 2004, there were approximately 150,000 female student-athletes, a number up dramatically from 1971, when there were only about 30,000 women participating in collegiate athletics.[a] Male participation has grown much more slowly, while the number of women's teams in the National Collegiate Athletic Association nearly doubled between 1971 and 2002, from 4,776 to 8,414.[b] A major source of that difference? The passage in 1972 of legislation popularly known as Title IX, which prohibits discrimination against girls and women in federally funded education, including athletic programs. This legislation mandates that "No person in the United States shall, on the basis of sex, be excluded from participation in, be denied the benefits of, or be subjected to discrimination under any education program or activity receiving federal financial assistance." It wasn't until December 1978—six years after passage of Title IX—that the Office for Civil Rights in the Department of Health, Education, and Welfare released a policy interpretation of the law, dealing largely with the section that concerned intercollegiate athletics.[c] More than thirty pages of text were devoted to dealing with a hundred or so words from the statute. Football was recognized as unique, because of the huge revenues it produces, so it could be inferred that male-dominated football programs could continue to outspend women's athletic programs. The more than sixty women's groups that had lobbied for equality of spending were outraged and turned their efforts toward seeking more favorable rulings on the construction of the statute from the courts.

Increased emphasis on Title IX enforcement has led many women to file lawsuits to force compliance. In 1991, in an effort to trim expenses, Brown University cut two men's and two women's teams from its varsity roster. Several women students filed a Title IX complaint against the school, arguing that it violated the act by not providing women varsity sport opportunities in relation to their population in the university. The women also argued that cutting the two women's programs saved $62,000, whereas the men's cuts saved only $16,000. Thus, the women's varsity programs took a bigger hit, in violation of federal law.

A U.S. district court refused to allow Brown to cut the women's programs. A U.S. court of appeals upheld that action, concluding that Brown had failed to provide adequate opportunities for its female students to participate in athletics.[d] In 1997, in *Brown University* v. *Cohen,* the U.S. Supreme Court declined to review the appeals court's decision.[e] This put all colleges and universities on notice that discrimination against women would not be tolerated, even when, as in the case of Brown University, the university had expanded sports opportunities for women tremendously since the passage of Title IX.

Women have made significant strides on all college campuses, but true equity in athletics is still a long way away at many colleges and universities. Although the number of women participating in college level sports is increasing, the proportion of women coaches is decreasing (at the same time the pool of women who could be coaches is increasing). Most colleges still provide far fewer opportunities to women, given their numbers in most universities, and enforcement still lags. This disparity has required groups including the National Women's Law Cen-

Photo courtesy: Doug Mills/The New York Times

Women's Participation in college sports such as soccer has increased dramatically since passage of Title IX.

ter to take the lead in the *Brown* case and to spend millions of dollars in legal fees to press for fuller enforcement, because Title IX is not self-enforcing.[f] Individual colleges and universities must comply with the law, aggrieved students must complain of inequities, and the Department of Education's Office of Civil Rights must enforce the law. This may become more difficult, given the mixed messages being put out by the Bush administration. In 2002, for example, the National Wrestling Coaches Association filed suit against the Department of Education, arguing that Title IX guidelines force universities to discriminate against low-profile men's sports such as wrestling. To the surprise of many women's rights organizations, the Bush administration asked the court to dismiss the wrestling challenge. The government brief, however, offered no praise or support for Title IX, leaving its supporters wary of future administration actions. This case was later dismissed on procedural grounds.

In early 2003, after holding hearings on Title IX throughout the United States, a commission appointed by the Bush administration recommended to the secretary of education that enforcement of Title IX's requirements that provide opportunities for women in athletics be weakened to account for perceived differences in interest in athletics between male and female college students. The recommendation was greeted with protest from women members of the House, who held their own hearings in support of Title IX. Public support for Title IX is quite high. A 2003 Roper poll found that 61 percent of the public viewed Title IX favorably.[g]

[a]*Intercollegiate Athletics: Status of Efforts to Promote Gender Equity,* General Accounting Office, October 25, 1996.

[b]Bill Pennington, "Colleges: More Men's Teams Benched as Colleges Level the Playing Field," *New York Times* (May 9, 2002): A1.

[c]See Joyce Gelb and Marian Lief Palley, *Women and Public Policies* (Charlottesville: University of Virginia Press, 1996), ch. 5.

[d]*Cohen* v. *Brown University,* 101 F.3d 155 (1996).

[e]520 U.S. 1186 (1997).

[f]http://www.edc.org/WomensEquity/resource/title9/report/athletic.html.

[g]Public Opinion Online, Accession Numbers 0418720 and 0418721.

Simulation
You Are a Federal
Administrator

ties be given the opportunity to submit written arguments and facts relevant to the rule; and, (3) the statutory purpose and basis of the rule be stated. Once rules are written, thirty days generally must elapse before they take effect.

Sometimes an agency is required by law to conduct a formal hearing before issuing rules. Evidence is gathered, and witnesses testify and are cross-examined by opposing interests. The process can take weeks, months, or even years, at the end of which agency administrators must review the entire record and then justify the new rules. Although cumbersome, the process has reduced criticism of some rules and bolstered the deference given by the courts to agency decisions. Many Americans are unaware of the opportunities available to them to influence government at this stage. As illustrated in On Campus: Enforcing Gender Equity in College Athletics, women's groups and female athletes testified at hearings held around the country urging Secretary of Education Rodney Paige not to revise existing Title IX regulations. Change could have affected their ability to play sports or receive college athletic scholarships.[23]

administrative adjudication
A quasi-judicial process in which a bureaucratic agency settles disputes between two parties in a manner similar to the way courts resolve disputes.

Administrative Adjudication.   **Administrative adjudication** is a quasi-judicial process in which a bureaucratic agency settles disputes between two parties in a manner similar to the way courts resolve disputes. Administrative adjudication is referred to as *quasi* (Latin for "seemingly") judicial, because law-making by any body other than Congress or adjudication by any body other than the judiciary would be a violation of the constitutional principle of separation of powers.

Agencies regularly find that persons or businesses are not in compliance with the federal laws the agencies are charged with enforcing, or that they are in violation of an agency rule or regulation. To force compliance, some agencies resort to administrative adjudication, which generally is less formal than a trial. Several agencies and boards employ administrative law judges to conduct the hearings. Although these judges are employed by the agencies, they are strictly independent and cannot be removed except for gross misconduct. Congress, for example, empowers the Federal Trade Commission (FTC) to determine what constitutes an unfair trade practice.[24] Its actions, however, are reviewable in the federal courts. So are the findings of the EEOC and Social Security judges.

■ Internal Revenue Service Commissioner Charles O. Rossotti appears before the Senate Finance Committee during a congressional probe into alleged abuses of taxpayers by employees of the IRS. As a result of the hearings, numerous positive changes were made in the way the IRS deals with the public.

MAKING AGENCIES ACCOUNTABLE

Photo courtesy: Joe Marquette/AP/Wide World Photos
Honorable Rossotti

THE QUESTION OF to whom bureaucrats should be responsible is one that continually comes up in any debate about governmental accountability. Should the bureaucracy be answerable to itself? To organized interest groups? To its clientele? To the president? To Congress? Or to some combination of all of these? At times an agency becomes so removed from the public it serves that Congress must step in. This is what happened with the Internal Revenue Service (IRS). Throughout 1997 and 1998, Congress held extensive hearings about abuses at the IRS, one of the most hated and feared federal agencies in America. Senate hearings in particular exposed abuses of ordinary citizens who found themselves in a nightmare of bureaucratic red tape and agency employee abuse of power. As a result of these hearings, Congress ordered the new IRS commissioner to overhaul the way the IRS deals with the public.[25] The IRS's attempt to ease online tax filing in 2002 was another example of the use of technology to improve relations with the public. The IRS also redesigned its Web site, http://www.irs.gov. The public responded positively to

---

TABLE 9.3   Making Agencies Accountable

The president has the authority to:
- Appoint and remove agency heads and a few additional top bureaucrats.
- Reorganize the bureaucracy (with congressional approval).
- Make changes in an agency's annual budget proposals.
- Ignore legislative initiatives originating within the bureaucracy.
- Initiate or adjust policies that would, if enacted by Congress, alter the bureaucracy's activities.
- Issue executive orders.
- Reduce an agency's annual budget.

Congress has the authority to:
- Pass legislation that alters the bureaucracy's activities.
- Abolish existing programs.
- Investigate bureaucratic activities and compel bureaucrats to testify about them.
- Influence presidential appointments of agency heads and other top bureaucratic officials.
- Write legislation to limit the bureaucracy's discretion.

The judiciary has the authority to:
- Rule on whether bureaucrats have acted within the law and require policy changes to comply with the law.
- Force the bureaucracy to respect the rights of individuals through hearings and other proceedings.
- Rule on the constitutionality of all rules and regulations.

---

these changes, and by 2002, 67 percent of the American public reported that they had confidence in the IRS.[26]

Although many critics of the bureaucracy might argue that federal employees should be responsive to the public interest, the public interest is difficult to define. As it turns out, several factors work to control the power of the bureaucracy, and to some degree, the same kinds of checks and balances that operate among the three branches of government serve to check the bureaucracy (see Table 9.3).

Many political scientists argue that the president should be in charge of the bureaucracy because it is up to him to see that popular ideas and expectations are translated into administrative action. But, under our constitutional system, the president is not the only actor in the policy process. Congress creates the agencies, funds them, and establishes the broad rules of their operation. Moreover, Congress continually reviews the various agencies through oversight committee investigations, hearings, and its power of the purse. And, the federal judiciary, as in most other matters, has the ultimate authority to review administrative actions.

Executive Control

As the size and scope of the American national government, in general, and of the executive branch and the bureaucracy, in particular, have grown, presidents have delegated more and more power to bureaucrats. But, most presidents have continued to try to exercise some control over the bureaucracy, although they have often found that task more difficult than they first envisioned. As president, John F. Kennedy, for example, once lamented that to give anyone at the Department of State an instruction was comparable to putting your request in a dead-letter box.[27] No response would ever be forthcoming.

Recognizing these potential problems, presidents try to appoint the best possible persons to carry out their wishes and policy preferences. Presidents make hundreds of appointments to the executive branch; in doing so, they have the opportunity to appoint individuals who share their views on a range of policies. Although presidential appointments make up a very small proportion of all federal jobs, presidents or the Cabinet secretaries usually fill most top policy-making positions.

Presidents, with the approval of Congress, can reorganize the bureaucracy. They also can make changes in an agency's annual budget requests and ignore legislative initiatives originating within the bureaucracy. Several presidents have made it a priority to try to tame the bureaucracy to make it more accountable. Thomas Jefferson was the

E-GOVERNMENT

In 1992, the White House first went up on the World Wide Web. Now all government agencies and bureaus have Web sites and provide a plethora of information to the American public that formerly would have taken numerous trips to the library or even Washington, D.C., to obtain.

By 1998, the Government Paperwork Elimination Act required that federal agencies allow persons transacting business with the government to have the option of submitting information or transacting business with them electronically. It is from this act that you or members of your family now have the option of submitting your tax returns electronically.

In 2002, the Bush administration took additional advantage of changing technologies and the increasing number of Americans' access to it, whether in their homes, at local public libraries, or at Internet cafes. The E-Government Act of 2002 was an effort to mandate that all government agencies use "Internet-based information technologies to enhance citizens' access to government information and services."[a]

According to the E-Gov Web site, E-Gov is not simply about putting forms online; its major purpose is to harness technology to make it easier for citizens to learn more about government services. GovBenefits.gov, for example, has been created so that citizens can find answers to a range of questions dealing with their individual circumstances and will immediately receive a list of government programs for which they may be eligible. Recreation.gov allows individuals to find out about national parks and recreation sites and to make online reservations at those facilities.

The newest addition to the e-government effort under the Bush administration is its eRulemaking Initiative. Managed by the Environmental Protection Agency, this new use of technology is designed to transform "the federal rule-making process by enhancing the public's ability to participate in their government's regulatory decision making."[b] Regulations.gov was launched in 2002 to allow the public to "search, view, and comment on proposed federal regulations open for comment."[c] While the regulatory process almost exclusively involved interest groups and affected industries, this new initiative allows the public to search proposed regulations easily. Agencies are in the process of posting their proposed regulations on this central site, although some agencies still have their own sites. One 2004 study revealed that some agencies had failed to post proposed regulations on the central site, but efforts are being made to remedy these lapses.

By 2006, individuals should be able to track and comment on regulations from the 173 rule-making entities of the federal government as each of these units adapts to this new technology. OMB Watch, a nonprofit group that monitors government actions as they affect citizen participation, has applauded the notion of a centralized, one-stop method to allow concerned citizens input into the policy process.

1. Will the bureaucracy become more responsive to citizens and less captured by special interests as e-government increases?

2. Is there any downside to eRulemaking?

---

[a]About E-Gov, http://www.whitehouse.gov/omb/egov/about_leg.htm.

[b]http://www.regulations.gov.

[c]http://www.regulations.gov.

---

first president to address the issue of accountability. He attempted to cut waste and bring about a "wise and frugal government." But, it wasn't until the Progressive era (1890–1920) that calls for reform began to be taken seriously. Later, President Calvin Coolidge urged spending cuts and other reforms. His Correspondence Club was designed to reduce bureaucratic letter writing by 30 percent.[28]

As discussed in chapter 8, presidents also can shape policy and provide direction to bureaucrats by issuing executive orders.[29] **Executive orders** are rules or regulations issued by the president that have the effect of law. All executive orders must be published in the *Federal Register*. Even before Congress acted to protect women from discrimination by the federal government, for example, the National Organization for Women convinced President Lyndon B. Johnson to sign a 1967 executive order that amended an earlier one prohibiting the federal government from discriminating on the basis of race, color, religion, or national origin in the awarding of federal contracts, by adding to it the category of "gender." Although the president signed the order, the Office of Federal Contract Compliance, part of the Department of Labor's Employment Standards Administration, failed to draft appropriate guidelines for implementation of the order until several years later.[30] A president can direct an agency to act, but it may take some time for the order to be carried out. Given the many jobs of any president, few can ensure that all their orders will be carried out or that they will like all the rules that are made.

executive orders

Rules or regulations issued by the president that have the effect of law. All executive orders must be published in the *Federal Register*.

Congressional Control

Congress, too, plays an important role in checking the power of the bureaucracy. Constitutionally, it possesses the authority to create or abolish departments and agencies as well as to transfer agency functions, as was recently the case in the protracted debate over the creation of the Department of Homeland Security. In addition, it can expand or contract bureaucratic discretion. The Senate's authority to confirm (or reject) presidential appointments also gives Congress a check on the bureaucracy. Congress exercises considerable oversight over the bureaucracy in several ways. Table 9.4 contains data from a study conducted by the Brookings Institution detailing this authority.

Congress uses many of its constitutional powers to exercise control over the bureaucracy. These include its investigatory powers. It is not at all unusual for a congressional committee or subcommittee to hold hearings on a particular problem and then direct the relevant agency to study the problem or find ways to remedy it. Representatives of the agencies also appear

Photo courtesy: © Peter Jones/Reuters/Corbis

before these committees on a regular basis to inform members about agency activities and ongoing investigations.

Political scientists distinguish between two different forms of congressional oversight: police patrol and fire alarm oversight.[31] As the names imply, police patrol oversight is proactive and allows Congress to set its own agenda for programs or agencies to review. In contrast, fire alarm oversight is reactive and generally involves a congressional response to a complaint filed by a constituent or politically significant actor.

Given the prevalence of iron triangles, issue networks, and policy coordinating committees, it is not surprising that the most frequently used form of oversight and the most effective is communication between house staffers and agency personnel. Various forms of program evaluations make up the next most commonly used forms of congressional control. Congress and its staff routinely conduct evaluations of programs and conduct oversight hearings.

■ U.S. Secretary of State Designate Condoleezza Rice shakes hands with Senator Christopher Dodd (D–CT), as Senator Joseph Biden (DE) and Senator Barack Obama (D–IL) look on, after her second day of testimony before the U.S. Senate Foreign Relations Committee during her confirmation hearings. On January 19, 2005, Rice was confirmed as Secretary of State by the committee.

TABLE 9.4	Frequency and Effectiveness of Oversight Techniques in a Single Congress	
Oversight Technique	Number of Cases in Which Technique Was Used	Effectiveness Ranking
Staff communication with agency personnel	91	1
Member communication with agency personnel	86	2
Program reauthorization hearings	73	3
Oversight hearings	89	4
Hearings on bills to amend ongoing programs	70	5
Staff investigations	90	6
Program evaluations done by committee staff	89	7
Program evaluations done by congressional support agencies	89	8
Legislative veto	82	9
Analysis of proposed agency rules and regulations	90	10
Program evaluations done by outsiders	88	11
Agency reports required by Congress	91	12
Program evaluations done by the agencies	87	13
Review of casework	87	14

Source: Joel Aberbach, *Keeping a Watchful Eye* (Washington, DC: Brookings Institution, 1990), 132, 135.

THE EPA AND LEAD IN WATER

OVERVIEW: Government bureaucracies influence life in the United States in many beneficial and, sometimes, not so beneficial ways. Most are charged with securing the common good and are dedicated to serving the American public. Administrative agencies, however, do not operate in a vacuum—they have mandates from the government and are ultimately subject to congressional, executive, and judicial supervision. The idea of bureaucratic oversight is to ensure that agencies and departments are held accountable for their activities. These administrative units have more or less discretion and freedom of action depending on their mandates. But, though considered expert in their respective policy domains, bureaucracies may receive from the government ill-conceived or poorly researched directives that can interfere with an agency's mission or hinder proper administrative functioning. As with any organization under human control, they also reflect the effect of human foibles and corruption. Nevertheless, because of the unique nature of government bureaucracies in that they can affect the lives of millions, there must be accountability when bureaucracies fail in their mission.

In February 2004, it was revealed that the District of Columbia's drinking water contained dramatically increased levels of lead, which can increase the risk of cancer. The problem affected approximately 23,000 residences in the District. It was later determined that the District's Water and Sewer Authority (WASA) neglected to follow the Environmental Protection Agency's (EPA) mandated language when informing citizens of high lead levels in D.C.'s water supply, and that WASA also neglected to do follow-up water testing

in areas where lead service pipes had been partially replaced. And, the EPA stands accused of neglecting oversight of WASA by taking too long to notice and act on the violations, some of which occurred in 2002.

Ironically, the increased lead levels were caused by the Army Corps of Engineers' attempt in 2000 to increase the quality of the water supply. The Army Corps of Engineers oversees the Washington Aqueduct that supplies drinking water to the city, while WASA manages operations of the water supply. In 2000, the Army Corps of Engineers sought to improve water quality by switching from chlorine to chloramine (a combination of chlorine and ammonia) to purify water. This change had the unintended effect of further corroding lead pipes and thus increasing the amount of lead in the water supply. Once word of the problem became public, the EPA had the Corps of Engineers replace chloramine with chlorine, and lead levels dropped immediately and significantly.

What is the lesson to be learned from this case? Where does accountability lie—with the EPA, with WASA, or with the Corps of Engineers? With all? All of these agencies were pursuing a public good: lower lead levels in the water supply that could reduce the risk of cancer for D.C. residents. Should motive and intent be taken into account when determining accountability? On the one hand, doesn't the fact that the water supply was immediately fixed demonstrate bureaucratic accountability? On the other, WASA was demonstrably negligent when informing D.C. residents of the problem by ignoring federal language guidelines in notices, pamphlets, and public service announcements, and WASA was negligent as well for not doing follow-up testing after replacing pipes, as required by EPA guidelines. Additionally, a Cato Institute scholar accused the EPA of

Congress also has the power of the purse. To control the bureaucracy, Congress uses its ability to fund or not to fund an agency's activities like the proverbial carrot and stick. The House Appropriations Committee routinely holds hearings to allow agency heads to justify their budget requests. Authorization legislation originates in the various legislative committees that oversee particular agencies (such as Agriculture, Veterans Affairs, Education, and Labor) and sets the maximum amounts that agencies can spend on particular programs. While some authorizations, such as those for Social Security, are permanent, others, including the Departments of State and Defense procurements, are watched closely and are subject to annual authorizations.

Once funds are authorized, they must be appropriated before they can be spent. Appropriations originate with the House Appropriations Committee, not the specialized legislative committees. Often the Appropriations Committee allocates sums smaller than those authorized by legislative committees. Thus, the Appropriations Committee, a budget cutter, has an additional oversight function.

To help Congress's oversight of the bureaucracy's financial affairs, in 1921 Congress created the General Accounting Office, now the General Accountability Office (GAO), at the same time that the Office of the Budget, now the Office of Management and Budget (OMB), was created in the executive branch. With the establishment bowing to interest-group pressure to replace chlorine with chloramine—pressure that advocated change based on questionable science and experience. Should bureaucracies heed private interests outside government?

Arguments for EPA Accountability

- **Accountability is ultimately the responsibility of the agency in question.** In the end, the parent agency is responsible for ensuring oversight and the proper functioning of all bureaucratic agencies and departments within its purview. Since the EPA is the ultimate authority for protecting the water supply, it should be held accountable.
- **Agencies are accountable for the science and methods used.** If science or methodology has not been scrupulously proved safe or effective, change should not be implemented until the science or methods have been demonstrated to be sound.
- **Government bureaucracies should not be influenced by interest groups.** If it is true that the EPA bowed to the wishes of interest groups—in this case, the environmental lobby—it is not performing its function as intended. Bureaucracies are accountable to the government, not outside interests.

Arguments Against EPA Accountability

- **Those in charge of regulation may sometimes be unaware of mid- and low-level problems.** Many times lower-level bureaucrats hide their actions from superiors in order to protect themselves. It is unreasonable to expect senior managers to know what is consciously being hidden at lower departmental levels. Those directly culpable should be disciplined accordingly.
- **The EPA was following federal law.** According to National Public Radio, weak federal laws regulating drinking water are to blame for water quality in the United States. What happened in the District of Columbia is to be expected when those engaged in oversight have little knowledge and understanding of, or little concern for, the domain being regulated. Ultimately, bureaucracies are to be held accountable to established law.
- **Bureaucratic efficiency and quality are only as good as current research and science.** The EPA cannot be held accountable for acting on possibly flawed science. The intent behind changing the water purification system in D.C. was to reduce the risk of cancer and affiliated illness. Practice showed the change to chloramine caused increased lead levels, and once the problem was noticed, it was fixed.

Questions

1. What agency or agencies were at fault in the above case study? What would be a means to determine accountability?
2. Should Congress be more diligent in exercising its oversight authority? If so, is the government not ultimately accountable?

Selected Readings

John Burke. *Bureaucratic Responsibility*. Baltimore, MD: Johns Hopkins University Press, 1988.

David Osborne and Peter Plastrik. *Banishing Bureaucracy: Five Strategies for Reinventing Government*. Boston: Addison Wesley, 1997.

of the GAO, the Congressional Research Service (CRS), and later, the Congressional Budget Office (CBO), Congress essentially created its own bureaucracy to keep an eye on what the executive branch and bureaucracy were doing. Today, the GAO not only tracks how money is spent in the bureaucracy, but it also monitors how policies are implemented. The CBO also conducts oversight studies. If it or the GAO uncovers problems with an agency's work, Congress is notified immediately.

Legislators also augment their formal oversight of the executive branch by allowing citizens to appeal adverse bureaucratic decisions to agencies, Congress, and even the courts. Congressional review, a procedure adopted by the 104th Congress, by which agency regulations can be nullified by joint resolutions of legislative disapproval, is another method of exercising congressional oversight. This form of oversight is discussed in greater detail in chapter 7.

Judicial Control

Whereas the president's and Congress's ongoing control over the actions of the bureaucracy is very direct, the judiciary's oversight function is less apparent. Still, federal judges, for example, can directly issue injunctions or orders to an executive agency even before a rule is promulgated formally, giving the federal judiciary a potent check on the bureaucracy. The courts also have ruled that agencies must give all affected individuals their due process rights guaranteed by the U.S. Constitution. A Social Security recipient's checks cannot be stopped, for example, unless that individual is provided with reasonable notice and an opportunity for a hearing. On a more informal, indirect level, litigation, or even the threat of litigation, often exerts a strong influence on bureaucrats. Injured parties can bring suit against agencies for their failure to enforce the law, and can challenge agency interpretations of the law. In general, however, the courts give great weight to the opinions of bureaucrats and usually defer to their expertise.[32]

Research by political scientists shows that government agencies are strategic. They often implement Supreme Court decisions "based on the costs and benefits of alternative policy choices." Specifically, the degree to which agencies appear to respond to Supreme Court decisions is based on the "specificity of Supreme Court opinions, agency policy preferences, agency age, and *amicus curiae* support."[33]

The development of specialized courts has altered the relationship of some agencies with the federal courts, apparently resulting in less judicial deference to agency rulings. Research by political scientists reveals that specialized courts such as the Court of International Trade, because of their expertise, defer less to agency decisions than do more generalized federal courts. Conversely, decisions from executive agencies are more likely to be reversed than those from more specialized independent regulatory commissions.[34]

SUMMARY

THE BUREAUCRACY plays a major role in America as a shaper of public policy, earning it the nickname the "fourth branch" of government. To explain the evolution and scope of bureaucratic power, in this chapter we have made the following points:

1. The Executive Branch and the Development of the Federal Bureaucracy

According to Max Weber, all bureaucracies have similar characteristics. These characteristics can be seen in the federal bureaucracy as it developed from George Washington's time, when the executive branch had only three departments—State, War, and Treasury—through the Civil War. Significant gains occurred in the size of the federal bureaucracy as the government geared up to conduct a war. As employment opportunities within the federal government increased, concurrent reforms in the civil service system assured that more and more jobs were filled according to merit and not by patronage. By the late 1800s, reform efforts led to further increases in the size of the bureaucracy, as independent regulatory commissions were created. In the wake of the Depression, many new agencies were created to get the national economy back on course as part of President Franklin D. Roosevelt's New Deal.

2. The Modern Bureaucracy

The modern bureaucracy is composed of nearly two million civilian workers from all walks of life. In general, bureaucratic agencies fall into four general types: departments, government corporations, independent agencies, and independent regulatory commissions.

3. How the Bureaucracy Works

The bureaucracy gets much of its power from the Congress delegating its powers. A variety of formal and informal mechanisms have been created to help the bureaucracy work more efficiently. These mechanisms help the bureaucracy and bureaucrats make policy.

4. Making Agencies Accountable

Agencies enjoy considerable discretion, but they are also subjected to many formal controls. The president, Congress, and the judiciary all exercise various degrees of control over the bureaucracy

KEY TERMS

administrative adjudication, p. 334
administrative discretion, p. 332
bureaucracy, p. 314
civil service system, p. 317
departments, p. 327
executive orders, p. 335
Federal Employees Political Activities Act, p. 320
government corporation, p. 329
Hatch Act, p. 320
implementation, p. 330
independent executive agency, p. 329
independent regulatory commission, p. 317
interagency councils, p. 331
iron triangles, p. 330
issue networks, p. 331
merit system, p. 317
patronage, p. 317

SELECTED READINGS

Aberbach, Joel D., and Bert A. Rockman. *In the Web of Politics: Three Decades of the U.S. Federal Executive.* Washington, DC: Brookings Institution, 2000.

Borrelli, MaryAnne. *The President's Cabinet: Gender, Power, and Representation.* Boulder, CO: Lynne Rienner, 2002.

Brehm, John, and Scott Gates. *Working, Shirking, and Sabotage: Bureaucratic Response to a Democratic Public.* Ann Arbor: University of Michigan Press, 1997.

Derthick, Martha, and Paul J. Quirk. *The Politics of Deregulation.* Washington, DC: Brookings Institution, 1985.

Dolan, Julie A., and David H. Rosenbloom. *Representative Bureaucracy: Continued Cases and Controversies.* Armonk, NY: M. E. Sharpe, 2003.

Felbinger, Claire L., and Wendy A. Haynes, eds. *Outstanding Women in Public Administration: Leaders, Mentors, and Pioneers.* Armonk, NY: M. E. Sharpe, 2004.

Goodsell, Charles T. *The Case for Bureaucracy: A Public Administration Polemic,* 4th ed. Washington, DC: CQ Press, 2003.

Gormley, William T., and Steven J. Balla. *Bureaucracy and Democracy: Accountability and Performance.* Washington, DC: CQ Press, 2003.

Handler, Joel F. *Down the Bureaucracy: The Ambiguity of Privatization and Empowerment.* Princeton, NJ: Princeton University Press, 1996.

Ingraham, Patricia Wallace. *The Foundation of Merit: Public Service in American Democracy.* Baltimore, MD: Johns Hopkins University Press, 1995.

Kerwin, Cornelius M. *Rulemaking: How Government Agencies Write Law and Make Policy,* 3rd ed. Washington, DC: CQ Press, 2003.

Peters, B. Guy. *The Politics of Bureaucracy,* 5th ed. New York: Routledge, 2001.

Richardson, William D. *Democracy, Bureaucracy and Character.* Lawrence: University Press of Kansas, 1997.

Stivers, Camilla. *Gender Images in Public Administration: Legitimacy and the Administrative State.* Thousand Oaks, CA: Sage, 2002.

Twight, Charlotte. *Dependent on DC: The Rise of Federal Control over the Lives of Ordinary Americans.* New York: Palgrave Macmillan, 2002.

Wilson, James Q. *Bureaucracy: What Government Agencies Do and Why They Do It,* reprint ed. New York: Basic Books, 2000.

WEB EXPLORATIONS

For more about the Women's Bureau in the Department of Labor, see
www.dol.gov/wb/

To examine the federal workforce by gender, race, and ethnicity, go to
www.opm.gov/feddata/factbook/

To see federal agency rules and regulations contained in the *Federal Register,* go to
www.gpoaccess.gov/fr/index.html

For more about the IRS and its modernization efforts, see
www.irs.gov

Photo courtesy: Rick Priedman/Corbis

The Judiciary

WHEN THE SUPREME COURT AGREED to hear the case of *Lawrence* v. *Texas* in late 2002, many social conservatives were stunned. Although legally, the petitioners only asked the justices to rule on the constitutionality of a Texas statute banning consensual sodomy between same-sex couples, the case had much broader practical implications. If the justices found the statute unconstitutional, the Court would be able to redefine the gay rights movement in the United States and perhaps open the door for equal rights for homosexuals in areas such as marriage and adoption.

Speculation about how the Court would decide the case, and how broad this decision would be, continued until the Court handed down its final decision on June 26, 2003. In this opinion, written by Justice Anthony Kennedy, the Court ruled that the Texas statute violated John Geddes Lawrence's Fourteenth Amendment right to due process of the law, as well as to his right to privacy. This decision also rendered unconstitutional the laws of thirteen other states. It also established a new national standard for the regulation of private sexual activity, to say nothing of bringing the gay rights struggle into the spotlight for the 2004 election cycle, which continued when the Court refused to hear an appeal challenging Massachusetts's decision to allow same-sex marriage.

The Supreme Court has not always played such a key role in setting the terms of constitutional debate in American society, nor have its members been able to make such broad legal policy. Today, however, the Court controls the fate of nearly every major policy made on the most significant local, state, and national social issues in our society, including abortion, the death penalty, the extent of the government's involvement in religion, and the scope of its right to resolve competing claims of domestic safety versus individual liberties.

Because the Court has usurped such tremendous policy-making power and is the final word on the meaning of the Constitution, many groups that believe that they cannot achieve policy change through traditional legislative means choose to bring their claims to the judiciary, especially the federal courts. This authority gives the nine men and women who sit on the Supreme Court unprecedented power in American society.

N 1787, WHEN ALEXANDER HAMILTON wrote to urge support of the U.S. Constitution, he firmly believed that the judiciary would prove to be the weakest of the three departments of government. In its formative years, the judiciary was, in Hamilton's words, "the least dangerous" branch. The judicial branch seemed so inconsequential that when the young national government made its move to the District of Columbia in 1800, Congress actually forgot to include any space to house the justices of the Supreme Court! Last-minute conferences with Capitol architects led to the allocation of a small area in the basement of the Senate wing of the Capitol building for a courtroom. No other space was allowed for the justices, however. Noted one commentator, "A stranger might traverse the dark avenues of the Capitol for a week, without finding the remote corner in which justice is administered to the American Republic."[1]

Today, the role of the courts, particularly the Supreme Court of the United States, is significantly different from that envisioned in 1788, the year the national government came into being. The "least dangerous branch" now is perceived by many as having too much power, and critics charge that the Framers would not recognize the scope of power of the current federal government, especially the judiciary.

Historically, too, Americans were unaware of the political power held by the courts. They were raised to think of the federal courts as above the fray of politics. That, however, has never been the case. Elected presidents nominate judges to the federal courts and justices to the Supreme Court, often to advance their personal politics, and elected senators ultimately confirm (or decline to confirm) presidential nominees to the federal bench. Not only is the selection process political, but the process by which cases ultimately get heard—if they are heard at all—by the Supreme Court often is political as well. Interest groups routinely seek out good test cases to advance their policy positions. Even the U.S. government, generally through the Department of Justice and the U.S. solicitor general (a political appointee in that department), seeks to advance its version of the public interest in court. Interest groups then often line up on opposing sides to advance their positions, much in the same way lobbyists do in Congress. More recent decisions of the Supreme Court, including *Bush* v. *Gore* (2000), which for many appeared to decide the outcome of the 2000 presidential election contest, propelled the power of the Court into the national consciousness.

In this chapter, we will explore these issues and the scope and development of judicial power:

- First, we will look at *the Constitution and the creation of the federal judiciary* as well as the Judiciary Act of 1789 and its establishment of the federal judicial system. Article III of the Constitution created a Supreme Court but left it to Congress to create any other federal courts, a task it took up quickly.

- Second, we will discuss *the American legal system* and the concepts of civil and criminal law.

- Third, we will discuss *the federal court system*. The federal court system is composed of specialized courts, district courts, courts of appeals, and the Supreme Court, which is the ultimate authority on all federal law.

- Fourth, we will examine *how federal court judges are selected*. All appointments to the federal district courts, courts of appeals, and the Supreme Court are made by the president and are subject to Senate confirmation.

- Fifth, we will take a look at *the Supreme Court today*. Only a few of the millions of cases filed in courts around the United States every year eventually make their way to the Supreme Court through the lengthy appellate process.

Protesters gathered outside the U.S. Supreme Court during arguments in *Bush v. Gore* (2000). The Court's decision, in effect, decided the outcome of the 2000 presidential election.

Photo courtesy: Sylvia Johnson/Woodfin Camp & Associates

- Sixth, we will examine *judicial philosophy and decision making* and discuss how judicial decision making is based on a variety of legal and extra-legal factors.
- Finally, we will discuss *judicial policy making and implementation*.

A note on terminology: When we refer to the "Supreme Court," the "Court," or the "high Court" here, we always mean the U.S. Supreme Court, which sits at the pinnacle of the federal and state court systems. The Supreme Court is referred to by the name of the chief justice who presided over it during a particular period (for example, the Marshall Court is the Court presided over by John Marshall from 1801 to 1835). When we use the term "courts," we refer to all federal or state courts unless otherwise noted.

THE CONSTITUTION AND THE CREATION OF THE FEDERAL JUDICIARY

THE DETAILED NOTES James Madison took at the Constitutional Convention in Philadelphia make it clear that the Framers devoted little time to the writing of, or the content of, Article III, which created the judicial branch of government. The Framers believed that a federal judiciary posed little of the threat of tyranny that they feared from the other two branches. One scholar has even suggested that, for at least some delegates to the Constitutional Convention, "provision for a national judiciary was a matter of theoretical necessity . . . more in deference to the maxim of separation [of powers] than in response to clearly formulated ideas about the role of a national judicial system and its indispensability."[2]

Alexander Hamilton argued in *Federalist No. 78* that the judiciary would be the least dangerous branch of government. Anti-Federalists, however, did not agree with Hamilton. They particularly objected to a judiciary whose members had life tenure and the ability to interpret what was to be "the supreme law of the land," a phrase that Anti-Federalists feared would give the Supreme Court too much power.

The Living Constitution

The Judges both of the supreme and inferior Courts, shall...receive for their Services, a Compensation, which shall not be diminished during their Continuance in Office.
—Article III, Section 1

This section of Article III simply posits the notion that the salaries of all federal judges cannot be reduced during their service on the bench. During the Constitutional Convention, there was considerable debate over how to treat the payment of federal judges. Some believed that Congress should have an extra check on the judiciary by being able to intimidate judges with the threat of reducing their salaries. This provision was a compromise after James Madison suggested that Congress have the authority to bar increases as well as decreases in the salaries of these unelected jurists. The delegates recognized that decreases, as well as no opportunity for raises, could negatively affect the pluses associated with life tenure.

There has not been much controversy over this clause of the Constitution. When the federal income tax was first enacted, some judges unsuccessfully challenged it as a diminution of their salaries. Much more recently, Chief Justice William H. Rehnquist often argued for increased salaries for federal judges, who earn less than some of their former clerks do as first-year associates in private law firms. As early as 1989, he noted that "judicial salaries were the single greatest problem facing the federal judiciary today." In 2002, not only did Rehnquist note the increased workload of each federal judge and the relative static salary of federal judges, but he also pointed out that while the salaries of those lawyers engaged in private practice has skyrocketed, the salaries of federal judges have stagnated, with judges receiving only small cost-of-living increases. This inequity is making it difficult to attract and retain top-flight judges, especially those who have children to put through college. He argued that inadequate pay undermines the strength of the independent judiciary.

More and more federal judges are leaving the bench for more lucrative private practice, which is a relatively recent phenomenon. While $150,000 may sound like a lot to most people, lawyers in large urban practices routinely earn more than double and often triple that amount each year.

As discussed in chapter 2, the Framers also debated the need for any federal courts below the level of the Supreme Court. Some argued in favor of deciding all cases in state courts, with only appeals going before the Supreme Court. Others argued for a system of federal courts. A compromise left the final choice to Congress, and Article III, section 1, begins simply by vesting "The judicial Power of the United States . . . in one supreme Court, and in such inferior Courts as the Congress may from time to time ordain and establish." Although there is some debate over whether the Court should have the power of **judicial review,** which allows the judiciary to review acts of the other branches of government and the states, the question was left unsettled in Article III—and not finally resolved until *Marbury* v. *Madison* (1803),[3] regarding acts of the national government and *Martin* v. *Hunter's Lessee* (1816), regarding state law, which upheld a

judicial review
Power of the courts to review acts of other branches of government and the states.

section of the Judiciary Act of 1789 authorizing Supreme Court review of state court actions interpreting the U.S. Constitution.[4]

Article III, section 1, also gave Congress the authority to establish other courts as it saw fit. Section 2 specifies the judicial power of the Supreme Court (see Table 10.1) and discusses the Court's original and appellate jurisdiction. This section also specifies that all federal crimes, except those involving impeachment, shall be tried by jury in the state in which the crime was committed. The third section of the article defines treason, and mandates that at least two witnesses appear in such cases.

Although it is the duty of the chief justice of the United States to preside over presidential impeachments, this is not mentioned in Article III. Instead, Article I, section 3, notes in discussing impeachment, "When the President of the United States is tried, the Chief Justice shall preside."

Had the Supreme Court been viewed as the potential policy maker it is today, it is highly unlikely that the Framers would have provided for life tenure with "good behavior" for federal judges in Article III. This feature was agreed on because the Framers did not want the justices (or any federal judges) subject to the whims of politics, the public, or politicians. Moreover, Alexander Hamilton argued in *Federalist No. 78* that the "independence of judges" was needed "to guard the Constitution and the rights of individuals." Because the Framers viewed the Court as quite powerless, Hamilton stressed the need to place federal judges above the fray of politics.

Some checks on the power of the judiciary were nonetheless included in the Constitution. The Constitution gives Congress the authority to alter the Court's jurisdiction (its ability to hear certain kinds of cases). Congress can also propose constitutional amendments that, if ratified, can effectively reverse judicial decisions, and it can impeach and remove federal judges. In one further check, it is the president who (with the "advice and consent" of the Senate) appoints all federal judges.

The Judiciary Act of 1789 and the Creation of the Federal Judicial System

In spite of the Framers' intentions, the pervasive role of politics in the judicial branch quickly became evident with the passage of the Judiciary Act of 1789. Congress spent nearly the entire second half of its first session deliberating the various provisions of the act to give form and substance to the federal judiciary. As one early observer noted, "The convention has only crayoned in the outlines. It left it to Congress to fill up and colour the canvas."[5]

TABLE 10.1   The Judicial Power of the United States Supreme Court

The following are the types of cases the Supreme Court was given the jurisdiction to hear as initially specified in the Constitution:

- All cases arising under the Constitution and laws or treaties of the United States
- All cases of admiralty or maritime jurisdiction
- Cases in which the United States is a party
- Controversies between a state and citizens of another state
- Controversies between two or more states
- Controversies between citizens of different states
- Controversies between citizens of the same states claiming lands under grants in different states
- Controversies between a state, or the citizens thereof, and foreign states or citizens thereof
- All cases affecting ambassadors or other public ministers

Judiciary Act of 1789
Established the basic three-tiered structure of the federal court system.

The **Judiciary Act of 1789** established the basic three-tiered structure of the federal court system. At the bottom are the federal district courts—at least one in each state—each staffed by a federal judge. If the people participating in a lawsuit (called litigants) were unhappy with the district court's verdict, they could appeal their case to one of three circuit courts. Each circuit court, initially created to function as a trial court for important cases, was composed of one district court judge and two itinerant Supreme Court justices who met as a circuit court twice a year. It wasn't until 1891 that circuit courts (also often called courts of appeals, as we know them today) took on their exclusively appellate function. The third tier of the federal judicial system fleshed out by the Judiciary Act of 1789 was the Supreme Court of the United States. Although the Constitution mentions "the supreme Court," it was silent on its size. In the Judiciary Act, Congress set the size of the Supreme Court at six—the chief justice plus five associate justices. After being reduced to five members in 1801, it later expanded and contracted, and finally the Court's size was expanded to nine in 1869.

When the justices met in their first public session in New York City in 1790, they were garbed magnificently in black and scarlet robes in the English fashion. The elegance of their attire, however, could not make up for the relative ineffectiveness of the Court. Its first session—presided over by John Jay, who was appointed chief justice of the United States by George Washington—initially had to be adjourned when a quorum of the justices failed to attend. Later, once a quorum assembled, the justices decided only one major case—*Chisholm* v. *Georgia* (1793) (discussed on the following page). Moreover, as an indication of its lowly status, one associate justice left the Court to become chief justice of the South Carolina Supreme Court. (Although such a move would be considered a step down today, keep in mind that in the early years of the United States, many viewed the states as more important than the new national government.)

Hampered by frequent changes in personnel, limited space for its operations, no clerical support, and no system of reporting its decisions, the Court and its meager activities did not impress many people. From the beginning, the circuit court duties of the Supreme Court justices presented problems for the prestige of the Court. Few good lawyers were willing to accept nominations to the high Court because circuit court duties entailed a substantial amount of travel—most of it on horseback over poorly maintained roads in frequently inclement weather. Southern justices often rode as many as 10,000 miles a year on horseback. President George Washington tried to prevail on several friends and supporters to fill vacancies on the Court as they appeared, but most refused the "honor." John Adams, the second president of the United States, ran into similar problems. When he asked John Jay to resume the position of chief justice after he resigned to become governor of New York, Jay declined the offer. Jay once had remarked of the Court that it lacked "energy, weight, and dignity" as well as "public confidence and respect."

In spite of all its problems, in its first decade, the Court took several actions to help mold the new nation. First, by declining to give George Washington advice on the legality of some of his actions, the justices attempted to establish the Supreme Court as an independent, nonpolitical branch of government. Although John Jay, as an individual, frequently gave the president private advice, the Court refused to answer questions Washington posed to it concerning the construction of international laws and treaties. The justices wanted to avoid the appearance of prejudging any issues that could arise later before them.

The early Court also tried to advance principles of nationalism and to maintain the national government's supremacy over the states. As circuit court jurists, the justices rendered numerous decisions on such matters as national suppression of the Whiskey Rebellion, which occurred in 1794 after a national excise tax was imposed on whiskey, and the constitutionality of the Alien and Sedition Acts, which made it a crime to criticize national governmental officials or their actions (see chapter 5).

During the ratification debates, Anti-Federalists had warned that Article III extended federal judicial power to controversies "between a State and Citizens of another State"—meaning that a citizen of one state could sue any other state in federal court, a prospect unthinkable to defenders of state sovereignty. Although Federalists, including Alexander Hamilton and James Madison, had scoffed at the idea, the nationalist Supreme Court quickly proved them wrong in *Chisholm* v. *Georgia* (1793). In *Chisholm,* the justices interpreted the Court's jurisdiction under Article III, section 2, to include the right to hear suits brought by a citizen against a state in which he did not reside. Writing in *Chisholm,* Justice James Wilson denounced the "haughty notions of state independence, state sovereignty, and state supremacy."[6] The states' reaction to this perceived attack on their authority led to passage and ratification (in 1798) of the Eleventh Amendment to the Constitution, which specifically limited judicial power by stipulating that the authority of the federal courts could not "extend to any suit . . . commenced or prosecuted against one of the United States by citizens of another State."

Finally, in a series of circuit and Supreme Court decisions, the justices paved the way for announcement of the doctrine of judicial review by the third chief justice, John Marshall.[7] Justices riding circuit occasionally held state laws unconstitutional because they violated the U.S. Constitution. In 1796, the Court for the first time evaluated the constitutionality of an act of *Congress,* finding the law, however, to be constitutional.[8]

The Chief Justice of the United States

The Marshall Court: *Marbury* v. *Madison* (1803) and Judicial Review

John Marshall, who headed the Court from 1801 to 1835, brought much-needed respect and prestige to the Court through his leadership in a progression of cases and a series of innovations. Marshall was appointed chief justice by President John Adams in 1801, three years after he declined to accept a nomination as associate justice (see Roots of Government: John Marshall). An ardent Federalist, Marshall has come to be considered the most important justice ever to serve on the high Court. Part of his reputation is the result of the duration of his service and the historical significance of this period in our nation's history.

As chief justice, Marshall instituted several innovations and led the Court to issue a number of important rulings that established the Court as a co-equal branch of government. First, the Marshall Court discontinued the practice of *seriatim* (Latin for "in a series") opinions, which was the custom of the King's Bench in Great

■ This 1881 wood engraving shows the Chief Justice and associate justices of the U.S. Supreme Court, clad in their traditional robes, as they pass from the robing room to the Court chamber.

Photo courtesy: Granger

Britain. Prior to the Marshall Court, the justices delivered their individual opinions in order. There was no single opinion of the Court, as we are accustomed to today. For the Court to take its place as an equal branch of government, Marshall strongly believed, the justices needed to speak as a Court and not as six individuals. In fact, during Marshall's first four years in office, the Court routinely spoke as one, and the chief justice wrote twenty-four of its twenty-six opinions.

The Marshall Court also established the authority of the Supreme Court over the judiciaries of the various states, including the Court's power to declare state laws invalid in a series of cases from 1810 to 1821 (*Fletcher* v. *Peck* [1810]; *Martin* v. *Hunter's Lessee* [1816]; and, *Cohens* v. *Virginia* [1821]), all cases in which states opposed the authority of the national government to review state actions.[9] In addition, the Court established the supremacy of the federal government and Congress over state governments through a broad interpretation of the necessary and proper clause in *McCulloch* v. *Maryland* (1819), discussed in detail in chapter 3.[10]

Finally, the Marshall Court claimed the right of judicial review, from which the Supreme Court derives much of its day-to-day power and impact on the policy process. This established the Court as the final arbiter of constitutional questions, with the right to declare congressional acts void (*Marbury* v. *Madison* [1803]).[11]

In *Federalist No. 78,* Alexander Hamilton first publicly endorsed the idea of judicial review, noting, "Whenever a particular statute contravenes the Constitution, it will be the duty of the judicial tribunals to adhere to the latter and disregard the former." Nonetheless, because the power of judicial review is not mentioned in the U.S. Constitution, the actual authority of the Supreme Court to review the constitutionality of acts of Congress was an unsettled question. But, in **Marbury v. Madison (1803),** Chief Justice John Marshall claimed this sweeping authority for the Court by asserting that the right of judicial review was a power that could be implied from the Constitution's supremacy clause.[12]

Marbury v. *Madison* arose amid a sea of political controversy. In the final hours of the Adams administration, William Marbury was appointed a justice of the peace for the District of Columbia. But, in the confusion of winding up matters, Adams's secretary of state failed to deliver Marbury's commission. Marbury then asked James Madison, Thomas Jefferson's secretary of state, for the commission. Under direct orders from Jefferson, who was irate over the Adams administration's last-minute appointment of several Federalist judges (quickly confirmed by the Federalist Senate), Madison refused to turn over the commission. Marbury and three other Adams appointees who were in the same situation then filed a writ of *mandamus* (a legal motion) asking the Supreme Court to order Madison to deliver their commissions.

Political tensions ran high as the Court met to hear the case. Jefferson threatened to ignore any order of the Court. Marshall realized that he and the prestige of the Court could be devastated by any refusal of the executive branch to comply with the decision. Responding to this challenge, in a brilliant opinion that in many sections reads more like a lecture to Jefferson than a discussion of the merits of Marbury's claim, Marshall concluded that although Marbury and the others were entitled to their commissions, the Court lacked the power to issue the writ sought by Marbury. In *Marbury* v. *Madison,* Marshall further ruled that the parts of the Judiciary Act of 1789 that extended the jurisdiction of the Court to allow it to issue writs were inconsistent with the Constitution and therefore unconstitutional.

Although the immediate effect of the decision was to deny power to the Court, its long-term effect was to establish the principle of judicial review. Said Marshall, writing for the Court, "it is emphatically the province and duty of the judicial department to say what the law is." Through judicial review, an implied power, the Supreme Court most dramatically exerts its authority to determine what the Constitution means. Since *Marbury,* the Court has routinely exercised the power of judicial review to determine the constitutionality of acts of Congress, the executive branch, and the states.

Marbury v. *Madison* (1803)
Case in which the Supreme Court first asserted the power of judicial review in finding that the congressional statute extending the Court's original jurisdiction was unconstitutional.

JOHN MARSHALL

A SINGLE person can make a major difference in the development of an institution. Such was the case with John Marshall, who dominated the Supreme Court during his thirty-four years as chief justice. As President James A. Garfield noted, "Marshall found the Constitution paper, and he made it power. He found a skeleton, and he clothed it with flesh and blood."

Who was this man still so revered today? John Marshall (1755–1835) was born in a log cabin in Virginia, the first of fifteen children of Welsh immigrants. Although tutored at home by two clergymen, Marshall's inspiration was his father, who introduced him to English literature and Sir William Blackstone's influential work, *Commentaries on the Laws of England*. After serving in the Continental Army and acquiring the rank of captain, Marshall taught himself the law. He attended only one formal course at the College of William & Mary before being admitted to the bar. Marshall practiced law in Virginia, where he and his wife lived and raised a family.

More of a politician than a lawyer, Marshall served as a delegate to the Virginia legislature from 1782 to 1785, 1787 to 1790, and 1795 to 1796, and he played an instrumental role in Virginia's ratification of the U.S. Constitution in 1787. As the leading Federalist in Virginia, Marshall was offered several positions in the Federalist administrations of George Washington and John Adams—including attorney general and associate justice of the Supreme Court—but he refused them all. Finally, in 1799, Washington persuaded him to run for the House of Representatives. Marshall was elected, but his career in the House was brief, for he became secretary of state in 1800

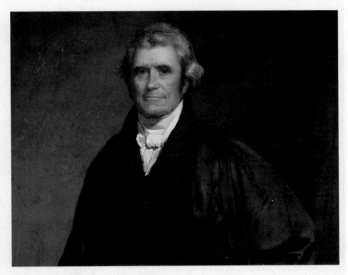

Photo courtesy: Boston Athenaeum

under John Adams. When Oliver Ellsworth resigned as chief justice of the United States in 1800, Adams nominated Marshall. Though Marshall was an ardent Federalist, he was a third cousin of Democratic-Republican President Thomas Jefferson, whose administration he faced head-on in *Marbury* v. *Madison* (1803).

Though Marshall had little legal experience when he came to the Court, he is regarded as one of the most significant chief justices in American history. He served on the Court until the day he died, participating in more than 1,000 decisions and authoring more than 500 opinions.

THE AMERICAN LEGAL SYSTEM

Comparing Judiciaries

THE JUDICIAL SYSTEM in the United States can best be described as a dual system consisting of the federal court system and the judicial systems of the fifty states, as illustrated in Figure 10.1 and also described in chapter 4. Cases may arise in either system. Both systems are basically three tiered. At the bottom of the system are **trial courts,** where litigation begins. In the middle are appellate courts in the state systems and the courts of appeals in the federal system. At the top of each pyramid sits a high court. (Some states call these supreme courts; New York calls it the Court of Appeals; Oklahoma and Texas call the highest state court for criminal cases the Court of Criminal Appeals.) The federal courts of appeals and Supreme Court as well as state courts of appeals and supreme courts are **appellate courts** that, with few exceptions, review on appeal only cases that already have been decided in lower courts. These courts generally hear matters of both civil and criminal law.

trial courts
Courts of original jurisdiction where cases begin.

appellate courts
Courts that generally review only findings of law made by lower courts.

351

JUDICIAL REVIEW

Constitutions are powerful documents. They establish who holds power in governments and where those powers begin and end. But, they are not necessarily unambiguous. Just what does "freedom of the press" mean? If Congress does not declare war, something it has done only five times and not since World War II, were the Korean War, Vietnam War, Persian Gulf War, and Iraq War all unconstitutional? Moreover, even when a constitution is clear as to what is meant by a word or phrase, it is not self-implementing. Some institution must have the binding authority to reach the conclusion that the constitution has been ignored or violated. That institution is the judiciary.

Constitutional democracies have taken two different approaches to creating courts with this power of judicial review. One approach is to give this power to the highest court in the country. The United States, Canada, India, and Australia employ this system. A second approach is to create a separate Constitutional Court, which exists apart from courts that hear criminal cases. Germany, France, Spain, and Greece use this judicial system. We can get a clearer idea of how the U.S. Supreme Court compares with other courts of final constitutional jurisdiction by taking a look at the German and Canadian examples—important points of comparison, since the United States was an important influence on each. In the case of Canada, it was the power of example, whereas in the case of Germany, American occupiers after World War II mandated the creation of a system of judicial review.

The Supreme Court of Canada has a chief justice and eight junior justices, all of whom are appointed by the governor-in-council. While Canada is an independent country, it is also part of the British Commonwealth, and the governor-in-council represents the British queen or king in Canada. The political reality is that the governor-in-council is a ceremonial figure and the actual selections are made by the prime minister. By law, three of the justices must come from Quebec, the predominately French province in Canada. By tradition, three judges come from Ontario, Canada's largest province; one comes from the Maritime provinces on the Atlantic Ocean; and two come from the Western provinces. Provincial superior court judges and lawyers who have belonged to a provincial bar for at least ten years are eligible to be selected.

The Supreme Court of Canada has both original jurisdiction for some cases and appellate jurisdiction. Most of its cases are heard on appeal, and decisions generally take the form of a single opinion written by the majority. Dissenting and concurrent opinions are also presented. For most of its history, the Supreme Court of Canada took a limited view of its power of judicial review and limited its decisions to questions of federalism. More recently it has begun to render decisions on matters of civil rights. Finally, in addition to making rulings of law, the Supreme Court of Canada also routinely gives advisory opinions on important political issues, unlike the U.S. federal courts.

The Constitutional Court of Germany is not part of the regular court system; instead, it is only a court of original jurisdiction on questions of constitutional interpretation. The full Constitutional Court is made up sixteen justices. In practice, it is divided into two panels of eight justices each. Three justices on each panel must be career judges, and the rest tend to be civil servants, politicians, or law professors. Justices serve a twelve-year term; they cannot be reappointed and must retire at age sixty-eight. Half are selected by a committee of the upper house of the German parliament that represents the states in the federal government, and the remainder are selected by a vote of all of the members of the lower house. In either case, in order to be selected, a candidate must receive a two-thirds vote.

A case comes before the Constitutional Court in three different ways. First, the federal government, a state government, or one-third of the members of the lower house of the German parliament can ask for a court ruling on the constitutionality of a law before it goes into effect. (The first chief justice of the United States, John Jay, rejected George Washington's request for this kind of advisory opinion.) Second, judges hearing a case in the regular court system can refer it to the Constitutional Court if they believe it raises constitutional issues. Third, and by far the most frequent way cases reach the Constitutional Court, petitions are filed by citizens. These cases of alleged violations of constitutional rights are screened by a committee of three justices and only about 3 percent are accepted.

Questions

1. Do you think the United States should create a separate constitutional court? Why or why not?
2. Which system for selecting justices do you think is best, the U.S., Canadian, or German approach? Explain your answer.

---

jurisdiction
Authority vested in a particular court to hear and decide the issues in any particular case.

Jurisdiction

Before a state or federal court can hear a case, it must have **jurisdiction,** which means the authority to hear and decide the issues in that case. The jurisdiction of the federal courts is controlled by the U.S. Constitution and by statute. Jurisdiction is conferred based on issues, money involved in a dispute, or the type of offense. Procedurally, we speak of two types of jurisdiction: original and appellate. **Original jurisdiction** refers to a court's authority to hear disputes as a trial court and may occur on the federal or state level. For example, the rape case against Los Angeles Laker Kobe Bryant was begun in a Colorado state trial court of original jurisdiction. In contrast, the legal battle over the constitutionality of the McCain-Feingold federal campaign finance reform law was begun in federal district court. More than 90 percent of all cases, whether state or federal, end in the court of original jurisdiction. **Appellate jurisdiction** refers to a court's ability to review cases already decided by a trial court. Appellate courts ordinarily do not review the factual record; instead, they review legal procedures to make certain that the law was applied properly to the issues presented in the case.

Criminal and Civil Law

Criminal law is the body of law that regulates individual conduct and is enforced by the state and national governments.[13] Crimes are graded as felonies, misdemeanors, or offenses, according to their severity. Some acts—for example, murder, rape, and robbery—are considered crimes in all states. Although all states outlaw murder, their penal, or criminal, codes treat the crime quite differently; the penalty for murder differs considerably from state to state. Other practices—such as gambling—are illegal only in some states.

Criminal law assumes that society itself is the victim of the illegal act; therefore, the government prosecutes, or brings an action, on behalf of an injured party (acting as a plaintiff) in criminal but not civil cases. For example, the murder charges against Scott Peterson, who was charged with killing his wife, Laci, was styled as *The State of California* v. *Scott Peterson*. Criminal cases are traditionally in the purview of the states. But, a burgeoning set of federal criminal laws is contributing significantly to delays in the federal courts.

Civil law is the body of law that regulates the conduct and relationships between private individuals or companies. Because the actions at issue in civil law do not constitute a threat to society at large, people who believe they have been injured by another party must take action on their own to seek judicial relief. Civil cases, then, involve lawsuits filed to recover something of value, whether it is the right to vote, fair treatment, or monetary compensation for an item or service that cannot be recovered. Most cases seen on television shows such as *Judge Judy* are civil cases.

Before a criminal or civil case gets to court, much has to happen. In fact, most legal disputes that arise in the United States never get to court. Individuals and companies involved in civil disputes routinely settle their disagreements out of court. Often these settlements are not reached until minutes before the case is to be tried. Many civil cases that go to trial are settled during the course of the trial—before the case can be handed over to the jury or submitted to a judge for a decision or determination of responsibility or guilt.

Each civil or criminal case has a plaintiff, or petitioner, who brings charges against a defendant, or respondent. Sometimes the government is the plaintiff. The government may bring civil charges on behalf of the citizens of the state or the national government against a person or corporation for violating the law, but it is always the government that brings a criminal case. When cases are initiated, they are known first by the name of the petitioner. In *Marbury* v. *Madison,* William Marbury was the plaintiff, suing the defendants, the U.S. government and James Madison as its secretary of state, for not delivering his judicial commission.

During trials, judges often must interpret the intent of laws enacted by Congress and state legislatures as they bear on the issues at hand. To do so, they read reports, testimony, and debates on the relevant legislation and study the results of other similar

original jurisdiction
The jurisdiction of courts that hear a case first, usually in a trial. Courts determine the facts of a case under their original jurisdiction.

appellate jurisdiction
The power vested in an appellate court to review and/or revise the decision of a lower court.

criminal law
Codes of behavior related to the protection of property and individual safety.

civil law
Codes of behavior related to business and contractual relationships between groups and individuals.

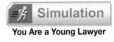
You Are a Young Lawyer

Photo courtesy: Greg Campbell/Wide World Photos

 During a news conference in October 2003, George Jackson talks about the alleged racial discrimination that he and his wife experienced while dining at a Cracker Barrel restaurant. Jackson and ten other African Americans filed a federal discrimination suit against Cracker Barrel, alleging that they received poor service compared to that of whites at some of the chain's restaurants in the South. The suit was settled in August 2004 when Cracker Barrel promised to take a number of steps to end its discriminatory practices but did not admit any wrongdoing and will pay no fines or penalties.

constitutional courts
Federal courts specifically created by the U.S. Constitution or by Congress pursuant to its authority in Article III.

legislative courts
Courts established by Congress for specialized purposes, such as the Court of Military Appeals.

Visual Literacy
Case Overload

legal cases. They also rely on the presentations made by lawyers in their briefs and at trial.

Another important component of most civil and criminal cases is the jury. This body acts as the ultimate finder of fact and plays an important role in determining the culpability of the individual on trial. The composition of juries has been the subject of much controversy in the United States. In the past, women and blacks often were excluded from jury service because many states selected jurors from those registered to vote. Although the Supreme Court ruled in 1888 that African American citizens could not be barred from serving as jurors,[14] it was not until 1975 that the Court extended this ruling to women.[15]

Until recently, however, it was not all that unusual for lawyers to use their peremptory challenges (those made without a reason) systematically to dismiss women or African Americans if they believed that they would be hostile to their case. In two opinions, however, the Supreme Court concluded that race or gender could not be used as reasons to exclude potential jurors.[16] Thus, today, juries are much more likely to be more representative of the community than in the past and capable of offering litigants in civil or criminal trial a jury of their peers.

THE FEDERAL COURT SYSTEM

THE FEDERAL DISTRICT COURTS, courts of appeals, and the Supreme Court are called **constitutional** (or Article III) **courts** because Article III of the Constitution either established them (as is the case with the Supreme Court) or authorizes Congress to establish them. Judges who preside over these courts are nominated by the president (with the advice and consent of the Senate), and they serve lifetime terms, as long as they engage in "good behavior."

In addition to constitutional courts, **legislative courts** are set up by Congress, under its implied powers, generally for special purposes. The U.S. territorial courts (which hear federal cases in the territories) and the U.S. Court of Veterans Appeals are examples of legislative courts, or what some call Article I courts. The judges who preside over these federal courts are appointed by the president (subject to Senate confirmation) and serve fixed, limited terms.

District Courts

As we have seen, Congress created U.S. district courts when it enacted the Judiciary Act of 1789. District courts are federal trial courts of original jurisdiction (see Figure 10.1). There are currently ninety-four federal district courts staffed by a total of 667 active judges, assisted by more than 300 retired judges who still hear cases on a limited basis. No district court cuts across state lines. Every state has at least one federal district court, and the most populous states—California, Texas, and New York—each have four (see Figure 10.2).[17]

Federal district courts, where the bulk of the judicial work takes place in the federal system, have original jurisdiction over only specific types of cases, as indicated in Figure 10.1. Although the rules governing district court jurisdiction can be complex,

FIGURE 10.1 The Dual Structure of the American Court System. ■

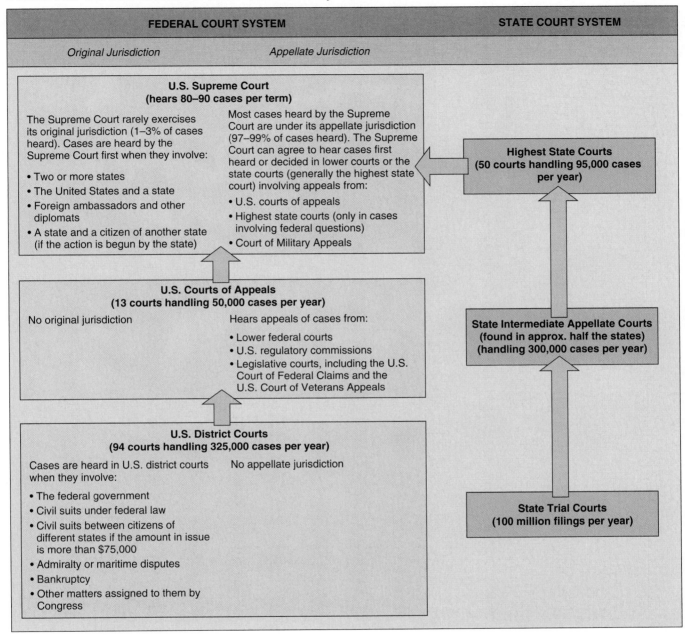

cases heard in federal district courts by a single judge (with or without a jury) generally fall into one of three categories:

1. They involve the federal government as a party.
2. They present a federal question based on a claim under the U.S. Constitution, a treaty with another nation, or a federal statute. This is called federal question jurisdiction and it can involve criminal or civil law.
3. They involve civil suits in which citizens are from different states, and the amount of money at issue is more than $75,000.[18]

FIGURE 10.2 The Federal Court System. ■

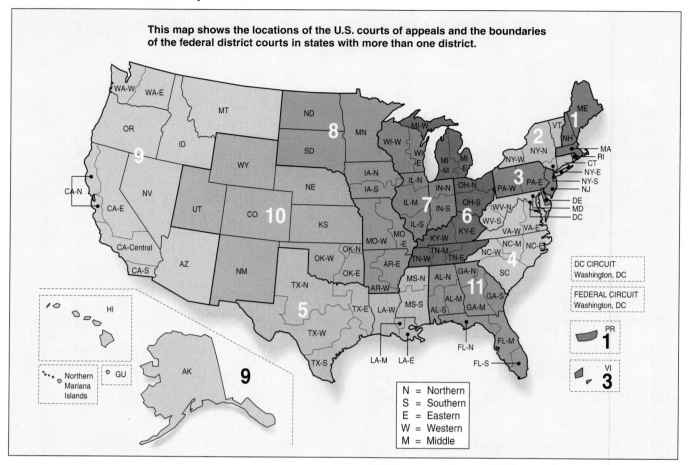

This map shows the locations of the U.S. courts of appeals and the boundaries of the federal district courts in states with more than one district.

N = Northern
S = Southern
E = Eastern
W = Western
M = Middle

DC CIRCUIT
Washington, DC

FEDERAL CIRCUIT
Washington, DC

Each federal judicial district has a U.S. attorney, who is nominated by the president and confirmed by the Senate. The U.S. attorney in each district is that district's chief law enforcement officer. The size of the staff and the number of assistant U.S. attorneys who work in each district depend on the amount of litigation in each district. U.S. attorneys, like district attorneys within the states, have a considerable amount of discretion as to whether they pursue criminal or civil investigations or file charges against individuals or corporations. These highly visible positions often serve as springboards for elective office. Former New York City Mayor Rudy Giuliani earlier was the U.S. attorney for the Southern District of New York.

The Courts of Appeals

The losing party in a case heard and decided in a federal district court can appeal the decision to the appropriate court of appeals. The United States courts of appeals (known as the circuit courts of appeals prior to 1948) are the intermediate appellate courts in the federal system and were established in 1789 to hear appeals from federal district courts. There are currently eleven numbered courts of appeals (see Figure 10.2). A twelfth, the D.C. Court of Appeals, handles most appeals involving federal regulatory commissions and agencies, including, for example, the National Labor Relations Board and the Securities and Exchange Commission. The thirteenth federal appeals court is the U.S. Court of Appeals for the Federal

Circuit, which deals with patents and contract and financial claims against the federal government.

In 2005, the U.S. courts of appeals were staffed by 167 active judges—assisted by more than eighty retired judges who still hear cases on a limited basis—who were appointed by the president, subject to Senate confirmation. The number of judges within each circuit varies—depending on the workload and the complexity of the cases—and ranges from six to nearly thirty. Each circuit is supervised by a chief judge, the most senior judge in terms of service below the age of sixty-five, who can serve no more than seven years. In deciding cases, judges are divided into rotating three-judge panels, made up of the active judges within the circuit, visiting judges (primarily district judges from the same circuit), and retired judges. In rare cases, all the judges in a circuit may choose to sit together (*en banc*) to decide a case by majority vote.

As shown in Figure 10.1, the courts of appeals have no original jurisdiction. Rather, Congress has granted these courts appellate jurisdiction over two general categories of cases: appeals from criminal and civil cases from the district courts, and appeals from administrative agencies. Criminal and civil case appeals constitute about 90 percent of the workload of the courts of appeals, with appeals from administrative agencies about 10 percent. Because so many agencies are located in Washington, D.C., the D.C. Circuit Court of Appeals hears an inordinate number of such cases. The D.C. Circuit Court of Appeals, then, is considered the second most important court in the nation because its decisions govern the regulatory agencies. Supreme Court Justices Antonin Scalia, Clarence Thomas, and Ruth Bader Ginsburg sat on that court before their nomination to the Supreme Court.

Once a decision is made by a federal court of appeals, a litigant no longer has an automatic right to an appeal. The losing party may submit a petition to the U.S. Supreme Court to hear the case, but the Court grants few of these requests. The courts of appeals, then, are the courts of last resort for almost all federal litigation. Keep in mind, however, that most cases, if they actually go to trial, go no further than the district court level.

In general, courts of appeals try to correct errors of law and procedure that have occurred in lower courts or administrative agencies. Courts of appeals hear no new testimony; instead, lawyers submit written arguments, in what is called a **brief** (also submitted in trial courts), and then appear to present and argue the case orally to the court.

Decisions of any court of appeals are binding on only the district courts within the geographic confines of the circuit, but decisions of the U.S. Supreme Court are binding throughout the nation and establish national **precedents.** This reliance on past decisions or precedents to formulate decisions in new cases is called *stare decisis* (a Latin phrase meaning "let the decision stand"). The principle of *stare decisis* allows for continuity and predictability in our judicial system. Although *stare decisis* can be helpful in predicting decisions, at times judges carve out new ground and ignore, decline to follow, or even overrule precedents in order to reach a different conclusion in a case involving similar circumstances. In one sense, that is why there is so much litigation in America today. Parties to a suit know that one cannot always predict the outcome of a case; if such prediction were possible, there would be little reason to go to court.

brief
A document containing the legal written arguments in a case filed with a court by a party prior to a hearing or trial.

precedents
Prior judicial decisions that serve as a rule for settling subsequent cases of a similar nature.

stare decisis
In court rulings, a reliance on past decisions or precedents to formulate decisions in new cases.

The Supreme Court

The U.S. Supreme Court, as we saw in the opening vignette, is often at the center of the storm of highly controversial issues that have yet to be resolved successfully in the political process. As the court of last resort at the top of the judicial pyramid, it reviews cases from the U.S. courts of appeals and state supreme courts (as well as other courts of last resort) and acts as the final interpreter of the U.S. Constitution. It not only decides major cases with tremendous policy significance each year, but it also ensures uniformity in the interpretation of national laws and the Constitution, resolves conflicts among the states, and maintains the supremacy of national law in the federal system (see Figure 10.3).

Since 1869, the U.S. Supreme Court has consisted of eight associate justices and one chief justice, who is nominated by the president specifically for that position. There is no special significance about the number nine, and the Constitution is silent about the size of the Court. Between 1789 and 1869, Congress periodically altered the size of the Court. The lowest number of justices on the Court was six; the most, ten. Through 2004, only 108 justices had served on the Court, and there had been fifteen chief justices (see Appendix IV).

FIGURE 10.3 **How a President Affects the Federal Judiciary**
This figure depicts the number of judges appointed by each president and how quickly a president can make an impact on the make-up of the Court. ■

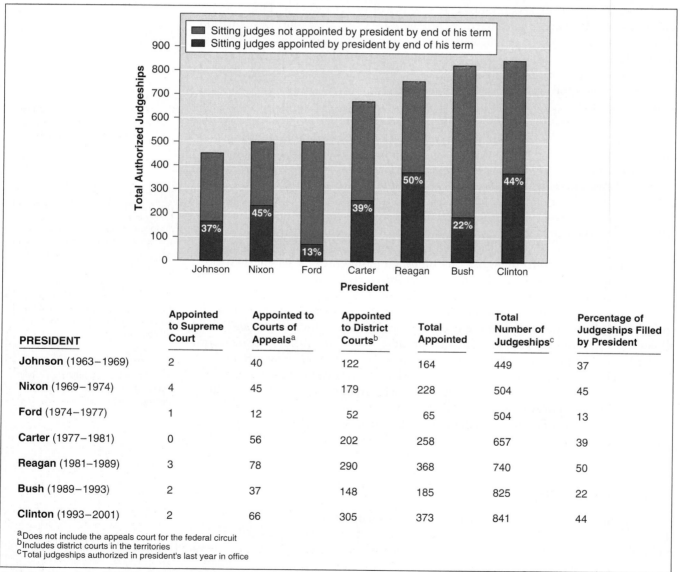

PRESIDENT	Appointed to Supreme Court	Appointed to Courts of Appeals[a]	Appointed to District Courts[b]	Total Appointed	Total Number of Judgeships[c]	Percentage of Judgeships Filled by President
Johnson (1963–1969)	2	40	122	164	449	37
Nixon (1969–1974)	4	45	179	228	504	45
Ford (1974–1977)	1	12	52	65	504	13
Carter (1977–1981)	0	56	202	258	657	39
Reagan (1981–1989)	3	78	290	368	740	50
Bush (1989–1993)	2	37	148	185	825	22
Clinton (1993–2001)	2	66	305	373	841	44

[a]Does not include the appeals court for the federal circuit
[b]Includes district courts in the territories
[c]Total judgeships authorized in president's last year in office

Source: "Imprints on the Bench," *CQ Weekly Report* (January 19, 2001): 173. Reprinted by permission of Copyright Clearance Center on behalf of Congressional Quarterly, Inc. Updated by author.

Compared with the president or Congress, the Supreme Court operates with few support staff. Along with the three or four clerks each justice employs, there are about 400 staff members at the Supreme Court.

HOW FEDERAL COURT JUDGES ARE SELECTED

THE SELECTION OF FEDERAL JUDGES is often a very political process with important political ramifications because judges are nominated by the president and must be confirmed by the U.S. Senate. During the administrations of Presidents Ronald Reagan and George Bush in the 1980s and early 1990s, for example, 553 mostly conservative Republican judges were appointed to the lower federal bench, remolding it in a conservative image (see Figure 10.3). The cumulative impact of this conservative block of judges led many liberal groups to abandon their efforts to achieve their policy goals through the federal courts.

Presidents, in general, try to select well-qualified men and women for the bench. But, these appointments also provide a president with the opportunity to put his philosophical stamp on the federal courts. Nominees, however, while generally members of the nominating president's party, usually are vetted through the senator's offices of the states where the district court or court of appeals vacancy occurs. In the Clinton White House, candidates for district court generally came from recommendations by Democratic senators, "or in the absence of a Democratic senator, from the Democratic members of the House of Representatives or other high ranking Democratic Party politicians."[19] This process, by which presidents generally defer selection of district court judges to the choice of senators of their own party who represent the state where the vacancy occurs, is known as **senatorial courtesy.**

Despite the Clinton administration's attempts to appoint moderate justices, so that they might win approval in a Republican-controlled Senate, the Senate leadership took steps to prevent many of these nominees from winning approval. Thus, when George W. Bush took office in 2001, his judicial nominees were immediately subject to extreme scrutiny. Almost immediately, Senate Democrats charged that many of Bush's appointees were too conservative, and even filibustered several nominations.

In later 2003, the Republican leadership attempted to counter these filibusters by holding a forty-hour talkathon to bring attention to the Senate's failure to confirm these nominees. Although this event received a good deal of press, it achieved little success. President George W. Bush further irritated Senate Democrats when he made several recess appointments of contested appointees, which allowed them to serve for the remainder of the 108th Congress. Finally, in 2004, President Bush and Senate Democrats reached an agreement that no further recess appointments would occur if the Senate confirmed twenty-five of the president's nominees.[20]

senatorial courtesy
Process by which presidents generally defer selection of district court judges to the choice of senators of their own party who represent the state where the vacancy occurs.

■ Senate Republican leader Bill Frist (R–TN) speaks to the press as Senate Republicans prepare to launch a forty-hour "Talkathon" session criticizing the Senate's failure to confirm judicial nominees selected by George W. Bush.

Photo courtesy: William Philpott/Corbis

Who Are Federal Judges?

Typically, federal district court judges have held other political offices, such as those of state court judge or prosecutor, as illustrated in Table 10.2. Most have been involved in politics, which is what usually brings them into consideration for a position on the federal bench. Griffin Bell, a former federal court of appeals judge (who later became U.S. attorney general in the Carter administration), once remarked, "For me, becoming a federal judge wasn't very difficult. I managed John F. Kennedy's presidential campaign in Georgia."[21]

Increasingly, most judicial nominees have had prior judicial experience. White males continue to dominate the federal courts, but since the 1970s, most presidents have pledged (with varying degrees of success) to do their best to appoint more African Americans, women, and other traditionally underrepresented groups to the federal bench (see Analyzing Visuals: Race/Ethnicity and Gender of District Court Appointees).

Appointments to the U.S. Supreme Court

The Constitution is silent on the qualifications for appointment to the Supreme Court (as well as to other constitutional courts), although Justice Oliver Wendell Holmes once remarked that a justice should be a "combination of Justinian, Jesus Christ and John Marshall."[22] However, like other federal court judges, the justices of the Supreme Court are nominated by the president and must be confirmed by the Senate.

Presidents always have realized how important their judicial appointments, especially their Supreme Court appointments, are to their ability to achieve all or many of their policy objectives. But, even though most presidents have tried to appoint jurists with particular political or ideological philosophies, they often have been wrong in their

TABLE 10.2	Characteristics of District Court Appointees from Carter to Bush				
	Carter Appointees	Reagan Appointees	Bush Appointees	Clinton Appointees	Bush Appointees[a]
Occupation					
Politics/government	5.0%	13.4%	10.8%	11.5%	8.4%
Judiciary	44.6	36.9	41.9	48.2	48.2
Lawyer	49.9	49.0	45.9	38.7	32.4
Other	0.5	0.7	1.4	2.6	4.8
Experience					
Judicial	54.0%	46.2%	46.6%	52.1%	53.0%
Prosecutorial	38.1	44.1	39.2	41.3	50.6
Neither	30.7	28.6	31.8	28.9	22.9
Political Affiliation					
Democrat	91.1%	4.8%	6.1%	87.5%	7.2%
Republican	4.5	91.7	88.5	6.2	83.1
Other/None	4.5	3.4	5.4	6.2	9.6
ABA Rating					
Extremely/Well Qualified	51.0%	53.5%	57.4%	59.0%	69.9%
Qualified	47.5	46.6	42.6	40.0	28.9
Not Qualified	1.5	—	—	1.0	1.2
Net Worth					
Under $200,000	35.8%	17.6%	10.1%	13.4%	4.8%
200,000–499,999	41.2	37.6	31.1	21.6	21.7
500,000–999,999	18.9	21.7	26.4	26.9	16.9
1,000,000+	4.0	23.1	32.4	32.4	56.6
Average age at nomination (years)	49.6	48.6	48.2	49.5	50.3
Total number of appointees	202	290	148	305	83

Note that percentages do not always add to 100 because some nominees fit in more than one category (i.e., they have been judges and prosecutors).

[a]George W. Bush appointee data are through January 1, 2003.

Source: Sheldon Goldman et al., "W. Bush Remaking the Judiciacry: Like Father like Son?" *Judicature* 86 (May–June 2003): 304.

Analyzing Visuals

RACE/ETHNICITY AND GENDER OF DISTRICT COURT APPOINTEES

Traditionally, white males have dominated federal court appointments. Of President Ronald Reagan's 290 appointees to federal district courts, for example, 92.4 percent were white males. Of President Bill Clinton's 305 appointments, however, the percentage of white males was only 52.1 percent. George W. Bush reversed the trend during the first eighteen months of his term; 68.7 percent of his appointees were white males. While most presidents in recent years have pledged to appoint more African Americans, women, and Hispanics to the federal bench, Clinton was the most successful. After reviewing the bar graph below, answer the following critical thinking questions: Is there a difference between appointments made by Democratic presidents (Carter and Clinton) and Republican presidents? Which group is most underrepresented in appointments? What factors do presidents consider, in addition to the nominee's gender and race/ethnicity, in making appointments to the federal bench? Should gender and race/ethnicity be considered by a president? Explain your answers.

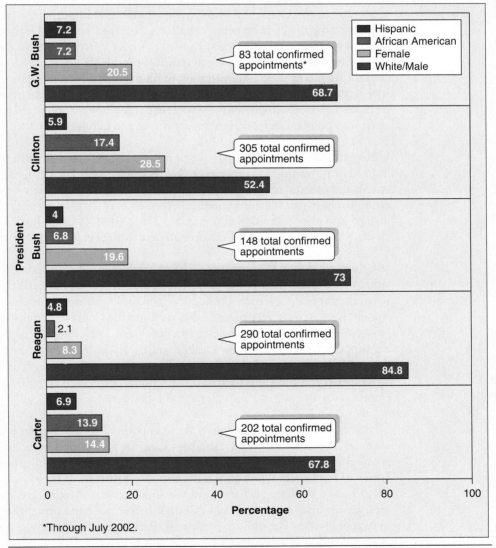

*Through July 2002.

Source: Sheldon Goldman et al., "W. Bush Remaking the Judiciary: Like Father like Son?" *Judicature* 86 (May–June 2003): 304.

assumptions about their appointees. President Dwight D. Eisenhower, a moderate conservative, was appalled by the liberal opinions written by his appointee to chief justice, Earl Warren, concerning criminal defendants' rights. Similarly, Justices John Paul Stevens, Sandra Day O'Connor, Anthony Kennedy, and David Souter, appointed by Presidents Gerald R. Ford, Ronald Reagan, and George Bush, are not as conservative as some predicted. Souter, in particular, has surprised many commentators with his moderate to liberal decisions in a variety of areas, including free speech, criminal rights, race and gender discrimination, and abortion.

Historically, because of the special place the Supreme Court enjoys in our constitutional system, its nominees have encountered more opposition than have district court or court of appeals nominees. As the role of the Court has increased over time, so too has the amount of attention given to nominees. With this increased attention has come greater opposition, especially to nominees with controversial views.

Nomination Criteria

Simulation
You Are Appointing a
Supreme Court Justice

Justice Sandra Day O'Connor once remarked that "You have to be lucky" to be appointed to the Court.[23] Although luck is certainly important, over the years nominations to the bench have been made for a variety of reasons. Depending on the timing of a vacancy, a president may or may not have a list of possible candidates or even a specific individual in mind. Until recently, presidents often have looked within their circle of friends or their administration to fill a vacancy. Nevertheless, whether the nominee is a friend or someone known to the president only by reputation, at least six criteria are especially important: competence, ideology or policy preferences, rewards, pursuit of political support, religion, and race and gender.

Competence.   Most prospective nominees are expected to have had at least some judicial or governmental experience. For example, John Jay, the first chief justice, was one of the authors of *The Federalist Papers* and was active in New York politics. Most nominees have had some prior judicial experience. In 2004, eight sitting Supreme Court justices had prior judicial experience (see Table 10.3). If Chief Justice Rehnquist's service as an associate justice is included, all nine justices enjoyed prior judicial experience.

Ideology or Policy Preferences.   Most presidents seek to appoint to the Court individuals who share their policy preferences, and almost all have political goals in mind when they appoint a justice. Presidents Franklin D. Roosevelt, Richard M. Nixon, and Ronald Reagan were very successful in molding the Court to their own political beliefs. Roosevelt was able to appoint eight justices from 1937 to his death in 1945, solidifying support for his liberal New Deal programs. In contrast, Presidents Nixon and Reagan publicly proclaimed that they would nominate only conservatives who favored a **strict constructionist** approach to constitutional decision making—that is, an approach emphasizing the original intentions of the Framers.

strict constructionist
An approach to constitutional interpretation that emphasizes the Framers' original intentions.

Rewards.   Historically, many of those appointed to the Supreme Court have been personal friends of presidents. Abraham Lincoln, for example, appointed one of his key political advisers to the Court. Lyndon B. Johnson appointed his longtime friend Abe Fortas to the bench. Most presidents also select justices of their own party affiliation. Chief Justice William H. Rehnquist was long active in Arizona Republican Party politics, as was Justice Sandra Day O'Connor before her appointment to the bench; both were appointed by Republican presidents. Party activism also can be used by presidents as an indication of a nominee's commitment to certain ideological principles.

Pursuit of Political Support.   During Ronald Reagan's successful campaign for the presidency in 1980, some of his advisers feared that the gender gap would hurt him. Polls repeatedly showed that he was far less popular with female voters than with men.

TABLE 10.3   The Supreme Court, 2004

Name	Year of Birth	Year of Appointment	Political Party	Law School	Appointing President	Religion	Prior Judicial Experience	Prior Government Experience
William H. Rehnquist	1924	1971/1986[a]	R	Stanford	Nixon	Lutheran	Associate justice U.S. Supreme Court	Assistant U.S. attorney general
John Paul Stevens	1920	1975	R	Chicago	Ford	Nondenominational Protestant	U.S. Court of Appeals	
Sandra Day O'Connor	1930	1981	R	Stanford	Reagan	Episcopalian	Arizona Court of Appeals	State legislator
Antonin Scalia	1936	1986	R	Harvard	Reagan	Catholic	U.S. Court of Appeals	
Anthony Kennedy	1936	1988	R	Harvard	Reagan	Catholic	U.S. Court of Appeals	
David Souter	1939	1990	R	Harvard	Bush	Episcopalian	U.S. Court of Appeals	New Hampshire assistant attorney general
Clarence Thomas	1948	1991	R	Yale	Bush	Catholic	U.S. Court of Appeals	Chair, Equal Employment Opportunity Commission
Ruth Bader Ginsburg	1933	1993	D	Columbia	Clinton	Jewish	U.S. Court of Appeals	
Stephen Breyer	1938	1994	D	Harvard	Clinton	Jewish	U.S. Court of Appeals	Chief counsel, Senate Judiciary Committee

[a]Promoted to chief justice by President Reagan in 1986.

To gain support from women, Reagan announced during his campaign that should he win, he would appoint a woman to fill the first vacancy on the Court. When Justice Potter Stewart, a moderate, announced his early retirement from the bench, under pressure from women's rights groups, President Reagan nominated Sandra Day O'Connor of the Arizona Court of Appeals to fill the vacancy. Similarly, it probably did not hurt President Bill Clinton that his first appointment (Ruth Bader Ginsburg) was a woman and Jewish (at a time when no Jews served on the Court).

Religion.   Ironically, religion, which historically has been an important issue, was hardly mentioned during the most recent Supreme Court vacancies. Some, however, hailed Clinton's appointment of Ginsburg, noting that the traditionally Jewish seat on the Court had been vacant since the retirement of Justice Abe Fortas in 1969.

Through 2004, of the 108 justices who served on the Court, almost all have been members of traditional Protestant faiths.[24] Only nine have been Catholic and only seven have been Jewish.[25] Twice during the Rehnquist Court, more Catholics—William Brennan, Antonin Scalia, and Anthony Kennedy, and then Scalia, Kennedy, and Clarence Thomas—served on the Court at one time than at any other period in history. Today, however, it is clear that religion cannot be taken as a sign of a justice's conservative or liberal ideology. When Brennan and fellow Catholic Scalia served on the Court together, they were at ideological polar extremes.

Race, Ethnicity, and Gender.   Through 2004, only two African Americans and two women have served on the Court. Race was undoubtedly a critical issue in the appointment of Clarence Thomas to replace Thurgood Marshall, the first African American justice. But, President George Bush refused to acknowledge his wish to retain a black seat on the Court. Instead, he announced that he was "picking the best man for the job on the merits," a claim that was met with considerable skepticism by many observers. Many

Photo courtesy: Frank Fournier/Contact Press Images

■ The scrutiny by the public and press of President Ronald Reagan's Supreme Court nominee Robert H. Bork set a new standard of inquiry into the values—political and personal—of future nominees. Bork's nomination was rejected by the Senate in 1987. Here, Kate Michelman, former president of NARAL Pro-Choice America, speaks at an anti-Bork rally.

assume that the next vacancy on the bench will go to a Hispanic in recognition of the growing proportion of Hispanics in the general population and their underrepresentation in national politics.

As discussed above, Sandra Day O'Connor pointedly was picked because of her gender. Ruth Bader Ginsburg's appointment, in contrast, surprised many because the Clinton administration initially appeared to be considering several men to fill the vacancy.

The Supreme Court Confirmation Process

The Constitution gives the Senate the authority to approve all nominees to the federal bench. Before 1900, about one-fourth of all presidential nominees to the Supreme Court were rejected by the Senate. In 1844, for example, President John Tyler sent six nominations to the Senate, and all but one were defeated. In 1866, Andrew Johnson nominated his brilliant attorney general, Henry Stanberry, but the Senate's hostility to Johnson led it to reduce the size of the Court from nine to six seats to prevent Johnson from filling any vacancies. Ordinarily, nominations are referred to the Senate Judiciary Committee. As detailed later, this committee investigates the nominees, holds hearings, and votes on its recommendation for Senate action. At this stage, the committee may reject a nominee or send the nomination to the full Senate for a vote. The full Senate then deliberates on the nominee before voting. A simple majority vote is required for confirmation.

Investigation. As a president begins to narrow the list of possible nominees to the Supreme Court, those names are sent to the Federal Bureau of Investigation before a nomination formally is made. At the same time, until George W. Bush became president, the names of prospective nominees were forwarded to the American Bar Association (ABA), the politically powerful organization that represents the interests of the legal profession. Republican President Dwight D. Eisenhower started this practice, believing it helped "insulate the process from political pressure."[26] After its own investigation, the ABA rated each nominee, based on his or her qualifications, as Well Qualified (previously "Highly Qualified"), Qualified, or Not Qualified. (The same system was used for lower federal court nominees; over the years, however, the exact labels have varied.)

David Souter, George Bush's first nominee to the Court, received a unanimous rating of Highly Qualified from the ABA, as did both of Bill Clinton's nominees, Ruth Bader Ginsburg and Stephen Breyer. In contrast, another Bush nominee, Clarence Thomas, was given only a Qualified rating (well before sexual harassment charges against him became public). Two ABA members even voted Not Qualified. Unlike the twenty-two previous successful nominees rated by the ABA, Thomas was the first to receive less than a unanimous Qualified rating.

Early in his administration, President George W. Bush announced that the ABA would no longer play this key role. Earlier, the 1996 Republican presidential candidate, Bob Dole, went so far as to pledge, if elected, he would remove the ABA from the selection process, viewing it as "another blatantly partisan liberal advocacy group."[27] Bush agrees with this view and instead has looked to the more conservative Federalist Society to vet his nominees, and to be a source of nominees as well.

After a formal nomination is made and sent to the Senate, the Senate Judiciary Committee begins its own investigation. (The same process is used for nominees to the lower federal courts, although such investigations generally are not nearly as extensive as for Supreme Court nominees.) To begin its task, the Senate Judiciary Committee asks each nominee to complete a lengthy questionnaire detailing previous work (dating as far back as high school summer jobs), judicial opinions written, judicial philosophy, speeches, and even all interviews ever given to members of the press. Committee staffers also contact potential witnesses who might offer testimony concerning the nominee's fitness for office.

Lobbying by Interest Groups.   Although historically the ABA was the only organization that was asked formally to rate nominees, other groups also are keenly interested in the nomination process. Until recently, interest groups played a minor and backstage role in most appointments to the Supreme Court. Although interest groups generally have not lobbied on behalf of any one individual, in 1981 women's rights groups successfully urged President Ronald Reagan to honor his campaign commitment to appoint a woman to the high Court.

It is more common for interest groups to lobby against a prospective nominee, as revealed in Table 10.4. Even this, however, is a relatively recent phenomenon. In 1987, the nomination of Robert H. Bork to the Supreme Court led liberal groups to launch the most extensive radio, television, and print media campaign against a nominee to the U.S. Supreme Court. These interest groups felt that Bork's actions as solicitor general, especially his firing of the Watergate special prosecutor at the request of President Richard M. Nixon, as well as his political beliefs, were abhorrent.

More and more, interest groups are also getting involved in district court and court of appeals nominations. They recognize that these appointments often pave the way for future nominees to the Supreme Court, as was the case with most of the members of the current Court. In 2002 and 2003, for example, the Senate Judiciary Committee, with the blessings of liberal groups including the Alliance for Justice and the Mexican American Legal Defense and Education Fund, delayed hearings on the nomination of Miguel Estrada to the U.S. Court of Appeals for the District of Columbia. These groups argued that Estrada is a "Latino Clarence Thomas and the darling of the right wing," and that his beliefs on abortion, criminal defendants' rights, and affirmative action were out of line with those of society.[28] Eventually, the staunch

---

TABLE 10.4 Interest Groups Appearing in Selected Senate Judiciary Committee Hearings

Nominee	Year	Liberal	Conservative	ABA Rating	Senate Vote
Stevens	1976	2	3	Well-Q	98–0
O'Connor	1981	8	7	Well-Q	99–0
Scalia	1986	5	7	Well-Q	98–0
Rehnquist	1986	6	13	Well-Q	68–36
Bork	1987	18	68	Well-Q[a]	42–58
Kennedy	1987	12	14	Well-Q	97–0
Souter	1990	13	18	Well-Q	90–9
Thomas	1991	30	46	Q[b]	52–48
Ginsburg	1993	6	5	Well-Q	96–3
Breyer	1994	8	3	Well-Q	87–9

[a]Four ABA committee members evaluated him as Not Qualified.
[b]Two ABA committee members evaluated him as Not Qualified.

Source: Karen O'Connor, "Lobbying the Justices or Lobbying for Justice," in Paul S. Herrnson, Ronald G. Shaiko, and Clyde Wilcox, eds., *The Interest Group Connection,* 2nd ed. (Washington, DC: CQ Press). Reprinted by permission of Chatham House Publishers, Inc.

SENATORIAL CONFIRMATION OF JUDICIAL NOMINATIONS

In May 2004, Senate Republican and Democratic leaders finally agreed to end a lengthy impasse over the confirmations of several judicial nominations to the federal courts made by President George W. Bush. In exchange for a commitment from Senate Democrats not to block twenty-five Bush nominees, the administration agreed not to make any more recess appointments. The Democrats, however, pledged to continue to block the confirmation of seven nominees who they believed are far too extreme to be on the federal bench.

"It's fair, it's balanced," said Republican Majority Leader Bill Frist (R–TN). The Democrats put a different spin on the agreement. Said Charles Schumer (D–NY) who sits on the Senate Judiciary Committee, "The White House waved the white flag here."[a]

This highly publicized dispute began when the Democrats perceived that President Bush was appointing high-profile, very conservative judges to vacancies on the federal courts. Still stinging from what they had perceived as unfair Republican treatment of several Clinton nominees to the federal bench (as well as other positions), the Democrats refused to allow votes to be taken on several nominees as they filibustered, or extended debate, to block the appointment of the few whom they found the most conservative. As the filibusters continued, the frustrated Bush administration appointed two of the most controversial nominees, William H. Pryor Jr. and Charles W. Pickering Sr., while the Senate was in recess. This action allows these men to serve as judges without Senate confirmation until the end of the congressional term. Pickering resigned rather than go through the process again. Unlike other federal judges, those appointed in this manner do not have a life term. Pryor, a devout Catholic, has characterized *Roe* v. *Wade* as "the worst abomination of constitutional law in our history," while Pickering drew the wrath of Democratic

senators and liberal interest groups for his actions to reduce the sentence of a man convicted of burning a cross in the yard of an interracial couple.[b] Pickering's nomination actually had been rejected by the Senate in 2001 when it was controlled by Democrats. After these appointments, outraged Democrats moved to stop consideration of all judicial nominees, even those who were uncontroversial. When they later agreed to allow noncontroversial nominees to be confirmed, however, Senate Democrats continued to block the nominations of the seven most controversial judges, five of whom were nominated to the courts of appeals. As these are seats just one step away from the U.S. Supreme Court, and the most common training ground for Supreme Court nominees, the Democrats believed that they had to take a stronger stand. And, by appearing to compromise with the White House on some nominees, they hoped to make judicial nominations less of an issue in the November elections.

In spite of their reduced numbers following the 2004 elections, Democratic senators, under the leadership of Harry Reid (D–NV), vowed to oppose any new appointees who hold what Democrats view as far too conservative views.

Questions

1. Do you think that the selection of federal court judges should be as political as it has become in recent years?
2. Should the president be able to appoint any qualified man or woman to the bench?

---

[a] Both quoted in Neil A. Lewis, "Deal Ends Impasse over Judicial Nominees," *New York Times* (May 19, 2004): A19.

[b] Mike Allen and Helen Dewar, "Bush Bypasses Senate on Judge; Pickering Named to Appeals Court During Recess," *Washington Post* (January 17, 2004): A1.

---

opposition of these groups and Democratic senators led Estrada to withdraw his nomination from consideration.

The Senate Committee Hearings and Senate Vote.   As the relatively uneventful 1994 hearings of Stephen Breyer attest, not all nominees inspire the kind of intense reaction that kept Bork from the Court and almost blocked the confirmation of Clarence Thomas. Until 1929, all but one Senate Judiciary Committee hearing on a Supreme Court nominee was conducted in executive session—that is, closed to the public. The 1916 hearings on Louis Brandeis, the first Jewish justice, were conducted in public and lasted nineteen days, although Brandeis himself never was called to testify. In 1939, Felix Frankfurter became the first nominee to testify in any detail before the committee.[29]

Since the 1980s, it has become standard for senators to ask the nominees probing questions. Most nominees have declined to answer most of these questions on the grounds that the issues raised ultimately might come before the Court.

After hearings are concluded, the Senate Judiciary Committee usually makes a recommendation to the full Senate. Any rejections of presidential nominees to the Supreme Court generally occur only after the Senate Judiciary Committee has recommended against a nominee's appointment. Few recent confirmations have been close; prior to Clarence

Thomas's 52–48 vote in 1991, William H. Rehnquist's nomination in 1971 as associate justice (68–26) and in 1986 as chief justice (65–33) were the closest in recent history (see Table 10.4).

THE SUPREME COURT TODAY

GIVEN THE JUDICIAL SYSTEM'S vast size and substantial, although often indirect, power over so many aspects of our lives, it is surprising that so many Americans know next to nothing about the judicial system, in general, and the U.S. Supreme Court, in particular.

Even today, after the unprecedented attention the Supreme Court received when the fate of the 2000 presidential election was in its hands, nearly two-thirds of those sampled in 2002 could not name one member of the Court; only 32 percent knew that the Court had nine members. In sharp contrast, 75 percent knew that there are three Rice Krispies characters. As revealed in Table 10.5, Sandra Day O'Connor, the first woman appointed to the Court, is the most well-known justice. Still, less than a quarter of those polled could name her. To fill in any gaps in your knowledge of the current Supreme Court, see Table 10.3.

While much of this ignorance can be blamed on the American public's lack of interest, the Court has also taken great pains to ensure its privacy and sense of decorum. Its rites and rituals contribute to the Court's mystique and encourage a "cult of the robe."[30] Consider, for example, the way Supreme Court proceedings are conducted. Oral arguments are not televised, and deliberations concerning the outcome of cases are conducted in utmost secrecy. In contrast, C-SPAN brings us daily coverage of various congressional hearings and floor debate on bills and important national issues, and Court TV (and sometimes other networks) provides gavel-to-gavel coverage of many important state court trials. The Supreme Court, however, remains adamant in its refusal to televise its proceedings—including public oral arguments, although it now allows the release of same-day audio tapes of oral arguments.

Deciding to Hear a Case

Almost 9,000 cases were filed at the Supreme Court in its 2003–2004 term; ninety were heard, and seventy-three were decided. In contrast, from 1790 to 1801, the Court heard only eighty-seven cases under its appellate jurisdiction.[31] In the Court's early years, the main of the justices' workload involved their circuit-riding duties. From 1862 to 1866, only 240 cases were decided. Creation of the courts of appeals in 1891 resulted in an immediate reduction in Supreme Court filings—from 600 in 1890 to 275 in 1892.[32] As recently as the 1940s, fewer than 1,000 cases were filed

TABLE 10.5 Don't Know Much About . . . the Supreme Court

	Percentage Responding Correctly
Rice Krispies Characters:	
Crackle	67
Snap	66
Pop	66
Supreme Court Justices:	
Sandra Day O'Connor	24
Clarence Thomas	19
William H. Rehnquist	11
Antonin Scalia	8
Ruth Bader Ginsburg	7
Anthony Kennedy	5
David Souter	5
Stephen Breyer	3
John Paul Stevens	2

Source: The Polling Company. Accessed May 30, 2002, http://www.pollingcompany.com/News.asp?FormMode=ViewReleases&ID=50. Reprinted by permission of the Polling Company.

FIGURE 10.4   **Supreme Court Caseload, 1950–2004 Terms**

Cases the Supreme Court chooses to hear (represented by blue bars below) represent a tiny fraction of the total number of cases filed with the Court (represented by red bars). The Court's caseload has remained fairly consistent from its 1992 through 2001 terms, although the Court accepted far fewer cases for its review than it did in earlier decades. Still, the Court decides only a small percentage of the cases filed. ■

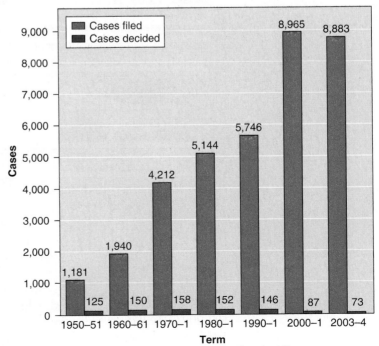

Source: Administrative Office of the Courts; Supreme Court Public Information Office.

FIGURE 10.5 This figure illustrates both how cases get on the Court's docket and what happens after a case is accepted for review. ■

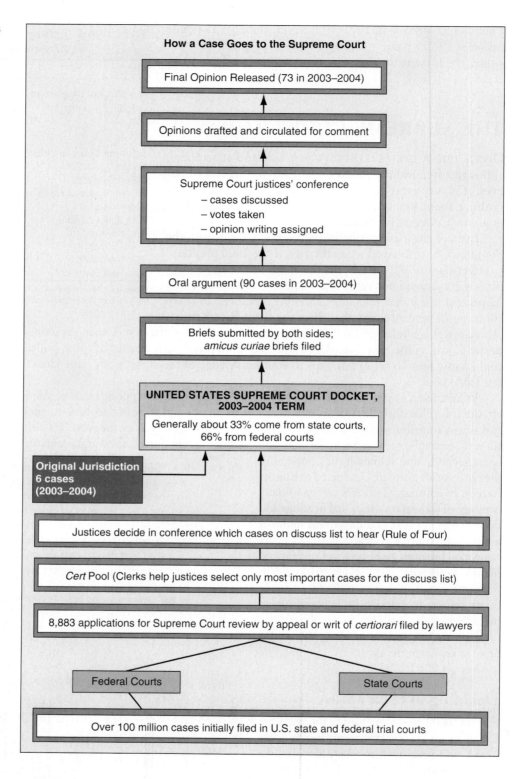

How a Case Goes to the Supreme Court

Final Opinion Released (73 in 2003–2004)

↑

Opinions drafted and circulated for comment

↑

Supreme Court justices' conference
– cases discussed
– votes taken
– opinion writing assigned

↑

Oral argument (90 cases in 2003–2004)

↑

Briefs submitted by both sides;
amicus curiae briefs filed

↑

UNITED STATES SUPREME COURT DOCKET, 2003–2004 TERM
Generally about 33% come from state courts, 66% from federal courts

Original Jurisdiction 6 cases (2003–2004)

Justices decide in conference which cases on discuss list to hear (Rule of Four)

Cert Pool (Clerks help justices select only most important cases for the discuss list)

8,883 applications for Supreme Court review by appeal or writ of *certiorari* filed by lawyers

Federal Courts   State Courts

Over 100 million cases initially filed in U.S. state and federal trial courts

annually. Since that time, filings increased at a dramatic rate until the mid 1990s and then shot up again in the late 1990s, as revealed in Figure 10.4, although there was a slight downturn in the 2003–2004 term. The process by which cases get to the Supreme Court is outlined in Figure 10.5.

Just as it is up to the justices to say what the law is, they can also exercise a significant role in policy making and politics by opting not to hear a case. For example, in late 2004 when it refused to hear an appeal of a Massachusetts Supreme Court decision requiring the state to sanction same-sex marriages, the Court prompted President George W. Bush and others to renew their calls for a constitutional amendment. The content of the Court's docket is, of course, every bit as significant as its size. During the 1930s, cases requiring the interpretation of constitutional law began to take a growing portion of the Court's workload, leading the Court to take a more important role in the policy-making process. At that time, only 5 percent of the Court's cases involved questions concerning the Bill of Rights. By the late 1950s, one-third of filed cases involved such questions; by the 1960s, half did.[33] More recently, 42 percent of the cases decided by the Court dealt with issues raised in the Bill of Rights.[34]

As discussed earlier in the chapter, the Court has two types of jurisdiction, as indicated in Figure 10.1. The Court has original jurisdiction in "all Cases affecting Ambassadors, other public Ministers and Consuls, and those in which a State shall be a party." It is rare for more than two or three of these cases to come to the Court in a year. The second kind of jurisdiction enjoyed by the Court is its appellate jurisdiction. The Court is not expected to exercise its appellate jurisdiction simply to correct errors of other courts. Instead, appeal to the Supreme Court should be taken only if the case presents important issues of law, or what is termed "a substantial federal question." Since 1988, nearly all appellate cases that have gone to the Supreme Court arrived there on a petition for a **writ of *certiorari*** (from the Latin "to be informed"), which is a request for the Supreme Court—at its discretion—to order up the records of the lower courts for purposes of review.

writ of *certiorari*
A request for the Court to order up the records from a lower court to review the case.

The Rule of Four.   The Supreme Court controls its own caseload through the *certiorari* process, deciding which cases it wants to hear, and rejecting most cases that come to it. All petitions for *certiorari* must meet two criteria:

1. The case must come from either a U.S. court of appeals, a special three-judge district court, or a state court of last resort.
2. The case must involve a federal question. Thus, the case must present questions of interpretation of federal constitutional law or involve a federal statute, action, or treaty. The reasons that the Court should accept the case for review and legal argument supporting that position are set out in the petition (also called a brief).

■ The Supreme Court at the begining of its 2004–2005 term. From left to right: Clarence Thomas, Antonin Scalia, Sandra Day O'Connor, Anthony Kennedy, David Souter, Stephen Breyer, John Paul Stevens, William H. Rehnquist, and Ruth Bader Ginsburg.

Photo courtesy: Ken Heinen/Pool/AP/Wide World Photos

The clerk of the Court's office transmits petitions for writs of *certiorari* first to the chief justice's office, where clerks review the petitions, and then to the individual justices' offices. On the Rehnquist Court, all of the justices except Justice John Paul Stevens (who allows his clerks great individual authority in selecting the cases for him to review) participated in what is called the *cert* pool.[35] Pool participants review their assigned fraction of petitions and share their notes with each other. Those cases that the justices deem noteworthy are then placed on what is called the discuss list prepared by the chief justice's clerks and circulated to the chambers of the other justices. All others are dead listed and go no further unless a justice asks that a case be removed from the dead list and discussed at conference. Only about 30 percent of submitted petitions make it to the discuss list. During one of the justices' weekly conference meetings, the cases on the discuss list are reviewed. The chief justice speaks first, then the rest of the justices, according to seniority. The decision process ends when the justices vote, and by custom, *certiorari* is granted according to the **Rule of Four**—when at least four justices vote to hear a case.

Rule of Four
At least four justices of the Supreme Court must vote to consider a case before it can be heard.

You Are a Clerk to a Supreme Court Justice

The Role of Clerks.   As early as 1850, the justices of the Supreme Court beseeched Congress to approve the hiring of a clerk to assist each justice. Congress denied the request, so when Justice Horace Gray hired the first law clerk in 1882, he paid the clerk himself. Justice Gray's clerk was a top graduate of Harvard Law School whose duties included cutting Justice Gray's hair and running personal errands. Finally, in 1886, Congress authorized each justice to hire a stenographer clerk for $1,600 a year.

Clerks typically are selected from candidates at the top of the graduating classes of prestigious law schools. They perform a variety of tasks, ranging from searching for arcane facts to playing tennis or taking walks with the justices. Clerks spend most of their time researching material relevant to particular cases, reading and summarizing cases, and helping justices write opinions. The clerks also make the first pass through the petitions that come to the Court, undoubtedly influencing which cases get a second look. Just how much help they provide in the writing of opinions is unknown.[36] (See Table 10.6 for more on what clerks do.)

Over time, the number of clerks employed by the justices has increased. Through the 1946 to 1969 terms, most justices employed two clerks. By 1970, most had three clerks, and by 1980 all but three justices had four clerks. In 2005, the nine justices employed a total of thirty-four clerks. This growth in the number of clerks has had many interesting ramifications for the Court. As the number of clerks has grown, so have the number and length of the Court's opinions.[37] And, until recently, the number of cases decided annually increased as more help was available to the justices.

The relationship between clerks and the justices for whom they work is close and confidential, and many aspects of the relationship are kept secret. Clerks may sometimes talk among themselves about the views and personalities of their justices, but rarely has a clerk leaked such information to the press. In 1998, a former clerk to Justice Harry A. Blackmun broke the silence. Edward Lazarus published a book that shocked many Court watchers by penning an insider's account of how the Court really works.[38] He also charged that the justices give their young, often ideological, clerks far too much power.

TABLE 10.6 What Do Supreme Court Clerks Do?

Supreme Court clerks are among the best and brightest recent law school graduates. Almost all first clerk for a judge on one of the courts of appeals. After their Supreme Court clerkship, former clerks are in high demand. Firms often pay signing bonuses of up to $80,000 to attract clerks, who often earn over $130,000 their first year in private practice.

Tasks of a Supreme Court clerk include the following:
- Perform initial screening of the 9,000 or so petitions that come to the Court each term
- Draft memos to summarize the facts and issues in each case, recommending whether the case should be accepted by the Court for full review
- Write a "bench memo" summarizing an accepted case and suggesting questions for oral argument
- Write the first draft of an opinion
- Be an informal conduit for communicating and negotiating between other justices' chambers as to the final wording of an opinion

How Does a Case Survive the Process?

It can be difficult to determine why the Court decides to hear a particular case. Sometimes it involves a perceived national emergency, as was the case with appeals concerning the outcome of the 2000 presidential election. The Court does not offer reasons, and "the standards by which the justices decide to grant or deny review are highly personalized and necessarily discretionary," noted former Chief Justice Earl Warren.[39] Political scientists nonetheless have attempted to determine the characteristics of the cases the Court accepts; not surprisingly, they are similar to those that help a case get on the discuss list. Among the cues are the following:

- The federal government is the party asking for review.
- The case involves conflict among the circuit courts.
- The case presents a civil rights or civil liberties question.
- The case involves ideological and/or policy preferences of the justices.
- The case has significant social or political interest, as evidenced by the presence of interest group *amicus curiae* briefs.

The Federal Government. One of the most important cues for predicting whether the Court will hear a case is the position the solicitor general takes on it. The **solicitor general,** appointed by the president, is the fourth-ranking member of the Department of Justice and is responsible for handling most appeals on behalf of the U.S. government to the Supreme Court. The solicitor's staff resembles a small, specialized law firm within the Department of Justice. But, because this office has such a special relationship with the Supreme Court, even having a suite of offices within the Supreme Court building, the solicitor general often is referred to as the Court's "ninth and a half member."[40] Moreover, the solicitor general, on behalf of the U.S. government, appears as a party or as an *amicus curiae* in more than 50 percent of the cases heard by the Court each term. ***Amicus curiae*** means friend of the court. *Amici* may file briefs or even appear to argue their interests orally before the Court.

This special relationship with the Court helps explain the overwhelming success the solicitor general's office enjoys before the Supreme Court. The Court generally accepts 70 to 80 percent of the cases where the U.S. government is the petitioning party, compared with about 5 percent of all others.[41] But, because of this special relationship, the solicitor general often ends up playing two conflicting roles: representing in Court both the president's policy interests and the broader interests of the United States. At times, solicitors find these two roles difficult to reconcile. Former Solicitor General Rex E. Lee (1981–1985), for example, noted that on more than one occasion he refused to make arguments in Court that had been advanced by the Reagan administration (a stand that ultimately forced him to resign his position).[42]

Conflict Among the Circuits. Conflict among the lower courts is apparently another reason that the justices take cases. When interpretations of constitutional or federal law are involved, the justices seem to want consistency throughout the federal court system.

Often these conflicts occur when important civil rights or civil liberties questions arise. As political scientist Lawrence Baum has commented, "Justices' evaluations of lower court decisions are based largely on their ideological position."[43] Thus, it is not uncommon to see conservative justices voting to hear cases to overrule liberal lower court decisions, or vice versa.

Interest Group Participation. A quick way for the justices to gauge the ideological ramifications of a particular civil rights or liberties case is by the nature and amount of

solicitor general
The fourth-ranking member of the Department of Justice; responsible for handling all appeals on behalf of the U.S. government to the Supreme Court.

amicus curiae
"Friend of the court"; *amici* may file briefs or even appear to argue their interests orally before the court.

■ This sketch by the Court artist shows Deputy Solicitor General Paul Clement arguing on behalf of the government before the Supreme Court in April 2004.

Photo courtesy: AP Photo/Dana Verkouteren

interest group participation. Richard C. Cortner has noted that "Cases do not arrive on the doorstep of the Supreme Court like orphans in the night."[44] Instead, most cases heard by the Supreme Court involve either the government or an interest group—either as the sponsoring party or as an *amicus curiae*. Liberal groups such as the ACLU, People for the American Way, or the NAACP Legal Defense Fund, and conservative groups including the Washington Legal Foundation, Concerned Women for America, or the American Center for Law and Justice, routinely sponsor cases or file *amicus* briefs either urging the Court to hear a case or asking it to deny *certiorari*.

Research by political scientists has found that "not only does [an *amicus*] brief in favor of *certiorari* significantly improve the chances of a case being accepted, but two, three and four briefs improve the chances even more."[45] Clearly, it's the more the merrier, whether or not the briefs are filed for or against granting review.[46] Interest group participation may highlight lower court and ideological conflicts for the justices by alerting them to the amount of public interest in the issues presented in any particular case.

Hearing and Deciding the Case

Once a case is accepted for review, a flurry of activity begins. Lawyers on both sides of the case begin to prepare their written arguments for submission to the Court. In these briefs, lawyers cite prior case law and make arguments as to why the Court should find in favor of their client.

More often than not, these arguments are echoed or expanded in *amicus curiae* briefs filed by interested parties, especially interest groups. (The vast majority of the cases decided by the Court in the 1990s, for example, had at least one *amicus* brief.)

Since the 1970s, interest groups increasingly have used the *amicus* brief as a way to lobby the Court. Because litigation is so expensive, few individuals have the money (or time or interest) to pursue a perceived wrong all the way to the U.S. Supreme Court. All sorts of interest groups, then, find that joining ongoing cases through *amicus* briefs is a useful way of advancing their policy preferences. Major cases such as *Brown* v. *Board of Education* (1954) (see chapter 6), *Planned Parenthood of Southeastern Pennsylvania* v. *Casey* (1992) (see chapter 5), and *Grutter* v. *Bollinger* (2003) (see chapter 6) all attracted large numbers of *amicus* briefs as part of interest groups' efforts to lobby the judiciary and bring about desired political objectives.[47] (See Table 10.7.)

Interest groups also provide the Court with information not necessarily contained in the major-party briefs, help write briefs, and assist in practice oral arguments during moot-court sessions. In these moot-court sessions, the lawyer who will argue the case before the nine justices goes through several complete rehearsals, with prominent lawyers and law professors role playing the various justices.

Oral Arguments.   Once a case is accepted by the Court for full review, and after briefs and *amicus* briefs are submitted on each side, oral argument takes place. The Supreme Court's annual term begins the first Monday in October, as it has since the late 1800s, and runs through late June or early July. Justices hear oral arguments from the beginning of the term until early April. Special cases, such as *U.S.* v. *Nixon* (1974), which involved President Richard M. Nixon's refusal to turn over tapes of Oval Office conversations to a special prosecutor investigating a break-in at the Democratic Party headquarters in the Watergate building, have been heard even later in the year.[48] During the term, "sittings," periods of about two weeks in which cases are heard, alternate with "recesses," also about two weeks long. Oral arguments usually are heard Monday through Wednesday.

Oral argument generally is limited to the immediate parties in the case, although it is not uncommon for the U.S. solicitor general to appear to argue orally as an *amicus curiae*. Oral argument at the Court is fraught with time-honored tradition and ceremony. At precisely ten o'clock every morning when the Court is in session, the Court

TABLE 10.7 *Amicus Curiae* Briefs in an Affirmative Action Case: *Grutter* v. *Bollinger* and *Gratz* v. *Bollinger* (2003)

Photo courtesy: Paul Sancya/AP/Wide World Photos

■ Barbara Grutter and Jennifer Gratz, two of the plaintiffs in The University of Michigan affirmative actions cases.

For the Petitioners

Asian American Legal Foundation
Cato Institute
Center for Equal Opportunity et al.
Center for Individual Freedom
Center for the Advancement of Capitalism
Center for New Black Leadership

Claremont Institute Center for Constitutional Jurisprudence
Law Professors
Massachusetts School of Law
Michigan Association of Scholars
National Association of Scholars

Pacific Legal Foundation
Reason Foundation
State of Florida and Governor Jeb Bush
United States
Ward Connerly

For the Respondents

65 Leading American Businesses
AFL-CIO
American Bar Association
American Council on Education et al.
American Educational Research Association et al.
American Jewish Committee et al.
American Law Deans Association
American Media Companies
American Psychological Association
American Sociological Association
Amherst College et al.
Arizona State University College of Law
Association of American Law Schools
Association of American Medical Colleges
Authors of the Texas Ten Percent Plan
Bay Mills Indian Community et al.
Black Women Lawyers Association of Greater Chicago
Boston Bar Association et al.
Carnegie Mellon University et al.
City of Philadelphia et al.
Clinical Legal Educational Association
Coalition for Economic Equity et al.
Columbia University et al.
Committee of Concerned Black Graduates of ABA Accredited Law Schools
Current Law Students at Accredited Law Schools

Deans of Law Schools
General Motors Corporation
Graduate Management Admission Council et al.
Harvard Black Law Students Association et al.
Harvard University et al.
Hayden Family
Hispanic National Bar Association
Howard University
Human Rights Advocates et al.
Indiana University
King County Bar Association
Latino Organizations
Lawyers Committee for Civil Rights Under Law et al.
Leadership Conference on Civil Rights et al.
Massachusetts Institute of Technology et al.
Members of Congress (3 briefs)
Members of the Pennsylvania General Assembly et al.
Michigan Black Law Alumni Association
Michigan Governor Jennifer Granholm
Military Leaders
MTV Networks
NAACP Legal Defense and Education Fund et al.
National Asian Pacific American Legal Consortium et al.
National Center for Fair and Open Testing

National Coalition of Blacks for Reparations in America et al.
National Education Association
National School Boards Association
National Urban League et al.
New America Alliance
New Mexico Hispanic Bar Association et al.
New York City Council Members
New York State Black and Puerto Rican Legislative Caucus
Northeastern University
NOW Legal Defense and Education Fund et al.
School of Law of the University of North Carolina
Social Scientists
Society of American Law Teachers
State of New Jersey
State of Maryland et al.
Students of Howard University Law School
UCLA School of Law Students of Color
United Negro College Fund et al.
University of Michigan Asian Pacific American Law Students Association
University of Pittsburgh et al.
Veterans of the Southern Civil Rights Movement et al.

For Neither Party

Anti-Defamation League
BP America
Criminal Justice Legal Foundation

Equal Employment Opportunity Council
Exxon Mobil Corporation

Join the Debate

SEPARATION OF POWERS AND THE SCALIA RECUSALS

OVERVIEW: The separation of powers is one of the fundamental tenets of the Constitution. Although the lines of authority among the legislative, executive, and judicial branches endlessly shift as the power of each increases or diminishes, each branch must retain its constitutional independence. Once a branch acts in collusion with another, American political theory argues, the door to corruption is opened. When it was learned that Justice Antonin Scalia went duck hunting with Vice President Dick Cheney a few months before the Supreme Court was to review the government's suit to compel the vice president to release documents concerning his secretive Energy Task Force, the question of conflict of interest arose. With this in mind, the Sierra Club filed a motion to formally ask that Justice Scalia recuse (or remove) himself from hearing the case in order to prevent undue influence. Justice Scalia refused to recuse himself and thus proffered an interesting ethical question.

It is historical and common practice for justices to socialize with the political and intellectual classes. For example, Justice Ruth Bader Ginsburg favored the position of the National Organization for Women's legal defense fund in a case before the Court and then spoke at NOW's lecture series two weeks later—these types of practices are considered proper. However, justices regularly recuse themselves if there is a conflict of interest. During the last five years, there have been nearly 500 recusals by the justices. Commentary in the *National Law Journal* argues that if a case before the Court involves an institutional issue, a justice's recusal is not necessary when a friend, family member, or acquaintance is involved. Because the issue in *Cheney* v. *U.S. District Court for the District of Columbia* concerns the separation of powers, the personal and political motives of the parties involved would seem irrelevant. However, public distrust of government, and of the Supreme Court in particular, has been increasing. Therefore, it could be argued, all who act in a political capacity should be meticulous in avoiding the appearance of impropriety or conflict of interest.

Should politicians and judges be held to higher ethical standards than the average citizen? Should members of the Supreme Court be allowed to participate in cases where acquaintances, friends, or family are involved? After all, some justices, such as Justices Sandra Day O'Connor and David Souter, recuse themselves as a matter of course if there is a hint of conflict of interest. Should the other justices be bound to do so as well? Is the issue of the public's trust in government so important that all Supreme Court justices should adhere to the highest ethical standard?

Arguments for Recusal

- **Justices should avoid the appearance of conflict of interest.** The current polarized political atmosphere

marshal, dressed in a formal morning coat, emerges to intone "Oyez! Oyez! Oyez!" as the nine justices emerge from behind a reddish-purple velvet curtain to take their places on the raised and slightly angled bench. The chief justice sits in the middle. The remaining justices sit alternating in seniority and right to left.

Almost all attorneys are allotted one half hour to present their cases, and this time includes that required to answer questions from the bench. As a lawyer approaches the mahogany lectern, a green light goes on, indicating that the attorney's time has begun. A white light flashes when five minutes remain. When a red light goes on, Court practice mandates that counsel stop immediately. One famous piece of Court lore told to all attorneys concerns a counsel who continued talking and reading from his prepared argument after the red light went on. When he looked up, he found an empty bench—the justices had risen quietly and departed while he continued to talk. On another occa-

and the American public's distrust of government and its institutions requires highly visible political figures such as Supreme Court justices to adhere to a rigorous ethical code to help the American people maintain confidence in their political and governmental establishments.

- **The principle of separation of powers must be maintained.** Situations may arise in which either intentional or unintentional collusion or influence occurs. The result could be an event or decision that is harmful to the national interest.
- **Justices must remain impartial.** If a justice's personal or political life might intrude on the decision-making process when rendering judgment, basic judicial ethics suggest that recusal is the proper remedy. Fairness and trust demand that a justice maintain impartiality when hearing a case.

Arguments Against Recusal

- **Questioning of judicial integrity may have a partisan basis.** Though oversight of the judiciary is indispensable, many charges against justices are partisan in nature. To bow to partisan pressure would further implicate the Court as being responsive to partisan politics.
- A recusal impairs the proper functioning of the Court. When a member of the Court is recused, the number of justices is reduced. One possibility is that the Court's decision may be evenly split, which effectually means the case is not decided. The Court might fail to reach a decision that could clarify or settle an important constitutional or political question.
- **It is unreasonable to expect justices to recuse themselves because of friendship.** It is the nature of the capital's professional, social, and political structure for justices to have social contact, address conferences and groups, and engage in political life. It is only natural that the justices over time would develop many different relationships outside the Court. To ask for a recusal in every instance in which a justice has a friend or acquaintance before the Court would be disabling.

Questions

1. What is the best way to ensure accountability in the federal judiciary? Should we expect our judges to be scrupulously apolitical?
2. What is the best way to ensure the independence of the judiciary? Are the lines that separate the branches becoming blurred, and is this a problem?

Selected Readings

Jeffrey Shaman et al. *Judicial Conduct and Ethics.* New York: Matthew Bender, 1990.

John T. Noonan, ed. *The Responsible Judge: Readings in Judicial Ethics.* New York: Praeger, 1993.

sion, Chief Justice Charles Evans Hughes stopped a leader of the New York bar in the middle of the word "if."

Although many Court watchers have tried to figure out how a particular justice will vote based on the questioning at oral argument, most find that the nature and number of questions asked do not help much in predicting the outcome of a case. Nevertheless, many believe that oral argument has several important functions. First, it is the only opportunity for even a small portion of the public (who may attend the hearings) and the press to observe the workings of the Court. Second, it assures lawyers that the justices have heard their case, and it forces lawyers to focus on arguments believed important by the justices. Last, it provides the Court with additional information, especially concerning the Court's broader political role, an issue not usually addressed in written briefs. For example, the justices can ask how many people might be affected by its decision or where the Court (and country) would be heading if a case were decided in a particular way. Justice Stephen Breyer also notes that oral arguments are a good way for the justices to try to highlight certain issues for other justices.

The Conference and the Vote.   The justices meet in closed conference once a week when the Court is hearing oral arguments. Since the ascendancy of Chief Justice Roger B. Taney to the Court in 1836, the justices have begun each conference session with a round of handshaking. Once the door to the conference room closes, no others are allowed to enter. The justice with the least seniority acts as the doorkeeper for the other eight, communicating with those waiting outside to fill requests for documents, water, and any other necessities.

Conferences highlight the importance and power of the chief justice, who presides over them and makes the initial presentation of each case. Each individual justice then discusses the case in order of his or her seniority on the Court, with the most senior justice speaking next. Most accounts of the decision-making process reveal that at this point some justices try to change the minds of others, but that most enter the conference room with a clear idea of how they will vote on each case. Although other Courts have followed different procedures, through 2004 the justices generally voted at the same time they discussed each case, with each justice speaking only once. Initial conference votes are not final, and justices are allowed to change their minds before final votes are taken later.

Writing Opinions.   After the Court has reached a decision in conference, the justices must formulate a formal opinion of the Court. If the chief justice is in the majority, he selects the justice who will write the opinion. This privilege enables him to wield tremendous power and is a very important strategic decision. If the chief justice is in the minority, the assignment falls to the most senior justice in the majority.

The opinion of the Court can take several different forms. Most decisions are reached by a majority opinion written by one member of the Court to reflect the views of at least five of the justices. This opinion usually sets out the legal reasoning justifying the decision, and this legal reasoning becomes a precedent for deciding future cases. The reasoning behind any decision is often as important as the outcome. Under the system of *stare decisis,* both are likely to be relied on as precedent later by lower courts confronted with cases involving similar issues.

In the process of creating the final opinion of the Court, informal caucusing and negotiation often take place, as justices may hold out for word changes or other modifications as a condition of their continued support of the majority opinion. This negotiation process can lead to divisions in the Court's majority. When this occurs, the Court may be forced to decide cases by plurality opinions, which attract the support of three or four justices. While these decisions do not have the precedential value of majority opinions, they nonetheless have been used by the Court to decide many major cases.

Justices who agree with the outcome of the case but not with the legal rationale for the decision may file concurring opinions to express their differing approach. For example, Justice Steven Breyer filed a concurring opinion in *Clinton* v. *Jones* (1997). Although a unanimous Court ruled that a sitting president was not immune to civil lawsuits, Breyer wanted to express his belief that a federal judge could not schedule judicial proceedings that might interfere with a president's public duties.[49]

Justices who do not agree with the outcome of a case file dissenting opinions. Although these opinions have little direct legal value, they can be an important indicator of legal thought on the Court and are an excellent platform for justices to note their personal and legal disagreements with other members of the Court. Justice

Antonin Scalia, for example, is often noted for writing particularly stinging dissents. In his dissent in *Webster* v. *Reproductive Health Services* (1989), for example, Scalia wrote that Justice Sandra Day O'Connor's "assertion that a fundamental rule of judicial restraint requires [the Court] to avoid reconsidering *Roe* [v. *Wade*] cannot be taken seriously."[50]

The process of crafting a final opinion is not an easy one, and justices often rely heavily on their clerks to do much of the revision. Neither is the process apolitical. Today, one vote on the Court can be the difference between two very different outcomes.

JUDICIAL PHILOSOPHY AND DECISION MAKING

JUSTICES DO NOT MAKE DECISIONS in a vacuum. Principles of *stare decisis* dictate that the justices follow the law of previous cases in deciding cases at hand. But, a variety of legal and extra-legal factors have also been found to affect Supreme Court decision making.

Judicial Philosophy, Original Intent, and Ideology

Legal scholars long have argued that judges decide cases based on the Constitution and their reading of various statutes. Determining what the Framers meant—if that is even possible today—often appears to be based on an individual jurist's philosophy.

One of the primary issues concerning judicial decision making focuses on what is called the activism/restraint debate. Advocates of **judicial restraint** argue that courts should allow the decisions of other branches to stand, even when they offend a judge's own sense of principles. Restraintists defend their position by asserting that the federal courts are composed of unelected judges, which makes the judicial branch the least democratic branch of government. Consequently, the courts should defer policy making to other branches of government as much as possible.

Restraintists refer to *Roe* v. *Wade* (1973), the case that liberalized abortion laws, as a classic example of **judicial activism** run amok. They maintain that the Court should have deferred policy making on this sensitive issue to the states or to the other branches of the federal government—the legislative and executive—because their officials are elected and therefore are more receptive to the majority's will.

Advocates of judicial restraint generally agree that judges should be strict constructionists; that is, they should interpret the Constitution as it was written and intended by the Framers. They argue that in determining the constitutionality of a statute or policy, the Court should rely on the explicit meanings of the clauses in the document, which can be clarified by looking at the intent of the Framers.

Advocates of judicial activism contend that judges should use their power broadly to further justice, especially in the areas of equality and personal liberty. Activists argue that it is the courts' appropriate role to correct injustices committed by the other branches of government. Explicit in this argument is the notion that courts need to protect oppressed minorities.[51]

Activists point to *Brown* v. *Board of Education* (1954) as an excellent example of the importance of judicial activism.[52] In *Brown*, the Supreme Court ruled that racial segregation in public schools violated the equal protection clause of the Fourteenth Amendment. Segregation nonetheless was practiced after passage of the Fourteenth Amendment. An activist would point out that if the Court had not reinterpreted pro-

judicial restraint
A philosophy of judicial decision making that argues courts should allow the decisions of other branches of government to stand, even when they offend a judge's own sense of principles.

judicial activism
A philosophy of judicial decision making that argues judges should use their power broadly to further justice, especially in the areas of equality and personal liberty.

visions of the amendment, many states probably would still have laws or policies mandating segregation in public schools.

Although judicial activists are often considered politically liberal and restraintists politically conservative, in recent years a new brand of conservative judicial activism has become prevalent. Unlike their liberal counterparts, whose activist decisions often expanded the rights of political and legal minorities, conservative activist judges view their positions as an opportunity to issue broad rulings that impose conservative political beliefs and policies on the country at large.

Some scholars argue that this increased conservative judicial activism has had an effect on the Court's reliance on *stare decisis* and adherence to precedent. Chief Justice William H. Rehnquist even noted that while "*stare decisis* is a cornerstone of our legal system . . . it has less power in constitutional cases."[53]

Models of Judicial Decision Making

Most political scientists who study what is called judicial behavior conclude that a variety of forces shape judicial decision making. Of late, many have attempted to explain how judges vote by integrating a variety of models to offer a more complete picture of how judges make decisions.[54] Many of those models attempt to take into account justices' individual behavioral characteristics and attitudes as well as the fact patterns of the case.

Behavioral Characteristics.   Originally, some political scientists argued that social background differences, including childhood experiences, religious values, education, earlier political and legal careers, and political party loyalties, are likely to influence how a judge evaluates the facts and legal issues presented in any given case. Justice Harry A. Blackmun's service at the Mayo Clinic often is pointed to as a reason that his opinion for the Court in *Roe* v. *Wade* (1973) was grounded so thoroughly in medical evidence. Similarly, Justice Potter Stewart, who was generally considered a moderate on most civil liberties issues, usually took a more liberal position on cases dealing with freedom of the press. Why? It may be that Stewart's early job as a newspaper reporter made him more sensitive to these claims.

The Attitudinal Model.   The attitudinal approach links judicial attitudes with decision making.[55] Simply stated, the attitudinal model holds that Supreme Court justices decide cases according to their personal preferences toward issues of public policy. Among some of the factors used to derive attitudes are a justice's party identification,[56] the party of the appointing president, and the liberal/conservative leanings of a justice.[57] For example, under the attitudinal model, a liberal justice appointed by a Democratic president would be more likely to decide an abortion case in favor of the pro-choice point of view. A conservative justice appointed by a Republican president, then, would most likely favor measures to support a free-market economy. Both justices would then manipulate the law to support these ideological beliefs.

The Strategic Model.   Some scholars who study the courts now are advocating the belief that judges act strategically, meaning that they weigh and assess their actions against those of other justices to optimize the chances that their preferences will be adopted by the whole Court.[58] Moreover, this approach seeks to explain not only a justice's vote but also the range of forces such as congressional/judicial relations and judicial/executive relations that also affect the outcome of legal disputes.

Public Opinion.   Many political scientists have examined the role of public opinion in Supreme Court decision making.[59] Not only do the justices read legal briefs and hear oral arguments, but they also read newspapers, watch television, and have some knowledge of public opinion—especially on controversial issues.

Whether or not public opinion actually influences some justices, public opinion can act as a check on the power of the courts as well as an energizing factor. Activist periods on the Supreme Court generally have corresponded to periods of social or economic crisis. For example, the Marshall Court supported a strong national government, much to the chagrin of a series of pro–states' rights Democratic-Republican presidents in the early crisis-ridden years of the republic. Similarly, the Court capitulated to political pressures and public opinion when, after 1936, it reversed many of its earlier decisions that had blocked President Franklin D. Roosevelt's New Deal legislation.

The courts, especially the Supreme Court, also can be the direct target of public opinion. When *Webster* v. *Reproductive Health Services* (1989) was about to come before the Supreme Court, the Court was subjected to unprecedented lobbying as groups and individuals on both sides of the abortion issue marched and sent appeals to the Court. Earlier, in the fall of 1988, Justice Harry A. Blackmun, author of *Roe v. Wade* (1973), had warned a law school audience that he feared the decision was in jeopardy.[60] This in itself was a highly unusual move; until recently, it was the practice of the justices never to comment publicly on cases or the Court.

Speeches such as Blackmun's put pro-choice advocates on guard. When the Court agreed to hear *Webster*, the pro-choice forces mounted one of the largest demonstrations in the history of the United States—more than 300,000 people marched from the Mall to the Capitol, just across the street from the Supreme Court. In addition, full-page advertisements appeared in prominent newspapers, and supporters of *Roe v. Wade* (1973) were urged to contact members of the Court to voice their support. Mail at the Court, which usually averaged about 1,000 pieces a day, rose to an astronomical 46,000 pieces per day, virtually paralyzing normal lines of communication.

The Court also is dependent on the public for its prestige as well as for compliance with its decisions. In times of war and other emergencies, for example, the Court frequently has decided cases in ways that commentators have attributed to the sway of public opinion and political exigencies. In *Korematsu* v. *U.S.* (1944), for example, the high Court upheld the obviously unconstitutional internment of Japanese American citizens during World War II.[61] Moreover, Chief Justice William H. Rehnquist himself once suggested that the Court's restriction on presidential authority in *Youngstown Sheet & Tube Co.* v. *Sawyer* (1952), which invalidated President Harry S Truman's seizure of the nation's steel mills,[62] was largely attributable to Truman's unpopularity and that of the Korean War.[63]

Public confidence in the Court, as with other institutions of government, has ebbed and flowed. Public support for the Court was highest after the Court issued *U.S.* v. *Nixon* (1974).[64] At a time when Americans lost faith in the presidency, they could at least look to the Supreme Court to do the right thing. Although the numbers of Americans with confidence in the courts has fluctuated over time, in 2004, 46 percent of those sampled by Gallup International had a "great deal" or "quite a bit" of confidence in the Supreme Court.[65]

The Supreme Court also appears to affect public opinion. Political scientists have found that the Court's initial rulings on controversial issues such as abortion or capital punishment positively influence public opinion in the direction of the Court's opinion. However, this research also finds that subsequent decisions have little effect.[66] As Table 10.8 reveals, the public and the Court often are in agreement on many controversial issues.

TABLE 10.8 The Supreme Court and the American Public

In recent years, the Court's rulings have agreed with or diverged from public opinion on various questions, such as:

Issue	Case	Court Decision	Public Opinion
Should homosexual relations between consenting adults be legal?	*Lawrence* v. *Texas* (2003)	Yes	Maybe (50%)
Should members of Congress be subject to term limits?	*U.S. Term Limits* v. *Thornton* (1995)	No	Yes (77% favor)
Is affirmative action constitutional?	*Grutter* v. *Bollinger* (2003) *Gratz* v. *Bollinger* (2003)	Yes	Yes (64%)
Before getting an abortion, whose consent should a teenager be required to gain?	*Williams* v. *Zbaraz* (1980)	One parent	Both parents (38%) One parent (37%) Neither parent (22%)
Is the death penalty constitutional?	*Gregg* v. *Georgia* (1976)	Yes	Yes (72% favor)

Source: Table compiled from R-Poll, LEXIS-NEXIS.

JUDICIAL POLICY MAKING AND IMPLEMENTATION

AS ILLUSTRATED in the opening vignette, all judges, whether they recognize it or not, make policy. The primary way federal judges, and the U.S. Supreme Court, in particular, make policy is through interpreting statutes or the Constitution. This occurs in a variety of ways. Judges can interpret a provision of a statute to cover matters previously not understood to be covered by the law, or they can discover new rights, such as that of privacy, from their reading of the Constitution. They also have literal power over life and death when they decide death penalty cases.

This power of the courts to make policy presents difficult questions for democratic theory, as noted by Justice Antonin Scalia in *Webster* v. *Reproductive Health Services* (1989), because democratic theorists believe that the power to make law resides only in the people or their elected representatives. Yet, court rulings, especially Supreme Court decisions, routinely affect policy far beyond the interests of the immediate parties.

Policy Making

One measure of the power of the courts and their ability to make policy is that more than one hundred federal laws have been declared unconstitutional. Although many of these laws have not been particularly significant, others have. For example, in *Ashcroft* v. *Free Speech Coalition* (2002), the Court ruled that the Child Online Protection Act, designed to prevent minors from viewing pornography over the Internet, was unconstitutional.[67]

Another measure of the policy-making power of the Supreme Court is its ability to overrule itself. Although the Court generally abides by the informal rule of *stare decisis*, by one count, it has overruled itself in more than 200 cases.[68] *Brown* v. *Board of Education* (1954), for example, overruled *Plessy* v. *Ferguson* (1896), thereby reversing years of constitutional interpretation concluding that racial segregation was not a violation of the Constitution. Moreover, in the past few years, the Court has repeatedly reversed earlier decisions in the areas of criminal defendants' rights, women's rights, and the establishment of religion, thus revealing its powerful role in determining national policy.

A measure of the growing power of the federal courts is the degree to which they now handle issues that had been considered political questions more appropriately left to the other branches of government to decide. Prior to 1962, for example, the Court refused to hear cases questioning the size (and population) of congressional districts, no matter how unequal they were.[69] The boundary of a legislative district was considered a political question. Then, in 1962, writing for the Court, Justice William Brennan, Jr. concluded that simply because a case involved a political issue, it did not necessarily involve a political question. This opened up the floodgates to cases involving a variety of issues that the Court formerly had declined to address.[70]

Implementing Court Decisions

President Andrew Jackson, annoyed about a particular decision handed down by the Marshall Court, is alleged to have said, "John Marshall has made his decision; now let him enforce it." Jackson's statement raises a question: how do Supreme Court rulings translate into public policy? In fact, although judicial decisions carry legal and even moral authority, all courts must rely on other units of government to carry out their directives. If the president or members of Congress, for example, don't like a particular Supreme Court ruling, they can underfund programs needed to implement a decision or seek only lax enforcement. **Judicial implementation** refers to how and whether judicial decisions are translated into actual public policies affecting more than the immediate parties to the lawsuit.

How well a decision is implemented often depends on how well crafted or popular it is. Hostile reaction in the South to *Brown v. Board of Education* (1954) and the absence of precise guidelines to implement the decision meant that the ruling went largely unenforced for years. The *Brown* experience also highlights how much the Supreme Court needs the support of both federal and state courts as well as other governmental agencies to carry out its judgments. For example, you probably graduated from high school after 1992, when the Supreme Court ruled that public middle school and high school graduations could not include a prayer, yet your own commencement ceremony may have included one.

The implementation of judicial decisions involves what political scientists call an implementing population and a consumer population.[71] The implementing population consists of those people responsible for carrying out a decision. It varies, depending on the policy and issues in question, but can include lawyers, judges, public officials, police officers and police departments, hospital administrators, government agencies, and corporations. In the case of school prayer, the implementing population could include teachers, school administrators, or school boards. The consumer population consists of those people who might be directly affected by a decision, that is, in this case, students and parents.

For effective implementation of a judicial decision, the first requirement is that the members of the implementing population must act to show that they understand the original decision. For example, the Supreme Court ruled in *Reynolds v. Sims* (1964) that

judicial implementation
Refers to how and whether judicial decisions are translated into actual public policies affecting more than the immediate parties to a lawsuit.

Photo courtesy: Joe Raedle/Newsmakers/Getty Images

■ This photo, taken in September 2000, illustrates the difficulty in implementing judicial decisions. Although the Supreme Court ruled in June 2000 that pre-game prayers at public high schools were unconstitutional, prayers continued at many public school sporting events across the country.

every person should have an equally weighted vote in electing governmental representatives.[72] This "one person, one vote" decision might seem simple enough at first glance,
but in practice it can be very difficult to understand. The implementing population in
this case consists chiefly of state legislatures and local governments, which determine
voting districts for federal, state, and local offices (see chapter 13). If a state legislature
draws districts in such a way that African American voters are spread thinly across a
number of separate constituencies, the chances are slim that any particular district will
elect a representative who is especially sensitive to blacks' concerns. Does that violate
"equal representation"? (In practice, through the early 1990s, courts and the Department of Justice intervened in many cases to ensure that elected officials would include
minority representation, only ultimately to be overruled by the Supreme Court.)[73]

The second requirement is that the implementing population actually must follow
Court policy. Thus, when the Court ruled that men could not be denied admission to
a state-sponsored nursing school, the implementing population—in this case, university administrators and the state board of regents governing the nursing school—had
to enroll qualified male students.[74]

Judicial decisions are most likely to be implemented smoothly if responsibility for
implementation is concentrated in the hands of a few highly visible public officials, such
as the president or a governor. By the same token, these officials also can thwart or
impede judicial intentions. Recall from chapter 6, for example, the effect of Governor
Orval Faubus's initial refusal to allow black children to attend all-white public schools
in Little Rock, Arkansas.

The third requirement for implementation is that the consumer population must
be aware of the rights that a decision grants or denies them. Teenagers seeking an abortion, for example, are consumers of the Supreme Court's decisions on abortion. They
need to know that most states require them to inform their parents of their intention
to have an abortion or to get parental permission to do so. Similarly, criminal defendants and their lawyers are consumers of Court decisions and need to know, for instance,
the implications of recent Court decisions for evidence presented at trial.

SUMMARY

THE JUDICIARY AND THE LEGAL PROCESS—on both the
national and state levels—are complex and play a far more
important role in the setting of policy than the Framers
ever envisioned. To explain the judicial process and its evolution, we have made the following points:

1. **The Constitution and the Creation of the Federal
   Judiciary**
   Many of the Framers viewed the judicial branch of government as little more than a minor check on the other
   two branches, ignoring Anti-Federalist concerns about
   an unelected judiciary and its potential for tyranny.
   The Judiciary Act of 1789 established the basic
   federal court system we have today. It was the Marshall
   Court (1801–1835), however, that interpreted the
   Constitution to include the Court's major power, that
   of judicial review.

2. **The American Legal System**
   Ours is a dual judicial system consisting of the federal
   court system and the separate judicial systems of the
   fifty states. In each system there are two basic types of
   courts: trial courts and appellate courts. Each type
   deals with cases involving criminal and civil law. Orig-

inal jurisdiction refers to a court's ability to hear a case
as a trial court; appellate jurisdiction refers to a court's
ability to review cases already decided by a trial court.

3. **The Federal Court System**
   The federal court system is made up of constitutional and
   legislative courts. Federal district courts, courts of appeals,
   and the Supreme Court are constitutional courts.

4. **How Federal Court Judges Are Selected**
   District court and court of appeals judges are nominated
   by the president and subject to Senate confirmation.
   Supreme Court justices are nominated by the president
   and must also win Senate confirmation. Presidents use
   different criteria for selection, but important factors
   include competence, standards, ideology, rewards, pursuit
   of political support, religion, race, ethnicity, and gender.

5. **The Supreme Court Today**
   Several factors go into the Court's decision to hear a case.
   Not only must the Court have jurisdiction, but at least
   four justices must vote to hear the case, and cases with
   certain characteristics are most likely to be heard. Once
   a case is set for review, briefs and *amicus curiae* briefs are
   filed and oral argument scheduled. The justices meet
   after oral argument to discuss the case, votes are taken,
   and opinions are written, circulated, and then announced.

6. Judicial Philosophy and Decision Making

Judges' philosophy and ideology have an extraordinary impact on how they decide cases. Political scientists consider these factors in identifying several models for how judges make decisions, including the behavioral, attitudinal, and strategic models.

7. Judicial Policy Making and Implementation

The Supreme Court is an important participant in the policy-making process. The process of judicial interpretation gives the Court powers never envisioned by the Framers.

KEY TERMS

amicus curiae, p. 371

appellate courts, p. 353

appellate jurisdiction, p. 353

brief, p. 357

civil law, p. 353

constitutional courts, p. 354

criminal law, p. 353

judicial activism, p. 377

judicial implementation, p. 381

judicial restraint, p. 377

judicial review, p. 346

Judiciary Act of 1789, p. 347

jurisdiction, p. 353

legislative courts, p. 354

Marbury v. *Madison* (1803), p. 350

original jurisdiction, p. 353

precedent, p. 357

Rule of Four, p. 370

senatorial courtesy, p. 359

solicitor general, p. 371

stare decisis, p. 357

strict constructionist, p. 362

trial courts, p. 353

writ of *certiorari*, p. 369

SELECTED READINGS

Abraham, Henry J. *The Judiciary: The Supreme Court in the Governmental Process*, 10th ed. New York: New York University Press, 1996.

Barrow, Deborah J., Gary Zuk, and Gerard S. Gryski. *The Federal Judiciary and Institutional Change*. Ann Arbor: University of Michigan Press, 1996.

Baum, Lawrence. *The Supreme Court*, 8th ed. Washington, DC: CQ Press, 2004.

Baum, Lawrence. *The Puzzle of Judicial Behavior*. Ann Arbor: University of Michigan Press, 1997.

Clayton, Cornell, and Howard Gillman, eds. *Supreme Court Decision-Making: New Institutionalist Approaches*. Chicago: University of Chicago Press, 1999.

Epstein, Lee, et al. *The Supreme Court Compendium*, 3rd ed. Washington, DC: Congressional Quarterly Inc., 2002.

Goldman, Sheldon. *Picking Federal Judges: Lower Court Selection from Roosevelt Through Reagan*. New Haven, CT: Yale University Press, 1997.

Hall, Kermit L., ed. *The Oxford Companion to the Supreme Court of the United States*, 2nd ed. New York: Oxford University Press, 2005.

Lazarus, Edward. *Closed Chambers: The First Eyewitness Account of the Epic Struggles Inside the Supreme Court*. New York: Times Books, 1998.

O'Brien, David M. *Storm Center: The Supreme Court in American Politics*, 6th ed. New York: Norton, 2002.

Perry, H. W. *Deciding to Decide: Agenda Setting in the United States Supreme Court*. Cambridge, MA: Harvard University Press, 1994.

Provine, Doris Marie. *Case Selection in the United States Supreme Court*. Chicago: University of Chicago Press, 1980.

Salokar, Rebecca Mae. *The Solicitor General: The Politics of Law*. Philadelphia: Temple University Press, 1992.

Slotnick, Elliot E., and Jennifer A. Segal. *Television News and the Supreme Court: All the News That's Fit to Air*. Boston: Cambridge University Press. 1998.

Spaeth, Howard, and Jeffrey A. Segal. *Majority Rule or Minority Will: Adherence to Precedent on the U.S. Supreme Court*. New York: Cambridge University Press, 2001.

Sunstein, Cass R. *One Case at a Time: Judicial Minimalism on the Supreme Court*, 2nd ed. Cambridge, MA: Harvard University Press, 2001.

Woodward, Bob, and Scott Armstrong. *The Brethren: Inside the Supreme Court*, reprint ed. New York: Avon, 1996.

WEB EXPLORATIONS

To learn more about the workings of the U.S. justice system, see
http://www.usdoj.gov/

To learn more about U.S. federal courts, see
http://www.uscourts.gov/UFC99.pdf

To take a virtual tour of the U.S. Supreme Court and examine current cases on its docket, go to
www.supremecourtus.gov

To learn about the U.S. Senate Judiciary Committee and judicial nominations currently under review, see
http://judiciary.senate.gov/

To learn the extent of the ABA's legislative and government advocacy, go to
http://www.abanet.org/

To examine the major Supreme Court decisions from the past to the present, go to
http://supct.law.cornell.edu/supct/index.htm/

To examine the recent filings of the office of solicitor general, go to
http://www.usdoj.gov/osg/

Photo courtesy: Bob Daemmrich/Stock Boston, LLC

Public Opinion and Political Socialization

AT 2:18 A.M. ON NOVEMBER 9, 2000, one of the major television networks made the call that George W. Bush would become the forty-third president of the United States. All the major networks quickly followed suit. But, as we all know now, that was not the end of it. As demands for recounts and litigation went on, one of the longest presidential elections in the nation's history became a field day for pollsters and their critics. In fact, the original call awarding Florida to Al Gore came early in the evening and was based not on actual vote totals, but on projections from the Voter News Service, an exit poll service used by a consortium of news organizations to hold down costs.

Pollsters sprang into action after Gore decided to retract the concession call he had made to Governor Bush. The Gallup Organization polled Americans to determine if they favored or opposed hand recounts in Florida. Nationwide, on November 11–12, 2000, 55 percent favored a recount, 85 percent of the Gore voters but only 20 percent of those who voted for Bush. Sixty percent believed that those votes should be included in the final totals.[1] On November 26, 2000, when asked whom they considered the real winner in Florida, 51 percent said Bush, but 32 percent were unsure. By then, only 15 percent thought Gore was the real winner. But, after the U.S. Supreme Court's decision that stopped all further vote counting, and, in essence, declared George W. Bush the winner, voters were asked on December 15–17, "Just your best guess, if the Supreme Court had allowed the vote recount to continue in Florida, who do you think would have ended up with the most votes in Florida?" Of the national sample, 46 percent said Gore; 45 percent said Bush.

As in the November 11–12 poll, there was a huge chasm between Bush and Gore voters. Nearly three-quarters (74 percent) of the Gore voters continued to believe that he was the rightful winner; 77 percent of the Bush voters believed that their man would have ended up the winner. The same poll found that only 51 percent of those sampled believed that the Electoral College outcome was "fair." Again, huge gaps were evident in Bush and Gore voters. Eighty-five percent of the Bush voters thought the election outcome was fair; only 23 percent of the Gore voters did. Nationally, 68 percent of black voters believed that their votes were less likely to have been counted fairly in Florida than the votes of whites. Still, 61 percent of the public reported their belief that George W. Bush would work hard to "represent the interests of all Americans," although only 22 percent of blacks polled agreed with this statement.

Polling gives us a unique view into the psyche of Americans. Politicians read the polls, as do their advisers. George W. Bush, who prided himself on his good relations with Hispanic and African American communities in Texas, undoubtedly was surprised by the feelings of Gore supporters and African Americans. Some might even argue that the diversity of Bush's first-term Cabinet appointments reflected his concern with bolstering his support among Hispanics, blacks, and even women. These efforts paid off in 2004, when he was able to capture more voters in all those groups.

CANDIDATES, NEWS SERVICES, and elected officials, including presidents, are not the only ones who look at poll data. Professional pollsters routinely question Americans from all walks of life about their beliefs and opinions on a variety of things from washing detergent to favorite television and radio programs to their attitudes about government and democracy. Americans hold myriad views on most issues. On many political issues they often are divided nearly evenly.

In 1787, John Jay wrote glowingly of the sameness of the American people. He and the other authors of *The Federalist Papers* believed that Americans had more in common than not. Wrote Jay in *Federalist No. 2*, we are "one united people—a people descended from the same ancestors, speaking the same language, professing the same religion, attached to the same principles of government, very similar in manners and customs." Many of those who could vote in Jay's time were of English heritage; almost all were Christian. Moreover, most believed that certain rights—such as freedom of speech, association, and religion—were rights that could not be revoked. Jay also spoke of shared public opinion and of the need for a national government that reflected American ideals.

Today, however, Americans are a far more heterogeneous lot. Election after election and poll after poll reveal this diversity, but, nonetheless, Americans appear to agree on many things. Most want less government, particularly at the national level. So did many citizens in 1787. Most want a better nation for their children. So did the Framers. But, the Framers did not have sophisticated public opinion polls to measure the citizens' views, nor did they have national news media to tell them the results of those polls. Today, many people wonder what shapes public opinion: poll results or people's opinions? Do the polls drive public opinion, or does public opinion drive the polls?

The role of public opinion in elections and its role in the making of public policy are just two issues we explore in this chapter.

- First, we will examine the question of *what is public opinion*. We offer a simple definition and then note the role of public opinion polls in determining public perception of political issues.

- Second, we will describe *efforts to influence and measure public opinion*. Since the writing of *The Federalist Papers*, parties, candidates, and public officials have tried to sway as well as gauge public opinion for political purposes.

- Third, we will discuss *how political socialization and other factors influence opinion formation* about political matters. We will also examine the role of political ideology in public opinion formation.

- Fourth, we will examine *why we form political opinions*.

By permission of Mike Luckovich and Creators Syndicate, Inc.

■ Fifth, we will analyze *how public opinion is measured* and note problems with various kinds of polling techniques.

■ Finally, we will look at *how polling and public opinion affect politicians, politics, and policy.*

WHAT IS PUBLIC OPINION?

AT FIRST GLANCE, **public opinion** seems to be a very straightforward concept: it is what the public thinks about a particular issue or set of issues at a particular time. Since the 1930s, governmental decision makers have relied heavily on **public opinion polls**—interviews with samples of citizens that are used to estimate what the public is thinking. According to George Gallup (1901–1983), an Iowan who is considered the founder of modern-day polling, polls have played a key role in defining issues of concern to the public, shaping administrative decisions, and helping "speed up the process of democracy" in the United States.[2]

According to Gallup, leaders must constantly take public opinion—no matter how short-lived—into account. Like the Jacksonians of a much earlier era, Gallup was distrustful of leaders who were not in tune with the common man. According to Gallup: "In a democracy we demand the views of the people be taken into account. This does not mean that leaders must follow the public's view slavishly; it does mean that they should have an available appraisal of public opinion and take some account of it in reaching their decision."[3]

Even though Gallup undoubtedly had a vested interest in fostering reliance on public opinion polls, his sentiments accurately reflect the feelings of many political thinkers concerning the role of public opinion and governance. Some, like Gallup, believe that the government should do what a majority of the public wants done. Others argue that the public as a whole doesn't have consistent opinions on day-to-day issues but that subgroups within the public often hold strong views on some issues. These pluralists believe that the government must allow for the expression of these minority opinions and that democracy works best when these different voices are allowed to fight it out in the public arena.

public opinion
What the public thinks about a particular issue or set of issues at any point in time.

public opinion polls
Interviews or surveys with samples of citizens that are used to estimate the feelings and beliefs of the entire population.

But, as we will see later in this chapter, what the public or even subgroups think about various issues is difficult to know with certainty, simply because public opinion can change so quickly. For example, two weeks before the United States invaded Iraq in March 2003, public opinion polls revealed that only 66 percent of the American public believed the United States should take military action against Iraq to remove Saddam Hussein from power. Several days after the invasion, however, 80 percent reported they approved of the United States' action. By July 2004, just 37 percent of those polled reported that they approved of George W. Bush's handling of the situation with Iraq.[4]

EFFORTS TO INFLUENCE AND MEASURE PUBLIC OPINION

YOU CAN HARDLY READ a newspaper or news magazine, watch television, or log on to the Internet without hearing the results of the latest public opinion poll on confidence in government, the war on terrorism, the economy, or the president's performance. But, even long before the existence of modern polling, politicians tried to mold and win public opinion. *The Federalist Papers* were one of the first major attempts to change public opinion—in this case, to gain public support for the newly drafted U.S. Constitution. Even prior to publication of *The Federalist Papers,* Thomas Paine's *Common Sense* and later *The Crisis* were distributed widely throughout the colonies to stimulate patriotic feelings and to increase public support for the Revolutionary War.

■ As part of "the world's greatest adventure in advertising," the Committee on Public Information created a vast gallery of posters designed to shore up public support for World War I.

Photo courtesy: Bettmann/Corbis

From the very early days of the republic, political leaders recognized the importance of public opinion and used all of the means at their disposal to manipulate it for political purposes (see The Living Constitution). By the early 1800s, the term public opinion frequently was being used by the educated middle class. As more Americans became educated, they became more vocal about their opinions and were more likely to, although suffrage was limited to white men. A more educated, reading public led to increased demand for newspapers, which in turn provided more information about the process of government. As the United States grew, there were more elections and more opportunities for citizens to express their political opinions through the ballot box. As a result of these trends, political leaders were forced more frequently to try to gauge public opinion to remain responsive to the wishes and desires of their constituents.

An example of the power of public opinion is the public's response to the 1851–1852 serialization of Harriet Beecher Stowe's *Uncle Tom's Cabin.* This novel was one of the most powerful anti-slavery tracts ever published. By the time the first shots of the Civil War were fired at Fort Sumter in 1861, more than 1 million copies of the book were in print. Only 31 million people lived in the United States at this time, and only 19 million lived in free states. Even though Stowe's words alone could not have caused the public outrage over slavery that contributed to northern support for the war, her book convinced the majority of northerners of the justness of the abolitionist cause and solidified public opinion in the North against slavery.

During World War I, some people argued that public opinion didn't matter at all. But, President Woodrow Wilson argued that public opinion would temper the actions of international leaders. Therefore, only eight days after the start of the war, Wilson created a Committee on Public Information. Run by a prominent journalist, the committee immediately undertook to unite U.S. public opinion behind

The Living Constitution

The Senate of the United States shall be composed of two Senators from each State, chosen by the legislature thereof, for six Years; and each Senator shall have one vote.

—Article I, Section 3, Clause 1

This section of the Constitution was designed to allow state legislatures to select their representatives to the U.S. Senate. Those in attendance at the Constitutional Convention were quite skeptical of the "common man's" ability to select the true statesmen that they envisioned would serve in the upper house of the new government. Fearing that senators would be too attuned to popular or public opinion, they not only opted to have senators serve for six year terms but placed their election out of the control of the masses.

Eventually, increasing public opinion against this method of selecting senators resulted in the ratification of the Seventeenth Amendment securing popular election of senators. As the size of the electorate grew, more and more individuals began to call for senators to be elected by the people, just as members of the lower house were and continue to be. Thus, the importance of the populace and public opinion in a democracy once again reaffirmed the intention of the Framers.

the war effort. It used all of the tools available—pamphlets, posters, and speakers who exhorted the patrons of local movie houses during every intermission—in an effort to garner support and favorable opinion for the war. In the words of the committee's head, it was "the world's greatest adventure in advertising."[5] After World War I, Walter Lippmann, a well-known journalist and author who was involved extensively in propaganda activities during the war, openly voiced his concerns about how easily governments could manipulate public opinion and voiced his reservations about the weight it should be given.

In an era of instantaneous communication, it is more difficult for the government to manage public opinion. Still, political leaders continue to view public opinion as an important policy-making tool, both internally and abroad. When the United States invaded Iraq in 2003, for example, the government received a great deal of criticism for allowing reporters to embed themselves in military units (see the opening vignette in chapter 15). Critics charged that these journalists, who ate, slept, and reported from the front lines, provided stories that were little more than propaganda, because many of their reports lacked critical analysis.

The growth of television and the Internet clearly adds another dimension to any efforts by the government to build effective propaganda campaigns. For example, newsmakers such as Michael Moore and his film *Farenheit 911* were poised to undo the Bush Administration's positive messages about the U.S.-led invasion of Iraq. Critics of the invasion were bolstered by accounts of the harsh realities of war as evidenced by the filmed beheading of several American and British hostages and the photos of prisoner abuse at Abu Ghraib prison in Iraq.

Timeline

War, Peace, and
Public Opinion

Early Efforts to Measure Public Opinion

Public opinion polling as we know it today did not begin to develop until the 1930s. Much of this growth was prompted by Walter Lippmann's seminal work *Public Opinion* (1922).

In this piece, Lippmann observed that research on public opinion was far too limited, especially in light of its importance. Researchers in a variety of disciplines, including political science, heeded Lippmann's call to learn more about public opinion. Some tried to use scientific methods to measure political thought through the use of surveys or polls. As methods for gathering and interpreting data improved, survey data began to play an increasingly important role in all walks of life, from politics to retailing.

As early as 1824, one Pennsylvania newspaper tried to predict the winner of that year's presidential contest. Later, in 1883, the *Boston Globe* sent reporters to selected election precincts to poll voters as they exited voting booths, in an effort to predict the results of key contests. In 1916, *Literary Digest,* a popular magazine, began mailing survey postcards to potential voters in an effort to predict election outcomes. *Literary Digest* drew its survey sample from "every telephone book in the United States, from the rosters of clubs and associations, from city directories, lists of registered voters [and] classified mail order and occupational data."[7] Using data from the millions of postcard ballots it received from all over the United States, *Literary Digest* correctly predicted every presidential election from 1920 to 1932.

Literary Digest used what were called **straw polls,** unscientific surveys used to gauge public opinion, to predict the popular vote in those four presidential elections. Its polling methods were hailed widely as "amazingly right" and "uncannily accurate."[8] In 1936, however, its luck ran out. *Literary Digest* predicted that Republican Alfred M. Landon would beat incumbent President Franklin D. Roosevelt by a margin of 57 percent to 43 percent of the popular vote. Roosevelt, however, won in a landslide election, receiving 62.5 percent of the popular vote and carrying all but two states.

Literary Digest's 1936 straw poll had three fatal errors. First, its sample was drawn from telephone directories and lists of automobile owners. This technique oversampled the upper middle class and the wealthy, groups heavily Republican in political orientation. Moreover, in 1936, voting polarized along class lines. Thus, the oversampling of wealthy Republicans was particularly problematic because it severely underestimated the Democratic vote.

Literary Digest's second problem was timing. Questionnaires were mailed in early September. It did not measure the changes in public sentiment that occurred as the election drew closer.

Its third error occurred because of a problem we now call self-selection. Only highly motivated individuals sent back the cards—a mere 22 percent of those surveyed responded. Those who respond to mail surveys (or today, online surveys) are quite different from the general electorate; they often are wealthier and better educated and care more fervently about issues. *Literary Digest,* then, failed to observe one of the now well-known cardinal rules of survey sampling: "One cannot allow the respondents to select themselves into the sample."[9]

At least one pollster, however, correctly predicted the results of the 1936 election: George Gallup. Gallup had written his dissertation in psychology at the University of Iowa on how to measure the readership of newspapers. He then expanded his research to study public opinion about politics. He was so confident about his methods that he gave all of his newspaper clients a money-back guarantee: if his poll predictions weren't closer to the actual election outcome than those of the highly acclaimed *Literary Digest,* he would refund their money. Although Gallup underpredicted Roosevelt's victory by nearly 7 percent, the fact that he got the winner right was what everyone remembered, especially given *Literary Digest*'s dramatic miscalculation.

Recent Efforts to Measure Public Opinion

Through the late 1940s, polling techniques became more sophisticated. The number of polling groups also dramatically increased, as businesses and politicians began to rely on polling information to market products and candidates. But, in 1948, the

straw polls

Unscientific surveys used to gauge public opinion on a variety of issues and policies.

FIGURE 11.1 The Success of the Gallup Poll in Presidential Elections, 1936–2004

As seen here, Gallup's final predictions have been remarkably accurate. Furthermore, in each of the years where there is a significant discrepancy between Gallup's prediction and the election's outcome, there was a prominent third candidate. In 1948, Strom Thurmond ran on the Dixiecrat ticket; in 1980, John Anderson ran as the American Independent Party candidate; in 1992, Ross Perot ran as an independent. ■

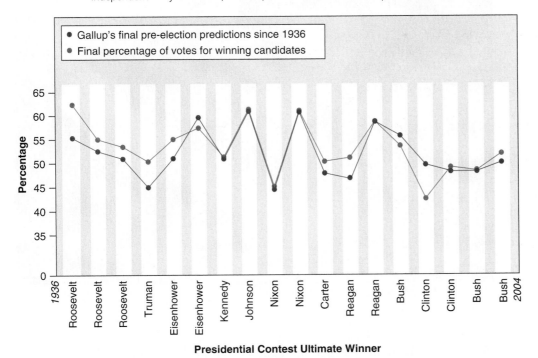

Presidential Contest Ultimate Winner

Sources: Marty Baumann, "How One Polling Firm Stacks Up," *USA Today* (October 27, 1992): 13A. 1996 data from Mike Mokrzycki, "Pre-election Polls' Accuracy Varied," *Atlanta Journal and Constitution* (November 8, 1996): A12. 2000 data from Gallup Organization, "Poll Releases" (November 7, 2000). 2004 data from *USA Today* and CNN/Gallup Tracking Poll, USAtoday.com.

polling industry suffered a severe, although fleeting, setback when Gallup and many other pollsters incorrectly predicted that Thomas E. Dewey would defeat President Harry S Truman.

Nevertheless, as revealed in Figure 11.1, the Gallup Organization, now co-chaired by George Gallup Jr., continues to predict the winners of the presidential popular vote successfully. But, as the 2000 presidential election reminded most Americans, it is the vote in the Electoral College—not the popular vote—that ultimately counts. Thus, while George W. Bush's lead in the polls continued to shrink in the final days of 2000 polling, he won a 271–266 vote in the Electoral College. On November 7, 2000, the Gallup Organization announced what turned out to be a major understatement: the election was too close to call. Ultimately, Bush got 48 percent of the popular vote; Gore 49 percent.

In 2004, although many polls were all over the place, Gallup predicted the winner while underpredicting George W. Bush's popular vote. Still, in spite of its reputation for accuracy, even the Gallup Organization is not immune from error, as is illustrated in Politics Now: Polling: When the Numbers Don't Add Up.

Recent efforts to measure public opinion also have been aided by social science surveys such as the National Election Study (NES), conducted by researchers at the University of Michigan since 1952. NES surveys focus on the political attitudes and the behavior of the electorate, and include questions about how respondents voted,

■ Not only did advance polls in 1948 predict that Republican nominee Thomas E. Dewey would defeat Democratic incumbent Harry S Truman, but based on early and incomplete vote tallies, some newspapers' early editions published the day after the election declared Dewey the winner. Here a triumphant Truman holds aloft the *Chicago Daily Tribune*.

Photo courtesy: Bettmann/Corbis

their party affiliation, and their opinions of major political parties and candidates. In addition, NES surveys include questions about interest in politics and political participation.

These surveys are conducted before and after midterm and presidential elections and often include many of the same questions. This format enables researchers to compile long-term studies of the electorate and facilitates political scientists' understanding of how and why people vote and participate in politics.

The Internet also has had an effect on how public opinion is measured. For example, one company used Internet polling to instantaneously measure the responses of potential voters to the 2000 Democratic presidential nomination acceptance of Al Gore.[10] Harris Interactive, an Internet-based marketing firm, used the Internet to achieve a 99 percent accuracy rate in seventy-three political contests in November 2000.[11] Still, critics charge that the Internet is far from perfect for polling. Many citizens, especially the poor and the elderly, are not online and therefore are undercounted in Internet polls.

HOW POLITICAL SOCIALIZATION AND OTHER FACTORS INFLUENCE OPINION FORMATION

political socialization
The process through which an individual acquires particular political orientations; the learning process by which people acquire their political beliefs and values.

POLITICAL SCIENTISTS BELIEVE that many of our attitudes about issues are grounded in our political values. We learn these values through **political socialization**, "the process through which an individual acquires his particular political orientations—his knowledge, feeling, and evaluations regarding his political world."[12]

Family, the mass media, school, and peers are often important influences or agents of political socialization. For example, try to remember your earliest memory of the president of the United States. It may have been George Bush or Bill Clinton (older students probably remember earlier presidents). What did you think of the president? Of the Republican or Democratic Party? It is likely that your earliest feelings or attitudes were shaped by what your parents thought about that particular president and his party. Your experiences at school and your friends also probably influence your political beliefs today. Similar processes also apply to your early attitudes about the American flag, or the police. Other factors, too, often influence how political opinions are formed or reinforced. These include political events; the social groups you belong to, including your church, synagogue, or mosque; your demographic group, including your race, gender, and age; and even the region of the country in which you live.

The Family

The influence of the family on political socialization can be traced to two factors: communication and receptivity. Children, especially during their preschool years, spend tremendous amounts of time with their parents; early on they learn their parents' political values, even though these concepts may be vague. One study, for example, found that the most important visible public figures for children under the age of ten were police officers and, to a much lesser extent, the president.[13] Young children almost uniformly view both as "helpful." But, by the age of ten or eleven, children become more selective in their perceptions of the president. By this age, children raised in Democratic households are much more likely to be critical of a Republican president than are those raised in Republican households. In 1988, for example, 58 percent of children in Republican households identified themselves as Republicans, and many had developed strong positive feelings toward Ronald Reagan, the Republican president. Support for and the popularity of Ronald Reagan translated into support for the Republican Party through the 1988 presidential election and also contributed to the decline of liberal ideological self-identification of first-year college students (see Figure 11.2).

School and Peers

Researchers report mixed findings concerning the role of schools in the political socialization process, which affects how individuals perceive events. There is no question that, in elementary school, children are taught respect for their nation and its symbols. Most school days begin with the Pledge of Allegiance, and patriotism and respect for country are important, although subtle, components of most school curricula. Support for flag and country create a foundation for national allegiance that prevails despite the negative views about politicians and government institutions that many Americans develop later in life. For example, though many Americans initially questioned action in Iraq in 2003, large numbers of schoolchildren prepared letters and packages to send to troops there and elsewhere. In some states, teachers were also encouraged to limit anti-war discussion.[14] Measures such as these, however controversial, help to build a sense of patriotism at a young age.

In 1994, Kids Voting USA was launched nationwide. This civic education project was designed to have a short-term impact on student political awareness and lead to a

Photo courtesy: Nancy O'Connor Zeigler

■ Political values are shaped in childhood.

higher voter turnout among parents. In 2002, Congress appropriated nearly $400,000 to Kids Voting USA to further teach "young people about the value of voting and democratic participation."[15] Over 2 million students participate annually, and adult turnout frequently goes up 3 to 5 percent in communities where the program operates.[16] Thus, a school-based program actually uses children to affect their parents.

The *Weekly Reader*, read by elementary students nationwide, not only attempts to present young students with newsworthy stories but also tries to foster political awareness and a sense of civic duty. In presidential election years, students get the opportunity to vote for actual presidential candidates in the nationwide *Weekly Reader* elections. These elections, which have been held since 1956, have been remarkably accurate. *Weekly Reader* has been wrong only once, in the 1992 election of Bill Clinton. These returns were skewed by prominent independent candidate Ross Perot.

A child's peers—that is, children about the same age—also seem to have an important effect on the socialization process. Whereas parental influences are greatest from birth to age five, a child's peer group becomes increasingly important as the child gets older, especially as he or she gets into middle school or high school.[17] Groups such as the Girl Scouts of the USA recognize the effect of peer pressure and are trying to influence more young women to participate in, and have a positive view of, politics. The

FIGURE 11.2 The Ideological Self-Identification of First-Year College Students

A majority of first-year college students describe themselves as middle of the road; this number has held fairly steady since the early 1990s. The number of students identifying themselves as liberal and far left declined dramatically during the 1970s and early 1980s, while the number of students identifying themselves as conservative and far right increased. But, by far, most students continue to identify their ideology as middle of the road. ■

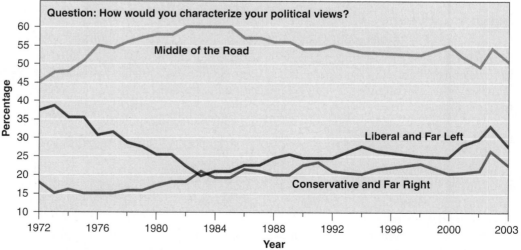

Sources: Reprinted from Howard W. Stanley and Richard G. Niemi, *Vital Statistics on American Politics, 2001–2002* (Washington, DC: CQ Press, 2001), 119. 2003 data from Cooperative Institutional Research Program (CIRP), "The American Freshman: National Norms for Fall 2003" (December 2003).

Girl Scouts' Ms. President merit badge encourages girls as young as five to learn "herstory" and to emulate women leaders.

High schools also can be important agents of political socialization. They continue the elementary school tradition of building good citizens and often reinforce textbook learning with trips to the state or national capital. They also offer courses on current U.S. affairs. Many high schools impose a compulsory service learning requirement, which some studies report positively affects later political participation.[18] Although the formal education of many people in the United States ends with high school, research shows that better-informed citizens vote more often as adults. Therefore, presentation of civic information is especially critical at the high school level, where it reinforces views about participation.

At the college level, teaching style often changes. Many college courses and texts like this one are designed in part to provide you with the information necessary to think critically about issues of major political consequence. It is common in college for students to be called on to question the appropriateness of certain political actions or to discuss underlying reasons for certain political or policy decisions. Therefore, most researchers believe that college has a liberalizing effect on students. Since the 1920s, studies have shown that students become more liberal each year they are in college.

Figure 11.2, however, reveals that students entering college in the 1980s were more conservative than in past years. The 1992 and 1996 victories of Bill Clinton and his equally youthful running mate Al Gore, who went out of their way to woo the youth vote, probably contributed to the small bump in the liberal ideological identification of first-year college students in those years. However, in 2003, 22.7 percent of freshmen identified themselves as conservative or far right; this was the highest percentage of conservative identifiiers in more than thirty years. The liberal label declined by a slightly larger percentage—from 25.3 to 24.2 percent. Nonetheless, more students continue to identify themselves as liberal than conservative, as they have done since studies of incoming freshmen began in 1965.[19]

Photo courtesy: Girl Scouts of the USA and The White House Project

■ To heighten young girls' interest in politics, Girl Scouts of the USA, in conjunction with The White House Project, has created a Ms. President merit badge.

The Mass Media

The media today are taking on a growing role as socialization agents. Adult Americans spend nearly thirty hours a week in front of their television sets; children spend even more.[20] Television has a tremendous impact on how people view politics, government, and politicians. TV talk shows, talk radio, and now even online newsletters and magazines are important sources of information about politics for many, yet the information that people get from these sources often is skewed. In 2004, one study estimated that more than 40 percent of those polled regularly learned about the election or candidates from alternative sources such as *The Tonight Show, The Late Show,* or *The Daily Show.*[21]

Television can serve to enlighten voters and encourage voter turnout. For example, MTV began coverage of presidential campaigns in 1992 and had reporters traveling with both major candidates to heighten young people's awareness of the stakes in the campaign. In addition, its "Choose or Lose" and "Rock the Vote" campaigns are designed to change the abysmal turnout rates of young voters.

Over the years, more and more Americans have turned away from traditional sources of news such as nightly news broadcasts on the major networks and daily newspapers in favor of different outlets. As one analyst put it, "Letterman, Jay Leno, Oprah

Join the Debate

TEACHING CIVICS IN AMERICAN HIGH SCHOOLS

OVERVIEW: Classical, Enlightenment, and contemporary political theories assert that a primary function of the state is the education of citizens; indeed, civic education is understood to be inseparable from public education. Civic education is considered an essential component of *political socialization*—the process whereby individuals acquire political knowledge, attitudes and beliefs. In many classrooms, for example, children elect the students who will erase chalkboards or serve as class leaders; by participating in classroom elections, students are thus socialized to accept electoral politics as part of legitimate political behavior. All mass democratic societies have some form of civic education, if only to teach citizens social norms, virtues, and the "rules of the game"—that is, governments teach individuals what is expected of them as citizens—be it voting in elections or accepting the dictates of arbitrary rule. It is generally understood that elections confer legitimacy to democratic regimes (remember, for example, the debate contending the legitimacy of George W. Bush's election to the presidency in 2000), so it follows that a significant decline in voter turnout and political participation may indicate fundamental dissatisfaction with the American regime. With this premise in mind, the public debate regarding civic education has taken on new importance in light of recent events. The debate over civic education in the United States is exacerbated by the increasing influence of the philosophies of relativism and identity politics, both of which argue that there is no one correct or right way to organize political society or governmental institutions.

It is obvious and accepted that civic education in secondary education has declined over the last thirty years. Many point to the Watergate scandal, the Vietnam War, and racial and social unrest during the civil rights movement as having a negative effect on the teaching of American history and government. The latest National Assessment of Educational Progress (NAEP) determined that only 26 percent of all high school seniors may be considered "proficient" in American political knowledge, and a Roper Survey discovered the majority of graduates from America's elite universities were incapable of identifying James Madison (a principal architect of the Constitution) or words from the Gettysburg Address (Lincoln's reaffirmation of American principles). With the decline in civic education, there seems to be a parallel decline in voter turnout and political participation. The Committee for the Study of the American Electorate reported that voter turnout in the 2000 primaries was only 16 percent of eligible voters—compare that to the 51 percent turnout in the 1966 midterm elections. It is telling that even motor-voter laws and relaxed rules of voter registration failed to increase voter turnout until 2004.

The noted nineteenth-century commentator on American political society Alexis de Tocqueville argued that without common values and virtues, there can be no common action and social stability. What is the best way to teach American history, government, and political principles so that all who have contributed to the American experiment are recognized? Is a common civic education necessary, or should political socialization be left to the family? What can be done to increase interest in democratic politics and participation, and how can civic knowledge be restored to the American electorate?

Arguments for Increased Civic Education in High Schools

- **There may be a relationship between the decline in political participation and the lack of civic education.** Research indicates there may be a correlation between

Winfrey, *Saturday Night Live*, and MTV became the deliverers of the news mainstream Americans want."[22] Several studies have found that the average media sound bite in the 2000 election was just seven seconds, three less than in 1998, which gives the electorate little opportunity to evaluate a candidate. In sharp contrast talk shows allow candidates ample time to discuss issues and present themselves as people. Thus, in 2004, both George W. Bush and John Kerry appeared on several popular shows and the public saw them unfiltered by packaging. Both candidates even appeared on *Dr. Phil* with their wives to talk about their families.

Former Secretary of State Colin Powell's ninety-minute appearance before a live audience on MTV is another example of how an administration can get its message out and sway public opinion. Powell's views on the conflict in Afghanistan were broadcast to over 370 million viewers worldwide.[23]

All of the major candidates in the 2004 presidential election used another form of media to sway and inform voters: the Internet, a form of campaigning that was con-the decline in political participation and civic education. A Carnegie Corporation study contends that student participation in the management of schools and classroom, as well as in simulations of democratic institutions and processes, may increase involvement in the American political process.

- **Civic education teaches citizens how to participate in democratic society.** Students become politically socialized by taking part in school elections, activities, and extra-curricular activities (such as participating in debate teams and publishing school newspapers). Civic education teaches not only cooperation but tolerance of dissent and opposing views, as well as the means of political compromise. This helps prepare students for the realities of pluralistic democratic life.

- **Civic education is a complement to political socialization.** The primary influence on one's political development comes from family and friends, and mass media and culture also help to shape political values and attitudes. The role of a formal civic education is to teach American history and governmental and political structures and principles, as well as to provide a forum for students to hone their political skills, practice public debate, and learn civic engagement.

Arguments Against Increased Civic Education in High Schools

- **Civic education is innately biased by promoting certain values over others.** In a free, multicultural society, it is inherently wrong to press upon individuals a certain political and social view. Modern democratic governments gather their strength from the many diverse cultures and political views that make up their respective social bodies. Teaching one sociopolitical view would stifle the contributions of those from different cultures.

- **Parents should be responsible for civic education.** One may assume a government-sanctioned education will be partial to its own interests and views. It is proper that parents introduce their children to political culture and socialization; this will help ensure a diversity of views in regard to the nature of government, thereby fostering debate and compromise in the marketplace of political ideas.

- **In a pluralist society it is difficult to determine what should constitute a civic education curriculum.** Which understanding of American history, politics, and government is to be taught? Different groups have different interpretations and understanding of the historical unfolding of American society. To promote the views of one group over another would be unfair, and to teach all views would be to overwhelm students with information; the effect may be actually to *discourage* political engagement by subjecting students to information overload.

Questions

1. Is there a correlation between the decline in civic participation and civic education? If so, why? If not, why not?

2. Is it the proper place of public schools to engage in civic education or is this the duty of family and friends?

Selected Readings

Stephen MacEdo. *Diversity and Distrust: Civic Education in a Multicultural Democracy*. Cambridge, MA: Harvard University Press, 2000.

Diane Ravitch, ed. *Making Good Citizens: Education and Civil Society*. New Haven, CT: Yale University Press, 2003.

sidered new in 1996. Each presidential and most other major and minor campaigns launched their own Internet sites, and the major networks and newspapers had their own Internet sites reporting on the election. For the first time, many political groups had Internet-based exhibits at the 2000 Republican and Democratic National Conventions. The outcome of the 2000 presidential election also was called online, prompting other forms of media to follow quickly.

One poll conducted after the 2000 election found that one in three voters followed the campaign online—three times the number who did in 1996. Nationwide, 11 percent of voters listed the Internet as their major source of information about campaign news; an additional 19 percent reported that they got some of their information about the election online. Forty-two percent of voters under age thirty reported that the Internet was their major source of information about the campaign. By the 2004 election cycle, more than 50 percent of those polled reported using the Internet to research candidates' positions on the issues.[24]

Social Groups

Group effects—certain characteristics that allow persons to be lumped into categories—also affect the development and continuity of political beliefs and opinions. Among the most important of these are religion, education level, income, and race. Researchers have learned that gender and age also are becoming increasingly important determinants of public opinion, especially on certain issues. Region, too, while not a social group, per se, appears to influence political beliefs and political socialization.

Religion.   Throughout our history, religion has played an extraordinary role in political life. Many colonists came to our shores seeking religious liberty, yet many quickly moved to impose their religious beliefs on others and some made participation in local politics contingent on religiosity. Since political scientists began to look at the role of religion, numerous scholars have found that organized religion influences the political beliefs and behaviors of its adherents. The effects of organized religion are magnified in today's society, as 67 percent of all Americans are members of a church or synagogue. This figure contrasts with 1776, when only one in five citizens was a member of such a group.

Through much of the twentieth century, social scientists found that faith-based political activity occurred largely on the left. From the civil rights movement, to efforts to improve the living standards of farmers and migrant workers, to abolition of the death penalty, religious leaders were evident. The civil rights movement, in particular, was led by numerous religious men, including the Reverend Martin Luther King Jr. and the Reverend Andrew Young (who later became mayor of Atlanta, Georgia, and the U.S. Ambassador to the United Nations), as well as more recently, the Reverend Jesse Jackson and the Reverend Al Sharpton.

In 1972, for the first time, a religious gap appeared in voting and public opinion. Richard M. Nixon's campaign was designed to appeal to what he termed "the Silent Majority," who wanted a return to more traditional values after the tumult of the 1960s. By the 1980s, conservative Christians could take credit for the election of Ronald Reagan. Throughout the 1980s, first the Moral Majority and then the Christian Coalition have played increasingly key roles in politics. Today, religion is the single largest predictor of the vote, after party identification. And, regular church-goers have conservative views and vote Republican by a 2 to 1 margin.

In 2004, 56 percent of Americans identified themselves as Protestant, 27 percent as Catholic, 2 percent as Jewish, and 7 percent as other. Only 8 percent claimed to have no religious affiliation. As shown in figure 11.3, Protestants, especially evangelicals, are the most conservative and Jews the most liberal. And, as liberals, Jews tend to vote

FIGURE 11.3 **The Ideological Self-Identification of Protestants, Catholics, and Jews.** ■

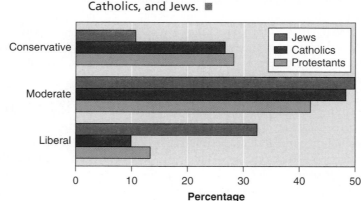

Source: Data compiled and analyzed by Alixandra Yanus from National American Election Studies 2002.

Democratic.[25] In 2004, for example, John Kerry and his running mate, John Edwards, captured 74 percent of the Jewish vote.[26]

Shared religious attitudes tend to affect voting and stances on particular issues. Catholics as a group, for example, favor aid to parochial schools, while many fundamentalist Protestants support organized prayer in public schools.

Race and Ethnicity.

Differences in political socialization of African Americans and whites appear at a very early age. Young black children, for example, generally show very positive feelings about the American society and political processes, but this attachment lessens considerably over time. Black children fail to hold the president in the esteem accorded him by white children; indeed, older African American children in the 1960s viewed the government primarily in terms of the U.S. Supreme Court.[27] These differences continue through adulthood.

During the murder trial of former football great turned actor O. J. Simpson in 1995, public opinion poll after public opinion poll revealed in stark numbers the immense racial divide that continued to exist in the nation. Blacks distrust governmental institutions far more than do whites, and are much more likely to question police actions. Not surprisingly, then, while a majority of whites believed that Simpson was guilty, a majority of blacks believed that he was innocent.

Photo courtesy: Arnold Gold/New Haven Register/The Image Works

■ Vice presidential candidate Joe Lieberman (D–CT) in the 2000 election became the first Jewish candidate to run for national office. Al Gore and Lieberman were defeated by George W. Bush and Dick Cheney in one of the closest presidential elections in American history. Many expected Lieberman would be the first Jewish candidate to be a strong contender for the presidency, but his 2004 candidacy attracted few primary voters.

Race and ethnicity are exceptionally important factors in elections and in the study of public opinion. The direction and intensity of African American opinion on a variety of hot-button issues often are quite different from those of whites. As revealed in Analyzing Visuals: Racial and Ethnic Attitudes on Selected Issues, whites are much more likely to support the war in Iraq than are blacks or Hispanics. Likewise, differences can be seen in other issue areas, including support for preferential treatment to improve the position of minorities.[28]

Hispanics, Asians/Pacific Islanders, and Native Americans are other identifiable ethnic minorities in the United States who often respond differently to issues than do whites. Generally, Hispanics and Native Americans hold similar opinions on many issues, largely because so many of them have low incomes and find themselves targets of discrimination. Government-sponsored health insurance for the working poor, for example, is a hot-button issue with Hispanic voters, with 94 percent favoring it. Unlike many other Americans, they also favor bilingual education and liberalized immigration policies.[29]

Within the Hispanic community, however, existing divisions often depend on national origin. Generally, Cuban Americans who cluster in Florida and in the Miami–Dade County area, in particular, are more likely to be conservative. They fled from communism and Fidel Castro in Cuba, and they generally vote Republican. In contrast, Hispanics of Mexican origin who vote in California, New Mexico, Arizona, Texas, or Colorado are more likely to vote Democratic.[30]

On issues directly affecting a particular group, sentiments often are markedly different. As our opening vignette illustrates, for example, black voters perceived the fairness of Florida vote counting procedures very differently from whites.

Analyzing Visuals

RACIAL AND ETHNIC ATTITUDES ON SELECTED ISSUES

Political opinions held by racial and ethnic groups in the United States differ on many issues. In the figure below, the opinions of whites, blacks, and Hispanics are compared on a number of political issues. After studying the bar graph and the material in this chapter on race, ethnicity, and public opinion, answer the following critical thinking questions: What do you observe about the differences and similarities in opinions among the different groups? On which issues do blacks and whites, Hispanics and blacks, and Hispanics and whites have similar or diverging opinions? What factors might explain these similarities and differences?

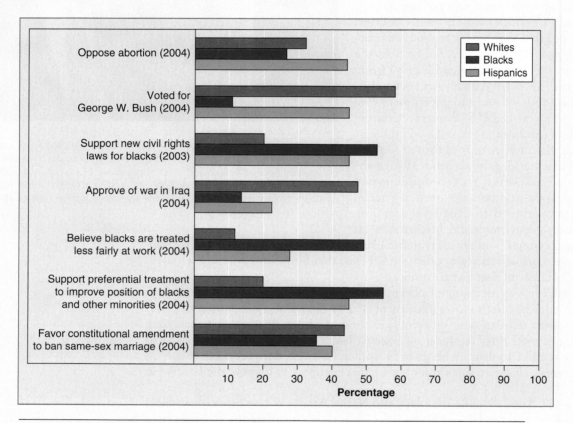

Source: *National Journal,* http://nationaljournal.com/members/polltrack.

Gender.   Poll after poll reveals that women hold very different opinions from men on a variety of issues, as shown in Analyzing Visuals: Gender Differences on Political Issues. These differences on political issues have often translated into substantial gaps in the way men and women vote. Women, and particularly unmarried women, are more likely to be Democrats, while white men are increasingly becoming the core of the Republican Party.[31]

Analyzing Visuals

GENDER DIFFERENCES ON POLITICAL ISSUES

Public opinion polls reveal that men and women hold different views on a number of political issues. Yet, on some political issues, little difference is evident. In the table below, the opinions of men and women on several political issues are compared. After studying the table and reading the material in this chapter on the impact of gender on public opinion, answer the following critical thinking questions: On which issues are the opinions of men and women the least different? What, if anything, do these issues have in common? On which issues are the opinions of men and women most different? What, if anything, do these issues have in common? How would you explain the results?

	Men (%)	Women (%)
Believe crime influences the way they live (2000)	47	66
Believe war on terrorism will spread (2002)	24	74
Have a favorable view of Saudi Arabia (2003)	42	23
Favor stricter laws against abortion (2003)	35	36
Believe books that contain dangerous ideas should be banned from public libraries (2003)	47	56
Consider prayer important in daily life (2003)	42	60
Voted for George W. Bush (2004)	55	48

Sources: Data from Gallup Organization, *Washington Post*/ABC Poll (May 7–10, 2000): http://nationaljournal.qpass.com/members/polltrack/2003/issues.htm.

From the time that the earliest public opinion polls were taken, women have been found to hold more positive attitudes about issues touching on social welfare concerns, such as education, juvenile justice, capital punishment, and the environment. Some analysts suggest that women's more nurturing nature and their prominent role as mothers lead women to have more liberal attitudes on issues affecting the family or children. Research by political scientists, however, finds no support for a maternal explanation.[32]

Historically, public opinion polls have also found that women hold more negative views about war and military intervention. However, the gender gap on military issues began to disappear in the late 1990s, when the United States intervened in Kosovo. Many speculated that this occurred because of the increased participation of women in the workforce and the military, the "sanitized nature of much of the war footage" shown on TV, and the humanitarian reasons for involvement.[33]

The gender gap in military affairs also was not visible following the terrorist attacks of 9/11. Right after the attacks, polls showed that 47 percent of women and 53 percent of men voiced their support for the operations in Afghanistan.[34] However, as the memory of 9/11 has receded, the war in Iraq has resulted in a renewed gender gap on foreign affairs. A May 2004 poll revealed that 31 percent of women and 62 percent of men favored staying in Iraq.[35] Many commentators speculate that this gap, as well as increased support for President George W. Bush in 2004 among women voters, may be the product of increasing concerns about terrorism abroad and national security at home.

FIGURE 11.4 Comparing Four Age Cohorts on Issues, 2003. ■

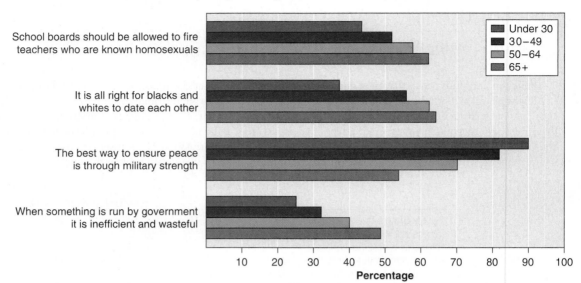

Source: Pew Research Center for the People and the Press, "Evenly Divided and Increasingly Polarized: 2004 Landscape," (November 5, 2003).

Age.   As Americans live longer, senior citizens are becoming a potent political force. In states such as Florida, to which many northern retirees have flocked seeking relief from cold winters and high taxes, the elderly have voted as a bloc to defeat school tax increases and to pass tax breaks for themselves. As a group, senior citizens are much more likely to favor an increased governmental role in the area of medical insurance and to oppose any cuts in Social Security benefits.

In the future, the graying of America will have major social and political consequences. As we discuss in chapter 13, those between sixty and seventy vote in much larger numbers than do their younger counterparts. Moreover, the fastest growing age group in the United States is that of citizens over the age of sixty-five. Thus, not only are there more people in this category, but they are more likely to be registered to vote, and often vote conservatively.

Age seems to have a decided effect on one's view of the proper role of government, with older people continuing to be affected by having lived through the Depression and World War II. One political scientist predicts that as Baby Boomers age, the age gap in political beliefs about political issues, especially governmental programs, will increase.[36] Young people, for example, resist higher taxes to fund Medicare, while the elderly resist all efforts to limit it or Social Security.

Region.   Regional and sectional differences have been important factors in the development and maintenance of public opinion and political beliefs since colonial times. As the United States developed into a major industrial nation, waves of immigrants with different religious traditions and customs entered the United States and often settled in areas where other immigrants from their region already lived. For example, thousands of Scandinavians settled in Minnesota, and many Irish settled in the urban centers of the Northeast, as did many Italians and Jews. All brought with them unique views about numerous issues, as well as about the role of government. Many of these regional differences continue to affect public opinion today and sometimes result in conflict at the national level.

One of the most long-standing and dramatic regional differences in the United States is that between the South and the North. Recall that during the Constitutional Convention most Southerners staunchly advocated a weak national government. Nearly

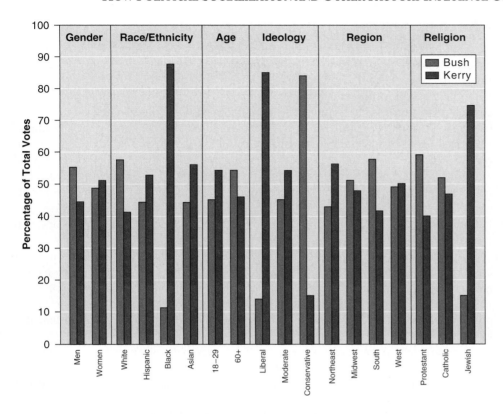

Source: CNN Exit Polls, http://www.cnn.com/election/2004/pages/results/states/us/p/00/epolls.0.html.

a hundred years later, the Civil War was fought in part because of basic differences in philosophy toward government (states' rights in the South versus national rights in the North). As we know from the results of modern political polling, the South has continued to lag behind the rest of the nation on support for civil rights, while continuing to favor return of power to the states at the expense of the national government.

The South also is much more religious than the rest of the nation, as well as more Protestant. Sixty-four percent of the South is Protestant (versus 39 percent for the rest of the nation), and 45 percent identify themselves as born-again Christians. Nearly half of all Southerners believe that "the United States is a Christian country, and the government should make laws to keep it that way."[37] Church attendance is highest in the South, where 38 percent report weekly visits. In contrast, only 26 percent of those living in the Midwest and 19 percent of those residing in the West go to church or synagogue on a weekly basis.[38] Given the South's higher churchgoing rates, it is not surprising that the Christian Coalition (discussed in chapter 16) has been very successful at mobilizing voters in that region.

Southerners also are much more supportive of a strong national defense. They accounted for 41 percent of the troops in the Persian Gulf in the early days of the 1991 Persian Gulf War, even though they made up only 28 percent of the general population.

The West, too, now appears different from other sections of the nation. Some people have moved there to avoid city life; other residents have an anti-government bias. Many who have sought refuge there are staunchly against any governmental action, especially on the national level. One need only look at a map of the vote distribution in the 2004 presidential election to see stark differences in candidate appeal. John Kerry carried almost every large city in America; George W. Bush carried 59 percent of the rural and small-town voters as well as most of America's heartland.[39] Republicans won the South, the West, and much of the Midwest; Democrats carried the Northeast and West Coast.

The Impact of Events

Key political events play a very important role in a person's political socialization. You probably have some professors who remember what they were doing on the day that President John F. Kennedy was killed—November 22, 1963. This dramatic event is indelibly etched in the minds of virtually all people who were old enough to be aware of it. Similarly, most college students today remember where they were when they heard of Princess Diana's death, or when they learned about the Oklahoma City bombing. Americans' collective memory of many events is fading, as is revealed in Table 11.1, but prior to 9/11, John F. Kennedy's assassination was the most compelling. No one old enough to have been aware of the events will ever forget where they were when they first heard about or saw the 2001 attacks on the World Trade Center and the Pentagon. These attacks on American shores evoked a profound sense of patriotism and national unity as American flags were displayed from windows, doors, balconies, and cars. For many Americans, the attacks were life-changing political events.

One has to go back to 1974 to find a political event that had such a dramatic effect on what people thought about the political process. President Richard M. Nixon's resignation in 1974 made a particular impression on young people, who were forced to realize that their government was not always right or honest. This general distrust of politicians was reignited during the highly publicized investigation of President Bill Clinton and his subsequent impeachment.

One problem in discussing political socialization is that many of the major studies on this topic were conducted in the aftermath of Watergate, which, along with the civil rights movement and the Vietnam War, produced a marked increase in Americans' distrust of government. The findings reported in Table 1.4 (see page 26) reveal the dramatic drop-off of trust in government that began in the mid-1960s and continued through the election of Ronald Reagan in 1980. In a study of Boston children conducted in the aftermath of the Watergate scandal, for example, one political scientist found that children's perception of the president went from that of a benevolent to a malevolent leader.[40] These findings are indicative of the low confidence most Americans had in government in the aftermath of Watergate and President Richard M. Nixon's ultimate resignation from office

---

TABLE 11.1 America's Collective Memory

Memories often define generations, and the memories (and experiencing) of key events often affect how individuals perceive other political events. Today, nearly all Americans know what they were doing when they first heard of the 9/11 attacks.

Early Events Fading		*Events Most Compelling*	
Percentage of public who remember hearing the news of:		*Percentage who remember what they were doing when they heard the news of:*[a]	
Princess Diana's death	87	John F. Kennedy's assassination	90
Oklahoma City bombing	86	Princess Diana's death	87
Challenger explosion	78	Oklahoma City bombing	86
Beginning of 1991 Persian Gulf War	75	Attack on Pearl Harbor	85
President Ronald Reagan shot by John Hinckley	67	*Challenger* explosion	82
Fall of Berlin Wall	59	Neil Armstrong walking on moon	80
Neil Armstrong walking on moon	54	End of World War II	79
President John F. Kennedy's assassination	53	Beginning of 1991 Persian Gulf War	76
President Richard M. Nixon's resignation	53	President Ronald Reagan shot by John Hinckley	72
Reverend Martin Luther King's assassination	43	Franklin D. Roosevelt's death	71
Tiananmen Square, China, massacre	41	President Richard M. Nixon's resignation	67
End of World War II	21	Reverend Martin Luther King's assassination	67
Attack on Pearl Harbor	18	Fall of Berlin Wall	60
President Franklin D. Roosevelt's death	17	N. Korea invading S. Korea	43
N. Korea invading S. Korea	15	Tiananmen Square, China, massacre	42
Paris falling to the Nazis	7	Paris falling to the Nazis	38
1929 stock market crash	4	1929 stock market crash	38

[a]Based on those who are old enough to remember.

Source: "Public Perspectives on the American Century," *1999 Millennium Survey* 1: Section 4, http://people-press.org/reports/display.ph3?PageID=283.

HOPES AND FEARS AROUND THE WORLD

Public opinion polls can be used to measure more than just political attitudes and beliefs. They can also provide us with a window on how people feel about a wide range of issues that affect their daily lives. In 2002, the Pew Global Attitudes Project published the results of a poll given to more than 38,000 people in forty-four countries. The results show points of global convergence and divergence in how people look at the world they deal with every day. Let's draw comparisons first by looking at what problems trouble people around the world and then by examining how people view the future.

In the public opinion poll, people were asked to identify the "very big" problems facing their country. Possible answers included crime, AIDS and other diseases, corrupt leaders, terrorism, ethnic conflict, poor drinking water, moral decline, poor schools, and immigration. In nineteen of the forty four countries, people identified crime as a very big problem more than any other problem. Only in Canada, Jordan, China, and South Korea was it viewed as a lesser problem. People in thirteen countries—including eight of ten African countries—rated AIDS and infectious diseases as the principle threats facing them. Clean water was identified as the greatest problem in Jordan, while in Senegal it was ethnic strife. None of the other problems listed above was ranked first in any of the countries.

"Very Big" National Problems Around the World

Country	Crime	AIDS and Other Diseases	Corrupt Leaders	Terrorism	Poor Drinking Water	Poor Schools
United States	48%	42%	46%	**50%**	17%	41%
Canada	26	31	**32**	19	18	25
Great Britain	**61**	30	21	23	7	32
Russia	**75**	63	61	65	35	29
Poland	**80**	37	70	45	28	14
Pakistan	**84**	63	61	65	35	37
Mexico	**81**	78	73	69	52	61
Honduras	**93**	**93**	84	62	66	71
Japan	**85**	54	85	68	47	40
Nigeria	84	83	**88**	65	66	65
South Africa	**96**	**96**	75	43	53	59

Note: Bold indicates highest-ranking problem

Source: Pew Global Attitudes Project, 2002

If the present is seen as full of problems, how do people look at the future? Are they pessimistic or optimistic? Asked to look five years into the future, people everywhere were more optimistic than pessimistic. To the right is a breakdown of how people in the countries listed above responded.

Global Pessimism and Optimism

Country	Pessimistic	Optimistic
United States	7%	61%
Canada	11	54
Great Britain	7	51
Russia	13	43
Poland	19	36
Pakistan	6	46
Mexico	15	49
Honduras	11	55
Japan	27	34
Nigeria	2	86
South Africa	21	59

Source: Pew Global Attitudes Project, 2002.

Questions

1. In your opinion, which of the very big problems is most easily solved? Which will be the hardest? What strategies would you use to solve these two problems?
2. How do you explain the differences in response by Canada, the United States, and Great Britain to the biggest problem they face?

to avoid impeachment. Confidence in government remained high during the Clinton scandal, although still down from the years preceding Watergate. But, the issues surrounding the Clinton impeachment raised concerns about their impact on young people, especially Generation Y. Some studies show that Generation Y's views toward the president and political affairs are significantly more negative than ever seen before—including during and immediately after Watergate.[41]

In times of war, however, the public generally rallies round the flag, which happened after the 1991 Persian Gulf War against Iraq as well as during the effort to remove the Taliban from Afghanistan in 2001. Children nationwide collected pennies as part of the Pennies for Patriots program announced by President George W. Bush in 2001, raised funds for the Red Cross, made flags, and expressed their patriotism in numerous ways, as did many of their parents and most of the rest of the nation. In fact, President Bush ran as a war president in 2004 and associated the war in Iraq with the struggle against terrorism. (See Global Perspective: Hopes and Fears Around the World). Many critics believe that this strategy was a major reason for his reelection.

Political Ideology and Public Opinion About Government

Comparative
Comparing Public
Opinion

As discussed in chapter 1, an individual's coherent set of values and beliefs about the purpose and scope of government is called his or her **political ideology.** Americans' attachment to strong ideological positions has varied over time. In sharp contrast to spur-of-the-moment responses, these sets of values, which are often greatly affected by political socialization, can prompt citizens to favor a certain set of policy programs and adopt views about the proper role of government in the policy process.

political ideology
The coherent set of values and beliefs about the purpose and scope of government held by groups and individuals.

Conservatives generally are likely to support smaller, less activist governments, limited social welfare programs, and reduced government regulation of business. Increasingly, they also have very strong views on social issues, including abortion and same-sex marriage. In contrast, liberals generally believe that the national government has an important role to play in a wide array of areas, including helping the poor and the disadvantaged. Unlike most conservatives, they generally favor activist governments. Most Americans today, however, identify themselves as moderates.

Visual Literacy
Who Are Liberals and
Conservatives? What's
the Difference?

Political scientists and politicians often talk in terms of conservative and liberal ideologies, and most Americans believe that they hold a conservative or liberal political ideology. When asked by the Roper Center, although 35 percent of Americans responded that their political beliefs were moderate, 29 percent labeled themselves as conservative. A similar number—30 percent—described themselves as liberal. Six percent of those polled "didn't know" or refused to label themselves. (For more information on political ideology, see Figure 1.4, page 24.)

WHY WE FORM POLITICAL OPINIONS

MANY OF US HOLD OPINIONS on a wide range of political issues, and our ideas can be traced to our social group and the different experiences each of us has had. Some individuals (called ideologues) think about politics and vote strictly on the basis of liberal or conservative ideology. Others vote according to party affiliation. Most people, however, do neither. Most people filter their ideas about politics through the factors discussed above, but they are also influenced by: (1) personal benefits; (2) political knowledge; and, (3) cues from various leaders or opinion makers.

Personal Benefits

Participation
Are You a Liberal or a
Conservative?

Most polls reveal that Americans are growing more and more "I" centered. This perspective often leads people to agree with policies that will benefit them personally. You've probably heard the adage, "People vote with their pocketbooks." Taxpayers generally favor lower taxes, hence the popularity of candidates pledging "No new taxes." Similarly, an elderly person is likely to support Social Security increases, while a member of Generation X, worried about the continued stability of the Social Security program, is not likely to be very supportive of federal retirement programs. Those born in Generation Y appear even less willing to support retirement programs. Similarly, an African American is likely to support strong civil rights laws and affirmative action programs, while a majority of nonminorities will not. In 2004, many women voted on their perception of national security.

Some government policies, however, don't really affect us individually. Legalized prostitution and the death penalty, for example, are often perceived as moral issues that directly affect few citizens. Individuals' attitudes on these issues often are based on underlying values they have acquired through the years.

When we are faced with policies that don't affect us personally and don't involve moral issues, we often have difficulty forming an opinion. Foreign policy is an area in which this phenomenon is especially true. Most Americans often know little of the world around them. Unless moral issues such as prisoner abuse in Iraq are involved, American public opinion is likely to be volatile in the wake of any new information.

Political Knowledge

Political knowledge and political participation have a reciprocal effect on one another— an increase in one will increase the other.[42] Knowledge about the political system is essential to successful political involvement, which, in turn, teaches citizens about politics and increases their interest in public affairs.[43]

Americans enjoy a relatively high literacy rate, and most Americans (82 percent) graduate from high school. Most Americans also have access to a range of higher education opportunities. In spite of that access to education, however, Americans' level of knowledge about history and politics is quite low. A 2002 Department of Education report found that most high school seniors had a poor grasp of history and that levels of knowledge haven't changed in nearly a decade.[44] Fifty-two percent didn't know that Russia was an ally of the United States in World War II, and 63 percent didn't know that President Richard M. Nixon opened diplomatic relations with China. According to the Department of Education, today's college graduates have less civic knowledge than high school graduates did fifty years ago.[45]

The lack of historical perspective hurts many Americans' understanding of current political events. Knowledge about current leaders or routine facts that everyone should know often is as abysmal as the answers given in Jay Leno's "Jaywalking" segments on the *Tonight Show*. As revealed in Table 11.2, in 2002, a majority of Americans could not identify the chief justice of the United States. Less than half could name their representative or the source of the phrase "government of the people, by the people, for the people."

Americans also don't appear to know much about foreign policy, and some critics would argue that many Americans are geographically illiterate. One National Geographic Society study done in late 2002, for example, showed that 87 percent of Americans age eighteen to twenty-four could not find Iraq on a map, despite the attention the nation received in the media. Similarly, an astounding 49 percent of young Americans could not find New York on a map, and 10 percent of all Americans could not locate the United States on a map.[46]

There are also significant gender differences in political knowledge. For example, one 2004 study done by the Annenberg Public Policy Center found that men were consistently more able than women to identify the candidates' issue positions.[47] This gender gap in knowledge, which has existed for the last fifty years, perplexes scholars, because women consistently vote in higher numbers than males of similar income and education levels.

In 1925, Walter Lippmann critiqued the American democratic experience and highlighted the large but limited role the population plays. Citizens, said Lippmann, cannot know everything about candidates and issues, but they can, and often do, know enough to impose their views and values as to the general direction the nation should take.[48] This generalized information often stands in contrast and counterbalance to the views held by more knowledgeable political elites inside the Washington, D.C., Beltway.

Cues from Leaders

As early as 1966, noted political scientist V. O. Key Jr. argued in *The Responsible Electorate* that voters "are not fools."[49] Still, low levels of knowledge can lead to rapid opinion shifts on issues. The ebb and flow of popular opinion can be affected dramatically (some

TABLE 11.2 Americans' Political Knowledge

	Percentage Unable to Identify
Number of senators	52
Representative in the House	53
Who has the power to declare war	60
Chief justice of the United States	69
Source of the phrase "government of the people, by the people, for the people"	78

Sources: "A Nation That Is in the Dark," *San Diego Union-Tribune* (November 3, 2002): E3; John Wilkens, "America Faces a Crisis of Apathy," *San Diego Union-Tribune* (November 3, 2002): E3.

cynics might say manipulated) by political leaders. Given the visibility of political leaders and their access to the media, it is easy to see the important role they play in influencing public opinion. Political leaders, members of the news media, and a host of other experts have regular opportunities to influence public opinion because of the lack of deep conviction with which most Americans hold many of their political beliefs.[50]

The president, especially, is often in a position to mold public opinion through effective use of the bully pulpit, as discussed in chapter 8.[51] Political scientist John E. Mueller concludes, in fact, that there is a group of citizens—called followers—who are inclined to rally to the support of the president no matter what he does.[52]

According to Mueller, the president's strength, especially in the area of foreign affairs (where public information is lowest), derives from the majesty of his office and his singular position as head of state. Recognizing this phenomenon, presidents often take to television in an effort to drum up support for their programs.[53] President George W. Bush, borrowing a page from Presidents Ronald Reagan and Bill Clinton, clearly realizes the importance of mobilizing public opinion. He took his case for his tax cut, as well as his plans for the war in Afghanistan and Iraq, directly to the public, urging citizens to support his efforts.

There is always a question, however, of who is leading, the president or the people? Bill Clinton, for example, often was criticized by Republicans for appearing to govern by public opinion poll. Still, according to one report, the Republican National Committee paid President George W. Bush's pollsters more than $1 million in 2002 to let him know the pulse of the people.[54]

HOW PUBLIC OPINION IS MEASURED

PUBLIC OFFICIALS AT ALL LEVELS use a variety of measures as indicators of public opinion to guide their policy decisions. These measures include election results; the number of telephone calls, faxes, or e-mail messages received pro and con on any particular issue; letters to the editor in hometown newspapers; and the size of demonstrations or marches. But, the most commonly relied-on measure of public sentiment continues to be the public opinion survey, more popularly called a public opinion poll. Opinion polls are big news—especially during an election year. However, even the most accurate polls can be very deceiving. In the past sixty years, polls have improved so much that we may be dazzled—and fooled—by their apparent statistical precision.

"Slight differences in question wording or in the placement of the questions in the interview can have profound consequences," says the vice president of the Gallup Organization. He points out that poll findings "are very much influenced by the polling process itself."[55] Consider, for instance, what researchers discovered in a 1985 national poll: only 19 percent of the public agreed that the country wasn't spending enough money on welfare. When the question contained the phrase "assistance to the poor" instead of "welfare,"

Simulation
You Are a Polling Consultant

■ How the questions in an opinion poll are worded can have a profound impact on the results of the poll. Here, the cartoonist questions the polling source itself.

Doonesbury

BY GARRY TRUDEAU

Photo courtesy: Doonesbury, copyright G. B. Trudeau. Reprinted with permission of Universal Press Syndicate. All rights reserved.

affirmative responses jumped to 63 percent. That 44 percent shift explains how people can make opposite—and equally vehement—claims about what polls show. The truth is that, at best, polls offer us flat snapshots of a three-dimensional world.

Traditional Public Opinion Polls

The polling process most often begins when someone says, "Let's find out about X and Y." Potential candidates for local office may want to know how many people have heard of them (the device used to find out is called a name recognition survey). Better-known candidates contemplating running for higher office might want to know how they might fare against an incumbent. Polls also can be used to gauge how effective particular ads are or if a candidate is being well (or negatively) perceived by the public. Political scientists have found that public opinion polls are critical to successful presidents and their staffs, who use polls to "create favorable legislative environment(s) to pass the presidential agenda, to win reelection, and to be judged favorably by history."[56] These polls and others have several key phases, including: (1) determining the content and phrasing the questions; (2) selecting the sample; and, (3) contacting respondents.

Determining the Content and Phrasing the Questions. Once a candidate, politician, or news organization decides to use a poll to measure the public's attitudes, special care has to be taken in constructing the questions to be asked. For example, if your professor asked you, "Do you think my grading procedures are fair?" rather than asking, "In general, how fair do you think the grading is in your American Politics course?" you might give a slightly different answer. The wording of the first question tends to put you on the spot and personalize the grading style; the second question is more neutral. Even more obvious differences appear in the real world of polling, especially when interested groups want a poll to yield particular results. Responses to highly emotional issues such as abortion, same-sex marriage, and affirmative action often are skewed depending on the wording of a particular question.

Selecting the Sample. Once the decision is made to take a poll, pollsters must determine the universe, or the entire group whose attitudes they wish to measure. This universe could be all Americans, all voters, all city residents, all Hispanics, or all Republicans. In a perfect world, each individual would be asked to give an opinion, but such comprehensive polling is not practical. Consequently, pollsters take a sample of the universe in which they are interested. One way to obtain this sample is by **random sampling.** This method of selection gives each potential voter or adult the same chance of being selected. In theory, this sounds good, but it is actually impossible to achieve because no one has lists of every person in any group. Thus, the method of poll taking is extremely important in determining the validity and reliability of the results.

As discussed earlier in the chapter, *Literary Digest* polls suffered from an oversampling of voters whose names were drawn from telephone directories and car registrations; this group was hardly representative of the general electorate in the midst of the Depression. Thus, the use of a nonstratified or nonrepresentative sample led to results that could not be used to predict accurately how the electorate would vote in 1936.

Perhaps the most common form of unrepresentative sampling is the kind of straw poll used today by local television news programs or online services. Many have regular features asking viewers to call in their sentiments (with one phone number for pro and another for con) or asking those logged on to indicate their preferences. The results of these unscientific polls are not very accurate because those who feel very strongly about the issue often repeatedly call in to vote more than once.

A more reliable method is a quota sample, in which pollsters draw their sample based on known statistics. Assume that a citywide survey has been commissioned. If the city is 30 percent African American, 15 percent Hispanic, and 55 percent white, interviewers will use those statistics to determine the proportion of particular groups

Peter Steiner

Photo courtesy: Peter Steiner/© Tribune Media Services, Inc. All rights reserved. Reprinted with permission.

■ Politicians' dependence on public opinion polls are well documented and can provide political cartoonists with an opportunity to poke fun at them, as this cartoon shows.

random sampling
A method of poll selection that gives each person in a group the same chance of being selected.

to be questioned. These kinds of surveys often are conducted in local shopping malls. Perhaps you've wondered why the man or woman with the clipboard has let you pass by but has stopped the next shopper. Now you know it is likely that you did not match the subject profile that the interviewer was instructed to locate. Although this kind of sampling technique can produce relatively accurate results, the degree of accuracy falls short of those surveys based on probability samples. Moreover, these surveys generally oversample the visible population, such as shoppers, while neglecting the stay-at-homes who may be glued to the Home Shopping Network or prefer to buy online.

stratified sampling
A variation of random sampling; census data are used to divide the country into four sampling regions. Sets of counties and standard metropolitan statistical areas are then randomly selected in proportion to the total national population.

Most national surveys and commercial polls use samples of 1,000 to 1,500 individuals and use a variation of the random sampling method called **stratified sampling.** Simple random, nonstratified samples are not very useful at predicting voting because they may undersample (or oversample) key populations that are not likely to vote. To avoid these problems, reputable polling organizations use stratified sampling (the most rigorous sampling technique) based on census data that provide the number of residences in an area and their location. Researchers divide the country into four sampling regions. They then randomly select a set of counties and standard metropolitan statistical areas in proportion to the total national population. Once certain primary sampling units are chosen, they often are used for many years, because it is cheaper for polling companies to train interviewers to work in fixed areas.

About twenty respondents from each primary sampling unit are picked to be interviewed. Generally four or five city blocks or areas are selected, and then four or five target families from each district are used. Large, sophisticated surveys such as the National Election Study and General Social Survey, which produce the data commonly used by political scientists, attempt to sample from lists of persons living in each household. The key to the success of the stratified sampling method is not to let people volunteer to be interviewed—volunteers as a group often have different opinions from those who do not volunteer.

Stratified sampling generally is not used by those who do surveys reported in the *New York Times* and *USA Today* or on network news programs. Instead, those organizations or pollsters working for them randomly place telephone calls to every tenth, hundredth, or thousandth person or household. If those individuals do not answer, they call the next person on the list.

Contacting Respondents. After selecting the methodology to conduct the poll, the next question is how to contact those to be surveyed. Television stations often ask people to call in, and some surveyors hit the streets. Telephone polls, however, are becoming the most frequently used mechanism by which to gauge the temper of the electorate.

The most common form of telephone polls are random-digit dialing surveys, in which a computer randomly selects telephone numbers to be dialed. Because it is estimated that as many as 95 percent of the American public have telephones in their homes, samples selected in this manner are likely to be fairly representative, although the increasing use of cell phones may eventually affect this. In spite of some problems (such as the fact that many people do not want to be bothered, especially at dinner time), most polls done for newspapers and news magazines are conducted in this way. Pollsters, notably, are exempt from federal and state do-not-call lists.

Individual, in-person interviews are conducted by some groups, such as the University of Michigan for the National Election Study. Some analysts favor such in-person surveys, but others argue that the unintended influence of the questioner or pollster is an important source of errors. How the pollster dresses, relates to the person being interviewed, and even asks the questions can affect responses. (Some of these factors, such as tone of voice or accent, can also affect the results of telephone surveys.)

Political Polls

As polling has become increasingly sophisticated and networks, newspapers, and magazines compete with each other to report the most up-to-the-minute changes in public opinion on issues or politicians, new types of polls have been suggested and put into

Model Introduction

Hello, my name is _____ and I'm calling from (company). Today/Tonight we are calling to gather opinions regarding (general subject), and are not selling anything. This study will take approximately (length) and may be monitored (and recorded) for quality purposes. We would appreciate your time. May I include your opinions?

Closing

- At the conclusion of the survey, thank the respondent for his/her time.

- Express the desired intention that the respondent had a positive survey experience and will be willing to participate in future market research projects.

- Remind the respondent that his/her opinions do count.

MODEL CLOSING

Thank you for your time and cooperation. I hope this experience was a pleasant one and you will participate in other market research projects in the future. Please remember that your opinion counts! Have a good day/evening.

Alternative: Participate in collecting respondent satisfaction data to improve survey quality.

Thank you very much for taking part in this survey. Because consumers like you are such a valued part of what we do, I'd like you to think about the survey you just participated in. On a scale from 1 to 10 where ten means "it was a good use of my time", and one means "it was not a good use of my time", which number between 1 and 10 best describes how you feel about your experience today? That's all the questions I have. Please remember that your opinion counts! Have a good day/evening.

Photo courtesy: Council for Marketing and Opinion Research

■ This script provides the general format for a survey conducted by the Council for Marketing and Opinion Research. Note that even in a telephone survey drawn from a random sample, the respondent has the opportunity to self-select out of the sample.

use. Each type of poll has contributed much to our knowledge of public opinion and its role in the political process.

Push Polls.   All good polls for political candidates contain push questions. These questions produce information that helps campaigns judge their own strengths and weaknesses as well as those of their opponents.[57] They might, for example, ask if you would be more likely to vote for candidate X if you knew that candidate was a strong environmentalist. These kinds of questions are accepted as an essential part of any poll, but there are concerns as to where to draw the line. Questions that go over the line result in **push polls,** which are telephone polls with an ulterior motive. Push polls are designed to give respondents some negative or even untruthful information about a candidate's opponent in order to push them away from that candidate toward the one paying for the poll. Reputable polling firms eschew these tactics. A typical push poll might ask a question such as "If you knew Candidate X beat his wife, would you vote for him?" Push poll takers don't even bother to record the responses because they are irrelevant. The questions are designed simply to push as many voters away from a candidate as possible. Push poll calls are made to thousands; legitimate polls survey much smaller samples.

Although campaign organizations generally deny conducting push polls, research shows that more than three-quarters of political candidates have been a victim of push polling. These numbers are likely to grow as the Internet becomes a more important campaign tool—unregulated online polls and mass e-mails have the potential to reach thousands of Internet users.

push polls
Polls taken for the purpose of providing information on an opponent that would lead respondents to vote against that candidate.

Tracking Polls.   During the 1992 presidential elections, **tracking polls,** which were taken on a daily basis by some news organizations, were first introduced to allow presidential candidates to monitor short-term campaign developments and the effects of their campaign strategies. Tracking polls involve small samples (usually of registered voters contacted at certain times of day) and are conducted every twenty-four hours. They usually are combined statistically with some other data to produce a statistical average to boost the sample size and therefore the statistical reliability.[58] Even though such one-day sur-

tracking polls
Continuous surveys that enable a campaign to chart its daily rise or fall in support.

veys are fraught with reliability problems and are vulnerable to bias, many major news organizations continue their use. As revealed in Figure 11.6, the 2004 tracking polls, in spite of receiving significant criticism for their performance in 2000, performed quite well and predicted a Bush victory.

exit polls
Polls conducted at selected polling places on Election Day.

Exit Polls.   **Exit polls** are polls conducted at selected polling places on Election Day. Generally, large news organizations send pollsters to selected precincts to sample every tenth voter as he or she emerges from the polling place. The results of these polls are used to help the media predict the outcome of key races, often just a few minutes after the polls close in a particular state and generally before voters in other areas—sometimes in a later time zone—have cast their ballots. They also provide an independent assessment of why voters supported particular candidates.

In 1980, President Jimmy Carter's own polling and the results of network exit polls led him to concede defeat three hours before the polls closed on the West Coast. Many Democratic party officials and candidates criticized Carter and network predictions for harming their chances at victories, arguing that with the presidential election already called, voters were unlikely to go to the polls. In the aftermath of that controversy, all networks agreed not to predict the results of presidential contests until all polling places were closed. Exit polls continue to be problematic. In 2000, they led newscasters to inaccurately call Florida in the Gore column, as discussed below. In 2004, mid-afternoon exit poll results that were leaked on the Internet made many believe a Kerry victory was at hand. Whether Republicans voted later, Democrats were more willing to be polled, or for other reasons, the exit polls were wrong.

Shortcomings of Polling

The information derived from public opinion polls has become an extremely important part of governance. When the results of a poll are accurate, they express the feelings of the electorate in unique way and help guide the creation of public policy. However, when the results of a poll are inaccurate, disastrous consequences often result.

For example, during the 2000 presidential election, Voter News Service (VNS), the conglomerate organization that provided the major networks with their exit poll data, made a host of errors in estimating the results of the election in Florida. Not only did VNS fail to estimate the number of voters accurately, but it also used an inaccurate exit poll model and incorrectly estimated the number of African American and Cuban voters. These errors came together in VNS's exit poll prediction and caused the major networks to call the state of Florida, and thus the entire presidential election, too early.

FIGURE 11.6 A Daily Tracking Poll for the 2004 Presidential Election. ■

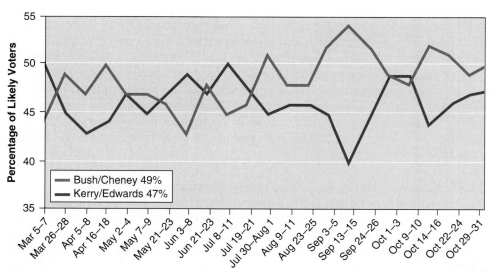

Source: USA Today and CNN/Gallup Poll results, http://www.usatoday.com/news/politicselections/nation/polls/usatodaypolls.htm.

It got worse in 2002. VNS, in spite of pledges to improve its act, announced mid-day that there would be no exit poll data revealed, leaving the networks with no data to project winners or discuss turnout or issues. Finally, in January 2003, VNS was disbanded. In November 2004, the major networks and the Associated Press joined in a new polling consortium, National Election Pool. Its data, like that of VNS, also were riddled with errors. Its subscribers were quite unhappy and the fate of exit polls on Election Day remains in doubt, given their poor track record in predicting winners in the past three national elections.

Sampling Error.   The accuracy of any poll depends on the quality of the sample that was drawn. Small samples, if properly drawn, can be very accurate if each unit in the universe has an equal opportunity to be sampled. If a pollster, for example, fails to sample certain populations, his or her results may reflect that shortcoming. Often the opinions of the poor and homeless are underrepresented because insufficient attention is given to making certain that these groups are sampled representatively. For example, in the case of tracking polls, if you choose to sample only on weekends or from 5 p.m. to 9 p.m., you may get more Republicans, who tend to have higher incomes and are less likely to be working shift work or multiple jobs. The 1992 CNN/Gallup poll, for example, used two different time periods—weekdays 5 p.m. to 9 p.m. and all day on the weekends. Midweek surveys produced candidate distributions that disproportionately favored George Bush over Bill Clinton, while weekend surveys showed the reverse. There comes a point in sampling, however, where increases in the size of the sample have little effect on a reduction of the **sampling error** (also called **margin of error**), the difference between the actual universe and the sample.

All polls contain errors. Standard samples of approximately 1,000 to 1,500 individuals provide fairly good estimates of actual behavior (in the case of voting, for example). Typically, the margin of error in a sample of 1,500 will be about 3 percent. If you ask 1,500 people "Do you like ice cream?" and 52 percent say yes and 48 percent say no, the results are too close to tell whether more people like ice cream than not. Why? Because the margin of error implies that somewhere between 55 percent (52 + 3) and 49 percent (52 − 3) of the people like ice cream, while between 51 percent (48 + 3) and 45 percent (48 − 3) do not. The margin of error in a close election makes predictions very difficult.

sampling error or margin of error
A measure of the accuracy of a public opinion poll.

Limited Respondent Options.   Polls can be inaccurate when they limit responses. If you are asked, "How do you like this class?" and are given only like or dislike options, your full sentiments may not be tapped if you like the class very much or feel only so-so about it.

Lack of Information.   Public opinion polls may also be inaccurate when they attempt to gauge attitudes about issues that some or even many individuals do not care about or about which the public has little information. For example, until the 2000 election, few Americans cared about the elimination of the Electoral College. If a representative sample had been polled prior to 2000, many would have answered pro or con without having given much consideration to the question.

Most academic public opinion research organizations, such as the National Election Study, use some kind of filter question that first asks respondents whether or not they have thought about the question. These screening procedures generally allow surveyors to exclude as many as 20 percent of their respondents, especially on complex issues like the federal budget. Questions on more personal issues such as moral values, drugs, crime, race, and women's role in society get far fewer no opinion or don't know responses.

Intensity.   Another shortcoming of polls concerns their inability to measure intensity of feeling about particular issues. Whereas a respondent might answer affirmatively to any question, it is likely that his or her feelings about issues such as abortion, the death penalty, or support for U.S. troops in Afghanistan or Iraq are much more intense than are his or her feelings about the Electoral College or types of voting machines.

HOW POLLING AND PUBLIC OPINION AFFECT POLITICIANS, POLITICS, AND POLICY

As EARLY AS THE FOUNDING PERIOD, the authors of *The Federalist Papers* noted that "all government rests on public opinion," and as a result, public opinion inevitably influences the actions of politicians and public officials. The public's perception of crime as a problem, for example, was the driving force behind the comprehensive crime bill President Bill Clinton submitted to Congress in 1994. The public's concern with crime skyrocketed to an all-time high in 1994, when 37 percent of the public rated crime as the nation's most important problem, and politicians at all levels were quick to convert that concern into a campaign issue.

Politicians and government officials spend millions of dollars each year taking the pulse of the public. Even the federal government spends millions annually on polls and surveys designed to evaluate programs and to provide information for shaping policies. But, as political scientist Benjamin Ginsberg noted, "the data reported by opinion polls are actually the product of an interplay between opinion and the survey instrument." They interact with each other in Ginsberg's opinion, and, can change the "character of the views receiving public expression."[60] In other words, even scientifically valid opinion polls have the potential to transform public opinion.

We know that politicians rely on polls, but it is difficult to say to what degree. Several political scientists have attempted to study whether public policy is responsive to public opinion, with mixed results.[61] As we have seen, public opinion can fluctuate, making it difficult for a politician or policy maker to assess. Some critics of polls and of their use by politicians argue that polls hurt democracy and make leaders weaker. Ginsberg, one of these critics, argues that widespread use of polling by politicians weakens democracy.[62] He claims that polls allow governments and politicians to say they have considered public opinion even though polls don't always measure the intensity of feeling on an issue or might overreflect the views of the public because of responders who lack sufficient information to make educated choices. Ginsberg further argues that democracy is better served by politicians' reliance on telephone calls and letters—active signs of interest—than on the passive voice of public opinion. Some observers worry that politicians rely on poll results rather than a thoughtful debate of the issues to determine their actions, arguing that the outcome of polls determines individual policy positions. In response to this argument, George Gallup retorted, "One might as well insist that a thermometer makes the weather."[63]

Polls can clearly distort the election process by creating what are called bandwagon and underdog effects. In a presidential campaign, an early victory in the Iowa caucuses or the New Hampshire primary, for example, can boost a candidate's standings in the polls as the rest of the nation begins to think of him or her in a more positive light. New supporters jump on the bandwagon. A strong showing in the polls, in turn, can generate more and larger donations, the lifeblood of any campaign. One political scientist has noted that "bad poll results, as well as poor primary and caucus standings, may deter potential donors from supporting a failing campaign."[64]

SUMMARY

PUBLIC OPINION is a subject constantly mentioned in the media, especially in presidential election years or when important policies are under consideration. What public opinion is, where it comes from, how it is measured, and how it is used are aspects of a complex subject. To that end, this chapter has made the following points:

1. What Is Public Opinion?

Public opinion is what the public thinks about an issue or a particular set of issues. Public opinion polls are used to estimate public opinion.

2. Efforts to Influence and Measure Public Opinion

Almost since the beginning of the United States, various attempts have been made to influence public opinion about particular issues or to sway elections. Modern-day polling did not begin until the 1930s, however. Over the years, polling to measure public opinion has become increasingly sophisticated and more accurate because pollsters are better able to sample the public in their effort to determine their attitudes and positions on issues. Pollsters recognize that their sample must reflect the population whose ideas and beliefs they wish to measure.

3. How Political Socialization and Other Factors Influence Opinion Formation

The first step in forming opinions occurs through a process called political socialization. Our family, school, peers, social groups—including religion, race, gender, and age—as well as where we live and the impact of events all affect how we view political events and issues. Our political ideology—whether we are conservative, liberal, or moderate—also provides a lens through which we filter our political views. Even the views of other people affect our ultimate opinions on a variety of issues, including race relations, the death penalty, abortion, and federal taxes.

4. Why We Form Political Opinions

Myriad factors enter our minds as we form opinions about political matters. These include a calculation about the personal benefits involved, degree of personal political knowledge, and cues from leaders.

5. How Public Opinion Is Measured

Measuring public opinion can be difficult. The most frequently used measure is the public opinion poll. Determining the content, phrasing the questions, selecting the sample, and choosing the right kind of poll are critical to obtaining accurate and useful data.

6. How Polling and Public Opinion Affect Politicians, Politics, and Policy

Knowledge of the public's views on issues is often used by politicians to tailor campaigns or to drive policy decisions. Polls, however, have several shortcomings, including sampling error and inadequate respondent information.

KEY TERMS

exit polls, p. 412
margin of error, p. 413
political ideology, p. 406
political socialization, p. 392
public opinion, p. 387
public opinion polls, p. 387
push polls, p. 411

random sampling, p. 409
sampling error, p. 413
stratified sampling, p. 410
straw polls, p. 390
tracking polls, p. 411

SELECTED READINGS

Alvarez, R. Michael, and John Brehm. *Easy Answers, Hard Choices: Values, Information, and American Public Opinion.* Princeton, NJ: Princeton University Press, 2002.

Asher, Herbert. *Polling and the Public: What Every Citizen Should Know,* 6th ed. Washington, DC: CQ Press, 2004.

Erikson, Robert S., and Kent L. Tedin. *American Public Opinion: Its Origins, Contents, and Impact,* 6th ed. New York: Longman, 2001.

Fishkin, James S. *The Voice of the People: Public Opinion and Democracy.* New Haven, CT: Yale University Press, 1997.

Herbst, Susan. *Numbered Voices: How Opinion Polling Has Shaped American Politics.* Chicago: University of Chicago Press, 1993.

Jamieson, Kathleen Hall. *Everything You Think You Know About Politics . . . And Why You Were Wrong.* New York: Basic Books, 2000.

Key, V. O., Jr. *Public Opinion and American Democracy.* New York: Knopf, 1961.

Manza, Jeff, ed. *Navigating Public Opinion: Polls, Policy, and the Future of American Democracy.* New York: Oxford University Press, 2002.

Mutz, Diana Carole. *Impersonal Influence: How Perceptions of Mass Collectives Affect Political Attitudes.* New York: Cambridge University Press, 1998.

Norrander, Barbara, and Clyde Wilcox, eds. *Understanding Public Opinion,* 2nd ed. Washington, DC: CQ Press, 2001.

Rubenstein, Sondra Miller. *Surveying Public Opinion.* Belmont, CA: Wadsworth, 1994.

Shafer, Byron E., and William J. M. Claggett. *The Two Majorities: The Issue Context of Modern American Politics.* Baltimore, MD: Johns Hopkins University Press, 1995.

Stimson, James A. *The Tides of Consent: How Public Opinion Shapes American Politics.* New York: Cambridge University Press, 2004.

Warren, Kenneth F. *In Defense of Public Opinion Polling.* Boulder, CO: Westview, 2001.

Zaller, John. *The Nature and Origins of Mass Opinions.* New York: Cambridge University Press, 1992.

WEB EXPLORATIONS

To learn more about the Gallup Organization and poll trends, see
http://www.gallup.com/
To use NES data sets,
http://www.umich.edu/~nes/
For the most recent Roper Center polls, see
http://www.ropercenter.uconn.edu/
To test your own political knowledge, go to
http://www.ablongman.com/oconnor
To see an example of a nonstratified poll, go to
http://www.cnn.com/

Photo courtesy: AP Photo/Victoria Arocho

Political Parties

IN THE SUMMER OF 2004, both major political parties held their national conventions. The primary focus of these conventions was the nomination of their presidential candidates. In July, the Democrats used the city of Boston to formally launch the nomination of John Kerry as their candidate for president of the United States. A few weeks later, from New York, the Republicans followed by renaming President George W. Bush their candidate. The televised convention proceedings and morning papers focused on the nominations of these two men and their personal attributes. Relatively little attention, however, was paid to something of similar importance: the passage at each convention of the party platform, which is an official statement that details the party's beliefs, as well as its positions on various policy issues. Party platforms are often taken for granted, certainly by the news media, and even by many political activists. They are not noted at all by most American voters, many of whom are cynical about the idea that parties stand for something.

How wrong the cynics are. The Democrats' platform, entitled "Strong at Home, Respected in the World," outlined substantial differences between their programs and those supported by the Bush administration. The platform focused specifically on foreign and domestic security, the economy, families, and communities. The Republicans' platform, "A Safer World and a More Hopeful America," also focused on security, the economy, families, and communities but added a section on private ownership that focused on tax relief, partial privatization of Social Security, and small business assistance. While the other topics were similar between the platforms, the content could not have been more different.

The Republicans strongly defended the policies of the previous four years, including the invasion of Iraq, a country they had considered a "great and gathering" danger to American interests at home and abroad. The Democrats pointed to the Bush administration's failure to find the weapons of mass destruction that had been said to constitute such a threat, and to the failure of the administration to bring peace to the region. The Republicans insisted that President Bush's 2001 and 2003 tax cuts were essential to rebuilding a weakened American economy. The Democrats argued that the tax cuts had created enormous national deficits to be paid off by future generations. In particular, Democrats deemed tax cuts fiscally irresponsible in light of rising defense costs because of continuing military action in

Afghanistan and Iraq. Republicans defended tax cuts by pointing to the reinvigorated stock market and the increase (albeit slow) in jobs. The Republicans continued their strong pro-life stance on the issue of abortion, their most recent success being a federal partial birth abortion ban. Staying committed to their pro-choice stance, Democrats made no mention of the partial birth abortion ban, thus supporting the most extreme form of abortion. They also reaffirmed their opposition to any Republican efforts to overturn *Roe v. Wade*. Republicans were opposed to marriage between homosexuals, and the party platform supported President Bush's call for a constitutional amendment to ban same-sex marriage. Democrats opposed amending the Constitution and asserted their belief that marriage should be defined at the state level.

The choice that Democrats made to criticize Bush on the economy was part of a strategy to appeal to a portion of their base, labor union members, who tend to favor more liberal economic plans but remain conservative on social issues. Since the nation's economic recovery had skipped the manufacturing sector, where unions were hurt the most, Democrats wanted to move labor attention away from their party's liberal social platform and toward a more manufacturing-sensitive economic platform. Meanwhile, Republicans focused on their social positions, satisfying their christian Conservative base while trying to lure labor away from the Democrats, and they remained optimistic about a national economic recovery. The battle for labor votes may seem narrow, since it focuses on one group located largely in one area, the upper Midwest. However, in the 2000 presidential election, margins of victory in these states for both parties were slim and the amount of electoral votes in states such as Pennsylvania and Michigan is high.

As this chapter will discuss, these party positions really matter, since they affect who will hold hundreds of elective offices across the nation. The winning party tries to act on the positions laid out in its platform. Platform positions are used as guidelines for the major legislative initiatives that will be enacted during the president's term. Given the results of the 2004 election, we can expect an aggressive, unilateralist foreign policy during President Bush's second term that nevertheless will continue cooperating militarily and otherwise with other nations to pursue terrorists, with an equally aggressive domestic policy against terrorism, as outlined in the Patriot Act. We can expect a continuation of pro-business policies and a preservation of the current tax cuts, with perhaps an extension of these cuts. We can expect conservative positions on a wide range of social issues, including opposition to abortion and same-sex marriage, and support for the return of organized prayer in schools.

Republican gains in both the House and the Senate will allow the Republican Party's platform to have a better chance of success in the 109th Congress. It is important to note, however, that the midterm elections during a president's second term often result in a loss of seats by that president's party. The public perception of legislation during the next two years will surely impact the 2006 election results.

A party's policies can affect millions of people. They are as important, if not more important, than the personal aspects of politics, which tend to dominate media coverage.

IT IS DIFFICULT TO REJECT the assertion that we are entering a new, more fluid era of party politics. But, while some analysts maintain that our two-party system is likely to be replaced by a chaotic multiparty system, or that on the horizon is a system in which presidential hopefuls bypass party nominations altogether and compete on their own, it is important to remember that political parties have been staples of American life since the late 1700s and, in one form or another, most likely will continue to be.

In this chapter we will address contemporary party politics by examining them from many vantage points. Our discussion of political parties will trace their development from their infancy in the late 1700s to their status today.

- First, we will answer the question, *what is a political party?*
- Second, we will look at *the evolution of American party democracy.*
- Third, we will examine *the functions of the American parties* in our political system.
- Fourth, we will present *the basic structure of American political parties.*
- Fifth, we will explore *the party in government,* the office holders and candidates who run under the party's banner.
- Sixth, we will examine *the modern transformation of party organization,* paying special attention to how political parties moved from labor-intensive, person-to-person operations toward the use of technology and communication strategies.
- Seventh, we will look at *the party in the electorate,* showing that a political party's reach extends well beyond the relative handful of men and women who are the party in government.
- Finally, we will discuss *third-partyism,* as well as independent and minor-party candidates and the history of party alignment in the United States.

Photo courtesy: Mary Altaffer/AP/Wide World Photos

- National security was a prominent theme at both parties' conventions in 2004. Here, delegates hold signs in support of President Bush at the Republican National Convention in New York City.

WHAT IS A POLITICAL PARTY?

AT THE MOST BASIC LEVEL, a **political party** is a group of office holders, candidates, activists, and voters who identify with a group label and seek to elect to public office individuals who run under that label. Notice how pragmatic this concept of party is. The goal is to win office, not just compete for it. Nevertheless, the party label can carry with it clear messages about ideology and issue positions. Although these especially exist for minor, less broad-based parties that have little chance of electoral success, they also apply to the Democrats and the Republicans, the national, dominant political parties in the United States.

Political scientists sometimes describe political parties as consisting of three separate but related entities: (1) the office holders and candidates who run under the party's banner (the **governmental party**); (2) the workers and activists who staff the party's formal organization (the **organizational party**); and, (3) the voters who consider themselves allied or associated with the party (the **party in the electorate**).[1] In this chapter, we examine all three components of political parties—the governmental party, the organizational party, and the party in the electorate. First, however, we turn to the history and development of political parties in the United States.

political party
A group of office holders, candidates, activists, and voters who identify with a group label and seek to elect to public office individuals who run under that label.

governmental party
The office holders and candidates who run under a political party's banner.

organizational party
The workers and activists who staff the party's formal organization.

party in the electorate
The voters who consider themselves allied or associated with the party.

THE EVOLUTION OF AMERICAN PARTY DEMOCRACY

IT IS ONE OF THE GREAT IRONIES of the early republic that George Washington's public farewell, which warned the nation against parties, marked the effective end of the

FIGURE 12.1 American Party History at a Glance. ■

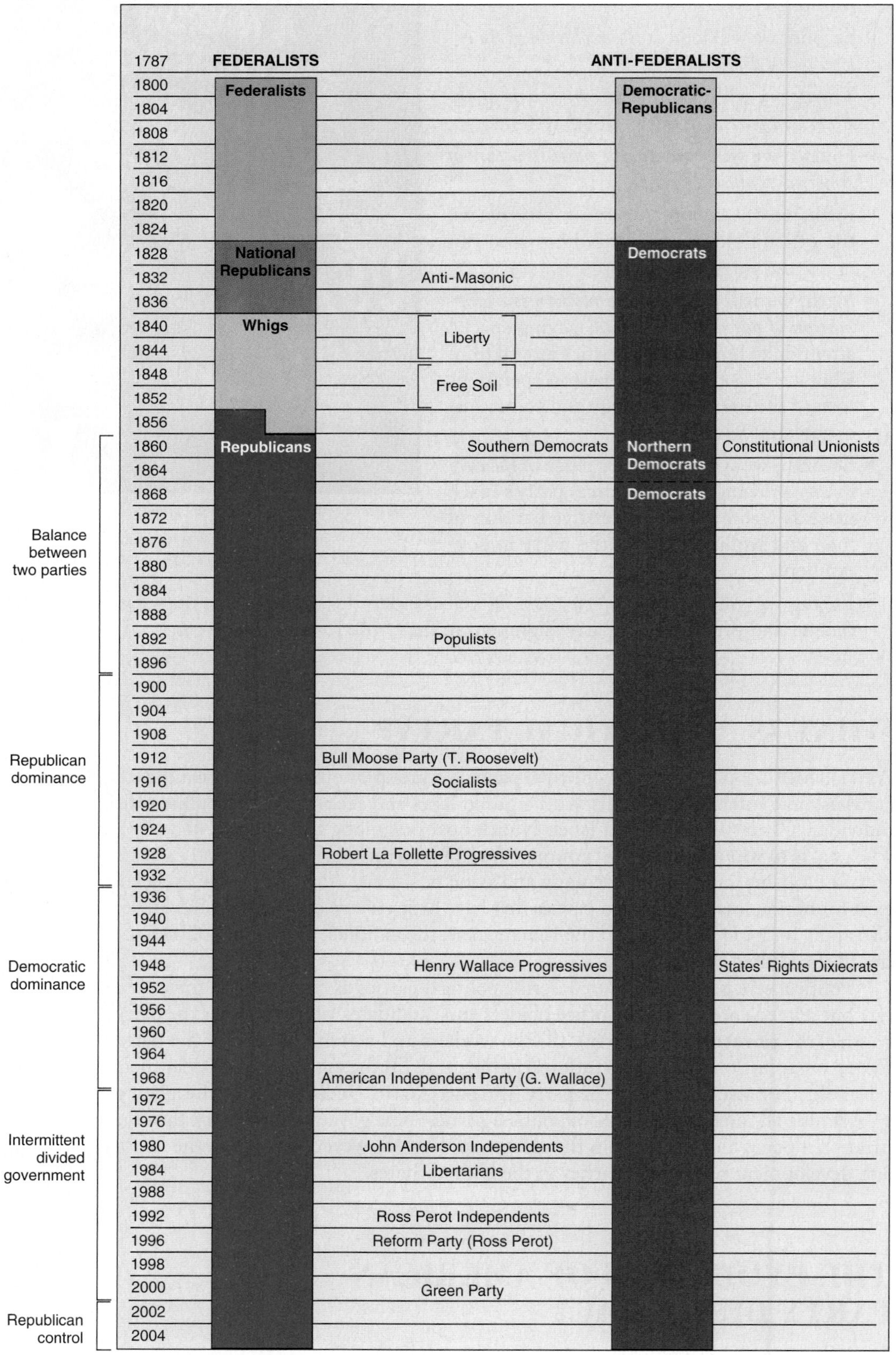

Year	Federalists line		Anti-Federalists line	
1787	**FEDERALISTS**		**ANTI-FEDERALISTS**	
1800	**Federalists**		**Democratic-Republicans**	
1804				
1808				
1812				
1816				
1820				
1824				
1828	**National Republicans**		**Democrats**	
1832		Anti-Masonic		
1836				
1840	**Whigs**			
1844		Liberty		
1848				
1852		Free Soil		
1856				
1860	**Republicans**	Southern Democrats	**Northern Democrats**	Constitutional Unionists
1864				
1868			**Democrats**	
1872				
1876				
1880				
1884				
1888				
1892		Populists		
1896				
1900				
1904				
1908				
1912		Bull Moose Party (T. Roosevelt)		
1916		Socialists		
1920				
1924				
1928		Robert La Follette Progressives		
1932				
1936				
1940				
1944				
1948		Henry Wallace Progressives		States' Rights Dixiecrats
1952				
1956				
1960				
1964				
1968		American Independent Party (G. Wallace)		
1972				
1976				
1980		John Anderson Independents		
1984		Libertarians		
1988				
1992		Ross Perot Independents		
1996		Reform Party (Ross Perot)		
1998				
2000		Green Party		
2002				
2004				

Left-margin era labels (aligned to year ranges):
- Balance between two parties
- Republican dominance
- Democratic dominance
- Intermittent divided government
- Republican control

brief era of partyless politics in the United States (see Figure 12.1). Washington's unifying influence ebbed as he stepped off the national stage, and his vice president and successor, John Adams, occupied a much less exalted position. Adams was allied with Alexander Hamilton. To win the presidency in 1796, Adams narrowly defeated Thomas Jefferson, Hamilton's former rival in Washington's Cabinet. Before ratification of the Constitution, Hamilton and Jefferson had been leaders of the Federalists and Anti-Federalists, respectively (see chapter 2). Over the course of Adams's single term, two competing congressional party groupings (or caucuses) gradually organized around these clashing men and their principles: Hamilton's Federalists supported a strong central government; the Democratic-Republicans of Thomas Jefferson and his ally James Madison inherited the mantle of the Anti-Federalists and preferred a federal system in which the states were relatively more powerful. (Jefferson actually preferred the simpler name "Republicans," a very different group from today's party of the same name, but Hamilton insisted on calling them "Democratic-Republicans" to link them to the radical democrats of the French Revolution.) In the presidential election of 1800, the Federalists supported Adams's bid for a second term, but this time the Democratic-Republicans prevailed with their nominee, Jefferson, who became the first U.S. president elected as the nominee of a political party (see The Living Constitution).

Jefferson was deeply committed to the ideas of his party, but not nearly as devoted to the idea of a party system. He regarded his party as a temporary measure necessary to defeat Adams and Hamilton. Neither Jefferson's party nor Hamilton's enjoyed widespread loyalty among the citizenry akin to that of today's Democrats and Republicans. Although Southerners were overwhelmingly partial to the Democratic-Republicans and New Englanders to the Federalists, no broad-based party organizations existed on either side to mobilize popular support. Rather, the congressional factions organized around Hamilton and Jefferson were primarily governmental parties designed to settle the dispute over how strong the new federal government would be.[2] Just as the nation was in its infancy, so, too, was the party system, and attachments to both parties were weak at first.

The Early Parties Fade

After the spirited confrontations of the republic's early years, political parties faded somewhat in importance for a quarter of a century. The Federalists ceased nominating presidential candidates by 1816, having failed to elect one of their own since Adams's victory in 1796, and by 1820 the party had dissolved. James Monroe's presidency from 1817 to 1825 produced the so-called Era of Good Feelings, when party politics was nearly suspended at the national level. Even during Monroe's tenure, though, party organizations continued to develop at the state level. Party growth was fueled in part by the enormous increase in the electorate that took place between 1820 and 1840, as the United States expanded westward and most states abolished property requirements as a condition of white male suffrage. During this twenty-year period, the number of votes cast in presidential contests rose from 300,000 to more than 2 million.

At the same time, U.S. politics was being democratized in other ways. By the 1820s, all the states except South Carolina had switched from state legislative selection of presidential electors to popular election of Electoral College members. This change helped transform presidential politics. No longer just the concern of society's upper crust, the election of the president became a matter for all qualified voters to decide.

Party membership broadened along with the electorate. After receiving criticism for being elitist and undemocratic, the small caucuses of congressional party leaders that had previously nominated candidates gave way to nominations at large party conventions. In 1832, the Democratic Party, which succeeded the old Jeffersonian Democratic-Republicans, held the first national presidential nomination convention. Formed around the charismatic populist President Andrew Jackson, the Democratic Party attracted most of the newly enfranchised voters, who were drawn to Jackson's style. His strong personality helped to polarize politics, and opposition to the president coalesced

The Living Constitution

It is difficult to imagine modern American politics without the political parties, but where in the text of Constitution do we find the provision to establish them?

Nowhere in the Constitution do we find a provision establishing political parties. Some might point out that the First Amendment establishes the right to assemble as a Constitutional right, and this right certainly helps to preserve and protect parties from governmental oppression during rallies and conventions. However, the right to assembly is not the same as permission for two organizations to mediate elections. Furthermore, James Madison, in Federalist No. 10, feared that one of the greatest dangers to the new American Republic was a majority tyranny created by the domination of a single faction fighting for one set of interests, so he hoped that extending the sphere of representation among many members of Congress would prevent a majority of representatives from coming together to vote as a bloc.

Of course, parties are *not* like the factions Madison describes. Parties today seem to embody Madison's principle of the extended sphere of representation. Neither party is monolithic in its beliefs; rather, both parties constantly reconsider their platforms in light of the changes of the various constituencies that they try to represent. The Republicans have both Senator Olympia Snow (ME), a pro-choice and pro-environmental Republican, and Representative Tom DeLay (TX), a pro-life and pro-business Republican. Democrats have both Representative Dennis Kucinich (OH), who advocates withdrawal from NAFTA, and Governor Bill Richardson (NM), who balances various racial/ethnic concerns and business interests while trying to protect the border between the U.S. and Mexico. Both comparisons yield differences in interests, the kind of things Madison wanted.

Finally, Madison himself actually belonged to two early American political parties during his public service, first the Federalists and later the Democratic-Republicans. In fact, it is because of the Federalist Party that we have a Constitution today. Federalists compromised with Anti-Federalists to provide a Bill of Rights so long as the Anti-Federalists would stop opposing ratification. So parties are not so much *in* the Constitution as *behind* the Constitution, first behind its ratification and, today, behind its preservation of diverse interests.

into the Whig Party, which was descended from the Federalists. Among its early leaders was Henry Clay, the speaker of the House from 1811 to 1820. The incumbent Jackson defeated Clay in the 1832 presidential contest. Jackson was the first chief executive who won the White House as the nominee of a truly national, popularly based political party.

The Whigs and the Democrats continued to strengthen after 1832, establishing state and local organizations almost everywhere. Their competition was usually fierce and closely matched, and they brought the United States the first broadly supported two-party system in the Western world.[3] Unfortunately for the Whigs, the issue of slavery sharpened the many divisive tensions within the party, which led to its gradual dissolution and replacement by the new Republican Party. Formed in 1854 by anti-slavery activists, the Republican Party set its sights on the abolition (or at least the containment) of slavery. After a losing presidential effort for John C. Frémont in 1856, the party was able to assemble enough support primarily from the Whigs and anti-slavery northern Democrats to win the presidency for Abraham Lincoln in a fragmented 1860 vote. In that year, the South voted solidly Democratic, beginning a tradition so strong that not a single southern state voted Republican for president again until 1920.

Democrats and Republicans: The Golden Age

From the presidential election of 1860 to this day, the same two major parties, the Republicans and the Democrats, have dominated elections in the United States, and control of an electoral majority has seesawed between them. Party stability, as well as the dominance of party organizations in local and state governments and the impact of those organizations on the lives of millions of voters, were the central traits of the era called the "Golden Age" of political parties.

This era, which spanned the years 1874–1912, from the end of post–Civil War Reconstruction until the reforms of the Progressive Era, featured remarkable stability in the identity of the two major political parties. Such stability has been exceptionally rare around the world as one looks at other democratic republics. Parties typically come and go, flourish and fall apart, whether it is the Liberals in Great Britain or the Christian Democrats in Italy.

Emigration from Europe (particularly from Ireland, Italy, and Germany) fueled the development in America of big-city party organizations that gained control of local and state government during this time. These big-city party organizations were called **machines.** A political machine is a party organization that uses tangible incentives to recruit its members. Machines are characterized by a high degree of leadership control over member activity, and party machines were a central element of life for millions of people in the United States during the Golden Age. For city-dwellers, their party and their government were virtually interchangeable during this time. Party organizations sponsored community events, such as parades and picnics, and provided social services, such as helping new immigrants settle in and giving food and temporary housing to those in immediate need, all in exchange for votes.

Political parties thus not only served the underlying political needs of the society but also supplemented the population's desire for important services. In addition to providing housing, employment, and even food to many voters, parties in most major cities provided entertainment by organizing torchlight parades, weekend picnics, socials, and the like. Many citizens—even those who weren't particularly "political"—attended, thereby gaining some allegiance to one party or the other. The parties offered immigrants not just services but also the opportunity for upward social mobility as they rose in the organization. Because they held the possibility of social advancement, the parties engendered intense devotion among their supporters and office holders that helped to produce startlingly high voter turnouts—75 percent or better in all presidential elections from 1876 to 1900—compared with today's 50–55 percent.[4] The strength of parties during the Golden Age also fostered the greatest party-line voting ever achieved in Congress and many state legislatures.[5]

machine
A party organization that recruits its members with tangible incentives and is characterized by a high degree of control over member activity.

The Modern Era Versus the Golden Age: Is the Party Over?

The modern era seems very different from the Golden Age of parties. Many social, political, technological, and governmental changes have contributed to party decline since the 1920s. Historically, the government's gradual assumption of important functions previously performed by the parties, such as printing ballots, conducting elections, and providing social welfare services, had a major impact. Beginning in the 1930s with Franklin Roosevelt's New Deal, social services began to be seen as a right of citizenship rather than as a privilege extended in exchange for a person's support of a party. Also, as the flow of immigrants slowed dramatically in the 1920s, party organizations gradually withered in most places.

PLUNKITT OF TAMMANY HALL

TAMMANY HALL was a powerful New York City political organization during the mid-nineteenth and early twentieth centuries. Originally formed as a social club in 1797, it had been transformed into an influential political machine by 1850, with membership including most of the city's prominent Democrats.

Of all the organization's politicians, one of the most renowned at the turn of the twentieth century was ward boss George Washington Plunkitt. Starting as a teenager, this son of Irish immigrants worked his way up through the ranks of the organization to become the leader of the city's Fifteenth Assembly District. (An assembly district is made up of many smaller units, called election districts.) He is remembered as one of the shrewdest politicians of his time. Plunkitt was born poor but died a millionaire, acquiring most of his wealth through what he called "honest graft," a term best described in his own candid words:

> My party's in power in the city, and its goin' to make a lot of public improvements. Well, I'm tipped off, say, that they're going to lay out a new park at a certain place.
>
> I see my opportunity and I take it. I go to that place and I buy up all the land I can in the neighborhood. Then the board of this or that makes it public, and there is a rush to get my land, which nobody cared particular for before.
>
> Ain't it perfectly honest to charge a good price and make a profit on my investment and foresight? Of course, it is. Well, that's honest graft.

For Plunkitt, there was a difference between dishonest and honest graft, "between [dishonest] political looters and [honest] politicians who make a fortune out of politics by keepin' their eyes wide open":

> The looter goes in for himself alone without considerin' his organization or his city. The politician looks after his own interests, the organization's interests, and the city's interests all at the same time.

Plunkitt certainly looked after his constituents' interests. During Tammany's reign, the population of New York City was made up predominantly of poor immigrants, mostly Irish, for whom Plunkitt and his fellow district leaders served as a bridge between the Old and New Worlds and also as a way out of the slums. Besides assimilating these newcomers into life in the United States and acquainting them with the processes of self-government, the ward bosses used the patronage at their disposal to provide tangible benefits. Be it a job, liquor, a pushcart license, or even cash, the ward boss was always happy to help out a needy constituent—in exchange, of course, for loyalty at the ballot box during election time.

In contrast to the issue-oriented or image-appeal politics we know today, Plunkitt's politics were personal. As Plunkitt put it, "[I] learned how to reach the hearts of the great mass of voters. I don't bother about reaching their heads." Plunkitt understood the value of this personalized, community-oriented politics to both voters and leaders. His advice to aspiring politicians was simply to know and study the members of their communities and to "study human nature and act accordin'."

Source: William L. Riordon, *Plunkitt of Tammany Hall* (New York: Dutton, 1963), 11, 89.

---

direct primary
The selection of party candidates through the ballots of qualified voters rather than at party nomination conventions.

civil service laws
These acts removed the staffing of the bureaucracy from political parties and created a professional bureaucracy filled through competition.

issue-oriented politics
Politics that focuses on specific issues rather than on party, candidate, or other loyalties.

ticket-split
To vote for candidates of different parties for various offices in the same election.

A **direct primary** system, in which party nominees were determined by the ballots of qualified voters rather than at party conventions, gained widespread adoption by the states in the first two decades of the twentieth century. Direct primaries removed the power of nomination from party leaders and workers and gave it instead to a much broader and more independent electorate, thus loosening the tie between party nominees and the party organization.

Reforms championed by the Progressive movement, which flourished in the first two decades of the twentieth century, also contributed to the loss of party influence in the United States. **Civil service laws,** for example, which require appointment on the basis of merit and competitive examinations, removed opportunities for much of the patronage used by the parties to reward their followers.

In the post–World War II era, extensive social changes also contributed to the move away from strong parties. Higher levels of education gave rise to **issue-oriented politics,** politics that focuses on specific issues, such as civil rights, tax cutting, or environmentalism, rather than on party labels. Issue politics tends to cut across party lines and encourages voters to **ticket-split,** that is, to vote for candidates of different parties for various offices in the same election (a phenomenon we discuss in greater depth in chapter 13). Another post–World War II social change that has affected the parties is the shift from urban to suburban locales. Millions of people have moved from the cities to the suburbs, where a sense of privacy and detachment can deter the most energetic party organizers. In addition, population growth in the last half-century has created districts with far more people, making it unfeasible to knock on every door or shake every hand.

Politically, many other trends have contributed to the parties' decline. Television, which has come to dominate U.S. politics, naturally emphasizes personalities rather than abstract concepts such as party labels. Other technological advances such as the autodialer, a computer that leaves prerecorded messages on voters' answering machines, have often alienated voters and further eroded precinct organization. It is little wonder that many candidates and office holders who have reached their posts without much help from their parties consider themselves as free as possible of party ties.

The Parties Endure

Despite the challenges described in the preceding section, the parties' decline can easily be exaggerated. Viewing parties in the broad sweep of U.S. history, several strengths of parties become clear. First, although political parties have evolved considerably and changed form from time to time, they usually have been reliable vehicles for mass participation in a representative democracy. In fact, parties orchestrated the gradual but steady expansion of suffrage in order to incorporate new supporters into the party fold.[6] Keep in mind, however, the notable exceptions in which parties attempted to contract the electorate. Southern Democrats, for example, worked to exclude black political participation from the end of Reconstruction through the civil rights movement of the 1960s, in an effort to maintain their political power in the region.

Photo courtesy: AP Wirephoto

■ One of the last of the big-city party bosses, Chicago Mayor Richard J. Daley (left) controlled a powerful political machine for over twenty-five years. Here, at a 1974 political rally, his son Richard M. Daley displays remarkably similar mannerisms.

PARTY, ISSUE, OR CANDIDATE?

Some college students may find it hard to believe that universities were once centers of political activism and controversy. Throughout the 1960s, students marched in favor of extending civil rights to African Americans and to women. After the federal government reinstituted the draft, students protested the Vietnam War as a war of imperialism fought by the disadvantaged who could not afford exemptions, while others counter-protested that the spread of communism into Vietnam was against American interests. Students joined party-sponsored campus organizations such as College Democrats and Young Republicans as a way of linking ideological fervor to a grassroots political process. In part because of these groups, youth turnout at the voting booth during that decade was at its highest, at 55 percent.[a]

Since 1972, however, turnout has dropped to 42 percent for eighteen- to twenty-four-year-olds, but not for lack of political controversy affecting young voters. Young Americans are just as affected by the debate over abortion rights and same-sex marriage, the hot-button social issues for 2004, and political parties remain opposed over how these issues should be handled. Perhaps young Americans have become more practical. Young voters are more concerned about unemployment, the economy, and national security in 2004 than in recent years.[b] While these issues no doubt matter as much to an average twenty-year-old as they do to an average fifty-year-old, economic issues do not seem to produce the same level of intensity as social issues—for example, civil rights for students in the 1960s.

Now that young people's interests are more similar to those of older voters, they also have more similar voting patterns. In 1996, voters eighteen to twenty-nine years of age voted 53 percent for the Democratic candidate, President Bill Clinton, and only 34 percent for Republican Senator Bob Dole. However, in 2000, eighteen- to twenty-nine-year-olds voted 48 percent for Gore and 46 percent for Bush. The partisan divide between young voters may have closed once the MTV-savvy Bill "Boxers or Briefs" Clinton could no longer run. This trend may indicate that young voters are more candidate-sensitive and less loyal to a political party than are older voters. When faced with a third-party candidate, young voters are less likely to flinch.[c] In March 2004, young voters had the highest support for Ralph Nader, at 12 percent of their vote, but in November 2004, when young voters went to the polls, only 5 percent ended up voting for him.[d]

Could it be that the 1960s were an anomaly? Do young voters have largely the same interests as older voters but merely focus more on the candidate and less on the party? It is hard to tell, since this age bracket has only recently begun attracting attention again. If parties could once again find an issue that captures the imagination of young voters, then perhaps young voters might become more loyal to a party. Rather than merely being attracted by a candidate's personality, young people might have a genuine sense that a party represents them on issues meaningful to them. What kinds of issues might those be?

[a]The Center for Information and Research on Civic Learning and Engagement, http://www.civicyouth.org/quick/youth_voting.htm.

[b]Ipsos News Center, http://www.ipsos-na.com/news/pressrelease.cfm?id=2068.

[c]James W. Ceaser and Andrew E. Busch, *The Perfect Tie: The True Story of the 2000 Presidential Election* (Lanham, MD: Rowman and Littlefield), 159.

[d]*Newsweek*/Ipsos poll, March 23, 2004. http://ipsos-na.com/news/pdf/media/mr040323-1tb.pdf.

Second, the parties' journey through U.S. history has been characterized by the same ability to adapt to prevailing conditions that is often cited as the genius of the Constitution. Both major parties exhibit flexibility and pragmatism, which help ensure their survival and the success of the society they serve.

Third, despite massive changes in political conditions and frequent dramatic shifts in the electorate's mood, the two major parties not only have achieved remarkable longevity but also have almost always provided strong competition for each other and the voters at the national level. Of the thirty presidential elections from 1884 to 2004, for instance, the Republicans won seventeen and the Democrats fourteen. Even when calamities have beset the parties—the Great Depression in the 1930s or the Watergate scandal of 1973–1974 for the Republicans (see chapter 8), and the Civil War or left-wing McGovernism in 1972 for the Democrats—the two parties have proved tremendously resilient, sometimes bouncing back from landslide defeats to win the next election.

Fourth, although research indicated that parties were declining for much of the twentieth century, new research suggests that parties have begun to rebound from this period of decline. One reason for the rebound is that the two major parties in the United States are starting to stand for two starkly different pictures of political reality. The Democrats have become increasingly liberal, while the Republicans have become increasingly conservative. The Democrats are on the left end of the ideological spectrum and the Republicans are on the right end. This portrayal of course refers to office holders, since average citizens tend to be fairly moderate, whether they consider themselves Democrats, Republicans, or independents. But the office holders, who are nominated by the ideological activists of their party, are more likely to embrace the ideology held by those nominating them. Fewer liberal Republicans and conservative Democrats make it easier for voters to identify with the party that best represents their personal ideology.[7]

Perhaps most of all, history teaches us that the development of parties in the United States has been inevitable, as James Madison feared. Human nature alone guarantees conflict in any society; in a free state, the question is simply how to contain and channel conflict productively without infringing on individual liberties. The Founders' utopian hopes for the avoidance of partisan faction, Madison's chief concern, have given way to an appreciation of the parties' constructive contributions to conflict definition and resolution during the years of the American republic.

THE FUNCTIONS OF THE AMERICAN PARTIES

FOR 150 YEARS, the two-party system has served as the mechanism American society uses to organize and resolve social and political conflict. (Of course, third parties have periodically made important contributions to American politics, and they will be discussed later in the chapter.) Although political parties are less popular today than in previous times, it is important to remember that political parties often are the chief agents of change in our political system. They provide vital services to society and it would be difficult to envision political life without them.

Mobilizing Support and Gathering Power

Party affiliation is enormously helpful to elected leaders. They can count on support among their fellow party members not just in times of trouble and times when they need to gather support for tight votes, but also on general political and legislative matters. Therefore the parties aid office holders by giving them room to develop their policies and by mobilizing support for them. When the president addresses the nation and requests support for his policies, for example, his party's members are usually the first to respond to the call, perhaps by flooding Congress with telegrams urging action on the president's agenda. Additionally, a recent study found that the more liberal and competitive the Democratic Party is in a state, the greater the level of mobilization and voter turnout among the lower classes. The lower classes, after activation by the Democrats, presumably then vote and participate in ways favorable to that state's Democratic Party or their position on relevant issues.[8]

Because there are only two major parties, citizens who are interested in politics or public policy are mainly attracted to one or the other party, creating natural majorities or near majorities for party office holders to command. The party generates a community of interest that bonds disparate groups over time into a **coalition.** This continuing mutual interest eliminates the necessity of forming a new coalition for every campaign or every issue. Imagine the constant chaos and mad scrambles for public support that would ensue without the continuity provided by the parties.

coalition
A group of interests or organizations that join forces for the purpose of electing public officials.

A Force for Stability and Moderation

As mechanisms for organizing and containing political change, the parties are a potent force for stability. They represent continuity in the wake of changing issues and personalities, anchoring the electorate in the midst of the storm of new political policies and people. Because of its unyielding, practical desire to win elections (not just to contest them), each party in a sense acts to moderate public opinion. The party tames its own extreme elements by pulling them toward an ideological center in order to attract a majority of votes on Election Day.

The parties encourage stability in the type of coalitions they form. There are inherent contradictions in these coalitions that, oddly enough, strengthen the nation even as they strain party unity. Franklin D. Roosevelt's Democratic New Deal coalition, for example, included many African Americans and most southern whites, opposing groups nonetheless joined in common political purpose by economic hardship and, in the case of better-off Southerners, in longtime voting habits. A recent study determined that the liberalization of the formerly conservative southern Democratic Party was a direct result of the growth of the viable and conservative southern Republican Party, and the extension of greater voting rights to African Americans.[9] As many white Southerners abandoned the Democratic Party for the GOP, the Democrats became even more dependent on black votes, and their policy positions changed in order to retain those votes.[10]

Unity, Linkage, and Accountability

Parties are the glue that holds together the disparate elements of the fragmented U.S. governmental and political apparatus. The Framers designed a system that divides and subdivides power, making it possible to preserve individual liberty but difficult to coordinate and produce action in a timely fashion. Parties help compensate for this drawback by linking all the institutions of power one to another. Although rivalry between the executive and legislative branches of U.S. government is inevitable, the partisan affiliations of the leaders of each branch constitute a common basis for cooperation, as the president and his fellow party members in Congress usually demonstrate daily. When President George W. Bush proposed a major new program of tax cuts, Republican members of Congress were the first to speak up in favor of the program and to orchestrate efforts for its passage. Not surprisingly, presidential candidates and presidents are inclined to push policies similar to those advocated by their party's congressional leaders.[11]

Even within each branch, there is intended fragmentation, and the party once again helps narrow the differences between the House of Representatives and the Senate, or between the president and the department heads in the executive bureaucracy. Similarly, the division of national, state, and local governments, while always an invitation to conflict, is made more workable and more easily coordinated by the intersecting party relationships that exist among office holders at all levels. Party affiliation, in other words, is a basis for mediation and negotiation laterally among the branches and vertically among the layers.

The party's linkage function does not end there. Party identification and organization foster communication between the voter and the candidate, as well as between the voter and the office holder. The party con-

■ Among the many reasons the California recall campaign was so fascinating was how it brought the Democratic "royal family," the Kennedys, together with a Republican, albeit liberal, candidate for governor, Arnold Schwarzenegger. His wife (left), Maria Shriver, is a member of the Kennedy family.

Photo courtesy: Rachel Epstein/The Image Works

nection is one means of increasing accountability in election campaigns and in government. Candidates on the campaign trail and elected party leaders in office are required from time to time to account for their performance at party-sponsored forums, nominating primaries, and conventions.

Political parties, too, can take some credit for unifying the nation by dampening sectionalism. Because parties must form national majorities in order to win the presidency, any single, isolated region is guaranteed minority status unless it establishes ties with other areas. The party label and philosophy build the bridge that enables regions to join forces; in the process, a national interest, rather than a merely sectional one, is created and served.

The Electioneering Function

The election, proclaimed author H. G. Wells, is "democracy's ceremonial, its feast, its great function," and the political parties assist this ceremony in essential ways. First, the parties funnel eager, interested individuals into politics and government. Thousands of candidates are recruited each year by the two parties, as are many of the candidates' staff members—the people who manage the campaigns and go on to serve in key governmental positions once the election has been won.

Elections can have meaning in a democracy only if they are competitive, and in the United States they probably could not be competitive without the parties. (When we use the term *competitive*, we mean that both parties have enough organization, money, and people to run a vigorous election campaign, and to sustain their arguments through the period of governance.) Even in the South, traditionally the least politically competitive U.S. region, the parties today regularly produce reasonably vigorous contests at the state (and increasingly the local) level.

Party as a Voting and Issue Cue

A voter's party identification acts as an invaluable filter for information, a perceptual screen that affects how he or she digests political news. Parties try to cultivate a popular image and help inform the public about issues through advertising and voter contact. Therefore, party affiliation provides a useful cue for voters, particularly for the least informed and least interested, who can use the party as a shortcut or substitute for interpreting issues and events they may not fully comprehend. Better-educated and more involved voters also find party identification helpful. After all, no one has the time to study every issue carefully or to become fully knowledgeable about every candidate seeking public office.

Policy Formulation and Promotion

As discussed at the beginning of this chapter, the **national party platform** is the most visible instrument that parties use to formulate, convey, and promote public policy. Every four years, each party writes for the presidential nominating conventions a lengthy platform explaining its positions on key issues. Platforms have considerable impact. About two-thirds of the promises in the victorious party's presidential platform have been completely or mostly implemented. Even more astounding, one-half or more of the pledges of the losing party find their way into public policy (with the success rate depending on whether the party controls one, both, or neither house of Congress).[12] The party platform also has great influence on a new presidential administration's legislative program and on the president's State of the Union Address. While party affiliation is normally the single most important determinant of voting in Congress and in state legislatures,[13] the party–vote relationship is even stronger when party platform issues come up on the floor of Congress.

national party platform
A statement of the general and specific philosophy and policy goals of a political party, usually promulgated at the national convention.

State Control and National Platforms

■ Senator Huey Long (D–LA) campaigned for the presidency in 1935 on a populist platform, arguing in fiery speeches that neither of the major parties' policies had the people's best interests at heart.

Photo courtesy: Bettmann/CORBIS

Besides mobilizing Americans on a permanent basis, then, the parties convert the cacophony of hundreds of identifiable social and economic groups into a two-part semi-harmony that is much more comprehensible, if not always on key and pleasing to the ears. The simplicity of two-party politics may be deceptive, given the enormous variety in public policy choices, but a sensible system of representation in the American context might be impossible without it.

THE BASIC STRUCTURE OF AMERICAN POLITICAL PARTIES

ALTHOUGH THE DISTINCTIONS might not be as clear today as they were two or three decades ago, the two major parties remain fairly simply organized, with national, state, and local branches (see Figure 12.2). The different levels of each party represent diverse interests in Washington, D.C., state capitals, and local governments throughout the nation.

The pyramid shown in Figure 12.2 illustrates the hierarchy of party organization in the United States, and it will help you to see how parties operate in a general sense. This very simple diagram, however, is deceptive in one important way: not shown is that the national, state, and local parties overlap. Frequently, state and local parties have more influence than the national party in their region, and their decisions can override those of the national party.

National Committees

The first national party committees were skeletal and formed some years after the creation of the presidential nominating conventions in the 1830s. First the Democrats in 1848 and then the Republicans in 1856 established national governing bodies—the

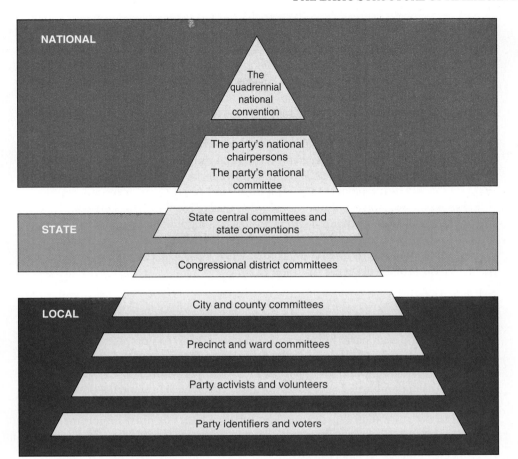

Democratic National Committee, or DNC, and the Republican National Committee, or RNC—to make arrangements for the conventions and to coordinate the subsequent presidential campaigns. The DNC and RNC were each composed of one representative from each state; this was expanded to two in the 1920s after the parties established the post of state committeewoman. The states had complete control over the selection of their representatives to the national committees. In addition, to serve their interests, the congressional party caucuses in both houses organized their own national committees, loosely allied with the DNC and RNC. The National Republican Congressional Committee (NRCC) was started in 1866 when the Radical Republican congressional delegation was feuding with Abraham Lincoln's moderate successor, President Andrew Johnson, and wanted a counterweight to his control of the RNC. At the same time, House and Senate Democrats set up a similar committee.

After the popular election of U.S. senators was initiated in 1913 with the ratification of the Seventeenth Amendment, both parties organized separate Senate campaign committees. This three-part arrangement of national party committee, House party committee, and Senate party committee has persisted in both parties to the present day, and each party's three committees are located together in Washington, D.C. There is, however, an informal division of labor among the national committees. Whereas the DNC and RNC focus primarily on aiding presidential campaigns and conducting general party-building activities, the congressional campaign committees work primarily to maximize the number of seats held by their respective parties in Congress. In the past two decades, all six national committees have become major, service-oriented organizations in American politics.[14]

Leadership

The key national party official is the chairperson of the national committee. Although the chair is formally elected by the national committee, he or she is usually selected by the sitting president or newly nominated presidential candidate, who is accorded the right to name the individual for at least the duration of his or her campaign. Only the post-campaign, out-of-power party committee actually has the authority to appoint a chairperson independently. The committee-crowned chairpersons generally have the greatest impact on the party, because they come to their posts at times of crisis when a leadership vacuum exists. (A defeated presidential candidate is technically the head of the national party until the next nominating convention, but the reality is naturally otherwise as a party attempts to shake off a losing image.) The chair often becomes the prime spokesperson and arbitrator for the party during the four years between elections. He or she is called on to damp down factionalism, negotiate candidate disputes, raise money, and prepare the machinery for the next presidential election. Balancing the interests of all potential White House contenders is a particularly difficult job, and strict neutrality is normally expected from the chair.

National Conventions

national convention
A party conclave (meeting) held in the presidential election year for the purposes of nominating a presidential and vice presidential ticket and adopting a platform.

Every four years, each party holds a **national convention** to nominate its presidential and vice presidential candidates. Much of any party chairperson's work involves planning the presidential nominating convention, the most publicized and vital event on the party's calendar. Until 1984, gavel-to-gavel coverage was standard practice on all national television networks. Recently, however, television networks have cut back their air time to no more than one hour a day, during which the most important speaker speaks as much to viewers as he or she does to convention attendees. In addition to nominating the presidential ticket, the convention also fulfills its role as the ultimate governing body for the party. The rules adopted and the platform passed at the quadrennial conclave are durable guidelines that steer the party for years after the final gavel has been brought down.

Most of the recent party chairpersons, in cooperation with the incumbent president or likely nominee, have tried to orchestrate every minute of the conventions in order to project just the right image to voters. By and large, they have succeeded, though at the price of draining some spontaneity and excitement from the convention process.

States and Localities

Although national committee activities of all kinds attract most of the media attention, the party is structurally based not in Washington, D.C., but in the states and localities. Except for the campaign finance arena, virtually all governmental regulation of political parties is left to the states, for example, and most elected officials give their allegiance to the local party divisions they know best. Most importantly, the vast majority of party leadership positions are filled at subnational levels.

The pyramid arrangement of party committees provides for a broad base of support. The smallest voting unit, the precinct, usually takes in a few adjacent neighborhoods and is the fundamental building block of the party. Each of the more than 100,000 precincts in the United States potentially has a committee member to represent it in each party's councils. The precinct committee members are the foot soldiers of any party, and their efforts are supplemented by party committees above them in the wards, cities, counties, towns, villages, and congressional districts.

The state governing body supervising this collection of local party organizations is usually called the state central (or executive) committee. Its members come from all major geographic units, as determined by and selected under state law. Generally, state parties are free to act within the limits set by their state legislatures without interfer-

Photo courtesy: Eric Risberg/AP/Wide World Photos

■ Gay rights has become an issue in presidential politics, affecting Democrats and Republicans both personally and politically. Here, former presidential nominee and Representative Dick Gephardt campaigns with his openly gay daughter, Chrissy. Mary Cheney, daughter of Vice President Dick Cheney, is also openly gay.

ence from the national party, except in the selection and seating of presidential convention delegates. National Democrats have been particularly inclined to regulate this aspect of party life. With the decline of big-city political machines, few local parties are strong enough to defy national party policy positions or to select nominees against the national party's wishes.

Although weaker in respect to how they affect the national party, state and local parties have become significantly more effective over the past three decades in terms of fund-raising, campaign events, registration drives, publicity of party and candidate activity, and the distribution of campaign literature.[15] Examining separately the national, state, and local parties should not lead us to overlook the increasing integration of these committees. The national parties have also become fund-raising powerhouses during the last two decades, and they now channel significant financial support—much of it in soft money—to state parties. This financial support has given the national parties considerable leverage over the state committees—many of which have become dependent on the funding—and the national parties have increasingly used the state committees to help execute national campaigns.

The growing reliance of state parties on national party funding has changed fundamentally the balance of power in the American party system. Whereas power previously flowed up from the state and local parties to the national committees, the national committees now enjoy considerable leverage over state and local parties.[16] That said, the relationships among the national, state, and local party committees are now being altered because of the passage of the Bipartisan Campaign Reform Act that took effect following the 2002 midterm elections (see chapter 14 for details of the Bipartisan Campaign Reform Act). New organizations have been formed that are hybrids of national, state, and local action; many of them had prominent positions in the 2004 campaign. The 527 groups, named after a provision of the federal tax code, were formed to circumvent the new regulations. Prominent 527s in 2004 included MoveOn.org, The Media Fund, and Swift Boat Veterans for Truth.

Informal Groups

The formal structure of party organization is supplemented by numerous official, semi-official, and unaffiliated groups that both coordinate and clash with the parties in countless ways. Both the DNC and RNC have affiliated organizations of state and local party women (the National Federation of Democratic Women and the National Federation of Republican Women). The youth divisions (the Young Democrats of America and the Young Republicans' National Federation) have a generous definition of "young," up to and including age thirty-five. In 1991, Bill Clinton used his chairmanship of the Democratic Leadership Council as a stepping stone to his successful presidential bid. The state governors in each party have their own party associations, too.

Just outside the party orbit are the supportive interest groups and associations that often provide money, labor, or other forms of assistance to the parties. Labor unions, progressive political action committees (PACs), teachers, African American and liberal women's groups, and the Americans for Democratic Action are some of the Democratic Party's organizational groups. Business PACs, the U.S. Chamber of Commerce, fundamentalist Christian organizations, and some anti-abortion groups work closely with the Republicans. Similar party–interest group pairings occur in other countries; for example, in Britain, trade unions have aligned themselves with the Labour Party, providing the bulk of the party's contributions, and business has been closely allied with the Conservatives.

think tank
Institutional collection of policy-oriented researchers and academics who are sources of policy ideas.

Each U.S. party has several institutionalized sources of policy ideas. Though unconnected to the parties in any official sense, these **think tanks** (institutional collections of policy-oriented researchers and academics) influence party positions and platforms.

Finally, there are extra-party organizations that form for various purposes, including "reforming" a party or moving it ideologically to the right or left. In New York City, for example, Democratic reform clubs were established in the late 1800s to fight the Tammany Hall machine, the city's dominant Democratic organization at the time. About seventy clubs still prosper by attracting well-educated activists committed to various liberal causes. Over the past decade, informal groups allied with the two parties have become more fully (if informally) integrated into the increasingly complex party network, often working closely with the national and state parties in conducting campaigns. Indeed, as one observer noted, parties and interest group allies now work together so closely that "the traditional lines of demarcation between parties and interest groups are no longer clear."[17]

THE PARTY IN GOVERNMENT

IN ADDITION to their role as grassroots organizations of voters, political parties are used to organize the branches and layers of American government.

The Congressional Party

In no segment of U.S. government is the party more visible or vital than in the Congress. In this century, the political parties have dramatically increased the sophistication and impact of their internal congressional organizations. Prior to the beginning of every session, the parties in both houses of Congress gather (or "caucus") separately to select party leaders (House speaker and minority leader, Senate majority and minority leaders, party whips, and so on) and to arrange for the appointment of members of each chamber's committees. In effect, then, the parties organize and operate the Congress. Their management systems have grown quite elaborate; the web of deputy and assistant whips for

House Democrats now extends to about one-fourth of the party's entire membership. Although not invulnerable to pressure from the minority, the majority party in each house generally holds sway, even fixing the size of its majority on all committees—a proportion frequently in excess of the percentage of seats it holds in the house as a whole.

Congressional party leaders enforce a degree of discipline in their party members in various ways. Even though seniority usually determines most committee assignments, an occasional choice plum may be given to the loyal or withheld from the rebellious. The Senate majority leader can decide whether a member's bill is given priority in the legislative agenda or will be dismissed without so much as a hearing. Pork barrel projects—government projects yielding rich patronage benefits that sustain many a legislator's electoral survival—may be included or deleted during the appropriations process. Small favors and perquisites (such as the allocation of desirable office space or the scheduling of floor votes for the convenience of a member) can also be useful levers. Then, too, there are the campaign aids at the command of the leadership: money from party sources, endorsements, appearances in the district or at fund-raising events, and so on. On rare occasions the leaders and their allies in the party caucus may even impose sanctions of various sorts (such as stripping away seniority rights or prized committee berths) in order to punish recalcitrant lawmakers.[18]

Photo courtesy: Matthew Cavanaugh/AP/Wide World Photos

■ Senate Majority Leader Bill Frist (R–TN) witnessed his party's margin of control increase by four seats in the 2004 election. Frist has been mentioned frequently as a possible Republican presidential candidate in 2008.

There are, however, limits to coordinated, cohesive party action. For example, the separate executive branch, the bicameral power sharing, and the extraordinary decentralization of Congress's work all constitute institutional obstacles to effective party action. Moreover, party discipline is hurt by the individualistic nature of U.S. politics: campaigns that are candidate centered rather than party oriented; diverse electoral constituencies to which members of Congress must understandably be responsive; the largely private system of election financing that indebts legislators to wealthy individuals and nonparty interest groups more than to their parties; and the importance to lawmakers of attracting the news media's attention—often more easily done by showmanship than by quiet, effective labor within the party system.

Indeed, given the barriers to coordinated party activity, it is impressive to discover that party labels have consistently been the most powerful predictor of congressional roll-call voting. In the last few years, party voting has increased noticeably, as reflected in the upward trend by both Democrats and Republicans shown in Figure 12.3. Although not

FIGURE 12.3 Congressional Party Unity Scores, 1959–2003

Note how party-based voting has increased conspicuously since the 1970s. ■

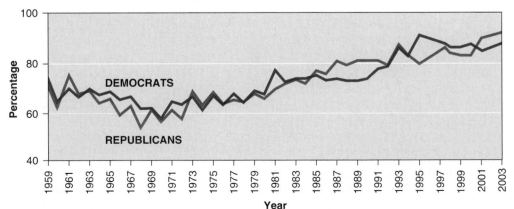

Source: Congressional Quarterly Almanacs (Washington, DC: CQ Press).

invariably predictive, as in strong parliamentary systems, a member's party affiliation has proven to be the indicator of his or her votes more than 70 percent of the time in recent years; that is, the average representative or senator sides with his or her party on about 70 percent of the votes that divide a majority of Democrats from a majority of Republicans. In most recent years, more than half of the roll-call votes in the House and Senate also found majorities of Democrats and Republicans on opposite sides.

There are many reasons for the recent growth of congressional party unity and cohesion. Some are the result of long-term political trends. Both congressional parties, for instance, have gradually become more ideologically homogeneous and internally consistent. Southern Democrats today are more moderate and much closer philosophically to their northern counterparts than the South's legislative barons of old ever were. Similarly, there are few liberal Republicans left in either chamber of Congress, and GOP House members from all regions of the country are—with a few exceptions—moderately to solidly conservative. As each party became more ideologically homogeneous, rank-and-file members of Congress (especially in the House) delegated to party leaders enhanced powers with which to push through the party's agenda.[19]

The recent defections of legislators from both parties ironically support the strengthening of party cohesion. Conservative Democratic Representative Virgil Goode of Virginia left the Democratic Party in January 2000 and is now a Republican. Similarly, liberal Republican Senator Jim Jeffords bolted the GOP and became an independent in spring 2001, shifting control of the Senate to the Democrats until the 2002 elections. These and other defections underscore that the polarization of the electorate is continuing. Liberals are moving more firmly into the Democratic camp, and conservatives are aligning strongly with the Republican Party. Rather than consistently vote against the party with which they were identified on Election Day, legislators are crossing over to the party that more accurately reflects their own ideology and, in most cases, the ideology of their constituents.

The political party campaign committees have also played a role in the renewed cohesiveness observed within Congress. Each national party committee has been recruiting and training House and Senate candidates as never before, and devising common themes for all nominees in election seasons—work that may help to produce a consensual legislative agenda for each party. Party money and campaign services, such as media advertisements and polling, may also help convert candidates into team players. The evidence for this, however, is mixed, with some research showing that party money increases party loyalty among House members[20] whereas other research reveals no such effect.[21]

The Presidential Party

Political parties may be more central to the operation of the legislative branch than the executive branch, but it is the party of the president that captures the public imagination and shapes the electorate's opinion of the two parties. In our very personalized politics, voters' perceptions of the incumbent president and the presidential candidates determine to a large extent how citizens perceive the parties.

The chief executive's successes are his party's successes; his failures are borne by the party as much as by the individual. The image a losing presidential candidate projects is incorporated into the party's contemporary portrait, whether wanted or not. As the highest elected candidate of the national party, the president naturally assumes the role of party leader, as does the nominee of the other party (at least during the campaign).

It is not easy for a president to juggle contradictory roles. Expected to bring the country together as ceremonial chief of state and also to forge a ruling consensus as head of government, the president must also be an effective commander of a sometimes divided party. Along with the inevitable headaches party leadership brings, though, are clear and compelling advantages. Foremost among them is a party's ability to mobilize support among voters for a president's program. Also, the executive's legislative agenda might be derailed more quickly without the common tie of party label between the chief executive and many members of Congress; all presidents appeal for some congressional support on the basis of shared party affiliation, and—depending on circumstances and their executive skill—they generally receive it.

Presidents reciprocate the support they get in many ways. In addition to compiling a record for the party and giving substance to its image, presidents appoint many activists to office, recruit candidates, raise money for the party treasury, campaign extensively for party nominees during election seasons, and occasionally provide some popular support for the candidates of the president's party.

Some presidents take their party responsibilities more seriously than others. Democrats Woodrow Wilson and Franklin D. Roosevelt were dedicated to building their party electorally and governmentally. Republican Ronald Reagan exemplified the "pro-party" presidency. Reagan was one of the most party-oriented presidents of recent times.[22] In 1983 and 1984, during his own reelection effort, Reagan made more than two dozen campaign and fund-raising appearances for all branches of the party organization and candidates at every level. He taped more than 300 television endorsements as well, including one for an obscure Honolulu city council contest. Reagan also showed a willingness to get involved in the nitty-gritty of candidate recruitment, frequently calling strong potential candidates to urge them to run. Reagan was willing to attempt a popularity transfer to his party and to campaign for Republicans whether or not they were strongly loyal to him personally. He was willing to put his prestige and policies to the test on the campaign trail; spent time and effort helping underdogs and long-shot candidates, not just likely winners; signed more than seventy fund-raising appeals for party committees; and took a personal interest in the further strengthening of his party's organizational capacity.

George W. Bush is also considered a pro-party president. Having lost the popular vote and only narrowly captured a majority in the Electoral College, George W. Bush came into the White House with one of the weakest and most bitterly contested mandates in recent history. When Bush took office in January 2001, the Republicans held a six-seat majority in the House and tie-breaking control of a Senate tied 50–50. For the first time in forty-six years, Republicans controlled (however slightly) both branches of the legislature and the White House.

In the aftermath of September 11, 2001, a new political landscape emerged. All of Bush's energy went into helping the country recover from the attacks and preparing the nation for the pursuit of terrorists in Afghanistan and beyond, and he did so with near universal bipartisan support. By the summer of 2002, George W. Bush's approval ratings were still hovering around 70 percent, as he and Vice President Dick Cheney campaigned and raised more money for their party than any previous president and vice president. President Bush was able to swing voter sentiment toward the Republicans, allowing them to win crucial races across the country and regain a majority in the Senate. However, Bush's bipartisan support eroded as his popularity and job favorability witnessed a decline, as the end of major combat in Iraq produced an apparently endless and violent insurgency, and as the 2004 election approached. As long as political parties compete for elected offices, efforts for bipartisanship will always remain contingent on whether such collaboration will help win the next election.

Most modern American chief executives have been cast in an entirely different mold from the pro-party presidents of more recent times. Dwight D. Eisenhower elevated "nonpartisanship" to a virtual art

■ Being in a political party means interacting with your supporters who are also your constituents. Here, we see a striking image of John Kerry surrounded by firefighters, whose support is significant because of the image of firefighters around President Bush at Ground Zero shortly after 9/11.

Photo courtesy: Rick Friedman/Corbis

form; while this may have preserved his personal popularity, it proved a disaster for his party. Despite his full two-term occupancy of the White House, the Republican Party remained mired in minority status among the electorate, and Eisenhower never really attempted to transfer his high ratings to the party. Lyndon Johnson, Richard Nixon, and Jimmy Carter all showed similar neglect of their parties, often drawing on their party's organization for personal uses. Clearly, then, some presidents have taken their party responsibilities more seriously than have others. In general, most presidents since Franklin D. Roosevelt have been less supportive of their respective political parties than were earlier presidents.[23] However, given the actions of Ronald Reagan and George W. Bush, it is possible that future presidents will take more involved roles as party leaders.

The Parties and the Judiciary

Many Americans view the judiciary as "above politics" and certainly as nonpartisan, and many judges are quick to agree. Yet, not only do members of the judiciary sometimes follow the election returns and allow themselves to be influenced by popular opinion, but they are also products of their party identification and possess the same partisan perceptual screens as all other politically aware citizens.

Legislators are much more partisan than judges, but it is wrong to assume that judges reach decisions wholly independently of partisan values. First, judges are creatures of the political process, and their posts are considered patronage plums. Judges who are not elected are appointed by presidents or governors for their abilities but also as members of the executive's party and increasingly as representatives of a certain philosophy of or approach to government. Most recent presidents have appointed judges overwhelmingly from their own party. Furthermore, Democratic executives are naturally inclined to select for the bench liberal individuals who may be friendly to social programs or critical of some business practices. Republican executives generally lean toward conservatives for judicial posts, hoping they will be tough on criminal defendants, opposed to abortion, and restrained in the use of court power. President George W. Bush saw many of his judicial appointments, such as Miguel Estrada and Priscilla Owens, blocked by Senate Democrats, who refused to allow a vote on the nominations. This tactic provided not only a way for Democrats to exact revenge on the Republicans, who had used similar measures during the Clinton administration, but also a means to forestall ideological changes that can last far beyond the next election cycle.

Research has long indicated that party affiliation is a moderately good predictor of judicial decisions in some areas.[24] One specific example involves judicial approval of new congressional districts created by state legislatures every ten years based on the U.S. Census. Judges tend to favor redistricting plans passed by their partisans in state legislatures rather than those of the opposition party.[25] In other words, party matters in the judiciary just as it does in the other two branches of government.

Many judges appointed to office have had long careers in politics as loyal party workers or legislators. Supreme Court Justice Sandra Day O'Connor, for example, was an active member of the National Republican Women's Club and is a former Republican state legislator. Jurists who are elected to office are even more overtly political. In a majority of states, at least some judicial positions are filled by election, and seventeen states hold outright partisan elections, with both parties nominating opposing candidates and running hard-hitting campaigns. In some rural counties across the United States, local judges are not merely partisan elected figures; they are the key public officials, controlling many patronage jobs and the party machinery.

The Parties and State Governments

Most of the conclusions just discussed about the party's relationship to the legislature, the executive, and the judiciary apply to those branches at the state level as well. The national parties, after all, are organized around state units, and the basic structural arrangement of party and government is much the same in Washington and the state capitals. Remarkably, too, the major national parties are the dominant political forces in all fifty states. This has been true consistently; unlike Great Britain or Canada, the United States has no regional or state parties that displace one or both of the national parties in local contests. Occasionally in U.S. history, a third party has proven locally potent, as did Minnesota's Farmer-Labor Party and Wisconsin's Progressives, both of which elected governors and state legislative majorities in the twentieth century. But, over time, no such party has survived,[26] and every state's two-party system mirrors national party dualism, at least as far as labels are concerned.

Photo courtesy: Reed Saxon/AP/Wide World Photos

■ In 2004, female candidates across the country were victorious in races at the local, state, and federal level. In South Dakota, where President Bush won by 21 percent, Stephanie Herseth (D) won the state's only U.S. House seat. Above, Herseth addresses supporters at the Democratic campaign headquarters in Sioux Falls, shortly after being declared the winner in November 2004.

Parties and Governors.   The powerful position of governor is a natural launching pad for a presidential candidacy. Just since 1900, Woodrow Wilson, Franklin D. Roosevelt, Jimmy Carter, Ronald Reagan, Bill Clinton, and most recently George W. Bush have all gone from statehouses to the White House.

Governors in many states have greater influence over their parties' organizations and legislators than do presidents. Many governors have more patronage positions at their command than does a president, and these material rewards and incentives give governors added clout with party activists and office holders. In addition, tradition in some states permits the governor to play a role in selecting the legislature's committee chairs and party floor leaders, and some state executives even attend and help direct the party legislative caucuses, activities no president would ever undertake. Moreover, forty-one governors possess the power of the line-item veto, which permits the governor to veto single items (such as pork barrel projects) in appropriations bills. The line-item veto has given governors enormous leverage with legislators, as they can now remove pork barrel projects from members who oppose the governor's agenda.

Parties and State Legislatures.   State legislatures are nearly evenly split between the two parties, with neither party having a significant advantage overall. However, parties have greater legislative influence at the state level than at the national level. Most state legislatures surpass the U.S. Congress in partisan unity and cohesion. Even though fewer than half of congressional roll calls in the post–World War II era have produced majorities of the two parties on opposite sides, a number of state legislatures (including Massachusetts, New York, Ohio, and Pennsylvania) have achieved party voting levels of 70 percent or better in some years. Not all states display party cohesion of this magnitude, of course. Nebraska has a nonpartisan legislature, elected without party labels on the ballot.

One other party distinction is notable in many state legislatures. Compared with the Congress, state legislative leaders have much more authority and power; this is one reason party unity is usually higher in the state capitols.[27] The strict seniority system that frequently controls committee assignments in Congress is less absolute in most states, and legislative leaders often have considerable discretion in appointing the committee chairs and members. The party caucuses, too, are usually more active and influential in state legislatures than in their Washington counterparts. In some legislatures, the caucuses meet weekly or even daily to work out strategy and count votes, and nearly one-fourth of the caucuses bind all the party members to support the group's decisions on key issues (such as appropriations measures, tax issues, and procedural questions).

Party leaders and caucuses as well as the party organizations have more influence over legislators at the state level. State legislators depend on their state and local parties for election assistance much more than their congressional counterparts. Whereas members of Congress have large government-provided staffs and lavish perquisites to assist (directly or indirectly) their reelection efforts, state legislative candidates need party workers and, increasingly, the party's financial support and technological resources at election time.

THE MODERN TRANSFORMATION OF PARTY ORGANIZATION

BOTH MAJOR POLITICAL PARTIES have substituted modern technological and communication strategies for the labor-intensive, person-to-person operations of the first half of the century, and both parties are similar in the objectives they pursue to achieve political power. Nevertheless, each party has its strengths and weaknesses.

Until 1992, the modern Republican Party thoroughly outclassed its Democratic rival in almost every category of campaign service and fund-raising. There are several explanations for this disparity. From 1932 until 1980, the Republicans were almost perennially disappointed underdogs, especially in congressional contests; they therefore felt the need to give extra effort. The GOP had the willingness, and enough electoral frustrations, to experiment with new campaign technologies that might hold the key to elusive victories. Also, since Democrats held most of the congressional offices and thus had most of the benefits of incumbency and staff, Republican nominees were forced to rely more on their party to offset built-in Democratic advantages. The party staff, in other words, compensated for the Democratic congressional staff, and perhaps also for organized labor's divisions of election troops, which were usually at the beck and call of Democratic candidates. Then, too, one can argue that the business and middle-class base of the modern GOP has a natural managerial and entrepreneurial flair, demonstrated by the party officers drawn from that talented pool.

■ Staffers call on the party faithful to vote on Election Day. Phone banks, like the ones shown here, have become a major part of party-related activity around election time.

Photo courtesy: Lou Dematteis/Reuters/Corbis

Whatever the causes, the contemporary national Republican Party has considerable organizational prowess, surpassing the Democrats in fund-raising by large margins in recent election cycles—never by less than two to one and usually by a considerably higher ratio (see Figure 12.4). Democrats must struggle to raise enough money to meet the basic needs of most of their candidates, while, in the words of a past chairman of the Democratic Senatorial Campaign Committee, "The single biggest problem the Republicans have is how to legally spend the money they have."[28] In 2004, Republicans still outspent the Democrats in Senate and House races, but the Democrats came closer to matching the Republicans than in any other modern election season. Either way, a party or candidate with a considerable financial advantage can daunt opponents. Recent empirical evidence shows that large campaign war chests of incumbents act to deter high-quality challengers from entering political races. Faced with the prospect of raising huge sums of money to match incumbents, many potentially competitive opposition candidates simply decide to sit races out.[29]

Republicans raise so much money because they have developed networks of donors reached by a variety of methods. Republicans have a highly successful mail solicitation list, started back in the early 1960s and accelerated in the mid-1970s, when postage and production costs were relatively low. The national Republican Party has expanded its mailing list of proven donors to several million, producing about three-fourths of total revenue, and they do so with an average contribution of less than $35. Republicans also pioneered the use of interactive tech-

FIGURE 12.4 **Political Party Finances, 1978–2004: Total Receipts**

Note how the Republican Party has consistently taken in substantially higher receipts than their Democratic competitors, especially in the 1980s, when the Republican Party consolidated and prospered during Ronald Reagan's administration. Not until 1996 did Democrats reach levels long enjoyed by the Republicans. ■

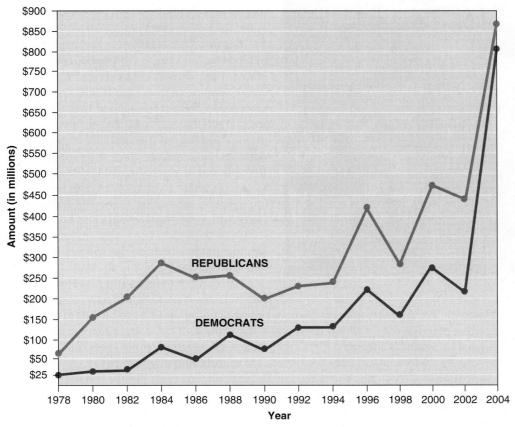

Source: Federal Election Commission, and opensecrets.org.

nologies to attract voters. The RNC's award-winning "Main Street" Internet site has offered "chats" with the RNC chair and links to sites of interest to voters. Former Democratic presidential candidate Howard Dean used an Internet Web site to coordinate "meet-ups" and to bring in campaign money. When his candidacy ended in defeat, Dean and his network of activist-contributors became a fund-raising resource for Democrats.

The national Republican committees have spent millions of dollars for national, state, and local public opinion surveys, and they have accumulated an enormous storehouse of data on American attitudes in general and on marginal districts in particular. Many of the surveys are provided to GOP nominees at a cut-rate cost. In important contests, the party frequently commissions tracking polls to chart its daily rise or fall. The information provided in such polls is invaluable in the tense concluding days of an election. The GOP also operates a sophisticated in-house media division that specializes in the design and production of television advertisements for party nominees at all levels. The party trains many of the political volunteers and paid operatives who manage the candidates' campaigns. Since 1976, the Republicans have held annually about a half-dozen week-long "Campaign Management Colleges" for staffers. In 1986, the party launched an ambitious million-dollar "Congressional Campaign Academy" that offers two-week, all-expenses-paid training courses for prospective campaign managers, finance directors, and press relations staff. Early in each election cycle, the national party staff also prepares voluminous research reports on Democratic opponents, analyzing their public statements, votes, and attendance records. The reports are made available to GOP candidates and their aides.

Simulation

You Are a Professional Campaign Manager

Photo courtesy: Tom Tingle/AP/Wide World Photos

■ The Bush-Cheney campaign received nearly $300 million in donations from individuals, PACs, and parties in 2004. Here President Bush seeks the support of a group of senior citizens in Phoenix, Arizona.

Despite its noted financial edge and service sophistication, however, all is not well in the Republican organization. Success has bred self-satisfaction and complacency, encouraged waste, and led the party to place too much reliance on money and technology and not enough on the foundation of any party movement—people.

Because Democrats were the majority party in Congress for decades throughout the twentieth century, they likely never saw the need to create such programs. Recent electoral defeats have made Democrats realize that their party must change to survive, that it must dampen internal ideological disputes and begin to revitalize its organization. Thus was born, with the Republican Party's accomplishments as a model, the commitment to technological and fund-raising modernization that drives the Democratic Party today. If the Republicans become too secure in their slim but stable majority status, Democrats may become the party that leads in new election strategies.

For now, Democrats still trail the Republicans by virtually every significant measure of party activity. Yet, the party finances (receipts) graphed in Figure 12.4 can be read in a different way. Although the GOP has consistently maintained an enormous edge, the Democrats have considerably increased their total receipts, raising many times more than just a few years ago. More importantly, Democrats are contributing much more to their candidates and have actually come close to the GOP's larger total recently. But the real strength of the Democratic party is in the number of party activists. The decision in 1981 to begin a direct-mail program for the national party was a turning point for Democrats. From a list of only 25,000 donors before the program began, the DNC's support base has grown to 500,000. The Democrats have imitated the Republicans not just in fund-raising but also in the uses to which the money is put.

THE PARTY IN THE ELECTORATE

A POLITICAL PARTY is much more than its organizational shell, however dazzling the technologies at its command, and its reach extends well beyond the relative handful of men and women who are the party in government. Although it is true that the organizations of both parties have grown stronger over time, this strength makes up only a small part of their overall level of significance. In any democracy, where power is derived directly from the people, the party's real importance and strength must come from the citizenry it attempts to mobilize. The party in the electorate—the mass of potential voters who identify with the Democratic or Republican labels—is the most important element of the political party, providing the foundation for the organizational and governmental parties. But, in some crucial respects, it is the weakest of the components of the U.S. political party system. In recent decades, fewer citizens have been willing to pledge their fealty to the major parties, and many of those who have declared their loyalties have done so with less intensity. Moreover, voters of each partisan stripe are increasingly casting ballots for some candidates of the opposing party. Partisan identification is a less reliable indicator of likely voting choices today than it once was. (For a more detailed explanation of patterns in American vote choice, see chapter 13.)

Analyzing Visuals
POLITICAL PARTY FINANCES, 1978–2004

Both major parties give money—a small portion of what they actually raise—directly to specific candidates, and they also provide millions of dollars in coordinated expenditures (which are federally limited) on behalf of the candidates. The Republican Party historically has raised and spent far more campaign money than the Democratic Party (notice the especially large difference in the 1980s). But, since the 1990s, the Democrats have made tremendous strides in fund-raising and contributions to candidates and are now much more competitive with their opponents. Democrats also receive an invisible boost from labor unions. After studying the graph, answer the following critical

thinking questions: What general trend do you notice about fund-raising and spending by both parties over time? What appears to be significant about 1994 and 1998? Drawing on what you know about recent election results, does there seem to be a strong correlation between which party spends the most money and which party wins on Election Night?

The graph includes totals for national, senatorial, and congressional committees as well as all other reported national, state, and local spending; all presidential, Senate, and House candidates are included. Not included are "soft money" expenditures. The 2002 amount includes monies spent between January 1, 2001, and October 16, 2002.

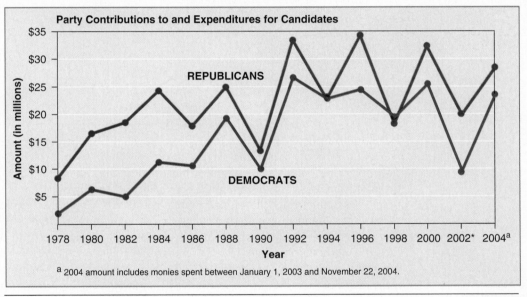

Source: Federal Election Commission.

Party Identification

Most American voters identify with a party but do not belong to it. Universal party membership does not exist in the United States: the voter pays no prescribed dues; no formal rules govern an individual's party activities; and voters assume no enforceable obligations to the party even when they consistently vote for its candidates. A party has no real control over or even an accurate accounting of its adherents, and the party's voters subscribe to few or none of the commonly accepted tenets of organizational membership, such as regular participation and some measure of responsibility for the group's welfare. Rather, **party identification** or affiliation is an informal and impressionistic exercise whereby a citizen acquires a party label and accepts its standard as a summary of his or her political views and preferences. (See Figure 12.5 for trends in party identification.)

party identification
A citizen's personal affinity for a political party, usually expressed by his or her tendency to vote for the candidates of that party.

FIGURE 12.5 Party Identification, 1952–2004

Simply defined, party identification is the response a voter gives to the poll question, "With what political party do you identify?" Notice how, despite the varying party of the president over time, party identification has remained fairly stable from the 1950s to the early 1990s. Not until an era of acute partisan strife in the mid-1990s have the independents made significant gains in party identification. ■

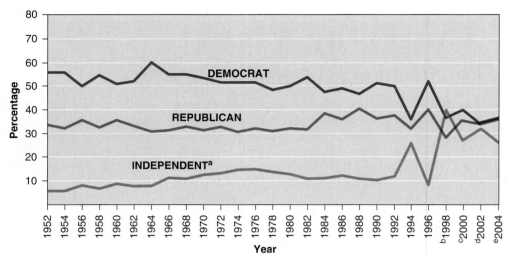

Note: Partisan totals do not add up to 100 percent because "apolitical" and "other" responses were deleted. Sample size varied from poll to poll, from a low of 1,130 to a high of 2,850.

a Pure Independents only. Independent "leaners" have been added to Democratic and Republican totals.

b 1998 figures were provided from a Gallup Poll. Due to differences in wording from the Center for Political Studies Poll, the Gallup Poll may overstate the number of Independents.

c 2000 figures based on Voter News Service exit poll.

d 2002 figures were provided from a November 4, 2002, Gallup Poll survey.

e 2004 figures based on National Election Pool exit poll.

Source: Leon D. Epstein, *Political Parties in the American Mold* (Madison: University of Wisconsin Press, 1986), table 8.1, 257. Data for 1996 provided by exit poll conducted by Voter Research and Surveys.

Participation

Deciding on a Political Party

However, that partisan identification is acquired informally through socialization does not mean that it is unimportant. The party label becomes a voter's central political reference symbol and perceptual screen, a prism or filter through which the world of politics and government flows and is interpreted. For many Americans, party identification is a significant aspect of their political personality and a way of defining and explaining themselves to others. The loyalty generated by the label can be as intense as any enjoyed by sports teams and alma maters; in a few areas of the country, "Democrat" and "Republican" are still fighting words (see Politics Now: The Limits of Red and Blue).

On the whole, Americans regard their partisan affiliation as a convenience rather than a necessity. Individual party identifications are reinforced by the legal institutionalization of the major parties. Because of restrictive ballot laws, campaign finance rules, the powerful inertia of political tradition, and many other factors, voters for all practical purposes are limited to a choice between a Democrat and a Republican in almost all elections—a situation that naturally encourages the pragmatic choosing up of sides. About half of the states require a voter to state a party preference (or independent status) when registering to vote, and they restrict voting in a party primary only to registrants in that particular party, making it an incentive for voters to affiliate themselves with a party.[30]

Sources of Party Identification.   Whatever the societal and governmental forces responsible for party identification, the explanations of partisan loyalty at the individual's level are understandably more personal. Not surprisingly, parents are the single greatest influence in establishing a person's first party identification. Politically active parents with the same party loyalty raise children who will be strong party identifiers, whereas parents without party affiliations or with mixed affiliations produce offspring more likely to be independents (see chapter 11).

Early socialization is hardly the last step in an individual's acquisition and maintenance of a party identity; marriage and other aspects of adult life can change one's loyalty. So can charismatic political personalities, particularly at the national level (such as

THE LIMITS OF RED AND BLUE

Journalists, pundits, and their ilk generally assumed that the growing political divisions in the United States, one between so-called "blue" and "red" states. Blue states are largely composed of New England, New York, the Pacific Coast, and a few midwestern states. Red States make up the South, the Midwest, Southwest, the Rockies, and Alaska. The origins of the colors come from the electoral map of the 2000 presidential election, which showed a striking geographical continuity (with the exception of a blue New Mexico and a red New Hampshire). Many supposed that the stark contrast on the political map indicates a growing division among the American people.

Of course, the belief that the American people are divided into two camps is not new. Conservative and liberal ideologues constantly refer to a cultural war perpetrated by the other side trying to subvert the appropriate path for America. Typically, conservatives point to the liberal news media, activist judges, and certain (inevitably Democratic) politicians trying to corrupt the traditional American values found in places like the South and Midwest that keep us free. Liberals respond with claims that talk radio hosts, reactionary judges, and certain (inevitably Republican) politicians are trying to stop greater social tolerance and the expansion of civil liberties found in places like Massachusetts and Oregon. The traditional economic conflicts of the twentieth century have given way to the moral conflicts of the twenty-first, with battle-lines drawn in the swing states.

Recently, however, scholars have taken issue with associating political divisions with cultural ones, claiming that there is a big difference between the greater political organization one sees in the growing divisions between red and blue states and the existing moral consensus shared among all of them.[a] They posit that the culture war is largely a consequence of the "misinterpretation of election returns, lack of hard examination of polling data, systematic and self-serving misrepresentation by issue activists, and selective coverage by an uncritical media more concerned with news value than with getting the story right."[b] The image of a culture war is actually more a function of how right-leaning communities vote in hard right candidates far right of the community's values, just as left-leaning communities vote in candidate on their ideological extreme. The extreme positions of successful candidates hides rather reveals the general moral consensus among Americans.

There is a tendency for people to pay more attention to those who make the most noise; subsequently, activists and extremists receive more attention, giving us the impression that everyone is an activist and an extremist. Nevertheless, according to exit polls, 22 percent of 2004 voters cited "moral values" as their primary issue while voting, and these voters voted 80 percent in favor of Bush. With data likes these, it is hard to discount entirely the belief in a cultural division among Americans; however, the peace in the streets after the 2004 election demonstrates that Americans at least share the principles of peace and democracy in spite of their different interpretations.

[a]Morris P. Fiorina et al., *Culture War? The Myth of a Polarized America*. New York: Longman, 2005.
[b]Ibid 5.

Franklin D. Roosevelt and Ronald Reagan), cataclysmic events (the Civil War and the Great Depression are the best examples), and maybe intense social issues (for instance, abortion). Interestingly, social class is not an especially strong indicator of likely partisan choice in the United States, at least in comparison with Western European democracies. Not only are Americans less inclined than Europeans to perceive class distinctions, preferring instead to see themselves and most other people as members of an exceedingly broad middle class, but other factors, including sectionalism and candidate-oriented politics, tend to blur class lines in voting.

Declining Loyalty?

Over the past two decades, numerous political scientists as well as other observers, journalists, and party activists have become increasingly anxious about a perceived decline in partisan identification and loyalty, since parties traditionally provide political information and serve as the means of political participation. Many public opinion surveys have shown a significant growth in independents at the expense of the two major parties. The

■ Simple messages and catchy phrases have earned campaign buttons a permanent place in American politics. These popular campaign novelties serve to increase candidate name recognition in the general public and to reinforce the support of the button wearer. These buttons from the 2004 presidential election reflect George W. Bush's attempts to appeal to a variety of prospective voters.

Photo courtesy: Ted Soqui/Corbis

Center for Political Studies/Survey Research Center (CPS/SRC) of the University of Michigan, for instance, has charted the rise of self-described independents from a low of 19 percent in 1958 to a peak of 38 percent in 1978, with percentages at the end of the 1990s hovering just below that high-water mark at 37 percent. Current surveys show the number of independents declining, but only slightly, with figures at or above 30 percent. Before the 1950s (although the evidence for this research is more circumstantial because of the scarcity of reliable survey research data), independents were far fewer in number and party loyalties were considerably firmer than is the case today.

Currently, the Democratic and Republican parties can claim a roughly equal percentage of self-identified partisans, with levels fluctuating around one-third of the population each. This can seem inconsistent with voting behavior and election results, but one must pay close attention to the manner in which these data are collected. When pollsters ask for party identification information, they generally proceed in two stages. First, they inquire whether a respondent considers himself or herself to be a Democrat, Republican, or independent. Then the party identifiers are asked to categorize themselves as "strong" or "not very strong" supporters, while the independents are pushed to reveal their leanings with a question such as "Which party do you normally support in elections, the Democrats or the Republicans?" (See Figure 12.5.) It may be true that some independent respondents are thereby prodded to pick a party under the pressure of the interview situation, regardless of their true feelings. But, research has demonstrated that independent "leaners" in fact vote very much like real partisans, in some elections more so than the "not very strong" party identifiers. There is reason to count the independent leaners as closet partisans, though voting behavior is not the equivalent of real partisan identification.

In fact, the reluctance of leaners to admit their real party identities is in itself worrisome, because it reveals a change in attitudes about political parties and their role in our society. Being a socially acceptable, integrated, and contributing member of one's community once almost demanded partisan affiliation; it was a badge of good citizenship signifying that one was a patriot. Today, voters consider such labels an offense to their individualism, and a vast majority of Americans insist that they vote for "the person, not the party."

The reasons for these anti-party attitudes are not hard to find. The growth of issue-oriented politics that cut across party lines for voters who feel intensely about certain policy matters is partly the cause. So, too, is the emphasis on personality politics by the mass media (especially television) and political consultants. Party splits have also played a role. Fiscal conservatives in the GOP often have little in common with social conservatives who care most about the abortion issue, for example. Underlying these causes, though, are two much more disturbing and destructive long-term phenomena: the perceived loss of party credibility, and the decline of the party's tangible connections to the lives of everyday citizens.

Although the underlying partisanship of the American people has not declined significantly since 1952, voter-admitted partisanship has dropped considerably. From 1952 to 1964 about three-fourths or more of the electorate volunteered a party choice without prodding, but since 1970 an average of less than two-thirds has been willing to do so. Professed independents (including leaners) have increased from around one-fifth of the electorate in the 1950s to one-third or more during the last three decades. Also cause for concern is the marginal decline in strong Democrats and strong Republicans. Strong partisans are a party's backbone, the source of its volunteer force, candidates, and dependable voters.

Group Affiliations

Just as individuals vary in the strength of their partisan choice, so, too, do groups vary in the degree to which they identify with the Democratic Party or the Republican Party. There are enormous variations in party identification from one region or demographic group to another, particularly in geographic region, gender, race and ethnicity, age, social and economic status, religion, marital status, and ideology.

Geographic Region.   While all other geographic regions in the United States are relatively closely contested between the parties, the South still exhibits some of the Democratic Party affinity cultivated in the nineteenth century and hardened in the fires of the Civil War. This is still true only in local elections, however, and even there, it is changing rapidly. In the 2004 election, for instance, Southerners elected Republicans to a majority of the U.S. House seats in the states of the old Confederacy, and dozens of sheriffs won under the GOP banner, too. In all regions, party strengths vary by locality, with central cities almost everywhere heavily Democratic, the swelling suburbs serving as the main source of GOP partisans, and the small-town and rural areas split evenly between the two major parties.

Gender.   Some political scientists argue that the difference in the way men and women vote first emerged in 1920, when newly enfranchised women registered overwhelmingly as Republicans. It was not until the 1980 presidential election, however, that a noticeable and possibly significant gender gap emerged. This time, the Democratic Party was the apparent beneficiary. When Ronald Reagan trounced incumbent Democratic President Jimmy Carter, he did so with the support of 54 percent of the men who voted but only 46 percent of the women voters.

The 2004 exit polls showed that the gender gap was smaller but still present. While polls leading up to November 2, 2004, hinted at a possible change, the results illustrated that women still favored Democrats, and men still favored Republicans. George W. Bush received 55 percent of the men's vote versus 44 percent for Kerry, while Bush received only 48 percent of the female vote versus Kerry's 51 percent.

Analyzing Visuals

THE GENDER GAP—WHERE MEN AND WOMEN VOTE DIFFERENTLY

For over twenty years, the voting behaviors of men and women have shown a clear difference in their support of the two major parties and their nominees for president. The election of 2004 proved no different, as women supported Senator John Kerry in greater numbers, and men supported President George Bush at a higher rate. This gender gap is illustrated state by state on the map below, based on exit polls from the 2000 election. Take a few moments to compare the gender gaps in the individual states. You will notice that while the national gender gap appears to be a moderate, reasonable number, several states exhibit extreme differences between male and female voting. After examining the various states and regions, answer the following critical thinking questions: Are there any apparent geographical gender gap trends? What issues do you think play a significant role in creating and maintaining this disparity? Drawing on what you have learned about the 2004 election results in each state, how do you think the gender gap will affect the campaign strategies of future candidates?

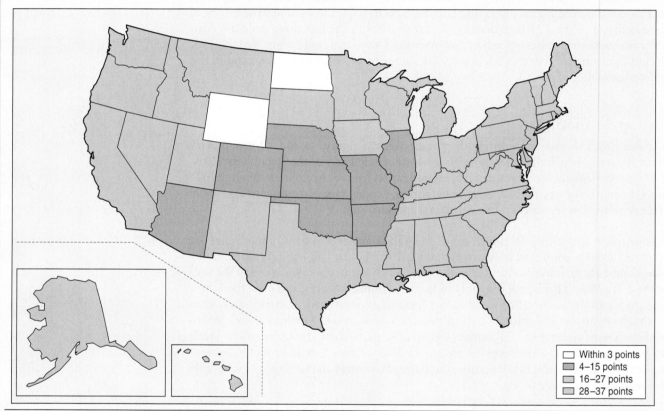

Legend:
- ☐ Within 3 points
- ■ 4–15 points
- ☐ 16–27 points
- ☐ 28–37 points

Source: Michigan State University Map Library, http://www.lib.msu.edu/coll/main/maps/vote/gendergap.jpg.

One of the biggest challenges facing Republicans is how to gain the support of women without alienating their male base. Besides abortion and women's rights issues, women's concerns for peace and social justice may provide much of the gap's distance. For instance, women are usually much less likely than men to favor American military action. One recent study has pointed the finger not at Republican Party difficulties in attracting female voters, but rather at the Democratic Party's inability to attract the votes of males. In other words, the gender gap exists because of the lack of support for the Democratic Party among men, and the corresponding male preference for the Republican Party, stemming from differences in opinions about social welfare and military issues.[31]

Race and Ethnicity.   African Americans are the most dramatically split population subgroup in party terms. The 80-percent-plus advantage they offer the Democrats dwarfs the edge given to either party by any other segment of the electorate, and their proportion of strong Democrats (about 40 percent) is three times that of whites. African Americans account almost entirely for the slight lead in party affiliation that Democrats normally enjoy over Republicans, since the GOP has recently been able to attract a narrow majority of whites to its standard. Perhaps as a reflection of the massive party chasm separating blacks and whites, the two races differ greatly on many policy issues, with blacks overwhelmingly on the liberal side and whites closer to the conservative pole. The belief of most blacks that their fate is linked causes upper-income blacks generally to vote the same as lower-income blacks. Whites see no such class-based obligation.[32] An exception, incidentally, is abortion, where religious beliefs may lead African Americans to adopt a more conservative pro-life stance.

Hispanics supplement African Americans as a Democratic stalwart; by more than three to one, Hispanics prefer the Democratic label. Voting patterns of Puerto Ricans are very similar to African Americans, while Mexican Americans favor the Democrats by smaller margins. An exception is the Cuban American population, whose anti–Fidel Castro tilt leads to support for the Republican Party. Republicans have fought to make inroads with Hispanic voters. President Bush made a high-ranking Hispanic appointment when he selected former Texas Supreme Court Justice Alberto Gonzales to serve as attorney general. Governor Jeb Bush of Florida, President Bush's brother, speaks fluent Spanish and often campaigns with non-Cuban Hispanic groups on behalf of the Republican Party.

Age.   Young people are once again becoming more Democratic. Polls in 1972 indicated that the group of eighteen- to twenty-four-year-olds, particularly students, was the only age group to support Democratic presidential nominee George McGovern. But, by the 1990s, the eighteen- to twenty-four-year-old age group was the most Republican of all. Perhaps because of the bad economy from 1990 to 1992, which reduced the jobs available to college graduates, young people swung back to the Democrats in 1992. Bill Clinton ran strongly among eighteen- to twenty-four-year-olds, and they were among his best groups in the electorate. In 2004, John Kerry won the youth vote by almost ten points, garnering 54 percent to George W. Bush's 45 percent. Elderly white males were the most Republican of all groups.

Social and Economic Factors.   Occupation, income, and education also influence party affiliation. The GOP remains predominant among executives, professionals, and white-collar workers, whereas the Democrats lead substantially among blue-collar workers and the unemployed. Labor union members are also Democratic by two-and-a-half to one. The more conservative, retired population leans Republican. Women who do not work outside the home are less liberal and Democratic than those who do. Occupation, income, and education are closely related, of course, so many of the same partisan patterns appear in all three classifications. Democratic support usually drops steadily as one climbs the income scale. Similarly, as years of education increase, identification with the Republican Party climbs; in graduate school, however, the Democrats reverse the trend and outnumber GOP partisans.

Religion.   Party preferences by religion are also traditional, but with modern twists. Protestants—especially Methodists, Presbyterians, and Episcopalians—favor the Republicans, whereas Catholics and, even more so, Jews are predominantly Democratic in affiliation. Decreased polarization is apparent all around, though.[33] Democrats have made inroads among many liberal Protestant denominations over the past three decades, and Republicans can now sometimes claim up to 25 percent of the Jewish population and nearly 40 percent of Catholics. Fundamentalist Christians, who received much attention in the 1990s, are somewhat less Republican than commonly believed. The GOP usually has just about a 10 percent edge among them, primarily because so many blacks classify themselves as members of this group.

Marital Status.   Even marital status reveals something about partisan affiliation. People who are married, a traditionally more conservative group, and people who have never married, a segment weighted toward the premarriage young who currently lean toward the Republicans, are closely divided in party loyalty. But, the widowed are Democratic in nature, probably because there are many more widows than widowers; here, the gender gap is again expressing itself. The divorced and the separated, who may be experiencing economic hardship and appear to be more liberal than the married population, are a substantially Democratic group.

Ideology.   Ideologically, there are few surprises. Lending credence to the belief that both parties are now relatively distinct philosophically, liberals are overwhelmingly Democratic and conservatives are staunchly Republican in most surveys and opinion studies.

However, as party identification has weakened, so, too, has the likelihood that voters will cast ballots predictably and regularly for their party's nominees. (Chapter 13 discusses this in some detail.) In the present day, as at the founding of the republic, Americans are simply not wedded to the idea or the reality of political parties, and the dealigning patterns we have witnessed in recent times are likely to remain the norm in the foreseeable future.

THIRD-PARTYISM

Timeline

Third Parties in American History

third-partyism
The tendency of third parties to arise with some regularity in a nominally two-party system.

THE TWO-PARTY SYSTEM has not gone unchallenged. At the state level, two-party competition was severely limited or nonexistent in much of the country for most of the twentieth century.[34] Formerly, in the one-party Democratic states of the Deep South and the rock-ribbed Republican states of Maine, New Hampshire, and Vermont, the dominant party's primary nomination was often equivalent to election, and the only real contest was an unsatisfying intraparty one in which colorful personalities often dominated and a half-dozen major candidacies in each primary proved confusing to voters.[35] Even in most two-party states, many cities and counties had a massive majority of voters aligned with one or the other party and thus were effectively one-party in local elections.

Third partyism, or the rise of alternative minor parties based on a single cause neglected by the major parties, has had an important impact on American politics, even if its existence has been sporadic and intermittent. Third parties find their roots in sectionalism (as did the South's states' rights Dixiecrats, who broke away from the Democrats in 1948); in economic protest (such as the agrarian revolt that fueled the Populists, an 1892 prairie-states party); in specific issues (such as the Green Party's support of the environment); in ideology (the Socialist, Communist, and Libertarian Parties are examples); and in appealing, charismatic personalities (Theodore Roosevelt's affiliation with the Bull Moose Party is perhaps the best case). Many minor parties have drawn strength from a combination of these sources. The American Independent Party enjoyed a measure of success because of a dynamic leader (George Wallace), a firm geographic base (the South), and an emotional issue (civil rights). In 1992, Ross Perot, the billionaire with a folksy Texas manner, was a charismatic leader whose campaign was fueled by the deficit issue (as well as by his personal fortune).

The 2000 election saw Green Party nominee Ralph Nader, the environmentalist and consumer advocate who ran for president in 1996, lead a nationwide grassroots, anti-establishment campaign to oppose the corporate-backed main party candidates, Vice President Al Gore and Texas Governor George W. Bush. Although Nader collected just 2.86 million votes (or 2.72 percent nationwide, well below the 5 percent

Global Perspective

THE EMERGENCE OF NEW PARTIES

As we have seen in this chapter, the American political party system essentially is a two-party system. Occasionally, third parties or independent candidates surface and make a bid to win public office, but for all practical purposes, Americans remain wedded to the Republican and Democratic parties. The same allegiance has not occurred in Western Europe. Here, support for new political parties (those founded since 1960) has been growing steadily over the past four decades at the expense of older established political parties, regardless of whether we look at presidential systems or parliamentary ones. The emergence of these new parties is tied to voter dissatisfaction with existing parties and the ability of new parties to tap into very specific complaints and concerns on the part of citizens.

In the 1960s, new parties received only 3.9 percent of the vote across Western Europe. They were most successful in France (16.3 percent) and least successful in Great Britain (0 percent) and Ireland (0.3 percent). Their percentage of the vote increased to 9.7 percent in the 1970s and to 15.3 percent in the 1980s. In the 1990s, new parties received 23.7 percent of all votes cast in Western Europe—a 19.8 percent increase.

The following table shows the growth of support for new parties in selected West European states. Only in Great Britain have they failed to increase their share of the vote.

Mean Percentage of Vote Recieved by New Parties

Country	1960s	1970s	1980s	1990s
Finland	1.6	8.2	13.7	22.3
France	16.3	29.1	27.1	41.7
Germany	4.3	0.5	7.5	13.9
Great Britain	0	0.8	11.6	2.3
Italy	9.5	3.3	7.1	66.8
Netherlands	2.3	26.6	44.5	45.9

Even more significant than the growth in support for new parties in Western Europe is the growing support over the past two decades for extremist parties—political parties at the ideological ends of the political spectrum. Those on the political left are most easily identified today as Green Parties. They advocate a clearly defined and aggressive pro-environmental agenda. Those on the political right tend to be more difficult to classify. Many of the most visible ones, such

as the National Front in France, advocate strongly nationalistic and anti-immigration policies.

On balance, Greens have not mounted a significant electoral challenge to the traditional ruling parties of Western Europe. But this is only part of the story. Greens have succeeded in influencing the political agenda in many countries and have become part of governing coalitions in France, Germany, Italy, and Finland. Whereas the appeal of the Greens throughout Western Europe is fairly even, the appeal of right-wing parties is quite varied. In many countries it is almost totally absent, while in others it has some support. And, in three countries—Austria, Italy, and France—extreme right-wing parties have come to represent real challenges to traditional parties. Unlike the Green Parties that are seen as very democratic in outlook, right-wing parties bring back memories of fascism in Europe and concerns about how willing these parties are to abide by democratic norms and procedures. The following table shows the vote totals for Green and right-wing extremist parties in the same countries profiled above. Because of the newness of many of these parties, data are only from the 1980s and 1990s.

Mean Percentage of Vote Recieved by Extremist Parties

Country	Green Vote 1980s	Green Vote 1990s	Right-Wing Vote 1980s	Right-Wing Vote 1990s
Finland	2.7	7.0	0	0.3
France	0.9	8.4	6.7	14.2
Germany	5.1	6.4	0.3	2.5
Great Britain	0.3	0.3	0.1	0
Italy	1.3	2.7	6.6	20.9
Netherlands	1.1	5.6	0.6	1.8

Questions

1. Under what conditions can you see new parties developing in the United States and getting the type of support that they have in Western Europe?
2. Which type of extremist parties do you see as more likely to become electorally successful in the United States, ones on the political left or the political right?

Source: Hans Keman, ed., *Comparative Democratic Politics* (London: Sage, 2002), 134, 137.

required for the Green Party to receive matching federal funding in 2004), there is little question that Nader cost Democrat Al Gore the presidency in 2000. Nader received 97,488 votes in the critical state of Florida, most of which, according to exit polls, would

Comparing Political Parties

Join the Debate

THIRD PARTIES: GOOD OR BAD FOR THE AMERICAN POLITICAL SYSTEM?

> **OVERVIEW:** Third parties are a recurring political phenomenon in the United States, and they originate for one of two reasons: (1) to express an alternative political platform to those held by the two major parties or (2) to launch an alternative candidate for public office.

The Socialist Party favored a dismantling of the American capitalist system and a complete overhaul of the government. The Dixiecrats, who believed in continued racial segregation, broke from the Democratic Party because it was beginning to abandon this position. These parties emerged to express ideas lacking support in the Republican and Democratic Parties.

The Reform Party and the Bull Moose Party illustrate how third parties can offer an alternative presidential candidate. In 1992 Ross Perot founded the Reform Party with the sole purpose of running for president. Similarly, in 1911 the Bull Moose Party—known officially as the Progressive Party—was conceived to support Theodore Roosevelt's 1912 presidential campaign. These parties, and the candidates that bore their standard, gained popularity and support based on a dissatisfaction with the candidates and trends in the two major parties at the time. They offered alternatives to the established Republican and Democratic Parties, and they claimed to have nominees who would achieve greater success as president due to their lack of strong party ties.

While single issues and popular candidates are successful ingredients for the creation of third parties, they lack the power to sustain a party's viability over time. In addition, the trouble with single-issue parties is that the issue is usually specific to a certain group of people or a certain area of the nation that is too small to impact a national election. If this kind of third party were to fight for more local or state representation, then they would have better chances of winning,

as the Vermont Socialists did in seeing one of their own, Independent Bernie Sanders, elected to the U.S. House of Representatives in 1990. Sanders defeated both Democratic and Republican candidates, and he has been reelected ever since, now possessing a secure seat. (Sanders caucuses with the Democrats but retains the Socialist identification.)

The trouble with candidate-oriented third parties is that they depend utterly on their candidate. When interest in Ross Perot declined, the support for the Reform Party seemed to evaporate with it, until former professional wrestler and popular independent governor of Minnesota, Jesse Ventura, became the new candidate on which the party could focus. When arch-conservative and former Republican insider Pat Buchanan received the Reform Party nomination for president, in hopes that he could also shine beneath the party's limelight, Ventura and his independent voters backed out, leaving the Reform Party in ruins.

Arguments for Third Parties

- **Third parties benefit the United States because they allow for a greater diversity of opinion, beyond that of Democrats and Republicans.** Often the issues promoted by third parties and the candidates that represent them gain popular support, and the major parties are then forced to address them. For example, several of the reforms proposed by the GOP's 1994 "Contract with America" had been part of Ross Perot's campaign platform in 1992. In cases like this, third parties are essential in guaranteeing that all voices are heard.
- **The two-party system is not integral to a successful representative democracy.** While American democracy quickly evolved into a political system characterized by two major parties, many other successful democracies

have gone to Gore if Nader had not run. While recent research in political science raises the chicken-or-egg question of which comes first, political dissatisfaction leading to third parties[36] or third-party movements leading to political dissatisfaction,[37] the accepted conclusion that third parties are at some point linked to discontent with government and party leaders is widely accepted.

In addition, minor-party and independent candidates are not limited to presidential elections. Many also run in congressional elections, and the numbers appear to be growing. In the 2004 congressional elections, for example, more than 800 minor-party and independent candidates ran for seats in the House and Senate—almost eight times as many as in 1968 and close to three times the number that ran in 1980. A recent study shows that minor-party candidates for the House are most likely to emerge under three operate with multiparty systems. Countries such as Spain, Germany, South Korea, and Israel have stable democratic governments that continue to provide successful leadership and progress for their citizens.

- **Third parties can provide useful solutions to political problems on the local and regional level.** While the major parties must incorporate a broad range of issues in order to maintain national appeal, third parties are able to focus on a single issue or on a few issues specific to a state or locality. While there has never been a third-party president, and currently there is only one member of the U.S. House of Representatives and one member of the U.S. Senate who do not belong to either major party, there have been several third-party state governors in recent history.

Arguments Against Third Parties

- **Third parties can be composed of political extremists who are uninterested in real politics.** With an intense focus on a specific issue or agenda, some groups and candidates that arise as alternatives to the major, mainstream political parties have been known to disregard the idea of compromise that characterizes the American political system and is the basis for progress. Instead, they use rhetoric and emotional appeals to energize supporters, which often serve to repulse as much support as they attract, resulting in disenchantment with the system and less participation in the process.
- **Some third parties contain strongly anti-democratic sentiments.** In the 1940s, the Dixiecrats wanted to preserve the Jim Crow South, where African Americans were legally discriminated against and states required businesses and public buildings to separate white patrons from black patrons. While this sounds outrageous today, it was the sole issue behind the Dixiecrats at the time. Earlier in the twentieth century, the Bull Moose Party nearly became a cult of personality

for Theodore Roosevelt. His supporters' hero worship went beyond political support and prevented the party from focusing simply on the issue positions that he represented.

- **Third parties may impact elections and produce an outcome contrary to the popular sentiment.** Frequently a third-party movement will arise out of dissatisfaction within a major party on a specific issue, or among individuals with political leanings in a particular direction. As a result, this third party can drain support disproportionately from voters of that party on Election Day, leading to a victory for a candidate who would not have had a majority of support in a two-candidate race. Ross Perot is often credited with costing then-President George Bush a second term in 1992, by appealing to a large number of conservative voters who might otherwise have voted for Bush. Likewise, in the 2000 presidential election, many recognize Ralph Nader as the primary reason for Al Gore's defeat, because he pulled much of his support from liberal voters.

Questions

1. In what ways has the current political climate benefited from the presence of third parties? How have third parties harmed the system?
2. How did the presence or absence of third party candidates impact the outcome of the 2004 presidential election? Do you think this had anything to do with the outcome of recent previous elections?

Selected Readings

Steven J. Rosenstone, Roy L. Behr, and Edward H. Lazarus. *Third Parties in America.* Princeton, NJ: Princeton University Press, 1996.

John Bibby and L. Sandy Maisel. *Two Parties—Or More? The American Party System.* Boulder, CO: Westview, 2002.

conditions: (1) when a House seat becomes open; (2) when a minor party candidate has previously competed in the district; and, (3) when partisan competition between the two major parties in the district is close.[38]

Above all, third parties make electoral progress in direct proportion to the failure of the two major parties to incorporate new ideas or alienated groups or to nominate attractive candidates as their standard-bearers. Third parties do best when declining trust in the two major political parties plagues the electorate.[39] Usually, though, third parties are eventually co-opted by one of the two major parties, each of them eager to take the politically popular issue that gave rise to the third party and make it theirs in order to secure the allegiance of the third party's supporters. For example, the Republicans of the 1970s absorbed many of the "states' rights" planks of George Wallace's

1968 presidential bid. Both parties have also more recently attempted to attract independent voters by sponsoring reforms of the governmental process, such as limitations on the activities of Washington lobbyists.

Why Third Parties Tend to Remain Minor

Third parties in the United States are akin to shooting stars that appear briefly and brilliantly but do not long remain visible in the political constellation. In fact, the United States is the only major Western nation that does not have at least one significant, enduring national third party. There are a number of explanations for this. Unlike many European countries that use **proportional representation** (awarding legislative seats according to the percentage of votes a political party receives), the United States has a "single-member, plurality" electoral system. The U.S. system requires a party to get one more vote than any other party in a legislative district or in a state's presidential election in order to win. In contrast, countries that use proportional representation often guarantee parliamentary seats to any faction securing as little as 5 percent of the vote. To paraphrase the legendary football coach Vince Lombardi, finishing first is not everything, it is the *only* thing in U.S. politics; placing second, even by a smidgen, doesn't count. This condition encourages the grouping of interests into as few parties as possible (the democratic minimum being two). Moreover, the two parties will often move to the left or right on issues in order to gain popular support. Some observers claim that parties in the United States have no permanent positions at all, only permanent interests—winning elections. Regardless of one's position on this issue, it is clear that the adaptive nature of the two parties further forestalls the growth of third parties in the United States. We should not write off the possibility that an enduring third party will emerge, but other institutional and historical factors also promote the two-party system:

- Most states have laws that require third parties to secure a place on the ballot by gathering large numbers of signatures, whereas the Democratic and Republican Parties are often granted automatic access.

- Democrats and Republicans in the state legislatures may have little in common, but both want to make sure that the political pie is cut into only two sizeable pieces, not three or more smaller slices.

- The public funding of campaigns (financing from taxpayer dollars), where it exists, is much more generous for the two major parties. At the national level, for instance, third-party presidential candidates receive money only after the general election, if they have garnered more than 5 percent of the vote, and only in proportion to their total vote; the major-party candidates, by contrast, get large, full general-election grants immediately upon their summer nominations. (This funding difference does not affect wealthy politicians or those who are very successful fundraisers. Both John Kerry and George W. Bush rejected public funding for their primary races in 2004.)

- The news media give relatively little coverage to minor parties compared with that given to major-party nominees. The media's bias is legitimate—it only reflects political reality, and it would be absurd to expect them to offer equal time to all comers. Still, this is a vicious cycle for minor-party candidates: A lack of broad-based support produces slight coverage, which minimizes their chances of attracting more adherents. Of course, once a third-party candidate becomes prominent, the media flock to his appearances and clamor to schedule him on their news shows.

- Voters tend to flirt with independent candidates early in the election process, but they routinely return to the two-party fold by late fall.

proportional representation
A voting system that apportions legislative seats according to the percentage of the vote won by a particular political party.

- Independents and third-party candidates suffer from a "can't win" syndrome. Voters tell pollsters that they like the non-major-party candidate but ultimately decide not to cast their vote for him or her if they suspect the candidate cannot win. In other words, many voters are hesitant to "waste" their vote on a third-party candidate.

The passion for power and victory that drives both Democrats and Republicans overrides ideology and prevents rigidity. Unless a kind of rigor mortis takes hold in the future in one or both major parties—with, say, the capture of the party organization by unyielding extremists of right or left—it is difficult to imagine any third party becoming a major, permanent force in U.S. politics. The corollary of this axiom, though, is that the major parties must be eternally vigilant if they are to avoid ideologically inspired takeovers.

For the foreseeable future, however, third parties likely will continue to play useful supporting roles similar to those they have performed in the past. They can popularize ideas that might not receive a hearing otherwise. They can serve as vehicles of popular discontent with the major parties and thereby induce change in major-party behavior and platforms. They may presage and assist party realignments in the future as they have sometimes done in the past. In a few states, third parties will also continue to take a unique part in political life, as the Conservative and Liberal Parties of New York State do. But, in a two-party political system that includes institutionalized means of expressing dissent and registering political opposition (court challenges and interest group organizing, for example), third parties will probably continue to have a limited future in the United States.

SUMMARY

A POLITICAL PARTY is a group of office holders, candidates, activists, and voters who identify with a group label and seek to elect to public office individuals who run under that label. Parties encompass three separate components: (1) the governmental party comprises office holders and candidates who run under the party's banner; (2) the electoral party comprises the workers and activists who staff the party's formal organization; and, (3) the party in the electorate refers to the voters who consider themselves allied or associated with the party. In this chapter, we have made the following points:

1. What Is a Political Party?
A political party is a group of office holders, candidates, activists, and voters who identify with a group label and seek to elect to public office individuals who run under that label. The goal of American political parties is to win office. This objective is in keeping with the practical nature of Americans and the country's long-standing aversion to most ideologically driven, "purist" politics.

2. The Evolution of American Party Democracy
The evolution of U.S. political parties has been remarkably smooth, and the stability of the Democratic and Republican groupings, despite name changes, is a wonder, considering all the social and political tumult in U.S. history.

3. The Functions of the American Parties
For 150 years, the two-party system has served as the mechanism American society uses to organize and resolve social and political conflict. The Democratic and Republican Parties, through lengthy nominating processes, provide a screening mechanism for those who aspire to the presidency, helping to weed out unqualified individuals, expose and test candidates' ideas on important policy questions, and ensure a measure of long-term continuity and accountability.

4. The Basic Structure of American Political Parties
While the distinctions might not be as clear today as they were two or three decades ago, the basic structure of the major parties remains simple and pyramidal. The state and local parties are more important than the

national ones, though campaign technologies and fund-raising concentrated in Washington, D.C., are invigorating the national party committees.

5. The Party in Government

Political parties are not restricted to their role as grass-roots organizations of voters; they also have another major role *inside* government institutions. The party in government comprises the office holders and candidates who run under the party's banner.

6. The Modern Transformation of Party Organization

Political parties have moved from labor-intensive, person-to-person operations toward the use of modern technologies and communication strategies. Nevertheless, the capabilities of the party organizations vary widely from place to place.

7. The Party in the Electorate

The party in the electorate refers to the voters who consider themselves allied or associated with the party. This is the most significant element of the political party, providing the foundation for the organizational and governmental parties.

8. Third-Partyism

The U.S. party system is uniquely a two-party system. Although periods of third-partyism or independent activism (such as the 1992 Perot phenomenon) can arise, the greatest proportion of all federal, state, and local elections are contests between the Republican and Democratic Parties only.

KEY TERMS

civil service laws, p. 424
coalition, p. 427
direct primary, p. 424
governmental party, p. 419
issue-oriented politics, p. 425
machine, p. 423
national convention, p. 432
national party platform, p. 429
organizational party, p. 419
party identification, p 443
party in the electorate, p. 419
political party, p. 419
proportional representation, p. 454
think tank, p. 434
third-partyism, p. 450
ticket-split, p. 425

SELECTED READINGS

Abramowitz, Alan, and Jeffrey A. Segal. *Senate Elections*. Ann Arbor: University of Michigan Press, 1997.

Aldrich, John Herbert. *Why Parties? The Origin and Transformation of Political Parties in America*. Chicago: University of Chicago Press, 1995.

Beck, Paul Allen, and Marjorie Randon Hershey. *Party Politics in America*, 10th ed. New York: Pearson Longman, 2002.

Broder, David S. *The Party's Over*. New York: Harper and Row, 1971.

Ceaser, James W. *Reforming the Reformers: A Critical Analysis of the Presidential Selection Process*. Cambridge, MA: Ballinger, 1982.

Chambers, William Nisbet, and Walter Dean Burnham, eds. *The American Party Systems: Stages of Political Development*, 2nd ed. New York: Oxford University Press, 1975.

Cox, Gary, and Mathew McCubbins. *Legislative Leviathan: Party Government in the House*. Berkeley: University of California Press, 1994.

Epstein, Leon. *Political Parties in the American Mold*. Madison: University of Wisconsin Press, 1986.

Fiorina, Morris P. *Divided Government*. Boston: Allyn and Bacon, 1996.

Gierzynski, Anthony. *Legislative Party Campaign Committees in the American States*. Lexington: University Press of Kentucky, 1992.

Kayden, Xandra, and Eddie Mahe. *The Party Goes On*. New York: Basic Books, 1985.

Key, V. O., Jr. *Politics, Parties, and Pressure Groups*, 5th ed. New York: Crowell, 1964.

Klinkner, Philip A. *The Losing Parties: Out-Party National Committees, 1956–1993*. New Haven, CT: Yale University Press, 1994.

Maisel, L. Sandy, ed. *The Parties Respond*, 4th ed. Boulder, CO: Westview, 2002.

Mayhew, David R. *Placing Parties in American Politics*. Princeton, NJ: Princeton University Press, 1986.

Milkis, Sidney M. *The President and the Parties: The Transformation of the American Party System Since the New Deal*. New York: Oxford University Press, 1993.

Patterson, Kelly D. *Political Parties and the Maintenance of Liberal Democracy*. New York: Columbia University Press, 1996.

Polsby, Nelson W. *Consequences of Party Reform*, 2nd ed. New York: Oxford University Press, 1983.

Pomper, Gerald M. *Passions and Interests: Political Party Concepts of American Democracy*. Lawrence: University Press of Kansas, 1992.

Price, David E. *Bringing Back the Parties*. Washington, DC: CQ Press, 1984.

Ranney, Austin. *Curing the Mischiefs of Faction: Party Reform in America*. Berkeley: University of California Press, 1975.

Reichley, James. *The Life of the Parties: A History of American Political Parties*. Lanham, MD: Rowman and Littlefield, 2000.

Riordan, William L., ed. *Plunkitt of Tammany Hall*. New York: Dutton, 1963.

Rohde, David W. *Parties and Leaders in the Postreform House.* Chicago: University of Chicago Press, 1991.

Sabato, Larry J., and Bruce A. Larson. *The Party's Just Begun: Shaping Political Parties for America's Future,* 2nd ed. New York: Longman, 2002.

Schattschneider, E. E. *Party Government.* New York: Holt, Rinehart and Winston, 1942.

Shafer, Byron E. *Quiet Revolution: The Struggle for the Democratic Party and the Shaping of Post-Reform Politics.* New York: Russell Sage, 1983.

Shea, Daniel M. *Transforming Democracy: Legislative Campaign Committees and Political Parties.* Albany: SUNY Press, 1995.

Sifry, Micah L. *Spoiling for a Fight: Third-Party Politics in America.* New York: Routledge, 2002.

Sundquist, James L. *Dynamics of the Party System,* rev. ed. Washington, DC: Brookings Institution, 1983.

Wattenberg, Martin P. *The Decline of American Political Parties, 1952–1996.* Cambridge, MA: Harvard University Press, 1998.

WEB EXPLORATIONS

To evaluate how the "Big Two" political parties portray their platform issues and use political language to present their policies, go to
www.domocrats.org/ and www.rnc.org

To explore the partisan and ideological agendas of unaffiliated think tanks and search for connections to specific parties or politicians, go to
www.heritage.org/
www.cato.org/
www.brookings.org/

To learn about the informal factions and interest groups that strive for influence with the major parties, go to
www.adaction.org/
www.cc.org

To compare the planks of several minor parties and find one that represents your views, go to
www.reformparty.org/
www.greens.org/gpusa/
www.lp.org/
www.natural-law.org/

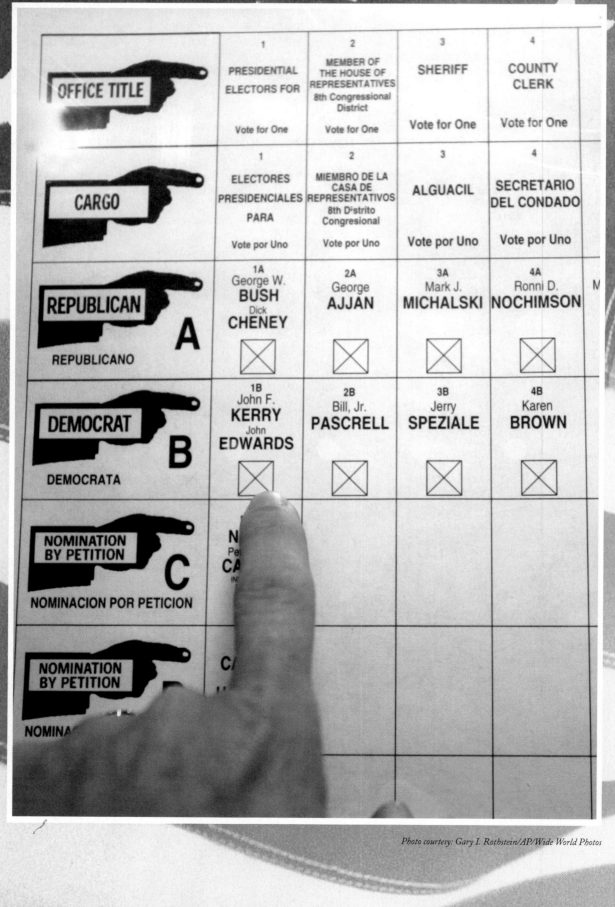

Photo courtesy: Gary I. Rothstein/AP/Wide World Photos

Voting and Elections

DURING THE MONTHS LEADING UP TO THE 2004 presidential election, no one doubted that the election between Republican President George W. Bush and the Democratic challenger, Massachusetts Senator John Kerry, would be close. The question everyone wanted answered was exactly how close it would be. Although the presidential election is national, both candidates focused on specific states that showed either narrow margins or even ties. Many of these so-called "battleground states" were located in the Rust Belt—Wisconsin, Michigan, Ohio, and Pennsylvania; however, others were spread across the country, such as Minnesota, Iowa, Florida, New Hampshire, New Mexico, and even Hawaii.

Of these several battleground states, three stood out as the most valuable because of their razor-thin margins of victory in 2000 and their large number of electoral votes. Pennsylvania, a state the 2000 Democratic Candidate Al Gore had won by 220,000 votes, had twenty-one electoral votes. Florida, with the minuscule and heavily contested 537 vote margin for Bush in 2000, had twenty-seven electoral votes up for grabs. Finally, there was Ohio with twenty electoral votes, a state no Republican candidate has lost and still been able to go on to win the presidency. By Election Day, it was conventional wisdom that a candidate had to win at least two of these three states in order to win the election. By early evening, it was clear that Bush would take Florida by a much wider margin than in 2000, and Kerry would narrowly win Pennsylvania. This left the election up to Ohio, which both candidates had visited more than twenty-five times in 2004. Throughout the night, Bush appeared to hold a 2 percent voter margin over Kerry, leading some networks—Fox News and NBC—to call the state for Bush, while others—such as ABC, CBS, and CNN—left it too close to call. However, fears that Ohio might become the 2004 version of Florida quickly abated when it became clear that Kerry could not rely on the provisional and absentee ballots to overtake Bush's voter lead. By the morning after Election Day, Bush took Ohio.

Bush also won the battleground states of New Mexico and Iowa (states Gore carried in 2000), but he lost New Hampshire to Kerry. The remaining battleground states also went to Kerry, but they did not collectively have enough Electoral College votes for him to win. When looking at how the 2004 Electoral College map changed from the 2000 map, one can see that the division of coastal "blue" (Democratic) states and "red" (Republican) states became even more contiguous. Like the Pacific states (except Alaska), New England is now completely Democratic in terms of Electoral College votes, while the South from Florida to Arizona is solidly Republican. Because of these geographical differences, many students of politics raise questions about whether blue-state and red-state Americans see America the same way, or if America is actually two nations fighting a culture war within the midwest battlegrounds, a question the 2008 presidential elections may help to answer.

EVERY FOUR YEARS, on the Tuesday following the first Monday in November, a plurality of voters, simply by casting ballots peacefully across a continent-sized nation, reelects or replaces politicians at all levels of government—from the president of the United States, to members of the U.S. Congress, to state legislators. A number of other countries do not have the luxury of a peaceful transition of political power. We tend to take this process for granted, but in truth it is a marvel. American political institutions have succeeded in maintaining peaceful elections, even when they are as closely contested as the high-stakes 2000 presidential election. Fortunately, most Americans, though not enough, understand why and how elections serve their interests. Elections take the pulse of average people and gauge their hopes and fears; the study of elections permits us to trace the course of the American Revolution over 200 years of voting.

Today, the United States of America is a democratic paradise in many respects, because it probably conducts more elections for more offices more frequently than any other nation on earth. Moreover, in recent times, the U.S. electorate (those citizens eligible to vote) has been the most inclusive in the country's history; no longer can one's race or sex or creed prevent participation at the ballot box. But, challenges still remain. After all the blood spilled and energy expended to expand the suffrage (as the right to vote is called), little more than half the potentially eligible voters bother to go to the polls.

This chapter focuses on the purposes served by elections, the various kinds of elections held in the United States, and patterns of voting over time. We concentrate in particular on presidential and congressional contests, both of which have rich histories that tell us a great deal about the American people and their changing hopes and needs. We conclude by returning to contemporary presidential elections and addressing some topics of electoral reform.

- First, we will examine *the purposes of elections*, pointing out that they confer a legitimacy on regimes better than any other method of change.
- Second, we will analyze different *kinds of elections*, including the many different types of elections held at the presidential and congressional levels.
- Third, we will take a closer look at the elements of *presidential elections*, including primaries, conventions, and delegates.
- Fourth, we will explore how *congressional elections*, although they share similarities with presidential elections, are really quite different.
- Fifth, we will discuss *voting behavior*, focusing on distinct patterns in voter turnout and vote choice.
- Finally, we will present arguments for *reforming the electoral process* for the most powerful official in the world, the president of the United States.

THE PURPOSES OF ELECTIONS

BOTH THE BALLOT and the bullet are methods of governmental change around the world, and surely the former is preferable to the latter. Although the United States has not escaped the bullet's awful effects, the election process is responsible for most leadership change in this country. Regular free elections guarantee mass political action and enable citizens to influence the actions of their government. Election campaigns may often seem unruly, unending, harsh, and even vicious, but imagine the stark alternatives: violence and social disruption. Societies that cannot vote their leaders out of office are left with little choice other than to force them out by means of strikes, riots, or coups d'état.

Popular election confers on a government the legitimacy that it can achieve no other way. Even many authoritarian systems around the globe, including Singapore, Syria, and China, recognize this. From time to time, they hold "referenda" to endorse their regimes or one-party elections, even though these so-called elections offer no real choice that would ratify their rule. The symbolism of elections as mechanisms to legitimize change, then, is important, but so is their practical value. After all, elections are the means to fill public offices and staff the government. The voters' choice of candidates and parties helps to organize government as well. Because candidates advocate certain policies, elections also involve a choice of platforms and point the society in certain directions on a wide range of issues, from abortion to civil rights to national defense to the environment.

Regular elections also ensure that government is accountable to the people it serves. At fixed intervals the **electorate,** citizens eligible to vote, is called on to judge those in power. If the judgment is favorable, and the incumbents are reelected, the office holders may continue their policies with renewed resolve. Should the incumbents be defeated and their challengers elected, however, a change in policies will likely result. Either way, the winners will claim a **mandate** (literally, a command) from the people to carry out their platform.

Sometimes the claim of a mandate is suspect because voters are not so much endorsing one candidate and his or her beliefs as rejecting his or her opponent. Frequently, this occurs because the electorate is exercising retrospective judgment; that is, voters are rendering judgment on the performance of the party in power. This judgment makes sense because voters can evaluate the record of office holders much better than they can predict the future actions of the out-of-power challengers.

At other times, voters might use **prospective judgment;** that is, they vote based on what a candidate pledges to do about an issue if elected. This forward-looking approach to choosing candidates voters believe will best serve their interests requires that the electorate examine the views that the rival candidates have on the issues of the day and then cast a ballot for the person they believe will best handle these matters. Unfortunately, prospective voting requires lots of information about issues and candidates. Voters who cast a vote prospectively must seek out information and learn about issues and how each candidate stands on them. Three requirements exist in order for voters to engage in prospective voting: (1) voters must have an opinion on an issue; (2) voters must have an idea of what action, if any, the government is taking on the issue; and, (3) voters must see a difference between the two parties on the issue.[1] Only a small minority of voters could meet these requirements, although scholars studying more recent elections have found voters better equipped to engage in prospective voting than they had thought.[2] Consider for a moment how voters retrospectively and prospectively judged recent presidential administrations in reaching their ballot decisions:

- *1980:* Burdened by difficult economic times and the Iranian hostage crisis (one year before Election Day, Iranian militants had seized fifty-three Americans, whom they held until January 20, 1981, Inauguration Day), Carter became a one-term president as the electorate rejected the Democrat's perceived weak leadership. Many voters did not view Ronald Reagan, at age sixty-nine, as the ideal replacement, nor

electorate
Citizens eligible to vote.

mandate
A command, indicated by an electorate's votes, for the elected officials to carry out their platforms.

retrospective judgment
A voter's evaluation of the performance of the party in power.

prospective judgment
A voter's evaluation of a candidate based on what he or she pledges to do about an issue if elected.

did a majority agree with some of his conservative principles. But, the retrospective judgment on Carter was so harsh, and the prospective outlook of four more years under his stewardship so glum, that an imperfect alternative was considered preferable to another term of the Democrat.

- *1984:* A strong economic recovery from a midterm recession and an image of strength derived from a defense buildup and a successful military venture in Grenada combined to produce a satisfied electorate whose retrospective judgment granted Ronald Reagan four more years. A forty-nine-state landslide reelected Reagan over Jimmy Carter's vice president, Walter Mondale.

- *1988:* Continued satisfaction with Reagan, a product of strong economic expansion and superpower summitry, produced an electoral endorsement of Reagan's vice president, George Bush. Bush was seen as Reagan's understudy and natural successor; the Democratic nominee, Michael Dukakis, offered too few convincing reasons to alter the voters' retrospective judgment.

- *1992:* A prolonged recession, weak job growth, and Ross Perot's candidacy—which split the Republican base—denied a second term to George Bush, despite many significant foreign policy triumphs. In the end, voters decided to vote retrospectively and gamble on little-known Arkansas Governor Bill Clinton.

- *1996:* Similar to 1984, only with the party labels reversed, a healthy economy prompted Americans to retrospectively support President Bill Clinton in his quest for reelection over Bob Dole. Voters also looked prospectively at the two candidates and again registered their support for President Clinton and his vision for the country's future.

- *2000:* Eight years of peace and record economic prosperity should have worked in favor of Vice President Al Gore. While he received more votes than any Democratic candidate in U.S. history, Gore's Clinton-era baggage and credibility questions helped to nullify any advantage over Texas Governor George W. Bush, an opponent with an undistinguished record but no significant liabilities. Given the unusual circumstances of the actual election, it is difficult to say more precisely to what extent the outcome represents a retrospective or prospective political opinion.

- *2004:* Ordinarily, incumbent reelections become a referendum on the incumbent's performance, making Americans likely to think retrospectively. For issues like the economy—which was in a slow recovery—and the post 9/11 war on terror, this was largely the case. However, the ongoing war in Iraq also led voters to consider how their choice of president would affect the next four years of American Military Policy. Finally, President Bush, the incumbent, encouraged retrospective opinion on his opponent, John Kerry, claiming his Senate voting record showed tax increases that hindered economic progress.

Whether we agree or disagree with these election results, there is a rough justice at work. When parties and presidents please the electorate, they are rewarded; when they preside over hard times, they are punished. Presidents usually are not responsible for all the good or bad developments that occur on their watch, but the voters nonetheless hold them accountable, not an unreasonable way for citizens to behave in a democracy.

On rare occasions, off-year congressional elections can produce mandates. In 1994, backlash against Clinton's decision to push liberal policies like national health care and a large government stimulus package helped Representative Newt Gingrich (R–GA) lead Republicans to gain control of the House of Representatives and claim a mandate for limiting government. Voters in 2002 expressed their strongly positive feelings toward President George W. Bush's performance as president by electing enough senators for Republicans to reclaim both houses of Congress, giving Bush the go-ahead to propose his program, and bucking the trend for voters to elect more candidates from the opposing party in federal off-year elections.

Photo courtesy: Kirk Condyles

■ Controversy over vote counting in the 2000 presidential election brought people to West Palm Beach, Florida, to protest on behalf of Al Gore and George W. Bush.

KINDS OF ELECTIONS

SO FAR, WE HAVE REFERRED mainly to presidential elections, but in the U.S. system, elections come in many varieties: primary elections, general elections, initiatives, referenda, and recalls.

Primary Elections

In **primary elections,** voters decide which of the candidates within a party will represent the party's ticket in the general elections. There are different kinds of primaries. For example, **closed primaries** allow only a party's registered voters to cast a ballot, and **open primaries** allow independents and sometimes members of the other party to participate. (Figure 13.1 shows the states with open and closed primaries for presidential delegate selection.) Closed primaries are considered healthier for the party system because they prevent members of one party from influencing the primaries of the opposition party. On the one hand, studies of open primaries indicate that **crossover voting**—participation in the primary of a party with which the voter is not affiliated—occurs frequently.[3] On the other hand, the research shows little evidence of much **raiding**—an *organized* attempt by voters of one party to influence the primary results of the other party.[4]

When none of the candidates in the initial primary secures a majority of the votes, most states have a **runoff primary,** a contest between the two candidates with the greatest number of votes. One final type of primary, used in Nebraska and Louisiana (in statewide, nonpresidential primaries), and in hundreds of cities large and small across America, is the **nonpartisan primary,** which is used to select candidates without regard to party affiliation. A nonpartisan primary could produce two final candidates of the same party from a slate of several candidates from many parties.

primary election
Election in which voters decide which of the candidates within a party will represent the party in the general election.

closed primary
A primary election in which only a party's registered voters are eligible to vote.

open primary
A primary in which party members, independents, and sometimes members of the other party are allowed to vote.

crossover voting
Participation in the primary of a party with which the voter is not affiliated.

raiding
An organized attempt by voters of one party to influence the primary results of the other party.

runoff primary
A second primary election between the two candidates receiving the greatest number of votes in the first primary.

nonpartisan primary
A primary used to select candidates regardless of party affiliation.

FIGURE 13.1 Methods of Selecting Democratic Party Presidential Delegates. ■

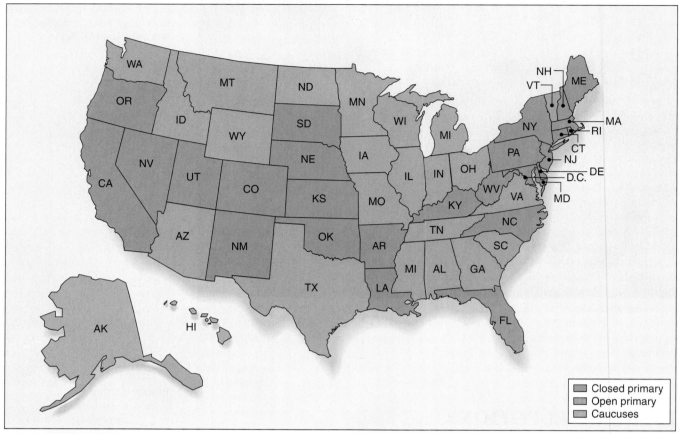

Note: Methods of selection current as of January 2004, and reflect the Democratic Presidential nomination process in each state, as there was no significant competition for the Republican nomination.

General Elections

general election
Election in which voters decide which candidates will actually fill elective public offices.

Once party members vote for their party candidates for various offices, each state holds its general election. In the **general election,** voters decide which candidates will actually fill the nation's elective public offices. These elections are held at many levels, including municipal, county, state, and national. Whereas primaries are contests between the candidates within each party, general elections are contests between the candidates of opposing parties.

In sizing up presidential candidates, voters look for leadership and character, and they base their judgments partly on foreign policy and defense issues that do not arise in state and local elections. Leadership qualities are vital for gubernatorial and mayoral candidates, as are the nuts-and-bolts issues (such as taxes, schools, and roads) that dominate the concerns of state and local governments. Citizens often choose their congressional representatives very differently from the way they select presidents. Knowing much less about the candidates, people will sometimes base a vote on simple name identification, visibility, or party identification. This way of deciding one's vote obviously helps incumbents and therefore to some degree explains the high reelection rates of incumbent U.S. representatives. Since World War II, 92 percent of all U.S. House members seeking another term have won; in several recent election years, the proportion has been above 95 percent. In 2004, fully 98 percent of the lawmakers who sought reelection won. However, greater name recognition is probably not the most important factor driving the incumbency advantage. More important is that incumbents are typically able to cultivate more favorable public images than are challengers.[5]

Initiative, Referendum, and Recall

Three other types of elections are the initiative, the referendum, and the recall. Used in twenty-four states and the District of Columbia, initiatives involve voting on issues (as opposed to voting for candidates). An **initiative** is a process that allows citizens to propose legislation and submit it to the state electorate for popular vote, as long as they get a certain number of signatures on petitions supporting the proposal. Ballot initiatives have been the subject of growing controversy in the past decades. Critics charge that the initiative—which was intended to give citizens more direct control over policy making—is now unduly influenced by interest groups and "the initiative industry"—"law firms that draft legislation, petition management firms that guarantee ballot access, direct-mail firms, and campaign consultants who specialize in initiative contests."[6] Colorado's Amendment 36, one of the more publicized and controversial initiatives, failed to receive a majority of votes in 2004. This proposed amendment to the state constitution would have changed Colorado's election law so that the state's nine electoral votes would be awarded proportionally, according to the popular vote.

A **referendum** is an election whereby the state legislature submits proposed legislation to the state's voters for approval. Although both the referendum and the initiative provide for more direct democracy, they are not problem free. In the 1990 elections, for instance, California had so many referenda and initiatives on its ballot that the state printed a lengthy two-volume guide to explain them all to voters. In addition, the wording of the question can have an enormous impact on the outcome. In some cases, a "yes" vote will bring about a policy change; in other cases, a "no" vote will cause a change.[7]

There are additional problems with initiatives and referenda. Among other things, referenda are imperfect representations of the public will because only a small, self-selected portion of the voting public chooses to participate in the referenda voting process. Those who decide to study and form an opinion on the numerous questions are generally of higher socio-economic class, and therefore the votes of the lower classes are underrepresented. Also, the expense of first getting thousands of signatures to place a question on the ballot, and then waging a political campaign for it, dissuades private citizens from taking part. Thus, referenda are not the voice of the people, but rather the voice of well-funded special interest groups who can afford the cost and time commitment of a major campaign.[8]

The third type of election (or "deelection") found in many states is the recall, in which voters can remove an incumbent from office by popular vote. Recall elections are very rare, and sometimes they are thwarted by the official's resignation or impeachment prior to the vote. In 2003, under intense national media attention, Californians recalled Governor Grey Davis (a Democrat) and replaced him with action star (and Republican) Arnold Schwarzenegger. Davis, who had won reelection against a weak Republican candidate, Bill Simon, faced intense criticism for his handling of the state's slumping economy and looming energy crisis. Preceding the recall election were sideshows, such as TV star Gary Coleman declaring his candidacy and columnist Arianna Huffington attacking Schwarzenegger during a debate for his alleged mistreatment of women. Immediately following the recall, commentators feared that voters in California had set a precedent for the people of a state to recall governors whenever things are not going well. Their fears appeared to be justified when Nevada resident Tony Dane tried to petition the recall of Nevada Governor Kenny Guinn, a Republican. However, after Dane submitted his petition with only three verified signatures, it appeared that there would be no wave of governor recalls.

initiative
An election that allows citizens to propose legislation and submit it to the state electorate for popular vote.

referendum
An election whereby the state legislature submits proposed legislation to the state's voters for approval.

Timeline
The Initiative and Referendum

NATIONAL ELECTIONS 2004

In 2004 Americans voted in two national elections. Both were held the same day, November 2. One election was for president. In the other, voters elected members to Congress. These were only two of one hundred national elections scheduled to take place in 2004 around the world. This number is up only slightly from previous years.

There were ninety-seven national elections held in 2003 and ninety-three in 2002. A look at where these elections were held shows that they were fairly evenly distributed around the world. The U.S. held two of fourteen elections held in the Americas. The largest number of elections was held in Europe (including Russia and the other countries that became independent when the Soviet Union collapsed), and the fewest elections were held in the Middle East. By far the two most frequent purposes of elections were to elect parliaments (forty-one) and presidents (thirty-eight). There were also eight national referenda, something that does not happen in the United States.

Referenda generally address three different issues. One is constitutional reform, such as amending an election system. A second set of issues deals with allowing provinces to have more autonomy or joining a federation or international organization such as the European Union. The third set of issues involves moral questions such as permitting divorce or legalizing abortion.

These one hundred elections were not held in one hundred different countries. In some countries, no national elections were held; in others, citizens went to the polls for more than one. In the 2002–2004 time period, Americans voted in three national elections. They were the presidential and congressional elections in 2004 and the 2002 congressional election. Voters in Portugal, Venezuela, and Egypt did not vote in national elections. Voters in Cuba (legislative election, 2003) and Iraq (referendum, 2002) went to the polls in national elections once.

Voters in France went to the polls the most often in any single year. They voted four times in 2002. This is because of the way in which their national elections are set up. In both presidential and National Assembly elections, a candidate must get an absolute majority (over 50 percent) in order to be declared the winner. Failing that, a second election is held in which the candidate with the most votes wins. The presidential run-off election is between the two leading vote-getters in the first round. For the National Assembly run-off

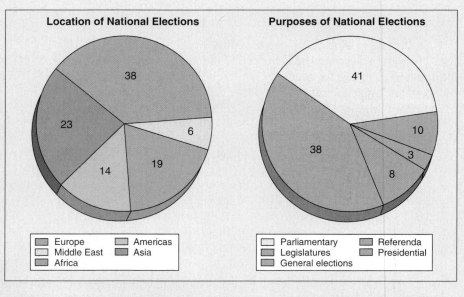

election, only those candidates who got more than 12.5 percent of the vote in the first round may compete. Voters in Serbia, a country that emerged out of the break-up of Yugoslavia, went to the polls most frequently between 2002–2004. They voted in the following:

- First-round presidential election in September 2002.
- Second-round presidential election in October 2002.
- Presidential rerun election in December 2002.
- First-round presidential election in early November 2003.
- Second-round presidential election in late November 2003.
- Parliamentary elections in December 2003.
- Presidential election in June 2004.

What is not clear is whether these frequent elections signal that democracy is strong in Serbia or if they are a sign that not all is well and that democracy is in danger because political institutions are weak. Concerns have been raised as well about the use of referenda. Are they ways for the public to express its voice, or do referenda short circuit the process of government by taking power away from elected representatives?

Questions

1. How often should elections be held? Can they be held too frequently?
2. Should the United States make use of national referenda?

Source: http://www.ifes.org/eguide.

PRESIDENTIAL ELECTIONS

VARIETY ASIDE, no U.S. election can compare to the presidential contest. This spectacle, held every four years, brings together all the elements of politics and attracts the most ambitious and energetic politicians to the national stage. Voters in a series of state primary elections and caucuses select delegates who will attend each party's national convention. After the primary elections (or caucuses) held in the winter and spring and the national convention for each party held in mid and late summer, there is a final set of fifty separate state elections all held on the Tuesday after the first Monday in November to select the president. This lengthy process exhausts candidates and voters alike, but it allows the diversity of the United States to be displayed in ways a shorter, more homogeneous presidential election process could not.

The state party organizations use several types of primary elections or caucuses to elect national convention delegates:

1. *Winner-take-all primary:* Under this system the candidate who wins the most votes in a state secures all of that state's delegates. The Democrats moved away from this mode of delegate selection in 1976 and no longer permit its use because of the arguable unfairness. Republicans generally prefer the way in which this primary enables a GOP candidate to amass a majority of delegates more quickly, especially since California alone has over one-fifth of the delegates needed to nominate.

2. *Proportional representation primary:* Under this system, candidates who secure a threshold percentage of votes are awarded delegates in proportion to the number of popular votes won. Democrats now strongly favor this system and use it in many states' Democratic primaries, where they award delegates to anyone who wins more than 15 percent in any congressional district. Although proportional representation is probably the fairest way of allocating delegates to candidates, its downfall is that it renders majorities of delegates more difficult to accumulate and thus can lengthen the contest for the presidential nomination.

3. *Proportional representation with bonus delegates primary; beauty contest with separate delegate selection; delegate selection with no beauty contest:* Used rarely, the first of these, proportional representation with bonus delegates, awards delegates to candidates in proportion to the popular vote won and then gives one bonus delegate to the winner of each district. The second, a "beauty contest" primary with separate delegate selection, serves as an indication of popular sentiment for the conventions to consider as they choose the actual delegates. Democrats bind delegates to the decision of the party members during the primary, while adding "superdelegates" who do not have that commitment. Republicans do not bind delegates to select the candidate the party members chose during the primary; thus, delegates can vote against the will of the state party. Under the third system, delegate selection with no beauty contest, the primary election chooses delegates to the national conventions who are not linked on the ballot to specific presidential contenders.

4. *Caucus:* Under this system, party members meet in small groups throughout a state to select the party's delegates to the national convention.

Primaries Versus Caucuses

The mix of preconvention contests has changed over the years, with the most pronounced trend being the shift from caucuses to primaries. Only seventeen states held presidential primaries in 1968; the number increased to thirty-eight in 1992, forty-two in 1996, forty-three in 2000, and thirty-six in 2004. Figure 13.1 shows which states use primaries (open and closed) and which use caucuses to select presidential delegates.

The caucus is the oldest, most party-oriented method of choosing delegates to the national conventions. Traditionally, the caucus was a closed meeting of party activists in each state who selected the party's choice for presidential candidate. In the late-nineteenth and early twentieth centuries, however, many people viewed these caucuses as elitist and anti-democratic, and reformers succeeded in replacing them with direct primaries in most states. Although there are still presidential nominating caucuses today (in Iowa, for example), they are now more open and attract a wider range of the party's membership. Indeed, new participatory caucuses more closely resemble primary elections than they do the old, exclusive party caucuses.[9]

Some people support the increase in the number of primaries because they believe that this type of election is more democratic. The primaries are open not only to party activists, but also to anyone, wealthy or poor, urban or rural, northern or southern, who wants to vote. Theoretically, then, representatives of all these groups have a chance of winning the presidency. Related to this idea, advocates argue that presidential primaries are the most representative means by which to nominate presidential candidates. They are a barometer of a candidate's popularity with the party rank and file. While conventional wisdom holds that both primaries and caucuses attract more extreme voters in each party, recent research posits that primaries help nominate more moderate and appealing candidates—those that primary voters believe can win in the general election. One scholar, for instance, describes "sophisticated voting," where primary voters vote for their second or third choice because they believe the candidate will more easily win in November than will their first choice—perhaps because of less extreme policy positions.[10] Finally, the proponents of presidential primaries claim that they constitute a rigorous test for the candidates, a chance to display under pressure some of the skills needed to be a successful president.

Critics of presidential primaries argue that although primaries may attract more participants than do caucuses, this quantity does not substitute for the quality of information held by caucus participants. Compared with the unenlightening minutes spent at the primary polls, caucus attendees spend several hours learning about politics and the party. Caucus attendees do not make their decision about which candidate to select by campaign advertisements or popularity among the media elite. Instead, they listen to speeches by candidates or their representatives and take advice from party leaders and elected officials, then cast a well-informed vote more valuable than any single vote during a primary.

Critics also argue that the unfair scheduling of primaries affects their outcomes. For example, the earliest primary takes place in the small, atypical state of New Hampshire, which is heavily white and conservative, and it receives much more media coverage than it warrants simply because it is first. Such excessive coverage undoubtedly skews voter opinions in more populous states that hold their primaries later. Additionally, critics believe that the qualities tested by the primary system are by no means a complete list of those a president needs to be successful. For instance, skill at playing the media game is by itself no guarantee of an effective presidency. Similarly, the exhausting schedule of the primaries may be a better test of a candidate's stamina than of his or her brain power.

The primary proponents have obviously had the better of the arguments so far, though the debate continues, as do efforts to experiment with the schedule of primaries. From time to time, proposals are made for **regional primaries.** Under this system, the nation would be divided into five or six geographic regions (such as the South or the Midwest). All the states in each region would hold their primary elections on the same day, with perhaps one regional election day per month from February through June of presidential election years. This change would certainly cut down on candidate wear and tear. Moreover, candidates would be inspired to focus more on regional issues. On the other hand, regional primaries would continue to favor wealthy candidates who can afford to advertise on television throughout the large regions, and the system might needlessly amplify the differences and create divisive rifts among the nation's regions.

regional primary
A proposed system in which the country would be divided into five or six geographic areas and all states in each region would hold their presidential primary elections on the same day.

Occasionally, parties adopt a regional plan (although sometimes coming into conflict with states). In 1988, for instance, fourteen southern and border South states joined together to hold simultaneous primaries on "Super Tuesday" (March 8) in order to maximize the South's impact on presidential politics. This was an attempt by conservative Democrats to influence the choice of the party nominee. Their effort failed, however, since the two biggest winners of Super Tuesday were liberals Jesse Jackson (who won six southern states) and Michael Dukakis, who carried the megastates of Texas and Florida. This outcome occurred because, in general, the kinds of citizens who voted in Democratic primaries in the South then were not greatly different from those who cast ballots in northern Democratic primaries—most tended to be liberal. This trend was repeated in the 1996 "Yankee Primary," when five of the six New England states (Massachusetts, Connecticut, Rhode Island, Vermont, and Maine) held their contests on March 5, followed by New York on March 7, and a scaled-down Super Tuesday on March 12.

Photo courtesy: © Kevin Lamarque/Reuters/Corbis

■ Senator John Kerry (D–MA) and former Governor Howard Dean of Vermont shake hands at a joint rally. Governor Dean, the early frontrunner in the 2004 Democratic primaries, later on supported Kerry, who eventually won the nomination.

front-loading
The tendency of states to choose an early date on the primary calendar.

The primary schedule has also been altered by a process called **front-loading,** the tendency of states to choose an early date on the primary calendar. Seventy percent of all the delegates to both party conventions are now chosen before the end of March. This trend is hardly surprising, given the added press emphasis on the first contests and the voters' desire to cast their ballots before the competition is decided. The focus on early contests (such as the Iowa caucus and the New Hampshire primary), coupled with front-loading, can result in a party's selecting a nominee too quickly, before press scrutiny and voter reflection separate the wheat from the chaff. Front-loading has also had other important effects on the nomination process. First, a front-loaded primary schedule generally benefits the front-runner, since opponents have little time to turn the contest around once they fall behind. Second, front-loading gives an advantage to the candidate who can raise the bulk of the money *before* the nomination season begins, since there will be little opportunity to raise money once the primaries begin and since candidates will need to finance campaign efforts simultaneously in many states. In 2004, Internet fund-raising emerged as a means to soften this advantage; its use will continue and expand in future elections. Finally, front-loading has amplified the importance of the "invisible primary"—the year or so prior to the start of the official nomination season when candidates begin raising money and unofficially campaigning.[11]

The Party Conventions

The seemingly endless nomination battle does have a conclusion: the national party convention held in the summer of presidential election years. The out-of-power party traditionally holds its convention first, in late July, followed in mid-August by the party holding the White House. Preempting an hour or more of prime-time network television for four nights and monopolizing the cable networks such as CNN, Fox News, and C-SPAN, these remarkable conclaves are difficult for the public to ignore, giving the civically engaged viewer a chance to learn about the candidate and the apathetic viewer something to complain about.

Yet, the conventions once were much more: they were composed of party members who made actual decisions, where party leaders held sway and deals were sometimes cut in "smoke-filled rooms" to deliver nominations to little-known contenders called "dark horses." This era predated the modern emphasis on reform, primaries, and proportional representation, all of which have combined to make conventions the place where parties choose one of several nominees who has been preselected through the various primaries and caucuses.[12]

The Anti-Masonic Party held the first national convention in 1831. In 1832, the first Democratic National Convention ratified Andrew Jackson's nomination for reelection. Just four years later, in 1836, Martin Van Buren became the first nonincumbent candidate nominated by a major party convention (the Democrats) to win the presidency.

From the 1830s to the mid-twentieth century, the national conventions remained primarily under the control of the important state and local party leaders, the so-called bosses or kingmakers, who would bargain within a splintered, decentralized party. During these years, state delegations to the convention consisted mostly of *uncommitted delegates* (that is, delegates who had not pledged to support any particular candidate). These delegates were selected by party leaders, a process that enabled the leaders to broker agreements with prominent national candidates. Under this system, a state party leader could exchange delegation support for valuable political plums—for instance, a Cabinet position or even the vice presidency—for an important state political figure.

Today, the convention is fundamentally different from what it was in the past. First, its importance as a party conclave, at which compromises on party leadership and policies can be worked out, has diminished. Second, although the convention still formally selects the presidential ticket, most nominations are settled well in advance. Third, three preconvention factors have lessened the role of the current parties and conventions: delegate selection, national candidates and issues, and the news media.

Delegate Selection.   The selection of delegates to the conventions is no longer the function of party leaders but of primary elections and grassroots caucuses. Moreover, recent reforms, especially by the Democratic Party, have generally weakened any remaining control by local party leaders over delegates. A prime example of such reform is the Democrats' abolition of the **unit rule,** a traditional party practice under which the majority of a state delegation (say, twenty-six of fifty delegates) could force the minority to vote for its candidate. Another new Democratic Party rule decrees that a state's delegates be chosen in proportion to the votes cast in its primary or caucus (so that, for example, a candidate who receives 30 percent of the vote gains about 30 percent of the convention delegates). This change has had the effect of requiring delegates to indicate their presidential preference at each stage of the selection process. Consequently, the majority of state delegates now come to the convention already committed to a candidate. Again, this diminishes the discretionary role of the convention and the party leaders' capacity to bargain.

In sum, the many complex changes in the rules of delegate selection have contributed to the loss of decision-making powers by the convention. Even though the Democratic Party initiated many of these changes, the Republicans were carried along as many Democratic-controlled state legislatures enacted the reforms as state laws. There have been new rules to counteract some of these changes, however. For instance, since 1984, the number of delegate slots reserved for elected Democratic Party officials—called **superdelegates**—has been increased in the hope of adding stability to the Democratic convention. Before 1972, most delegates to a Democratic National Convention were not bound by primary results to support a particular candidate for president. This freedom to maneuver meant that conventions could be exciting and somewhat unpredictable gatherings, where last-minute events and deals could sway wavering delegates. Superdelegates are supposed to be party professionals concerned with winning the general election contest, not simply amateur ideologues concerned mainly with satisfying their policy appetites. All Democratic governors and 80 percent of the congressional Democrats, among others, are now included as voting delegates at the convention.

unit rule
A traditional party practice under which the majority of a state delegation can force the minority to vote for its candidate.

superdelegate
Delegate slot to the Democratic Party's national convention that is reserved for an elected party official.

Photo courtesy: Matt York/AP/Wide World Photos
■ Democratic presidential candidates are introduced to the audience prior to their October, 2003 debate in Phoenix, Arizona.

Photo courtesy: M. Spencer Green/AP/Wide World Photos
■ President George W. Bush and Vice President Dick Cheney. In 2004, Bush faced no national opposition for the Republican Party presidential nomination.

Two studies of the role of superdelegates in the Democratic Party offer differing conclusions about the usefulness of those party insiders in the nomination process. One scholar posits that if the superdelegate rule had been relaxed in 1984, as it was in 1992, Walter Mondale, the candidate for nomination overwhelmingly favored by party insiders, may not have won.[13] Using data on the views of both regular and superdelegates to the 1988 Democratic convention, another scholar argues that regular delegates and superdelegates are more similar to each other than previously believed.[14]

National Candidates and Issues. The political perceptions and loyalties of voters are now influenced largely by national candidates and issues, a factor that has undoubtedly served to diminish the power of state and local party leaders at the convention. The national candidates have usurped the autonomy of state party leaders with their preconvention ability to garner delegate support. Issues, increasingly national in scope, are significantly more important to the new, issue-oriented party activists than to the party professionals, who, prior to the late 1960s, had a monopoly on the management of party affairs.

The News Media. The media have helped transform the national conventions into political extravaganzas for the television audience's consumption. They have also helped to preempt the convention, by keeping count of the delegates committed to the candidates; as a result, well before the convention, the delegates and even the candidates have much more information about nomination politics than they did in the past. From the strategies of candidates to the commitments of individual delegates, the media cover it all. Even the bargaining within key party committees, formerly done in secret, is now subject to some public scrutiny, thanks to open meetings.

Television coverage has shaped the business of the convention. Desirous of presenting a unified image to kick off a strong general election campaign, the parties assign important roles to attractive speakers, and most crucial party affairs are saved for prime-time viewing hours. During the 1990s, the networks gradually began to reduce their convention coverage, citing low viewer ratings.

In 2004, the major networks changed their coverage slightly, providing no prime-time coverage on some days, and extending coverage to as much as three hours on the final day of each convention. While this likely reflects a change in the political culture away from meaningful convention activity overall, the increased final-night coverage indicates a greater interest in the candidates themselves. Fortunately, C-SPAN still gives gavel-to-gavel coverage.

Extensive media coverage of the convention has its pros and cons. On the one hand, such exposure helps the party launch its presidential campaign with fanfare, usually providing a boost to the party's candidate. President George Bush went from a 17-point deficit to a slim lead following the 1988 Republican convention. On the other hand, it can expose rifts within a party, as happened in 1968 at the Democratic convention in Chicago. Dissension was obvious when "hawks," supporting the Vietnam War and President Lyndon B. Johnson, clashed with the anti-war "doves" both on the convention floor and in street demonstrations outside the convention hall. Whatever the case, it is obvious that saturation media coverage of preelection events has led to the public's loss of anticipation and exhilaration about convention events.

Some reformers have spoken of replacing the conventions with national direct primaries, but it is unlikely that the parties would agree to this. Although its role in nominating the presidential ticket has often been reduced to formality, the convention is still valuable. After all, it is the only real arena where the national political parties can command a nearly universal audience while they celebrate past achievements and project their hopes for the future.

Who Are the Delegates?   In one sense, party conventions are microcosms of the United States: every state, most localities, and all races and creeds find some representation there. (For some historic "firsts" for women at the conventions, see Table 13.1.) Yet, delegates are an unusual and unrepresentative collection of people in many ways. It is not just their exceptionally keen interest in politics that distinguishes delegates. These activists also are ideologically more to the right or left and financially better off than most Americans.

In 2004, for example, both parties drew their delegates from an elite group that had income and educational levels far above the average American's; however, the parties also showed their differences. Nearly 40 percent of delegates at the Democratic convention were minorities, and half were also women. Only 17 percent of the delegates to the Republican convention were minorities; however, this actually marks the GOP's concerted effort to increase minority representation at its convention, since only 9 percent of the 2000 delegates were minorities.

The contrast in the two parties' delegations is no accident; it reflects not only the differences in the party constituencies, but also conscious decisions made by party leaders. After

---

TABLE 13.1 Historic Moments for Women at the Conventions

Since 1980, Democratic Party rules have required that women constitute 50 percent of the delegates to its national convention. The Republican Party has no similar quota. Nevertheless, both parties have tried to increase the role of women at the convention. Some "firsts" and other historic moments for women at the national conventions include:

1876	First woman to address a national convention
1890	First women delegates to conventions of both parties
1940	First woman to nominate a presidential candidate
1951	First woman asked to chair a national party
1972	First woman keynote speaker
1984	First major-party woman nominated for vice president (Democrat Geraldine Ferraro)
1996	Wives of both nominees make major addresses
2000	Daughter of a presidential candidate nominates her father
2004	Both candidates introduced by their daughters

Source: Center for American Women in Politics. Updated by authors.

the tumultuous 1968 Democratic National Convention (which, as noted above, was torn by dissent over the Vietnam War), Democrats formed a commission to examine the condition of the party and to propose changes in its structure. As a direct consequence of the commission's work, the 1972 Democratic convention was the most broadly representative ever of women, African Americans, and young people, because the party required these groups to be included in state delegations in rough proportion to their numbers in the population of each state. (State delegations failing this test were not seated.) This new mandate was very controversial, and it has since been watered down considerably. Nonetheless, women and blacks are still more fully represented at Democratic conventions than at Republican conventions. GOP leaders have placed much less emphasis on proportional representation; instead of procedural reforms, Republicans have concentrated on strengthening their state organizations and fund-raising efforts, a strategy that has clearly paid off at the polls in the elections of 1980, 1984, and 1988, which saw Republicans elected as president. Yet, overall, the representation of women and minorities at the convention is largely symbolic, as delegates no longer have a great deal of power in selecting the nominee.

Photo courtesy: Stephan Savoia/AP/Wide World Photos

■ Kweisi Mfume, former president of the National Association for the Advancement of Colored People, addresses the 2004 Democratic National Convention in Boston. Mfume is also a former U.S. Congressman from Maryland.

The delegates in each party also exemplify the philosophical gulf separating the two parties. Democratic delegates are well to the left of their own party's voters on most issues, and even farther away from the opinions held by the nation's electorate as a whole. Republican delegates are a mirror image of their opponents—considerably to the right of GOP voters and even more so of the entire electorate. Although it is sometimes said that the two major parties do not present U.S. citizens with a "clear choice" of candidates, it is possible to argue the contrary. Our politics are perhaps too polarized, with the great majority of Americans, moderates and pragmatists overwhelmingly, left underrepresented by parties too fond of ideological purity. Political scientists conducted a study of 1980 Iowa caucus and convention delegates for both the Republican and Democratic parties that confirms the above conclusion. Among the Democrats, the delegates to the state convention were the most liberal of the group of voters studied, followed closely by Democratic caucus attendees. Republican delegates, similarly, were the most conservative members of the group studied, followed closely by Republican caucus attendees. While both groups of party decision makers were more ideological than other party members, Republican Party leaders were "closer to their followers in representativeness of opinions than were Democratic leaders and followers,"[15] although the difference was small. The philosophical divergence is usually reflected in the party platforms, even in years such as 1996 and 2004, when both parties attempted to water down their rhetoric and smooth over ideological differences.

The Electoral College: How Presidents Are Elected

Given the enormous amount of energy, money, and time expended to nominate two major-party presidential contenders, it is difficult to believe that the general election could be more arduous than the nominating contests, but it usually is. The actual campaign for the presidency (and other offices) is described in chapter 14, but the object of the exercise is clear: winning a majority of the **Electoral College.** This uniquely American institution consists of representatives of each state who cast the final ballots that actually elect a president. The total number of **electors**—the members of the Electoral College—for each state is equivalent to the number of senators and representatives that state has in the U.S. Congress. And, the District of Columbia is accorded three electoral votes.

Electoral College
Representatives of each state who cast the final ballots that actually elect a president.

elector
Member of the Electoral College chosen by methods determined in each state.

The Living Constitution

No Person shall be a Representative who shall not have attained to the Age of twenty five Years.

—Article I, Section 2

No Person shall be a Senator who shall not have attained to the Age of thirty Years.

—Article I, Section 3

neither shall any person be eligible to that Office [of the Presidency] who shall not have attained to the Age of thirty-five Years.

—Article II, Section 1

Age Qualifications for National Elected Office

There was little debate among the Framers at the Constitutional Convention that elected officials should have enough experience in life and in politics before being qualified to take on the responsibility of representing the interests of the nation and of their district or state. It is likely that they concurred, as they so often did, with John Locke, who stated in section 118 of his *Second Treatise of Government*, "a Child is born a Subject of no Country or Government. He is under his Father's Tuition and Authority, till he come to Age of Discretion." However, a minor, who is not subject to the authority of the state in the same way as a full citizen, also could not possibly be qualified to possess it. The Framers added age requirements higher than the age when one becomes a full citizen as a guarantee that statesmen would be elected. Notice how the age limits scale upward according to the amount of deliberation and decision-making that the position involves. House members only need to be twenty-five, but the president must be at least thirty-five, giving whoever would run for that office plenty of time to acquire the political experience necessary for the central role he or she will play.

State governments usually employ similar requirements. For instance, Virginia requires that candidates for the state's House of Delegates and Senate be at least twenty-one years old, while candidates for the state's three most powerful executive positions—governor, lieutenant governor, and attorney general—must be at least thirty years old. South Dakota, however, sets the minimum age limit for its most important executive officers—governor and lieutenant governor—at twenty-one.

Amazingly, the Framers did not impose an age limit on Supreme Court justices, not even the chief justice. Perhaps the Framers thought that the president was not likely to appoint minors to the bench, or at least that they would not be approved by the Senate. Looking at the nine justices today, it is obvious that the Framers were right not to worry.

The Electoral College was the result of a compromise between Framers such as Roger Sherman and Elbridge Gerry, who argued for selection of the president by the Congress, and those such as James Madison, James Wilson, and Gouverneur Morris, who favored selection by direct popular election. The Electoral College compromise, although not a perfect solution, had practical benefits. Since there were no mass media in those days, common citizens, even reasonably informed ones, were unlikely to know much about a candidate from another state. On the one hand, this situation could have left voters with no choice but to vote for someone from their own state, thus making it improbable that any candidate would secure a national majority. On the other hand, the electors would be men of character with a solid knowledge of national politics who were able to identify, agree on, and select prominent national statesmen. There are three essentials to understanding the Framers' design of the Electoral College. The system was constructed (1) to work without political parties; (2) to cover both the nominating and electing phases of presidential selection; and, (3) to produce a nonpartisan president.

The Electoral College machinery was somewhat complex. Each state designated electors (through appointment or popular vote) equal in number to the sum of its representation in the House and Senate. (Figure 13.2 shows a map of the United States drawn in proportion to each state's 2004 Electoral College votes.) The electors met in

Visual Literacy

American Electoral Rules: How Do They Influence Campaigns?

FIGURE 13.2 **The States Drawn in Proportion to Their Electoral College Votes**
This map visually represents the respective electoral weights of the fifty states in the 2004 presidential election. For each state, the gain or loss of Electoral College votes based on the 2000 Census is indicated in parentheses. ■

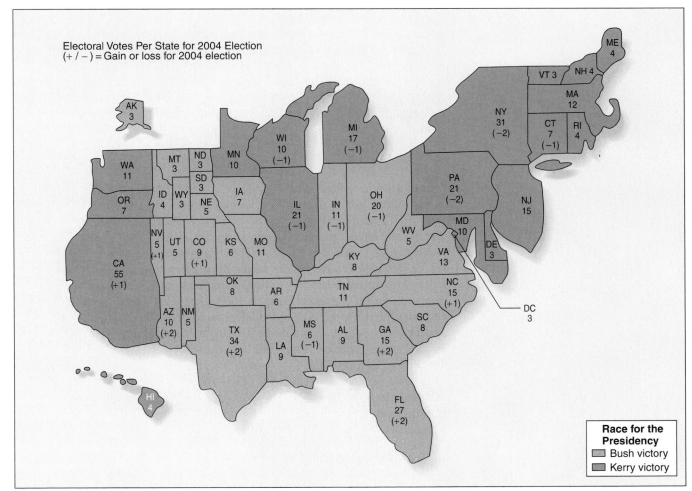

Note: States drawn in proportion to number of electoral votes. Total electoral votes: 538.
Source: New York Times 2004 Election Guide, http://www.nytimes.com/packages/htmlpolitics/2004_ELECTIONGUIDE_GRAPHIC/.

their respective states. Each elector had two votes to cast in the Electoral College's selection for the president and vice president, although electors could not vote for more than one candidate from their state. The rules of the college stipulated that each elector was allowed to cast only one vote for any single candidate, and by extension obliged each elector to use his second vote for another candidate. There was no way to designate votes for president or vice president; instead, the candidate with the most votes (provided he also received votes from a majority of the electors) won the presidency and the runner-up won the vice presidency. If two candidates received the same number of votes and both had a majority of electors, the election was decided in the House of Representatives, with each state delegation acting as a unit and casting one vote. If no candidate secured a majority, the election would also be decided in the House, with each state delegation casting one vote for any of the top five electoral vote-getters. In both these scenarios, the candidate needed a majority of the total number of states for victory.

This system seems almost insanely unpredictable, complex, and unwieldy until one remembers that the Framers devised it specifically for the type of political system that existed when they framed the Constitution and that they (erroneously) foresaw for America in perpetuity: a nonpartisan (one-party), consensus-based, indirectly representative, multicandidate system. In such a system, the Electoral College would function admirably. In practice, the Framers hoped that electors with a common basic political understanding would arrive at a consensus preference for president, and most, if not all, would plan to cast one of their votes for that candidate, thereby virtually guaranteeing one clear winner, who would become president; a tie was an unlikely and unhappy outcome. Each would then plan to cast his remaining vote for another candidate, the one whom the elector implicitly preferred for vice president. Consensus on the vice presidency would presumably be less clear than for the more important position of president, so there might be a closer spread among the runners-up; but, in any case, the eventual president and vice president—indeed, all the candidates—would still have been members of the same one party.

The Framers' idea of nonpartisan presidential elections, however, lasted barely a decade, ending for the most part after George Washington's two terms. In 1796, their arrangement for presidential selection produced a president and vice president with markedly different political philosophies, a circumstance much less likely in modern times.

The Electoral College in the Nineteenth Century

The republic's fourth presidential election revealed a flaw in the Framers' Electoral College plan. In 1800, Thomas Jefferson and Aaron Burr were, respectively, the presidential and vice presidential candidates advanced by the Democratic-Republican Party, and supporters of the Democratic-Republican Party controlled a majority of the Electoral College. Accordingly, each Democratic-Republican elector in the states cast one of his two votes for Jefferson and the other one for Burr, a situation that resulted in a tie for the presidency between Jefferson and Burr, since there was no way under the constitutional arrangements for electors to earmark their votes separately for president and vice president. Even though most understood Jefferson to be the actual choice for president, the Constitution mandated that a tie be decided by the House of Representatives. It was, of course, and in Jefferson's favor, but only after much energy was expended to persuade lame-duck Federalists not to give Burr the presidency.

The Twelfth Amendment, ratified in 1804 and still the constitutional foundation for presidential elections, was an attempt to remedy the confusion between the selection of vice presidents and presidents that beset the election of 1800. The amendment provided for separate elections for each office, with each elector having only one vote to cast for each. In the event of a tie or when no candidate received a majority of the total number of electors, the election still went to the House of Representatives; now, however, each state delegation would have one vote to cast for one of the three candidates who had received the greatest number of electoral votes.

The Electoral College modified by the Twelfth Amendment has fared better than the college as originally designed, but it has not been problem free. For example, in the 1824 election between John Quincy Adams and Andrew Jackson, neither presidential candidate secured a majority of electoral votes, once again throwing the election into the House. Although Jackson had more electoral and popular votes than Adams, the House voted for the latter as president. On two other occasions in the nineteenth century, the presidential candidate with fewer popular votes than his opponent won the presidency. In the 1876 contest between Republican Rutherford B. Hayes and Democrat Samuel J. Tilden, no candidate received a majority of electoral votes; the House decided in Hayes's favor even though he had only one more (disputed) electoral vote and 250,000 fewer popular votes than Tilden. In the election of 1888, President Grover Cleveland secured about 100,000 more popular votes than did Benjamin Harrison, yet Harrison won a majority of the Electoral College vote, and with it the presidency.

The Electoral College Today

Several near crises pertaining to the Electoral College occurred in the twentieth century. The election of 1976 was almost a repeat of those nineteenth-century contests in which the candidate with fewer popular votes won the presidency: Even though Democrat Jimmy Carter received about 1.7 million more popular votes than Republican Gerald Ford, a switch of some 8,000 popular votes in Ohio and Hawaii would have secured for Ford enough votes to win the Electoral College, and hence the presidency. Had Ross Perot stayed in the 1992 presidential contest, he could have thrown the election into the House of Representatives. His support had registered from 30 percent to 36 percent in the polls in early 1992. When he reentered the race, some of that backing had evaporated, and he finished with 19 percent of the vote and carried no states. However, Perot drained a substantial number of Republican votes from George Bush, thus splitting the GOP base and enabling Clinton to win many normally GOP-leaning states.

"And the Winner Is . . ."
Close Calls in
Presidential Elections

Throughout the 2000 presidential campaign, many analysts foresaw that the election would likely be the closest since the 1960 race between John F. Kennedy and Richard M. Nixon. Few realized, however, that the election would be so close that the winner would not be officially declared for more than five weeks after Election Day, and that a mere 500 votes in Florida would effectively decide the presidency of the United States. With the margin of the Electoral College results so small (271 for Bush, 267 for Gore), a Gore victory in any number of closely contested states, including Arkansas, Tennessee, West Virginia, or New Hampshire, could have given him a majority in the Electoral College.

Keep in mind that the representation of states in the Electoral College is altered every ten years to reflect population shifts. The number of congressional seats has been fixed at 435 since 1910 (with a temporary increase to 437 in 1959 to accommodate the entrance of Hawaii and Alaska to the union). Since that time, the average size of congressional districts has tripled in population, from 211,000 following the 1910 Census to 647,000 in the 2000 Census. Following the 2000 Census, Arizona, Florida, Georgia, and Texas each gained two congressional districts, and therefore two additional seats in the House of Representatives and two additional votes in the Electoral College. California, Colorado, Nevada, and North Carolina each picked up one seat and one vote. Two states, New York and Pennsylvania, each lost two seats and two votes, while eight states each lost a single seat and electoral vote: Connecticut, Illinois, Indiana, Michigan, Mississippi, Ohio, Oklahoma, and Wisconsin. The Census figures show a sizable population shift from the Northeast to the South and West. (Figure 13.2 shows the gains and losses in Electoral College votes per state.)

Recent reapportionment has favored the Republicans. With the exception of California, George W. Bush carried all of the states that gained seats in 2000. Had Bush won the same states in 2004 that he won in 2000, and if Kerry had won all of the Gore

The Electoral College

states from 2000, Bush would have had 278 electoral votes rather than the 271 he officially received in 2000, and Kerry would have received 267 (instead of 260).

Given the periodically recurring dissatisfaction expressed by the public, especially in the wake of the 2000 election, reformers have seized the opportunity to suggest several proposals for improving the American Electoral College system. Three major reform ideas have developed; each is described below.

Abolition.

This reform would abolish the Electoral College entirely and have the president selected by popular vote. George W. Bush's election in 2000 marked the fourth time in U.S. history that a president was elected without the majority of the popular vote. Many critics believe that the Electoral College is archaic and that the only way to have a true democracy in the United States is to have the president elected directly by a popular vote. This reform is by far the most unlikely to succeed, given that the Constitution of the United States would have to be amended to change the Electoral College. Even assuming that the House of Representatives could muster the two-third majority necessary to pass an amendment, the proposal would almost certainly never pass the Senate. Small states have the same representation in the Senate as populous ones, and the Senate thus serves as a bastion of equal representation for all states, regardless of population—a principle generally reinforced by the existing configuration of the Electoral College, which ensures a minimum of electoral influence for even the smallest states. In addition, the likelihood of engaging a national recount in the event of a close election would wreak havoc on our electoral system.

Congressional District Plan.

Under this plan, each candidate would receive one electoral vote for each congressional district that he or she wins in a state, and the winner of the overall popular vote in each state would receive two bonus votes (one for each senator) for that state. Take for example Virginia, which has eleven representatives and two senators for a total of thirteen electoral votes. If the Democratic candidate wins five congressional districts, and the Republican candidate wins the other six districts and also the statewide majority, the Democrat wins five electoral votes and the Republican wins a total of eight. This reform could be adopted without a constitutional amendment. This electoral system currently exists only in Maine and Nebraska; neither state has had to split its votes. Any state can adopt this system on its own because the Constitution gives states the right to determine the place and manner by which it selects its electors.

The congressional district plan has some unintended consequences. First, the winner of the overall election might change in some circumstances. Under a congressional district plan, Richard M. Nixon would have won the 1960 election instead of John F. Kennedy. George W. Bush would have likely won by a wider margin if the entire nation used this system in 2000. Second, this reform would further politicize the redistricting process that takes place every ten years according to U.S. Census results. Fair and objective redistricting already suffers at the hands of many political interests; if electoral votes were at stake, it would suffer further as the parties made nationwide efforts to maximize the number of safe electoral districts for their presidential nominee while minimizing the number of competitive districts. The third consequence of state-by-state adoption is that the nation would quickly come to resemble a patchwork of different electoral methods, with some states being awarded by congressional districts and some states awarded solely by popular vote.

Finally, candidates would quickly learn to focus their campaigning on competitive districts while ignoring secure districts, since secure districts would contribute electoral votes only through the senatorial/statewide-majority component. In the end, the United States and its democracy might be better served by preserving the more uniform system that currently prevails, despite its other shortcomings.

Keep the College, Abolish the Electors.   This proposal calls for the preservation of the college as a statistical electoral device but would remove all voting power from actual human electors and their legislative appointers. It would eliminate the threat of so-called faithless electors—that is, electors who are appointed by state legislators to vote for the candidate who won that state's vote, but who then choose, for whatever reason, to vote for the other candidate. Most Americans are comfortable with making this change, although—perhaps even because—the problem of faithless electors is only a secondary and little-realized liability of the Electoral College.

While the fate of these three reform proposals has yet to be determined, any change in the existing system would inevitably have a profound impact on the way that candidates go about the business of seeking votes for the U.S. presidency.

Patterns of Presidential Elections

The Electoral College results reveal more over time than simply who won the presidency. They show which party and which regions are coming to dominance and how voters may be changing party allegiances in response to new issues and generational changes.

Party Realignments.   Usually such movements are gradual, but occasionally the political equivalent of a major earthquake swiftly and dramatically alters the landscape. During these rare events, called **party realignments,**[16] existing party affiliations are subject to upheaval: many voters may change parties, and the youngest age group of voters may permanently adopt the label of the newly dominant party. The existing party cleavage fades over time, allowing new issues to emerge. Until recent times, at least, party realignments occurred about thirty-six years apart in the U.S. experience.

Preceding a major realignment are one or more **critical elections,** which may polarize voters around new issues and personalities in reaction to crucial developments, such as a war or an economic depression. In Britain, for example, the first postwar election held in 1945 was critical, since it ushered the Labour Party into power for the first time and introduced to Britain a new interventionist agenda in the fields of economic and social welfare policies.

In the entire history of the United States, there have been six party realignments. Three tumultuous eras in particular have produced significant elections (see Figure 13.3). First, during the period leading up to the Civil War, the Whig Party gradually dissolved and the Republican Party developed and won the presidency in 1860. Second, the populist radicalization of the Democratic Party in the 1890s enabled the Republicans to greatly strengthen their majority status and make lasting gains in voter attachments. Third, the Great Depression of the 1930s propelled the Democrats to power, causing large numbers of voters to repudiate the GOP and embrace the Democratic Party. Each of these cases resulted in fundamental and enduring alterations in the party equation.

The last confirmed major realignment, then, happened in the 1928–1936 period, as Republican Herbert Hoover's presidency was held to one term because of voter anger about the Depression. In 1932, Democrat Franklin D. Roosevelt swept to power as the electorate decisively rejected Hoover and the Republicans. This dramatic vote of "no confidence" was followed by substantial changes in policy by the new president, who demonstrated in fact or at least in appearance that his policies were effective. The people responded to his success, accepted his vision of society, and ratified their choice of the new president's party in subsequent presidential and congressional elections.

With the aid of timely circumstances, realignments take place in two main ways.[17] Some voters are converted from one party to the other by the issues and candidates of the time. New voters may also be mobilized into action: immigrants, young voters, and

party realignment
A shifting of party coalition groupings in the electorate that remains in place for several elections.

critical election
An election that signals a party realignment through voter polarization around new issues.

FIGURE 13.3 Electoral College Results for Three Realigning Presidential Contests

This figure shows the electoral votes in three crucial U.S. elections. ■

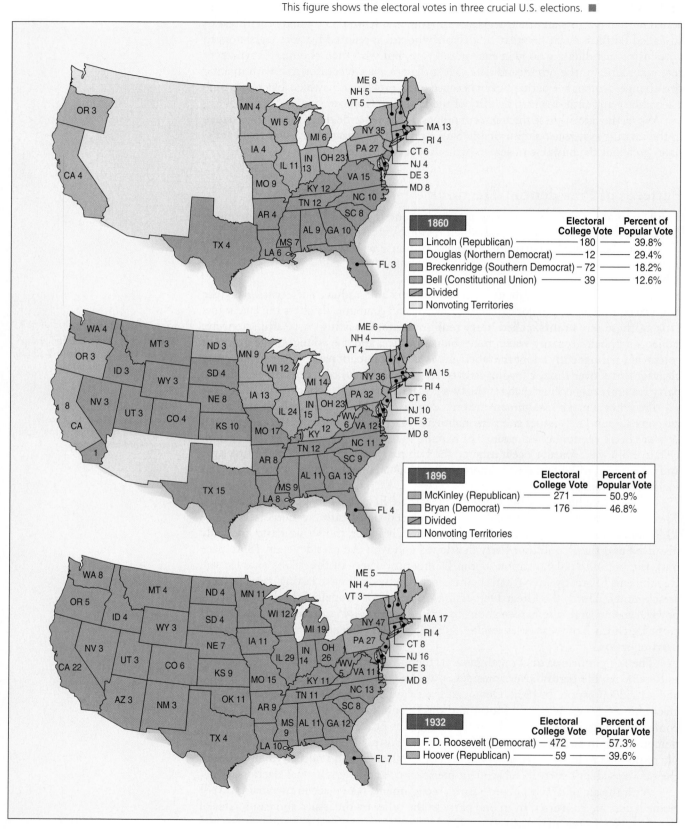

1860	Electoral College Vote	Percent of Popular Vote
Lincoln (Republican)	180	39.8%
Douglas (Northern Democrat)	12	29.4%
Breckenridge (Southern Democrat)	72	18.2%
Bell (Constitutional Union)	39	12.6%
Divided		
Nonvoting Territories		

1896	Electoral College Vote	Percent of Popular Vote
McKinley (Republican)	271	50.9%
Bryan (Democrat)	176	46.8%
Divided		
Nonvoting Territories		

1932	Electoral College Vote	Percent of Popular Vote
F. D. Roosevelt (Democrat)	472	57.3%
Hoover (Republican)	59	39.6%

previous nonvoters may become motivated and then absorbed into a new governing majority, especially if they have been excluded previously. However vibrant and potent party coalitions may be at first, as they age, tensions increase and grievances accumulate. The majority's original reason for existing fades, and new generations neither remember the traumatic events that originally brought about the realignment nor possess the stalwart party identifications of their ancestors. New issues arise, producing conflicts that can be resolved only by a breakup of old alignments and a reshuffling of individual and group party loyalties. Viewed from historical perspective, party realignments ensure stability by adapting to changes in American politics.

A critical realigning era is not the only occasion when changes in partisan affiliation are accommodated. In truth, every election produces realignment to some degree, since some individuals are undoubtedly pushed to change parties by events and by their reactions to the candidates. Research suggests that partisanship is much more responsive to current issues and personalities than had been believed earlier, and that major realignments are just extreme cases of the kind of changes in party loyalty registered every year.[18]

Secular Realignment.   Although the term *realignment* is usually applied only if momentous events such as war or economic depression produce enduring and substantial alterations in the party coalitions, political scientists have long recognized that a more gradual rearrangement of party coalitions can occur.[19] Called **secular realignment,** this piecemeal process depends not on convulsive shocks to the political system, but on slow, almost barely discernible demographic shifts—the shrinking of one party's base of support and the enlargement of the other's, for example—or simple generational replacement (that is, the dying off of the older generation and the maturing of the younger generation). According to one version of this theory, termed "rolling realignment,"[20] in an era of weaker party attachments (such as we currently are experiencing), a dramatic, full-scale realignment may not be possible. Still, a critical mass of voters may be attracted for years to one party's banner in waves or streams, if that party's leadership and performance are consistently exemplary.

The decline of party affiliation has in essence left the electorate dealigned and incapable of being realigned as long as party ties remain tenuous for so many voters.[21] Voters shift with greater ease between the parties during dealignment, but little permanence or intensity exists in identifications made and held so lightly. If nothing else, the calendar may indicate the error in realignment theory; if major realignments occur roughly every thirty-six years, then we are long overdue. The last major realignment took place between 1928 and 1936, thus the next one might have been expected in the late 1960s and early 1970s.

As the trends toward ticket-splitting, partisan independence, and voter volatility suggest, there is little question that we have been moving through an unstable and somewhat "dealigned" period at least since the 1970s. The foremost political question today is whether dealignment will continue (and in what form) or whether a major realignment is in the offing. Each previous dealignment has been a precursor of realignment,[22] but realignment need not succeed dealignment, especially under modern conditions.

secular realignment
The gradual rearrangement of party coalitions, based more on demographic shifts than on shocks to the political system.

CONGRESSIONAL ELECTIONS

MANY SIMILAR ELEMENTS are present in different kinds of elections. Candidates, voters, issues, and television advertisements are constants. But, there are distinctions among the various kinds of elections as well. Compared with presidential elections, congressional elections are a different animal. Unlike major-party presidential contenders, most candidates for Congress labor in relative obscurity. There are some celebrity nominees for Congress—television stars, sports heroes, even local TV news anchors. In 2000, First Lady Hillary Rodham Clinton's historic senatorial campaign gained the nation's attention. The vast majority of party nominees, however, are little-known state legislators and local office holders who receive remarkably little coverage in many states and communities. For them, just getting known, establishing name identification, is the biggest battle.

The Incumbency Advantage

The current circumstances enhance the advantages of incumbency (that is, already being in office), and a kind of electoral inertia takes hold: those people in office tend to remain in office. Every year, the average member of the U.S. House of Representatives receives about $750,000 in taxpayer funds to run his or her office. Much of this money directly or indirectly promotes the legislator by means of mass mailings and *constituency services*, the term used to describe a wide array of assistance provided by a member of Congress to voters in need (for example, tracking a lost Social Security check, helping a veteran receive disputed benefits, or finding a summer internship for a college student). Having a responsive constituent service program contributes strongly to incumbency. If a House incumbent helped solve a problem for a constituent, that constituent rated the incumbent more favorably than constituents who were not assisted by the incumbent,[23] therefore providing the incumbent a great advantage over any challenger.

In addition to these institutional means of self-promotion, most incumbents are highly visible in their districts. They have easy access to local media, cut ribbons galore, attend important local funerals, and speak frequently at meetings and community events. Nearly a fourth of the people in an average congressional district claim to have met their representative, and about half recognize their legislator's name without prompting. This spending and visibility pay off. Reelection rates for sitting House members range above 95 percent in most election years, and research shows district attentiveness is at least partly responsible for incumbents' electoral safety.[24]

Recent research also identifies an indirect advantage of incumbency: the ability of the office holder to fend off challenges from strong opposition candidates, something two scholars call the "scare-off" effect. Incumbents have the ability to scare off high-quality challengers because of the institutional advantages of office, such as high name recognition, large war chests, staffs attached to legislative offices, and overall experience in running a successful campaign. Potential strong challengers facing this initial uphill battle will wait until the incumbent retires rather than challenge him or her. This tendency only strengthens the arguments for advantages to reelection related to incumbency.[25]

The 2004 congressional elections provided evidence of the tremendous power of incumbency. Although not as turbulent an election as the Republican takeover of Congress in 1994, the results illustrate the disadvantage faced by challengers. Only one incumbent senator, Democrat Tom Daschle from South Dakota, lost a reelection bid, and just seven incumbent House members were ousted. Two of these Congressmen were defeated by other incumbents, the result of a partisan redistricting plan in Texas.

Frequently, the reelection rate for senators is as high, but not always. In a "bad" year for House incumbents, "only" 88 percent will win (as in the Watergate year of 1974), but the senatorial reelection rate can drop much lower on occasion (to 60 percent in the 1980 Reagan landslide, for example). There is a good reason for this lower senatorial reelection rate. A Senate election is often a high-visibility contest; it receives much more publicity than a House race. So, while House incumbents remain protected and insulated in part because few voters pay attention to their little-known challengers, a Senate-seat challenger

■ U.S. Senator Edward Kennedy (D–MA) knows full well the advantages of incumbency. Elected to the Senate in 1962 to complete the term of his brother, President John F. Kennedy, Edward Kennedy has been reelected every term since. His name recognition and campaign war chest enabled him to handily defeat Republican challenger Jack Robinson 73 percent to 13 percent in the 2000 election.

Photo courtesy: David McNew/Newsmakers/Getty Source

can become well known more easily and thus be in a better position to defeat an incumbent. In addition, studies show that the quality of the challengers in Senate races is higher than in House races, making it more likely that an incumbent could be upset.[26]

Redistricting, Scandals, and Coattails

For the relatively few incumbent members of Congress who lose their reelection bids, there are three major reasons: redistricting, scandals, and coattails.

Redistricting. Every ten years, after the U.S. Census, all congressional district lines are redrawn (in states with more than one representative) so that every legislator represents about the same number of citizens. The U.S. Constitution requires that a census, which entails the counting of all Americans, be conducted every ten years. Until the first U.S. Census could be taken, the Constitution fixed the number of representatives in the House at sixty-five. In 1790, then, one member represented 30,000 people. As the population of the new nation grew and states were added to the union, the House became larger and larger. In 1910, it expanded to 435 members, and in 1929, its size was fixed at that number by statute.

Because the Constitution requires that representation in the House be based on state population, and that each state have at least one representative, congressional districts must be redrawn by state legislatures to reflect population shifts, so that each member in Congress will represent approximately the same number of residents. Exceptions to this rule are states such as Wyoming and Vermont, whose statewide populations are less than average congressional districts. This process of redrawing congressional districts to reflect increases or decreases in seats allotted to the states, as well as population shifts within a state, is called redistricting. When shifts occur in the national population, states gain or lose congressional seats through a process called *reapportionment*. The 2000 U.S. Census showed the largest population growth in American history. Between 1990 and 2000, the U.S. population had increased 13.2 percent, from 248.7 million people to an estimated 281.4 million people, with western and southern states (the sunbelt) gaining residents at the expense of the Northeast. This has been a trend since the 1960 Census, causing the Northeast to lose congressional seats in every recent decade.

Redistricting is a largely political process that the majority party in a state uses to ensure formation of voting districts that retain or expand their majority. For example, in 2003, ten Texas Democratic state senators left the capitol in Austin for Albuquerque, New Mexico, in order to break the Senate quorum necessary to pass the Republican-sponsored redistricting bill that would give Texas Republicans a sizeable majority in their state delegation to the U.S. House. At one point, state police were ordered to begin a search for any errant state senators. The efforts of the ten Democrats failed after one of them, State Senator John Whitmire, returned to the Texas Senate, believing that the Democrats were going to lose any future legal action against them. Some states, however, including Iowa and Arizona, hope to avoid this sort of political high theater by appointing nonpartisan commissions or using some independent means of drawing district lines. Although the processes vary in detail, most states require legislative approval of the plans.

This redistricting process, which has gone on since the first U.S. Census in 1790, often involves what is called **gerrymandering** (see Figure 13.4). Because of the enormous population growth, the partisan implications of redistricting, and the requirement under the Voting Rights Act for minorities to have special "majority-minority districts" in order to get an equal chance to elect candidates of their choice, legislators end up drawing oddly shaped districts to achieve their goals.[27] Redistricting plans routinely meet with court challenges across the country. Following the 2000 Census and the subsequent redistricting in 2002, courts have thrown out legislative maps in a half-dozen states, primarily because of state constitutional concerns about compactness.

Simulation
You Are Redrawing the Districts in Your State

gerrymandering
The legislative process through which the majority party in each statehouse tries to assure that the maximum number of representatives from its political party can be elected to Congress through the redrawing of legislative districts.

The circuitous boundaries of improper districts often cut across county lines or leap over natural barriers and split counties and long-standing communities.[28] Despite the obviously abnormal shape of many districts (including Texas's 6th district, Illinois's 17th district, and North Carolina's 12th district), gerrymandering is very difficult to prove and its interpretation often depends on partisan factors.

Over the years, the Supreme Court has ruled that:

- Congressional as well as state legislative districts must be apportioned on the basis of population.[29]

- Purposeful gerrymandering of a congressional district to dilute minority strength is illegal under the Voting Rights Act of 1965.[30]

- Redrawing of districts for obvious racial purposes to enhance minority representation is constitutional if race is not the "predominate" factor over all other factors that are part of traditional redistricting, including compactness.[31]

New software has made it easier to draw more politically reliable electoral maps, which have reduced partisan contention. Until the 1990s, legislators had to draw districts using colored pens on acetate sheets spread out on large maps. Computers appeared before the 1990s, but only a few states could afford the big, sophisticated ones that could handle demographic data. Now the U.S. Census Bureau makes available digitized maps, and new geographic information systems for mapping and analyzing demographic data can draw up partisan maps automatically. These developments have changed redistricting (and gerrymandering) from an art into a science.[32] Yet, the process requires more resources and takes more time than ever.

Recent research has added yet another actor into the redistricting process: the individual member of a legislature. In an analysis of 1992 redistricting in North Carolina, Paul Gronke maintains that members' partisanship is balanced with their own ambition. He finds that "individual ambition generally outweighs partisan loyalty." If, in other words,

FIGURE 13.4 **Gerrymandering**

Two drawings—one a mocking cartoon, the other all too real—show the bizarre geographical contortions that result from gerrymandering. ■

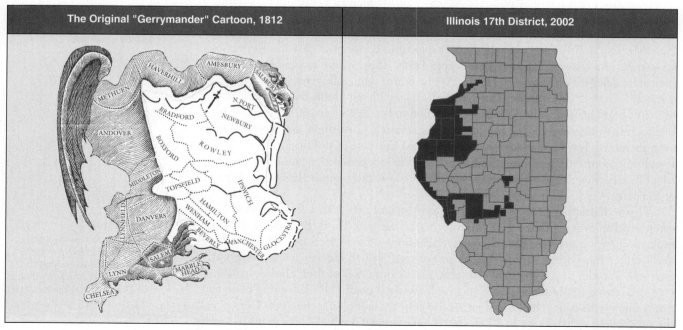

| The Original "Gerrymander" Cartoon, 1812 | Illinois 17th District, 2002 |

Sources: David Van Biema, "Snakes or Ladders?" *Time* (July 12, 1993) © 1993, Time Inc. Reprinted by permission. Illinois General Assembly.

voting for the other party's district lines will help individual members obtain higher office, they will vote in their own self-interest over the better interests of their party.[33]

The dominant party often uses redistricting to make their incumbents safer. But redistricting can also be used to punish the out-of-power party. Some incumbents can be put in the same districts as other incumbents, or the base of other representatives can be weakened by adding territory favorable to the opposition party. In 1992, ten incumbents were paired together to compete against each other in redrawn districts—five therefore lost—and about a dozen more incumbents were defeated in part because of unfavorable redistricting. The number of incumbents who actually lose their reelections because of redistricting is lessened by the strategic behavior of redistricted members—who often choose to retire rather than wage an expensive (and likely unsuccessful) reelection battle.[34]

In one innovative study, researchers created a post-1990 redistricting model of partisan support in each congressional district by pretending all seats were open seats, eliminating incumbency as a factor. Their projections based on this model gave the Republicans twenty more seats than before the redistricting. Republicans took over dominance from the Democrats in three districts and gained dominance in seventeen districts that were previously evenly divided. When the researchers included incumbency in the model, however, strong Democratic incumbents in the newly formed districts suppressed the projected Republican gain from the new redistricting, and the parties came out even. This conclusion partially explains the Republican rise in congressional power after the 1990 redistricting. The eventual retirement of these Democratic incumbents made the next elections open in a district strongly favor Republicans. As the model predicted, Republicans won the open races. In short, redistricting along party lines obviously affects the make-up of the U.S. Congress, a fact that explains the lengths those ten Texan state senators went to stop it.[35]

Scandals. Scandals come in many varieties in this age of investigative journalism. The old standby of financial impropriety (bribery and payoffs, for example) has been supplemented by other forms of career-ending incidents, such as personal improprieties (sexual escapades, for instance). Incumbents implicated in scandals typically do not lose reelections—because they simply choose to retire rather than face defeat.[36] The power of incumbency is so strong, however, that many legislators survive even serious scandal to win reelection. One of the more famous recent political scandals is that of New Jersey Governor Jim McGreevey. In August 2004, the Garden State's first-term Democratic governor announced that he would be resigning from office effective November 15, in response to a sexual harassment lawsuit being prepared by a former security aide. Although the suit was never filed, it alleged that while working as the governor's lead homeland security adviser, Golan Cipel was the subject of improper sexual conduct and intimidating behavior by McGreevey. Cipel, an Israeli citizen, initially resigned in 2002 but was kept on the state payroll for several months afterward.

Coattails. The defeat of a congressional incumbent can also occur as a result of the presidential coattail effect. Successful presidential candidates usually carry into office congressional candidates of the same party in the year of their election. Notice the overall decline in the strength of the coattail effect in modern times, however, as party identification has weakened and the powers and perks of incumbency have grown. Whereas Harry S Truman's party gained seventy-six House seats and nine additional Senate seats in 1948, George Bush's party actually lost three House seats and one Senate berth in 1988, despite Bush's handsome 54 percent majority. The gains can be minimal even in presidential landslide reelection years, such as 1972 (Nixon) and 1984 (Reagan). Occasionally, though, when the issues are emotional and the voters' desire for change is strong enough, as in Reagan's original 1980 victory, the coattail effect can still be substantial.

Analyzing Visuals

CONGRESSIONAL ELECTION RESULTS, 1948–2004

Take a few moments to study the table, which indicates whether or not the president's party gained or lost seats in each election since 1948, and then answer the following critical thinking questions: Are there any striking patterns in the outcomes of congressional elections that occur in presidential election years? Are there any striking patterns in the outcomes of congressional elections that occur in nonpresidential (midterm) election years? Drawing on what you've learned from this chapter, how might you explain the patterns in midterm elections?

GAIN (+) OR LOSS (–) FOR PRESIDENT'S PARTY

PRESIDENTIAL ELECTION YEARS			NONPRESIDENTIAL ELECTION YEARS		
President/Year	House	Senate	Year	House	Senate
Truman (D): 1948	+76	+9	1950	–29	–6
Eisenhower (R): 1952	+24	+2	1954	–18	–1
Eisenhower (R): 1956	–2	0	1958	–48	–13
Kennedy (D): 1960	–20	–2	1962	–4	+3
Johnson (D): 1964	+38	+2	1966	–47	–4
Nixon (R): 1968	+7	+5	1970	–12	+2
Nixon (R): 1972	+13	–2	Ford (R): 1974	–48	–5
Carter (D): 1976	+2	0	1978	–15	–3
Reagan (R): 1980	+33	+12	1982	–26	+1
Reagan (R): 1984	+15	–2	1986	–5	–8
G. Bush (R): 1988	–3	–1	1990	–9	–1
Clinton (D): 1992	–10	0	1994	–52	–9[a]
Clinton (D): 1996	+10	–2	1998	+5	0
G. W. Bush (R): 2000	–2	–4	2002	+6	+2
G. W. Bush (R): 2004	+3	+4			

[a]Includes the switch from Democrat to Republican of Alabama U.S. Senator Richard Shelby.

Midterm Congressional Elections

midterm election
Election that takes place in the middle of a presidential term.

Elections in the middle of presidential terms, **midterm elections,** present a threat to incumbents. This time it is the incumbents of the president's party who are most in jeopardy. Just as the presidential party usually gains seats in presidential election years, it usually loses seats in off years. The problems and tribulations of governing normally cost a president some popularity, alienate key groups, or cause the public to want to send the president a message of one sort or another. An economic downturn or a scandal can underline and expand this circumstance, as the Watergate scandal of 1974 and the recession of 1982 demonstrated. The 2002 midterm elections, however, bucked that trend, marking the first time since 1934 and Franklin D. Roosevelt that a first-term president gained seats for his party in a midterm election.

Most apparent from the midterm statistics presented in Analyzing Visuals: Congressional Elections Results, 1948–2004, is the tendency of voters to punish the president's party much more severely in the sixth year of an eight-year presidency, a phenomenon associated with retrospective voting. After only two years, voters are still willing to "give the guy a chance," but after six years, voters are often restless for change.

In 1994, the United States seemed to experience a sixth-year itch in the second year of a presidency, such was the dissatisfaction with the Clinton administration. To their credit, Democrats, despite the scandals that plagued Clinton's presidency, avoided a true sixth-year itch in 1998. During this midterm election, Democrats actually gained five seats in the U.S. House of Representatives.

Senate elections are less inclined to follow these off-year patterns than are House elections. The idiosyncratic nature of Senate contests is due to their intermittent scheduling (only one-third of the seats come up for election every two years) and the existence of well-funded, well-known candidates who can sometimes swim against whatever political tide is rising. Also worth remembering is that midterm elections in recent history have a much lower voter turnout than presidential elections. A midterm election may draw only 35 percent to 40 percent of adult Americans to the polls, whereas a presidential contest usually attracts between 50 percent and 55 percent (see Analyzing Visuals: Voter Turnout in Presidential and Midterm Congressional Elections).

As noted, the 1994 midterm elections were extraordinary, a massacre for the Democrats and a dream come true for the Republicans. Not since Harry S Truman's loss in 1946 had a Democratic president lost both houses of Congress in a midterm election, but such was President Clinton's fate. For the first time since popular elections for the U.S. Senate began in the early 1900s, the entire freshman Senate class (that is, all newly elected senators) was Republican. Moreover, every incumbent House member, senator, and governor who was defeated for reelection was a Democrat. Even the speaker of the House, Thomas Foley (D–WA), fell in the onslaught. Republican George Nethercutt became the first person to unseat a House speaker since 1862. Looking specifically at the House, Republicans scored their impressive victory in 1994 "by fielding (modestly) superior candidates who were on the right side of the issues that were important to voters in House elections and by persuading voters to blame a unified Democratic government for government's failures."[37]

Republicans had just as much success at the state level. The GOP took control of nineteen houses in state legislatures, securing a majority of the legislative bodies. From just nineteen governors before the election, Republicans wound up with thirty governorships, including eight of the nine largest. (Only Florida, which reelected Democratic Governor Lawton Chiles, resisted the trend.)

Cynics frequently say that elections do not matter, but the 1998 midterm elections effectively and dramatically refuted the cynics. A loss of just five seats for the Republicans in the U.S. House of Representatives toppled a speaker, and not just any speaker of the House, but one of the most powerful speakers of the twentieth century—Newt Gingrich of Georgia. The Republicans were expected to gain seats in both the House of Representatives and, especially, in the Senate, as well as a few governorships. They, however, did not do so, for several reasons. First, Republicans had pushed hard for severe punishment against President Clinton because of the Monica Lewinsky scandal. While the public disapproved of President Clinton's embarrassing and demeaning behavior in that scandal, most Americans believed that impeachment was simply too severe a penalty. Second, the Republicans had made a strategic miscalculation by shifting into neutral governmentally; that is, Republicans accomplished virtually nothing in the second session of the 105th Congress. Their assumption was that the Clinton scandal would be enough to deliver substantial gains for the GOP, and they bet wrong. President Clinton's Democratic Party scored a moral victory by actually gaining five seats in the U.S. House of Representatives and maintaining their share of seats in the Senate. The most surprising election result of all, however, occurred on the Friday after the November 3 election, when Gingrich shocked the nation by announcing his resignation from the speakership and from Congress itself.

The 2002 Midterm Elections

As discussed earlier, the president's party historically loses congressional seats in midterm elections. George. W. Bush's first midterm election, however, was a remarkable exception. In the previous fourteen midterms, the opposing party had lost an average of twenty-six seats in the House and four in the Senate. It was more than a statistical anomaly, however, when the Republicans gained a handful of seats in House

Analyzing Visuals

VOTER TURNOUT IN PRESIDENTIAL AND MIDTERM ELECTIONS

Various factors influence voter turnout in the United States. The high percentages of 1876 and 1960 both occurred in open races (that is, when no incumbent was running). In the latter, the new TV debates energized and engaged the electorate. Following the historic 2000 presidential election, many anticipated high voter turnout in 2004. Take a few moments to study the graph below, and then answer the following critical thinking questions: What general trend do you notice about voter turnout during the twentieth century? What is generally true about turnout in midterm elections as opposed to turnout in presidential elections? Drawing on what you've learned from this and other chapters, why do you think voter turnout, generally speaking, increased over the course of the nineteenth century? Why do you think voter turnout declined during the twentieth century?

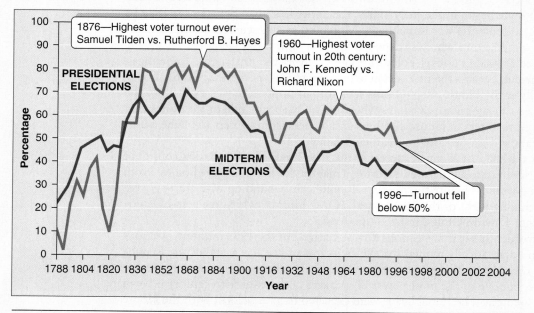

Source: Adapted from Harold W. Stanley and Richard G. Niemi, *Vital Statistics on American Politics, 2001–2002* (Washington, DC: CQ Press, 2001), figure 1-1, 12. Updated by the authors.

and Senate races. This year marks the first time since 1934 that a first-term president picked up seats in both houses of Congress. How did this occur? While there is no definitive answer, we must consider the remarkable time and energy President George W. Bush devoted to stumping for Republican candidates in key battleground states (under White House strategist Karl Rove's watchful direction). Between April and November, Bush and Vice President Dick Cheney raised more than $141 million campaigning for Republican candidates, capitalizing on Bush's approval ratings, which remained high more than a year after the September 11, 2001, terrorists attacks. Some Democrats believed that the war on terrorism and the administration's focus on impending hostility with Iraq constrained the voice of opposition by monopolizing the political agenda, preventing Democratic candidates from gaining ground on a weak economy, corporate scandals, and traditionally Democratic domestic issues. In addition, the D.C.-area snipers dominated media coverage, quite justifiably becoming a fixture of public consciousness that eclipsed virtually all political discourse until the final twelve days before the election.

Following the 2000 election, the Senate was tied at 50–50 with Republicans holding leadership capacity because of Vice President Dick Cheney's tie-breaking vote. In May 2001, the defection of Senator Jim Jeffords of Vermont allowed Democrats to take control of the Senate by the smallest of margins, while Republicans narrowly held a six-vote majority in the House. The near parity of the balance of power in the Senate and House produced an election where even marginal gains for either side made a crucial difference. In 2002, thirty-four Senate seats, thirty-six governorships, and the entire House were up for grabs. Republicans capitalized on a late wave that expanded their House majority by six seats and regained control of the Senate, 51–49, possibly giving Bush the mandate that eluded him in the 2000 election. The Louisiana Senate election was decided in a December 7 runoff in which Democratic incumbent Mary Landrieu defeated Republican Suzanne Haik Terrell. The runoff was a result of Louisiana election law that requires winners to post fifty percent or more of the vote; Landrieu had secured only 46 percent of the vote in an election that featured nine candidates.

Consistent with historical norms, most contests tended to favor incumbents regardless of party. Only four incumbent governors lost, and only three incumbent senators who were on the Election Day ballot lost: Democrats Jean Carnahan of Missouri and Max Cleland of Georgia, and Republican Tim Hutchinson of Arkansas. (In addition, Republican Senator Bob Smith of New Hampshire was defeated in the primary.) Because many of the Republican governors elected in the 1994 GOP landslide and reelected in 1998 were restricted by term limits, Democrats were expected to make big gains in several open gubernatorial races. Wins by Republicans in heavily Democratic Massachusetts and Maryland, as well as the surprise victory of Republican Sonny Perdue over the Georgia governor, helped mute the number of Democratic increases in state executive positions, leaving the Republicans with twenty-six governorships and the Democrats with twenty-four when the dust settled.

The 2002 elections were unique not only for delivering big wins for the incumbent president, but also for the unusual and unexpected conditions that preceded a number of contests. In Minnesota, Senator Paul Wellstone, along with members of his family and several staff members, died tragically in a plane crash while campaigning on October 25, only days before the November elections. Amid the disbelief, Minnesotans desperately scanned the political landscape for a qualified replacement. Former Vice President Walter Mondale accepted the Democratic Party's appointment but lost the race to Republican Norm Coleman, who capitalized on a remarkable backlash to Senator Wellstone's memorial service, which was seen by some as a Democratic pep rally. In New Jersey, former Senator Frank Lautenberg became the Democrats' late nominee when Senator Robert Torricelli abruptly withdrew his candidacy after a wave of criticism over professional ethics made it clear that he was not likely to win the election. Following a decisive ruling by the New Jersey Supreme Court, Lautenberg was permitted to replace Torricelli on the ballot, ultimately defeating his Republican opponent, Douglas Forrester.

By and large, control by the Republicans over the two branches of elected government hastened the flow of legislative business and improved the ability of the White House to promote and control the agenda. For the remainder of the term, Representative Tom Delay (R–TX), newly elected as majority leader in the House, was able to help promote Republican legislation. After the 2004 election, Republicans increased their majorities to 29 seats in the House and 10 seats in the Senate, and President George W. Bush proposed a bold legislative agenda for his second term, including significant Social Security reform. Democrats are looking to House Minority Leader Nancy Pelosi (D–CA) and Senate Minority Leader Harry Reid (D–NV) to organize their opposition.

TABLE 13.2   Results of Selected Elections, 2004

State	Contest	Winner	Loser	Significance
Alaska	Senate	Lisa Murkowski (R)	Tony Knowles (D)	Murkowski, daughter of the current Alaska governor who appointed her to replace him in the Senate, suffered from claims of nepotism but eked out a victory against strong challenger Knowles. Both candidates set the record for the most expensive race in Alaskan history.
Colorado	Senate	Ken Salazar (D)	Pete Coors (R)	Piles of money and name recognition could not counteract the bad taste that Coors's conservative agenda left in the mouths of both Democrats and moderate Republicans, who preferred the more experienced Colorado Attorney General Salazar.
Florida	Senate	Mel Martinez (R)	Betty Castor (D)	Former Secretary of Housing Martinez won by the smallest of margins against the former state education commissioner, after the two spent $40 million in television ads. Martinez joins Colorado's Salazar in a growing Hispanic presence in the U.S. Senate.
Georgia	House	John Barrow (D)	Max Burns (R)	Freshman Representative Burns lost to Barrow in a close election, giving Georgia Republicans in the House only a very slight 7–6 advantage, in spite of Georgia's increasing Republican leanings.
Illinois	Senate	Barack Obama (D)	Alan Keyes (R)	Both African Americans, State Senator Obama and former Ambassador Keyes waged a lopsided campaign. Obama, an immensely popular figure, was featured during a prime time spot at the Democratic convention. Keyes was a last-minute substitute for Jack Ryan, who left the race after it was revealed he asked his ex-wife, celebrity Jerry Ryan, to sex clubs.
Kentucky	House	Geoff Davis (R)	Nick Clooney (D)	Davis, a military veteran who lost a House election only two years before, defeated Clooney, the father of actor George Clooney.
Louisiana	Senate	David Vitter (R)	several candidates	In the Bayou State's open primary system, a candidate must garner over 50 percent of the vote in order to avoid a run-off in December. Vitter— the only Republican in the race—did just that in defeating four Democratic opponents.
Montana	Governor	Brian Schweitzer (D)	Bob Brown (R)	Schweitzer, a rancher, beat a more experienced secretary of state in the heavily Republican state of Montana by effectively campaigning to independent voters as a political outsider.
New Hampshire	Governor	John Lynch (D)	Craig Benson (R)	For the second time in seventy-eight years, New Hampshire voters ousted a freshman governor. Lynch won among college graduates and women, who turned out in large numbers to defeat the incumbent.
North Carolina	Senate	Jim Burr (R)	Erskine Bowles (D)	In the race for the vacated seat of Democratic vice presidential nominee John Edwards, Jim Burr resigned his House seat and defeated the former Clinton chief of staff, who also lost the 2002 Senate race to Elizabeth Dole.
Oklahoma	Senate	Tom Coburn (R)	Brad Carson (D)	In what was expected to be a close race between a current and a former member of Congress, Coburn won by 12 percentage points in a state that voted heavily for Bush.
South Carolina	Senate	Jim DeMint (R)	Inez Tenenbaum (D)	Former Representative Jim DeMint, from the 4th Congressional District of the Palmetto State, benefited from Bush's strong showing to defeat the former state superintendent of education.
South Dakota	Senate	John Thune (R)	Tom Daschle (D)	The popular former Congressman Thune unseated Senate Minority Leader Daschle in a bitter and expensive upset. After Thune nearly defeated Senator Tim Johnson (D) in 2000, Daschle seemed weak in a state becoming increasingly Republican, making him an easy target for Thune in 2004.
Texas	House	Peter Sessions (R)	Martin Frost (D)	After redistricting in Texas, Frost's original district no longer existed, forcing the leader of the Texas Democrats in the House to run against Sessions. Both were incumbents, but district lines obviously favored the Republican candidate, who won easily.

VOTING BEHAVIOR

RESEARCH ON VOTING BEHAVIOR seeks primarily to explain two phenomena: voter turnout (that is, what factors contribute to an individual's decision to vote or not to vote) and vote choice (once the decision to vote has been made, what leads voters to choose one candidate over another). Table 13.2 shows some of the choices voters made in 2004 elections. In this section, we will discuss patterns in voter turnout and analyze the recent decline in voter turnout; we will then turn our attention to similar patterns in vote choice. Finally, we will discuss ticket-splitting, a new development in American politics.

Patterns in Voter Turnout

Turnout is the proportion of the voting-age public that votes. About 40 percent of the eligible adult population in the United States votes regularly, whereas 25 percent are occasional voters. Thirty-five percent rarely or never vote. According to the Federal Election Commission, this places us far beneath nations such as Turkey (77 percent in 2002) and Sweden (80 percent in 2002). Turnout is important because voters have the ability to influence election outcomes. The presidential election of 2000 will forever be the classic example of the power of an individual's single vote. As recount succeeded recount in several states, and the fate of the presidency rested on razor-thin margins representing perhaps a handful of ballots, many nonvoters in Florida, New Mexico, and Oregon must have wished they had taken the trouble to exercise their right to choose their leader. (For the various methods citizens use once they turn out to vote, see Table 13.3.) Some of the factors known to influence voter turnout include education, income, age, race and ethnicity, and interest in politics.

turnout
The proportion of the voting-age public that votes.

**Voting Turnout:
Who Votes?**

Education. People who vote are usually more highly educated than nonvoters. Other things being equal, college graduates are much more likely to vote than those with less education. People with more education tend to learn more about politics, are less hindered by registration requirements, and are more self-confident about their ability to affect public life. Therefore, one might argue that institutions of higher education provide citizens with opportunities to learn about and become interested in politics.

Income. There is also a relationship between income and voting. A considerably higher percentage of citizens with annual incomes over $40,000 vote than do citizens with incomes under $10,000. Income level, to some degree, is connected to education level, as wealthier people tend to have more opportunities for higher education, and more education also may lead to higher income. Wealthy citizens are more likely than poor ones to think that the "system" works for them and that their votes make a difference. People with higher income also find the opportunity cost of participation cheaper than do the poor and are more likely to have a direct financial stake in the decisions of the government, thus spurring them into action.[38]

TABLE 13.3 How America Votes

The U.S. voting system relies on a patchwork of machines to tally voters' choices, with different metheods used even within each state. The following table illustrates the type of voting machines used in each of the ten largest counties in Ohio, one of the important battleground states of the 2004 election.

County	Registered Voters	Equipment
Cuyahoga	861,113	Punch card
Franklin	706,668	Electronic
Hamilton	522,307	Punch card
Montgomery	334,787	Punch card
Summit	334,515	Punch card
Lucas	281,500	Optical scan
Stark	246,562	Punch card
Mahoning	177,445	Electronic
Lorain	166,092	Punch card
Lake	150,137	Electronic

Source: "The e-Book on Election Law," Moritz College of Law at Ohio State University, November 2004, http://moritzlaw.osu.edu/electionlaw/.

SHOULD THE VOTING AGE BE LOWERED TO SIXTEEN?

> **OVERVIEW:** In Baltimore, Maryland, hundreds of six-teen- and seventeen-year-olds have registered to vote. Laws governing elections require only that voters be eighteen the day of the election and not when they register. Interestingly, the addition of these young voters could potentially affect the city's future council elections, which have been historically narrow con-tests: in 1979, Kweisi Mfume, who later seved in the U.S. Congress and as a president of the National Asso-ciation for the Advancement of Colored People, was elected to the city council by three votes."[a]

In California, some legislators have proposed giving partial voting rights to teens; fourteen-year-olds would receive a one-quarter vote and sixteen-year-olds would receive a half vote. Internationally, Germany and Austria have already low-ered their voting ages to sixteen. The Electoral Commission in Great Britain recommended in April 2004 that the voting age for British citizens be lowered from eighteen to sixteen. Stu-dents and elected officials in Tanzania have made demands to lower the voting age from eighteen, both because Tanzanians finish their education at fourteen and, sadly, because of falling life expectancy rates due to the African AIDS epidemic.

Throughout its history, the United States has expanded voting rights, starting with removing restrictions based on property ownership and later passing the Fifteenth and Nine-teenth Amendments to grant suffrage respectively to African American men and all women. The Civil Rights Act of 1964 put an end to racial restrictions imposed on voters by Jim Crow laws. And, passage of the Twenty-Sixth Amendment lowered the voting age to eighteen. Should we continue to expand voting rights by lowering the voting age still further?

Arguments for Lowering the Voting Age to Sixteen

- **The government must represent the interests of all Americans, but we cannot guarantee that it will if we do not lower the age limit.** There are issues that uniquely affect young voters that the government can overlook unless teens hold it accountable.
- **There is no magical transformation one undergoes when one turns eighteen.** By sixteen, a person has more

By contrast, lower-income citizens often feel alienated from politics, possibly believing that conditions will remain the same no matter for whom they vote. Ameri-can political parties may contribute to this feeling of alienation. Unlike parties in many other countries that tend to associate themselves with specific social classes, U.S. polit-ical parties do not attempt to link themselves closely to one major class (such as the "working class"). Therefore, the feelings of alienation and apathy about politics preva-lent among many lower-income Americans should not be unexpected.

Age. A strong correlation exists between age and voter participation rates. The Twenty-Sixth Amendment, ratified in 1971, lowered the voting age to eighteen. While this amendment obviously increased the number of *eligible* voters, it did so by enfran-chising the group that is least likely to vote. A much higher percentage of citizens age thirty and older vote than do citizens younger than thirty, although voter turnout decreases over the age of seventy, primarily because of physical infirmity, which makes it difficult to get to the polling location. Regrettably, less than half of eligible eighteen-to twenty-four-year-olds are even registered to vote. The most plausible reason for this is that younger people are more mobile; they have not put down roots in a community. Because voter registration is not automatic, people who relocate have to make an effort to register. Therefore, the effect of adding this low-turnout group to the electorate has been to lower the overall turnout rate. As young people marry, have children, and set-tle down in a community, their likelihood of voting increases.[39]

Race and Ethnicity. Another pattern in voter turnout is related to race: whites tend to vote more regularly than do African Americans. This was evident in the 2004 presidential election. Although turnout was up for both races—from the 51 percent of 2000 to a little over 60 percent in 2004—turnout increased less among African Americans than among whites. Turnout among whites was slightly over 60 percent

492

or less developed intellectually, and some sixteen-year-olds have more maturity than some adults, so they should not be bound by an arbitrary date.

- **The earlier young people are exposed to politics, the more likely they will participate when they're older.** We should socialize American youth into better citizens by introducing them to the great ceremony of democracy, the election, to try to raise future turnout.

Arguments Against Lowering the Voting Age to Sixteen

- **In most states, the age of legal majority, or the age when one acquires the rights and responsibilities of an adult, is currently eighteen years.** In a strict legal sense, young people are not recognized as independent members of society until they turn eighteen, after which the right to vote is a natural entitlement.

- **High school students often do not complete their civics and American government education until their junior and senior years in high school.** Participation in the political process, especially voting, is only effective if individuals have a proper foundation in the privileges

and responsibilities of citizenship. Youth civic engagement must be improved before consideration can be given to a lower voting age.

- **Lowering the voting age will not make any difference in the outcomes of elections.** Most sixteen-year-olds are not interested in politics and likely would not vote. It might be worse if they did, since they would not have a very good idea of what they were doing.

Selected Readings

Patricio Aylwin Azocar et al., *Youth Voter Participation: Involving Today's Young in Tomorrow's Democracy.* Stockholm: International IDEA, 1999.

Henry A. Giroux, *The Abandoned Generation: Democracy Beyond the Culture of Fear.* New York: Palgrave Macmillan, 2003.

Selected Web Sites

http://www.youthrights.org/votingage.shtml.
http://votesforadults.typepad.com/votes_for_adults/2004/04/.

[a]Robert Redding Jr., "Baltimore 16-year-olds to Vote," *Washington Times* (August 21, 2003), http://www.washtimes.com/metro/20030820-094324-4992r.htm.

---

in 2004; among African Americans, it hovered in the mid-50-percent range, depending on the locality.

This difference is due primarily to the relative income and educational levels of the two racial groups. African Americans tend to be poorer and have less formal education than whites; as mentioned earlier, both of these factors affect voter turnout. Significantly, though, highly educated and wealthier African Americans are as likely to vote as whites of similar background, and sometimes more likely.

Race also helps explain why the South has long had a lower turnout than the rest of the country (see Figure 13.5). In the wake of Reconstruction, the southern states made it extremely difficult for African Americans to register to vote, and only a small percentage of the eligible African American population was registered throughout the South. The Voting Rights Act (VRA) of 1965 helped to change this situation. The VRA was intended to guarantee voting rights to African Americans nearly a century after passage of the Fifteenth Amendment. Often now heralded as the most successful piece of civil rights legislation ever passed, the VRA targeted states that had used literacy or morality tests or poll taxes to exclude blacks from the polls. The act bans any voting device or procedure that interferes with a minority citizen's right to vote and requires approval for any changes in voting qualifications or procedures in certain areas where minority registration was not in pro-

■ Maria Gonzales Mabbutt, Director of Idaho Latino Vote, holds a sample ballot flyer from Nampa, Idaho. The project "Get the Vote Out" was created to inform the Hispanic community where and when to vote, as well as who the candidates are.

Photo courtesy: Matt Lilley/AP/Wide World Photos

FIGURE 13.5 The South Versus the Non-South for Presidential Voter Turnout
After a century-long discrepancy caused by discrimination against African American voters in the South, regional voting turnouts have grown much closer together with the increasing enfranchisement of these voters. ■

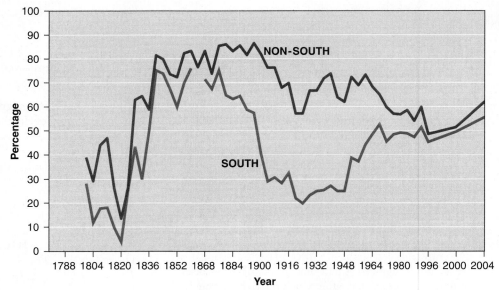

Source: Compiled from data contained in the Center for the Study of the American Electorate 2004 Election Report, November 4, 2004, http://www.fairvote.org/reports/CSEA2004electionreport.pdf.

portion to the racial composition of the district. It also authorized the federal government to monitor all elections in areas where discrimination was found to be practiced or where less than 50 percent of the voting-age public was registered to vote in the 1964 election.

The impact of the act was immediate. African American voter registration sky-rocketed, as did the number of African Americans elected to office. For example, in 1965 there were 280 black elected officials at any level in the United States. Since 1965, African American voters have used their strength at the ballot box to elect more black officials at all levels of government. But, while the results have been encouraging, the percentage of elected offices held by African Americans in the eleven southern states covered by the VRA remains relatively small.

The 2000 Census revealed that the Hispanic community in the United States is slightly larger in size than the African American community; thus, Hispanics have the potential to wield enormous political power. In California, Texas, Florida, Illinois, and New York, five key electoral states, Hispanic voters have emerged as powerful allies for candidates seeking office. However, just as voter turnout among African Americans is historically much lower than whites, the turnout among Hispanics is much lower than that among African Americans. In 2004, 55 percent of African Americans voted in the presidential election; only 38 percent of Hispanics turned out to vote.[40]

Like any voting group, Hispanics and Latinos are not easily categorized and voting patterns cannot be neatly generalized. However, several major factors play out as key deci-sion-making variables: one's point of origin, length of time in the United States, and income levels. Although Hispanics and Latinos share a common history of Spanish colo-nialism and similar nation building, they differ in political processes and agendas. Despite having citizenship, Puerto Ricans can vote in a presidential election only if they live on the mainland and establish residency. Cuban Americans are concentrated in south Florida and tend to be conservative and vote for GOP candidates. Mexican American voting pat-terns are very issue-oriented, divided according to income levels and generation.[41]

As more Hispanic candidates run for office, the excitement level and participation of Hispanic voters is likely to increase. The 2004 elections featured several high-pro-file Hispanic candidates, including Colorado's Salazar brothers, Ken, who won a Sen-ate seat, and John, who won a seat in the House. Mel Martinez ran for a Senate seat in Florida and won as well.

Interest in Politics.   Although socio-economic factors undoubtedly influence voter par-ticipation rates, an interest in politics must also be included as an important factor for voter turnout. Many citizens who vote have grown up in families interested and active in politics, and they in turn stimulate their children to take an interest. Additionally, research has determined that interest in politics does not depend on an especially mobilizing candidate. Those citizens involved in the process remain so even if their favored candidate loses; as one political scientist observes, "preconvention mobilization into presidential politics tends to increase participation on behalf of House candidates," even if the candidate for which the individual was mobilized lost the party's presidential nomination.[42] Voters become mobilized for later party work and support after participating in presidential nominating campaigns, whether their favored candidate won or lost. Such workers care more about the outcome of elections and the political process than they do about individual candidates.[43] Conversely, many nonvoters simply do not care about politics or the outcome of elections, never having been taught their importance at a younger age.

People who are highly interested in politics constitute only a small minority of the U.S. population. For example, the most politically active Americans—party and issue-group activists—make up less than 5 percent of the country's more than 285 million people. Those who contribute time or money to a party or a candidate during a campaign make up only about 10 percent of the total population. On the other hand, although these percentages appear low, they translate into millions of Americans who contribute more than just votes to the system.

Why Is Voter Turnout So Low?

The United States has one of the lowest voter participation rates of any nation in the industrialized world. In 1960, 62 percent of the eligible electorate voted in the presidential election, but by 1996, American voter participation had fallen to a record low of 48.8 percent—the lowest general presidential election turnout since 1824. In 2004, participation climbed to 59 percent, the highest it has been since 1968. In contrast, turnout for postwar British elections has fluctuated between 72 percent and 84 percent. Figure 13.6 shows several reasons U.S. nonvoters give for not voting. A number of contributing factors are discussed below.

Too Busy.   Over 39 million eligible voters did not cast a ballot in the 2002 midterm elections. According to the U.S. Census Bureau, 27 percent of registered non-voters surveyed said that they did not vote because they were too busy or had conflicting work or school schedules. Another 13 percent said that they did not vote because they were ill, disabled, or had a family emergency. While these reasons seem to account for a large portion of the people surveyed, they may also reflect the respondents' desire not to seem uneducated about the candidates and issues or apathetic about the political process. Although some would-be voters are undoubtedly busy, infirm, or otherwise unable to make it to the polls, it is likely that many of these nonvoters are offering an easy excuse and have another reason for failing to vote.

Difficulty of Registration.   Of those citizens who are registered, the overwhelming majority vote. The major reason for lack of participation in the United States seems to be that a relatively low percentage of the adult population is registered to vote. There are several reasons for the low U.S. registration rate. First, while nearly every other democratic country places the burden of registration on the government rather than on the individual, in the United States the registration process requires individual initiative—a daunting impediment in this age of political apathy. Thus, the cost (in terms of time and effort) of registering to vote is higher in the United States than it is in other industrialized democracies. Second, many nations automatically register all of their citizens to vote. In the United States, however, citizens must jump the extra hurdle of remembering on their own to register. Indeed, it is no coincidence that voter participation rates dropped markedly after reformers pushed through strict voter registration laws in the early part of the twentieth century. Correspondingly, several recent studies of the effects of relaxed state voter registration laws show that easier registration leads to higher levels of turnout. When states

FIGURE 13.6 Why People Don't Vote

According to the U.S. Census Bureau's Current Population Survey taken after the 2002 elections, "too busy" was the single biggest reason Americans gave for not voting on Election Day. Anger toward politicians and disenchantment with the current political system also drove Americans away from the polls. ∎

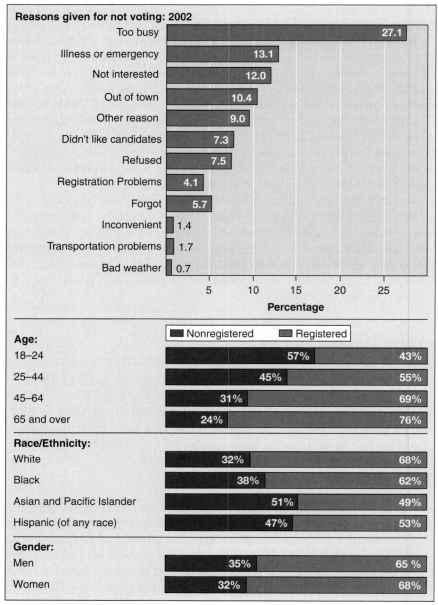

Source: U.S. Census Bureau, Current Population Survey, July 2004.

adopted Election Day registration of new voters, large and significant improvements in turnout occurred among younger voters and the poor.[44] States with a "motor voter" law (allowing citizens to register to vote at the Department of Motor Vehicles) had significantly higher levels of registration and turnout than did states lacking such a law.[45]

Difficulty of Absentee Voting.   Stringent absentee ballot laws are another factor in low voter turnout for the United States. Many states, for instance, require citizens to apply in person for absentee ballots, a burdensome requirement given that one's inability to be present in his or her home state is often the reason for absentee balloting in the first place. Recent literature in political science links liberalized absentee voting rules and higher turnout. One study, for instance, concluded that lax absentee voting restrictions reduced the "costs of voting" and increased turnout when the parties mobilized their followers to take advantage of new lenient absentee voting laws.[46]

Number of Elections.   Another explanation for low voter turnout in this country is the sheer number and frequency of elections, which few if any other democracies can

Comparative

Comparing Voting and Elections

match. Yet, an election cornucopia is the inevitable result of federalism and the separation of powers, which result in layers of often separate elections on the local, state, and national levels.

Voter Attitudes.   Although some of the reasons for low voter participation are due to the institutional factors we have just described, voter attitudes play an equally important part. Some nations, such as Australia and Belgium, try to get around the effects of voter attitudes with compulsory voting laws. Not surprisingly, voter turnout rates in Australia and Belgium are often greater than 95 percent. Other nations fine citizens who do not vote.

As noted previously, some voters are alienated, and others are just plain apathetic, possibly because of a lack of pressing issues in a particular year, satisfaction with the status quo, or uncompetitive (even uncontested) elections. Furthermore, many citizens may be turned off by the quality of campaigns in a time when petty issues and personal mudslinging are more prevalent than ever. Divided government affects voter turnout, with turnout declining by 2 percent in each consecutive election conducted when the presidency and Congress are controlled by different parties.[47] Finally, perhaps turnout has declined because of rising levels of distrust of government. More and more people are telling pollsters that they lack confidence in political leaders. In the past, some scholars argued that there is no correlation between distrust of political leaders and nonvoting. But, as the levels of distrust rise, these preliminary conclusions might need to be revisited.

Photo courtesy: Ron Edmonds/AP/Wide World Photos

■ Citizen Change was one of many organizations that endeavored to educate, register, and turn out young voters in 2004. Here, Sean "P. Diddy" Combs is seen wearing a shirt featuring the group's much-publicized slogan.

Weak Political Parties.   Political parties today are no longer as effective as they once were in mobilizing voters, ensuring that they are registered, and getting them to the polls. As we discussed in chapter 12, the parties once were grassroots organizations that forged strong party-group links with their supporters. Today, these bonds have been stretched to the breaking point for many. Candidate-centered campaigns and the growth of expansive party bureaucracies have resulted in a somewhat more distant party with which most people do not identify very strongly.

How Can the United States Improve Voter Turnout?

Reformers have proposed many ideas to increase voter turnout in the United States. Always on the list is raising the political awareness of young citizens, a reform that inevitably must involve our nation's schools. The rise in formal education levels among Americans has played a significant role in preventing an even greater decline in voter turnout.[48] No less important, and perhaps simpler to achieve, are institutional reforms, though many of the reforms discussed below, if enacted, may result in only a marginal increase in turnout.

The Prepared Voter Kit

Easier Registration and Absentee Voting.   Registration laws vary by state, but in every state except North Dakota, people must register before they can vote. Many observers believe that voter turnout could be increased if registering to vote were made simpler for citizens. The typical thirty-days-before-an-election registration deadline could be shortened to a week or ten days. After all, most people become more interested in voting as Election Day nears. Indeed, allowing citizens to register on the same day as they vote would boost national turnout by five percentage points.[49] Better yet, all U.S. citizens could be registered automatically at the age of eighteen. States could make it easier to obtain absentee ballots by eliminating the in-person requirement.

STUDENTS AND VOTING

In the 2004 presidential election, young voters—those between eighteen and twenty-nine years old—made up only 17 percent of all voters.[a] This should disturb young voters, since their low turnout directly impacts what issues state and federal governments address. Now that the United States has intervened militarily with nations suspected of harboring or assisting terrorists, the government may need to increase the number of soldiers in the military, perhaps by resurrecting the draft. Many state governments are still recovering from the one-two punch of the economic recession resulting from the 9/11 attacks and technology boom-gone-bust, forcing them to cut back or not increase higher education spending. That forces state universities to raise tuitions, a move that might force students to start a (second) job, take out more loans, or even drop out. The stakes are high for young voters, so why aren't they voting?

According to one survey, young voters said they did not vote because they believed their vote does not make a difference, they did not have enough information to make a decision, or they were too busy.[b] Furthermore, nearly half of the students sampled claimed not to discuss politics with their parents, and over half of them believe that schools did not sufficiently educate them on how to vote! Of course, if you do not know how to vote, then you do not vote, and if you never vote, then you never discover that your vote does make a difference.

A number of get-out-the-vote efforts (GOTV) focus on informing young voters about how to vote. Rock the Vote, for instance, provides young voters registration kits and election schedules. However, those with the most to gain from securing the young vote, the two major political parties, remain on the sidelines. Another study shows that over 53 percent of undergraduates claim that neither party contacted them during the 2004 presidential campaign.[c] If one of the parties chooses to fill this gap, it could tilt the balance in their favor in future elections. That would not just be good for the party; it would be good for young voters, since they could use their influence to affect legislation.

[a]National Election Pool exit poll, http://www.cnn.com/ELECTION/2004/pages/results/states/US/P/00/epolls.0.html.

[b]http://www.stateofthevote.org/factsheet.html.

[c]CIRCLE Fact Sheet: College Students in the 2004 Election, Richard Niemi and Michael Hamner, http://www.civicyouth.org/PopUps/FactSheets/FS_College_Voting.pdf.

In 1993, Congress, with support from President Clinton, passed the so-called motor-voter bill, which required states to permit individuals to register by mail, not just in person. The law also allows citizens to register to vote when they visit any motor vehicles office, public assistance agency, or military recruitment division. Proponents of the law said at the time that it would result in the registration of roughly 49 million Americans of voting age with driver's licenses or identification cards. Opponents claimed the law was yet another unfunded federal mandate burdening state governments. Motor-voter registration has not increased voter turnout but rather has slowed the rate of decrease. Recently, states with motor-voter registration have experienced a 6 percent decrease in voter turnout, while those without experienced nearly a 10 percent decrease.[50] Although not the definitive solution for decreasing voter turnout, motor-voter registration still helps while proving the value of innovative election reform for state and federal lawmakers.

Make Election Day a Holiday.   Besides removing an obstacle to voting (the busy workday), making Election Day a national holiday might focus more voter attention on the contests in the critical final hours.

Strengthen Parties.   Reformers have long argued that strengthening the political parties would increase voter turnout, because parties have historically been the organizations in the United States best suited for and most successful at mobilizing citizens to vote. During the late 1800s and early 1900s, the country's "Golden Age" of powerful political parties, one of their primary activities was getting out the vote on Election Day. Even today, the parties' Election Day get-out-the-vote drives increase voter turnout by as many as several million in national contests.

■ A worker at a state motor vehicles office displays the form that makes it easy to register to vote.

Photo courtesy: Dennis Brack/Black Star

Other Suggestions.   Other ideas to increase voter turnout are less practical or feasible. For example, holding fewer elections might sound appealing, but it is difficult to see how this could be accomplished without diluting many of the central tenets of federalism and separation of powers that the Framers believed essential to the protection of liberty. Still other reforms might increase voter turnout, including proportional representation of the congressional vote to encourage third parties and combat voter apathy toward the two major parties, changing Election Day to Saturday or Sunday, and making voting mandatory, which has benefits that far outweigh most Americans' aversion to the idea.[51]

Does Low Voter Turnout Matter?

Some political observers have argued that nonvoting is not a critical problem. For example, some believe that the preferences of nonvoters are not much different from those who do vote. If this is true, the results would be about the same if everyone voted. Others contend that because laws forbid the denial of the vote to previously disfranchised groups—African Americans, women, Hispanics—nonvoting is voluntary. Some say that nonvoters are indicating their acceptance of things as they are, or that we should not attempt to make voting easier for people characterized as apathetic and lazy. Finally, some claim that low voter turnout is a positive benefit, based on the dubious supposition that less-educated people are more easily swayed. Thus, low turnout supposedly increases the stability of the system.

We should not be too quick to accept these arguments, which have much in common with the early nineteenth-century view that the Nineteenth Amendment to the Constitution (which enfranchised women) need not be passed because husbands could protect the interests of their wives. First, voters do not represent nonvoters; the social make-up and attitudes of present-day nonvoters are significantly different from those of voters. Nonvoters tend to be low income, younger, blue collar, less educated, and more heavily minority. Even if their expressed preferences about politics do not look very distinctive, their objective circumstances and their need for government services differ from the majority of those who do vote. These people—who require the most help from government—currently lack a fair share of electoral power. A political system that actively seeks to include and mobilize these people might well produce broader-based policies that differ from those we have today.

In 2004, nationwide voter turnout was just under 60 percent of the voting-age population, nearly 9 percentage points up from 51 percent in 2000. The sudden surge in voter turnout surprised no one. The major political parties and nonpartisan groups had been registering voters throughout the year and in unprecedented numbers. Voters also had much to motivate them with the election predicted to be as close as in 2000 and featuring critical issues such as the war in Iraq, the fate of Social Security, and possible appointments to the Supreme Court (an issue highlighted after Supreme Court Justice William H. Rehnquist underwent thyroid cancer surgery a week before the election). With nearly 60 million viewers watching the first presidential debate, voters also acquainted themselves with the candidates and their stances on the issues. For the first time in decades, the American people seemed politically engaged, and the stakes were high.

This significant improvement from the 2000 election is encouraging, and hopefully the beginning of a trend toward an increased level of participation. The 2000 outcome had offered a mixed message of idealism and cynicism, and we learned anew how one vote really can make a difference. An older generation of Americans learned this in 1960 in the extremely close election where an average of one vote per precinct in the United States made John F. Kennedy the president of the United States. This was so few votes in a handful of states that the power of the individual vote became clear, and perhaps this is a lesson that Americans need to learn and relearn.

On the other hand, the carelessness with which the media handled the 2000 election in its early stages, especially in Florida, did nothing to dispel the doubly false belief of many Americans that their votes would be no more important than usual. Of course, there is bitterness from the realization that for many Americans who did trouble to vote, their vote went uncounted. Thousands of ballots were discarded because of machine or human error; several thousand ballots from Americans living overseas or serving in the military were not counted in the initial tabulation; some polling stations may have unfairly turned away rightful voters. Some of the same problems occurred in 2004 as well.

Turnout in some states exceeded even the national average in 2004. South Dakota experienced a 78 percent turnout of registered voters, very likely because of the high-stakes race between the then Senate minority leader and a popular challenger. Even states with fewer high-profile races saw a huge increase in voter turnout. Maine reached a 73 percent voter turnout, only the third time the state passed the 70 percent mark in its history. Such a sharp increase in voter participation is exciting and undoubtedly good for democracy, but it is uncertain whether such gains are permanent or simply unique to this highly contested presidential race. One test is the level of turnout in the 2006 midterm elections.

Patterns in Vote Choice

Just as there are certain predictable patterns when it comes to American voter turnout (discussed above), so, too, are there predictable patterns of vote choice. One of the most prominent and consistent correlates of vote choice is partisan identification, which is discussed in the previous chapter. Some other consistent and notable correlates of vote choice include race and ethnicity, gender, income, ideology, and issues and campaign-specific developments.

Race and Ethnicity.   Different racial and ethnic groups vote differently from each other. While whites have shown an increasing tendency to vote Republican in recent elections, African American voters remain overwhelmingly Democratic in both their partisan identification and in their voting decisions. Despite the best efforts of the Republican Party to garner African American support, this pattern shows no signs of waning. In 2004, for example, 88 percent of the votes cast by African Americans were cast for Kerry, while Bush received a mere 11 percent of the African American vote.[52]

Hispanics also tend to identify with and vote for Democrats, although not as monolithically as do African Americans.[53] In 2004, for example, Kerry received 53 percent of the votes cast by Hispanics; Bush received only 44 percent. These exit poll data indicate that, in fact, Bush is closing the Democratic lead among Hispanics; however, new research has raised questions as to whether the exit poll data may have been skewed.

The Asian American segment of the electorate is less monolithic and more variable in its voting than either the Hispanic or the African American communities. It is worth noting the considerable political diversity within this group: Chinese Americans tend to prefer Democratic candidates, but Vietnamese Americans, with a strong anticommunist leaning, tend to support Republicans. A typical voting split for the Asian American community in general, though, might run about 60 percent Democratic and 40 percent Republican, though it can reach the extreme of a 50–50 split, depending on the election.

Gender.   There have been elections throughout the twentieth century in which gender was a factor, although precise data are not always available to prove the conventional wisdom. For example, journalists in 1920 claimed that women—in their first presidential election after the passage of the Nineteenth Amendment granted women suffrage—were especially likely to vote for Republican presidential candidate Warren G. Harding. In the sexist view of the day, women were supposedly taken in by the handsome Harding's charm. Recent evidence indicates that women act and react differently from men to some candidacies, including those of other women. For instance, Democratic women were more likely than Democratic men to support Walter Mondale's presidential ticket in 1984 because of former Vice President Mondale's selection of Representative Geraldine Ferraro (D–NY) for the second slot on his presidential ticket. However, Republican women at the time were more likely than GOP men to support Ronald Reagan's candidacy because of Ferraro's presence on the Democratic ticket; Republican women were opposed to Ferraro's liberal voting record and views. Since 1980, the so-called "gender gap" (the difference between the voting choices of men and women) has become a staple of American politics.

Simply put, in most elections today, women are more likely to support the Democratic candidate and men are more likely to support the Republican candidate. The size of the gender gap varies considerably from election to election, though normally the gender gap is between 5 and 7 percentage points. That is, women support the average Democrat 5 to 7 percent more than men support the average Republican candidate. Some elections result in an expanded gender gap though, such as the presidential election of 1996, where the gender gap was an enormous 17 percentage points, about 10 points larger than in 1992. Bob Dole narrowly won among men in 1996, while Bill Clinton scored a landslide among women. In 2004, Bush won 55 percent of the male vote, while Kerry received 51 percent of the female vote. Of importance here is the fact that women now constitute a majority of the adult population in all the American states, and they are a majority of the registered electorate in virtually all of those states. This trend has made it increasingly important for both Democrats and Republicans to seek the votes and support of women.

Income.   Over the years, income has been a remarkably stable correlate of vote choice. The poor vote less often and more Democratic, the well-to-do vote more often and heavily Republican.[55] Indeed, in the 2004 presidential election, those voters who earned less than $15,000 yearly voted for Kerry over Bush by 63 percent to 36 percent, whereas those voters who earned more than $100,000 yearly supported Bush over Kerry by 59 to 41 percent.[56]

Ideology.   Ideology represents one of the most significant cleavages in contemporary American politics. Liberals, generally speaking, favor government involvement in society to try to solve problems, and they are committed to the ideals of tolerance and diversity. Conservatives, on the other hand, think individuals and private organizations, *not* government, should be responsible for solving most problems, and they are dedicated to the promotion of traditional and family values. Moderates, as the name implies, lie somewhere between liberals and conservatives on the ideological spectrum.

Not surprisingly, ideology is very closely related to vote choice. Liberals tend to vote for Democrats, and conservatives tend to vote for Republicans. In 2004, 85 percent of self-described liberals voted for Kerry, whereas only 13 percent voted for Bush. Conservatives, on the other hand, voted for Bush over Kerry at a rate of 84 to 15 percent.[57]

Issues and Campaign-Specific Developments.   In addition to the underlying influences on vote choice discussed above, issues and campaign-specific developments can have important effects on vote choice in any given election year. In the 1992 presidential election, aid to the disadvantaged and the admission of open homosexuals to the military were issues critical to a voter's choice between Bill Clinton or George Bush.[58]

The 2004 election had two major campaign-specific issues, Iraq and the war on terrorism. Early in the campaign, George W. Bush attempted to link the two issues together with the hope that the general support he received in his handling the war on terrorism could help boost flagging ratings for his handling of the war in Iraq. The Kerry campaign's efforts to keep the two issues separate, however, succeeded. Exit polls showed that voters who considered terrorism the most important issue voted 86 to 14 percent for Bush, while those who considered Iraq the most important issue voted 73 to 26 percent for Kerry. Amazingly, while terrorism and Iraq dominated the 2004 election, and even the 2004 Democratic primaries, voters actually cited the economy (20 percent of respondents) and moral values (22 percent) as the most important issues. Terrorism and Iraq were cited by 19 and 15 percent, respectively. Those voters citing the economy as most important voted 82 to 18 percent in favor of Kerry, and those stating moral values as most important voted 80 to 20 percent in favor of Bush. In the end, the campaign-specific issues ran side by side with the perennial problems Americans and their representatives face every day.

Ticket-Splitting

ticket-splitting
Voting for candidates of different parties for various offices in the same election.

Citizens have been increasingly deserting their party affiliations in the polling booths. The practice of **ticket-splitting,** voting for candidates of different parties for various offices in an election, rose dramatically since the 1950s, but has leveled off and started to decline since the early 1990s.[60] The evidence of this development abounds. As already mentioned, Republican presidential landslides in 1956, 1972, 1980, and 1984 were accompanied by the election of substantial Democratic majorities in the House of Representatives. Divided government, with the presidency held by one party and one or both houses of Congress held by the other party, has never been as frequent in U.S. history as it has been recently. From 1920 to 1944, about 15 percent of the congressional districts voted for presidential and House candidates of different parties. But, from 1960 to 1996, at least 25 percent of the districts cast split tickets in any presidential year; in 1984, nearly 50 percent of the districts did so.

Similarly, at the statewide level, only 17 percent of the states electing governors in presidential years between 1880 and 1956 elected state and national executives from different parties. Yet, from 1960 to 1992, almost 40 percent of states holding simultaneous presidential and gubernatorial elections recorded split results. (In 1992 and 1996, this proportion was somewhat lower, just 25 percent and 27 percent, respectively.) Whereas the proportion of states voting for a governor of a party different from that of the president was up in 2000 (to 45 percent), the proportion of congressional districts that voted for a presidential candidate of one party and a congressional candidate of a different party was down to 18 percent,[61] an indication that some voters are increasingly willing to vote a straight party ticket. The 2004 election saw a continued decline in ticket-splitting, resulting in a greater coattail effect for President Bush.

These percentages actually understate the degree of ticket-splitting by individual voters. The Gallup poll has regularly asked its respondents, "For the various political offices, did you vote for all the candidates of one party, that is, a straight ticket, or did you vote for the candidates of different parties [ticket-splitting]?" Since 1968, the proportion of voters who have ticket-split in presidential years has consistently been around 60 percent of the total.[62] Other polls and researchers have found reduced straight-ticket balloting and significant ticket-splitting at all levels of elections, especially since 1952.

Not surprisingly, the intensity of party affiliation is a major determinant of a voter's propensity to split the ticket. Strong party identifiers are the most likely to cast a straight-party ballot; pure independents are the least likely. Somewhat greater proportions of ticket-splitters are found among high-income and better-educated citizens, but there is little difference in the distribution by gender or age. African Americans exhibit the highest straight-party rate of any population subgroup; about three-quarters of all black voters stay in the Democratic Party column from the top to the bottom of the ballot.

Scholars have posited several potential explanations for ticket-splitting. One explanation is that voters split their tickets, consciously or not, because they trust neither party to govern.[63] Under this interpretation, ticket-splitters are aware of the differences between the two parties and split their tickets to augment the checks and balances already present in the Constitution. Alternatively, voters split their tickets possibly because partisanship has become less relevant as a voting cue.[64] Other explanations for ticket-splitting abound. The growth of issue-oriented politics, the mushrooming of single-interest groups, the greater emphasis on candidate-centered personality politics, and broader-based education are all often cited. A strong independent presidential candidacy also helps to loosen party ties among many voters. So, too, does the marked gain in the value of incumbency. Thanks in part to the enormous fattening of congressional constituency services, incumbent U.S. representatives and senators have been able to attract a steadily increasing share of the other party's identifiers.[65]

REFORMING THE ELECTORAL PROCESS

MOST PROPOSALS FOR ELECTORAL REFORM in America center on the Electoral College, as discussed earlier. Abolition of the Electoral College, the establishment of a congressional district plan, and the elimination of electors are at once the most dramatic and apparently urgent reforms, especially in light of the events of the 2000 election—and the least likely to succeed, given the many entrenched interests they serve and the difficulty of amending the Constitution. Changes to the Electoral College, however, are not the only ways in which the election of public officials in America might be improved.

Another possible electoral reform, one that focuses on the nomination rather than the general election in presidential elections, is the idea of holding a series of regional primaries throughout the United States during the first week of each month, beginning in February of a presidential election year. Under this system, the country would be divided into five regions: the Southeast, Southwest, Far West, Midwest, and Northeast. In December of the year prior to the presidential election, states would hold a lottery to determine the order of the primaries, with all regional contests held on the first of every month from February through June. The goals of this reform would be twofold. First, it would end the current "permanent campaign" by preventing candidates from "camping out" in Iowa and New Hampshire for one to two years in the hopes of winning or doing better than expected in these small, unrepresentative states. Second, some rational order would be imposed on the electoral process, allowing candidates to focus on each region's concerns and people in turn.

Another area of electoral reform that has gained attention in recent years involves campaign finance. The Bipartisan Campaign Reform Act, sponsored by Senators John McCain (R–AZ) and Russ Feingold (D–WI), was signed into law in March 2002. This legislation bans unregulated "soft-money" donations to political parties, restricts the use of political ads, and increases political contribution limits for private individuals. Supporters heralded its passage as a major victory in lessening the influence of big money on politics. Unfortunately, political consultants have already found ways around the new legislation, leaving many voters to wonder what change the legislation will effect, if any. Campaign finance will be discussed more thoroughly in chapter 14.

These possible reform ideas should convince you that although individual elections may sometimes be predictable, the electoral system in the United States is anything but static. New generations, and party changers in older generations, constantly remake the political landscape. At least every other presidential election brings a change of administration and a focus on new issues. Every other year, at least a few fresh personalities and perspectives infuse the Congress, as newly elected U.S. senators and representatives claim mandates and seek to shake up the established order. Each election year, tumult and transformation take place in the fifty states and in thousands of localities.

The welter of elections may seem like chaos, but from this chaos comes the order and often explosive productivity of a democratic society. Indeed, the source of all change in the United States, just as Hamilton and Madison predicted, is the individual citizen who goes to the polls and casts a ballot.

In the nineteenth century, political parties ran the elections, supplying not only paper ballots but also many of the poll watchers and election judges. This was a formula for fraud, of course—there was not even a truly secret ballot, as people voted on ballots of different colors, depending on their choice of party. The twentieth century saw widespread improvements in election practices and technology. The states now oversee the election process through official state boards of election, and the use of voting machines, nearly universal in America by the 1970s, permits truly secret mechanical voting. These measures helped effect enormous reductions in fraud and electoral ambiguity—though as the problems of the 2000 and 2004 elections proved, there is still a long way to go.

As more and more Americans become computer savvy, and as computer technology continues to evolve, Internet voting has become a likely way to cast votes in the coming years. Rightly or wrongly, Internet voting equates in the minds of many Americans with the ideals of instant democracy and greater citizen input in major decisions. Many states are formally studying the feasibility and impact of Internet voting. In 2000, Arizona pioneered online balloting by allowing citizens to vote via the Internet in the state's Democratic presidential primary. Opponents and proponents alike recognize potential problems, but technical solutions draw ever nearer.

The use of mail-in ballots, whereby registered voters are mailed ballots and given several weeks to mail them back with their votes, increases participation but delays final tabulation of the ballots for several weeks. Oregon, the only state that votes entirely by mail-in ballots, did not have its 2000 presidential results finalized until several weeks after Election Day. The state of Washington, which has

■ New electronic voting systems are being rolled out across the country as an alternative to traditional paper and punch card balloting. Here, the ESlate System is demonstrated in Austin, Texas.

Photo courtesy: Bob Daemmrich/The Image Works

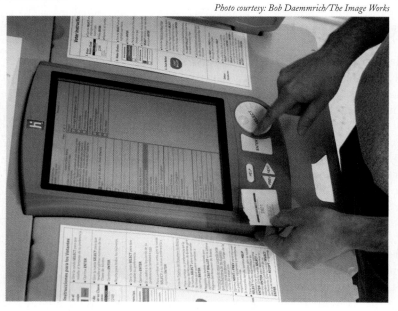

Is California the New Florida?

During the Florida vote recount of the 2000 presidential election, average Americans learned an unsettling truth: the technology they use to vote affects the likelihood that their vote will be counted. One technology in particular, the punch-card ballot, contributed to the confusion over who would be our president, George W. Bush or Al Gore. Politicians, pundits, and voters called for improving voting technology, but which technology a county should pick became a difficult question. The two leading electronic choices were optical scanning technology, the same kind employed on standardized tests, and Digital Recording Electronic devices (DREs), computers that use a touch-screen or keypad interface and record ballots on a hard drive.

Many counties chose DREs. Not only did they fit in with the American love of the "new" and the digital technology boom, but DREs, it was argued, would avoid the perils of punch-card ballots: overvoting and undervoting. DRE software would reject any mistaken attempt to vote for two candidates for the same office, thus preventing overvoting. And, since the machines do not use paper, they would have no risk of "hanging chads" (the bits that adhere to ballot cards when voters don't completely punch out their selections), thus eliminating undervoting. Advocates also argued that the arrangement of candidate names in a big font on a bright screen would make the ballot easier to read than on a punch-card ballot. They also noted that counting votes would take less time than in many other voting systems, since the DRE operator merely dials into a central server and transfers ballots digitally in a matter of seconds. Once all the votes are in, the server instantly has the error-free results.

However, during the 2004 California primaries, DREs were put to the test throughout the state and failed. San Diego County was the most extreme case. One-third of the machines failed when the batteries powering the DREs ran out of juice the night before the election. When the DREs would not turn on the morning of the primaries, officials were at a loss since they had no backup plan. It also turned out that many of the DRE manufacturers were "rejigging and patching their software without heed to the lengthy certification process prescribed by law."[a]

Optical scanning technology, the road not taken in voting technology reform, may actually be preferable to DREs. Researchers from Caltech and MIT tested all existing voting technology and discovered that optical scanning technology recorded votes correctly all but 1.6 percent of the time. Astonishingly, punch-card ballots and DREs both scored a 3 percent error-rate, meaning that counties that exchanged punch-cards for touch-screen systems spent a bunch of taxpayer money to miscount the same number of votes. However, optical scanning is not perfect; the researchers found "in Hawaii in 1998, 7 out of the 361 optical scanners failed to operate properly."[b]

As with any technology, however, it may simply take time for DREs to be perfected and for Americans to get used to them. In the meantime, if you use a punch-card ballot, check the back for hanging chads, and if you're an election official in charge of DREs, please check the batteries the night before the election!

---

[a]Andrew Gumbel, "Out of Touch," *Los Angeles City Beat* (April 29, 2004), http://www.lacitybeat.com/article.php?id=863&IssueNum=47.
[b]Caltech/MIT Voting Technology Project, "Residual Votes Attributable to Technology: An Assessment of the Reliability of Existing Voting Equipment," Version 2, March 30, 2001.

---

extremely liberal laws regarding mail-in votes, was also much later than the rest of the country in announcing its presidential and congressional winners.

The nation also lacks a standardized method by which votes should be recounted in close elections. Many reformers favor a national uniform ballot system for the entire country—every voting locale would use the same kind of ballot. A national ballot is highly unlikely, however. If the federal government mandates a ballot form, it would almost certainly have to pay for it, at a price tag of up to several billion dollars. In addition, there are over 41,000 voting localities in states and jurisdictions across the United States, electing hundreds of thousands of officials, making it extremely difficult to create a uniform type of ballot.

Another change likely to result from the chaos of the 2000 election addresses the technology of the ballot itself. America can look forward to the elimination of the "butterfly ballot," which featured prominently in the heavily contested county of Palm Beach, Florida. Although the ballot was approved for use, it gained national attention because of its confusing layout. After the debacle of ambiguously punched ballots, Americans can also expect to see fewer stylus punch-card ballots, a technologically

Democracy and the Internet

obsolete method of voting whereby voters use increasingly antiquated and faulty voting machines to stamp out a small bit of paper, or chad, to indicate their vote.

Many Americans believe that the federal government should assist states in updating outdated and faulty voting equipment. Some localities across the country use computerized touch-screen machines, which are expensive but much more secure and accurate than the older mechanical devices still in widespread use. An analysis of Florida's voting machines found that older, punch-card machines failed to indicate a vote for president on 1.5 percent of the ballots, while newer, optical-scanning machines failed on only 0.3 percent of the ballots. Additionally, older, error-ridden machines are commonly assigned to low-income and African American precincts, a practice that reintroduces a troublesome discriminatory dimension into the voting process. Indeed, prior to the 2002 midterm elections the Florida legislature undertook massive voting reforms, including banning punch-card ballots and investing $30 million in new touch-screen voting systems, with the individual counties spending tens of millions more. Unfortunately, the tragic scene of election 2000 was replayed in south Florida on September 12, 2002, as problems plagued the Democratic gubernatorial primary. Confusion abounded as voters and poll workers misused the expensive new machines. Election administrators had difficulty tabulating the electronic votes, leading to a week-long delay in naming an official winner. Florida was once again the electoral laughingstock of the nation, and everyone learned an important lesson: technology is not a panacea that will cure all election problems.

Updating election equipment and ensuring fair elections across the country should be a legislative priority, but emphasis must be placed on training poll workers, administrators, and voters how to effectively use the new equipment. As Charles M. Vest, the president of the Massachusetts Institute of Technology, said, "A nation that can send a man to the moon, that can put a reliable ATM machine on every corner, has no excuse not to deploy a reliable, affordable, easy-to-use voting system."

SUMMARY

THE EXPLOSION OF ELECTIONS we have experienced in over 200 years of voting has generated much good and some harm. But, all of it has been done, as Hamilton insisted, "on the solid basis of the consent of the people." In our efforts to explain the complex and multilayered U.S. electoral system, we covered these points in this chapter:

1. **The Purposes of Elections**
   Regular elections guarantee mass political action and governmental accountability. They also confer legitimacy on regimes better than any other method of change.

2. **Kinds of Elections**
   When it comes to elections, the United States has an embarrassment of riches. There are various types of primary elections in the country, as well as general elections, initiatives, referenda, and recall elections. In presidential elections, primaries are sometimes replaced by caucuses, in which party members choose a candidate in a closed meeting, but recent years have seen fewer caucuses and more primaries.

3. **Presidential Elections**
   Variety aside, no U.S. election can compare to the presidential contest. This spectacle, held every four years, brings together all the elements of politics and attracts the most ambitious and energetic politicians to the national stage.

4. **Congressional Elections**
   Many similar elements are present in different kinds of elections. Candidates, voters, issues, and television advertisements are constants. But, there are distinctive aspects of each kind of election as well. Compared with presidential elections, congressional elections are a different animal.

5. **Voting Behavior**
   Whether they are casting ballots in congressional or presidential elections, voters behave in certain distinct ways and exhibit unmistakable patterns to political scientists who study them.

6. **Reforming the Electoral Process**
   The American political system uses indirect electoral representation in the form of the Electoral College. Events of the 2000 election have renewed a longstanding debate over the legitimacy and efficacy of this institution and sparked controversial calls for change. Other suggested reforms are regional primaries and campaign finance limits. Some states have promoted new voting technologies to eliminate problems with punch-card ballots and protect against voter fraud.

KEY TERMS

closed primary, p. 463
critical election, p. 479
crossover voting, p. 463
elector, p. 473
Electoral College, p. 473
electorate, p. 461
front-loading, p. 469
general election, p. 464
gerrymandering p. 483
initiative, p. 465
mandate, p. 461
midterm election, p. 486
nonpartisan primary, p. 463
open primary, p. 463
party realignment, p. 479
primary election, p. 463
prospective judgment, p. 461
raiding, p. 463
referendum, p. 465
regional primary, p. 468
retrospective judgment, p. 461
runoff primary, p. 463
secular realignment, p. 481
superdelegate, p. 470
ticket-splitting, p. 502
turnout, p. 490
unit rule, p. 470

SELECTED READINGS

Bartels, Larry M. *Presidential Primaries and the Dynamics of Public Choice.* Princeton, NJ: Princeton University Press, 1988.

Berelson, Bernard R., Paul F. Lazarsfeld, and William N. McPhee. *Voting: A Study of Opinion Formation in a Presidential Campaign,* reprint ed. Chicago: University of Chicago Press, 1986.

Burnham, Walter Dean. *Critical Elections and the Mainsprings of American Politics.* New York: Norton, 1970.

Campbell, Angus, Philip E. Converse, Warren E. Miller, and Donald E. Stokes, reprint ed. *The American Voter.* Chicago: University of Chicago, 1980.

Carroll, Susan J. *Women as Candidates in American Politics.* Bloomington: Indiana University Press, 1994.

Conway, M. Margaret. *Political Participation in the United States,* 3rd ed. Washington, DC: CQ Press, 2000.

Darcy, Robert, Susan Welch, and Janet Clark. *Women, Elections, and Representation,* 2nd ed. Lincoln: University of Nebraska Press, 1994.

Fiorina, Morris P. *Retrospective Voting in American National Elections.* New Haven, CT: Yale University Press, 1999.

Herrnson, Paul S. *Congressional Elections: Campaigning at Home and in Washington,* 3rd ed. Washington, DC: CQ Press, 2000.

Jacobson, Gary C. *The Electoral Origins of Divided Government.* Boulder, CO: Westview, 1990.

Jacobson, Gary C. *The Politics of Congressional Elections,* 5th ed. New York: HarperCollins, 2000.

Key, V. O., Jr., with Milton C. Cummings. *The Responsible Electorate.* Cambridge, MA: Harvard University Press, 1966.

Nie, Norman H., Sidney Verba, and John R. Petrocik. *The Changing American Voter.* Cambridge, MA: Harvard University, 1980.

Patterson, Thomas E. *The Vanishing Voter: Public Involvement in an Age of Uncertainty.* New York: Vintage, 2003.

Sabato, Larry J. *Midterm Madness: The Elections of 2002.* Lanham, MD: Rowman and Littlefield, 2003.

Sabato, Larry J., Howard R. Ernst, and Bruce A. Larson. *Dangerous Democracy?: The Battle over Ballot Initiatives in America.* Lanham, MD: Rowman and Littlefield, 2001.

Sundquist, James L. *Dynamics of the Party System: Alignment and Realignment of Political Parties in the United States.* Washington, DC: Brookings Institution, 1983.

Teixeira, Ruy. *The Disappearing American Voter.* Washington, DC: Brookings Institution, 1992.

Verba, Sidney, Norman H. Nie, and Jae-on Kim. *Participation and Political Equality.* Chicago: University of Chicago Press, 1987.

Verba, Sidney, Kay Lehman Schlozman, and Henry E. Brady. *Voice and Equality: Civic Voluntarism in American Politics.* New York: Belknap Press, 1996.

Wayne, Stephen J. *The Road to the White House,* 6th ed. New York: Wadsworth, 2003.

Weisberg, Herbert F., ed. *Democracy's Feast: Elections in America.* Chatham, NJ: Chatham House, 1995.

WEB EXPLORATIONS

To select, evaluate, and debate upcoming referenda or initiatives currently under consideration in California, the "Referendum State," see
http://www.calvoter.org/

To see how presidential candidates presented themselves in the technology age of the 2004 race, see the official sites of some of the past, and possibly future, candidates.
http://www.johnkerry.com/
http://www.gop.com/

To learn about the functions of the Federal Election Commission, the government agency that monitors and enforces campaign finance and election laws, see
http://www.fec.gov/

To access the most up-to-date, high-quality data on voting, public opinion, and political participation, go to
http://www.gallup.com/

To learn more about the Electoral College, go to
http://www.fec.gov/pages/ecmenu2.htm

To learn more about candidates you have supported in the past or to familiarize yourself with other political candidates so you can make informed choices, go to
http://www.vote-smart.org/

To look at what voters said before going to the polls and whom they actually voted for, go to
http://www.pollingreport.com/

Photo courtesy: © Kate Wade/San Francisco Chronicle/Corbis

The Campaign Process

BY OCTOBER 2003, Senator John Kerry (D–MA) was second to former Governor Howard Dean (D–VT) in cash raised for the Democratic presidential primary. Kerry had amassed about $20 million; Dean, $25 million. Dean had the advantage and the momentum, but he and his campaign team, it seems, did not have a clue as to how to use them. While both Dean and Kerry spent about $1 million in Iowa, Kerry spent twice as much in New Hampshire on political advertisements. Pouring money into a campaign is not everything, however. Dean made foolish mistakes, such as spending $50,000 on a $1,500-a-plate Carly Simon fund-raising dinner. Although the event made $200,000, it cost far more than it might have—the money spent could well have gone to something far more important. In fact, Dean became known for throwing money around. One journalist reflected that the Dean campaign lacked attention to the big picture (winning), being more worried about custom-made Louisville Sluggers and fleece pullovers than poll numbers.[1] Dean's mistakes eventually led to his downward slide and Kerry's nomination.

Nevertheless, Dean made Kerry spend much of his money merely to keep up, leaving Kerry so strapped that he had to take out a loan of $6 million. Kerry's fund-raising picked up as it became clear he would be the Democrats' nominee. But, President George W. Bush had $200 million to Kerry's $110 million, even though Kerry's fund-raising began to exceed Bush's in dollars per day. Kerry contemplated not accepting the Democratic Party's nomination until well after the party's national convention, so that he could spend all the money he raised himself before being limited to public matching funds while Bush spent freely. Bush had proven to be a perfect fund-raising machine, leaving Kerry to engage in creative funding techniques just to stay in the race.

By June, however, it became clear that Kerry was not as badly off as he seemed. Liberal groups such as MoveOn and Media Fund had aired anti-Bush television spots 56,627 times in contested states alone.[2] Meanwhile, Michael Moore's editorial documentary *Fahrenheit 9/11* presented an intensely critical portrayal of how Bush handled the terrorist attacks of September 11, 2001, and speculated about Bush connections to possible supporters of Osama bin Laden. Although Kerry had nothing to do with the production of the film or with the groups producing the anti-Bush ads, he benefited. *Fahrenheit 9/11*, for example, served as the negative advertising Kerry would otherwise have had to consider running. In addition, the film—at one point holding the highest ticket sales of any movie in the nation—reached a huge audience, a large portion of which were young potential voters, who are notoriously uninformed about politics. MoveOn, Media Fund, and Moore had effectively campaigned for Kerry throughout June, and Kerry didn't pay a cent but stayed above the fray, announcing Senator John Edwards as his vice presidential candidate and preparing for what would turn out to be a heated general election campaign in the fall.

UP TO THIS POINT in the book, we have focused on the election decision and have said little about the campaign conducted prior to the balloting. Today many critics denounce electioneering and politicians for their negative use of the airwaves and the perceived disproportionate influence of a few wealthy donors and a handful of well-endowed and well-organized political action committees and interest groups. Nonetheless, the basic purpose of modern electioneering remains intact: one person asking another for support, an approach unchanged since the dawn of democracy.

The art of campaigning involves the science of polls, the planning of sophisticated mass mailings, and the coordination of electronic telephone banks—and, recently, the creation of a campaign Web site coordinated with e-mail updates to reach potential voters and donors. More importantly, it also involves the diplomatic skill of unifying disparate individuals and groups to achieve a fragile but election-winning majority. How candidates perform this exquisitely difficult task is the subject of this chapter, in which we discuss the following topics:

- First, we will explore the *structure of a campaign,* the process of seeking and winning votes in the run-up to an election, which consists of five separate components: the nomination campaign, the general election campaign, the personal campaign, the organizational campaign, and the media campaign.

- Second, we will look at the *media and campaigns* and how candidates make use of both paid and free media.

- Third, we will analyze *campaign finance,* the features and potential implications of the Bipartisan Campaign Reform Act of 2002, and possible finance reform in the future.

- Finally, we will discuss the *2004 presidential campaign and election* and assess its importance.

THE STRUCTURE OF A CAMPAIGN

A CAMPAIGN FOR HIGH OFFICE (such as the presidency, a governorship, or a U.S. Senate seat) is a highly complex effort akin to running a multimillion-dollar business. Campaigns for local offices are usually less complicated, but all campaigns, no matter what their size, have common characteristics. Each election campaign consists of several smaller campaigns that balance one another. They are:

nomination campaign
That part of a political campaign aimed at winning a primary election.

- The **nomination campaign.** During the nomination campaign, the candidate targets the leaders and activists who choose nominees in primaries or conventions. Party leaders are concerned with electability, while party activists are often ideologically and issue oriented, so a candidate must appeal to both bases. The nomination campaign begins as soon as the candidate has decided to run—sometimes as much as two years prior to an official announcement—and ends the night of the party primary or convention.

- The **general election campaign.** A farsighted candidate never forgets the ultimate goal: winning the general election. Therefore the candidate tries to avoid taking stands that, however pleasing to party activists in the primary, will alienate a majority of the larger general election constituency. Sometimes, if the candidate is a clear frontrunner, he or she may transition the nomination campaign into a general election campaign before the nomination is official.

- The **personal campaign.** Candidates must be seen by the voters, and they must cultivate a positive image. Therefore, the candidate and his or her family and supporters make appearances, meet voters, hold press conferences, and give speeches. The personal campaign begins as soon as the candidate wants to run for office, since it lays the groundwork for the organizational and media campaigns discussed below.

- The **organizational campaign.** In contrast to the public nature of the personal campaign, the organizational campaign consists of behind-the-scenes efforts to ensure the campaign is running effectively. For fund-raising, voter contact, and the media campaign, a candidate needs a strong campaign organization. The organizational campaign begins once the candidate has been able to drum up the capital and personnel to invest in what will hopefully turn into more money, volunteers, and—most importantly—votes.

- The **media campaign.** The goal of this aspect of campaigning is for the candidate to reach out to the voters—whether in person, or via the media—in order to create a positive impression and ultimately gain votes. On television and radio, the candidate's paid advertisements air frequently in an effort to convince the public that the candidate is the best person for the job. Meanwhile, campaigners attempt to influence press coverage of the campaign by the print and electronic news reporters.

Photo courtesy: Playboy *magazine, reproduced by special permission.* *Copyright 1992 by Playboy*

■ "Next time, why don't you run? You're a well-known figure, people seem to like you, and you haven't had an original idea in years." Name recognition is often more important than political ideology for winning campaigns.

general election campaign
That part of a political campaign aimed at winning a general election.

personal campaign
That part of a political campaign concerned with presenting the candidate's public image.

organizational campaign
That part of a political campaign involved in fund-raising, literature distribution, and all other activities not directly involving the candidate.

media campaign
That part of a political campaign in which the candidate reaches out to the voters, in person or via the media, to create a positive impression and gain votes.

The Nomination Campaign

The nomination campaign gives new candidates an opportunity to get their sea legs early on. As they seek their party's nomination, candidates learn to adjust to the pressure of being in the spotlight day in and day out. This is the time for the candidates to learn that a single careless phrase could end the campaign or guarantee a defeat. This is also the time to seek the support of party leaders and interest groups and to test out themes, slogans, and strategies. The press and public take much less notice of shifts in strategy at this time than they will later in the general election campaign.

The nomination campaign is a critical time for gaining and maintaining the aura of support both within the party and with the larger electorate. A study of the weeks leading up to the 1988 Republican convention found that Vice President George Bush, the eventual Republican nominee for president, converted support from other Republican candidates through a variety of means. Much of this new support, therefore, grew out of Bush's previous success and a sense of inevitability, not necessarily out of support for his issue positions or campaign themes.[3] These principles also clearly apply to the

Photo courtesy: Jim West/The Image Works

■ Former Vermont Governor Howard Dean addresses a rally during his presidential primary campaign in November, 2003. Dean was the early front-runner for the Democratic nomination.

2004 campaign. For example, John Kerry campaigned with his former competitors for the Democratic ticket, such as Dick Gephardt and Howard Dean, and even named John Edwards, Kerry's toughest opponent during the primaries, as his vice presidential nominee.

A danger that is not widely recognized by candidates during the nomination campaign is that in the quest to win the party's nomination, a candidate can move too far to the right or the left and become too extreme for the November electorate. Diehard activists voters, who are often more extreme than other members of their own party, tend to participate in primaries and caucuses. If a candidate tries too hard to appeal to their interests, he or she jeopardizes the ultimate goal of winning the election. Conservative Barry Goldwater, the 1964 Republican nominee for president, and liberal George McGovern, the 1972 Democratic nominee for president, both fell victim to this phenomenon in seeking their party's nomination—Goldwater going too far right, and McGovern going too far left—and they were handily defeated in the general elections by Presidents Lyndon B. Johnson and Richard M. Nixon, respectively.

The General Election Campaign

After earning the party's nomination, candidates embark on the general election campaign (see The Living Constitution). They must seek the support of groups and voters and decide on the issues they will emphasize. When courting interest groups, a candidate seeks both money and endorsements, although the results are mainly predictable: liberal, labor, and minority groups usually back Democrats, while conservative and business organizations support Republicans. The most active groups often coalesce around emotional issues such as abortion and gun control, and these organizations can produce a bumper crop of money and activists for favored candidates.

Virtually all candidates adopt a brief theme, or slogan, to serve as a rallying cry in their quest for office. In 2004, the Kerry-Edwards campaign adopted the slogan "A Stronger America" in order to emphasize the security issue. Most slogans can fit many candidates ("She thinks like us," "He's on our side," "She hears you," "You know where he stands"). Candidates try to avoid controversy in their selection of slogans, and some openly eschew ideology. (An ever-popular one of this genre is "Not left, not right—forward!") The clever candidate also attempts to find a slogan that cannot be lampooned easily. In 1964, Barry Goldwater's handlers may have regretted their choice of "In your heart, you know he's right" when Lyndon B. Johnson's supporters quickly converted it into "In your guts, you know he's nuts." (Democrats were trying to portray Goldwater as a warmonger after the Republican indicated a willingness to use nuclear weapons.)

In addition to deciding on the issues to focus on during the campaign, the candidate must also define his or her stance on other topics of interest to voters. A variety of factors influence candidates' positions and core issues, including personal conviction, party platform, and experience in a certain area. Candidates also utilize public opinion polling to gauge whether or not the issues that they care about are issues that the voters care about.

Roots of Government

STUMP SPEECHES PAST AND PRESENT

SENATOR JOHN EDWARDS (D–NC) gave one of the most memorable stump speeches of the 2004 presidential election. In the speech, called "The Two Americas," Edwards discussed how the wealthy minority of Americans live in stark contrast to the majority of working and middle-class Americans. The contrast was not to provoke a "hate-the-rich" politics of envy but to demonstrate how the disparity between the two groups was too great and could be closed only by improving state services, repealing tax breaks for the rich, and giving greater tax relief to the middle class. On the stump, President George W. Bush often imbues his speeches with a religious tone as an expression of his faith and how it affects his conceptions of liberty.

Themes of economic inequality and religion are not unique to our present political situation but operate in a long tradition of stump speeches. President Andrew Jackson, the first president not from either Massachusetts or Virginia, was the first to engage large crowds with speeches. The times had changed since the westward expansion of the United States and the loosening of voting rights standards took power away from the ruling elite that had governed since the nation's founding. Jackson gave his speeches in common-man style, making use of his war hero status and opposition to the Second Bank of the United States, believed to be an institution favoring the rich.

In 1896, William Jennings Bryan continued the Jacksonian tradition in his legendary Cross of Gold speech, in which he harangued the Democratic Party for considering using gold as the standard by which to set American currency, a move that would benefit, in Bryan's opinion, wealthy city dwellers while hurting the agricultural base of the Democratic Party. "There are two ideas of government," Bryan said.

"There are those who believe that, if you only legislate to make the well-to-do prosperous, their prosperity will leak through on those below. The Democratic idea, however, has been that if you legislate to make the masses prosperous, their prosperity will find its way up through every class which rests upon them." Clearly, when Edwards says, "We shouldn't have two tax systems, one for the special interests, the big corporations, many of whom pay no taxes at all, and one for all those families who just work hard every year and pay their taxes and carry the tax burden in America," he honors Bryan's concept of the "two ideas of government" and a long-standing tradition of Democratic stump speeches.

Bush, in defense of his invasion of Iraq, stated: "liberty is not America's gift to the world—liberty and freedom are God's gift to every man and woman who lives in this world."[a] His religious conception of liberty is also part of a tradition of stump speeches, one easily traceable to Abraham Lincoln, who asked a September 11, 1858, Edwardsville audience, "What constitutes the bulwark of our own liberty and independence?" He then answered, "Our reliance is in the *love of liberty* which God has planted in our bosoms." For some, Bush's frequent use of "God talk" is disquieting, while others find it reassuring.

Obviously, the 2004 presidential election candidates stood on the shoulders of giants, but they themselves have contributed to the ever growing tradition of stump speeches, both by operating within the tradition and by slightly changing its course—Edwards by making inequality a need to uplift and Bush by making piety into a foreign policy.

---

[a]George W. Bush, "Remarks via Satellite by the President to the National Association of Evangelicals Convention," Washington, DC, March 3, 2004.

The Personal Campaign

In the effort to show voters that they are hardworking, thoughtful, and worthy of the office they seek, candidates try to meet personally as many citizens as possible in the course of a campaign. To some degree, these personal campaign events are symbolic, especially for presidential candidates, since it is possible to have direct contact with only a limited number of people. But, one cannot underestimate the value of visiting numerous localities to increase media coverage and to motivate local activists who are working for the candidate's campaign.

In a typical campaign, a candidate for high office maintains an exhausting schedule. The day may begin at 5 a.m. at the entrance gate to an auto plant with an hour or two of handshaking, followed by similar glad-handing at subway stops until 9 a.m. Strategy sessions with key advisers and preparation for upcoming presentations and forums may fill the rest of the morning. A luncheon talk, afternoon fundraisers, and a

■ Right-wing 1964 Republican candidate Barry Goldwater's famous slogan, "In your heart, you know he's right," was quickly lampooned by incumbent Democratic opponent President Lyndon B. Johnson's campaign as "In your guts, you know he's nuts."

Photo courtesy: Bettmann/Corbis

series of television and print interviews crowd the afternoon agenda. Cocktail parties are followed by a dinner speech, perhaps telephone or neighborhood canvassing of voters, and a civic-forum talk or two. More meetings with advisers and planning for the next day's events can easily take a candidate past midnight. Following only a few hours of sleep, the candidate starts all over again. After months of this grueling pace, the candidate may be functioning on automatic pilot and sometimes momentarily may be unable to think clearly.

Beyond the strains this fast-lane existence adds to a candidate's family life, the hectic schedule leaves little time for reflection and long-range planning. Is it any wonder that under these conditions many candidates commit gaffes?

The Organizational Campaign

The organizational campaign is the behind-the-scenes business effort that funds and supports the candidate. It raises money from supporters, which is then spent on the campaign infrastructure: a staff, offices, television advertising production and airing, direct mail, fund-raising dinners, and public opinion polling that helps reveal to campaign managers which issues the public cares about.

Also, volunteers walk the streets of their neighborhoods, going door to door to solicit votes, while other volunteers use computerized telephone banks to call targeted voters with scripted messages. Both contact methods are termed **voter canvass.** Most canvassing, or direct solicitation of support, takes place in the month before the election,

voter canvass
The process by which a campaign reaches individual voters, either by door-to-door solicitation or by telephone.

The Living Constitution

Congress shall make no law . . .
abridging the freedom of speech. . .

—First Amendment

When the Founding Fathers set about writing the Constitution and the Bill of Rights, they were not specific in their definition of free speech in the First Amendment. Therefore it has been up to subsequent Congresses, presidents, Supreme Courts, and others to interpret and expand on their very simple, elegant definition. Today, we have an elaborate campaign finance system that balances free speech with the need to prevent political corruption. The Supreme Court has repeatedly addressed that difficult balance in cases such as *Buckley* v. *Valleo* (1976) and *McConnell* v. *Federal Election Commission* (2003).

Essentially, the Founders looked at campaigning as crass and beneath the dignity of office holders. At least theoretically, they believed that the office should seek the person, although in practice many of them were very ambitious and intensely sought high elected office. They did not do so in the context of a mass electorate, but rather by means of the aristocratic gentry that acted through the Electoral College to select our presidents and vice presidents.

In this era of ultra-democracy, when everyone expects to have a voice, even if not bothering to cast a ballot, the system must operate very differently. As a result, candidates campaign by raising hundreds of millions of dollars, visiting television studio after television studio for news coverage, holding media events, taping paid television and radio advertisements, and using the Internet for communication with their supporters.

The candidates' free speech is augmented by the free speech of those who have interests in seeing one candidate elected and the other defeated in a particular race. Thus, there are the political parties, raising money and doing everything described in chapter 12. There are political action committees (PACs)—the contributing arms of special interest groups on the left, on the right, and in the middle. There also are the so-called "527 committees," a recent creation that stems from the effects of the Bipartisan Campaign Finance Act of 2002, generally created to attack the opposing candidates through television and radio ads, as well as individual voter contact. And, finally, there are completely independent political committees that can raise and spend whatever they want, for whatever interests they support and prefer—so long as they have no direct or indirect contact with any campaign organizations.

It is amazing that all of these aspects have developed from the powerful words of the First Amendment. The Founders could hardly have imagined what massive enterprises campaigns would become, and what the few words they penned on parchment would create with the passing of two centuries.

Photo courtesy: Brooks Kraft/Corbis

■ Democratic Presidential nominee John Kerry responds to supporters at a rally in Pittsburgh, Pennsylvania in July, 2004. During his speech, Kerry announced that Senator John Edwards would be his vice presidential running mate.

get-out-the-vote (GOTV)
A push at the end of a political campaign to encourage supporters to go to the polls.

campaign manager
The individual who travels with the candidate and coordinates the many different aspects of the campaign.

campaign consultant
The private-sector professionals and firms who sell to a candidate the technologies, services, and strategies required to get that candidate elected.

finance chair
A professional who coordinates the fund-raising efforts for the campaign.

pollster
A professional who takes public opinion surveys that guide political campaigns.

direct mailer
A professional who supervises a political campaign's direct-mail fund-raising strategies.

You Are a Presidential Campaign Consultant

when voters are paying attention. Close to Election Day, the telephone banks begin vital **get-out-the-vote (GOTV)** efforts, reminding supporters to vote and arranging for their transportation to the polls if necessary. As the media become less effective in encouraging political education and participation, candidates increasingly realize the value of identifying base voters and getting them to the polls.

Depending on the level of the office sought, the organizational staff can consist of a handful of volunteers or hundreds of paid specialists supplementing and directing the work of thousands of volunteers. Presidential campaign organizations have the most elaborate structure. At the top of the chart is the **campaign manager,** who coordinates and directs the campaign. The campaign manager is the person closest to the candidate, the person who delivers the good and bad news about the condition of the campaign and makes the essential day-to-day decisions, such as whom to hire and when to air which television ad.

Campaign consultants are the private-sector professionals and firms who sell to a candidate the technologies, services, and strategies required to get that candidate elected to his or her office of choice. Their numbers have grown exponentially since they first appeared in the 1930s, and their specialties and responsibilities have increased accordingly, to the point that they are now an obligatory part of campaigns at almost any level of government. Candidates hire generalist consultants to oversee their entire campaign from beginning to end. Alongside the generalist consultant are more specialized consultants who focus on the new and complex technologies for only one or two areas, such as fund-raising, polling, mass mailings, media relations, advertising, and speech writing.

Figure 14.1 shows the organizational chart for the George W. Bush reelection campaign. The reelection committee is headed by Ken Mehlman, who worked at the White House for three years before resigning in mid-2003 to head the reelection committee. An important player in the campaign is not on the chart. Perhaps the key political person in the White House staff is Karl Rove, a long-time friend and colleague of Bush. Rove masterminded Bush's nomination and general election in 2000 and performed the same function in 2004 while remaining in the White House. Mehlman clearly answered to Rove.

Other key positions include the **finance chair,** who is responsible for bringing in the large contributions that fund the campaign, the **pollster,** who takes public opinion surveys to learn what issues voters want candidates to address in speeches, and the **direct mailer,** who supervises direct-mail fund-raising.

Many critics claim that consultants strip campaigns of substance and reduce them to a clever bag of tricks for sale. Others insist that despite the prevalence of consultants, running for office is still the bread and butter of campaigns: shaking hands, speaking persuasively, and listening to the voters. Voters, they say, are smart enough to tell the difference between a good candidate and a bad one, regardless of the smoke and mirrors erected by their consultants. Nevertheless, consultants do make a difference. In campaigns for the U.S. House of Representatives, for example, the use of professional campaign consultants has been shown to have a positive impact on candidates' fund-raising ability[4] and on candidates' final vote shares.[5]

The Media Campaign

The media campaign is as complex as it is essential for a candidate to win election. The various elements that make up the media (television, radio, the Internet, newspapers,

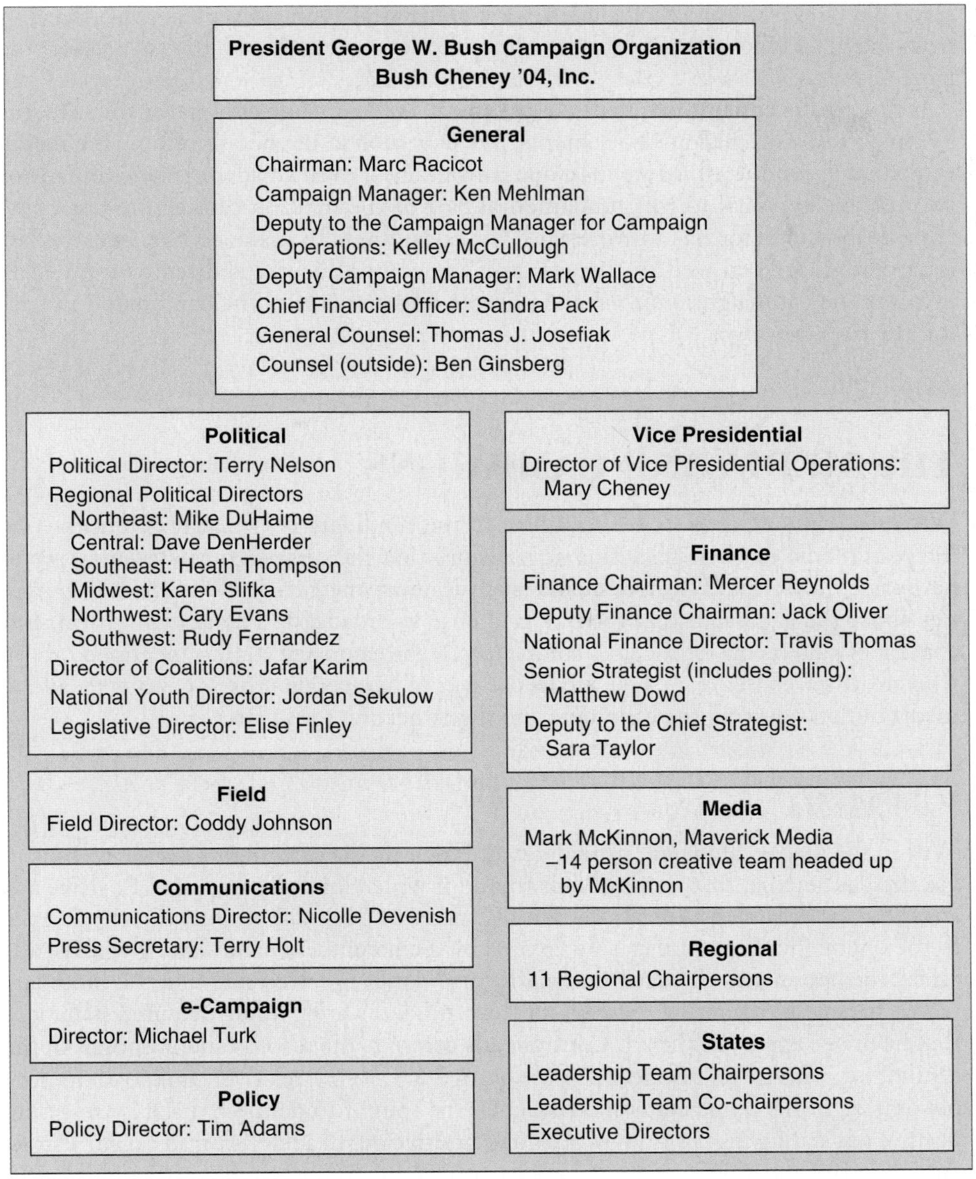

FIGURE 14.1 Bush Campaign
Organizational Chart. ■

**President George W. Bush Campaign Organization
Bush Cheney '04, Inc.**

General

Chairman: Marc Racicot

Campaign Manager: Ken Mehlman

Deputy to the Campaign Manager for Campaign
  Operations: Kelley McCullough

Deputy Campaign Manager: Mark Wallace

Chief Financial Officer: Sandra Pack

General Counsel: Thomas J. Josefiak

Counsel (outside): Ben Ginsberg

Political

Political Director: Terry Nelson

Regional Political Directors
  Northeast: Mike DuHaime
  Central: Dave DenHerder
  Southeast: Heath Thompson
  Midwest: Karen Slifka
  Northwest: Cary Evans
  Southwest: Rudy Fernandez

Director of Coalitions: Jafar Karim

National Youth Director: Jordan Sekulow

Legislative Director: Elise Finley

Vice Presidential

Director of Vice Presidential Operations:
  Mary Cheney

Finance

Finance Chairman: Mercer Reynolds

Deputy Finance Chairman: Jack Oliver

National Finance Director: Travis Thomas

Senior Strategist (includes polling):
  Matthew Dowd

Deputy to the Chief Strategist:
  Sara Taylor

Field

Field Director: Coddy Johnson

Media

Mark McKinnon, Maverick Media
  –14 person creative team headed up
  by McKinnon

Communications

Communications Director: Nicolle Devenish

Press Secretary: Terry Holt

Regional

11 Regional Chairpersons

e-Campaign

Director: Michael Turk

States

Leadership Team Chairpersons

Leadership Team Co-chairpersons

Executive Directors

Policy

Policy Director: Tim Adams

---

and magazines) are the best methods available to candidates to get their message to every potential voter. Candidates employ a network of staff to manage the different kinds of media.

The **communications director** develops the overall media strategy for the candidate, carefully blending press coverage with paid TV, radio, and mail media. A candidate cannot merely buy an election by blasting major media markets with political advertising. That is both an inefficient and extremely expensive method. A candidate cannot rely entirely on the attention of the press, since the press interests are capricious and never align with those of the candidate. The communications director develops a strategy of using both paid and free media to market a candidate most effectively to voters, such as airing negative ads in areas recently visited by the competing candidate.

The **press secretary** is charged with interacting and communicating with journalists on a daily basis. We are all familiar with the campaign press secretary, since it is his or her job to be quoted in the newspapers or on TV explaining the candidate's positions or reacting to the actions of the opposing candidate. Good news is usually announced by the candidate. Bad news, including attacks from the other side, is the preserve of the press secretary (better to have someone not on the ballot doing the dirty work of the campaign). The press secretary's position is a stressful one, as he or she must be available at all hours,

communications director
The person who develops the overall media strategy for the candidate, blending the free press coverage with the paid TV, radio, and mail media.

press secretary
The individual charged with interacting and communicating with journalists on a daily basis.

seven days a week, holidays included, for a demanding, voracious press corps that fills news shows and files print or Internet edition stories at all hours. This is not a job for the faint-hearted.

The **media consultant,** as discussed above, is the outside contractor who designs TV and radio and mail advertisements. We now look at the details of how the media campaign is conducted. More than one consultant or even an advertising company or two may be assigned to this fundamental part of the modern campaign. The communications director has to work with the consultants to make certain that the key issues are addressed well in the ads, and the communications director frequently involves the campaign manager, the pollster, and sometimes the candidate in crafting the paid messages.

media consultant
A professional who produces candidates' television, radio, and print advertisements.

You Are a Media Consultant to a Political Candidate

THE MEDIA AND CAMPAIGNS

WHAT VOTERS ACTUALLY SEE and hear of the candidate is primarily determined by the **paid media** (such as television advertising) that the campaign creates and pays to have disseminated, and the **free media** (such as newspaper articles) that result from stories about the campaign that the media choose to broadcast. The amount, form, and content of paid media are dictated completely by the campaign staffers mentioned above who create advertisements. Free media consists of independent press coverage—all the media outlets covering the candidate and his or her run for office.

paid media
Political advertisements purchased for a candidate's campaign.

free media
Coverage of a candidate's campaign by the news media.

Paid Media

Within the media campaign, candidates and their media consultants decide on how to use the paid media; that is, which ads to air for which kind of campaign. **Positive ads** stress the candidate's qualifications, family, and issue positions with no direct reference to the opponent. These are usually favored by the incumbent candidate. **Negative ads** attack the opponent's character and platform and may not even mention the candidate who is paying for the airing—except for the candidate's brief, legally required statement that he or she approved the ad. **Contrast ads** compare the records and proposals of the candidates, with a bias toward the sponsor. In 2004, Kerry, relatively unknown to people outside of his home state of Massachusetts, sought to define himself by releasing positive ads stating his position on taxes and health care. In a television ad called "Patriot Act," the Bush campaign sought to use contrast ads to portray Kerry as weak by his reversal of support for the Patriot Act after receiving criticism from fellow Democrats. All three kinds of ads can inject important (as well as trivial) issues into a campaign.

Most paid advertisements are short **spot ads** that range from ten to sixty seconds long, though some may run as long as thirty minutes and take the form of documentaries. Although negative advertisements have grown dramatically in number during the past two decades, they have been a part of American campaigns for some time. In 1796, Federalists portrayed presidential candidate Thomas Jefferson as an atheist and a coward. In Jefferson's bid for a second term in 1800, Federalists again attacked him, this time spreading a rumor that he was dead. The effects of negative advertising are well documented. Voters frequently vote *against* the other candidate, and negative ads can provide the critical justification for such a vote.

Before the 1980s, well-known incumbents usually ignored negative attacks from their challengers, believing that the proper stance was to be above the fray. But, after some well-publicized defeats of incumbents in the early 1980s in which negative television advertising played a prominent role,[6] incumbents began attacking their challengers in earnest. The new rule of politics became "An attack unanswered is an attack agreed to." In a further attempt to stave off brickbats from challengers, incumbents began anticipating the substance of their opponents' attacks and airing **inoculation ads**

positive ad
Advertising on behalf of a candidate that stresses the candidate's qualifications, family, and issue positions, without reference to the opponent.

negative ad
Advertising on behalf of a candidate that attacks the opponent's platform or character.

contrast ad
Ad that compares the records and proposals of the candidates, with a bias toward the sponsor.

spot ad
Television advertising on behalf of a candidate that is broadcast in sixty-, thirty-, or ten-second duration.

inoculation ad
Advertising that attempts to counteract an anticipated attack from the opposition before the attack is launched.

Photo courtesy: Swiftvets/AP/Wide World Photos

■ Rear Admiral Roy Hoffman, who commanded a Swiftboat during the Vietnam War, appearing in an ad by Swiftboat Veterans for Truth. These ads, which attacked John Kerry's character and service in Vietnam and questioned his honor and truthfulness, had a significant impact on the 2004 election.

early in the campaign to protect themselves in advance from the other side's spots. (Inoculation advertising attempts to counteract an anticipated attack from the opposition before such an attack is launched.) For example, a senator who fears a broadside about her voting record on Social Security issues might air advertisements featuring senior citizens praising her support of Social Security.

Although paid advertising remains the most controllable aspect of a campaign's strategy, the news media are increasingly having an impact on it. Major newspapers throughout the country have taken to analyzing the accuracy of television advertisements aired during campaigns—a welcome and useful addition to journalists' scrutiny of politicians.

Free Media

While candidates have control over what advertisements are run (paid media), they do not have total control over how journalists will cover their campaign and convey it to voters. In this section, we look at how the media report on campaigns and how campaigns attempt to control the media.

How the News Media Cover Campaigns. During campaign season, the news media constantly report political news. What they report is largely based on news editors' decisions of what is newsworthy, what is "fit to print." Often, the press will simply report what candidates are doing, such as giving speeches, holding fundraisers, or meeting with party leaders. Even better, the news media can report on a candidate's success, perhaps giving that candidate the brand of a "winner," making him or her that much more difficult to beat. On the other hand, the reporters may run stories on a candidate's darker past, such as run-ins with the law or a failed marriage.

Many analysts observe that not all media practices in campaigns are conducive to fair and unbiased coverage. For example, the news media often regard political candidates with suspicion—looking for possible deception even when a candidate is simply

Analyzing Visuals

MISSION ACCOMPLISHED

If ever there has been a double-edged sword in presidential public relations, it is the famous example of President George W. Bush heralding the end of the "hot war" in Iraq, by landing on the deck of the aircraft carrier *Abraham Lincoln,* and giving a speech to enthusiastic military personnel on board. On May 1, 2003, Bush gave a speech saluting the troops and congratulating them on their quick victory in Iraq, with a giant banner headlined "Mission Accomplished" in the background, as the photo shows. Even though Bush in his speech was careful to note that the work in Iraq was not finished, the picture overwhelmed his own words.

Most Americans remember the event mainly because of the Mission Accomplished controversy, since it was only a matter of weeks before a tough guerrilla war, which has since then taken more than a thousand American lives, broke out in Iraq. At the time, almost every observer saw the aircraft carrier speech as a brilliant stroke, and one that would nearly guarantee Bush's reelection in 2004. As it happened, though, in the fullness of time, the Mission Accomplished banner became a metaphor for the increasingly difficult struggle in Iraq, which critics called "Vietnam without the jungle."

How did the Mission Accomplished banner get so prominently placed? White House spokesperson Scott McClellan stated that Navy officials asked for it, and the administration agreed to create it. "We took care of the production of it. We have people to do those things. But the Navy actually put it up," said McClellan in an interview with CNN months later.

In the presidency, the occupant of the Oval Office is responsible for these mishaps, whether or not he knew about the proposed actions in advance, and whether or not

Photo courtesy: J. Scott Applewhite/AP/Wide World Photos

he agreed with them. As Harry Truman used to say during his term in the White House, "The buck stops here," and that axiom is the real lesson of Mission Accomplished.

In looking at this photo from the speech, what do you think about the strategy behind the staging of the event? In this age of the Internet and the twenty-four-hour news cycle, how can political figures avoid similar predicaments in future?

Source: http://www.usatoday.com/news/world/iraq/2003-05-01-lincoln_x.htm.

trying to share his or her message with the public. This attitude makes it difficult for candidates to appear in a positive light or to have a genuine opportunity to explain their basic ideas via the news media without being on the defensive. In addition, many studies have shown that the media are obsessed with the horse-race aspect of politics—who's ahead, who's behind, who's gaining—to the detriment of the substance of the candidates' issues and ideas. Public opinion polls, especially tracking polls, many of them taken by the news outlets themselves, dominate coverage, especially on network television, where only a few minutes a night are devoted to politics.

The media's expectations can have an effect on how the public views the candidates. Using poll data, journalists often predict the margins by which they expect contenders to win or lose. A clear victory of 5 percentage points can be judged a setback if the candidate had been projected to win by 12 or 15 points. The tone of the media coverage—that a candidate is either gaining or losing support in polls—can affect whether people decide to give money and other types of support to a candidate.[7]

One final area in which the media tend to portray candidates in a biased way is in overemphasizing trivial parts of the campaign, such as a politician's minor gaffe or private-life indiscretions. This superficial coverage displaces serious journalism on the issues. These subjects are taken up again in the next chapter, which deals specifically with the news media.

Campaign Strategies.   Candidates, of course, want favorable media coverage. Voters tend to find the news media more credible sources of information than paid advertisements. A favorable editorial can carry more weight than a campaign ad. In an effort to obtain favorable coverage, candidates and their media consultants use various strategies to attempt to influence the press.

First, the campaign staff members often seek to isolate the candidate from the press, thus reducing the chances that reporters will bait a candidate into saying something that might damage his or her cause. Naturally, journalists are frustrated by such a tactic, and they demand open access to candidates.

Second, the campaign stages media events—activities designed to include brief, clever quotes called *sound bites* and staged with appealing backdrops so that they will be run on the television news and in the newspaper. In this fashion, the candidate's staff can successfully fill the news hole reserved for campaign coverage.

Third, the handlers and consultants have cultivated a technique termed *spin*—that is, they put the most favorable possible interpretation for their candidate (and the most negative for their opponent) on any circumstance occurring in the campaign, and they work the press to sell their point of view or at least to ensure that it is included in the reporters' stories. Early in the 2004 Democratic primaries, Howard Dean was the frontrunner, a position he won by portraying himself as the indignant or "angry" candidate, which worked well with the Democratic base voting in the primaries; yet, he lost the Iowa caucus vote. Dean tried to spin the loss as playing to his strengths, since Dean only achieved frontrunner status by starting at the back of the pack. Spin can spin both ways, however, and Dean's spin spun out of control after he tried to show strength in rallying his supporters by letting out a high-pitched yelp. While the yelp certainly helped rally the troops, it also gave competing candidates the proof they needed to spin Dean as not the angry candidate but the "crazy" candidate.[8]

Fourth, candidates have found ways to circumvent the news media by appearing on talk shows such as *The Oprah Winfrey Show* and *Larry King Live*, where they have an opportunity to present their views and answer questions in a less critical forum.

Fifth, **candidate debates** are an established feature of campaigns for president, governor, U.S. senator, and many other offices. Candidates and their staffs recognize their importance as a tool not only for consolidating their voter base but for correcting misperceptions about the candidate's suitability for office. However, while candidates have complete control over what they say in debates, they do not have control over what the news media will highlight and focus on from the debates. Therefore, even though candidates prepare themselves by rehearsing their responses, they cannot avoid the perils of spontaneity. Errors or slips of the tongue in a debate can affect election outcomes. President Gerald R. Ford's erroneous insistence during an October 1976 debate with Jimmy Carter that Poland was not under Soviet domination (when, in fact, it was) may have cost him a close election. In an effort to put the best possible spin on debates, teams of staffers for each participant swarm the press rooms to declare victory even before their candidates finish their closing statements.

A study showed that 16 percent of viewers of the 1976 debates more strongly supported their choice for president, and 10 percent switched candidate allegiance altogether.[9] A 1980 study found significant shifts occurred in candidate preference among viewers with low levels of political knowledge.[10] The debates of 2004 reinforced and added to these studies, as public opinion surveys showed that Kerry's strong

candidate debate
Forum in which political candidates face each other to discuss their platforms, records, and character.

Timeline

Television and Presidential Campaigns

performance in the first debate spurred him to a temporary lead in the polls. So, while debates do not directly alter the results of elections, they do tend to increase knowledge about the candidates and their respective personalities and issue positions, especially among voters who have not previously paid attention to the campaign. Voters, once knowing more about candidates and their positions, might then change their mind or finally decide for whom they will vote, meaning that debates may indirectly affect the results of elections.

Sometimes debates affect voters only by confirming or denying the public preconceptions of the candidates. The two major presidential contenders in 2004 offered a classic example of spin before and after their first debate. In 2000, George W. Bush was widely believed to have benefited from low expectations. Al Gore was expected to perform better in the debate, so Bush's exceeding the low expectations set for him added to the generally positive evaluation of his performance. The Bush and Kerry campaigns remembered this phenomenon, and each attempted to paint the opponent as a superior debater going into the debate. Bush strategist Matthew Dowd called Kerry "the best debater since Cicero." The Kerry campaign countered that Bush had never lost a debate. Each campaign tried to spin the press to call its opponent the superior debater, hoping that its candidate would come out as "exceeding expectations." Candidates take part in debates to disprove the preconceptions the public holds for them while hoping that their opposition will perform according to the public's negative preconception.

Technology and Campaign Strategy

Timeline

Major Technological Innovations That Have Changed the Political Landscape

Since candidates began using electronic media (Franklin D. Roosevelt and radio, John F. Kennedy and television, Howard Dean and the Internet) to reach out directly to voters, the nature of campaigns has changed drastically. Labor-intensive community activities have been replaced by carefully targeted messages disseminated through the mass media, and candidates today are able to reach voters more quickly than at any time in our nation's history. Consequently, the well-organized party machine is no longer essential to winning an election. The results of this technological transformation are candidate-centered campaigns in which candidates build well-financed, finely tuned organizations centered around their personal aspirations.

At the heart of the move toward today's candidate-centered campaigns is an entire generation of technological improvements. Contemporary campaigns have an impressive new array of weapons at their disposal: faster printing technologies, instantaneous

■ Presidential debates have come a long way—at least in terms of studio trappings—since the ill-at-ease Richard M. Nixon was visually bested by John F. Kennedy in the first televised debate. John Kerry's strong performances in the three presidential debates of 2004 helped him stay within striking distance of President Bush's lead going into the final weeks of the campaign.

Photos courtesy: left, Bettmann/Corbis; right, Rick Wilking/Reuters/Corbis

PRESIDENTIAL DEBATES: COMING TO A CAMPUS NEAR YOU?

Televised presidential debates offer the American electorate a unique opportunity to see and hear the candidates for the presidency. It is a means by which millions of Americans gather information regarding each candidate's personality and platform. Recognizing the profound educational value of these debates to the voting public, two bipartisan national study groups recommended that steps be taken to establish an organization whose main function was the sponsorship of presidential and vice presidential debates during the general election period. In response to the recommendations put forward by the two study groups, the Commission on Presidential Debates (CPD) was established in 1987.

The CPD's formal charge is to ensure that debates are a permanent part of every general election and that they provide the best possible information to viewers and listeners. The organization sponsored all the presidential debates since 1988, heavily favoring institutions of higher learning as the host sites. The last five presidential elections have included seventeen debates sponsored by the CPD, thirteen of which have been held on college campuses. In 2004, the CPD selected the University of Miami, Case Western Reserve, Washington University in St. Louis, and Arizona State University as sites for presidential debates.

Prospective debate hosts must conform to a rigorous set of criteria as dictated by the CPD. The selection criteria encompass a broad range of categories, including the physical structure of the debate hall (over 17,000 square feet with a 35-foot ceiling and 65-foot stage), the transportation and lodging networks available, and the ability to raise $550,000 to cover production costs.

Why would a college or university go through so much trouble to host a presidential debate? The answer is that the benefits are plentiful and diverse. The host sites inevitably bring in revenue with masses of people migrating into town, purchasing community services and products. The colleges gain immediate international exposure, perhaps becoming a more attractive option to prospective students. Students and professors benefit from firsthand exposure to a very important aspect of the American political process.

Source: Commission on Presidential Debates, http://www.debates.org.

Internet publishing and mass e-mail, fax machines, video technology, and enhanced telecommunications and teleconferencing. As a result, candidates can gather and disseminate information better than ever.

One outcome of these changes is the ability of candidates to employ "rapid-response" techniques: the formulation of prompt and informed responses to changing events on the campaign battlefield. In response to breaking news of a scandal or issue, for example, candidates can conduct background research, implement an opinion poll and tabulate the results, devise a containment strategy and appropriate "spin," and deliver a reply. This makes a strong contrast with the campaigns of the 1970s and early 1980s, dominated primarily by radio and TV advertisements, which took much longer to prepare and had little of the flexibility enjoyed by contemporary campaigners.

The first widespread use of the Internet in national campaigning came in 1996. Republican presidential candidate Bob Dole urged voters to log onto his Web site, and many did. According to one source, 26 percent of the public in 1996 regularly logged onto the Internet to get campaign and election information. On Election Day 2004, traffic on the CNN Web site increased by 110 percent, while the Fox News site saw a 134 percent jump.[11] All of the candidates for the 2004 presidential campaign started up Web sites, even when their candidacies were only in the exploratory stage, before their formal declarations. Candidate Web sites typically present the candidate's platform and offer information on how to get involved in the campaign and how to contribute money. As bandwidth on the Internet continues to improve, real-time video clips enable Web users to view candidate's speeches, press conferences, and other typically "live" events at their own convenience, independent of the schedule of the original television coverage or rebroadcast. Campaign sites often offer the text of speeches, as well as multiple video and audio versions of the real public event.

In the campaigns of 2002, many candidates increasingly turned to recorded phone messages targeted to narrow constituencies. Fundraisers also experimented with voice

■ Both the Kerry-Edwards campaign and the Bush-Cheney campaign used the Internet extensively in 2004 to raise money and disseminate information. Here, the Kerry-Edwards Web site displays John Kerry's concession speech on November 3, 2004.

John Kerry's Remarks to Supportsers at Faneuil Hall in Boston

"Earlier today, I spoke to President Bush, and I offered him and Laura our congratulations on their victory. We had a good conversation and we talked about the danger of division in our country and the need - the desperate need - for unity, for finding the common ground, coming together. Today, I hope that we can begin the healing. In America it is vital that every vote count, and that every vote be counted. But the outcome should be decided by voters, not a protracted legal process.

"I would not give up this fight if there was a chance that we would prevail. But it is now clear that even when all the provisional ballots are counted, which they will be, there won't be enough outstanding votes for us to be able to win Ohio. And, therefore, we can

Photo courtesy: www.JohnKerry.com

messages from high-profile figures such as former President Bill Clinton. Florida Governor Jeb Bush used a fund-raising technique many might question; the governor recorded a message asking for money, which was autodialed to contributors to the 2000 presidential campaign of his brother, George W. Bush. Jeb Bush's victory is due, in part, to the cohesive use of this kind of new and effective tactic. This practice was much more widespread in 2004, as both parties used politicians and celebrities to contact voters through pre-recorded phone messages. Democrats heard from John Kerry, Bill Clinton, Wesley Clark, and comedian Chris Rock; Republicans heard from Rudy Giuliani, Arnold Schwarzenegger, and actress Janine Turner.[12]

While candidates use such technologies to gain access to voters, they also seek to convey to voters that they are technologically savvy and have a rich depth of resources. These new technologies are currently reshaping the campaign landscape. Political parties might use new technologies to organize and manage massive voter bases, in an effort to return to an older mode of campaign that supports the party, rather than just one individual candidate. Another possible scenario is that the Web allows greater interactivity among independents or third-party organizers, perhaps providing a new medium of communication and organization for those who find no representation within the two-party system.

CAMPAIGN FINANCE

CAMPAIGN FINANCE REFORM has been a major source of discussion among politicians and pundits in recent years. For the past thirty years, campaign finance has been governed by the provisions of the Federal Election Campaign Act (FECA). The most recent bout of reforms were set in motion by Senator John McCain, who ran for the 2000 Republican presidential nomination on a platform to take elections out of the hands of the wealthy. McCain lost to Bush, who ironically used soft money in the primaries to defeat McCain. However, McCain's credibility on the issue skyrocketed. Once corporate soft-money donors at Enron, WorldCom, and Global Crossing (to name a few) became embroiled in accounting scandals and alleged criminal behavior, the possibility of corruption became too strong for Congress to ignore. Senators John McCain (R–AZ) and Russ Feingold (D–WI) co-sponsored the Bipartisan Campaign Reform Act of 2002 (BCRA) in the Senate, while Representatives Chris Shays (R–CT) and Martin Meehan (D–MA) sponsored the House version. On Valentine's Day, the bills passed, and in March 2002, President George W. Bush signed BCRA into law, which has altered the campaign finance landscape in ways we perhaps have yet to discover.

Included within BCRA was a "fast track" provision that any suits challenging the constitutionality of the reforms would be immediately placed before a U.S. District Court, and giving appellate powers to the U.S. Supreme Court. The reason for this provision was simple: to thwart the numerous lobbying groups and several high-profile elected officials who threatened to tie up BCRA in the courts for as long as they could, until they could find a judge who would kill it. No sooner did Bush sign BCRA than U.S. Senator Mitch McConnell (R–KY) and the National Rifle Association separately filed lawsuits claiming that BCRA violated free speech rights, specifically by equating financial contributions with symbolic political speech.

In May 2003, a three-judge panel of the U.S. District Court in the District of Columbia found that the BCRA restrictions on soft-money donations violated free speech rights, although the BCRA restrictions on political advertising did not. The decision was immediately appealed to the Supreme Court, which stayed the district court's decision. After oral arguments in September, the Court handed down its 5–4 decision, *McConnell* v. *FEC*, in December, concluding that the government's interest in preventing political-party corruption overrides the free speech rights to which the parties would otherwise be entitled. In other words, the Supreme Court very narrowly upheld the BCRA measures restricting speech both in the form of political contributions and in political advertising. There are some serious questions about whether the Court has really solved the problem of campaign finance reform, since the attempt to avoid the corruption that so often plagues a democracy necessarily means limiting the political speech necessary to sustain democracy. For now, we will investigate the compromise over campaign finance laws that the federal government has most recently struck.

Sources of Political Contributions

To run all aspects of a campaign successfully requires a great deal of money. More than $1.6 billion was raised by the Democratic and Republican parties through November 2004, a 37 percent increase in fund-raising over the totals of the 2000 midterm election cycle. Democratic incumbents in the Senate raised an average of $9.7 million, while Republican incumbents in the Senate raised an average of $6.7 million. Their challengers, in contrast, raised an average of $889,000.[13] As humorist Will Rogers once remarked early in the twentieth century, "Politics has got so expensive that it takes lots of money even to get beat with."

Political money is now regulated by the federal government under the terms of the Bipartisan Campaign Reform Act (BRCA), which supplanted most of the provisions of the Federal Election Campaign Act (FECA) in 2002. Table 14.1 summarizes some of the important provisions of this law, which limits the amounts that individuals, interest groups, and political parties can give to candidates for president, U.S. senator, and U.S. representative. The goal of all limits is the same: to prevent any single group or individual from gaining too much influence over elected officials, who naturally feel indebted to campaign contributors.

TABLE 14.1 Contribution Limits for Congressional Candidates Before and After Bipartisan Campaign Reform Act, 2002

Contributions from	Given to Candidate (per election)[a]	Given to National Party (per calendar year)	Total Allowable Contributions (per calendar year)
	Before/After	**Before/After**	**Before/After**
Individual	$1,000/$2,000	$20,000/$25,000	$25,000/$47,500 each year per two-year cycle
Political action committee[b]	$5,000/$5,000	$15,000/$15,000	No limit/No Limit
Any political party committee[c]	$5,000/$10,000	No limit/No limit	No limit/No limit
All national and state party committees taken together	To House candidates: $30,000 plus "coordinated expenditures"[d] To Senate candidates: $27,500 plus "coordinated expenditures"[d]		

Note: The regulations under the Bipartisan Campaign Reform Act did not take effect until after the 2002 election.
[a]Each of the following is considered a separate election: primary (or convention), runoff, general election.
[b]Multicandidate PACs only. Multicandidate committees have received contributions from at least fifty persons and have given to at least five federal candidates.
[c]Multicandidate party committees only. Multicandidate committees have received contributions from at least fifty persons and have given to at least five federal candidates.
[d]Coordinated expenditures are party-paid general election campaign expenditures made in consultation and coordination with the candidate under the provisions of section 441(a)(d) of the Federal Code.

Given the cash flow required by a campaign and the legal restrictions on political money, raising the funds necessary to run a modern campaign is a monumental task. Consequently, presidential and congressional campaigns have squads of fundraisers on staff. These professionals rely on several standard sources of campaign money.

Individual Contributions. Individual contributions are donations from individual citizens. Citizens typically donate because they like the candidate or party or a particular stand on issues they care about, or to feel involved in the political process, or because they want access to the candidate. The maximum allowable contribution under federal law for congressional and presidential elections is $2,000 per election to each candidate, with primary and general elections considered separately. Individuals are also limited to a total of $47,500 in gifts to all candidates combined in each calendar year. Most candidates receive a majority of all funds directly from individuals, and most individual gifts are well below the maximum level. Finally, individuals who spend over $10,000 to air "electioneering communication," that is, "any broadcast, cable, or satellite communication which refers to a clearly identified candidate for Federal office" that airs within sixty days of a general election or thirty days of a primary election, is now subject to a strict disclosure law. The rationale behind the last regulation is that spending any more on an ad favoring a candidate is effectively the same as a contribution to the candidate's campaign and requires the same scrutiny as other large donations.

political action committee (PAC)
Federally mandated, officially registered fund-raising committee that represents interest groups in the political process.

Political Action Committee (PAC) Contributions. When interest groups such as labor unions, corporations, trade unions, and ideological issue groups seek to make donations to campaigns, they must do so by establishing **political action committees (PACs).** PACs are officially recognized fund-raising organizations that are allowed by federal law to participate in federal elections. (Some states have similar requirements for state elections.) Approximately 4,000 PACs are registered with the Federal Election Commission—the governmental agency charged with administering the election laws. In 2004, PACs contributed $294 million to Senate and House candidates, while individuals donated $693 million. On average, PAC contributions account for 57 percent of the war chests (campaign funds) of House candidates and 67 percent of the treasuries of Senate candidates. Incumbents benefit the most from PAC money; incumbents received $228 million, much more than the $66 million given to challengers during the 2004 election cycle.[14] By making these contributions, PACs hope to secure entrée to the candidate after he or she has been elected in order to influence them on issues important to the PAC, since a candidate might reciprocate campaign donations with loyalty to the cause. Therefore, PACs give primarily to incumbents because incumbents tend to win.

Because donations from a small number of PACs make up such a large proportion of campaign war chests, PACs have influence disproportionate to that of individuals. Studies, in fact, have shown that PACs effectively use contributions to punish legislators and affect policy, at least in the short run.[15] Legislators who vote contrary to the wishes of a PAC see their donations withheld, but those who are successful in legislating as the PAC wishes are rewarded with even greater donations.[16] (Interest groups are treated in more detail in chapter 16.)

In an attempt to control PACs, BCRA has a limit on the way PACs attempt to influence campaigns. The law strictly forbids PACs from using corporate or union funds for the electioneering communications discussed earlier. PACs can only use corporate or labor contributions for administrative costs. The purpose of the limit is to prevent corporations or unions from having an undue influence on the outcome of elections, as they have in the past, by heavily advertising toward specific audiences in the weeks leading up to elections.

Political Party Contributions. Candidates also receive donations from the national and state committees of the Democratic and Republican Parties. As mentioned in chapter 12, political parties can give substantial contributions to their congressional nominees. In 2004, the Republicans and the Democrats funneled over $52 million to their standard-bearers, via direct contributions and cooordinated expenditures. In competitive races, the parties may provide 15–17 percent of their candidates' total war chests. In addition to helping elect party members, campaign contributions from political parties have another, less obvious benefit: helping to ensure party discipline in voting. One study of congressional voting behavior in the 1980s, for instance, found that those members who received a large percentage of their total campaign funds from their party voted with their party more often than they were expected to.[17]

FIGURE 14.2 Expenditures by PACs in 2004 Election Cycle

Notice how PACs use a majority of their expenditures to support congressional candidates. Of independent expenditures by PACs, a majority of the money is spent positively to support candidates and only a small fraction to attack opponents in presidential campaigns. Notice how PAC spending has a slight bias toward Republican candidates and a strong bias toward incumbents. ■

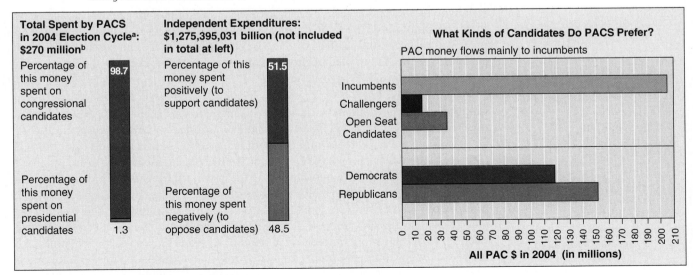

ᵃThe amount is the total from January 1, 2003 to June 30, 2004.
ᵇTotal amount spent by PACs does not include $21 million in independent expenditures.
Source: Federal Election Commission

Source: Federal Election Commission.

"*And, if elected, I will take the money out of politics and put it into a portfolio of high-yielding instruments.*"

Photo courtesy: © The New Yorker Collection 2000 Bernard Schoenbaum from Cartoonbank.com. All Rights Reserved.

Some nations favor contributions to the party over contributions to individual campaigns. Parliamentary forms of government are much less candidate oriented and much more party oriented; therefore, the political monies raised flow to the *party coffers*. For example, in Great Britain, rather than receiving direct contributions, candidates for prime minister obtain campaign funds through party donations.

Member-to-Candidate Contributions.   In Congress and in state legislatures, well-funded, electorally secure incumbents now often contribute campaign money to their party's needy incumbent and nonincumbent legislative candidates.[18] This activity began in some state legislatures (notably California), but it is now well-established at the congressional level.[19] Generally, members contribute to other candidates in one of two ways. First, some members have established their own PACs—informally dubbed "leadership" PACs—through which they distribute campaign support to candidates. For example, through the 2004 general election cycle, a PAC established by then Senate Minority Leader Tom Daschle and Vermont Senator Patrick Leahy allowed them to contribute to 221 House and 19 Senate candidates. In total, their PAC spent over $3 million in an attempt to help the Democrats win back the Senate and House.[20] Second, individual members can give up to $2,000 per candidate per election and $10,000 per candidate for each cycle: $5,000 for the primary election and $5,000 for the general election from a leadership PAC.

These contributions from members, whether individually or via a PAC, can add up. In 2004, the U.S. House race in South Dakota saw a tremendous influx of member-to-candidate money, with Republican challenger Larry Diedrich receiving the most, at over $423,000. He lost the race to first-term Democratic incumbent Stephanie Herseth, who recived an impressive $293,00 of these donations.[21] In general, members give their contributions to the same candidates who receive the bulk of congressional campaign committee resources. Thus, member contributions at the congressional level have emerged as a major supplement to the campaign resources contributed by the party campaign committees.[22]

Candidates' Personal Contributions.   Candidates and their families may donate to the campaign. The Supreme Court ruled in 1976 in *Buckley* v. *Valeo* that no limit could be placed on the amount of money candidates can spend from their own families' resources, since such spending is considered a First Amendment right of free speech.[23] For wealthy politicians, this allowance may mean personal spending in the millions. In 2004, the number of million-dollar self-contributors increased, but no one approached the level of Democratic U.S. Senate hopeful Blair Hull from Illinois. The wealthy former investment broker sank $29 million into his campaign, but he lost in the primary election. In 2002, twenty candidates for House or Senate seats spent over $1 million of their own money to finance their campaigns; only one of the candidates, Frank Lautenberg (D–NJ), was victorious. The man Lautenberg beat, Republican Douglas Forrester, spent $7 million of his own money in the race. While self-financed candidates often garner a great deal of attention, most candidates commit much less than $100,000 in family resources to their election bids.

Public Funds.   **Public funds** are donations from general tax revenues. Only presidential candidates (and a handful of state and local contenders) receive public funds. Under the terms of the FECA (which first established public funding of presidential campaigns), a candidate for president can become eligible to receive public funds during the nominating contest by raising at least $5,000 in individual contributions of $250 or less in each of twenty states. The candidate can apply for federal **matching funds,** whereby every dollar raised from individuals in amounts less than $251 is matched by the federal treasury on a dollar-for-dollar basis. Of course, this assumes there is enough money in the Presidential Election Campaign Fund to do so. The fund is accumulated by taxpayers who designate $3 of their taxes for this purpose each year when they send in their federal tax returns. (Only about 20 percent of taxpayers check off the appropriate box, even though participation does not increase their tax burden.) During the 2004 Democratic primaries, John Kerry and Howard Dean, like George W. Bush in 2000, both opted out of the federal matching funds, allowing them to raise considerably more money than the government would have provided.

For the general election, the two major-party presidential nominees can accept a $75 million lump-sum payment from the federal government after the candidate accepts his or her nomination. If the candidate accepts the money, it becomes the sole source for financing the campaign. A candidate could refuse the money and be free from the spending cap the government attaches to it. John Kerry considered doing just that in order to help finance general election campaign operations. Because the Democratic convention, during which Kerry accepted his nomination, occurred five weeks before the Republican convention, Kerry actually had five weeks more than Bush during which he had to stretch out the $75 million the government provided. Kerry first considered not accepting his party's nomination until after the Republican convention, a possibility that proved unpopular.[24]

A third-party candidate receives a smaller amount proportionate to his or her November vote total if that candidate gains a minimum of 5 percent of the vote. Note that in such a case, the money goes to third-party campaigns only *after* the election is over; no money is given in advance of the general election. Only two third-party candidates have qualified for public campaign funding: John B. Anderson in 1980, gaining 7 percent of the vote, and colorful Texas billionaire Ross Perot in 1992, gaining 19 percent of the vote.

Independent Expenditures.   Because of two Supreme Court decisions,[25] individuals, PACs, and now political parties may spend unlimited amounts of money directly advocating the election or defeat of a candidate as long as these expenditures are not made in coordination with the candidate's campaign. For example, a group may create and run television advertisements urging voters to support or defeat a candidate. In October 2004, the Planned Parenthood Action Fund launched a three-part television ad campaign costing $1 million, aimed at promoting the Kerry campaign among women and criticizing the Bush administration for cutting family planning programs.[26] However, because independent expenditure advertisements expressly advocate the election or defeat of a specific federal candidate, they must be paid for with **hard money**— that is, with money raised under the FECA guidelines (see Figure 14.3).

The Internet

The Internet, like campaign finance reform, has the potential to alter radically the way candidates raise funds for their campaigns. After all, making an online appeal for campaign contributions costs significantly less than raising funds through expensive direct-

public funds
Donations from the general tax revenues to the campaigns of qualifying presidential candidates.

matching funds
Donations to presidential campaigns from the federal government that are determined by the amount of private funds a qualifying candidate raises.

hard money
Legally specified and limited contributions that are clearly regulated by the Federal Election Campaign Act and by the Federal Election Commission.

FIGURE 14.3 How the Bipartisan Campaign Reform Act of 2002 Alters Money Flow. ■

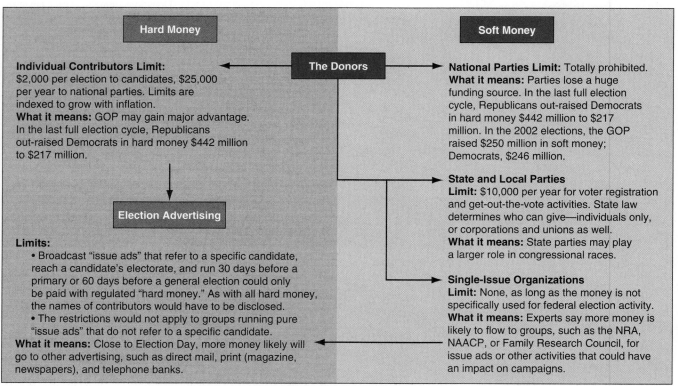

Hard Money

The Donors

Soft Money

Individual Contributors Limit: $2,000 per election to candidates, $25,000 per year to national parties. Limits are indexed to grow with inflation.
What it means: GOP may gain major advantage. In the last full election cycle, Republicans out-raised Democrats in hard money $442 million to $217 million.

Election Advertising

Limits:
• Broadcast "issue ads" that refer to a specific candidate, reach a candidate's electorate, and run 30 days before a primary or 60 days before a general election could only be paid with regulated "hard money." As with all hard money, the names of contributors would have to be disclosed.
• The restrictions would not apply to groups running pure "issue ads" that do not refer to a specific candidate.
What it means: Close to Election Day, more money likely will go to other advertising, such as direct mail, print (magazine, newspapers), and telephone banks.

National Parties Limit: Totally prohibited.
What it means: Parties lose a huge funding source. In the last full election cycle, Republicans out-raised Democrats in hard money $442 million to $217 million. In the 2002 elections, the GOP raised $250 million in soft money; Democrats, $246 million.

State and Local Parties
Limit: $10,000 per year for voter registration and get-out-the-vote activities. State law determines who can give—individuals only, or corporations and unions as well.
What it means: State parties may play a larger role in congressional races.

Single-Issue Organizations
Limit: None, as long as the money is not specifically used for federal election activity.
What it means: Experts say more money is likely to flow to groups, such as the NRA, NAACP, or Family Research Council, for issue ads or other activities that could have an impact on campaigns.

Source: http://www.opensecrets.org/bigpicture/ptytots.asp?cycle=2002.

mail campaigns or pricey fund-raising events—the standard means of attaining campaign resources. Nevertheless, the potential weaknesses of Internet fund-raising are unlikely to stop candidates from experimenting with it. Former Republican presidential candidate John McCain became the first political candidate to raise over $1 million online in forty-eight hours after his victory in the New Hampshire primary in 2000. The Internet converted McCain's momentum into money and volunteers virtually overnight. McCain eventually took in over $5 million online—nearly 25 percent of his total contributions.

In 2004, the Internet had an immediate impact during the Democratic primary season, and in the months of preparation that led up to it. Former Vermont Governor Howard Dean surged to an early lead in the polls thanks in large part to a tremendously successful Internet-based fund-raising strategy. The Dean campaign used thousands of young, eager volunteers to solicit tens of thousands of small online donations that eventually totaled over $50 million by the end of the campaign. These tactics were mimicked by candidates and party organizations on both sides, as well as PACs and special interest groups, and as a result, fund-raising records from previous years were easily surpassed.[27]

The Internet also promises to create headaches for the Federal Election Commission. The FEC had to rule on issues such as whether a business site link to a campaign site constitutes in-kind contribution from the business to the campaign, and whether funds raised online by presidential candidates are eligible to be matched with public funds from the Presidential Election Campaign Fund. (In the first case, the FEC ruled yes; in the second case, it ruled no.) Clearly, these issues are only the beginning of a seemingly limitless plethora of concerns regarding the Internet and campaign finance which the FEC will be asked to address. Campaign finance experts question whether the agency has the resources to regulate and monitor the newly unfolding campaign activity on the Internet.[28]

Soft Money and Issue Advocacy Advertisements

Soft money is campaign money raised and spent by political parties for expenses such as overhead and administrative costs and for grassroots activities such as political education and GOTV efforts. In a 1978 advisory opinion, the Federal Election Commission ruled that political parties could raise these funds without regulation. Then, in 1979, Congress passed an amendment allowing parties to *spend* unlimited sums on these same activities.[29] In the years immediately following the rule changes, the national parties began raising five- and six-figure sums from individuals and interest groups to pay for expenses such as rent, employee salaries, and building maintenance. The national parties also began transferring large sums of soft money to state parties in order to help pay for grassroots activities (such as get-out-the-vote drives) and campaign paraphernalia (such as yard signs and bumper stickers).

However, the line separating expenditures that influence federal elections from those that do not proved to be quite blurry, and this blurriness resulted in a significant campaign finance loophole. The largest controversy came in the area of campaign advertisements. The federal courts have ruled that only campaign advertisements that use explicit words—for example, "vote for," "vote against," "elect," or "support"—qualify as *express advocacy* advertisements. Political advertisements that do not use these words are considered *issue advocacy* advertisements.[30] The distinction here is crucial. Because express advocacy advertisements were openly intended to influence federal elections, they could only be paid for with strictly regulated hard money. Issue advocacy advertisements, on the other hand, were paid for with unregulated soft money. The parties' response to these rules was to create issue advocacy advertisements that very much resemble express advocacy ads, for such advertisements call attention to the voting record of the candidate supported or opposed and are replete with images of the candidate. However, the parties ensured that the magic words "vote for" or "vote against" were never uttered in the advertisements, allowing them to be paid for with soft rather than hard money.

Soft-money donations are now prohibited under BCRA, and third-party issue ads, if coordinated with a federal candidate's campaign, can now be considered campaign contributions, thus regulated by the FEC. The last election cycle for the parties to use soft money was 2001–2002, and the amount raised, nearly $430 million for Republican and Democrats combined,[31] highlights why the reform seemed necessary. Republicans raised $219 million in soft money from pharmaceutical, insurance, and energy companies. Democrats came in just under $211 million in soft money from unions and law firms. With soft money banned, wealthy donors and interest groups now lack the privileged and potentially corrupting influence on parties and candidates. Like every other citizen, they must donate within the hard-money limits placed on individuals and PACs. With BCRA in place and supported by the courts in *McConnell* v. *FEC,* the reforms appear to be working. A preliminary study of the effects of BCRA on the 2004 Democratic primaries revealed that hard-money donations have increased and are increasingly used for grassroots efforts.[32] However, reforms usually necessitate more reform, since the correction of one problem usually creates a new one.

Post-election financial reports revealed that hard-money fund-raising and spending increased greatly during the 2004 campaign, mainly because of the increased contribution limits and the ban on soft money. While individual campaigns and PACs receive hard money as well, political party organizations account for the largest chunks of hard money, and in 2004 they used it to counter some of the impact of the new campaign finance legislation. Independent expenditures—the money spent on express advocacy advertisements without a candidate's cooperation—jumped by $173.3 million for the Democratic Party and $86.5 million for the Republican Party. Overall, the hard money raised by both parties in 2004 eclipsed the combined hard-money and soft-money totals from any prior election.

The most significant unintended result of the BRCA in 2004 was the emergence of single-issue entities known as 527 political committees. These are discussed in greater detail later in this chapter, but they are essentially unregulated interest groups that focus

soft money
The virtually unregulated money funneled by individuals and political committees through state and local parties.

on a specific cause or policy position and attempt to influence the decision of voters. Money that would have entered the system as unregulated soft money in previous election cycles ended up in the hands of these organizations, so in a sense the BCRA created a new place for soft money, rather than eliminating it completely.[33]

Are PACs Good or Bad for the Process?

Of all the forms of campaign spending, probably the most controversial is that involving PAC money. Some observers claim that PACs are the embodiment of corrupt special interests that use campaign donations to buy the votes of legislators. Furthermore, they argue that the less affluent and minority members of our society do not enjoy equal access to these political organizations.

These charges are serious and deserve consideration. Although the media relentlessly stress the role of money in determining policy outcomes, the evidence that PACs buy votes is less than overwhelming.[34] Political scientists have conducted many studies to determine the impact of interest group PAC contributions on legislative voting, and the conclusions reached by these studies have varied widely.[35] Whereas some studies have found that PAC money affects legislators' voting behavior, other studies have uncovered no such correlation. It may be, of course, that interest group PAC money has an impact at earlier stages of the legislative process. One innovative study found that PAC money had a significant effect on legislators' participation in congressional committees on legislation important to the contributing group.[36] Thus, interest group PAC money may mobilize something more important than votes—the valuable time and energy of members.

Also serious is the charge that some interests are significantly better represented by the PAC system than are others. This view was put forth by a political scientist who argues that laws regulating PAC activity inherently favor PACs with parent organizations—corporate, labor, and trade PACs—over citizen-based PACs without parent organizations.[37] Thus, he argues that any campaign finance reform should raise substantially the limits on the amount of money an individual may contribute to a PAC—to the point where a single person could underwrite a citizen group's formation and maintenance costs.

FIGURE 14.4 **PACs**

Created in the early 1970s, PACs allowed individuals to collect money and contribute to political campaigns. PACs saw explosive growth in the 1980s, but their numbers have declined in recent years, although their ability to raise money has increased. ■

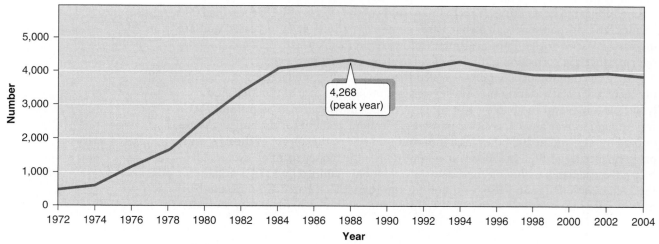

Note: Numbers are as of December 31 of every other year, starting in 1972.

*Source:*http://www.fec.gov.press/press2004/20040202paccount.html.

FIGURE 14.5 Growth in Total Contributions by PACs to House and Senate Candidates
The growth of campaign spending by PACs has roughly paralleled the increasing number of PACs over their thirty-year history. ■

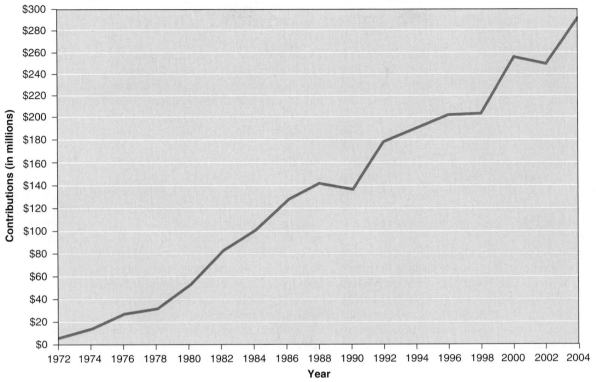

Note: Contributions are for two-year election cycles ending in years shown.

Source: Center for Responsive Politics, http://www.opensecrets.org.

Although a good number of PACs of all persuasions existed prior to the 1970s, it was during the 1970s—the decade of campaign reform—that the modern PAC era began. Spawned by the Watergate-inspired revisions of the campaign finance laws, PACs grew in number from 113 in 1972 to 4,268 by the late 1980s (see Figure 14.4), and their contributions to congressional candidates multiplied almost thirty-fold, from $8.5 million in 1971 and 1972 to $294 million in 2004 (see Figure 14.5). But, these numbers should not obscure a basic truth about the PAC system: that a very small group of PACs conducts the bulk of total PAC activity. Indeed, as political scientist Paul Herrnson observes, a mere 6 percent of all PACs contributed a full 62 percent of the total dollars given to congressional candidates by PACs during the 2001–2002 election cycle.[38]

Some people argue that PACs are newfangled inventions that have flooded the political system with money. Although the widespread use of the PAC structure is new, special-interest money of all types has always found its way into politics. Before the 1970s, it did so in less traceable and much more disturbing and unsavory ways, because little of the money given to candidates was regularly disclosed to public inspection. Although it is true that PACs contribute a massive sum to candidates in absolute terms, it is not clear that there is proportionately more interest group money in the system than earlier. The proportion of House and Senate campaign funds provided by PACs has certainly increased since the early 1970s, but individuals, most of whom are unaffiliated with PACs, together with the political parties still supply more than 60 percent of all the money spent by or on behalf of House candidates, 75 percent of the campaign expenditures for Senate contenders, and 85 percent of the campaign expenditures for presidential candidates. So, while the importance of PAC spending has grown, PACs clearly remain secondary as a source of election funding and therefore pose no overwhelming threat to the system's legitimacy.

THE IMPACT OF FUNDING AND FREE AND FAIR ELECTIONS ON THE CAMPAIGN PROCESS

Few Americans would argue with the proposition that for elections to matter they must be free and fair. But, what is a "free and fair" election? Although no clear answer exists to this question, we can identify conditions that contribute to making an election free and fair. Elections are likely to be free to the extent that we find freedom of speech, freedom of association, freedom from coercion, free access to the polls, and the freedom to vote in secret. Elections are likely to be fair when elections are administered in a nonpartisan fashion, there is balanced reporting by the media, votes are counted in an open and transparent fashion, and there is equitable access to the resources needed to run a campaign.

This last point, access to campaign funds, is particularly problematic today, given the high costs of running for office. Some election observers have concluded that corruption related to the financing of parties and candidates is among the most common dangers facing democracies around the world today. The negative consequences of unequal access to campaign funds include the beliefs that only the rich can run for public office, that large contributors get preferential treatment by public officials, and that because incumbents can raise money more easily than challengers they do not have to be responsive to voters.

Many different ways exist for trying to ensure that there exists an evenhanded access to campaign funds for all parties and candidates. In some cases this involves limiting the amount of money that can be spent. New Zealand forbids parties from spending more than $1 million plus $20,000 per candidate nominated by the party in the three months preceding the election. Some countries try to limit the source of campaign funds. Canadian parties and candidates may accept contributions only from Canadian citizens or permanent residents—corporations and associations not doing business in Canada are not allowed to make contributions. France places limits on the size of campaign contributions and reimburses some of the costs. Individuals may not contribute more than $5,000 to a legislative race (corporations and other organizations may not make contributions). All parties that get more than 5 percent of the vote are reimbursed the cost of the paper and printing of their official ballots, posters, and campaign circulars.

Other nations employ a combination of measures. Brazil seeks to limit the length of the election campaign and the amount of money spent, and provides reasonable access to the media. All elections at the national, regional, and local level are held on the first Sunday in October. Election materials can be distributed only after July 5. Candidates may buy advertising space in newspapers, but radio and television airtime is free and allocated equally among the registered political parties. Limits are placed on how many candidates a party may run in an election. They may only field candidates equal to 150 percent of the positions to be filled in an election.

Japan also seeks to put multiple restrictions in place. Here a distinction is made between political activities that try to make the public aware of a party's position on issues and political activity designed to obtain votes for a particular candidate. Door-to-door political canvassing is illegal. Campaign materials cannot be posted until six months before one's term has expired or one day after parliament is dissolved. All candidates receive a specified amount of free advertising in newspapers. In 1996 this was five ads.

Political parties in Japan face more lenient restrictions, however. Neither candidates nor parties may advertise in the mass media until twelve days before the election. But, there is no limit on how much can be spent in these twelve days—in 1996 political parties spent an estimated $100 million. Japanese parties are required to report all campaign contributions of more than $500, and their recipients. Political contributions from corporations and organizations are banned. Japanese parties are eligible to obtain public funding if they have at least five members in the lower house of parliament or have received at least 2 percent of the vote in a recent national election.

To be effective, laws must be enforced. Even on paper, great variation exists. In Brazil, a court reviews compliance with campaign laws but there are no legal or financial penalties. In Japan, failure to report contributions by individuals can result in a five-year prison term and a $10,000 fine.

Questions

1. Which do you think is the most effective way to make an election fair: regulate the source of campaign funds, limit campaign expenditures, or require greater public disclosure of sources?
2. How does the United States compare with other countries in regard to the above criteria for having free and fair elections?

The election outlays of PACs, like the total amount expended in a single election season, seem huge. In the past, the cost of elections in the United States has been less than or approximately the same as in some other nations, measured on a per-voter basis. However, in the current era of increased spending, American elections are outpacing those of comparable nations. For example, the cost of Canada's 2004 elections is estimated at $265 million—a significant increase form 2000, but still well below U.S. numbers. Still, the cost of all elections in the United States taken together is less than the amount many individual private corporations spend on advertising their cereals, dog food, cars, and toothpaste. These days, it is expensive to communicate, whether the message is political or commercial. The costs of television time, polling, consultants, and other items have soared over and above the inflation rate.[39]

Comparative

Comparing Political
Campaigns

Future Campaign Finance Reform

Despite the overblown promises of campaign finance nirvana by some of those pushing the McCain-Feingold Bipartisan Campaign Reform Act, many problems remain in this complicated area of politics and constitutional law. For example, the McCain-Feingold law banned donations of "soft-money" to the political parties (as explained earlier in the chapter). Did that money disappear? Of course not! Much of it has shown up in new "527 political committees"—the number 527 comes from the provision of the Internal Revenue tax code that gives life to these committees.

Participation

The Debate
over Campaign
Finance Reform

The 527s exist on all sides of the political fence, though the Democrats were first to aggressively pursue them in 2004. Two of the largest Democratic committees are the Media Fund and Americans Coming Together (ACT), both run by allies of presidential nominee John Kerry and raising millions of dollars from people who desired to see President Bush defeated, such as billionaire George Soros. These committees bought TV, radio, and print advertising to sell their message, focusing on the battleground or "swing" states that were not firmly in the Bush or Kerry camps. Ohio is an excellent example: in that state, not only did the groups air thousands of media ads, but they also helped organize many thousands of volunteers who went door to door, recruiting voters and volunteers for Democratic campaigns. Even though most political observers predicted that President Bush would easily outspend Senator Kerry in the presidential contest, the Democratic 527s considerably aided the Democratic campaign. Through the end of the 2004 election, Democratic 527 groups spent $115 million, nearly double that of their Republican counterparts, who reported $62 million in expenditures. Groups on both sides saw large donations from wealthy individuals, including Soros, who gave $23.7 million to Democratic organizations, and Texas developer Bob Perry, who donated $9.6 million to Republican groups.[40] As fundraising records in almost every category were shattered in 2004, the campaign reform law clearly had no effect on overall spending.

It is easy to see that reformers will once again attempt to reform their reforms. The next target may well be the 527s. Their abolition is highly unlikely—and the money supporting them would simply reappear in some other form—but there is a need for greater transparency. The 527s have far less required disclosure than other forms of finance committees, and that does cry out for a legislative fix. Overall, however, the lesson of McCain-Feingold is obvious. No amount of clever legislating will rid the American system of campaign money. Interested individuals and groups will always give lots of cash. The challenge is to find a way to get that cash disclosed in a timely fashion for the press and the public. As always, disclosure and its sunshine are the ultimate check on potential misbehavior in the realm of political money.

CAMPAIGN FINANCE: FREEDOM OF SPEECH OR LICENSE TO CORRUPT

OVERVIEW: Campaigns are not free. A candidate has to employ an army of staff to engage in a number of activities, from scheduling campaign stops to ordering pizza deliveries. Unless a candidate is massively wealthy, the money to pay for campaign staff and services has to come from other people, namely donors. Aside from the instrumental value of money, there is a symbolic value. Many donors believe that their contributions make a larger statement about their beliefs. The question is, therefore, whether campaign finance regulations are merely controlling the sources and use of money to prevent political corruption or are also prohibiting the right to free speech that belongs to all Americans.

Both the National Rifle Association and the American Civil Liberties Union agree that the regulation of campaign contributions amounts to a government violation of the very rights the government is supposed to protect. If organizations wish to air ads on behalf of an issue that interests them, then they should be able to do so under the First Amendment. Organizations such as Common Cause, however, say that the problem with the "money equals speech" argument is that money actually replaces speech. Too often, groups lacking funds are squeezed out of meetings with elected officials, who need the money for reelec-

tion more than they need to hear about the complaints of constituents.

Disallowing organizations from engaging in the political process is by definition an infringement of political freedom, but perhaps it was a freedom so thoroughly abused that it had to be taken away to protect the republic. Furthermore, there is no guarantee that increasing government regulation will make the process any more democratic, just more regulated, meaning more complicated and bureaucratic. The scope of campaign finance is broad, and the implications of regulating it are far reaching.

Arguments for Campaign Finance Reform

- **A government beholden to a small group of wealthy and mobilized interest is, by definition, an oligarchy and un-American.** With millions of dollars to spare, large organizations such as unions and corporations can control candidate agendas by demanding loyalty in exchange for donations. The result is that a candidate, once elected, represents not ordinary constituents but those who got him or her elected. This is nothing more than bribery.
- **Prohibiting large organizations from dominating the attention of elected officials creates greater grassroots**

BRINGING IT TOGETHER: THE 2004 PRESIDENTIAL CAMPAIGN AND ELECTIONS

The 2004 election for president may go down in history for how extremely it divided the nation. An entire month before the election, polls showed that only 3% of Americans remained undecided on a candidate. Despite his status as an incumbent, implementation of tax cuts, and reputation for decisiveness, President George W. Bush faced an incredibly heated race against Massachusetts Senator John Kerry. At the most basic level, Americans knew that John Kerry had the knowledge and experience to serve in the highest office in the nation. Many were also unhappy with the situation in Iraq, job losses, and health care costs. However, Americans were casting their first presidential vote in the post-9/11 world, and they also had reservations about electing a president whose leadership during a national security crisis had not yet been proven.

The Party Nomination Battle

Although few Americans may have remembered after the election, the Republican Party *did* hold presidential primaries in 2004. Few noticed, as is usually the case when there is an incumbent candidate, because there was no significant opposition within the party to George W. Bush's reelection.

political involvement. If candidates cannot count on big donors to finance their elections, they will have to find ways of appealing to larger numbers of people. That forces candidates back into their local communities to listen to their concerns and promise to address them. Then, communities can organize to fund-raise for certain candidates. The winner is bound to address the local community's interests, which is what representative government is supposed to do in the first place.

- **Campaign finance reform opens up the door for new challengers.** Curbing the influence of wealthy interests creates an even playing field for candidates. If incumbents must run against strong challengers, they become more accountable and, if necessary, more easily replaced.

Arguments Against Campaign Finance Reform

- **Campaign contributions are political speech, the most hallowed and protected speech under the First Amendment.** All Americans have a right to freely state their political beliefs; just because one group has more money than another doesn't make a difference.
- **Bureaucracy is never the better answer to a market-driven problem.** While the intentions behind campaign finance reform are usually good, they are based on the false assumption that the way to solve all political problems is with more government. More government means a forever expanding labyrinth of quickly out-of-date rules that only years of debate and wrangling will fix, fol-

lowed by implementing more quickly outgrown rules requiring another round of wrangling. Regulation is a dog chasing its tail.

- **Campaign finance reform actually assists incumbents, not challengers.** Incumbents benefit from free media, since they have name recognition and greater credibility from their experience "on the Hill." A challenger needs money to counteract this and other advantages of incumbency. Regulating campaign finance limits a challenger's competitiveness, making the government less democratic as a result.

Questions

1. Can money, in the form of campaign contributions, be considered protected speech under the First Amendment? Why or why not?
2. Is it more democratic to centralize control of elections in order to allow more interests to be heard, or to let interests compete for attention without government interference?

Selected Readings

Bradley A. Smith. *Unfree Speech: The Folly of Campaign Finance Reform.* Princeton, NJ: Princeton University Press, 2001.

Dan Clawson, Alan Neustadtl, and Mark Weller. *Dollars and Votes: How Business Campaign Contributions Subvert Democracy.* Philadelphia: Temple University Press, 1998.

The Democrats, meanwhile, would have ten candidates competing for their party's nomination. Democratic Party veterans Representative Dick Gephardt (MO), Senator and 2000 vice presidential nominee Joseph Lieberman (CT), Senator Bob Graham (FL), and Senator John Kerry (MA) joined the five other "original" candidates. Senator John Edwards (NC), former Illinois Senator Carol Moseley-Braun, the first African American woman in the Senate, former Governor Howard Dean, Representative Dennis Kucinich (OH), and the Reverend Al Sharpton, an African American activist from New York. Retired General Wesley Clark entered late in the race after some Democrats ran a "Draft Clark" effort.

The Democratic candidates spent the spring and summer of 2003 in the typical primary season fashion: fund-raising, debating, giving speeches, and concentrating on the key states of Iowa and New Hampshire. By autumn, Senator Graham had dropped out of the race, citing fund-raising problems. Autumn also brought the rise of the once "fringe" candidate Howard Dean. His solid stance against the Iraq War and harsh criticism of President Bush appealed to Democratic partisans, providing him with impressive grassroots support and a large war chest. Although in the spring of 2003 Democratic insiders were predicting that John Kerry would emerge as the front-runner, the fall brought Howard Dean the endorsements of party leaders such as Iowa Senator Tom Harkin and former Vice President Al Gore.

Initially, the Democrats' campaigns were focused on contrasting themselves with President Bush. However, as Dean emerged as the apparent front-runner, his rivals began aiming many of their attacks in his direction rather than at the president. The former governor's third-place finish in the Iowa caucuses, behind both John Kerry and John Edwards, may have partially been attributed to these attacks. Others blamed the Iowa upset on the campaign's mismanagement of Dean's resources—not spending enough on ads and appearances and overspending on other items. Dean would win only one primary, in Vermont, and he dropped out of the race by February.

After Iowa, the race centered on Kerry and Edwards. The appeal of Gephardt and of Lieberman proved narrow, the former dropping out after Iowa and the latter after losing in Arizona. Edwards dropped out of the race in March, leaving Senator John Kerry of Massachusetts as the "presumptive" Democratic candidate. Democrats appeared united, at least in their determination to defeat George W. Bush in the general election. For this reason, many suggest, they chose a candidate quickly and channeled their energies toward winning in the fall.

The 2004 election indicated that left-leaning voters had become risk-averse after their experience in 2000. The "Nader effect" was a mere 1% nationally, not enough to swing any states. Whereas in 2000 some left-leaning voters complained that there was not much of a difference between Bush and Gore and thus voted for Nader, four years of a Bush presidency contributed to a mentality that came to be known as "anything but Bush." Anything-but-Bush adherents were not necessarily enthusiastic about John Kerry, but they were so determined to get President Bush out of office that they gave Kerry their votes. Low levels of third party voting therefore did not necessarily indicate increased popularity of the major parties; rather, they demonstrated that Florida had made liberal voters unwilling to take the risk of voting for a third party.

The Democratic Convention

With Kerry entering the national convention in a virtual tie with George W. Bush, he and Edwards would take this opportunity to define their candidacy, woo new voters, and rally their party faithful at the July 26-29 Democratic National Convention. The convention was held in Boston, Massachusetts, Kerry's home state and solid Democratic territory.

The first night started with a flourish, with former Presidents Bill Clinton and Jimmy Carter taking center stage, joined by former Vice President Al Gore. With polls that showed Americans giving Bush higher marks than Kerry on national security issues, Clinton sought to highlight the Democratic nominee's credentials in this area.

Photo courtesy: AP Photo/Matt York, Pool

■ At a debate held in Phoenix, Arizona on Ocober 3, 2003, several members of the Democratic primary field discussed their ideas with the audience.

TABLE 14.2 2004 Democratic Candidates and Their Strategies

Wesley Clark: to use his record as Supreme Allied Commander in Europe from 1997–2000, during which time he successfully managed a multilateral military effort ousting Serbian dictator Slobodan Milosevic, to neutralize Bush's claim to expertise in national defense and foreign diplomacy; to appeal to male voters who otherwise tend to vote Republican.

Howard Dean: to relieve the dissatisfaction of many Democratic interest groups that had begun to tire of the dominance of moderates in party decision making; to tap into desire for true liberalism; to capitalize on the newest form of political organization and fund-raising, the Internet.

John Edwards: to market himself as a fresh, new leader unconnected to inside-the-Beltway disputes and corruption; to represent the South, a necessary group of states to capture in order to win.

Richard Gephardt: to capitalize on his long experience in public office (in Congress since 1977; presidential candidate in 1988, minority leader in U.S. House 1995–2002); to capture the imagination of the Democratic Party with a startlingly comprehensive health care package.

Bob Graham: to capitalize on the Democratic obsession with the state of Florida that emerged following the close presidential election in 2000; to put forward a dovish foreign policy.

John Kerry: to use both his military service in Vietnam and significant foreign policy experience in the Senate to convince voters that he had the credentials to challenge President Bush on any issue in the general election.

Dennis Kucinich: to use anti-Bush rhetoric in order to stir up far-left support and Democratic voter base.

Joseph Lieberman: to capitalize on his service as vice presidential candidate in 2000 presidential election; to satisfy interests of conservative Democrats with his morally conservative views and as a foreign policy hawk.

Carol Mosley Braun: to capitalize on her historic position as the first African American woman elected to the Senate; to promote the roles of minorities and women in Democratic office.

Al Sharpton: to present hmself as the new Jesse Jackson to have a "seat at the table" for decision making within the party; to advocate African American interests within the Democratic Party.

The second night of the convention featured a diverse series of speakers. The most surprising speaker was Ron Reagan, son of the late Republican President Ronald Reagan. His speech focused on the controversial topic of embryonic stem cell research. In 2001 President Bush limited the use of federal funds for this practice, which was opposed by some conservatives who linked it to abortion. Reagan's speech detailed stem cell research's potential to cure disease, labeling it the "future of medicine," and implored voters to vote for Kerry, who supported this type of research.

If Ron Reagan were the most unlikely speaker of the second night, it was Barack Obama, a Democratic Senate candidate from Illinois, who really stole the spotlight. The multiracial son of a Kenyan immigrant father and poor, Kansas-born mother, Obama used his own story, of "a skinny kid with a funny name who believes that America has a place for him too," to illustrate his party's hope for creating opportunity and unity in America. This appearance launched Obama into fame on the national political scene.

The next night, Senator John Edwards addressed the delegates. True to form, Edwards delivered a populist pitch for his and John Kerry's candidacy. He returned to his primary race theme of "two different Americas." "John Kerry and I believe that we shouldn't have two different economies in America: one for people who are set for life . . . and then one for most Americans, people who live paycheck to paycheck." His speech's refrain, "Hope is on the way," summarized his pledge to the nation to improve their everyday lives.

The overarching theme of the Democrats' convention was, "Respected abroad, stronger at home." This emphasis of national security was most prominent on the final night of the convention, which featured testimonials from former Senator Max Cleland and Kerry's Vietnam Swiftboat crewmates. In Kerry's speech, foreign affairs and his personal biography vastly overshadowed other topics. The biographical portion was most likely in response to polls that showed Kerry as not yet having established a personal connection with Americans. Kerry also used his speech as an opportunity to defend against GOP accusations that he "flip flops." In one of his most direct attacks on the integrity of President Bush, Kerry pledged that his leadership would "start by telling the truth to the American people."

THE DEAN FUND-RAISING NETWORK

As a Democratic presidential candidate, former Vermont Governor Howard Dean was a revelation to politicians, pundits, and fellow candidates alike. Dean and his campaign manager Joe Trippi devised a fund-raising strategy that defied convention. Ordinarily, when politicians must raise money for a campaign, they call big donors who call other big donors. Then, the candidate holds large dinners and banquets, or even a concert, at which the big donors write checks. This method alienates less wealthy voters, who feel unable to catch a candidate's attention without first unloading the cash.

Dean challenged this fund-raising approach by focusing on the Internet as a new medium for donations. First, the Internet is cheap, since a Web site is easy to create and maintain, requiring only a few webmasters to update content and troubleshoot. Second, the Internet is fast—contributions come in almost instantly, making them immediately accessible as cash on hand for the candidate. Third, the Internet is interactive. Not only did Dean take in donations, but he also made small donors feel as though they were part of a movement. Frequently, Dean set a fund-raising goal and had his webmasters continually update the amount reached. All the while, Dean supporters gathered together through a Web-based organizing tool called MeetUp, posted messages on numerous Dean campaign-based message boards, and wrote Web journals ("blogs") on their political views. The sense of community gave many Dean supporters the feeling that their money was going somewhere, simultaneously making Internet fund-raising a grassroots effort, a far cry from the alienation most citizens feel with more conventional fund-raising methods.

The feeling of community is necessary, however, since matching a small number of large donations requires a large number of small donations. In July 2003, Dean averaged $53 per contribution. By October, his average donation had only gone up to $74 with 169,000 donors on his list. On the other hand, President George W. Bush averaged $280 per donation with 262,000 donors. Bush's number obviously exceeds Dean's, but what matters in this comparison is that Dean was an unknown in January 2003, while Bush was a popular president. Dean's jump from former governor of a small state to leading Democratic fundraiser demonstrated the potency of the Internet as a fund-raising tool. In fact, even though Dean eventually lost the nomination, he has become an important player in fund-raising and speech-making for the Democratic Party.

There are still some doubts about Internet fund-raising as the wave of the future. First, the Internet is not universally accessible—some donors, such as many African Americans and seniors, remain cut out.[a] Second, there is some belief that Dean's success had more to do with Dean than with the Internet as an organizing and fundraising tool. Dean's antiwar rhetoric and progressive social positions may have particularly appealed to heavy Internet users in ways that John Kerry or George W. Bush may not. Finally, unlike conventional donations, Internet donations are not always secure and could be hacked or stolen.

If President John F. Kennedy was the first television president, Dean may be the first true Internet candidate. Perhaps future candidates must have what it takes to sustain an Internet movement, or maybe Dean resembles the Internet companies of the late 1990s that showed so much promise but eventually faded from view as investors looked for more stable investments.

[a] Liz Marlantes, "Web May Revolutionize Fundraising," *Christian Science Monitor* (July 31, 2003), http://www.csmonitor.com/2003/0731/p02s01-uspo.html.

Despite what most analysts considered a solid performance, Kerry-Edwards did not receive any significant post-convention "bounce." This was unusual in that there had not been another candidate since George McGovern in 1972 whose convention had not yielded at least a small bounce. In their candidate's defense, the Kerry campaign argued that challengers historically run behind incumbents by about 15 points heading into a convention, whereas Kerry entered the convention already polling neck and neck with Bush.

The Republican Convention

The Republican National Convention was held from August 30th to September 2nd, beginning a full month after the Democratic National Convention ended. It was held in Madison Square Garden in New York City, considered to be one of the most heavily liberal, Democratic locales in the nation and most certainly Kerry territory. It was clear that the GOP picked New York City not to win over its residents, but rather in an effort to use the symbolism of the 9/11 terrorist attacks to their advantage.

Under the theme, "A Nation of Courage," the 2004 Republican National Convention had an unmistakable focus on showcasing moderate Republicans. The right-wing branch of the Republican Party that had captured the stage at past conventions would

Analyzing Visuals

JOHN KERRY WINDSURFS

On the one hand, John Kerry looked athletic and Kennedy-esque while windsurfing off the coast of Nantucket, Massachusetts, in August 2004, which was no doubt the effect that he and his advisers wanted. On the other hand, windsurfing is not exactly a common sport, and many of Kerry's aides had privately wished he had gone bowling instead. Blue-collar workers, who ended up defecting from Kerry in large numbers in November 2004, are bowlers, not windsurfers. In Kerry's own mind, he was simply being himself, believing that this genuineness would override any projected elitist image. But, to his chagrin, Kerry found that his windsurfing was interpreted as the act of an upper-class, out-of-touch northeastern liberal Democrat.

Moreover, less than three weeks later, it became the focus of a thirty-second television advertisement entitled simply "Windsurfing," aired on national cable channels and in select local markets by the Bush-Cheney campaign, In the ad, the narrator claimed that Kerry's positions on the war in Iraq, health care reform, education, and other important issues shifted "whichever way the wind blows."

As with the Bush Mission Accomplished banner, this photo op cut both ways. But, in the end, it became a negative commentary on the Democratic nominee and his electoral chances.

Photo courtesy: Reuters/Landov

After looking at the photo, what do you think about John Kerry's decision to choose windsurfing as a way to identify with voters? Is a candidate's choice of leisure activities a fair target for his opponent? Do you think Kerry's experience will make future candidates think carefully about every move they make in their spare time?

stand aside as the more moderate Arnold Schwarzenegger, Rudy Giuliani, and John McCain spoke on behalf of their party and President Bush. The convention would be a delicate balancing act between reaching out to the swing voters (who were charmed in 2000 by Bush's "compassionate conservative" agenda) without alienating the socially conservative Republican base.

The second night of the Republican convention saw less emphasis on national security and more on domestic issues, such as education and health care, under the banner "People with Compassion." Former movie actor and bodybuilder Arnold Schwarzenegger, who had become governor of California less than a year earlier used his star power and reputation as a moderate to bring support to President Bush. Schwarzenegger peppered his speech with references to his films, asserting that Bush would "terminate" terrorism and referring to the Democratic Convention as "True Lies."

If Ron Reagan were most surprising speaker at the Democratic National Convention, his equivalent at the Republican National Convention was undoubtedly Georgia Democratic Senator Zell Miller. Miller, who was by then thought of as a Democrat in name only, sharply attacked John Kerry and the Democratic Party's positions on national defense. Vice President Dick Cheney also took the stage on the third night of the Republican National Convention, accepting his party's nomination for a second term. In harmony with the Bush campaign strategy, he sought to portray Kerry as a "flip-flopper." "On Iraq, Senator Kerry has disagreed with many of his fellow Democrats. But Senator Kerry's liveliest disagreement is with himself," he said. Although the vice president made mention if domestic issues such as reforming medical liability laws, job creation and health care, his speech had the same general focuses as did the entire convention: the War on Terror, Iraq, and Homeland Security.

President George W. Bush, Vice President Dick Cheney and their wives wave to supporters during a victory rally in Washington, D.C. on November 3, 2004.

Photo courtesy: Mark Wilson/Getty Images

The final night was reserved for the Republican Party's official nomination of George W. Bush for a second term as president. In addition to his vows to stay the course on terrorism, he discussed education, health care, jobs, and taxes. Bush also took advantage of his location—New York City—to remind voters of his handling of the crisis and reawaken the emotion, unity and fear surrounding the 9/11 attacks. "My fellow Americans, for as long as our country stands, people will look to the resurrection of New York City and they will say: Here buildings fell, and here a nation rose," he said.

The 2004 Republican National Convention was not only a depiction of the Republican Party's agenda and campaign strategy, but also a vivid demonstration of how polarized the nation had become this election season. Thousands of New Yorkers and protesters from other states took to the streets during the convention for primarily peaceful protests against Bush, the Iraq War, and the Republican Party. Still, the GOP had reason to be pleased with its convention performance. Whereas the Democratic National Convention did not give Kerry a "bounce" in public opinion polls, Bush left New York with the prize of a modest 2 percent postconvention bounce, giving him the support of 52% of likely voters.

The Presidential Debates

The first debate took place on September 30, 2004, in Coral Gables, Florida. The candidates' format for this event featured questions posed by the moderator, PBS host Jim Lehrer, with responses and rebuttals by the candidates. During the discussion on foreign policy, Bush and Kerry clashed sharply on the war in Iraq and on fighting terrorism. Television ratings were exceptionally high, with the first debate being watched

TABLE 14.3 2004 Election Results (Popular Vote Percentage)

State	Bush (%)	Kerry (%)	State	Bush (%)	Kerry (%)
Alabama	63	37	Montana	59	39
Alaska	62	35	Nebraska	66	33
Arizona	55	44	Nevada	51	48
Arkansas	54	45	New Hampshire	49	50
California	45	54	New Jersey	46	53
Colorado	52	47	New Mexico	50	49
Connecticut	44	54	New York	40	58
Delaware	46	53	North Carolina	56	44
District of Columbia	9	90	North Dakota	63	36
Florida	52	47	Ohio	51	49
Georgia	58	41	Oklahoma	66	34
Hawaii	45	54	Oregon	48	52
Idaho	68	30	Pennsylvania	49	51
Illinois	45	55	Rhode Island	39	60
Indiana	60	39	South Carolina	58	41
Iowa	50	49	South Dakota	60	39
Kansas	62	37	Tennessee	57	43
Kentucky	60	40	Texas	61	38
Louisiana	57	42	Utah	71	27
Maine	45	54	Vermont	39	59
Maryland	43	56	Virginia	54	45
Massachusetts	37	62	Washington	46	53
Michigan	48	51	West Virginia	56	43
Minnesota	48	51	Wisconsin	49	50
Mississippi	60	40	Wyoming	69	29
Missouri	54	46			

Source: Official election results from CNN, http://www.cnn.com/ELECTION/2004/.

by 62.5 million viewers, the most since 1992. Viewers generally found Kerry to have won the debate, and many pundits commented on Bush's lack of energy and focus.

A town hall format was used for the second presidential debate, wherein voters found to be undecided by the Gallup polling organization were allow to ask questions of each candidate in turn. Reacting against the criticism that he seemed tired and unfocused, Bush was extremely forthright and energetic throughout the night. The candidates met for the last time on October 13 in Tempe, Arizona. This debate followed a structure similar to that for the first debate, with the candidates standing behind podiums and answering questions in turn from CBS News anchor Bob Schieffer. For the first time during the debates, the questions were geared toward domestic issues. The last debate was generally considered to have been won by Kerry by the public and media commentators. Ultimately, Kerry—with his debate performances—seemed to even the playing field going into the final days of the campaign.

The Fall Campaign and General Election

In the final weeks of the campaign, public opinion was deadlocked, and many Americans began to fear that the closeness and uncertainty of 2000 were again possible in 2004. There was even the real possibility of a tie in the Electoral College, which would throw the election into the House of Representatives. The election was especially close in the key battleground states of Ohio, Florida, Pennsylvania, New Mexico, Iowa, and Wisconsin.

Bush stayed on message during the last days of the campaign, emphasizing the need to continue the effort in Iraq and to strongly prosecute the war on terrorism. Kerry continued to hack away at the president's choice to invade Iraq as misguided and without a plan for victory. Kerry especially criticized Bush's handling of foreign relations, mentioning the bad blood in Europe and around the world created out of his Iraq policy. Kerry promised a change in international relations in which the United States would be more attuned to the concerns of allies and would expend more effort building alliances to fight the global war on terrorism. In a number of television commercials, and in public appearances, Bush fought back, attempting to paint Kerry as a "flip-flopper" who constantly switched his positions to better fit public opinion. To attack Kerry's credibility on defense, Bush also used a *New York Times* interview in which Kerry likened terrorism before 9/11 to a "nuisance" like illegal gambling or prostitution.

Despite the efforts of each campaign, public opinion remained very divided in key states like Ohio and Florida up until the election. Realizing this, both candidates made a marathon sprint through battleground states in the last few days before the election. Bush covered several states in the final week, but spent seven consecutive days traveling through Ohio, including Election Day. Kerry visited Michigan, Wisconsin, Florida, and Ohio in the final days of the campaign. After voting in his home state of Texas, Bush flew back to Washington to await the election results. Kerry returned to Massachusetts to cast his vote and follow an Election Day tradition of lunch at a Boston oyster bar. With the election close, and both candidates confident of their chances, the afternoon wore on in anticipation of the first exit polls.

Election Results

With the painful memories of 2000 still fresh in their minds, network and cable news bureaus proceeded with caution on election night. As the night wore on and more states began to close their polls, Bush began to show a convincing lead in the key battleground state of Florida. However, the networks remained extremely cautious, only calling the states that had given a clear and commanding victory to either candidate. As Election Day approached midnight, Florida had been called for Bush, but Ohio still remained too close to call for some networks, despite a significant lead by the president. By early the next morning, neither candidate had yet to capture the necessary 270 electoral votes. Despite a lead of over a hundred thousand votes for Bush in Ohio, the Kerry campaign believed there might be enough late votes to turn the tide.

By later that morning, the Bush campaign was confident that they had carried the election, and they informed the Kerry campaign that they would be declaring victory. Allowing Kerry the courtesy of giving his concession speech first, the Bush campaign waited until the early afternoon for Kerry to speak. Kerry then conceded formally at the historic Faneuil Hall in Boston, emphasizing the need for unity after such a divisive campaign. About an hour later, Bush gave his victory speech at the Ronald Reagan building in Washington, D.C., also speaking of the need for unity but emphasizing his victory as ratification by the people of his policies.

Turnout in the 2004 Election

The 2004 election had the highest voter turnout rate since 1968, with 59.6% of eligible citizens participating, or an estimated 120 million votes. Fifteen million more Americans voted in 2004 than in 2000, despite long lines that kept some voters waiting for over 7 hours. Not surprisingly, the largest turnouts occurred in "swing states," where a majority of campaign time and resources were spent. The major partisan divide is seen as a primary cause for such high numbers. Despite the highly publicized youth vote campaign on both sides, increases among college-attending youth were seen only in the battleground states, and there only slightly. Across the board, young people accounted for 17 percent of the overall turnout, exactly the same percentage as 2000.

Because of such a polarized campaign and election, the third party factor was almost completely nonexistent in 2004. A little over 1 million votes went to the four third-party candidates. If this political division between Republican and Democrats were to continue, the role of the third party would decline. However, this same divide that brought about such large turnouts may prove to be temporary if such polarization does not exist in the future.

SUMMARY

WITH THIS CHAPTER, we switched our focus from the election decision and turned our attention to the actual campaign process. What we have seen is that while modern campaigning makes use of dazzling new technologies and a variety of strategies to attract voters, campaigns still tend to rise and fall on the strength of the individual candidate. In this chapter we have stressed the following observations:

1. **The Structure of a Campaign**
   A campaign, the process of seeking and winning votes in the run-up to an election, consists of five separate components: the nomination campaign, in which party leaders and activists are courted to ensure that the candidate is nominated in primaries or conventions; the general election campaign, in which the goal is to appeal to the nation as a whole; the personal campaign, in which the candidate and his or her family make appearances, meet voters, hold press conferences, and give speeches; the organizational campaign, in which volunteers telephone voters, distribute literature, organize events, and raise money; and the media campaign waged on television and radio and in newspapers and magazines.

   Campaign staffs combine volunteers, a manager to oversee them, and key political consultants including media consultants, a pollster, and a direct mailer.

   In recent years media consultants have assumed greater and greater importance, partly because the cost of advertising has skyrocketed, so that campaign media budgets consume the lion's share of available resources.

2. **The Media and Campaigns**
   Candidates for public office primarily win by gaining access to media. They gain access with paid media, purchasing ad time on television and ad space in print media, and with free media, television and print media news coverage. Because candidates cannot easily control media coverage, they cannot rely on free media alone. Candidates, therefore, must spend campaign dollars on creating advertisements that deliver campaign messages without media criticism. The Internet increasingly makes this possible, since candidates can use it as a cheap medium to relate directly to voters and activists.

3. **Campaign Finance**
   Since the 1970s, campaign financing has been governed by the terms of the Federal Election Campaign Act (FECA). Because of the rise of soft money, the FECA was amended in 2002 by the Bipartisan Campaign Finance Reform Act, which was promptly challenged and upheld with very few exceptions by the Supreme Court.

4. Bringing It Together: The 2004 Presidential Campaign and Election

A very competitive Democratic primary season, that had Howard Dean leading for much of the winter, ended in victory for John Kerry in Iowa. Kerry's momentum carried him on to a quick primary victory, and began the unofficial general campaign far in advance of the summer. Public opinion remained extremely close until the conventions, where President Bush benefited from a well orchestrated effort by the Republicans. Bush's slight lead over Kerry was diminished by a lackluster performance during three televised debates and the end of the race was a photo finish. Turnout was very brisk, and President Bush managed a close but convincing win in both the Electoral College and the popular vote.

KEY TERMS

campaign consultant, p. 516
campaign manager, p. 516
candidate debate, p. 521
communications director, p. 517
contrast ad, p. 518
direct mailer, p. 516
finance chair, p. 516
free media, p. 518
general election campaign, p. 511
get-out-the-vote (GOTV), p. 516
hard money, p. 529
inoculation ad, p. 518
matching funds, p. 529
media campaign, p. 511
media consultant, p. 518
negative ad, p. 518
nomination campaign, p. 510
organizational campaign, p. 511
paid media, p. 518
personal campaign, p. 511
political action committee (PAC), p. 526
pollster, p. 516
positive ad, p. 518
press secretary, p. 517
public funds, p. 529
soft money, p. 531
spot ad, p. 518
voter canvass, p. 514

SELECTED READINGS

Abramson, Paul R., John H. Aldrich, and David W. Rohde. *Change and Continuity in the 2000 and 2002 Elections.* Washington, DC: CQ Press, 2003.

Ansolabehere, Stephen, and Shanto Iyengar. *Going Negative: How Political Ads Shrink and Polarize the Electorate.* New York: Free Press, 1997.

Ceaser, James W., and Andrew E. Busch. *Losing to Win: The 1996 Elections and American Politics.* Lanham, MD: Rowman and Littlefield, 1997.

Ceaser, James W., and Andrew E. Busch. *The Perfect Tie: The True Story of the 2000 Presidential Election.* Lanham, MD: Rowman and Littlefield, 2001.

Fenno, Richard F., Jr. *Senators on the Campaign Trail: The Politics of Representation.* Norman: University of Oklahoma Press, 1998.

Greive, R. R. Bob. *The Blood, Sweat, and Tears of Political Victory . . . And Defeat.* Lanham, MD: University Press of America, 1996.

Herrnson, Paul S. *Congressional Elections: Campaigning at Home and in Washington,* 4th ed. Washington, DC: CQ Press, 2003.

Holbrook, Thomas M. *Do Campaigns Matter?* Thousand Oaks, CA: Sage, 1996.

Kern, Montague. *30-Second Politics: Political Advertising in the Eighties.* New York: Praeger, 1989.

Mayer, William G., ed. *In Pursuit of the White House 2000: How We Choose Our Presidential Nominees.* Chatham, NJ: Chatham House, 2000.

Nelson, Michael, ed. *The Elections of 1996.* Washington, DC: CQ Press, 1997.

Pomper, Gerald M., ed. *The Election of 2000: Reports and Interpretations.* Washington, DC: CQ Press, 2001.

Sabato, Larry J., ed. *Campaigns and Elections: A Reader in Modern American Politics.* Glenview, IL: Scott, Foresman, 1989.

Sabato, Larry J., *Paying for Elections: The Campaign Finance Thicket.* New York: Priority Press for the Twentieth Century Fund, 1989.

Sabato, Larry J., *Toward the Millennium: The Elections of 1996.* New York: Prentice Hall, 1997.

Sabato, Larry J., *Overtime! The Election 2000 Thriller.* New York: Longman, 2001.

Sabato, Larry J., and Glenn R. Simpson. *Dirty Little Secrets: The Persistence of Corruption in American Politics.* New York: Random House, 1996.

Sorauf, Frank J. *Inside Campaign Finance,* reissue ed. New Haven, CT: Yale University Press, 1994.

Thurber, James A., and Candice J. Nelson. *Campaign Warriors: Political Consultants in Elections.* Washington, D.C.: Brookings Institution, 2000.

Troy, Gil. *See How They Ran: The Changing Role of the Presidential Candidate,* revised ed. Cambridge, MA: Harvard University Press, 1996.

WEB EXPLORATIONS

To compare the development of presidential candidates, go to
http://www.cnn.com/ALLPOLITICS/
To find out what Americans have to say on a range of political issues and to experience poll-taking firsthand, go to
www.gallup.com
To get an insider's look at the detail and urgency with which campaigns are now covered, go to
http://www.cnn.com/ELECTION/2004/
To get involved and find out what you can do about campaign reform, go to
http://www.house.gov/shays/reform/cfr3526-sum.htm
http://www.cnn.com/2004/ALLPOLITICS/02/24/elec04.prez.bush.marriage/index.html

Photo courtesy: David Guttenfelder/AP/Wide World Photos

The Media

AT THE END OF MARCH 2003, following months of intense diplomacy and military buildup, a U.S.-led coalition sent military forces into Iraq to remove Saddam Hussein's government from power. Among the battalions were "embedded journalists," men and women employed by a variety of news media and hailing from across the globe. These journalists underwent some basic training and were deployed along with forces such as Kurdish militias in Northern Iraq as well as the U.S. 101st Airborne. Their stories ranged in subjects from patriotic profiles of individual soldiers to biting criticism over long and possibly vulnerable supply lines out of Kuwait. News commentators repeatedly said that the news media were "going to war." They were right. A year later, nineteen journalists reporting from Iraq were dead, and two were missing and presumed dead.

Journalists were not the only media casualties of war; reputations were, too. In April 2003, for example, *New York Times* journalist Jayson Blair admitted to fabricating stories about homefront events related to the war in Iraq and resigned, along with his editor Howell Raines. The *Times* subsequently created a "public editor" position that was intended to keep *Times* journalists accountable for their stories. Daniel Okrent, writing as the public editor, published an article criticizing *Times* editors and reporters for relying on uncorroborated claims made by anonymous sources for front-page stories about Iraq. Their reliance solely on anonymous sources placed speed as a priority over truth but allowed reporters to publish stories before those at competing newspapers. "The failure was not individual, but institutional," Okrent stated. In other words, Blair was the logical outcome of a system built to produce news quickly instead of correctly.

The U.S. military completed its major combat mission in Iraq with relatively few losses, and film of U.S. forces assisting Iraqis in pulling down a large statue of Saddam Hussein projected an image of the U.S. as liberators. Months later, however, the U.S. military had a different image, one of Pfc. Lyndee England holding a naked Iraqi prisoner by a leash in Abu Ghraib prison. The prisoner abuse scandal, begun with the release to the media of photographs taken within the military prison, gave the media as an institution a chance to redeem themselves. Reporters rapidly uncovered that soldiers from the 372nd military police company were acting against the U.S. Army's official policies regarding treatment of prisoners, while others in the media searched for whether commanding officers and even Secretary of Defense Donald Rumsfeld knew of the abuse.

THE MEDIA have the potential to exert enormous influence over Americans. Not only do they tell us what is important by setting the agenda for what we will watch and read, but they can also influence what we think about issues through the content of their news stories. The simple words of the First Amendment, "Congress shall make no law…abridging the freedom of speech, or of the press," have shaped the American republic as much as or more than any others in the Constitution. With the Constitution's sanction, as interpreted by the Supreme Court over two centuries, a vigorous and highly competitive press has emerged. This freedom has been crucial in facilitating the political discourse and education necessary to maintain democracy. But, does this freedom also entail responsibility on the part of the press and other media? Have the media, over the years, met their obligation to provide objective, issue-based coverage of our politicians and political events, or do they tend to focus on the trivial and sensational, ignoring important issues and contributing to voter frustration with government and politicians?

This chapter traces the historical development of the press in the United States and then explores the contemporary media scene. It also explores the ways in which government controls the organization and operation of the media, attempting to promote a balance between freedom and responsibility on the one hand, and competitiveness and consumer choice on the other. In discussing the changing role and impact of the media, we will address the following:

1. First, we will discuss *the evolution of journalism in the United States,* from the founding of the country up to modern times.
2. Second, we will examine *the U.S. media today.*
3. Third, we will consider *how the media cover politicians and government,* including how politicians and the media interact.
4. Fourth, we will investigate *the media's influence on the public,* and whether public opinion is significantly swayed by media coverage.
5. Fifth, we will examine *the public's perception of the media.*
6. Finally, we will explain *government regulation of the electronic media* and identify the motivations for and evolution of such control.

THE EVOLUTION OF JOURNALISM IN THE UNITED STATES

JOURNALISM—the process and profession of collecting and disseminating the news (that is, new information about subjects of public interest)—has existed in some form since the dawn of civilization.[1] (See Table 15.1 for a history of the media in the United States.) Yet, its practice has often been remarkably uncivilized, and it was much more so at the beginning of the American republic than it is today.

The first newspapers were published in the American colonies in 1690. The number of newspapers grew throughout the 1700s, as colonists began to realize the value of a press free from government oversight and censorship. The battle between Federalists and Anti-Federalists, discussed in chapter 2, played out in various partisan newspapers. Thus, it was not surprising that one of the Anti-Federalists' demands during our country's constitutional debate was to include an amendment guaranteeing the freedom of the press in the final version of the Constitution. A free press is a necessary component of a democratic society because it informs the public, giving them the information they

TABLE 15.1 Landmarks of the American Media	
1760	First newspaper published.
1789	First party newspapers circulated.
1833	First penny press.
1890	Yellow journalism spreads.
1900	Muckraking in fashion.
1928	First radio broadcast of election.
1948	First election results to be covered by television.
1952	First presidential campaign advertisements aired on television.
1960	Televised presidential campaign debates.
1979	The Cable Satellite Public Affairs Network (C-SPAN) is founded, providing live, round-the-clock coverage of politics and government.
1980	Cable News Network (CNN) is founded by media mogul Ted Turner, making national and international events available instantaneously around the globe.
1992	Talk-show television circumvents the news, allowing candidates to go around journalists to reach the voting public directly,
1996	Official candidate home pages containing, among other things, candidate profiles, issue positions, campaign strategy and slogans, and e-mail addresses appear on the World Wide Web.
2000	Explosion of World Wide Web as a primary campaign tool for candidates, and a continuous twenty-four-hour news cycle.
2004	Web logs, or "blogs," create a popular forum for the disbursement of political news and commentary.

need in order to choose their leaders and influence the direction of public policy. In fact, the American media have been called the "fourth branch of government" because their influence is often as great as that of the three constitutional branches: the executive, the legislative, and the judiciary. However, this term is misleading because the American media are composed of many competing private enterprises.

During his presidency, George Washington escaped the sort of harsh press scrutiny that presidents experience today, but he detested journalists nonetheless because his battle tactics in the Revolutionary War had been much criticized in print. An early draft of his "Farewell Address to the Nation" at the end of his presidency (1796) contained a savage condemnation of the press.[2] The partisan press eventually gave way to the penny press. In 1833, Benjamin Day founded the *New York Sun*, which cost a penny at the newsstand. Because it was not tied to one party, it was politically more independent than the party papers. The *Sun*, the forerunner of modern newspapers, relied on mass circulation and commercial advertising to produce profit. By 1861, the penny press had so supplanted partisan papers that President Abraham Lincoln announced that his administration would have no favored or sponsored newspaper.

Although the press was becoming less partisan, it was not necessarily becoming more respectable. Mass-circulation dailies sought wide readership, attracting readers with the sensational and the scandalous. The sordid side of politics became the entertainment of the times. One of the best-known examples occurred in the presidential campaign of 1884, when the *Buffalo Evening Telegraph* headlined "A Terrible Tale" about Grover Cleveland, the Democratic nominee.[3] In 1871, while sheriff of Buffalo, Cleveland had allegedly fathered a child. Even though paternity was indeterminate because the child's mother had been seeing other men, Cleveland willingly accepted responsibility, since all the other men were married, and he had dutifully paid child support for years. The strict Victorian moral code that dominated American values at the time made the story even more shocking than it would be today. Fortunately for Cleveland, another newspaper, the *Democratic Sentinel*, broke a story that helped to offset this scandal: Republican presidential nominee James G. Blaine and his wife had had their first child just three months after their wedding.

Timeline

Three Centuries of American Mass Media

The Living Constitution

Congress shall make no law respecting an establishment of religion, or prohibiting the free exercise thereof; or abridging the freedom of speech, or of the press; or the right of the people peaceably to assemble, and to petition the government for a redress of grievances.

—First Amendment

The Founders knew that no democracy is easy, that a republic requires a continuous battle for rights and responsibilities. One of those rights is the freedom of the press, preserved in the First Amendment to the Constitution. To protect the press, the Founders were wise enough to keep the constitutional language simple—and a good thing, too. Their view of the press, and its required freedom, was almost certainly less broad than we conceive of the press today.

It is difficult today to appreciate what a leap of faith it was for the Founders to grant freedom of the press when James Madison brought the Bill of Rights before Congress. Newspapers were largely run by disreputable people, since at the time editors and reporters were judged as merely purveyors of rumor and scandal, the reason Madison, as well as Alexander Hamilton and John Jay, published their newspaper articles advocating the ratification of the Constitution, *The Federalist Papers,* under the pseudonym "Publius."

The printed word was one of the few media of political communication in the young nation—it was critical for keeping Americans informed about issues. Therefore, the Founders had to hope that giving freedom for the press to print all content, although certain to give rise to tabloids, would also produce high-quality newspapers. Nevertheless, we should note that the Founders were not above using journalism as a way of promoting their political agendas. For example, Thomas Jefferson created a newspaper, the *National Gazette,* to report news favoring his Democratic-Republican Party. Giving the press freedom was also giving opposing politicians an open forum to attack each other.

Not much has changed since the Founders instituted the free press. We still have tabloids and partisan publicans in which politicians attack each other, and we still rely on the press to give us important political information with which we make voting decisions. The First Amendment declares the priority of free expression. The Founders recognized that all kinds of information would have to be allowed, in order to create as many opportunities for solid information to be reported, the fear being that regulations in response to what offends some people might be the first step on the slippery slope to censorship. In other words, protecting the *New York Times* means protecting the "paparazzi" or else we will have neither. Although the vices and virtues of a free press have not changed, the number of media has, but the simple yet powerful protection the Founders created in the First Amendment made their invention and implementation merely a continuation of a freedom we all enjoy.

In the late 1800s and early 1900s, the era of the intrusive press was in full flower. Pioneered by prominent publishers such as William Randolph Hearst and Joseph Pulitzer, **yellow journalism**—the name strictly derived from printing the comic strip "Yellow Kid" in color—featured pictures, comics, and color designed to capture a share of the burgeoning immigrant population market. These newspapers also oversimplified and sensationalized many news developments. The front-page editorial crusade became common, the motto for which frequently seemed to be: "Damn the truth, full speed ahead."

After the turn of the twentieth century, the muckrakers—so named by President Theodore Roosevelt after a special rake designed to collect manure[4]—took charge of a number of newspapers and nationally circulated magazines. **Muckraking** journalists searched out and exposed misconduct by government, business, and politicians in order to stimulate reform.[5] There was no shortage of corruption to reveal, of course, and much good came from these efforts. In particular, muckrakers stimulated demands for the increased regulation of public trusts. But, an unfortunate side effect of the emphasis on crusades and investigations was the frequent publication of gossip and rumor without sufficient proof.

The modern press corps may also be guilty of this offense, but it has achieved great progress on another front. Throughout the nineteenth century, payoffs to the press were common. Andrew Jackson, for instance, gave one in ten of his early appointments to loyal reporters.[6] During the 1872 presidential campaign, the Republicans slipped cash to about 300 newsmen.[7] Wealthy industrialists also sometimes purchased investigative cease-fires for tens of thousands of dollars. Examples of such press corruption in the United States are exceedingly rare today.

As the news business grew, its focus gradually shifted from passionate opinion to corporate profit. Newspapers, hoping to maximize profit, were more careful to avoid alienating the advertisers and readers who produced their revenues, and the result was less harsh, more objective reporting. Meanwhile, media barons such as Joseph Pulitzer and William Randolph Hearst became pillars of the establishment; for the most part, they were no longer the anti-establishment insurgents of yore.

yellow journalism

A form of newspaper publishing in vogue in the late-nineteenth century that featured pictures, comics, color, and sensationalized, oversimplified news coverage.

muckraking

A form of journalism, in vogue in the early twentieth century, concerned with reforming government and business conduct.

Photo courtesy: Stock Montage, Inc.

■ "Uncle Sam's Next Campaign—the War Against the Yellow Press." In this 1898 cartoon in the wake of the Spanish-American War, yellow journalism is attacked for its threats, insults, filth, grime, blood, death, slander, gore, and blackmail, all of which are "lies." The cartoonist suggests that, after winning the foreign war, the government ought to attack its own yellow journalists at home.

Technological advances had a major impact on this transformation in journalism. High-speed presses and more cheaply produced paper made mass-circulation dailies possible. The telegraph and then the telephone made news gathering easier and much faster. When radio became widely available in the 1920s, millions of Americans could hear national politicians instead of merely reading about them. With television—first introduced in the late 1940s, and nearly a universal fixture in U.S. homes by the mid-1950s—citizens could see and hear candidates and presidents. The supplanting of newspapers and magazines as the foremost conduits between politicians and voters had profound effects on the electoral process, as we discuss shortly.

THE U.S. MEDIA TODAY

THE EDITORS of the first partisan newspapers could scarcely have imagined what their profession would become more than two centuries later. The number and diversity of media outlets existing today are stunning. The **print press** consists of many thousands of daily and weekly newspapers, periodicals, magazines, newsletters, and journals. The **electronic media** are radio and television stations and networks, and the Internet.

Print Media

The growth of the political press corps is obvious to anyone familiar with government or campaigns. Since 1983, for example, the number of print (newspaper and magazine) reporters accredited at the U.S. Capitol has jumped from 2,300 to more than 4,100; the gain for broadcast (television and radio) journalists was equally impressive and proportionately larger, from about 1,000 in 1983 over 3,200 in 2004.[8] On the campaign trail, a similar phenomenon has occurred. In the 1960s, a presidential candidate in the primaries would attract a press entourage of at most a few dozen reporters, but today a hundred or more journalists can be seen tagging along with a front-runner. When a victorious candidate reaches the White House, he doesn't simply see the media for big events; in 2004, sixty-three journalists were credentialed as daily White House correspondents.[9] Consequently, a politician's every public utterance is reported and intensively scrutinized and interpreted in the media.

Although there are more journalists, they are not necessarily attracting a larger audience, at least on the print side. Readers of daily newspapers among the top fifty markets (these top fifty markets reflect an overall trend for daily newspaper readers) fell from 58 percent in 1998 to 54 percent in 2003.[10] This number conceals more than it reveals—68 percent of Americans over age sixty-five read daily newspapers, while only 40 percent of readers age eighteen to twenty-four and 41 percent of readers between age twenty-five to thirty-four do. In spring of 2004, the Newspaper Association of America sought new methods to retain and grow readership, such as posting content on newspaper Web sites and focusing on local events.[11]

Along with the relative decline of readership has come a drop in the overall level of competition. In 1923, over 500 cities had competing daily newspapers; by 2004, that number was down to a mere twelve.[12] Most of the dailies are owned by large media conglomerates called chains, such as Gannett, Hearst, Knight-Ridder, and Newhouse. The thirteen largest chains account for 54 percent of daily circulation, while only 300 of the nearly 1,480 daily newspapers are independently owned; thus, chains own over 80 percent of the daily newspapers.[13] Chain ownership usually reduces the diversity of editorial opinions and can result in the homogenization of the news.

Radio and Television

The advent of radio in the early part of the twentieth century was a media revolution and a revelation to the average American—who rarely, if ever had heard the voice of a president, governor, or senator. The radio became the center of most homes in the evening, when national networks broadcast the news as well as entertainment shows.

print press
The traditional form of mass media, comprising newspapers, magazines, and journals.

electronic media
The broadcast and cable media, including television, radio, and the Internet.

Simulation
You Are a News Editor

Calvin Coolidge was the first president to appear on radio on a regular basis, but President Franklin D. Roosevelt made the radio appearance a must-listen by presenting "fireside chats" to push his New Deal, to allay the fears of some citizens that his program was too radical, and to calm Americans as the country entered World War II. The soothing voice of Roosevelt made it difficult for most Americans to dispute that what the president wanted could be anything other than what was best for America. By the late 1950s, however, television expanded into most homes throughout the United States and thus took from radio the central role of providing the news.

Radio took a back seat to television until the development of AM talk radio in the mid-1980s. Controversial radio host Rush Limbaugh began the trend with his unabashed conservative views, opening the door for other conservative commentators such as Sean Hannity and Michael Reagan. Statistics show that these conservative radio hosts have resurrected the radio as a news medium by giving the information that they share a strong ideological bent. In 1997, 12 percent of Americans claimed to get their news from talk radio, but by 2004, 17 percent did.[14]

Despite radio's reach, however, there is simply no more important source of news and information than television. Use of the Internet is growing, especially among younger people, but the commercial and cable television networks provide most Americans with the news they get each day.

One cause of the newspapers' declining audience is the increased numbers of television sets and cable and satellite television subscribers. In the early 1960s, a substantial majority of Americans reported that they got most of their news from newspapers. Forty years later, 83 percent of Americans claimed to get their news from television, whereas only a little over 50 percent read newspapers (Figure 15.1). There is, however, an important distinction between network and cable news stations. Network news has lost viewers since 1980, with the loss becoming even steeper after the advent of cable news. Between 2000 and 2004, viewership for all network news programming declined from 45 percent to 35 percent.[15] Cable news has seen an increase in viewership, from 34 percent in 2000 to 38 percent in 2004. This increase is due in large part because of the

Visual Literacy
The Media and the
American Public

FIGURE 15.1 **Distribution of News Source Usage by Individuals**
While the dominant, mainstream media outlets are still used by the greatest number of consumers, the only growth areas are ethnic, alternative, and online media. ■

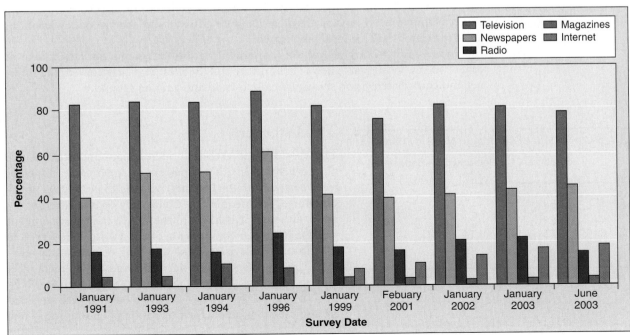

Source: Pew Research Center for the People and the Press, "Strong Opposition to Media Cross-Ownership Emerges: Public Wants Neutrality and Pro-American Point of View," accessed August 13, 2004, http://www.stateofthenewsmedia.org/narrative_overview_audience.asp?media=1.

increased availability of services providing the twenty-four-hour news channels. By 2004, 67 percent of all U.S. households were wired for basic cable, with 18 percent of households using a direct broadcast satellite (such as DirectTV or DISH).[16] Thus, the vast majority of Americans receive cable news in addition to their broadcast stations.

Within the realm of cable news, the two ratings leaders, CNN and Fox News, have begun engaging in *niche journalism*—that is, both stations cater particularly to specific groups of people. The two stations divide audiences by ideology. Fox News increasingly favors a more conservative view and CNN a more liberal one, although the Fox view is much more pronounced.[17] (Table 15.2 indicates where Republicans, Democrats, and independents prefer to get their news about political campaigns.) Despite its many drawbacks (such as simplicity, brevity, and entertainment orientation), television news, especially cable news, is "news that matters." It has the power to affect greatly which issues viewers say are important.[18]

Cable and satellite providers also give consumers access to a less glitzy and more unfiltered source of news with C-SPAN. C-SPAN is a basic cable channel that offers coverage of congressional proceedings, major political events, and events sponsored by political groups. It also produces some of its own programming, such as *Washington Journal,* which invites scholars and journalists to speak about topics pertaining to their areas of expertise. C-SPAN expanded its brand to include C-SPAN2 and C-SPAN3, which air programming such as academic seminars and book presentations in a series titled *BookTV.* C-SPAN benefits from having no sponsors distracting (with commercials or banners) or possibly affecting what it broadcasts. Because the content of C-SPAN can be erudite, technical, and sometimes downright tedious (such as the fixed camera shot of the Senate during a roll call vote), audiences tend to be very small, but they are very loyal and give C-SPAN its place as a truly content-driven medium.

Local television reporters often outnumber the national television news corps on the campaign trail. Satellite technology has provided any of the 1,300 local stations willing to invest in the hardware an opportunity to beam back reports from the field. Consequently, local news can tie national events to local issues in ways national network and cable news cannot. It is no surprise, then, that Americans prefer local news to the national coverage of the broadcast and cable networks, 42 percent of them watching their local news programs for news. This number has, however, dropped from 48 percent in 2000, perhaps because of the increased access to cable news and the subsequent fragmentation of news sources. Unfortunately, however, studies also show that local news, compared to newspapers and network reports, contains the least substantive coverage. National news reports are more likely to criticize and analyze policy positions and candidates than are local broadcasts.[19]

Increasingly, young people are abandoning traditional media outlets in favor of other sources. While cable news networks are still the most regularly viewed, the Internet and comedy television shows are close behind and gaining ground.[20]

TABLE 15.2 Main Source of Campaign News by Party	Republican %	Democratic %	Independent %
Newspapers	38	43	36
ABC/CBS/NBC	24	40	30
CNN	20	27	20
Fox News	29	14	17
Radio	20	12	13
Internet	11	12	16

Note: Figures add to more than 100% because respondents could list more than one source.

Source: Pew Research Center for the People and the Press, Early January 2004 Political Communications Study.

The Internet

The World Wide Web is an increasingly important source of information. In 2000, 9 percent of Americans claimed to receive news from the Internet, whereas 13 percent do now.[21] Of course, few people rely exclusively on the Internet for news, although it is likely in the future that many citizens will use the video components of the World Wide Web to substitute for television news watching or newspaper reading. Already, many major networks and newspapers offer their news online. Major cable news stations, such as CNN, MSNBC, and Fox News, each have their own Web sites that are also used to promote their television programming as well

WHERE DO YOUNG VOTERS GET THEIR CAMPAIGN NEWS?

In January 2004, the Pew Research Center for the People and the Press stated in a press release[a] that Americans increasingly believed there is partisan bias in cable news; also buried in the release was the report that young voters (age eighteen to twenty-nine) increasingly rely on two sources for campaign news—the Internet and comedy television shows, such as *The Daily Show* and *Saturday Night Live*. Twenty-one percent of young voters, 16 percent of voters age thirty to forty-nine, and 7 percent of voters age fifty or older use the Internet for campaign news; 21 percent of young voters use comedy television shows, much higher than the 6 percent of those between thirty to forty-nine and 3 percent of those fifty or older. Very quickly, the fact that young voters might make voting decisions based on a quip from Steven Colbert or Seth Meyers's impression of John Kerry upset many in the media, generating a flurry of articles. One journalist called the age bracket "the Young and the Newsless."[b]

But there is more to the data than reported. What Pew actually revealed was that where voters get their news affects how well informed they are. For voters of all ages, if the regular source of 2004 campaign news was a television comedy show, they were very badly informed about the campaign. For voters using new Internet Web sites as their regular source of campaign news, knowledge of the campaign was actually higher than average. Pew raises the issue of age because

young voters use both comedy shows and the Internet more frequently than any other age demographic, a finding indicating that well-informed young voters gravitate to newer technologies for learning about politics. At the same time, while comedy viewers may claim to get their news from sketches and satire, it is clear that the content is only entertaining and not informing them.

So when Jon Stewart reminds the audience, as he often does, that he anchors a fake news show, the audience will listen and perhaps, after "the Moment of Zen," check the headlines at a major news Web site or even pick up a local newspaper. After all, when told that *The Daily Show* could be confused with an old form of satire or a new kind of journalism, Stewart said, "Well, then, that either speaks to the sad state of comedy or the sad state of the news."[c]

---

[a] Pew Research Center for the People and the Press, "Cable and Internet Loom Large in Fragmented Political News Universe: Perceptions of Partisan Bias Seen as Growing, Especially by Democrats," January 11, 2004, http://www.pewinternet.org/pdfs/PIP_Political_Info_Jan04.pdf.

[b] Melanie McFalrand, "Young People Turning Comedy Shows into Serious News Source," *Seattle Post-Intelligencer*, January 22, 2004, http://seattlepi.nwsource.com/tv/157538_tv22.html.

[c] Bill Moyers, "Bill Moyers Interviews Jon Stewart," *NOW*, July 11, 2003, http://www.pbs.org/now/transcript/transcript_stewart.html.

---

as provide up-to-date news. The *New York Times* and *Washington Post* are available online for free to users who register. Access to older articles requires a fee. Political magazines such as the *National Review* and the *Nation* provide all online content free of charge; like the online newspapers, they earn revenue from advertising through pop-up and banner ads.

Many people wonder if newspapers and television stations currently offering free Web sites are cutting into their own subscription revenues. However, there is very little evidence that this is happening. By and large, the people who use media Web sites are highly informed voters who devour additional information about politics and government and use the Web for updates and supplements to their traditional media services. Indeed, a recent study discovered that out of light, medium, and heavy users of online news sites, heavy users read newspapers the most, while light users read newspapers the least. In short, heavy users, those most interested in the news, will take their news any way they can get it.[22]

In an attempt to assert an online presence, the U.S. government provides its own news, frequently publishing its press releases on Web sites it has set up for its major departments, as well as for both houses of Congress and the president. These Web sites offer basic information regarding the history, function, and current issues before their respective body. Also, Web users who access the Senate or House site can enter their zip code to find out the identity of their representative. In addition, users can access the complete voting record of their members of Congress on the Senate and House sites and use the contact information found there to e-mail their representative or senator.

Analyzing Visuals

MORE MEN THAN WOMEN SEEK POLITICAL CONTENT ONLINE

According to a study released recently as part of the Pew Internet and Public Life Project, 63 percent of Americans—or 126 million—go online, as of August 2003. While the number of individuals searching for political news and information on the Internet grew by over 17 million between 2000 and 2002, the percentage of men using the Internet to locate such data (43 percent) is still greater than that of women (36 percent). This gap has remained consistent as measured over the two years contained in the study report, and it appears to be continuing.

During the 2002 midterm elections, more than four in ten Internet users reported looking for political news and information online, with 64 percent of searches focused on candidates and their positions on issues. The highest proportion of these political information seekers are not surprisingly found in the highest education and income groups, and those with significant Internet experience or broadband connections are among the most likely to get this kind of information online.

Interestingly, nearly half of Internet users (45 percent) who searched for political news or information claimed not to have found the material they were seeking. Only 22 percent of health information seekers and 20 percent of government Web site visitors had the same complaint.

After examining the bar graph, answer the following critical thinking questions: Why do you think there is a

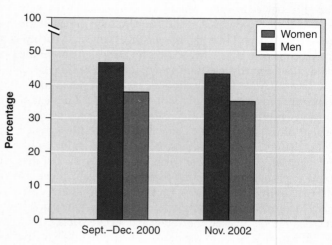

gap between men and women when it comes to using the Internet to obtain political information? Is there something about the Internet that appeals more to men than to women? What are some possible explanations for the slight decline in the percentages for both men and women in 2002?

Source: http://www.pewinternet.org/pdfs/PIP_Online_Pursuits_Final.PDF.

The Internet also offers access to foreign news media previously unavailable to most Americans. The British Broadcasting Channel (BBC) has a Web site entirely devoted to news and available in over forty languages. International newspapers offer online content, although usually in their native languages. Al-Jazeera, a major Arabic television news source, has an English-language Web site providing news concerning Arabs and Muslims in the Middle East (see Global Perspective: Al-Jazeera: The CNN of the Arab World?). For those many Americans with access to the Internet, these alternative sources of information may shed a different perspective on global issues.

National Influence of the Media

Every newspaper, radio station, television station, and Web site is influential in its own area, but only a handful of media outlets are influential nationally. The United States has no nationwide daily newspapers to match the influence of Great Britain's *Times,*

AL-JAZEERA: THE CNN OF THE ARAB WORLD?

Few Americans other than those of Arabic descent had heard of al-Jazeera before October 7, 2001. On that day, less than one month following the terrorist attacks on the World Trade Center and the Pentagon, Osama bin Laden spoke to the world for six and one-half minutes. It was not the first time al-Jazeera carried his image or his words, nor would it be the last. In June 1999 it broadcast a ninety-minute interview with him, and several bin Laden tapes have been aired since then. Many have taken these interviews as evidence that al-Jazeera is little more than a mouthpiece for al-Qaeda's anti-American propaganda, or at least an accomplice, allowing bin Laden periodically to emerge from hiding and speak to his followers through embedded messages. But what is al-Jazeera, and why is it so influential in the Arab world?

Al-Jazeera means "the island" or "the peninsula" in Arabic. It is an independent station that broadcasts from the tiny oil-rich and Islamic country of Qatar in the Persian Gulf. Qatar is a member of the Organization of Petroleum Exporting Countries (OPEC) and is ruled by a progressive emir (prince) who is pro-Western. The emir allowed American troops to use Qatar as a staging point for the 1991 Persian Gulf War and the Iraqi War. He also funded al-Jazeera when it was founded in 1996. Al-Jazeera emerged out of the failure of a British Broadcasting Corporation (BBC) news service, after a Saudi Arabian–owned radio and television network reportedly terminated its financial support because the news service had aired a documentary about executions in Saudi Arabia.

Al-Jazeera immediately set a course that separated it from its competitors in the region. Most of them were owned either by Middle Eastern governments or by powerful individuals within these countries, and their standard offerings emphasized entertainment and limited news that amounted to state propaganda. A typical newscast would do little more than follow the morning-to-night public schedule of a leading official. Sensitive political and social issues were ignored for fear of the controversy they would create.

In contrast, the trail that al-Jazeera chose to follow was pioneered by Cable News Network (CNN). Like CNN, al-Jazeera focuses its political reporting on two staples. The first is on-the-scene coverage of conflict. Just as CNN was the only television network to broadcast out of Baghdad in the Persian Gulf War, al-Jazeera had a monopoly of live reporting from Kabul during the war in Afghanistan against the Taliban. Three Western news agencies, including CNN, also received permission from the Taliban government in 1999 to establish offices in Afghanistan, but only al-Jazeera did so. Al-Jazeera also covers the Palestinian conflict extensively, receiving heavy criticism from the West for referring to Palestinians killed by Israeli forces as martyrs and showing extensive footage of Palestinian casualties.

The second staple is political talk shows that often feature call-ins from viewers. Among the most popular are *The Opposite Direction,* a live weekly two-hour show modeled after CNN's *Crossfire,* and *Without Frontiers,* in which an individual discusses a current event topic in depth. Shows such as these have often angered Middle Eastern governments where there is little tradition of free press. Libya and Kuwait both threatened to recall their ambassadors to Qatar in protest over critical stories aired by al-Jazeera. Saudi Arabia did so and prohibited al-Jazeera from covering the pilgrimage to Mecca. The government of Algeria created a blackout in the capital city to prevent the airing of a story on its civil war. Saddam Hussein once criticized al-Jazeera's broadcasts as too "pro-American" and expelled two al-Jazeera reporters during the Iraq War because of its coverage. Yasser Arafat criticized al-Jazeera for carrying an interview with Sheikh Ahmed Yassin, head of Hamas and his longtime rival for leadership among the Palestinians.

Not only Arabs appear on al-Jazeera news shows: U.S., British, and Israeli leaders, including President George W. Bush, Prime Minister Tony Blair, Secretary of State Colin Powell, and National Security Advisor Condoleezza Rice, have all been interviewed by al-Jazeera.

Questions

1. Spend some time looking at the Web site of al-Jazeera (aljazeera.net). How does its coverage compare with that of American networks?
2. On balance, is the United States better off or worse off in the Middle East because of al-Jazeera?

Guardian, and *Daily Telegraph,* all of which are avidly read in virtually every corner of the United Kingdom. The national orientation of the British print media can be traced to the smaller size of the country and also to London's role as both the national capital and the largest cultural metropolis. The vastness of the United States and the existence of many large cities effectively preclude a nationally united print medium in this country.

network

An association of broadcast stations (radio or television) that share programming through a financial arrangement.

affiliates

Local television stations that carry the programming of a national network.

wire service

An electronic delivery of news gathered by the news service's correspondents and sent to all member news media organizations.

However, the *New York Times*, the *Wall Street Journal, USA Today,* and the *Christian Science Monitor* are distributed nationally, and other newspapers, such as the *Washington Post* and the *Los Angeles Times,* have substantial influence from coast to coast. These six newspapers also have a pronounced effect on what the five major national **networks** (ABC, CBS, NBC, CNN, and Fox) broadcast on their evening news programs—or, in the case of cable news (MSNBC, CNBC, CNN, and Fox News), air on cable around the clock. A major story that breaks in one of these papers is nearly guaranteed to be featured on one or more of the network news shows. These news shows are carried by hundreds of local stations—called **affiliates**—that are associated with the national networks and may choose to carry their programming. A **wire service,** such as the Associated Press (AP) (established in 1848), also nationalizes the news. Most newspapers subscribe to the service, which not only produces its own news stories but also puts on the wire major stories produced by other media outlets.

Several national news magazines, whose subscribers number in the millions, supplement the national newspapers, wire services, and broadcast networks. *Time, Newsweek,* and *U.S. News & World Report* bring the week's news into focus and headline one event or trend for special treatment. Other news magazines stress commentary from an ideological viewpoint, including the *Nation* (left-wing), *New Republic* (moderate-liberal), and the *Weekly Standard* (conservative). These last three publications have much smaller circulations, but because their readerships are composed of activists and opinion leaders, they have disproportionate influence. There are now some good, exclusively Web-based magazines, such as salon.com and slate.com. These Web sites direct their content to a hipper, college-educated audience by emphasizing cultural forces at work within day-to-day political events.

The future relationship between the Internet and politics remains hard to predict. Some analysts believe that as the current generation of computer-literate children and young people become adult voters, the Web is likely to become the primary means by which America informs itself about politics and government. (Table 15.3 shows the public's media choices by age group.) Others assert that "it appears unlikely that more than a small portion of the existing audience for traditional news media will abandon those media for Internet news sources."[23] Scholars debate whether all the information

TABLE 15.3 The News Generation Gap

	18–29 %	30–49 %	50–64 %	65+ %
Did yesterday				
Watched TV news	40	52	62	73
Local TV news	28	41	49	52
Network evening	17	25	38	46
Cable TV news	16	23	30	35
Morning news	11	16	21	27
Read a newspaper	26	37	52	59
Listened to radio news	34	49	42	29
No news yesterday	33	19	15	12
Watch/listen/read regularly				
Local TV news	46	54	64	69
Cable TV news	23	31	42	38
Nightly network news	19	23	45	53
Network TV magazines	15	22	30	33
Network morning news	16	22	23	31
Call-in radio shows	16	19	20	10
National Public Radio	14	18	15	11
Time/Newsweek/US News	12	13	15	13
Online news 3+ times/week	31	30	24	7

Source: Pew Research Center for the People and the Press, "Public's Habits Little Changed by September 11," June 9, 2002, http://people-press.org.

available on the Web will be good for politics or not. Some believe that the availability of all this information makes for a better informed and more active electorate, whereas others think that this remains to be seen. One obvious question is whether citizens will devote the time necessary to find valid and balanced data amid the almost unlimited information available through the Internet, or if instead they will refer to only a few favorite sites that support their views.

HOW THE MEDIA COVER POLITICIANS AND GOVERNMENT

THE NEWS MEDIA focus much attention on our politicians and the day-to-day operations of our government. In this section, we will discuss media coverage of government and politics and show how the tenor of this coverage has changed since the Watergate scandal of the early 1970s.

How the Press and Public Figures Interact

The type of communication between elected officials or public figures and the media may take different forms. A **press release** is a written document offering an official comment or position on an issue or news event; it is usually printed on paper and handed directly to reporters, or increasingly, released by e-mail or fax. A **press briefing** is a relatively restricted live engagement with the press, with the range of questions limited to one or two specific topics. In a press briefing, a press secretary or aide represents the elected official or public figure, who does not appear in person. In a full-blown **press conference,** an elected official appears in person to talk with the press at great length about an unrestricted range of topics. Press conferences provide a field on which reporters struggle to get the answers they need and public figures attempt to retain control of their message and spin the news and issues in ways favorable to them.

On some occasions, candidates and their aides will go on background to give trusted newspersons juicy morsels of negative information about rivals. **On background**—meaning that none of the news can be attributed to the source—is one of several journalistic devices used to elicit information that might otherwise never come to light. **Deep background** is another such device; whereas background talks can be attributed to unnamed senior officials, deep background news must be completely unsourced, with the reporter giving the reader no hint about the origin of the information. A journalist may also obtain information **off the record,** which means that nothing the official says may be printed. (If a reporter can obtain the same information elsewhere, however, he or she is free to publish it.) By contrast, if a session is **on the record,** as in a formal press conference, every word an official utters can be printed—and used against that official. It is no wonder that office holders often prefer the nonpublishable alternatives! Clearly, these rules are necessary for reporters to do their basic job—informing the public. Ironically, the same rules keep the press from fully informing their readers and viewers. Every public official knows that journalists are pledged to protect the confidentiality of their sources, and therefore the rules can sometimes be used to an official's own benefit.

Although the media are powerful actors in any election campaign, they can also be used and manipulated by politicians in a variety of ways. For example, many politicians hire campaign consultants who use focus groups and polling in an attempt to gauge how to present the candidate to the media and to the public. Additionally, politicians can attempt to bypass the national news media through paid advertising and by appearing on talk shows and local news programs. (Some of these and other techniques for dealing with the media during a campaign are discussed in greater detail in chapter 14.) Politicians also use the media to attempt to retain a high level of name recognition and to build support for their ideological and policy ideas.

press release
A document offering an official comment or position.

press briefing
A relatively restricted session between a press secretary or aide and the press.

press conference
An unrestricted session between an elected official and the press.

on background
Information provided to a journalist that will not be attributed to a named source.

deep background
Information provided to a journalist that will not be attributed to any source.

off the record
Information provided to a journalist that will not be released to the public.

on the record
Information provided to a journalist that can be released and attributed by name to the source.

Covering the Presidency

The three branches of the U.S. government—the executive, the legislative, and the judicial—are roughly equal in power and authority, but in the world of media coverage the president is first among equals. All television cables lead to the White House, and a president can address the nation on all networks almost at will. On television, Congress and the courts appear to be divided and confused institutions—different segments contradicting others—whereas the commander in chief is in clear focus as chief of state and head of government. The situation is scarcely different in other democracies. In Great Britain, for example, all media eyes are on No. 10 Downing Street, the office and residence of the prime minister.

Since Franklin D. Roosevelt's time, chief executives have used the office and presidential press conference as a bully pulpit to shape public opinion and explain their actions (see Figure 15.2). The presence of the press in the White House enables a president to appear even on very short notice and to televise live, interrupting regular programming. The White House's press briefing room is a familiar sight on the evening news, not just because presidents use it so often, but also because the presidential press secretary has almost daily question-and-answer sessions there.

The post of press secretary to the president has existed only since Herbert Hoover's administration (1929–1933), and the individual holding it is the president's main disseminator of information to the press. For this vital position, some presidents choose close aides with whom they have worked previously and who are familiar with their thinking. Jimmy Carter chose his longtime Georgia associate Jody Powell. Press secretaries are not always close aides, however; George W. Bush did not know his first press secretary, Ari Fleischer, when he hired him, but he respected Fleischer's strong experience in public relations and his communication skills. Press secretaries must be very adept at dealing with the press; some worked as journalists prior to becoming a press secretary, and many go on to press jobs after their stint in the White House. For example, Lyndon B. Johnson's press secretary, Bill Moyers, now hosts many PBS documentaries. The first female press secretary, Dee Dee Myers, served under President Clinton and has also used her experience to launch a career into political punditry.

In deciding what *does* become news, presidents and the press engage in a continuous "debate about newsworthiness." This debate occurs not only between the White House and the news media but within the two entities as well, and it involves "what gets covered, who gets asked about a story, and how and for how long the story is covered."[24]

FIGURE 15.2 Presidential Press Conferences. ■

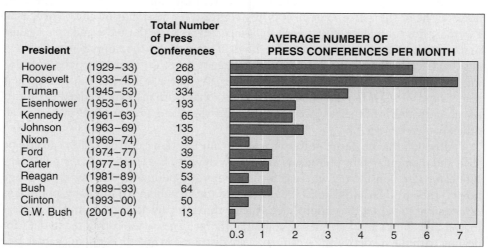

Source: White House press office.

Although the president receives the vast majority of the press's attention, much of this focus is unfavorable. Since the advent of televising press conferences in the 1960s, press coverage of the president has become dramatically more negative. Dwight Eisenhower once opened up a press conference by inviting the press to "nail him to the cross" as they usually did, and this approach suggests the way most presidents approach their formal encounters with the press. A study in the early 1990s found coverage of George Bush's handling of important national problems was almost solely negative.[25] The media have faced a more difficult challenge in covering the administration of George W. Bush, a president who prides himself on the tight-lipped, no leaks nature of his White House. No member of his staff appears on television or in print without prior permission, while Bush himself has held a record low number of thirteen formal press conferences during his first term. Compared to his father, who held sixty-four during his four years as president, Bush clearly has tried to control his image by controlling how much the press directly encounters him.

Photo courtesy: Charles Dharapak/AP/Wide World Photos

■ White House spokesperson Scott McClellan fields from the press inquiries about White House involvement in releasing the name of an undercover CIA operative married to former Ambassador and Bush critic Joseph Wilson.

Covering Congress

The size of Congress (535 members) and its decentralized nature (bicameralism, the committee system, and so on) make it difficult for the media to survey. Nevertheless, the congressional press corps has more than 3,000 members.[26] Most news organizations solve the size and decentralization problems by concentrating coverage on three groups of individuals. First, the leaders of both parties in both houses receive the lion's share of attention because only they can speak for a majority of their party's members. Usually the majority and minority leaders in each house and the speaker of the House are the preferred spokespersons, but the whips also receive a substantial share of air time and column inches. Second, key committee chairs command center stage when subjects in their domain are newsworthy. Heads of the most prominent committees (such as Ways and Means or Armed Services) are guaranteed frequent coverage, but even the chairs and members of minor committees or subcommittees can achieve fame when the time and issue are right. Third, local newspapers and broadcast stations normally devote some resources to covering their local senators and representatives, even when these legislators are junior and relatively lacking in influence. Most office holders, in turn, are mainly concerned with meeting the needs of their local media contingents, since these reporters are the ones who directly and regularly reach the voters in their home constituencies. Coverage of Congress has been greatly expanded through cable channels C-SPAN and C-SPAN2, which provide gavel-to-gavel coverage of House and Senate sessions as well as many committee hearings. For the first time, Americans can watch their representatives in action twenty-four hours a day.

As with coverage of the president, media coverage of Congress is disproportionately negative. Much media attention given to the House and Senate focuses on conflict between members. Some political scientists believe that such reporting is at least partially responsible for the public's negative perceptions of Congress.[27]

One other kind of congressional news coverage is worth noting: investigative committee hearings. Occasionally, a sensational scandal leads to televised congressional committee hearings that transfix and electrify the nation. In the early 1950s, Senator

Photo courtesy: C-SPAN Archive

■ During the Clinton impeachment hearings, C-SPAN provided extensive live congressional coverage for cable viewers across the United States.

Joseph R. McCarthy (R–WI) held a series of hearings to root out what he claimed were Communists in the Department of State and other U.S. government agencies, as well as in Hollywood's film industry. The senator's style of investigation, which involved many wild charges made without proof and the smearing and labeling of opponents as Communists, gave rise to the term *McCarthyism*. In 2002, congressional committees were heavily involved in investigating several high-profile corporate scandals, including the collapse of prominent companies such as Enron and WorldCom. Many Democrats and Republicans had received contributions from these corporations they were suddenly scrutinizing, and most representatives from both parties returned the contributions to avoid future political liabilities and the appearance of impropriety.[28]

Congressional investigation became its own subject after the photographs depicting abuse of Iraqi prisoners in Abu Ghraib were released to the press in 2004. Democrats questioned why the Republican majority in both houses refused to perform any real investigation of prison abuse, citing their obvious political alliance with President Bush. In short, Democrats wanted an investigation of the abuse and of the lack of investigation. Republican Senator Charles Grassley (R–IA) attributed Republican failure less to partisan interests and more to the fact that "oversight can be tedious, unglamorous work, and that it sometimes takes years to tease out problems buried deep in the bureaucracy."[29] If Grassley's assertion is correct, it could take years for Congress to get to the bottom of this matter.

Media Coverage of Local Elections

Many of the principles involving national news apply as well to local elections. The media can have a strong impact on local elections, candidates, and issues. Because of the increasing nationalization of media chains, however, the news frequently omits local issues.

Relatively few independent sources cover local contests with sufficient means of communicating local political events to the relevant audiences. At most, one might find a two- or three-minute story on the twenty-two-minute local news broadcast, which is hardly enough time to learn anything but the most general information. If the local area is fortunate, several small weekly newspapers may publish articles about local issues, but this is not the case everywhere. For these reasons, it remains difficult for candidates for local office to communicate their platforms to voters. Candidates often must go door to door in their localities to spread their message to voters or, if they can afford it, pay for radio ads and direct mail to substitute for the lack of media coverage.

Favorable name identification is critical in local races, and the most credible way for candidates to achieve name recognition is through independent newspaper and television coverage. Thus, those media outlets covering local contests in detail wield a great deal of political influence. Newspaper editorials endorsing candidates for city council and school board can have disproportionate impact, both because of the absence of other information and because most voters who frequently read newspapers tend to vote.

Investigative Journalism and the Character Issue

In a field as powerful and as pervasive as the news media, it is inevitable that certain controversies would develop over time—controversies that would interest large numbers of Americans and attract the growing stable of media critics throughout the United States. In this section and the next, we will focus on three issues:

- Investigative journalism, whereby reporters go beyond headlines and scrutinize public officials and public policy in order to find wrongdoing.

- The "character issue," referring to what some see as a press obsession with the sins and foibles of our politicians.

- Press bias, the debate about whether the press in its coverage leans to the left or the right and therefore misleads the public.

The Watergate scandal of the Nixon administration had a profound impact on press conduct. Watergate began a chain reaction that today allows for intense media scrutiny of public officials' private lives and shifted the orientation of journalism away from mere description (providing an account of happenings) and toward prescription—helping to set the campaign's (and society's) agenda by focusing attention on the candidates' shortcomings as well as on certain social problems. After Watergate, people increasingly saw the press as the most powerful agent to keep government accountable through sustaining the constant threat of finding and exposing political corruption.

The sizeable financial and personnel investments many major news organizations make in investigative units almost guarantee that they give greater attention to scandals, and that they uncover more of them than in the pre-Watergate years in journalism.

Another clear consequence of Watergate has been the increasing emphasis by the press on the character of candidates. The issue of character has always been present in U.S. politics—George Washington was not made the nation's first president for his policy positions but because he was esteemed as the general who won the Revolutionary War—but rarely if ever has character been such an issue as it has in elections since

Photo courtesy: AP/Wide World Photos

■ *Washington Post* reporters Bob Woodward, right, and Carl Bernstein won a Pulitzer Prize for their reporting of the Watergate scandal.

Watergate. In 2004, the character issue appeared in the form of questions about each candidate's military service. President Bush's National Guard tenure was examined, while Senator Kerry's conduct in Vietnam drew significant attention. This shift in focus from issues to character is the result of the shift from newspaper to television news. Unlike print, television is a visual medium, which best portrays faces and images. As a result, voters who receive their political information from television are significantly more likely to rely on candidate traits (rather than issue positions) in casting their ballots than are voters who receive their political information primarily from newspapers.[30]

The character trend in reporting is supported by certain assumptions held by the press. First, the press has mainly replaced the political parties as the screening committee that winnows the field of candidates and filters out the weaker contenders. (This fact may be another reason to support the strengthening of the political parties. Politicians are in a much better position than the press to provide professional peer review of colleagues who are seeking the presidency.) Second, many journalists believe it necessary to publicize a candidate's foibles that might affect his or her public performance. Third, the press believes that it is giving the public what it wants and expects. Finally, scandal sells papers and attracts television viewers.[31]

In the past, a reporter would think twice about filing a story critical of a politician's character, and the editors probably would have killed the story had the reporter been foolish enough to do so. The reason? Fear of a libel suit. (Recall from chapter 5 that libel is written defamation of character that unjustly injures a person's reputation.) The first question editors would ask about even an ambiguous or suggestive phrase about a public official was, "If we're sued, can you prove beyond a doubt what you've written?"

Such inhibitions were ostensibly lifted in 1964, when the Supreme Court ruled in ***New York Times Co.* v. *Sullivan*** that simply publishing a defamatory falsehood is not enough to justify a libel judgment.[32] Henceforth, a public official would have to prove "actual malice," a requirement extended three years later to all public figures, such as Hollywood stars and prominent athletes.[33] The Supreme Court declared that the First Amendment requires elected officials and candidates to prove that the publisher either believed the challenged statement was false or at least entertained serious doubts about its truth and acted recklessly in publishing it in the face of those doubts. The actual malice rule has made it very difficult for public figures to win libel cases.

New York Times Co. v. *Sullivan* (1964)
The Supreme Court concluded that "actual malice" must be proved to support a finding of libel against a public figure.

Participation
Are the Media Biased?

Media Bias

Whenever the media break an unfavorable story about a politician, the politician usually counters with a cry of "biased reporting"—a claim that the press has told an untruth, has told only part of the truth, or has reported facts out of the complete context of the event (see Join the Debate: Media Bias: Is the News Affected by an Ideological Bias?). Who is right? Are the news media biased? The answer is simple and unavoidable. Of course they are. Journalists are fallible human beings who inevitably have values, preferences, and attitudes galore—some conscious, others subconscious, but all reflected at one time or another in the subjects selected for coverage or the slant of that coverage. Given that the press is biased, in what ways is it biased and when and how are the biases shown?

For much of the 1980s and 1990s, the argument was that the media were liberally biased because of the sheer number of journalists who leaned to the left. Studies in the 1980s showed that professional journalists were drawn heavily from the ranks of highly educated social and political liberals.[34] Journalists are substantially Democratic in party affiliation and voting habits, progressive and anti-establishment in political orientation, and well to the left of the general public on most economic, foreign policy, and social issues (such as abortion, affirmative action, gay rights, and gun control). Indeed, a 2001 survey revealed that, whereas 35 percent of the general public describes themselves as being ideologically conservative, only 6 percent of those in the media would do the same.[35] In addition, dozens of the most influential reporters and executives entered (or reentered) journalism after stints of partisan participation in campaigns or government; studies in the 1980s showed that a substantial majority worked for Democrats.[36]

Some scholars argue that corporate interests play a significant role in what journalists report. During legislative debate over the Telecommunications Act of 1996, the passage of which would benefit media corporations with television holdings, scholars found that articles appearing in newspapers owned by media corporations with television interests typically failed to report the possible negative impact resulting from passage of the act. These scholars concluded that "very different pictures of the likely effects of this legislation were being painted by the different newspapers examined, pictures that served to further the interests of the newspapers' corporate owners rather than the interests of their readers in a fair and complete coverage of an important policy issue."[37]

Many liberal media critics have focused on the national news media's lack of skepticism about the Bush administration's arguments for waging a war in Iraq during the run-up to that conflict. As we now know, those in the administration who believed the Iraqis would acquiesce to a U.S. occupation were dead wrong, and terrorists have had a field day in and out of Iraq. It is probably true that the *New York Times*, the *Washington Post*, the networks, and other news outlets did not question the administration enough about their evidence for Iraqi weapons of mass destruction and ties to terrorism.

It seems that much of the more recent media bias is intentional and a response to increasing fragmentation and competition among media. Uncovering media bias may no longer be necessary, since it is no longer something the media (whether the journalists or the corporate executive) wish to hide but rather something they very intentionally market to gain a competitive edge. A comprehensive study of the news media reports that audiences seek out particular perspectives in the news they consume. While "mainstream, general interest newspapers, network television and local television news" are slowly losing audiences, "online, ethnic and alternative media are growing markedly" and "share the same strength—the opportunity for audiences to select tailored content and, in the case of the Internet, to do it on demand."[38] In order for various media to compete, they have to differentiate themselves from the rest, and their current method of choice is in the bias infused within their content.

■ Bill O'Reilly, host of the Fox News Channel's *The O'Reilly Factor*, is one of the country's most visible conservative commentators.

Photo courtesy: Marc Asnin/Corbis/Saba

Recent survey data show that 27 percent of Democrats watch CNN, while only 20 percent of Republicans do. Meanwhile, 29 percent of Republicans watch Fox News, but a mere 14 percent of Democrats do.[39] With cable news becoming a crowded field fighting over audience share, stations have tried to differentiate themselves in order to attract audiences. The trend, however, goes beyond cable news. Research shows that 40 percent of Democrats watch network news, while only 20 percent of Republicans do. Republicans listen to the radio for news more than Democrats, 20 to 12 percent, respectively. This number may even hide the divisions existing among stations—National Public Radio (NPR) typically catering to a more liberal palette and talk radio to a more conservative one. Finally, there is only a small disparity in newspaper reading between Republicans and Democrats (38 to 43 percent, respectively). However, like radio, newspapers can be subdivided by ideology; for instance, the *Washington Times* offers more conservative fare than its rival the *Washington Post*.

The ideological fragmentation of the media should give pause to those who believe that mass media are essential to providing the facts to educate the public about policies our local, state, and federal government consider. If those facts are reported with bias (or worse, not reported at all because of bias),

MEDIA BIAS: IS THE NEWS AFFECTED
BY AN IDEOLOGICAL BIAS?

OVERVIEW: Throughout the second half of the twentieth century, the national news media made the claim that their journalists had fully developed the professionalism they needed to be objective in their reporting. Journalistic objectivity is the reporting of the facts of an event without imposing a political or ideological slant. The objectivity of journalists is crucial, since the vast majority of Americans rely on the news media for the information they need to make political decisions. To charge bias against the news media, then, is to explode a whole learning model for American citizenship. Rather than allowing American citizens to make political decisions based on facts, the media would make the decisions for them by either reporting only certain aspects of a story or not reporting the story at all. The media would control what you know or how you know it, making all the political decisions of average Americans merely an outcome of the original bias.

But is there a systemic bias? Conservative critics charge that up to 90 percent of journalists vote Democratic,[a] and that many of the political reporters and analysts are hired not merely because of their political experience but also because of their Democratic experience. For example, ABC News hired former Clinton White House adviser George Stephanopoulos to host the Sunday morning political talk show *This Week*. Liberals argue in return that conservatives have no right to talk, since Fox News reports news for conservatives.[b] Moreover, the corporate interests of companies that own the media, regarded as fiscally conservative and strongly hesitant to criticize possible sponsors, operate as much stronger biases than do the personal beliefs of journalists.[c]

The difficulty of proving bias is that it often requires one to believe it exists before one can prove it. While conservative watchdog group Accuracy in Media believes that the media reported stories of Iraqi violence too often, liberal watchdog group Fairness and Accuracy in Reporting believes that media intentionally suppressed stories about Iraqi civilian casualties and prisoner abuse. However, editors have to make decisions on what to report based on newsworthiness and audience demand, not merely their own politics, in order to keep viewers watching or readers reading. Otherwise, editors would simply drive their paper or program into the ground. Therefore, to prove bias, one must disprove alternatives, such as newsworthiness, a standard as frustratingly subjective as bias itself.

Arguments Asserting Media Bias

- **Since journalists have their own personal bias, claims of professional objectivity are absurd.** Journalistic professionalism is a myth sustained only by those who wish to conceal a personal agenda. Even if journalists feel bound to be objective, it is hard to believe that all of them are all of the time, especially when audiences have no other information with which to corroborate stories the media report. Since they are unaccountable, journalists may be fearless in imposing their beliefs on unsuspecting American audiences.
- **Corporate demands for the news media to make profits preclude the reporting of otherwise newsworthy stories.** Huge corporations demand that papers, television programs, and Web sites report only the stories that attract viewers rather than educating them, and that attract sponsors rather than holding them accountable.

then portions of the public only learn the facts they want to learn, making consensus among the public and, thus, their representatives increasingly difficult.

The Internet now features Web sites openly devoted to ideological rabble rousing and rumor mongering. The right-leaning Drudge Report pioneered the spreading of newsworthy rumors during the second Clinton administration and has inspired a Web site, the Drudge Retort, devoted to debunking its counterpart's less reliable content. MoveOn has established itself as the leading Web site for liberal activists against the Bush administration. Thousands of individuals host Weblogs—known commonly as "blogs"—that contain daily entries espousing that individual's political opinions and, in some cases, gain a significant following from those with similar political perspectives. These "bloggers" (those who keep blogs) link their sites to sites with ideologically like-minded bloggers, creating a network for those who read daily entries.

The result is that tabloid journalists report on minor scandals and not on Iraqi human rights abuse or threats from corporate mergers, leading to further audience ignorance of important issues.

- **Ideological bias aside, the American media insufficiently report news from other regions of the world.** Americans lack sufficient knowledge about global events. This void is dangerous, since these events directly affect American interests. On television, reports on world news usually come packaged as "Around the World in 80 Seconds," while newspapers typically relegate world news not immediately pertaining to American interests to the back pages. This downplay creates an unfounded bias among audiences that places America at the center of world affairs.

Arguments Denying Media Bias

- **Bias is not systemic but a problem only with particular journalists.** Even if a certain journalist is unprofessional, it does not follow that all journalists are. Accusations of systemic bias could be themselves the product of bias, since the vast majority of journalists have done nothing to lead us to believe that they are somehow politically biased. The practice of uncovering media bias is nothing more than a witch hunt.

- **Bias is a misunderstanding of the niche journalism trend.** Recently, all news media have begun tailoring their content to specific audiences because audiences for news have fractured into tinier and tinier pieces. Some media direct content toward specific ideologies. Calling certain newspapers or cable stations biased is wrong, not because it is not factually true, but because the stations, rather openly, have begun presenting information about matters important to liberals or to conservatives. That's how the free market works.

- **There are simply too many sources of news for an audience to suffer the influence of media bias.** Perhaps there was once a media bias, when there were only a few television stations and national newspapers from which to derive political information. Now, however, there are dozens of magazines, news Web sites, and smaller circulation newspapers that allow audiences different views of subjects. Bias, in this context, is understood. Audiences merely must learn about opposing positions on an issue and decide for themselves where they stand.

Questions

1. What other kinds of biases might exist in the news media, aside from a regional or ideological one? Do these seriously impact American audiences? If so, how could these biases be corrected without violating the First Amendment?
2. What does it mean for a journalist to be "objective"?

Selected Readings

Shanto Iyengar and Richard Reeves. *Do the Media Govern? Politicians, Voters, and Reporters in America.* Newbury Park, CA: Sage, 1997.

Bernard Goldberg. *Bias: A CBS Insider Exposes How the Media Distort the News.* Washington, DC: Regnery, 2001.

[a]According to Accuracy in Media, a conservative watchdog group, http://www.aim.org/static/19_0_7_0_C.

[b]The Pew Research Center for the People and the Press. "News Audiences Increasingly Politicized: Online News Audience Larger, More Diverse," June 8, 2004, http://people-press.org/reports/display.php3?PageID=834.

[c]According to Fairness and Accuracy in Reporting, a liberal watchdog group, http://www.fair.org/media-woes/corporate.html.

The deepest bias most political journalists have is the desire to get to the bottom of a good campaign story—which is usually negative news about a candidate. The fear of missing a good story, more than bias, leads all media outlets to develop the same headlines and to adopt the same slant. In the absence of a good story, news people may attempt to create a horse race where none exists. News people, whose lives revolve around the current political scene, naturally want to add spice and drama, minimize their boredom, and increase their audience. While the horse-race components of elections are intrinsically interesting, the limited time that television has to devote to politics is disproportionately devoted to the competitive aspects of politics, leaving less time for adequate discussion of public policy.

Other human biases are also at work in reporting on politics. Whether the press likes or dislikes a candidate personally is often vital. In 2000, the press gave Senator

John McCain considerable amounts of favorable coverage, making him a more viable although inevitably defeated candidate for the Republican presidential nomination. Former Governor Howard Dean became a media darling during the 2004 Democratic primaries because his fiery speeches made for good stories, putting him on the cover of *Time* and other news magazines. His rapid fall from grace after his poor showing in Iowa and his subsequent and much criticized "scream" at a rally gave rise to the speculation that the press can make then break their favorite candidates. Richard M. Nixon and Jimmy Carter—both aloof politicians—were disliked by many reporters who covered them, and they suffered from a harsh and critical press. The higher a politician's profile, the more open he or she is to scrutiny, and the more care he or she must take in handling the press.

Some research suggests that candidates may charge the media with bias as a strategy for dealing with the press, and that bias claims are part of the dynamic between elected officials and reporters. If a candidate can plausibly and loudly decry bias in the media as the source of his negative coverage, for example, reporters might temper future negative stories or give the candidate favorable coverage to mitigate the calls of bias.[40]

One other source of bias in the press, or at least of nonobjectivity, is the increasing celebrity status of many people who report the news. In an age of media stardom and blurring boundaries between forms of entertainment, journalists in prominent media positions have unprecedented opportunities to attain fame and fortune, of which they often take full advantage. Already commanding multimillion-dollar salaries, these celebrity journalists can often secure lucrative speaker's fees. Especially in the case of journalists with highly ideological perspectives, close involvement with wealthy or powerful special-interest groups can blur the line between reporting on policy issues and influencing them. Some journalists find work as political consultants or members of government—which seems reasonable, given their prominence, abilities, and expertise, but which can become problematic when they move between spheres not once, but repeatedly. A good example of this revolving-door phenomenon is the case of Pat Buchanan, who has repeatedly and alternately enjoyed prominent positions in media (as a host of CNN's *Crossfire* and later as a commentator on MSNBC) and politics (as a perennial presidential candidate). If American journalism is to retain the watertight integrity for which it is justly renowned, it is essential that key distinctions between private and media enterprise and conscientious public service continue to command our respect.

THE MEDIA'S INFLUENCE ON THE PUBLIC

HOW MUCH INFLUENCE do the media have on the public? In most cases the press has surprisingly little effect. To put it bluntly, people tend to see what they want to see; that is, human beings will focus on parts of a report that reinforce their own attitudes and ignore parts that challenge their core beliefs. Most people also selectively tune out or ignore reports that contradict their preferences in politics and other fields. Therefore, a committed Democrat will remember certain portions of a televised news program about a current campaign—primarily the parts that reinforce his or her own choice—and an equally committed Republican will recall very different sections of the report or remember the material in a way that supports the GOP position. In other words, most voters are not empty vessels into which the media can pour their own beliefs. This fact dramatically limits the ability of news organizations to sway public opinion.

However, this is not the only view. Some political scientists argue that the content of network television news accounts for a large portion of the volatility and change in policy preferences of Americans, when measured over relatively short periods of time.[41] These changes are called **media effects.** Let's examine how these media-influenced changes might occur.

media effects
The influence of news sources on public opinion.

First, reporting can sway people who are uncommitted and have no strong opinion in the first place. So, for example, the media have a greater influence on political independents than on strong partisans.[42] Indeed, many studies from the 1940s and 1950s, an era when partisanship was very strong, suggested that the media had no influence at all on public opinion. During the last forty years, however, the rapid decline in political partisanship[43] has opened the door to greater media influence. On the other hand, the sort of politically unmotivated individual who is subject to media effects is probably unlikely to vote in a given election, and therefore the media influence is of no particular consequence.

Second, the media have a much greater impact on topics far removed from the lives and experiences of its readers and viewers. News reports can probably shape public opinion about events in foreign countries fairly easily. Yet, what the media say about domestic issues such as rising prices, neighborhood crime, or child rearing may have relatively little effect, because most citizens have personal experience of and well-formed ideas about these subjects.

Third, news organizations can help tell us what to think about, even if they cannot determine what we think. Indeed, the press often sets the agenda for a campaign or for government action by focusing on certain issues or concerns. For example, nationwide in 2003, the media reported the abduction and recovery of fifteen-year old Utah resident Elizabeth Smart. Many in the press and in Utah government attributed the success in finding Smart to the AMBER alert—a system in which law enforcement uses the media to notify the public of a kidnapping—set off in the state of Utah. Soon after, there were calls for a national AMBER alert system, which Congress quickly passed as the Protection Act of 2003 and the president just as quickly signed. Before the Smart story, child kidnapping had not been a national issue. It was only after sustained media coverage put Smart and the AMBER alert system in headlines that the problem received national attention.

Thus, perhaps not so much in *how* they cover an event, but in *what* they choose to cover, the media make their effect felt. By deciding to focus on one event while ignoring another, the media can determine to a large extent the country's agenda. Unfortunately, the media have increasingly focused on the horse-race aspects of a campaign, rather than giving candidates a chance to address issues in more than a six-second sound bite.

The media's power to shape citizens' perceptions—though limited—can influence a politician's success. For example, voters' choices in presidential elections are often related to their assessments of the economy. In general, a healthy economy motivates voters to reelect the incumbent president, whereas a weak economy motivates voters to choose the challenger. Hence, if the media paint a consistently dismal picture of the economy, that picture may well hurt the incumbent president seeking reelection. In fact, one study convincingly shows that the media's relentlessly negative coverage of the economy in 1992 shaped voters' retrospective assessments of the economy, which in turn helped lead to George Bush's defeat in the 1992 presidential election.[44]

Finally, in light of the debacle of the media coverage of Election Night 2000, it is worth remarking on one very particular way in which the media can influence public behavior. On Election Night 2000, all the networks assigned Florida to Al Gore's list of wins fairly early in the evening. In fact, their call was extremely premature, and their actions had disastrous consequences for the dignity and credibility of both the networks and the election. (For a more detailed description of the media debacle, see chapter 13.) One pollster concluded that the early calls made by the media depressed voter turnout in the Florida panhandle, which still had polls open for another hour because it sits in the Central Time Zone. Perhaps his conclusion was moot, since he estimates that without the early call, Bush would have won an additional 5,000 votes, thus winning simply by a larger margin.[45] In the end, the networks must shoulder the blame for hasty, premature reporting, with all the ensuing implications.

WHEN THE MEDIA BECOME THE STORY

The purpose of the news media is to cover the news, not to make the news. But, every now and then, whether journalists like it or not, they become the story. Partly, this reality reflects the critical importance of news media coverage in campaigns. Candidates are elected or defeated in many cases based on their media image, created by news coverage of their issue positions and personal qualities. Moreover, the news media are such a massive part of the political process today that it is almost impossible for journalists not to stumble into the story, at least on occasion. A classic example, and one that will live for many years to come, occurred in September 2004 when CBS news anchor Dan Rather, reporting on *60 Minutes II*, took center stage in the presidential contest in a way that he and his network had not intended.

For years, George W. Bush's service in the National Guard during the Vietnam War had percolated in the political system, occasionally becoming front-page news but generally lying below the surface. In 2000, when Bush was campaigning for the presidency, reporters naturally asked about his National Guard posting, by which he avoided military service in Vietnam. This was a product, in part, of the extensive coverage in the 1992 campaign given to Bill Clinton, who rather openly evaded the draft and never served in either the active military or the National Guard during the Vietnam War. Bush insisted in 2000 that he had served honorably and fulfilled all of his obligations, and his Democratic opponent, Al Gore, who had served in Vietnam for a brief period, decided not to make it an issue. The topic gradually faded and was not even a minor factor in the 2000 outcome.

The issue of Bush's military record resurfaced in 2004, however, when John Kerry, a certified war hero from his service in Vietnam, was nominated as the Democrats' presidential candidate. Kerry's service contrasted with Bush's decision not to go to Vietnam. But, attacks by a group named Swift Boat Veterans for Truth and other supporters of Bush's candidacy questioned whether Kerry deserved some of his medals and particularly broadsided Kerry on his anti-war comments to the U.S. Senate and the news media after he returned from Vietnam. Democrats countered that Bush had not fulfilled all of his National Guard obligations.

Enter Dan Rather and CBS. Mary Mapes, a producer for *60 Minutes II* and a close associate of Rather, had long been interested—critics say obsessed—with the Bush National Guard episode and had been collecting information for years. Then, Bill Burkett, a Texan who had served in the National Guard about the same time as Bush and knew some of the key players, turned over documents that apparently showed Bush had violated the terms of his National Guard agreement relating to the scheduling of a physical examination and reporting for drill. In a hastily prepared piece, broadcast at a critical juncture in the campaign, Rather reported that "Mr. Bush may have received preferential treatment in the Guard after not fulfilling his commitments." Within hours of the broadcast, conservative bloggers had dissected the documents and were claiming that they were produced on computers unavailable in the early 1970s. As evidence, they cited the small superscript "th" after several unit numbers and the variable-width font that appeared to be Times New Roman, a font not in existence at the time.

Initially, Rather and CBS held firm, saying, "you couldn't have a starker contrast between the multiple layers of check and balances [at *60 Minutes*] and a guy sitting in his living room in his pajamas writing." But, when media reporters from major outlets such as the *Washington Post* and *USA Today* soon revealed that the bloggers were right, CBS launched a major investigation headed by former Attorney General Richard Thornburgh, who had served as Republican governor of Pennsylvania in the 1980s. The investigation report indicated that CBS had been negligent and that Rather and Mapes had not fulfilled their journalistic obligations in verifying the authenticity of the documents provided by Burkett. Several CBS employees lost their jobs as a result. Rather had announced his retirement even before the report was released.

This disaster for CBS, and the news media in general, will rank with other major gaffes in modern times, including *Washington Post* reporter Janet Cooke's invented stories of a nine-year-old heroin addict that won a Pulitzer Prize, and *New York Times* reporter Jayson Blair's articles about places he had never visited and people he had never interviewed. The credibility of the news media—once sky-high—was brought low by these and other events. And, especially after the Rather incident, media outlets will almost invariably be seen as having some degree of partisan leaning—and many voters will get their information only from the sources that they most identify with.

Increasing Use of Experts

Most journalists know a little bit about most major subjects but do not specialize in any one. Therefore, especially at the network level, the news media like to employ on a consulting basis experts from a number of different disciplines ranging from medical ethics to political campaigning. Which experts you see depends on which issues dominate the news at that time. For example, during the 9/11 Commission proceedings and after the release of their report on how to improve intelligence gathering, one could not turn on the television or read a newspaper without encountering a stable full of former intelligence officers and other intelligence experts giving their thoughts.

Scholars measuring the effects of televised experts have found that experts have a significant impact on shaping the views of Americans toward foreign policy. One 1992 study says that "news from experts or research studies is estimated to have almost as great an impact [as anchorpersons, reporters in the field, or special commentators]." These scholars consider the findings concerning experts to be both good and bad for Americans. On the one hand, the "strong effects by commentators and experts are compatible with a picture of a public that engages in collective deliberation and takes expertise seriously." On the other, "one might argue that the potency of media commentators and of ostensibly nonpartisan TV 'experts' is disturbing. Who elected them to shape our views of the world? Who says they are insightful or even unbiased?"[46]

The lesson is clear. Viewers and readers must rely on the networks and newspapers to choose experts wisely. Rarely is there much discussion of the backgrounds and the credentials of the individuals who are placed on the screen. There may be hidden biases unknown to the public, but there is little the public can do about that.

Group Media and Narrowcasting

In our increasingly diverse society, one recent trend is group media—media aimed at major populations. For example, several television networks and newspapers are focusing on burgeoning Hispanic/Latino groups. There is also the Black Entertainment Television cable network, as well as many African American newspapers, such as the *Richmond Free Press,* which competes with the white-dominated *Richmond Times-Dispatch.* Women's ENEWS is a daily online newsletter targeted at women.

All of these examples are forms of narrowcasting, an attempt by a particular station, network, or newspaper to communicate with a specific segment of the population. This is neither good nor bad, although it is important for individual constituencies to receive broad coverage of news and not just the parts that are most appealing to their personal views. In addition, with groups paying greater attention to these focused sources, the chances are greater that undue influence could be exerted over viewers and readers. At the same time, narrowcasting can help to promote the interests of parts of the population, especially minorities that may ordinarily be left out of the mainstream American media coverage.

THE PUBLIC'S PERCEPTION OF THE MEDIA

THE NEWS MEDIA have long been subject to greater public discontent and criticism than other institutions essential to the operation of the American government. When asked in the summer of 2002 how much confidence they had in various institutions, only 11 percent of the public said they had a great deal of confidence in the media, ranking them just behind the Internal Revenue Service. By comparison, 50 percent had a great deal of confidence in the president, and 71 percent felt the same way about the military.[47] The Pew Research Center for the People and the Press, which has been studying public opinion of the media since 1985, found that survey participants when asked to describe the national news media use the words "biased" and "sensational" nearly as often as "good" and "informative."[48] A majority of Americans perceive the media to be politically biased, believe the media stand in the way of solving society's problems, and think the media usually report inaccurately and are unwilling to admit mistakes. In a recent survey, Americans found media election coverage biased, but those Americans most likely to report a bias were on the ideological extremes, liberal Democrats reporting a Republican bias and conservative Republicans reporting a Democratic bias.[49] The public perception of the media is as much a function people's ideological stance as it is a response to media content.

Despite the obvious displeasure that the majority of Americans express about political bias and sensationalism, credibility ratings for the national news media have remained relatively high. Broadcast news outlets tend to get higher believability ratings than print, with CNN, C-SPAN, and the major networks leading the way. Anchors Tom Brokaw, Dan Rather, and Peter Jennings rate as the most trusted journalists (around 80 percent positive ratings), while cable journalist Geraldo Rivera ranks at the bottom (less than 9 percent believe all or most of what he says).[50] The main exception to the domination of broadcast outlets is the *Wall Street Journal*, which consistently ranks with CNN at the top of credibility polls.

The terrorist attacks of September 11, 2001, caused a temporary shift in the public's attitude toward the media—Americans followed the news more closely and relied heavily on cable network coverage of the attacks and the war on terrorism. Among Americans polled, 69 percent believed that the news media defend America abroad, and the professionalism rating of the news media soared to 73 percent. During this period of extreme stress, however, Americans appeared simply to have united behind their institutions against an unknown threat. After all, the bounce in media popularity was short lived. By July 2002, less than a year after the attacks, the public's perception and support of the media were essentially the same as pre-9/11 levels. However, Americans continue to value the watchdog role that the media serve, with 59 percent believing that press scrutiny keeps political leaders from doing things they should not do. In addition, a substantial majority thinks that the media's influence is increasing, rather than decreasing.[51]

TABLE 15.4 Top Problems Facing Journalism

	National		Local	
	1999 %	2004 %	1999 %	2004 %
Quality of Coverage	**44**	**41**	**39**	**33**
Reporting accurately	10	8	10	10
Not relevant/Out of touch	12	7	6	7
Sensationalism	8	8	12	5
Lack of depth/context	—	6	—	4
Reporting objectively/Balance	12	5	6	4
Business and Financial	**25**	**30**	**25**	**35**
Decline in audience/readership	14	9	11	8
Lack of resources/cutbacks	3	8	4	9
Bottom-line emphasis	8	5	7	9
Corporate owners/consolidation	2	5	2	4
Commercial/ratings pressure	6	3	6	4
Loss of Credibility with Public	**30**	**28**	**34**	**23**
Credibility problem	23	22	28	17
Lack of trustworthiness	6	5	8	4
Changing Media Environment	**24**	**15**	**19**	**7**
Too much competition	17	5	15	2
Need to adapt to changes	—	3	—	2
Speed/pace of reporting	—	5	—	2
Ethics and Standards	**11**	**5**	**10**	**6**

Source: Pew Research Center for the People and the Press, May 23, 2004.

Analyzing Visuals

PARTISAN BIAS IN MEDIA REPORTING?

Late in the summer of 2004, the Center for Media and Public Affairs conducted a study of the media's coverage of the presidential campaign by comparing the number of positive and negative stories on each candidate. They examined the evening news programs on the major broadcast television networks, and on the Fox News Channel, a cable news outlet that debuted in 1996 and quickly reached a level of viewership comparable to—and sometimes better than—that of CNN.

While the question of media bias is not a new one, several incidents in 2004 brought greater attention to the issue and heightened the debate over whether a news organization or its journalists favored one candidate over another and the degree to which that favoritism is evidenced. In September

2004, CBS faced harsh criticism for airing a story based on forged documents that would have painted a negative picture of President Bush's National Guard service. In October 2004, Fox News was forced to apologize for several unflattering quotes attributed to John Kerry, that were actually fabricated by one of its correspondents.

After examining the graph of positive stories aired about each candidate, answer the following critical thinking questions: What do you notice about the results for each network? Given that data were collected from each network during the same time period, what explanations might exist for the differences you see in the graph? Should it always be the goal of a network to have an equal number of positive and negative stories about each candidate?

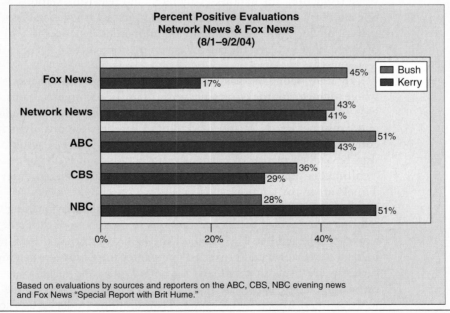

**Percent Positive Evaluations
Network News & Fox News
(8/1–9/2/04)**

Fox News — Bush 45%, Kerry 17%
Network News — Bush 43%, Kerry 41%
ABC — Bush 51%, Kerry 43%
CBS — Bush 36%, Kerry 29%
NBC — Bush 28%, Kerry 51%

Based on evaluations by sources and reporters on the ABC, CBS, NBC evening news and Fox News "Special Report with Brit Hume."

Source: Center for Media and Public Affairs, "Campaign 2004: The Media Agenda," September 9, 2004, http://www.cmpa.com/documents/04.09.08.Summer.Campaign.pdf.

Table 15.4 illustrates journalists' perceptions of the problems they face in their field. National journalists continue to cite coverage quality as their primary concern, while local journalists now mention business and financial problems just as frequently.

Numerous polling organizations and scholarly centers (such as the Pew Research Center for the People and the Press) survey voters to gather and analyze public opinion regarding the news media in order to understand why American audiences use the media the way they do and how the media can, then, understand and improve their relationship with their audiences. Several major newspapers and magazines, including the

Washington Post and the *Boston Globe,* have media critics, who assess how the media are performing their duties. Some nonprofits, such as the Center for Media and Public Affairs in Washington, D.C., conduct scientific studies of the news and entertainment media. Other groups, including the conservative watchdog group Accuracy in Media and its liberal counterpart Fairness and Accuracy in Reporting (FAIR), critique news stories and attempt to set the record straight on important issues that they believe have received biased coverage. All of these organizations have a role in ensuring that the media provide fair and balanced coverage of topics that are of importance to citizens.

GOVERNMENT REGULATION OF THE ELECTRONIC MEDIA

THE U.S. GOVERNMENT REGULATES the electronic component of the media. Unlike radio or television, the print media are exempt from most forms of government regulation, although even print media must not violate community standards for obscenity, for instance. There are two reasons for this unequal treatment. First, the airwaves used by the electronic media are considered public property and are leased by the federal government to private broadcasters. Second, those airwaves are in limited supply; without some regulation, the nation's many radio and television stations would interfere with one another's frequency signals. It was not, in fact, the federal government but rather private broadcasters, frustrated by the numerous instances in which signal jamming occurred, that initiated the call for government regulation in the early days of the electronic media.

In 1996, Congress passed the sweeping Telecommunications Act, deregulating whole segments of the electronic media. The Telecommunications Act sought to provide an optimal balance of competing corporate interests, technological innovations, and consumer needs. It appeared to offer limitless opportunities for entrepreneurial companies to provide enhanced services to consumers. The result of this deregulation was the sudden merger of previously distinct kinds of media in order to create a more "multimedia" approach to communicating information and entertainment, such as TimeWarner and Comcast.

In June 2003, the FCC further deregulated media by pushing through a series of reforms that enabled media corporations to own more of different kinds of media in a given media market. For instance, the FCC overturned a 1975 regulation that had banned newspapers and broadcast companies from cross-ownership. They also overturned a 1970 rule that similarly prevented radio and television stations from cross-ownership. These bans were replaced with a formula based on the number of outlets in the market. Also, the FCC granted corporations, under certain conditions, the ability to own two ("duopoly") or even three ("triopoly") television stations in a given market, effectively allowing corporations to own all or nearly all of the television content in those markets.[52] Finally, the FCC increased the limit to the total national audience a corporation could reach, from 35 percent to 45 percent. Since total national audience is measured by how many stations a corporation owns, the increase allows corporations to own more television stations. All this deregulation makes it possible for one media corporation to own large chunks of the radio, print, and television audiences in a community.

Both Republicans and Democrats in Congress opposed the FCC changes, arguing that the country needs more and not less media diversification, given the increasing media outlet consolidation. Furthermore, many ideologically opposing groups also argued against media consolidation; conservative religious groups believe that large media corporations purvey immoral content, and liberal groups believe that less diversification kills community-based media. Finally, there was a general public outcry, with legislators receiving angry letters and e-mails demanding Congress stop the FCC.[53] By July 2003, a huge bipartisan majority voted 400–21 to block the FCC policy changes. By December, Congress passed an appropriations bill that raised the 35 percent cap on a national audience to 39 percent, a compromise that allows the largest corporations to retain their current share—the largest corporation, Viacom, had 38.9 percent of the national audience—but prohibited any further expansion.[54]

Although the Senate moved quickly to reverse the FCC decision, similar legislation was blocked in the House. Community radio station proponent Prometheus Radio Project, along with several advocacy groups, then successfully petitioned a stay on the FCC decision at the 3rd Circuit U.S. Court of Appeals in Philadelphia.

Content Regulation

The government subjects the electronic media to substantial **content regulation** that, again, does not apply to the print media. Charged with ensuring that the airwaves "serve the public interest, convenience, and necessity," the FCC has attempted to promote equity in broadcasting. For example, the **equal time rule** requires that broadcast stations sell air time equally to all candidates in a political campaign if they choose to sell it to any, which they are under no obligation to do. An exception to this rule is a political debate: stations may exclude from this event less well-known and minor-party candidates.

Until 2000, FCC rules required broadcasters to give candidates the opportunity to respond to personal attacks and to political endorsements by the station. In October 2000, however, a federal court of appeals found these rules, long attacked by broadcasters as having a chilling effect on free speech, to be unconstitutional when the FCC was unable to justify these regulations to its satisfaction.

Perhaps the most controversial FCC regulation was the **fairness doctrine.** Implemented in 1949 and in effect until 1985, the fairness doctrine required broadcasters to be "fair" in their coverage of news events—that is, they had to cover the events adequately and present contrasting views on important public issues. Many broadcasters disliked this rule, claiming that fairness is simply too difficult to define and that the rule abridged their First Amendment freedoms. They also argued that it ultimately forced broadcasters to decrease coverage of controversial issues out of fear of a deluge of requests for air time from interest groups involved in each matter.

The 1969 U.S. Supreme Court case of *Red Lion Broadcasting Co., Inc.* v. *FCC* confirmed the power and legitimacy of the fairness doctrine. In that case, a station in Pennsylvania, licensed by Red Lion Co., had aired a "Christian Crusade" program wherein an author, Fred J. Cook, was attacked. When Cook requested time to reply in keeping with the fairness doctrine, the station refused. Upon appeal to the FCC, the commission declared that there was a personal attack and the station had failed to meet its obligation. The station appealed and eventually the case wound its way to the Supreme Court. The court ruled for the FCC, giving sanction to the fairness doctrine.[55]

In a hotly debated 1985 decision, the FCC, without congressional consent, abolished the fairness doctrine (and subsequently won a 1986 appeal), arguing that the growth of the electronic media in the United States during the preceding forty years had created enough diversity among the stations to render unnecessary the ordering of diversity within them. Congress passed a bill to write the fairness doctrine into law, but President Reagan vetoed it, citing his First Amendment concerns about government regulation of the news media. The abolition of the fairness doctrine has by no means ended debate over its merit, however. Proponents, still trying to reinstate the doctrine, argue that its elimination results in a reduction of quality programming

content regulation
Government attempts to regulate the electronic media.

equal time rule
The rule that requires broadcast stations to sell air time equally to all candidates in a political campaign if they choose to sell it to any.

fairness doctrine
Rule in effect from 1949 to 1985 requiring broadcasters to cover events adequately and to present contrasting views on important public issues.

on public issues. Opponents of the fairness doctrine, on the other hand, continue to call for decreased regulation, arguing that the electronic media should be as free as the print media.

Efforts to Regulate Media Practices

As discussed in the introduction of this chapter, during and after major combat in Iraq, journalists were trained by the military and placed among different sections of the military to report what they saw. When reading or listening to the stories of embedded journalists, however, one had to wonder to what extent these reporters were limited to topics and information approved by U.S. military personnel. When considering whether the media in Iraq are as free to report the news as they should be, we must also wonder whether the news we receive is news at all. After all, even the generally accepted "newspaper of record," the *New York Times,* cannot escape the highly unprofessional reliance on anonymous sources and the downright condemnable manufacturing of false accounts. These issues are just part of the larger issue of how to regulate the media and yet preserve their freedom.

In the United States, only government officials can be prosecuted for divulging classified information; no such law applies to journalists. Nor can the government, except under extremely rare and confined circumstances, impose prior restraints on the press—that is, the government cannot censor the press. This principle was clearly established in *New York Times Co. v. U.S.* (1971).[56] In this case, the Supreme Court ruled that the government could not prevent publication by the *New York Times* of the Pentagon Papers, classified government documents about the Vietnam War that had been stolen, photocopied, and sent to the *Times* and the *Washington Post* by Daniel Ellsberg, a government employee. "Only a free and unrestrained press can effectively expose deception in the government," Justice Hugo Black wrote in a concurring opinion for the Court. "To find that the President has 'inherent power' to halt the publication of news by resort to the courts would wipe out the First Amendment."

Similar concerns arose in the United States during the 1991 Persian Gulf War. Reporters were upset that the military was not forthcoming about events on and off the battlefield, while some Pentagon officials and many persons in the general public accused the press of telling the enemy too much in their dispatches. The U.S. government had little recourse but to attempt to isolate offending reporters by keeping them away from the battlefield. Even this maneuver was highly controversial and very unpopular with news correspondents because it directly interfered with their job of reporting the news. Critics of the military's public affairs strategy resent its emphasis on controlling information as a tool for manipulating public support. Both civilian and military officials alike have a keen awareness of and desire to avoid the "Vietnam syndrome," where popular resistance to the war, some would argue, grew out of the media's great freedom to frame events.

When U.S.-led forces invaded Iraq in 2003, the Bush administration gave journalists the opportunity to be embedded with various parts of the military and report about the experiences of each unit. The arrangement proved a strange one. Fox News correspondent Geraldo Rivera, embedded with the 101st Airborne, drew a map on the ground, identifying the location of the division and where they were next going to attack. Rivera was promptly removed from his embedded position. Rivera's error may have compromised the mission for the 101st, putting in danger both the division and Rivera himself.

Organizations such as the Project for Excellence in Journalism found that embedded journalists typically provided only anecdotal stories, lacked the overall context of the war, and stressed American successes without much coverage of Iraqi civilian casualties. While conceding these limitations, some scholars maintain that an embedded journalist is better than no journalist at all, especially since journalists of foreign news organizations will cover the events from different perspectives.[57]

Such arguments are an inevitable part of the landscape in a free society. Whatever their specific quarrels with the press, most Americans would probably prefer that the media tell them too much rather than not enough. Totalitarian and authoritarian societies have a tame journalism, after all, so media excesses may be the price of unbridled freedom. In the United States, freedom is secured mainly by the Constitution's basic guarantees and institutions. But, freedom is also ensured by the thousands of independently owned and operated newspapers, magazines, and broadcast stations, although consolidation among independent media corporations may begin to reduce the number of these independent voices vital to American democracy.

Efforts to Regulate Media Practices Around the World

Comparative
Comparing News Media

Throughout the world, mass media are organized around different principles from those in the United States and can serve different purposes. In dictatorships, the media serve as a carefully controlled outlet for "approved" messages from those in charge to those being governed without consent. In constitutional monarchies, the media cooperate with the monarchy in a mutually beneficial relationship. The media get interesting stories about the royal family, while the family helps support the media. In the Middle East, there may be no more influential network than al-Jazeera, which now has a global audience thanks both to satellite television and to an English-language Web site covering regional events from an Arab perspective. Al-Jazeera is monitored by experts in the Pentagon to gauge reactions to U.S. actions in the Middle East.

One of the world's oldest democracies, Great Britain, owns that nation's main electronic medium, the British Broadcasting Company (BBC). The BBC, along with the privately owned media, is subjected to unusually strict regulation on the publication of governmental secrets. For example, the sweeping Official Secrets Act of 1911 makes it a criminal offense for a Briton to publish any facts, material, or news collected in that person's capacity as a public minister or civil servant. The act was invoked when the British government banned the publication of *Spy Catcher*, a 1987 novel written by Peter Wright, a former British intelligence officer, who undoubtedly collected much of the book's information while on the job. On the other hand, the UK applies a far more liberal standard of indecency to its broadcasters, who exercise considerably more freedom than Americans with regard to explicit content. To assist the media in determining what is and is not publishable, Great Britain provides a system called D-notice, which allows journalists to submit questionable material to a review committee before its publication.

SUMMARY

THE SIMPLE WORDS of the First Amendment, that "Congress shall make no law…abridging the freedom of speech, or of the press," have shaped the American republic as much as or more than any others in the Constitution. With the Constitution's sanction, as interpreted by the Supreme Court over two centuries, a vigorous and highly competitive press has emerged. In this chapter we examined the following topics:

1. **The Evolution of Journalism in the United States**
Journalism—the process and profession of collecting and disseminating the news—was introduced in America in 1690 with the publication of the nation's first newspaper. Until the mid- to late 1800s, when independent papers first appeared, newspapers were partisan; that is, they openly supported a particular party. In the twentieth century, first radio in the late 1920s and then television in the late 1940s revolutionized the

transmission of political information, leading to more candidate-centered, entrepreneurial politics in the age of television.

2. The U.S. Media Today

The modern media consist of print press (many thousands of daily and weekly newspapers, magazines, newsletters, and journals) and electronic media (television and radio stations and networks as well as the Internet). In the United States, the media are relatively uncontrolled and free to express many views.

3. How the Media Cover Politicians and Government

Media coverage of politics has shifted focus from investigative journalism in the Watergate era toward the more recent attention to character issues. While there are useful aspects to both kinds of coverage, excesses have occurred, especially unnecessary invasions of privacy and the publication and broadcast of unsubstantiated rumor. Politicians constantly try to manipulate and influence media coverage; some officials pass along information off the record, in the hopes of currying favor or producing stories favorable to their interests.

4. The Media's Influence on the Public

Studies have shown that by framing issues for debate and discussion, the media have clear and recognizable effects on voters. For example, people who are relatively uninformed about a topic can be more easily swayed by media coverage about that topic. However, in most cases, the media have surprisingly little effect on people's views.

5. The Public's Perception of the Media

Studies consistently show that although Americans generally believe the information that reputable media outlets provide, most dislike the sensationalism and perceived political bias presented by the media. The 9/11 terrorist attacks caused a temporary shift in the public's attitude toward the media, but within a year after the attacks, the media's popularity and support returned to the pre-9/11 levels.

6. Government Regulation of the Electronic Media

The government has gradually loosened restrictions on the media. The Federal Communications Commission (FCC) licenses and regulates broadcasting stations but has been quite willing to grant and renew licenses and has reduced its regulation of licensees. Content regulations have loosened, with the courts using a narrow interpretation of libel. The Telecommunications Act of 1996 further deregulated the communications landscape, and the rise of imbedded journalists during the Iraq War in 2003 showed the government's willingness to cooperate with the media.

KEY TERMS

affiliates, p. 558
content regulation, p. 575
deep background, p. 559
electronic media, p. 552
equal time rule, p. 575
fairness doctrine, p. 575
media effects, p. 568
muckraking, p. 551
network, p. 558
New York Times Co. v. *Sullivan* (1964), p. 564
off the record, p. 559
on background, p. 559
on the record, p. 559
press briefing, p. 559
press conference, p. 559
press release, p. 559
print press, p. 552
wire service, p. 558
yellow journalism, p. 551

SELECTED READINGS

Arterton, F. Christopher. *Media Politics: The News Strategies of Presidential Campaigns.* Lexington, MA: Lexington Books, 1984.

Berkman, Ronald, and Laura W. Kitch. *Politics in the Media Age.* New York: McGraw-Hill, 1986.

Broder, David S. *Behind the Front Page,* reprint ed. New York: Simon and Schuster, 2000.

Cook, Timothy E. *Making Laws and Making News: Media Strategies in the U.S. House of Representatives,* reprint ed. Washington, DC: Brookings Institution, 1995.

Crouse, Timothy. *The Boys on the Bus,* reprint ed. New York: Random House, 2003.

Farnsworth, Stephen J., and S. Robert Lichter. *The Nightly News Nightmare: Network Television's Coverage of U. S. Presidential Elections, 1988–2000.* Lanham, MD: Rowman and Littlefield, 2002.

Garment, Suzanne. *Scandal.* New York: Random House, 1991.

Graber, Doris A. *Mass Media and American Politics,* 6th ed. Washington, DC: CQ Press, 2001.

Graber, Doris A. *Media Power in Politics,* 4th ed. Washington, DC: CQ Press, 2000.

Grossman, Michael Baruch, and Martha Joynt Kumar. *Portraying the President: The White House and the News Media.* Baltimore: Johns Hopkins University Press, 1981.

Hamilton, John Maxwell. *Hold the Press: The Inside Story on Newspapers,* reprint ed. Baton Rouge: Louisiana State University Press, 1997.

Iyengar, Shanto, and Donald R. Kinder. *News That Matters,* reprint ed. Chicago: University of Chicago Press, 1989.

Jamieson, Kathleen Hall, and Paul Waldman. *The Press Effect: Politicians, Journalists, and the Stories That Shape the Political World.* Oxford: Oxford University Press, 2002.

Kerbel, Matthew Robert. *Remote and Controlled: Media Politics in a Cynical Age,* 2nd ed. Boulder, CO: Westview, 1998.

Lichter, S. Robert, Stanley Rothman, and Linda S. Lichter. *The Media Elite,* reprint ed. Bethesda, MD: Adler and Adler, 1990.

Linsky, Martin. *Impact: How the Press Affects Federal Policymaking.* New York: Norton, 1988.

McChesney, Robert W. *The Problem of the Media: U.S. Communication Politics in the Twenty-First Century.* New York: Monthly Review Press, 2004.

Patterson, Thomas E. *Out of Order: An Incisive and Boldly Original Critique of the News Media's Domination of America's Political Process,* reprint ed. New York: Vintage, 1994.

Press, Charles, and Kenneth VerBurg. *American Politicians and Journalists.* Glenview, IL: Scott, Foresman, 1988.

Ranney, Austin. *Channels of Power: The Impact of Television on American Politics.* New York: Basic Books, 1983.

Sabato, Larry J. *Feeding Frenzy: Attack Journalism and American Politics,* updated ed. Baltimore: Lanahan, 2000.

Starr, Paul. *The Creation of the Media.* New York: Basic Books, 2004.

Stephens, Mitchell. *A History of News: From the Drum to the Satellite.* New York: Viking, 1989.

West, Darrell M. *Air Wars: Television Advertising in Election Campaigns, 1952–1996.* Washington, DC: CQ Press, 2000.

Zaller, John. *The Nature and Origins of Mass Opinion.* Cambridge: Cambridge University Press, 1992.

WEB EXPLORATIONS

For examples of nineteenth-century yellow journalism, go to
alt.tnt.tv/movies/tntoriginals/roughriders/jour.home.html
To see how the media are diversifying and repackaging themselves through the use of pundits, go to
www.publicagenda.org/specials/cjrpolls/cjrdec.htm
To see which newspapers, magazines, and networks have a Web presence and how that complements their standard coverage, go to
www.nationaljournal.com
www.washingtonpost.com
www.cnn.com/ALLPOLITICS
To learn more about thre debate on cameras in the courtroom, particularly the Supreme Court, go to
5pj.org/news.asp?REF=68
To compare news coverage on a particular news story for evidence of political bias, go to
hometown.aol.com/gopbias/
and
new.mrc.org/cyberalerts/1999/cyb19990125.asp#1

Roy Hoffmann
Rear Admiral
Distinguished Service Medal, Silver Star
www.swiftvets.com

Photo courtesy: Swiftvets/AP/Wide World Photos

Interest Groups

SOON AFTER THE DEMOCRATIC NATIONAL CONVENTION in July 2004, an interest group calling itself Swift Boat Veterans for Truth aired a television advertisement charging that Democratic presidential nominee John Kerry was lying about his military service record. Most specifically, the ad asserted that Senator Kerry (D–MA) had exaggerated the severity of the wounds that led to his first Purple Heart. Less than a week after this ad hit the airwaves, another organized interest, MoveOn.org, countered the Swift Boat Veterans ad with a commercial attacking the many gaps in President George W. Bush's military record. "George Bush used his father to get into the National Guard," the ad charged, "and when the chips were down, went missing. Now he's allowing false advertising that attacks John Kerry, a man who served with dignity and heroism."[1]

Although personal attacks are not unusual in modern American politics, it is important to ask who these groups are, and how they came to have such substantial influence in the 2004 presidential election. Swift Boat Veterans for Truth is a loose association of Vietnam veterans who first came together in 2000 to attack the military service record of Senator John McCain (R–AZ) during the South Carolina presidential primary.[2] MoveOn.org is an organization founded by a group of Silicon Valley financiers in 1998 to protest the impeachment of President Bill Clinton.

Both groups became major players in American politics following the 2002 Bipartisan Campaign Reform Act commonly known as the McCain-Feingold Act. After that law banned all soft money donations from corporations and political action committees to political parties and candidates, political elites began to look for new ways to remain influential players in electoral politics. Groups quickly discovered a loophole in the 2002 law that allows for tax-exempt organizations—known as 527s, for the section of the Internal Revenue Code that governs them—to raise unlimited money for the purposes of voter mobilization and issue advocacy as long as they do not expressly advocate the election of a particular candidate.[3]

This loophole, which many expect to be closed by 2008, allows 527s to air almost unlimited ads attacking candidates for their character, career choices, or policies, so long as the advertisements never explicitly state, for example, "Vote for John Kerry." MoveOn.org spent more than $21 million during the 2004 election cycle on print, radio, and television ads that both raised questions about members of the Bush administration and voiced support for liberal stances such as legalized same-sex marriage and opposition to outsourcing American jobs. However, even after a slow start, conservative 527s managed to spend almost $62 million on advertisements criticizing John Kerry. In an attempt to maximize their impact, the groups aired most of these ads in America's largest and most contentious media markets.

THE FACE OF INTEREST GROUP POLITICS in the United States is changing as quickly as laws, political consultants, and technology allow. Big business and trade groups are increasing their activities and engagement in the political system at the same time that there is conflicting evidence concerning whether ordinary citizens join political groups. In an influential 1995 essay and later in a 2000 book, political scientist Robert Putnam argued that fewer Americans are joining groups, a phenomenon he labelled "bowling alone."[4] Others have faulted Putnam, concluding that America is in the midst of an "explosion of voluntary groups, activities and charitable donations [that] is transforming our towns and cities."[5] Although bowling leagues, which were a very common means of bringing people together, have withered, other groups such as soccer associations, health clubs, and environmental groups are flourishing. Older groups such as the Elks Club and the League of Women Voters, whose membership was tracked by Putnam, no longer are attracting members, but this does not necessarily mean that people aren't joining groups; they just aren't joining the ones studied by Putnam.

Why is this debate so important? Political scientists believe that involvement in these kinds of community groups and activities enhances the level of **social capital,** "the web of cooperative relationships between citizens that facilitates resolution of collective action problems."[6] The more social capital that exists in a given community, the more citizens are engaged in its governance and well-being, and the more likely they are to work for the collective good.[7] This tendency to form small-scale associations for the public good, or **civic virtue,** as Putnam calls it, creates fertile ground within communities for improved political and economic development.[8] In studying community involvement in local politics in Italy, for example, Putnam found that good government was a by-product of singing groups and soccer clubs.[9] Thus, if Americans truly are joining fewer groups, we might expect the overall quality of government and its provision of services to suffer.

Although the debate continues over whether America is still the nation of joiners that French political philosopher Alexis de Tocqueville found in the 1830s, it is clear that people are reporting more individual acts—many of them designed to pressure policy makers at all levels of government. Newer types of groups have replaced those that were common in the past, and some commentators believe that political scientists trained in the 1960s and 1970s overlook the kinds of contributions made by young people today, such as involvement in voluntary community service work. Young people often don't see participation in groups such as Habitat for Humanity or working in a soup kitchen as political, but frequently it is. Similarly, other studies have noted that involvement in church groups, especially for women, can be an important part of political activism.[10]

Interest groups often fill voids left by the traditional political parties and give Americans another opportunity to take their claims directly to the government (see Table 16.1). Interest groups give the unrepresented or underrepresented an opportunity to have their voices heard, thereby making the government and its policy-making process more representative of diverse populations and perspectives. Additionally, interest groups offer powerful and wealthy interests even greater access to, or influence on, pol-

social capital

The myriad relationships that individuals enjoy that facilitate the resolution of community problems through collective action.

civic virtue

The tendency to form small-scale associations for the public good.

icy makers at all levels of government. To explore this phenomenon, in this chapter we will look at the following issues:

- First, we will answer the question, *what are interest groups?*

- Second, we will explore *the roots and development of American interest groups.*

- Third, we will answer the question *what do interest groups do* by looking at the various strategies and tactics used by organized interests.

- Finally, we will analyze *what makes an interest group successful.*

TABLE 16.1   Reported Acts Designed to Influence Policy Makers (in the last year)

Political Activity	Total
Direct Contacting	
Phoned, wrote, or visited a government official	22
Joining/Attending	
Attended a meeting about community or schools	30
Belonged to an organization other than local church or synagogue	43
Participated in a march or protest	3
Contributing	
Contributed money to a candidate	7
Contributed money to a political party	8
Contributed money to any other group	7
Contributed to church or charity	75

Source: Data from 2002 National Election Study.

WHAT ARE INTEREST GROUPS?

INTEREST GROUPS go by various names: special interests, pressure groups, organized interests, nongovernmental organizations (NGOs), political groups, lobby groups, and public interest groups. Originally, most political scientists used the term "pressure group" because it best described what these groups do. Today, most political scientists use the terms interest group and organized interest. David Truman, one of the first political scientists to study interest groups, defines an organized interest as "any group that, on the basis of one or more shared attitudes, makes certain claims upon other groups in society for the establishment, maintenance, or enhancement of forms of behavior that are implied by shared attitudes."[11]

Truman further posed what he termed **disturbance theory** to explain why interest groups form.[12] He hypothesized that groups arise, in part, to counteract the activities of other groups or of organized special interests. According to Truman, the government's role is to provide a forum in which the competing demands of groups and the majority of the U.S. population can be heard and balanced. He argued that the government's role in managing competing groups is to balance their conflicting demands.

Political scientist Robert Salisbury expanded on Truman's theories by arguing that groups form when resources—be they clean air, women's rights, or rights of the unborn, for example—are inadequate or scarce. Unlike Truman, Salisbury stresses the role that leaders, or what he terms "entrepreneurs," play in the formation of groups.[13]

interest groups
Organized groups that try to influence public policy.

disturbance theory
Political scientist David B. Truman's theory that interest groups form in part to counteract the efforts of other groups.

Kinds of Organized Interests

In this book, we use interest group as a generic term to describe the numerous organized groups that try to influence government policy. Thus, interest groups can be what we normally think of as organized interests such as public interest groups, individual businesses and corporations, or economic interest groups; they may also be governmental units such as state and local governments and political action committees, as well as other groups formed to affect the outcome of elections. These groups can be further delineated as single or multi-issue.

With the exception of political action committees (PACs), most of these groups lobby on behalf of their members. Many also hire D.C.-based lobbying firms to lead or supplement their efforts.

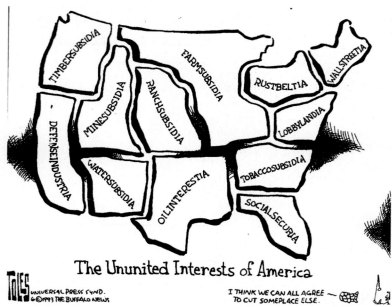

The Ununited Interests of America

TOLES UNIVERSAL PRESS SYND.
© 1993 THE BUFFALO NEWS

I THINK WE CAN ALL AGREE —
TO CUT SOMEPLACE ELSE.

Photo courtesy: Toles © The Buffalo News. Reprinted with
permission of Universal Press Syndicate. All rights reserved

public interest groups
Organizations that seek a collective
good that will not selectively and
materially benefit group members.

economic interest group
A group with the primary purpose
of promoting the financial interests
of its members.

political action committees (PACs)
Federally mandated, officially registered fund-raising committees that
represent interest groups in the
political process.

Public Interest Groups.

Political scientist Jeffrey M. Berry defines **public interest groups** as organizations "that seek a collective good, the achievement of which will not selectively and materially benefit the membership or activists of the organization."[14] Public interest groups do not tend to be particularly motivated by the desire to achieve goals that necessarily benefit their members. For example, many Progressive era groups were created by upper- and middle-class women to solve the varied problems of new immigrants and the poor. Today, civil rights and liberties groups, environmental groups, good government groups such as Common Cause, peace groups, church groups, and groups that speak out for those who cannot (such as children, the mentally ill, or animals) and even MoveOn.org are examples of public interest groups.

Economic Interest Groups.

Most groups have some sort of economic agenda, even if it only involves acquiring enough money in donations to pay the telephone bill or to send out the next mailing. **Economic interest groups** are, however, a special type of interest group: Their primary purpose is to promote the economic interests of their members. Historically, the big three of economic interest groups were business groups (including trade and professional groups such as the American Medical Association), labor organizations (such as the AFL-CIO), and organizations representing the interests of farmers. The influence of farmers and labor unions is on the decline, however, as big businesses such as Halliburton and Philip Morris spend increasingly large amounts contributing to campaigns and hiring lobbyists.

Groups that mobilize to protect particular economic interests generally are the most fully and effectively organized of all the types of interest groups.[15] They exist to make profits and to obtain economic benefits for their members. To achieve these goals, however, they often find that they must resort to political means rather than trust the operation of economic markets to produce outcomes favorable for their members.

Governmental Units.

State and local governments are becoming strong organized interests as they lobby the federal government or even charitable foundations for money for a vast array of state and local programs. The big intergovernmental associations and state and local governments want to make certain that they get their fair share of federal dollars in the form of block grants or pork-barrel projects. Most states retain lobbyists in Washington, D.C., to advance their interests or to keep them informed about legislation that could affect them as they seek money from the federal budget designated to go back to the states in a variety of forms, including money for roads, schools, and poverty programs.

Political Action Committees.

In 1974, amendments to the Federal Election Campaign Act made it legal for corporations, labor unions, and interest groups to form what were termed **political action committees (PACs),** which could make contributions to candidates for national elections (see chapter 14 for more on this subject). Technically, a PAC is a political arm of a business, labor, trade, professional, or other interest group legally authorized to raise funds on a voluntary basis from employees or members in order to contribute to a political candidate or party. PAC money changed the face of U.S. elections as corporate interests and organized interests tried to maximize the effect of their campaign contributions.[16] Unlike interest groups, PACs do not have formal

■ Ted Nugent, a member of the National Rifle Association board of directors and an avid hunter, talks with NRA President Kayne Robinson before delivering a speech to conventioneers at the 133rd Annual NRA Convention in Pittsburgh, PA, in April 2004. Over four acres of firearms were on display and the event was expected to bring $7 million to the organization.

Photo courtesy: Jeff Swensen/Getty Images

TABLE 16.2   Profiles of Selected Interest Groups

Name (Founded)	Single- or Multi-Issue	Members	PAC	2003–2004 Election Cycle PAC Donation
Economic Groups				
AFL-CIO (1886)	M	13 million	AFL-CIO	$1.2 million
American Medical Association (AMA) (1847)	M	300,000	AMA PAC	$3.1 million
Association of Trial Lawyers of America (1946)	M	65,000	ATLA PAC	$2 million
National Association of Manufacturers (NAM) (1895)	M	18 million	Inactive	
U.S. Chamber of Commerce (1912)	M	3 million companies	U.S. Chamber of Commerce PAC	$155,805
Public Interest Groups				
AARP (1958)	M	35 million	no	
Amnesty International U.S.A. (1961)	S	386,000	no	
League of United Latin American Citizens (LULAC) (1929)	M	115,000	no	
NARAL Pro-Choice America (1969)	S	500,000	NARAL- Pro Choice America PAC	$2.47 million
National Association for the Advancement of Colored People (NAACP) (1909)	M	500,000	no	
Human Rights Campaign (1980)	S	450,000	HRC PAC	$1.37 million
National Right to Life Committee	S	400,000	National Right to Life PAC	$1.36 million
Environmental Groups				
Environmental Defense Fund (1967)	S	300,000	no	
Greenpeace USA (1971)	S	350,000	no	
Sierra Club (1892)	S	700,000	Sierra Club Political Committee	$650,000
Good Government Groups				
Common Cause (1970)	S	200,000	no	
Public Citizen, Inc. (1971)	M	150,000	no	
MoveOn.org (1998)	M	1,000,000	MoveOn PAC	$20.9 milion

Source: http://www.opensecrets.org.

members; they simply have contributors who seek to influence public policy by electing legislators sympathetic to their aims. In contrast, 527 political groups, discussed in the opening vignette and in chapter 14, have members.

Multi-Issue Versus Single-Issue Groups.   Political scientists often talk of interest groups as single-issue or multi-issue. Many organizations, while founded around a single guiding principle such as the NAACP's interest in advancing the cause of civil rights, or the Christian Coalition's concern with Christian family values, actually are involved in a wide range of issue areas, including education (school vouchers, organized prayer in schools), television ratings, and abortion. Thus, they must divide some of their energies as they lobby for varied policies in diverse forums. Similarly, the National Organization for Women (NOW) supports issues such as abortion and reproductive rights, affirmative action, economic equity, and same-sex marriage. Multi-issue groups often must have expertise in a wide array of areas and be prepared to work on the local, state, and national levels to advance their interests.

Single-issue groups differ from multi-issue groups in both the range and intensity of their interests. Concentration on one area generally leads to greater zeal in a group's lobbying efforts. Probably the most visible single-issue groups today are those organized on either side of the abortion and gun control debates. Right-to-life groups such as the Army of God and pro-choice groups such as NARAL Pro-Choice America are good examples of single-issue groups, as are the National Rifle Association (NRA) and the Brady Campaign to Prevent Gun Violence. Table 16.2 categorizes a number of prominent interest groups by their issue concentration.

THE ROOTS AND DEVELOPMENT OF AMERICAN INTEREST GROUPS

POLITICAL SCIENTISTS HAVE LONG DEBATED how and why interest groups arise, their nature, and their role in a democratic society. Do they contribute to the betterment of society, or are they an evil best controlled by government? From his days in the Virginia Assembly, James Madison knew that factions occurred in all political systems and that the struggle for influence and power among such groups was inevitable in the political process. This knowledge led him and the other Framers to tailor a governmental system of multiple pressure points to check and balance these factions, or what today we call interest groups, in the natural course of the political process. As we discuss in chapter 2, Madison and many of the other Framers were intent on creating a government of many levels—local, state, and national—with the national government consisting of three branches. It was their belief that this division of power would prevent any one individual or group of individuals from becoming too influential. They also believed that decentralizing power would neutralize the effect of special interests, who would not be able to spread their efforts throughout so many different levels of government. Thus, the "mischief of faction" could be lessened. But, farsighted as they were, the Framers could not have envisioned the vast sums of money or technology that would be available to some interest groups as the nature of these groups evolved over time (see The Living Constitution).

National Groups Emerge (1830–1889)

Although all kinds of local groups proliferated throughout the colonies and in the new states, it was not until the 1830s, as communications networks improved, that the first groups national in scope emerged. Many of these first national groups were single-issue groups deeply rooted in the Christian religious revivalism that was sweeping the nation. Concern with humanitarian issues such as temperance (total abstinence from alcoholic beverages), peace, education, and slavery led to the founding of numerous associations

The Living Constitution

Congress shall make no law respecting. . .the right of the people peaceably to assemble, and to petition the Government for a redress of grievances.

—First Amendment

This amendment prohibits the national government from enacting laws dealing with the right of individuals to join together to make their voices known about their positions on a range of political issues. There was little debate on this clause in the U.S. House of Representatives and none was recorded in the Senate. James Madison, however, warned of the perils of "discussing and proposing abstract propositions," which this clause was for many years.

The concept of freedom of association, a key concept that allows Americans to organize and join a host of political groups, grew out of a series of cases decided by the Supreme Court in the 1950s and 1960s when many southern states were trying to limit the activities of the National Association for the Advancement of Colored People (NAACP). From the right to assemble and petition the government, along with the freedom of speech, the Supreme Court construed the right of people to come together to support or to protest government actions. First, the Court ruled that states could not compel interest groups to provide their membership lists to state officials. Later, the Court ruled that Alabama could not prohibit the NAACP from urging its members and others to file lawsuits challenging state discriminatory practices. Today, although states and localities can require organized interests to apply for permits to picket or protest, they cannot in any way infringe on their ability to assemble and petition in peaceable ways.

dedicated to solving these problems. Among the first of these groups was the American Anti-Slavery Society, founded in 1833 by William Lloyd Garrison.

After the Civil War, more groups were founded. For example, the Women's Christian Temperance Union (WCTU) was created in 1874 with the goal of outlawing the sale of liquor. Its members, many of them quite religious, believed that the consumption of alcohol was an evil injurious to family life because many men drank away their paychecks, leaving no money to feed or clothe their families. The WCTU's activities took conventional and nonconventional forms, including organizing prayer groups, lobbying for prohibition legislation, conducting peaceful marches, and engaging in more violent protests such as the destruction of saloons. Like the WCTU, the Grange also was formed during the period following the Civil War, as an educational society for farmers to teach them about the latest agricultural developments. Although its charter formally stated that the Grange was not to become involved in politics, in 1876 it formulated a detailed plan to pressure Congress to enact legislation favorable to farmers.

Perhaps the most effective organized interest of the day was the railroad industry. In a move that couldn't take place today because of its clear impropriety, the Central Pacific Railroad sent its own **lobbyist** to Washington, D.C., in 1861, where he eventually became the clerk (staff administrator) of the committees of both houses of Congress

lobbyist
Interest group representative who seeks to influence legislation that will benefit his or her organization through political persuasion.

that were charged with overseeing regulation of the railroad industry. Subsequently, Congress awarded the Central Pacific Railroad (later called the Southern Pacific) vast grants of lands along its route and large subsidized loans. The railroad company became so powerful that it later went on to have nearly total political control of the California state legislature.

After the Civil War, business interests began to play even larger roles in both state and national politics. A popular saying of the day noted that the Standard Oil Company did everything to the Pennsylvania legislature except refine it. Increasingly large trusts, monopolies, business combinations, and corporate conglomerations in the oil, steel, and sugar industries became sufficiently powerful to control many representatives in the state and national legislatures.

The Progressive Era (1890–1920)

By the 1890s, a profound change had occurred in the nation's political and social outlook. Rapid industrialization, an influx of immigrants, and monopolistic business practices created a host of problems including crime, poverty, squalid and unsafe working conditions, and widespread political corruption. Many Americans began to believe that new measures would be necessary to impose order on this growing chaos and to curb some of the more glaring problems. The political and social movement that grew out of these concerns was called the Progressive movement.

Not even the Progressives themselves could agree on what the term "progressive" actually meant, but their desire for reform led to an explosion of all types of interest groups, including single-issue, trade, labor, and the first public interest groups. Politically, the movement took the form of the Progressive Party, which sought on many fronts to limit or end the power of the industrialists' near-total control of the steel, oil, railroad, and other key industries.

In response to the pressure applied by Progressive-era groups, the national government began to regulate business. Because businesses had a vested interest in keeping wages low and costs down, more business groups organized to consolidate their strength and to counter Progressive moves. Not only did governments have to mediate Progressive and business demands, but they also had to accommodate the role of organized labor, which often allied itself with Progressive groups against big business.

Organized Labor.   Until the creation of the American Federation of Labor (AFL) in 1886, there was not any real national union activity. The AFL brought skilled workers from several trades together into one stronger national organization for the first time. As the AFL grew in power, many business owners began to press individually or collectively to quash the unions. As business interests pushed states for what are called open shop laws to outlaw unions in their factories, the AFL became increasingly political. It also was forced to react to the success of big businesses' use of legal injunctions to prohibit union organization. In 1914, massive lobbying by the AFL and its members led to passage of the Clayton Act, which labor leader Samuel Gompers hailed as the Magna Carta of the labor movement. This law allowed unions to organize free from prosecution and also guaranteed their right to strike, a powerful weapon against employers.

Business Groups and Trade Associations.   The National Association of Manufacturers (NAM) was founded in 1895 by manufacturers who had suffered business reverses in the economic panic of 1893 and who believed that they were being affected adversely by the growth of organized labor. NAM first became active politically in 1913 when a major tariff bill was under congressional consideration. NAM's tactics were "so insistent and abrasive" and its expenditures of monies so lavish that President Woodrow Wilson was forced to denounce its lobbying tactics as an "unbearable situation."[17] Congress immediately called for an investigation of NAM's activities but found no member of Congress willing to testify that he had ever even encountered a member of NAM (probably because many members of Congress had received illegal contributions and gifts).

The second major business organization came into being in 1912, when the U.S. Chamber of Commerce was created with the assistance of the Department of Commerce and Labor. (The chamber was created before that department was split into the Department of Commerce and the Department of Labor.) NAM, the Chamber of Commerce, and other **trade associations** representing specific industries were effective spokespersons for their member companies. They were unable to defeat passage of the Clayton Act, but groups such as the Cotton Manufacturers planned elaborate and successful campaigns to overturn key provisions of the act in the courts.[18] Aside from the Clayton Act, innumerable pieces of pro-business legislation were passed by Congress, whose members continued to insist that they had never been contacted by business groups.

In 1928, the bubble burst for some business interests. At the Senate's request, the Federal Trade Commission (FTC) undertook a massive investigation of the lobbying tactics of the business community. The FTC's examination of Congress revealed extensive illegal lobbying by yet another group, the National Electric Light Association (NELA). Not only did NELA lavishly entertain members of Congress, but it also went to great expense to educate the public on the virtues of electric lighting. Books and pamphlets were produced and donated to schools and public libraries to sway public opinion. Needy teachers and ministers who were willing to advocate electricity were helped with financial grants. Many considered these tactics unethical and held business in disfavor. These kinds of activities led the public to view lobbyists in a negative light.

trade association
A group that represents a specific industry.

The Rise of the Interest Group State

During the 1960s and 1970s, the Progressive spirit reappeared in the rise of public interest groups. Generally, these groups devoted themselves to representing the interests of African Americans, women, the elderly, the poor, and consumers, or to working on behalf of the environment. Many of their leaders and members had been active in the civil rights and anti–Vietnam War movements of the 1960s. Other groups, such as the American Civil Liberties Union (ACLU) and the NAACP gained renewed vigor. Many of them had as their patron the liberal Ford Foundation, which helped to bankroll numerous groups, including the Women's Rights Project of the ACLU, the Mexican American Legal Defense and Education Fund, the Puerto Rican Legal Defense and Education Fund, and the Native American Rights Fund (as discussed in chapter 6).[19] The American Association of Retired Persons, now simply called AARP, also came to prominence in this era.

The civil rights and anti-war struggles left many Americans feeling cynical about a government that they believed failed to respond to the will of the majority. They also believed that if citizens banded together, they could make a difference. Thus, two major new public interest groups—Common Cause and Public Citizen, Inc.—were founded. Common Cause, a good-government group that acts as a watchdog over the federal government, is similar to some of the early Progressive movement's public interest groups. Common Cause effectively has challenged aspects of the congressional seniority system, successfully urged the passage of sweeping campaign financing reforms, and played a major role in the enactment of legislation authorizing federal financing of presidential campaigns. It continues to lobby for accountability in government and for more efficient and responsive governmental structures and practices.

Perhaps more well known than Common Cause is Public Citizen, Inc., the collection of groups headed by Ralph Nader (who later went on to run as a candidate for president in 1996, 2000, and 2004). In 1965, the publication of Nader's *Unsafe at Any Speed* thrust the young lawyer into the limelight. In this book, he charged that the Corvair, a

2004 Christian Coalition
VOTER GUIDE

PRESIDENTIAL
Election

George W. Bush (R)	ISSUES	John F. Kerry (D)
Supports	Passage of a Federal Marriage Protection Amendment	Opposes
Supports	Permanent Extension of the $1,000 Per Child Tax Credit	Opposes
Supports	Educational Choice for Parents (Vouchers)	Opposes
Opposes	Unrestricted Abortion on Demand	No Response
Supports	Federal Funding for Faith-Based Charitable Organizations	No Response
Supports	Permanent Elimination of the Marriage Penalty Tax	Opposes
Supports	Permanent Elimination of the Death Tax	Opposes
Supports	Banning Partial Birth Abortions	Opposes
Opposes	Public Financing of Abortions	Supports
Opposes	Federal Firearms Registration & Licensing of Gun Owners	No Response
Opposes	Adoption of Children by Homosexuals	No Response
Supports	Prescription Drug Benefits for Medicare Recipients	Supports
Opposes	Placing US Troops Under UN Control	No Response
Opposes	Affirmative Action Programs that Provide Preferential Treatment	Supports
Supports	Allowing Younger Workers to Invest a Portion of their Social Security Tax in a Private Account	Opposes

www.georgewbush.com   www.johnkerry.com

Each candidate was sent a 2004 Federal Issue Survey by certified mail and/or facsimile machine. When possible, positions of candidates on issues were verified or determined using voting records and/or public statements.

Authorized by the Christian Coalition of America; PO Box 37030 - Washington, DC 20013

The Christian Coalition of America is a pro-family, citizen action organization. This voter guide is provided for educational purposes only and is not to be construed as an endorsement of any candidate or party.

Please visit our website at www.cc.org, and the Texas website at www.texascc.org

Vote on November 2   F

Photo courtesy: Christian Coalition of America

■ Voter guides like this one were distributed in conservative churches around the United States as well as at public places and events to let voters see the major candidates' positions on a variety of issues of concern to the Christian Coalition.

General Motors (GM) car, was unsafe to drive; he produced voluminous evidence of how the car could flip over at average speeds on curved roads. In 1966, he testified about auto safety before Congress and then learned that GM had spied on him in an effort to discredit his work. The $250,000 that GM subsequently paid to Nader in an out-of-court settlement allowed him to establish the Center for the Study of Responsive Law in 1969. The center analyzed the activities of regulatory agencies and concluded that few of them enforced anti-trust regulations or cracked down on deceptive advertising practices. Nader then turned again to lobbying Congress, which led him to create Public Citizen, Inc., which would act as an umbrella organization for what was to be called the "Nader Network" of groups.

Conservative Backlash: Religious and Ideological Groups.
During the 1960s and 1970s, various public interest groups and civil rights and women's rights movements grew and achieved success in shaping and defining the public agenda. Conservatives, concerned by the activities of these liberal groups, responded by forming religious and ideological groups that became a potent force in U.S. politics. In 1978, the Reverend Jerry Falwell founded the first major new religious group, the Moral Majority. The Moral Majority was widely credited with assisting in the election of Ronald Reagan as president in 1980 as well as with the defeats of several liberal Democratic senators that same year. Falwell claimed to have sent 3 to 4 million newly registered voters to the polls.[20]

In 1990, televangelist Pat Robertson, host of the popular television program *The 700 Club*, formed a new group, the Christian Coalition. Since then, it has grown in power and influence. The Christian Coalition played an important role in the Republicans' winning control of the Congress in 1994. In 2004, the group distributed more than 100 million voter guides in churches throughout the United States. The Christian Coalition also lobbies Congress and the White House. The group had the sympathetic ear of President George W. Bush, whom it helped elect. In fact, one of Bush's first moves as president was to create an Office of Faith-Based and Community Initiatives to work with religious groups to effect policy change.

The Christian Coalition is not the only conservative interest group to play an important role in the policy process as well as in elections at the state and national level. The National Rifle Association (NRA), an active opponent of gun control legislation, saw its membership rise in recent years (see Figure 16.1), as well as its importance in Washington, D.C. The NRA and its political action committee spent $20 million to reelect President George W. Bush in 2004. Before the 2000 election, an NRA vice president had boasted: "We'll have a president . . . where we work out of their office—unbelievably friendly relations."[21]

Business Groups, Corporations, and Associations.
Conservative, religious-based groups were not the only ones organized in the 1970s to advance conservative

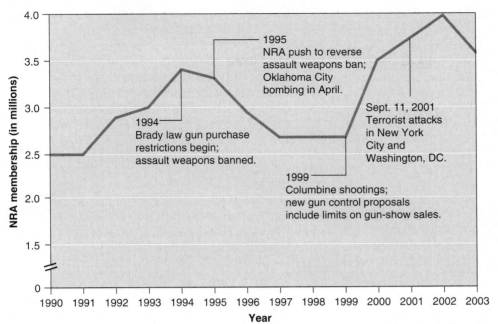

1994
Brady law gun purchase
restrictions begin;
assault weapons banned.

1995
NRA push to reverse
assault weapons ban;
Oklahoma City
bombing in April.

1999
Columbine shootings;
new gun control proposals
include limits on gun-show sales.

Sept. 11, 2001
Terrorist attacks
in New York
City and
Washington, DC.

FIGURE 16.1 NRA Membership
The National Rifle Association (NRA),
a single-issue interest group, lobbies
against any law that would restrict
an individual's right to bear arms.
NRA membership tends to increase
in reaction to proposed
gun control legislation or near an
election. Interestingly, following the
Columbine High School shooting in
1999, in which twelve people were
killed and several others were
wounded, membership increased
dramatically. Its membership also
took a jump after the 9/11 terrorist
attacks but then declined. ■

Sources: Genevieve Lynn, "How the NRA Membership Has Risen," *USA Today* (May 18, 2000): 1A. © 2000, USA Today. Reprinted with permission. Updated by the authors. Stephanie Strom, "A Deficit of $100 Million Is Confronting the N.R.A.," *New York Times* (December 21, 2003).

views. Many business people, dissatisfied with the work of the National Association of Manufacturers or the Chamber of Commerce, decided to start new, more politically oriented organizations to advance their political and financial interests in Washington, D.C. The Business Roundtable, for example, was created in 1972. The Roundtable, whose members head about 150 large corporations, is "a fraternity of powerful and prestigious business leaders that tells 'business's side of the story' to legislators, bureaucrats, White House personnel, and other interested public officials."[22] It urges its members to engage in direct lobbying to influence the course of policy formation. In 1998, for example, the Business Roundtable's Environment Task Force lobbied hard against the Kyoto Protocol on Climate Change out of concern over its impact on American businesses. These efforts ultimately paid off when George W. Bush announced that his administration would not support the Kyoto agreement. Another indication of the Roundtable's close ties to the federal government is the new communications network the group set up to enable its member CEOs to communicate with appropriate government officials in the wake of another terrorist attack.[23]

Most large corporations, in addition to having their own governmental affairs departments, employ D.C.-based lobbyists to keep them apprised of legislation that may affect them, or to lobby bureaucrats for government contracts. In the past, large corporations also gave significant sums of soft money to favored politicians or political candidates. While campaign finance reforms (discussed in greater detail in chapter 14) have prohibited such corporate donations, businesses still channel money to favored candidates through political action committees, 527s, and individual donations from employees and their families, as well as through state parties. In the 2004 election, for example, 527 groups, which receive corporate as well as individual donations, contributed $409 million to candidates for president and other national offices.[24]

These corporate interests also have far-reaching tentacles and ties to lawmakers. A number of congressional spouses as well as sons, daughters, and in-laws, are registered lobbyists.

SPEAKING UP

Many conservative college students believe that their voices are being stifled on campuses across the United States. Some charge that there is discrimination by professors and a lack of respect of diverse views in the classroom. Others say that the hiring process favors liberal professors. Some charge a bias in the selection of campus speakers and funding of groups.

A 2002 study by the Center for the Study of Popular Culture revealed that at the nation's top thirty-two universities, Democratic professors greatly outnumbered Republicans. Said Harvey Mansfield, a conservative Harvard political scientist, "We have sixty members in the department of government. Maybe three are Republicans. How could that be just by chance? How could that be fair?"[a]

The Center for the Study of Popular Culture has drafted an Academic Bill of Rights that it is urging colleges and universities to adopt. This document requests institutions of higher learning to "include both liberal and conservative viewpoints in their selection of campus speakers and syllabuses for courses and to choose faculty members 'with a view toward fostering a plurality of methodologies and perspectives.'"[b] It also notes a variety of ways in which students' academic freedom can be compromised, including:

- Mocking national or religious leaders.
- Forcing students to take a particular point of view in assignments.
- Requiring readings that cover only one side of an issue.

Several state legislators have considered enacting legislation suggesting that publicly funded state colleges and universities adhere to this statement of principles. Representative Jack Kingston (R–GA) introduced a nonbinding resolution along these lines in the U.S. House of Representatives, on which the Congress took no action.

University administrators, as well as the American Association of University Professors (AAUP) have been nearly unanimous in their disapproval of the center's proposed Academic Bill of Rights. "The danger of such guidelines," says the AAUP, "is that they invite diversity to be measured by political standards that diverge from the academic criteria of the scholarly profession." The AAUP points out that to comply with this Academic Bill of Rights, a professor professing a Nazi philosophy would need to be hired even "if that philosophy is not deemed a reasonable scholarly option within the discipline."[c]

The Center for the Study of Popular Culture is working closely with Students for Academic Freedom, a national coalition of student organizations whose goal is to bring dual viewpoints to campuses; the center also works with College Republican groups on some campuses. At some schools, including the University of Colorado, students can post alleged discrimination by liberal professors on special student-created Web sites.[d] The University of Texas at Austin has a "Professor Watch List," and Students for Academic Freedom and NoIndoctrination.org allow students from all over the country to post complaints about particular professors. Many professors view this as a form of blacklisting similar to that which existed in the 1950s when professors who were suspected of being members of or sympathetic to the Communist Party were barred from teaching positions.

Questions

1. How do interest groups such as Students for Academic Freedom benefit from working in coalition with other groups?
2. Getting issues on the public agenda is often as important for groups as the actual passage of legislation or rules. How successful have conservative student groups been on your campus in having issues of classroom bias addressed?

[a]Quoted in Yilu Zhao, "Taking the Liberalism Out of Liberal Arts," *New York Times* (April 3, 2004): B9.

[b]Zhao, "Taking the Liberalism Out."

[c]http://www.aaup.org.

[d]Dave Curtin, "Students' Site Solicits Allegations of CU Bias," *Denver Post* (January 20, 2004): A1.

Organized Labor. As revealed in Figure 16.2, membership in labor unions held steady throughout the early and mid-1900s and then skyrocketed toward the end of the Depression. By then, organized labor began to be a potent political force as it was able to turn out its members in support of particular political candidates.

Labor became a stronger force in U.S. politics when the American Federation of Labor merged with the Congress of Industrial Organizations in 1955. Concentrating its efforts largely on the national level, the new AFL-CIO immediately turned its energies to pressuring the government to protect concessions won from employers at the bargaining table and to other issues of concern to its members, including minimum wage laws, the environment, civil rights, medical insurance, and health care.

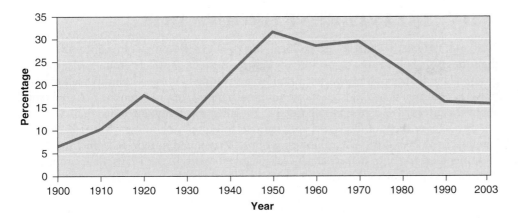

FIGURE 16.2 Labor Union Membership

After reaching an all-time high in 1950, labor union membership and political clout have steadily declined. ■

Source: Harold W. Stanley and Richard G. Niemi, eds., *Vital Statistics on American Politics, 2001–2002* (Washington, DC: CQ Press, 2001), 402. Updated by the authors.

More recently, the once fabled political clout of organized labor has been on the wane at the national level. As Figure 16.2 shows, union membership has plummeted as the nation has changed from a land of manufacturing workers and farmers to a nation of white-collar professionals and service workers. Thus, unions and agricultural organizations no longer have the large memberships or the political clout they once held in governmental circles.

Organized labor recognizes its troubles and has tried to recapture some of its lost political clout within the rank-and-file members of the Democratic Party. Nevertheless, its electoral weaknesses were clearly evident in the 2004 Democratic presidential primaries. In spite of significant labor backing, Representative Dick Gephardt (D–MO) was forced to withdraw from the presidential race when he came in fourth in the Iowa caucuses.

Photo courtesy: Rick Friedman/Corbis

■ Former House Majority (and then Minority) Leader Dick Gephardt (D–MO) relied heavily on the support of labor in his unsuccessful bid to win his party's nomination for president in 2004. In the end, labor support was not enough and he withdrew from the race.

WHAT DO INTEREST GROUPS DO?

NOT ALL INTEREST GROUPS are political, but they may become politically active when their members believe that a government policy threatens or affects group goals. Interest groups also enhance political participation by motivating like-minded individuals to work toward a common goal. Legislators often are much more likely to listen to or be concerned about the interests of a group as opposed to the interests of any one individual.

Just as members of Congress are assumed to represent the interests of their constituents in Washington, D.C., interest groups are assumed to represent the interests of their members to policy makers at all levels of government. In the 1950s, for example, the National Association for the Advancement of Colored People (NAACP) was able to articulate and present the interests of African Americans to national decision makers even though as a group they had little or no electoral clout, especially in the South. Without the efforts of the civil rights groups discussed in chapter 6, it is unlikely that either the courts or Congress would have acted as quickly to make discrimination illegal. By banding together with others who have similar interests, all sorts of individuals—from railroad workers to women to physical therapists to campers to homosexuals to mushroom growers—can advance their collective interests. Getting celebrity support or hiring a lobbyist to advocate those interests in Washington, D.C., or a state capital also increases the likelihood that issues of concern to them will be addressed and acted on favorably.

There is a downside to interest groups, however. Because groups make claims on society, they can increase the cost of public policies. The elderly can push for more costly health care and Social Security programs; people with disabilities, for improved access to public buildings; industry, for tax loopholes; and veterans, for improved benefits. Many Americans believe that interest groups exist simply to advance their own selfish interests, with little regard for the rights of other groups or, more importantly, of people not represented by any organized group.

Whether good or bad, interest groups play an important role in U.S. politics. In addition to enhancing the democratic process by providing increased representation and participation, they increase public awareness about important issues, help frame the public agenda, and often monitor programs to guarantee effective implementation. Most often, they accomplish these things through some sort of lobbying activities as well as participating in elections (see Global Perspective: Global Lobbying and Environmental Issues). But, as the rich and powerful appear to be spending far more than those groups representing poor and working-class interests, there is cause for concern.

Comparative
Comparing Interest Groups

lobbying
The activities of a group or organization that seeks to influence legislation and persuade political leaders to support the group's position.

■ Julia Roberts testifies before the House Appropriations Committee of Labor, Health and Human Services and Education Committee, to appeal for money to fight Rett's Syndrome. Several stars including Michael J. Fox and the late Christopher Reeve used their celebrity status to lobby Congress on behalf of issues of concern to them personally.

Photo courtesy: Dennis Cook/AP/Wide World Photos

Lobbying

Most interest groups put lobbying at the top of their agendas. **Lobbying** is the process by which interest groups attempt to assert their influence on the policy-making process. The term *lobbyist* refers to any representative of a group that attempts to influence a policy maker by one or more of the tactics listed in Table 16.3. Note that not only do large, organized interests have their own lobbyists, but other groups, including colleges, trade associations, cities, states, and even foreign nations, also hire lobbying firms (some law firms have lobbying specialists) to represent them in the halls of Congress or to get through the bureaucratic maze.

Most politically active groups use lobbying to make their interests heard and understood by those who are in a position to influence or cause change in governmental policies (see Roots of Government: Pressure Politics of the Past). Depending on the type of group and on the role it is looking to play, lobbying can take many forms. You probably have never thought of the Boy Scouts or Girl Scouts as political. Yet, when Congress

GLOBAL LOBBYING AND ENVIRONMENTAL ISSUES

Environmental problems do not recognize national boundaries. We do not need to look far to see evidence of this. Carbon dioxide released from aging manufacturing plants in the U.S. northeast and Ohio River Valley contribute to the destruction of forests in Canada. The United States and Canada quarrel over water diversion programs involving the Great Lakes. The United States and Mexico have been at odds over the Rio Grande River regarding levels of water flow, agrochemical pollution, and salination. Mexico and the United States also have been involved in a dispute over fishing practices. The United States banned the importing of tuna from Mexico because Mexican fishing fleets used nets that also trapped and killed dolphins protected under the U.S. Marine Mammal Protection Act.

If we look farther away, evidence of transnational environmental problems is even more abundant. Consider just the issue of clean water. Presently, in about twenty-five countries—with a combined population of 232 million people—water is considered to be scarce. It is estimated that 3 billion people will face shortages of freshwater by 2025. Complicating matters further is the fact that over 200 river basins are international in scope. Thirteen rivers, including the Danube, Nile, Zaire, Amazon, and Mekong, pass through more than five countries each. The situation is most dangerous in the Middle East, where experts speak of the possibility of water wars.

National solutions to these problems are unlikely to be successful. Regional and international cooperation among countries would seem to be necessary—in fact, is taking place. One consequence of the shift from approaching environmental issues strictly from a national perspective to approaching them internationally is that interest groups have also gone international in their efforts to influence environmental policy. And, they are not alone. Transnational groups —public advocacy groups whose activities cross national boundaries— have grown dramatically in number. Their influence is felt in areas such as human rights, environmental protection, promotion of democracy, and improving global health care. By one estimate, they have doubled since 1985 and now total over 47,000. At the United Nations, over 21,000 such groups are officially recognized and hold consultative status. In 1992, there were 928; in 1952, only 222 existed.

Large numbers do not necessarily bring influence or policy success, however. For example, in European Union (EU)

decision-making circles, environmental and consumer groups are not as well represented as business and labor groups. The eight largest European environmental groups lobby the EU through an umbrella organization, the Green-8. In its 2003 evaluation of EU policies, the Green-8 concluded that only in the area of protecting the environment had advances been made. The worst performance was in waste and transportation policies. Overall, the Green-8 judged the performance of the EU to be deteriorating.

Dissatisfaction with government policies has led some transnational environmental groups to adopt a confrontational strategy in dealing with governments and businesses. One of the best known of these groups is Greenpeace (which is also a member of the Green-8). This nonprofit organization has a presence in forty countries in Europe, Asia, and the Americas. Greenpeace has been active in protecting the environment and promoting environmental consciousness since 1971. Among the recent environmental victories it claims are:

- Pressuring companies in Great Britain not to apply for application to grow genetically engineered maize for commercial planting, after the British government had given its approval for this practice.

- Getting the United Nations Maritime Organization to designate the Baltic Sea as a "particularly sensitive sea area" over the strong opposition of the shipping companies and the oil industry.

- Pressuring McDonalds in Denmark to open the first restaurants that use no climate-killing chemicals for refrigeration.

- Having the United Nations place sanctions on Liberia for illegal logging.

Questions

1. Which strategy, quiet negotiation or public confrontation, do you think is better for an interest group to follow? Why?
2. How much influence should transnational or foreign interest groups have on the United States as it makes decisions about the environment and related issues?

began debating the passage of legislation dealing with discrimination in private clubs, representatives of both organizations testified in an attempt to persuade Congress to allow them to remain single-sex organizations. Similarly, you probably don't often think of golf clubs as political. Yet, when the Augusta National Golf Course refused to allow women to become members, the National Council of Women's Organizations, an umbrella organization of more than 200 organizations, made that decision political by contacting sponsors of the Masters Tournament and asking them to withdraw their sponsorship.

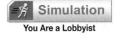

You Are a Lobbyist

TABLE 16.3   Groups and Lobbyists Using Each Lobbying Technique (percentage)

Technique	STATE-BASED GROUPS Lobbyists (n = 595)	STATE-BASED GROUPS Organizations (n = 301)	WASHINGTON, D.C.- BASED GROUPS (n = 175)
1. Testifying at legislative hearings	98	99	99
2. Contacting government officials directly to present point of view	98	97	98
3. Helping to draft legislation	96	88	85
4. Alerting state legislators to the effects of a bill on their districts	96	94	75
5. Having influential constituents contact legislator's office	94	92	80
6. Consulting with government officials to plan legislative strategy	88	84	85
7. Attempting to shape implementation of policies	88	85	89
8. Mounting grassroots lobbying efforts	88	86	80
9. Helping to draft regulations, rules, or guidelines	84	81	78
10. Raising new issues and calling attention to previously ignored problems	85	83	84
11. Engaging in informal contacts with officials	83	81	95
12. Inspiring letter-writing or telegram campaigns	82	83	84
13. Entering into coalitions with other groups	79	93	90
14. Talking to media	73	74	86
15. Serving on advisory commissions and boards	58	76	76
16. Making monetary contributions to candidates	—	45	58
17. Attempting to influence appointment to public office	44	42	53
18. Doing favors for officials who need assistance	41	36	56
19. Filing suit or otherwise engaging in litigation	36	40	72
20. Working on election campaigns	—	29	24
21. Endorsing candidates	—	24	22
22. Running advertisements in media about position	18	21	31
23. Engaging in protests or demonstrations	13	21	20

Sources: State-Based Groups: Anthony J. Nownes and Patricia Freeman, "Interest Group Activity in the States," *Journal of Politics* 60 (1998): 92. Washington, DC–Based Groups: Kay Lehman Schlozman and John Tierney, "More of the Same: Washington Pressure Group Activity in a Decade of Change," *Journal of Politics* 45 (1983): 358.

As Table 16.3 indicates, there are at least twenty-three ways for lobbyists and organizations to lobby on the state and national level. Lobbying allows interest groups to try to convince key governmental decision makers and the public of the correctness of their positions. Almost all interest groups lobby by testifying at hearings and contacting legislators. Other groups also provide information that decision makers might not have the time, opportunity, or interest to gather on their own. Of course, information these groups provide is designed to present the group's position in a favorable light, although a good lobbyist for an interest group also will note the downside to proposed legislation. Interest groups also file lawsuits to lobby the courts, and some even engage in protests or demonstrations as a form of lobbying public opinion or decision makers. In 2004, a coalition of several pro-choice groups sponsored one of the largest marches ever held in Washington, D.C., to draw attention to the reproductive rights at stake in the 2004 elections and to motivate and energize its base (see Politics Now: The March for Women's Lives).

Lobbying Congress.   Members of Congress are the targets of a wide variety of lobbying activities: congressional testimony on behalf of a group, individual letters from interested constituents, campaign contributions, trips, speaking fees, or the outright payment of money for votes. Of course, the last item is illegal, but there are numerous documented instances of money changing hands for votes. Because lobbying plays such an important role in Congress, many effective lobbyists often are former members of that body, former staff aides, former White House officials or Cabinet officers, or other Washington insiders. This type of lobbyist frequently drops in to visit members of Congress or their staff members and often takes them to lunch, to play golf, or to parties. Although much of that activity may be ethically questionable, most is not illegal. Many lobbying firms pay millions yearly to former lawmakers to lobby their old colleagues.

PRESSURE POLITICS OF THE PAST

THE EXACT ORIGIN of the term lobbying is disputed. In mid-seventeenth-century England, there was a room located near the floor of the House of Commons where members of Parliament would congregate and could be approached by their constituents and others who wanted to plead a particular cause. Similarly, in the United States, people often waited outside the chambers of the House and Senate to speak to members of Congress as they emerged. Because they waited in the lobbies to argue their cases, by the nineteenth century they were commonly referred to as lobbyists. Another piece of folklore explains that when Ulysses S. Grant was president, he would frequently walk from the White House to the Willard Hotel on Pennsylvania Avenue just to relax in its comfortable and attractive lobby. Interest group representatives and those seeking favors from Grant would crowd into that lobby and try to press their claims. Soon they were nicknamed lobbyists.

Congress began to regulate some aspects of lobbying in 1946 with the Regulation of Lobbying Act, which required paid lobbyists to register with the House and Senate and to file quarterly financial reports, including an account of all contributions and expenditures as well as the names and addresses of those to whom they gave $500 or more. Organizations also were required to submit financial reports, although they did not have to register officially.

The purpose of the act was to publicize the activities of lobbyists and to remove some of the uncertainty surrounding the influence of lobbying on legislation. In 1954, however, a lower court ruled the act unconstitutional. Although the Supreme Court reversed the decision, it ruled that the act was applicable

Photo courtesy: Bettmann/CORBIS

Women lobby for the suffrage amendment.

only to persons or organizations that solicited, collected, or received money for the principal purpose of influencing legislation by directly lobbying members of Congress. Consequently, many lobbyists did not register at all. The National Association of Manufacturers, for example, was formed in 1895 but did not register as a lobbying group until 1975.

For example, former Senators Robert Dole (R–KS) and George Mitchell (D–ME) earn well over a million dollars a year in a Washington, D.C., law firm specializing in lobbying for a wide array of clients.[25]

Lobbying Congress and issue advocacy are skills that many people have developed over the years. In 1869, for example, women gathered in Washington, D.C., for the second annual meeting of the National Woman Suffrage Association and marched to Capitol Hill to hear one of their members (unsuccessfully) ask Congress to pass legislation to enfranchise women under the terms of the Fourteenth Amendment. Practices such as these floor speeches are no longer permitted.

Today, lobbyists try to develop close relationships with senators and House members in an effort to enhance their access to the policy-making process. A symbiotic relationship between members of Congress, interest group representatives, and affected bureaucratic agencies often develops. In these iron triangles (discussed in chapter 9), congressional representatives and their staff members, who face an exhausting workload and legislation they frequently know little about, often look to lobbyists for information. "Information is the currency on Capitol Hill, not dollars," said one lobbyist.[26] According to one aide: "My boss demands a speech and a statement for the *Congressional Record* for every bill we introduce or co-sponsor—and we have a lot of bills. I just can't do it all

THE MARCH FOR WOMEN'S LIVES

On Sunday, April 25, 2004, women and men from all over the United States gathered in Washington, D.C., to show support for abortion rights and to highlight what march organizers called the Bush administration's "war against reproductive rights and health." It was the largest women's rights march in history and came at a time when many were doubting the current vitality of the women's movement and effectiveness of individual women's rights groups. The event also marked a new effort by women's groups to place the abortion rights issue in a wider context, equating it with the need to improve access to reproductive education and health care, access to emergency contraception, and affordable prenatal care.

March organizers, who had requested a permit for at least 750,000 people, estimated that more than 1 million attended. This peaceful march was the culmination of months of planning and the concerted activity of several pro-choice organizations, including NARAL Pro-Choice America, the National Organization for Women, the Planned Parenthood Federation of America, the Feminist Majority, the American Civil Liberties Union, the Black Women's Health Imperative, and the National Latina Institute for Reproductive Health. There was a donor gathering at the home of House Minority Leader Nancy Pelosi (D–CA), an afternoon tea highlighted by singer and songwriter Carole King, and a breakfast sponsored by Senator Hillary Rodham Clinton (D–NY). Attracting additional media attention to the event, actresses Whoopi Goldberg, Cybill Shepherd, and Ashley Judd and singers Ani DiFranco and Moby joined the marchers, along with members of Congress and former executive-branch officials such as former Secretary of State Madeleine Albright, for a day of speeches on the Mall.

As they attempted to expand the agenda from abortion rights to a wider array of reproductive rights, organizers had especially targeted young, college-age women and were heartened that busloads of students from many colleges and universities attended. In addition to student groups, more than 1,400 groups nationwide, including the NAACP, signed on

Photo courtesy: Krista Kennell/Zuma/Corbis

to send members to Washington, D.C. Longtime abortion rights advocates, many of them now in their late fifties and early sixties, are particularly conscious of the need to recruit and energize new members. Interest groups and social movements cannot maintain themselves without new recruits, and the march, while demonstrating the ability of a wide array of organized interests to come together, also attracted a new cohort of reproductive rights activists who, organizers hope, not only will spread the word around the nation, but also will become the next generation of leaders of myriad pro-choice, reproductive rights organizations.

Questions

1. How did efforts made by interest groups to engage young people translate into an energized youth vote?
2. How effective is the use of celebrity advocates as a strategy in helping an interest group achieve its goals?

---

myself. The better lobbyists, when they have a proposal they are pushing, bring it to me along with a couple of speeches, a *Record* insert, and a fact sheet."[27]

Not surprisingly, lobbyists work most closely with representatives who share their interests.[28] A lobbyist from the NRA, for example, would be unlikely to try to influence a liberal representative who was on record as strongly in favor of gun control. It is much more effective for a group such as the NRA to provide useful information for its supporters and to those who are undecided. Good lobbyists also can encourage members to file amendments to bills favorable to their interests. They also can urge their supporters in Congress to make speeches (often written by the group) and to pressure their colleagues in the chamber.

A lobbyist's effectiveness depends largely on his or her reputation for fair play and provision of accurate information. No member of Congress wants to look uninformed. As one member noted: "It doesn't take very long to figure out which lobbyists are straightforward, and which ones are trying to snow you. The good ones will give you the weak points as well as the strong points of their case. If anyone ever gives me false or misleading information, that's it—I'll never see him again."[29]

Attempts to Reform Congressional Lobbying.   In 1946, in an effort to limit the power of lobbyists, Congress passed the Federal Regulation of Lobbying Act, which required anyone hired to lobby any member of Congress to register and file quarterly financial reports. Few lobbyists actually filed these reports. For years, numerous good government groups argued for the strengthening of lobbying laws. Civil liberties groups such as the ACLU, however, argue that registration provisions violate the First Amendment's freedom of speech and the right of citizens to petition the government.

But, according to public opinion polls, many Americans believed that the votes of numerous members of Congress were available to the highest bidder. In late 1995, after nearly fifty years of inaction, Congress passed the first effort to regulate lobbying since the 1946 act. The Lobbying Disclosure Act employs a strict definition of lobbyist (one who devotes at least 20 percent of a client's or employer's time to lobbying activities). It also requires lobbyists to: (1) register with the clerk of the House and the secretary of the Senate; (2) report their clients and issues and the agency or house they lobbied; and, (3) estimate the amount they are paid by each client (see Join the Debate: Should There Be Limits on Interest Group Participation?).

These reporting requirements make it easier for watchdog groups or the media to monitor lobbying activities. In fact, the first comprehensive analysis by the Center for Responsive Politics revealed that by June 1999, 20,512 lobbyists were registered. The number of organizations that reported spending more than $1 million a year on lobbying also jumped dramatically. In 2004, nearly $4 million was spent on lobbying for every member of Congress.[30]

As revealed in Analyzing Visuals: Top Lobbying Expenditures, medical interests not only were among the top spenders for lobbying activities but also were the source of significant campaign contributions to both Republicans and Democrats. Although contributing huge sums does not necessarily mean that votes are being bought, political scientists have found a strong correlation between a group's campaign contributions and a member's involvement in certain kinds of legislation or a representative's responsiveness to big business.[31]

Lobbying the Executive Branch.   As the scope of the federal government has expanded and legislation often originates in the executive branch, lobbying that branch has increased in importance and frequency. Groups often target one or more levels of the executive branch because there are so many potential access points, including the president, White House staff, and the numerous levels of the executive-branch bureaucracy. Groups try to work closely with the administration to influence policy decisions at their formulation and later implementation stages. As with congressional lobbying, the effectiveness of a group often depends on its ability to provide decision makers with important information and a sense of where the public stands on the issue.

Photo courtesy: Mike Luckovich and Creators Syndicate, Inc., by permission

Analyzing Visuals
TOP LOBBYING EXPENDITURES

For most interest groups, lobbying is their most important activity. Successful lobbying efforts require spending large amounts of money, as shown in the bar graph. Based on the narrow definition of lobbying used under the Lobbying Disclosure Act, the reported expenditures account for money spent to contact members of Congress and executive-branch officials but do not include money spent for state-level lobbying, public relations work, legal work, or congressional testimony. Interest groups also supplement their lobbying efforts with campaign contributions to congressional candidates. After studying the bar graph, answer the following critical thinking questions: What is the correlation, if any, between an interest group's expenditures for lobbying and its expenditures for campaign contributions? Which interest groups are most likely to contribute to Republican candidates? Which interest groups are most likely to contribute to Democratic candidates? What do you think explains the differences in these groups' contribution tendencies?

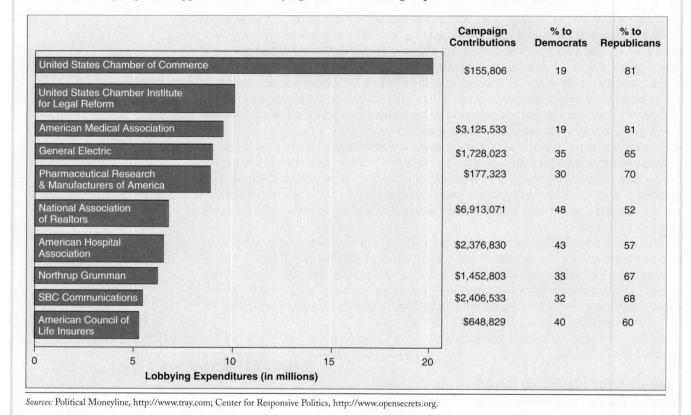

	Campaign Contributions	% to Democrats	% to Republicans
United States Chamber of Commerce	$155,806	19	81
United States Chamber Institute for Legal Reform			
American Medical Association	$3,125,533	19	81
General Electric	$1,728,023	35	65
Pharmaceutical Research & Manufacturers of America	$177,323	30	70
National Association of Realtors	$6,913,071	48	52
American Hospital Association	$2,376,830	43	57
Northrup Grumman	$1,452,803	33	67
SBC Communications	$2,406,533	32	68
American Council of Life Insurers	$648,829	40	60

Lobbying Expenditures (in millions)

Sources: Political Moneyline, http://www.tray.com; Center for Responsive Politics, http://www.opensecrets.org.

Historically, group representatives have met with presidents or their staff members to urge policy directions. In 1992, representatives of the auto industry accompanied President George Bush to lobby the Japanese for more favorable trade regulations. Most presidents also have set up staff positions to provide interest groups or organizations with access to the administration. Many of these offices, such as those dealing with consumer affairs, the environment, minority affairs, or women's issues, are routinely the target of organized interests.

An especially strong link exists between interest groups and regulatory agencies (see chapter 9). Although these agencies are ostensibly independent of Congress and the president, interest groups often have clout there. Because of the highly technical aspects of much regulatory work, many groups employ Washington attorneys and lobbying firms to deal directly with the agencies. So great is interest group influence in the decision-making process of these agencies that many people charge that the agencies have been captured by the interest groups.

Groups often monitor the implementation of the laws or policies they advocated. The National Women's Law Center, for example, has been instrumental in seeing that Title IX, which was passed by Congress to mandate educational equity for women and girls, be enforced fully. It has successfully sued several colleges and universities that have failed to provide equity in athletic funding for men and women.

Often, executive branch employees leave their positions to take much more lucrative jobs as lobbyists. The Ethics in Government Act (see Table 16.4) attempted to curtail questionable moves by barring members of the executive branch from representing any clients before their agency for one year after leaving governmental service. Thus, someone who worked in Title IX enforcement in the Department of Education and then went to work for a university or the National Collegiate Athletic Association would have to wait a year before lobbying his or her old agency. Members of Congress aren't under these kinds of restrictions.

Lobbying the Courts.   The courts, too, have proved a useful target for interest groups.[32] Although you might think that the courts decide cases that affect only the parties involved or that they should be immune from political pressures, interest groups for years have recognized the value of lobbying the courts, especially the Supreme Court, and many political scientists view it as a form of political participation.[33] As shown in Table 16.3, 72 percent of the Washington-based groups surveyed participated in litigation as a lobbying tool.

Generally, interest group lobbying of the courts can take two forms: direct sponsorship or the filing of *amicus curiae* briefs. When cases come to the Supreme Court that raise issues a particular organization is interested in but not actually sponsoring, the organization often will file an *amicus* brief—either alone or with other like-minded groups—to inform the justices of their policy preference, generally offered in the guise of legal arguments. Over the years, as the number of both liberal and conservative groups viewing litigation as a useful tactic has increased, so has the number of briefs submitted to the Court. Most major cases noted in this book have been sponsored by an interest group, or one or both of the parties in the case have been supported by an *amicus curiae* brief.

In addition to litigating, interest groups try to influence who is nominated to the federal courts. They also play an important role in Senate confirmation hearings, as discussed in chapter 10. In 1991, for example, 112 groups testified or filed prepared statements for or against the controversial nomination of Clarence Thomas to the U.S. Supreme Court.[34] Upon hearing news of Chief Justice William H. Rehnquist's illness in late 2004, moreover, interest groups immediately began to gear up for another bruising nomination battle.

TABLE 16.4   The Ethics in Government Act

In 1978, in the wake of Watergate, Congress passed the Ethics in Government Act. Its key provisions dealt with: (1) financial disclosure; and, (2) employment after government service.

(1) Financial disclosure: The president, vice president, and top-ranking executive employees must file annual public financial disclosure reports that list:
- The source and amount of all earned income; all income from stocks, bonds, and property; any investments or large debts; the source of a spouse's income, if any.
- Any position or offices held in any business, labor, or nonprofit organizations.

(2) Employment after government services: Former executive branch employees may not:
- Represent anyone before an agency for two years after leaving government service on matters that came within the former employees' sphere or responsibility (even if they were not personally involved in the matter).
- Represent anyone on any matter before their former agency for one year after leaving it, even if the former employees had no connection with the matter while in the government.

Source: Congressional Quarterly Weekly Report (October 28, 1978): 3121.

Grassroots Lobbying. As the term implies, grassroots lobbying is a form of pressure-group activity that attempts to involve individuals who contact their representatives directly in an effort to affect policy.[35] Although it often involves door-to-door informational or petition drives—a tried and true method of lobbying—the term also encompasses more modern forms such as fax and Internet lobbying of lawmakers. As early as the 1840s, women (who could not vote) used petition campaigns to persuade state legislators to enact Married Women's Property Acts that gave women control of their earnings and a greater legal say in the custody of their children. Petitioning has come a long way since then. It is now routine for interest groups to e-mail their members and to provide a direct Web link as well as suggested text that citizens can use to lobby their legislators.

Interest groups regularly try to inspire their members to engage in grassroots activity, hoping that lawmakers will respond to those pressures and the attendant publicity. In essence, the goal of many organizations is to persuade ordinary voters to serve as their advocates. In the world of lobbying, there are few things more useful than a list of committed supporters. Radio talk-show hosts such as Rush Limbaugh try to stir up their listeners by urging them to contact their representatives in Washington, D.C. Other interest groups now run carefully targeted and costly television advertisements pitching one side of an argument. Some of these undefined masses, as they join together on the Internet or via faxes, may be mobilized into one or more groups.

Protest Activities. Most groups have few members so devoted as to put everything on the line for their cause. Some will risk jail or even death, but it is much more usual for a group's members to opt for more conventional forms of lobbying or to influence policy through the electoral process. When these forms of pressure-group activities are unsuccessful or appear to be too slow to achieve results, however, some groups (or individuals within groups) resort to more forceful legal as well as illegal measures to attract attention to their cause. Since the Revolutionary War, violent, illegal protest has been one tactic of organized interests. The Boston Tea Party, for example, involved breaking all sorts of laws, although no one was hurt physically. Other forms of protest, such as Shays's Rebellion, ended in tragedy for some participants. Much more recently, anti-war protestors have been willing to march and risk detention and jail in the United States.

During the civil rights movement, as discussed in chapter 6, Reverend Martin Luther King Jr. and his followers frequently resorted to nonviolent marches to draw attention to the plight of African Americans in the South. These forms of organized group activity were legal. The groups obtained proper parade permits and notified government officials. The protesters who tried to stop the freedom marchers, however, were engaging in illegal protest activity. Today, protesters regularly try to picket or protest meetings of the International Monetary Fund or the World Bank. Political conventions as well as inaugurations also routinely are targeted by protesters (see Politics Now: The March for Women's Lives).

Election Activities

In addition to trying to achieve their goals (or at least draw attention to them) through the conventional and unconventional forms of lobbying and protest activity, many interest groups also become involved more directly in the electoral process. The 2004 Republican and Democratic

Simulation
You Are the Leader of Concerned Citizens for World Justice

■ Protesters with People for the Ethical Treatment of Animals (PETA) wear fur coats smudged with fake blood as they demonstrate in front of the building that houses *Vogue* magazine, in June 2003. PETA was protesting what it claimed was the magazine's policy of not accepting paid anti-fur advertisements while continually promoting fur in its pages.

Photo courtesy: Mary Altaffer/AP/Wide World Photo

presidential nominating conventions were the targets of significant organized interest group protest concerning each party's stance on a variety of issues, including the U.S.-led war in Iraq, same-sex marriage, the environment, gun control laws, and reproductive rights, among others.

Candidate Recruitment and Endorsements.   Many interest groups claim to be nonpolitical. But, some interest groups recruit, endorse, and/or provide financial or other forms of support for political candidates. EMILY's List (EMILY stands for "Early money is like yeast—it makes the dough rise") was founded to support pro-choice Democratic women candidates, especially during party primary election contests. It now, however, like its Republican counterpart the WISH List (WISH stands for Women in the House and Senate), recruits and trains candidates in addition to contributing to their campaigns. EMILY's List, in 2004, for example, solicited volunteers to work on Betty Castor's campaign in Florida for the U.S. Senate. It paid the airfare and expenses for hundreds of volunteers from all over the nation to work in Florida in the four days leading up to the election.

Getting Out the Vote.   Many interest groups believe they can influence public policy by putting like-minded representatives in office. To that end, many groups across the ideological spectrum, such as the Christian Coalition and EMILY's List, launch massive get-out-the-vote (GOTV) efforts. These include identifying prospective voters and getting them to the polls on Election Day. Well-financed interest groups such as MoveOn.org and Swift Boat Veterans for Truth often produce issue-oriented ads for newspapers, radio, and television designed to educate the public as well as increase voter interest in election outcomes, as was the case with the groups discussed in our opening vignette.

Rating the Candidates or Office Holders.   Many liberal and conservative ideological groups rate candidates to help their members (and the general public) evaluate the voting records of members of Congress. The American Conservative Union (conservative) and the Americans for Democratic Action (liberal)—two groups at ideological polar extremes—routinely rate candidates and members of Congress based on their votes on key issues (see Analyzing Visuals: Interest Group Ratings of Selected Members of Congress). These scores help voters know more about their representatives' votes on issues that concern them.

Political Action Committees.   In 1974, Congress passed legislation to allow corporations, labor unions, and interest groups to form political action committees (PACs). PACs allow these interests to raise money to contribute to political candidates in national elections. Unlike some contributions to interest groups, contributions to PACs are not tax deductible, and PACs generally don't have members who call legislators; instead, PACs have contributors who write checks specifically for the purpose of campaign donations. PAC money plays a significant role in the campaigns of many congressional incumbents, often averaging over half a House candidate's total campaign spending. PACs generally contribute to those who have helped them before and who serve on committees or subcommittees that routinely consider legislation of concern to that group.

Political scientists have found a strong relationship between committee assignments of members of the House and Senate and PAC contributions.[36] Systematic research has failed to find a significant relation between PAC contributions and floor voting, but other research shows that group expenditures are more likely to have an effect in committee votes; most often affected is the degree of a member's involvement with proposed legislation, not how the member votes.[37] Moreover, studies by economists find that "campaign contributions are made to support politicians with the 'right' beliefs . . . [not to] buy politicians' votes."[38] (PACs are discussed in greater detail in chapter 14.)

Timeline

Interest Groups and
Campaign Finance

Analyzing Visuals

INTEREST GROUP RATINGS OF SELECTED MEMBERS OF CONGRESS

Among the election activities of interest groups are the endorsement of candidates for public office and the rating of candidates and incumbents. Interest groups inform their members, as well as the public generally, of the voting records of office holders, helping voters make an informed voting decision. The table displays the 2003 ratings of selected members of Congress by seven interest groups that vary greatly in their ideological tendencies. Each group rates the members of Congress on issues that are important to the group. For example, the AFL-CIO bases its rating on a member's votes in support of labor unions. After reviewing the table, answer the following critical thinking questions: Which members of the Senate would you consider the most liberal? Which groups' ratings did you use to reach your conclusion? Which members of the House would you consider the most conservative? Which groups' ratings did you use to reach your conclusion? Would it be important to know which of a representative's votes were used by each group to determine the rating? Explain your answer.

Member	ACU	ACLU	ADA	AFL-CIO	CC	CoC	LCV
Senate							
Dianne Feinstein (D–CA)	20	60	80	92	20	55	80
Bill Frist (R–TN)	100	20	0	15	100	100	0
Kay Bailey Hutchison (R–TX)	100	25	5	23	100	95	4
Ted Kennedy (D–MA)	0	60	100	100	0	29	84
House							
Mary Bono (R–CA)	71	27	10	11	75	95	9
John Conyers (D–MI)	0	93	100	100	14	21	91
Tom DeLay (R–TX)	92	7	0	0	100	95	0
Sheila Jackson Lee (D–TX)	4	93	100	100	0	26	68

Key
ACU = American Conservative Union
ACLU = American Civil Liberties Union
ADA = Americans for Democratic Action
AFL-CIO = American Federation of Labor–Congress of Industrial Organizations
CC = Christian Coalition
CoC = Chamber of Commerce
LCV = League of Conservation Voters
Members are rated on a scale from 1 to 100, with 1 being the lowest and 100 being the highest support of a particular group's policies.

WHAT MAKES AN INTEREST GROUP SUCCESSFUL?

THROUGHOUT OUR NATION'S HISTORY, all kinds of interests in society have organized to pressure the government for policy change. Some have been successful, and some have not. Political scientist E. E. Schattschneider once wrote, "Pressure politics is essentially the politics of small groups. . . . Pressure tactics are not remarkably successful in mobilizing general interests."[39] He was correct; historically, corporate interests often prevail over the concerns of public interest groups such as environmentalists.

All of the groups discussed in this chapter have one thing in common: They all want to shape the public agenda, whether by winning elections, maintaining the status quo, or obtaining favorable legislation or rulings from Congress, executive agencies, or the courts.[40] For powerful groups, simply making sure that certain issues never get discussed may be the goal. In contrast, those opposed to random stops of African American drivers or those of Middle Eastern appearance win when the issue becomes front-page news and law enforcement officials feel pressured to investigate, if not to stop altogether, the discriminatory practice of racial profiling.

Groups often claim credit for winning legislation, court cases, or even elections individually or in coalition with other groups.[41] They also are successful when their leaders become elected officials or policy makers in any of the three branches of the government. For example, Representative Rosa DeLauro (D–CT) was a former political director of EMILY's List, and Senator Hillary Clinton (D–NY) was a former board member of the Children's Defense Fund. Associate Justice Ruth Bader Ginsburg was a former ACLU board member and the director of its Women's Rights Project. President George W. Bush's Secretary of the Interior Gale Norton was formerly with the Mountain States Legal Foundation, a conservative public interest law firm, as was Rex E. Lee, the U.S. solicitor general in the Reagan administration. Lynne Cheney, the wife of George W. Bush's vice president, Dick Cheney, is a senior fellow at the conservative American Enterprise Institutute and a former board member of the conservative Independent Women's Forum.

Political scientists have studied several phenomena that contribute in varying degrees—individually and collectively—to particular groups' successes. These include: (1) leaders; (2) patrons and funding; and, (3) a solid membership base.

Leaders. Interest group theorists frequently acknowledge the key role that leaders play in the formation, viability, and success of interest groups while noting that leaders often vary from rank-and-file members on various policies. Without the powerful pen of William Lloyd Garrison in the 1830s, who knows whether the abolitionist movement would have been as successful? Other notable prime movers include Frances Willard of the WCTU, Marian Wright Edelman of the Children's Defense Fund in 1968, and Pat Robertson of the Christian Coalition in the 1990s. Most successful groups, especially public interest groups, are led by charismatic individuals who devote most of their energies to the cause.

The role of an interest-group leader is similar to that of an entrepreneur in the business world. Leaders of groups must find ways to attract members. As in the marketing of a new product, an interest-group leader must offer something attractive to persuade members to join. Potential members of the group must be convinced that the benefits of joining outweigh the costs. Union members, for example, must be persuaded that the cost of their union dues will be offset by the union's winning higher wages for them. Other groups, such as the American Automobile Association (AAA), offer what political scientists term material benefits. The AAA, for example, offers roadside assistance and trip planning services to its members. Similarly, AARP offers a wide range of discount programs to its 35 million members over the age of fifty. Many of those members do not necessarily support all of the group's positions but simply want to take advantage of its discounts.

Patrons and Funding. All interest groups require adequate funding to build their memberships as well to advance their policy objectives. Governments, foundations, and wealthy individuals can serve as **patrons,** providing crucial start-up funds for groups, especially public interest groups. Advertising, litigating, and lobbying are expensive. Without financiers, few public interest groups could survive their initial start-up period. Many interest groups rely on membership dues, direct-mail solicitations, and patrons to remain in business. Charismatic leaders often are especially effective fundraisers and recruiters of new members.

patrons
Persons who finance groups.

Members. Organizations are usually composed of three kinds of members. At the top are a relatively small number of leaders who devote most of their energies to the single group. The second tier of members is generally involved psychologically as well as organizationally. They are the workers of the group—they attend meetings, pay dues, and chair committees to see that things get done. In the bottom tier are the rank and file, members who don't actively participate. They pay their dues and call

SHOULD THERE BE LIMITS ON INTEREST GROUP PARTICIPATION?

OVERVIEW: The First Amendment to the Constitution guarantees the right to freedom of speech, press, association and the right to "petition the government for a redress of grievances." These are necessary rights in a democracy because they guarantee the right of the people—within the framework of law—to have their voice heard by the government. Grievances can be political or social in nature, and all citizens have the right to petition the government to have their (sometimes narrow) interest or issue addressed, and this right includes expressing policy preferences. Nevertheless, political speech and activity are regulated by law, as are the actions of the government (so as to prevent undue influence and corruption), and the line between constitutional regulation and rights violations is difficult to discern. Additionally, in order for government to fulfill its functions, it must attempt to balance fairly the claims of very diverse competing interests—take, for example, the legal, economic, and rights claims of music and video file-sharers and of the entertainment industry. Because the framework within which interest groups and government must operate is contentious, so regulation is necessary. But, when a group lobbies to change government policies, can the government require full disclosure of the group's activities and finances?

citizens to verify accountability of both group and government activity—this allows government watchdog groups such as OpenSecrets to correlate lobbying activities with perceived government response. Moreover, insisting that groups disclose information will allow both government and the public to know who or what is behind a lobby's agenda. For example, billionaire George Soros has given $15.8 million to interest groups such as MoveOn.org, the Campaign for America's Future, and other organizations, to fund political activities. This information is relevant to discerning motive and assigning accountability behind an interest's political action.

The political nature of lobbying activity may mean that interest groups are subject to a higher standard of disclosure and scrutiny. Just as the American people demand transparency in government activity, it seems reasonable that they be provided with information regarding those interest groups monitoring (or supporting) the government. To that end, requiring disclosure of group information is rational. But what about the right to privacy? Should interest groups have the same right to privacy as individuals? After all, citizens are not required to disclose the reasons behind their votes or why they engage in political activity the way they do. Why should interest groups be denied this standard of privacy?

Depending on what is done with the information gathered from interest group disclosure requirements, the government may be acting in the public interest. For example, part of the mandate from the Lobbying Disclosure Act of 1995 (LDA) is to facilitate public access to information about lobbying groups as well as about the government's knowledge of their activities. The goal is to allow concerned

Arguments for Regulating Interest Group Activities

- **Interest groups are not given a constitutional role to make or influence policy.** Though individuals and groups have the right to lobby the government, they have no unrestricted right to do so. Given literally thousands of interests, the government must have some means to

themselves group members, but they do little more. Most group members fall into this last category.

In 1960, E. E. Schattschneider noted that the interest group system in the United States had a decidedly "upper-class bias," and he concluded that 90 percent of the population did not participate in an interest group, or what he called the pressure-group system.[42] Since the 1960s, survey data have revealed that group membership is drawn primarily from people with higher income and education levels. Individuals who are wealthier can afford to belong to more organizations because they have more money and, often, more leisure time. Money and education also are associated with greater confidence that one's actions will bring results, a further incentive to devote time to organizing or supporting interest groups. These elites often are more involved in politics and hold stronger opinions on many political issues.

People who do belong to groups often belong to more than one. Overlapping memberships often can affect the cohesiveness of a group. Imagine, for example, that you are an officer in the College Republicans. If you call a meeting, people may not attend prioritize and determine the legitimacy of various groups. For example, should a local 4H group have the same voice and access to national policy makers as the National Dairy Association?

- **Regulation is necessary to ensure the public knows why and in what capacity an interest group is acting.** LDA's regulatory mandate is to ensure accountability in the lobbying process. The American public needs to know about corruption or misinformation not only coming from the government, but coming from interest groups as well. For instance, the Rainbow Push Coalition has been implicated in lobbying the City of Chicago to keep a dangerous after-hours dance club open in which a fire subsequently caused twenty-one deaths. The club owners, Rainbow Push, and certain Chicago politicians were known to have a business relationship.
- **Regulation of interest groups allows the government to level the playing field.** Research published by the American Political Science Association (APSA) contends that inequality and unequal access to wealth harms the American democratic process. APSA implies that wealthier groups have a larger voice and thus more access to policy makers. By regulating interest groups, the federal government can ensure relative equality of access—and voice—to policy makers.

Arguments Against Regulating Interest Group Activities

- **Government regulation of interest groups may stifle political speech.** For example, the U.S. Supreme Court upheld the new Bipartisan Campaign Reform Act's provision prohibiting groups from issue advertising sixty days prior to a general election. Many scholars and legal experts believe that this is a fundamental violation of political speech rights, as it is now believed that money gives "voice" to the political process—and to deny groups the right to political advertisement is to deny political speech.
- **Regulation of groups essentially creates approved speech and politics.** By using regulation to determine which groups have the right to lobby the government, the government is in effect establishing which groups are legitimate (in both their activities and speech) and which are not. It is not the government's role to conclude whether a group's political activity and speech are more or less legitimate or important.
- **Government regulation of interest groups is not necessary.** In an open, pluralistic society, interest groups are subject to market dynamics. That is, those groups that truly represent broad or important interests will have their views heard over those that do not. Thus, a natural voice is given to those groups deemed by the American people to represent important interests and issues.

Questions

1. Is compelling disclosure of group information a violation of privacy rights? How can this be reconciled with the public's right to know?
2. Does the political nature of lobbyist activity demand a higher level of governmental scrutiny?

Selected Readings

Kevin Phillips. *Arrogant Capital: Washington, Wall Street, and the Frustration of American Politics.* Boston: Back Bay Books, 1995.
Luigi Graziano. *Lobbying, Pluralism and Democracy.* London: Palgrave Macmillan, 2001.

---

because they have academic, athletic, or social obligations. Divided loyalties and multiple group memberships frequently can affect the success of a group, especially if any one group has too many members who simply fall into the dues-paying category.

Groups vary tremendously in their ability to enroll what are called potential members (see Table 16.5). According to economist Mancur Olson Jr., all groups provide some **collective good**—that is, something of value, such as money, a tax write-off, a good feeling, or a better environment, that can't be withheld from a nonmember.[43] If one union member at a factory gets a raise, for example, all other workers at that factory will, too. Therefore, those who don't join or work for the benefit of the group still reap the rewards of the group's activity. The downside of this phenomenon is called the **free rider problem.** As Olson asserts, potential members may be unlikely to join a group because they realize that they will receive many of the benefits the group achieves, regardless of their participation. Not only is it irrational for free riders to join any group, but the bigger the group, the greater the free rider problem. Thus, groups need to provide a variety of other incentives to convince potential members to join. These can be newsletters, discounts, or simply a good feeling.

collective good
Something of value that cannot be withheld from a nonmember of a group, for example, a tax write-off or a better environment.

free rider problem
Potential members fail to join a group because they can get the benefit, or collective good, sought by the group without contributing the effort.

TABLE 16.5	Potential Versus Actual Interest Group Members		

The goal of most groups is to mobilize all potential members, but as Mancur Olson Jr. points out, the larger the group, the more difficult it is to mobilize. To illustrate the potential versus actual membership phenomenon, here are several examples of groups and their potential memberships.

Population	Group	Number of Potential Members	Number of Actual Members
Governors	National Governors Association (includes territories)	55	55
Political Science Faculty	American Political Science Association	17,000	14,000
African Americans	National Association for the Advancement of Colored People (NAACP)	37,000,000	500,000
Physicians	American Medical Association (AMA)	690,000	300,000
Women	National Organization for Women (NOW)	147,000,000	500,000

Several scholars examining why individuals join groups have found that a group's attempt to pursue a collective good is not always a mere by-product of the group's ability to provide selective material incentives, as Olson has argued. Specifically, they found that several factors help groups overcome the free rider problem. One factor is that members representing other groups or institutions are much more likely than individuals to value efforts to obtain collective goods. Another factor is that once a policy environment appears to threaten existing rights, many individuals come to realize those threats and join groups in exchange for only collective benefits.[44] Moreover, Olson, an economist, fails to consider that many political, D.C.-based groups count other groups, and not just individuals, as their members. These alliances often are considered carefully by organized interests much in the way some individuals calculate their membership in groups.[45]

These alliances have important implications.[46] Although interest groups do work together in alliances, they also carve out policy niches to differentiate themselves to potential members as well as policy makers. While the National Women's Law Center, for example, vigorously pursues enforcement of Title IX through litigation, the National Organization for Women, although very supportive of Title IX, is more involved in welfare reform as it affects women. Similarly, one study of gay and lesbian groups found that they avoided direct competition by developing different issue niches.[47] Some concentrate on litigation; others lobby for marriage law reform or open inclusion of gays in the military.

Small groups often have an organizational advantage because, for example, in a small group such as the National Governors Association, any individual's share of the collective good may be great enough to make it rational for him or her to join. Patrons, be they large foundations such as the Ford Foundation or individuals such as wealthy financier George Soros (who contributed over $15.8 million to new progressive organizations, including Americans Coming Together, MoveOn.org, and Campaign for America's Future, in an effort to defeat President George W. Bush in 2004), often eliminate the free rider problem for public interest groups.[48] They make the costs of joining minimal because they contribute much of the group's necessary financial support.[49]

SUMMARY

INTEREST GROUPS LIE at the heart of the American social and political system. National groups first emerged in the 1830s. Since that time, the type, nature, sophistication, and tactics of groups have changed dramatically. In this chapter, we have made the following points:

1. What Are Interest Groups?

Those who study interest groups have offered a variety of definitions to explain what they are. Most definitions revolve around notions of associations or groups of individuals who share some sort of common interest or attitude and who try to influence or engage in activity to affect governmental policies or the people in government. Political scientists find it helpful to categorize interest groups in several ways. They study multi-issue versus single-issue groups. They also examine economic, public interest, and governmental units as participants in the interest group process.

2. The Roots and Development of American Interest Groups

Interest groups, national in scope, did not begin to emerge until around the 1830s. Later, from 1890 to 1920, the Progressive movement emerged. The 1960s saw the rise of a wide variety of liberal interest groups. By the 1970s through the 1980s, legions of conservatives were moved to form new groups to counteract those efforts. Business groups, corporations, and unions established their presence in Washington, D.C.

3. What Do Interest Groups Do?

Interest groups often fill voids left by the major political parties and give Americans opportunities to make claims, as a group, on government. The most common activity of interest groups is lobbying, which takes many forms. Groups routinely pressure members of Congress and their staffs, the president and the bureaucracy, and the courts; they use a variety of techniques to educate and stimulate the public to pressure key governmental decision makers. Interest groups also attempt to influence the outcome of elections; some run their own candidates for office. Others rate elected officials to inform their members how particular legislators stand on issues of importance to them. Political action committees (PACs), a way for some groups to contribute money to candidates for office, are another method of gaining support from elected officials and ensuring that supportive officials stay in office. Reaction to public criticism of this influence led Congress to pass the first major lobbying reforms in fifty years.

4. What Makes an Interest Group Successful?

Interest group success can be measured in a variety of ways, including a group's ability to get its issues on the public agenda, winning key pieces of legislation in Congress or executive branch or judicial rulings, or backing successful candidates. Several factors contribute to interest group success, including leaders and patrons, funding, and committed members.

KEY TERMS

civic virtue, p. 582
collective good, p. 607
disturbance theory, p. 583
economic interest group, p. 584
free rider problem, p. 607
interest groups, p. 583
lobbying, p. 594
lobbyist, p. 587
patrons, p. 605
political action committees (PACs), p. 584
public interest groups, p. 584
social capital, p. 582
trade associations, p. 589

SELECTED READINGS

Baumgartner, Frank, and Beth Leech. *Basic Interests*. Princeton, NJ: Princeton University Press, 1998.
Berry, Jeffrey M. *The Interest Group Society*, 4th ed. New York: Addison Wesley, 2001.
Cigler, Allan J., and Burdett A. Loomis, eds. *Interest Group Politics*, 6th ed. Washington, DC: CQ Press, 2002.
Grossman, Gene M., and Elhanan Helpman. *Special Interest Politics*. Cambridge, MA: MIT Press, 2001.
Herrnson, Paul S., Ronald G. Shaiko, and Clyde Wilcox, eds. *The Interest Group Connection*, 4th ed. Washington, DC: CQ Press, 2005.
Kollman, Ken. *Outside Lobbying: Public Opinion and Interest Group Strategies*. Princeton, NJ: Princeton University Press, 1998.
McGlen, Nancy E., et al. *Women, Politics, and American Society*, 4th ed. Upper Saddle River, NJ: Prentice Hall, 2004.
Olson, Mancur, Jr. *The Logic of Collective Action: Public Good and the Theory of Groups*. Cambridge, MA: Harvard University Press, 1965.
Truman, David B. *The Governmental Process: Political Interests and Public Opinion*. New York: Knopf, 1951.
Wright, John R. *Interest Groups and Congress: Lobbying, Contributions, and Influence*. New York: Longman, 2002.

WEB EXPLORATIONS

For more on NOW and the NRA, see
www.now.org/
www.nra.org/
For more about Common Cause and Public Citizen, Inc., see
www.commoncause.org
www.publiccitizen.org/
For more on the Christian Coalition of America and other conservative groups, see
www.cc.org/
www.heritage.org/
www.cbn.com/
To join Rock the Vote, go to
www.rockthevote.org
For more on the AFL-CIO, see
www.aflcio.org/
For information on interest groups that watch over lobbyists' activities, see
www.comoncause.org/special/pisites.htm#3
To experience how the lobbying process works, go to
www.meyersandassociates.com/lobbyist.html
To learn more about the issue positions of selected groups mentioned in this chapter, see
www.adaction.org/
www.conservative.org/
www.aclu.org/

Appendix I

The Declaration of Independence

In Congress, July 4, 1776
The Unanimous Declaration of the Thirteen United States of America

When in the Course of human events it becomes necessary for one people to dissolve the political bands which have connected them with another, and to assume, among the powers of the earth, the separate and equal station to which the Laws of Nature and of Nature's God entitle them, a decent respect to the opinions of mankind requires that they should declare the causes which impel them to the separation.

We hold these truths to be self-evident, that all men are created equal, that they are endowed by their Creator with certain unalienable Rights, that among these are Life, Liberty and the pursuit of Happiness. That to secure these rights, Governments are instituted among Men, deriving their just powers from the consent of the governed. That whenever any Form of Government becomes destructive of these ends, it is the Right of the People to alter or to abolish it, and to institute new Government, laying its foundation on such principles and organizing its powers in such form, as to them shall seem most likely to effect their Safety and Happiness. Prudence, indeed, will dictate that Governments long established should not be changed for light and transient causes; and accordingly all experience hath shewn that mankind are more disposed to suffer, while evils are sufferable, than to right themselves by abolishing the forms to which they are accustomed. But when a long train of abuses and usurpations, pursuing invariably the same Object evinces a design to reduce them under absolute Despotism, it is their right, it is their duty, to throw off such Government, and to provide new Guards for their future security.—Such has been the patient sufferance of these Colonies; and such is now the necessity which constrains them to alter their former Systems of Government. The history of the present King of Great Britain is a history of repeated injuries and usurpations, all having in direct object the establishment of an absolute Tyranny over these States. To prove this, let Facts be submitted to a candid world.

He has refused his Assent to Laws, the most wholesome and necessary for the public good.

He has forbidden his Governors to pass Laws of immediate and pressing importance, unless suspended in their operation till his Assent should be obtained; and when so suspended, he has utterly neglected to attend to them.

He has refused to pass other Laws for the accommodation of large districts of people, unless those people would relinquish the right of Representation in the Legislature, a right inestimable to them and formidable to tyrants only.

He has called together legislative bodies at places unusual, uncomfortable, and distant from the depository of their Public Records, for the sole purpose of fatiguing them into compliance with his measures.

He has dissolved Representative Houses repeatedly, for opposing with manly firmness his invasions on the rights of the people.

He has refused for a long time, after such dissolutions, to cause others to be elected; whereby the Legislative Powers, incapable of Annihilation, have returned to the People at large for their exercise, the State remaining in the mean time exposed to all the dangers of invasion from without, and convulsions within.

He has endeavored to prevent the population of these States; for that purpose obstructing the Laws of Naturalization of Foreigners; refusing to pass others to encourage their migration hither, and raising the conditions of new Appropriations of Lands.

He has obstructed the Administration of Justice, by refusing his Assent to Laws for establishing Judiciary powers.

He has made Judges dependent on his Will alone, for the tenure of their offices, and the amount and payment of their salaries.

He has erected a multitude of New Offices, and sent hither swarms of Officers to harass our people, and eat out their substance.

He has kept among us, in times of peace, Standing Armies without the Consent of our legislatures.

He has affected to render the Military independent of and superior to the Civil power.

He has combined with others to subject us to a jurisdiction foreign to our constitution, and unacknowledged by our laws, giving his Assent to their Acts of pretended Legislation:

For quartering large bodies of armed troops among us:

For protecting them, by a mock Trial, from punishment for any Murders which they should commit on the Inhabitants of these States:

For cutting off our Trade with all parts of the world:

For imposing Taxes on us without our Consent:

For depriving us in many cases, of the benefits of Trial by Jury:

For transporting us beyond Seas to be tried for pretended offences:

For abolishing the free System of English Laws in a neighboring Province, establishing therein an Arbitrary government, and enlarging its Boundaries so as to render it at once an example and fit instrument for introducing the same absolute rule into these Colonies:

For taking away our Charters, abolishing our most valuable Laws, and altering fundamentally the Forms of our Governments:

For suspending our own Legislatures, and declaring themselves invested with power to legislate for us in all cases whatsoever.

He has abdicated Government here, by declaring us out of his Protection and waging War against us.

He has plundered our seas, ravaged our Coasts, burnt out towns, and destroyed the lives of our people.

He is at this time transporting large Armies of foreign Mercenaries to compleat the works of death, desolation and tyranny, already begun with circumstances of Cruelty and perfidy scarcely paralleled in the most barbarous ages, and totally unworthy the Head of a civilized nation.

He has constrained our fellow Citizens taken Captive on the high Seas to bear Arms against their Country, to become the executioners of their friends and Brethren, or to fall themselves by their Hands.

He has excited domestic insurrections amongst us, and has endeavored to bring on the inhabitants of our frontiers, the merciless Indian Savages, whose known rule of warfare, is an undistinguished destruction of all ages, sexes and conditions.

In every stage of these Oppressions We have Petitioned for Redress in the most humble terms: Our repeated Petitions have been answered only by repeated injury: A Prince, whose character is thus marked by every act which may define a Tyrant, is unfit to be the ruler of a free people.

Nor have We been wanting in attention to our British brethren. We have warned them from time to time of attempts by their legislature to extend an unwarrantable jurisdiction over us. We have reminded them of the circumstances of our emigration and settlement here. We have appealed to their native justice and magnanimity; and we have conjured them by the ties of our common kindred to disavow these usurpations, which would inevitably interrupt our connections and correspondence. They too have been deaf to the voice of justice and consanguinity. We must, therefore, acquiesce in the necessity, which denounces our Separation, and hold them, as we hold the rest of mankind, Enemies in War, in Peace Friends.

We, therefore, the Representatives of the United States of America, in General Congress, Assembled, appealing to the Supreme Judge of the world for the rectitude of our intentions, do, in the Name, and by Authority of the good People of these Colonies, solemnly publish and declare, That these United Colonies are, and of Right ought to be Free and Independent States; that they are Absolved from all Allegiance to the British Crown, and that all political connection between them and the State of Great Britain, is and ought to be totally dissolved: and that as Free and Independent States, they have full power to levy War, conclude Peace, contract Alliances, establish Commerce, and to do all other Acts and Things which Independent States may of right do. And for the support of this Declaration, with a firm reliance on the protection of Divine Providence, we mutually pledge to each other our Lives, our Fortunes and our sacred Honor.

JOHN HANCOCK

NEW HAMPSHIRE
Josiah Bartlett
William Whipple
Matthew Thornton

MASSACHUSETTS BAY
Samuel Adams
John Adams
Robert Treat Paine
Elbridge Gerry

RHODE ISLAND
Stephen Hopkins
William Ellery

CONNECTICUT
Roger Sherman
Samuel Huntington
William Williams
Oliver Wolcott

NEW YORK
William Floyd
Philip Livingston
Francis Lewis
Lewis Morris

NEW JERSEY
Richard Stockton
John Witherspoon
Francis Hopkinson
John Hart
Abraham Clark

PENNSYLVANIA
Robert Morris
Benjamin Rush
Benjamin Franklin
John Morton
George Clymer
James Smith
George Taylor
James Wilson
George Ross

DELAWARE
Caesar Rodney
George Read
Thomas McKean

MARYLAND
Samuel Chase
William Paca
Thomas Stone
Charles Carroll

VIRGINIA
George Wythe
Richard Henry Lee
Thomas Jefferson
Benjamin Harrison
Thomas Nelson, Jr.
Francis Lightfoot Lee
Carter Braxton

NORTH CAROLINA
William Hooper
Joseph Hewes
John Penn

SOUTH CAROLINA
Edward Rutledge
Thomas Heyward, Jr.
Thomas Lynch, Jr.
Arthur Middleton

GEORGIA
Button Gwinnett
Lyman Hall
George Walton

Federalist No. 10

November 22, 1787
James Madison

TO THE PEOPLE OF THE STATE OF NEW YORK.

Among the numerous advantages promised by a well constructed Union, none deserves to be more accurately developed than its tendency to break and control the violence of faction. The friend of popular governments, never finds himself so much alarmed for their character and fate, as when he contemplates their propensity to this dangerous vice. He will not fail therefore to set a due value on any plan which, without violating the principles to which he is attached, provides a proper cure for it. The instability, injustice and confusion introduced into the public councils, have in truth been the mortal diseases under which popular governments have every where perished; as they continue to be the favorite and fruitful topics from which the adversaries to liberty derive their most specious declamations. The valuable improvements made by the American Constitutions on the popular models, both ancient and modern, cannot certainly be too much admired; but it would be an unwarrantable partiality, to contend that they have as effectually obviated the danger on this side as was wished and expected. Complaints are every where heard from our most considerate and virtuous citizens, equally the friends of public and private faith, and of public and personal liberty; that our governments are too unstable; that the public good is disregarded in the conflicts of rival parties; and that measures are too often decided, not according to the rules of justice, and the rights of the minor party; but by the superior force of an interested and overbearing majority. However anxiously we may wish that these complaints had no foundation, the evidence of known facts will not permit us to deny that they are in some degree true. It will be found indeed, on a candid review of our situation, that some of the distresses under which we labor, have been erroneously charged on the operation of our governments; but it will be found, at the same time, that other causes will not alone account for many of our heaviest misfortunes; and particularly, for that prevailing and increasing distrust of public engagements, and alarm for private rights, which are echoed from one end of the continent to the other. These must be chiefly, if not wholly, effects of the unsteadiness and injustice, with which a factious spirit has tainted our public administrations.

By a faction I understand a number of citizens, whether amounting to a majority or minority of the whole, who are united and actuated by some common impulse of passion, or of interest, adverse to the rights of other citizens, or to the permanent and aggregate interests of the community.

There are two methods of curing the mischiefs of faction: the one, by removing its causes; the other, by controlling its effects.

There are again two methods of removing the causes of faction: the one by destroying the liberty which is essential to its existence; the other, by giving to every citizen the same opinions, the same passions, and the same interests.

It could never be more truly said than of the first remedy, that it is worse than the disease. Liberty is to faction, what air is to fire, an aliment without which it instantly expires. But it could not be a less folly to abolish liberty, which is essential to political life, because it nourishes faction, than it would be to wish the annihilation of air, which is essential to animal life, because it imparts to fire its destructive agency.

The second expedient is as impracticable, as the first would be unwise. As long as the reason of man continues fallible, and he is at liberty to exercise it, different opinions will be formed. As long as the connection subsists between his reason and his self-love, his opinions and his passions will have a reciprocal influence on each other; and the former will be objects to which the latter will attach themselves. The diversity in the faculties of men from which the rights of property originate, is not less an insuperable obstacle to a uniformity of interests. The protection of these faculties is the first object of Government. From the protection of different and unequal faculties of acquiring property, the possession of different degrees and kinds of property immediately results: and from the influence of these on the sentiments and views of the respective proprietors, ensues a division of the society into different interests and parties.

The latent causes of faction are thus sown in the nature of man; and we see them every where brought into different degrees of activity, according to the different circumstances of civil society. A zeal for different opinions concerning religion, concerning Government and many other points, as well of speculation as of practice; an attachment to different leaders ambitiously contending for pre-eminence and power; or to persons of other descriptions whose fortunes have been interesting to the human passions, have in turn divided mankind into parties, inflamed them with mutual animosity, and rendered them much more disposed to vex and oppress each other, than to cooperate for their common good. So strong is this propensity of mankind to fall into mutual animosities, that where no substantial occasion presents itself, the most frivolous and fanciful distinctions have been sufficient to kindle their unfriendly passions, and excite their most violent conflicts. But the most common and durable source of factions, has been the various and unequal distribution of property. Those who hold, and those who are without property, have ever formed distinct interests in society. Those who are creditors, and those who are debtors, fall under a like discrimination. A landed interest, a manufacturing interest, a mercantile interest, a monied interest, with many lesser interests, grow up of necessity in civilized nations, and divide them into different classes, actuated by different sentiments and views. The regulation of these various and interfering interests forms the principal task of modern Legislation, and involves the spirit of party and faction in the necessary and ordinary operations of Government.

No man is allowed to be a judge in his own cause; because his interest would certainly bias his judgment, and, not improbably, corrupt his integrity. With equal, nay with greater reason, a body of men, are unfit to be both judges and parties, at the same time; yet, what are many of the most important acts of legislation, but so many judicial determinations, not indeed concerning the rights of single persons, but concerning the rights of large bodies of citizens, and what are the different classes of legislators, but advocates and parties to the causes which they determine? Is a law proposed concerning private debts? It is a question to which the creditors are parties on one side, and the debtors on the other. Justice ought to hold the balance between them. Yet the parties are and must be themselves the judges; and the most numerous party, or, in other words, the most powerful faction must be expected to prevail. Shall domestic manufactures be encouraged, and in what degree, by restrictions on foreign manufactures? are questions which would be differently decided by the landed and the manufacturing classes; and probably by neither, with a sole regard to justice and the public good. The apportionment of taxes on the various descriptions of property, is an act which seems to require the most exact impartiality; yet, there is perhaps no legislative act in which greater opportunity and temptation are given to a predominant party, to trample on the rules of justice. Every shilling with which they over-burden the inferior number, is a shilling saved to their own pockets.

It is in vain to say, that enlightened statesmen will be able to adjust these clashing interests, and render them all subservient to the public good. Enlightened statesmen will not always be at the helm: Nor, in many cases, can such an adjustment be made at all, without taking into view indirect and remote considerations, which will rarely prevail over the immediate interest which one party may find in disregarding the rights of another, or the good of the whole.

The inference to which we are brought, is, that the *causes* of faction cannot be removed; and that relief is only to be sought in the means of controlling its *effects*.

If a faction consists of less than a majority, relief is supplied by the republican principle, which enables the majority to defeat its sinister views by regular vote: It may clog the administration, it may convulse the society; but it will be unable to execute and mask its violence under the forms of the Constitution. When a majority is included in a faction, the form of popular government on the other hand enables it to sacrifice to its ruling passion or interest, both the public good and the rights of other citizens. To secure the public good, and private rights, against the danger of such a faction, and at the same time to preserve the spirit and the form of popular government, is then the great object to which

our enquiries are directed: Let me add that it is the great desideratum, by which alone this form of government can be rescued from the opprobrium under which it has so long labored, and be recommended to the esteem and adoption of mankind.

By what means is this object attainable? Evidently by one of two only. Either the existence of the same passion or interest in a majority at the same time, must be prevented; or the majority, having such co-existent passion or interest, must be rendered, by their number and local situation, unable to concert and carry into effect schemes of oppression. If the impulse and the opportunity be suffered to coincide, we well know that neither moral nor religious motives can be relied on as an adequate control. They are not found to be such on the injustice and violence of individuals, and lose their efficacy in proportion to the number combined together; that is, in proportion as their efficacy becomes needful.

From this view of the subject, it may be concluded, that a pure Democracy, by which I mean, a Society, consisting of a small number of citizens, who assemble and administer the Government in person, can admit of no cure for the mischiefs of faction. A common passion or interest will, in almost every case, be felt by a majority of the whole; a communication and concert results from the form of Government itself; and there is nothing to check the inducements to sacrifice the weaker party, or an obnoxious individual. Hence it is, that such Democracies have ever been spectacles of turbulence and contention; have ever been found incompatible with personal security, or the rights of property; and have in general been as short in their lives, as they have been violent in their deaths. Theoretic politicians, who have patronized this species of Government, have erroneously supposed, that by reducing mankind to a perfect equality in their political rights, they would, at the same time, be perfectly equalized and assimilated in their possessions, their opinions, and their passions.

A republic, by which I mean a government in which the scheme of representation takes place, opens a different prospect, and promises the cure for which we are seeking. Let us examine the points in which it varies from pure democracy, and we shall comprehend both the nature of the cure and the efficacy which it must derive from the union.

The two great points of difference, between a democracy and a republic, are, first, the delegation of the government, in the latter, to a small number of citizens, elected by the rest; secondly, the greater number of citizens, and greater sphere of country, over which the latter may be extended.

The effect of the first difference is, on the one hand, to refine and enlarge the public views, by passing them through the medium of a chosen body of citizens, whose wisdom may best discern the true interest of their country, and whose patriotism and love of justice, will be least likely to sacrifice it to temporary or partial considerations. Under such a regulation, it may well happen, that the public voice, pronounced by the representatives of the people, will be more consonant to the public good, than if pronounced by the people themselves, convened for the purpose. On the other hand the effect may be inverted. Men of factious tempers, of local prejudices, or of sinister designs, may by intrigue, by corruption, or by other means, first obtain the suffrages, and then betray the interest of the people. The question resulting is, whether small or extensive republics are most favorable to the election of proper guardians of the public weal, and it is clearly decided in favor of the latter by two obvious considerations.

In the first place, it is to be remarked that, however small the republic may be, the representatives must be raised to a certain number, in order to guard against the cabals of a few; and that however large it may be, they must be limited to a certain number, in order to guard against the confusion of a multitude. Hence, the number of representatives in the two cases not being in proportion to that of the constituents, and being proportionally greatest in the small republic, it follows, that if the proportion of fit characters be not less in the large than in the small republic, the former will present a greater option, and consequently a greater probability of a fit choice.

In the next place, as each Representative will be chosen by a greater number of citizens in the large than in the small Republic, it will be more difficult for unworthy candidates to practise with success the vicious arts, by which elections are too often carried; and the suffrages of the people being more free, will be more likely to center on men who possess the most attractive merit, and the most diffusive and established characters.

It must be confessed, that in this, as in most other cases, there is a mean, on both sides of which inconveniences will be found to lie. By enlarging too much the number of electors, you render the representatives too little acquainted with all their local circumstances and lesser interests; as by reducing it too much, you render him unduly attached to these, and too little fit to comprehend and pursue great and national objects. The Federal Constitution forms a happy combination in this respect; the great and aggregate interests being referred to the national, the local and particular, to the state legislatures.

The other point of difference is, the greater number of citizens and extent of territory which may be brought within the compass of Republican, than of Democratic Government; and it is this circumstance principally which renders factious combinations less to be dreaded in the former, than in the latter. The smaller the society, the fewer probably will be the distinct parties and interests composing it; the fewer the distinct parties and interests, the more frequently will a majority be found of the same party; and the smaller the number of individuals composing a majority, and the smaller the compass within which they are placed, the more easily will they concert and execute their plans of oppression. Extend the sphere, and you take in a greater variety of parties and interests; you make it less probable that a majority of the whole will have a common motive to invade the rights of other citizens; or if such a common motive exists, it will be more difficult for all who feel it to discover their own strength, and to act in unison with each other. Besides other impediments, it may be remarked, that where there is a consciousness of unjust or dishonorable purposes, communication is always checked by distrust, in proportion to the number whose concurrence is necessary.

Hence it clearly appears, that the same advantage, which a Republic has over a Democracy, in controlling the effects of faction, is enjoyed by a large over a small Republic—is enjoyed by the Union over the States composing it. Does this advantage consist in the substitution of Representatives, whose enlightened views and virtuous sentiments render them superior to local prejudices, and to schemes of injustice? It will not be denied, that the Representation of the Union will be most likely to possess these requisite endowments. Does it consist in the greater security afforded by a greater variety of parties, against the event of any one party being able to outnumber and oppress the rest? In an equal degree does the increased variety of parties, comprised within the Union, increase this security? Does it, in fine, consist in the greater obstacles opposed to the concert and accomplishment of the secret wishes of an unjust and interested majority? Here, again, the extent of the Union gives it the most palpable advantage.

The influence of factious leaders may kindle a flame within their particular States, but will be unable to spread a general conflagration through the other States: a religious sect, may degenerate into a political faction in a part of the Confederacy but the variety of sects dispersed over the entire face of it, must secure the national Councils against any danger from that source: a rage for paper money, for an abolition of debts, for an equal division of property, or for any other improper or wicked project, will be less apt to pervade the whole body of the Union, than a particular member of it; in the same proportion as such a malady is more likely to taint a particular county or district, than an entire State.

In the extent and proper structure of the Union, therefore, we behold a Republican remedy for the diseases most incident to Republican Government. And according to the degree of pleasure and pride, we feel in being Republicans, ought to be our zeal in cherishing the spirit, and supporting the character of Federalists.

PUBLIUS

Appendix III

Federalist No. 51

February 6, 1788
James Madison

TO THE PEOPLE OF THE STATE OF NEW YORK.

To what expedient then shall we finally resort for maintaining in practice the necessary partition of power among the several departments, as laid down in the constitution? The only answer that can be given is, that as all these exterior provisions are found to be inadequate, the defect must be supplied, by so contriving the interior structure of the government, as that its several constituent parts may, by their mutual relations, be the means of keeping each other in their proper places. Without presuming to undertake a full development of this important idea, I will hazard a few general observations, which may perhaps place it in a clearer light, and enable us to form a more correct judgment of the principles and structure of the government planned by the convention.

In order to lay a due foundation for that separate and distinct exercise of the different powers of government, which to a certain extent, is admitted on all hands to be essential to the preservation of liberty, it is evident that each department should have a will of its own; and consequently should be so constituted, that the members of each should have as little agency as possible in the appointment of the members of the others. Were this principle rigorously adhered to, it would require that all the appointments for the supreme executive, legislative, and judiciary magistracies, should be drawn from the same fountain of authority, the people, through channels, having no communication whatever with one another. Perhaps such a plan of constructing the several departments would be less difficult in practice than it may in contemplation appear. Some difficulties however, and some additional expense, would attend the execution of it. Some deviations therefore from the principle must be admitted. In the constitution of the judiciary department in particular, it might be inexpedient to insist rigorously on the principle; first, because peculiar qualifications being essential in the members, the primary consideration ought to be to select that mode of choice, which best secures these qualifications; secondly, because the permanent tenure by which the appointments are held in that department, must soon destroy all sense of dependence on the authority conferring them.

It is equally evident that the members of each department should be as little dependent as possible on those of the others, for the emoluments annexed to their offices. Were the executive magistrate, or the judges, not independent of the legislature in this particular, their independence in every other would be merely nominal.

But the great security against a gradual concentration of the several powers in the same department, consists in giving to those who administer each department, the necessary constitutional means, and personal motives, to resist encroachments of the others. The provision for defense must in this, as in all other cases, be made commensurate to the danger of attack. Ambition must be made to counteract ambition. The interest of the man must be connected with the constitutional right of the place. It may be a reflection on human nature, that such devices should be necessary to control the abuses of government. But what is government itself but the greatest of all reflections on human nature? If men were angels, no government would be necessary. If angels were to govern men, neither external nor internal controls on government would be necessary. In framing a government which is to be administered by men over men, the great difficulty lies in this: You must first enable the government to control the governed; and in the next place, oblige it to control itself. A dependence on the people is no doubt the primary control on the government; but experience has taught mankind the necessity of auxiliary precautions.

This policy of supplying by opposite and rival interests, the defect of better motives, might be traced through the whole system of human affairs, private as well as public. We see it particularly displayed in all the subordinate distributions of power; where the constant aim is to divide and arrange the several offices in such a manner as that each may be a check on the other; that the private interest of every individual, may be a sentinel over the public rights. These inventions of prudence cannot be less requisite in the distribution of the supreme powers of the state.

But it is not possible to give to each department an equal power of self defense. In republican government the legislative authority, necessarily, predominates. The remedy for this inconveniency is, to divide the legislature into different branches; and to render them by different modes of election, and different principles of action, as little connected with each other, as the nature of their common functions, and their common dependence on the society, will admit. It may even be necessary to guard against dangerous encroachments by still further precautions. As the weight of the legislative authority requires that it should be thus divided, the weakness of the executive may require, on the other hand, that it should be fortified. An absolute negative, on the legislature, appears at first view to be the natural defense with which the executive magistrate should be armed. But perhaps it would be neither altogether safe, nor alone sufficient. On ordinary occasions, it might not be exerted with the requisite firmness; and on extraordinary occasions, it might be prefidiously abused. May not this defect of an absolute negative be supplied, by some qualified connection between this weaker department, and the weaker branch of the stronger department, by which the latter may be led to support the constitutional rights of the former, without being too much detached from the rights of its own department? If the principles on which these observations are founded be just, as I persuade myself they are, and they be applied as a criterion, to the several state constitutions, and to the federal constitution, it will be found, that if the latter does not perfectly correspond with them, the former are infinitely less able to bear such a test.

There are moreover two considerations particularly applicable to the federal system of America, which place that system in a very interesting point of view.

First. In a single republic, all the power surrendered by the people, is submitted to the administration of a single government; and usurpations are guarded against by a division of the government into distinct and separate departments. In the compound republic of America, the power surrendered by the people, is first divided between two distinct governments, and then the portion allotted to each, subdivided among distinct and separate departments. Hence a double security arises to the rights of the people. The different governments will control each other; at the same time that each will be controlled by itself.

Second. It is of great importance in a republic, not only to guard the society against the oppression of its rulers; but to guard one part of the society against the injustice of the other part. Different interests necessarily exist in different classes of citizens. If a majority be united by a common interest, the rights of the minority will be insecure. There are but two methods of providing against this evil: The one by creating a will in the community independent of the majority, that is, of the society itself, the other by comprehending in the society so many separate descriptions of citizens, as will render an unjust combination of a majority of the whole, very improbable, if not impracticable. The first method prevails in all governments possessing an hereditary or self appointed authority. This at best is but a precarious security; because a power independent of the society may as well espouse the unjust views of the major, as the rightful interests, of the minor party, and may possibly be turned against both parties. The second method will be exemplified in the federal republic of the United States. While all authority in it will be derived from and dependent on the society, the society itself will be broken into so many parts, interests and classes of citizens, that the rights of individuals or of the minority, will be in little danger from interested combinations of the majority. In a free government, the security for civil rights must be the same as for religious rights. It consists in the one case in the multiplicity of interests, and in the other, in the multiplicity of sects. The degree of security in both cases will depend on the number of interests and sects; and this may be presumed to depend on the extent of country and number of people comprehended under the same government. This view of the subject must particularly recommend a proper federal system to all the sincere and considerate friends of republican government: Since it shows that in exact proportion as the territory of the union may be formed into more circumscribed confederacies or states, oppressive combinations of a majority will be facilitated, the best security under the republican form, for the rights of every class of citizens, will be diminished; and consequently, the stability and independence of some member of the government, the only other security, must be proportionally increased. Justice is the end of government. It is the end of civil society. It ever has been, and ever will be pursued, until it be obtained, or until liberty be lost in the pursuit. In a society under the forms of which the stronger faction can readily unite and oppress the weaker, anarchy may as truly be said to reign, as in a state of nature where the weaker individual is not secured against the violence of the stronger: And as in the latter state even the stronger individuals are prompted by the uncertainty of their condition, to submit to a government which may protect the weak as well as themselves: So in the former state, will the more powerful factions or parties be gradually induced by a like motive, to wish for a government which will protect all parties, the weaker as well as the more powerful. It can be little doubted, that if the state of Rhode Island was separated from the confederacy, and left to itself, the insecurity of rights under the popular form of government within such narrow limits, would be displayed by such reiterated oppressions of factious majorities, that some power altogether independent of the people would soon be called for by the voice of the very factions whose misrule had proved the necessity of it. In the extended republic of the United States, and among the great variety of interests, parties and sects which it embraces, a coalition of a majority of the whole society could seldom take place on any other principles than those of justice and the general good; and there being thus less danger to a minor from the will of the major party, there must be less pretext also, to provide for the security of the former, by introducing into the government a will not dependent on the latter; or in other words, a will independent of the society itself. It is no less certain than it is important, notwithstanding the contrary opinions which have been entertained, that the larger the society, provided it lie within a practicable sphere, the more duly capable it will be of self government. And happily for the *republican cause*, the practicable sphere may be carried to a very great extent, by a judicious modification and mixture of the *federal principle*.

PUBLIUS

Appendix IV

Presidents, Congresses, and Chief Justices: 1789–2005

Term	President and Vice President	Party of President	Congress	Majority Party		Chief Justice of the United States
				House	Senate	
1789–1797	**George Washington** John Adams	None	1st 2nd 3rd 4th	(N/A) (N/A) (N/A) (N/A)	(N/A) (N/A) (N/A) (N/A)	John Jay (1789–1795) John Rutledge (1795) Oliver Ellsworth (1796–1800)
1797–1801	**John Adams** Thomas Jefferson	Federalist	5th 6th	(N/A) Fed	(N/A) Fed	Oliver Ellsworth (1796–1800) John Marshall (1801–1835)
1801–1809	Thomas Jefferson Aaron Burr (1801–1805) George Clinton (1805–1809)	Democratic-Republican	7th 8th 9th 10th	Dem-Rep Dem-Rep Dem-Rep Dem-Rep	Dem-Rep Dem-Rep Dem-Rep Dem-Rep	John Marshall (1801–1835)
1809–1817	**James Madison** George Clinton (1809–1812)[a] Elbridge Gerry (1813–1814)[a]	Democratic-Republican	11th 12th 13th 14th	Dem-Rep Dem-Rep Dem-Rep Dem-Rep	Dem-Rep Dem-Rep Dem-Rep Dem-Rep	John Marshall (1801–1835)
1817–1825	**James Monroe** Daniel D. Tompkins	Democratic-Republican	15th 16th 17th 18th	Dem-Rep Dem-Rep Dem-Rep Dem-Rep	Dem-Rep Dem-Rep Dem-Rep Dem-Rep	John Marshall (1801–1835)
1825–1829	**John Quincy Adams** John C. Calhoun	National-Republican	19th 20th	Nat'l Rep Dem	Nat'l Rep Dem	John Marshall (1801–1835)
1829–1837	**Andrew Jackson** John C. Calhoun (1829–1832)[c] Martin Van Buren (1833–1837)	Democrat	21st 22nd 23rd 24th	Dem Dem Dem Dem	Dem Dem Dem Dem	John Marshall (1801–1835) Roger B. Taney (1836–1864)
1837–1841	**Martin Van Buren** Richard M. Johnson	Democrat	25th 26th	Dem Dem	Dem Dem	Roger B. Taney (1836–1864)
1841	**William H. Harrison**[a] John Tyler (1841)	Whig				Roger B. Taney (1836–1864)
1841–1845	**John Tyler** (VP vacant)	Whig	27th 28th	Whig Dem	Whig Whig	Roger B. Taney (1836–1864)
1845–1849	**James K. Polk** George M. Dallas	Democrat	29th 30th	Dem Whig	Dem Dem	Roger B. Taney (1836–1864)
1849–1850	**Zachary Taylor**[a] Millard Fillmore	Whig	31st	Dem	Dem	Roger B. Taney (1836–1864)

Term	President and Vice President	Party of President	Congress	Majority Party House	Majority Party Senate	Chief Justice of the United States
1850–1853	**Millard Fillmore** (VP vacant)	Whig	32nd	Dem	Dem	Roger B. Taney (1836–1864)
1853–1857	**Franklin Pierce** William R. D. King (1853)[a]	Democrat	33rd 34th	Dem Rep	Dem Dem	Roger B. Taney (1836–1864)
1857–1861	**James Buchanan** John C. Breckinridge	Democrat	35th 36th	Dem Rep	Dem Dem	Roger B. Taney (1836–1864)
1861–1865	**Abraham Lincoln**[a] Hannibal Hamlin (1861–1865) Andrew Johnson (1865)	Republican	37th 38th	Rep Rep	Rep Rep	Roger B. Taney (1836–1864) Salmon P. Chase (1864–1873)
1865–1869	**Andrew Johnson** (VP vacant)	Republican	39th 40th	Union Rep	Union Rep	Salmon P. Chase (1864–1873)
1869–1877	**Ulysses S. Grant** Schuyler Colfax (1869–1873) Henry Wilson (1873–1875)[a]	Republican	41st 42nd 43rd 44th	Rep Rep Rep Dem	Rep Rep Rep Rep	Salmon P. Chase (1864–1873) Morrison R. Waite (1874–1888)
1877–1881	**Rutherford B. Hayes** William A. Wheeler	Republican	45th 46th	Dem Dem	Rep Dem	Morrison R. Waite (1874–1888)
1881	**James A. Garfield**[a] Chester A. Arthur	Republican	47th	Rep	Rep	Morrison R. Waite (1874–1888)
1881–1885	**Chester A. Arthur** (VP vacant)	Republican	48th	Dem	Rep	Morrison R. Waite (1874–1888)
1885–1889	**Grover Cleveland** Thomas A. Hendricks (1885)[a]	Democrat	49th 50th	Dem Dem	Rep Rep	Morrison R. Waite (1874–1888) Melville W. Fuller (1888–1910)
1889–1893	**Benjamin Harrison** Levi P. Morton	Republican	51st 52nd	Rep Dem	Rep Rep	Melville W. Fuller (1888–1910)
1893–1897	**Grover Cleveland** Adlai E. Stevenson	Democrat	53rd 54th	Dem Rep	Dem Rep	Melville W. Fuller (1888–1910)
1897–1901	**William McKinley**[a] Garret A. Hobart (1897–1899)[a] Theodore Roosevelt (1901)	Republican	55th 56th	Rep Rep	Rep Rep	Melville W. Fuller (1888–1910)
1901–1909	**Theodore Roosevelt** (VP vacant, 1901–1905) Charles W. Fairbanks (1905–1909)	Republican	57th 58th 59th 60th	Rep Rep Rep Rep	Rep Rep Rep Rep	Melville W. Fuller (1888–1910)
1909–1913	**William Howard Taft** James S. Sherman (1909–1912)[a]	Republican	61st 62nd	Rep Dem	Rep Rep	Melville W. Fuller (1888–1910) Edward D. White (1910–1921)
1913–1921	**Woodrow Wilson** Thomas R. Marshall	Democrat	63rd 64th 65th 66th	Dem Dem Dem Rep	Dem Dem Dem Rep	Edward D. White (1910–1921)
1921–1923	**Warren G. Harding**[a] Calvin Coolidge	Republican	67th	Rep	Rep	William Howard Taft (1921–1930)
1923–1929	**Calvin Coolidge** (VP vacant, 1923–1925) Charles G. Dawes (1925–1929)	Republican	68th 69th 70th	Rep Rep Rep	Rep Rep Rep	William Howard Taft (1921–1930)
1929–1933	**Herbert Hoover** Charles Curtis	Republican	71st 72nd	Rep Dem	Rep Rep	William Howard Taft (1921–1930) Charles Evans Hughes (1930–1941)

Term	President and Vice President	Party of President	Congress	Majority Party House	Majority Party Senate	Chief Justice of the United States
1933–1945	**Franklin D. Roosevelt**[a] John Nance Garner (1933–1941) Henry A. Wallace (1941–1945) Harry S Truman (1945)	Democrat	73rd 74th 75th 76th 77th 78th	Dem Dem Dem Dem Dem Dem	Dem Dem Dem Dem Dem Dem	Charles Evans Hughes (1930–1941) Harlan F. Stone (1941–1946)
1945–1953	**Harry S Truman** (VP vacant, 1945–1949) Alben W. Barkley (1949–1953)	Democrat	79th 80th 81st 82nd	Dem Rep Dem Dem	Dem Rep Dem Dem	Harlan F. Stone (1941–1946) Frederick M. Vinson (1946–1953)
1953–1961	**Dwight D. Eisenhower** Richard M. Nixon	Republican	83rd 84th 85th 86th	Rep Dem Dem Dem	Rep Dem Dem Dem	Frederick M. Vinson (1946–1953) Earl Warren (1953–1969)
1961–1963	**John F. Kennedy**[a] Lyndon B. Johnson (1961–1963)	Democrat	87th	Dem	Dem	Earl Warren (1953–1969)
1963–1969	**Lyndon B. Johnson** (VP vacant, 1963–1965) Hubert H. Humphrey (1965–1969)	Democrat	88th 89th 90th	Dem Dem Dem	Dem Dem Dem	Earl Warren (1953–1969)
1969–1974	**Richard M. Nixon**[b] Spiro Agnew (1969–1973)[c] Gerald R. Ford (1973–1974)[d]	Republican	91st 92nd	Dem Dem	Dem Dem	Earl Warren (1953–1969) Warren E. Burger (1969–1986)
1974–1977	**Gerald R. Ford** Nelson A. Rockefeller	Republican	93rd 94th	Dem Dem	Dem Dem	Warren E. Burger (1969–1986)
1977–1981	**Jimmy Carter** Walter Mondale	Democrat	95th 96th	Dem Dem	Dem Dem	Warren E. Burger (1969–1986)
1981–1989	**Ronald Reagan** George Bush	Republican	97th 98th 99th 100th	Dem Dem Dem Dem	Rep Rep Rep Dem	Warren E. Burger (1969–1986) William H. Rehnquist (1986–)
1989–1993	**George Bush** Dan Quayle	Republican	101st 102nd	Dem Dem	Dem Dem	William H. Rehnquist (1986–)
1993–2001	**Bill Clinton** Al Gore	Democrat	103rd 104th 105th 106th	Dem Rep Rep Rep	Dem Rep Rep Rep	William H. Rehnquist (1986–)
2001–2005	**George W. Bush** Dick Cheney	Republican	107th 108th 109th 110th	Rep Rep Rep	Dem Rep Rep	William H. Rehnquist (1986–)

[a]Died in office.
[b]Resigned from the presidency.
[c]Resigned from the vice presidency.
[d]Appointed vice president.

Selected Supreme Court Cases

- *Agostini* v. *Felton* **(1997):** The Court agreed to permit public school teachers to go into parochial schools during school hours to provide remedial education to disadvantaged students because it was not an excessive entanglement of church and state.

- *Alden* v. *Maine* **(1999):** In another case involving sovereign immunity, the Court ruled that Congress lacks the authority to abrogate a state's immunity in its own courts.

- *Ashcroft* v. *Free Speech Coalition* **(2002):** The Court ruled that the Child Online Protection Act of 1998 was unconstitutional because it was too vague in its reliance on "community standards" to define what is harmful to minors.

- *Avery* v. *Midland* **(1968):** The Court declared that the one-person, one-vote standard applied to counties as well as congressional and state legislative districts.

- *Baker* v. *Carr* **(1962):** Watershed case establishing the principle of one-person, one-vote, which requires that each legislative district within a state have the same number of eligible voters so that representation is equitably based on population.

- *Barron* v. *Baltimore* **(1833):** Decision that limited the application of the Bill of Rights to the actions of Congress alone.

- *Benton* v. *Maryland* **(1969):** Incorporated the Fifth Amendment's double jeopardy clause.

- *Board of Regents* v. *Southworth* **(2000):** Unanimous ruling from the Supreme Court which stated that public universities could charge students a mandatory activities fee that could be used to facilitate extracurricular student political speech so long as the programs are neutral in their application.

- *Boerne* v. *Flores* **(1997):** The Court ruled that Congress could not force the Religious Freedom Restoration act upon the state governments.

- *Bowers* v. *Hardwick* **(1986):** Unsuccessful attempt to challenge Georgia's sodomy law.

- *Boy Scouts of America* v. *Dale* **(2000):** The Court ruled that the Boy Scouts could exclude gays from serving as scoutmasters because a private group has the right to set its own moral code.

- *Bradwell* v. *Illinois* **(1873):** In this case, a woman argued that Illinois's refusal to allow her to practice law despite the fact that she had passed the bar violated her citizenship rights under the privileges and immunities clause of the Fourteenth Amendment; the justices denied her claim.

- *Bragdon* v. *Abbott* **(1998):** The Court ruled that individuals infected with HIV but not sick enough to qualify as having AIDS were protected from discrimination by the 1990 Americans with Disabilities Act (ADA).

- *Brandenburg* v. *Ohio* **(1969):** The Court fashioned the direct incitement test for deciding whether certain kinds of speech could be regulated by the government. This test holds that advocacy of illegal action is protected by the First Amendment unless imminent action is intended and likely to occur.

- *Brown* v. *Board of Education* **(1954):** U.S. Supreme Court decision holding that school segregation is inherently unconstitutional because it violates the Fourteenth Amendment's guarantee of equal protection; marked the end of legal segregation in the United States.

- *Brown* v. *Board of Education II* **(1955):** Follow-up to *Brown* v. *Board of Education*, this case laid out the process for school desegregation and established the concept of dismantling segregationist systems "with all deliberate speed."

- *Brown University* v. *Cohen* **(1997):** Landmark Title IX case that put all colleges and universities on notice that discrimination against women would not be tolerated, even when, as in the case of Brown University, the university had tremendously expanded sports opportunities for women.

- *Buckley* v. *Valeo* **(1976):** The Court ruled that money spent by an individual or political committee in support or opposition of a candidate (but independent of the candidate's campaign) was a form of symbolic speech, and therefore could not be limited under the First Amendment.

- *Bush* v. *Gore* **(2000):** Controversial 2000 election case that made the final decision on the Florida recounts, and thus, the result of the 2000 election. The Rehnquist Court broke from tradition in this case by refusing to defer to the state court's decision.

- *Cantwell* v. *Connecticut* (1940): The case in which the Supreme Court incorporated the freedom of religion, ruling that the freedom to believe is absolute, but the freedom to act is subject to the regulation of society.

- *Chandler* v. *Miller* (1997): The Supreme Court refused to allow Georgia to require all candidates for state office to pass a urinalysis thirty days before qualifying for nomination or election, concluding that this law violated the search-and-seizure clause.

- *Chaplinsky* v. *New Hampshire* (1942): Established the Supreme Court's rationale for distinguishing between protected and unprotected speech.

- *Chicago, B&O R.R. Co.* v. *Chicago* (1897): Incorporated the Fifth Amendment's just compensation clause.

- *Chisholm* v. *Georgia* (1793): The Court interpreted its jurisdiction under Article III, section 2, of the Constitution to include the right to hear suits brought by a citizen of one state against another state.

- *Civil Rights Cases* (1883): Name attached to five cases brought under the Civil Rights Act of 1875. In 1883, the Supreme Court decided that discrimination in a variety of public accommodations, including theaters, hotels, and railroads, could not be prohibited by the act because it was private and not state discrimination.

- *Clinton* v. *City of New York* (1998): The Court ruled that the line-item veto was unconstitutional because it gave powers to the president denied him by the U.S. Constitution.

- *Clinton* v. *Jones* (1997): The Court refused to reverse a lower court's decision that allowed Paula Jones's civil case against President Bill Clinton to proceed.

- *Cohens* v. *Virginia* (1821): The Court defined its jurisdiction to include the right to review all state criminal cases; additionally, this case built on *Martin* v. *Hunter's Lessee*, clarifying the Court's power to declare state laws unconstitutional.

- *Colorado Republican Federal Campaign Committee* v. *Federal Election Commission* (1996): The Supreme Court extended its ruling in *Buckley* v. *Valeo* to also include political parties.

- *Cooper* v. *Aaron* (1958): Case wherein the court broke with tradition and issued a unanimous decision against the Little Rock School Board ruling that the district's evasive schemes to avoid the *Brown II* decision were illegal.

- *Craig* v. *Boren* (1976): The Court ruled that keeping drunk drivers off the roads may be an important governmental objective, but allowing women aged eighteen to twenty-one to drink alcoholic beverages while prohibiting men of the same age from drinking is not substantially related to that goal.

- *Cruzan by Cruzan* v. *Director, Missouri Department of Health* (1990): The Court rejected any attempt to extend the right to privacy into the area of assisted suicide. However, the Court did note that individuals could terminate medical treatment if they were able to express, or had done so in writing, their desire to have medical treatment terminated in the event they became incompetent.

- *DeJonge* v. *Oregon* (1937): Incorporated the First Amendment's right to freedom of assembly.

- *Doe* v. *Bolton* (1973): In combination with *Roe* v. *Wade*, established a woman's right to an abortion.

- *Dred Scott* v. *Sandford* (1857): Concluded that the U.S. Congress lacked the constitutional authority to bar slavery in the territories; this decision narrowed the scope of national power while it enhanced that of the states. This case marks the first time since *Marbury* v. *Madison* that the Supreme Court found an act of Congress unconstitutional.

- *Duncan* v. *Louisiana* (1968): Incorporated the Sixth Amendment's trial by jury clause.

- *Engel* v. *Vitale* (1962): The Court ruled that the recitation in public classrooms of a nondenominational prayer was unconstitutional and a violation of the establishment clause.

- *Fletcher* v. *Peck* (1810): The Court ruled that state legislatures could not make laws that voided contracts or grants made by earlier legislative action.

- *Florida Prepaid* v. *College Savings Bank* (1999): The Court ruled that Congress does not have the authority under the commerce clause or the patent clause to change patent laws in a manner that would negatively affect a state's right to assert its immunity from suit.

- *Furman* v. *Georgia* (1972): The Supreme Court used this case to end capital punishment, at least in the short run. (The case was overturned by *Gregg* v. *Georgia* in 1976.)

- *Garcia* v. *San Antonio Metropolitan Transport Authority* (1985): In this case, the court ruled that Congress has the broad power to impose its will on state and local governments, even in areas that have traditionally been left to state and local discretion.

- *Gibbons* v. *Ogden* (1824): The Court upheld broad congressional power over interstate commerce.

- *Gideon* v. *Wainwright* (1963): Granted indigents the right to counsel.

- *Gitlow* v. *New York* (1925): Incorporated the free speech clause of the First Amendment, ruling that the states were not completely free to limit forms of political expression.

- *Gratz* v. *Bollinger* (2003): The Court struck down the University of Michigan's undergraduate point system, which gave minority applicants twenty automatic points simply because they were minorities.

- *Gray* v. *Sanders* (1963): Court held that voting by unit systems was unconstitutional.

- *Gregg* v. *Georgia* (1976): Overturning *Furman* v. *Georgia*, the case ruled that Georgia's rewritten death penalty statute was constitutional.

- *Griswold* v. *Connecticut* (1965): Supreme Court case that established the Constitution's implied right to privacy.

- *Grutter* v. *Bollinger* (2003): The Court voted to uphold the constitutionality of the University of Michigan's law school policy, which gave preference to minority students.

- *Harris* v. *Forklift Systems* (1993): The Court ruled that a federal civil rights law created a "broad rule of workplace equality."

- *Hoyt* v. *Florida* (1961): The Court ruled that an all-male jury did not violate a woman's rights under the Fourteenth Amendment.

- *Hunt* v. *Cromartie* (1999, 2001): Continuation of redistricting litigation begun with *Shaw* v. *Reno* (1993). The Court reversed district court conclusions that the North Carolina legislature had used race-driven criteria in violation of the equal protection clause to redraw district lines.

- *Immigration and Naturalization Service* v. *Chadha* (1983): The Court ruled that the legislative veto as it was used in many circumstances was unconstitutional because it violated the separation of powers principle.

- *Klopfer* v. *North Carolina* (1967): Incorporated the Sixth Amendment's right to a speedy trial.

- *Korematsu* v. *U.S.* (1944): In this case, the Court ruled that the internment of Japanese Americans during World War II was not unconstitutional.

- *Lawrence* v. *Texas* (2003): The Court reversed its 1986 ruling in *Bowers* v. *Hardwick* by finding a Texas statute that banned sodomy to be unconstitutional.

- *Lemon* v. *Kurtzman* (1971): The Court determined that direct government assistance to religious schools was unconstitutional. In the majority opinion, the Court created what has become known as the "Lemon Test" for deciding if a law is in violation of the establishment clause.

- *Lynch* v. *Donnelly* (1984): In a defeat for the ACLU, the Court held that a city's inclusion of a crèche in its annual Christmas display in a private park did not violate the establishment clause.

- *Malloy* v. *Hogan* (1964): Incorporated the Fifth Amendment's self-incrimination clause.

- *Mapp* v. *Ohio* (1961): Incorporated a portion of the Fourth Amendment by establishing that illegally obtained evidence cannot be used at trial.

- *Marbury* v. *Madison* (1803): Supreme Court case in which the Court first asserted the power of judicial review in finding that a congressional statute extending the Court's original jurisdiction was unconstitutional.

- *Martin* v. *Hunter's Lessee* (1816): The Court's power of judicial review in regard to state law was clarified in this case.

- *Ex parte McCardle* (1869): Post–Civil War case that reinforced Congress's power to determine the jurisdiction of the Supreme Court.

- *McCleskey* v. *Kemp* (1987): The Court ruled that the imposition of the death penalty did not violate the equal protection clause.

- *McCleskey* v. *Zant* (1991): On this appeal of the 1987 *McCleskey* case, the Court produced new standards designed to make it much more difficult for death-row inmates to file repeated appeals.

- *McCulloch v. Maryland* **(1819):** Supreme Court upheld the power of the national government and denied the right of a state to tax the bank. The Court's broad interpretation of the necessary and proper clause paved the way for later rulings upholding expansive federal powers.

- *Miller v. California* **(1973):** Case wherein the Supreme Court began to formulate rules designed to make it easier for states to regulate obscene materials and to return to communities a greater role in determining what is obscene.

- *Minor v. Happersett* **(1875):** The Supreme Court once again examined the privileges and immunities clause of the Fourteenth Amendment, ruling that voting was not a privilege of citizenship.

- *Miranda v. Arizona* **(1966):** The Fifth Amendment requires that individuals arrested for a crime must be advised of their right to remain silent and to have counsel present.

- *Morrison v. U.S.* **(2000):** The Court ruled that Congress has no authority under the commerce clause to enact a provision of the Violence Against Women Act providing a federal remedy to victims of gender-motivated violence.

- *Muller v. Oregon* **(1908):** Case that ruled Oregon's law barring women from working more than ten hours a day was constitutional; also an attempt to define women's unique status as mothers to justify their differential treatment.

- *Near v. Minnesota* **(1931):** By ruling that a state law violated the freedom of the press, the Supreme Court incorporated the free press provision of the First Amendment.

- *New York v. Smith* **(1992):** A section of the Low-Level Waste Act that required states to dispose of radioactive waste within their borders was found unconstitutional because it would force states into the service of the federal government.

- *New York Times Co. v. Sullivan* **(1964):** Supreme Court decision ruling that simply publishing a defamatory falsehood is not enough to justify a libel judgment. "Actual malice" must be proved to support a finding of libel against a public figure.

- *New York Times Co. v. U.S.* **(1971):** Also called the Pentagon Papers case; the Supreme Court ruled that any attempt by the government to prevent expression carried "a heavy presumption" against its constitutionality.

- *NLRB v. Jones and Laughlin Steel Co.* **(1937):** Case that upheld the National Labor Relations Act of 1935, marking a turning point in the Court's ideology toward the programs of President Franklin D. Roosevelt's New Deal.

- *In re Oliver* **(1948):** Incorporated the Sixth Amendment's right to a public trial.

- *Palko v. Connecticut* **(1937):** Set the Court's rationale of selective incorporation, a judicial doctrine whereby most but not all of the protections found in the Bill of Rights are made applicable to the states via the Fourteenth Amendment.

- *Parker v. Gladden* **(1966):** Incorporated the Sixth Amendment's right to an impartial trial.

- *Planned Parenthood v. Casey* **(1992):** An unsuccessful attempt to challenge Pennsylvania's restrictive abortion regulations.

- *Plessy v. Ferguson* **(1896):** *Plessy* challenged a Louisiana statute requiring that railroads provide separate accommodations for blacks and whites. The Court found that separate but equal accommodations did not violate the equal protection clause of the Fourteenth Amendment.

- *Pointer v. Texas* **(1965):** Incorporated the Sixth Amendment's right to confrontation of witnesses.

- *Printz v. U.S.* **(1997):** The Court found that Congress lacks the authority to compel state officers to execute federal laws, specifically relating to background checks on handgun purchasers.

- *Quilici v. Village of Morton Grove* **(1983):** The Supreme Court refused to review a lower court's ruling upholding the constitutionality of a local ordinance banning handguns against a Second Amendment challenge.

- *R.A.V. v. City of St. Paul* **(1992):** The Court concluded that St. Paul, Minnesota's Bias-Motivated Crime Ordinance violated the First Amendment because it regulated speech based on the content of the speech.

- *Reed v. Reed* **(1971):** Turned the tide in terms of constitutional litigation, ruling that the equal protection clause of the Fourteenth Amendment prohibited unreasonable classifications based on sex.

- *Regents of the University of California* v. *Bakke* (1978): A sharply divided Court concluded that the university's rejection of Bakke as a student had been illegal because the use of strict affirmative action quotas was inappropriate.

- *Reno* v. *American Civil Liberties Union* (1997): The Court ruled that the 1996 Communications Decency Act prohibiting transfer of obscene or indecent materials over the Internet to minors violated the First Amendment because it was too vague and overbroad.

- *Reynolds* v. *Sims* (1964): In this case, the Court decided that every person should have an equally weighted vote in electing governmental representatives.

- *Robinson* v. *California* (1962): Incorporated the Eighth Amendment's right to freedom from cruel and unusual punishment.

- *Roe* v. *Wade* (1973): The Supreme Court found that a woman's right to an abortion was protected by the right to privacy that could be implied from specific guarantees found in the Bill of Rights and the Fourteenth Amendment.

- *Romer* v. *Evans* (1996): A Colorado constitutional amendment precluding any legislative, executive, or judicial action at any state or local level designed to bar discrimination based on sexual preference was ruled not rational or reasonable.

- *Roth* v. *U.S.* (1957): The Court held that in order to be obscene, material must be "utterly without redeeming social value."

- *Santa Fe Independent School District* v. *Doe* (2000): The Court ruled that student-led, student-initiated prayer at high school football games violated the establishment clause.

- *Schenck* v. *U.S.* (1919): Case in which the Supreme Court interpreted the First Amendment to allow Congress to restrict speech that was "of such a nature as to create a clear and present danger that will bring about the substantive evils that Congress has a right to prevent."

- *Seminole Tribe* v. *Florida* (1996): Congress cannot impose a duty on states forcing them to negotiate with Indian tribes; the state's sovereign immunity protects it from a congressional directive about how to do business.

- *Shaw* v. *Reno* (1993): First in a series of redistricting cases in which the North Carolina legislature's reapportionment of congressional districts based on the 1990 Census was contested because the plan included an irregularly-shaped district in which race seemed to be a dominant consideration. The Court ruled that districts created with race as the dominant consideration violated the equal protection clause of the Fourteenth Amendment.

- *In re Sindram* (1991): The Court chastised Michael Sindram for filing his petition *in forma pauperis* to require the Maryland courts to expedite his request to expunge a $35 speeding ticket from his record.

- *The Slaughterhouse Cases* (1873): The Court upheld Louisiana's right to create a monopoly on the operation of slaughterhouses, despite the Butcher's Benevolent Association's claim that this action deprived its members of their livelihood and the privileges and immunities granted by the Fourteenth Amendment.

- *South Dakota* v. *Dole* (1987): The Court ruled that it was permissible for the federal government to require states that wanted transportation funds to pass laws setting twenty-one as the legal drinking age.

- *Stenberg* v. *Carhart* (2000): The Court ruled that a Nebraska "partial birth" abortion statute was unconstitutionally vague and unenforceable, calling into question the laws of twenty-nine other states.

- *Stromberg* v. *California* (1931): The Court overturned the conviction of a director of a Communist youth camp under a state statute prohibiting the display of a red flag.

- *Swann* v. *Charlotte-Mecklenberg School District* (1971): The Supreme Court ruled that all vestiges of *de jure* discrimination must be eliminated at once.

- *Texas* v. *Johnson* (1989): Case in which the Court overturned the conviction of a Texas man found guilty of setting fire to an American flag.

- *Tinker* v. *Des Moines Independent School District* (1969): Upheld student's rights to express themselves by wearing black armbands symbolizing protest of the Vietnam War.

- *U.S. v. Curtiss-Wright Export Corporation* **(1936):** The Court upheld the rights of Congress to grant the president authority to act in foreign affairs and to allow the president to prohibit arms shipments to participants in foreign wars.

- *U.S. v. Lopez* **(1995):** The Court invalidated a section of the Gun Free School Zones Act, ruling that regulating guns did not fall within the scope of the commerce clause, and therefore the powers of the federal government. Only states have the authority to ban guns in school zones.

- *U.S. v. Miller* **(1939):** The last time the Supreme Court addressed the constitutionality of the Second Amendment; ruled that the Amendment was only intended to protect a citizen's right to own ordinary militia weapons.

- *U.S. v. Nixon* **(1974):** In a case involving President Richard M. Nixon's refusal to turn over tape recordings of his conversations, the Court ruled that executive privilege does not grant the president an absolute right to secure all presidential documents.

- *U.S. Term Limits* v. *Thornton* **(1995):** The Supreme Court ruled that states do not have the authority to enact term limits for federal elected officials.

- *Washington* v. *Texas* **(1967):** Incorporated the Sixth Amendment's right to a compulsory trial.

- *Webster* v. *Reproductive Health Services* **(1989):** In upholding several restrictive abortion regulations, the Court opened the door for state governments to enact new restrictions on abortion.

- *Weeks* v. *U.S.* **(1914):** Case wherein the Supreme Court adopted the exclusionary rule, which bars the use of illegally obtained evidence at trial.

- *Wesberry* v. *Sanders* **(1964):** Established the principal of one person, one vote for congressional districts.

- *Wolf* v. *Colorado* **(1949):** The Court ruled that illegally obtained evidence did not necessarily have to be eliminated from use during trial.

- *Youngstown Sheet & Tube Co.* v. *Sawyer* **(1952):** The Court invalidated President Harry S Truman's seizure of the nation's steel mills.

- *Zelman* v. *Simmons-Harris* **(2002):** The Court concluded that governments can give money to parents to allow them to send their children to private or religious schools.

Notes

CHAPTER 1

1. Thomas Byrne Edsall, "The Era of Bad Feelings," *Civilization* (March/April 1996): 37.
2. Jack C. Plano and Milton Greenberg, *The American Political Dictionary*, 6th ed. (New York: Holt, Rinehart and Winston, 1982).
3. Frank Michelman, "The Republican Civic Tradition," *Yale Law Journal* 97 (1988): 1503.
4. The United States Agency for International Development, "Agency Objectives: Civil Society."
5. Thomas Carothers, "Democracy Promotion: A Key Focus in a New World Order," *Issues of Democracy* (May 2000): online.
6. Susan A. MacManus, *Young v. Old: Generational Combat in the 21st Century* (Boulder, CO: Westview Press, 1995), 3.
7. MacManus, *Young v. Old*, 4.
8. "Sixty-Five Plus in the United States," http://www.census.gov/socdemo/www/agebrief.html.
9. See William Strauss and Neil Howe, *Generations: The History of America's Future, 1984–2069* (New York: William Morrow, 1991), and Fernando Torres-Gil, *The New Aging: Politics and Generational Change in America* (New York: Auburn House, 1992).
10. William R. Buck and Tracey Rembert, "Not Just Doing It: Generation X Proves That Actions Speak Louder than Words," *Earth Action Network* (September 19, 1997): 28.
11. Buck and Rembert, "Not Just Doing It."
12. Buck and Rembert, "Not Just Doing It."
13. Teresa Gubbins, "Teens Push Aside the Boomers, Emerge As New Kings of Cool," *Times-Picayune* (April 11, 1999): B3.
14. Kavita Varma, "Family Values," *USA Today* (March 11, 1997): 6D.
15. "New Poll Finds a Majority of Americans See Illegal Immigration as a Serious Problem," Roper Poll, March 2003, http://www.NPG.org/immpoll.html.
16. Plano and Greenberg, *The American Political Dictionary*, 6th ed., 10.
17. William Safire, *Safire's New Political Dictionary* (New York: Random House, 1993), 144–45.
18. Jack C. Plano and Milton Greenberg, *The American Political Dictionary*, 9th ed. (Fort Worth, TX: Harcourt Brace, 1993), 16.
19. Safire, *Safire's New Political Dictionary*.
20. Plano and Greenberg, *The American Political Dictionary*, 6th ed., 16.
21. Philip E. Converse, "The Nature of Belief Systems in Mass Publics," in David E. Apter, ed., *Ideology and Discontent* (New York: Free Press, 1964), 206–21.
22. David Broder and Richard Morin, "Americans See 2 Distinct Bill Clintons," *Washington Post* (August 23, 1998): A10.
23. Howard Wilkinson and Patrick Crowly, "Campaign '98: Races Offer Definite Choices." *Cincinnati Enquirer* (September 7, 1998): Bl.
24. "Apathetic Voters? No, Disgusted," *Ledger* (July 12, 1998): A14.
25. Scott Shepard, "Non-voters: Too Busy or Apathetic?" *Palm Beach Post* (August 1998): 6A.

CHAPTER 2

1. See Richard B. Bernstein with Jerome Agel, *Amending America* (New York: New York Times Books, 1993), 138–40.
2. *Oregon* v. *Mitchell*, 400 U.S. 112 (1970).
3. Bernstein with Agel, *Amending America*, 139.
4. For an account of the early development of the colonies, see D. W. Meining, *The Shaping of America*, vol. 1: *Atlantic America, 1492–1800* (New Haven, CT: Yale University Press, 1986).
5. For an excellent chronology of the events leading up to the writing of the Declaration of Independence and the colonists' break with

Great Britain, see Calvin D. Lonton, ed., *The Bicentennial Almanac* (Nashville, TN: Thomas Nelson, 1975).
6. See Garry Wills, *Inventing America: Jefferson's Declaration of Independence* (New York: Random House, 1978). Wills argues that the Declaration was signed solely to secure foreign aid for the ongoing war effort.
7. See Gordon S. Wood, *The Creation of the American Republic, 1776–1787*, reissue ed. (New York: Norton, 1993).
8. For more about the Articles of Confederation, see Merrill Jensen, *The Articles of Confederation* (Madison: University of Wisconsin Press, 1940).
9. Charles A. Beard, *An Economic Interpretation of the Constitution of the United States*, reissue ed. (New York: Free Press, 1996).
10. Quoted in Richard N. Current et al., *American History: A Survey*, 6th ed. (New York: Knopf, 1983), 170.
11. John Patrick Diggins, "Power and Authority in American History: The Case of Charles A. Beard and His Critics," *American Historical Review* 86 (October 1981): 701–30; Robert Brown, *Charles Beard and the Constitution: A Critical Analysis of "An Economic Interpretation of the Constitution"* (Princeton, NJ: Princeton University Press, 1956)).
12. Jackson Turner Main, *The Anti-Federalists* (Chapel Hill: University of North Carolina, 1961).
13. Wood, *Creation of the American Republic*.
14. Quoted in Doris Faber and Harold Faber, *We the People* (New York: Charles Scribner's Sons, 1987), 31.
15. For more on the political nature of compromise at the convention, see Calvin C. Jillson, *Constitution Making: Conflict and Consensus in the Federal Constitution of 1787* (New York: Agathon, 1988).
16. Quoted in Current et al., *American History*, 168.
17. Bernard Bailyn, *The Ideological Origins of the American Revolution* (Cambridge, MA: Belknap Press, 1967).
18. *U.S. Term Limits* v. *Thornton*, 514 U.S. 779 (1995).
19. Richard E. Neustadt, *Presidential Power: The Politics of Leadership from FDR to Carter* (New York: Macmillan, 1980), 26.
20. Quoted in Faber and Faber, *We the People*, 51–52.
21. Federal Republicans favored a republican or representative form of government (do not confuse this term with the modern Republican Party, which came into being in 1854; see chapter 12). Ultimately, the word *federal* referred to the form of government embodied in the new Constitution, and *confederation* referred to a "league of states," as under the Articles, and later was applied in the "Confederacy" of 1861–1865.
22. See Ralph Ketcham, ed., *The Anti-Federalist Papers and the Constitutional Debates* (New York: New American Library, 1986).
23. See Herbert J. Storing, *What the Anti-Federalists Were For* (Chicago: University of Chicago Press, 1981), for a fuller discussion of Anti-Federalist views.
24. See Alan P. Grimes, *Democracy and the Amendments to the Constitution* (Lexington, MA: Lexington Books, 1978).
25. David E. Kyvig, *Repealing National Prohibition* (Chicago: University of Chicago Press, 1978).
26. See Jane J. Mansbridge, *Why We Lost the ERA* (Chicago: University of Chicago Press, 1986).
27. Molly Peterson, "Senate Panel Approves Constitutional Ban on Flag Desecration," LEGI-SLATE, http://www.legislate.com/xp/p-daily/i-19990422101/a-924733492/article.view.
28. *Marbury* v. *Madison*, 5 U.S. 137 (1803).
29. Speech by Attorney General Edwin Meese III before the American Bar Association, July 9, 1985, Washington, DC. See also

Antonin Scalia and Amy Gutman, eds. *A Matter of Interpretation: Federal Courts and the Law* (Princeton, NJ: Princeton University Press, 1998).

30. Speech by William J. Brennan Jr. at Georgetown University, Text and Teaching Symposium, October 10, 1985, Washington, DC.

31. Mark V. Tushnet, *Taking the Constitution Away from the Courts.* Princeton, NJ: Princeton University Press, 2000.

32. Bruce Ackerman, *We the People: Foundations* (Cambridge, MA: Belknap Press, 1991).

CHAPTER 3

1. T. R. Reid, "States Feel Less Pinch in Budgets, Services," *Washington Post* (May 9, 2004): A3. This vignette draws heavily from this work.

2. Reid, "States Feel Less Pinch."

3. Reid, "States Feel Less Pinch."

4. Alan Ehrenhalt, "Every Government's Mandate," *New York Times* (April 27, 2003), D13.

5. Kris Hundley, "Health Costs Are up 8.7%," *St. Petersburg Times* (January 3, 2003): 1E.

6. In *City of Burbank* v. *Lockheed Air Terminal,* 411 U.S. 624 (1973), the U.S. Supreme Court ruled that the city could not impose curfews on plane takeoff or landing times. The Court said that one uniform national standard was critical for safety and the national interest.

7. *Missouri* v. *Holland,* 252 U.S. 416 (1920).

8. Oral argument in *Baker by Thomas* v. *General Motors Corporation,* 522 U.S. 222 (1998), noted in Linda Greenhouse, "Court Weighs Whether One State Must Obey Another's Courts," *New York Times* (October 16, 1997): A25.

9. Catherine F. Klein, "Full Faith and Credit: Interstate Enforcement of Protection Orders Under the Violence Against Women Act of 1994," *Family Law Quarterly* 29 (1995): 253.

10. Nancy Plevin, "Ohio Frees Indian-Rights Activist 'Little Rock' Reed," *Santa Fe New Mexican* (March 12, 1999): B1.

11. *New Mexico ex rel. Ortiz* v. *Reed,* 524 U.S. 151 (1998).

12. *New Jersey* v. *New York,* 523 U.S. 767 (1998).

13. John Mountjoy, "Interstate Cooperation: Interstate Compacts Make a Comeback," *Council of State Governments,* available online at http://www.csg.org.

14. *McCulloch* v. *Maryland,* 17 U.S. 316 (1819).

15. *Gibbons* v. *Ogden,* 22 U.S. 1 (1824).

16. *Dred Scott* v. *Sandford,* 60 U.S. 393 (1857).

17. *Plessy* v. *Ferguson,* 163 U.S. 537 (1896).

18. *Panhandle Oil Co.* v. *Knox,* 277 U.S. 218, 223 (1928).

19. *Indian Motorcycle Co.* v. *U.S.,* 238 U.S. 570 (1931).

20. *Pensacola Telegraph* v. *Western Union,* 96 U.S. 1 (1877).

21. *U.S.* v. *E. C. Knight,* 156 U.S. 1 (1895).

22. *Pollock* v. *Farmers Loan and Trust,* 157 U.S. 429 (1895); and *Springer* v. *U.S.,* 102 U.S. 586 (1881).

23. John O. McGinnis, "The State of Federalism," testimony before the Senate Government Affairs Committee, May 5, 1999.

24. *NLRB* v. *Jones and Laughlin Steel Co.,* 301 U.S. 1 (1937).

25. *U.S.* v. *Darby Lumber Co.,* 312 U.S. 100 (1941).

26. *Wickard* v. *Filburn,* 317 U.S. 111 (1942).

27. Morton Grodzins, "Centralization and Decentralization in the American Federal System," in Robert A. Goldwin, ed., *A Nation of States* (Chicago: Rand McNally, 1963), 3–4.

28. Alice M. Rivlin, *Reviving the American Dream* (Washington, DC: Brookings Institution, 1992), 92.

29. Rivlin, *Reviving the American Dream,* 98.

30. Richard P. Nathan et al., *Reagan and the States* (Princeton, NJ: Princeton University Press, 1987), 4.

31. "Devolutionary Thinking Is Now Part of a Larger Critique of Modern Governmental Experience," *Public Perspective* (April/May 1995): 28.

32. Richard Wolf, "States Bracing for Leaner Times," *USA Today* (July 10, 2000): 1A.

33. Reid, "States Feel Less Pinch."

34. David S. Broder, "So, Now Bigger Is Better?" *Washington Post* (January 12, 2003): B1.

35. Marianne Arneberg, "Cuomo Assails Judicial Hodgepodge," *Newsday* (August 15, 1990): 15.

36. *Webster* v. *Reproductive Health Services,* 492 U.S. 490 (1989).

37. *Planned Parenthood of Southeastern Pennsylvania* v. *Casey,* 505 U.S. 833 (1992).

38. *Stenberg* v. *Carhart,* 530 U.S. 914 (2000).

39. *U.S.* v. *Lopez,* 514 U.S. 549 (1995).

40. *Seminole Tribe* v. *Florida,* 517 U.S. 44 (1996).

41. *Boerne* v. *Flores,* 521 U.S. 507 (1997).

42. *Printz* v. *U.S.,* 521 U.S. 898 (1997).

43. *Florida Prepaid* v. *College Savings Bank,* 527 U.S. 627 (1999).

44. *Bush* v. *Gore,* 531 U.S. 98 (2000).

45. Linda Greenhouse, "In a Momentous Term, Justices Remake the Law and the Court," *New York Times* (July 1, 2003): A18.

46. *Nevada Department of Human Resources* v. *Hibbs,* 538 U.S. 72 (2003).

CHAPTER 4

1. Terry McCarthy, "Can the Terminator Save California," *Time* (July 14, 2003): 38–39.

2. Roger Simon, "Coastal Disturbance," *U.S. News and World Report* (September 22, 2003): 20.

3. Karen Tumulty, "The Five Meanings of Arnold," *Time* (October 20, 2003): 27.

4. Peter K. Eisinger, *The Rise of the Entrepreneurial State* (Madison: University of Wisconsin Press, 1988).

5. Albert L. Sturm, "The Development of American State Constitutions," *Publius* 12 (Winter 1982): 62–68.

6. Albert L. Kohlmeier, *The Old Northwest As the Keystone of the Arch of the American Federal Union* (Bloomington, IN: Principia Press, 1938), and *Pathways to the Old Northwest* (Indianapolis: Indiana Historical Society, 1988).

7. George E. Mowry, *The Progressive Era, 1900–1920* (Washington, DC: American Historical Association, 1972).

8. Janice C. May, "Constitutional Amendment and Revision Revisited," *Publius* 12 (Winter 1982): 153–79.

9. Charles Wiggins, "Executive Vetoes and Legislative Overrides in the American States," *Journal of Politics* 54 (November 1980): 42. Also see Glenn Abney and Thomas Lauth, "The Line-Item Veto in the States," *Public Administration Review* 45 (January/February 1985): 66–79.

10. F. Ted Hebert, Jeffrey L. Brudney, and Deil S. Wright, "Gubernatorial Influence and State Bureaucracy," *American Politics Quarterly* 11 (April 1983): 37–52; and Abney and Lauth, "The Governor As Chief Administrator," *Public Administration Quarterly* 3 (January/February 1983): 40–49.

11. Thad L. Beyle and Robert Dalton, "Appointment Power: Does It Belong to the Governor?" *State Government* 54(1) (Winter 1981): 6.

12. Leon W. Blevins, *Texas Government in National Perspective* (Englewood Cliffs, NJ: Prentice Hall, 1987), 169.

13. James L. Garnett, *Reorganizing State Government: The Executive Branch* (Boulder, CO: Westview, 1980), 8–9; and Diane Kincaid Blair, "The Gubernatorial Appointment Power: Too Much of a Good Thing?" *State Government* 55 (Summer 1982): 88–91.

14. Timothy O'Rourke, *The Impact of Reapportionment* (New Brunswick, NJ: Transaction Books, 1980).

15. Council of State Governments, *Book of the States, 2000–2001* (Lexington, KY: Council of State Governments, 2000), 49.

16. "Schwarzenegger Wants Part-time Legislature," *SFGate.com,* posted April 7, 2004, http://sfgate.com/cgi-bin/article.cgi?file=/news/archive/2004/04/07/state0515EDT0029.DTL.

17. Gerald Benjamin and Michael J. Malin, eds., *Limiting Legislative Terms* (Washington, DC: CQ Press, 1992).

18. Diana Gordon, "Citizen Legislators—Alive and Well," *State Legislatures* 20 (January 1994): 24–27.

19. Earl M. Maltz, "Federalism and State Court Activism," *Intergovernmental Perspective* (Spring 1987): 23–26.

20. Thomas E. Cronin, *Direct Democracy* (Cambridge, MA: Harvard University Press, 1989); and David B. Magleby, *Direct Legislation* (Baltimore, MD: Johns Hopkins University Press, 1984).

21. Patrick McMahon, "Voters Like Recall Idea, but Few Want One," *USA Today* (October 14, 2003): 3A; Andy Bowers, "Can You Recall Your Governor?" *Slate,* July 30, 2003, http://slate.msn.com/id/2086409/.

22. Alexis de Tocqueville, *Democracy in America,* ed. Phillips Bradley (New York: Knopf, 1945), 40.

23. *City of Clinton* v. *Cedar Rapids and Missouri River Railroad Co.* (Iowa, 1868).

24. Steven P. Erie, *Rainbow's End: Irish-Americans and the Dilemmas of Urban Machine Politics, 1840–1985* (Berkeley: University of California Press, 1988); Alfred Steinberg, *The Bosses* (New York: New American Library, 1972); Seymour Mandelbaum, *Boss Tweed's New York* (New York: Wiley, 1955); and Milton Rakove, *Don't Make No Waves—Don't Back No Losers: An Insider's Analysis of the Daley Machine* (Bloomington: Indiana University Press, 1975).

25. Samuel P. Hays, "The Politics of Reform in Municipal Government in the Progressive Era," *Pacific Northwest Quarterly* 55 (October 1964): 157–66.

26. Raymond Wolfinger, "Reputation and Reality in the Study of Community Power," *American Sociological Review* 25 (October 1960): 636–44; Nelson Polsby, *Community Power and Political Theory* (New Haven, CT: Yale University Press, 1963); and Robert E. Agger, Daniel Goldrich, and Bert Swanson, *The Rulers and the Ruled: Political Power and Impotence in American Communities* (New York: Wiley, 1964).

27. Laura R. Woliver, *From Outrage to Action: The Politics of Grass-Roots Dissent* (Urbana: University of Illinois Press, 1993); and Matthew A. Crenson, *Neighborhood Politics* (Cambridge, MA: Harvard University Press, 1983).

28. Sharon O'Brien, *American Indian Tribal Governments* (Norman: University of Oklahoma Press, 1989), 261–97.

29. U.S. Census Bureau, *Government Finances in 1993–1994* (Washington, DC: Government Printing Office, 1994), 12–19.

30. http://www.nga.org/center/divisions/1,1188,C_ISSUE_BRIEF^D_2915,00.html.

31. Dennis Cauchon, "States Getting Budgets Under Control," *USA Today* (November 12, 2003): 3A.

32. Steven Ginsberg and Chris L. Jenkins, "Vote Quiets Anti-Tax Clarion Call in Virginia," *Washington Post* (April 29, 2004): A1.

CHAPTER 5

1. Janny Scott, "Protesters Are Denied Potent Tactic of the Past," *New York Times* (February 13, 2003): B1.

2. "Restrictions Overreach," *USA Today* (May 27, 2003): 14A.

3. Charles Lane, "Court Made Dramatic Shifts in Law," *Washington Post* (June 30, 2002): A6.

4. The absence of a bill of rights led Mason to refuse to sign the proposed Constitution, noting that he "would sooner chop off his right hand than put it to the Constitution as it now stands." Quoted in Eric Black, *Our Constitution: The Myth That Binds Us* (Boulder, CO: Westview, 1988), 75.

5. Quoted in Jack N. Rakove, "Madison Won Passage of the Bill of Rights but Remained a Skeptic," *Public Affairs Report* (March 1991): 6.

6. *Barron* v. *Baltimore,* 32 U.S. 243 (1833).

7. *Allgeyer* v. *Louisiana,* 165 U.S. 578 (1897).

8. *Gitlow* v. *New York,* 268 U.S. 652 (1925).

9. *Near* v. *Minnesota,* 283 U.S. 697 (1931). For more about *Near,* see Fred W. Friendly, *Minnesota Rag: The Dramatic Story of the Landmark Case That Gave New Meaning to Freedom of the Press* (New York: Random House, 1981).

10. *Palko* v. *Connecticut,* 302 U.S. 319 (1937).

11. Continental Congress to the People of Great Britain, October 21, 1774, in Philip Kurland and Ralph Lerner, eds., *The Founders' Constitution,* vol. 5 (Chicago: University of Chicago Press, 1987), 61.

12. *Reynolds* v. *U.S.,* 98 U.S. 145 (1879).

13. *Cantwell* v. *Connecticut,* 310 U.S. 296 (1940).

14. *Zobrest* v. *Catalina Foothills School District,* 506 U.S. 813 (1992).

15. *Engel* v. *Vitale,* 370 U.S. 421 (1962).

16. *Lee* v. *Weisman,* 505 U.S. 577 (1992).

17. *Santa Fe Independent School District* v. *Doe,* 530 U.S. 290 (2000).

18. *Elk Grove* v. *Newdow,* 124 S.Ct. 2301 (2004).

19. *Lemon* v. *Kurtzman,* 403 U.S. 602 (1971).

20. "An Eternal Debate," *Omaha World-Journal* (November 27, 2002): 6B.

21. *Widmar* v. *Vincent,* 454 U.S. 263 (1981).

22. *Board of Education* v. *Mergens,* 496 U.S. 226 (1990).

23. *Lamb's Chapel* v. *Center Moriches Union Free School District,* 508 U.S. 384 (1993).

24. *Rosenberger* v. *University of Virginia,* 515 U.S. 819 (1995).

25. *Agostini* v. *Felton,* 521 U.S. 203 (1997).

26. *Mitchell* v. *Helms,* 530 U.S. 793 (2000).

27. *Zelman* v. *Simmons-Harris,* 536 U.S. 639 (2002).

28. Charles Lane, "Court Upholds Ohio School Vouchers," *Washington Post* (June 28, 2002): A1, A11.

29. *Employment Division, Dept. of Human Resources of Oregon* v. *Smith,* 494 U.S. 872 (1990).

30. *Boerne* v. *Flores,* 521 U.S. 507 (1997).

31. *Church of the Lukumi Babalu Aye* v. *Hialeah,* 508 U.S. 525 (1993).

32. *U.S.* v. *Seeger,* 380 U.S. 163 (1965).

33. *Cruz* v. *Beto,* 405 U.S. 319 (1972).

34. *O'Lone* v. *Shabazz,* 482 U.S. 342 (1987).

35. Tony Mauro, "Stern's Raunch Is Better than Silence," *USA Today* (May 12, 2004): 13A.

36. *Ex parte McCardle,* 74 U.S. 506 (1869).

37. David M. O'Brien, *Constitutional Law and Politics,* vol. 2: *Civil Rights and Civil Liberties* (New York: Norton, 1991), 345.

38. See Frederick Siebert, *The Rights and Privileges of the Press* (New York: Appleton-Century, 1934), 886, 931–40.

39. *Schenck* v. *U.S.,* 249 U.S. 47 (1919).

40. *Brandenburg* v. *Ohio,* 395 U.S. 444 (1969).

41. *New York Times Co.* v. *Sullivan,* 403 U.S. 713 (1971).

42. *Nebraska Press Association* v. *Stuart,* 427 U.S. 539 (1976).

43. *Abrams* v. *U.S.,* 250 U.S. 616 (1919).

44. *Stromberg* v. *California,* 283 U.S. 359 (1931).

45. *Tinker* v. *Des Moines Independent Community School District,* 393 U.S. 503 (1969).

46. *Texas* v. *Johnson,* 491 U.S. 397 (1989).

47. *U.S.* v. *Eichman,* 496 U.S. 310 (1990).

48. Harry Kalven Jr., *Negro and the First Amendment* (Chicago: University of Chicago Press, 1966).

49. Henry Louis Gates Jr., "Why Civil Liberties Pose No Threat to Civil Rights," *New Republic* (September 20, 1993).

50. *R.A.V.* v. *City of St. Paul,* 505 U.S. 377 (1992).

51. *Virginia* v. *Black,* 538 U.S. 343 (2003).

52. *Chaplinsky* v. *New Hampshire,* 315 U.S. 568 (1942).

53. *New York Times Co.* v. *Sullivan,* 376 U.S. 254 (1964).

54. *Masson* v. *New Yorker Magazine,* 501 U.S. 496 (1991).

55. "Making It Official," *Pittsburgh Post Gazette,* December 4, 2001, LEXIS.

56. *Chaplinsky* v. *New Hampshire,* 315 U.S. 568 (1942).

57. *Cohen* v. *California,* 403 U.S. 15 (1971).

58. *Regina* v. *Hicklin,* L.R. 2 Q.B. 360 (1868).

59. *Roth* v. *U.S.,* 354 U.S. 476 (1957).

60. *Miller* v. *California,* 413 U.S. 15 (1973).

61. *Barnes* v. *Glen Theater,* 501 U.S. 560 (1991).

62. *National Endowment for the Arts* v. *Finley,* 524 U.S. 569 (1998).

63. *Reno* v. *American Civil Liberties Union*, 521 U.S. 844 (1997).
64. *Ashcroft* v. *Free Speech Coalition*, 535 U.S. 234 (2002).
65. David G. Savage, "Ban on 'Virtual' Child Porn Is Upset by Court," *Los Angeles Times* (April 17, 2002): A1.
66. Lyle Denniston, "Court Puts 2D Pornography Law on Hold: A Majority Doubt Giving Localities an Internet Veto," *Boston Globe* (May 14, 2002): A2.
67. Nick Anderson and Elizabeth Levin, "Crime Bill Passes Easily in Congress: Measure Includes Expansion of Amber Alert System," *Los Angeles Times* (April 11, 2003): A36.
68. *Ashcroft* v. *American Civil Liberties Union*, 124 S.Ct. 2783 (2004).
69. *DeJonge* v. *Oregon*, 229 U.S. 353 (1937).
70. *Barron* v. *Baltimore*, 32 U.S. 243 (1833).
71. *Dred Scott* v. *Sandford*, 60 U.S. 393 (1857).
72. *U.S.* v. *Miller*, 307 U.S. 174 (1939).
73. *Quilici* v. *Village of Morton Grove*, 104 U.S. 194 (1983).
74. *Printz* v. *U.S.*, 514 U.S. 898 (1997).
75. *Stein* v. *New York*, 346 U.S. 156 (1953).
76. *Wilson* v. *Arkansas*, 514 U.S. 927 (1995).
77. *U.S.* v. *Sokolov*, 490 U.S. 1 (1989).
78. *U.S.* v. *Knights*, 534 U.S. 112 (2001).
79. *U.S.* v. *Matlock*, 415 U.S. 164 (1974).
80. *Johnson* v. *U.S.*, 333 U.S. 10 (1948).
81. *Winston* v. *Lee*, 470 U.S. 753 (1985).
82. *South Dakota* v. *Neville*, 459 U.S. 553 (1983).
83. *Michigan* v. *Tyler*, 436 U.S. 499 (1978).
84. *Hester* v. *U.S.*, 265 U.S. 57 (1924).
85. *Kyllo* v. *U.S.*, 533 U.S. 27 (2001).
86. David G. Savage, "Court Says No to Home Snooping," *Los Angeles Times* (June 12, 2001): A1.
87. *Carroll* v. *U.S.*, 267 U.S. 132 (1925).
88. *U.S.* v. *Arvizu*, 534 U.S. 266 (2002).
89. *Skinner* v. *Railway Labor Executives' Association*, 489 U.S. 602 (1989).
90. *Vernonia School District* v. *Acton*, 515 U.S. 646 (1995).
91. *Board of Education of Independent School District No. 92 of Pottawatomie County* v. *Earls*, 536 U.S. 822 (2002).
92. *Ferguson* v. *City of Charleston*, 532 U.S. 67 (2001).
93. *Chandler* v. *Miller*, 520 U.S. 305 (1997).
94. John Wefing, "Employer Drug Testing: Disparate Judicial and Legislative Responses," *Albany Law Review* 63 (2000): 799–801.
95. *Counselman* v. *Hitchcock*, 142 U.S. 547 (1892).
96. *Brown* v. *Mississippi*, 297 U.S. 278 (1936).
97. *Lynumm* v. *Illinois*, 372 U.S. 528 (1963).
98. *Rhode Island* v. *Innis*, 446 U.S. 291 (1980).
99. *Arizona* v. *Fulminante*, 500 U.S. 938 (1991).
100. *Dickerson* v. *U.S.*, 530 U.S. 428 (2000).
101. *Weeks* v. *U.S.*, 232 U.S. 383 (1914).
102. *Mapp* v. *Ohio*, 367 U.S. 643 (1961).
103. *Stone* v. *Powell*, 428 U.S. 465 (1976).
104. *Johnson* v. *Zerbst*, 304 U.S. 458 (1938).
105. *Powell* v. *Alabama*, 287 U.S. 45 (1932).
106. *Gideon* v. *Wainwright*, 372 U.S. 335 (1963).
107. *Argersinger* v. *Hamlin*, 407 U.S. 25 (1972).
108. *Scott* v. *Illinois*, 440 U.S. 367 (1979).
109. *Alabama* v. *Shelton*, 536 U.S. 654 (2002).
110. *Strauder* v. *West Virginia*, 100 U.S. 303 (1880).
111. *Taylor* v. *Louisiana*, 419 U.S. 522 (1975).
112. *Batson* v. *Kentucky*, 476 U.S. 79 (1986).
113. *Maryland* v. *Craig*, 497 U.S. 836 (1990).
114. *Hallinger* v. *Davis*, 146 U.S. 314 (1892).
115. *O'Neil* v. *Vermont*, 144 U.S. 323 (1892).
116. See Michael Meltsner, *Cruel and Unusual: The Supreme Court and Capital Punishment* (New York: Random House, 1973).
117. *Furman* v. *Georgia*, 408 U.S. 238 (1972).
118. *Gregg* v. *Georgia*, 428 U.S. 153 (1976).
119. *McCleskey* v. *Kemp*, 481 U.S. 279 (1987).

120. *McCleskey* v. *Zant*, 499 U.S. 467 (1991).
121. *Atkins* v. *Virginia*, 536 U.S. 304 (2002).
122. Joan Biskupic, "Retarded Convicts Can't Be Executed," *USA Today* (June 21, 2002): 1A.
123. Henry Weinstein, "Inmate Seeks to Halt Execution for DNA Tests," *Los Angeles Times* (April 28, 2002): A20.
124. Henry Weinstein, "Judge Leans Toward Declaring Death Penalty Unconstitutional," *Los Angeles Times* (April 26, 2002): A22.
125. *Olmstead* v. *U.S.*, 277 U.S. 438 (1928).
126. *Griswold* v. *Connecticut*, 381 U.S. 481 (1965).
127. *Eisenstadt* v. *Baird*, 410 U.S. 113 (1972).
128. *Roe* v. *Wade*, 410 U.S. 113 (1973).
129. *Beal* v. *Doe*, 432 U.S. 438 (1977); and *Harris* v. *McRae*, 448 U.S. 297 (1980).
130. *Webster* v. *Reproductive Health Services*, 492 U.S. 490 (1989).
131. *Planned Parenthood of Southeastern Pennsylvania* v. *Casey*, 502 U.S. 1056 (1992).
132. Karen O'Connor, *No Neutral Ground: Abortion Politics in an Age of Absolutes* (Boulder, CO: Westview, 1996).
133. "House Sends Partial Birth Abortion Bill to Clinton," *Politics USA* (March 28, 1996): 1.
134. *Stenberg* v. *Carhart*, 530 U.S. 914 (2000).
135. *Hill* v. *Colorado*, 530 U.S. 703 (2000).
136. *Bowers* v. *Hardwick*, 478 U.S. 186 (1986).
137. *Lawrence* v. *Texas*, 539 U.S. 558 (2003).
138. *Boy Scouts of America* v. *Dale*, 530 U.S. 640 (2000).
139. Charles Lane, "Poll: Americans Say Court Is 'About Right,'" *Washington Post* (July 7, 2002): A15.
140. Lane, "Poll."
141. *Cruzan* v. *Director, Missouri Dept. of Health*, 497 U.S. 261 (1990).
142. *Vacco* v. *Quill*, 521 U.S. 793 (1997).
143. Office of the Attorney General, Memorandum for Asa Hutchinson, Administrator, the Drug Enforcement Administration, November 6, 2001.
144. William McCall, "Oregon Suicide Law Gets Longer Reprieve: Court Allows US Senate 5 Months to Ready Arguments," *Boston Globe* (November 21, 2001): A8.
145. *Oregon* v. *Ashcroft*, 192 F. Supp. 2d 1077 (2002); and Kim Murphy, "U.S. Cannot Block Oregon Suicide Law, Judge Rules," *Los Angeles Times* (April 18, 2002): A1.

CHAPTER 6

1. Michael Cooper, "Officers in Bronx Fire 41 Shots, and an Unarmed Man Is Killed," *New York Times* (February 5, 1999): A1.
2. Amy Wilentz, "New York: The Price of Safety in a Police State," *Los Angeles Times* (April 11, 1999): M1.
3. N. R. Kleinfield, "Veterans of 60's Protests Meet the Newly Outraged in a March," *New York Times* (April 16, 1999): B8.
4. *Civil Rights Cases*, 109 U.S. 3 (1883).
5. *Plessy* v. *Ferguson*, 163 U.S. 537 (1896).
6. Jack Greenburg, *Judicial Process and Social Change: Constitutional Litigation* (St. Paul, MN: West, 1976), 583–86.
7. Juan Williams, *Eyes on the Prize: America's Civil Rights Years, 1954–1965* (New York: Penguin, 1987), 10.
8. *Williams* v. *Mississippi*, 170 U.S. 213 (1898); *Cummins* v. *Richmond County Board of Education*, 175 U.S. 528 (1899).
9. *Muller* v. *Oregon*, 208 U.S. 412 (1908).
10. *Missouri* ex rel. *Gaines* v. *Canada*, 305 U.S. 337 (1938).
11. Richard Kluger, *Simple Justice* (New York: Vintage, 1975), 268.
12. *Sweatt* v. *Painter*, 339 U.S. 629 (1950); and *McLaurin* v. *Oklahoma*, 339 U.S. 637 (1950).
13. *Sweatt* v. *Painter*, 339 U.S. 629 (1950).
14. *Brown* v. *Board of Education*, 347 U.S. 483 (1954).
15. But see Gerald Rosenberg, *Hollow Hope: Can Courts Bring About Social Change* (Chicago: University of Chicago Press, 1991).
16. Quoted in Williams, *Eyes on the Prize*, 10.

17. *Brown* v. *Board of Education II,* 349 U.S. 294 (1955).
18. Quoted in Williams, *Eyes on the Prize,* 37.
19. *Cooper* v. *Aaron,* 358 U.S. 1 (1958).
20. *Heart of Atlanta Motel* v. *U.S.,* 379 U.S. 241 (1964).
21. *Swann* v. *Charlotte-Mecklenburg School District,* 402 U.S. 1 (1971).
22. *Freeman* v. *Pitts,* 498 U.S. 1081 (1992); *Missouri* v. *Jenkins,* 515 U.S. 70 (1995).
23. Gary Orfield, "Turning Back to Segregation" in Gary Orfield, S. Eaton, and the Harvard Project on Desegregation, eds., *Dismantling Desegregation* (New York: New Press, 1996).
24. *Griggs* v. *Duke Power Co.,* 401 U.S. 424 (1971).
25. Jo Freeman, *The Politics of Women's Liberation* (New York: Longman, 1975), 57.
26. *Hoyt* v. *Florida,* 368 U.S. 57 (1961).
27. Betty Friedan, *The Feminine Mystique* (New York: Dell, 1963).
28. *Korematsu* v. *U.S.,* 323 U.S. 214 (1944). This is the only case involving race-based distinctions applying the strict scrutiny standard where the Court has upheld the restrictive law.
29. *Reed* v. *Reed,* 404 U.S. 71 (1971).
30. *Craig* v. *Boren,* 429 U.S. 190 (1976).
31. *Mississippi University for Women* v. *Hogan,* 458 U.S. 718 (1982).
32. *Craig* v. *Boren,* 429 U.S. 190 (1976).
33. *Orr* v. *Orr,* 440 U.S. 268 (1979).
34. *JEB* v. *Alabama* ex rel. *TB,* 440 U.S. 268 (1979).
35. *U.S.* v. *Virginia,* 518 U.S. 515 (1996).
36. *Nguyen* v. *INS,* 533 U.S. 53 (2001).
37. *Rostker* v. *Goldberg,* 453 U.S. 57 (1981).
38. *Michael M.* v. *Superior Court of Sonoma County,* 450 U.S. 464 (1981).
39. *Rostker* v. *Goldberg,* 453 U.S. 57 (1981).
40. *U.S.* v. *Virginia,* 518 U.S. 515 (1996).
41. "How Much Will the Wage Gap Cost You?" http://www.aflcio.org/issuespolitics/women/equalpay/equalpay.cfm. Accessed May 18, 2004.
42. *Meritor Savings Bank* v. *Vinson,* 477 U.S. 57 (1986).
43. *Oncale* v. *Sundowner Offshore Services, Inc.,* 523 U.S. 75 (1998).
44. *Hishon* v. *King & Spalding,* 467 U.S. 69 (1984).
45. *Johnson* v. *Transportation Agency,* 480 U.S. 616 (1987).
46. *Davis* v. *Monroe County Board of Education,* 526 U.S. 629 (1999).
47. Joyce Gelb and Marian Lief Palley, *Women and Public Policies* (Charlottesville: University of Virginia Press, 1996).
48. Ernesto B. Virgil, *The Crusade for Justice* (Madison: University of Wisconsin Press, 1999).
49. F. Chris Garcia, *Latinos and the Political System* (Notre Dame, IN: University of Notre Dame Press, 1988), 1.
50. *White* v. *Register,* 412 U.S. 755 (1973).
51. *San Antonio Independent School District* v. *Rodriguez,* 411 U.S. 1 (1973).
52. *Plyler* v. *Doe,* 457 U.S. 202 (1982).
53. *Edgewood Independent School District* v. *Kirby,* 777 SW.2d 391 (1989).
54. "MALDEF 'Pleased with Settlement of California Public Schols Inequity Case, *Williams* v. *California,*" August 13, 2004.
55. Rennard Strickland, "Native Americans," in Kermit Hall, ed., *The Oxford Companion to the Supreme Court of the United States* (New York: Oxford University Press, 1992), 557.
56. Strickland, "Native Americans," 579.
57. Dee Brown, *Bury My Heart at Wounded Knee* (New York: Holt, Rinehart and Winston, 1971).
58. Hugh Dellios, "Rites by Law: Indians Seek Sacred Lands," *Chicago Tribune* (July 4, 1993): C1.
59. *Employment Division of the Oregon Department of Human Resources* v. *Smith,* 494 U.S. 872 (1990).
60. *Boerne* v. *Flores,* 521 U.S. 507 (1997).
61. *Cobell* v. *Norton,* 204 F.3d 1081 (2001). For more on the Indian trust, see http://www.indiantrust.com/overview.cfm.
62. Richard Luscombe, "Tribes Go on Legal Warpath," *The Observer* (April 25, 2004): 20.

63. Diane Helene Miller, *Freedom to Differ: The Shaping of the Gay and Lesbian Struggle for Civil Rights* (New York: New York University Press, 1998).
64. Sarah Brewer, David Kaib, and Karen O'Connor, "Sex and the Supreme Court: Gays, Lesbians, and Justice," in Craig A. Rimmerman, Kenneth D. Wald, and Clyde Wilcox, eds., *The Politics of Gay Rights* (Chicago: University of Chicago Press, 2000).
65. Evan Gerstmann, *The Constitutional Underclass: Gays, Lesbians, and the Failure of Class-Based Equal Protection* (Chicago: University of Chicago Press, 1999).
66. Deborah Ensor, "Gay Veterans Working for Change," *San Diego Union* (April 13, 2002): B1.
67. *Romer* v. *Evans,* 517 U.S. 620 (1996).
68. *Lawrence* v. *Texas,* 539 U.S. 558 (2003).
69. Joan Biskupic, "Court's Opinion on Gay Rights Reflects Trends," *USA Today* (July 18, 2003): 2A.
70. David Pfeiffer, "Overview of the Disability Movement: History, Legislative Record and Political Implications," *Policy Studies Journal* (Winter 1993): 724–42; and "Understanding Disability Policy," *Policy Studies Journal* (Spring 1996): 157–74.
71. Joan Biskupic, "Supreme Court Limits Meaning of Disability," *Washington Post* (June 23, 1999): A1.
72. *Sutton* v. *United Air Lines, Inc.,* 527 U.S. 471 (1999).
73. *Tennessee* v. *Lane,* 2004 U.S. LEXIS 3386 (2004).
74. CNN/*USA Today*/Gallup Poll, May 30, 2003, NEXIS.
75. *Regents of the University of California* v. *Bakke,* 438 U.S. 265 (1978).
76. *Johnson* v. *Santa Clara County,* 480 U.S. 616 (1987).
77. Ruth Marcus, "Hill Coalition Aims to Counter Court in Job Bias," *Washington Post* (February 8, 1990): A10.
78. *Adarand Constructors* v. *Pena,* 515 U.S. 200 (1995).
79. Cert. denied, *Texas* v. *Hopwood,* 518 U.S. 1033 (1996). See also Terrance Stutz, "UT Minority Enrollment Tested by Suit: Fate of Affirmative Action in Education Is at Issue," *Dallas Morning News* (October 14, 1995).
80. *Grutter* v. *Bollinger,* 539 U.S. 306 (2003).
81. *Gratz* v. *Bollinger,* 539 U.S. 306 (2003).
82. *Grutter* v. *Bollinger,* 539 U.S. 306 (2003).
83. Michael Markowitz, "Gay Rights: Shareholders' Power Is the New Weapon in the Fight for Workplace Equality." *Newsday* (January 4, 2004): F10.
84. Victoria Colliver, "Class Action Considered in Wal-Mart Suit," *San Francisco Chronicle* (September 25, 2003): B1.
85. "Wal-Mart's Immigrant Labor Problem," *Tampa Tribune* (November 14, 2003): 10.

CHAPTER 7

1. For an outstanding account of Pelosi's campaign for the whip post, see Juliet Eilperin, "The Making of Madam Whip: Fear and Loathing—and Horse Trading—The Race for the House's No. 2 Democrat," *Washington Post* (January 6, 2002): W27.
2. "Mother of All Whips," *Pittsburgh Post-Gazette* (February 9, 2002): A11.
3. Sue Thomas, *How Women Legislate* (New York: Oxford University Press, 1994); and Karen O'Connor, ed., *Women and Congress: Running, Winning and Ruling* (New York: Haworth Press, 2002).
4. Barbara Hinckley, *Stability and Change in Congress,* 3rd ed. (New York: Harper and Row, 1983), 166.
5. Katharine Seelye, "Congressional Memo: New Speaker, New Style, Old Problem," *New York Times* (March 12, 1999): A18.
6. Karen Foerstel, "Hastert and the Limits of Persuasion," *CQ Weekly* (September 30, 2000): 2252.
7. Barbara Sinclair, "The Struggle over Representation and Lawmaking in Congress: Leadership Reforms in the 1990s," in James A. Thurber and Roger H. Davidson, eds., *Remaking Congress: Change and Stability in the 1990s* (Washington, DC: CQ Press, 1995), 105.

8. Quoted in Donald R. Matthews, *U.S. Senators and Their World* (Chapel Hill: University of North Carolina Press, 1960), 97–8.

9. Steven S. Smith and Eric D. Lawrence, "Party Control of Congress in the Republican Congress," in Lawrence C. Dodd and Bruce I. Oppenheimer, eds., *Congress Reconsidered*, 6th ed. (Washington, DC: CQ Press, 1997), 163–4. For more on the role of parties in the organization of Congress, see Forrest Maltzman, *Competing Principals: Committees, Parties, and the Organization of Congress* (Ann Arbor: University of Michigan Press, 1997).

10. "What Is the Democratic Caucus?" http://dcaucusweb.house.gov/about/what_is.asp.

11. Woodrow Wilson, *Congressional Government: A Study in American Government* (New York: Meridian Books, 1956; originally published in 1885), 79.

12. Roger H. Davidson, "Congressional Committees in the New Reform Era: From Combat to the Contract," in Thurber and Davidson, *Remaking Congress*. 28.

13. See E. Scott Adler, *Why Congressional Reforms Fail: Reelection and the House Committee System* (Chicago: University of Chicago Press, 2002).

14. For more about committees, see Christopher Deering and Steven S. Smith, *Committees in Congress*, 3rd ed. (Washington, DC: CQ Press, 1997).

15. Woodrow Wilson, *Congressional Government*. (New York: Houghton Mifflin, 1885).

16. Kenneth A. Shepsle, *The Giant Jigsaw Puzzle: Democratic Committee Assignments in the Modern House* (Chicago: University of Chicago Press, 1978).

17. Cal Thomas, "It's Hog Season on the Hill," *New York Times* (April 1, 2004): A25.

18. Tim Groseclose and Charles Stewart III, "The Value of Committee Seats in the House, 1947–91," *American Journal of Political Science* 42 (April 1998): 453–74.

19. Jim VandeHi and Juliet Eilperin, "GOP Leaders Tighten Hold in the House; Hastert, DeLay Reward Loyalty over Seniority," *Washington Post* (January 13, 2003): A1.

20. Charles S. Bullock III, "House Careerists: Changing Patterns of Longevity and Attrition," *American Political Science Review* 66 (December 1972): 1295–1300.

21. Michael K. Moore and John R. Hibbing. "Situational Dissatisfaction in Congress: Explaining Voluntary Departures," *Journal of Politics* 4 (November 1998): 1088–1107.

22. Helen Dewar, "Retiring Senators Look Beyond the Beltway; Eschewing Washington's Revolving Door, Many Instead Turn to Home-State Classrooms," *Washington Post* (December 29, 1996): A4.

23. Juliet Eilperin, "Ex Lawmakers' Edge Is Access," *Washington Post* (September 13, 2003): A1.

24. Jeffrey H. Birnbaum, "Lawmaker-Turned-Lobbyist a Growing Trend on the Hill," *Washington Post* (July 11, 2004): A1.

25. Richard F. Fenno Jr., "U.S. House Members in Their Constituencies: An Exploration," 71 *American Political Science Review* 3 (September 1977): 883–917.

26. Richard F. Fenno Jr., *Home Style: House Members in Their Districts* (Boston: Little, Brown, 1978), 32.

27. Hedrick Smith, *The Power Game* (New York: Ballantine Books, 1989), 108.

28. Gary W. Cox and Jonathan N. Katz, "Why Did the Incumbency Advantage in U.S. House Elections Grow?" *American Journal of Political Science* 40 (May 1996): 478–97; and Kenneth N. Bickers and Robert M. Stein, "The Electoral Dynamics of the Federal Pork Barrel," *American Journal of Political Science* 40 (November 1996): 1300–26.

29. Marjorie Randon Hershey, "Congressional Elections," in Gerald M. Pomper et al., *The Election of 1992: Reports and Interpretations* (Chatham, NJ: Chatham House, 1993), 159.

30. Alan I. Abramowitz, "Incumbency, Congressional Spending, and the Decline of Competition in House Elections," *Journal of Politics* 53 (February 1991): 34–56.

31. Mildred L. Amer, "Membership of the 108th Congress: A Profile." Congressional Research Service (March 20, 2003).

32. Amy Keller, "The Roll Call 50 Richest: For Richer or Poorer Thanks to Spouses, Kerry Keeps Top Spot and Clinton Joins List," *Roll Call* (September 9, 2002).

33. Amer, "Membership of the 108th Congress."

34. Warren E. Miller and Donald Stokes, "Constituency Influence in Congress," *American Political Science Review* 57 (March 1963): 45–57.

35. Public Opinion Online, Accession Number 0363310, Question Number 054, June 14–18, 2000, R-Poll (NEXIS).

36. Nancy E. McGlen, et al., *Women, Politics and America Society*, 4th ed. (New York: Longman, 2004).

37. See also Cindy Simon Rosenthal, *Women Transforming Congress* (Norman: University of Oklahoma Press, 2003); O'Connor, *Women and Congress;* and Susan J. Carroll, ed., *The Impact of Women in Public Office* (Bloomington: Indiana University Press, 2002).

38. Michele L. Swers, *The Difference Women Make* (Chicago: University of Chicago Press, 2002).

39. *Congressional Quarterly Weekly Report* (January 6, 2001).

40. Norman Ornstein, "GOP Moderates Can Impact Policy—If They Dare," *Roll Call* (February 12, 2003).

41. Byron York, "Bored by Estrada? Owen May Be a Reprise," *The Hill* (March 19, 2003): 43.

42. See L. Martin Overby, "The Senate and Justice Thomas: A Note on Ideology, Race, and Constituent Pressures," *Congress and the Presidency* 21 (Autumn 1994): 131–6.

43. John W. Kingdon, *Congressmen's Voting Decisions*, 3rd ed. (Ann Arbor: University of Michigan Press, 1989).

44. Kingdon, *Congressmen's Voting Decisions.* See also Lee Sigelman, Paul J. Wahlbeck, and Emmett H. Buell Jr., "Vote Choice and the Preference for Divided Government: Lessons of 1992," *American Journal of Political Science* 41 (July 1997): 879–94.

45. Ken Kollman, "Inviting Friends to Lobby: Interest Groups, Ideological Bias, and Congressional Committees," *American Journal of Political Science* 41 (April 1997): 519–44. See also Marie Hojnacki and David C. Kimball, "Organized Interests and the Decision of Whom to Lobby in Congress," *American Political Science Review* 92 (December 1998): 775–90.

46. Robert Beirsack, Paul Herrnson, and Clyde Wilcox, *After the Revolution: PACs, Lobbies and the Republican Congress* (Boston: Allyn and Bacon, 1999).

47. Barbara S. Romzek and Jennifer A. Utter, "Congressional Legislative Staff: Political Professionals or Clerks?" *American Journal of Political Science* 41 (October 1997): 1251–79; and Susan Webb Hammond, "Recent Research on Legislative Staffs," *Legislative Studies Quarterly* (November 1996): 543–76.

48. Keith Krehbiel, "Cosponsors and Wafflers from A to Z." *American Journal of Political Science* 39 (November 1995): 906–23.

49. Don Phillips, "Biden Stalls Transportation Picks," *Washington Post* (March 28, 2002): A4.

50. David E. Sanger, "Rounding Out a Clear Clinton Legacy," *New York Times* (May 25, 2000): A1.

51. Sanger, "Rounding Out," A1, A10.

52. Eric Schmitt, "How a Hard-Driving G.O.P. Gave Clinton a Trade Victory," *New York Times* (May 26, 2000): A1.

53. John Burgess, "A Winning Combination: Money, Message, and Clout," *Washington Post* (May 25, 2000): A4.

54. David E. Rosenbaum, "With Smiles and Cell Phones, a Last-Minute Assault on the Undecided," *New York Times* (May 25, 2000): A11.

55. Schmitt, "How a Hard-Driving."

56. Schmitt, "How a Hard-Driving."

57. Sanger, "Rounding Out," A1, A10.

58. Andrew Beadle, "Up Against a Wall? Election-Year Politics and a New Trade Dispute Pose a Challenge to Otherwise Strong Relations Between the US and China," *Journal of Commerce* (April 5, 2004): 24.

59. Joel D. Aberbach, *Keeping a Watchful Eye: The Politics of Congressional Oversight* (Washington, DC: Brookings Institution, 1990).

60. William F. West, "Oversight Subcommittees in the House of Representatives, *Congress and the Presidency* 25 (Autumn 1998): 147–60.

61. This discussion draws heavily on Steven J. Balla, "Legislative Organization and Congressional Review," paper delivered at the 1999 meeting of the Midwest Political Science Association.

62. *Wall Street Journal* (April 13, 1973): 10.

63. Craig Gilbert, "Use of Force Is President's Call," *Milwaukee Journal Sentinel* (April 18, 2002): A8.

64. Quoted in Stewart M. Powell, "Lee Fight Signals Tougher Battles Ahead on Nomination," *Commercial Appeal* (December 21, 1997): A15.

CHAPTER 8

1. "Two Hundred Years of Presidential Funerals," *Washington Post* (June 10, 2004): C14.

2. "The Fold: Presidential Funerals; Farewell to the Chiefs," *Newsday* (June 9, 2004): A38.

3. Gail Russell Chaddock, "The Rise of Mourning in America," *Christian Science Monitor* (June 11, 2004): 1.

4. Richard E. Neustadt, *Presidential Power and the Modern Presidency* (New York: Free Press, 1991).

5. Edward S. Corwin, *The President: Office and Powers, 1787–1957,* 4th ed. (New York: New York University Press, 1957), 5.

6. Quoted in Corwin, *The President,* 11.

7. Winston Solberg, *The Federal Convention and the Formation of the Union of the American States* (Indianapolis, IN: Bobbs-Merrill, 1958), 235.

8. James P. Pfiffner, "Recruiting Executive Branch Leaders," *Brookings Review* 19 (Spring 2001): 41–3.

9. Benjamin I. Page and Mark P. Petracca, *The American Presidency* (New York: McGraw-Hill, 1983), 262.

10. Page and Petracca, *The American Presidency,* 268.

11. Todd Shields and Chi Huang, "Executive Vetoes: Testing Presidency Versus President Centered Perspectives of Presidential Behavior," *American Politics Quarterly* (October 1997): 431–2.

12. Quoted in Solberg, *The Federal Convention,* 91.

13. *Clinton v. City of New York,* 524 U.S. 417 (1998).

14. "War Powers: Resolution Grants Bush Power He Needs," *Rocky Mountain News* (September 15, 2001): B6.

15. *Public Papers of the Presidents* (1963), 889.

16. Quoted in Neustadt, *Presidential Power,* 9.

17. Quoted in Paul F. Boller Jr., *Presidential Anecdotes* (New York: Penguin Books, 1981), 78.

18. Lyn Ragsdale and John Theis III, "The Institutionalization of the American Presidency, 1924–1992," *American Journal of Political Science* 41 (October 1997): 1280–1318.

19. Quoted in Page and Petracca, *The American Presidency,* 57.

20. Alfred Steinberg, *The First Ten: The Founding Presidents and Their Administrations* (New York: Doubleday, 1967), 59.

21. See Louis Fisher, *Constitutional Conflicts Between Congress and the President,* 4th ed. (Lawrence: University Press of Kansas, 1997).

22. Franklin D. Roosevelt, Press Conference, July 23, 1937.

23. Lyndon B. Johnson, *The Vantage Point* (New York: Holt, Rinehart and Winston, 1971), 448.

24. Morris Fiorina, *Divided Government,* 2nd ed. (New York: Macmillan, 1995).

25. See Lance LeLoup and Steven Shull, *The President and Congress: Collaboration and Conflict in National Policymaking* (Boston: Allyn and Bacon, 1999).

26. See Cary Covington, J. Mark Wrighton, and Rhonda Kinney, "A 'Presidency-Augmented' Model of Presidential Success on House Roll Call Votes," *American Journal of Political Science* 39 (November 1995): 1001–24; and Wayne P. Steger, "Presidential Policy Initiation and the Politics of Agenda Control," *Congress and the Presidency* 24 (Spring 1997): 102–14.

27. Quoted in Thomas E. Cronin, *The State of the Presidency,* 2nd ed. (Boston: Little, Brown, 1980), 169.

28. Robert A. Caro, *Master of the Senate: The Years of Lyndon Johnson* (New York: Knopf, 2002).

29. Paul C. Light, *The President's Agenda: Domestic Policy Choice from Kennedy to Carter* (Baltimore, MD: Johns Hopkins University Press, 1983).

30. Mary Leonard, "Bush Begins Talks on Human Cloning," *Boston Globe* (January 17, 2002): A6.

31. "Resisting Secrecy," *Plain Dealer* (April 30, 2002): B8.

32. Richard Reeves, "Writing History to Executive Order," *New York Times* (November 16, 2001): A25.

33. Samuel Kernell, *New Strategies of Presidential Leadership,* 2nd ed. (Washington, DC: CQ Press, 1993), 3.

34. Jeffrey Cohen, "Presidential Rhetoric and the Public Agenda," *American Journal of Political Science* 39 (February 1995): 87–107.

35. Brian Kates and Kenneth R. Bazinet, "Crisis Forges a New Bush First-Year," *Daily News* (January 20, 2002): 9.

36. George Reedy, *The Twilight of the Presidency* (New York: New American Library), 38–9.

37. Reedy, *Twilight of the Presidency,* 33.

38. Neustadt, *Presidential Power,* 1–10.

39. Michael Waldman, "Bush's Presidential Power," *Washington Post* (December 26, 2000): A29.

40. Samuel Kernell, *Going Public: New Strategies of Presidential Leadership,* 3rd ed. (Washington, DC: CQ Press, 1996).

41. Dan Balz, "Strange Bedfellows: How Television and Presidential Candidates Changed American Politics," *Washington Monthly* (July 1993).

42. William E. Gibson, "Job Approval Ratings Steady: Personal Credibility Takes a Hit," *News and Observer* (August 19, 1998): A16.

43. Michael R. Kagay, "History Suggests Bush's Popularity Will Ebb," *New York Times* (May 22, 1991): A10.

CHAPTER 9

1. Thomas Frank, "Homeland Security: Terror Warnings Not Coordinated," *Newsday* (May 28, 2004): A4.

2. Stephen Barr, "Users Mostly Rate Agencies Favorably," *Washington Post* (April 13, 2000): A29.

3. Harold D. Lasswell, *Politics: Who Gets What, When and How* (New York: McGraw-Hill, 1938).

4. H. H. Gerth and C. Wright Mills, *From Max Weber* (New York: Oxford University Press, 1958).

5. Office of Personnel Management, *The Fact Book.* Available online at http://www.opm.gov/feddata/03factbk.pdf. The Postal Service, like the rest of the federal government, continues to downsize. "20,000 Job Cuts at Postal Service," *Newsday* (January 9, 2002): A38.

6. Quoted in Robert C. Caldwell, *James A. Garfield* (Hamden, CT: Archon Books, 1965).

7. "Federal News: Hatch Act," *Inc.: Government Employee Relations Report* (October 11, 1993): 1317.

8. Avram Goldstein, "Teacher to Lose Job Under Hatch Act," *Washington Post* (April 15, 2002): A8.

9. David Osborne and Ted Gaebler, *Reinventing Government* (Reading, MA: Addison-Wesley, 1992), 20–21.

10. John Erlichman, "Government Reform: Will Al Gore's Package of Changes Succeed Where Others Failed? Washington's 'Iron Triangles,'" *Atlanta Journal and Constitution* (September 16, 1993): A15.

11. Office of Personnel Management, *2003 Fact Book*. See also Julie Dolan, "The Senior Executive Service: Gender, Attitudes and Representative Bureaucracy," *Journal of Public Administration Research and Theory* 10(3) (2003): 513–29.

12. Stephen Barr, "Some Trainees Voice Frustration with Presidential Management Intern Program," *Washington Post* (November 26, 2001): B2.

13. Kenneth J. Cooper, "U.S. May Repay Loans for College," *Washington Post* (December 13, 2001): A45.

14. Edward Walsh, "OMB Details 'Outsourcing' Revisions; Unions Denounce New Rules Aimed at Competition," *Washington Post* (May 30, 2003): A24.

15. "A Century of Government Growth," *Washington Post* (January 3, 2000): A17. On the difficulty of counting the exact number of government agencies, see David Nachmias and David H. Rosenbloom, *Bureaucratic Government: U.S.A.* (New York: St. Martin's Press, 1980).

16. For the EPA to become a department and its head a formal member of the president's Cabinet, Congress would have to act.

17. The classic work on regulatory commissions is Marver Bernstein, *Regulating Business by Independent Commission* (Princeton, NJ: Princeton University Press, 1955).

18. *Humphrey's Executor* v. *U.S.*, 295 U.S. 602 (1935).

19. Karen DeYoung, "Saudis Detail Steps on Charities; Kingdom Seeks to Quell Record on Terrorist Financing," *Washington Post* (December 3, 2002): A1.

20. Mike Allen, "White House to Defer to NASA Investigation; Work on Space Policy to Await Probe's End," *Washington Post* (February 5, 2003): A14.

21. Michael Lipsky, *Street-Level Bureaucracy: Dilemmas of the Individual in Public Services* (New York: Russell Sage Foundation, 1980).

22. Cornelius M. Kerwin, *Rulemaking: How Government Agencies Write Law and Make Policy*, 2nd ed. (Washington, DC: CQ Press, 1999), xv.

23. David J. Lorenzo, "Countering Popular Misconceptions of Federal Bureaucracies in American Government Classes," *PS: Political Science and Politics* 4 (December 1999): 743–7.

24. Jack C. Plano and Milton Greenberg, *The American Political Dictionary*, 6th ed. (New York: Holt, Rinehart and Winston, 1982), 236.

25. Stephen Barr, "For IRS, a Deadline to Draft a Smile," *Washington Post* (January 31, 1999): H1.

26. Public Opinion Online, FOX News, Opinion Dynamics Poll, April 4, 2002.

27. Quoted in Arthur Schlesinger Jr., *A Thousand Days* (Greenwich, CT: Fawcett Books, 1967), 377.

28. Thomas V. DiBacco, "Veep Gore Reinventing Government—Again!" *USA Today* (September 9, 1993): 13A.

29. George A. Krause, "Presidential Use of Executive Orders, 1953–1994," *American Politics Quarterly* 25 (October 1997): 458–81.

30. Irene Murphy, *Public Policy on the Status of Women* (Lexington, MA: Lexington Books, 1974).

31. Matthew McCubbins and Thomas Schwartz, "Congressional Oversight Overlooked: Police Patrols Versus Fire Alarms," *American Journal of Political Science* 28 (1987): 165–79.

32. Rosemary O'Leary, *Environmental Change: Federal Courts and the EPA* (Philadelphia: Temple University Press, 1993).

33. James F. Spriggs III, "The Supreme Court and Federal Administrative Agencies: A Resource-Based Theory and Analysis of Judicial Impact," *American Journal of Political Science* 40 (November 1996): 1122.

34. Wendy Hansen, Renee Johnson, and Isaac Unah, "Specialized Courts, Bureaucratic Agencies, and the Politics of U.S. Trade Policy," *American Journal of Political Science* 39 (August 1995): 529–57.

CHAPTER 10

1. Bernard Schwartz, *The Law in America* (New York: American Heritage, 1974), 48.

2. Julius Goebel Jr., *History of the Supreme Court of the United States*, vol. 1: *Antecedents and Beginnings to 1801* (New York: Macmillan, 1971), 206.

3. *Marbury* v. *Madison*, 5 U.S. 137 (1803).

4. *Martin* v. *Hunter's Lessee*, 14 U.S. 304 (1816).

5. Quoted in Goebel, *History of the Supreme Court*, 280.

6. *Chisholm* v. *Georgia*, 2 U.S. 419 (1793).

7. Oliver Ellsworth served from 1796 to 1800.

8. In *Hylton* v. *U.S.*, 3 U.S. 171 (1796), the Court ruled that a congressional tax on horse-drawn carriages was an excise tax and not a direct tax and therefore it need not be apportioned evenly among the states (as direct taxes must be, according to the Constitution).

9. *Fletcher* v. *Peck*, 10 U.S. 87 (1810); *Martin* v. *Hunter's Lessee*, 14 U.S. 304 (1816); *Cohens* v. *Virginia*, 19 U.S. 264 (1821).

10. *McCulloch* v. *Maryland*, 17 U.S. 316 (1819).

11. *Marbury* v. *Madison*, 5 U.S. 137 (1803).

12. *Marbury* v. *Madison*, 5 U.S. 137 (1803).

13. This discussion draws heavily on Jack C. Plano and Milton Greenberg, *The American Political Dictionary*, 10th ed. (Fort Worth, TX: Harcourt Brace, 1996), 247.

14. *Strauder* v. *West Virginia*, 100 U.S. 303 (1888).

15. *Duren* v. *Missouri*, 439 U.S. 357 (1979).

16. *Batson* v. *Kentucky*, 476 U.S. 79 (1986) (African Americans), and *JEB* v. *Alabama*, 511 U.S. 127 (1994) (women).

17. David W. Neubauer, *Judicial Process: Law, Courts, and Politics* (Pacific Grove, CA: Brooks/Cole, 1991), 57.

18. Cases involving citizens from different states can be filed in state or federal court.

19. Sheldon Goldman and Elliot E. Slotnick, "Clinton's First Term Judiciary: Many Bridges to Cross," *Judicature* (May/June 1997): 254–55.

20. Neil Lewis, "Deal Ends Impasse over Judicial Nominees," *New York Times* (May 19, 2004): A19.

21. Quoted in Nina Totenberg, "Will Judges Be Chosen Rationally?" *Judicature* (August/September 1976): 93.

22. Quoted in Judge Irving R. Kaufman, "Charting a Judicial Pedigree," *New York Times* (January 24, 1981): A23.

23. Quoted in Lawrence Baum, *The Supreme Court*, 3rd ed. (Washington, DC: CQ Press, 1989), 108.

24. See Barbara A. Perry, *A Representative Supreme Court? The Impact of Race, Religion, and Gender on Appointments* (New York: Greenwood Press, 1991).

25. Clarence Thomas was raised a Catholic but attended an Episcopalian church at the time of his appointment, having been barred from Catholic sacraments because of his remarriage. He again, however, is attending Roman Catholic services.

26. Amy Goldstein, "Bush Set to Curb ABA's Role in Court Appointments," *Washington Post* (March 18, 2001): A2.

27. Saundra Torry, "ABA's Judicial Panel Is a Favorite Bipartisan Target," *Washington Post* (April 29, 1996): F7.

28. Lawrence M. O'Rourke, "Judicial Nomination Sparks Partisan Fight," *Sacramento Bee* (April 22, 2002): A1.

29. Subsequent revelations about Brandeis's secret financial payments to Frankfurter to allow him to handle cases of social interest to Brandeis (while Brandeis was on the Court and couldn't handle them himself) raise questions about the fitness of both Frankfurter and Brandeis for the bench. Still, no information about Frankfurter's legal arrangements with Brandeis was unearthed during the committee's investigations or Frankfurter's testimony.

30. John Brigham, *The Cult of the Court* (Philadelphia: Temple University Press, 1987).

31. Stephen L. Wasby, *The Supreme Court in the Federal Judicial System*, 4th ed. (Chicago: Nelson-Hall, 1988), 194.

32. Wasby, *The Supreme Court in the Federal Judicial System*, 194.

33. Wasby, *The Supreme Court in the Federal Judicial System*, 199. Much of this change occurred as the result of an increase in state criminal cases, of which nearly 100 percent concerned constitutional questions.

34. Data compiled by authors for 2001–2002 term of the Court.

35. Justice Stevens chooses not to join this pool. According to one former clerk, "He wanted an independent review," but Stevens examines only about 20 percent of the petitions, leaving the rest to his clerks. Tony Mauro, "Ginsburg Plunges into the Cert Pool," *Legal Times* (September 6, 1993): 8.

36. Paul Wahlbeck, James F. Spriggs II, and Lee Sigelman, "Ghostwriters on the Court? A Stylistic Analysis of U.S. Supreme Court Opinion Drafts," *American Politics Research 30* (March 2002): 166–92. Wahlbeck, Spriggs, and Sigelman note that "between 1969 and 1972—the period during which the justices each became entitled to a third law clerk . . . .the number of opinions increased by about 50 percent and the number of words tripled."

37. Richard A. Posner, *The Federal Courts: Crisis and Reform* (Cambridge, MA: Harvard University Press, 1985), 114.

38. Edward Lazarus, *Closed Chambers: The First Eyewitness Account of the Epic Struggles Inside the Supreme Court* (New York: Random House, 1998).

39. "Retired Chief Justice Warren Attacks . . . Freund Study Group's Composition and Proposal," *American Bar Association Journal* 59 (July 1973): 728.

40. Kathleen Werdegar, "The Solicitor General and Administrative Due Process," *George Washington Law Review* (1967–1968): 482.

41. Rebecca Mae Salokar, *The Solicitor General: The Politics of Law* (Philadelphia: Temple University Press, 1992), 3.

42. Quoted in Elder Witt, *A Different Justice: Reagan and the Supreme Court* (Washington, DC: CQ Press, 1986), 133.

43. Lawrence Baum, *The Supreme Court*, 4th ed. (Washington, DC: CQ Press, 1992), 106.

44. Richard C. Cortner, *The Supreme Court and Civil Liberties* (Palo Alto, CA: Mayfield, 1975), vi.

45. Gregory A. Caldeira and John R. Wright, "*Amicus Curiae* Before the Supreme Court: Who Participates, When and How Much?" *Journal of Politics* 52 (August 1990): 803.

46. See also John R. Hermann, "American Indians in Court: The Burger and Rehnquist Years," Ph.D. dissertation, Emory University, 1996.

47. *Brown* v. *Board of Education*, 347 U.S. 483 (1954); *Planned Parenthood of Southeastern Pennsylvania* v. *Casey*, 585 U.S. 833 (1992); *Grutter* v. *Bollinger*, 539 U.S. 306 (2003).

48. *U.S.* v. *Nixon*, 418 U.S. 683 (1974).

49. *Clinton* v. *Jones*, 520 U.S. 681 (1997).

50. *Webster* v. *Reproductive Health Services*, 492 U.S. 490 (1989).

51. Donald L. Horowitz, *The Courts and Social Policy* (Washington, DC: Brookings Institution, 1977), 538.

52. *Brown* v. *Board of Education*, 347 U.S. 483 (1954).

53. *Webster* v. *Reproductive Health Services*, 492 U.S. 490 (1989).

54. See, for example, Tracy E. George and Lee Epstein, "On the Nature of Supreme Court Decision Making," *American Political Science Review* 86 (1992): 323–37; Melinda Gann Hall and Paul Brace, "Justices' Responses to Case Facts: An Interactive Model," *American Politics Quarterly* (April 1996): 237–61; Lawrence Baum, *The Puzzle of Judicial Behavior* (Ann Arbor: University of Michigan Press, 1997); and Gregory N. Flemming, David B. Holmes, and Susan Gluck Mezey, "An Integrated Model of Privacy Decision Making in State Supreme Courts," *American Politics Quarterly* 26 (January 1998): 35–58.

55. Jeffrey A. Segal and Harold J. Spaeth, *The Supreme Court and the Attitudinal Model Revisited* (New York: Cambridge University Press, 2002).

56. Gerard Gryski, Eleanor C. Main, and William Dixon, "Models of State High Court Decision Making in Sex Discrimination Cases," *Journal of Politics* 48 (1986): 143–55; and C. Neal Tate and Roger Handberg, "Time Binding and Theory Building in Personal Attribute Models of Supreme Court Voting Behavior, 1916–1988," *American Political Science Review* 35 (1991): 460–80.

57. Donald R. Songer and Sue Davis, "The Impact of Party and Region on Voting Decisions in the U.S. Courts of Appeals, 1955–86," *Western Political Quarterly* 43 (1990): 830–44.

58. See, generally, Lee Epstein and Jack Knight, "Field Essay: Toward a Strategic Revolution in Judicial Politics: A Look Back, a Look Ahead," *Political Research Quarterly* 53 (September 2000): 663–76.

59. Thomas R. Marshall, "Public Opinion, Representation and the Modern Supreme Court," *American Politics Quarterly* 16 (1988): 296–316.

60. Curtis J. Sitomer, "High Court to Rethink Abortion?" *Christian Science Monitor* (September 16, 1988): 3.

61. *Korematsu* v. *U.S.*, 323 U.S. 214 (1944).

62. *Youngstown Sheet & Tube Co.* v. *Sawyer*, 343 U.S. 579 (1952).

63. The Supreme Court ruled that President Truman's seizure and operation of U.S. steel mills in the face of a strike threat were unconstitutional, because the Constitution implied no such broad executive power. See Alan Westin, *Anatomy of a Constitutional Law Case* (New York: Macmillan, 1958); and Maeva Marcus, *Truman and the Steel Seizure Case* (New York: Columbia University Press, 1977).

64. *U.S.* v. *Nixon*, 418 U.S. 683 (1984).

65. Gallup Poll, *Public Opinion Online.* (May 21–24, 2004).

66. Timothy R. Johnson and Andrew D. Martin, "The Public's Conditional Response to Supreme Court Decisions," *American Political Science Review* 92 (June 1998): 299–309.

67. *Ashcroft* v. *Free Speech Coalition*, 535 U.S. 234 (2002).

68. "Supreme Court Cases Overruled by Subsequent Decision," U.S. Government Printing Office. Accessed online at http://www.gpoaccess.gov/constitution/pdf/con041.pdf.

69. See *Colegrove* v. *Green*, 328 U.S. 549 (1946), for example.

70. *Baker* v. *Carr*, 369 U.S. 186 (1962).

71. Charles Johnson and Bradley C. Canon, *Judicial Policies: Implementation and Impact*, 2nd ed. (Washington, DC: CQ Press, 1998), ch. 1.

72. *Reynolds* v. *Sims*, 377 U.S. 533 (1964).

73. *Hunt* v. *Cromartie*, 546 U.S. 541 (1999).

74. *Mississippi University for Women* v. *Hogan*, 458 U.S. 718 (1982).

CHAPTER 11

1. The Gallup Organization, "Poll Releases: The Florida Recount Controversy from the Public's Perspective: 25 Insights," http://www.gallup.com/poll/releases. All data discussed here are drawn from this compendium of polls concerning the Florida recount.

2. Allan M. Winkler, "Public Opinion," in Jack Greene, ed., *The Encyclopedia of American Political History* (New York: Charles Scribner's Sons, 1988), 1038.

3. Quoted in *Public Opinion Quarterly* 29 (Winter 1965–1966): 547.

4. CBS News/*New York Times* Poll, July 11–15, 2004.

5. Winkler, "Public Opinion," 1035.

6. Gina Kim and Marc Ramirez, "Judging Embedded Reporting: The Experts," *Seattle Times* (March 26, 2003).

7. *Literary Digest* 122 (August 22, 1936): 3.

8. *Literary Digest* 125 (November 14, 1936): 1.

9. Robert S. Erikson, Norman Luttbeg, and Kent Tedin, *American Public Opinion: Its Origin, Contents, and Impact* (New York: Wiley, 1980), 28.

10. Steve Marantz, "Dotcom Finds a Future Cyber Polling," *Boston Herald* (September 25, 2000): 21.

11. "2000 Election Winners: George W. Bush and Online Polling," *Business Wire* (December 14, 2000).

12. Richard Dawson et al., *Political Socialization*, 2nd ed. (Boston: Little, Brown, 1977), 33.

13. Robert D. Hess and David Easton, "The Child's Changing Image of the President," *Public Opinion Quarterly* 14 (Winter 1960): 632–42; and Fred I. Greenstein, *Children and Politics* (New Haven, CT: Yale University Press, 1965).

14. Laura Pappano, "Potential War Poses Threat to Teachers," *Boston Globe* (March 9, 2003): B9.

15. "Kids Voting USA Gains Support in Two Congressional Actions: Rep. Pastor Praised for His Continued Efforts," http://www.kidsvoteusa.org/march1502.htm.

16. "Kids Voting USA."

17. James Simon and Bruce D. Merrill, "Political Socialization in the Classroom Revisited: The Kids Voting Program," *Social Science Journal* 35 (1998): 29–42.

18. Simon and Merrill, "Political Socialization in the Classroom Revisited."

19. Linda J. Sax et al., *The American Freshman: National Norms for Fall 2003*, University of California, Los Angeles, December 2003.

20. *Statistical Abstract of the United States, 1997* (Washington, DC: Government Printing Office, 1997), 1011.

21. Princeton Research Survey Associates Poll, accessed through LEXIS, Question ID USPSRA.011104, R19, December 19, 2003–January 3, 2004.

22. Julie Mason, "Avalanche of Politico-tainment Seems to Benefit Presidential Candidates," *Houston Chronicle* (October 1, 2000): A38; and Lois Romano, "For the Candidates, It's Showtime," *Washington Post* (October 20, 2000): A11.

23. Sean H. Smith, "Breaking News: ABC Had It Right," *Washington Post* (March 29, 2002): A23.

24. Princeton Research Survey Associates Poll, accessed through LEXIS, Question ID USPSRA.032504, RIT06B, March 17–21, 2004.

25. Steven M. Cohen and Charles S. Liebman, "American Jewish Liberalism," *Public Opinion Quarterly* 61 (1997): 405–30.

26. USA Today and CNN/Gallup Tracking Poll, USAToday.com.

27. Edward S. Greenberg, "The Political Socialization of Black Children," in Edward S. Greenberg, ed., *Political Socialization* (New York: Atherton Press, 1970), 181.

28. Elaine J. Hall and Myra Marx Ferree, "Race Differences in Abortion Attitudes," *Public Opinion Quarterly* 50 (Summer 1986): 193–207; and Jon Hurwitz and Mark Peffley, "Public Perceptions of Race and Crime: The Role of Racial Stereotypes," *American Journal of Political Science* 41 (April 1997): 375–401.

29. Elaine S. Povich, "Courting Hispanics: Group's Votes Could Shift House Control," *Newsday* (April 21, 2002): A4.

30. Alejandro Portes and Rafael Mozo, "The Political Adaptation Process of Cubans and Other Ethnic Minorities in the United States: A Preliminary Analysis," in F. Chris Garcia, ed., *Latinos and the Political System* (Notre Dame, IN: University of Notre Dame Press, 1988), 161.

31. Pamela Johnson Conover and Virginia Sapiro, "Gender, Feminist Consciousness, and War," *American Journal of Political Science* 37 (November 1993): 1079–99.

32. Margaret Trevor, "Political Socialization, Party Identification, and the Gender Gap," *Public Opinion Quarterly* 63 (Spring 1999): 62–89.

33. Alexandra Marks, "Gender Gap Narrows over Kosovo," *Christian Science Monitor* (April 30, 1999): 1.

34. Pew Research Center for People and the Press (2002).

35. Pew Research Center for People and the Press, "Iraq Prison Scandal Hits Home, but Most Reject Troop Pullout," May 12, 2004, http://people-press.org/reports/display.php37REportID=213.

36. Susan A. MacManus, *Young v. Old: Generational Combat in the 21st Century* (Boulder, CO: Westview, 1995).

37. Richard Morin, "Southern Exposure," *Washington Post* (July 14, 1996): A18.

38. "Church Pews Seat More Blacks, Seniors, and Republicans," http://www.gallup.com/POLL_ARCHIVES/970329.html.

39. CNN Exit Polls, www.cnn.com/election/2004/pages/results/states/us/p/oo/epolls.o.html.

40. F. Christopher Arterton, "The Impact of Watergate on Children's Attitudes Toward Political Authority," *Political Science Quarterly* 89 (June 1974): 273.

41. Diana Owen and Jack Dennis, "Kids and the Presidency: Assessing Clinton's Legacy," *Public Perspective* (April 1999): NEXIS.

42. Suzanne Soule, "Will They Engage? Political Knowledge, Participation and Attitudes of Generations X and Y," paper prepared for the 2001 German and American Conference, 6.

43. Soule, "Will They Engage?" quoting Richard G. Niemi and Jane Junn, *Civic Education* (New Haven, CT: Yale University Press, 1998).

44. Tamara Henry, "Kids Get 'Abysmal' Grade in History," *USA Today* (May 10, 2002): 1A.

45. "Don't Know Much About . . . " *Christian Science Monitor* (May 16, 2002): 8.

46. "Don't Know Much About History, Geography . . . " *Pittsburgh Post-Gazette* (January 22, 2003): E2; Laurence D. Cohen, "Geography for Dummies," *Hartford Courant* (December 8, 2002): C3.

47. "Gender Gap in Political Knowledge Persists in 2004, National Annenberg Election Survey Shows," http://www.nacs.org/.

48. Quoted in Everett Carl Ladd, "Fiskin's 'Deliberative Poll' Is Flawed Science and Dubious Democracy," *Public Perspective* (December/January 1996): 41.

49. V. O. Key Jr., *The Responsible Electorate: Rationality in Presidential Voting, 1936–1960* (Cambridge, MA: Belknap Press of Harvard University, 1966).

50. Richard Nodeau et al., "Elite Economic Forecasts, Economic News, Mass Economic Judgments and Presidential Approval," *Journal of Politics* 61 (February 1999): 109–35.

51. Michael Towle, Review of *Presidential Responsiveness and Public Policy-making: The Public and the Policies* by Jeffrey E. Cohen, *Journal of Politics* 61 (February 1999): 230–2.

52. John E. Mueller, *War, Presidents, and Public Opinion* (New York: Wiley, 1973), 69.

53. Roderick P. Hart, *The Sound of Leadership: Presidential Communication in the Modern Age* (Chicago: University of Chicago Press, 1987).

54. Dana Milbank, "At the White House, 'The People' Have Spoken—Endlessly," *Washington Post* (June 4, 2002): A15.

55. David W. Moore, *The Superpollsters: How They Measure and Manipulate Public Opinion in America*, 2nd ed. (New York: Four Walls Eight Windows, 1995).

56. Diane J. Heith, "Staffing the White House Public Opinion Apparatus 1969–1988," *Public Opinion Quarterly* 62 (Summer 1998): 165.

57. Francis J. Connolly and Charley Manning, "What 'Push Polling' Is and What It Isn't," *Boston Globe* (August 16, 2001): A21.

58. Michael W. Traugott, "The Polls in 1992: Views of Two Critics: A Good General Showing, but Much Work Needs to Be Done," *Public Perspective* 4 (November/December 1992): 14–16.

59. Adam Berinsky, "A Tale of Two Elections: An Investigation of Pre-election Polling in Biracial Contests," paper presented at the 1999 annual meeting of the Midwest Political Science Association.

60. Benjamin Ginsberg, "How Polls Transform Public Opinion," in Michael Margolis and Gary A. Mauser, eds., *Manipulating Public Opinion* (Pacific Grove, CA: Brooks/Cole, 1989), 273.

61. See, for example, Benjamin Page and Robert Shapiro, "Effects of Public Opinion on Policy," *American Political Science Review* 57

(March 1983): 175–90; Alan D. Monroe, "Public Opinion and Public Policy, 1980–1993," *Public Opinion Quarterly* 62 (Spring 1998): 6–28; and Kathleen M. McGraw, Samuel Best, and Richard Timpone, "'What They Say or What They Do?' The Impact of Elite Explanation and Policy Outcomes on Public Opinion," *American Journal of Political Science* 39 (February 1995): 53–74.

62. Benjamin Ginsberg, *The Captive Public* (New York: Basic Books, 1986), ch. 4.

63. "George Gallup Is Dead at 82," *New York Times* (July 28, 1984): A1.

64. Herbert Asher, *Polling and the Public: What Every Citizen Should Know* (Washington, DC: CQ Press, 1988), 109.

CHAPTER 12

1. This conception of a political party was originally put forth by V. O. Key in *Politics, Parties, and Pressure Groups* (New York, Crowell, 1958).

2. John H. Aldrich, *Why Parties? The Origin and Transformation of Party Politics in America* (Chicago: University of Chicago Press, 1995).

3. By contrast, Great Britain did not develop truly national, broad-based parties until the 1870s.

4. See *Historical Statistics of the United States: Colonial Times to 1970*, part 2, series Y-27-28 (Washington, DC: Government Printing Office, 1975), based on unpublished data prepared by Walter Dean Burnham.

5. Frank J. Sorauf, *Party Politics in America*, 5th ed. (Boston: Little, Brown, 1984), 22.

6. Elmer E. Schattschneider, *Party Government* (New York: Farrar and Rinehart, 1942).

7. Marc J. Heatherington, "The Effect of Political Trust on the Presidential Vote, 1968–1996," *American Political Science Review* 93 (June 1999): 311–26.

8. Kim Hill and Jan Leighley, "Political Parties and Class Mobilization in Contemporary United States Elections," *American Journal of Political Science* 40 (August 1996): 787–804.

9. M. V. Hood, Quentin Kidd, and Irwin L. Morris, "Of Byrds and Bumpers: Using Democratic Senators to Analyze Political Change in the South, 1960–1995," *American Journal of Political Science* 43 (April 1999): 465–87.

10. Earl Black and Merle Black, *The Rise of Southern Republicans* (Cambridge, MA: Harvard University Press, 2002).

11. Kelly D. Patterson, *Political Parties and the Maintenance of Liberal Democracy* (New York: Columbia University Press, 1996).

12. See David E. Price, *Bringing Back the Parties* (Washington, DC: CQ Press, 1984), 284–8.

13. See, for example, Sarah McCally Morehouse, "Legislatures and Political Parties," *State Government* 59 (1976): 23.

14. Paul S. Herrnson, "National Party Organizations at Century's End," in L. Sandy Maisel, ed., *The Parties Respond: Changes in American Parties and Campaigns*, 3rd ed. (Boulder, CO: Westview, 1998).

15. Cornelius P. Cotter, James L. Gibson, John F. Bibby, and Robert J. Huckshorn, *Party Organizations in American Politics* (Pittsburgh: University of Pittsburgh Press, 1989).

16. John F. Bibby, "Party Networks: National-State Integration, Allied Groups, and Issue Activists," in John C. Green and Daniel M. Shea, eds., *The State of the Parties: The Changing Role of Contemporary American Parties*, 3rd ed. (Lanham, MD: Rowman and Littlefield, 1999).

17. Bibby, "Party Networks."

18. Such cases are few, but a deterrent nonetheless. Several U.S. senators were expelled from the Republican Caucus in 1925 for having supported the Progressive candidate for president the previous year. In 1965, two southern House Democrats lost all their committee seniority because of their 1964 endorsement of GOP presidential nominee Barry Goldwater, as did another southerner in 1968 for backing George Wallace's third-party candidacy. In early 1983, the House Democratic Caucus removed Texas Representative Phil Gramm from his Budget Committee seat because of his "disloyalty" in working more closely with Republican committee members than with his own party leaders. (Gramm resigned his seat in Congress, changed parties, and was reelected as a Republican. He then used the controversy to propel himself into the U.S. Senate in 1984.)

19. David W. Rohde, *Parties and Leaders in the Postreform House* (Chicago: University of Chicago Press, 1991); and John A. Aldrich and David W. Rohde, "The Transition to Republican Rule in the House: Implications for Theories of Congressional Politics," *Political Science Quarterly* 112 (1997–1998): 541–67.

20. Kevin M. Leyden and Stephen A. Borrelli, "An Investment in Goodwill: Party Contributions and Party Unity Among U.S. House Members in the 1980s," *American Politics Quarterly* 22 (1994): 421–52.

21. Richard A. Clucas, "Party Contributions and the Influence of Campaign Committee Chairs on Roll-Call Voting," *Legislative Studies Quarterly* 22 (1997): 179–94; and David M. Cantor and Paul S. Herrnson, "Party Campaign Activity and Party Unity in the U.S. House of Representatives," *Legislative Studies Quarterly* 22 (1997): 393–415.

22. Rhodes Cook, "Reagan Nurtures His Adopted Party to Strength," *Congressional Quarterly Weekly Report* 43 (September 28, 1985): 1927–30.

23. Sidney M. Milkis, *The President and the Parties: The Transformation of the American Party System Since the New Deal* (New York: Oxford University Press, 1993).

24. See S. Sidney Ulmer, "The Political Party Variable on the Michigan Supreme Court," *Journal of Public Law* 11 (1962): 352–62; Stuart Nagel, "Political Party Affiliation and Judges' Decisions," *American Political Science Review* 55 (1961): 843–50; David W. Adamany, "The Party Variable in Judges' Voting: Conceptual Notes and a Case Study," *American Political Science Review* 63 (1969): 57–73; Sheldon Goldman, "Voting Behavior on the United States Courts of Appeals, 1961–1964," *American Political Science Review* 60 (1966): 374–83; and Robert A. Carp and C. K. Rowland, *Policymaking and Politics in the Federal District Courts* (Knoxville: University of Tennessee Press, 1983).

25. Randall D. Lloyd, "Separating Partisanship from Party in Judicial Research: Reapportionment in the U.S. District Courts," *American Political Science Review* 89 (June 1995): 413–20.

26. The Farmer-Labor Party did survive in a sense; having endured a series of defeats, it merged in 1944 with the Democrats, and Minnesota's Democratic candidates still officially bear the standard of the Democratic-Farmer-Labor (DFL) Party. At about the same time, also having suffered severe electoral reversals, the Progressives stopped nominating candidates in Wisconsin. The party's members either returned to the Republican Party, from which the Progressives had split early in the century, or became Democrats.

27. Morehouse, "Legislatures and Political Parties," 19–24.

28. Senator George J. Mitchell (D–ME), as quoted in the *Washington Post* (February 9, 1986): A14.

29. Janet M. Box-Steffensmeier, "A Dynamic Analysis of the Role of War Chests in Campaign Strategy," *American Journal of Political Science* 40 (May 1996): 352–71.

30. See Steven E. Finkel and Howard A. Scarrow, "Party Identification and Party Enrollment: The Difference and the Consequence," *Journal of Politics* 47 (May 1985): 620–42.

31. Karen M. Kaufmann and John R. Petrocik, "The Changing Politics of American Men: Understanding the Sources of the Gender Gap," *American Journal of Political Science* 43 (July 1999): 864–87.

32. Michael Dawson, *Behind the Mule: Race and Class in African-American Politics* (Princeton, NJ: Princeton University Press, 1994); and

Louis Bolce, Gerald DeMaio, and Douglas Muzzio, "Blacks and the Republican Party: The 20 Percent Solution," *Political Science Quarterly* 107 (Spring 1992): 63–79.

33. The presidential election of 1960 may be an extreme case, but John F. Kennedy's massive support among Catholics and Nixon's less substantial but still impressive backing by Protestants demonstrates the polarization that religion could once produce. See Philip E. Converse, "Religion and Politics: The 1960 Election," in Angus Campbell et al., *Elections and the Political Order* (New York: Wiley, 1966), 96–124.

34. See V. O. Key Jr., *American State Politics: An Introduction* (New York: Knopf, 1956).

35. See V. O. Key Jr., *Southern Politics in State and Nation* (New York: Knopf, 1949).

36. Todd Donovan, Shaun Bowler, and Tammy Terrio, "Support for Third Parties in California," *American Politics Quarterly* 28 (January 2000): 50–71.

37. Jeffrey Koch, "The Perot Candidacy and Attitudes Toward Government and Politics," *Political Research Quarterly* 51 (March 1998): 141–54.

38. Christian Collet and Martin P. Wattenberg, "Strategically Unambitious: Minor Party and Independent Candidates in the 1996 Congressional Elections," in John C. Green and Daniel M. Shea, eds., *The State of the Parties: The Changing Role of Contemporary American Parties*, 3rd ed. (Lanham, MD: Rowman and Littlefield, 1999).

39. Marc J. Heatherington, "The Effect of Political Trust on the Presidential Vote, 1968–1992," *American Political Science Review* 93 (1999): 311–26.

CHAPTER 13

1. Angus Campbell, Philip E. Converse, Warren E. Miller, and Donald E. Stokes, *The American Voter* (New York: Wiley, 1960).

2. Paul Abramson, John H. Aldrich, and David W. Rohde, *Change and Continuity in the 1996 Elections* (Washington, DC: CQ Press, 1998).

3. Paul Allen Beck, *Party Politics in America*, 8th ed. (New York: Longman, 1998); David Adamany, "Cross-over Voting and the Democratic Party's Reform Rules," *American Political Science Review* 70 (1976): 536–41; Ronald Hedlund and Meredith W. Watts, "The Wisconsin Open Primary: 1968 to 1984," *American Politics Quarterly* 14 (1986): 55–74; and Gary D. Wekkin, "The Conceptualization and Measurement of Crossover Voting," *Western Political Quarterly* 41 (1988): 105–14.

4. Beck, *Party Politics in America;* Alan Abromowitz, John McGlennon, and Ronald Rapoport, "A Note on Strategic Voting in a Primary Election," *Journal of Politics* 43 (1981): 899–904; and Gary D. Wekken, "Why Crossover Voters Are Not 'Mischievous' Voters," *American Politics Quarterly* 19 (1991): 229–47.

5. Gary C. Jacobson, *The Politics of Congressional Elections*, 5th ed. (New York: Addison Wesley, 2000), 107–8.

6. Shaun Bowler, Todd Donovan, and Caroline Tolbert, eds., *Citizens as Legislators: Direct Democracy in the United States* (Columbus: Ohio State University Press, 1998).

7. For a more in-depth discussion of initiative, referendum, and recall voting, see Larry J. Sabato, Howard R. Ernst, and Bruce Larson, *Dangerous Democracy: The Battle over Ballot Initiatives in America* (Lanham, MD: Rowman and Littlefield, 2001); and David S. Broder *Democracy Derailed: Initiative Campaigns and the Power of Money* (New York: Harcourt, 2000).

8. Edward L. Lascher Jr., Michael G. Hagen, and Steven A. Rochlin, "Gun Behind the Door?" *Journal of Politics* 58 (August 1996): 766–75.

9. Elaine Ciulla Kamarck and Kenneth M. Goldstein, "The Rules Matter: Post-Reform Presidential Nominating Politics," in L.

Sandy Maisel, *The Parties Respond: Changes in American Parties and Campaigns* (Boulder, CO: Westview, 1994), 174.

10. Paul R. Abramson, John H. Aldrich, Phil Paolino, and David W. Rohde, "'Sophisticated' Voting in the 1998 Presidential Primaries," *American Political Science Review* 86 (March 1992): 55–69.

11. Larry J. Sabato, "Presidential Nominations: The Front-loaded Frenzy of 1996," in Larry J. Sabato, ed., *Toward the Millennium: The Elections of 1996* (New York: Allyn and Bacon, 1997).

12. Byron Shafer, *Bifurcated Politics: Evolution and Reform in the National Party Convention* (Cambridge, MA: Harvard University Press, 1988).

13. Priscilla Southwell, "Rules as 'Unseen Participants,'" *American Politics Quarterly* 20 (January 1992): 54–68.

14. Richard Herrera, "Are 'Superdelegates' Super?" *Political Behavior* 16 (March 1994): 79–92.

15. James L. Hutter and Steven E. Schier, "Representativeness: From Caucus to Convention in Iowa," *American Politics Quarterly* 12 (October 1984): 431–48.

16. On the subject of party realignment, see Walter Dean Burnham, *Critical Elections and the Mainsprings of American Politics* (New York: Norton, 1970); Kristi Andersen, *The Creation of a Democratic Majority* (Chicago: University of Chicago Press, 1979); and John R. Petrocik, "Realignment: New Party Coalitions and the Nationalization of the South," *Journal of Politics* 49 (May 1987): 347–75.

17. Barbara Farah and Helmut Norpoth, "Trends in Partisan Realignment, 1976–1986: A Decade of Waiting," paper prepared for the annual meeting of the American Political Science Association, Washington, DC, August 27–31, 1986.

18. Morris P. Fiorina, *Retrospective Voting in American National Elections* (New Haven, CT: Yale University Press, 1981); and Charles H. Franklin and John E. Jackson, "The Dynamics of Party Identification," *American Political Science Review* 77 (1983): 957–73.

19. See, for example, V. O. Key Jr., "A Theory of Critical Elections," *Journal of Politics* 17 (February 1955): 3–18.

20. The less dynamic term "creeping realignment" is also sometimes used by scholars and journalists.

21. Everett Carl Ladd, "Like Waiting for Godot: The Uselessness of 'Realignment' for Understanding Change in Contemporary American Politics," in Byron Shafer, ed., *The End of Realignment? Interpreting American Electoral Eras* (Madison: Wisconsin, 1991).

22. See Paul Allen Beck, "The Dealignment Era in America," in Russell J. Dalton et al., *Electoral Change in Advanced Industrial Democracies: Realignment or Dealignment?* (Princeton, NJ: Princeton University Press, 1984), 264. See also Philip M. Williams, "Party Realignment in the United States and Britain," *British Journal of Political Science* 15 (January 1985): 97–115.

23. George Serra, "What's in It for Me? The Impact of Congressional Casework on Incumbent Evaluation," *American Politics Quarterly* 22 (1994): 403–20.

24. Glenn R. Parker and Suzanne L. Parker, "Correlates and Effects of Attention to District by U.S. House Members," *Legislative Studies Quarterly* 10 (May 1985): 223–42.

25. Gary W. Cox and Jonathan N. Katz, "Why Did the Incumbency Advantage in U.S. House Elections Grow?" *American Journal of Political Science* 40 (May 1996): 478–97.

26. Jonathan Krasno, *Challengers, Competition and Reelection: Comparing Senate and House Elections* (New Haven, CT: Yale University Press, 1994).

27. "How to Rig an Election," *The Economist* (April 25, 2002).

28. Matthew Mosk and Lori Montgomery, "Md. Court Spurns Assembly Map: Glendening Plan Ruled Unconstitutional; Judges to Redraw Lines," *Washington Post* (June 12, 2002).

29. *Wesberry* v. *Sanders*, 376 U.S. 1 (1964).

30. *Thornburg* v. *Gingles*, 478 U.S. 30 (1986).

31. *Shaw* v. *Reno*, 113 S.Ct. 2816 (1993).

32. "How to Rig an Election," *The Economist* (April 25, 2002).

33. Paul Gronke and J. Wilson, "Competing Plans as Evidence of Political Motives: The North Carolina Case," *American Politics Quarterly* 27 (April 1999): 147–76.

34. Sunhil Ahuja et al., "Modern Congressional Election Theory Meets the 1992 House Elections," *Political Research Quarterly* 47 (1994): 909–21; and Paul S. Herrnson, *Congressional Elections: Campaigning at Home and in Washington,* 2nd ed. (Washington, DC: CQ Press, 1998).

35. John W. Swain, Stephen A. Borrelli, and Brian C. Reed, "Partisan Consequences of the Post-1990 Redistricting for the U.S. House of Representatives," *Political Research Quarterly* 51 (December 1998): 945–67.

36. Gary C. Jacobson and Michael A. Dimock, "Checking Out: The Effects of Bank Overdrafts on the 1992 House Elections," *American Journal of Political Science* 38 (1994): 601–24; and Herrnson, *Congressional Elections.*

37. Gary C. Jacobson, "The 1994 House Elections in Perspective," *Political Science Quarterly* 111 (1996): 203–23.

38. Steven J. Rosenstone and John Mark Hanson, *Mobilization, Participation, and Democracy in America* (New York: Macmillan, 1993).

39. See, for example, Laura Stoker and M. Kent Jennings, "Life-Cycle Transitions and Political Participation: The Case of Marriage," *American Political Science Review* 89 (1995): 421–36; and Abramson et al., *Change and Continuity in the 1996 Elections.*

40. U.S. Census Bureau, http://www.census.gov/prod/2002pubs/p20-542.pdf.

41. League of United Latin American Citizens, http://www.lulac.org.

42. James A. McCann, Randall W. Partin, Ronald B. Rapoport, and Walter J. Stone, "Presidential Nomination Campaigns and Party Mobilization: An Assessment of Spillover Effects," *American Journal of Political Science* 40 (August 1996): 756–67.

43. Walter Stone, Lonna Rae Atkeson, and Ronald B. Rapoport, "Turning On or Turning Off? Mobilization and Demobilization Effects of Participation in Presidential Nomination Campaigns," *American Journal of Political Science* 36 (August 1992): 665–91.

44. Stephen Knack and J. White, "Election-Day Registration and Turnout Inequality," *Political Behavior* 22 (March 2000): 29–44.

45. Daniel Franklin and Eric Grier, "Effects of Motor Voter Legislation: Voter Turnout, Registration, and Partisan Advantage in the 1992 Presidential Election," *American Politics Quarterly* 25 (January 1997): 104–17.

46. J. Eric Oliver, "The Effects of Eligibility Restrictions and Party Activity on Absentee Voting and Overall Turnout," *American Journal of Political Science* 40 (May 1996): 498–513.

47. Marg N. Franklin and Wolfgang P. Hirczy, "Separated Powers, Divided Government, and Turnout in U.S. Presidential Elections," *American Journal of Political Science* 42 (January 1998): 316–26.

48. Steven J. Rosenstone and John Marc Hansen, *Mobilization, Participation, and Democracy in America* (New York: Macmillan, 1993).

49. Mark J. Fenster, "The Impact of Allowing Day of Registration Voting on Turnout in U.S. Elections from 1960 to 1992: A Research Note," *American Politics Quarterly* 22 (January 1994): 74–87.

50. Stephen Knack, "Drivers Wanted: Motor Voter and the Election of 1996," *PS: Political Science and Politics* 32 (June 1999): 237–43.

51. Arend Lijphart, "Unequal Participation: Democracy's Unsolved Dilemma," *American Political Science Review* 91 (March 1997): 1–14.

52. http://www.cnn.com/ELECTION/2004/pages/results/states/US/P/00/epolls.0.html

53. Warren E. Miller and J. Merrill Shanks, *The New American Voter* (Cambridge, MA: Harvard University Press, 1996), 256.

54. Voter News Service Exit Poll, http://www.CNN.com.

55. Miller and Shanks, *The New American Voter,* 270.

56. Voter News Service Exit Poll, http://www.CNN.com.

57. Voter News Service Exit Poll, http://www.CNN.com.

58. Warren E. Miller and J. Merrill Shanks, "Multiple-Stage Explanation of Political Preferences," in Richard G. Niemi and Herbert F. Weisberg, eds., *Controversies in Voting Behavior* (Washington, DC: CQ Press, 2001), 227–32.

59. Charles Babington, "Campaigns Matter: The Proof of 2000," in Larry J. Sabato, ed., *Overtime! The Election 2000 Thriller* (New York: Longman, 2002), 65.

60. Gary C. Jacobson, *The Politics of Congressional Elections,* 5th ed. (New York: Addison Wesley, 2000.)

61. Barry C. Burden and David C. Kimball, *Why Americans Split Their Tickets: Campaigns, Competition, and Divided Government* (Ann Arbor: University of Michigan Press, 2002).

62. Cited in Everett Carl Ladd Jr., "On Mandates, Realignments, and the 1984 Presidential Election," *Political Science Quarterly* 100 (Spring 1985): 23.

63. Morris P. Fiorina, *Divided Government* (Boston: Allyn and Bacon, 1996).

64. Martin P. Wattenberg, *The Decline of American Political Parties, 1952–1994* (Cambridge, MA: Harvard University Press, 1996).

65. Thomas E. Mann and Raymond E. Wolfinger, "Candidates and Parties in Congressional Elections," *American Political Science Review* 74 (September 1980): 617–32; Albert D. Cover, "One Good Term Deserves Another: The Advantage of Incumbency in Congressional Elections," *American Journal of Political Science* 21 (August 1977): 535; and Gary C. Jacobson, *The Politics of Congressional Elections,* 2nd ed. (Boston: Little, Brown, 1987), 86.

CHAPTER 14

1. Holly Bailey, "Where Did the Money Go?" MSNBC.com, February 12, 2004, http://msnbc.msn.com/id/4252087/site/newsweek/.

2. Howard Kurtz, "Kerry Invests $2 Million in Ads to Court Black Voters," *Washington Post* (July 15, 2004): A08, http://www.washingtonpost.com/wp-dyn/articles/A50181-2004Jul14.html.

3. Patrick J. Kenney and Tom W. Rice, "The Psychology of Political Momentum," *Political Research Quarterly* 47 (December 1994): 923–38.

4. Paul S. Herrnson, "Campaign Professionalism and Fundraising in Congressional Elections," *Journal of Politics* 54 (1992): 859–70.

5. Stephen K. Medvic and Silvo Lenart, "The Influence of Political Consultants in the 1992 Congressional Elections," *Legislative Studies Quarterly* 22 (February 1997): 61–77.

6. Five liberal Democratic U.S. senators, including George McGovern of South Dakota, were defeated in this way in 1980, for example.

7. Diana C. Mutz, "Effects of Horse-Race Coverage on Campaign Coffers: Strategic Contributing in Presidential Primaries," *Journal of Politics* 57 (November 1995): 1015–42.

8. Carla Marinucci, "'Iowa Yell' Stirring Doubts About Dean" *San Francisco Chronicle* (January 21, 2004): A1.

9. John G. Geer, "The Effects of Presidential Debates on the Electorate's Preferences for Candidates," *American Politics Quarterly* 16 (October 1988): 486–501.

10. David J. Lanoue, "One That Made a Difference: Cognitive Consistency, Political Knowledge, and the 1980 Presidential Debate," *Public Opinion Quarterly* 56 (Summer 1992): 168–84.

11. http://www.cyberjournalist.net/news/001705.php.

12. Dennis J. Willard et al, "Quiet Push Wins Ohio for GOP," *Akron Beacon Journal* (November 4, 2004). http://www.ohio.com/mld/ohio/news/politics/10096916.htm?1c.

13. opensecrets.org (http://www.opensecrets.org/overview/incumbs.asp?cycle=2004).

14. opensecrets.org (http://www.opensecrets.org/overview/stats.asp?cycle=2004).

15. Steven T. Engel and David J. Jackson, "Wielding the Stick Instead of Its Carrot: Labor PAC Punishment of Pro-NAFTA Democrats," *Political Research Quarterly* 51 (September 1998): 813–28.

16. Janet M. Box-Steffensmeier and J. Tobin Grant, "All in a Day's Work: The Financial Rewards of Legislative Effectiveness," *Legislative Studies Quarterly* 24 (November 1999): 511–23.

17. Kevin M. Leyden and Stephen A. Borrelli, "An Investment in Goodwill: Party Contributions and Party Unity Among U.S. House Members in the 1980s," *American Politics Quarterly* 22 (October 1994): 421–52.

18. Amy Keller, "Helping Each Other Out: Members Dip into Campaign Funds for Fellow Candidates," *Roll Call* (June 15, 1998): 1.

19. For member contribution activity at the state level, see Jay K. Dow, "Campaign Contributions and Intercandidate Transfers in the California Assembly," *Social Science Quarterly* 75 (1994): 867–80. For member contribution activity at the congressional level, see Bruce A. Larson, "Ambition and Money in the U.S. House of Representatives: Analyzing Campaign Contributions from Incumbents' Leadership PACs and Reelection Committees" (Ph.D. dissertation, University of Virginia, 1998). For a briefer account, see Paul S. Herrnson, "Money and Motives: Spending in House Elections," in Lawrence C. Dodd and Bruce I. Oppenheimer, eds., *Congress Reconsidered*, 6th ed. (Washington, DC: CQ Press, 1997).

20. Federal Election Commission. www.fec.gov.

21. Open secrets.org 2004 Election Overview: Candidate to Candidate Giving. http://www.opensecrets.org/overview/cand2cand.asp?cycle=2004.

22. Larson, "Ambition and Money in the U.S. House of Representatives."

23. *Buckley* v. *Valeo*, 424 U.S. 1 (1976).

24. Marisa Katz, "Matching Funds" *New Republic Online*, July 13, 2004, http://www.tnr.com/doc.mhtml?i=express&s=katz071304.

25. *Buckley* v. *Valeo*, 424 U.S. 1 (1976); *Colorado Republican Federal Campaign Committee* v. *Federal Election Commission*, 116 S.Ct. 2309 (1996).

26. Meg Kinnard and Jennifer Koons, "Issue Groups Target Women, Question Kerry's Character," NationalJournal.com, October 22, 2004. Http://nationaljournal.com/members/adspotlight/2004/10/1022wh1.htm.

27. Thomas B. Edsall and Derek Willis, "Fundraising Records Broken by Both Major Political Parties," *Washington Post*, December 3, 2004, page A07.

28. Amy Keller, "Experts Wonder About FEC's Internet Savvy: Regulating Web Is a Challenge for Watchdog Agency," *Roll Call* (May 6, 1999): 1, 21.

29. Anthony Corrado, "Party Soft Money," in Anthony Corrado et al., eds., *Campaign Finance Reform: A Sourcebook* (Washington, DC: Brookings Institution, 1997).

30. Trevor Potter, "Issue Advocacy and Express Advocacy," in Anthony Corrado et al., eds., *Campaign Finance Reform: A Sourcebook* (Washington, DC: Brookings Institution, 1997).

31. http://www.commoncause.org/laundromat/stat/topdonors01.htm.

32. Thomas E. Mann and Norman J. Ornstein, "Separating Myth from Reality in *McConnell v. FEC*," *Election Law Journal* (March 2004): 14. Taken from the Brookings Institute Web site, http://www.brook.edu/views/articles/mann/20040204.pdf.

33. Federal Election Commission Release, "Party Finacial Activity Summarized," December 14, 2004. http://www.fec.gov/press/press2004/20041214party/20041214party.html

34. Frank Sorauf, *Inside Campaign Finance: Myths and Realities* (New Haven, CT: Yale University Press, 1992), ch. 6.

35. Richard A. Smith, "Interest Group Influence in the U.S. Congress," *Legislative Studies Quarterly* 20 (1995): 89–139. See also Janet Grenzke, "PACs and the Congressional Supermarket: The Currency Is Complex," *American Journal of Political Science* 33 (1989): 1–24.

36. Richard L. Hall and Frank W. Wayman, "Buying Time: Moneyed Interests and the Mobilization of Bias in Congressional Committees," *American Political Science Review* 84 (1990): 797–820.

37. Thomas Gais, *Improper Influence: Campaign Finance Law, Political Interest Groups, and the Problem of Equality* (Ann Arbor: University of Michigan Press, 1996).

38. http://www.opensecrets.org/overview/stats.asp?cycle=2004.

39. "What an Election Costs," Canadian Broadcasting Corporation, March 17, 2004. http://www.cbc.ca/canadavotes/thecampaign/electioncosts.html

40. Michael Janofsky, "Advocacy Groups Spent Record Amount on 2004 Election," New York Times, December 17, 2004.

CHAPTER 15

1. See Mitchell Stephens, *A History of News: From the Drum to the Satellite* (New York: Viking, 1989).

2. Charles Press and Kenneth VerBurg, *American Politicians and Journalists* (Glenview, IL: Scott, Foresman, 1988), 8–10.

3. For a delightful rendition of this episode, see Shelley Ross, *Fall from Grace* (New York: Ballantine, 1988), ch. 12.

4. Doris A. Graber, *Mass Media and American Politics*, 3rd ed. (Washington, DC: CQ Press, 1989), 12.

5. See Thomas C. Leonard, *The Power of the Press: The Birth of American Political Reporting* (New York: Oxford University Press, 1986), ch. 7.

6. Richard L. Rubin, *Press, Party, and Presidency* (New York: Norton, 1981), 38–9.

7. Stephen Bates, *If No News, Send Rumors* (New York: St. Martin's Press, 1989), 185.

8. U.S. Senate press gallery and U.S. House of Representatives radio-television correspondents gallery.

9. Washingtonpost.com. List of White House Correspondents, http://www.washingtonpost.com/wp-svr/politics/administration/whbriefing/correspondents.html.

10. Data complied by the Newspaper Association of America, http://www.naa.org/marketscope/pdfs/DailyReadership1964-Present.pdf.

11. *PR Newswire*, "NAA Finds Newspaper Readership Steady in Top 50 Markets," May 3, 2004.

12. Newspaper Association of America.

13. Brasch, "Synergizing America."

14. Pew Research Center for the People and the Press, "Cable and Internet Loom Large in Fragmented Political News Universe: Perceptions of Partisan Bias Seen as Growing, Especially by Democrats," January 11, 2004.

15. Pew Research Center, "Cable and Internet Loom Large."

16. Katy Bachman, "Direct Broadcast Satellite Gains Users; Cable Wanes," mediaweek.com, April 7, 2004.

17. Andrew Kohut, *The Biennial Pew Media Survey: How News Habits Changed in 2004*, Brookings/Pew Research Center Forum, Washington, DC, June 8, 2004, http://www.brookings.edu/dybdocroot/comm/events/20040608.pdf.

18. This was the fundamental conclusion of Shanto Iyengar and Donald R. Kinder, *News That Matters* (Chicago: University of Chicago Press, 1987).

19. M. Just, T. Buhr, and A. Crigler, "Voice, Substance, and Cynicism in Presidential Campaign Media," *Political Communication* 16 (January 1999): 25–44.

20. Pew Research Center for the People and the Press, Political Communications Study, January 11, 2004, http://people-press.org/reports/display.php3?PageID=774.

21. Pew Research Center, "Cable and Internet Loom Large."

22. UCLA Center for Communication Policy, "The UCLA Internet Report: Surveying the Digital Future," January 2003; PEJ Research.

23. Scott L. Althaus and David Tewksbury, "Patterns of Internet and Traditional News Media Use in a Networked Community," *Political Communication* 17 (2000): 21–45.

24. Timothy E. Cook and Lyn Ragsdale, "The President and the Press: Negotiating Newsworthiness at the White House," in Michael Nelson, ed., *The Presidency and the Political System*, 5th ed. (Washington DC: CQ Press, 1998), 323.

25. Thomas Patterson, *Out of Order* (New York: Vintage, 1994).

26. Harold W. Stanley and Richard G. Niemi, *Vital Statistics on American Politics*, 4th ed. (Washington, DC: CQ Press, 1994), 28.

27. John Hibbing and Elizabeth Theiss-Morse, *Congress As Public Enemy: Political Attitudes Toward American Political Institutions* (New York: Cambridge University Press, 1995).

28. Hibbing and Theiss-Morse, *Congress As Public Enemy*.

29. Carl Hulse, "Even Some in G.O.P. Call for More Oversight of Bush," *New York Times* (May 30, 2004): A1.

30. Roderick Hart, *Seducing America: How Television Charms the Modern Voter* (New York: Oxford University Press, 1995).

31. Larry Sabato, *Feeding Frenzy: Attack Journalism and American Politics* (Baltimore: Lanahan, 2000).

32. *New York Times Co. v. Sullivan*, 376 U.S. 254 (1964). See also Steven Pressman, "Libel Law: Finding the Right Balance," *Editorial Research Reports* 2 (August 18, 1989): 462–71.

33. *Curtis Publishing Co. v. Butts*, 388 U.S. 130 (1967); *Associated Press v. Walker*, 388 U.S. 130 (1967).

34. American Society of Newspaper Editors, *The Changing Face of the Newsroom* (Washington, DC: ASNE, 1989), 33; William Schneider and I. A. Lewis, "Views on the News," *Public Opinion* 8 (August/September 1985): 6–11, 58–9; and S. Robert Lichter, Stanley Rothman, and Linda S. Lichter, *The Media Elite* (Bethesda, MD: Adler and Adler, 1986).

35. National Survey of the Role of Polls in Policymaking, survey conducted by the Kaiser Family Foundation, http://www.kff.org/content/2001/3146/toplines.pdf.

36. See Dom Bonafede, "Crossing Over," *National Journal* 21 (January 14, 1989): 102; Richard Harwood, "Tainted Journalists," *Washington Post* (December 4, 1988): L6; Charles Trueheart, "Trading Places: The Insiders Debate," *Washington Post* (January 4, 1989): D1, 19; and Kirk Victor, "Slanted Views," *National Journal* 20 (June 4, 1988): 1512.

37. Martin Gilens and Craig Hertzman. "Corporate Ownership and News Bias: Newspaper Coverage of the 1996 Telecommunication Act," *Journal of Politics* 62 (May 2000), 369–86.

38. See http://www.stateofthenewsmedia.org/narrative_overview_audience.asp?media=1.

39. Pew Research Center, "Cable and Internet Loom Large."

40. David Domke, David P. Fan, Dhavan V. Shah, and Mark D. Watts, "The Politics of Conservative Elites and the 'Liberal Media' Argument," *Journal of Communication* 49 (Fall 1999): 35–58.

41. Benjamin I. Page, Robert Y. Shapiro, and Glenn R. Dempsey, "What Moves Public Opinion?" *American Political Science Review* 81 (March 1987): 23–44.

42. Iyengar and Kinder, *News That Matters*.

43. Martin P. Wattenberg, *The Decline of American Political Parties, 1952–1994* (Cambridge, MA: Harvard University Press, 1996).

44. Marc Hetherington, "The Media's Role in Forming Voters' National Economic Evaluations in 1992," *American Journal of Political Science* 40 (May 1996): 372–95.

45. Stuart Polk, "Panhandle Poll Summary: Networks' Wrong Florida Call for Gore Cost Bush Votes," John McLaughlin and Associates, November 20, 2000, http://www.mclaughlinonline.com/newspoll/np2001/001120panh.htm.

46. Donald L. Jorand and Benjamin I. Page. "Shaping Foreign Policy Opinions: The Role of TV News." *Journal of Conflict Resolution* 36 (June, 1992), 227–41.

47. Fox News/Opinion Dynamic Poll, conducted June 18–19, 2002.

48. Pew Research Center for the People and the Press, "Internet News Takes Off: Event Driven News Audiences," June 8, 1998, http://people-press.org.

49. Pew Research Center, "Cable and Internet Loom Large."

50. Pew Research Center for the People and the Press, "News Media's Improved Image Proves Short-Lived," August 4, 2002, http://people-press.org.

51. Pew Research Center, "News Media's Improved Image Proves Short-Lived."

52. FCC News Release, "FCC Sets Limits on Media Concentration: Unprecedented Public Record Results in Enforceable and Balanced Broadcast Ownership Rules," June 2, 2003.

53. Christopher Stern, "FCC Chairman's Star a Little Dimmer," *Washington Post* (July 25, 2003): E01, http://www.washingtonpost.com/ac2/wp-dyn?pagename=article&contentId=A43044-2003Jul24&notFound=true.

54. Mark K. Miller. "On Hold; Rankings Change Little as Regulatory Uncertainty Keeps Station Trading in Neutral," *Broadcasting and Cable* (April, 19, 2004): 50.

55. See http://www.museum.tv/archives/etv/F/htmlF/fairnessdoct/fairnessdoct.htm.

56. *New York Times Co. v. U.S.*, 403 U.S. 713 (1971).

57. Jillian Harrison, "Embedded Journalism Limited in Perspective, Tufts U. Professors Say," *University Wire*, April 15, 2003.

CHAPTER 16

1. Howard Kurtz, "MoveOn.org's Swift Boat Response to Anti-Kerry Ad," *Washington Post* (August 17, 2004): A8.

2. Kurtz, "MoveOn.org's Swift Boat Response."

3. "Campaign Finance Reform Led to Birth of 527s," *Seattle Times* (July 25, 2004): A18.

4. Robert D. Putnam, "Bowling Alone: America's Declining Social Capital," *Journal of Democracy* 6 (1995): 650–65; and Putnam, *Bowling Alone: The Collapse and Revival of American Community* (New York: Simon and Schuster, 2000).

5. Everett Carll Ladd, quoted in Richard Morin, "Who Says We're Not Joiners," *Washington Post* (May 2, 1999): B5.

6. John Brehm and Wendy Rahn, "Individual-Level Evidence for the Causes and Consequences of Social Capital," *American Journal of Political Science* 41 (July 1997): 999.

7. Mark Schneider et al., "Institutional Arrangements and the Creation of Social Capital: The Effects of Public School Choice," *American Political Science Review* 91 (March 1997): 82–93.

8. Nicholas Lemann, "Kicking in Groups," *Atlantic Monthly* (April 1996), NEXIS.

9. Robert D. Putnam et al., *Making Democracy Work: Civic Traditions in Modern Italy* (Princeton NJ: Princeton University Press, 1994).

10. Kay Lehman Schlozman, Nancy Burns, and Sidney Verba, "Gender and the Pathways to Participation: The Role of Resources," *Journal of Politics* 56 (1994): 963–90.

11. David B. Truman, *The Governmental Process: Political Interests and Public Opinion* (New York: Knopf, 1951), 33.

12. Truman, *The Governmental Process*, ch. 16.

13. Robert H. Salisbury, "An Exchange Theory of Interest Groups," *Midwest Journal of Political Science* 13 (1969): 1–32.

14. Jeffrey M. Berry, *Lobbying for the People: The Political Behavior of Public Interest Groups* (Princeton, NJ: Princeton University Press, 1977), 7.

15. Jeffrey M. Berry, *Lobbying for the People*, 7.

16. Neil J. Mitchell, Wendy L. Hansen, and Eric M. Jepsen, "The Determinants of Domestic and Foreign Corporate Political Activity," *Journal of Politics* 59 (November 1997): 1096–1113.

17. Quoted in Grant McConnell, "Lobbies and Pressure Groups," in Jack Greene, ed., *Encyclopedia of American Political History*, vol. 2 (New York: Macmillan, 1984), 768.

18. Lee Epstein, *Conservatives in Court* (Knoxville: University of Tennessee Press, 1985).

19. Jack L. Walker, "The Origins and Maintenance of Interest Groups in America," *American Political Science Review* 77 (June 1983): 390–406.

20. Peter Steinfels, "Moral Majority to Dissolve: Says Mission Accomplished," *New York Times* (June 12, 1989): A14.

21. Robert Scheer, "The NRA-Friendly Candidate: Bush's Stance on Guns Proves That He Is No Compassionate Conservative," *Pittsburgh Post-Gazette* (May 11, 2000): A29.

22. David Mahood, *Interest Groups Participation in America: A New Intensity* (Englewood Cliffs, NJ: Prentice Hall, 1990), 23.

23. Bill Miller, "CEOs Plan Network to Link Them in Attack," *Washington Post* (March 13, 2002): E1.

24. Political Moneyline, www.tray.com.

25. Sam Loewenberg, "Now, The Tricky Part: Dividing Profits," *Legal Times* (May 31, 1999): 4.

26. Michael Wines, "For New Lobbyists, It's What They Know," *New York Times* (November 3, 1993): B14.

27. Quoted in Kay Lehman Schlozman and John T. Tierney, *Organized Interests and American Democracy* (New York: Harper and Row, 1986), 85.

28. Ken Kollman, "Inviting Friends to Lobby: Interest Groups, Ideological Bias, and Congressional Committees," *American Journal of Political Science* 41 (April 1997): 519–44.

29. Quoted in Norman J. Ornstein and Shirley Elder, *Interest Groups, Lobbying and Policy Making* (Washington, DC: CQ Press, 1978), 77.

30. Center for Responsive Politics, http://www.opensecrets.org.

31. Richard L. Hall and Frank W. Wayman, "Buying Time: Moneyed Interests and the Mobilization of Bias in Congress," *American Political Science Review* 84 (September 1990): 797–820.

32. Some political scientists speak of "iron rectangles," reflecting the growing importance of a fourth party, the courts, in the lobbying process.

33. Clement E. Vose, "Litigation As a Form of Pressure Group Activity," *Annals* 319 (September 1958): 20–31.

34. Karen O'Connor, "Lobbying the Justices or Lobbying for Justice?" in Paul Herrnson, Ronald G. Shaiko, and Clyde Wilcox, eds., *The Interest Group Connection* (Chatham, NJ: Chatham House, 1998), 267–88.

35. Robert A. Goldberg, *Grassroots Resistance: Social Movement in Twentieth Century America* (Belmont, CA: Wadsworth, 1991).

36. Thomas Romer and James M. Snyder, "An Empirical Investigation of the Dynamics of PAC Contributions," *American Journal of Political Science* 38 (August 1994): 745–69.

37. Hall and Wayman, "Buying Time"; and Jack R. Wright, "Contributions, Lobbying, and Committee Voting in the U.S. House of Representatives," *American Political Science Review* 84 (June 1990): 417–38.

38. D. Bruce La Pierre, "A Little Problem of Constitutionality: . . .But the Court May Not Save the Day," *St. Louis Post-Dispatch* (March 27, 2002): B7.

39. E. E. Schattschneider, *The Semi-Sovereign People* (New York: Holt, Rinehart, and Winston, 1960), 51.

40. Ken Kollman, *Outside Lobbying: Public Opinion and Interest Group Strategies* (Princeton, NJ: Princeton University Press, 1998); and Karen O'Connor, *Women's Organizations' Use of the Courts* (Lexington, MA: 1980).

41. Marie Hojnacki, "Interest Groups' Decisions to Join Alliances or Work Alone," *American Journal of Political Science* 41 (January 1997): 61–87.

42. Schattschneider, *The Semi-Sovereign People*, 35.

43. Mancur Olson Jr., *The Logic of Collective Action: Public Goods and the Theory of Groups* (Cambridge, MA: Harvard University Press, 1965).

44. David C. King and Jack L. Walker, "The Provision of Benefits by Interest Groups in the United States," *Journal of Politics* 54 (May 1992): 394.

45. Hojnacki, "Interest Groups' Decisions."

46. William Browne, "Organized Interests and Their Issue Niches: A Search for Pluralism in a Policy Domain," *Journal of Politics* 52 (May 1990): 477.

47. Donald P. Haider-Markel, "Interest Group Survival: Shared Interests Versus Competition for Resources," *Journal of Politics* 59 (August 1997): 903–12.

48. Leslie Wayne, "And for his Next Feat, Billionaire Sets Sights on Bush," *New York Times* (May 31, 2004): A14.

49. Walker, "The Origins and Maintenance of Interest Groups," 390–406.

Glossary

A

administrative adjudication: A quasi-judicial process in which a bureaucratic agency settles disputes between two parties in a manner similar to the way courts resolve disputes.

administrative discretion: The ability of bureaucrats to make choices concerning the best way to implement congressional intentions.

advisory referendum: A process in which voters cast nonbinding ballots on an issue or proposal.

affiliates: Local television stations that carry the programming of a national network.

affirmative action: Policies designed to give special attention or compensatory treatment to members of a previously disadvantaged group.

al-Qaeda: Worldwide terrorist organization led by Osama bin Laden, responsible for numerous attacks against U.S. interests, including 9/11 attacks against the World Trade Center and the Pentagon.

American dream: An American ideal of a happy, sucessful life, which often includes wealth, a house, a better life for one's children, and, for some, the ability to grow up to be president.

amicus curiae: "Friend of the court"; a third party to a lawsuit who files a legal brief for the purpose of raising additional points of view in an attempt to influence a court's decision.

Anti-Federalists: Those who favored strong state governments and a weak national government; opposed the ratification of the U.S. Constitution.

appellate court: Court that generally reviews only findings of law made by lower courts.

appellate jurisdiction: The power vested in an appellate court to review and/or revise the decision of a lower court.

apportionment: The proportional process of allotting congressional seats to each state following the decennial census.

allotment: The proportional process of allotting congressional seats to each state following the decennial census.

Articles of Confederation: The compact among the thirteen original states that was the basis of their government. Written in 1776, the Articles were not ratified by all the states until 1781.

at-large election: Election in which candidates for office must compete throughout the jurisdiction as a whole.

B

bicameral legislature: A legislature divided into two houses; the U.S. Congress and the state legislatures are bicameral except Nebraska, which is unicameral.

bill: A proposed law.

bill of attainder: A law declaring an act illegal without a judicial trial.

Bill of Rights: The first ten amendments to the U.S. Constitution, which largely guarantee specific rights and liberties.

Black Codes: Laws denying most legal rights to newly freed slaves; passed by southern states following the Civil War.

blanket primary: A primary in which voters may cast ballots in either party's primary (but not both) on an office-by-office basis.

block grant: Broad grant with few strings attached; given to states by the federal government for specified activities, such as secondary education or health services.

brief: A document containing the legal written arguments in a case filed with a court by a party prior to a hearing or trial.

Brown v. Board of Education (1954): U.S. Supreme Court decision holding that school segregation is inherently unconstitutional because it violates the Fourteenth Amendment's guarantee of equal protection; marked the end of legal segregation in the United States.

bureaucracy: A set of complex hierarchical departments, agencies, commissions, and their staffs that exist to help a chief executive officer carry out his or her duties. Bureaucracies may be private organizations of governmental units.

C

Cabinet: The formal body of presidential advisers who head the fifteen executive departments. Presidents often add others to this body of formal advisers.

campaign consultant: The private-sector professionals and firms who sell to a candidate the technologies, services, and strategies required to get that candidate elected.

campaign manager: The individual who travels with the candidate and coordinates the many different aspects of the campaign.

candidate debate: Forum in which political candidates face each other to discuss their platforms, records, and character.

categorical grant: Grant for which Congress appropriates funds for a specific purpose.

charter: A document that, like a constitution, specifies the basic policies, procedures, and institutions of a municipality.

checks and balances: A governmental structure that gives each of the three branches of government some degree of oversight and control over the actions of the others.

citizen: Member of the political community to whom certain rights and obligations are attached.

city charter: A document similar to a constitution, setting out city government structure and powers and its political processes.

city council: The legislature in a city government.

civic virtue: The tendency to form small-scale associations for the public good.

civil law: Codes of behavior related to business and contractual relationships between groups and individuals.

civil liberties: The personal guarantees and freedoms that the federal government cannot abridge by law, constitution, or judicial interpretation.

civil rights: The government-protected rights of individuals against arbitrary or discriminatory treatment by governments or individuals based on categories such as race, sex, national origin, age, religion, or sexual orientation.

Civil Rights Act of 1964: Legislation passed by Congress to outlaw segregation in public facilities and racial discrimination in employment, education, and voting; created the Equal Employment Opportunity Commission.

Civil Rights Cases (1883): Name attached to five cases brought under the Civil Rights Act of 1875. In 1883, the Supreme Court decided that discrimination in a variety of public accommodations, including theaters, hotels, and railroads, could not be prohibited by the act because it was private, not state, discrimination.

civil service laws: These acts removed the staffing of the bureaucracy from political parties and created a professional bureaucracy filled through competition.

civil service system: The system created by civil service laws by which many appointments to the federal bureaucracy are made.

civil society: Society created when citizens are allowed to organize and express their views publicly as they engage in an open debate about public policy.

clear and present danger test: Test articulated by the Supreme Court in *Schenck v. U.S.* (1919) to draw the line between protected and unprotected speech; the Court looks to see "whether the words used…" could "create a clear and present danger that they will bring about substantive evils" that Congress seeks "to prevent."

closed primary: A primary election in which only a party's registered voters are eligible to vote.

cloture: Mechanism requiring sixty senators to vote to cut off debate.

coalition: A group of interests or organizations that join forces for the purpose of electing public officials.

coattail effect: The tendency of lesser-known or weaker candidates lower on the ballot to profit in an election by the presence on the party's ticket of a more popular candidate.

collective good: Something of value that cannot be withheld from a nonmember of a group, for example, a tax write-off or a better environment.

commission: Form of local government in which several officials are elected to top positions that have both legislative and executive responsibilities.

Committees of Correspondence: Organizations in each of the American colonies created to keep colonists abreast of developments with the British; served as powerful molders of public opinion against the British.

communications director: The person who develops the overall media strategy for the candidate, blending the free press coverage with the paid TV, radio, and mail media.

commute: The action of a governor to cancel all or part of the sentence of someone convicted of a crime, while keeping the conviction on the record.

compact: A formal, legal agreement between a state and a tribe.

concurrent powers: Authority possessed by both the state and national governments that may be exercised concurrently as long as that power is not exclusively within the scope of national power or in conflict with national law.

confederation: Type of government where the national government derives its powers from the states; a league of independent states.

conference committee: Joint committee created to iron out differences between Senate and House versions of a specific piece of legislation.

congressional review: A process whereby Congress can nullify agency regulations by a joint resolution of legislative disapproval.

congressionalist: One who believes that Article II's provision that the president should ensure "faithful execution of the laws" should be read as an injunction against substituting presidential authority for legislative intent.

conservative: One thought to believe that a government is best that governs least and that big government can only infringe on individual, personal, and economic rights.

Constitution: A document establishing the structure, functions, and limitations of a government.

constitutional courts: Federal courts specifically created by the U.S. Constitution or by Congress pursuant to its authority in Article III.

content regulation: Governmental attempts to regulate the electronic media.

contrast ad: Ad that compares the records and proposals of the candidates, with a bias toward the sponsor.

cooperative federalism: The relationship between the national and state governments that began with the New Deal.

county: A geographic district created within a state with a government that has general responsibilities for land, welfare, environment, and, where appropriate, rural service policies.

criminal law: Codes of behavior related to the protection of property and individual safety.

critical election: An election that signals a party realignment through voter polarization around new issues.

crossover voting: Participation in the primary of a party with which the voter is not affiliated.

D

de facto **discrimination:** Racial discrimination that results from practice (such as housing patterns or other social factors) rather than the law.

de jure **discrimination:** Racial segregation that is a direct result of law or official policy.

Declaration of Independence: Document drafted by Thomas Jefferson in 1776 that proclaimed the right of the American colonies to separate from Great Britain.

deep background: Information provided to a journalist that will not be attributed to any source.

delegate: Role played by elected representatives who vote the way their constituents would want them to, regardless of their own opinions.

democracy: A system of government that gives power to the people, whether directly or through their elected representatives.

departments: Major administrative units with responsibility for a broad area of government operations. Departmental status usually indicates a permanent national interest in a particular governmental function, such as defense, commerce, or agriculture.

Dillon's Rule: A court ruling that local governments do not have any inherent sovereignty but instead must be authorized by state government.

direct democracy: A system of government in which members of the polity meet to discuss all policy decisions and then agree to abide by majority rule.

direct incitement test: A test articulated by the Supreme Court in *Brandenberg* v. *Ohio* (1969) that holds that advocacy of illegal action is protected by the First Amendment unless imminent lawless action is intended and likely to occur.

direct initiative: A process in which voters can place a proposal on a ballot and enact it into law without involving the legislature or the governor.

direct mailer: A professional who supervises a political campaign's direct-mail fund-raising strategies.

direct (popular) referendum: A process in which voters can veto a bill recently passed in the legislature by placing the issue on a ballot and expressing disapproval.

direct primary: The selection of party candidates through the ballots of qualified voters rather than at party nomination conventions.

discharge petition: Petition that gives a majority of the House of Representatives the authority to bring an issue to the floor in the face of committee inaction.

district-based election: Election in which candidates run for an office that represents only the voters of a specific district within the jurisdiction.

disturbance theory: Political scientist David B. Truman's theory that interest groups form in part to counteract the efforts of other groups.

divided government: The political condition in which different political parties control the White House and Congress.

domestic dependent nation: A type of sovereignty that makes an Indian tribe in the United States outside the authority of state governments but reliant on the federal government for the definition of tribal authority.

dual federalism: The belief that having separate and equally powerful levels of government is the best arrangement.

due process clause: Clause contained in the Fifth and Fourteenth Amendments. Over the years, it has been construed to guarantee to individuals a variety of rights ranging from economic liberty to criminal procedural rights to protection from arbitrary governmental action.

due process rights: Procedural guarantees provided by the Fourth, Fifth, Sixth, and Eighth Amendments for those accused of crimes.

E

economic interest group: A group with the primary purpose of promoting the financial interests of its members.

Eighth Amendment: Part of the Bill of Rights that states: "Excessive bail shall not be required, nor excessive fines imposed, nor cruel and unusual punishments inflicted."

elector: Member of the Electoral College chosen by methods determined in each state.

Electoral College: Representatives of each state who cast the final ballots that actually elect a president.

electorate: Citizens eligible to vote.

electronic media: The broadcast and cable media, including television, radio, and the Internet.

enumerated powers: Seventeen specific powers granted to Congress under Article I, section 8, of the U.S. Constitution; these powers include taxation, coinage of money, regulation of commerce, and the authority to provide for a national defense.

Equal Employment Opportunity Commission: Federal agency created to enforce the Civil Rights Act of 1964, which forbids discrimination on the basis of race, creed, national origin, religion, or sex in hiring, promotion, or firing.

equal protection clause: Section of the Fourteenth Amendment that guarantees that all citizens receive "equal protection of the laws."

Equal Rights Amendment: Proposed amendment that would bar discrimination against women by federal or state governments.

equal time rule: The rule that requires broadcast stations to sell air time equally to all candidates in a political campaign if they choose to sell it to any.

establishment clause: The first clause in the First Amendment; it prohibits the national government from establishing a national religion.

ex post facto **law:** Law passed after the fact, thereby making previously legal activity illegal and subject to current penalty; prohibited by the U.S. Constitution.

exclusionary rule: Judicially created rule that prohibits police from using illegally seized evidence at trial.

executive agreement: Formal government agreement entered into by the president that does not require the advice and consent of the U.S. Senate.

Executive Office of the President (EOP): Establishment created in 1939 to help the president oversee the executive branch bureaucracy.

executive order: A rule or regulation issued by the president that has the effect of law. All executive orders must be published in the *Federal Register*.

executive privilege: An implied presidential power that allows the president to refuse to disclose information regarding confidential conversations or national security to Congress or the judiciary.

exit polls: Polls conducted at selected polling places on Election Day.

extradite: To send someone against his or her will to another state to face criminal charges.

F

fairness doctrine: Rule in effect from 1949 to 1985 requiring broadcasters to cover events adequately and to present contrasting views on important public issues.

Federal Employees Political Activities Act: 1993 liberalization of the Hatch Act. Federal employees are now allowed to run for office in nonpartisan elections and to contribute money to campaigns in partisan elections.

federal system: System of government where the national government and state governments derive all authority from the people.

federalism: The philosophy that describes the governmental system created by the Framers; see also **federal system**.

The Federalist Papers: A series of eighty-five political papers written by John Jay, Alexander Hamilton, and James Madison in support of ratification of the U.S. Constitution.

Federalists: Those who favored a stronger national government and supported the proposed U.S. Constitution; later became the first U.S. political party.

Fifteenth Amendment: One of the three Civil War amendments; specifically enfranchised newly freed male slaves.

Fifth Amendment: Part of the Bill of Rights that imposes a number of restrictions on the federal government with respect to the rights of persons suspected of committing a crime. It provides for indictment by a grand jury, protection against self-incrimination, and prevents the national government from denying a person life, liberty, or property without the due process of law. It also prevents the national government from taking property without fair compensation.

fighting words: Words that, "by their very utterance inflict injury or tend to incite an immediate breach of peace." Fighting words are not subject to the restrictions of the First Amendment.

filibuster: A formal way of halting action on a bill by means of long speeches or unlimited debate in the Senate.

finance chair: A professional who coordinates the fund-raising efforts for the campaign.

First Amendment: Part of the Bill of Rights that imposes a number of restrictions on the federal government with respect to the civil liberties of the people, including freedom of religion, speech, press, assembly, and petition.

First Continental Congress: Meeting held in Philadelphia from September 5 to October 26, 1774, in which fifty-six delegates (from every colony except Georgia) adopted a resolution in opposition to the Coercive Acts.

Fourteenth Amendment: One of the three Civil War amendments; guarantees equal protection and due process of the laws to all U.S. citizens.

Fourth Amendment: Part of the Bill of Rights that reads: "The right of the people to be secure in their persons, houses, papers, and effects, against unreasonable searches and seizures, shall not be violated, and no Warrants shall issue, but upon probable cause, supported by Oath or affirmation, and particularly describing the place to be searched, and the persons or things to the seized."

free exercise clause: The second clause of the First Amendment. It prohibits the U.S. government from interfering with a citizen's right to practice his or her religion.

free media: Coverage of a candidate's campaign by the news media.

free rider problem: Potential members fail to join a group because they can get the benefit, or collective good, sought by the group without contributing to the effort.

front-loading: The tendency of states to choose an early date on the primary calendar.

full faith and credit clause: Portion of Article IV of the Constitution that ensures judicial decrees and contracts made in one state will be binding and enforceable in any other state.

fundamental freedoms: Those rights defined by the Court to be essential to order, liberty, and justice.

G

general election: Election in which voters decide which candidates will actually fill elective public offices.

general election campaign: That part of a political campaign aimed at winning a general election.

gerrymandering: The legislative process through which the majority party in each statehouse tries to assure that the maximum number of representatives from its political party can be elected to Congress through the redrawing of legislative districts.

get-out-the-vote (GOTV): A push at the end of a political campaign to encourage supporters to go to the polls.

Gibbons v. Ogden (1824): The Court upheld broad congressional power over interstate commerce. The Court's broad interpretation of the Constitution's commerce clause paved the way for later rulings upholding expansive federal powers.

government: A collective of individuals ad institutions, the formal vehicles through which policies are made and affairs of state are conducted.

government corporations: Businesses established by Congress that perform functions that could be provided by private businesses (such as the U.S. Postal Service).

governmental party: The office holders and candidates who run under a political party's banner.

governor: Chief elected executive in state government.

grandfather clause: Voting qualification provision in many Southern states that allowed only those whose grandfathers had voted before Reconstruction to vote unless they passed a wealth or literacy test.

Great Compromise: A decision made during the Constitutional Convention to give each state the same number of representatives in the Senate regardless of size; representation in the House was determined by population.

H

hard money: Legally specified and limited contributions that are clearly regulated by the Federal Election Campaign Act and by the Federal Election Commission.

Hatch Act: Law enacted in 1939 to prohibit civil servants from taking activist roles in partisan campaigns. This act prohibited federal employees from making political contributions, working for a particular party, or campaigning for a particular candidate.

hold: A tactic by which a senator asks to be informed before a particular bill is brought to the floor. This stops the bill from coming to the floor until the hold is removed.

I

impeachment: The power delegated to the House of Representatives in the Constitution to charge the president, vice president, or other "civil officers," including federal judges, with "Treason, Bribery, or other High Crimes and Misdemeanors." This is the first step in the constitutional process of removing such government officials from office.

implementation: The process by which a law or policy is put into operation by the bureaucracy.

implied powers: Powers derived from the enumerated powers and the necessary and proper clause. These powers are not stated specifically but are considered to be reasonably implied through the exercise of delegated powers.

inclusion: The principle that state courts will apply federal laws when those laws directly conflict with the laws of a state.

incorporation doctrine: An interpretation of the Constitution that holds that the due process clause of the Fourteenth Amendment requires that state and local governments also guarantee those rights.

incumbency: The fact that being in office helps a person stay in office because of a variety of benefits that go with the position.

incumbency factor: The fact that being in office helps a person stay in office because of a variety of benefits that go with the position.

independent executive agencies: Governmental units that closely resemble a Cabinet department but have a narrower area of responsibility (such as the Central Intelligence Agency) and are not part of any Cabinet department.

independent regulatory commission: An agency created by Congress that is generally concerned with a specific aspect of the economy.

indirect initiative: A process in which the legislature places a proposal on a ballot and allows voters to enact it into law, without involving the governor or further action by the legislature.

indirect (representative) democracy: A system of government that gives citizens the opportunity to vote for representatives who will work on their behalf.

inherent powers: Powers of the president that can be derived or inferred from specific powers in the Constitution.

initiative: A process that allows citizens to propose legislation and submit it to the state electorate for popular vote.

inoculation ad: Advertising that attempts to counteract an anticipated attack from the opposition before the attack is launched.

interagency councils: Working groups created to facilitate coordination of policy making and implementation across a host of governmental agencies.

interest group: An organized group that tries to influence public policy.

interstate compacts: Contracts between states that carry the force of law; generally now used as a tool to address multistate policy concerns.

iron triangles: The relatively stable relationships and patterns of interaction that occur among an agency, interest groups, and congressional committees or subcommittees.

issue networks: The loose and informal relationships that exist among a large number of actors who work in broad policy areas.

issue-oriented politics: Politics that focuses on specific issues rather than on party, candidate, or other loyalties.

J

Jim Crow laws: Laws enacted by southern states that discriminated against blacks by creating "whites only" schools, theaters, hotels, and other public accommodations.

joint committee: Includes members from both houses of Congress, conducts investigations or special studies.

judicial activism: A philosophy of judicial decision making that argues judges should use their power broadly to further justice, especially in the areas of equality and personal liberty.

judicial implementation: Refers to how and whether judicial decisions are translated into actual public policies affecting more than the immediate parties to a lawsuit.

judicial restraint: A philosophy of judicial decision making that argues courts should allow the decisions of other branches of government to stand, even when they offend a judge's own sense of principles.

judicial review: Power of the courts to review acts of other branches of government and the states.

Judiciary Act of 1789: Established the basic three-tiered structure of the federal court system.

jurisdiction: Authority vested in a particular court to hear and decide the issues in any particular case.

L

legislative courts: Courts established by Congress for specialized purposes, such as the Court of Military Appeals.

libel: False written statements or written statements tending to call someone's reputation into disrepute.

liberal: One considered to favor extensive governmental involvement in the economy and the provision of social services and to take an activist role in protecting the rights of women, the elderly, minorities, and the environment.

libertarian: One who favors a free market economy and no governmental interference in personal liberties.

line-item veto: The authority of a chief executive to delete part of a bill passed by the legislature that involves taxing or spending. The legislature may override a veto, usually with a two-thirds majority of each chamber.

lobbying: The activities of a group or organization that seeks to influence legislation and persuade political leaders to support the group's position.

lobbyist: Interest group representative who seeks to influence legislation that will benefit his or her organization through political persuasion.

logrolling: Vote trading; voting yea to support a colleague's bill in return for a promise of future support.

Louisiana Purchase: The 1803 land purchase authorized by President Thomas Jefferson, which expanded the size of the United States dramatically.

M

machine: A party organization that recruits its members with tangible incentives and is characterized by a high degree of control over member activity.

majority leader: The elected leader of the party controlling the most seats in the House of Representatives or the Senate; is second in authority to the speaker of the House and in the Senate is regarded as its most powerful member.

majority party: The political party in each house of Congress with the most members.

majority rule: The central premise of direct democracy in which only policies that collectively garner the support of a majority of voters will be made into law.

manager: A professional executive hired by a city council or county board to manage daily operations and to recommend policy changes.

mandate: A command, indicated by an electorate's votes, for the elected officials to carry out their platforms.

Marbury v. Madison (1803): Supreme Court first asserted the power of judicial review in finding that the congressional statute extending the Court's original jurisdiction was unconstitutional.

margin of error: A measure of the accuracy of a public opinion poll.

matching funds: Donations to presidential campaigns from the federal government that are determined by the amount of private funds a qualifying candidate raises.

mayor: Chief elected executive of a city.

McCulloch **v.** *Maryland* **(1819):** The Supreme Court upheld the power of the national government and denied the right of a state to tax the bank. The Court's broad interpretation of the necessary and proper clause paved the way for later rulings upholding expansive federal powers.

media campaign: That part of a political campaign in which the candidate reaches out to the voters, in person or via the media, to create a positive impression and gain votes.

media consultant: A professional who produces political candidates' television, radio, and print advertisements.

media effects: The influence of news sources on public opinion.

mercantilism: An economic theory designed to increase a nation's wealth through the development of commercial industry and a favorable balance of trade.

merit system: The system by which federal civil service jobs are classified into grades or levels, to which appointments are made on the basis of performance on competitive examinations.

midterm election: Election that takes place in the middle of a presidential term.

minority leader: The elected leader of the party with the second highest number of elected representatives in the House of Representatives or the Senate.

minority party: The political party in each house of Congress with the second most members.

Miranda **rights:** Statements that must be made by the police informing a suspect of his or her constitutional rights protected by the Fifth Amendment, including the right to an attorney provided by the court if the suspect cannot afford one.

Miranda **v.** *Arizona* **(1966):** A landmark Supreme Court ruling that held the Fifth Amendment requires that individuals arrested for a crime must be advised of their right to remain silent and to have counsel present.

Missouri (Merit) Plan: A method of selecting judges in which a governor must appoint someone from a list provided by an independent panel. Judges are then kept in office if they get a majority of "yes" votes in general elections.

monarchy: A form of government in which power is vested in hereditary kings and queens who govern in the interests of all.

muckraking: A form of journalism, in vogue in the early twentieth century, concerned with reforming government and business conduct.

municipality: A government with general responsibilities, such as a city, town, or village government, that is created in response to the emergence of relatively densely populated areas.

N

national convention: A party conclave (meeting) held in the presidential election year for the purposes of nominating a presidential and vice presidential ticket and adopting a platform.

national party platform: A statement of the general and specific philosophy and policy goals of a political party, usually promulgated at the national convention.

natural law: A doctrine that society should be governed by certain ethical principles that are part of nature and, as such, can be understood by reason.

necessary and proper clause: The final paragraph of Article I, section 8, of the U.S. Constitution, which gives Congress the authority to pass all laws "necessary and proper" to carry out the enumerated powers specified in the Constitution; also called the elastic clause.

negative ad: Advertising on behalf of a candidate that attacks the opponent's platform or character.

network: An association of broadcast stations (radio or television) that share programming through a financial arrangement.

New Deal: The name given to the program of "Relief, Recovery, Reform" begun by President Franklin D. Roosevelt in 1933 to bring the United States out of the Great Depression.

New Federalism: Federal/state relationship proposed by Reagan administration during the 1980s; hallmark is returning administrative powers to the state governments.

New Jersey Plan: A framework for the Constitution proposed by a group of small states; its key points were a one-house legislature with one vote for each state, the establishment of the acts of Congress as the "supreme law" of the land, and a supreme judiciary with limited power.

New York Times Co. **v.** *Sullivan* **(1964):** The Supreme Court concluded that "actual malice" must be proved to support a finding of libel against a public figure.

Nineteenth Amendment: Amendment to the Constitution that guaranteed women the right to vote.

Ninth Amendment: Part of the Bill of Rights that reads "The enumeration in the Constitution, of certain rights, shall not be construed to deny or disparage others retained by the people."

nomination campaign: That part of a political campaign aimed at winning a primary election.

nonpartisan election: A contest in which candidates run without formal identification or association with a political party.

nonpartisan primary: A primary used to select candidates regardless of party affiliation.

O

off the record: Information provided to a journalist that will not be released to the public.

off-year election: Election that takes place in the middle of a presidential term.

Office of Management and Budget (OMB): The office that prepares the president's annual budget proposal, reviews the budget and programs of the executive departments, supplies economic forecasts, and conducts detailed analyses of proposed bills and agency rules.

oligarchy: A form of government in which the right to participate is conditioned on the possession of wealth, social status, military position, or achievement.

on background: Information provided to a journalist that will not be attributed to a named source.

on the record: Information provided to a journalist that can be released and attributed by name to the source.

one-person, one-vote: The principle that each legislative district within a state should have the same number of eligible voters so that representation is equitably based on population.

open primary: A primary in which party members, independents, and sometimes members of the other party are allowed to vote.

organizational campaign: That part of a political campaign involved in fund-raising, literature distribution, and all other activities not directly involving the candidate.

organizational party: The workers and activists who staff the party's formal organization.

original jurisdiction: The jurisdiction of courts that hear a case first, usually in a trial. Courts determine the facts of a case under their original jurisdiction.

oversight: Congressional review of the activities of an agency, department, or office.

P

package or general veto: The authority of a chief executive to void an entire bill that has been passed by the legislature. This veto applies to all bills, whether or not they have taxing or spending components, and the legislature may override this veto, usually with a two-thirds majority of each chamber.

paid media: Political advertisements purchased for a candidate's campaign.

pardon: The authority of a government to cancel someone's conviction of a crime by a court and to eliminate all sanctions and punishments resulting from conviction.

parole: The authority of a governor to release a prisoner before his or her full sentence has been completed and to specify conditions that must be met as part of the release.

party caucus or conference: A formal gathering of all party members.

party identification: A citizen's personal affinity for a political party, usually expressed by his or her tendency to vote for the candidates of that party.

party in the electorate: The voters who consider themselves allied or associated with the party.

party realignment: A shifting of party coalition groupings in the electorate that remains in place for several elections.

patrons: Persons who finance a group or individual activity.

patronage: Jobs, grants, or other special favors that are given as rewards to friends and political allies for their support.

Pendleton Act: Reform measure that created the Civil Service Commission to administer a partial merit system. The act classified the federal service by grades, to which appointments were made based on the results of a competitive examination. It made it illegal for federal political appointees to be required to contribute to a particular political party.

personal campaign: That part of a political campaign concerned with presenting the candidate's public image.

personal liberty: A key characteristic of U.S. democracy. Initially meaning freedom from governmental interference, today it includes demands for freedom to engage in a variety of practices free from governmental discrimination.

Plessy **v.** *Ferguson* **(1896):** Plessy challenged a Louisiana statute requiring that railroads provide separate accommodations for blacks and whites. The Court found that separate but equal accommodations did not violate the equal protection clause of the Fourteenth Amendment.

pocket veto: If Congress adjourns during the ten days the president has to consider a bill passed by both houses of Congress, without the president's signature, the bill is considered vetoed.

political action committee (PAC): Federally mandated, officially registered fund-raising committee that represents interest groups in the political process.

political culture: Commonly shared attitudes, beliefs, and core values about how government should operate.

political ideology: The coherent set of values and beliefs about the purpose and scope of government held by groups and individuals.

political machine: An organization designed to solicit votes from certain neighborhoods or communities for a particular political party in return for services and jobs if that party wins.

political party: A group of office holders, candidates, activists, and voters who identify with a group label and seek to elect to public office individuals who run under that label.

political socialization: The process through which an individual acquires particular political orientations; the learning process by which people acquire their political beliefs and values.

politico: Role played by elected representatives who act as trustees or as delegates, depending on the issue.

politics: The study of who gets what, when, and how—or how policy decisions are made.

pollster: A professional who takes public opinion surveys that guide political campaigns.

popular consent: The idea that governments must draw their powers from the consent of the governed.

popular sovereignty: The right of the majority to govern themselves.

pork: Legislation that allows representatives to bring home the bacon to their districts in the form of public works programs, military bases, or other programs designed to benefit their districts directly.

positive ad: Advertising on behalf of a candidate that stresses the candidate's qualifications, family, and issue positions, without reference to the opponent.

precedent: Prior judicial decision that serves as a rule for settling subsequent cases of a similar nature.

preemption: A concept derived from the Constitution's supremacy clause that allows the national government to override or preempt state or local actions in certain areas.

presidentialist: One who believes that Article II's grant of executive power is a broad grant of authority allowing a president wide discretionary powers.

press briefing: A relatively restricted session between a press secretary or aide and the press.

press conference: An unrestricted session between an elected official and the press.

press release: A document offering an official comment or position.

press secretary: The individual charged with interacting and communicating with journalists on a daily basis.

primary election: Election in which voters decide which of the candidates within a party will represent the party in the general election.

print press: The traditional form of mass media, comprising newspapers, magazines, and journals.

prior restraint: Constitutional doctrine that prevents the government from prohibiting speech or publication before the fact; generally held to be in violation of the First Amendment.

privilegs and immunites clause: Part of Article IV of the Constitution guaranteeing that the citizens of each state are afforded the same rights as citizens of all other states.

Progressive movement: Advocated measures to destroy political machines and instead have direct participation by voters in the nomination of candidates and the establishment of public policy.

progressive tax: The tax level increases with the wealth or ability of an individual or business to pay.

proportional representation: A voting system that apportions legislative seats according to the percentage of the vote won by a particular political party.

prospective judgment: A voter's evaluation of a candidate based on what he or she pledges to do about an issue if elected.

public corporation (authority): Government organization established to provide a particular service or to run a particular facility that is independent of other city or state agencies is to be operated like a business. Examples include a port authority or a mass transit system.

public funds: Donations from the general tax revenues to the campaigns of qualifying presidential candidates.

public interest group: An organization that seeks a collective good that will not selectively and materially benefit the members of the group.

public opinion: What the public thinks about a particular issue or set of issues at any point in time.

public opinion polls: Interviews or surveys with samples of citizens that are used to estimate the feelings and beliefs of the entire population.

push polls: "Polls" taken for the purpose of providing information on an opponent that would lead respondents to vote against that candidate.

R

raiding: An organized attempt by voters of one party to influence the primary results of the other party.

random sampling: A method of poll selection that gives each person in a group the same chance of being selected.

recall: A process in which voters can petition for a vote to remove office holders between elections.

redistricting: The redrawing of congressional districts to reflect increases or decreases in seats allotted to the states, as well as population shifts within a state.

referendum: An election whereby the state legislature submits proposed legislation to the state's voters for approval.

regional primary: A proposed system in which the country would be divided into five or six geographic areas and all states in each region would hold their presidential primary elections on the same day.

regressive tax: The tax level increases as the wealth or ability of an individual or business to pay decreases.

regulations: Rules that govern the operation of a particular government program that have the force of law.

republic: A government rooted in the consent of the governed; a representative or indirect democracy.

reserve (or police) powers: Powers reserved to the states by the Tenth Amendment that lie at the foundation of a state's right to legislate for the public health and welfare of its citizens.

reservation land: Land designated in a treaty that is under the authority of an Indian nation and is exempt from most state laws and taxes.

restrictive constitution: Constitution that incorporates detailed provisions in order to limit the powers of government.

retrospective judgment: A voter's evaluation of the performance of the party in power.

right-of-rebuttal rule: A Federal Communications Commission regulation that people attacked on a radio or television broadcast be offered the opportunity to respond.

right to privacy: The right to be let alone; a judicially created doctrine encompassing an individual's decision to use birth control or secure an abortion.

Roe v. *Wade* (1973): The Supreme Court found that a woman's right to an abortion was protected by the right to privacy that could be implied from specific guarantees found in the Bill of Rights applied to the states through the Fourteenth Amendment.

rule making: A quasi-legislative administrative process that has the characteristics of a legislative act.

Rule of Four: At least four justices of the Supreme Court must vote to consider a case before it can be heard.

runoff primary: A second primary election between the two candidates receiving the greatest number of votes in the first primary.

S

sampling error or margin of error: A measure of the accuracy of a public opinion poll.

Second Continental Congress: Meeting that convened in Philadelphia on May 10, 1775, at which it was decided that an army should be raised and George Washington of Virginia was named commander in chief.

secular realignment: The gradual rearrangement of party coalitions, based more on demographic shifts than on shocks to the political system.

segregated funds: Money that comes in from a certain tax or fee and then is restricted to a specific use, such as a gasoline tax that is used for road maintenance.

select (or special) committee: Temporary committee appointed for specific purpose, such as conducting a special investigation or study.

selective incorporation: A judicial doctrine whereby most but not all of the protections found in the Bill of Rights are made applicable to the states via the Fourteenth Amendment.

senatorial courtesy: A process by which presidents, when selecting district court judges, defer to the senator in whose state the vacancy occurs.

seniority: Time of continuous service on a committee.

separation of powers: A way of dividing power among three branches of government in which members of the House of Representatives, members of the Senate, the president, and the federal courts are selected by and responsible to different constituencies.

Seventeenth Amendment: Made senators directly elected by the people; removed their selection from state legislatures.

Shays's Rebellion: A 1786 rebellion in which an army of 1,500 disgruntled and angry farmers led by Daniel Shays marched to Springfield, Massachusetts, and forcibly restrained the state court from foreclosing mortgages on their farms.

Sixteenth Amendment: Authorized Congress to enact a national income tax.

Sixth Amendment: Part of the Bill of Rights that sets out the basic requirements of procedural due process for federal courts to follow in criminal trials. These include speedy and public trials, impartial juries, trials in the state where crime was committed, notice of the charges, the right to confront and obtain favorable witnesses, and the right to counsel.

slander: Untrue spoken statements that defame the character of a person.

social capital: The myriad relationships that individuals enjoy that facilitate the resolution of community problems through collective action.

social contract: An agreement between the people and their government signifying their consent to be governed.

social contract theory: The belief that people are free and equal by God-given right and that this in turn requires that all people give their consent to be governed; espoused by John Locke and influential in the writing of the Declaration of Independence.

soft money: The virtually unregulated money funneled by individuals and political committees through state and local parties.

solicitor general: The fourth-ranking member of the Department of Justice; responsible for handling all appeals on behalf of the U.S. government to the Supreme Court.

sovereign immunity: The right of a state to be free from lawsuit unless it gives permission to the suit. Under the Eleventh Amendment, all states are considered sovereign.

speaker of the House: The only officer of the House of Representatives specifically mentioned in the Constitution; elected at the beginning of each new Congress by the entire House; traditionally a member of the majority party.

special district: A local government that is responsible for a particular function, such as K–12 education, water, sewerage, or parks.

spoils system: The firing of public-office holders of a defeated political party and their replacement with loyalists of the newly elected party.

spot ad: Television advertising on behalf of a candidate that is broadcast in sixty-, thirty-, or ten-second duration.

Stamp Act Congress: Meeting of representatives of nine of the thirteen colonies held in New York City in 1765, during which representatives drafted a document to send to the king listing how their rights had been violated.

standing committee: Committee to which proposed bills are referred.

stare decisis: In court rulings, a reliance on past decisions or precedents to formulate decisions in new cases.

state constitution: The document that describes the basic policies, procedures, and institutions of the government of a specific state, much as the U.S. Constitution does for the federal government.

stewardship theory: The theory that holds that Article II confers on the president the power and the duty to take whatever actions are deemed necessary in the national interest, unless prohibited by the Constitution or by law.

stratified sampling: A variation of random sampling; Census data are used to divide a country into four sampling regions. Sets of counties and standard metropolitan statistical areas are then randomly selected in proportion to the total national population.

straw polls: Unscientific surveys used to gauge public opinion on a variety of issues and policies.

strict constructionist: An approach to constitutional interpretation that emphasizes the Framers' original intentions.

strict scrutiny: A heightened standard of review used by the Supreme Court to determine the constitutional validity of a challenged practice.

substantive due process: Judicial interpretation of the Fifth and Fourteenth Amendments' due process clause that protects citizens from arbitrary or unjust laws.

suffrage movement: The drive for voting rights for women that took place in the United States from 1890 to 1920.

superdelegate: Delegate slot to the Democratic Party's national convention that is reserved for an elected party official.

supremacy clause: Portion of Article VI of the U.S. Constitution mandating that national law is supreme to (that is, supercedes) all other laws passed by the states or by any other subdivision of government.

suspect classification: Category or class, such as race, that triggers the highest standard of scrutiny from the Supreme Court.

symbolic speech: Symbols, signs, and other methods of expression generally also considered to be protected by the First Amendment.

T

Taftian theory: The theory that holds that the president is limited by the specific grants of executive power found in the Constitution.

Tenth Amendment: The final part of the Bill of Rights that defines the basic principle of American federalism in stating: "The powers not delegated to the United States by the Constitution, nor prohibited by it to the States, are reserved to the States respectively, or to the people."

term limits: Restrictions that exist in some states about how long an individual may serve in state or local elected offices.

third-partyism: The tendency of third parties to arise with some regularity in a nominally two-party system.

Thirteenth Amendment: One of the three Civil War amendments; specifically bans slavery in the United States.

Three-Fifths Compromise: Agreement reached at the Constitutional Convention stipulating that each slave was to be counted as three-fifths of a person for purposes of determining population for representation in the U.S. House of Representatives.

ticket-split: To vote for candidates of different parties for various offices in the same election.

Title IX: Provision of the Educational Amendments of 1972 that bars educational institutions receiving federal funds from discriminating against female students.

totalitarianism: An economic system in which the government has total control over the economy.

town meeting: Form of local government in which all eligible voters are invited to attend a meeting at which budgets and ordinances are proposed and voted on.

tracking polls: Continuous surveys that enable a campaign to chart its daily rise or fall in support.

trade associations: A group that represents a specific industry.

trial court: Court of original jurisdiction where a case begins.

trust land: Land owned by an Indian nation and designated by the federal Bureau of Indian Affairs as exempt from most state laws and taxes.

trust relationship: The legal obligation of the United States federal government to protect the interests of Indian tribes.

trustee: Role played by elected representatives who listen to constituents' opinions and then use their best judgment to make final decisions.

turnout: The proportion of the voting-age public that votes.

Twenty-Fifth Amendment: Adopted in 1967 to establish procedures for filling vacancies in the office of president and vice president as well as providing for procedures to deal with the disability of a president.

Twenty-Second Amendment: Adopted in 1951, prevents a president from serving more than two terms or more than ten years if he came to office via the death or impeachment of his predecessor.

U

unfunded mandates: National laws that direct states or local governments to comply with the federal rules or regulations (such as clean air or water standards) but contain no federal funding to defray the cost of meeting these requirements.

unitary system: System of government where the local and regional governments derive all authority from a strong national government.

unit rule: A traditional party practice under which the majority of a state delegation can force the minority to vote for its candidate.

U. S. v. Nixon (1974): Key Supreme Court ruling on power of the president, finding that there is no absolute constitutional executive privilege to allow a president to refuse to comply with a court order to produce information needed in a criminal trial.

V

veto: Formal constitutional authority of the president to reject bills passed by both houses of the legislative body, thus preventing their becoming law without further congressional activity.

veto power: The formal, constitutional authority of the president to reject bills passed by both houses of Congress, thus preventing their becoming law without further congressional action.

Virginia Plan: The first general plan for the Constitution, proposed by James Madison. Its key points were a bicameral legislature, an executive chosen by the legislature, and a judiciary also named by the legislature.

voter canvass: The process by which a campaign gets in touch with individual voters, either by door-to-door solicitation or by telephone.

W

War Powers Act: Passed by Congress in 1973; the president is limited in the deployment of troops overseas to a sixty-day period in peacetime (which can be extended for an extra thirty days to permit withdrawal) unless Congress explicitly gives its approval for a longer period.

whip: One of several representatives who keep close contact with all members and take nose counts on key votes, prepare summaries of bills, and in general act as communications links within the party.

wire service: An electronic delivery of news gathered by the news service's correspondents and sent to all member news media organizations.

writ of certiorari: A request for the Court to order up the records from a lower court to review the case.

Y

yellow journalism: A form of newspaper publishing in vogue in the late-nineteenth century that featured pictures, comics, color, and sensationalized, oversimplified news coverage.

664 INDEX